A Guide to

European Union Law

as amended by the
Treaty of Lisbon

A Guide to
European Union Law

as amended by the Treaty of Lisbon

Tenth Edition

By

P.S.R.F. Mathijsen

Advocaat
Professor of Law, University of Brussels.
Former Director-General with the Commission of the European
Communities

SWEET & MAXWELL

First edition 1972
Second edition 1975
Third edition 1980
Fourth edition 1985
Fifth edition 1990
Sixth edition 1995
Seventh edition 2001
Eighth edition 2004
Ninth edition 2007
Tenth edition 2010

Published in 2010 by Thomson Reuters (Legal) Limited
(Registered in England & Wales Company No 1679046,
Registered Office and address for service:
100 Avenue Road, London, NW3 3PF) trading as
Sweet & Maxwell
For further information on our products and services,
visit//www.sweetandmaxwell.co.uk

Typeset by LBJ Typesetting Ltd of Kingsclere
Printed in the UK by
CPI William Clowes Beccles NR34 7TL

No natural forests were destroyed to make this product; only farmed timber was used
and replanted.

A CIP catalogue record for this book is available from the British Library.

ISBN 978–1847–03744–2

In memoriam

Daphné
Olivier

Acknowledgments

By starting, back in May 2008,[1] to update the 9th edition of this book, and including in it all the modifications provided for by the Treaty of Lisbon, I took quite a risk, and so did Sweet & Maxwell. As is well known, it was indeed not until November 2009, that this Treaty was finally ratified by all the Member States and could enter into force on December 1, 2009. I am therefore particularly grateful to the publisher and publishing editor (Nicola Thurlow) for having stood by me all that time. I also want to thank the editorial staff for their patience, understanding and indispensable help: they produced the many tables and the index, without which this book would be much less useful. For editing, correcting and improving the manuscript and proofs my thanks go to Michelle Afford.

Community activities have developed tremendously over the past years, more so probably than before. Some tasks also became more technical, more complicated. I realised I needed some outside help and was particularly lucky in finding the required experts ready to assist me. In the first place there is my university colleague, Prof. Tony Joris, who once again accepted to review the chapters concerning the institutions. Ms Katia Bodard helped me updating the chapter on Intellectual Property Rights (IPR) and, above all, Ms Bettina Bognár, my assistant at the law firm, who, for months, researched, rechecked and reread the many drafts!

I have freely made use of information published by the Union institutions on the Internet and elswhere and have always made reference to the place where I found it. I remain particularly grateful to the Office for Official Publications of the European Union in Luxembourg and the Court of Justice for graciously supplying me with needed documents and publications.

For morale and physical support nothing equals, as always, my wife Beverly. She gracefully accepted the consequences of prolonged absences at the office during drafting, including weekends.

P. Mathijsen
February 2010

---

[1] The consolidated versions of the Treaty on European Union and the Treaty on the functioning of the European Union were published in the *Official Journal* on May 9, 2008 (CIIJ).

Introduction to the "After Lisbon" Edition

Readers who now approach "European law" for the first time are to be envied in a certain way since they start out with the new terminology, article numbering, concepts, treaty contents, etc. They will get to know "Europe" under its new "cloak"! However, they need to know what went on before the Treaty of Lisbon became applicable in order not to be utterly confused when confronted with former expressions, numbers, etc. One example will make this clear: "Community" was the term universally used to designate the enterprise to unify Europe, that started after World War II at the beginning of the 1950s, which is now referred to as "Union". The term "Community" was used all over the world for more than 50 years but has now been discarded and replaced; it is, however, to be expected that the term "Community" won't totally disappear from one day to the next as by magic; and, furthermore, the *acquis communautaire*[1] remains and must constantly be dealt with. The same applies to the many other changes; the European newcomer might, therefore, find it more than useful to have some knowledge about what went on before the Treaty of Lisbon.

It seems necessary to start by briefly mentioning some of the major technical and material modifications introduced by the Treaty of Lisbon, leaving the substantive changes for the chapters of this book dealing with the various structures and activities of the Union. The reader should not be surprised that modifications were introduced, after all this has happened over and over again in the past: the first modification was introduced back in 1952 and since then some 17 modifications have been introduced by treaty or act.

- At one point there existed four legal and institutional European "structures": the 1951 Coal and Steel Community (ECSC); the 1957 European Economic Community (EEC), which became the European Community (EC); the 1957 European Atomic Energy Community (Euratom); and the 1993 European Union (EU).

  The ECSC was established for 50 years only and has, therefore, now ceased to exist, but it should be remembered that it was during that time that the basis of the present European law was developed: the case law of those first years (1951–1958) is very important indeed. Euratom today plays a rather minor role (only some aspects are discussed in this book) and until the end of 2008 the emphasis lay mostly with the EC, while the EU acquired, over the years, more and more importance within the European structure and is now the major player on the world scene.

  Although the three Treaties continue to exist,[2] politically speaking the accent now lies with the Treaty on European Union, which gives its name to the whole European endeavour. As indicated above, the term "Community" disappears from the European vocabulary and although the EU and TFEU Treaties have the same legal value,[3] the EC Treaty was made into an instrument for accomplishing the tasks set out in the EU Treaty[4] and is now referred to as the Treaty

---

[1] All the legal texts that have been adopted (acquired) by the European institution over the past 58 years and are still applicable.

[2] Contrary to the "Constitutional" draft treaty, which would have merged the three Treaties into one.

[3] art.1, 3 EU.

[4] It even lost its legal personality in favour of the European Union!

on the Functioning of the European Union (TFEU). Nonetheless, it still constitutes the basis for practically all the Union's activities.

- The EU Treaty lays down the objectives of the Union, the values and principles on which it is based (conferral of powers, subsidiarity, proportionality, democracy, etc.), the institutional structure and its main competences; it provides for enhanced co-operation, external action and common foreign and security policy, the creation of a permanent Council chairman and of a High Representative of the Union for Foreign Affairs and Security Policy, and a defence policy. The fact that the EU Treaty now contains all those basic provisions concerning the Union as a whole, makes it necessary to include the provisions of that Treaty in this book; the previous editions were more or less limited to the EC Treaty (now TFEU).

- As for the TFEU, it constitutes, as mentioned, the legal basis for practically all the Union's activities. It defines the Union's competences, which are either exclusive, shared with the Member States or the object of co-ordination, it establishes the "citizenship" of the Union, the internal market and, as mentioned, all the activities of the Union. It also contains the details of the institutional set up, the voting procedures, the maximum number of members, etc. All those subjects are discussed in the following chapters of this book.

- Another important technical change is the, already mentioned, new numbering of the provisions of the Treaties: in the EU Treaty not all numbers were modified, but in the TFEU the numbering of every single article has changed. The newcomer should be aware of the fact that this is the fourth time that article numbers have been modified, with most disturbing consequences for the study of, for instance, the case law of the European courts. A simple example will make this clear: the provisions concerning competition rules applying to undertakings were, in the ECSC Treaty (for cartels) art.65 and (for abuse of a dominant position) art.66; in the EEC Treaty they were respectively arts 85 and 86; in the EC Treaty they became arts 81 and 82; and, now, in the TFEU they are arts 100 and 101! In order to give some help to the reader, the numbers of the EC Treaty are, in this edition, indicated in brackets after each present article number and in the quoted texts, including the case law, they have simply been replaced by the new numbers, but in brackets.

Those changes mean that when consulting the European courts case law, for instance, attention must be paid to the year in which the case was initiated, although the courts have indicated in their judgments, but necessarily only since the first modification, the previous numbering. Supposedly the courts shall now in some cases have to mention the last two changes!

So, maybe, when writing that the "newcomer to European law is to be envied" because he is introduced right away to the new terminology and numbering—which certainly is an enormous advantage—special attention is required by them when studying older acts, whether emanating from the Council, the Commission, Parliament or the courts. Indeed, although the content of the Treaties' provisions remained, for the most part, unchanged, the references in those acts to Treaty articles will not correspond to the ones having that number in the new TFEU. Many European acts, although more than 55 years old, are still applicable today and are often the object of courts' interpretation; studying them without the above warning in mind could be most confusing.[5]

---

[5] *The Official Journal* [2007] C306 contains tables of correspondence between the new and the old numbers.

- Some texts that were in one Treaty are now to be found in another: this is the case, for instance with "Judicial Co-operation in Criminal Matters", which used to be in the EU Treaty and is now in the TFEU. On the other hand, some provisions that were in the EC Treaty are now in the EU Treaty.
- The names of the Union acts have changed in so far that some names have disappeared and only the traditional Regulation, Directive and Decision are now used.
- The three so-called pillars (the European Treaties, Justice and Home Affairs and Foreign Affairs and Security) on which the Union was based[6], were merged and incorporated into one of the two Treaties: EU or TFEU; undoubtedly this constitutes an important simplification.

Changes Introduced by the Treaty of Lisbon in the European Material Law

- Generally speaking, the material law (in other words the provisions concerning the activities of the Union, such as the internal market, competition, agriculture, environment, social policy, regional policy, consumer protection, etc.) is practically unchanged, except for the introduction of extended provisions on the "external action" of the Union.

    Having learned, probably, from the traumatic consequences of the rejection of the "Constitution", the Treaty of Lisbon provides for a simplified Treaty revision procedure.

Changes Introduced by the Treaty of Lisbon in the European Institutional Law

- This is where most modifications were introduced, which is not surprising since the main purpose of modifying (once again) the Treaties was to make the Union institutions capable of functioning with 27 Member States, the existing institutional set-up was devised for six members!

    Besides the, probably by now well known, creation of a Presidency (chairmanship) of the European Council (now one of the seven institutions and not to be confused with "the Council" [of Ministers]) for a duration of 2½ years, renewable once, and of a High Representative of the Union for Foreign Affairs and Security Policy, more fundamental changes were introduced.

    They concern, in the first place, a new rule of double majority for decision-taking in the Council, to be introduced step-by-step until November 1, 2014; from that date on, all decisions will be taken by qualified majority based on the number of votes assigned to each Member State when accepted by 55 per cent of the members of the Council, and representing Member States comprising at least 65 per cent of the population of the Union. A blocking minority has to include at least four Member States.[7] This will facilitate the creation of majorities and, therefore, decision-taking.

---

[6] See the 1992 Maastricht or European Union Treaty.

[7] However, in order to win over Poland, the so-called informal "Ioannina compromise" was maintained in the following manner: if one-third of the Member States or 25 per cent of the population are opposed to a decision without attaining the "blocking minority", all the Member States commit to seeking a solution to rally opponents, while reserving the option to vote at any time.

Secondly, practically all decisions are now taken by the European Parliament and the Council acting together; this so-called codecision procedure, now referred to as the "ordinary legislative procedure" was extended to many new areas.

Thirdly, the role of citizens and of national parliaments, in the decision-making process, is increased.

Fourthly, the competences of the institutions are more strictly defined as "exclusive competences", "competences shared with the Member States" and "actions to support, coordinate or supplement the actions of the Member States".

The modifications introduced by the Treaty of Lisbon are examined hereunder, in some detail, in the corresponding chapters.

Table of Contents

Acknowledgments   vii
Introduction to the "After Lisbon" Edition   ix
Table of Cases   xxix
Table of Treaties and Conventions   cxv
Table of Secondary Legislation of the European Union   cxxxv
Table of National Legislation   cxcix
Basic Statistics   cci
Abbreviations   ciii

PART ONE: THE EUROPEAN UNION, THE TREATIES, THE
ACTS AND THE LAW   1

Chapter One: The European Treaties   3
Introduction   3
  1. The EU Treaty and the Treaty on the Functioning of the
     European Union (TFEU)   4
  2. Enhanced Co-operation   6
  3. The Treaty on the Functioning of the European Union   8
  4. Modification of the Treaties   10
  5. Countries to which the European Treaties Apply and
     Territorial Scope of these Treaties   11

Chapter Two: History   13
  1. Churchill's Speech   13
  2. Marshall Plan—OEEC   13
  3. Robert Schuman: May 9, 1950   14
  4. The European Coal and Steel Community (ECSC)   14
  5. The European Defence Community   15
  6. The European Economic Community (EEC) and the European
     Atomic Energy Community (Euratom)   15
  7. The Treaty Establishing a Single Council and a Single Commission   16
  8. The Customs Union   16
  9. The Community's (now Union's) Own Resources   16
 10. The British, Danish and Irish Membership   16
 11. The Enlargement to Greece, Portugal and Spain   17
 12. The Direct Election of Parliament and the Declaration on
     Democracy and Fundamental Rights   17
 13. The Secession of Greenland   18
 14. The Completion of the Internal Market by 1992   18
 15. The Single European Act (SEA)   19
 16. The Treaty on European Union or Maastricht Treaty (EU Treaty)   19
 17. The European Economic Area (EEA) and the European Free
     Trade Association (EFTA)   20
 18. The Accession of Austria, Finland and Sweden   21
 19. The Treaty of Amsterdam   22
 20. The Treaty of Nice   23

21. The Accession of 10 New Member States	23
22. The European Convention on the Future of the European Union and the Draft Constitution	23
23. The Accession of Bulgaria and Romania	24
24. The Treaty of Lisbon	25
25. Ireland and the Treaty of Lisbon	26
26. The Czech Republic and the Treaty of Lisbon	27

Chapter Three: The Legal Acts of the Union — 28

1. Binding Acts Provided for in the Treaties: Legal Acts/Legislative Acts	30
2. Regulations, Directives and Decisions must be Reasoned	36
3. Publication and Entry into Force	37
4. Enforcement of Pecuniary Obligations	38
5. Binding Acts not Provided for Under TFEU Article 288	39
6. Other Forms of Union "Acts"	40

Chapter Four: Union Law — 42

1. Direct Applicability	43
2. Direct Effect	44
3. Precedence or Primacy of Union Law	46
4. Member States' Liability for Breach of Union Law	51
5. Infringement of Union Law by Natural/Legal Persons	52
6. Sources of Community Law	52
7. Application of National and International Law by the European Courts	54
8. Application of Union Law by the National Courts	55
9. Conclusions	56

PART TWO: THE INSTITUTIONS AND BODIES OF THE UNION AND THE FINANCING OF ITS ACTIVITIES — 59

Introduction — 59

Chapter Five: The European Parliament — 61

1. The Members of Parliament	61
(1) Election of the Members	62
(2) The Member's Mandate	63
(a) Privileges and Immunity	64
(b) Performance of Duties	65
2. Tasks and Powers of Parliament	65
(1) Exercise, Jointly with the Council, Legislative Functions	66
(a) Consultation	66
(b) The Ordinary Legislative Procedure	68
First Reading	68
Second Reading	69
Conciliation	69
Third Reading	70
Special Provisions	70
Type of Act to be Adopted	70
Implementing Measures	71

(c) The Special Legislative Procedure	71
(d) Consent Procedure	71
(2) Setting up of a Temporary Committee of Inquiry	72
(3) Right of Petition and Appointment of an Ombudsman	72
(4) Questions to the Council, the Commission and the ECB	73
(5) The Adoption of the Rules of Procedure	74
(6) The General Report	75
(7) The Motion of Censure	76
(8) Approval of the President and Members of the Commission	76
(9) Participation in the Budgetary Procedure	77
(10) Procedures before the Court of Justice	79
(11) Participation in other Union Activities	80
3. Internal Organisation of Parliament	80
(1) The Political Groups	80
(2) Parliamentary Committees	81
(3) The Bureau	82
(4) Sessions and Meeting Place(s)	83
(5) The Conference of European Affairs Committees of (national) Parliaments of the European Union (COSAC)	83
(6) Parliament's Secretariat	84
4. Conclusion	84
Chapter Six: The European Council	85
Introduction	85
The European Council	85
(1) History	85
(2) Composition	86
(3) The President of the European Council	86
(4) Voting	86
(5) Tasks	87
(6) Existence of a "serious and persistent breach" by a Member State of the Union's Values	87
(7) Organisation	88
Chapter Seven: The Council	90
Introduction—the Objectives of the Treaties and the Means to Achieve Them: the Role of the Council	90
1. Members of the Council	91
2. Tasks and Powers of the Council	92
(1) Decision-making	92
(a) Principles	92
(b) Scope	94
(c) Voting Procedure	95
(i) Simple Majority	96
(ii) Qualified Majority	96
(iii) Unanimity	98
(2) Co-ordination of Economic Policies: Broad Guidelines of the Economic Policies of the Member States and the Union	99

    (3) Guidelines on Employment Policy   101
  3. Organisational Aspects of the Council   101
    (1) Configurations of the Council   101
    (2) COREPER (COmite REpresents PERmanents—
        Committee of Permanent Representatives)   102
    (3) The Rules of Procedure   104
    (4) The Secretariat   105

Chapter Eight: The Commission   106
  1. The Members of the European Commission   107
    (1) The Number of Commissioners   107
    (2) The Choice of Members of the Commission   107
    (3) The Nomination Procedure of Members of the Commission   108
  2. The Commission's Tasks and Powers   109
    (1) "Ensure the application of the Treaties and of
        measures adopted by the institutions pursuant to
        them" and "oversee the application of Union law
        under the control of the Court of Justice of the
        European Union"   110
        (a) With Regard to Member States   110
        (b) With Regard to acts of Institutions and Other
            Bodies   113
        (c) With Regard to Legal or Natural Persons   113
    (2) "Adopt regulations, directives, decisions,
        recommendations and opinions"   113
    (3) Exercise of Powers delegated by Legislative Act   115
    (4) Participation in the Legislative Process   118
    (5) External Relations   121
    (6) Implementation of the Community Budget   122
    (7) Publication of the Annual General Report   123
  3. Rules of Procedure and the Commission's Staff   123
  4. Access to Documents   124

Chapter Nine: The Court of Justice of the European Union   125
I. The Court of Justice ("Court")   127
  1. The Judges and Advocates-General   127
  2. The Task of the Advocates-General   128
  3. The Court's Jurisdiction   129
    (1) Finding that a Member State has failed to fulfil
        an obligation under the Treaties   130
    (2) Unlimited Jurisdiction with regard to Penalties
        provided for in Regulations   131
    (3) Review of the Legality of an Act and of the Failure of an
        Institution to Act   132
        (a) Appeal for Annulment   132
           (i)   Acts Submitted to the Control of Legality   133
           (ii) Who may Lodge an Appeal for Annulment?   133
           (iii) Grounds for Annulment   137
           (iv) Consequences of the Annulment of an Act
               by the Court   140
        (b) Appeal against Failure of an Institution to Act   141

(4) Preliminary Ruling 142
(5) Compensation for Damages caused by Institutions 149
(6) Union Industrial Property Rights 151
(7) The Objection of Illegality 151
(8) Other Cases within the Court's Jurisdiction 152
(9) European Investment Bank (EIB) and the European
    Central Bank (ECB) 153
(10) Attribution of Competence 154
(11) Appellate Jurisdiction 154
4. The Procedure 155
(1) The Written Procedure 156
(2) The Oral Procedure 159
(3) Costs 160
(4) Special Forms of Procedure 161
(5) Time Limit 165
II. The General Court (GC) 165
1. Members of the General Court 166
2. Jurisdiction 167
3. Procedure before the General Court 169
III. Specialised Courts/Judicial Panels—The Civil Service
Tribunal (CST) 169

Chapter Ten: The Court of Auditors 173
1. Members of the Court of Auditors 173
2. Tasks of the Court of Auditors 174

Chapter Eleven: The European Central Bank 176
1. The European System of Central Banks and the
   European Central Bank 176
2. Institutional Provisions concerning the ESCB and
   the ECB 176
3. Tasks of the ECB 177

Chapter Twelve: Other Bodies of the Union 180
1. The Economic and Social Committee (ESC) 180
2. The Committee of the Regions 181
3. The Scientific and Technical Committee of Euratom 182
4. Euratom's Supply Agency 182
5. The Group of the European Investment Bank (EIB) 182
(1) Task 182
(2) Procedure for Granting Loans or Guarantees 184
(3) Internal Structure of the EIB 185
6. The European Investment Fund 186
7. The European Body for the Enhancement of Judicial
   Co-operation (Eurojust) 186
8. The European Police Office (Europol) 187
9. The European Institute of Innovation and
   Technology (EIT) 188
10. The Economic and Financial Committee 188
11. The European Data Protection Supervisor 189

Chapter Thirteen: Decentralised Bodies of the Union   191
General Remarks   191
I   Decentralised Union Agencies   192
   1.   The European Centre for the Development of Vocational
        Training (Cedefop)   192
   2.   The European Foundation for the Improvement of Living and
        Working Conditions (Eurofound)   192
   3.   The European Environment Agency (EEA)   192
   4.   The European Training Foundation (ETF)   193
   5.   The European Monitoring Centre for Drugs and Drug
        Addiction (EMCDDA)   194
   6.   The European Medicines Agency (EMEA)   194
   7.   The Office for Harmonisation in the Internal Market
        (Trade Marks, Designs and Models) (OHIM)   195
   8.   Translation Centre for Bodies of the European Union (CDT)   196
   9.   The Union Plant Variety Office (CPVO)   197
   10.   The European Agency for Safety and Health at Work
        (COSHA)   197
   11.   The European Agency for Reconstruction (EAR)   198
   12.   The European Food Safety Authority (EFSA)   198
   13.   The European Maritime Safety Agency (EMSA)   199
   14.   The European Aviation Safety Agency (EASA)   199
   15.   The European Network and Information Security
        Agency (ENISA)   200
   16.   The European Centre for Disease Prevention and
        Control (ECDC)   200
   17.   The European Railway Agency (ERA)   201
   18.   The European GNSS (Global Navigation Satellite System)
        Supervisory Authority   201
   19.   The European Agency for the Management of Operational
        Co-operation at the External Borders of the Member States
        of the European Union (FRONTEX)   202
   20.   The Union of Fisheries Control Agency (CFCA)   202
   21.   The European Institute for Gender Equality   203
   22.   The European Chemicals Agency   203
   23.   The European Union Agency for Fundamental Rights   204
   24.   The European Institute for Innovation and Technology (EIT)   205
II   Union Agencies   205
   1.   The European Defence Agency (EDA)   205
   2.   The European Union Satellite Centre (EUSC)   206
   3.   The European Police College (CEPOL)   206
   4.   Eurojust (The European Body for the Enhancement of
        Judicial Co-operation)   207
   5.   The European Union Institute for Security Studies (ISS)   207
   6.   The European Police Office (Europol)   208
   7.   The Agency for Co-operation of Energy Regulators   208
III   Executive Agencies   209
   1.   The European Research Council Executive Agency (ERC)   209
   2.   The Trans-European Transport Network Executive Agency   209
   3.   The Education, Audio-Visual and Culture Executive Agency
        (EACEA)   210

    4. The Executive Agency for Competetiveness and Innovation
        (EACI)   210
    5. The Research Executive Agency (REA)   210
    6. The Executive Agency for Health and Consumers (formerly
        the Public Health Executive Agency)   211
IV Joint Undertakings and Other Structures   212
V   Inter-Institutional Office: The Publications Office   212

Chapter Fourteen: Financing Union Activities   214
    1. Financial Contributions of the Member States and the
        Union's own Resources   214
    2. The Union Budget, Revenue and Expenditure   216
        (1) Commitment and Payment Appropriations   217
        (2) Compulsory and Non-compulsory Expenditure   217
    3. Financial Framework and Inter-institutional Agreement   218
    4. Protection of the Union's Financial Interests   219

PART THREE: THE INTERNAL MARKET   221

Introduction   221

Chapter Fifteen: The Free Movement of Goods   223
    1. The Customs Union   224
        (1) Prohibition of Customs Duties and Charges having
             Equivalent Effect   225
        (2) The Common Customs Tariff (CCT)   225
    2. Prohibition of Quantitative Restrictions   227
    3. Prohibition of Discriminating or Protective Taxation   231
    4. Exceptions to the Free Movement of Goods   232
    5. Technical Standards   234
    6. Theory and Reality of the Free Movement of Goods   235

Chapter Sixteen: The Free Movement of Persons   238
Introduction   238
I   The Free Movement of Citizens   239
II The Free Movement of Workers   243
    1. Obstacles to the Free Movement of Workers and their
        Remedies   245
    2. Freedom of Movement of Workers after the 2004
        Enlargement   252
    3. Exceptions to the Free Movement of Workers   253
    4. Workers from Third Countries   254
III An Area of Freedom, Security and Justice—The Free
    Movement of Third-Country Nationals   255
    1. Policies on Border Checks, Asylum and
        Immigration   256
    2. Judicial Co-operation in Civil and Commercial
        Matters   258
    3. Judicial Co-operation in Criminal Matters   261
    4. Police Co-operation   263

IV The Free Movement of Students   264

Chapter Seventeen: Freedom of Establishment/Company Law   266
   1.   Introduction: Free Movement of Self-Employed
       Persons   266
   2.   Freedom of Establishment/Company Law   268
   3.   Students   270
   4.   Required Qualifications for Natural Persons   270
       (1) The "Regulated Professions"   272
             (i)   Doctors of Medicine   272
             (ii) Nurses responsible for general care   273
             (iii) Dental Practitioners   273
             (iv) Veterinary surgeons   273
             (v)   Midwives   273
             (vi) Pharmacists   274
             (vii) Architects   274
             (viii)Lawyers   274
       (2) The non-regulated Professions   275
       (3) Recognition of Professional Experience   277
   5.   Required Qualifications for Legal
       Persons/Company Law   278
       (1) The European Company: Societas Europaea (SE)   282
       (2) The European Co-operative Society   283
       (3) The Private European Company (Sociatas Privata
            Europaea)   283
   6.   Exceptions to the Freedom of Establishment   284

Chapter Eighteen: Freedom to Provide Services/Financial Services   286
   1.   Required Qualifications   287
   2.   Definition of "Services"   288
   3.   The Exceptions, the Directives and Companies and Firms   290
   4.   Financial Services (referred to in the Treaty as
       "Banking services")   291
   5.   Investment Services   293
   6.   Insurance   295
   7.   Future Developments   297

Chapter Nineteen: Free Movement of Capital and Payments   298

Chapter Twenty: Intellectual Property Rights (IPR)   301
   1.   Exhaustion   303
   2.   Patents   303
   3.   Copyrights and Related Rights   304
   4.   Trade marks   305
   5.   Community and Industrial Design   306
   6.   Counterfeit Goods and Piracy   307
   7.   Licensing   307
   8.   Protected Geographical Indications and Designations
       of Origin   308
   9.   International Treaties   308

Chapter Twenty-one: Public Procurement 309
1. Public Works, Public Supply and Public Services Contracts
   are regulated in a Single Directive 311
2. The Water, Electricity, Transport and Postal Services Sectors 314
3. The Remedies Directive 316

PART FOUR: OTHER UNION POLICIES 317

Chapter Twenty-two: Competition Policy 319
Introduction 319
I. Competition Rules Applying to Undertakings 319
1. Cartels (Agreements, Decisions of Associations of
   Undertakings and Concerted Practices) 320
   (1) The Prohibition 321
       (a) Agreements and Concerted Practices 321
       (b) Decisions by Associations of Undertakings 322
       (c) Undertakings 323
       (d) Which may affect Trade between Member States 324
       (e) "Which have as their object or effect" 325
       (f) "Prevention, restriction or distortion of
           competition" 325
       (g) "Within the internal market" 326
   (2) The Nullity 327
   (3) Exemptions from the Prohibition 328
       (a) Individual Exemptions 328
       (b) Exemptions for Categories of Agreements 329
           (i) Vertical Agreements and Concerted Practices 329
           (ii) Certain Categories of Vertical Agreement and
                Concerted Practices in the Motor Vehicle Sector 331
           (iii) Specialisation Agreements 332
           (iv) Research and Development Agreements 333
           (v) Technology Transfer Agreements 334
       (c) De Minimis 336
2. Abuse of a Dominant Position 337
   (1) Dominant Position/joint dominant position 337
   (2) Abuse 340
3. Competition Rules Applying to Various Branches of
   the Economy 341
   (1) Agriculture 341
   (2) Transport 342
       (a) Maritime Transport 342
       (b) Air Transport 343
       (c) International Aviation 344
       (d) Rail Transport 344
   (3) Telecommunications 345
   (4) Postal Service 347
   (5) Insurance—Financial Sector 349
   (6) Intellectual Property Rights 350
   (7) Energy 350
   (8) Coal and Steel 350

4. Implementation of the Rules on Competition 350
   (1) Role of the Member States and the European
       Competition Network 351
   (2) Role of the Commission 353
   (3) Limitation Periods 358
   (4) Hearings 358
   (5) Implementing Provisions 360
   (6) Consequences of the Entering into Force of the
       New Regulation for other Regulations in the
       Competition Field 363
5. Control of Concentrations—The Merger Regulation 363
   Joint or Colletive Dominance 365
6. Commission Notices of a General Nature 370
   (1) Exclusive Dealing Contracts made with Commercial
       Agents 370
   (2) Co-operation Agreements 370
   (3) Subcontracting Agreements 371
   (4) Agreements of Minor Importance 372
   (5) Access to the Files 372
7. Relationship between Union and National
   Competition Rules 373
8. International Co-operation 374
II. Competition Rules Applying to Member States 375
1. State Monopolies 375
2. Public Undertakings/Services of General Economic
   Interest 376
   Services of General Economic Interest 378
3. Aids Granted by States 379
   (1) The Notion of Aid 379
      (a) "advantage an undertaking" 379
      (b) "granted by a Member State or through State
          resources" 379
      (c) "specificity": Favour "certain" Undertakings or the
          Production of "certain" Goods 380
      (d) "distort competition and affect trade between
          Member States" 381
   (2) Aids Compatible or Declared Compatible with the
      Common Market 382
      (a) Regional Development Aids 383
      (b) Sectoral Aids 385
         (i) Shipbuilding 385
         (ii) Steel 385
         (iii) Coal 385
         (iv) Motor Vehicle Industry 386
         (v) Synthetic Fibre Industry 386
         (vi) Transport 387
         (vii) Agriculture and Fisheries 388
         (viii) Financial Sector 389
         (ix) Broadcasting 389
      (c) Horizontal Aids 389
         (i) R & D 390

(ii)   Employment and Training 390
(iii) Environment 390
(iv)   Small and Medium-Sized Enterprises 391
(v)   Rescue and Reconstruction 391
(vi)   Aid to Firms in Under-privileged Urban
       Areas 391
(vii) General Aid Schemes 392
(viii) Financial Transfers to Public Undertakings 392
(ix)   Direct Business Taxation 392
(x)   State Guarantees 392
(xi)   The State Aid Action Plan 393
(xii) The General Block Exemption Regulation 393
(xiii) Special Measures to Combat the 2008/2009
       World Crisis 394
   (d) Procedural Rules 394
   (e) Recovery of Aid 395
4. Competition Rules of the European Coal and Steel
    Community 397

Chapter Twenty-three: Agriculture 399
1. The Common Agricultural Policy (CAP) 401
   (1) A Bit of History: Mixed Results of the Successive
        Reforms of the CAP 402
   (2) The Single Common Market Organisation (CMO) 404
      (a) Plant Products 404
         (i)   Cereals 404
         (ii)   Wine 405
         (iii) Olive oil and table olives 405
         (iv)   Fresh fruit and vegetables 405
         (v)   Processed fruit and vegetables 406
         (vi)   Raw tobacco 406
         (vii) Sugar 406
         (viii) Rice 406
         (ix)   Cotton 406
         (x)   Hops 407
         (xi)   Bananas 407
      (b) Animal Products 407
         (i)   Milk and milk Products 407
         (ii)   Beef and veal 407
         (iii) Sheep-meat and goat-meat 408
         (iv)   Pig-meat 408
         (v)   Poultry-meat 408
         (vi)   Eggs 408
         (vii) Honey 408
   (3) The Structural Measures 409
      (a) Organic Farming 409
      (b) Genetically Modified Food and Feed 410
      (c) Food Safety 410
2. Rural Development 411
3. Financing the CAP and Rural Development 411

Chapter Twenty-four: The Common Fisheries Policy (CFP) and Marine Policy   414
  1. Access to Fishing Grounds   415
  2. Conservation of Fish Stocks   415
  3. Monitoring Fishing Activities   417
  4. Aquaculture   417
  5. The Common Organisation of the Market   418
  6. Agreements with Third Countries and International Conventions   419
  7. Structural Measures—The European Fisheries Fund   420
  8. Marine Environmental Policy   422

PART FIVE: POLICIES OF THE UNION AND THE MEMBER STATES   423

Chapter Twenty-five: Taxation   425
  1. Indirect taxation   427
    (1) Value Added Tax (VAT)   427
    (2) Excise Duties   428
  2. Direct taxes   430

Chapter Twenty-six: Approximation of Laws   434

Chapter Twenty-seven: Transport   438
Introduction   438
  1. New European Transport Policy: Adapt the Mobility System to New Challenges   439
  2. Special Features of Transport   440
  3. Application of Competition Rules to Transport   443
  4. Road transport   443
  5. Rail transport   446
  6. Air transport   449
    (1) Single European Skye   451
    (2) Safety Assessment of Foreign Aircraft (SAFA)   453
    (3) International Agreements   453
  7. Inland waterway transport   454
  8. Maritime transport   454
  9. Intermodality   457
  10. Trans-European Transport Network   457
  11. Conclusion with Regard to a "Common Transport Policy"   458

Chapter Twenty-eight: Economic and Monetary Union (Policy) 459
  1. Economic Policy   460
    (1) Co-ordination of the Economic Policies of the Member States   461
    (2) Excessive Government Deficits   462
    (3) Prohibition of "overdraft facilities" and "privileged access to financial institutions"   463
  2. Monetary Policy   463
  3. Provisions specific to Member States whose Currency is the Euro—the Euro Group   464
  4. Institutional Provisions   465

5. Transitional Provisions 465
6. Stability and Growth Pact 466
   (1) The Strengthening of Budgetary Surveillance and
       Co-ordination of Economic Policies 466
   (2) Speeding up and Clarifying the Implementation of
       the Excessive Deficit Procedure 467
   (3) Global Financial Crisis and the Stability and Growth Pact 468
   (4) The European Response to the Financial Crises 468

Chapter Twenty-nine: Social Policy and Education 470
1. Social Provisions 471
   (1) Union Action Supporting and Complementing
       Member States' Activities 472
   (2) Consultation of Management and Labour 475
   (3) Encouraging Co-operation between the Member
       States and Facilitating Co-ordination of their Action 476
   (4) The Principle of Equal Opportunity and Equal
       Treatment of Men and Women 477
       Equal Pay 478
2. The European Social Fund 479
3. Education, Vocational Training, Youth and Sports 480
   (1) Education 480
   (2) Vocational Training 483
   (3) Youth 484
   (4) Sports 484
4. Employment 485
5. The Social Agenda (2005–2010) 486

Chapter Thirty: Culture, Public Health, Consumer Protection 487
1. Culture 488
   Culture and Audio-visual Media 489
   Culture and Regional Development 489
   Culture and Research and Technological Development 489
   Culture and Agriculture 489
   Culture and the Information Society 490
   Culture and the Environment 490
2. Public Health 491
   (1) Food Safety 494
   (2) Medicinal Products 495
3. Consumer Protection 496
   Product Liability 497
   Protection of Personal Data 500

Chapter Thirty-one: Enterprise and Industrial Policy/Information Society 502
General Remarks 502
1. The Lisbon Strategy/Programme 502
2. Industrial Policy 504
   Promoting Open Standards 507
3. Information Society 507
   (1) Implementation of the Information Society Policies 508
       (a) The Internet 508

(b) The i2010   508
(c) Telecommunications   509
(d) Electronic Commerce   511
(e) Information Society Technology (IST)   511
(f) Protection of Personal Data   511
(g) Network Security   512
(h) International Dimension   512
(2) Framework Programmes   512
4. Enterprise Policy—(Micro) Small and Medium-Sized
    Enterprises (SMEs)   513
5. Trans-European Networks   515
6. Judicial Co-operation in Civil and Commercial Matters 517

Chapter Thirty-two: Regional Policy/Economic, Social and
Territorial Cohesion   519
Generalities   519
1. Structural Operations   522
2. Objectives of the Structural Funds   523
3. Allocation of Financial Support   524
    (1) Convergence Objective   525
    (2) Regional Competitiveness and Employment Objective 525
    (3) European Territorial Co-operation Objective   525
    (4) Specific Types of Areas   526
4. Eligibility   526
        (i)   Additionality   526
        (ii)   Consistency   526
        (iii) Co-ordination   526
        (iv)   Programmes   527
        (v)   Partnership   527
        (vi)   Global Resources   527
        (vii) Reporting   528
        (viii) Rates of Assistance   528
        (ix)   Administration and Financial Management of
               Structural Funds   528
5. The Cohesion Fund   529

Chapter Thirty-three: Research and Technological Development
and Space   530
1. Introduction   530
2. The Seventh Framework Programme (2007–2013)   531
3. The European Research Area   534
4. The European Space Policy   535
5. Co-operation with Third Countries   536
6. Dissemination of Results   537
7. The Joint Research Centre (JRC)   537

Chapter Thirty-four: Environment   540
1. The Treaty Provisions   540
2. Guiding Principles   541
3. Environmental Action Programmes   543
4. The Sixth Environmental Action Programme   543

5. Civil Liability 548
6. Protection of the Environment through Criminal Law 549
7. External Co-operation 549
8. The European Environmental Agency 550
9. Financial Instruments 550
10. Competition 551

Chapter Thirty-five: Energy Policy 552
1. Security of Energy Supply and International Co-operation 553
2. Integrating Energy Markets 555
3. Promoting Energy Technology Development 556
4. Sectoral Aspects 556
5. Nuclear Energy—Euratom's Supply Agency and Safeguards 558
6. Nuclear Safety 560

**PART SIX: EXTERNAL ACTION BY THE UNION, THE COMMON
FOREIGN AND SECURITY POLICY AND ENLARGEMENT** 561

Introduction 561

**Chapter Thirty-six: General Provisions concerning the Union's
External Action** 563
Co-operation with Third Countries and Humanitarian Aid 567
I   Economic, Financial and Technical Co-operation with
     Third Countries
II   Humanitarian Aid 568
III Restrictive Measures 569
IV   International Agreements 569
V   The Union's Relations with International Organisations
     and Third Countries and the Union's Delegations 572
VI   Solidarity Clause 573
VII The European Neighbourhood Policy (ENP) 573

Chapter Thirty-seven: The Common Foreign and Security Policy (CFSP) 575
1. The Common Security and Defence Policy (CSDP) 577
2. The High Representative 579

**Chapter Thirty-eight: Common Commercial Policy and Relations
with Third Countries** 580
General Principles 580
1. Commercial Policy Instruments and Import and
   Export Arrangements 582
   (1) Liberalisation and Export Policy 582
   (2) Measures to Protect Trade 583
2. Relations with Other European Countries 585
   (1) The European Economic Area (EEA) 585
   (2) Other European Countries 586
   (3) Central and Eastern European Countries (CEECs) 586
   (4) The New Independent States (NIS) 587

3. Relations with Major Industrialised Countries 587
    (1) The United States 587
    (2) Canada 589
    (3) Japan 590
    (4) Russia 591
    (5) China 591
    (6) Australia 592
    (7) New Zealand 592
4. Relations with Mediterranean Countries 593
5. Relations with Asia 594
    (1) South Korea 595
    (2) India 595
    (3) Other Asian Countries 596
6. Latin-America 596
7. Africa 597
8. Euratom's External Relations 597
9. Multilateral Relations 598
    (1) GATT 598
    (2) The World Trade Organisation (WTO) 598
    (3) The Doha Negotiations for a New Round 598

Chapter Thirty-nine: Development Co-operation 600
1. General Remarks 600
2. Relations with the African, Caribbean and Pacific
    Countries (ACP) 604
3. Association of the Overseas Countries and Territories (OCT) 608

Chapter Forty: Enlargement 609
1. Financial and Economic Assistance 610
2. Candidate Countries 610
    (1) Turkey 610
    (2) Croatia 611
    (3) Macedonia (former Yugoslav Republic of) 612
    (4) Iceland 613
2. Potential Candidate Countries 613
    (1) Albania 613
    (2) Bosnia and Herzegovina 614
    (3) Serbia and Montenegro 615
         (a) Montenegro 615
         (b) Serbia 616

Index 617

Table of Cases

Court of Justice (ECJ) of the European Union
Chronological List of Cases

3/54 Associazione Industrie Siderurgiche Italiane (ASSIDER) v High Authority of the European Coal and Steel Community [1954–1955] E.C.R. 63 ECJ 54, 140

4/54 Industrie Siderurgiche Associate (ISA) v High Authority of the European Coal and Steel Community [1954–56] E.C.R. 91 37

6/54 Netherlands v High Authority [1954–56] E.C.R. 103 67

8/55 Fédération Charbonnière de Belgique v High Authority [1954–1956] E.C.R. 245 . . . . 94, 138

7/56, 3/57, 4/57, 5/57, 6/57 and 7/57 Algera v Common Assembly [1957–1958] E.C.R. 39 ECJ 54

9/56 Meroni & Co., Industrie Metallurgiche, SpA v High Authority of the European Coal and Steel Community [1957 and 1958] E.C.R. 133 . . . . 115, 151

15/57 Compagnie des Hauts Fourneaux de Chasse v High Authority of the European Coal and Steel Community [1957–1958] E.C.R. 211 151

18/57 Firme J Nold KG v High Authority of the European Coal and Steel Community [1959] E.C.R. 41 ECJ 37, 54

1/58 Friedrich Stork & Cie v High Authority of the European Coal and Steel Community [1959] E.C.R. 17 54

36/59–38/59 and 40/59 Geitling v High Authority [1960] E.C.R. 423 . . . . 36, 54

43/59, 45/59 and 48/59 Eva von Lachmüller, Bernard Peuvrier, Roger Ehrhardt v Commission of the European Economic Community [1960] E.C.R. 463 59

10/61 Commission of the European Economic Community v Italy; sub nom. Italian Customs Duties on Radio Valves, Re [1962] E.C.R. 1; [1962] C.M.L.R. 187 ECJ 53

17/61 and 20/61 Klöckner-Werke AG and Hoesch AG v High Authority of the European Coal and Steel Community [1962] E.C.R. 325 54

16/62 Confederation Nationale des Producteurs de Fruits et Legumes v Council of the European Economic Community [1962] E.C.R. 471; [1963] C.M.L.R. 160 ECJ 30, 137

24/62 Germany v Commission of the European Economic Community; sub nom. Tariff Quota on Wine, Re [1963] E.C.R. 63; [1963] C.M.L.R. 347 ECJ 36

25/62 Plaumann & Co v Commission of the European Economic Community [1963] E.C.R. 95; [1964] C.M.L.R. 29 ECJ . . . 135, 149

26/62 NV Algemene Transport- en Expeditie Onderneming van Gend en Loos v Nederlandse Administratie der Belastingen [1963] E.C.R. 1; [1963] C.M.L.R. 105 ECJ 8, 9, 42, 225

28/63 Koninklijke Nederlandsche Hoogovens en Staalfabrieken NV v High Authority of the European Coal and Steel Community [1963] E.C.R. 231; [1964] C.M.L.R. 125 ECJ . . . 34, 36

73/63 NV Internationale Credieten Handelsvereniging Rotterdam v Minister van Landbouw en Visserij [1964] E.C.R. 1; [1964] C.M.L.R. 198 ECJ 37

75/63 Unger v Bestuur der Bedrijfsvereniging voor Detailhandel en Ambachten [1964] E.C.R. 177; [1964] C.M.L.R. 319 ECJ 143

90/63 Commission of the European Economic Community v Belgium; sub nom. Import of Milk Products, Re [1964] E.C.R. 625; [1965] C.M.L.R. 58 ECJ 111, 138

101/63 Wagner v Fohrmann [1964] E.C.R. 383; [1964] E.C.R. 195; [1964] C.M.L.R. 245 ECJ 83

6/64 Costa v Ente Nazionale per l'Energia Elettrica (ENEL) [1964] E.C.R. 585; [1964] C.M.L.R. 425 ECJ 8, 42, 44, 48, 142, 143, 145

56/64 and 58/64 Etablissements Consten Sarl v Commission of the European Economic Community; Grundig-Verkaufs GmbH v Commission of the European Economic Community [1966] E.C.R. 299; [1966] C.M.L.R. 418 ECJ 228, 324, 325, 328

9/65 and 58/65 Acciaierie San Michele SpA (in liquidation) v High Authority ofthe ECSC [1967] E.C.R. 1 48

56/65 Société Technique Minière v Maschinenbau Ulm GmbH [1966] E.C.R. 235; [1966] C.M.L.R. 357 ECJ 321, 324, 325, 326

61/65 Vaassen (nee Gobbels) v Beambtenfonds voor het Mijnbedrijf [1966] E.C.R. 261; [1966] C.M.L.R. 508 ECJ 144

24/67 Parke Davis & Co v Probel [1968] E.C.R. 55; [1968] C.M.L.R. 47; [1968] F.S.R. 393 ECJ 301, 302

27/67 Firma Fink-Frucht GmbH v Hauptzollamt München-Landsbergerstrasse [1968] E.C.R. 223; [1968] C.M.L.R. 187 425

28/67 Molkerei-Zentrale Westfalen/Lippe GmbH v Hauptzollamt Paderborn [1968] E.C.R. 143; [1968] C.M.L.R. 187 ECJ 45, 142, 426

7/68 Commission of the European Communities v Italy; sub nom. Export Tax on Art Treasures, Re [1968] E.C.R. 423; [1969] C.M.L.R. 1 ECJ 224, 232

14/68 Wilhelm v Bundeskartellamt [1969] E.C.R. 1; [1969] C.M.L.R. 100 ECJ 37

1/69 Italy v Commission of the European Communities; sub nom. Preferential Freight Rates, Re [1969] E.C.R. 277; [1970] C.M.L.R. 17 ECJ 36

5/69 Volk v Etablissements J Vervaecke SPRL [1969] E.C.R. 295; [1969] C.M.L.R. 273 ECJ 143, 326

6/69 Commission of the European Communities v France; sub nom. Export Credits, Re [1969] E.C.R. 523; [1970] C.M.L.R. 43 ECJ 137

41/69 ACF Chemiefarma v Commission of the European Communities [1970] E.C.R. 661 ECJ 67, 94, 322

43/69 Brauerei A Bilger Sohne GmbH v Jehle [1970] E.C.R. 127; [1974] 1 C.M.L.R. 382 ECJ 324

48/69 Imperial Chemical Industries (ICI) Ltd v Commission of the European Communities [1972] E.C.R. 619; [1972] C.M.L.R. 557 ECJ 322, 324

77/69 Commission of the European Communities v Belgium; sub nom. Stamp Tax on Timber, Re [1970] E.C.R. 237; [1974] 1 C.M.L.R. 203 ECJ 425

817/69 Buyl v Commission of the European Communities [1982] E.C.R. 245 67

9/70 Grad v Finanzamt Traunstein [1970] E.C.R. 825; [1971] C.M.L.R. 1 ECJ 32, 34

11/70, 25/70, 26/70 and 30/70 Internationale Handelsgesellschaft mbH v Einfuhr- und Vorratsstelle fur Getreide und Futtermittel; Einfuhr und Vorratsstelle fur Getreide und Futtermittel v Firma Koster, Berodt & Co; Einfuhr und Vorratsstelle fur Getreide und Futtermittel v Firma Gunther Henck; Firma Ottoscheer v Einfuhr und Vorratsstelle fur Getreide und Futtermittel [1970] E.C.R. 1125; [1972] C.M.L.R. 255 ECJ 48, 53, 115

73/74 Groupement des Fabricants de Papiers Peints de Belgique v Commission of the European Communities [1976] E.C.R. 1491; [1975] E.C.R. 1491; [1976] 1 C.M.L.R. 589 ECJ 36

3/75 RI Johnson & Firth Brown v Commission of the European Communities [1975] E.C.R. 1; [1975] 1 C.M.L.R. 638 ECJ ... 162, 163

32/75 Fiorini v Societe Nationale des Chemins de Fer Francais; Cristini (Anita) v Societe Nationale des Chemins de Fer Francais (SNCF); sub nom. Fiorini v SNCF [1975] E.C.R. 1085; [1976] 1 C.M.L.R. 573 ECJ 249

36/75 Rutili v Ministre de l'Iinterieur [1975] E.C.R. 1219; [1976] 1 C.M.L.R. 140 ECJ ... 246, 253

38/75 Douaneagent der NV Nederlandse Spoorwegen v Inspector der Invoerrechten en Accijnzen [1976] E.C.R. 1439; [1975] E.C.R. 1439 ECJ 255, 566

43/75 Defrenne v SA Belge de Navigation Aerienne (SABENA); sub nom. Defrenne v SABENA [1981] 1 All E.R. 122; [1976] E.C.R. 455; [1976] 2 C.M.L.R. 98 ECJ 44, 45, 141, 478

48/75 Belgium v Royer; sub nom. Procureur du Roi v Royer [1976] E.C.R. 497; [1976] 2 C.M.L.R. 619 ECJ 238, 244, 247

51/75, 86/75 and 96/75 EMI Records Ltd v CBS United Kingdom Ltd; EMI v CBS Grammofon A/S; EMI v CBS Schallplatten GmbH [1976] E.C.R. 811; [1976] 2 C.M.L.R. 235 ECJ 303

86/75 EMI Records Ltd v CBS Grammofon A/S [1976] E.C.R. 871 303

87/75 Conceria Daniele Bresciani v Amministrazione delle Finanze [1976] E.C.R. 129; [1976] 2 C.M.L.R. 62 ECJ 570

96/75 EMI Records Ltd v CBS Schallplatten GmbH [1976] A.C.R. 913 303

104/75 Officier van Justitie v De Peijper; sub nom. De Peijper (Managing Director of Centrafarm BV), Re [1976] E.C.R. 613; [1976] 2 C.M.L.R. 271 ECJ 232

111/75 Impresa Costruzioni Comm Quirino Mazzalai v Ferrovia Del Renon [1976] E.C.R. 657; [1977] 1 C.M.L.R. 105 ECJ 32

118/75 Italy v Watson and Belmann [1976] E.C.R. 1185; [1976] 2 C.M.L.R. 552 ECJ 244, 247

119/75 Terrapin (Overseas) Ltd v Terranova Industrie CA Kapferer & Co [1975] E.C.R. 1039; [1976] E.C.R. 1039 ECJ ... 301, 302, 303

10/76 Public Works Directive 1971, Re; sub nom. Commission of the European Communities v Italy [1976] E.C.R. 1359; [1976] 2 C.M.L.R. 699 ECJ 313

13/76 Dona v Mantero [1976] E.C.R. 1333; [1976] 2 C.M.L.R. 578 ECJ 248

20/76 Schottle & Sohne OHG v Finanzamt Freudenstadt [1977] E.C.R. 247; [1977] 2 C.M.L.R. 98 ECJ 425

27/76 United Brands Co v Commission of the European Communities [1978] E.C.R. 207; [1978] 1 C.M.L.R. 429 ECJ ... 132, 324, 339

33/76 Rewe Zentralfinanz eG v Landwirtschaftskammer fur das Saarland [1976] E.C.R. 1989; [1977] 1 C.M.L.R. 533 ECJ ... 44, 45, 55, 56, 143, 231

41/76 Criel v Procureur de la République au Tribunal de Grande Instance (Lille) [1976] E.C.R. 1921; [1977] 2 C.M.L.R. 535 ECJ 581

46/76 Bauhuis v Netherlands [1977] E.C.R. 5 ECJ 230

51/76 Verbond van Nederlandse Ondernemingen v Inspecteur der Invoerrechten en Accijnzen; sub nom. Federation of Dutch Industries v Inspector of Customs and Excise [1977] E.C.R. 113; [1977] 1 C.M.L.R. 413 ECJ ... 32, 50

74/76 and 78/76 Iannelli & Volpi SpA v Ditta Paolo Meroni; Firma Steinike und Weinlig v Bundesamt fur Ernahrung und Forstwirtschaft [1977] E.C.R. 595; [1977] E.C.R. 557; [1977] 2 C.M.L.R. 688 ECJ 381

76/76 Di Paolo v Office National de l'Emploi [1977] E.C.R. 315; [1977] 2 C.M.L.R. 59 ECJ 251

83/76 Bayerische HNL Vermehrungsbetriebe GmbH & Co KG v Commission of the European Communities [1978] E.C.R. 1209; [1978] 3 C.M.L.R. 566 ECJ 33, 149, 150

85/76 F Hoffmann La Roche & Co AG v Commission of the European Communities [1979] E.C.R. 461; [1979] 3 C.M.L.R. 211; [1980] F.S.R. 13 ECJ 322, 324, 339, 340, 359

89/76 Commission of the European Communities v Netherlands; sub nom. Inspection Fees on Exported Plants, Re [1977] E.C.R. 1355; [1978] 3 C.M.L.R. 630 ECJ 225

107/76 F Hoffmann La Roche & Co AG v Centrafarm Vertriebsgesellschaft Pharmazeutischer Erzeugnisse mbH [1977] E.C.R. 957; [1977] 2 C.M.L.R. 334 ECJ 146

126/76 Firma Gebruder Dietz v Commission of the European Communities (No.1); sub nom. Firma Dietz Gebr v Commission of the European Communities (No.1) [1977] E.C.R. 2431; [1978] 2 C.M.L.R. 608 ECJ 150

5/77 Tedeschi v Denkavit Commerciale Srl [1977] E.C.R. 1555; [1978] 1 C.M.L.R. 1 ECJ ... 145, 233

31/77 Pig Production Subsidies, Re; sub nom. Commission of the European Communities v United Kingdom [1977] E.C.R. 921; [1977] 2 C.M.L.R. 359 ECJ 163

35/77 Beerens v Rijksdienst voor Arbiedsvoorziening; sub nom. Ermin v Rijksdienst voor Arbeidsvoorziening [1977] E.C.R. 2249; [1978] 2 C.M.L.R. 320 ECJ 251

38/77 Enka BV v Inspecteur der Invoerrechten en Accijnzen [1977] E.C.R. 2203; [1978] 2 C.M.L.R. 212 ECJ 50

41/77 R. v National Insurance Commissioner Ex p. Warry; sub nom. R. v National Insurance Commissioner Ex p. Insurance Officer [1978] Q.B. 607; [1978] 3 W.L.R. 99; [1977] E.C.R. 2085 ECJ 251

58/77 Ireland v France [1977] O.J. C142/8 130

61/77 Commission of the European Communities v Ireland; sub nom. Sea Fishery Restrictions, Re [1978] E.C.R. 417; [1978] 2 C.M.L.R. 466 ECJ 49, 163

65/77 Razanatsimba, Re [1977] E.C.R. 2229; [1978] 1 C.M.L.R. 246 ECJ 570

75/77 Mollet v Commission of the European Communities [1978] E.C.R. 897 ECJ 36

77/77 Benzine en Petroleum Handelsmaatschappij BV v Commission of the European Communities [1978] E.C.R. 1513; [1978] 3 C.M.L.R. 174 ECJ 134

80/77 and 81/77 Societe Les Commissionnaires Reunis Sarl v Receveur des Douanes; Les Fils de Henri Ramel v Receveur des Douanes [1978] E.C.R. 927 ECJ 223

82/77 Openbaar Ministerie v Van Tiggele [1978] E.C.R. 25; [1978] 2 C.M.L.R. 528 ECJ 227

106/77 Amministrazione delle Finanze dello Stato v Simmenthal SpA; sub nom. Italian Tax and Revenue Administration v SA Simmenthal, Monza (Italy) [1978] E.C.R. 629; [1978] 3 C.M.L.R. 263 .... 49, 140

113/77 NTN Toyo Bearing Co Ltd v Council of Ministers of the European Communites (No.1); sub nom. Japanese Bearings Cases; NTN Toyo Bearing Co Ltd v Commission of the European Communities [1977] E.C.R. 1721 ECJ 162, 163

142/77 Statens Kontrol med Aedle Metaller v Larsen [1978] E.C.R. 1543; [1979] 2 C.M.L.R. 680 ECJ 232, 425

3/78 Centrafarm BV v American Home Products Corp [1978] E.C.R. 1823; [1979] 1 C.M.L.R. 326 ECJ 302

7/78 R. v Thompson (Ernest George); R. v Johnson (Brian Albert); R. v Woodiwiss (Colin Alex) [1980] Q.B. 229; [1980] 2 W.L.R. 521; [1978] E.C.R. 2247; [1979] E.C.R. 2247 ECJ ... 232, 299

13/78 Firma Joh Eggers Sohn & Co v Freie Hansestadt Bremen [1978] E.C.R. 1935; [1979] 1 C.M.L.R. 562 ECJ 309

21/78 Delkvist v Anklagemyndigheden Ex p. Landsnaevuet for Omnibuskorsel [1978] E.C.R. 2327; [1979] R.T.R. 161; [1979] 1 C.M.L.R. 372 ECJ 45

30/78 Distillers Co Ltd v Commission of the European Communities [1980] E.C.R. 2229; [1980] 3 C.M.L.R. 121; [1980] F.S.R. 589 ECJ 326

83/78 Pigs Marketing Board (Northern Ireland) v Redmond [1978] E.C.R. 2347; [1979] 1 C.M.L.R. 177 ECJ ... 323, 375, 400

92/78 Simmenthal SpA v Commission of the European Communities [1979] E.C.R. 777; [1980] 1 C.M.L.R. 25 ECJ 140, 151

98/78 Firma A Racke v Hauptzollamt Mainz [1979] E.C.R. 69 ECJ 37

99/78 Weingut Gustav Decker AG v Hauptzollamt Landau [1979] E.C.R. 101 ECJ 37

101/78 Granaria BV v Hoofdproduktschap voor Akkerbouwprodukten [1979] E.C.R. 623; [1979] 3 C.M.L.R. 124 ECJ 150

110/78 and 111/78 Ministère Public and Chambre Syndicale des Agents Artistiques et Impresarii de Belgique Asbl v van Wesemael and Poupaert; Ministere Public, Chambre Syndicale des Agents Artistiques et Impresarii de Belgique Asbl v Follachio and Leduc [1979] E.C.R. 35; [1979] 3 C.M.L.R. 87 ECJ 143, 290

115/78 Knoors v Secretary of State for Economic Affairs [1979] E.C.R. 399; [1979] 2 C.M.L.R. 357 ECJ 267

120/78 Rewe-Zentral AG v Bundesmonopolverwaltung für Branntwein; sub nom. Cassis de Dijon, Re [1979] E.C.R. 649; [1979] 3 C.M.L.R. 494 ECJ 228, 229, 230, 267, 275, 436

122/78 Buitoni SA v Fonds d'Orientation et de Regularisation des Marches Agricoles [1979] E.C.R. 677; [1979] 2 C.M.L.R. 665 ECJ 139

128/78 Tachographs, Re; sub nom. Commission of the European Communities v United Kingdom [1979] E.C.R. 419; [1979] R.T.R. 321; [1979] 2 C.M.L.R. 45 ECJ 30, 47, 48

130/78 Salumificio di Cornuda SpA v Amministrazione delle Finanze dello Stato [1979] E.C.R. 867; [1979] 3 C.M.L.R. 561 ECJ 37

141/78 Fishing Net Mesh Sizes, Re); sub nom. France (Commission of the European Communities intervening) v United Kingdom [1979] E.C.R. 2923; [1980] 1 C.M.L.R. 6 ECJ ... 130, 414

159/78 Customs Agents, Re; sub nom. Commission of the European Communities v Italy [1979] E.C.R. 3247; [1980] 3 C.M.L.R. 446 .... 49, 54

168/78 Commission of the European Communities v France; sub nom. French Taxation of Spirits, Re [1980] E.C.R. 347; [1981] 2 C.M.L.R. 631 ECJ 426

169/78 Commission of the European Communities v Italy; sub nom. Italian Taxation of Spirits, Re [1980] E.C.R. 385; [1981] 2 C.M.L.R. 673 ECJ 231, 232

175/78 R. v Saunders (Vera Ann) [1980] Q.B. 72; [1979] 3 W.L.R. 359; [1979] E.C.R. 1129 ECJ ... 239

209/78 Heintz van Landewyck Sarl v Commission of the European Communities [1980] E.C.R. 3125; [1981] 3 C.M.L.R. 134 ECJ 321, 322

230/78 SpA Eridania-Zuccherifici Nazionali SpA and Societa Italiana per l'Industria degli Zuccheri SpA Minister of Agriculture and Forestry, Minister for Industry, Trade and Craft and Zuccherifici Meridionali SpA [1979] E.C.R. 2749 ECJ 31, 49

251/78 Denkavit Futtermittel GmbH v Minister fur Ernahrung, Landwirtschaft und Forsten des Landes Nordrhein-Westfalen [1979] E.C.R. 3369; [1980] 3 C.M.L.R. 513 ECJ 230

268/78 Pennartz v Caisse Primaire d'Assurance Maladie des Alpes-Maritimes [1979] E.C.R. 2411; [1980] 1 C.M.L.R. 682 ECJ 251

3/76, 4/76 and 6/76 Officier van Justitie v Kramer; Officier van Justitie v Van Den Berg; Officier van Justitie v Kramer en Bais & Co [1976] E.C.R. 1279; [1976] 2 C.M.L.R. 440 ECJ 565, 566

9/79 Worsdorfer (nee Koschniske) v Raad van Arbeid [1979] E.C.R. 2717; [1980] 1 C.M.L.R. 87 ECJ 37

16/79–20/79 Criminal proceedings against Joseph Danis [1979] E.C.R. 3327 230

33/79 and 75/79 Richard Kuhner v Commission of the European Communities [1980] E.C.R. 1677 140

34/79 R. v Henn (Maurice Donald); R.v Darby (John Frederick) [1980] 2 W.L.R. 597; [1979] E.C.R. 3795; [1980] 1 C.M.L.R. 246 ECJ 139, 232

44/79 Hauer v Land Rheinland-Pfalz [1979] E.C.R. 3727; [1980] 3 C.M.L.R. 42 ECJ 53

52/79 Procureur du Roi v Debauve [1980] E.C.R. 833; [1981] 2 C.M.L.R. 362 ECJ 44, 289, 291

53/79 Office National des Pensions pour Travailleurs Salaries v Damiani [1980] E.C.R. 273; [1981] 1 C.M.L.R. 548 ECJ 143

61/79 Amministrazione delle Finanze dello Stato v Denkavit Italiana Srl [1980] E.C.R. 1205; [1981] 3 C.M.L.R. 694 ECJ 144, 379

69/79 Jordens-Vosters v Bestuur van de Bedrijfsvereniging voor de Leder- en Lederverwerkende Industrie [1980] E.C.R. 75; [1980] 3 C.M.L.R. 412 ECJ 251

91/79 Commission of the European Communities v Italy; sub nom. Detergents Directive, Re [1980] E.C.R. 1099; [1981] 1 C.M.L.R. 331 ECJ 540

95/79 and C-96/79 Procureur du Roi v Kefer; Procureur du Roi v Delmelle [1980] E.C.R. 103; [1982] 2 C.M.L.R. 77 ECJ 143

98/79 Pecastaing v Belgium [1981] E.C.R. 691; [1980] E.C.R. 691; [1980] 3 C.M.L.R. 685 ECJ 253

99/79 Lancôme SA v Etos BV; Cosparfrance Nederland BV v Albert Heijn Supermart BV [1981] E.C.R. 2511; [1980] E.C.R. 2511; [1981] 2 C.M.L.R. 164 ECJ 326

104/79 Foglia v Novello [1981] E.C.R. 745; [1980] E.C.R. 745; [1981] 1 C.M.L.R. 45 ECJ 143

106/79 Vereeniging ter Bevordering van de Belangen des Boekhandels v Eldi Records BV [1980] E.C.R. 1137; [1980] 3 C.M.L.R. 719 ECJ 143

108/79 Salvatore Belfiore v Commission of the European Communities [1980] E.C.R. 1769 158

138/79 Roquette Frères SA v Council of Ministers of the European Communities 1980] E.C.R. 3333 ECJ 68, 80

139/79 Maizena GmbH v Council of Ministers of the European Communities [1980] E.C.R. 3393 ECJ 68, 80, 138, 158

140/79 Chemial Farmaceutici SpA v DAF SpA [1981] E.C.R. 1; [1981] 3 C.M.L.R. 350 ECJ 426

145/79 Roquette Frères SA v French State Customs Administration [1980] E.C.R. 2917 ECJ . . . 144

155/79 Australian Mining & Smelting Europe Ltd v Commission of the European Communities; sub nom. AM&S Europe Ltd v Commission of the European Communities [1983] Q.B. 878; [1983] 3 W.L.R. 17; [1982] E.C.R. 1575 ECJ 354

730/79 Philip Morris Holland BV v Commission of the European Communities [1980] E.C.R. 2671; [1981] 2 C.M.L.R. 321 ECJ 137, 381

789/79 and 790/79 Calpak SpA v Commission of the European Communities; Societa Emiliana Lavorazione SpA v Commission of the European Communities [1980] E.C.R. 1949; [1981] 1 C.M.L.R. 26 ECJ 30

792/79 R Camera Care Ltd v Commission of the European Communities [1980] E.C.R. 119; [1981] E.C.R. 119; [1980] 1 C.M.L.R. 334 ECJ 353

811/79 Amministrazione delle Finanze dello Stato v Ariete SpA, Rome [1981] E.C.R. 2545; [1980] E.C.R. 2545; [1981] 1 C.M.L.R. 316 ECJ 143

27/80 Criminal Proceedings against Fietje; sub nom. Fietje, Re [1980] E.C.R. 3839; [1981] 3 C.M.L.R. 722 ECJ 126, 230

31/80 L'Oreal NV v De Nieuwe AMCK PVBA [1980] E.C.R. 3775; [1981] 2 C.M.L.R. 235 ECJ 339

53/80 Officier van Justitie v Koninblijke Kaasfabriek Eyssen BV [1981] E.C.R. 409; [1982] 2 C.M.L.R. 20 ECJ 230

55/80 Musik-Vertrieb Membran GmbH v GEMA; sub nom. Musik-Vertrieb Membran GmbH v Gesellschaft fur Musikalische Auffuhrungs- und Mechanische Vervielfaltigungsrechte (GEMA) [1981] E.C.R. 147; [1981] 2 C.M.L.R. 44 ECJ 304

58/80 Dansk Supermarked A/S v Imerco A/S [1981] E.C.R. 181; [1981] 3 C.M.L.R. 590 ECJ 229

66/80 International Chemical Corp SpA v Amministrazione delle Finanze dello Stato [1981] E.C.R. 1191; [1983] 2 C.M.L.R. 593 ECJ 144

96/80 Jenkins v Kingsgate (Clothing Productions) Ltd [1981] 1 W.L.R. 972; [1981] E.C.R. 911; [1981] 2 C.M.L.R. 24 ECJ 245

100/80, 103/80 and 101/80 Musique Diffusion Francaise SA v Commission of the European Communities; Pioneer High Fidelity (GB) Ltd v Commission of the European Communities; Pioneer Electronic (Europe) NV v Commission of the European Communities (102/80); C Melchers & Co v Commission of the European Communities [1983] E.C.R. 1825; [1983] 3 C.M.L.R. 221 ECJ 321

126/80 Salonia v Poidamani; Salonia v Baglieri (nee Giglio) [1981] E.C.R. 1563; [1982] 1 C.M.L.R. 64 ECJ 145

130/80 Criminal proceedings against Fabriek voor Hoogwaardige Voedingsprodukten Kelderman BV [1981] E.C.R. 527 230

138/80 Borker, Re [1980] E.C.R. 1975; [1980] 3 C.M.L.R. 638 ECJ 144

155/80 Oebel, Re [1981] E.C.R. 1993; [1983] 1 C.M.L.R. 390 ECJ 229

158/80 Rewe-Handelsgesellschaft Nord mbH v Hauptzollamt Kiel; Rewe Markt Steffen v Hauptzollamt Kiel [1981] E.C.R. 1805; [1982] 1 C.M.L.R. 449 ECJ 37

188/80 France v Commission of the European Communities; sub nom. Public Undertakings, Re [1982] E.C.R. 2545; [1982] 3 C.M.L.R. 144 ECJ 114

197–200, 243 245, and 247/80 Ludwigshafener Walzmühle Erling KG v Council and Commission of the European Communities [1981] E.C.R. 3211 149

246/80 Broekmeulen v Huisarts Registratie Commissie; sub nom. Broekmeulen v Committee for the Registration of General Medical Practitioners [1981] E.C.R. 2311; [1982] 1 C.M.L.R. 91 ECJ 144, 273

256/80 Birra Wührer SpA v Council of Ministers and Commission of the European Communities [1982] E.C.R. 85 ECJ 150

258/80   SpA Metallurgica Rumi v
Commission of the European
Communities [1982] E.C.R. 487
ECJ 151

279/80   Criminal   Proceedings
against Webb [1981] E.C.R.
3305; [1982] 1 C.M.L.R. 719
ECJ 44, 309,
                            310

6/81   Industrie Diensten Groep BV
v JA Beele Handelmaatschappij
BV [1982] E.C.R. 707; [1982] 3
C.M.L.R. 102 ECJ 227

21/81   Openbaar Ministerie v Bout
[1982] E.C.R. 381; [1982] 2
C.M.L.R. 371 ECJ 139

22/81   R. v Social Security Commissioner Ex p. Browning [1981]
E.C.R. 3357; [1982] 1 C.M.L.R.
427 ECJ 251

51/81   De Franceschi SpA Monfalcone v Council and Commission
of the European Communities
[1982] E.C.R. 117 ECJ 149

53/81   Levin v Staatssecretaris van
Justitie; sub nom. Levin v Secretary of State for Justice [1982]
E.C.R. 1035; [1982] 2 C.M.L.R.
454 ECJ 143, 238,
                        244, 245,
                            247

60/81   IBM Corp v Commission of
the European Communities; sub
nom. International Business
Machines Corp v Commission of
the European Communities
[1981] E.C.R. 2639; [1981] 3
C.M.L.R. 635 ECJ 28, 133,
                            138

61/81   Commission of the European Communities v United
Kingdom; sub nom. Equal Pay
for Equal Work, Re [1982]
E.C.R. 2601; [1982] 3 C.M.L.R.
284 ECJ 478

62 and 63/81   Société anonyme de
droit français Seco and Société
anonyme de droit français
Desquenne & Giral v Etablissement d'assurance contre la vieillesse et l'invalidité [1982] E.C.R.
223 .... 286, 309

65/81   Reina v Landeskreditbank
Baden-Wurttemberg   [1982]
E.C.R. 33; [1982] 1 C.M.L.R.
744 ECJ 143, 251

76/81   Transporoute et Travaux SA
v Minister of Public Works
[1982] E.C.R. 417; [1982] 3
C.M.L.R. 382 ECJ 309, 313

102/81   Nordsee   Deutsche
Hochseefischerei GmbH v Reed-
erei Mond Hochseefischerei
Nordstern AG & Co KG [1982]
E.C.R. 1095; [1982] Com. L.R.
154 ECJ 144

104/81   Hauptzollamt Mainz v CA
Kupferberg & Cie KG aA [1982]
E.C.R. 3641; [1983] 1 C.M.L.R.
1 ECJ 570

144/81   Keurkoop BV v Nancy
Kean Gifts BV [1982] E.C.R.
2853; [1983] 2 C.M.L.R. 47
ECJ 232, 303

216/81   Compagnia Generale Interscamsi SpA (COGIS) v Amministrazione delle Finanze dello Stato
[1982] E.C.R. 2701; [1983] 1
C.M.L.R. 685 ECJ 232

230/81   Luxembourg v European
Parliament [1983] E.C.R. 255;
[1983] 2 C.M.L.R. 726 ECJ ... 83, 134

256/81   Pauls Agriculture Ltd v
Council of Ministers and Commission of the European Communities [1983] E.C.R. 1707;
[1983] 3 C.M.L.R. 176 ECJ 150

262/81   Coditel SA v Cine Vog
Films SA [1982] E.C.R. 3381;
[1983] 1 C.M.L.R. 49 ECJ 289

267/81   Amministrazione   delle
Finanze dello Stato v Societa
Petrolifera Italiana SpA [1983]
E.C.R. 801; [1984] 1 C.M.L.R.
354 ECJ 566

290/81 and C-291/81   Compagnia
Singer SpA v Amministrazione
delle Finanze dello Stato; Geigy
SpA v Amministrazione delle
Finanze dello Stato [1983]
E.C.R. 847 ECJ 39, 566

310/81   Ente Italiano di Servizio
Sociale v Commission of the
European Communities [1984]
E.C.R. 1341; [1985] 1 C.M.L.R.
550 ECJ 150

7/82   Gesellschaft zur Verwertung
von   Leistungsschutzrechten
mbH (GVL) v Commission of
the European Communities
[1983] E.C.R. 483; [1983] 3
C.M.L.R. 645 ECJ 339

35/82 and 36/82 Morson v Netherlands; Jhanjan v Netherlands [1982] E.C.R. 3723; [1983] 2 C.M.L.R. 221 ECJ 146

40/82 Commission of the European Communities v United Kingdom; sub nom. Imports of Poultry Meat, Re [1982] E.C.R. 2793; [1982] 3 C.M.L.R. 497 ECJ 233

86/82 Hasselblad (GB) Ltd v Commission of the European Communities [1984] E.C.R. 883; [1984] 1 C.M.L.R. 559 ECJ 39

152/82 Forcheri v Belgium [1983] E.C.R. 2323; [1984] 1 C.M.L.R. 334 ECJ 249

159/82 Angélique Verli-Wallace v Commission of the European Communities [1983] E.C.R. 2711 53

165/82 Commission of the European Communities v United Kingdom; sub nom. Equal Treatment, Re [1984] 1 All E.R. 353; [1983] E.C.R. 3431; [1984] 1 C.M.L.R. 44 ECJ 478

181/82 Roussel Laboratoria BV v Netherlands [1983] E.C.R. 3849; [1985] 1 C.M.L.R. 834 ECJ 229

228/82 R Ford Werke AG v Commission of the European Communities; Ford of Europe Inc v Commission of the European Communities [1982] E.C.R. 2849; [1982] E.C.R. 3091; [1982] 3 C.M.L.R. 673 ECJ 353

286/82 Luisi v Ministero del Tesoro [1984] E.C.R. 377; [1985] 3 C.M.L.R. 52 ECJ 288, 299

319/82 Société de Vente de Ciments et Betons de L'Est SA v Kerpen & Kerpen GmbH & Co KG [1983] E.C.R. 4173; [1985] 1 C.M.L.R. 511 ECJ 141, 325

13/83 European Parliament v Council of Ministers of the European Communities [1987] E.C.R. 1513; [1985] E.C.R. 1513; [1986] 1 C.M.L.R. 138 ECJ 80, 142, 442

16/83 Criminal Proceedings against Prantl [1984] E.C.R. 1299; [1985] 2 C.M.L.R. 238 ECJ 228, 230

29/83 Compagnie Royale Asturienne des Mines SA v Commission of the European Communities [1984] E.C.R. 1679; [1985] 1 C.M.L.R. 688 ECJ 322

59/83 Biovilac SA v Commission of the European Communities [1984] E.C.R. 4057; [1987] 2 C.M.L.R. 881 ECJ 150

72/83 Campus Oil Ltd v Minister for Industry and Energy [1984] E.C.R. 2727; [1984] 3 C.M.L.R. 544 ECJ 143, 233

107/83 Ordre des Advocats au Barreau de Paris (Paris Bar Council) v Rechtsanwalt Onno Klopp; sub nom. Ordre des Advocats au Barreau de Paris v Klopp [1985] Q.B. 711; [1985] 2 W.L.R. 1058; [1984] E.C.R. 2971 ECJ 269

108/83 Luxembourg v European Parliament (No.2) [1984] E.C.R. 1945; [1986] 2 C.M.L.R. 507 ECJ 83, 133, 134

123/83 Bureau National Interprofessionel du Cognac (BNIC) v Clair [1985] E.C.R. 391; [1985] 2 C.M.L.R. 430 ECJ 322

145/83 & C-53/84 Adams v Commission of the European Communities (No.1); Adams (Stanley George) v Commission of the European Communities (No.2) [1986] Q.B. 138; [1986] 2 W.L.R. 367; [1985] E.C.R. 3539 ECJ 150

180/83 Moser v Land Baden-Württemberg [1984] E.C.R. 2539; [1984] 3 C.M.L.R. 720 ECJ 239

207/83 Commission of the European Communities v United Kingdom [1985] E.C.R 1207 ... 230

220/83 Commission of the European Communities v France; sub nom. Co-Insurance Services, Re [1986] E.C.R. 3663; [1987] 2 C.M.L.R. 113 ECJ 287

240/83 Procureur de la République v Association de défense des brûleurs d'huiles usagées (ADBHU) [1985] E.C.R. I-531 ... 540

270/83 Commission of the European Communities v France; sub nom. Tax Credits, Re [1986] E.C.R. 273; [1987] 1 C.M.L.R. 401 ECJ 430

274/83 Public Works Contracts,
Re; sub nom. Commission of the
European Communities v Italy
[1985] E.C.R. 1077; [1987] 1
C.M.L.R. 345 ECJ 313

293/83 Gravier v Liege [1985]
E.C.R. 593; [1985] 3 C.M.L.R. 1
ECJ 249

294/83 Parti Ecologiste Les Verts v
European Parliament; sub nom.
Les Verts, Parti Ecologiste v
European Parliament [1986]
E.C.R. 1339; [1987] 2 C.M.L.R.
343 ECJ 125

19/84 Pharmon BV v Hoechst AG
[1985] E.C.R. 2281; [1985] 3
C.M.L.R. 775 ECJ 302, 336

42/84 Remia BV v Commission of
the European Communities
[1985] E.C.R. 2545; [1987] 1
C.M.L.R. 1 ECJ 324

60/84 & C-61/84 Cinéthèque SA v
Federation Nationale des Cinemas Francais [1985] E.C.R.
2065; [1985] E.C.R. 2605;
[1986] 1 C.M.L.R. 365 ECJ 229

73/84 Denkavit Futtermittel
GmbH v Land Nordrhein-Westfalen [1985] E.C.R. 1013;
[1986] 2 C.M.L.R. 482 ECJ 230

112/84 Humblot v Directeur des
Services Fiscaux [1987] E.C.R.
1367; [1985] E.C.R. 1367;
[1986] 2 C.M.L.R. 338 ECJ 426

152/84 Marshall v Southampton
and South West Hampshire AHA
[1986] Q.B. 401; [1986] 2 W.L.R.
780; [1986] E.C.R. 723 ECJ 33

169/84 Societe CdF Chimie Azote
et Fertilisants SA v Commission
of the European Communities
[1990] E.C.R. I-3083; [1992] 1
C.M.L.R. 177 ECJ 137

178/84 Commission of the European Communities v Germany;
sub nom. Purity Requirements
for Beer, Re [1987] E.C.R. 1227;
[1988] 1 C.M.L.R. 780 ECJ 139

209/84 Ministere Public v Asjes
[1986] E.C.R. 1425; [1986] 3
C.M.L.R. 173 ECJ 343, 450

234/84 Aid to Meura SA, Re; sub
nom. Belgium v Commission of
the European Communities
[1986] E.C.R. 2263; [1988] 2
C.M.L.R. 331 ECJ 379

248/84 Germany v Commission of
the European Communities; sub
nom. Regional Aid Plans, Re
[1987] E.C.R. 4013; [1989] 1
C.M.L.R. 591 ECJ 384

262/84 Beets-Proper v F Van Lanschot Bankiers NV [1986]
E.C.R. 773; [1987] 2 C.M.L.R.
616 ECJ 33

292/84 TP F Bolognese v H Scharf
and Commission of the European Communities [1987]
E.C.R. 3563 164

53/85 AKZO Chemie BV v Commission of the European Communities [1986] E.C.R. 1965;
[1987] 1 C.M.L.R. 231 ECJ 359

89/85 A Ahlstrom Osakeyhtio v
Commission of the European
Communities [1988] E.C.R.
5193; [1988] 4 C.M.L.R. 901
ECJ 53, 327

118/85 Commission of the
European Communities v Italy;
sub nom. Amministrazione
Autonoma dei Monopoli di
Stato, Re [1987] E.C.R. 2599;
[1988] 3 C.M.L.R. 255 ECJ 377

131/85 Emir Gül v Regierungspräsident [1986] E.C.R. 1573;
[1987] 1 C.M.L.R. 501 ECJ 249

149/85 Wybot v Faure [1986]
E.C.R. 2391; [1987] 1 C.M.L.R.
819 ECJ 64, 83

167/85 Associazione Industrie
Siderurgiche Italiane (Assider) v
Commission of the European
Communities [1987] E.C.R.
1701; [1988] 2 C.M.L.R. 783
ECJ 142

193/85 Cooperativa Co-frutta Srl v
Amministrazione delle Finanze
dello Stato [1987] E.C.R. 2085
ECJ 425

199/85 Commission of the European Communities v Italy [1987]
E.C.R. 1039 312

227/85 Commission of the European Communities v Belgium;
sub nom. Directives On Waste,
Re [1988] E.C.R. 1; [1989] 2
C.M.L.R. 797 ECJ 111

237/85 Rummler v Dato-Druck
GmbH [1986] E.C.R. 2101;
[1987] 3 C.M.L.R. 127
ECJ 478

239/85 Toxic and Dangerous Waste, Re; sub nom. Commission of the European Communities v Belgium [1986] E.C.R. 3645; [1988] 1 C.M.L.R. 248 ECJ 32

314/85 Firma Foto Frost v Hauptzollamt Lübeck-Ost [1987] E.C.R. 4199; [1988] 3 C.M.L.R. 57 ECJ 145

358/85 Brussels Meetings, Re; sub nom. France v European Parliament [1986] E.C.R. 2149; [1988] 3 C.M.L.R. 786 ECJ ... 83, 134

12/86 Demirel v Stadt Schwabisch Gmund [1987] E.C.R. 3719; [1989] 1 C.M.L.R. 421 ECJ 570

34/86 Council of the European Communities v European Parliament; sub nom. 1986 Budget, Re [1986] E.C.R. 2155; [1986] 3 C.M.L.R. 94 ECJ 134

51/86 France v European Parliament [1988] E.C.R. 4846; [1990] 2 C.M.L.R. 406 134

65/86 Maschinenfabrik Hennecke GmbH v Sullhofer [1988] E.C.R. 5249; [1990] 4 C.M.L.R. 182 ECJ 304

85/86 Commission of the European Communities v Board of Governors of the European Investment Bank (EIB) [1988] E.C.R. 1281; [1989] 1 C.M.L.R. 103 ECJ 153, 185

247/86 Societe Alsacienne et Lorraine de Telecommunications et d'Electronique (Alsatel) v Novasam SA [1988] E.C.R. 5987; [1990] 4 C.M.L.R. 434 ECJ 340

263/86 Belgium v Humbel [1988] E.C.R. 5365; [1989] 1 C.M.L.R. 393 ECJ 249, 288

297/86 Confederazione Italiana Dirigenti di Azienda (CIDA) v Council of Ministers of the European Communities [1988] E.C.R. 3531; [1989] 3 C.M.L.R. 851 ECJ 180

302/86 Commission of the European Communities v Denmark [1988] E.C.R. 4627 229

386/86 Dreyfus v Commission of the European Communities [1998] E.C.R. I–2309 ..... 135, 136

3/87 R. v Ministry of Agriculture, Fisheries and Food Ex p. Agegate Ltd [1990] 2 Q.B. 151; [1990] 3 W.L.R. 226; [1989] E.C.R. 4459 ECJ 416

31/87 Gebroeders Beentjes BV v Netherlands [1988] E.C.R. 4635; [1990] 1 C.M.L.R. 287 ECJ 309, 313

42/87 Commission of the European Communities v Belgium; sub nom. Higher Education Funding, Re [1988] E.C.R. 5445; [1989] 1 C.M.L.R. 457 ECJ 249

45/87 Commission of the European Communities v Ireland; sub nom. Dundalk Water Supply Scheme, Re (No.3) [1988] E.C.R. 4929; 44 B.L.R. 1; [1989] 1 C.M.L.R. 225 ECJ 309, 310

46/87 Hoechst AG v Commission of the European Communities [1989] E.C.R. 2859; [1991] 4 C.M.L.R. 410 ECJ 53, 354

53/87 Consorzio Italiano della Componentistica di Ricambio per Autoveicoli v Regie Nationale des Usines Renault; Maxicar v Regie Nationale des Usines Renault [1988] E.C.R. 6039; [1990] 4 C.M.L.R. 265; [1990] F.S.R. 544 ECJ 301

81/87 R. v HM Treasury Ex p. Daily Mail; R. v Customs and Excise Commissioners Ex p. Daily Mail [1989] Q.B. 446; [1989] 2 W.L.R. 908; [1988] E.C.R. 5483 ECJ 269, 278

87/87 R Dow Chemical Nederland BV v Commission of the European Communities [1987] E.C.R. 4367; [1988] 4 C.M.L.R. 439 ECJ 354

106/87 Asteris AE v Greece [1988] E.C.R. 5515; [1990] 1 C.M.L.R. 575 ECJ 150

131/87 Commission of the European Communities v Council of Ministers of the European Communities; sub nom. Trade in Animal Glands, Re [1989] E.C.R. 3743; [1991] 1 C.M.L.R. 780 ECJ 137

Table of Cases

165/87 Commission of the European Communities v Council of Ministers of the European Communities; sub nom. Harmonised Commodity Descriptions, Re [1988] E.C.R. 5545; [1990] 1 C.M.L.R. 457 ECJ 70

186/87 Cowan v Trésor Public [1989] E.C.R. 195; [1990] 2 C.M.L.R. 613 ECJ 289

216/87 R. v Ministry of Agriculture, Fisheries and Food Ex p. Jaderow Ltd [1990] 2 Q.B. 193; [1990] 3 W.L.R. 265; [1989] E.C.R. 4509 ECJ 416

226/87 Commission of the European Communities v Greece; sub nom. Public Sector Insurance, Re [1988] E.C.R. 3611; [1989] 3 C.M.L.R. 569 ECJ 34

235/87 Matteucci v Communaute Française de Belgique [1988] E.C.R. 5589; [1989] 1 C.M.L.R. 357 ECJ 249

238/87 Volvo AB v Erik Veng (UK) Ltd [1988] E.C.R. 6211; [1989] 4 C.M.L.R. 122 ECJ 307

242/87 Commission of the European Communities v Council of Ministers of the European Communities; sub nom. Erasmus Legislation, Re [1989] E.C.R. 1425; [1991] 1 C.M.L.R. 478 ECJ 93, 134

275/87 Commission of the European Communities v Council [1988] E.C.R. 259 141

344/87 Bettray v Staatssecretaris van Justitie [1989] E.C.R. 1621; [1991] 1 C.M.L.R. 459 ECJ 245

374/87 Orkem v Commission of the European Communities [1989] E.C.R. 3350 354

103/88 Fratelli Costanzo SpA v Comune di Milano [1989] E.C.R. 1839; [1990] 3 C.M.L.R. 239 ECJ 313

109/88 Handels- og Kontorfunktionaerernes Forbund i Danmark v Dansk Arbejdsgiverforening Ex p. Danfoss A/S; sub nom. Union of Clerical and Commercial Employees v Danish Employers Association Ex p. Danfoss A/S [1989] E.C.R. 3199; [1991] 1 C.M.L.R. 8 ECJ 144, 478

18/90 Office national de l'emploi v Bahia Kziber [1991] E.C.R. I-221 45

149/96 Portuguese Republic v Council of the European Union [1999] E.C.R. I-8395 55

17/98 Emesa Sugar (Free Zone) NV v Aruba [2000] E.C.R. I-665 .... 128, 129

165/99 Austria v Commission Unpublished 2001 158

C-277/87 Sandoz prodotti farmaceutici SpA v Commission of the European Communities [1990] E.C.R. I-45 321

C-301/87 France v Commission of the European Communities [1990] E.C.R. I-307 395

C-302/87 European Parliament v Council of Ministers of the European Communities [1988] E.C.R. 5615 ECJ 80, 141

C-341/87 EMI Electrola GmbH v Patricia Im- und Export Verwaltungsgesellschaft mbH [1989] E.C.R. 79; [1989] 2 C.M.L.R. 413; [1989] 1 F.S.R. 544 ECJ ... 302

C-2/88 JJ Zwartveld [1990] E.C.R. I-3365 142

C-3/88 Commission of the European Communities v Italy; sub nom. Data Processing Contracts, Re [1989] E.C.R. 4035; [1991] 2 C.M.L.R. 115 ECJ 309, 310

C-21/88 Du Pont de Nemours Italiana SpA v Unità sanitaria locale N° 2 di Carrara [1990] E.C.R. I-889 .... 309, 310

C-30/88 Greece v Commission of the European Communities; sub nom. Aid to Turkey, Re [1989] E.C.R. 3711; [1991] 2 C.M.L.R. 169 ECJ 53

C-64/88 Commission of the European Communities v France [1991] E.C.R. I-2727 111

C-70/88 European Parliament v Council of Ministers of the European Communities [1990] E.C.R. I-2041; [1992] 1 C.M.L.R. 91 ECJ 134

C-114/88 Delbar v Caisse d'allocations familiales de Roubaix-Tourcoing [1989] E.C.R. 4067 251

C-143/88 Zuckerfabrik Suderdithmarschen AG v Hauptzollamt Itzehoe; Zuckerfabrik Soest GmbH v Hauptzollamt Paderborn (C-92/89) [1991] E.C.R. I-415; [1993] 3 C.M.L.R. 1 ECJ 31

C-202/88 France v Commission of the European Communities [1991] E.C.R. I–1223 ..... 314, 325

C-262/88 Barber v Guardian Royal Exchange Assurance Group [1991] 1 Q.B. 344; [1991] 2 W.L.R. 72 ECJ 478

C-322/88 Grimaldi v Fonds des Maladies Professionnelles [1989] E.C.R. 4407; [1991] 2 C.M.L.R. 265; [1990] I.R.L.R. 400 ECJ 34

C-326/88 Anklagemyndigheden (Public Prosecutor) v Hansen & Son [1990] E.C.R. I-2911; [1992] I.C.R. 277 ECJ 52

C-331/88 R. v Ministry of Agriculture, Fisheries and Food Ex p. Federation Europeene de la Sante Animale (FEDESA) [1990] E.C.R. I-4023; [1991] 1 C.M.L.R. 507 ECJ 36, 37

C-337/88 Societa Agricola Fattoria Alimentaire SpA v Amministrazione delle Finanze dello Stato [1990] E.C.R. I-1; [1991] 1 C.M.L.R. 872 ECJ 37

C-366/88 France v Commission of the European Communities [1990] E.C.R. I–3595; [1992] 1 C.M.L.R. 2 133

C-10/89 Cnl-Sucal NV SA v Hag GF AG [1990] E.C.R. I-3711; [1990] 3 C.M.L.R. 571 ECJ 302

C-32/89 R Commission of the European Communities v Greece; sub nom. FEOGA Accounts, Re [1989] E.C.R. 985; [1991] 1 C.M.L.R. 377 ECJ 162

C-35/89 R Extramet Industrie SA v Council of Ministers of the European Communities [1990] E.C.R. I-431; [1990] 2 C.M.L.R. 406 ECJ 136

C-104/89 and C-37/90 Mulder v Council and Commission [1992] E.C.R. 3131 149

C-113/89 Rush Portuguesa Ldª v Office national d'immigration [1990] E.C.R. I–1417 309

C-172/89 Vandemoortele NV v Commission of the European Communities [1990] E.C.R. I–4677 140

C-192/89 Sevince v Staatssecretaris van Justitie [1990] E.C.R. I-3461; [1992] 2 C.M.L.R. 57 ECJ 133

C-213/89 R. v Secretary of State for Transport Ex p. Factortame Ltd [1990] 2 Lloyd's Rep. 351; [1990] E.C.R. I-2433; [1990] 3 C.M.L.R. 1 ECJ 47, 56, 140

C-216/89 Beate Reibold v Bundesanstalt für Arbeit [1990] E.C.R. I–4163 247

C-221/89 R. v Secretary of State for Transport Ex p. Factortame Ltd [1992] Q.B. 680; [1992] 3 W.L.R. 288; [1991] E.C.R. I-3905 ECJ 416

C-234/89 Delimitis v Henninger Brau AG [1991] E.C.R. I-935; [1992] 5 C.M.L.R. 210 ECJ 373

C-238/89 Pall Corp v PJ Dahlhausen & Co [1990] E.C.R. 4827 302

C-243/89 Commission of the European Communities v Denmark [1993] E.C.R. I–3353 309

C-246/89 Commission of the European Communities v United Kingdom; sub nom. Nationality of Fishermen, Re [1991] E.C.R. I-4585; [1991] 3 C.M.L.R. 706 ECJ 416

C-292/89 R. v Immigration Appeal Tribunal Ex p. Antonissen [1991] E.C.R. I-745; [1991] 2 C.M.L.R. 373; (1991) 135 S.J. 6 ECJ 247

C-297/89 Rigsadvokaten v Ryborg [1991] E.C.R. I-1943; [1993] 1 C.M.L.R. 218 ECJ 269

C-300/89 Commission of the European Communities v Council of the European Communities; sub nom. Titanium Dioxide Directive, Re [1991] E.C.R. I-2867; [1993] 3 C.M.L.R. 359 ECJ ... 36, 70

C-305/89 Italy v Commission of the European Communities [1991] E.C.R. I–1603 379

C-360/89 Commission of the European Communities v Italy [1992] E.C.R. I-3401 309

C-370/89 Société Générale d'En-
treprises Electro-Mécaniques SA
(SGEEM) and Roland Etroy v
European Investment Bank
[1992] E.C.R. I–6211 113,
                                    185
C-376/89 Giagounidis v Reutlin-
gen [1991] E.C.R. I-1069;
[1993] 1 C.M.L.R. 537 ECJ 247
C-470/89 Universale-Bau AG,
Bietergemeinschaft: 1) Hintereg-
ger & Söhne Bauges.m.b.H.
Salzburg, 2) ÖSTÜ-STETTIN
Hoch- und Tiefbau GmbH v
Entsorgungsbetriebe Simmering
GmbH [2002] E.C.R. I–11617 ... 309
C-2/90 Commission of the Euro-
pean Communities v Belgium
[1992] E.C.R. I–4466 224
C-6/90 and C-9/90 Francovich v
Italy; Bonifacti v Italy [1991]
E.C.R. I-5357; [1993] 2
C.M.L.R. 66 ECJ 33, 51,
                          112, 310,
                               474
C-41/90 Höfner v Macrotron
GmbH [1991] E.C.R. I-1979;
[1993] 4 C.M.L.R. 306 ECJ 338
C-42/90 Criminal proceedings
against Jean-Claude Bellon
[1990] E.C.R. I–4863 ..... 229, 232
C-48/90 and C-66/90 Netherlands
v Commission of the European
Communities [1992] E.C.R.
I–565 .... 377, 378
C-48/90 Netherlands v Commis-
sion of the European Communi-
ties. *See* Koninklijke PTT
Nederland NV v Commission
of the European Communities
(C-66/90)
C-63/90 and C-67/90 Portuguese
Republic and Kingdom of Spain
v Council of the European
Communities [1992] E.C.R.
I–5073 416
C-66/90 and C-48/90 Koninklijke
PTT Nederland NV v Commis-
sion of the European Communi-
ties; PTT Post BV v Commission
of the European Communities
[1991] E.C.R. I-2723; [1993] 5
C.M.L.R. 316 ECJ 139, 347
C-167/90 Commission of the Euro-
pean Communities v Belgium
[1991] E.C.R. I–2535 274

C-185/90 P Rev Walter Gill v
Commission of the European
Communities [1992] E.C.R.
I–993 164
C-271/90 Spain v Commission of
the European Communities
[1992] E.C.R. I-5833 ECJ 314
C-303/90 France v Commission of
the European Communities
[1991] E.C.R. I–5340 133
C-320/90 Telemarsicabruzzo SpA v
CircostelTelemarsicabruzzo SpA
v Ministerio delle Poste e
Telecommunicazioni [1993]
E.C.R. I-393 ECJ 146
C-354/90 Federation Nationale du
Commerce Exterieur des Pro-
duits Alimentaires v France
[1991] E.C.R. I-5505 ECJ 395
C-65/91 European Parliament v
Council of Ministers of the
European Communities [1992]
E.C.R. I-4593 ECJ 67, 121
C-66/91 Emerald Meats Ltd v
Commission of the European
Communities [1991] E.C.R.
I–1143 133
C-260/91 Diversinte SA and Iber-
lacta SA v Administracion Princi-
pal de Aduanas E Impuestos
Especiales de la Junquera [1993]
E.C.R. I-1885 ECJ 37
C-267/91 and C-268/91 Criminal
Proceedings against Keck;
Criminal Proceedings against
Mithouard [1993] E.C.R.
I-6097; [1995] 1 C.M.L.R. 101
ECJ 52, 230, 231,
                          375, 426
C-272/91 Commission of the Euro-
pean Communities v Italy [1994]
E.C.R. I–1409 309,
                               314
C-320/91 Criminal Proceedings
against Corbeau, Re [1993]
E.C.R. I-2533; [1995] 4
C.M.L.R. 621 ECJ 347
C-325/91 France v Commission
of the European Communities
[1993] E.C.R. I-3283 ECJ ... 35, 133,
                               378
C-49/92 P Commission of the
European Communities v Anic
Partecipazioni SpA [1999]
E.C.R. I-4125; [2001] 4
C.M.L.R. 17 ECJ 321

C-53/92 P Hilti AG v Commission of the European Communities [1994] E.C.R. I-667; [1994] 4 C.M.L.R. 614; [1994] F.S.R. 760 ECJ 155

C-73/92 Commission of the European Communities v Spain [1993] E.C.R. I–5997; [1997] S.T.C. 700 ECJ 312

C-91/92 Faccini Dori v Recreb Srl [1994] E.C.R. I-3325; [1994] 1 C.M.L.R. 665 32

C-157/92 Pretore di Genova v Banchero [1993] E.C.R. I-1085 ECJ 143

C-188/92 TWD Textilwerke Deggendorf GmbH v Germany [1994] E.C.R. I-833; [1995] 2 C.M.L.R. 145 ECJ 147

C-234/92 Teresa Fernández de Bobadilla v Museo Nacional del Prado, Comité de Empresa del Museo Nacional del Prado and Ministerio Fiscal [1999] E.C.R. I–4773 271

C-328/92 Commission of the European Communities v Spain [1994] E.C.R. I–1569 312

C-387/92 Banco Exterior de Espana SA v Ayuntamiento de Valencia; sub nom. Banco de Credito Industrial SA v Ayuntamiento de Valencia [1994] E.C.R. I-877; [1994] 3 C.M.L.R. 473 ECJ 347, 379

C-393/92 Gemeente Almelo v Energiebedrijf Ijssellmij NV; sub nom. Commune d'Almelo ea v NV Energiebedrijf Ijsselmij; Municipality of Almelo v NV Energibedrijf Ijsselmij [1994] E.C.R. I-1477; [1994] 2 C.E.C. 281 ECJ 338

C-39/93 P Syndicat Francais de l'Express International (SFEI) v Commission of the European Communities [1994] E.C.R. I-2681 ECJ 133

C-41/93 France v Commission of the European Communities; sub nom. Pentachlorophenol, Re [1994] E.C.R. I-1829; [1995] 3 C.M.L.R. 733 ECJ 436

C-43/93 Raymond Vander Elst v Office des Migrations Internationales [1994] E.C.R. I–3803 . . . 310

C-46/93 and C-48/93 Brasserie du Pêcheur SA v Germany; R. v Secretary of State for Transport Ex p. Factortame Ltd [1996] Q.B. 404; [1996] 2 W.L.R. 506; [1996] E.C.R. I-1029 ECJ 33, 112, 310

C-65/93 European Parliament v Council of Ministers of the European Communities; sub nom. Generalised Tariff Preferences, Re [1995] E.C.R. I-643; [1996] 1 C.M.L.R. 4 ECJ 67, 68

C-69/93 and C-258/93 Punto Casa SpA v Sindaco del Comune di Capena et Comune di Capena and Promozioni Polivalenti Venete Soc coop arl (PPV) v Sindaco del Comune di Torri di Quartesolo and Comune di Torri di Quartesolo [1994] E.C.R. I–2355 231

C-131/93 Commission of the European Communities v Germany; sub nom. Crayfish Imports, Re [1994] E.C.R. I-3303; [1995] 2 C.M.L.R. 278 ECJ 139

C-135/93 Spain v Commission of the European Communities [1995] E.C.R. I-1651 ECJ 386

C-279/93 Finanzamt Koln-Altstadt v Schumacker [1996] Q.B. 28; [1995] 3 W.L.R. 498; [1995] E.C.R. I-225 ECJ 431

C-308/93 Bestuur van de Sociale Verzekeringsbank v JM Cabanis-Issarte [1996] E.C.R. I–2097 141

C-312/93 Peterbroeck Van Campenhout & Cie SCS v Belgium [1996] All E.R. (E.C.) 242; [1995] E.C.R. I-4599; [1996] 1 C.M.L.R. 793 ECJ 45, 56

C-319/93, C-40/94 C-399/93 and Dijkstra v Friesland (Frico Domo) Cooperatieve BA; Van Roessel v de Cooperatie Vereniging Zuivelcooperatie Campina Melkunie BA; Luttikhuis v Verenigde Cooperatieve Melkindustrie Coberco BA [1995] E.C.R. I-4471; [1996] 5 C.M.L.R. 178 ECJ 342

C-324/93   R. v Secretary of State
   for the Home Department Ex p.
   Evans Medical Ltd [1995] All
   E.R. (E.C.) 481; [1995] E.C.R.
   I-563; [1996] 1 C.M.L.R. 53
   ECJ 566
C-349/93   Commission of the Euro-
   pean Communities v Italy [1995]
   E.C.R. I–343 396
C-358/93 and C-416/93   Ministerio
   Fiscal v Bordessa; Ministerio Fis-
   cal v Mellado [1995] All E.R.
   (E.C.) 385; [1995] E.C.R. I-361;
   [1996] 2 C.M.L.R. 13 ECJ 299
C-387/93   Banchero, Re [1995]
   E.C.R.   I-4663;   [1996]   1
   C.M.L.R. 829 ECJ 375
C-392/93   R. v HM Treasury Ex p.
   British Telecommunications Plc
   [1996] Q.B. 615; [1996] 3
   W.L.R. 203; [1996] E.C.R.
   I-1631 ECJ 112
C-415/93   Union Royale Belge des
   Societes de Football Association
   (ASBL) v Bosman; sub nom.
   Union des Associations Euro-
   peennes de Football (UEFA) v
   Bosman; Royal Club Liegois SA
   v Bosman [1996] All E.R. (EC)
   97; [1995] E.C.R. I-4921;
   [1996] 1 C.M.L.R. 645 ECJ 244
C-418/93   Semeraro Casa Uno Srl v
   Sindaco del Comune di Erbusco
   [1996] E.C.R. I-2975; [1996] 3
   C.M.L.R. 648 ECJ 230, 231
C-426/93   Germany v Council of
   Ministers [1995] E.C.R. I-3723 ... 110
C-427/93, C-436/93 and C-429/93
   Bristol Myers Squibb Co v Para-
   nova A/S; Bayer AG v Paranova
   A/S; CH Boehringer Sohn v Para-
   nova A/S [2003] Ch. 75; [2002]
   3 W.L.R. 1746; [1996] E.C.R.
   I-3457 ECJ 232, 305
C-430/93 and C-431/93   Van Schi-
   jndel v Stichting Pensioenfonds
   voor Fysiotherapeuten; Van Veen
   v Stichting Pensioenfonds voor
   Fysiotherapeuten [1996] All E.R.
   (E.C.) 259; [1995] E.C.R. I-
   4705; [1996] 1 C.M.L.R. 801
   ECJ 45,56
C-435/93   Dietz v Stichting Thuis-
   zorg Rotterdam [1996] E.C.R.
   I-5223; [1997] 1 C.M.L.R. 199
   ECJ 477

C-441/93   Pafitis v Trapeza Ken-
   trikis Ellados AE [1996] E.C.R.
   I-1347; [1996] 2 C.M.L.R. 551;
   [1997] C.E.C. 646 ECJ 164, 278
C-450/93   Eckhard Kalanke v Freie
   Hansestadt Bremen [1995]
   E.C.R. I-3051 477
C-465/93   Atlanta Fruchthandels-
   gesellschaft mbH v Bundesamt
   fur   Ernahrung   und
   Forstwirtschaft [1996] All E.R.
   (E.C.) 31; [1995] E.C.R. I-3761;
   [1996] 1 C.M.L.R. 575 ECJ 145
C-473/93   Commission of the Euro-
   pean Communities v Luxem-
   bourg; sub nom. Public Service
   Employment, Re [1996] E.C.R.
   I-3207; [1996] 3 C.M.L.R. 981
   ECJ 254
C-479/93   Francovich v Italy
   [1995] E.C.R. I-3843; [1997] 2
   B.C.L.C. 203 ECJ 473
C-499/93   Rockfon A/S v Specialar-
   bejderforbundet i Danmark
   [1995] E.C.R. I-4291; [1996]
   C.E.C. 224 ECJ 473
C-5/94   R. v Ministry of Agriculture,
   Fisheries and Food Ex p. Hedley
   Lomas (Ireland) Ltd [1997] Q.B.
   139; [1996] 3 W.L.R. 787; [1996]
   E.C.R. I-2553 ECJ 110, 112
C-16/94   Edouard Dubois et Fils SA
   v Garonor Exploitation SA;
   General Cargo Services SA v
   Garonor Exploitation SA [1995]
   All E.R. (E.C.) 821; [1995]
   E.C.R. I-2421; [1995] 2
   C.M.L.R. 771 ECJ 225
C-17/94   Criminal Proceedings
   against Gervais [1995] E.C.R.
   I-4353 ECJ 375
C-25/94   Commission of the Euro-
   pean Communities v Council of
   the European Union [1996]
   E.C.R. I-1469 ECJ 415, 565
C-39/94   Syndicat Francais de l'Ex-
   press International (SFEI) v La
   Poste [1996] All E.R. (EC) 685;
   [1996] E.C.R. I-3547; [1996] 3
   C.M.L.R. 369 ECJ ... 337, 380, 396
C-55/94   Gebhard v Consiglio
   dell'Ordine degli Avvocati e
   Procuratori di Milano [1996] All
   E.R. (EC) 189; [1995] E.C.R.
   I-4165; [1996] 1 C.M.L.R. 603
   ECJ 267, 289

C-58/94 Netherlands v Council of the European Union [1996] E.C.R. I-2169; [1996] 2 C.M.L.R. 996 ECJ 104

C-68/94 and C-30/95 France v Commission of the European Communities; Societe Commerciale des Potasses et de l'Azote (SCPA) v Commission of the European Communities [1998] E.C.R. I-1375; [1998] 4 C.M.L.R. 829 ECJ 365

C-80/94 Wielockx v Inspecteur der Directe Belastingen [1996] 1 W.L.R. 84; [1995] All E.R. (E.C.) 769; [1995] E.C.R. I-2493 ECJ ... 431

C-85/94 Groupement des Producteurs, Importateurs et Agents Generaux d'Eaux Minerales Etrangeres Asbl (PIAGEME) v Peeters NV); sub nom. PIAGEME Asbl v Peeters NV [1995] E.C.R. I-2955 ECJ 499

C-87/94 Commission of the European Communities v Belgium [1996] E.C.R. I–2043 ... 309, 310, 313

C-90/94 Haahr Petroleum Ltd v Abenra Havn [1997] E.C.R. I-4085; [1998] 1 C.M.L.R. 771 ECJ 425

C-113/94 Jacquier v Directeur Général des Impots [1995] E.C.R. I–4203 426

C-114/94 Intelligente Systemen, Database toepassingen, Elektronische diensten BV (IDE) v Commission of the European Communities [1997] E.C.R. I–803 154

C-126/94 Société Cadi Surgelés v Ministre des Finances [1996] E.C.R. I-5647; [1997] 1 C.M.L.R. 795 ECJ 225

C-155/94 Wellcome Trust Ltd v Customs and Excise Commissioners [1996] All E.R. (EC) 589; [1996] E.C.R. I-3013; [1996] 2 C.M.L.R. 909 ECJ 427

C-157/94 Commission of the European Communities v Netherlands, Italy, France and Spain [1997] E.C.R. I–5699 376

C-163/94 Criminal Proceedings against Sanz de Lera [1995] E.C.R. I-4821; [1996] 1 C.M.L.R. 631 ECJ 299

C-171/94 and C-172/94 Merckx v Ford Motors Co Belgium SA; Neuhuys v Ford Motors Co Belgium SA [1996] All E.R. (EC) 667; [1996] E.C.R. I-1253 ECJ ... 473

C-173/94 Commission of the European Communities v Belgium [1996] E.C.R. I–3265 254

C-178/94, C-190/94, C-189/94, C-188/94 and C-179/94 Dillenkofer v Germany; Knor v Germany; Heuer v Germany; Schulte v Germany; Erdmann v Germany [1997] Q.B. 259; [1997] 2 W.L.R. 253; [1996] E.C.R. I-4845 ECJ 112, 361

C-192/94 El Corte Ingles SA v Blazquez Rivero [1996] E.C.R. I-1281; [1996] 2 C.M.L.R. 507 ECJ 33

C-194/94 CIA Security International SA v Signalson SA [1996] All E.R. (EC) 557; [1996] E.C.R. I-2201; [1996] 2 C.M.L.R. 781 ECJ 234

C-214/94 Boukhalfa v Germany [1996] E.C.R. I-2253; [1996] 3 C.M.L.R. 22 ECJ 43

C-232/94 MPA MPA Pharma GmbH v Rhône-Poulenc Pharma GmbH [1996] E.C.R. I–3671 ... 306

C-233/94 Germany v European Parliament; sub nom. Deposit Guarantee Directive, Re [1997] E.C.R. I-2405; [1997] 3 C.M.L.R. 1379 ECJ 292

C-238/94 José García v Mutuelle de Prévoyance Sociale d'Aquitaine [1996] E.C.R. I–1673 296

C-241/94 France v Commission of the European Communities; sub nom. Kimberly Clark, Re [1996] E.C.R. I-4551; [1997] 1 C.M.L.R. 983; [1997] I.R.L.R. 415 ECJ 381

C-244/94 Federation Francaise des Société d'Assurance v Ministere de l'Agriculture et de la Peche [1995] E.C.R. I-4013; [1996] 4 C.M.L.R. 536 ECJ 323

C-278/94 Commission of the European Communities v Belgium; sub nom. Access to Special Employment Programmes, Re (C-278/94) [1996] E.C.R. I-4307; [1997] 1 C.M.L.R. 1040 ECJ 249

C-293/94 Criminal Proceedings against Brandsma [1996] All E.R. (EC) 837; [1996] E.C.R. I-3159; [1996] 3 C.M.L.R. 904 ECJ 232

C-298/94 Henke v Gemeinde Schierke [1997] All E.R. (EC) 173; [1996] E.C.R. I-4989; [1997] 1 C.M.L.R. 373 ECJ 473

C-302/94 R. v Secretary of State for Trade and Industry Ex p. British Telecommunications Plc [1996] E.C.R. I-6417; [1997] 1 C.M.L.R. 424 ECJ 314

C-305/94 Rotsart de Hertaing v J Benoidt SA (In Liquidation) [1997] All E.R. (E.C.) 40; [1996] E.C.R. I-5927; [1997] 1 C.M.L.R. 329 ECJ 473

C-318/94 Commission of the European Communities v Germany [1996] E.C.R. I–1949 311

C-319/94 Jules Dethier Equipement SA v Dassy; Jules Dethier Equipement SA v Sovam Sprl [1998] All E.R. (EC) 346; [1998] E.C.R. I-1061; [1998] 2 C.M.L.R. 611 ECJ 473

C-333/94 P Tetra Pak International SA v Commission of the European Communities [1997] All E.R. (EC) 4; [1996] E.C.R. I-5951; [1997] 4 C.M.L.R. 662 ECJ 341

C-3/95 Reisebüro Broede v Sandker [1996] E.C.R. I-6511; [1997] 1 C.M.L.R. 224 ECJ 268, 287

C-4/95 and C-5/95 Stöber v Bundesanstalt für Arbeit; Pereira v Bundesanstalt für Arbeit [1997] E.C.R. I-511; [1997] 2 C.M.L.R. 213 ECJ 267

C-7/95 P John Deere Ltd v Commission of the European Communities; John Deere Ltd v Commission of the European Communities [1998] All E.R. (E.C.) 481 (Note); [1998] E.C.R. I-3111; [1998] 5 C.M.L.R. 311 ECJ 168

C-8/95 P New Ford Holland v Commission of the European Communities. *See* John Deere Ltd v Commission of the European Communities (C-7/95 P)

C-12/95 P(R) Transacciones Maritimas SA (Tramasa) v Commission of the European Communities [1995] E.C.R. I-467; [1996] 2 C.M.L.R. 580 ECJ 336, 396

C-13/95 Ayse Süzen v Zehnacker Gebäudereinigung GmbH Krankenhausservice [1997] All E.R. (EC) 289; [1997] E.C.R. I-1259 ECJ 473

C-28/95 A Leur-Bloem v Inspecteur der Belastingdienst/Ondernemingen Amsterdam 2 [1997] E.C.R. I-4161 148

C-32/95 P Commission of the European Communities v Lisrestal [1996] E.C.R. I-5373; [1997] 2 C.M.L.R. 1 ECJ 139

C-42/95 Siemens AG v Henry Nold [1996] E.C.R. I–6017 278

C-58/95 Gallotti, Re; sub nom. Criminal Proceedings against Gallotti, Re [1996] E.C.R. I-4345; [1997] 1 C.M.L.R. 32 ECJ 33

C-65/95 and C-111/95 R. v Secretary of State for the Home Department Ex p. Shingara; R. v Secretary of State for the Home Department Ex p. Radiom [1997] All E.R. (EC) 577; [1997] E.C.R. I-3343; [1997] 3 C.M.L.R. 703 ECJ 253

C-66/95 R. v Secretary of State for Social Security Ex p. Sutton [1997] All E.R. (EC) 497; [1997] E.C.R. I-2163; [1997] 2 C.M.L.R. 382 ECJ 112

C-77/95 Züchner v Handelskrankenkasse (Ersatzkasse) Bremen [1997] All E.R. (EC) 359; [1996] E.C.R. I-5689; [1997] 3 C.M.L.R. 263 ECJ 477

C-91/95 P Tremblay v Commission of the European Communities [1996] E.C.R. I-5547; [1997] 4 C.M.L.R. 211 ECJ 56, 155

C-104/95 Kontogeorgas v Kartonpak AE [1996] E.C.R. I-6643; [1997] 1 C.M.L.R. 1093 ECJ ... 267

C-107/95 P Bundesverband der Bilanzbuchhalter eV v Commission of the European Communities [1997] E.C.R. I-947; [1997] 5 C.M.L.R. 432; [1997] 3 C.M.L.R. 1189 ECJ 378

C-110/95 Yamanouchi Pharmaceuticals Co Ltd v Comptroller-General of Patents, Designs and Trade Marks [1997] E.C.R. I-3251; [1997] 3 C.M.L.R. 749 ECJ 195

C-120/95 Decker v Caisse de Maladie des Employés Privés [1998] All E.R. (E.C.) 673; [1998] E.C.R. I-1831; [1998] 2 C.M.L.R. 879 ECJ 251

C-127/95 Norbrook Laboratories Ltd v Ministry of Agriculture, Fisheries and Food [1998] E.C.R. I-1531; [1998] 3 C.M.L.R. 809 ECJ 112

C-143/95 P Commission of the European Communities v Sociedade de Curtumes a Sul do Tejo Ldª (Socurte), Revestimentos de Cortiça Ldª (Quavi) and Sociedade Transformadora de Carnes Ldª (Stec) [1997] E.C.R. I-1 132

C-149/95 P(R) Commission of the European Communities v Atlantic Container Line AB [1995] All E.R. (EC) 853; [1995] E.C.R. I-2165; [1997] 5 C.M.L.R. 167 ECJ 162, 163

C-178/95 Wiljo NV v Belgische Staat [1997] E.C.R. I–585 147

C-180/95 Draehmpaehl v Urania Immobilienservice OHG [1997] All E.R. (E.C.) 719; [1997] E.C.R. I-2195; [1997] 3 C.M.L.R. 1107 ECJ 474

C-181/95 Biogen Inc v SmithKline Beecham Biologicals SA (Intervention in Preliminary Ruling) [1996] E.C.R. I-717; [1997] 1 C.M.L.R. 704 ECJ 148

C-189/95 Criminal Proceedings against Franzén [1997] E.C.R. I-5909; [1998] 1 C.M.L.R. 1231 ECJ 376

C-229/95 Parodi v Banque H Albert de Bary [1997] E.C.R. I–3899 293

C-235/95 Assedic Pas-de-Calais AGS v Dumon [1998] E.C.R. I-4531; [1999] 2 C.M.L.R. 113 ECJ 473

C-241/95 R. v Intervention Board for Agricultural Produce Ex p. Accrington Beef Co Ltd [1996] E.C.R. I-6699; [1997] 1 C.M.L.R. 675 ECJ 147

C-264/95 P Commission of the European Communities v Union Internationale des Chemins de Fer (UIC) [1997] E.C.R. I-1287; [1997] 5 C.M.L.R. 49 ECJ 342

C-265/95 Commission of the European Communities v France [1997] E.C.R. I–6959 ECJ 236

C-278/95 P Siemens SA v Commission of the European Communities [1997] E.C.R. I-2507; [1997] C.E.C. 1267 ECJ 392

C-286/95 P Commission of the European Communities v ICI Plc [2001] All E.R. (EC) 439; [2000] E.C.R. I-2341; [2000] 5 C.M.L.R. 413 ECJ 114

C-300/95 Commission of the European Communities v United Kingdom; sub nom. Product Liability Directive, Re [1997] All E.R. (EC) 481; [1997] E.C.R. I-2649; [1997] 3 C.M.L.R. 923 ECJ 498

C-321/95 P Stichting Greenpeace Council (Greenpeace International) v Commission of the European Communities [1998] All E.R. (E.C.) 620; [1998] E.C.R. I-1651; [1998] 3 C.M.L.R. 1 ECJ 135, 136

C-343/95 Diego Calì & Figli Srl v Servizi ecologici porto di Genova SpA (SEPG) [1997] E.C.R. I–1547 377

C-344/95 Commission of the European Communities v Belgium [1997] E.C.R. I-1035; [1997] 2 C.M.L.R. 187 ECJ 244

C-345/95 France v European Parliament [1997] E.C.R. I-5215 . 83

C-352/95 Phytheron International SA v Jean Bourdon SA [1997] E.C.R. I-1729; [1997] 3 C.M.L.R. 199 ECJ 305

C-357/95 P Empresa Nacional de Uranio SA (ENU) v Commission of the European Communities [1997] E.C.R. I-1329; [1997] 3 C.M.L.R. 95 ECJ 182

C-359/95   P Commission of the
European   Communities   v
Ladbroke   Racing   Ltd;
France v Ladbroke Racing
Ltd [1997] E.C.R. I-6265;
[1998]   4   C.M.L.R.   27
ECJ 377
C-367/95   P Commission of the
European Communities v Sys-
traval and Brink's France [1998]
E.C.R. I–1719 138,
395
C-368/95   Vereinigte Familiapress
Zeitungsverlags- und vertriebs
GmbH v Heinrich Bauer Verlag
[1997] E.C.R. I–3689 229
C-388/95   Belgium v Spain [2000]
E.C.R.   I-3123;   [2002]   1
C.M.L.R. 26 ECJ 130
C-400/95   Handels- og Kontor-
funktionærernes Forbund i Dan-
mark, acting on behalf of Helle
Elisabeth Larsson v Dansk Han-
del & Service, acting on behalf
of Føtex Supermarked A/S
[1997] E.C.R. I-2757; [1979] 2
C.M.L.R. 915 478
C-408/95   Eurotunnel   SA   v
SeaFrance [1997] E.C.R. I–6315 ... 147
C-22/96   European Parliament v
Council of the European Union
[1998] E.C.R. I–3231 141
C-35/96   Commission of the Euro-
pean Communities v Italy; sub
nom. Customs Agents, Re [1998]
E.C.R.   I-3851;   [1998]   5
C.M.L.R. 889 ECJ 323
C-44/96   Mannesmann Anlagenbau
Austria AG v Strohal Rotations-
druck GmbH [1998] E.C.R.
I-73; [1998] 2 C.M.L.R. 805
ECJ 309
C-45/96   Bayerische Hypotheken-
und Wechselbank AG v Dietzinger
[1998] 1 W.L.R. 1035; [1998] All
E.R. (EC) 332; [1998] E.C.R.
I-1199; [1998] 2 C.M.L.R. 499
ECJ 293
C-51/96 and C-191/97 Christelle
Deliège v Ligue francophone de
judo et disciplines associées
ASBL, Ligue belge de judo ASBL,
Union européenne de judo;
François Pacquée [2000] E.C.R.
I–2549 290

C-54/96   Dorsch   Consult   Inge-
nieurgesellschaft mbH v Bundes-
baugesellschaft Berlin mbH
[1998] All E.R. (EC) 262; [1997]
E.C.R.   I-4961;   [1998]   2
C.M.L.R. 237 ECJ 316
C-55/96   Job Centre Coop arl, Re
[1997] E.C.R. I-7119; [1998] 4
C.M.L.R. 708; [1998] C.E.C.
507 ECJ 341
C-69/96 to C79/96   Garofalo v
Ministero della Sanita; Garofalo
v Unita Sanitaria Locale (USL)
No.58 di Palermo [1997] E.C.R.
I-5603; [1998] 1 C.M.L.R. 1087
ECJ 144, 273
C-85/96   María Martínez Sala v
Freistaat Bayern [1998] E.C.R.
I–2691 246
C-97/96   Verband   deutscher
Daihatsu-Händler eV v Daihatsu
Deutschland   GmbH   [1997]
E.C.R. I–6843 278
C-114/96   Criminal   proceedings
against René Kieffer and Romain
Thill [1997] E.C.R. I–3629 ... 227, 230
C-116/96   Reisebüro   Binder
GmbH v Finanzamt Stuttgart-
Körperschaften [1998] E.C.R.
I–1891 148
C-129/96   Inter-Environnement Wal-
lonie ASBL v Region Wallonie;
sub nom. Inter-Environnement
Wallonie Asbl v Region Wallonne;
Inter-Environnement   Wallonie
Asbl v Region Wallone [1998] All
E.R. (E.C.) 155; [1997] E.C.R.
I-7411; [1998] 1 C.M.L.R. 1057
ECJ 33
C-157/96   R. v Ministry of Agricul-
ture, Fisheries and Food Ex p.
National Farmers' Union [1998]
E.C.R. I-2211 541
C-162/96   A Racke GmbH & Co v
Hauptzollamt   Mainz   [1998]
E.C.R. I–3655 .... 138, 144, 582
C-174/96   P Orlando Lopes v
Court of Justice of the European
Communities   [1996]   E.C.R.
I–6401 157
C-176/96   Jyri Lehtonen and Cas-
tors Canada Dry Namur-Braine
ASBL v Fédération royale belge
des sociétés de basket-ball ASBL
(FRBSB) [2000] E.C.R. I–2714 ... 290

C-253/96 and C-257/96 Kampelmann v Landschaftsverband Westfalen-Lippe; Stadtwerke Witten GmbH v Schade; Haseley v Stadtwerke Altena GmbH (C-258/96) [1997] E.C.R. I-6907; [1998] 2 C.M.L.R. 131 ECJ 474

C-278/96 Comité des Salines [1996] E.C.R. 2410 392

C-290/96 Commission of the European Communities v Hellenic Republic [1996] E.C.R. I–3285 . 254

C-298/96 Oelm Ühle Hamburg AG v Bundesanstalt fur Landwirtschaft und Ernahrung [1998] E.C.R. I-4767; [1999] 2 C.M.L.R. 492 ECJ . 396

C-323/96 Commission of the European Communities v Belgium [1998] E.C.R. I–5063 313

C-355/96 Silhouette International Schmied GmbH & Co KG v Hartlauer Handelsgesellschaft mbH [1999] Ch. 77; [1998] 3 W.L.R. 1218; [1998] E.C.R. I-4799 ECJ .. 306

C-360/96 Gemeente Arnhem v BFI Holding BV; sub nom. BFI Holding BV v Municipality of Arnhem [1999] All E.R. (EC) 709; [1998] E.C.R. I-6821; [2001] 1 C.M.L.R. 6 ECJ 314

C-364/96 Verein für Konsumenteninformation v Österreichische Kreditversicherungs AG [1999] All E.R. (EC) 183; [1998] E.C.R. I-2949; [1999] 1 C.M.L.R. 1430 ECJ 498

C-367/96 Alexandros Kefalas v Elliniko Dimosio (Greek State) and Organismos Oikonomikis Anasygkrotisis Epicheiriseon AE (OAE) [1998] E.C.R. I–2843 ... 278

C-385/96 Criminal Proceedings against Goerres [1998] E.C.R. I-4431 ECJ 499

C-395/96 P and C-396/96 P Compagnie Maritime Belge Transports SA v Commission of the European Communities; Dafra-Lines A/S v Commission of the European Communities; sub nom. Cie Maritime Belge Transports SA v Commission of the European Communities [2000] All E.R. (EC) 385; [2000] E.C.R. I-1365; [2000] 4 C.M.L.R. 1076 ECJ 338

C-402/96 European Information Technology Observatory, Europäische Wirtschaftliche Interessenvereinigung [1997] E.C.R. I–7515 283

C-415/96 Spain v Commission of the European Communities [1998] E.C.R. I-6993; [1999] 1 C.M.L.R. 304 ECJ 160

C-6/97 Italy v Commission of the European Communities [1999] E.C.R. I–2981 .... 380, 381

C-7/97 Oscar Bronner GmbH & Co KG v Mediaprint Zeitungs- und Zeitschriftenverlag GmbH & Co KG [1998] E.C.R. I-7791; [1999] 4 C.M.L.R. 112 ECJ 341

C-38/97 Autotrasporti Librandi Snc di Librandi F&C v Cuttica spedizioni e servizi internationali Srl 378, 444

C-39/97 Canon Kabushiki Kaisha v Metro Goldwyn Mayer Inc [1998] All E.R. (EC) 934; [1998] E.C.R. I-5507; [1999] 1 C.M.L.R. 77 ECJ 306

C-70/97 P Kruidvat BVBA v Commission of the European Communities [1998] E.C.R. I-7183; [1999] 4 C.M.L.R. 68 ECJ 137

C-76/97 Togel v Niederosterreichische Gebietskrankenkasse [1998] E.C.R. I-5357; [1998] 3 C.M.L.R. 768 ECJ 316

C-95/97 Région wallonne v Commission of the European Communities [1997] E.C.R. I–1787 134

C-110/97 Netherlands v Council of the European Union [1997] E.C.R. I–1795 150

C-121/97 Commission of the European Communities v Germany [1990] E.C.R. I-2721 550

C-161/97 P Kernkraftwerke Lippe-Ems GmbH v Commission of the European Community [1999] E.C.R. I-2057; [2000] 2 C.M.L.R. 489 ECJ 182, 559

C-180/97 Regione Toscana v Commission of the European Communities [1997] E.C.R. I–5247 134

C-185/97 Coote v Granada Hospitality Ltd [1998] All E.R. (EC) 865; [1998] E.C.R. I-5199; [1998] 3 C.M.L.R. 958; [1999] C.E.C. 515 ECJ 474

C-200/97 Ecotrade Srl v Altiforni e Ferriere di Servola SpA (AFS) [1998] E.C.R. I–7907 380

C-215/97 Barbara Bellone v Yokohama SpA [1998] E.C.R. I–2191 267

C-241/97 Försäkringsaktiebolaget Skandia [1999] E.C.R. I–1879 296

C-258/97 Hospital Ingenieure Krankenhaustechnik Planungs-Gesellschaft mbH (HI) v Landeskrankenanstalten-Betriebsgesellschaft [1999] E.C.R. I–1405 316

C-310/97 P Commission of the European Communities v AssiDoman Kraft Products AB [1999] All E.R. (EC) 737; [1999] E.C.R. I-5363; [1999] 5 C.M.L.R. 1253 ECJ 140

C-323/97 Commission of the European Communities v Belgium [1998] E.C.R. I-4291 .... 4, 240

C-333/97 Lewen v Denda [2000] All E.R. (EC) 261; [1999] E.C.R. I-7243; [2000] 2 C.M.L.R. 38 ECJ 472

C-342/97 Lloyd Schuhfabrik Meyer & Co GmbH v Klijsen Handel BV [1999] All E.R. (EC) 587; [1999] E.C.R. I-3819; [1999] 2 C.M.L.R. 1343 ECJ ... 306

C-387/97 Commission of the European Communities v Greece [2000] E.C.R. I-5047; [2001] Env. L.R. D2 ECJ 131

C-424/97 Haim v Kassenzahnärztliche Vereinigung Nordrhein [2000] E.C.R. I-5123; [2002] 1 C.M.L.R. 11 ECJ 112

C-437/97 Evangelischer Krankenhausverein Wien v Abgabenberufungskommission Wien and Wein & Co. HandelsgesmbH v Oberösterreichische Landesregierung [2000] E.C.R. I–1157 141

C-16/98 Commission of the European Communities v France [2000] E.C.R. I–831 309

C-49/98, C-69/98, C-68/98, C-54/98, C-53/98, C-52/98, C-50/98, C-71/98 and C-70/98 Finalarte Sociedade de Construcao Civil Lda v Urlaubs- und Lohnausgleichskasse der Bauwirtschaft; Urlaubs- und Lohnausgleichskasse der Bauwirtschaft v Santos & Kewitz Construcoes Lda; Urlaubs- und Lohnausgleichskasse der Bauwirtschaft v Duarte dos Santos Sousa; Urlaubs- und Lohnausgleichskasse der Bauwirtschaft v Turiprata Construcoes Civil SA; Urlaubs- und Lohnausgleichskasse der Bauwirtschaft v Tecnamb-Tecnologia do Ambiente Lda; Urlaubs- und Lohnausgleichskasse der Bauwirtschaft v Tudor Stone Ltd; Urlaubs- und Lohnausgleichskasse der Bauwirtschaft v Amilcar Oliveira Rocha; Engil Sociedade de Construcao Civil SA v Urlaubs- und Lohnausgleichskasse der Bauwirtschaft; Portugaia Construcoes Lda v Urlaubs- und Lohnausgleichskasse der Bauwirtschaft [2001] E.C.R. I-7831; [2003] 2 C.M.L.R. 11 ECJ 309

C-81/98 Alcatel Austria AG v Bundesministerium fur Wissenschaft und Verkehr [1999] E.C.R. I-7671; (2000) 2 T.C.L.R. 894 ECJ 316

C-83/98 P France v Ladbroke Racing Ltd [2000] E.C.R. I-3271; [2000] 3 C.M.L.R. 555 ECJ 381

C-99/98 Austria v Commission of the European Communities [2001] E.C.R. I–1101 395

C-107/98 Teckal Srl v Comune di Viano and Azienda Gas-Acqua Consorziale (AGAC) di Reggio Emilia [1999] E.C.R. I–8121 310

C-108/98 RI.SAN. Srl v Comune di Ischia, Italia Lavoro SpA and Ischia Ambiente SpA [1999] E.C.R. I–5219 314

C-186/98 Criminal Proceedings against Nunes; sub nom. Nunes, Re [1999] E.C.R. I-4883; [1999] 2 C.M.L.R. 1403 ECJ 480

C-207/98 Mahlburg v Land Mecklenburg Vorpommern [2000] E.C.R. I-549; [2001] 3 C.M.L.R. 40 ECJ 477

C-210/98 Salzgitter AG, formerly Preussag Stahl AG v Commission of the European Communities [2000] E.C.R. I–5843 385

C-225/98 Commission of the European Communities v France [2000] E.C.R. I–7445 312

C-240/98–C-244/98 Océano Grupo Editorial SA v Quintero; Salvat Editores SA v Feliu Salvat Editores SA v Berroane); Salvat Editores SA v Badillo; Salvat Editores SA v Prades [2000] E.C.R. I-4941; [2002] 1 C.M.L.R. 43 ECJ 56, 451

C-254/98 Schutzverband gegen unlauteren Wettbewerb v TK-Heimdienst Sass GmbH [2000] E.C.R. I–151 143

C-275/98 Unitron Scandinavia A/S and 3-S A/S, Danske Svineproducenters Serviceselskab v Ministeriet for Fødevarer, Landbrug og Fiskeri [1999] E.C.R. I-8291 309

C-300/98 and C-392/98 Parfums Christian Dior SA v Tuk Consultancy BV; Assco Geruste GmbH v Wilhelm Layher GmbH & Co KG [2000] E.C.R. I-11307; [2001] E.T.M.R. 26 ECJ 54

C-322/98 Bärbel Kachelmann v Bankhaus Hermann Lampe KG [2000] E.C.R. I-7505 474

C-324/98 Telaustria Verlags GmbH and Telefonadress GmbH v Telekom Austria AG [2000] E.C.R. I–10745 314

C-343/98 Collino v Telecom Italia SpA [2001] All E.R. (EC) 405; [2000] E.C.R. I-6659; [2002] 3 C.M.L.R. 35 ECJ 473

C-359/98 P Ca' Pasta Srl v Commission of the European Communities [2000] E.C.R. I–3977 155

C-403/98 Azienda Agricola Monte Arcosu Srl v Regione Autonoma della Sardegna [2001] E.C.R. I-103; [2002] 2 C.M.L.R. 14 ECJ ... 31

C-407/98 Abrahamsson v Fogelqvist [2000] E.C.R. I-5539; [2002] I.C.R. 932 ECJ 477

C-456/98 Centrosteel Srl v Adipol GmbH [2000] E.C.R. I-6007; [2000] 3 C.M.L.R. 711 ECJ ... 129, 370

C-466/98 Commission of the European Communities v United Kingdom; sub nom. Open Skies Agreement, Re [2002] E.C.R. I-9427; [2003] 1 C.M.L.R. 6 ECJ 344, 453

C-468/98 Commission of the European Communities v Sweden [2002] E.C.R. I-9575 581

C-16/99 Ministre de la Santé v Jeff Erpelding [2000] E.C.R. I–6821 ... 273

C-29/99 Commission of the European Communities v Council of the European Union [2002] E.C.R. I–11221 560

C-37/99 Criminal proceedings against Roelof Donkersteeg [2000] E.C.R. I–10223 234

C-51/99 P Hercules Chemicals NV v Commission of the European Communities [1999] E.C.R. I–4225 155

C-62/99 Betriebsrat der Bofrost Josef H Boquoi Deutschland West GmbH & Co KG v Bofrost Josef H Boquoi Deutschland West GmbH & Co KG [2001] E.C.R. I-2579; [2004] 2 C.M.L.R. 53 ECJ 474

C-94/99 ARGE Gewässerschutz v Bundesministerium für Land- und Forstwirtschaft [2000] E.C.R. I–11037 ECJ 310

C-153/99P Commission of the European Communities v Gianni [2000] E.C.R. I–2891 140

C-172/99 Oy Liikenne AB v Liskojarvi; sub nom. Liskojarvi v Oy Liikenne AB [2001] All E.R. (EC) 544; [2001] E.C.R. I-745; [2001] 3 C.M.L.R. 37 ECJ 473

C-184/99 Grzelczyk v Centre Public d'Aide Sociale d'Ottignies Louvain la Neuve [2003] All E.R. (EC) 385; [2001] E.C.R. I-6193; [2002] 1 C.M.L.R. 19 ECJ 129

C-202/99 Commission of the European Communities v Italy [2001] E.C.R. I–9319 271

C-228/99 Silos e Mangimi Martini SpA v Ministero delle Finanze [2001] E.C.R. I-8401 37

C-262/99 Paraskevas Louloudakis v Elliniko Dimosio [2001] E.C.R. I–5547 269

C-267/99 Christiane Adam, épouse Urbing v Administration de l'enregistrement et des domaines [2001] E.C.R. I–7467 271

C-286/99 Impresa Lombardini SpA – Impresa Generale di Costruzioni v ANAS – Ente nazionale per le strade and Società Italiana per Condotte d'Acqua SpA (C-285/99); Impresa Ing. Mantovani SpA v ANAS – Ente nazionale per le strade and Ditta Paolo Bregoli [2001] E.C.R. I–9233 313

C-290/99 Council of the European Union v Bangemann 108

C-306/99 Banque internationale pour l'Afrique occidentale SA (BIAO) v Finanzamt für Großunternehmen in Hamburg [2003] E.C.R. I–1 279

C-310/99 Italy v Commission of the European Communities [2002] E.C.R. I–2289 390

C-340/99 TNT Traco SpA v Poste Italiane SpA [2001] E.C.R. I–4109 .... 145, 340

C-413/99 Baumbast v Secretary of State for the Home Department [2002] E.C.R. I–7091; [2002] 3 C.M.L.R. 23 ECJ 248

C-459/99 Mouvement contre le Racisme, l'Antisemitisme et la Xenophobie ASBL (MRAX) v Belgium [2003] 1 W.L.R. 1073; [2002] E.C.R. I-6591; [2002] 3 C.M.L.R. 25 ECJ 248

C-541/99 and C-542/99 Cape SNC v Idealservice Srl; Idealservice MN RE SAS v OMAI Srl [2002] All E.R. (EC) 657; [2001] E.C.R. I-9049; [2003] 1 C.M.L.R. 42 ECJ . 498

C-6/00 Abfall Service AG (ASA) v Bundesminister für Umwelt, Jugend und Familie [2002] E.C.R. I-1961 ECJ 546

C-11/00 Commission of the European Communities v European Central Bank [2003] E.C.R. I-7147 79

C-31/00 Conseil national de l'ordre des architectes v Nicolas Dreessen [2002] E.C.R. I–663 .... 274, 276

C-50/00 P Union de Pequenos Agricultores v Council of the European Union [2003] Q.B. 893; [2003] 2 W.L.R. 795; [2002] E.C.R. I-6677 ECJ 135

C-53/00 Ferring SA v Agence centrale des organismes de sécurité sociale (ACOSS) [2001] E.C.R. I–9067 382

C-59/00 Vestergaard v Spottrup Boligselskab [2001] E.C.R. I-9505; [2002] 2 C.M.L.R. 42 ECJ 311

C-62/00 Marks & Spencer Plc v Customs and Excise Commissioners [2003] Q.B. 866; [2003] 2 W.L.R. 665; [2002] E.C.R. I-6325 ECJ 140

C-79/00 Telefonica de Espana SA v Administracion General del Estado [2001] E.C.R. I-10075; [2002] 4 C.M.L.R. 22 ECJ 510

C-92/00 Hospital Ingenieure Krankenhaustechnik Planungs-Gesellschaft mbH (HI) v Stadt Wien [2002] E.C.R. I–5553 316

C-104/00 P DKV Deutsche Krankenversicherung AG v Office for Harmonisation in the Internal Market (Trade Marks and Designs) (OHIM) [2002] E.C.R. I-7561; [2003] E.T.M.R. 20 ECJ 196

C-168/00 Simone Leitner v TUI Deutschland GmbH & Co KG [2002] E.C.R. I-26321 498

C-183/00 María Victoria González Sánchez v Medicina Asturiana SA [2002] E.C.R. I-3901 498

C-187/00 Kutz-Bauer v Freie und Hansestadt Hamburg [2003] E.C.R. I-2741; [2005] 2 C.M.L.R. 35 ECJ 56

C-208/00 Überseering BV v Nordic Construction Company Baumanagement GmbH (NCC) [2002] E.C.R. I–9919 ... 268

C-209/00 Commission of the European Communities v Germany [2002] E.C.R. I–11695 393

C-218/00 Cisal Cisal di Battistello Venanzio & C. Sas v Istituto nazionale per l'assicurazione contro gli infortuni sul lavoro (INAIL) [2002] E.C.R. I–691 ECJ 323

C-242/00 Germany v Commission of the European Communities [2002] E.C.R. I–5603 139

C-245/00 Stichting ter Exploitatie van Naburige Rechten (SENA) v Nederlandse Omroep Stichting (NOS) [2003] E.C.R. I–12151 .. 301

C-280/00 Altmark Trans GmbH v Nahverkehrsgesellschaft Altmark GmbH [2005] All E.R. (EC) 610; [2003] E.C.R. I-7747; [2003] 3 C.M.L.R. 12 ECJ 382, 389

C-305/00 Christian Schulin v Saatgut-Treuhandverwaltungsgesellschaft mbH [2003] E.C.R. I–3525 197

C-378/00 Commission of the European Communities v Parliament and Council [2003] E.C.R. I-937 .... 116, 118, 550

C-411/00 Felix Swoboda GmbH v Österreichische Nationalbank [2002] E.C.R. I–10567 312

C-453/00 Kûhne & Heitz NV v Productschap voor Pluimvee en Eieren [2004] E.C.R. I-837; [2006] 2 C.M.L.R. 17 ECJ 50, 140

C-465/00 Rechnungshof v Österreichischer Rundfunk [2003] E.C.R. I-4989; [2003] 3 C.M.L.R. 10 ECJ 501

C-20/01 and C-28/01 Commission of the European Communities v Germany [2003] E.C.R. I–3609 . 311

C-56/01 Inizan v Caisse Primaire d'Assurance Maladie des Hauts de Seine) [2003] E.C.R. I-12403; [2006] 1 C.M.L.R. 20 ECJ 146

C-57/01 Makedoniko Metro and Michaniki AE v Elliniko Dimosio [2003] E.C.R. I–1091 316

C-83/01 P, C-93/01 P and C-94/01 P Chronopost SA v Union Francaise de l'Express (UFEX); La Poste v Union Francaise de l'Express (UFEX); France v Union Francaise de l'Express (UFEX) [2003] E.C.R. I-6993; [2003] 3 C.M.L.R. 11 ECJ 382

C-186/01 R Alexander Dory v Bundesrepublik Deutschland [2001] E.C.R. I–7823 146

C-187/01 amd C-385/01 Criminal Proceedings against Hüseyin Gözütok; Criminal Proceedings against Klaus Brügge [2003] E.C.R. I-1345; [2003] 2 C.M.L.R. 2 ECJ 243

C-216/01 Budejovicky Budvar Narodni Podnik v Rudolf Ammersin GmbH [2003] E.C.R. I-13617; [2005] 1 C.M.L.R. 56 ECJ 55

C-224/01 Köbler v Austria [2004] Q.B. 848; [2004] 2 W.L.R. 976; [2004] All E.R. (EC) 23; [2003] E.C.R. I-10239; [2003] 3 C.M.L.R. 28 ECJ 51, 112

C-228/01 Criminal Proceedings against Bourrasse; Criminal Proceedings against Perchicot; sub nom. Bourasse v Ministere Public [2003] All E.R. (EC) 465; [2002] E.C.R. I-10213 ECJ 444

C-241/01 National Farmers' Union v Secrétariat général du gouvernement [2002] E.C.R. I–9079 137

C-285/01 Isabel Burbaud v Ministère de l'Emploi et de la Solidarité [2003] E.C.R. I-8219; [2003] 3 C.M.L.R. 21 276

C-290/01 Receveur principal des douanes de Villepinte v Derudder & Cie SA, and Tang Frères [2004] E.C.R. I–2041 224

C-349/01 Betriebsrat der ADS Anker GmbH v ADS Anker GmbH [2004] E.C.R. I-6803; [2004] 3 C.M.L.R. 14 ECJ 474

C-349/01 Betriebsrat der Firma ADS Anker GmbH v ADS Anker GmbH [2004] E.C.R. I–6819 ... 282

C-418/01 IMS Health GmbH & Co OHG v NDC Health GmbH & Co KG [2004] All E.R. (EC) 813; [2004] E.C.R. I–5039 307

C-421/01 Traunfellner GmbH v Österreichische Autobahnen- und Schnellstraβen-Finanzierungs-AG (Asfinag) [2003] E.C.R. I–11941 313

C-486/01 P Front National v European Parliament [2004] E.C.R. I-6289; [2004] 2 C.M.L.R. 51 ECJ 81

C-19/02 Hlozek v Roche Austria GmbH [2004] E.C.R. I-11491; [2005] 1 C.M.L.R. 28 ECJ 478

C-25/02 Katharina Rinke v Ärztekammer Hamburg [2003] E.C.R. I–8349 273

C-30/02 Recheio – Cash & Carry SA v Fazenda Pública/Registo Nacional de Pessoas Colectivas, and Ministério Público [2004] E.C.R. I–6051 140

C-167/02 P Rothley v European Parliament [2004] E.C.R. I-3149; [2004] 2 C.M.L.R. 11 ECJ 64

C-184/02 and C-223/02 Spain and Finland v European Parliament and Council of the European Union [2004] E.C.R. I–7789 . 140, 446

C-201/02 R. (on the application of Wells) v Secretary of State for Transport, Local Government and the Regions; sub nom. Wells v Secretary of State for Transport, Local Government and the Regions [2005] All E.R. (EC) 323; [2004] E.C.R. I-723; [2004] 1 C.M.L.R. 31 ECJ 32, 140

C-212/02 Commission of the European Communities v Austria Unpublished, 2004 316

C-222/02 Paul v Germany [2004] E.C.R. I-9425; [2006] 2 C.M.L.R. 62 ECJ 51, 292

C-277/02 EU-Wood-Trading GmbH v Sonderabfall-Management-Gesellschaft Rheinland-Pfalz mbH [2004] E.C.R. I-11957 546

C-284/02 Land Brandenburg v Sass [2004] E.C.R. I-11143; [2005] 1 C.M.L.R. 27 ECJ 479

C-304/02 Commission of the European Communities v France; sub nom. Control Measures for Fishing Activities, Re [2005] E.C.R. I-6263; [2005] 3 C.M.L.R. 13 ECJ 111, 131

C-313/02 Wippel v Peek & Cloppenburg GmbH & Co KG [2004] E.C.R. I-9483; [2005] 1 C.M.L.R. 9 ECJ 479

C-347/02 Commission of the European Communities v France [2004] E.C.R. I–7557 295

C-377/02 Léon Van Parys NV v Belgisch Interventie- en Restitutiebureau (BIRB) [2005] E.C.R I-1465 55

C-387/02 Criminal Proceedings against Berlusconi [2005] E.C.R. I-3565; [2005] 2 C.M.L.R. 32 ECJ 278

C-434/02 Arnold André GmbH & Co KG v Landrat des Kreises Herford [2004] E.C.R. I-11825 ECJ 36

C-435/02 and C-103/03 Axel Springer AG v Zeitungsverlag Niederrhein GmbH & Co. Essen KG and Hans-Jürgen Weske [2004] E.C.R. I–8663 ..... 279, 292

C-460/02 Commission of the European Communities v Italy [2004] E.C.R. I-7335 451

C-6/03 Deponietzweckverband Eiterköpfe v Land Rheinland-Pfalz [2005] E.C.R. I-2753; [2005] 2 C.M.L.R. 52 ECJ 542

C-17/03 Vereniging voor Energie, Milieu en Water v Directeur van de Dienst uitvoering en toezicht energie [2005] E.C.R. I-49831 ... 555

C-23/03, C-52/03, C-133/03, C-337/03 and C-473/03 Criminal proceedings against Michel Mulliez and Giuseppe Momblano; Alessandro Nizza and Giacomo Pizzi); Fabrizio Barra; Adelio Aggio [2006] E.C.R. I-3923 33

C-26/03 Stadt Halle v Arbeitsgemeinschaft Thermische Restabfall- und Energieverwertungsanlage TREA Leuna [2005] E.C.R. I–1; [2006] 1 C.M.L.R. 39 ECJ ... 313, 316

C-39/03 Commission of the European Communities v Artegodan GmbH [2003] E.C.R. I–7885 ... 162

C-70/03 Commission of the European Communities v Spain [2004] E.C.R. I-7999 .... 451, 498

C-81/03 Commission of the European Communities v Austria Unpublished 266

C-110/03 Belgium v Commission of the European Communities; sub nom. Legality of Regulation 2204/2002, Re [2005] E.C.R. I-2801; [2006] 2 C.M.L.R. 5 ECJ 379, 390

C-131/03 P RJ Reynolds Tobacco Holdings Inc v Commission of the European Communities [2006] E.C.R. I-7795; [2007] 1 C.M.L.R. 1 ECJ 113

C-138/03, C-324/03 and C-431/03 Italy v Commission of the European Communities [2005] E.C.R. I–10043 134

C-147/03 Commission of the European Communities v Austria [2005] E.C.R. I–5969 270

C-160/03 Spain v Eurojust [2005] E.C.R. I-2077 191

C-173/03 Traghetti del Mediterraneo SpA (In Liquidation) v Italy [2006] All E.R. (EC) 983; [2006] E.C.R. I-5177; [2006] 3 C.M.L.R. 19 ECJ 51, 112

C-176/03 Commission of the European Communities v Council of the European Union [2006] All E.R. (EC) 1; [2005] E.C.R. I-7879; [2005] 3 C.M.L.R. 20; [2006] Env. L.R. 18 ECJ 548, 549

C-188/03 Junk v Kuhnel [2005] E.C.R. I-885; [2005] 1 C.M.L.R. 42 ECJ 473

C-191/03 North Western Health Board v McKenna [2006] All E.R. (EC) 455; [2005] E.C.R. I-7631; [2006] 1 C.M.L.R. 6 ECJ 474

C-209/03 R. (on the application of Bidar) v Ealing LBC [2005] Q.B. 812; [2005] 2 W.L.R. 1078; [2005] E.C.R. I-2119 ECJ 270

C-213/03 Syndicat professionnel coordination des pêcheurs de l'étang de Berre et de la région v Électricité de France (EDF) July 15, 2004 40

C-215/03 Oulane v Minister voor Vreemdelingenzaken en Integratie [2005] Q.B. 1055; [2005] 3 W.L.R. 543; [2005] E.C.R. I-1215 ECJ 240

C-231/03 Consorzio Aziende Metano (Coname) v Comune di Cingia de' Botti [2005] E.C.R. I–7287 310

C-265/03 Simutenkov v Ministerio de Educacion y Cultura [2006] All E.R. (EC) 42; [2005] E.C.R. I-2579; [2005] 2 C.M.L.R. 11 ECJ 591

C-276/03 P Scott SA v Commission of the European Communities [2005] E.C.R. I–8437 .... 337, 396

C-327/03 Germany v Isis Multimedia Net GmbH & Co KG [2005] E.C.R. I-8877; [2006] 4 C.M.L.R. 1 ECJ 510

C-329/03 Trapeza tis Ellados AE v Banque Artesia [2005] E.C.R. I–9341 298

C-330/03 Colegio de Ingenieros de Caminos, Canales y Puertos v Administracion del Estado [2006] E.C.R. I-801; [2006] 2 C.M.L.R. 26 ECJ 275

C-350/03 AJ Schulte v Deutsche Bausparkasse Badenia AG [2005] E.C.R. I–9178 161

C-350/03 Schulte v Deutsche Bausparkasse Badenia AG [2006] All E.R. (EC) 420; [2005] E.C.R. I-9215; [2006] 1 C.M.L.R. 11 ECJ 497

C-364/03 Commission of the European Communities v Greece [2005] E.C.R. I-6159; [2006] Env. L.R. 9 ECJ 546

C-402/03 Skov Æg v Bilka Lavprisvarehus A/S and Bilka Lavprisvarehus A/S v Jette Mikkelsen and Michael Due Nielsen [2006] E.C.R. I-199 498

C-436/03 European Parliament v Council of the European Union; sub nom. Validity of Regulation 1435/2003, Re [2006] E.C.R. I-3733; [2006] 3 C.M.L.R. 3 ECJ... 436

C-443/03 Leffler v Berlin Chemie AG [2006] All E.R. (EC) 692; [2005] E.C.R. I-9611 ECJ 259

C-445/03 Commission of the European Communities v Luxembourg; sub nom. Law on Work Permits for Foreign Workers Employed by Cross Border Service Providers, Re [2004] E.C.R. I-10191; [2005] 1 C.M.L.R. 22 ECJ 254

C-458/03 Parking Brixen GmbH v Gemeinde Brixen [2006] All E.R. (EC) 779; [2005] E.C.R. I-8612; [2006] 1 C.M.L.R. 3; [2006] C.E.C. 144 ECJ 311

C-459/03 Commission of the European Communities v Ireland; sub nom. Dispute over MOX Plant, Re [2006] All E.R. (EC) 1013; [2006] E.C.R. I-4635; [2006] 2 C.M.L.R. 59 ECJ 131

C-461/03 Gaston Schul Douane-
expediteur BV v Minister van
Landbouw, Natuur en Voedselk-
walitei [2005] E.C.R. I–10513 ... 145
C-462/03 Strabag AG (and Kost-
mann GmbH v Österreichische
Bundesbahnen [2005] E.C.R.
I–5397 312
C-477/03 Commission of the Euro-
pean Communities v Germany
November 17, 2004 ...... 447, 448
C-478/03 Celtec Ltd v Astley; sub
nom. Astley v Celtec Ltd [2005]
E.C.R. I-4389; [2005] 3 C.M.L.R.
9 ECJ 473
C-481/03 Commission of the European Communities v Luxem-
bourg [2004] O.J. C284/6 448
C-483/03 Commission of the Euro-
pean Communities v United
Kingdom [2004] O.J. C300/23 ... 448
C-503/03 Commission of the Euro-
pean Communities v Spain
[2007] All E.R. (EC) 797; [2006]
E.C.R. I-1097 ECJ 243,
                              253
C-507/03 Commission of the Euro-
pean Communities v Ireland; sub
nom. Irish Post Office Contract,
Re [2007] E.C.R. I-9777; [2008]
1 C.M.L.R. 34; [2008] C.E.C.
782 ECJ 311, 314
C-520/03 José Vicente Olaso
Valero v Fondo de Garantía
Salarial (Fogasa) [2004] E.C.R.
I-12065 473
C-524/03 Commission of the
European Communities v G&E
Gianniotis EPE 164
C-540/03 European Parliament v
Council of the European Union;
sub nom. Validity of Directive
2003/86, Re [2007] All E.R.
(EC) 193; [2006] E.C.R. I-5769;
[2006] 3 C.M.L.R. 28 ECJ 140
C-550/2003 Commission of the
European Communities v Greece
[2004] O.J. C300/24 448
C-3/04 Poseidon Chartering BV v
Marianne Zeeschip Vof [2007]
Bus. L.R. 446; [2006] 2 Lloyd's
Rep. 105; [2006] E.C.R. I-2505
ECJ 267
C-07/04 Commission of the Euro-
pean Communities v Akzo and
Ackros [2004] E.C.R. I-8739 ... 354

C-29/04 Commission of the Euro-
pean Communities v Austria; sub
nom. Modling Waste Disposal
Contract, Re [2005] E.C.R.
I-9705; [2006] 1 C.M.L.R. 40
ECJ 312
C-30/04 Ursel Koschitzki v Istituto
nazionale della previdenza sociale
(INPS) [2005] E.C.R. I–7389 251
C-66/04 United Kingdom v Euro-
pean Parliament; sub nom.
Validity of Regulation
2065/2003, Re [2006] All E.R.
(EC) 487; [2005] E.C.R.
I-10553; [2006] 3 C.M.L.R. 1
ECJ 436
C-112/04 Commission of the Euro-
pean Communities v Germany
(Volkswagen law) [2007] E.C.R.
I-8995 298
C-122/04 Commission of the Euro-
pean Communities v Parliament
and Council [2006] E.C.R.
I-2001 116
C-127/04 O'Byrne v Sanofi Pasteur
MSD Ltd (formerly Aventis Pas-
teur MSD Ltd) [2006] 1 W.L.R.
1606; [2006] All E.R. (EC) 674;
[2006] E.C.R. I-1313 ECJ 497
C-128/04 Criminal Proceedings
against Raemdonck [2005]
E.C.R. I-2445; [2005] R.T.R. 25
ECJ 442
C-131/04, C-257/04 and C-257/04
Robinson-Steele v RD Retail Ser-
vices Ltd; Clarke v Frank Stad-
don Ltd; Caulfield v Hanson
Clay Products Ltd [2006] All
E.R. (EC) 749; [2006] E.C.R.
I-2531; [2006] 2 C.M.L.R. 34
ECJ 476
C-141/04 Michail Peros v Tech-
niko Epimelitirio Ellados [2005]
E.C.R. I–7165 276
C-145/04 Spain v United Kingdom;
sub nom. Gibraltar European
Elections, Re [2007] All E.R.
(EC) 486; [2006] E.C.R. I-7917;
[2007] 1 C.M.L.R. 3 ECJ 63
C-167/04 P JCB Service v Commis-
sion of the European Communi-
ties [2006] E.C.R. I-8935; [2006]
5 C.M.L.R. 23 ECJ 29
C-170/04 Rosengren v Riksakla-
garen [2009] All E.R. (EC) 455;
[2007] 3 C.M.L.R. 10 ECJ 376

C-212/04 Adeneler v Ellinikos Organismos Galaktos (ELOG) [2007] All E.R. (EC) 82; [2006] E.C.R. I-6057; [2006] 3 C.M.L.R. 30 ECJ 34

C-213/04 Burtscher v Stauderer [2005] E.C.R. I-10309; [2006] 2 C.M.L.R. 13 ECJ 298

C-217/04 United Kingdom v European Parliament; sub nom. Validity of Regulation 460/2004, Re [2006] E.C.R. I-3771; [2006] 3 C.M.L.R. 2 ECJ 200, 435

C-234/04 Kapferer v Schlank & Schick GmbH [2006] E.C.R. I-2585; [2006] 2 C.M.L.R. 19 ECJ 50

C-317/04 and C-318/04 European Parliament v Council of the European Union; European Parliament v Council of the European Union [2007] All E.R. (EC) 278; [2006] E.C.R. I-4721; [2006] 3 C.M.L.R. 9 ECJ 501

C-340/04 Carbotermo SpA v Comune di Busto Arsizio [2006] E.C.R. I-4137; [2006] 3 C.M.L.R. 7 ECJ 311

C-341/04 Eurofood IFSC Ltd [2006] E.C.R. I-3813 260

C-344/04 R. (on the application of International Air Transport Association (IATA)) v Department of Transport [2006] E.C.R. I-403; [2006] 2 C.M.L.R. 20 ECJ 451

C-348/04 Boehringer Ingelheim KG v Swingward Ltd [2008] All E.R. (EC) 411; [2007] E.C.R. I-3391; [2007] 2 C.M.L.R. 52 ECJ 305

C-354/04 P Gestoras Pro Amnistia v Council of the European Union [2008] All E.R. (EC) 65; [2007] E.C.R. I-1579; [2007] 2 C.M.L.R. 22 ECJ 263

C-356/04 Lidl Belgium GmbH & Co KG v Etablissementen Franz Colruyt NV [2007] Bus. L.R. 492; [2006] E.C.R. I-8501; [2007] 1 C.M.L.R. 9 ECJ 496

C-374/04 Germany v Commission of the European Communities [2006] E.C.R. I-11673 547

C-392/04 and C-422/04 I-21 Germany GmbH v Germany; Arcor AG & Co KG (formerly ISIS Multimedia Net GmbH & Co KG v Germany [2006] E.C.R. I-8559; [2007] 1 C.M.L.R. 10 ECJ 510

C-434/04 Criminal Proceedings against Ahokainen; sub nom. Ahokainen v Virallinen Syyttaja [2006] E.C.R. I-9171; [2007] 1 C.M.L.R. 11 ECJ 232

C-479/04 Laserdisken ApS v Kulturministeriet [2007] All E.R. (EC) 549; [2006] E.C.R. I-8089; [2007] 1 C.M.L.R. 6 ECJ 303

C-506/04 Wilson v Ordre des Avocats du Barreau de Luxembourg [2007] All E.R. (EC) 403; [2006] E.C.R. I-8613; [2007] 1 C.M.L.R. 7 ECJ 275

C-523/04 Commission of the European Communities v Netherlands; sub nom. Dutch Air Transport Agreement, Re [2007] E.C.R. I-3267; [2007] 2 C.M.L.R. 48 ECJ 450

C-1/05 Jia v Migrationsverket [2007] Q.B. 545; [2007] 2 W.L.R. 1005; [2007] 1 C.M.L.R. 41 ECJ 248, 249

C-5/05 Staatssecretaris van Financien v Joustra [2008] S.T.C. 2226; [2006] E.C.R. I-11075; [2007] 1 C.M.L.R. 30 ECJ 429

C-19/05 Commission of the European Communities v Denmark [2007] E.C.R. I-8597 215

C-20/05 Criminal proceedings against Karl Josef Wilhelm Schwibbert [2007] E.C.R. I-9447 234

C-39/05 P and C-52/05 P Sweden v Council of the European Union; Turco v Council of the European Union [2009] Q.B. 269; [2009] 2 W.L.R. 867; [2008] E.C.R. I-4723 ECJ 104

C-61/05 Commission of the European Communities v Portugal [2006] E.C.R. I-6779; [2006] 3 C.M.L.R. 36 ECJ 301

C-77/05 United Kingdom v Council of the European Union [2007] E.C.R. I-11459; [2008] 2 C.M.L.R. 11 ECJ 202

C-110/05   Commission of the European Communities v Italy; sub
nom. Motorcycle Trailers, Re
[2009] All E.R. (EC) 796; [2009]
2 C.M.L.R. 3 ECJ 231
C-127/05   Commission of the European Communities v United
Kingdom [2007] E.C.R. I–4619;
[2007] All E.R. (EC) 986; [2007]
3 C.M.L.R. 20 ECJ 251
C-142/05   Änklagaren v Mickelson
[2009] All E.R. (EC) 842 ECJ ... 231
C-168/05   Mostaza Claro v Centro
Movil Milenium SL [2006] E.C.R.
I-10421; [2007] 1 C.M.L.R. 22
ECJ 498
C-243/05   P Agraz SA v Commis-
sion of the European Communi-
ties [2006] E.C.R. I-10833;
[2007] 1 C.M.L.R. 27 ECJ 150
C-278/05   Robins v Secretary of
State for Work and Pensions
[2007] All E.R. (EC) 648; [2007]
2 C.M.L.R. 13 ECJ 34
C-283/05   ASML Netherlands BV v
Semiconductor Industry Services
GmbH (Semis) [2007] 1 All
E.R. (Comm) 949; [2006] E.C.R.
I-12041 ECJ 258
C-288/05   Kretzinger v Hauptzol-
lamt Augsburg [2007] E.C.R.
I-6441; [2007] 3 C.M.L.R. 43
ECJ 242
C-291/05   Minister voor Vreemdelin-
genzaken en Integratie v Eind
[2008] All E.R. (EC) 371; [2008]
2 C.M.L.R. 1 ECJ 248,
                            249
C-295/05   Asociacion Nacional de
Empresas Forestales (ASEMFO)
v Transformacion Agraria SA
(TRAGSA)   [2007]   E.C.R.
I-2999; [2007] 2 C.M.L.R. 45
ECJ 310
C-303/05   Advocaten   voor   de
Wereld VZW v Leden van de
Ministerraad [2008] All E.R.
(EC) 317; [2007] 3 C.M.L.R. 1
ECJ 261
C-305/05   Ordre   des   Barreaux
Francophones et Germanophone
v Conseil des Ministres [2007]
All E.R. (EC) 953; [2007] E.C.R.
I-5305; [2007] 3 C.M.L.R. 28
ECJ 293

C-316/05   Nokia Corp v Wardell
[2006] E.C.R. I-12083; [2007] 1
C.M.L.R. 37; [2007] C.E.C.
393; [2007] E.T.M.R. 20; [2007]
Bus. L.R. D16 ECJ 195
C-356/05   Farrell v Whitty [2007] 2
C.M.L.R. 46; [2007] C.E.C. 718
ECJ 296, 445
C-380/05   Centro Europa 7 Srl v
Ministero delle Comunicazioni e
Autorita per le Garanzie nelle
Comunicazioni [2008] E.C.R.
I-349; [2008] 2 C.M.L.R. 18
ECJ 289, 346,
                            347
C-385/05   Cofédération   Generale
du Travail (CGT) v Prime Minis-
ter (C-385/05); sub nom. Con-
federation Generale du Travail
(CGT) v Premier Ministre [2007]
E.C.R. I-611; [2007] 2 C.M.L.R.
6 ECJ 282, 473
C-386/05   Color   Drack   GmbH   v
Lexx   International   Vertriebs
GmbH [2008] All E.R. (EC)
1044; [2008] 1 All E.R. (Comm)
169;   [2007]   E.C.R.   I-3699
ECJ 258
C-403/05   European   Parliament   v
Commission of the European
Communities; sub nom. Validity
of Philippine Border, Re [2007]
E.C.R.   I-9045;   [2008]   All
E.R. (EC) 526; [2008] 1 C.M.L.R.
20 137
C-411/05   Palacios   de   la   Villa   v
Cortefiel Servicios SA [2008] All
E.R. (EC) 249; [2007] E.C.R.
I-8531; [2008] 1 C.M.L.R. 16
ECJ 479
C-429/05   Rampion   v   Franfinance
SA [2008] Bus. L.R. 715; [2007]
E.C.R. I-8017; [2008] 1 C.M.L.R.
8 ECJ 498
C-430/05   Ntionik Anonymi Etaireia
Emporias H/Y, Logismikou kai
Paroxis Ypiresion Michanografisis
and Ioannis Michail Pikoulas v
Epitropi Kefalaiagoras [2007]
E.C.R. I-5835 281
C-431/05   Merck Genericos Produ-
tos Farmaceuticos Lda v Merck
& Co Inc [2008] All E.R. (EC)
40; [2007] E.C.R. I-7001; [2007]
3 C.M.L.R. 49 ECJ 55

C-432/05 Unibet (London) Ltd v Justitiekanslern [2008] All E.R. (EC) 453; [2007] E.C.R. I-2271; [2007] 2 C.M.L.R. 30 ECJ 46

C-438/05 International Transport Workers' Federation v Viking Line ABP) [2008] All E.R. (EC) 127; [2007] E.C.R. I-10779; [2008] 1 C.M.L.R. 51 ECJ 470

C-440/05 Commission of the European Communities v Council of the European Union [2008] All E.R. (EC) 489; [2007] E.C.R. I-9097; [2008] 1 C.M.L.R. 22; [2008] Env. L.R. 12 ECJ 549

C-446/05 Criminal Proceedings against Doulamis [2008] E.C.R. I-1377; [2008] 5 C.M.L.R. 4 ECJ 146

C-465/05 Commission of the European Communities v Italy; sub nom. Private Security Guards, Re [2007] E.C.R. I-11091; [2008] 2 C.M.L.R. 3 ECJ 287

C-467/05 Criminal Proceedings against dell'Orto [2007] 3 C.M.L.R. 29 ECJ 290

C-02/06 Willy Kempter KG v Hauptzollamt Hamburg-Jonas [2008] E.C.R. I–411 144

C-50/06 Commission of the European Communities v Netherlands; sub nom. Expulsion of Foreign Nationals, Re [2006] E.C.R. I-4383; [2007] 3 C.M.L.R. 8 ECJ 239

C-55/06 Arcor AG & Co KG v Bundesrepublik Deutschland [2008] E.C.R. I-2931 ECJ 509

C-98/06 Freeport Plc v Arnoldsson [2008] Q.B. 634; [2008] 2 W.L.R. 853; [2007] E.C.R. I-8319 ECJ 258

C-125/06 P Commission of the European Communities v Infront WM AG [2008] E.C.R. I-1451; [2008] 2 C.M.L.R. 28 ECJ ... 135, 136

C-158/06 Stichting ROM-Projecten v Staatssecretaris van Economische Zaken [2007] 3 C.M.L.R. 21 ECJ 396

C-161/06 Skoma-Lux sro v Celni Reditelstvi Olomouc [2007] E.C.R. I-10841; [2008] 1 C.M.L.R. 50 ECJ 37

C-195/06 Kommunikationsbehorde Austria (KommAustria) v Östereichischer Rundfunk (ORF) [2007] E.C.R. I-8817; [2008] Bus. L.R. D85 ECJ 513

C-197/06 Confederatie van Immobilien-Beroepen van Belgie VZW v Van Leuken [2008] E.C.R. I-2627; [2008] 2 C.M.L.R. 48 ECJ 275

C-202/06 P Cementbouw Handel & Industrie BV v Commission of the European Communities [2007] E.C.R. I-12129; [2008] 4 C.M.L.R. 17 ECJ 367

C-210/06 Cartesio Oktato es Szolgaltato bt; sub nom. Application Brought by Cartesio Oktato es Szolgaltato bt [2009] Ch. 354; [2009] 3 W.L.R. 777; [2009] 1 C.M.L.R. 50 ECJ 278

C-231/06, C-233/06 and C-232/06 National Pensions Office v Jonkman; Permesaen v National Pensions Office; National Pensions Office v Vercheval [2008] All E.R. (EC) 1017; [2007] 3 C.M.L.R. 25 ECJ 147

C-246/06 Velasco Navarro v Fondo de Garantia Salarial (Fogasa) [2008] All E.R. (EC) 361; [2008] E.C.R. I-105; [2008] 2 C.M.L.R. 6 ECJ 34

C-249/06 Commission of the European Communities v Sweden [2010] All E.R. (EC) 185; [2009] 2 C.M.L.R. 49 ECJ 55

C-262/06 Deutsche Telekom AG v Germany [2007] E.C.R. I-10057; [2008] 4 C.M.L.R. 9 ECJ 346, 509, 517

C-266/06 Evonik Degussa GmbH v Commission of the European Communities [2008] E.C.R.I-81 ... 356

C-267/06 Maruko v Versorgungsanstalt der Deutschen Buhnen [2008] All E.R. (EC) 977; [2008] E.C.R. I-1757; [2008] 2 C.M.L.R. 32; [2008] I.R.L.R. 450; [2008] Pens. L.R. 22 ECJ 479

C-269/06 Commission of the European Communities v the Translation Centre [2007] E.C.R. I-187 167

C-275/06 Productores de Musica
de Espana (Promusicae) v Tele-
fonica de Espana SAU [2008] All
E.R. (EC) 809; [2008] E.C.R.
I-271; [2008] 2 C.M.L.R. 17
ECJ 32, 303, 307, 497, 511

C-280/06 Autorità Garante della
Concorrenza e del Mercato v
Ente tabacchi italiani – ETI SpA
and Philip Morris Products SA v
Autorità Garante della Concor-
renza e del Mercato [2007]
E.C.R. I–10893 143

C-286/06 Commission of the European Communities v Spain [2008]
E.C.R. I-8025 275

C-303/06 Coleman v Attridge Law
[2008] All E.R. (EC) 1105;
[2008] E.C.R. I-5603 ECJ 479

C-306/06 01051 Telecom GmbH v
Deutsche Telekom AG [2008]
E.C.R. I-1923; [2008] Bus. L.R.
D116 ECJ 498

C-308/06 International Association
of Independent Tanker Owners
(Intertanko) v Secretary of State
for Transport; sub nom. Proceedings Brought by International
Association of Independent
Tanker Owners; R. (on the application of International Association of Independent Tanker
Owners) v Secretary of State for
Transport [2008] 2 Lloyd's Rep.
260; [2008] E.C.R. I-4057;
[2008] 3 C.M.L.R. 9; [2009] Env.
L.R. 14 ECJ 55

C-311/06 Consiglio Nazionale
degli Ingegneri v Ministero della
Giustizia and Marco Cavallera
[2009] E.C.R. I-415 272

C-329/06 Wiedemann v Land
Baden-Wurttemberg [2008]
E.C.R. I-4635; [2008] 3 C.M.L.R.
18 ECJ 445

C-345/06 Proceedings Brought by
Heinrich [2009] 3 C.M.L.R. 7
ECJ 37, 200, 452

C-346/06 Dirk Rüffert v Land
Niedersachsen [2008] All E.R.
(EC) 902; [2008] E.C.R. I-1989;
[2008] 2 C.M.L.R. 39 ECJ 476

C-353/06 Grunkin v Grunkin-Paul
[2008] E.C.R. I-7639; [2009] 1
C.M.L.R. 10; [2009] C.E.C. 263
ECJ 239

C-363/06 P Comunidad Autónoma
de Valencia – Generalidad Valenciana v Commission of the European Communities February 20,
2008 157

C-383/06, C-384/06, C-385/06 and
C-386/06 Vereniging Nation-
aal Overlegorgaan Sociale
Werkvoorziening; Gemeente Rot-
terdam v Minister van Sociale
Zaken en Werkgelegenheid and
Sociaal Economische Samen-
werking West-Brabant v
Algemene Directie voor de Arbei-
dsvoorziening [2008] E.C.R.
I–1597 421

C-398/06 Commission of the European Communities v Nether-
lands [2008] E.C.R. I-56 247

C-404/06 Quelle AG v Bundesverband der Verbraucherzentralen
und Verbraucherverbande [2008]
E.C.R. I-2685; [2008] 2 C.M.L.R.
49 ECJ 497

C-412/06 Hamilton v Volksbank
Filder eG [2008] E.C.R. I-2383;
[2008] 2 C.M.L.R. 46 ECJ 497

C-435/06 C (A Child), Re; sub
nom. C, Appellant [2008] Fam.
27; [2008] 3 W.L.R. 419; [2007]
E.C.R. I-10141 ECJ 259

C-439/06 Citiworks AG [2008]
E.C.R. I-3913 552

C-452/06 R. (on the application of
Synthon BV) v Licensing Author-
ity [2008] E.C.R. I-7681 195

C-460/06 Paquay v Societe d'Architectes Hoet + Minne SPRL [2007]
E.C.R. I-851; [2008] 1 C.M.L.R.
12 ECJ 472, 474

C-463/06 FBTO Schadeverzekerin-
gen NV v Odenbreit; sub nom.
Odenbreit v FBTO Schadev-
erzekeringen NV [2008] 2 All
E.R. (Comm) 733; [2007] E.C.R.
I-11321 ECJ 258

C-498/06 Maira María Robledillo
Núñez v Fondo de Garantía
Salarial (Fogasa) [2008] E.C.R.
I-921 473

C-499/06 Nerkowska v Zaklad
Ubezpieczen Spolecznych Odd-
zial w Koszalinie [2008] E.C.R.
I-3993; [2008] All E.R. (EC)
885; [2008] 3 C.M.L.R. 8
ECJ 240

C-516/06 P Commission of the European Communities v Ferriere Nord SpA; sub nom. Welded Steel Mesh Cartel Appeal, Re [2007] E.C.R. I-10685; [2008] 4 C.M.L.R. 10 ECJ 356

C-520/06 and C-350/06 Stringer v Revenue and Customs Commissioners; Schultz-Hoff v Deutsche Rentenversicherung Bund [2009] All E.R. (EC) 906; [2009] 2 C.M.L.R. 27 ECJ 476

C-524/06 Huber v Germany [2009] All E.R. (EC) 239; [2009] 1 C.M.L.R. 49 ECJ 501

C-14/07 Ingenieurburo Michael Weiss und Partner GbR v Industrie- und Handelskammer Berlin [2008] E.C.R. I-3367; [2009] C.E.C. 3 ECJ 259

C-14/07 Lodato Gennaro & C. SpA v Istituto nazionale della previdenza sociale (INPS) and SCCI April 2, 2009 390

C-19/07 Chevassus-Marche's Heirs v Groupe Danone [2008] Bus. L.R. 1290; [2008] 2 All E.R. (Comm) 1093; [2008] 1 Lloyd's Rep. 475; [2008] 2 C.M.L.R. 13 ECJ 267

C-27/07 Banque Federative du Crédit Mutuel v Ministre de l'Economie, des Finances et de l'Industrie [2008] S.T.C. 2192; [2008] 2 C.M.L.R. 33 ECJ 281, 431

C-33/07 Ministerul Administratiei si Internelor – Directia Generala de Pasapoarte Bucuresti v Jipa [2008] E.C.R. I-5157; [2008] 3 C.M.L.R. 23 ECJ 239

C-45/07 Commission of the European Communities v Greece [2009] 1 Lloyd's Rep. 425; [2009] 2 C.M.L.R. 38 ECJ 567

C-49/07 Motosykletistiki Omospondia Ellados NPID (MOTOE) v Greece [2009] All E.R. (EC) 150; [2008] E.C.R. I-4863; [2008] 5 C.M.L.R. 11 ECJ 323

C-54/07 Centrum voor gelijkheid van kansen en voor racismebestrijding v Firma Feryn NV [2008] E.C.R. I-5187 479

C-55/07 and C-56/07 Othmar Michaeler, Subito GmbH and Ruth Volgger v Amt für sozialen Arbeitsschutz and Autonome Provinz Bozen [2008] E.C.R. I-3135 476

C-68/07 Sundelind Lopez [2007] E.C.R. I-10403 259

C-73/07 Tietosuojavaltuutettu v Satakunnan Markkinaporssi Oy [2007] E.C.R I–7075; [2010] All E.R. (EC) 213 ECJ 148

C-88/07 Commission of the European Communities v Spain; sub nom. Marketing of Herbal Medicines, Re [2009] 2 C.M.L.R. 52 ECJ 195

C-121/07 Commission of the European Communities v France [2008] E.C.R. 9159; [2009] Env. L.R. 23 ECJ 111

C-138/07 Belgium v Cobelfret NV [2009] S.T.C. 1127; [2009] 2 C.M.L.R. 43 ECJ 281, 431

C-152–154/07 Arcor AG & Co KG; Communication Services TELE2 GmbH; Firma 01051 Telekom GmbH v Bundesrepublik Deutschland. [2008] E.C.R. I-5959 ECJ 32, 33

C-173/07 Emirates Airlines Direktion fur Deutschland v Schenkel [2009] All E.R. (EC) 436; [2008] E.C.R. I-5237; [2008] 3 C.M.L.R. 20 ECJ 451

C-185/07 Allianz SpA (formerly Riunione Adriatica di Sicurta SpA) v West Tankers Inc; Front Comor, The; sub nom. West Tankers Inc v Allianz SpA (formerly Riunione Adriatica di Sicurta SpA) [2009] 1 A.C. 1138; [2009] 3 W.L.R. 696 ECJ 258

C-188/07 Commune de Mesquer v Total France SA [2009] All E.R. (EC) 525; [2008] 2 Lloyd's Rep. 672; [2008] E.C.R. I-4501; [2008] 3 C.M.L.R. 16; [2009] Env. L.R. 9 ECJ 546

C-200/07 Marra v De Gregorio [2008] E.C.R. I-7929; [2009] 1 C.M.L.R. 15 ECJ 65

C-205/07 Criminal Proceedings against Gysbrechts [2009] All E.R. (EC) 711; [2009] 2 All E.R. (Comm) 951; [2009] 2 C.M.L.R. 2 ECJ 497

C-209/07 Competition Authority v Beef Industry Development Society Ltd [2009] All E.R. (EC) 367; [2008] E.C.R. I-8637; [2009] 4 C.M.L.R. 6 ECJ 326

C-239/07 Julius Sabatauskas [2008] E.C.R. I-7523 557

C-240/07 Sony Music Entertainment (Germany) GmbH v Falcon Neue Medien Vertrieb GmbH [2009] E.C.D.R. 12 ECJ 304

C-261/07 and C-299/07 VTB-VAB NV v Total Belgium NV; Galatea BVBA v Sanoma Magazines Belgium NV [2009] 3 C.M.L.R. 17 ECJ 496

C-265/07 Caffaro Srl v Azienda Unità Sanitaria Locale RM/C [2008] E.C.R. I-7095 498

C-297/07 Bourquain [2008] E.C.R. 9425 242

C-298/07 Bundesverband der Verbraucherzentralen und Verbraucherverbande – Verbraucherzentrale Bundesverband eV v Deutsche Internet versicherung AG [2009] 1 All E.R. (Comm) 938; [2008] E.C.R. I-7841; [2008] Info. T.L.R. 387 ECJ 497

C-313/07 Kirtruna SL v Red Elite de Electrodomesticos SA [2008] E.C.R. I-7907; [2009] 1 C.M.L.R. 14 ECJ 473

C-324/07 Coditel Brabant SA v Commune d'Uccle [2008] E.C.R. I-8457; [2009] 1 C.M.L.R. 29 ECJ 311

C-336/07 Kabel Deutschland Vertrieb und Service GmbH & Co KG v Niedersachsische Landesmedienanstalt fur Privaten Rundfunk [2009] 2 C.M.L.R. 6 ECJ 346, 509

C-339/07 Seagon v Deko Marty Belgium NV [2009] 1 W.L.R. 2168; [2009] Bus. L.R. 1151; [2009] B.C.C. 347; [2009] I.L.Pr. 25 ECJ 260

C-364/07 Spyridon Vassilakis v Dimos Kerkyraion [2008] E.C.R. I-90 34

C-372/07 Hassett v South Eastern Health Board [2008] E.C.R. I-7403; [2009] C.E.C. 390 ECJ 258

C-394/07 Gambazzi v Daimler-Chrysler Canada Inc [2009] 1 Lloyd's Rep. 647; [2009] I.L.Pr. 38 ECJ 258

C-404/07 Győrgy Katz v István Roland Sós [2008] E.C.R. I-7607 261

C-461/07 P(I) Provincia di Ascoli Piceno v Council of the European Union; sub nom. Provincia di Ascoli Piceno v Sun Sang Kong Yuen Shoes Factory (Hui Yang) Corp Ltd [2008] E.C.R. I-11; [2008] 2 C.M.L.R. 15 ECJ . . . 163

C-465/07 Elgafaji v Staatssecretaris van Justitie [2009] 1 W.L.R. 2100; [2009] All E.R. (EC) 651; [2009] 2 C.M.L.R. 45 ECJ 257

C-466/07 Klarenberg v Ferrotron Technologies GmbH [2009] I.C.R. 1263; [2009] I.R.L.R. 301 ECJ 473

C-489/07 Pia Messner v Firma Stefan Krüger September 3, 2009 497

C-509/07 Luigi Scarpelli v NEOS Banca SpA April 23, 2009 498

C-523/07 Proceedings Brought by A; sub nom. A (Area of Freedom, Security and Justice), Re [2009] I.L.Pr. 39; [2009] 2 F.L.R. 1 ECJ . . . 259

C-533/07 Falco Privatstiftung and Thomas Rabitsch v Gisela Weller-Lindhorst [2009] E.C.R. 23.04.09 258

C-549/07 Wallentin-Hermann v Alitalia – Linee Aeree Italiane SpA [2009] Bus. L.R. 1016; [2009] 1 Lloyd's Rep. 406; [2009] 2 C.M.L.R. 9 ECJ 55

C-552/07 Commune de Sausheim v Azelvandre [2009] All E.R. (EC) 1028; [2009] 2 C.M.L.R. 44 ECJ 198, 410

C-553/07 College van Burgemeester en Wethouders van Rotterdam v Rijkeboer [2009] 3 C.M.L.R. 28 ECJ 501

C-568/07 Commission of the European Communities v Greece June 4, 2009 131

C-8/08 T-Mobile Netherlands BV v Raad van Bestuur van de Nederlandse Mededingingsautoriteit [2010] Bus. L.R. 158; [2009] 5 C.M.L.R. 11 ECJ 321, 322

C-19/08 Migrationsverket v Petrosian [2009] 2 C.M.L.R. 33; [2009] I.N.L.R. 258 ECJ 256

C-46/08 Proceedings concerning the execution of a European arrest warrant issued against Szymon Kozłowski [2008] E.C.R. I-6041 263

C-97/08 Akzo Nobel NV v Commission of the European Communities September 10, 2009 ... 355

C-127/08 Metock v Minister for Justice, Equality and Law Reform [2009] Q.B. 318; [2009] 2 W.L.R. 821; [2008] E.C.R. I-6241 ECJ 148, 240

C-132/08 Lidl Magyarorszag Kereskedelmi bt v Nemzeti Hirkozlesi Hatosag Tanacsa [2009] 3 C.M.L.R. 23 ECJ 498

C-195/08 PPU Proceedings brought by Rinau; sub nom. Rinau v Rinau [2009] 2 W.L.R. 972; [2008] All E.R. (EC) 1145; [2008] E.C.R. I-5271 ECJ ... 148, 259

C-201/08 Plantanol GmbH & Co KG v Hauptzollamt Darmstadt September 10, 2009 148

C-243/08 Pannon GSM Zrt v Erzsébet Sustikné Győrf June 4, 2009 ECJ 498

C-249/08 Commission of the European Communities v Italian Republic [2009] E.C.R. 29.10.09 418

C-296/08 PPU Extradition Proceedings against Santesteban Goicoechea [2008] E.C.R. I-6307; [2008] 3 C.M.L.R. 40 ECJ 263

C-301/08 Irène Bogiatzi, married name Ventouras v Deutscher Luftpool, Société Luxair, société luxembourgeoise de navigation aérienne SA, European Communities, Grand Duchy of Luxembourg, Foyer Assurances SA [2009] E.C.R. 22.10.09 452

C-449/08 G. Elbertsen v Minister van Landbouw, Natuur en Voedselkwaliteit [2009] E.C.R. 22.10.09 445

C-559/08 Deepak Rajani (Dear! Net Online) v Office for Harmonisation in the Internal Market Order January 21, 2009 161

Court of First Instance (CFI) [now General Court (GC)] of the European Union

Chronological List of Cases

T-42/89 Wolfdieter Graf Yorck von Wartenburg v European Parliament [1990] E.C.R. II–31 169

T-51/89 Tetra Pak Rausing SA v Commission of the European Communities [1990] E.C.R. II–309 142

T-68/89, T-77/89 and T-78/89 Societe Italiano Vetro SpA v Commission of the European Communities; Fabbrica Pisana SpA v Commission of the European Communities; Vernante Pennitalia v Commission of the European Communities; sub nom. Italian Flat Glass, Re [1992] E.C.R. II-1403; [1992] 5 C.M.L.R. 302 CFI 338

T-69/89 Radio Telefis Eireann v Commission of the European Communities [1991] E.C.R. II-485; [1991] 4 C.M.L.R. 586 ECJ 338

T-113/89 Nederlandse Associatie van de Farmaceutische Industrie "Nefarma" and Bond van Groothandelaren in het Farmaceutische Bedrijf v Commission of the European Communities [1990] E.C.R. II–797; [1991] 2 C.M.L.R. 818 134

T-24/90 Automec Srl v Commission of the European Communities [1992] E.C.R. II-2223; [1992] 5 C.M.L.R. 431 CFI 360

T-83/91 Tetra Pak International SA v Commission of the European Communities [1994] E.C.R. II-755; [1997] 4 C.M.L.R. 726 CFI... 341

T-114/92 Bureau Européen des Médias de l'Industrie Musicale v Commission of the European Communities [1995] E.C.R. II–147 360

T-24/93, T-25/93 and T-26/93 Compagnie Maritime Belge Transports SA v Commission of the European Communities [1996] E.C.R. II–1201; [1977] 4 C.M.L.R. 273 .... 338, 343

T-49/93 Société Internationale de Diffusion et d'Edition (SIDE) v Commission of the European Communities [1995] E.C.R. II–2501 395

T-244/93 Textilwerke Deggendorg GmbH (TWD) v Commission of the European Communities [1995] E.C.R. II-2265; [1996] 1 C.M.L.R. 332 ECJ 396

T-447/93, T-448/93 and T-449/93 Associazione Italiana Tecnico Economica del Cemento v Commission of the European Communities [1995] E.C.R. II–1971 ECJ 392

T-450/93 Lisrestal – Organização Gestão de Restaurantes Colectivos Ld™ v Commission of the European Communities [1994] E.C.R. II–1177 359

T-458/93 and T-523/93 Empresa Nacional de Urânio SA (ENU) v Commission of the European Communities [1995] E.C.R. II-2459 557

T-459/93 Siemens SA v Commission of the European Communities [1995] E.C.R. II-1675 CFI 335, 396

T-480/93 and T-483/93 Antilian Rice Mills NV v Council of the European Union [1995] E.C.R. II–2310 .... 134, 140

T-485/93 Societe Louis Dreyfus & Cie v Commission of the European Communities [1996] E.C.R. II-1101; [1997] 1 C.M.L.R. 1008 CFI...................... 150

T-504/93 Tiercé Ladbroke SA v Commission of the European Communities [1997] E.C.R. II–923 307

T-528/93 Metropole Television SA v Commission of the European Communities [1996] E.C.R. II-649; [1996] 5 C.M.L.R. 386; [1996] C.E.C. 794; [1998] E.M.L.R. 99 ECJ 322

T-575/93 Koelman v Commission of the European Communities [1996] E.C.R. II-1; [1996] 4 C.M.L.R. 636; [1996] E.M.L.R. 555 CFI 353

T-589/93 Susan Ryan-Sheridan v European Foundation for the Improvement of Living and Working Conditions [1996] E.C.R. II–77 192

T-20/94 Johannes Hartmann v Council of the European Union and Commission of the European Communities [1997] E.C.R. II–595 149

T-85/94 Eugenio Branco Lda v Commission of the European Communities [1995] E.C.R. II-45 CFI 164

T-115/94 Opel Austria GmbH v Council of the European Union [1997] E.C.R. II–39 139

T-149/94 Kernkraftwerke Lippe-EMS GmbH v Commission of the European Communities. See Kernkraftwerke Lippe-EMS GmbH v Commission of the European Communities (T-181/94)

T-154/94 Comite des Salines de France v Commission of the European Communities [1996] E.C.R. II-1377; [1997] 1 C.M.L.R. 943 CFI 133, 152

T-181/94 and T-149/94 Kernkraftwerke Lippe-EMS GmbH v Commission of the European Communities; sub nom. Kernkraftwerke Lippe-EMS GmbH v Commission of the European Communities [1997] E.C.R. II-161; [1997] 3 C.M.L.R. 136 CFI 182

T-194/94 Carvel v Council of the European Union; Guardian Newspapers Ltd v Council of Ministers of the European Communities [1996] All E.R. (E.C.) 53; [1995] E.C.R. II-2765; [1995] 3 C.M.L.R. 359; [1996] C.E.C. 282 CFI 104

T-260/94 Air Inter SA v Commission of the European Communities [1997] E.C.R. II-997; [1997] 5 C.M.L.R. 851 CFI 344, 378

T-271/94 Eugénio Branco v Commission of the European Communities [1998] E.C.R. II–3761 161

T-309/94 NV Koninklijke KNP BT v Commission of the European Communities [1998] E.C.R. II–1007 324

T-327/94 SCA Holding Ltd v Commission of the European Communities [1998] E.C.R. II–1373 .... 322, 357

T-336/94 Efisol SA v Commission of the European Communities [1996] E.C.R. II–1343 139

T-347/94 Mayr-Melnhof Kartongesellschaft mbH v Commission of the European Communities [1998] E.C.R. II–1751 321

T-371/94 and T-394/94 British Airways plc, Scandinavian Airlines System Denmark-Norway-Sweden, Koninklijke Luchtvaart Maatschappij NV, Air UK Ltd, Euralair international, TAT European Airlines SA and British Midland Airways Ltd v Commission of the European Communities [1998] E.C.R. II–2405 .... 378, 387

T-380/94 Association Internationale des Utilisateurs de Fils de Filaments Artificiels et Synthetiques et de Soie Naturelle (AIUFFASS) v Commission of the European Communities [1996] E.C.R. II-2169; [1997] 3 C.M.L.R. 542 CFI 323

T-387/94 Asia Motor France SA v Commission of the European Communities [1996] E.C.R. II-961; [1996] 5 C.M.L.R. 537 CFI 324, 360

T-395/94 Atlantic Container Line AB v Commission of the European Communities [2002] E.C.R. II-875 343

T-86/95 Compagnie Générale Maritime v Commission of the European Communities [2002] E.C.R. II–1011 343

T-174/95 Svenska Journalistforbundet v Council of the European Union [1998] All E.R. (E.C.) 545; [1998] E.C.R. II-2289; [1998] 3 C.M.L.R. 645 ECJ 104, 161

T-175/95 BASF Coating AG v Commission of the European Communities [1999] E.C.R. II-1581; [2000] 4 C.M.L.R. 33 CFI 330

T-227/95 AssiDoman Kraft Products AB v Commission of the European Communities [1997] All E.R. (EC) 769; [1997] E.C.R. II-1185; [1997] 5 C.M.L.R. 364 CFI 357

T-25/96 Arbeitsgemeinschaft Deutscher Luftfahrt-Unternehmen and Hapag-Lloyd Fluggesellschaft mbH v Commission of the European Communities [1997] E.C.R. II-363 ECJ 323

T-41/96 R Bayer AG v Commission of the European Communities [1996] E.C.R. II-381; [1996] 5 C.M.L.R. 290 CFI 162

T-95/96 Gestevision Telecinco SA v Commission of the European Communities [1998] All E.R. (EC) 918; [1998] E.C.R. II-3407; [1998] 3 C.M.L.R. 1112 CFI 395

T-102/96 Gencor Ltd v Commission of the European Communities (Applications to Intervene) [1997] E.C.R. II-879; [1998] 1 C.M.L.R. 142; [1997] 5 C.M.L.R. 290 CFI 369

T-124/96 Interporc Im- und Export GmbH v Commission of the European Communities [1998] E.C.R. II-231; [1998] 2 C.M.L.R. 82 ECJ 124

T-191/96 CAS Succhi di Frutta SpA v Commission of the European Communities [1999] E.C.R II–3181 309

T-18/97 Atlantic Container Line AB v Commission of the European Communities [2002] E.C.R. II–395 343

T-46/97 SIC – Sociedade Independente de Comunicação SA v Commission of the European Communities [2000] E.C.R. I-2125 .... 379, 395

T-83/97 SA de Traverses en Beton Arme (SATEBA) v Commission of the European Communities [1997] E.C.R. II-1523; [1998] 4 C.M.L.R. 528 CFI 110

T-159/97 R Luis Manuel Chaves Fonseca Ferrão v Office for Harmonisation in the Internal Market [1997] E.C.R. II–1049 196

T-182/97 Smanor SA, Hubert Ségaud and Monique Ségaud v Commission of the European Communities [1998] E.C.R. II-271 110

T-188/97 Rothmans International BV v Commission of the European Communities [1999] E.C.R. II-2463; [1999] 3 C.M.L.R. 66 CFI 117

T-207/97 Georges Berthu v Council of the European Union [1998] E.C.R. II-509 456

T-228/97 Irish Sugar Plc v Commission of the European Communities [2000] All E.R. (EC) 198; [1999] E.C.R. II-2969; [1999] 5 C.M.L.R. 1300 CFI 338, 341

T-256/97 Bureau européen des unions des consommateurs (BEUC) v Commission of the European Communities [2000] E.C.R. II-101 583

T-282/97 and T-57/98 Antonio Giannini v Commission of the European Communities [1999] E.C.R. II-151 140

T-288/97 Regione autonoma Friuli Venezia Giulia v Commission of the European Communities [1999] E.C.R. II–1871 134

T-609/97 Regione Puglia v Commission of the European Communities and Kingdom of Spain [1998] E.C.R. II–4051 136

T-73/98 Société chimique Prayon-Rupel SA v Commission of the European Communities [2001] E.C.R. II–867 395

T-112/98 Mannesmannröhren-Werke AG v Commission of the European Communities [2001] E.C.R. II–729 354

T-128/98 Aéroports de Paris v Commission of the European Communities [2000] E.C.R. II-3929; [2001] 4 C.M.L.R. 38 ECJ 344

T-173/98 Unión de Pequeños Agricultores (UPA) v Council of the European Union [1999] E.C.R. II–3357 .... 135, 136, 151

T-186/98 Compañía Internacional de Pesca y Derivados (Inpesca) SA v Commission of the European Communities [2001] E.C.R. II-557 115

T-188/98 Kuijer v Council of the European Union [2000] E.C.R. II-1959; [2000] 2 C.M.L.R. 400 CFI 104

T-18/99 Cordis Obst und Gemüse Großhandel GmbH v Commission of the European Communities [2001] E.C.R. II-913 .... 39, 54

T-25/99 AJ Colin and Valerie Roberts v Commission of the European Communities [2001] E.C.R. II-1881 161

T-38/99 and T-50/99 Sociedade Agricola dos Arinhos, Ldª v Commission of the European Communities [2001] E C.R II–585 137

T-55/99 Confederación Española de Transporte de Mercancías (CETM) v Commission of the European Communities [2000] E.C.R. II–3207 380

T-69/99 Danish Satellite TV (DSTV) A/S (Eurotica Rendez-vous Television) v Commission of the European Communities [2000] E.C.R. II–4039 134

T-106/99 Karl L Meyer v Commission of the European Communities [1999] E.C.R. II-3273 124

T-127/99, T-129/99 and T-148/99 Territorio Histórico de Álava – Diputación Foral de Álava; Comunidad Autónoma del País Vasco and Gasteizko Industria Lurra, SA; Daewoo Electronics Manufacturing España, SA v Commission of the European Communities [2002] E.C.R. II-1275 380

T-208/99 Bangemann v Council of the European Union [2001] E.C.R. I-9183 108

T-228/99 and T-233/99 Westdeutsche Landesbank Girozentrale and Land Nordrhein-Westfalen v Commission of the European Communities E.C.R. II–435 393

T-342/99 Airtours Plc v Commission of the European Communities [2002] All E.R. (EC) 783; [2002] E.C.R. II-2585 CFI 338

T-11/00 Michel Hautem v European Investment Bank [2000] E.C.R. II–4036 150

T-17/00 Rothley v European Parliament [2002] E.C.R. II-579; [2002] 2 C.M.L.R. 30 CFI 64, 134

T-69/00 Fabbrica Italiana Accumulatori Motocarri Montecchio Spa (FIAMM) v Council of the European Union [2005] E.C.R. II-5393; [2006] 2 C.M.L.R. 9 ECJ 55

T-220/00 Cheil Jedang Corp v Commission of the European Communities [2003] E.C.R. II–2481 355

T-377/00, T-380/00 and T-379/00 Philip Morris International Inc v Commission of the European Communities; Japan Tobacco Inc v Commission of the European Communities; RJ Reynolds Tobacco Holdings Inc v Commission of the European Communities [2003] All E.R. (EC) 1008; [2003] E.C.R. II-1; [2003] 1 C.M.L.R. 21 ECJ 113

T-18/01 R Goldstein v Commission of the European Communities [2001] E.C.R. II–1147 157

T-33/01 Infront WM AG v Commission of the European Communities [2005] E.C.R. II-5897 513

T-82/01 VOF Josanne v Commission of the European Communities [2003] E.C.R. II-2013 454

T-110/01 Vedial SA v Office for Harmonisation in the Internal Market (Trade Marks and Designs) (OHIM) [2002] E.C.R. II-5275; [2004] E.T.M.R. 102 CFI 196

T-168/01 GlaxoSmithKline Services Unlimited v Commission of the European Communities [2006] E.C.R. II-2969; [2006] 5 C.M.L.R. 29 ECJ 326

T-177/01 Jego-Quere et Cie SA v Commission of the European Communities [2003] Q.B. 854; [2003] 2 W.L.R. 783; [2002] E.C.R. II-2365 ECJ 135

T-310/01 Schneider Electric SA v Commission of the European Communities [2004] All E.R. (EC) 314; [2002] E.C.R. II-4071; [2003] 4 C.M.L.R. 17 CFI 369

T-325/01 Daimlerchrysler AG v Commission of the European Communities [2005] E.C.R. II-3319; [2007] 4 C.M.L.R. 15 CFI 324

T-5/02 Tetra Laval BV v Commission of the European Communities [2002] E.C.R. II-4381 369

T-44/02 Dresdner Bank AG v Commission of the European Communities [2006] E.C.R. II–3567; [2007] 4 C.M.L.R. 13 ECJ 164

T-144/02 Eagle v Commission of the European Communities [2004] E.C.R. II-3381 149

T-211/02 Tideland Signal Ltd v Commission of the European Communities [2002] E.C.R. II-3781; [2002] 3 C.M.L.R. 33 CFI 169, 314

T-317/02 Fédération des industries condimentaires de France (FICF) v Commission of the European Communities [2004] E.C.R. II-4325 585

T-27/03 SP SpA v Commission of the European Communities; sub nom. Reinforcing Bars Cartel Appeal, Re [2007] E.C.R. II-4331; [2008] 4 C.M.L.R. 5 ECJ 14

T-54/03 Lafarge SA v Commission of the European Communities [2008] E.C.R. II-120 355

T-125/03 and T-253/03 Akzo Nobel Chemicals Ltd v Commission of the European Communities; Akzo Nobel Chemicals Ltd v Commission of the European Communities [2008] Bus. L.R. 348; [2008] All E.R. (EC) 1; [2007] E.C.R. II-3523; [2008] 4 C.M.L.R. 3 ECJ 354

T-273/03 Merck Sharp & Dohme Ltd v Commission of the European Communities [2006] E.C.R. II-141 195

T-289/03 British United Provident Association Ltd (BUPA) v Commission of the European Communities [2008] E.C.R. II-81; [2009] 2 C.M.L.R. 41 CFI 139

T-410/03 Hoechst GmbH v Commission of the European Communities [2008] E.C.R. II-881; [2008] 5 C.M.L.R. 12 ECJ 357

T-155/04 Selex Sistemi Integrati SpA v Commission of the European Communities [2006] E.C.R. II-4797; [2007] 4 C.M.L.R. 10 CFI 164

T-229/04 Sweden v Commission of the European Communities [2007] E.C.R. II-2437 197

T-276/04 Compagnie Maritime Belge SA v Commission of the European Communities [2008] E.C.R. II-1277; [2009] 4 C.M.L.R. 21 CFI 161, 353

T-339/04 France Télécom v Commission of the European Communities [2007] E.C.R. II-521; [2008] 5 C.M.L.R. 6 CFI 355

T-360/04 FG Marine SA v Commission of the European Communities July 19, 2007 149

T-439/04 Eurohypo AG v Office for Harmonisation in the Internal Market (Trade Marks and Designs) (OHIM) [2006] E.C.R. II-1269 305

T-474/04 Pergan Hilfsstoffe fur Industrielle Prozesse v Commission of the European Communities; sub nom. Organic Peroxides Cartel Appeal, Re [2007] E.C.R. II-4225; [2008] 4 C.M.L.R. 4 ECJ 359

T-101/05 BASF AG v Commission of the European Communities; UCB SA v Commission of the European Communities; sub nom. Choline Chloride Sector Cartel, Re [2007] E.C.R. II-4949; [2008] 4 C.M.L.R. 13 CFI 356

T-112/05 Akzo Nobel NV v Commission of the European Communities; sub nom. Choline Chloride Cartel, Re [2007] E.C.R. II-5049; [2008] 4 C.M.L.R. 12 CFI 355

T-216/05 Mebrom NV v Commission of the European Communities [2007] E.C.R. II-1507 139

T-319/05 Confédération Suisse v Commission of the European Communities [2006] E.C.R. II-2073 164

T-357/05 Comunidad Autónoma de Valencia – Generalidad Valenciana v Commission of the European Communities [2006] E.C.R. II-2015 157

T-376/05 and T-383/05 TEA-CEGOS, SA, Services techniques globaux (STG) SA and GHK Consulting Ltd v Commission of the European Communities [2006] E.C.R. II–205 139

T-95/06 Federación de Cooperativas Agrarias de la Comunidad Valenciana v Community Plant Variety Office (CPVO) [2008] E.C.R. II-31 197

T-109/06 Vodafone Espana SA v Commission of the European Communities [2007] E.C.R. II-5151; [2008] 4 C.M.L.R. 19 CFI 346, 509

T-116/06 R Oakley Inc v Office for Harmonisation in the Internal Market (Trade Marks and Designs) (OHIM) [2006] E.C.R. II-2627 ECJ 162

T-223/06 European Parliament v Ole Eistrup [2007] E.C.R. II-1581 171

T-345/08 Ashley Neil Mote v European Parliament October 15, 2008 65

Alphabetical List of Cases

01051 Telecom GmbH v Deutsche Telekom AG (C-306/06) [2008] E.C.R. I-1923; [2008] Bus. L.R. D116 ECJ 498

A Ahlstrom Osakeyhtio v Commission of the European Communities (89/85) [1988] E.C.R. 5193; [1988] 4 C.M.L.R. 901 ECJ 53, 327

A Leur-Bloem v Inspecteur der Belastingdienst/Ondernemingen Amsterdam 2 (C-28/95) [1997] E.C.R. I–4161 148

A Racke GmbH & Co. v Hauptzollamt Mainz (162/96) [1998] E.C.R. I–3655 .... 138, 144, 582

ACF Chemiefarma v Commission of the European Communities (41/69) [1970] E.C.R. 661 ECJ 67, 94, 322

AJ Colin and Valerie Roberts v Commission of the European Communities (T-25/99) [2001] E.C.R. II-1881 161

AJ Schulte v Deutsche Bausparkasse Badenia AG (C-350/03) [2005] E.C.R. I–9178 161

AKZO Chemie BV v Commission of the European Communities (53/85) [1986] E.C.R. 1965; [1987] 1 C.M.L.R. 231 ECJ 359

ARGE Gewässerschutz v Bundesministerium für Land-und Forstwirtschaft (C-94/99) [2000] E.C.R. I–11037 ECJ 310

ASML Netherlands BV v Semiconductor Industry Services GmbH (Semis) (C-283/05) [2007] 1 All E.R. (Comm) 949; [2006] E.C.R. I-12041 ECJ 258

Abfall Service AG (ASA) v Bundesminister für Umwelt, Jugend und Familie (C-6/00) [2002] E.C.R. I-1961 ECJ 546

Abrahamsson v Fogelqvist (C-407/98) [2000] E.C.R. I-5539; [2002] I.C.R. 932 ECJ 477

Acciaierie San Michele SpA (in liquidation) v High Authority of the ECSC (9/65 and 58/65) [1967] E.C.R. 1 48

Accord Européen de Transport (European Transport Agreement) AETR (22/70). *See* Commission of the European Communities v Council of the European Communities (22/70)

Adams v Commission of the European Communities (No.1) (C-145/83); Adams (Stanley George) v Commission of the European Communities (No.2) (53/84) [1986] Q.B. 138; [1986] 2 W.L.R. 367; [1985] E.C.R. 3539 ECJ 150

Adeneler v Ellinikos Organismos Galaktos (ELOG) (C-212/04) [2007] All E.R. (EC) 82; [2006] E.C.R. I-6057; [2006] 3 C.M.L.R. 30 ECJ 34

Advocaten voor de Wereld VZW v Leden van de Ministerraad (C-303/05) [2008] All E.R. (EC) 317; [2007] 3 C.M.L.R. 1 ECJ 261

Aéroports de Paris v Commission of the European Communities (T-128/98) [2000] E.C.R. II-3929; [2001] 4 C.M.L.R. 38 ECJ 344

Agraz SA v Commission of the European Communities (C-243/05 P) [2006] E.C.R. I-10833; [2007] 1 C.M.L.R. 27 ECJ 150

Ählström v Commission of the European Communities. *See* A Ahlstrom Osakeyhtio v Commission of the European Communities (89/85)

Aid to Meura SA, Re (C-234/84); sub nom. Belgium v Commission of the European Communities (234/84) [1986] E.C.R. 2263; [1988] 2 C.M.L.R. 331 ECJ 379

Air Inter SA v Commission of the European Communities (T-260/94) [1997] E.C.R. II-997; [1997] 5 C.M.L.R. 851 CFI 344, 378

Airtours Plc v Commission of the European Communities (T-342/99) [2002] All E.R. (EC) 783; [2002] E.C.R. II-2585 CFI 338

Aktien-Zuckerfabrik Schöppenstedt v Council of the European Communities (5/71) [1971] E.C.R. 975 149

Akzo Nobel Chemicals Ltd v Commission of the European Communities (T-125/03); Akzo Nobel Chemicals Ltd v Commission of the European Communities (T-253/03) [2008] Bus. L.R. 348; [2008] All E.R. (EC) 1; [2007] E.C.R. II-3523; [2008] 4 C.M.L.R. 3 ECJ 354

Akzo Nobel NV v Commission of the European Communities (C-97/08) September 10, 2009 ... 355

Akzo Nobel NV v Commission of the European Communities (T-112/05); sub nom. Choline Chloride Cartel, Re (T-112/05) [2007] E.C.R. II-5049; [2008] 4 C.M.L.R. 12 CFI 355

Alcatel Austria AG v Bundesministerium fur Wissenschaft und Verkehr (C-81/98) [1999] E.C.R. I-7671; (2000) 2 T.C.L.R. 894 ECJ 316

Alexander Dory v Bundesrepublik Deutschland (C-186/01 R) [2001] E.C.R. I–7823 146

Alexandros Kefalas v Elliniko Dimosio (Greek State) and Organismos Oikonomikis Anasygkrotisis Epicheiriseon AE (OAE) (C-367/96) [1998] E.C.R. I–2843 278

Algera v Common Assembly (7/56, 3/57, 4/57, 5/57, 6/57 and 7/57) [1957–1958] E.C.R. 39 ECJ 54

Allianz SpA (formerly Riunione Adriatica di Sicurta SpA) v West Tankers Inc (C-185/07); Front Comor, The; sub nom. West Tankers Inc v Allianz SpA (formerly Riunione Adriatica di Sicurta SpA) (C-185/07) [2009] 1 A.C. 1138; [2009] 3 W.L.R. 696 ECJ 258

Altmark Trans GmbH v Nahverkehrsgesellschaft Altmark GmbH (C-280/00) [2005] All E.R. (EC) 610; [2003] E.C.R. I-7747; [2003] 3 C.M.L.R. 12 ECJ 382, 389

Amedeo Chevalley v Commission of the European Communities (15/70) [1970] E.C.R. 975 ...... 30, 142

Amministrazione delle Finanze dello Stato v Ariete SpA, Rome (811/79) [1981] E.C.R. 2545; [1980] E.C.R. 2545; [1981] 1 C.M.L.R. 316 ECJ 143

Amministrazione delle Finanze dello Stato v Denkavit Italiana Srl (61/79) [1980] E.C.R. 1205; [1981] 3 C.M.L.R. 694 ECJ ... 144, 379

Amministrazione delle Finanze dello Stato v Simmenthal SpA (106/77); sub nom. Italian Tax and Revenue Administration v SA Simmenthal, Monza (Italy) (106/77) [1978] E.C.R. 629; [1978] 3 C.M.L.R. 263 .... 49, 140

Amministrazione delle Finanze dello Stato v Societa Petrolifera Italiana SpA (267/81) [1983] E.C.R. 801; [1984] 1 C.M.L.R. 354 ECJ 566

Angélique Verli-Wallace v Commission of the European Communities (159/82) [1983] E.C.R. 2711 53

Änklagaren v Mickelson (C-142/05) [2009] All E.R. (EC) 842 ECJ ... 231

Anklagemyndigheden (Public Prosecutor) v Hansen & Son (C-326/88) [1990] E.C.R. I-2911; [1992] I.C.R. 277 ECJ 52

Antilian Rice Mills NV v Council of the European Union (T-480/93 and T-483/93) [1995] E.C.R. II–2310 .... 134, 140

Antonio Giannini v Commission of the European Communities (T-282/97 and T-57/98) [1999] E.C.R. II-151 140

Arbeitsgemeinschaft Deutscher Luftfahrt-Unternehmen and Hapag-Lloyd Fluggesellschaft mbH v Commission of the European Communities (T-25/96) [1997] E.C.R. II-363 ECJ 323

Arcor AG & Co KG (C-152/07); Communication Services TELE2 GmbH (C-153/07); Firma 01051 Telekom GmbH v Bundesrepublik Deutschland (C-154/07) [2008] E.C.R. I-5959 ECJ ... 32, 33

Arcor AG & Co KG v Bundesrepublik Deutschland (C-55/06) [2008] E.C.R. I-2931 ECJ 509

Arnold André GmbH & Co KG v Landrat des Kreises Herford (C-434/02) [2004] E.C.R. I-11825 ECJ 36

Ashley Neil Mote v European Parliament (T-345/08) October 15, 2008 65

Asia Motor France SA v Commission of the European Communities (T-387/94) [1996] E.C.R. II-961; [1996] 5 C.M.L.R. 537 CFI 324, 360

Asociacion Nacional de Empresas Forestales (ASEMFO) v Transformacion Agraria SA (TRAGSA) (C-295/05) [2007] E.C.R. I-2999; [2007] 2 C.M.L.R. 45 ECJ 310

Assedic Pas-de-Calais AGS v Dumon (C-235/95) [1998] E.C.R. I-4531; [1999] 2 C.M.L.R. 113 ECJ 473

AssiDoman Kraft Products AB v Commission of the European Communities (T-227/95) [1997] All E.R. (EC) 769; [1997] E.C.R. II-1185; [1997] 5 C.M.L.R. 364 CFI 357

Association Internationale des Utilisateurs de Fils de Filaments Artificiels et Synthetiques et de Soie Naturelle (AIUFFASS) v Commission of the European Communities (T-380/94) [1996] E.C.R. II-2169; [1997] 3 C.M.L.R. 542 CFI 323

Associazione Industrie Siderurgiche Italiane (Assider) v Commission of the European Communities (167/85) [1987] E.C.R. 1701; [1988] 2 C.M.L.R. 783 ECJ 142

Associazione Industrie Siderurgiche Italiane (ASSIDER) v High Authority of the European Coal and Steel Community (3/54) [1954–1955] E.C.R. 63 ECJ 54, 140

Associazione Italiana Tecnico Economica del Cemento v Commission of the European Communities (T-447/93, T-448/93 and T-449/93) [1995] E.C.R. II–1971 ECJ 392

Asteris AE v Greece (106/87) [1988] E.C.R. 5515; [1990] 1 C.M.L.R. 575 ECJ 150

Atlanta Fruchthandelsgesellschaft mbH v Bundesamt fur Ernahrung und Forstwirtschaft (C-465/93) [1996] All E.R. (E.C.) 31; [1995] E.C.R. I-3761; [1996] 1 C.M.L.R. 575 ECJ 145

Atlantic Container Line AB v Commission of the European Communities (T-395/94) [2002] E.C.R. II-875 343

Atlantic Container Line AB v Commission of the European Communities (T-18/97) [2002] E.C.R. II–395 343

Australian Mining & Smelting Europe Ltd v Commission of the European Communities (155/79); sub nom. AM&S Europe Ltd v Commission of the European Communities (155/79) [1983] Q.B. 878; [1983] 3 W.L.R. 17; [1982] E.C.R. 1575 ECJ 354

Austria v Commission (165/99) Unpublished 2001 158

Austria v Commission of the European Communities (C-99/98) [2001] E.C.R. I–1101 395

Automec Srl v Commission of the European Communities (T-24/90) [1992] E.C.R. II-2223; [1992] 5 C.M.L.R. 431 CFI 360

Autorità Garante della Concorrenza e del Mercato v Ente tabacchi italiani – ETI SpA and Philip Morris Products SA v Autorità Garante della Concorrenza e del Mercato (C-280/06) [2007] E.C.R. I–10893 143

Autotrasporti Librandi Snc di Librandi F&C v Cuttica spedizioni e servizi internationali Srl (C-38/97) [1998] E.C.R. I–5955 .... 378, 444

Axel Springer AG v Zeitungsverlag Niederrhein GmbH & Co. Essen KG and Hans-Jürgen Weske (C-435/02 and C-103/03) [2004] E.C.R. I–8663 .... 279, 292

Ayse Süzen v Zehnacker Gebäudereinigung GmbH Krankenhausservice (C-13/95) [1997] All E.R. (EC) 289; [1997] E.C.R. I-1259 ECJ 473

Azienda Agricola Monte Arcosu Srl v Regione Autonoma della Sardegna (C-403/98) [2001] E.C.R. I-103; [2002] 2 C.M.L.R. 14 ECJ 31

BASF AG v Commission of the European Communities (T-101/05); UCB SA v Commission of the European Communities (T-111/05); sub nom. Choline Chloride Sector Cartel, Re (T-101/05) [2007] E.C.R. II-4949; [2008] 4 C.M.L.R. 13 CFI 356

BASF Coating AG v Commission of the European Communities (T-175/95) [1999] E.C.R. II-1581; [2000] 4 C.M.L.R. 33 CFI 330

Balkan Import Export GmbH v
Hauptzollamt Berlin Packhof
(5/73) [1973] E.C.R. 1091
ECJ 401
Banchero, Re (C-387/93) [1995]
E.C.R. I-4663; [1996] 1
C.M.L.R. 829 ECJ 375
Banco Exterior de Espana SA v
Ayuntamiento de Valencia
(C-387/92); sub nom. Banco de
Credito Industrial SA v Ayun-
tamiento de Valencia (C-387/92)
[1994] E.C.R. I-877; [1994] 3
C.M.L.R. 473 ECJ 347,
379
Bangemann v Council of the Euro-
pean Union (T-208/99) [2001]
E.C.R. I-9183 108
Banque Federative du Crédit Mutuel
v Ministre de l'Economie, des
Finances et de l'Industrie
(C-27/07) [2008] S.T.C. 2192;
[2008] 2 C.M.L.R. 33 ECJ 281,
431
Banque internationale pour l'Afrique
occidentale SA (BIAO) v Finan-
zamt für Groβunternehmen in
Hambur (C-306/99) [2003]
E.C.R. I–1 279
Barbara Bellone v Yokohama SpA
(C-215/97) [1998] E.C.R.
I–2191 267
Bärbel Kachelmann v Bankhaus
Hermann Lampe KG (C-322/98)
[2000] E.C.R. I-7505 474
Barber v Guardian Royal Exchange
Assurance Group (C-262/88)
[1991] 1 Q.B. 344; [1991] 2
W.L.R. 72 ECJ 478
Bauhuis v Netherlands (46/76)
[1977] E.C.R. 5 ECJ 230
Baumbast v Secretary of State for the
Home Department (C-413/99)
[2002] E.C.R. I-7091; [2002] 3
C.M.L.R. 23 ECJ 248
Bayer AG v Commission of the Euro-
pean Communities (T-41/96 R)
[1996] E.C.R. II-381; [1996] 5
C.M.L.R. 290 CFI 162
Bayerische HNL Vermehrungsbe-
triebe GmbH & Co KG v
Commission of the European
Communities (83/76) [1978]
E.C.R. 1209; [1978] 3 C.M.L.R.
566 ECJ 33,
149, 150

Bayerische Hypotheken- und Wech-
selbank AG v Dietzinger
(C-45/96) [1998] 1 W.L.R. 1035;
[1998] All E.R. (EC) 332; [1998]
E.C.R. I-1199; [1998] 2
C.M.L.R. 499 ECJ 293
Beate Reibold v Bundesanstalt für
Arbeit (C-216/89) [1990] E.C.R.
I–4163 247
Beerens v Rijksdienst voor
Arbiedsvoorziening (C-35/77);
sub nom. Ermin v Rijksdienst
voor Arbeidsvoorziening (35/77)
[1977] E.C.R. 2249; [1978] 2
C.M.L.R. 320 ECJ 251
Beets-Proper v F Van Lanschot
Bankiers NV (262/84) [1986]
E.C.R. 773; [1987] 2 C.M.L.R.
616 ECJ 33
Belgische Radio en Televisie v
SABAM SV (127/73) (No.2)
[1974] E.C.R. 313; [1974] 2
C.M.L.R. 238 ECJ 145
Belgium v Cobelfret NV (C-138/07)
[2009] S.T.C. 1127; [2009] 2
C.M.L.R. 43 ECJ 281, 431
Belgium v Commission of the Euro-
pean Communities (C-110/03);
sub nom. Legality of Regulation
2204/2002, Re (C-110/03)
[2005] E.C.R. I-2801; [2006] 2
C.M.L.R. 5 ECJ 379, 390
Belgium v Commission of the European Communities. *See* Aid to
Meura SA, Re (C-234/84)
Belgium v Humbel (263/86) [1988]
E.C.R. 5365; [1989] 1 C.M.L.R.
393 ECJ 249,
288
Belgium v Royer (48/75); sub nom.
Procureur du Roi v Royer
(48/75) [1976] E.C.R. 497;
[1976] 2 C.M.L.R. 619 ECJ ... 238,
244, 247
Belgium v Spain (C-388/95) [2000]
E.C.R. I-3123; [2002] 1 C.M.L.R.
26 ECJ 130
Benzine en Petroleum Handels-
maatschappij BV v Commission
of the European Communities
(77/77) [1978] E.C.R. 1513;
[1978] 3 C.M.L.R. 174 ECJ 134
Bestuur van de Sociale Verzekeringsbank v JM Cabanis-Issarte
(C-308/93) [1996] E.C.R.
I–2097 141

Betriebsrat der ADS Anker GmbH v ADS Anker GmbH (C-349/01) [2004] E.C.R. I-6803; [2004] 3 C.M.L.R. 14 ECJ 474

Betriebsrat der Bofrost Josef H Boquoi Deutschland West GmbH & Co KG v Bofrost Josef H Boquoi Deutschland West GmbH & Co KG (C-62/99) [2001] E.C.R. I-2579; [2004] 2 C.M.L.R. 53 ECJ 474

Betriebsrat der Firma ADS Anker GmbH v ADS Anker GmbH (C-349/01) [2004] E.C.R. I–6819 282

Bettray v Staatssecretaris van Justitie (344/87) [1989] E.C.R. 1621; [1991] 1 C.M.L.R. 459 ECJ 245

Biogen Inc v SmithKline Beecham Biologicals SA (C-181/95) (Intervention in Preliminary Ruling) [1996] E.C.R. I-717; [1997] 1 C.M.L.R. 704 ECJ 148

Biovilac SA v Commission of the European Communities (59/83) [1984] E.C.R. 4057; [1987] 2 C.M.L.R. 881 ECJ 150

Birra Wührer SpA v Council of Ministers and Commission of the European Communities (256/80) [1982] E.C.R. 85 ECJ 150

Boehringer Ingelheim KG v Swingward Ltd (C-348/04) [2008] All E.R. (EC) 411; [2007] E.C.R. I-3391; [2007] 2 C.M.L.R. 52 ECJ 305

Boehringer Mannheim GmbH v Commission of the European Communities (7/72) [1972] E.C.R. 1281; [1973] C.M.L.R. 864 ECJ 373

Borker, Re (138/80) [1980] E.C.R. 1975; [1980] 3 C.M.L.R. 638 ECJ 144

Boukhalfa v Germany (C-214/94) [1996] E.C.R. I-2253; [1996] 3 C.M.L.R. 22 ECJ 43

Bourquain (C-297/07) [2008] E.C.R. 9425 242

Brasserie du Pêcheur SA v Germany (C-46/93); R. v Secretary of State for Transport Ex p. Factortame Ltd (C-48/93) [1996] Q.B. 404; [1996] 2 W.L.R. 506; [1996] E.C.R. I-1029 ECJ 33, 112, 310

Brauerei A Bilger Sohne GmbH v Jehle (43/69) [1970] E.C.R. 127; [1974] 1 C.M.L.R. 382 ECJ 324

Bristol Myers Squibb Co v Paranova A/S (C-427/93); Bayer AG v Paranova A/S (C-436/93); CH Boehringer Sohn v Paranova A/S (C-429/93) [2003] Ch. 75; [2002] 3 W.L.R. 1746; [1996] E.C.R. I-3457 ECJ 232, 305

British Airways plc, Scandinavian Airlines System Denmark-Norway-Sweden, Koninklijke Luchtvaart Maatschappij NV, Air UK Ltd, Euralair international, TAT European Airlines SA and British Midland Airways Ltd v Commission of the European Communities (T-371/94 and T-394/94) [1998] E.C.R. II–2405 .... 378, 387

British United Provident Association Ltd (BUPA) v Commission of the European Communities (T-289/03) [2008] E.C.R. II-81; [2009] 2 C.M.L.R. 41 CFI 139

Broekmeulen v Huisarts Registratie Commissie (246/80); sub nom. Broekmeulen v Committee for the Registration of General Medical Practitioners [1981] E.C.R. 2311; [1982] 1 C.M.L.R. 91 ECJ 144, 273

Brussels Meetings, Re (358/85); sub nom. France v European Parliament (358/85) [1986] E.C.R. 2149; [1988] 3 C.M.L.R. 786 ECJ 83, 134

Budejovicky Budvar Narodni Podnik v Rudolf Ammersin GmbH (C-216/01) [2003] E.C.R. I-13617; [2005] 1 C.M.L.R. 56 ECJ 55

Buitoni SA v Fonds d'Orientation et de Regularisation des Marches Agricoles (122/78) [1979] E.C.R. 677; [1979] 2 C.M.L.R. 665 ECJ 139

Bundesverband der Bilanzbuchhalter eV v Commission of the European Communities (C-107/95 P) [1997] E.C.R. I-947; [1997] 5 C.M.L.R. 432; [1997] 3 C.M.L.R. 1189 ECJ 378

Bundesverband der Verbraucherzentralen und Verbraucherverbande – Verbraucherzentrale Bundesverband eV v Deutsche Internet versicherung AG (C-298/07) [2009] 1 All E.R. (Comm) 938; [2008] E.C.R. I-7841; [2008] Info. T.L.R. 387 ECJ 497

Bureau Européen des Médias de l'Industrie Musicale v Commission of the European Communities (T-114/92) [1995] E.C.R. II–147 360

Bureau européen des unions des consommateurs (BEUC) v Commission of the European Communities (T-256/97) [2000] E.C.R. II-101 583

Bureau National Interprofessionel du Cognac (BNIC) v Clair (123/83) [1985] E.C.R. 391; [1985] 2 C.M.L.R. 430 ECJ 322

Burtscher v Stauderer (C-213/04) [2005] E.C.R. I-10309; [2006] 2 C.M.L.R. 13 ECJ 298

Buyl v Commission of the European Communities (817/69) [1982] E.C.R. 245 67

C (A Child), Re (C-435/06); sub nom. C, Appellant (C-435/06) [2008] Fam. 27; [2008] 3 W.L.R. 419; [2007] E.C.R. I-10141 ECJ 259

CAS Succhi di Frutta SpA v Commission of the European Communities (T-191/96) [1999] E.C.R II–3181 309

CIA Security International SA v Signalson SA (C-194/94) [1996] All E.R. (EC) 557; [1996] E.C.R. I-2201; [1996] 2 C.M.L.R. 781 ECJ 234

CILFIT Srl v Ministero della Sanita (283/81); sub nom. CILFIT Srl v Ministro della Sanita (283/81) [1982] E.C.R. 3415; [1983] 1 C.M.L.R. 472 ECJ 145

Ca' Pasta Srl v Commission of the European Communities (C-359/98 P) [2000] E.C.R. I–3977 155

Caffaro Srl v Azienda Unità Sanitaria Locale RM/C (C-265/07) [2008] E.C.R. I-7095 498

Calpak SpA v Commission of the European Communities (789/79); Societa Emiliana Lavorazione SpA v Commission of the European Communities (790/79) [1980] E.C.R. 1949; [1981] 1 C.M.L.R. 26 ECJ 30

Camera Care Ltd v Commission of the European Communities (792/79 R) [1980] E.C.R. 119; [1981] E.C.R. 119; [1980] 1 C.M.L.R. 334 ECJ 353

Campus Oil Ltd v Minister for Industry and Energy (72/83) [1984] E.C.R. 2727; [1984] 3 C.M.L.R. 544 ECJ 143, 233

Canon Kabushiki Kaisha v Metro Goldwyn Mayer Inc (C-39/97) [1998] All E.R. (EC) 934; [1998] E.C.R. I-5507; [1999] 1 C.M.L.R. 77 ECJ 306

Cape SNC v Idealservice Srl (C-541/99); Idealservice MN RE SAS v OMAI Srl (C-542/99) [2002] All E.R. (EC) 657; [2001] E.C.R. I-9049; [2003] 1 C.M.L.R. 42 ECJ 498

Carbotermo SpA v Comune di Busto Arsizio (C-340/04) [2006] E.C.R. I-4137; [2006] 3 C.M.L.R. 7 ECJ 311

Cartesio Oktato es Szolgaltato bt (C-210/06); sub nom. Application Brought by Cartesio Oktato es Szolgaltato bt (C-210/06) [2009] Ch. 354; [2009] 3 W.L.R. 777; [2009] 1 C.M.L.R. 50 ECJ 278

Carvel v Council of the European Union (T-194/94); Guardian Newspapers Ltd v Council of Ministers of the European Communities [1996] All E.R. (E.C.) 53; [1995] E.C.R. II-2765; [1995] 3 C.M.L.R. 359; [1996] C.E.C. 282 CFI 104

Cassis de Dijon, Re (120/78). See Rewe-Zentral AG v Bundesmonopolverwaltung für Branntwein (120/78)

Celtec Ltd v Astley (C-478/03); sub nom. Astley v Celtec Ltd (C-478/03) [2005] E.C.R. I-4389; [2005] 3 C.M.L.R. 9 ECJ 473

Cementbouw Handel & Industrie BV v Commission of the European Communities (C-202/06 P) [2007] E.C.R. I-12129; [2008] 4 C.M.L.R. 17 ECJ 367

Cementhandelaren v Commission of the European Communities. *See* Vereeniging van Cementhandelaren v Commission of the European Communities (8/72)

Centrafarm BV v American Home Products Corp (3/78) [1978] E.C.R. 1823; [1979] 1 C.M.L.R. 326 ECJ 302

Centrafarm BV v Sterling Drug Inc (15/74); Centrafarm BV v Winthrop BV (16/74) [1974] E.C.R. 1183; [1974] E.C.R. 1147; [1974] 2 C.M.L.R. 480 ECJ 302

Centro Europa 7 Srl v Ministero delle Comunicazioni e Autorita per le Garanzie nelle Comunicazioni (C-380/05) [2008] E.C.R. I-349; [2008] 2 C.M.L.R. 18 ECJ 289, 346, 347

Centrosteel Srl v Adipol GmbH (C-456/98) [2000] E.C.R. I-6007; [2000] 3 C.M.L.R. 711 ECJ ... 129, 370

Centrum voor gelijkheid van kansen en voor racismebestrijding v Firma Feryn NV (C-54/07) [2008] E.C.R. I-5187 479

Charmasson v Minister for Economic Affairs and Finance (48/74) [1974] E.C.R. 1383; [1975] 2 C.M.L.R. 208 ECJ 400

Chaves Fonsica Ferrao v OHIM (T-159/97 R). *See* Luis Manuel Chaves Fonseca Ferrão v Office for Harmonisation in the Internal Market

Cheil Jedang Corp v Commission of the European Communities (T-220/00) [2003] E.C.R. II-2481 355

Chemial Farmaceutici SpA v DAF SpA (140/79) [1981] E.C.R. 1; [1981] 3 C.M.L.R. 350 ECJ 426

Chevassus-Marche's Heirs v Groupe Danone (C-19/07) [2008] Bus. L.R. 1290; [2008] 2 All E.R. (Comm) 1093; [2008] 1 Lloyd's Rep. 475; [2008] 2 C.M.L.R. 13 ECJ 267

Christelle Deliège v Ligue francophone de judo et disciplines associées ASBL, Ligue belge de judo ASBL, Union européenne de judo (C-51/96); François Pacquée (C-191/97). [2000] E.C.R. I-2549 290

Christian Schulin v Saatgut-Treuhandverwaltungsgesellschaft mbH (C-305/00) [2003] E.C.R. I-3525 197

Christiane Adam, épouse Urbing v Administration de l'enregistrement et des domaines (C-267/99) [2001] E.C.R. I-7467 271

Christini v SNCF (32/75). *See* Fiorini v Societe Nationale des Chemins de Fer Francais (32/75)

Chronopost SA v Union Francaise de l'Express (UFEX) (C-83/01 P); La Poste v Union Francaise de l'Express (UFEX) (C-93/01 P); France v Union Francaise de l'Express (UFEX) (C-94/01 P) [2003] E.C.R. I-6993; [2003] 3 C.M.L.R. 11 ECJ 382

Cinéthèque SA v Federation Nationale des Cinemas Francais (60/84 & 61/84) [1985] E.C.R. 2065; [1985] E.C.R. 2605; [1986] 1 C.M.L.R. 365 ECJ 229

Cisal Cisal di Battistello Venanzio & C. Sas v Istituto nazionale per l'assicurazione contro gli infortuni sul lavoro (INAIL) (C-218/00) [2002] E.C.R. I-691 ECJ 323

Citiworks AG (C-439/06) [2008] E.C.R. I-3913 552

Cnl-Sucal NV SA v Hag GF AG (C-10/89) [1990] E.C.R. I-3711; [1990] 3 C.M.L.R. 571 ECJ 302

Coditel Brabant SA v Commune d'Uccle (C-324/07) [2008] E.C.R. I-8457; [2009] 1 C.M.L.R. 29 ECJ 311

Coditel SA v Cine Vog Films SA (262/81) [1982] E.C.R. 3381; [1983] 1 C.M.L.R. 49 ECJ 289

Colegio de Ingenieros de Caminos, Canales y Puertos v Administracion del Estado (C-330/03) [2006] E.C.R. I-801; [2006] 2 C.M.L.R. 26 ECJ 275

Coleman v Attridge Law (C-303/06) [2008] All E.R. (EC) 1105; [2008] E.C.R. I-5603 ECJ 479

College van Burgemeester en Wethouders van Rotterdam v Rijkeboer (C-553/07) [2009] 3 C.M.L.R. 28 ECJ 501

Collino v Telecom Italia SpA (C-343/98) [2001] All E.R. (EC) 405; [2000] E.C.R. I-6659; [2002] 3 C.M.L.R. 35 ECJ 473

Color Drack GmbH v Lexx International Vertriebs GmbH (C-386/05) [2008] All E.R. (EC) 1044; [2008] 1 All E.R. (Comm) 169; [2007] E.C.R. I-3699 ECJ 258

Comité des Salines (C-278/96) [1996] E.C.R. 2410 392

Comite des Salines de France v Commission of the European Communities (T-154/94) [1996] E.C.R. II-1377; [1997] 1 C.M.L.R. 943 CFI 133, 152

Commercial Solvents (6/73 and 7/73). *See* Istituto Chemioterapico Italiano SpA v Commission of the European Communities (6/73)

Commission of the European Communities v Akzo and Ackros (C-07/04) [2004] E.C.R. I-8739 354

Commission of the European Communities v Anic Partecipazioni SpA (C-49/92 P) [1999] E.C.R. I-4125; [2001] 4 C.M.L.R. 17 ECJ 321

Commission of the European Communities v Artegodan GmbH (C-39/03) [2003] E.C.R. I–7885 162

Commission of the European Communities v AssiDoman Kraft Products AB (C-310/97 P) [1999] All E.R. (EC) 737; [1999] E.C.R. I-5363; [1999] 5 C.M.L.R. 1253 ECJ 140

Commission of the European Communities v Atlantic Container Line AB (C-149/95 P(R)) [1995] All E.R. (EC) 853; [1995] E.C.R. I-2165; [1997] 5 C.M.L.R. 167 ECJ 162, 163

Commission of the European Communities v Austria (C-212/02) Unpublished, 2004 316

Commission of the European Communities v Austria (C-81/03) Unpublished 266

Commission of the European Communities v Austria (C-147/03) [2005] E.C.R. I–5969 270

Commission of the European Communities v Austria (C-29/04); sub nom. Modling Waste Disposal Contract, Re (C-29/04) [2005] E.C.R. I-9705; [2006] 1 C.M.L.R. 40 ECJ 312

Commission of the European Communities v Belgium (77/69); sub nom. Stamp Tax on Timber, Re (77/69) [1970] E.C.R. 237; [1974] 1 C.M.L.R. 203 ECJ 425

Commission of the European Communities v Belgium (227/85); sub nom. Directives On Waste, Re [1988] E.C.R. 1; [1989] 2 C.M.L.R. 797 ECJ 111

Commission of the European Communities v Belgium (42/87); sub nom. Higher Education Funding, Re [1988] E.C.R. 5445; [1989] 1 C.M.L.R. 457 ECJ 249

Commission of the European Communities v Belgium (C-2/90) [1992] E.C.R. I–4466 224

Commission of the European Communities v Belgium (C-167/90) [1991] E.C.R. I–2535 274

Commission of the European Communities v Belgium (C-173/94) [1996] E.C.R. I–3265 254

Commission of the European Communities v Belgium (C-278/94); sub nom. Access to Special Employment Programmes, Re (C-278/94) [1996] E.C.R. I-4307; [1997] 1 C.M.L.R. 1040 ECJ 249

Commission of the European Communities v Belgium (C-344/95) [1997] E.C.R. I-1035; [1997] 2 C.M.L.R. 187 ECJ 244

Commission of the European Communities v Belgium (C-323/96) [1998] E.C.R. I–5063 313

Commission of the European Communities v Belgium (C-323/97) [1998] E.C.R. I-4291 .... 4, 240

Commission of the European Communities v Belgium (C-87/94) [1996] E.C.R. I–2043 .... 309, 310, 313

Commission of the European Communities v Belgium. *See* Toxic and Dangerous Waste, Re (C-239/85)

Commission of the European Communities v Board of Governors of the European Investment Bank (EIB) (85/86) [1988] E.C.R. 1281; [1989] 1 C.M.L.R. 103 ECJ 153, 185

Commission of the European Communities v Council (275/87) [1988] E.C.R. 259 141

Commission of the European Communities v Council of Ministers of the European Communities (C-131/87); sub nom. Trade in Animal Glands, Re (131/87) [1989] E.C.R. 3743; [1991] 1 C.M.L.R. 780 ECJ 137

Commission of the European Communities v Council of Ministers of the European Communities (165/87); sub nom. Harmonised Commodity Descriptions, Re (165/87) [1988] E.C.R. 5545; [1990] 1 C.M.L.R. 457 ECJ 70

Commission of the European Communities v Council of Ministers of the European Communities (C-242/87); sub nom. Erasmus Legislation, Re (242/87) [1989] E.C.R. 1425; [1991] 1 C.M.L.R. 478 ECJ 93, 134

Commission of the European Communities v Council of the European Communities (22/70); sub nom. European Road Transport Agreement, Re (22/70) [1971] E.C.R. 263; [1971] C.M.L.R. 335 ECJ 36, 59, 94, 133, 446, 564, 565, 566

Commission of the European Communities v Council of the European Communities (C-300/89); sub nom. Titanium Dioxide Directive, Re (C-300/89) [1991] E.C.R. I-2867; [1993] 3 C.M.L.R. 359 ECJ 36, 70

Commission of the European Communities v Council of the European Union (C-25/94) [1996] E.C.R. I-1469 ECJ 415, 565

Commission of the European Communities v Council of the European Union (C-29/99) [2002] E.C.R. I–11221 560

Commission of the European Communities v Council of the European Union (C-176/03) [2006] All E.R. (EC) 1; [2005] E.C.R. I-7879; [2005] 3 C.M.L.R. 20; [2006] Env. L.R. 18 ECJ . . . 548, 549

Commission of the European Communities v Council of the European Union (C-440/05) [2008] All E.R. (EC) 489; [2007] E.C.R. I-9097; [2008] 1 C.M.L.R. 22; [2008] Env. L.R. 12 ECJ 549

Commission of the European Communities v Denmark (302/86) [1988] E.C.R. 4627 229

Commission of the European Communities v Denmark (C-243/89) [1993] E.C.R. I–3353 309

Commission of the European Communities v Denmark (C-19/05) [2007] E.C.R. 8597 215

Commission of the European Communities v European Central Bank (C-11/00) [2003] E.C.R. I-7147 . . . 79

Commission of the European Communities v Ferriere Nord SpA (C-516/06 P); sub nom. Welded Steel Mesh Cartel Appeal, Re (C-516/06 P) [2007] E.C.R. I-10685; [2008] 4 C.M.L.R. 10 ECJ 356

Commission of the European Communities v France (6/69); sub nom. Export Credits, Re (6/69) [1969] E.C.R. 523; [1970] C.M.L.R. 43 ECJ 137

Commission of the European Communities v France (7/71); sub nom. Euratom Supply Agency, Re (7/71) [1971] E.C.R. 1003; [1972] C.M.L.R. 453 ECJ 559

Commission of the European Communities v France (167/73); sub nom. French Merchant Seamen, Re (167/73) [1974] E.C.R. 359; [1974] 2 C.M.L.R. 216 ECJ 49, 450

Commission of the European Communities v France (168/78); sub nom. French Taxation of Spirits, Re (168/78) [1980] E.C.R. 347; [1981] 2 C.M.L.R. 631 ECJ 426

Commission of the European Communities v France (220/83); sub nom. Co-Insurance Services, Re [1986] E.C.R. 3663; [1987] 2 C.M.L.R. 113 ECJ 287

Commission of the European Communities v France (270/83); sub nom. Tax Credits, Re (270/83) [1986] E.C.R. 273; [1987] 1 C.M.L.R. 401 ECJ 430

Commission of the European Communities v France (C-64/88) [1991] E.C.R. I-2727 111

Commission of the European Communities v France (C-265/95) [1997] E.C.R. I–6959 ECJ 236

Commission of the European Communities v France (C-225/98) [2000] E.C.R. I–7445 312

Commission of the European Communities v France (C-16/98) [2000] E.C.R. I–831 309

Commission of the European Communities v France (C-304/02); sub nom. Control Measures for Fishing Activities, Re (C-304/02) [2005] E.C.R. I-6263; [2005] 3 C.M.L.R. 13 ECJ 111, 131

Commission of the European Communities v France (C-347/02) [2004] E.C.R. I–7557 295

Commission of the European Communities v France (C-121/07) [2008] E.C.R. 9159; [2009] Env. L.R. 23 ECJ 111

Commission of the European Communities v G&E Gianniotis EPE (C-524/03) 164

Commission of the European Communities v Germany (178/84); sub nom. Purity Requirements for Beer, Re (178/84) [1987] E.C.R. 1227; [1988] 1 C.M.L.R. 780 ECJ 139

Commission of the European Communities v Germany (C-131/93); sub nom. Crayfish Imports, Re [1994] E.C.R. I-3303; [1995] 2 C.M.L.R. 278 ECJ 139

Commission of the European Communities v Germany (C-318/94) [1996] E.C.R. I–1949 311

Commission of the European Communities v Germany (C-121/97) [1990] E.C.R. I-2721 550

Commission of the European Communities v Gianni (C-153/99P) [2000] E.C.R. I–2891 140

Commission of the European Communities v Germany (C-209/00) [2002] E.C.R. I–11695 393

Commission of the European Communities v Germany (C-20/01 and C-28/01) [2003] E.C.R. I-3609 311

Commission of the European Communities v Germany (C-477/03) November 17, 2004 ...... 447, 448

Commission of the European Communities v Germany (Volkswagen law) (C-112/04) [2007] E.C.R. I-8995 298

Commission of the European Communities v Greece (226/87); sub nom. Public Sector Insurance, Re (226/87) [1988] E.C.R. 3611; [1989] 3 C.M.L.R. 569 ECJ 34

Commission of the European Communities v Greece (C-32/89 R); sub nom. FEOGA Accounts, Re (C-32/89 R) [1989] E.C.R. 985; [1991] 1 C.M.L.R. 377 ECJ 162

Commission of the European Communities v Greece (C-387/97) [2000] E.C.R. I-5047; [2001] Env. L.R. D2 ECJ 131

Commission of the European Communities v Greece (C-364/03) [2005] E.C.R. I-6159; [2006] Env. L.R. 9 ECJ 546

Commission of the European Communities v Greece (C-550/03) [2004] O.J. C300/24 448

Commission of the European Communities v Greece (C-45/07) [2009] 1 Lloyd's Rep. 425; [2009] 2 C.M.L.R. 38 ECJ 567

Commission of the European Communities v Greece (C-568/07) June 4, 2009 131

Commission of the European Communities v Hellenic Republic (C-290/96) [1996] E.C.R. I–3285 ... 254

Commission of the European Communities v ICI Plc (C-286/95 P) [2001] All E.R. (EC) 439; [2000] E.C.R. I-2341; [2000] 5 C.M.L.R. 413 ECJ 114

Commission of the European Communities v Infront WM AG (C-125/06 P) [2008] E.C.R. I-1451; [2008] 2 C.M.L.R. 28 ECJ 135, 136

Commission of the European Communities v Ireland (61/77); sub nom. Sea Fishery Restrictions, Re (61/77) [1978] E.C.R. 417; [1978] 2 C.M.L.R. 466 ECJ 49, 163

Commission of the European Communities v Ireland (45/87); sub nom. Dundalk Water Supply Scheme, Re (No.3) (45/87) [1988] E.C.R. 4929; 44 B.L.R. 1; [1989] 1 C.M.L.R. 225 ECJ 309, 310

Commission of the European Communities v Ireland (C-459/03); sub nom. Dispute over MOX Plant, Re (C-459/03) [2006] All E.R. (EC) 1013; [2006] E.C.R. I-4635; [2006] 2 C.M.L.R. 59 ECJ 131

Commission of the European Communities v Ireland (C-507/03); sub nom. Irish Post Office Contract, Re (C-507/03) [2007] E.C.R. I-9777; [2008] 1 C.M.L.R. 34; [2008] C.E.C. 782 ECJ 311, 314

Commission of the European Communities v Italian Republic (C-249/08); [2009] E.C.R. 29.10.09 418

Commission of the European Communities v Italy (7/68); sub nom. Export Tax on Art Treasures, Re (7/68) [1968] E.C.R. 423; [1969] C.M.L.R. 1 ECJ 224, 232

Commission of the European Communities v Italy (159/78). *See* Customs Agents, Re (159/78)

Commission of the European Communities v Italy (169/78); sub nom. Italian Taxation of Spirits, Re (169/78) [1980] E.C.R. 385; [1981] 2 C.M.L.R. 673 ECJ . . . 231, 232

Commission of the European Communities v Italy (91/79); sub nom. Detergents Directive, Re (91/79) [1980] E.C.R. 1099; [1981] 1 C.M.L.R. 331 ECJ 540

Commission of the European Communities v Italy (274/83). *See* Public Works Contracts, Re (C-274/83)

Commission of the European Communities v Italy (C-118/85); sub nom. Amministrazione Autonoma dei Monopoli di Stato, Re (118/85) [1987] E.C.R. 2599; [1988] 3 C.M.L.R. 255 ECJ 377

Commission of the European Communities v Italy (C-3/88); sub nom. Data Processing Contracts, Re (C-3/88) [1989] E.C.R. 4035; [1991] 2 C.M.L.R. 115 ECJ 309, 310

Commission of the European Communities v Italy (199/85) [1987] E.C.R. 1039 312

Commission of the European Communities v Italy (C-360/89) [1992] E.C.R. I–3401 309

Commission of the European Communities v Italy (C-272/91) [1994] E.C.R. I–1409 . . . . . 309, 314

Commission of the European Communities v Italy (C-349/93) [1995] E.C.R. I–343 396

Commission of the European Communities v Italy (C-35/96); sub nom. Customs Agents, Re (C-35/96) [1998] E.C.R. I-3851; [1998] 5 C.M.L.R. 889 ECJ 323

Commission of the European Communities v Italy (C-202/99) [2001] E.C.R. I–9319 271

Commission of the European Communities v Italy (C-460/02) [2004] E.C.R. I-7335 451

Commission of the European Communities v Italy (C-110/05); sub nom. Motorcycle Trailers, Re (C-110/05) [2009] All E.R. (EC) 796; [2009] 2 C.M.L.R. 3 ECJ 231

Commission of the European Communities v Italy (C-465/05); sub nom. Private Security Guards, Re (C-465/05) [2007] E.C.R. I-11091; [2008] 2 C.M.L.R. 3 ECJ 287

Commission of the European Communities v Italy. *See* Public Works Directive 1971, Re (10/76)

Commission of the European Communities v Ladbroke Racing Ltd (C-359/95 P); France v Ladbroke Racing Ltd (C-379/95 P) [1997] E.C.R. I-6265; [1998] 4 C.M.L.R. 27 ECJ 377

Commission of the European Communities v Lisrestal (C-32/95 P) [1996] E.C.R. I-5373; [1997] 2 C.M.L.R. 1 ECJ 139

Commission of the European Communities v Luxembourg (C-473/93); sub nom. Public Service Employment, Re (C-473/93) [1996] E.C.R. I-3207; [1996] 3 C.M.L.R. 981 ECJ 254

Commission of the European Communities v Luxembourg (C-445/03); sub nom. Law on Work Permits for Foreign Workers Employed by Cross Border Service Providers, Re (C-445/03) [2004] E.C.R. I-10191; [2005] 1 C.M.L.R. 22 ECJ 254

Commission of the European Communities v Luxembourg (C-481/03) [2004] O.J. C284/6 ... 448

Commission of the European Communities v Netherlands (C-89/76); sub nom. Inspection Fees on Exported Plants, Re (89/76) [1977] E.C.R. 1355; [1978] 3 C.M.L.R. 630 ECJ 225

Commission of the European Communities v Netherlands (C-523/04); sub nom. Dutch Air Transport Agreement, Re (C-523/04) [2007] E.C.R. I-3267; [2007] 2 C.M.L.R. 48 ECJ 450

Commission of the European Communities v Netherlands (C-50/06); sub nom. Expulsion of Foreign Nationals, Re (C-50/06) [2006] E.C.R. I-4383; [2007] 3 C.M.L.R. 8 ECJ 239

Commission of the European Communities v Netherlands (C-398/06) [2008] E.C.R. I-56 ... 247

Commission of the European Communities v Netherlands, Italy, France and Spain (C-157/94) [1997] E.C.R. I–5699 376

Commission of the European Communities v Parliament and Council (C-378/00) [2003] E.C.R. I-937 .... 116, 118, 550

Commission of the European Communities v Parliament and Council (C-122/04) [2006] E.C.R. I-2001 116

Commission of the European Communities v Portugal (C-61/05) [2006] E.C.R. I-6779; [2006] 3 C.M.L.R. 36 ECJ 301

Commission of the European Communities v Sociedade de Curtumes a Sul do Tejo Ld™ (Socurte), Revestimentos de Cortiça Ld™ (Quavi) and Sociedade Transformadora de Carnes Ld™ (Stec) (C-143/95 P) [1997] E.C.R. I–1 132

Commission of the European Communities v Spain (C-73/92) [1993] E.C.R. I–5997; [1997] S.T.C. 700 ECJ 312

Commission of the European Communities v Spain (C-328/92) [1994] E.C.R. I–1569 312

Commission of the European Communities v Spain (C-70/03) [2004] E.C.R. I-7999 .... 451, 498

Commission of the European Communities v Spain (C-503/03) [2007] All E.R. (EC) 797; [2006] E.C.R. I-1097 ECJ 243, 253

Commission of the European Communities v Spain (C-286/06) [2008] E.C.R. I-8025 275

Commission of the European Communities v Spain (C-88/07); sub nom. Marketing of Herbal Medicines, Re (C-88/07) [2009] 2 C.M.L.R. 52 ECJ 195

Commission of the European Communities v Sweden (C-468/98) [2002] E.C.R. I-9575 581

Commission of the European Communities v Sweden (C-249/06) [2010] All E.R. (EC) 185; [2009] 2 C.M.L.R. 49 ECJ 55

Commission of the European Communities v Systraval and Brink's France (C-367/95 P) [1998] E.C.R. I–1719 .... 138, 395

Commission of the European Communities v the Translation Centre (C-269/06) [2007] E.C.R. I-187 167

Commission of the European Communities v Union Internationale des Chemins de Fer (UIC) (C-264/95 P) [1997] E.C.R. I-1287; [1997] 5 C.M.L.R. 49 ECJ 342

Commission of the European Communities v United Kingdom (C-31/77 R). *See* Pig Production Subsidies, Re (C-31/77)

Commission of the European Communities v United Kingdom (C-61/81); sub nom. Equal Pay for Equal Work, Re (61/81) [1982] E.C.R. 2601; [1982] 3 C.M.L.R. 284 ECJ 478

Commission of the European Communities v United Kingdom (40/82); sub nom. Imports of Poultry Meat, Re (40/82) [1982] E.C.R. 2793; [1982] 3 C.M.L.R. 497 ECJ 233

Commission of the European Communities v United Kingdom (165/82); sub nom. Equal Treatment, Re (165/82) [1984] 1 All E.R. 353; [1983] E.C.R. 3431; [1984] 1 C.M.L.R. 44 ECJ 478

Commission of the European Communities v United Kingdom (207/83) [1985] E.C.R 1207 230

Commission of the European Communities v United Kingdom (C-246/89); sub nom. Nationality of Fishermen, Re (C-246/89) [1991] E.C.R. I-4585; [1991] 3 C.M.L.R. 706 ECJ 416

Commission of the European Communities v United Kingdom (C-466/98); sub nom. Open Skies Agreement, Re (C-466/98) [2002] E.C.R. I-9427; [2003] 1 C.M.L.R. 6 ECJ 344, 453

Commission of the European Communities v United Kingdom (C-300/95); sub nom. Product Liability Directive, Re (C-300/95) [1997] All E.R. (EC) 481; [1997] E.C.R. I-2649; [1997] 3 C.M.L.R. 923 ECJ 498

Commission of the European Communities v United Kingdom (C-483/03) [2004] O.J. C300/23 448

Commission of the European Communities v United Kingdom (C-127/05) [2007] E.C.R. I-4619; [2007] All E.R. (EC) 986; [2007] 3 C.M.L.R. 20 ECJ 251

Commission of the European Communities v United Kingdom. *See* Tachographs, Re (128/78)

Commission of the European Economic Community v Belgium (90/63); sub nom. Import of Milk Products, Re (90/63) [1964] E.C.R. 625; [1965] C.M.L.R. 58 ECJ 111, 138

Commission of the European Economic Community v Italy (10/61); sub nom. Italian Customs Duties on Radio Valves, Re (10/61) [1962] E.C.R. 1; [1962] C.M.L.R. 187 ECJ 53

Commune de Mesquer v Total France SA (C-188/07) [2009] All E.R. (EC) 525; [2008] 2 Lloyd's Rep. 672; [2008] E.C.R. I-4501; [2008] 3 C.M.L.R. 16; [2009] Env. L.R. 9 ECJ 546

Commune de Sausheim v Azelvandre (C-552/07) [2009] All E.R. (EC) 1028; [2009] 2 C.M.L.R. 44 ECJ 198, 410

Compagnia Generale Interscamsi SpA (COGIS) v Amministrazione delle Finanze dello Stato (216/81) [1982] E.C.R. 2701; [1983] 1 C.M.L.R. 685 ECJ 232

Compagnia Singer SpA v Amministrazione delle Finanze dello Stato (290/81); Geigy SpA v Amministrazione delle Finanze dello Stato (291/81) [1983] E.C.R. 847 ECJ 39, 566

Compagnie des Hauts Fourneaux de Chasse v High Authority of the European Coal and Steel Community (15/57) [1957–1958] E.C.R. 211 151

Compagnie Générale Maritime v Commission of the European Communities (T-86/95) [2002] E.C.R. II–1011 343

Compagnie Maritime Belge SA v Commission of the European Communities (T-276/04) [2008] E.C.R. II-1277; [2009] 4 C.M.L.R. 21 CFI 161, 353

Compagnie Maritime Belge Trans-
ports SA v Commission of
the European Communities
(T-24/93, T-25/93 and T-26/93)
[1996] E.C.R. II–1201; [1977] 4
C.M.L.R. 273 338,
                              343
Compagnie Maritime Belge Trans-
ports SA v Commission of
the European Communities
(C-395/96 P); Dafra-Lines A/S v
Commission of the European
Communities (C-396/96 P);
sub nom. Cie Maritime Belge
Transports SA v Commission of
the European Communities
(C-395/96 P) [2000] All E.R.
(EC) 385; [2000] E.C.R. I-1365;
[2000] 4 C.M.L.R. 1076
ECJ 338
Compagnie Royale Asturienne des
Mines SA v Commission of the
European Communities (29/83)
[1984] E.C.R. 1679; [1985] 1
C.M.L.R. 688 ECJ 322
Compañía Internacional de Pesca
y Derivados (Inpesca) SA v
Commission of the European
Communities (T-186/98) [2001]
E.C.R. II-557 115
Competition Authority v Beef Indus-
try Development Society Ltd (C-
209/07) [2009] All E.R. (EC)
367; [2008] E.C.R. I-8637;
[2009] 4 C.M.L.R. 6 ECJ 326
Comunidad Autónoma de Valencia –
Generalidad Valenciana v Com-
mission of the European
Communities (C-363/06 P)
February 20, 2008 157
Comunidad Autónoma de Valencia –
Generalidad Valenciana v Com-
mission of the European Com-
munities (T-357/05) [2006]
E.C.R. II-2015 157
Conceria Daniele Bresciani v
Amministrazione delle Finanze
(87/75) [1976] E.C.R. 129;
[1976] 2 C.M.L.R. 62
ECJ 570
Confederación Española de
Transporte de Mercancías
(CETM) v Commission of
the European Communities
(T-55/99) [2000] E.C.R.
II–3207 380

Confederatie van Immobilien-
Beroepen van Belgie VZW v Van
Leuken (C-197/06) [2008] E.C.R.
I-2627; [2008] 2 C.M.L.R. 48
ECJ 275
Confédération Generale du Travail
(CGT) v Prime Minister
(C-385/05); sub nom. Con-
fédération Generale du Travail
(CGT) v Premier Ministre
(C-385/05) [2007] E.C.R. I-611;
[2007] 2 C.M.L.R. 6 ECJ ... 282, 473
Confederation Nationale des Produc-
teurs de Fruits et Legumes v
Council of the European Eco-
nomic Community (16/62)
[1962] E.C.R. 471; [1963]
C.M.L.R. 160 ECJ 30, 137
Confédération Suisse v Commission
of the European Communities
(T-319/05) [2006] E.C.R.
II–2073 164
Confederazione Italiana Dirigenti di
Azienda (CIDA) v Council of
Ministers of the European Com-
munities (297/86) [1988] E.C.R.
3531; [1989] 3 C.M.L.R. 851
ECJ 180
Conseil national de l'ordre des archi-
tectes v Nicolas Dreessen (C-31/
00) [2002] E.C.R. I–663 .... 274, 276
Consiglio Nazionale degli Ingegneri v
Ministero della Giustizia and
Marco Cavallera (311/06) [2009]
E.C.R. I-415 272
Consorzio Aziende Metano
(Coname) v Comune di Cingia
de' Botti (C-231/03) [2005]
E.C.R. I–7287 310
Consorzio Italiano della Componentistica di Ricambio per Autoveicoli v Regie Nationale des
Usines Renault (C-53/87); Maxicar v Regie Nationale des Usines
Renault (C-53/87) [1988] E.C.R.
6039; [1990] 4 C.M.L.R. 265;
[1990] F.S.R. 544 ECJ 301
Cooperatieve Vereniging Suiker Unie
UA v Commission of the European Communities (40/73); sub
nom. European Sugar Cartel, Re
(40/73); Suiker Unie v Commission of the European Communities (40/73) [1975] E.C.R. 1663;
[1976] 1 C.M.L.R. 295 ECJ 322,
                                    325

Cooperativa Co-frutta Srl v Amministrazione delle Finanze dello Stato (193/85) [1987] E.C.R. 2085 ECJ 425

Coote v Granada Hospitality Ltd (C-185/97) [1998] All E.R. (EC) 865; [1998] E.C.R. I-5199; [1998] 3 C.M.L.R. 958 ECJ 474

Cordis Obst und Gemüse Großhandel GmbH v Commission of the European Communities (T-18/99) [2001] E.C.R. II-913 .... 39, 54

Costa v Ente Nazionale per l'Energia Elettrica (ENEL) (6/64) [1964] E.C.R. 585; [1964] C.M.L.R. 425 ECJ 8, 42, 44, 48, 142, 143, 145

Council of the European Communities v European Parliament (34/86); sub nom. 1986 Budget, Re (34/86) [1986] E.C.R. 2155; [1986] 3 C.M.L.R. 94 ECJ 134

Council of the European Union v Bangemann (C-290/99) 108

Cowan v Trésor Public (186/87) [1989] E.C.R. 195; [1990] 2 C.M.L.R. 613 ECJ 289

Criel v Procureur de la République au Tribunal de Grande Instance (Lille) (41/76) [1976] E.C.R. 1921; [1977] 2 C.M.L.R. 535 ECJ 581

Criminal Proceedings against Ahokainen (C-434/04); sub nom. Ahokainen v Virallinen Syyttaja (C-434/04) [2006] E.C.R. I-9171; [2007] 1 C.M.L.R. 11 ECJ 232

Criminal proceedings against Aldo Bordessa (C-358/9 and C-416/93). *See* Ministerio Fiscal v Bordessa (C-358/93)

Criminal Proceedings against Berlusconi (C-387/02) [2005] E.C.R. I-3565; [2005] 2 C.M.L.R. 32 ECJ 278

Criminal Proceedings against Bourrasse (C-228/01); Criminal Proceedings against Perchicot (C-289/01); sub nom. Bourasse v Ministere Public (C-228/01) [2003] All E.R. (EC) 465; [2002] E.C.R. I-10213 ECJ 444

Criminal Proceedings against Brandsma (C-293/94) [1996] All E.R. (EC) 837; [1996] E.C.R. I-3159; [1996] 3 C.M.L.R. 904 ECJ 232

Criminal Proceedings against Corbeau, Re (C-320/91) [1993] E.C.R. I-2533; [1995] 4 C.M.L.R. 621 ECJ 347

Criminal Proceedings against dell'Orto (C-467/05) [2007] 3 C.M.L.R. 29 ECJ 290

Criminal Proceedings against Doulamis (C-446/05) [2008] E.C.R. I-1377; [2008] 5 C.M.L.R. 4 ECJ 146

Criminal proceedings against Fabriek voor Hoogwaardige Voedingsprodukten Kelderman BV (130/80) [1981] E.C.R. 527 230

Criminal Proceedings against Fietje (27/80); sub nom. Fietje, Re [1980] E.C.R. 3839; [1981] 3 C.M.L.R. 722 ECJ 126, 230

Criminal Proceedings against Franzén (C-189/95) [1997] E.C.R. I-5909; [1998] 1 C.M.L.R. 1231 ECJ 376

Criminal Proceedings against Gervais (C-17/94) [1995] E.C.R. I-4353 ECJ 375

Criminal Proceedings against Goerres (C-385/96) [1998] E.C.R. I-4431 ECJ 499

Criminal Proceedings against Gysbrechts (C-205/07) [2009] All E.R. (EC) 711; [2009] 2 All E.R. (Comm) 951; [2009] 2 C.M.L.R. 2 ECJ 497

Criminal Proceedings against Hüseyin Gözütok (C-187/01); Criminal Proceedings against Klaus Brügge (C-385/01) [2003] E.C.R. I-1345; [2003] 2 C.M.L.R. 2 ECJ 243

Criminal proceedings against Jean-Claude Bellon (C-42/90) [1990] E.C.R. I-4863 .... 229, 232

Criminal proceedings against Joseph Danis (16/79–20/79) [1979] E.C.R. 3327 230

Criminal proceedings against Karl Josef Wilhelm Schwibbert (C-20/05) [2007] E.C.R. I-9447 234

Criminal Proceedings against Keck (C-267/91); Criminal Proceedings against Mithouard (C-268/91) [1993] E.C.R. I-6097; [1995] 1 C.M.L.R. 101 ECJ 52, 230, 231, 375, 426

Criminal proceedings against Michel Mulliez and Giuseppe Momblano (C-23/03 and C-52/03); Alessandro Nizza and Giacomo Pizzi (C-133/03); Fabrizio Barra (C-337/03); Adelio Aggio (C-473/03) [2006] E.C.R. I-3923 33

Criminal Proceedings against Nunes (C-186/98); sub nom. Nunes, Re (C-186/98) [1999] E.C.R. I-4883; [1999] 2 C.M.L.R. 1403 ECJ 480

Criminal Proceedings against Prantl (16/83) [1984] E.C.R. 1299; [1985] 2 C.M.L.R. 238 ECJ ... 228, 230

Criminal Proceedings against Raemdonck (C-128/04) [2005] E.C.R. I-2445; [2005] R.T.R. 25 ECJ ... 442

Criminal proceedings against René Kieffer and Romain Thill (C-114/96) [1997] E.C.R. I-3629 .... 227, 230

Criminal proceedings against Roelof Donkersteeg (C-37/99) [2000] E.C.R. I-10223 234

Criminal Proceedings against Sanz de Lera (C-163/94) [1995] E.C.R. I-4821; [1996] 1 C.M.L.R. 631 ECJ 299

Criminal Proceedings against Webb (279/80) [1981] E.C.R. 3305; [1982] 1 C.M.L.R. 719 ECJ 44, 309, 310

Customs Agents, Re (159/78); sub nom. Commission of the European Communities v Italy (159/78) [1979] E.C.R. 3247; [1980] 3 C.M.L.R. 446 ..... 49, 54

DKV Deutsche Krankenversicherung AG v Office for Harmonisation in the Internal Market (Trade Marks and Designs) (OHIM) (C-104/00 P) [2002] E.C.R. I-7561; [2003] E.T.M.R. 20 ECJ 196

Daihatsu-Händler v Daihatsu Deutschland (C-97/96). *See* Verband deutscher Daihatsu-Händler eV v Daihatsu Deutschland GmbH

Daimlerchrysler AG v Commission of the European Communities (T-325/01) [2005] E.C.R. II-3319; [2007] 4 C.M.L.R. 15 CFI 324

Danish Satellite TV (DSTV) A/S (Eurotica Rendez-vous Television) v Commission of the European Communities (T-69/99) [2000] E.C.R. II-4039 134

Dansk Supermarked A/S v Imerco A/S (58/80) [1981] E.C.R. 181; [1981] 3 C.M.L.R. 590 ECJ 229

De Franceschi SpA Monfalcone v Council and Commission of the European Communities (51/81) [1982] E.C.R. 117 ECJ 149

Decker v Caisse de Maladie des Employés Privés (C-120/95) [1998] All E.R. (E.C.) 673; [1998] E.C.R. I-1831; [1998] 2 C.M.L.R. 879 ECJ 251

Decker v Hauptzollamt Landau (99/78). *See* Weingut Gustav Decker AG v Hauptzollamt Landau (C-99/78)

Deepak Rajani (Dear!Net Online) v Office for Harmonisation in the Internal Market (C-559/08) Order January 21, 2009 161

Defrenne v Belgium (80/70) [1971] E.C.R. 445; [1974] 1 C.M.L.R. 494 ECJ 478

Defrenne v SA Belge de Navigation Aerienne (SABENA) (43/75); sub nom. Defrenne v SABENA (43/75) [1981] 1 All E.R. 122; [1976] E.C.R. 455; [1976] 2 C.M.L.R. 98 ECJ 44, 45, 141, 478

Delbar v Caisse d'allocations familiales de Roubaix-Tourcoing (C-114/88) [1989] E.C.R. 4067 251

Delimitis v Henninger Brau AG (C-234/89) [1991] E.C.R. I-935; [1992] 5 C.M.L.R. 210 ECJ 373

Delkvist v Anklagemyndigheden Ex p. Landsnaevuet for Omnibuskorsel (21/78) [1978] E.C.R. 2327; [1979] R.T.R. 161; [1979] 1 C.M.L.R. 372 ECJ 45

Demirel v Stadt Schwabisch Gmund (12/86) [1987] E.C.R. 3719; [1989] 1 C.M.L.R. 421 ECJ 570

Denkavit Futtermittel GmbH v Land Nordrhein-Westfalen (73/84) [1985] E.C.R. 1013; [1986] 2 C.M.L.R. 482 ECJ 230

Denkavit Futtermittel GmbH v Minister fur Ernahrung, Landwirtschaft und Forsten des Landes Nordrhein-Westfalen (251/78) [1979] E.C.R. 3369; [1980] 3 C.M.L.R. 513; [1981] F.S.R. 53 ECJ 230

Deponietzweckverband Eiterköpfe v Land Rheinland-Pfalz (C-6/03) [2005] E.C.R. I-2753; [2005] 2 C.M.L.R. 52 ECJ 542

Deutsche Grammophon Gesellschaft GmbH v Metro SB Grossmarkte GmbH & Co KG (78/70) [1971] E.C.R. 487; [1971] C.M.L.R. 631 ECJ 54, 304

Deutsche Telekom AG v Germany (C-262/06) [2007] E.C.R. I-10057; [2008] 4 C.M.L.R. 9 ECJ 346, 509, 517

Deutscher Komponistenverband eV v Commission of the European Communities (8/71) [1971] E.C.R. 705; [1973] C.M.L.R. 902 ECJ 141

Di Paolo v Office National de l'Emploi (76/76) [1977] E.C.R. 315; [1977] 2 C.M.L.R. 59 ECJ 251

Diego Calì & Figli Srl v Servizi ecologici porto di Genova SpA (SEPG) (C-343/95) [1997] E.C.R. I–1547 377

Dietz v Stichting Thuiszorg Rotterdam (C-435/93) [1996] E.C.R. I-5223; [1997] 1 C.M.L.R. 199 ECJ 477

Dijkstra v Friesland (Frico Domo) Cooperatieve BA (C-319/93); Van Roessel v de Cooperatie Vereniging Zuivelcooperatie Campina Melkunie BA (C-40/94); Luttikhuis v Verenigde Cooperatieve Melkindustrie Coberco BA (C-399/93) [1995] E.C.R. I-4471; [1996] 5 C.M.L.R. 178 ECJ 342

Dillenkofer v Germany (C-178/94); Knor v Germany (C-190/94); Heuer v Germany (C-189/94); Schulte v Germany (C-188/94); Erdmann v Germany (C-179/94) [1997] Q.B. 259; [1997] 2 W.L.R. 253; [1996] E.C.R. I-4845 ECJ 112, 361

Diputation Foral de Alava v Commission (T-127/99, T-129/99 and T-148/99 and T-92/00 and T-103/99). *See* Territorio Histórico de Álava – Diputación Foral de Álava (T-127/99)

Dirk Rüffert v Land Niedersachsen (C-346/06) [2008] All E.R. (EC) 902; [2008] E.C.R. I-1989; [2008] 2 C.M.L.R. 39 ECJ 476

Distillers Co Ltd v Commission of the European Communities (30/78) [1980] E.C.R. 2229; [1980] 3 C.M.L.R. 121; [1980] F.S.R. 589 ECJ 326

Diversinte SA and Iberlacta SA v Administracion Principal de Aduanas E Impuestos Especiales de la Junquera (C-260/91) [1993] E.C.R. I-1885 ECJ 37

Dona v Mantero (13/76) [1976] E.C.R. 1333; [1976] 2 C.M.L.R. 578 ECJ 248

Donckerwolcke v Procureur de la République. *See* Criel v Procureur de la République au Tribunal de Grande Instance (Lille)

Dorsch Consult Ingenieurgesellschaft mbH v Bundesbaugesellschaft Berlin mbH (C-54/96) [1998] All E.R. (EC) 262; [1997] E.C.R. I-4961; [1998] 2 C.M.L.R. 237 ECJ 316

Douaneagent der NV Nederlandse Spoorwegen v Inspector der Invoerrechten en Accijnzen (38/75) [1976] E.C.R. 1439; [1975] E.C.R. 1439 ECJ 255, 566

Dow Chemical Nederland BV v Commission of the European Communities (87/87 R) [1987] E.C.R. 4367; [1988] 4 C.M.L.R. 439 ECJ 354

Draehmpaehl v Urania Immobilienservice OHG (C-180/95) [1997] All E.R. (E.C.) 719; [1997] E.C.R. I-2195; [1997] 3 C.M.L.R. 1107 ECJ 474

Dresdner Bank AG v Commission of the European Communities (T-44/02) [2006] E.C.R. II–3567; [2007] 4 C.M.L.R. 13 ECJ 164

Dreyfus v Commission of the European Communities (386/86) [1998] E.C.R. I–2309 ..... 135, 136

Du Pont de Nemours Italiana SpA v Unità sanitaria locale N° 2 di Carrara (C-21/88) [1990] E.C.R. I–889 .... 309, 310

EMI Electrola GmbH v Patricia Im- und Export Verwaltungsge- sellschaft mbH (C-341/87) [1989] E.C.R. 79; [1989] 2 C.M.L.R. 413; [1989] 1 F.S.R. 544 ECJ 302

EMI Records Ltd v CBS Grammofon A/S (86/75) [1976] E.C.R. 871 ... 303

EMI Records Ltd v CBS Schallplat- ten GmbH (96/75) [1976] A.C.R. 913 303

EMI Records Ltd v CBS United King- dom Ltd (51/75); EMI v CBS Grammofon A/S (86/75); EMI v CBS Schallplatten GmbH (96/75) [1976] E.C.R. 811; [1976] 2 C.M.L.R. 235 ECJ 303

EU-Wood-Trading GmbH v Sonder- abfall-Management-Gesellschaft Rheinland-Pfalz mbH (C-277/02) [2004] E.C.R. I-11957 546

Eagle v Commission of the European Communities (T-144/02) [2004] E.C.R. II–3381 149

Eckhard Kalanke v Freie Hansestadt Bremen (C-450/93) [1995] E.C.R. I-3051 477

Ecotrade Srl v Altiforni e Ferriere di Servola SpA (AFS) (C-200/97) [1998] E.C.R. I–7907 380

Edouard Dubois et Fils SA v Garonor Exploitation SA (C-16/94); Gen- eral Cargo Services SA v Garonor Exploitation SA [1995] All E.R. (E.C.) 821; [1995] E.C.R. I-2421; [1995] 2 C.M.L.R. 771 ECJ 225

Efisol SA v Commission of the Euro- pean Communities (T-336/94) [1996] E.C.R. II–1343 139

Einfuhr und Vorratsstelle fur Getreide und Futtermittel v Firma Koster, Berodt & Co (25/70). *See* Interna- tionale Handelsgesellschaft mbH v Einfuhr- und Vorratsstelle fur Getreide und Futtermittel (11/70)

El Corte Ingles SA v Blazquez Rivero (C-192/94) [1996] E.C.R. I-1281; [1996] 2 C.M.L.R. 507 ECJ 33

Elgafaji v Staatssecretaris van Justitie (C-465/07) [2009] 1 W.L.R. 2100; [2009] All E.R. (EC) 651; [2009] 2 C.M.L.R. 45 ECJ 257

Emerald Meats Ltd v Commission of the European Communities (C-66/91) [1991] E.C.R. I–1143 133

Emesa Sugar (Free Zone) NV v Aruba (17/98) [2000] E.C.R. I–665 .... 128, 129

Emir Gül v Regierungspräsident (131/85) [1986] E.C.R. 1573; [1987] 1 C.M.L.R. 501 ECJ 249

Emirates Airlines Direktion fur Deutschland v Schenkel (C-173/07) [2009] All E.R. (EC) 436; [2008] E.C.R. I-5237; [2008] 3 C.M.L.R. 20 ECJ 451

Empresa Nacional de Uranio SA (ENU) v Commission of the Euro- pean Communities (C-357/95 P) [1997] E.C.R. I-1329; [1997] 3 C.M.L.R. 95 ECJ 182

Empresa Nacional de Urânio SA (ENU) v Commission of the European Communities (T-458/ 93 and T-523/930 [1995] E.C.R. II-2459 557

Enka BV v Inspecteur der Invoerrechten en Accijnzen (38/77) [1977] E.C.R. 2203; [1978] 2 C.M.L.R. 212 ECJ 50

Ente Italiano di Servizio Sociale v Commission of the European Communities (310/81) [1984] E.C.R. 1341; [1985] 1 C.M.L.R. 550 ECJ 150

Eridania v Minister of Agriculture and Forestry (230/78). *See* SpA Eridania-Zuccherifici Nazionali SpA and Societa Italiana per l'Industria degli Zuc- cheri SpA Minister of Agricul- ture and Forestry, Minister for Industry, Trade and Craft and Zuccherifici Meridionali SpA (230/78)

Etablissements Consten Sarl v Com- mission of the European Economic Community (56/64); Grundig-Verkaufs GmbH v Commission of the European Economic Community (58/64) [1966] E.C.R. 299; [1966] C.M.L.R. 418 ECJ 228, 324, 325, 328

Eugenio Branco Lda v Commission of the European Communities (T-85/94) [1995] E.C.R. II-45 CFI 164

Eugénio Branco v Commission of the European Communities (T-271/94) [1998] E.C.R. II-3761 ... 161

Eurofood IFSC Ltd (C-341/04) [2006] E.C.R. I-3813 260

Eurohypo AG v Office for Harmonisation in the Internal Market (Trade Marks and Designs) (OHIM) (T-439/04) [2006] E.C.R. II-1269 305

European Information Technology Observatory, Europäische Wirtschaftliche Interessenvereinigung (C-402/96) [1997] E.C.R. I–7515 283

European Parliament v Commission of the European Communities (C-403/05); sub nom. Validity of Philippine Border, Re (C-403/05) [2007] E.C.R. I-9045; [2008] All E.R. (EC) 526; [2008] 1 C.M.L.R. 20 137

European Parliament v Council of Ministers of the European Communities (13/83) [1987] E.C.R. 1513; [1985] E.C.R. 1513; [1986] 1 C.M.L.R. 138 ECJ 80, 142, 442

European Parliament v Council of Ministers of the European Communities (C-302/87) [1988] E.C.R. 5615 ECJ 80, 141

European Parliament v Council of Ministers of the European Communities (C-65/91) [1992] E.C.R. I-4593 ECJ 67, 121

European Parliament v Council of Ministers of the European Communities (C-65/93); sub nom. Generalised Tariff Preferences, Re [1995] E.C.R. I-643; [1996] 1 C.M.L.R. 4 ECJ 67, 68

European Parliament v Council of Ministers of the European Communities (C-70/88) [1990] E.C.R. I-2041; [1992] 1 C.M.L.R. 91 ECJ 134

European Parliament v Council of the European Union (C-22/96) [1998] E.C.R. I–3231 141

European Parliament v Council of the European Union (C-317/04); European Parliament v Council of the European Union (C-318/04) [2007] All E.R. (EC) 278; [2006] E.C.R. I-4721; [2006] 3 C.M.L.R. 9 ECJ 501

European Parliament v Council of the European Union (C-436/03); sub nom. Validity of Regulation 1435/2003, Re (C-436/03) [2006] E.C.R. I-3733; [2006] 3 C.M.L.R. 3 ECJ 436

European Parliament v Council of the European Union (C-540/03); sub nom. Validity of Directive 2003/86, Re (C-540/03) [2007] All E.R. (EC) 193; [2006] E.C.R. I-5769; [2006] 3 C.M.L.R. 28 ECJ 140

European Parliament v Ole Eistrup (T-223/06) [2007] E.C.R. II-1581 171

Europemballage Corp v Commission of the European Communities (6/72) [1973] E.C.R. 215; [1973] C.M.L.R. 199 ECJ 324

Eurotunnel SA v SeaFrance (C-408/95) [1997] E.C.R. I–6315 147

Eva von Lachmüller, Bernard Peuvrier, Roger Ehrhardt v Commission of the European Economic Community (43/59, 45/59 and 48/59) [1960] E.C.R. 463 59

Evangelischer Krankenhausverein Wien v Abgabenberufungskommission Wien and Wein & Co. HandelsgesmbH v Oberösterreichische Landesregierung (C-437/97) [2000] E.C.R. I–1157 141

Evonik Degussa GmbH v Commission of the European Communities (C-266/06) [2008] E.C.R.I-81 356

Extradition Proceedings against Santesteban Goicoechea (C-296/08 PPU) [2008] E.C.R. I-6307; [2008] 3 C.M.L.R. 40 ECJ 263

Extramet Industrie SA v Council of Ministers of the European Communities (C-35/89 R) [1990] E.C.R. I-431; [1990] 2 C.M.L.R. 406 ECJ 136

F Bolognese v H Scharf and Commission of the European Communities (292/84 TP) [1987] E.C.R. 3563 ... 164

F Hoffmann La Roche & Co AG v Centrafarm Vertriebsgesellschaft Pharmazeutischer Erzeugnisse mbH (107/76) [1977] E.C.R. 957; [1977] 2 C.M.L.R. 334 ECJ 146

F Hoffmann La Roche & Co AG v Commission of the European Communities (85/76) [1979] E.C.R. 461; [1979] 3 C.M.L.R. 211; [1980] F.S.R. 13 ECJ 322, 324, 339, 340, 359

FBTO Schadeverzekeringen NV v Odenbreit (C-463/06); sub nom. Odenbreit v FBTO Schadeverzekeringen NV (C-463/06) [2008] 2 All E.R. (Comm) 733; [2007] E.C.R. I-11321 ECJ 258

FG Marine SA v Commission of the European Communities (T-360/04) July 19, 2007 149

Fabbrica Italiana Accumulatori Motocarri Montecchio Spa (FIAMM) v Council of the European Union (T-69/00) [2005] E.C.R. II-5393; [2006] 2 C.M.L.R. 9 ECJ 55

Faccini Dori v Recreb Srl (C-91/92) [1994] E.C.R. I-3325; [1994] 1 C.M.L.R. 665 32

Falco Privatstiftung and Thomas Rabitsch v Gisela Weller-Lindhorst (C-533/07) [2009] E.C.R.23.04.09 258

Familiapress v Bauer Verlag (C-368/95). See Vereinigte Familiapress Zeitungsverlags- und vertriebs GmbH v Heinrich Bauer Verlag (C-368/95)

Farrell v Whitty (C-356/05) [2007] 2 C.M.L.R. 46; [2007] C.E.C. 718 ECJ 296, 445

Federación de Cooperativas Agrarias de la Comunidad Valenciana v Community Plant Variety Office (CPVO) (T-95/06) [2008] E.C.R. II-31 197

Fédération Charbonnière de Belgique v High Authority (8/55) [1954–1956] E.C.R. 245 ... 94, 138

Fédération des industries condimentaires de France (FICF) v Commission of the European Communities (T-317/02) [2004] E.C.R. II-4325 585

Federation Francaise des Société d'Assurance v Ministere de l'Agriculture et de la Peche (C-244/94) [1995] E.C.R. I-4013; [1996] 4 C.M.L.R. 536 ECJ 323

Federation Nationale du Commerce Exterieur des Produits Alimentaires v France (C-354/90) [1991] E.C.R. I-5505 ECJ 395

Felix Swoboda GmbH v Österreichische Nationalbank (C-411/00) [2002] E.C.R. I–10567 312

Fernandez de Bovadilla v Museo Nacional del Prado (C-234/92). See Teresa Fernández de Bobadilla v Museo Nacional del Prado, Comité de Empresa del Museo Nacional del Prado and Ministerio Fiscal (C-234/92)

Ferring SA v Agence centrale des organismes de sécurité sociale (ACOSS) (C-53/00) [2001] E.C.R. I–9067 382

Finalarte Sociedade de Construcao Civil Lda v Urlaubs- und Lohnausgleichskasse der Bauwirtschaft (C-49/98); Urlaubs- und Lohnausgleichskasse der Bauwirtschaft v Santos & Kewitz Construcoes Lda (C-69/98); Urlaubs- und Lohnausgleichskasse der Bauwirtschaft v Duarte dos Santos Sousa (C-68/98); Urlaubs- und Lohnausgleichskasse der Bauwirtschaft v Turiprata Construcoes Civil SA (C-54/98); Urlaubs- und Lohnausgleichskasse der Bauwirtschaft v Tecnamb-Tecnologia do Ambiante Lda (C-53/98); Urlaubs- und Lohnausgleichskasse der Bauwirtschaft v Tudor Stone Ltd (C-52/98); Urlaubs- und Lohnausgleichskasse der Bauwirtschaft v Amilcar Oliveira Rocha (C-50/98); Engil Sociedade de Construcao Civil SA v Urlaubs- und Lohnausgleichskasse der Bauwirtschaft (C-71/98); Portugaia Construcoes Lda v Urlaubs- und Lohnausgleichskasse der Bauwirtschaft (C-70/98) [2001] E.C.R. I-7831; [2003] 2 C.M.L.R. 11 ECJ 309

Finanzamt Koln-Altstadt v Schumacker (C-279/93) [1996] Q.B. 28; [1995] 3 W.L.R. 498; [1995] E.C.R. I-225 ECJ 431

Fiorini v Societe Nationale des Chemins de Fer Francais (32/75); Cristini (Anita) v Societe Nationale des Chemins de Fer Francais (SNCF) (32/75); sub nom. Fiorini v SNCF (32/75) [1975] E.C.R. 1085; [1976] 1 C.M.L.R. 573 ECJ 249

Firma A Racke v Hauptzollamt Mainz (98/78) [1979] E.C.R. 69 ECJ 37

Firma C Mackprang Jr v EC Commission (15/71); sub nom. Firma Mackprang (C) Jr v Commission of the European Communities (15/71) [1971] E.C.R. 797; [1972] C.M.L.R. 52 ECJ 142

Firma Fink-Frucht GmbH v Hauptzollamt München-Landsbergerstrasse (27/67) [1968] E.C.R. 223; [1968] C.M.L.R. 187 425

Firma Foto Frost v Hauptzollamt Lübeck-Ost (314/85) [1987] E.C.R. 4199; [1988] 3 C.M.L.R. 57 ECJ 145

Firma Gebruder Dietz v Commission of the European Communities (126/76) (No.1); sub nom. Firma Dietz Gebr v Commission of the European Communities (126/76) (No.1) [1977] E.C.R. 2431; [1978] 2 C.M.L.R. 608 ECJ 150

Firma Joh Eggers Sohn & Co v Freie Hansestadt Bremen (13/78) [1978] E.C.R. 1935; [1979] 1 C.M.L.R. 562 ECJ 309

Firme J Nold KG v High Authority of the European Coal and Steel Community (18/57) [1959] E.C.R. 41 ECJ 37, 54

Fishing Net Mesh Sizes, Re (141/78); sub nom. France (Commission of the European Communities intervening) v United Kingdom (141/78) [1979] E.C.R. 2923; [1980] 1 C.M.L.R. 6 ECJ ... 130, 414

Foglia v Novello (104/79) [1981] E.C.R. 745; [1980] E.C.R. 745; [1981] 1 C.M.L.R. 45 ECJ 143

Forcheri v Belgium (152/82) [1983] E.C.R. 2323; [1984] 1 C.M.L.R. 334 ECJ 249

Ford Werke AG v Commission of the European Communities (228/82 R); Ford of Europe Inc v Commission of the European Communities [1982] E.C.R. 2849; [1982] E.C.R. 3091; [1982] 3 C.M.L.R. 673 ECJ 353

Försäkringsaktiebolaget Skandia (C-241/97) [1999] E.C.R. I–1879 296

France Télécom v Commission of the European Communities (T-339/04) [2007] E.C.R. II-521; [2008] 5 C.M.L.R. 6 CFI 355

France v Commission of the European Communities (188/80); sub nom. Public Undertakings, Re (188/80) [1982] E.C.R. 2545; [1982] 3 C.M.L.R. 144 ECJ 114

France v Commission of the European Communities (C-301/87) [1990] E.C.R. I–307 395

France v Commission of the European Communities (C-202/88) [1991] E.C.R. I–1223 .... 314, 325

France v Commission of the European Communities (C-366/88) [1990] E.C.R. I–3595; [1992] 1 C.M.L.R. 2 133

France v Commission of the European Communities (C-241/94); sub nom. Kimberly Clark, Re (C-241/94) [1996] E.C.R. I-4551; [1997] 1 C.M.L.R. 983; [1997] I.R.L.R. 415 ECJ 381

France v Commission of the European Communities (C-303/90) [1991] E.C.R. I–5340 133

France v Commission of the European Communities (C-325/91) [1993] E.C.R. I-3283 ECJ 35, 133, 378

France v Commission of the European Communities (C-41/93); sub nom. Pentachlorophenol, Re [1994] E.C.R. I-1829; [1995] 3 C.M.L.R. 733 ECJ 436

France v Commission of the European Communities (C-68/94); Societe Commerciale des Potasses et de l'Azote (SCPA) v Commission of the European Communities (C-30/95) [1998] E.C.R. I-1375; [1998] 4 C.M.L.R. 829 ECJ 365

France v Commission of the European Communities (C-304/02). *See* Commission of the European Communities v France (C-304/02)

France v European Parliament (358/85 and 51/86) [1988] E.C.R. 4846; [1990] 2 C.M.L.R. 406 134

France v European Parliament (C-345/95) [1997] E.C.R. I-5215 ... 83

France v Ladbroke Racing Ltd (C-83/98 P) [2000] E.C.R. I-3271; [2000] 3 C.M.L.R. 555 ECJ 381

France v United Kingdom (141/78). *See* Fishing Net Mesh Sizes, Re (141/78)

Francovich v Italy (C-479/93) [1995] E.C.R. I-3843; [1997] 2 B.C.L.C. 203 ECJ 473

Francovich v Italy (C-6/90); Bonifacti v Italy (C-9/90) [1991] E.C.R. I-5357; [1993] 2 C.M.L.R. 66 ECJ 33, 51, 112, 310, 474

Fratelli Costanzo SpA v Comune di Milano (103/88) [1989] E.C.R. 1839; [1990] 3 C.M.L.R. 239 ECJ 313

Freeport Plc v Arnoldsson (C-98/06) [2008] Q.B. 634; [2008] 2 W.L.R. 853; [2007] E.C.R. I-8319 ECJ 258

Friedrich Stork & Cie v High Authority of the European Coal and Steel Community (1/58) [1959] E.C.R. 17 54

Frilli v Belgium (1/72) [1972] E.C.R. 457; [1973] C.M.L.R. 386 ECJ 251

Front National v European Parliament (C-486/01 P) [2004] E.C.R. I-6289; [2004] 2 C.M.L.R. 51 ECJ 81

G. Elbertsen v Minister van Landbouw, Natuur en Voedselkwaliteit (C-449/08) [2009] E.C.R. 22.10.09 445

Gallotti, Re (C-58/95); sub nom. Criminal Proceedings against Gallotti, Re (C-58/95) [1996] E.C.R. I-4345; [1997] 1 C.M.L.R. 32 ECJ 33

Gambazzi v DaimlerChrysler Canada Inc (C-394/07) [2009] 1 Lloyd's Rep. 647; [2009] I.L.Pr. 38 ECJ 258

Garofalo v Ministero della Sanita (C-69/96); Garofalo v Unita Sanitaria Locale (USL) No.58 di Palermo (C-69/96 to C79/96) [1997] E.C.R. I-5603; [1998] 1 C.M.L.R. 1087 ECJ 144, 273

Gaston Schul Douane-expediteur BV v Minister van Landbouw, Natuur en Voedselkwalitei (C-461/03) [2005] E.C.R. I-10513 145

Gebhard v Consiglio dell'Ordine degli Avvocati e Procuratori di Milano (C-55/94) [1996] All E.R. (EC) 189; [1995] E.C.R. I-4165; [1996] 1 C.M.L.R. 603 ECJ 267, 289

Gebroeders Beentjes BV v Netherlands (31/87) [1988] E.C.R. 4635; [1990] 1 C.M.L.R. 287 ECJ 309, 313

Geitling v High Authority (36/59–38/59 and 40/59) [1960] E.C.R. 423 .... 36, 54

Gemeente Almelo v Energiebedrijf Ijssellmij NV (C-393/92); sub nom. Commune d'Almelo ea v NV Energiebedrijf Ijsselmij (C-393/92); Municipality of Almelo v NV Energibedrijf Ijsselmij (C-393/92) [1994] E.C.R. I-1477; [1994] 2 C.E.C. 281 ECJ 338

Gemeente Arnhem v BFI Holding BV (C-360/96); sub nom. BFI Holding BV v Municipality of Arnhem (C-360/96) [1999] All E.R. (EC) 709; [1998] E.C.R. I-6821; [2001] 1 C.M.L.R. 6 ECJ 314

Gencor Ltd v Commission of the European Communities (T-102/96) (Applications to Intervene) [1997] E.C.R. II-879; [1998] 1 C.M.L.R. 142; [1997] 5 C.M.L.R. 290 CFI 369

Georges Berthu v Council of the European Union (T-207/97) [1998] E.C.R. II-509 456

Germany v Commission of the European Communities (248/84); sub nom. Regional Aid Plans, Re (248/84) [1987] E.C.R. 4013; [1989] 1 C.M.L.R. 591 ECJ 384

Germany v Commission of the European Communities (C-242/00) [2002] E.C.R. I-5603 139

Germany v Commission of the European Communities (C-374/04) [2006] E.C.R. I-11673 547

Germany v Commission of the European Economic Community (24/62); sub nom. Tariff Quota on Wine, Re (24/62) [1963] E.C.R. 63; [1963] C.M.L.R. 347 ECJ 36

Germany v Council of Ministers (C-426/93) [1995] E.C.R. I-3723 110

Germany v European Parliament (C-233/94); sub nom. Deposit Guarantee Directive, Re (C-233/94) [1997] E.C.R. I-2405; [1997] 3 C.M.L.R. 1379 ECJ 292

Germany v Isis Multimedia Net GmbH & Co KG (C-327/03) [2005] E.C.R. I-8877; [2006] 4 C.M.L.R. 1 ECJ 510

Gesellschaft zur Verwertung von Leistungsschutzrechten mbH (GVL) v Commission of the European Communities (7/82) [1983] E.C.R. 483; [1983] 3 C.M.L.R. 645 ECJ 339

Gestevision Telecinco SA v Commission of the European Communities (T-95/96) [1998] All E.R. (EC) 918; [1998] E.C.R. II-3407; [1998] 3 C.M.L.R. 1112 CFI . . . 395

Gestoras Pro Amnistia v Council of the European Union (C-354/04 P) [2008] All E.R. (EC) 65; [2007] E.C.R. I-1579; [2007] 2 C.M.L.R. 22 ECJ 263

Giagounidis v Reutlingen (C-376/89) [1991] E.C.R. I-1069; [1993] 1 C.M.L.R. 537 ECJ 247

GlaxoSmithKline Services Unlimited v Commission of the European Communities (T-168/01) [2006] E.C.R. II-2969; [2006] 5 C.M.L.R. 29 ECJ 326

Goldstein v Commission of the European Communities (T-18/01 R) [2001] E.C.R. II–1147 157

Grad v Finanzamt Traunstein (9/70) [1970] E.C.R. 825; [1971] C.M.L.R. 1 ECJ 32, 34

Granaria BV v Hoofdproduktschap voor Akkerbouwprodukten (101/78) [1979] E.C.R. 623; [1979] 3 C.M.L.R. 124 ECJ 150

Gravier v Liege (293/83) [1985] E.C.R. 593; [1985] 3 C.M.L.R. 1 ECJ 249

Greece v Commission (32/89 R). *See* Commission of the European Communities v Greece (C-32/89 R)

Greece v Commission of the European Communities (C-30/88); sub nom. Aid to Turkey, Re (C-30/88) [1989] E.C.R. 3711; [1991] 2 C.M.L.R. 169 ECJ 53

Grimaldi v Fonds des Maladies Professionnelles (C-322/88) [1989] E.C.R. 4407; [1991] 2 C.M.L.R. 265; [1990] I.R.L.R. 400 ECJ 34

Groupement des Fabricants de Papiers Peints de Belgique v Commission of the European Communities (73/74) [1976] E.C.R. 1491; [1975] E.C.R. 1491; [1976] 1 C.M.L.R. 589 ECJ 36

Groupement des Producteurs, Importateurs et Agents Generaux d'Eaux Minerales Etrangeres Asbl (PIAGEME) v Peeters NV (C-85/94); sub nom. PIAGEME Asbl v Peeters NV (C-85/94) [1995] E.C.R. I-2955 ECJ 499

Grunkin v Grunkin-Paul (C-353/06) [2008] E.C.R. I-7639; [2009] 1 C.M.L.R. 10; [2009] C.E.C. 263 ECJ 239

Grzelczyk v Centre Public d'Aide Sociale d'Ottignies Louvain la Neuve (C-184/99) [2003] All E.R. (EC) 385; [2001] E.C.R. I-6193; [2002] 1 C.M.L.R. 19 ECJ 129

Győrgy Katz v István Roland Sós (C-404/07) [2008] E.C.R. I-7607 261

Haahr Petroleum Ltd v Abenra Havn (C-90/94) [1997] E.C.R. I-4085; [1998] 1 C.M.L.R. 771 ECJ 425

Haim v Kassenzahnarztliche Vereinigung Nordrhein (C-424/97) [2000] E.C.R. I-5123; [2002] 1 C.M.L.R. 11 ECJ 112

Hamilton v Volksbank Filder eG (C-412/06) [2008] E.C.R. I-2383; [2008] 2 C.M.L.R. 46 ECJ 497

Handels- og Kontorfunktionaererernes Forbund i Danmark v Dansk Arbejdsgiverforening Ex p. Danfoss A/S (109/88); sub nom. Union of Clerical and Commercial Employees v Danish Employers Association Ex p. Danfoss A/S (109/88) [1989] E.C.R. 3199; [1991] 1 C.M.L.R. 8 ECJ ... 144, 478

Handels- og Kontorfunktionærernes Forbund i Danmark, acting on behalf of Helle Elisabeth Larsson v Dansk Handel & Service, acting on behalf of Føtex Supermarked A/S (C-400/95) [1997] E.C.R. I-2757; [1979] 2 C.M.L.R. 915 478

Hasselblad (GB) Ltd v Commission of the European Communities (86/82) [1984] E.C.R. 883; [1984] 1 C.M.L.R. 559 ECJ 39

Hassett v South Eastern Health Board (C-372/07) [2008] E.C.R. I-7403; [2009] C.E.C. 390 ECJ 258

Hauer v Land Rheinland-Pfalz (44/79) [1979] E.C.R. 3727; [1980] 3 C.M.L.R. 42 ECJ 53

Hauptzollamt Bremerhaven v Massey-Ferguson GmbH (8/73) [1973] E.C.R. 897 ECJ 93

Hauptzollamt Mainz v CA Kupferberg & Cie KG aA (104/81) [1982] E.C.R. 3641; [1983] 1 C.M.L.R. 1 ECJ 570

Heintz van Landewyck Sarl v Commission of the European Communities (209/78) [1980] E.C.R. 3125; [1981] 3 C.M.L.R. 134 ECJ 321, 322

Henke v Gemeinde Schierke (C-298/94) [1997] All E.R. (EC) 173; [1996] E.C.R. I-4989; [1997] 1 C.M.L.R. 373 ECJ 473

Hercules Chemicals NV v Commission of the European Communities (C-51/99 P) [1999] E.C.R. I-4225 155

Hilti AG v Commission of the European Communities (C-53/92 P) [1994] E.C.R. I-667; [1994] 4 C.M.L.R. 614; [1994] F.S.R. 760 ECJ 155

Hlozek v Roche Austria GmbH (C-19/02) [2004] E.C.R. I-11491; [2005] 1 C.M.L.R. 28 ECJ 478

Hoechst AG v Commission of the European Communities (46/87) [1989] E.C.R. 2859; [1991] 4 C.M.L.R. 410 ECJ 53, 354

Hoechst GmbH v Commission of the European Communities (T-410/03) [2008] E.C.R. II-881; [2008] 5 C.M.L.R. 12 ECJ ... 357

Höfner v Macrotron GmbH (C-41/90) [1991] E.C.R. I-1979; [1993] 4 C.M.L.R. 306 ECJ 338

Hospital Ingenieure Krankenhaustechnik Planungs-Gesellschaft mbH (HI) v Landeskrankenanstalten-Betriebsgesellschaft (C-258/97) [1999] E.C.R. I–1405 316

Hospital Ingenieure Krankenhaustechnik Planungs-Gesellschaft mbH (HI) v Stadt Wien (C-92/00) [2002] E.C.R. I–5553 316

Huber v Germany (C-524/06) [2009] All E.R. (EC) 239; [2009] 1 C.M.L.R. 49 ECJ 501

Humblot v Directeur des Services Fiscaux (112/84) [1987] E.C.R. 1367; [1985] E.C.R. 1367; [1986] 2 C.M.L.R. 338 ECJ 426

I-21 Germany GmbH v Germany (C-392/04); Arcor AG & Co KG (formerly ISIS Multimedia Net GmbH & Co KG) v Germany (C-422/04) [2006] E.C.R. I-8559; [2007] 1 C.M.L.R. 10 ECJ 510

IBM Corp v Commission of the European Communities (60/81); sub nom. International Business Machines Corp v Commission of the European Communities (60/81) [1981] E.C.R. 2639; [1981] 3 C.M.L.R. 635 ECJ 28, 133, 138

IMS Health GmbH & Co OHG v NDC Health GmbH & Co KG (C–418/01) [2004] All E.R. (EC) 813; [2004] E.C.R. I–5039 307

Iannelli & Volpi SpA v Ditta Paolo Meroni (74/76); Firma Steinike und Weinlig v Bundesamt fur Ernahrung und Forstwirtschaft (78/76) [1977] E.C.R. 595; [1977] E.C.R. 557; [1977] 2 C.M.L.R. 688 ECJ 381

Imperial Chemical Industries (ICI) Ltd v Commission of the European Communities (48/69) [1972] E.C.R. 619; [1972] C.M.L.R. 557 ECJ 322, 324

Impresa Costruzioni Comm Quirino Mazzalai v Ferrovia Del Renon (111/75) [1976] E.C.R. 657; [1977] 1 C.M.L.R. 105 ECJ 32

Impresa Lombardini SpA – Impresa Generale di Costruzioni v ANAS – Ente nazionale per le strade and Società Italiana per Condotte d'Acqua SpA (C-285/99); Impresa Ing. Mantovani SpA v ANAS – Ente nazionale per le strade and Ditta Paolo Bregoli (C-286/99) [2001] E.C.R. I–9233 313

Industrie Diensten Groep BV v JA Beele Handelmaatschappij BV (6/81) [1982] E.C.R. 707; [1982] 3 C.M.L.R. 102 ECJ 227

Industrie Siderurgiche Associate (ISA) v High Authority of the European Coal and Steel Community (4/54) [1954–56] E.C.R. 91 37

Infront WM AG v Commission of the European Communities (T-33/01) [2005] E.C.R. II-5897 513

Ingenieurburo Michael Weiss und Partner GbR v Industrie- und Handelskammer Berlin (C-14/07) [2008] E.C.R. I-3367; [2009] C.E.C. 3 ECJ 259

Inizan v Caisse Primaire d'Assurance Maladie des Hauts de Seine (C-56/01) [2003] E.C.R. I-12403; [2006] 1 C.M.L.R. 20 ECJ 146

Intelligente Systemen, Database toepassingen, Elektronische diensten BV (IDE) v Commission of the European Communities (C-114/94) [1997] E.C.R. I–803 154

Inter-Environnement Wallonie ASBL v Region Wallonie (C-129/96); sub nom. Inter-Environnement Wallonie Asbl v Region Wallonne (C-129/96); Inter-Environnement Wallonie Asbl v Region Wallone (C-129/96) [1998] All E.R. (E.C.) 155; [1997] E.C.R. I-7411; [1998] 1 C.M.L.R. 1057 ECJ 33

International Association of Independent Tanker Owners (Intertanko) v Secretary of State for Transport (C-308/06); sub nom. Proceedings Brought by International Association of Independent Tanker Owners (C-308/06); R. (on the application of International Association of Independent Tanker Owners) v Secretary of State for Transport (C-308/06) [2008] 2 Lloyd's Rep. 260; [2008] E.C.R. I-4057; [2008] 3 C.M.L.R. 9; [2009] Env. L.R. 14 ECJ 55

International Chemical Corp SpA v Amministrazione delle Finanze dello Stato (66/80) [1981] E.C.R. 1191; [1983] 2 C.M.L.R. 593 ECJ 144

International Fruit Co NV v Produktschap voor Groenten en Fruit (No.3) (21/72) [1972] E.C.R. 1219; [1975] 2 C.M.L.R. 1 ECJ 39, 45, 53, 138, 144, 566

International Transport Workers' Federation v Viking Line ABP (C-438/05) [2008] All E.R. (EC) 127; [2007] E.C.R. I-10779; [2008] 1 C.M.L.R. 51 ECJ 470

Internationale Handelsgesellschaft mbH v Einfuhr- und Vorratsstelle fur Getreide und Futtermittel (11/70); Einfuhr und Vorratsstelle fur Getreide und Futtermittel v Firma Koster, Berodt & Co (25/70); Einfuhr und Vorratsstelle fur Getreide und Futtermittel v Firma Gunther Henck (26/70); Firma Ottoscheer v Einfuhr und Vorratsstelle fur Getreide und Futtermittel (30/70) [1970] E.C.R. 1125; [1972] C.M.L.R. 255 ECJ 48, 53, 115

Interporc Im- und Export GmbH v Commission of the European Communities (T-124/96) [1998] E.C.R. II-231; [1998] 2 C.M.L.R. 82 ECJ 124

Ireland v Council of the European Communities (151/73) [1974] E.C.R. 285; [1974] 1 C.M.L.R. 429 ECJ 134

Ireland v France (58/77) [1977]
O.J. C142/8 130
Irène Bogiatzi, married name
Ventouras v Deutscher Luftpool,
Société Luxair, société luxem-
bourgeoise de navigation aérienne
SA, European Communities,
Grand Duchy of Luxembourg,
Foyer Assurances SA (C-301/08)
[2009] E.C.R. 22.10.09 452
Irish Sugar Plc v Commission of
the European Communities
(T-228/97) [2000] All E.R. (EC)
198; [1999] E.C.R. II-2969;
[1999] 5 C.M.L.R. 1300 CFI 338,
341
Isabel Burbaud v Ministère de
l'Emploi et de la Solidarité (C-
285/01) [2003] E.C.R. I-8219;
[2003] 3 C.M.L.R. 21 276
Istituto Chemioterapico Italiano SpA
v Commission of the European
Communities (6/73); sub nom.
Commercial Solvents Corp v
Commission of the European
Communities (7/73) [1974]
E.C.R. 223; [1974] 1 C.M.L.R.
309 ECJ 324,
327
Italy v Commission of the European
Communities (1/69); sub nom.
Preferential Freight Rates, Re
(1/69) [1969] E.C.R. 277; [1970]
C.M.L.R. 17 ECJ 36
Italy v Commission of the European
Communities (C-305/89) [1991]
E.C.R. I-1603 379
Italy v Commission of the European
Communities (C-6/97) [1999]
E.C.R. I-2981 380,
381
Italy v Commission of the European
Communities (C-310/99) [2002]
E.C.R. I-2289 390
Italy v Commission of the European
Communities   (C-138/03,
C-324/03   C-431/03)   [2005]
E.C.R. I-10043 134
Italy v Sacchi (155/73) [1974] E.C.R.
409; [1974] 2 C.M.L.R. 177
ECJ 289
Italy v Watson and Belmann (118/75)
[1976] E.C.R. 1185; [1976] 2
C.M.L.R. 552 ECJ 244,
247

J Nold Kohlen- und Baustoff-
grosshandlung v Commission of
the European Communities
(4/73) [1975] E.C.R. 985; [1974]
E.C.R. 491; [1974] 2 C.M.L.R.
338 ECJ 48, 138, 139
JCB Service v Commission of the
European Communities (C-
167/04 P) [2006] E.C.R. I-8935;
[2006] 5 C.M.L.R. 23 ECJ 29
JJ Zwartveld (C-2/88) [1990] E.C.R.
I-3365 142
Jacquier v Directeur Général des
Impots   (C-113/94)   [1995]
E.C.R. I-4203 426
Jego-Quere et Cie SA v Commission
of the European Communities
(T-177/01) [2003] Q.B. 854;
[2003] 2 W.L.R. 783; [2002]
E.C.R. II-2365 ECJ 135
Jenkins v Kingsgate (Clothing Pro-
ductions) Ltd (96/80) [1981] 1
W.L.R. 972; [1981] E.C.R. 911;
[1981] 2 C.M.L.R. 24 ECJ 245
Jia v Migrationsverket (C-1/05)
[2007] Q.B. 545; [2007] 2
W.L.R. 1005; [2007] 1 C.M.L.R.
41 ECJ 248, 249
Job Centre Coop arl, Re (C-55/96)
[1997] E.C.R. I-7119; [1998] 4
C.M.L.R. 708; [1998] C.E.C.
507 ECJ 341
Johannes Hartmann v Council of the
European Union and Commis-
sion of the European Communi-
ties (T-20/94) [1997] E.C.R.
II-595 149
John Deere Ltd v Commission of the
European Communities (C-7/95
P); John Deere Ltd v Commis-
sion of the European Communities (C-7/95 P) [1998] All E.R.
(E.C.) 481 (Note); [1998] E.C.R.
I-3111; [1998] 5 C.M.L.R. 311
ECJ 168
Johnson & Firth Brown v Commis-
sion of the European Communities (3/75 RI) [1975] E.C.R. 1;
[1975] 1 C.M.L.R. 638 ECJ ... 162,
163
Jordens-Vosters v Bestuur van de
Bedrijfsvereniging voor de Leder-
en Lederverwerkende Industrie
(69/79) [1980] E.C.R. 75; [1980]
3 C.M.L.R. 412 ECJ 251

José García v Mutuelle de Prévoyance Sociale d'Aquitaine (C-238/94) [1996] E.C.R. I–1673 296

José Vicente Olaso Valero v Fondo de Garantía Salarial (Fogasa) (C-520/03) [2004] E.C.R. I-12065 473

Jules Dethier Equipement SA v Dassy (C-319/94); Jules Dethier Equipement SA v Sovam Sprl [1998] All E.R. (EC) 346; [1998] E.C.R. I-1061; [1998] 2 C.M.L.R. 611 ECJ 473

Julius Sabatauskas (C-239/07) [2008] E.C.R. I-7523 557

Junk v Kuhnel (C-188/03) [2005] E.C.R. I-885; [2005] 1 C.M.L.R. 42 ECJ 473

Jyri Lehtonen and Castors Canada Dry Namur-Braine ASBL v Fédération royale belge des sociétés de basket-ball ASBL (FRBSB) (C-176/96) [2000] E.C.R. I–2714 290

Kabel Deutschland Vertrieb und Service GmbH & Co KG v Niedersachsische Landesmedienanstalt fur Privaten Rundfunk (C-336/07) [2009] 2 C.M.L.R. 6 ECJ 346, 509

Kampelmann v Landschaftsverband Westfalen-Lippe (C-253/96); Stadtwerke Witten GmbH v Schade (C-257/96); Haseley v Stadtwerke Altena GmbH (C-258/96) [1997] E.C.R. I-6907; [1998] 2 C.M.L.R. 131 ECJ 474

Kapferer v Schlank & Schick GmbH (C-234/04) [2006] E.C.R. I-2585; [2006] 2 C.M.L.R. 19 ECJ 50

Karl L Meyer v Commission of the European Communities (T-106/99) [1999] E.C.R. II-3273 124

Katharina Rinke v Ärztekammer Hamburg (C-25/02) [2003] E.C.R. I–8349 273

Kernkraftwerke Lippe-Ems GmbH v Commission of the European Community (C-161/97 P) [1999] E.C.R. I-2057; [2000] 2 C.M.L.R. 489 ECJ 182, 559

Kernkraftwerke Lippe-EMS GmbH v Commission of the European Communities (T-181/94); sub nom. Kernkraftwerke Lippe-EMS GmbH v Commission of the European Communities (T-149/94) [1997] E.C.R. II-161; [1997] 3 C.M.L.R. 136 CFI 182

Keurkoop BV v Nancy Kean Gifts BV (144/81) [1982] E.C.R. 2853; [1983] 2 C.M.L.R. 47 ECJ ... 232, 303

Kirtruna SL v Red Elite de Electrodomesticos SA (C-313/07) [2008] E.C.R. I-7907; [2009] 1 C.M.L.R. 14 ECJ 473

Klarenberg v Ferrotron Technologies GmbH (C-466/07) [2009] I.C.R. 1263; [2009] I.R.L.R. 301 ECJ 473

Klöckner-Werke AG and Hoesch AG v High Authority of the European Coal and Steel Community (17/61 and 20/61) [1962] E.C.R. 325 54

Knoors v Secretary of State for Economic Affairs (115/78) [1979] E.C.R. 399; [1979] 2 C.M.L.R. 357 ECJ 267

Köbler v Austria (C-224/01) [2004] Q.B. 848; [2004] 2 W.L.R. 976; [2004] All E.R. (EC) 23; [2003] E.C.R. I-10239; [2003] 3 C.M.L.R. 28 ECJ 51, 112

Koelman v Commission of the European Communities (T-575/93) [1996] E.C.R. II-1; [1996] 4 C.M.L.R. 636; [1996] E.M.L.R. 555 CFI 353

Kommunikationsbehorde Austria (KommAustria) v Östereichischer Rundfunk (ORF) (C-195/06) [2007] E.C.R. I-8817; [2008] Bus. L.R. D85 ECJ 513

Koninklijke Nederlandsche Hoogovens en Staalfabrieken NV v High Authority of the European Coal and Steel Community (28/63) [1963] E.C.R. 231; [1964] C.M.L.R. 125 ECJ 34, 36

Koninklijke PTT Nederland NV v Commission of the European Communities (C-66/90); PTT Post BV v Commission of the European Communities (C-48/90) [1991] E.C.R. I-2723; [1993] 5 C.M.L.R. 316 ECJ 139, 347

Kontogeorgas v Kartonpak AE (C-104/95) [1996] E.C.R. I-6643; [1997] 1 C.M.L.R. 1093 ECJ ... 267

Kretzinger v Hauptzollamt Augsburg (C-288/05) [2007] E.C.R. I-6441; [2007] 3 C.M.L.R. 43 ECJ 242

Kruidvat BVBA v Commission of the European Communities (C-70/97 P) [1998] E.C.R. I-7183; [1999] 4 C.M.L.R. 68 ECJ 137

Kûhne & Heitz NV v Productschap voor Pluimvee en Eieren (C-453/00) [2004] E.C.R. I-837; [2006] 2 C.M.L.R. 17 ECJ 50, 140

Kuijer v Council of the European Union (T-188/98) [2000] E.C.R. II-1959; [2000] 2 C.M.L.R. 400 CFI 104

Kutz-Bauer v Freie und Hansestadt Hamburg (C-187/00) [2003] E.C.R. I-2741; [2005] 2 C.M.L.R. 35 ECJ 56

L'Oreal NV v De Nieuwe AMCK PVBA (31/80) [1980] E.C.R. 3775; [1981] 2 C.M.L.R. 235 ECJ 339

Lafarge SA v Commission of the European Communities (T-54/03) [2008] E.C.R. II-120 355

Lancôme SA v Etos BV (99/79); Cosparfrance Nederland BV v Albert Heijn Supermart BV [1981] E.C.R. 2511; [1980] E.C.R. 2511; [1981] 2 C.M.L.R. 164 ECJ 326

Land Brandenburg v Sass (C-284/02) [2004] E.C.R. I-11143; [2005] 1 C.M.L.R. 27 ECJ 479

Laserdisken ApS v Kulturministeriet (C-479/04) [2007] All E.R. (EC) 549; [2006] E.C.R. I-8089; [2007] 1 C.M.L.R. 6 ECJ 303

Leffler v Berlin Chemie AG (C-443/03) [2006] All E.R. (EC) 692; [2005] E.C.R. I-9611 ECJ ... 259

Léon Van Parys NV v Belgisch Interventie- en Restitutiebureau (BIRB) (C-377/02) [2005] E.C.R I-1465 55

Leonesio v Italian Ministry of Agriculture and Forestry (93/71); sub nom. Leonesio v Ministero dell'Agricoltura e Foreste (93/71) [1972] E.C.R. 287; [1973] C.M.L.R. 343 ECJ 31, 45

Levin v Staatssecretaris van Justitie (53/81); sub nom. Levin v Secretary of State for Justice (53/81) [1982] E.C.R. 1035; [1982] 2 C.M.L.R. 454 ECJ 143, 238, 244, 245, 247

Lewen v Denda (C-333/97) [2000] All E.R. (EC) 261; [1999] E.C.R. I-7243; [2000] 2 C.M.L.R. 38 ECJ 472

Lidl Belgium GmbH & Co KG v Etablissementen Franz Colruyt NV (C-356/04) [2007] Bus. L.R. 492; [2006] E.C.R. I-8501; [2007] 1 C.M.L.R. 9 ECJ 496

Lidl Magyarorszag Kereskedelmi bt v Nemzeti Hirkozlesi Hatosag Tanacsa (C-132/08) [2009] 3 C.M.L.R. 23 ECJ 498

Lisrestal – Organização Gestão de Restaurantes Colectivos Ld™ v Commission of the European Communities (T-450/93) [1994] E.C.R. II–1177 359

Lloyd Schuhfabrik Meyer & Co GmbH v Klijsen Handel BV (C-342/97) [1999] All E.R. (EC) 587; [1999] E.C.R. I-3819; [1999] 2 C.M.L.R. 1343 ECJ 306

Lodato Gennaro & C. SpA v Istituto nazionale della previdenza sociale (INPS) and SCCI (C-14/07) April 2, 2009 390

Louwage v Commission of the European Communities (148/73) [1974] E.C.R. 81 ECJ 139

Ludwigshafener Walzmühle Erling KG v Council and Commission of the European Communities (197–200, 243 245, and 247/80) [1981] E.C.R. 3211 149

Luigi Scarpelli v NEOS Banca SpA (C-509/07) April 23, 2009 498

Luis Manuel Chaves Fonseca Ferrão v Office for Harmonisation in the Internal Market (T-159/97 R) [1997] E.C.R. II–1049 196

Luisi v Ministero del Tesoro (286/82) [1984] E.C.R. 377; [1985] 3 C.M.L.R. 52 ECJ 288, 299

Luxembourg v European Parliament (230/81) [1983] E.C.R. 55; [1983] 2 C.M.L.R. 726 ECJ 83, 134

Luxembourg v European Parliament (No.2) (108/83) [1984] E.C.R. 1945; [1986] 2 C.M.L.R. 507 ECJ 83, 133, 134

MPA Pharma GmbH v Rhône-Poulenc Pharma GmbH (C-232/94 MPA) [1996] E.C.R. I–3671 306

Mahlburg v Land Mecklenburg Vorpommern (C-207/98) [2000] E.C.R. I-549; [2001] 3 C.M.L.R. 40 ECJ 477

Maira María Robledillo Núñez v Fondo de Garantía Salarial (Fogasa) (C-498/06) [2008] E.C.R. I-921 473

Maizena GmbH v Council of Ministers of the European Communities (139/79) [1980] E.C.R. 3393 ECJ 80, 138, 158

Maizena GmbH v Council of the European Communities (138/79) [1980] E.C.R. I-3149 .... 68, 80

Makedoniko Metro and Michaniki AE v Elliniko Dimosio (C-57/01) [2003] E.C.R. I–1091 316

Mannesmann Anlagenbau Austria AG v Strohal Rotationsdruck GmbH (C-44/96) [1998] E.C.R. I-73; [1998] 2 C.M.L.R. 805 ECJ 309

Mannesmannröhren-Werke AG v Commission of the European Communities (T-112/98) [2001] E.C.R. II–729 354

María Martínez Sala v Freistaat Bayern (C-85/96) [1998] E.C.R. I–2691 246

María Victoria González Sánchez v Medicina Asturiana SA (C-183/00) [2002] E.C.R. I-3901 498

Marimex SpA v Ministero delle Finanze (29/72); sub nom. SPA Marimex v Italian Finance Administration [1972] E.C.R. 1309; [1973] C.M.L.R. 486 ECJ 225

Marks & Spencer Plc v Customs and Excise Commissioners (C-62/00) [2003] Q.B. 866; [2003] 2 W.L.R. 665; [2002] E.C.R. I-6325 ECJ 140

Marra v De Gregorio (C-200/07) [2008] E.C.R. I-7929; [2009] 1 C.M.L.R. 15 ECJ 65

Marshall v Southampton and South West Hampshire AHA (152/84) [1986] Q.B. 401; [1986] 2 W.L.R. 780; [1986] E.C.R. 723 ECJ 33

Maruko v Versorgungsanstalt der Deutschen Buhnen (C-267/06) [2008] All E.R. (EC) 977; [2008] E.C.R. I-1757; [2008] 2 C.M.L.R. 32; [2008] I.R.L.R. 450; [2008] Pens. L.R. 22 ECJ 479

Maschinenfabrik Hennecke GmbH v Sullhofer (65/86) [1988] E.C.R. 5249; [1990] 4 C.M.L.R. 182 ECJ 304

Matteucci v Communaute Française de Belgique (235/87) [1988] E.C.R. 5589; [1989] 1 C.M.L.R. 357 ECJ 249

Mayr-Melnhof Kartongesellschaft mbH v Commission of the European Communities (T-347/94) [1998] E.C.R. II–1751 321

Mebrom NV v Commission of the European Communities (T-216/05) [2007] E.C.R. II-1507 ... 139

Merck Genericos Produtos Farmaceuticos Lda v Merck & Co Inc (C-431/05) [2008] All E.R. (EC) 40; [2007] E.C.R. I-7001; [2007] 3 C.M.L.R. 49 ECJ 55

Merck Sharp & Dohme Ltd v Commission of the European Communities (T-273/03) [2006] E.C.R. II-141 195

Merckx v Ford Motors Co Belgium SA (C-171/94); Neuhuys v Ford Motors Co Belgium SA (C-172/94) [1996] All E.R. (EC) 667; [1996] E.C.R. I-1253 ECJ 473

Meroni & Co., Industrie Metallurgiche, SpA v High Authority of the European Coal and Steel Community (9/56) [1957 and 1958] E.C.R. 133 .... 115, 151

Metock v Minister for Justice, Equality and Law Reform (C-127/08) [2009] Q.B. 318; [2009] 2 W.L.R. 821; [2008] E.C.R. I-6241 ECJ 148, 240

Metropole Television SA v Commission of the European Communities (T-528/93) [1996] E.C.R. II-649; [1996] 5 C.M.L.R. 386; [1996] C.E.C. 794; [1998] E.M.L.R. 99 ECJ 322

Michail Peros v Techniko Epimelitirio Ellados (C-141/04) [2005]
E.C.R. I–7165 276
Michel Hautem v European Invest-
ment Bank (T-11/00) [2000]
E.C.R. II–4036 150
Migrationsverket v Petrosian (C-
19/08) [2009] 2 C.M.L.R. 33;
[2009] I.N.L.R. 258 ECJ 256
Minister voor Vreemdelingenzaken
en Integratie v Eind (C-291/05)
[2008] All E.R. (EC) 371; [2008]
2 C.M.L.R. 1 ECJ 248, 249
Ministère Public and Chambre Syndi-
cale des Agents Artistiques et
Impresarii de Belgique Asbl v van
Wesemael and Poupaert (110/78);
Ministere Public, Chambre Syndi-
cale des Agents Artistiques et
Impresarii de Belgique Asbl v
Follachio and Leduc (111/78)
[1979] E.C.R. 35; [1979]
3 C.M.L.R. 87 ECJ 143, 290
Ministère Public v Asjes (209/84)
[1986] E.C.R. 1425; [1986] 3
C.M.L.R. 173 ECJ 343, 450
Ministère Public Luxembourgeois v
Muller (10/71) [1971] E.C.R.
723 . . . . 45, 143
Ministerio Fiscal v Bordessa (C-
358/93); Ministerio Fiscal v Mel-
lado (C-416/93) [1995] All E.R.
(E.C.) 385; [1995] E.C.R. I-361;
[1996] 2 C.M.L.R. 13 ECJ 299
Ministerul Administratiei si Inter-
nelor – Directia Generala de
Pasapoarte Bucuresti v Jipa (C-
33/07) [2008] E.C.R. I-5157;
[2008] 3 C.M.L.R. 23 ECJ 239
Ministre de la Santé v Jeff Erpelding
(C-16/99) [2000] E.C.R. I–6821. . . 273
Molkerei-Zentrale Westfalen/Lippe
GmbH v Hauptzollamt Pader-
born (28/67) [1968] E.C.R. 143;
[1968] C.M.L.R. 187 ECJ 45,
142, 426
Mollet v Commission of the European
Communities (75/77) [1978]
E.C.R. 897 ECJ 36
Morson v Netherlands (35/82);
Jhanjan v Netherlands (36/82)
[1982] E.C.R. 3723; [1983] 2
C.M.L.R. 221 ECJ 146
Moser v Land Baden-Württemberg
(180/83) [1984] E.C.R. 2539;
[1984] 3 C.M.L.R. 720 ECJ 239

Mostaza Claro v Centro Movil
Milenium SL (C-168/05) [2006]
E.C.R. I-10421; [2007] 1
C.M.L.R. 22 ECJ 498
Motosykletistiki Omospondia Ella-
dos NPID (MOTOE) v Greece
(C-49/07) [2009] All E.R. (EC)
150; [2008] E.C.R. I-4863;
[2008] 5 C.M.L.R. 11 ECJ 323
Mouvement contre le Racisme,
l'Antisemitisme et la Xenophobie
ASBL (MRAX) v Belgium
(C-459/99) [2003] 1 W.L.R. 1073;
[2002] E.C.R. I-6591; [2002] 3
C.M.L.R. 25 ECJ 248
Mulder v Council and Commission
(C-104/89 and C-37/90) [1992]
E.C.R. 3131 149
Murru v Caisse Regionale d'Assur-
ance Maladie de Paris (2/72)
[1972] E.C.R. 333; [1972]
C.M.L.R. 888 ECJ 251
Musik-Vertrieb Membran GmbH v
GEMA (C-55/80); sub nom.
Musik-Vertrieb Membran GmbH
v Gesellschaft fur Musikalische
Auffuhrungs- und Mechanische
Vervielfaltigungsrechte (GEMA)
(55/80) [1981] E.C.R. 147;
[1981] 2 C.M.L.R. 44 ECJ 304
Musique Diffusion Francaise SA v
Commission of the European
Communities (100/80); Pioneer
High Fidelity (GB) Ltd v Commis-
sion of the European Communi-
ties (103/80); Pioneer Electronic
(Europe) NV v Commission of the
European Communities (102/80);
C Melchers & Co v Commission
of the European Communities
(101/80) [1983] E.C.R. 1825;
[1983] 3 C.M.L.R. 221 ECJ 321
NTN Toyo Bearing Co Ltd v Council
of Ministers of the European
Communites (113/77) (No.1);
sub nom. Japanese Bearings
Cases (113/77); NTN Toyo Bear-
ing Co Ltd v Commission of the
European Communities (113/77)
[1977] E.C.R. 1721 ECJ . . . 162, 163
NV Algemene Transport- en Expeditie Onderneming van Gend en
Loos v Nederlandse Administratie der Belastingen (26/62)
[1963] E.C.R. 1; [1963]
C.M.L.R. 105 ECJ 8, 9, 42, 225

NV Internationale Credieten Handelsvereniging Rotterdam v Minister van Landbouw en Visserij (73/63) [1964] E.C.R. 1; [1964] C.M.L.R. 198 ECJ 37

NV Koninklijke KNP BT v Commission of the European Communities (T-309/94) [1998] E.C.R. II–1007 324

National Farmers' Union v Secrétariat général du gouvernement (C-241/01) [2002] E.C.R. I–9079 137

National Pensions Office v Jonkman (C-231/06); Permesaen v National Pensions Office (C-233/06); National Pensions Office v Vercheval (C-232/06) [2008] All E.R. (EC) 1017; [2007] 3 C.M.L.R. 25 ECJ 147

Nederlandse Associatie van de Farmaceutische Industrie "Nefarma" and Bond van Groothandelaren in het Farmaceutische Bedrijf v Commission of the European Communities (T-113/89 [1990] E.C.R. II–797; [1991] 2 C.M.L.R. 818 134

Nederlandse Spoorwegen v Inspecteur der Invoerrechten en Accijnzen. *See* Douaneagent der NV Nederlandse Spoorwegen v Inspector der Invoerrechten en Accijnzen (C-38/75)

Nerkowska v Zaklad Ubezpieczen Spolecznych Oddzial w Koszalinie (C-499/06) [2008] E.C.R. I-3993; [2008] All E.R. (EC) 885; [2008] 3 C.M.L.R. 8 ECJ 240

Netherlands v Commission (C-48/90 and C-66/90). *See* Koninklijke PTT Nederland NV v Commission of the European Communities (C-66/90)

Netherlands v Commission of the European Communities (C-48/90 and C-66/90) [1992] E.C.R. I–565 .... 377, 378

Netherlands v Council of the European Union (C-58/94) [1996] E.C.R. I-2169; [1996] 2 C.M.L.R. 996 ECJ 104

Netherlands v Council of the European Union (C-110/97) [1997] E.C.R. I–1795 150

Netherlands v High Authority (6/54) [1954–56] E.C.R. 103 67

New Ford Holland v Commission of the European Communities (C-8/95 P). *See* John Deere Ltd v Commission of the European Communities (C-7/95 P)

Nokia Corp v Wardell (C-316/05) [2006] E.C.R. I-12083; [2007] 1 C.M.L.R. 37; [2007] C.E.C. 393; [2007] E.T.M.R. 20; [2007] Bus. L.R. D16 ECJ 195

Norbrook Laboratories Ltd v Ministry of Agriculture, Fisheries and Food (C-127/95) [1998] E.C.R. I-1531; [1998] 3 C.M.L.R. 809 ECJ 112

Nordgetreide GmbH & Co KG v Commission of the European Communities (42/71) [1972] E.C.R. 105; [1973] C.M.L.R. 177 ECJ 135

Nordsee Deutsche Hochseefischerei GmbH v Reederei Mond Hochseefischerei Nordstern AG & Co KG (102/81) [1982] E.C.R. 1095; [1982] Com. L.R. 154 ECJ 144

Nordsee, Deutsche Hochseefischerei GmbH v Federal Republic of Germany and Land Rheinland-Pfalz (122/73) [1973] E.C.R. 1511 395

North Western Health Board v McKenna (C-191/03) [2006] All E.R. (EC) 455; [2005] E.C.R. I-7631; [2006] 1 C.M.L.R. 6 ECJ 474

Ntionik Anonymi Etaireia Emporias H/Y, Logismikou kai Paroxis Ypiresion Michanografisis and Ioannis Michail Pikoulas v Epitropi Kefalaiagoras (C-430/05) [2007] E.C.R. I-5835 281

O'Byrne v Sanofi Pasteur MSD Ltd (formerly Aventis Pasteur MSD Ltd) (C-127/04) [2006] 1 W.L.R. 1606; [2006] All E.R. (EC) 674; [2006] E.C.R. I-1313 ECJ 497

Oakley Inc v Office for Harmonisation in the Internal Market (Trade Marks and Designs) (OHIM) (T-116/06 R) [2006] E.C.R. II-2627 ECJ 162

Océano Grupo Editorial SA v Quintero (C-240/98); Salvat Editores SA v Feliu (C-244/98); Salvat Editores SA v Berroane (C-243/98); Salvat Editores SA v Badillo (C-242/98); Salvat Editores SA v Prades (C-241/98) [2000] E.C.R. I-4941; [2002] 1 C.M.L.R. 43 ECJ 56, 451

Oebel, Re (155/80) [1981] E.C.R. 1993; [1983] 1 C.M.L.R. 390 ECJ 229

Oelm Ühle Hamburg AG v Bundesanstalt fur Landwirtschaft und Ernahrung (C-298/96) [1998] E.C.R. I-4767; [1999] 2 C.M.L.R. 492 ECJ 396

Office national de l'emploi v Bahia Kziber (18/90) [1991] E.C.R. I-221 45

Office National des Pensions pour Travailleurs Salaries v Damiani (53/79) [1980] E.C.R. 273; [1981] 1 C.M.L.R. 548 ECJ 143

Officier van Justitie v De Peijper (104/75); sub nom. De Peijper (Managing Director of Centrafarm BV), Re (104/75) [1976] E.C.R. 613; [1976] 2 C.M.L.R. 271 ECJ ... 232

Officier van Justitie v Koninblijke Kaasfabriek Eyssen BV (53/80) [1981] E.C.R. 409; [1982] 2 C.M.L.R. 20 ECJ 230

Officier van Justitie v Kramer (3/76); Officier van Justitie v Van Den Berg (4/76); Officier van Justitie v Kramer en Bais & Co (6/76) [1976] E.C.R. 1279; [1976] 2 C.M.L.R. 440 ECJ 565, 566

Opel Austria GmbH v Council of the European Union (T-115/94) [1997] E.C.R. II–39 139

Openbaar Ministerie v Bout (21/81) [1982] E.C.R. 381; [1982] 2 C.M.L.R. 371 ECJ 139

Openbaar Ministerie v Van Tiggele (82/77) [1978] E.C.R. 25; [1978] 2 C.M.L.R. 528 ECJ 227

Ordre des Advocats au Barreau de Paris (Paris Bar Council) v Rechtsanwalt Onno Klopp (107/83); sub nom. Ordre des Advocats au Barreau de Paris v Klopp (107/83) [1985] Q.B. 711; [1985] 2 W.L.R. 1058; [1984] E.C.R. 2971 ECJ 269

Ordre des Barreaux Francophones et Germanophone v Conseil des Ministres (C-305/05) [2007] All E.R. (EC) 953; [2007] E.C.R. I-5305; [2007] 3 C.M.L.R. 28 ECJ 293

Orkem v Commission of the European Communities (374/87) [1989] E.C.R. 3350 354

Orlando Lopes v Court of Justice of the European Communities (C-174/96 P) [1996] E.C.R. I–6401 157

Oscar Bronner GmbH & Co KG v Mediaprint Zeitungs- und Zeitschriftenverlag GmbH & Co KG (C-7/97) [1998] E.C.R. I-7791; [1999] 4 C.M.L.R. 112 ECJ 341

Othmar Michaeler, Subito GmbH and Ruth Volgger v Amt für sozialen Arbeitsschutz and Autonome Provinz Bozen (C-55/07 and C-56/07) [2008] E.C.R. I-3135 ... 476

Oulane v Minister voor Vreemdelingenzaken en Integratie (C-215/03) [2005] Q.B. 1055; [2005] 3 W.L.R. 543; [2005] E.C.R. I-1215 ECJ 240

Oy Liikenne AB v Liskojarvi (C-172/99); sub nom. Liskojarvi v Oy Liikenne AB (C-172/99) [2001] All E.R. (EC) 544; [2001] E.C.R. I-745; [2001] 3 C.M.L.R. 37 ECJ 473

Pafitis v Trapeza Kentrikis Ellados AE (C-441/93) [1996] E.C.R. I-1347; [1996] 2 C.M.L.R. 551; [1997] C.E.C. 646 ECJ 164, 278

Palacios de la Villa v Cortefiel Servicios SA (C-411/05) [2008] All E.R. (EC) 249; [2007] E.C.R. I-8531; [2008] 1 C.M.L.R. 16 ECJ 479

Pall Corp v PJ Dahlhausen & Co (C-238/89) [1990] E.C.R. 4827 ... 302

Pannon GSM Zrt v Erzsébet Sustikné Győrf (C-243/08) June 4, 2009 ECJ 498

Paquay v Societe d'Architectes Hoet + Minne SPRL (C-460/06) [2007] E.C.R. I-851; [2008] 1 C.M.L.R. 12; [2008] I.C.R. 420 ECJ 472, 474

Paraskevas Louloudakis v Elliniko Dimosio (C-262/99) [2001] E.C.R. I–5547 269

Parfums Christian Dior SA v Tuk Consultancy BV (C-300/98); Assco Geruste GmbH v Wilhelm Layher GmbH & Co KG (C-392/98) [2000] E.C.R. I-11307; [2001] E.T.M.R. 26 ECJ 54

Parke Davis & Co v Probel (24/67) [1968] E.C.R. 55; [1968] C.M.L.R. 47; [1968] F.S.R. 393 ECJ 301, 302

Parking Brixen GmbH v Gemeinde Brixen (C-458/03) [2006] All E.R. (EC) 779; [2005] E.C.R. I-8612; [2006] 1 C.M.L.R. 3; [2006] C.E.C. 144 ECJ 311

Parodi v Banque H Albert de Bary (C-229/95) [1997] E.C.R. I-3899 293

Parti Ecologiste Les Verts v European Parliament (294/83); sub nom. Les Verts, Parti Ecologiste v European Parliament (294/83) [1986] E.C.R. 1339; [1987] 2 C.M.L.R. 343 ECJ 125

Paul v Germany (C-222/02) [2004] E.C.R. I-9425; [2006] 2 C.M.L.R. 62 ECJ 51, 292

Pauls Agriculture Ltd v Council of Ministers and Commission of the European Communities (256/81) [1983] E.C.R. 1707; [1983] 3 C.M.L.R. 176 ECJ 150

Pecastaing v Belgium (98/79) [1981] E.C.R. 691; [1980] E.C.R. 691; [1980] 3 C.M.L.R. 685 ECJ 253

Pennartz v Caisse Primaire d'Assurance Maladie des Alpes-Maritimes (268/78) [1979] E.C.R. 2411; [1980] 1 C.M.L.R. 682 ECJ 251

Pergan Hilfsstoffe fur Industrielle Prozesse v Commission of the European Communities (T-474/04); sub nom. Organic Peroxides Cartel Appeal, Re (T-474/04) [2007] E.C.R. II-4225; [2008] 4 C.M.L.R. 4 ECJ 359

Peterbroeck Van Campenhout & Cie SCS v Belgium (C-312/93) [1996] All E.R. (E.C.) 242; [1995] E.C.R. I-4599; [1996] 1 C.M.L.R. 793 ECJ 45, 56

Pharmon BV v Hoechst AG (19/84) [1985] E.C.R. 2281; [1985] 3 C.M.L.R. 775 ECJ 302, 336

Philip Morris Holland BV v Commission of the European Communities (730/79) [1980] E.C.R. 2671; [1981] 2 C.M.L.R. 321 ECJ 137, 381

Philip Morris International Inc v Commission of the European Communities (T-377/00); Japan Tobacco Inc v Commission of the European Communities (T-380/00); RJ Reynolds Tobacco Holdings Inc v Commission of the European Communities (T-379/00) [2003] All E.R. (EC) 1008; [2003] E.C.R. II-1; [2003] 1 C.M.L.R. 21 ECJ 113

Phytheron International SA v Jean Bourdon SA (C-352/95) [1997] E.C.R. I-1729; [1997] 3 C.M.L.R. 199 ECJ 305

Pia Messner v Firma Stefan Krüger (C-489/07) September 3, 2009 . . . 497

Pig Production Subsidies, Re (31/77); sub nom. Commission of the European Communities v United Kingdom (31/77) [1977] E.C.R. 921; [1977] 2 C.M.L.R. 359 ECJ 163

Pigs Marketing Board (Northern Ireland) v Redmond (83/78) [1978] E.C.R. 2347; [1979] 1 C.M.L.R. 177 ECJ 323, 375, 400

Plantanol GmbH & Co KG v Hauptzollamt Darmstadt (C-201/08) September 10, 2009 148

Plaumann & Co v Commission of the European Economic Community (25/62) [1963] E.C.R. 95; [1964] C.M.L.R. 29 ECJ . . . 135, 149

Politi Sas v Ministero delle Finanze (43/71) [1971] E.C.R. 1039; [1973] C.M.L.R. 60 ECJ 31

Portuguese Republic and Kingdom of Spain v Council of the European Communities (C-63/90 and C-67/90) [1992] E.C.R. I-5073 416

Portuguese Republic v Council of the European Union (149/96) [1999] E.C.R. I-8395 55

Poseidon Chartering BV v Marianne Zeeschip Vof (C-3/04) [2007] Bus. L.R. 446; [2006] 2 Lloyd's Rep. 105; [2006] E.C.R. I-2505 ECJ 267

Pretore di Genova v Banchero (C-157/92) [1993] E.C.R. I-1085 ECJ 143

Proceedings Brought by A (C-523/07); sub nom. A (Area of Freedom, Security and Justice), Re (C-523/07) [2009] I.L.Pr. 39; [2009] 2 F.L.R. 1 ECJ 259

Proceedings Brought by Heinrich (C-345/06) [2009] 3 C.M.L.R. 7 ECJ 37, 200, 452

Proceedings brought by Rinau (C-195/08 PPU); sub nom. Rinau v Rinau (C-195/08 PPU) [2009] 2 W.L.R. 972; [2008] All E.R. (EC) 1145; [2008] E.C.R. I-5271 ECJ 148, 259

Proceedings concerning the execution of a European arrest warrant issued against Szymon Kozłowski (C-46/08) [2008] E.C.R. I-6041 263

Procureur de la République v Association de défense des brûleurs d'huiles usagées (ADBHU) (240/83) [1985] E.C.R. I-531 ... 540

Procureur du Roi v Dassonville (8/74); sub nom. Dassonville v Commission of the European Communities (8/74) [1974] E.C.R. 837; [1974] 2 C.M.L.R. 436; [1975] F.S.R. 191 ECJ 227, 230, 436

Procureur du Roi v Debauve (52/79) [1980] E.C.R. 833; [1981] 2 C.M.L.R. 362 ECJ 44, 289, 291

Procureur du Roi v Kefer (95/79); Procureur du Roi v Delmelle (96/79) [1980] E.C.R. 103; [1982] 2 C.M.L.R. 77 ECJ 143

Productores de Musica de Espana (Promusicae) v Telefonica de Espana SAU (C-275/06) [2008] All E.R. (EC) 809; [2008] E.C.R. I-271; [2008] 2 C.M.L.R. 17 ECJ 32, 303, 307, 497, 511

Provincia di Ascoli Piceno v Council of the European Union (C-461/07 P(I)); sub nom. Provincia di Ascoli Piceno v Sun Sang Kong Yuen Shoes Factory (Hui Yang) Corp Ltd (C-461/07 P(I)) [2008] E.C.R. I-11; [2008] 2 C.M.L.R. 15 ECJ 163

Public Works Contracts, Re (274/83); sub nom. Commission of the European Communities v Italy (274/83) [1985] E.C.R. 1077; [1987] 1 C.M.L.R. 345 ECJ 313

Public Works Directive 1971, Re (10/76); sub nom. Commission of the European Communities v Italy (10/76) [1976] E.C.R. 1359; [1976] 2 C.M.L.R. 699 ECJ 313

Punto Casa SpA v Sindaco del Comune di Capena et Comune di Capena and Promozioni Polivalenti Venete Soc. coop. arl (PPV) v Sindaco del Comune di Torri di Quartesolo and Comune di Torri di Quartesolo (C-69/93 and C-258/93) [1994] E.C.R. I-2355 231

Quelle AG v Bundesverband der Verbraucherzentralen und Verbraucherverbande (C-404/06) [2008] E.C.R. I-2685; [2008] 2 C.M.L.R. 49 ECJ 497

R. v Henn (Maurice Donald) (34/79); R.v Darby (John Frederick) (34/79) [1980] 2 W.L.R. 597; [1979] E.C.R. 3795; [1980] 1 C.M.L.R. 246 ECJ 139, 232

R. v HM Treasury Ex p. British Telecommunications Plc (C-392/93) [1996] Q.B. 615; [1996] 3 W.L.R. 203; [1996] E.C.R. I-1631 ECJ 112

R. v HM Treasury Ex p. Daily Mail (81/87); R. v Customs and Excise Commissioners Ex p. Daily Mail (81/87) [1989] Q.B. 446; [1989] 2 W.L.R. 908; [1988] E.C.R. 5483 ECJ ... 269, 278

R. v Immigration Appeal Tribunal Ex p. Antonissen (C-292/89) [1991] E.C.R. I-745; [1991] 2 C.M.L.R. 373; (1991) 135 S.J. 6 ECJ 247

R. v Intervention Board for Agricultural Produce Ex p. Accrington Beef Co Ltd (C-241/95) [1996] E.C.R. I-6699; [1997] 1 C.M.L.R. 675 ECJ 147

R. v Ministry of Agriculture, Fisheries and Food Ex p. Agegate Ltd (3/87) [1990] 2 Q.B. 151; [1990] 3 W.L.R. 226; [1989] E.C.R. 4459 ECJ 416

R. v Ministry of Agriculture, Fisheries and Food Ex p. Federation Europeene de la Sante Animale (FEDESA) (C-331/88) [1990] E.C.R. I-4023; [1991] 1 C.M.L.R. 507 ECJ 36, 37

R. v Ministry of Agriculture, Fisheries and Food Ex p. Hedley Lomas (Ireland) Ltd (C-5/94) [1997] Q.B. 139; [1996] 3 W.L.R. 787; [1996] E.C.R. I-2553 ECJ 110, 112

R. v Ministry of Agriculture, Fisheries and Food Ex p. Jaderow Ltd (216/87) [1990] 2 Q.B. 193; [1990] 3 W.L.R. 265; [1989] E.C.R. 4509 ECJ 416

R. v Ministry of Agriculture, Fisheries and Food Ex p. National Farmers' Union (C-157/96) [1998] E.C.R. I-2211 541

R. v National Insurance Commissioner Ex p. Warry (41/77); sub nom. R. v National Insurance Commissioner Ex p. Insurance Officer (41/77) [1978] Q.B. 607; [1978] 3 W.L.R. 99; [1977] E.C.R. 2085 ECJ 251

R. v Saunders (Vera Ann) (175/78) [1980] Q.B. 72; [1979] 3 W.L.R. 359; [1979] E.C.R. 1129 ECJ 239

R. v Secretary of State for Social Security Ex p. Sutton (C-66/95) [1997] All E.R. (EC) 497; [1997] E.C.R. I-2163; [1997] 2 C.M.L.R. 382 ECJ 112

R. v Secretary of State for the Home Department Ex p. Evans Medical Ltd (C-324/93) [1995] All E.R. (E.C.) 481; [1995] E.C.R. I-563; [1996] 1 C.M.L.R. 53 ECJ 566

R. v Secretary of State for the Home Department Ex p. Shingara (C-65/95); R. v Secretary of State for the Home Department Ex p. Radiom (C-111/95) [1997] All E.R. (EC) 577; [1997] E.C.R. I-3343; [1997] 3 C.M.L.R. 703 ECJ 253

R. v Secretary of State for Trade and Industry Ex p. British Telecommunications Plc (C-302/94) [1996] E.C.R. I-6417; [1997] 1 C.M.L.R. 424 ECJ 314

R. v Secretary of State for Transport Ex p. Factortame Ltd (C-213/89) [1990] 2 Lloyd's Rep. 351; [1990] E.C.R. I-2433; [1990] 3 C.M.L.R. 1 ECJ 47, 56, 140

R. v Secretary of State for Transport Ex p. Factortame Ltd (C-221/89) [1992] Q.B. 680; [1992] 3 W.L.R. 288; [1991] E.C.R. I-3905 ECJ 416

R. v Social Security Commissioner Ex p. Browning (22/81) [1981] E.C.R. 3357; [1982] 1 C.M.L.R. 427 ECJ 251

R. v Thompson (Ernest George) (7/78); R. v Johnson (Brian Albert) (7/78); R. v Woodiwiss (Colin Alex) (7/78) [1980] Q.B. 229; [1980] 2 W.L.R. 521; [1978] E.C.R. 2247; [1979] E.C.R. 2247 ECJ 232, 299

R. (on the application of Bidar) v Ealing LBC (C-209/03) [2005] Q.B. 812; [2005] 2 W.L.R. 1078; [2005] E.C.R. I-2119 ECJ 270

R. (on the application of International Air Transport Association (IATA)) v Department of Transport (C-344/04) [2006] E.C.R. I-403; [2006] 2 C.M.L.R. 20 ECJ 451

R. (on the application of Synthon BV) v Licensing Authority (C-452/06) [2008] E.C.R. I-7681 195

R. (on the application of Wells) v Secretary of State for Transport, Local Government and the Regions (C-201/02); sub nom. Wells v Secretary of State for Transport, Local Government and the Regions (C-201/02) [2005] All E.R. (EC) 323; [2004] E.C.R. I-723; [2004] 1 C.M.L.R. 31 ECJ 32, 140

RI.SAN. Srl v Comune di Ischia, Italia Lavoro SpA and Ischia Ambiente SpA (C-108/98) [1999] E.C.R. I–5219 314

RJ Reynolds Tobacco Holdings Inc v Commission of the European Communities (C-131/03 P) [2006] E.C.R. I-7795; [2007] 1 C.M.L.R. 1 ECJ 113

Radio Telefis Eireann v Commission
of the European Communities
(T-69/89) [1991] E.C.R. II-485;
[1991] 4 C.M.L.R. 586 ECJ 338
Rampion v Franfinance SA (C-429/05)
[2008] Bus. L.R. 715; [2007]
E.C.R. I-8017; [2008] 1 C.M.L.R.
8 ECJ 498
Raymond Vander Elst v Office des
Migrations Internationales (C-
43/93) [1994] E.C.R. I-3803 310
Razanatsimba, Re (65/77) [1977]
E.C.R. 2229; [1978] 1 C.M.L.R.
246 ECJ 570
Receveur principal des douanes de
Villepinte v Derudder & Cie SA,
and Tang Frères (C-290/01)
[2004] E.C.R. I–2041 224
Recheio – Cash & Carry SA v Fazenda
Pública/Registo Nacional de
Pessoas Colectivas, and Ministério
Público (C-30/02) [2004] E.C.R.
I–6051 140
Rechnungshof v Österreichischer
Rundfunk (C-465/00) [2003]
E.C.R. I-4989; [2003] 3 C.M.L.R.
10 ECJ 501
Région wallonne v Commission of the
European Communities (C-95/97)
[1997] E.C.R. I–1787 134
Regione autonoma Friuli Venezia
Giulia v Commission of the Euro-
pean Communities (T-288/97)
[1999] E.C.R. II–1871 134
Regione Puglia v Commission of the
European Communities and
Kingdom of Spain (T-609/97)
[1998] E.C.R. II–4051 136
Regione Toscana v Commission of
the European Communities (C-
180/97) [1997] E.C.R. I–5247 ... 134
Reina v Landeskreditbank Baden-
Wurttemberg (65/81) [1982]
E.C.R. 33; [1982] 1 C.M.L.R.
744 ECJ 143, 251
Reisebüro Binder GmbH v Finanzamt
Stuttgart-Körperschaften (C-116/
96) [1998] E.C.R. I–1891 148
Reisebüro Broede v Sandker (C-3/95)
[1996] E.C.R. I-6511; [1997] 1
C.M.L.R. 224 ECJ 268, 287
Remia BV v Commission of the
European Communities (42/84)
[1985] E.C.R. 2545; [1987] 1
C.M.L.R. 1 ECJ 324

Rewe Zentralfinanz eG v Landwirtschaftskammer fur das Saarland (33/76) [1976] E.C.R.
1989; [1977] 1 C.M.L.R. 533
ECJ 44, 45, 55,
56, 143, 231
Rewe-Handelsgesellschaft   Nord
mbH v Hauptzollamt Kiel
(158/80); Rewe Markt Steffen v
Hauptzollamt Kiel [1981] E.C.R.
1805; [1982] 1 C.M.L.R. 449
ECJ 37
Rewe-Zentral   AG   v   Bundesmonopolverwaltung   für
Branntwein (120/78); sub nom.
Cassis de Dijon, Re (120/78)
[1979] E.C.R. 649; [1979] 3
C.M.L.R. 494 ECJ 228, 229,
230, 267,
275, 436
Reyners v Belgium (2/74) [1974]
E.C.R. 631; [1974] 2 C.M.L.R.
305 ECJ 44, 284, 290
Rheinmuhlen-Dusseldorf v Einfuhr-
und Vorratsstelle fur Getreide
und Futtermittel (166/73) [1974]
E.C.R. 33; [1974] 1 C.M.L.R.
523 ECJ 44, 145
Richard Kuhner v Commission of
the European Communities
(33/79 and 75/79) [1980] E.C.R.
1677 140
Rigsadvokaten v Ryborg (C-297/89)
[1991] E.C.R. I-1943; [1993] 1
C.M.L.R. 218 ECJ 269
Robins v Secretary of State for Work
and Pensions (C-278/05) [2007]
All E.R. (EC) 648; [2007] 2
C.M.L.R. 13 ECJ 34
Robinson-Steele v RD Retail Services
Ltd (C-131/04); Clarke v Frank
Staddon   Ltd   (C-257/04);
Caulfield v Hanson Clay Prod-
ucts Ltd (C-257/04) [2006] All
E.R. (EC) 749; [2006] E.C.R.
I-2531; [2006] 2 C.M.L.R. 34
ECJ 476
Rockfon A/S v Specialarbejderfor-
bundet i Danmark [1995] E.C.R.
I-4291; [1996] C.E.C. 224
ECJ 473
Roquette Frères SA v Council of
Ministers of the European Com-
munities (138/79) 1980] E.C.R.
3333 ECJ 68, 80

Roquette Frères SA v French State Customs Administration (145/79) [1980] E.C.R. 2917 ECJ 144

Rosengren v Riksaklagaren (C-170/04) [2009] All E.R. (EC) 455; [2007] 3 C.M.L.R. 10 ECJ 376

Rothley v European Parliament (C-167/02 P) [2004] E.C.R. I-3149; [2004] 2 C.M.L.R. 11 ECJ 64

Rothley v European Parliament (T-17/00) [2002] E.C.R. II-579; [2002] 2 C.M.L.R. 30 CFI64, 134

Rothmans International BV v Commission of the European Communities (T-188/97) [1999] E.C.R. II-2463; [1999] 3 C.M.L.R. 66 CFI 117

Rotsart de Hertaing v J Benoidt SA (In Liquidation) (C-305/94) [1997] All E.R. (E.C.) 40; [1996] E.C.R. I-5927; [1997] 1 C.M.L.R. 329 ECJ 473

Roussel Laboratoria BV v Netherlands (181/82) [1983] E.C.R. 3849; [1985] 1 C.M.L.R. 834 ECJ 229

Rummler v Dato-Druck GmbH (237/85) [1986] E.C.R. 2101; [1987] 3 C.M.L.R. 127 ECJ 478

Rush Portuguesa Ld™ v Office national d'immigration (C-113/89) [1990] E.C.R. I–1417 . . . 309

Rutili v Ministre de l'Iinterieur (36/75) [1975] E.C.R. 1219; [1976] 1 C.M.L.R. 140 ECJ 246, 253

SA de Traverses en Beton Arme (SATEBA) v Commission of the European Communities (T-83/97) [1997] E.C.R. II-1523; [1998] 4 C.M.L.R. 528 CFI 110

SCA Holding Ltd v Commission of the European Communities (T-327/94) [1998] E.C.R. II–1373 . . . 322, 357

SIC – Sociedade Independente de Comunicação SA v Commission of the European Communities (T-46/97) [2000] E.C.R. I–2125 . . 379, 395

SP SpA v Commission of the European Communities (T-27/03); sub nom. Reinforcing Bars Cartel Appeal, Re (T-27/03) [2007] E.C.R. II-4331; [2008] 4 C.M.L.R. 5 ECJ . . . 14

Salonia v Poidamani (126/80); Salonia v Baglieri (nee Giglio) [1981] E.C.R. 1563; [1982] 1 C.M.L.R. 64 ECJ 145

Salumificio di Cornuda SpA v Amministrazione delle Finanze dello Stato (130/78) [1979] E.C.R. 867; [1979] 3 C.M.L.R. 561 ECJ 37

Salvatore Belfiore v Commission of the European Communities (108/79) [1980] E.C.R. 1769 . . . 158

Salzgitter AG, formerly Preussag Stahl AG v Commission of the European Communities (C-210/98) [2000] E.C.R. I–5843 385

Sandoz prodotti farmaceutici SpA v Commission of the European Communities (C-277/87) [1990] E.C.R. I–45 321

Schluter v Hauptzollamt Lörrach (9/73) [1973] E.C.R. 1135 ECJ 40

Schneider Electric SA v Commission of the European Communities (T-310/01) [2004] All E.R. (EC) 314; [2002] E.C.R. II-4071; [2003] 4 C.M.L.R. 17 CFI 369

Schottle & Sohne OHG v Finanzamt Freudenstadt (20/76) [1977] E.C.R. 247; [1977] 2 C.M.L.R. 98 ECJ 425

Schulte v Deutsche Bausparkasse Badenia AG (C-350/03) [2006] All E.R. (EC) 420; [2005] E.C.R. I-9215; [2006] 1 C.M.L.R. 11 ECJ 497

Schutzverband gegen unlauteren Wettbewerb v TK-Heimdienst Sass GmbH (C-254/98) [2000] E.C.R. I–151 143

Scott SA v Commission of the European Communities (C-276/03 P) [2005] E.C.R. I–8437 . . . . . 337, 396

Seagon v Deko Marty Belgium NV (C-339/07) [2009] 1 W.L.R. 2168; [2009] Bus. L.R. 1151; [2009] B.C.C. 347; [2009] I.L.Pr. 25 ECJ 260

Selex Sistemi Integrati SpA v Commission of the European Communities (T-155/04) [2006] E.C.R. II-4797; [2007] 4 C.M.L.R. 10 CFI 164

Semeraro Casa Uno Srl v Sindaco del Comune di Erbusco (C-418/93) [1996] E.C.R. I-2975; [1996] 3 C.M.L.R. 648 ECJ 230, 231

Sevince v Staatssecretaris van Justitie (C-192/89) [1990] E.C.R. I-3461; [1992] 2 C.M.L.R. 57 ECJ 133

Siemens AG v Henry Nold (C-42/95) [1996] E.C.R. I–6017 278

Siemens SA v Commission of the European Communities (C-278/95 P) [1997] E.C.R. I-2507; [1997] C.E.C. 1267 ECJ 392

Siemens SA v Commission of the European Communities (T-459/93) [1995] E.C.R. II-1675 CFI 335, 396

Silhouette International Schmied GmbH & Co KG v Hartlauer Handelsgesellschaft mbH (C-355/96) [1999] Ch. 77; [1998] 3 W.L.R. 1218; [1998] E.C.R. I-4799 ECJ 306

Silos e Mangimi Martini SpA v Ministero delle Finanze (C-228/99) [2001] E.C.R. I-8401 37

Simmenthal SpA v Commission of the European Communities (92/78) [1979] E.C.R. 777; [1980] 1 C.M.L.R. 25 ECJ 140, 151

Simone Leitner v TUI Deutschland GmbH & Co KG (C-168/00) [2002] E.C.R. I-26321 498

Simutenkov v Ministerio de Educacion y Cultura (C-265/03) [2006] All E.R. (EC) 42; [2005] E.C.R. I-2579; [2005] 2 C.M.L.R. 11 ECJ 591

Sirena Srl v Eda Srl (40/70) [1971] E.C.R. 69; [1971] C.M.L.R. 260; [1971] F.S.R. 666 ECJ 301

Skoma-Lux sro v Celni Reditelstvi Olomouc (C-161/06) [2007] E.C.R. I-10841; [2008] 1 C.M.L.R. 50 ECJ 37

Skov Æg v Bilka Lavprisvarehus A/S and Bilka Lavprisvarehus A/S v Jette Mikkelsen and Michael Due Nielsen (C-402/03) [2006] E.C.R. I-199 498

Smanor SA, Hubert Ségaud and Monique Ségaud v Commission of the European Communities (T-182/97) [1998] E.C.R. II-271 110

Sociedade Agricola dos Arinhos, Ld™ v Commission of the European Communities (T-38/99 and T-50/99) [2001] E C.R II–585 ... 137

Societa Agricola Fattoria Alimentaire SpA v Amministrazione delle Finanze dello Stato (C-337/88) [1990] E.C.R. I-1; [1991] 1 C.M.L.R. 872 ECJ 37

Societe Alsacienne et Lorraine de Telecommunications et d'Electronique (Alsatel) v Novasam SA (247/86) [1988] E.C.R. 5987; [1990] 4 C.M.L.R. 434 ECJ 340

Société anonyme de droit français Seco and Société anonyme de droit français Desquenne & Giral v Etablissement d'assurance contre la vieillesse et l'invalidité (62 and 63/81) [1982] E.C.R. 223 ... 286, 309

Société Cadi Surgelés v Ministre des Finances (C-126/94) [1996] E.C.R. I-5647; [1997] 1 C.M.L.R. 795 ECJ 225

Societe CdF Chimie Azote et Fertilisants SA v Commission of the European Communities (169/84) [1990] E.C.R. I-3083; [1992] 1 C.M.L.R. 177 ECJ 137

Société chimique Prayon-Rupel SA v Commission of the European Communities (T-73/98) [2001] E.C.R. II–867 395

Société de Vente de Ciments et Betons de L'Est SA v Kerpen & Kerpen GmbH & Co KG (319/82) [1983] E.C.R. 4173; [1985] 1 C.M.L.R. 511 ECJ 141, 325

Société Générale d'Entreprises Electro-Mécaniques SA (SGEEM) and Roland Etroy v European Investment Bank (C-370/89) [1992] E.C.R. I–6211 ..... 113, 185

Société Internationale de Diffusion et d'Edition (SIDE) v Commission of the European Communities (T-49/93) [1995] E.C.R. II–2501 ... 395

Societe Italiano Vetro SpA v Commission of the European Communities (T-68/89); Fabbrica Pisana SpA v Commission of the European Communities (T-77/89); Vernante Pennitalia v Commission of the European Communities (T-78/89); sub nom. Italian Flat Glass, Re (T-68/89) [1992] E.C.R. II-1403; [1992] 5 C.M.L.R. 302 CFI 338

Societe Les Commissionnaires Reunis Sarl v Receveur des Douanes (80/77); Les Fils de Henri Ramel v Receveur des Douanes (81/77) [1978] E.C.R. 927 ECJ 223

Societe Louis Dreyfus & Cie v Commission of the European Communities (T-485/93) [1996] E.C.R. II-1101; [1997] 1 C.M.L.R. 1008 CFI 150

Société Technique Minière v Machienenbau Ulm GmbH (56/65) [1966] E.C.R. 235; [1966] C.M.L.R. 357 ECJ 321, 324, 325, 326

Sony Music Entertainment (Germany) GmbH v Falcon Neue Medien Vertrieb GmbH (C-240/07) [2009] E.C.D.R. 12 ECJ 304

Sotgiu v Deutsche Bundepost (152/73) [1974] E.C.R. 153 ECJ 245, 254

SpA Eridania-Zuccherifici Nazionali SpA and Societa Italiana per l'Industria degli Zuccheri SpA Minister of Agriculture and Forestry, Minister for Industry, Trade and Craft and Zuccherifici Meridionali SpA (230/78) [1979] E.C.R. 2749 ECJ 31, 49

SpA Metallurgica Rumi v Commission of the European Communities (258/80) [1982] E.C.R. 487 ECJ 151

Spain and Finland v European Parliament and Council of the European Union (C-184/02 and C-223/02) [2004] E.C.R. I–7789 ...... 140, 446

Spain v Commission of the European Communities (C-271/90) [1992] E.C.R. I-5833 ECJ 314

Spain v Commission of the European Communities (C-135/93) [1995] E.C.R. I-1651 ECJ 386

Spain v Commission of the European Communities (C-415/96) [1998] E.C.R. I-6993; [1999] 1 C.M.L.R. 304 ECJ 160

Spain v Eurojust (C-160/03) [2005] E.C.R. I-2077 191

Spain v United Kingdom (C-145/04); sub nom. Gibraltar European Elections, Re (C-145/04) [2007] All E.R. (EC) 486; [2006] E.C.R. I-7917; [2007] 1 C.M.L.R. 3 ECJ 63

Spyridon Vassilakis v Dimos Kerkyraion (C-364/07) [2008] E.C.R. I–90 34

Staatssecretaris van Financien v Joustra (C-5/05) [2008] S.T.C. 2226; [2006] E.C.R. I-11075; [2007] 1 C.M.L.R. 30 ECJ 429

Stadt Halle v Arbeitsgemeinschaft Thermische Restabfall- und Energieverwertungsanlage TREA Leuna (C-26/03) [2005] E.C.R. I–1; [2006] 1 C.M.L.R. 39 ECJ 313, 316

Statens Kontrol med Aedle Metaller v Larsen (142/77) [1978] E.C.R. 1543; [1979] 2 C.M.L.R. 680 ECJ 232, 425

Stichting Greenpeace Council (Greenpeace International) v Commission of the European Communities (C-321/95 P) [1998] All E.R. (E.C.) 620; [1998] E.C.R. I-1651; [1998] 3 C.M.L.R. 1 ECJ 135, 136

Stichting ROM-Projecten v Staatssecretaris van Economische Zaken (C-158/06) [2007] 3 C.M.L.R. 21 ECJ 396

Stichting ter Exploitatie van Naburige Rechten (SENA) v Nederlandse Omroep Stichting (NOS) (C-245/00) [2003] E.C.R. I–12151 301

Stöber v Bundesanstalt für Arbeit (C-4/95); Pereira v Bundesanstalt für Arbeit (C-5/95) [1997] E.C.R. I-511; [1997] 2 C.M.L.R. 213 ECJ 267

Strabag AG (and Kostmann GmbH v Österreichische Bundesbahnen (C-462/03) [2005] E.C.R. I–5397 312

Stringer v Revenue and Customs Commissioners (C-520/06); Schultz-Hoff v Deutsche Rentenversicherung Bund (C-350/06) [2009] All E.R. (EC) 906; [2009] 2 C.M.L.R. 27 ECJ 476

Suède v Commission of the European Communities (T-229/04). *See* Sweden v Commission of the European Communities (T-229/04)

Sundelind Lopez (C-68/07) [2007] E.C.R. I-10403 259

Susan Ryan-Sheridan v European Foundation for the Improvement of Living and Working Conditions (T-589/93) [1996] E.C.R. II–77 . . . 192

Svenska Journalistforbundet v Council of the European Union (T-174/95) [1998] All E.R. (E.C.) 545; [1998] E.C.R. II-2289; [1998] 3 C.M.L.R. 645 ECJ 104, 161

Sweden v Commission of the European Communities (T-229/04) [2007] E.C.R. II-2437 197

Sweden v Council of the European Union (C-39/05 P); Turco v Council of the European Union (C-52/05 P) [2009] Q.B. 269; [2009] 2 W.L.R. 867; [2008] E.C.R. I-4723 ECJ 104

Syndicat Francais de l'Express International (SFEI) v Commission of the European Communities (C-39/93 P) [1994] E.C.R. I-2681 ECJ 133

Syndicat Francais de l'Express International (SFEI) v La Poste (C-39/94) [1996] All E.R. (EC) 685; [1996] E.C.R. I-3547; [1996] 3 C.M.L.R. 369 ECJ . . . 337, 380, 396

Syndicat professionnel coordination des pêcheurs de l'étang de Berre et de la région v Électricité de France (EDF) (C-213/03) July 15, 2004 40

T-Mobile Netherlands BV v Raad van Bestuur van de Nederlandse Mededingingsautoriteit (C-8/08) [2010] Bus. L.R. 158; [2009] 5 C.M.L.R. 11 ECJ 321, 322

TEA-CEGOS, SA, Services techniques globaux (STG) SA and GHK Consulting Ltd v Commission of the European Communities (T-376/05 and T-383/05) [2006] E.C.R. II–205 139

TNT Traco SpA v Poste Italiane SpA (C-340/99) [2001] E.C.R. I-4109 . . . . 145, 340

TWD Textilwerke Deggendorf GmbH v Germany (C-188/92) [1994] E.C.R. I-833; [1995] 2 C.M.L.R. 145 ECJ 147

Tachographs, Re (128/78); sub nom. Commission of the European Communities v United Kingdom (128/78) [1979] E.C.R. 419; [1979] R.T.R. 321; [1979] 2 C.M.L.R. 45 ECJ 30, 47, 48

Teckal Srl v Comune di Viano and Azienda Gas-Acqua Consorziale (AGAC) di Reggio Emilia (C-107/98) [1999] E.C.R. I–8121 310

Tedeschi v Denkavit Commerciale Srl (5/77) [1977] E.C.R. 1555; [1978] 1 C.M.L.R. 1 ECJ . . . 145, 233

Telaustria Verlags GmbH and Telefonadress GmbH v Telekom Austria AG (C-324/98) [2000] E.C.R. I–10745 314

Telefonica de Espana SA v Administracion General del Estado (C-79/00) [2001] E.C.R. I-0075; [2002] 4 C.M.L.R. 22 ECJ 510

Telemarsicabruzzo SpA v Circostel (C-320/90); Telemarsicabruzzo SpA v Ministerio delle Poste e Telecommunicazioni (C-320/90) [1993] E.C.R. I-393 ECJ 146

Teresa Fernández de Bobadilla v Museo Nacional del Prado, Comité de Empresa del Museo Nacional del Prado and Ministerio Fiscal (C-234/92) [1999] E.C.R. I–4773 271

Terrapin (Overseas) Ltd v Terranova Industrie CA Kapferer & Co (119/75) [1975] E.C.R. 1039; [1976] E.C.R. 1039 ECJ 301, 302, 303

Territorio Histórico de Álava – Diputación Foral de Álava (T-127/99); Comunidad Autónoma del País Vasco and Gasteizko Industria Lurra, SA (T-129/99); Daewoo Electronics Manufacturing España, SA (T-148/99) v Commission of the European Communities [2002] E.C.R. II-1275 380

Tetra Laval BV v Commission of the European Communities (T-5/02) [2002] E.C.R. II–4381 369

Tetra Pak International SA v Commission of the European Communities (T-83/91) [1994] E.C.R. II-755; [1997] 4 C.M.L.R. 726 CFI 341

Tetra Pak International SA v Commission of the European Communities (C-333/94 P) [1997] All E.R. (EC) 4; [1996] E.C.R. I-5951; [1997] 4 C.M.L.R. 662 ECJ 341

Tetra Pak Rausing SA v Commission of the European Communities (T-51/89) [1990] E.C.R. II-309 142

Textilwerke Deggendorf GmbH (TWD) v Commission of the European Communities (T-244/93) [1995] E.C.R. II-2265; [1996] 1 C.M.L.R. 332 ECJ 396

Tideland Signal Ltd v Commission of the European Communities (T-211/02) [2002] E.C.R. II-3781; [2002] 3 C.M.L.R. 33 CFI ... 169, 314

Tiercé Ladbroke SA v Commission of the European Communities (T-504/93) [1997] E.C.R. II-923 307

Tietosuojavaltuutettu v Satakunnan Markkinaporssi Oy (C-73/07) [2007] E.C.R I-7075; [2010] All E.R. (EC) 213 ECJ 148

Togel v Niederosterreichische Gebietskrankenkasse (C-76/97) [1998] E.C.R. I-5357; [1998] 3 C.M.L.R. 768 ECJ 316

Toxic and Dangerous Waste, Re (239/85); sub nom. Commission of the European Communities v Belgium (239/85) [1986] E.C.R. 3645; [1988] 1 C.M.L.R. 248 ECJ 32

Traghetti del Mediterraneo SpA (In Liquidation) v Italy (C-173/03) [2006] All E.R. (EC) 983; [2006] E.C.R. I-5177; [2006] 3 C.M.L.R. 19 ECJ 51, 112

Transacciones Maritimas SA (Tramasa) v Commission of the European Communities (C-12/95 P(R)) [1995] E.C.R. I-467; [1996] 2 C.M.L.R. 580 ECJ 336, 396

Transporoute et Travaux SA v Minister of Public Works (76/81) [1982] E.C.R. 417; [1982] 3 C.M.L.R. 382 ECJ 309, 313

Trapeza tis Ellados AE v Banque Artesia (C-329/03) [2005] E.C.R. I-9341 298

Traunfellner GmbH v Österreichische Autobahnen- und Schnellstraβen-Finanzierungs-AG (Asfinag) (C-421/01) [2003] E.C.R. I-11941 313

Tremblay v Commission of the European Communities (C-91/95 P) [1996] E.C.R. I-5547; [1997] 4 C.M.L.R. 211 ECJ 56, 155

Überseering BV v Nordic Construction Company Baumanagement GmbH (NCC) (C-208/00) [2002] E.C.R. I-9919 268

Unger v Bestuur der Bedrijfsvereniging voor Detailhandel en Ambachten (75/63) [1964] E.C.R. 177; [1964] C.M.L.R. 319 ECJ 143

Unibet (London) Ltd v Justitiekanslern (C-432/05) [2008] All E.R. (EC) 453; [2007] E.C.R. I-2271; [2007] 2 C.M.L.R. 30 ECJ 46

Unión de Pequeños Agricultores (UPA) v Council of the European Union (T-173/98) [1999] E.C.R. II-3357 .... 135, 136, 151

Union de Pequenos Agricultores v Council of the European Union (C-50/00 P) [2003] Q.B. 893; [2003] 2 W.L.R. 795; [2002] E.C.R. I-6677 ECJ 135

Union Royale Belge des Societes de Football Association (ASBL) v Bosman (C-415/93); sub nom. Union des Associations Europeennes de Football (UEFA) v Bosman (C-415/93); Royal Club Liegois SA v Bosman (C-415/93) [1996] All E.R. (EC) 97; [1995] E.C.R. I-4921; [1996] 1 C.M.L.R. 645 ECJ 244

Union Syndicale v Council of the European Communities (175/73) [1974] E.C.R. 917; [1975] 1 C.M.L.R. 131 ECJ 139

Union Syndicale v Council of the European Communities (72/74) [1975] E.C.R. 401; [1975] 2 C.M.L.R. 181 ECJ 136

United Brands Co v Commission of the European Communities (27/76) [1978] E.C.R. 207; [1978] 1 C.M.L.R. 429 ECJ 132, 324, 339

United Kingdom v Council of the European Union (C-77/05) [2007] E.C.R. I-11459; [2008] 2 C.M.L.R. 11 ECJ 202

United Kingdom v European Parliament (C-217/04); sub nom. Validity of Regulation 460/2004, Re (C-217/04) [2006] E.C.R. I-3771; [2006] 3 C.M.L.R. 2 ECJ 200, 435

United Kingdom v European Parliament (C-66/04); sub nom. Validity of Regulation 2065/2003, Re (C-66/04) [2006] All E.R. (EC) 487; [2005] E.C.R. I-10553; [2006] 3 C.M.L.R. 1 ECJ 436

Unitron Scandinavia A/S and 3-S A/S, Danske Svineproducenters Serviceselskab v Ministeriet for Fødevarer, Landbrug og Fiskeri (C-275/98)[1999]E.C.R.I–8291 .. 309

Universale-Bau AG, Bietergemeinschaft: 1) Hinteregger & Söhne Bauges.m.b.H. Salzburg, 2) ÖSTÜ-STETTIN Hoch- und Tiefbau GmbH v Entsorgungsbetriebe Simmering GmbH (C-470/89) [2002] E.C.R. I–11617 ... 309

Ursel Koschitzki v Istituto nazionale della previdenza sociale (INPS) (C-30/04) [2005] E.C.R. I–7389 ... 251

VOF Josanne v Commission of the European Communities (T-82/01) [2003] E.C.R. II-2013 454

VTB-VAB NV v Total Belgium NV (C-261/07); Galatea BVBA v Sanoma Magazines Belgium NV (C-299/07) [2009] 3 C.M.L.R. 17 ECJ ... 496

Vaassen (nee Gobbels) v Beambtenfonds voor het Mijnbedrijf (61/65) [1966] E.C.R. 261; [1966] C.M.L.R. 508 ECJ 144

Van Binsbergen v Bestuur van de Bedrijfsvereniging voor de Metaalnijverheid (33/74) [1974] E.C.R. 1299; [1975] 1 C.M.L.R. 298 ECJ 287, 290

Van Duyn v Home Office (41/74) [1974] E.C.R. 1337; [1975] 1 C.M.L.R. 1 ECJ 138, 253

Van Schijndel v Stichting Pensioenfonds voor Fysiotherapeuten (C-430/93); Van Veen v Stichting Pensioenfonds voor Fysiotherapeuten (C-431/93) [1996] All E.R. (E.C.) 259; [1995] E.C.R. I-4705; [1996] 1 C.M.L.R. 801 ECJ 45, 56

Vandemoortele NV v Commission of the European Communities (C-172/89) [1990] E.C.R. I–4677 ... 140

Vedial SA v Office for Harmonisation in the Internal Market (Trade Marks and Designs) (OHIM) (T-110/01) [2002] E.C.R. II-5275; [2004] E.T.M.R. 102 CFI 196

Velasco Navarro v Fondo de Garantia Salarial (Fogasa) (C-246/06) [2008] All E.R. (EC) 361; [2008] E.C.R. I-105; [2008] 2 C.M.L.R. 6 ECJ ... 34

Verband deutscher Daihatsu-Händler eV v Daihatsu Deutschland GmbH (C-97/96) [1997] E.C.R. I–6843 278

Verbond van Nederlandse Ondernemingen v Inspecteur der Invoerrechten en Accijnzen (51/76); sub nom. Federation of Dutch Industries v Inspector of Customs and Excise (51/76) [1977] E.C.R. 113; [1977] 1 C.M.L.R. 413 ECJ ... 32, 50

Vereeniging ter Bevordering van de Belangen des Boekhandels v Eldi Records BV (106/79) [1980] E.C.R. 1137; [1980] 3 C.M.L.R. 719 ECJ 143

Vereeniging van Cementhandelaren v Commission of the European Communities (8/72) [1972] E.C.R. 977; [1973] C.M.L.R. 7 ECJ 115, 322

Verein für Konsumenteninformation v Österreichische Kreditversicherungs AG (C-364/96) [1999] All E.R. (EC) 183; [1998] E.C.R. I-2949; [1999] 1 C.M.L.R. 1430 ECJ 498

Vereinigte Familiapress Zeitungsverlags- und vertriebs GmbH v Heinrich Bauer Verlag (C-368/95) [1997] E.C.R. I–3689 229

Vereniging Nationaal Overlegorgaan Sociale Werkvoorziening; Gemeente Rotterdam v Minister van Sociale Zaken en Werkgelegenheid en Sociaal Economische Samenwerking West-Brabant v Algemene Directie voor de Arbeidsvoorziening (C-383/06, C-384/06, C-385/06 and C-386/06) [2008] E.C.R. I–1597 ... 421

Vereniging voor Energie, Milieu en Water v Directeur van de Dienst uitvoering en toezicht energie (C-17/03) [2005] E.C.R. I-49831 555

Vestergaard v Spottrup Boligselskab (C-59/00) [2001] E.C.R. I-9505; [2002] 2 C.M.L.R. 42 ECJ 311

Vodafone Espana SA v Commission of the European Communities (T-109/06) [2007] E.C.R. II-5151; [2008] 4 C.M.L.R. 19 CFI ... 346, 509

Volk v Etablissements J Vervaecke SPRL (5/69) [1969] E.C.R. 295; [1969] C.M.L.R. 273 ECJ 143, 326

Volvo AB v Erik Veng (UK) Ltd (238/87) [1988] E.C.R. 6211; [1989] 4 C.M.L.R. 122 ECJ 307

Wagner v Fohrmann (101/63) [1964] E.C.R. 383; [1964] E.C.R. 195; [1964] C.M.L.R. 245 ECJ 83

Wallentin-Hermann v Alitalia – Linee Aeree Italiane SpA (C-549/07) [2009] Bus. L.R. 1016; [2009] 1 Lloyd's Rep. 406; [2009] 2 C.M.L.R. 9 ECJ 55

Walrave v Association Union Cycliste Internationale (36/74) [1974] E.C.R. 1405; [1975] 1 C.M.L.R. 320 ECJ 146, 245

Walter Gill v Commission of the European Communities (C-185/90 P Rev) [1992] E.C.R. I–993 164

Weingut Gustav Decker AG v Hauptzollamt Landau (99/78) [1979] E.C.R. 101 ECJ 37

Wellcome Trust Ltd v Customs and Excise Commissioners (C-155/94) [1996] All E.R. (EC) 589; [1996] E.C.R. I-3013; [1996] 2 C.M.L.R. 909 ECJ 427

Westdeutsche Landesbank Girozentrale and Land Nordrhein-Westfalen v Commission of the European Communities (T-228/99 and T-233/99) E.C.R. II–435 393

Wiedemann v Land Baden-Wurttemberg (C-329/06) [2008] E.C.R. I-4635; [2008] 3 C.M.L.R. 18 ECJ 445

Wielockx v Inspecteur der Directe Belastingen (C-80/94) [1996] 1 W.L.R. 84; [1995] All E.R. (E.C.) 769; [1995] E.C.R. I-2493 ECJ 431

Wilhelm v Bundeskartellamt (14/68) [1969] E.C.R. 1; [1969] C.M.L.R. 100 ECJ 37

Wilhelm Werhahn Hansamuhle v Council of the European Communities (63/72) [1973] E.C.R. 1229 ECJ 118, 121

Wiljo NV v Belgische Staat (C-178/95) [1997] E.C.R. I–585 147

Willy Kempter KG v Hauptzollamt Hamburg-Jonas (C-02/06) [2008] E.C.R. I–411 144

Wilson v Ordre des Avocats du Barreau de Luxembourg (C-506/04) [2007] All E.R. (EC) 403; [2006] E.C.R. I-8613; [2007] 1 C.M.L.R. 7 ECJ 275

Wippel v Peek & Cloppenburg GmbH & Co KG (C-313/02) [2004] E.C.R. I-9483; [2005] 1 C.M.L.R. 9 ECJ 479

Wolfdieter Graf Yorck von Wartenburg v European Parliament (T-42/89) [1990] E.C.R. II–31 ... 169

Worsdorfer (nee Koschniske) v Raad van Arbeid (9/79) [1979] E.C.R. 2717; [1980] 1 C.M.L.R. 87 ECJ ... 37

Wünsche OHG v Einfuhr- und Vorratsstelle für Getreide und Futtermittel (50/71) [1972] E.C.R. 53; [1973] C.M.L.R. 35 54

Wybot v Faure (149/85) [1986] E.C.R. 2391; [1987] 1 C.M.L.R. 819 ECJ 64, 83

Yamanouchi Pharmaceuticals Co Ltd v Comptroller-General of Patents, Designs and Trade Marks (C-110/95) [1997] E.C.R. I-3251; [1997] 3 C.M.L.R. 749 ECJ 195

Züchner v Handelskrankenkasse (Ersatzkasse) Bremen (C-77/95) [1997] All E.R. (EC) 359; [1996] E.C.R. I-5689; [1997] 3 C.M.L.R. 263 ECJ 477

Zuckerfabrik Suderdithmarschen AG v Hauptzollamt Itzehoe (143/88); Zuckerfabrik Soest GmbH v Hauptzollamt Paderborn (92/89) [1991] E.C.R. I-415; [1993] 3 C.M.L.R. 1 ECJ 31

Commission Decisions

ACF Chemiefarma [1969] O.J. L192/5 322
ASPA [1970] O.J. L148/1 322
Airtours/First Choice Decision (IV/M.1524) [2000] O.J. L93/1 ... 338
Adalat/Bayer [1996] O.J. L201/1 ... 321
BL (British Leyland) [1984] O.J. L207/11 339
Boeing v McDonnell Douglas (IV/M 877) [1997] O.J. L336/16 374
Bomee-Stichting [1975] O.J. L329/30 322
Cecimo [1969] O.J. L69/13 322
Christiani and Nielsen [1969] O.J. L165/72 324

Ferrovie dello Stato (FS)/Georg
   Verkehrsorganisation (GVG) ... 345
General Electric/Honeywell (Case
   M.2220, Decision of July 3,
   2001) and Microsoft 374
Franco-Japanese Ballbearings Decision
   [1974] O.J. L 343/19 327
Irish Sugar Plc (IV/34.621) [1997]
   O.J. L258/1 338
Kodak Decision [1970] O.J.
   L147/24 324
Nestlé/Perrier Decision [1992] O.J.
   L356/1 113
Price Waterhouse/Coopers & Lybrand
   (IV/M.1016) 340
Price Waterhouse v Coopers &
   Lybrand [1999] O.J. L50/27 374
Reuter/BASF Decision [1976] O.J.
   L254/40 323
Rieckermann Decision [1968] O.J. L
   276/25 327
Sea Containers v Stena Sealink –
   Interim measures [1994] O.J.
   L15/8 341
Société Française de Messageries
   Chronopost and Securitpost
   I.P.(96)126 380
Trans-Atlantic Conference Agree-
   ment for abuse of a dominant
   position: press release IP/98/811
   of September 16, 1998 455
Welded Steel Mesh Cartel Decision
   [1989] O.J. L260/1 324

National Courts

Belgium

Belgian State v Fromagerie Franco-
   Suisse. *See* Minister for Eco-
   nomic Affairs v SA Fromagerie
   Franco-Suisse "Le Ski"

Minister for Economic Affairs v SA
   Fromagerie Franco-Suisse "Le
   Ski" [1972] C.M.L.R. 330 Cour
   de Cassation (Belgium) 49

France

Administration des Contributions
   Indirectes v Ramel [1971]
   C.M.L.R. 315 Cour de Cassation
   (F) 48
Administration des Douanes v
   Societe Cafes Jacques Vabre;
   Administration des Douanes v
   J Weigel et Compagnie Sarl; sub
   nom. J Weigel et Compagnie Sarl
   and La Societe des Cafes Jacques
   Vabre SA v Directeur General
   des Douanes et des Droits Indi-
   rects and L'Agent Judiciaire du
   Treso [1975] 2 C.M.L.R. 336
   Cour de Cassation (F)f 47, 49
Boisdet, Re [1991] 1 C.M.L.R. 3
   Conseil d'Etat (F) 49
Recueil Dalloz-Sirey Jurisprudence
   March 1, 1968 Conseil d'Etat ... 48
Ruling of March 1, 1968 ((1968)
   Recueil Dalloz-Sirey Jurispru-
   dence 286) the French Conseil
   d'Etat 48
Syndicat Général des Fabricants de
   Semoules v Direction des Indus-
   tries Agricoles [1970] C.M.L.R.
   395 Conseil d'Etat (F) 47

Table of Treaties and Conventions

1883 Paris Convention on the
Protection of Industrial
Property (March 20,
1883) 196, 301
1944 Chicago Convention
(December 7, 1944) . . . 440, 452
1949 North Atlantic Treaty
(Washington DC, April 4
1949) 578
Treaty establishing the
Council of Europe (May 5,
1949, London) 13
1950 European Convention for the
Protection of Human Rights
and Fundamental
Freedoms (November 4,
1950) 53, 139, 571
Art.8 248
1951 Geneva Convention (July 28,
1981) 256
Treaty establishing the
European Coal and Steel
Community (ECSC)
(April 18, 1951,
Paris) 8, 9, 14, 16, 42,
60, 62, 84, 107,
111, 134, 214, 350,
385, 397, 556, 557
Art.7 60
Art.9 . . . . 8, 107
(5) 8
(6) 8
Art.21(3) 62
Art.65 350
Art.66 350
Art.67 350
Art.85 558
Art.86 558
Art.88 111
Art.97 . . . . 42, 557
1957 Convention on certain
institutions common to the
three Communities
(March 25, 1957) 9
Treaty establishing the
European Atomic Energy
Community (EURATOM)
(March 25, 1957,
Rome) 3, 4, 9, 15, 16,
42, 168, 182, 214,
470, 557

Art.8(1) 537
Art.52(2)(b) 182, 559
Arts 53–56 182
Art.54 59
Art.101 597
Art.103 597
Art.134 182
Art.140a 168
Art.172(4) 123
Treaty establishing the
European Community
(EC Treaty, Treaty of
Rome) (formerly European
Economic Community
(EEC Treaty); modified
by the Treaty on European
Union and the Treaty of
Amsterdam 3, 4, 8, 15,
16, 26, 42, 47, 60, 90,
98, 106, 107, 176, 214,
222, 224, 243, 264, 297,
397, 479, 485, 504, 530, 553,
557, 561, 563, 568, 572, 604
Preamble 25
Art.1 6
Art.2 . . . 5, 90, 91, 98, 101, 540
Art.3 . . . . . . 5, 91, 99, 123, 437
(1) 541
(b) 580
(d) 414
(g) 438
(h) 434
(q) 488
Art.4 . . . 99, 123, 176, 460, 484
(1) 91, 460
(2) 460
(3) 74, 460
Art.5 603
(2) 100
Art.6 . . . . . . 438, 442, 542, 543
(1) 6
Art.7 59
(1) 126
(2) 59
Art.8 . . . . 16, 59, 176
Art.9 59
Art.10 . . . . . . 6, 31, 33, 44, 46,
49, 56, 142
(1) 43
Art.11 . . . . . 6, 7, 152, 167, 581
Arts 11–17 7

Art.11a 6, 7
Art.12 .... 93, 153,
244, 309, 475
Art.13 .... 66, 478
Art.14 .... 228, 435, 487
(1) 435
(2) 4, 19, 223, 503
Art.15 .... 223, 234
Art.16 222
Art.17 .... 40, 240,
241, 572
(1) 239
Arts 17–22 .... 4, 238
Art.18 239
(1) 4, 238
(2) 69, 239
Art.19 240
(1) 4
Art.20 .... 5, 241
Art.21 ...... 5, 73, 241, 572
(1) 74
Art.22 241
Art.23 224
(1) 580
(2) 228
Art.24 .... 224, 228
Art.25 225
Art.26 .... 93, 225, 581
Art.27a 580
a–b 6
Art.28 .... 224, 227,
233, 236, 302
Art.29 227
Arts 29–42 148
Art.30 .... 153, 187,
229, 232,
263, 299,
301, 302
Art.31 .... 153, 186,
195, 261, 262
(2) 224
Art.32 400
(1) 400
(2) 400
(3) 400, 414
(4) 400
Arts 32–38 414
Art.33(1) 401
(b) 401
(c) 401
(d) 401
(e) 401
(2)(a) 400
(b) 400
(3) 29
Art.34 404

(1) 400
(c) 400
Art.35 226
Art.36 .... 255, 310,
342, 573, 603
Art.38 114
Art.39 239
(2) 238, 246,
248, 254, 267
(3) 253, 299
(a) 247
(b) 247
(c) 247
(d) 250
(4) 253, 254, 284
Arts 39–42 243
Art.40 .... 180, 246, 248
Arts 40–40b 6
Art.42 250
(1) 180
(a) 250
(b) 250
Art.43 309
(1) 267, 268
(2) 266, 268, 269, 323
(3) 238
Arts 43–48 243
Art.44 .... 95, 268
(1) 278, 283
(2) 278
(c) 270
(e) 269
(f) 270
Art.45 .... 290, 310
(1) 284
(2) 285, 291
Art.46 299
(1) 284, 290, 299
Art.47 .... 271, 507
(1) 271, 291, 552
(2) 271, 513, 552
Art.48 .... 54, 153,
238, 515
(1) 238, 268,
278, 291
(2) 268
Art.49 .... 21, 153,
286, 287, 404
(1) 238, 267, 297
(2) 284, 286
Arts 49–55 .... 243, 286
Art.50 288
(1) 223, 289
(2) 290
(3) 223, 286,
287, 289

Art.51(1) 289
(2) 291
Art.54(1) 267
Art.55 . . . . 290, 299,
310, 507, 553
Art.56 289
(1) 298
Arts 56–60 289
Art.57(1) 298
(2) 298, 299
Art.58(1)(a) 299
(b) 299
Art.59 . . . . 189, 298
Art.60 . . . . 189, 255, 298
Art.61 255
Arts 61–69 238
Art.62 256
Arts 62–63 256
Art.63 257
(1) 267, 284
(5) 257
Arts 63–64 256
Art.64(1) 260
Art.65 258
Art.66 255
Art.67 298
Art.69(3) 257
Arts 70–80 438
Art.71 . . . . 440, 442, 443
(1) 181, 438
(c) 442
(2) 438
Art.72 . . . . 98, 439
Art.73 . . . . 443, 447
Art.75(1) 444
(3) 131
Art.77 114
Art.80 . . . . 439, 450
(2) 199, 343,
439, 440
Art.81 . . . . 110, 319, 320,
323, 334, 343,
438, 455, 507
(1) 326
(2) 327
(3) 114, 328,
331, 343, 455
Arts 81–85 319
Art.82 . . . . 110, 307,
319, 320, 337,
438, 455, 507
(2)(a) 131
Art.83 341
Art.85(2) 114
Art.86 . . . . 113, 443
(3) 34, 114

Art.87 443
(3)(a) 521
(b) 469
(d) 488
Art.88 . . . . 394, 395
(2) 98, 114, 167
(3) 110, 394, 395
Art.89 118
Art.90 36
(2) 425, 426
Art.91 427
Art.92 427
Art.93 . . . . 395, 427
Art.94 . . . . 228, 434, 437
Art.95 . . . . 228, 435,
436, 496, 507
(1) 434, 435, 436, 552
(2) 437
(3) 436
(4) 436
(5) 436, 542
(6) 542
(9) 436
Arts 95–97 434
Art.96 437
(2) 437
Art.97 . . . . 35, 100, 437
Arts 97–100 238
Art.98 99
Arts 98–104 460
Arts 98–124 459
Art.99 . . . . 35, 99,
100, 189, 461
(1) 101, 460
(2) 460
(3) 460, 461
(4) 461
(6) 461
Art.100 461
(1) 233
Art.101 . . . . 189, 461, 463
Art.102 . . . . 189, 461, 463
Art.103 . . . . 189, 461
Art.104 . . . . 189, 461,
462, 466, 525
(2) 462
(4) 462, 529
(5) 462
(6) 462, 467
(7) 29, 529
(9) 462
(10) 462
(11) 462, 468
(14) 462
Art.105 176
(1) 460

(3) 177
(5) 177
(6) 189
Arts 105–111 463
Art.106(2) 189
Art.107 59
(2) 177
(3) 176
(4) 189
Art.110 465
(1) 178, 465
(3) 465
Art.111 . . . . 189, 571
(2) 35, 100
(3) 563
(4) 189
Art.112(1) 177
Art.113(1) 177
Art.114 . . . . 59, 467
(1) 178
(2) 178, 465
Art.115 435
Art.116 100
Art.119 189
(1) 189
(2) 463
Art.120 189
Art.121 189
(1) 460
Art.122 189
Art.123 189
Art.125 100
Arts 125–130 . . . . 470, 485
Art.126 99
Art.127(5) 176
Art.128 99
(2) 66, 485
Art.129 . . . . . . 59, 93, 101, 437
Art.130 . . . . 66, 101
Art.131 580
Arts 131–134 580
Art.133 . . . . 167, 570, 581
(1) 581, 582
(3) 581
(4) 581
(5) 308, 582
(6) 582
(7) 308
Art.136 471
(1) 471
(2) 470, 480
(3) 471
Arts 136–145 470
Arts 136–150 470
Art.137 471
(1) 470

(3) 181
(4) 475
Art.138 . . . . 62, 101,
471, 475
Art.139 475
(2)(b) 470
Art.140 . . . . 114, 471, 477
(1) 192
Art.141 . . . . 471, 474,
477, 478
(2) 478
Art.145 75
Art.146 480
Arts 146–148 . . . . . . 470, 479
Art.149(1) 481
(3) 484
(4) 437
Art.150 . . . . 249, 483
(4) 35, 100, 181
Art.151 488
(1) 488
(5) 437
Art.152 . . . . 438, 491
(1) 442
(4) 181, 475
(c) 437
(5) 492
Art.153 . . . . 438, 442, 496
Art.154 554
(1) 181, 487, 515
(4) 488
Arts 154–156 508
Art.155 554
(2) 516
Art.156 . . . . 475, 516
Art.157 . . . . 502, 508
(1) 504
(2) 505
(3) 505
Art.158 . . . . 480, 487,
505, 519, 519
Arts 158–162 519
Art.159 . . . . 480, 519, 521
(2) 181, 528
(3) 181, 527
Art.161 . . . . 442, 525, 529
(1) 181
Art.162(1) 181
Art.163(1) 531
Arts 163–172 508
Arts 163–173 530
Art.164 531
(b) 531
(c) 531
(d) 531
Art.165(1) 530

Art.166 . . . . 40, 100
Arts 166–170 531
Art.167 535
Art.168 535
Art.169 . . . . 475, 535
Art.170 535
Art.171 . . . . 212, 533
Art.173 . . . . 122, 539
Art.174 . . . . 438, 541,
                                542, 550
  (2) 492
  (4) 549
Arts 174–176 540
Art.175 542
  (1) 181, 500, 548
  (2) 181, 543
  (3) 40, 543
Art.176 542
Art.177(3) 601
Arts 177–181 563
Art.179 602
  (2) 603
Art.180 . . . . 73, 603
Art.181 . . . . 484, 603
Art.181a 567
Art.182 . . . . 603, 604
Arts 182–188 608
Art.185 475
Art.187 . . . . 98, 605
Art.189 . . . . 61, 65
  (2) 61
Arts 189–201 61
Art.190(4) 65, 71
  (5) 65
Art.191 81
Art.192 . . . . 67, 68, 93, 118
Art.193 72
Art.194 . . . . 72, 241
Art.195 . . . . 72, 73
  (2) 128
Art.196 75
  (2) 83
Art.197 . . . . 73, 74
  (1) 82
Art.198 83
  (4) 73
Art.200 75
Art.201 76
Art.202 . . . . 91, 95
Art.203 91
Art.205(1) 87, 95,
                             96, 97, 98
  (2) 87, 96,
                            97, 98, 116
  (3) 98
Art.206 95

Art.207 96
  (1) 59, 103
  (2) 105
  (3) 104
Art.208 . . . . 67, 93, 96, 118
Art.210 96
Art.211 106
Art.212 123
Art.213(1) 107
  (2) 77, 108,
                             128, 166
  (3) 107
Art.214 . . . . 75, 76
  (1) 107
  (2) 40, 77, 108
Art.215 . . . . 76, 569, 571
Art.216 128
Art.217(2) 109
Art.218(2) 123
  (4) 121
Art.219(1) 114
Art.220 . . . . 57, 165
  (1) 165
Art.221 127
  (2) 127
Art.222(2) 166
Art.223 40
  (1) 125, 127
  (3) 127
  (6) 156, 159
Art.224 . . . . 88, 166
  (2) 166
  (3) 166
  (5) 167
  (6) 167
Art.225 . . . . 154, 167, 169
  (1) 130, 165
  (2) 155, 168, 171
  (3) 130, 168, 169
Art.225a 168, 169, 170
  (4) 170
  (5) 170
  (6) 170
Art.226 . . . . 110, 111, 112,
                  129, 182, 313, 547
Art.227 130
Art.228 . . . . 129, 131, 550
  (1) 93, 131
  (2) 111, 154, 547
Art.229 . . . . 129, 131, 151
Art.230 . . . . 37, 38, 39,
                        80, 94, 113,
                    129, 132, 133,
                    136, 138, 141,
                142, 151, 152, 153,
            167, 191, 465, 570

(1) 65
(3) 134, 158, 173
(4) 137
(5) 132, 151
(7) 132
Art.231 .... 140, 141, 144
Art.232 .... 67, 80, 93,
113, 129, 133, 141,
152, 157, 167, 442
(1) 173
Art.233 .... 133, 140, 141, 142
Art.234 .... 46, 54, 129,
133, 136, 142, 143,
144, 145, 566, 570
(1)(b) 143
(2) 145
Art.235 .... 129, 132, 149, 168
Art.236 .... 129, 132
Art.237 ..... 32, 129, 133, 153
(a) 113
Art.238 .... 129, 149, 154, 168
Art.239 .... 131, 154
Art.240 .... 129, 154
(3) 104
Art.241 .... 130, 132,
133, 136, 151
Art.242 .... 130, 154, 162
Art.243 .... 130, 154,
162, 163
Art.244 38
Art.245 155
Art.246 173
(1) 173
Art.247(2) 173
(4) 173
(6) 173
(7) 128, 166, 173
Art.248 .... 79, 122, 174
(1) 174
(2) 174
(3) 174
(4) 72, 174, 175
Art.249 .... 33, 88,
113, 114,
133, 434, 465
(2) 43
(3) 33, 51
Art.250 67
(1) 67, 69, 94, 98, 121
(2) 66, 94, 103, 120
Art.251 .... 11, 67, 68, 69,
70, 81, 95, 101,
131, 241, 256, 257,
261, 262, 263, 271,
285, 288, 435, 437,
438, 439, 461, 475,

478, 484, 488,
499, 521, 527,
535, 536, 542, 567
(4) 67, 98
(5) 67, 98
Art.253 .... 36, 66, 70, 92
Art.254 .... 37, 465
(3) 132
Art.255 .... 104, 169
Art.256 38
(4) 154
Art.257 180
Art.259 180
Art.263 .... 180, 181
Art.265(3) 181
(4) 181
Art.267 183
(a) 521
Art.268 .... 67, 98
(3) 215, 21
Art.272 .... 65, 67, 95,
98, 216, 217
(2) 122
(3) 122
Arts 272–280 77
Art.273 .... 67, 79, 98
Art.274 .... 79, 122
Art.275 .... 79, 122
Art.276 .... 79, 122
Art.279 122
Art.280(1) 219
Art.281 .... 59, 565
Art.282 .... 59, 60
Art.284 110
Art.286 97
(2) 189
Art.288 .... 54, 129,
132, 133, 141
(2) 150
Art.292 131
Art.296 233
(2) 98
Art.297 233
Art.298 233
Art.299 .... 11, 223
Art.300 .... 53, 80, 563,
570, 571, 603
(1) 60
(2) 60, 570
(3) 71
(6) 122, 565
Art.301 569
Arts 302–304 572
Art.303 488
Art.304 122
Art.307 .... 55, 566

Art.308 . . . . .93, 141, 436,
521, 540, 553
Art.310 . . . . 569, 570
Protocol (No.2) integrating
the Schengen *acquis* into
the framework of the
European Union [1997]
O.J. C340/93 242
Protocol No.18 on the Statute
of the European System of
Central Banks and the
European Central Bank 59
Art.34(1) 30

1959 European Convention on
Mutual Assistance in
Criminal Matters 264
1960 European Free Trade Association
Treaty (January 4, 1960)
Art.4 224
Paris Convention on Third-party
Liability in the Field of
Nuclear Energy 560
1961 European Social Charter 471
1964 Yaoundé Convention [1964]
O.J. 1431 . . . . 604, 605
1965 Treaty establishing a Single
Council and a Single
Commission of the
European Communities
(the Merger Treaty) (April 8,
1965) 9, 16, 60,
214, 319, 572
Art.1 60
Art.9 60
Art.11(2) 60
Art.18 75
Protocol on the Privileges and
Immunities of the European
Communities attached to the
Merger Treaty 64, 572
Art.9 64
Art.10 64
Art.18 65
1967 Protocol of January 31,
1967 256
1968 Convention on the mutual
recognition of companies and
legal persons (February 29,
1968) 148
Protocol concerning the
interpretation by the Court of
the Convention (September 27,
1968) 148
Art.5(1) 258
Art.27(1) 258
Art.43(1) 258

Convention on Early Notification
of a Nuclear Accident and on
Assistance in the Case of
Nuclear Accident or
Radiological Emergency . . . 560
1969 Vienna Convention on the
Law of Treaties 582
1970 Treaty amending certain
budgetary provisions
(April 22, 1970) 9
1972 British Accession Act
Art.28 12
Treaty on the Accession of
Denmark, Ireland and the
United Kingdom (Treaty
of Brussels) (January 22,
1972) 9, 17
Art.109 605
Art.115(1) 605
1973 International Convention for
the Prevention of Pollution
from Ships (MARPOL
73/78) 455
Munich Convention on the
Grant of European Patents
(European Patent Convention)
(October 5, 1973) . . . 303, 335
1974 Convention for the safety of
life at sea 456
1975 Lomé Convention I 604
Paris Convention for the
Prevention of Marine
Pollution from Land-
Based Sources [1975]
O.J. L194/5 549
Treaty amending Certain Financial
Provisions of the Treaties
establishing the European
Communities and the Merger
Treaty (July 22, 1975) [1977]
O.J. L359/1 . . . . . . 9, 173, 214
1976 Act concerning the direct
election of the European
Parliament (September 20,
1976) 9
Art.4(1) 81
Art.5 63
Art.6(1) 63, 83
(2) 63, 83
Treaty on the secession of
Greenland (September 20,
1976) 9
Act concerning the Election of the
Representatives of the Assembly
by Direct Universal Suffrage
[1976] O.J. L278/1 17

1977   Munich Convention on the
        European Patent (October
        1977) 301
1978   Convention on safety in
        shipping [1978] O.J.
        L194/17 456
        European Agreement
        concerning the work of
        crews of vehicles engaged
        in international road
        transport (AETR) [1978]
        O.J. L95/1 446
1979   Convention for safe
        containers [1979] O.J.
        L125/18 456
        Convention on standards of
        training, certification and
        watch-keeping for sea-farers
        [1979] O.J. L33/31 456
        Treaty on the accession of
        Greece (May 28, 1979)
        [1979] O.J. L291/1 ..... 9, 17
1980   Convention on the law
        applicable to contractual
        obligations, Rome
        Convention [1980] O.J.
        L266/1 .... 56, 260
        Lomé Convention II ... 604, 605
1982   Bonn Convention on the
        Conservation of Migratory
        Species of Wild Animals
        [1982] O.J. L210/10 549
        UN Convention on the Law
        of the Sea (Montego Bay,
        December 10, 1982) 455
1983   Convention on maritime
        Search and Rescue (SAR)
        [1983] O.J. L237/34 456
1985   Convention for the safety
        of fishing vessels, see
        Council Resolution [1985]
        O.J. L72 /110 456
        Schengen Agreement (June 14,
        1985) 241
        Treaty concerning the accession
        of Portugal and Spain
        (March 9/30, 1985) 9
        Art.187 216
        Art.374 216
1986   Convention on Early
        Notification of a Nuclear
        Accident and on Assistance
        in the Case of Nuclear
        Accident or Radiological
        Emergency 560
        Lomé Convention III ... 604, 605

        Single European Act (February
        17/28, 1986) 4, 9, 10, 19,
                    61, 65, 66, 71, 98,
                    99, 117, 118, 165,
                    221, 228, 402, 479,
                    505, 519, 530, 540, 542
        Art.8 71
        Art.9 71
        Art.11 165
1988   Montreal Protocol on
        Substances that Deplete
        the Ozone Layer [1988]
        O.J. L297/8 549
        Vienna Convention on the
        Protection of the Ozone
        Layer [1988] O.J. L297/8 .. 549
1989   Charter of the Fundamental
        Social Rights of Workers
        (Social Charter) 471
        Court of the Convention on
        the law applicable to
        contractual obligations
        [1989] O.J. L48/1 ... 148, 260
        Lomé Convention IV
        (ACP-EEC Convention,
        December 15, 1989) 80,
                            584, 596,
                            604, 605
        Madrid Protocol System
        for the International
        Registration of Trade
        Marks OAMI-ONLINE
        (Madrid, June 27, 1989) .. 196
1992   Agreement establishing the
        European Economic Area
        (EEA) (May 2, 1992) .. 20, 21,
                            80, 147,
                            156, 157, 192
        Treaty on European Union
        (Maastricht Treaty)
        (modified by the
        Amsterdam, Nice and
        Lisbon Treaties) [2008]
        O.J. C115/1 ...... 3, 4, 9, 10,
                    16, 19, 22, 27, 46,
                    53, 54, 66, 68, 71,
                    74, 87, 92, 96, 98,
                    99, 101, 106, 107,
                    119, 125, 126, 133,
                    139, 152, 173, 181,
                    205, 206, 208, 221,
                    233, 243, 246, 255,
                    289, 435, 458, 471,
                    480, 504, 506, 519,
                    530, 542, 553, 561, 563,
                    569, 576, 578, 602 EU

Preamble 573
  para.11 573
Title I 19
Title II 19
Title III 19
Title IV 6, 19, 569
Title V 3, 11
  Ch.I 561
Title VI 3, 187, 206,
                208, 243, 263,
                264, 547
Title VII 264
Art.A.2 3
Art.1 ...... 6, 9, 60, 100, 119
Art.2 .... 6, 9, 21, 87, 152
Art.3 .... 5, 60, 90,
                99, 176, 520
  (1)(a) 114
  (2) 90, 101
  (3) 90, 101, 222
  (4) 90
Art.4 .... 50, 92
  (3) 31, 33, 43,
                44, 46, 49, 50,
                51, 52, 56, 142
Art.5 487
  (1) 28, 92, 114
  (2) 28, 92, 137
  (3) 28, 100, 603
  (4) 28
Art.6(1) 53, 54,
                125, 139, 609
  (2) 53
  (3) 53
Art.7 .... 6, 95
  (1) 6, 71, 87
  (2) 87
  (3) 6
  (4) 6
Art.8 90
Art.9 60
  (1) 60
Art.10(4) 81
Art.11(2) 60
  (4) 241
Art.13(1) 5, 59, 85,
                176, 465
  (2) 65
Art.14 ...... 61, 62, 207, 435
  (1) 29, 65, 82
  (2) 62, 63, 71
  (3) 63
Art.15 29
  (1) 87
  (2) 104
  (3) 86, 92

  (4) 86
  (5) 86
  (6) 86
  (d) 74
Art.16(1) 91, 92
  (2) 91
  (3) 96
  (4) 87, 97, 98, 116
  (5) 96, 97, 98, 116
  (6) 87
  (8) 104
  (9) 86, 87, 102
Art.17 .... 77, 108
  (1) 106, 110, 114
  (2) 106
  (3) 107
  (4) 107
  (5) 107
  (6) 109
  (7) 109
  (8) 109
Art.18(1) 109
  (3) 102
  (4) 109
  (7) 71
Art.19 ...... 57, 125, 165, 169
  (1) 125, 165
  (2) 127, 166
  (3) 125
Art.20 6
  (1) 7
  (2) 7
Art.21 .... 561, 563, 603
  (1) 563
  (2) 564
Art.22 .... 561, 563, 564
Art.23 561
Arts 23–41 573
Arts 23–46 .... 561, 569
Art.24 563
  (1) 561, 573
  (2) 573
Art.25 576
Art.26 576
  (13) 87
Arts 23–46 .... 7, 153
Art.27 .... 7, 167, 579
  (1) 60
  (3) 572
Art.28 576
Art.29 .... 243, 255,
                262, 576
Arts 29–39 243
Art.31(1) 573
  (2) 576
Art.32 576

Art.34 264
(2) 576
(b) 264
Art.33 576
Art.35 .... 264, 576
Art.36 579
(1) 73
(2) 73, 74
Art.37 576
(2) 66
Art.38 576
Art.40 .... 7, 264, 573
Art.40a 264
Art.40b 264
Art.41 577
Art.42 .... 573, 577, 578
(1) 577
(2) 578
(3) 205, 577, 578
(4) 578
(6) 579
(7) 579
Arts 42–46 577
Art.43 .... 7, 578, 579
(2) 578
Arts 43–45 .... 7, 152, 167
Art.43b 7
Art.44 578
Art.45 205
Art.46 579
Art.47 4
Art.48 93
(2) 66
(2)–(5) 10
(6) 11, 66
(7) 11, 64
Art.49 .... 21, 71, 609
(1) 21
Art.50 223
Art.52 43
(1) 11
Art.54(1) 270
Art.67 284
Art.69 243
Art.90 45

1993   Basel Convention on the
Control of Transport of
Hazardous Waste [1993]
O.J. L39/1 549
Convention for the prevention
of pollution from ships
[1993] O.J. L194/5 456
Lugano Convention establishing
a Civil Liability Scheme for
Activities Dangerous to the
Environment 548

Rio de Janeiro Convention
on Biological Diversity
[1993] O.J. L309/1 549
1994   General Agreement on Trade
in Services (GATS) 512
New York Convention on
Climate Change [1994]
O.J. L33/11 549
Treaty concerning the
accession of Austria,
Finland, (Norway) and
Sweden (June 24, 1994) ... 9, 21
WTO Agreement on
Trade-Related Aspects
of Intellectual Property
(TRIPS) 308
Art.50 54
Vienna Convention on
Nuclear Safety 560
1995   Convention on the use of
information technology for
customs purposes and
Agreement on provisional
application between certain
Member States [1995]
O.J. C316/33 226
Europol Convention (Brussels,
26 July 1995) 187, 208
1996   Hague Convention on
Parental Responsibility and
Protection of Children 260
WIPO Copyright Treaty
(December 20, 1996) 308
WIPO Performances and
Phonograms Treaty
(December 20, 1996) 308
1997   Energy Charter Treaty 554
Protocol on the location of
the seats of the institutions
and certain bodies and
departments of the European
Union and of Europol
annexed to the Treaty on
European Union and the
Treaties establishing the
European Union and the
European Atomic Energy
Union [1997] O.J.
C340/112 106
Treaty of Amsterdam
(October 2, 1997) 3, 9,
22, 23, 61, 65,
66, 68, 71, 83, 87,
98, 125, 221, 242,
243, 270, 291, 298,
470, 479, 485, 487,

504, 506, 516, 530,
540, 541, 544, 549, 552
Preamble 221, 543
Art.2 543
(1) 243
2000 Charter of Fundamental
Rights of the European
Union (December 7,
2000) 26, 53,
135, 139
Convention Implementing the
Schengen Agreement (CISA)
[2000] O.J. L239/19 241
Arts 54–58 140
Art.96(2)(a) 243
Cotonou Agreement between
the members of the African,
Caribbean and Pacific Group
of States of the on part and
the European Community
and its Member States
of the other part (June 23,
2000) [2000] O.J.
L317/1 . . . . 80, 604, 605
Art.1 604
Art.16 607
Art.21 605
Art.23 605
Art.37 605
Art.44 606
Art.55 605
Art.62 606
Art.63 606
Art.74 605
Arts 84–90 606
Art.96 607
Art.98 607
2001 Convention for the Unification
of Certain Rules for
International Carriage
by Air (the Montreal
Convention) [2001] O.J.
L194/38 . . . . 55, 452, 453
Treaty of Nice (February 26,
2001) [2001] O.J. C80/1 3,
9, 23, 27,
37, 61, 65, 66,
68, 80, 98, 99,
165, 169, 174, 221,
473, 479, 504,
506, 548, 552
Art.2(17) 61
(34) 80
(38) 37
Protocol providing additional
measures for the purpose of

the fight against crime,
including organised crime,
money laundering and
financial crime; it concerns
information on bank
accounts held by persons
subject to criminal
investigation, on banking
transactions, fiscal offences,
etc. [2001] O.J. C326/3 . . . 264
2002 Agreement on Co-operation
and Customs Union, [2002]
O.J. L84/43 12
Protocol on the Statute
of the Court [2002] O.J.
L218/1 . . . . 147, 154, 155
2003 Treaty on the Accession of the
Czech Republic, Estonia,
Cyprus, Latvia, Lithuania,
Hungary, Malta, Poland,
Slovenia and the Slovak
Republic (April 16, 2003)
[2003] O.J. L326/1 . 9, 23, 252
2004 Agreement on trade in certain
steel products [2004] O.J.
L384/23 587
2005 Aarhus Convention on Access
to Information, Public
Participation in Decision-
making and Access to
Justice in Environmental
Matters 544, 550
Accession Treaty of Bulgaria
and Romania (April 25,
2005) 9, 24
Art.7(2) 62
Art.9 62
Art.24 62
International Convention for
the Protection of New
Varieties of Plants [2005]
O.J. L192/63 197
2007 Treaty of Lisbon 3, 9, 15,
25, 26, 27, 49, 60,
68, 93, 99, 107,
109, 112, 127, 131,
134, 136, 221, 223,
259, 382, 399,
465, 479, 535,
552, 569, 581
2008 Treaty on the Functioning
of the European Union
(May 9, 2008) 3, 4, 9,
11, 26, 27, 28,
29, 34, 39, 87,
90, 97, 100, 106,

125, 126, 138, 145, 152,
166, 176, 177, 186, 187,
188, 221, 223, 229, 233,
238, 244, 247, 255, 257,
258, 286, 290, 309, 320,
326, 399, 400, 415, 434,
435, 438, 460, 464, 470,
471, 485, 487, 489, 504,
520, 530, 557, 561, 567,
568, 569, 571, 573, 577,
580, 581, 582, 583, 601
Preamble 222
Recital (1) 222
Pt2 238
Title III 6, 11, 470, 487
  Pt 3 399
Title IV Ch.2 268
  Pt 3 238
Title V 148, 238, 243
Title VI 439
Title VII 425, 540
Title VIII 459
Title IX 485
Title X 485
Title XIX 530
Title XVI (Arts 170–172) .. 442
Art.2(4) 90
Art.3 .... 7, 90, 99, 123,
           222, 223, 435, 459
  (1) 28, 100, 320
    (a) 222
    (b) 222
    (c) 459
    (e) 580
  (3) 91
  (4) 434
Arts 3–6 .... 90, 541,
                 573, 577
Arts.4 .... 100, 123, 222,
            414, 437, 459
  (1)–(2) 90
  (2) 470
    (b) 470, 519
    (e) 519
    (g) 438
  (3) 91
  (4) 91, 567, 568
Art.5 .... 123, 434,
               437, 459
  (1) 460
  (4) 601
Art.6 .... 26, 100,
            123, 459, 471
  (c) 488
Art.11 ..... 438, 442, 542, 543
Art.12 .... 438, 442

Art.13(2) 59, 126
Art.14 222
  (2) 61
Art.15(3) 104
Art.16 189
  (3) 95
  (4) 97
Art.17 75
Art.18 .... 244, 309
  (2) 93
Art.19 .... 66, 478
Art.20(2) 239
  (a) 4
  (b) 4, 240
  (c) 5, 240
  (d) 241
  (3) 95
Arts 20–25 .... 4, 238
Art.21 .... 239, 240
  (1) 4, 238, 239
  (3) 69
Art.22(1) 240
  (2) 63
Art.23 .... 5, 241, 572
Art.24(1) 241
  (2) 5, 581
  (3) 5
Art.25(2) 241
Art.26 .... 228, 487
  (2) 4, 19, 223
Art.27 .... 44, 234
  (1) 223
Art.28 224
  (1) 580
  (2) 228
Art.29 .... 224, 228
Art.30 225
  (1)(d) 401
Art.31 .... 93, 225, 581
Art.32 580
Art.33(1) 399
Art.34 .... 224, 227, 232,
            233, 236, 302
Art.35 227
Art.36 .... 229, 232, 299,
            301, 302, 310
Art.37(2) 224
Art.38(1) 400
  (2) 400
  (3) 414
  (4) 400
Arts 38–44 414
Art.39 404
  (1) 401
    (b) 401
    (c) 401

(e) 401
(2) 269
   (a) 400
   (b) 400
   (c) 400
Arts 39–44 400
Art.40(1) 400
   (c) 400
Art.42 342
Art.43(2) 284, 404
Art.44 114
Art.45 239
  (2) 246, 248,
254, 267
  (3) 253, 299
   (a) 247
   (b) 247
   (c) 247
   (d) 250
  (4) 253, 284
Arts 45–48 .... 238, 243
Art.46 .... 180, 246, 248
Art.47 59
Art.48 250
  (1) 180
   (a) 250
   (b) 250
Art.49 309
  (1) 267, 268
  (2) 266, 268,
269, 323
Arts 49–54 243
Arts 49–55 238
Art.50(1) 278, 283
  (2) 278
   (c) 270
   (e) 268, 269
   (f) 270
Art.51 .... 290, 310
  (1) 284
  (2) 285, 290, 291
Art.52 .... 290, 299
  (1) 284, 299
Art.53 .... 507, 513
  (1) 271, 291, 552
  (2) 271, 552
Art.54 .... 54, 153,
238, 323, 515
  (1) 268, 278, 291
  (2) 268
Art.55(3) 223
Art.56 .... 153, 286,
287, 298, 310
  (1) 267, 284, 297
Arts 56–62 ..... 238, 243, 286
Art.57(1) 288, 289

(2) 223, 290
(3) 286, 287, 289
Art.58(1) 289
  (2) 291
Art.62 .... 290, 291, 299,
310, 507, 552
Art.63 289
  (1) 298
Arts 63–66 289
Art.64(1) 298
  (2) 298, 299
Art.65(1)(a) 299
  (b) 299
Art.66 .... 189, 298
Art.67 262
  (1) 255
  (2)–(4) 255
Art.68 255
Art.69 255
Art.70 255
Art.71 255
Art.72 260
Art.74 255
Art.75 .... 189, 255, 298
Art.76 255
Arts 67–89 .... 148, 238
Art.71 573
Art.77(2) 256
Arts 77–80 .... 238, 256
Art.78 256
Art.79 257
  (3) 257
  (5) 257
Art.81 258
Art.82(3) 261
Arts 82–86 .... 153, 261
Art.83 195
  (1) 115
  (3) 262
Art.84 262
Art.85 186
Art.86 262
  (4) 262
Art.87 263
  (3) 263
Arts 87–89 153
Art.88 187
Arts 90–100 438
Art.91 .... 440, 442, 443
  (1) 181, 438
   (c) 442
  (2) 438
Art.92 .... 98, 439
Art.93 .... 443, 447
Art.94 435
Art.95(1) 444

(3) 131
Art.97 114
Art.100 . . . . 439, 450
  (2) 199, 343, 439, 440
Art.101 . . . . 29, 110, 319,
                320, 323, 324,
                327, 334, 343,
                438, 455
  (1) 321, 326
  (2) 327
  (3) 114, 328,
                331, 343, 455
Arts 101–102 507
Arts 101–105 319
Art.102 . . . . 110, 307, 319,
            320, 337, 438, 455
Art.103(2)(a) 131
   (c) 341
Art.105(2) 114, 114
Art.106 . . . . 113, 443
  (3) 34, 114
Art.107 443
  (3)(b) 469
   (d) 488
Art.108 . . . . 394, 395
  (2) 98, 114, 167
  (3) 110, 394, 395
Art.109 118
Art.110 36
  (2) 425, 426
Art.111 427
Art.112 427
Art.113 . . . . 395, 397, 427
Art.114 . . . . 228, 436,
                496, 507
  (1) 434, 435,
                436, 552
  (2) 437
  (3) 436
  (4) 436
  (5) 436, 542
  (6) 542
  (9) 78, 436
Arts 114–118 434
Art.115 . . . . 228, 434, 437
Art.116 437
  (2) 437
Art.117 . . . . 35, 437
  (1) 100
Art.118(7) 571
  (8) 571
  (9) 571
Art.119 . . . . 99, 176, 460
  (1) 91, 460
  (2) 460
  (3) 460

Arts 199–144 459
Art.120 99
Arts 120–126 460
Art.121 . . . . 35, 189
  (1) 101
  (2) 99, 460
  (2)–(3) 100
  (3) 100, 460, 461
  (4) 461
  (6) 461
Art.122 461
  (1) 233
  (2) 463
Art.123 . . . . 461, 463
Arts 123–124 189
Art.124 . . . . 461, 463
Art.125 . . . . 189, 461
Art.126 . . . . 189, 462,
                466, 525
  (1) 461
  (2) 462
  (4) 462, 467
  (5) 462
  (6) 462, 529
  (7) 29, 529
  (9) 462
  (10) 462
  (11) 462, 468
  (14) 462
Art.127(1) 176, 460
  (3) 177
  (5) 176, 177
  (6) 189
Arts 127–133 463
Art.128(2) 189
Art.129(2) 177
  (3) 176
  (4) 189
Art.132 465
  (1) 178, 465
  (3) 465
Art.134 . . . . 59, 465, 467
  (1) 178
  (2) 178, 465
Arts 136–138 464
Art.137(3)(a) 521
Art.138 189
Art.139 100
  (1) 459
Art.140 189
  (1) 460
Art.143 . . . . 189, 463
Art.144 189
Art.145 100
Arts 145–150 485
Art.146(1) 99

Art.148(2) 66, 99, 485
Art.149 .... 101, 437
  (2) 93
Art.150 .... 66, 101
Art.151 471
  (1) 471
  (2) 470, 480
  (3) 471
Arts 151–161 470
Arts 151–164 470
Art.153 471
  (1) 470
  (2)(a) 472, 475
  (3) 181
  (4) 475
Art.154 .... 471, 475
Art.155 475
  (2)(b) 470
Art.156 .... 114, 471, 477
  (1) 192
Art.157 .... 471, 474,
                   477, 478
  (3) 527
Art.160(3) 114
Art.161 75
Art.162 480
Arts 162–164 .... 470, 479
Art.165 .... 470, 484
  (1) 481
  (2) 484
  (3) 484
  (4) 437, 481
Art.166 .... 249, 470, 483
  (4) 35, 100, 181, 437
Art.167 488
  (1) 488
  (3) 488
  (4) 488
  (5) 437
Art.168 .... 475, 491
  (1) 438, 442
  (4) 181
  (5) 437, 492
  (7) 491
Art.169 .... 442, 496
  (1) 438, 499
  (4) 475
Art.170 554
  (1) 487, 515
Arts 170–172 508
Art.171 554
  (2) 516
Art.172 .... 475, 516
  (1) 181
Art.173 .... 502, 508
  (1) 504

  (3) 505
Art.174 .... 480, 487, 505, 519
  (3) 520
Arts 174–178 519
Art.175 .... 181, 480, 519, 521
  (1) 520
  (2) 528
  (3) 181
Art.177 .... 442, 525, 529
  (1) 181
Art.178(1) 181
Art.179(1) 531
Arts 179–190 .... 508, 530
Art.180 ....
  (b) 531
  (c) 531
  (d) 531
Art.181(1) 530
Art.182 40
  (1) 100
Arts 182–186 531
Art.183 535
Art.184 535
Art.185 535
Art.186 535
Art.187 .... 212, 533, 535
Art.189 .... 475, 535, 571
  (2) 30, 435
Art.190 .... 122, 539
Art.191 .... 438, 541, 542, 550
  (2) 492
  (4) 549
Arts 191–193 540
Art.192 181
  (1) 181, 500, 542
  (2) 543
  (3) 40, 543
Art.193 542
Art.194 552
Art.198 .... 603, 604
Arts 198–204 608
Art.203 .... 98, 553, 605
Art.205 561
Arts 205–222 561
Art.206 .... 561, 580
Arts 206–207 580
Art.207 .... 167, 308,
                561, 570, 581
  (1) 582
  (3) 29
  (4) 581, 582
  (6) 582
Art.208(1) 601
  (2) 601
Art.208–211 .... 561, 563
Art.209(1) 602, 603

(2) 603
(3) 603
Art.210 215
(1) 603
(3) 73
Art.212 .... 561, 567
(1) 567
Art.213 .... 561, 567
Art.214 .... 561, 568
(1) 568
(2) 568
(5) 569
Art.215 .... 561, 569
(2) 67
(3) 569
Art.216(2) 570
Arts 216–219 .... 561, 569
Art.217 570
Art.218 .... 53, 60,
563, 570, 603
(6)(a) 71
(11) 80, 122, 571
Art.219 189
(1) 571
(2) 35, 100, 571
(3) 563, 571
(4) 571
Art.220 .... 561, 572
(1) 122, 488
(2) 572
Art.221 .... 561, 572
(1) 572
Art.222 .... 561, 573, 579
(4) 573
Art.223(1) 62, 63, 71
(2) 65
Arts 223–234 61
Art.224 81
Art.225 .... 67, 93, 118
Art.226(1) 72
(2) 72
(3) 72
Arts 226–334 6
Art.227 72
Art.228 .... 72, 241
(2) 128, 166
(4) 73
Art.229 75
(2) 83
Art.230(2) 73
(3) 74
Art.231 83
Art.233 75
Art.234 .... 76, 96, 109
(1) 76
Art.235(1) 95, 96

(3) 95
Art.236 101
(b) 86, 102
Art.238 7
(1) 96
(2) 87, 93, 97, 98
(3) 97, 98
Art.239 95
Art.240(1) 103
(2) 96, 105
(3) 59, 96, 104
Art.241 ...... 67, 93, 96, 118
Art.242 96
Art.245 108
(1) 77
(2) 108, 128, 166
(5) 167
(6) 167
Art.246 76
Art.247 .... 128, 166
Art.248 109
Art.249 .... 246, 261
(1) 123
(2) 123
Art.250 114
Art.251(2) 127
Arts 251–281 125
Art.252 166
Art.253 40
(1) 125, 127
(2) 127
(3) 127
(4) 127
(6) 156, 159
Art.254 166
(2) 166
(3) 166
Art.255 .... 104, 127
Art.256 167
(1) 165
(2) 155, 168, 171
(3) 130, 168, 169
Art.257 .... 168, 169, 170
(4) 170
(5) 170
(6) 170
Art.258 .... 110, 111,
112, 129,
154, 182, 313
(1) 547
(2) 111
Art.259 130
Art.260 .... 129, 550
(2) 131, 154, 547
(3) 112, 131
Art.261 .... 129, 131

Art.262 151
Art.263 .... 37, 38, 39, 65,
80, 94, 113,
120, 129, 132,
141, 142, 147,
151, 152, 167, 191,
  (1) 113, 133
  (2) 36, 138
  (3) 133, 134, 137,
151, 158, 173
  (4) 136, 153
  (5) 133, 152
  (6) 132
Art.264 .... 140, 141, 144
Art.265 .... 67, 80, 93,
113, 129, 141,
152, 157, 167, 442
  (1) 173
Art.266 .... 93, 141, 142
  (1) 140, 570
Art.267 .... 32, 46, 54,
129, 136, 142,
143, 144, 145,
566, 570
  (1)(b) 143
  (2) 145
Art.268 .... 129, 132,
149, 168
Art.269 152
Art.270 132
Art.271 .... 129, 153
  (a) 113
  (d) 154
Art.272 .... 129, 154, 168
Art.273 .... 131, 154
Art.274 .... 129, 154
Art.275 .... 153, 573
Art.276 153
Art.277 .... 130, 132,
136, 151
Art.278 .... 130, 154, 162
Art.279 .... 130, 154,
162, 163
Art.280 38
Art.281 155
Art.282 176
Art.283(1) 177
Art.285 173
  (1) 173
  (2) 173
Art.286(2) 173
  (4) 173
  (6) 128, 173
  (7) 173
Art.287 ..... 79, 122, 174, 465
  (1) 174

  (2) 174
  (3) 174
  (4) 72, 175
Art.288 .... 29, 88,
106, 133, 434
  (1) 30, 113
  (2) 30, 43
  (3) 33, 51
  (5) 114
Arts 288–292 28
Art.289 .... 115, 226
  (1) 30, 34, 66,
133, 239
  (2) 11, 34, 66,
71, 73, 77, 115,
133, 151, 240,
241, 263, 427, 542
  (3) 30, 133
Art.290 .... 71, 95,
115, 138
  (1) 115, 116, 117
Art.291(2) 167
Art.293(1) 67, 69,
94, 98, 121
  (2) 66, 94, 103, 120
Art.294 .... 11, 30, 68,
81, 95, 101, 115,
120, 131, 241, 256,
257, 262, 263, 271,
285, 288, 435, 437,
438, 439, 461, 475,
478, 484, 489, 491,
499, 521, 527, 535,
536, 542, 567, 569, 571
  (1) 177
  (2) 70
  (6) 70
  (9) 69, 70
  (10) 67, 98, 121
  (13) 67, 98, 121
Art.296(1) 70
  (2) 36, 66, 92
Art.297 .... 37, 465
  (3) 132
Art.299 .... 38, 154
Art.300 .... 59, 181
  (1) 121
  (2) 180
  (6) 121
  (7) 39
Art.301 180
  (1) 180
Arts 301–304 59
Art.302 180
Art.305 181
Arts 305–307 59

Art.307(3) 181
(4) 181
Art.308 .... 59, 93
Art.309 .... 59, 183
(a) 521
Art.310 .... 67, 98, 121
(1) 216
Art.312 .... 67, 98, 121
Art.313 .... 216, 217
Arts 313–316 65
Art.314 ..... 67, 98, 121, 122
Arts 314–316 77
Art.315 .... 79, 98
(2) 67
Art.317 .... 79, 122
Art.318 .... 79, 122
Art.319 .... 79, 122
Art.322 79
(1) 122
Art.325(4) 219
Art.326(1) 7
Arts 326–334 152
Art.328(1) 7
(2) 7
(4) 98
Art.329(1) 7
(2) 7
Art.330 7
Art.331 167
(1) 7
Art.332 8
Art.335 .... 59, 60
Art.336 .... 149, 153
Art.337 110
Art.340 .... 54, 129, 132
(2) 150
Art.344 131
Art.346 .... 141, 233
(2) 98
Art.347 233
Art.348 233
Art.349 11
Art.351 .... 55, 566
(2) 55
Art.352 .... 10, 93,
141, 436,
521, 540, 553
(1) 93
(3) 93
(4) 93
Art.354 .... 6, 88, 465
(1) 88
Art.355 .... 43, 223
(5)(a) 12
(b) 12
Annex I 414

Annex II 11, 400
Protocol No.1 64
Arts 1–2 64
Arts 9–10 64
Protocol No.2 .... 28, 64,
100, 542
Art.2 .... 29, 119
Art.3 118
Art.5 119
Art.7(3) 120
Protocol No.3 ... 125, 127, 147,
154, 155
Art.2 .... 125, 128
Art.3 128
Art.4 127
Art.7 170
Art.9,1 165
Art.14 165
Art.15 166
Art.16 .... 128, 166
Art.16.3 .... 128, 166
Art.16,5 166
Art.17 166
Art.19,1 157
Art.19,4 157
Art.20 ...... 129, 156, 159
Art.20,2 157
Art.20,4 .... 159, 160
Art.21 .... 157, 158
Art.21,2 157
Art.23,3 156
Art.24,3 147
Art.29 159
Art.29(3)6 156
Art.30 159
Art.31 160
Art.37,5 156
Art.38 161
Art.39 161
Art.40 164
Art.41 164
Art.42 164
Art.43 .... 150, 164
Art.45,2 158
Art.48 166
Art.49,1 166
Art.51 .... 152, 167
Art.54 155
Art.54,3 165
Art.56,1 154
Art.56,2 154
Art.57,1 154
Art.58 155
Art.61,2 169
Art.62a 171
Art.62b 171

Art.63 156
Protocol No.4 464
Protocol No.5 . . . . 182, 183
  Art.4 183
  Art.8 185
  Art.9(2) 185
  Art.10 185
Protocol No.7 124
  Art.10 572

Protocol No.12 462
Protocol No.14 465
Protocol No.19 242
Protocol No.33 478
Protocol No.34 608
Protocol No.36 . . . . 96, 97, 180
  Art.3(1) 96, 97, 98
    (2) 97, 98
    (4) 97

Table of Secondary Legislation of the European Union

Directives

1962 Dir.62/2005 fixing the maximum aid for cream, butter and concentrated butter for the 155th individual invitation to tender under the standing invitation to tender provided for in Regulation No.2571/97 [1962] O.J. L13/17 444

1964 Dir.64/221 on the co-ordination of special measures concerning the movement and residence of foreign nationals which are justified on grounds of public policy, public security or public health [1964] O.J. L56/850 ...... 239, 243, 253, 284

Dir.64/222 laying down detailed provisions concerning transitional measures in respect of activities in wholesale trade and activities of intermediaries in commerce, industry and small craft industries [1964] O.J. L56/857 277

Dir.64/224 concerning the attainment of freedom of establishment and freedom to provide services in respect of activities of intermediaries in commerce, industry and small craft industries [1964] O.J. L56/869 277

Dir.64/225 on the abolition of restrictions on freedom of establishment and freedom to provide services in respect of reinsurance and retrocession [1964] O.J. L56/878 296

Dir.64/427 laying down detailed provisions concerning transitional measures in respect of activities of self-employed persons in manufacturing and processing industries [1964] O.J. L1117/1863 277

Dir.64/428 concerning the attainment of freedom of establishment and freedom to provide services in respect of activities of self-employed persons in mining and quarrying [1964] O.J. L117/1871 277

Dir.64/429 concerning the attainment of freedom of establishment and freedom to provide services in respect of activities of self-employed persons in manufacturing and processing industries falling within ISIC Major Groups 23–40 (Industry and small craft industries) [1964] O.J. 117/1880 277

1965 Dir.65/65 on the approximation of provisions laid down by Law, Regulation or Administrative Action relating to proprietary medicinal products [1965] O.J. L 22/369 495

1967 Dir.67/548 on the approximation of laws, regulations and administrative provisions relating to the classification, packaging and labelling of dangerous substances [1967] O.J. L196/1 .... 492, 540, 546

1968 Dir.68/151 on co-ordination of safeguards which, for the protection of the interests of members and others, are required by Member States of companies within the meaning of the second paragraph of Article 58 of the Treaty, with a view to making such safeguards equivalent throughout the Community [1968] O.J. L65/8 278

Dir.68/360 on the abolition of restrictions on movement and residence within the Community for workers of Member States and their families [1968] O.J. L257/13 ...... 247, 248, 253

Art.2(2) 247
Dir.68/363 concerning the
  attainment of freedom of
  establishment and freedom
  to provide services in respect
  of activities of self-employed
  persons in retail trade [1968]
  L260/1 267
Dir.68/365 concerning the
  attainment of freedom of
  establishment and freedom
  to provide services in respect
  of activities of self-employed
  persons in the food
  manufacturing and
  beverage industries [1968]
  O.J. L260/9 277
Dir.68/366 laying down detailed
  provisions concerning
  transitional measures in
  respect of activities of self-
  employed persons in the
  food manufacturing and
  beverage industries [1968]
  O.J. L260/12 277
Dir.68/368 laying down detailed
  provisions concerning
  transitional measures in
  respect of activities of
  self-employed persons in the
  personal services sectors
  [1968] O.J. L260/19 267
1969 Dir.69/82 concerning the
  attainment of freedom of
  establishment and freedom to
  provide services in respect of
  activities of self-employed
  persons engaging in exploration
  (prospecting and drilling) for
  petroleum and natural gas
  [1969] O.J. L68/4 277
Dir.69/335 concerning indirect
  taxes on the raising of capital
  [1969] O.J. L249/25 431
1970 Dir.70/50 based on the
  provisions of Article 33 (7),
  on the abolition of measures
  which have an effect equivalent
  to quantitative restrictions on
  imports and are not covered by
  other provisions adopted in
  pursuance of the EEC Treaty
  [1970] O.J. L13/29 227
Dir.70/157 on the approximation
  of the laws of the Member
  States relating to the permissible

sound level and the exhaust
  system of motor vehicles
  [1970] O.J. L42/16 540
Dir.70/220 on the approximation
  of the laws of the Member
  States relating to measures to
  be taken against air pollution
  by gases from positive-
  ignition engines of motor
  vehicles 540
1971 Dir.71/18 laying down detailed
  provisions for the attainment
  of freedom of establishment
  in respect of self-employed
  persons providing
  agricultural and
  horticultural services
  [1971] O.J. L8/24 277
1972 Dir.72/166 on the approximation
  of the laws of Member States
  relating to insurance against
  civil liability in respect of the
  use of motor vehicles, and to
  the enforcement of the
  obligation to insure against
  such liability [1972]
  O.J. L103/1 296
1973 Dir.73/148 on the abolition of
  restrictions on movement
  and residence within the
  Community for nationals of
  Member States with regard
  to establishment and the
  provision of services [1973]
  O.J. L172/14 266,
                        269, 276,
                        287, 288
Dir.73/183 on the abolition of
  restrictions on freedom of
  establishment and freedom to
  provide services in respect of
  self-employed activities of
  banks and other financial
  institutions [1973]
  O.J. L194/1 292
Dir.73/239 on the coordination
  of laws, regulations and
  administrative provisions
  relating to the taking-up and
  pursuit of the business of
  direct insurance other than
  life assurance [1973]
  O.J. L228/3 296
Dir.73/240 abolishing restrictions
  on freedom of establishment in
  the business of direct insurance

other than life assurance
[1973] O.J. L228/20 296

1975 Dir.75/34 concerning the right
of nationals of a Member
State to remain in the
territory of another Member
State after having pursued
therein an activity in a
self-employed capacity
[1975] O.J. L14/10 269

Dir.75/117 on the approximation
of the laws of the Member
States relating to the application
of the principle of equal pay for
men and women [1975] O.J.
L45/19 .... 478, 479

Dir.75/129 on the approximation
of the laws of the Member
States relating to collective
redundancies [1975]
O.J. L48/29 473

Dir.75/319 on the approximation
of provisions laid down by Law,
Regulation or Administrative
Action relating to proprietary
medicinal products [1975]
O.J. L147/13 495

Dir.75/439 on the disposal of
waste oils [1975]
O.J. L194/23 .... 542, 546

Dir.75/440 concerning the quality
required of surface water
intended for the abstraction
of drinking water in the
Member States [1975]
O.J. L194/26 .... 492, 545

Dir.75/442 on waste [1975]
O.J. L194/39 546

1976 Dir.76/160 concerning the quality
of bathing water [1976] O.J.
L31/1 .... 492, 545

Dir.76/207 on the implementation
of the principle of equal
treatment for men and
women as regards access to
employment, vocational
training and promotion,
and working conditions
[1976] O.J. L39/40 474,
477, 478
Art.2(1) 474
Art.5(1) 474

Dir.76/308 on mutual assistance
for the recovery of claims
resulting from operations
forming part of the system of

financing the European
Agricultural Guidance and
Guarantee Fund, and of
the agricultural levies and
customs duties [1976]
O.J. L73/18 .... 428, 432

Dir.76/464 on pollution caused by
certain dangerous substances
discharged into the aquatic
environment of the Community
[1976] O.J. L129/23 545

Dir.76/769 on the approximation
of the laws, regulations and
administrative provisions of the
Member States relating to
restrictions on the marketing
and use of certain dangerous
substances and preparations
[1976] O.J. L262/201 492

Dir.76/796 approximation of laws
relating to the marketing and
use of certain dangerous
substances and preparations
[1976] O.J. L262/201 499

Dir.76/914 on the minimum level
of training for some road
transport drivers [1976]
O.J. L357/36 445

1977 Dir.77/91 on coordination of
safeguards which, for the
protection of the interests of
members and others, are
required by Member States of
companies within the meaning
of the second paragraph of
Article 58 of the Treaty, in
respect of the formation of
public limited liability
companies and the maintenance
and alteration of their capital,
with a view to making such
safeguards equivalent [1977]
O.J. L26/1 278
Art.25(1) 278
Art.29 278

Dir.77/92 on measures to
facilitate the effective exercise
of freedom of establishment
and freedom to provide
services in respect of the
activities of insurance agents
and brokers (ex ISIC Group
630) and, in particular,
transitional measures in respect
of those activities [1977]
O.J. L26/14 296

Directive 77/187 n the
approximation of the laws of
the Member States relating to
the safeguarding of employees'
rights in the event of transfers
of undertakings, businesses or
parts of businesses [1977]
O.J. L61/26 473
Dir.77/799 concerning mutual
assistance by the competent
authorities of the Member
States in the field of direct
taxation [1977] O.J.
L336/15 .... 429, 432, 432
Dir.77/249 to facilitate the
effective exercise by lawyers of
freedom to provide services
[1977] O.J. L78/17 275
Art.3 275
Art.4 275
Dir.77/388 on the harmonization
of the laws of the Member
States relating to turnover
taxes – Common system of
value added tax: uniform basis
of assessment [1977]
O.J. L145/1 12,
                      215, 427
Dir.77/452 concerning the mutual
recognition of diplomas,
certificates and other evidence
of the formal qualifications of
nurses responsible for general
care, including measures to
facilitate the effective exercise
of this right of establishment
and freedom to provide
services [1977]
O.J. L176/1 271
Dir.77/453 concerning the
coordination of provisions laid
down by Law, Regulation or
Administrative Action in respect
of the activities of nurses
responsible for general care
[1977] O.J. L176/8 271
Dir.77/486 on the education of
the children of migrant
workers [1977]
O.J. L199/32 249
Dir.77/799 concerning mutual
assistance by the competent
authorities of the Member
States in the field of direct
taxation [1977]
O.J. L336/15 428

Dir.77/780 on the coordination
of the laws, regulations and
administrative provisions
relating to the taking up and
pursuit of the business of
credit institutions [1977]
O.J. L322/30 293
1978 Dir.78/473 on the coordination
of laws, regulations and
administrative provisions
relating to Community
co-insurance [1978]
O.J. L151/25 296
Dir.78/631 on the approximation
of the laws of the Member
States relating to the
classification, packaging and
labelling of dangerous
preparations (pesticides)
[1978] O.J. L206/13 492
Dir.78/659 on the quality of
fresh waters needing protection
or improvement in order to
support fish life [1978]
O.J. L222/1 545
Dir.78/660 based on Article
54(3)(g) of the Treaty on the
annual accounts of certain
types of companies [1978]
O.J. L222/11 .... 279, 280,
                      292, 391
Dir.78/686 concerning the mutual
recognition of diplomas,
certificates and other evidence
of the formal qualifications of
practitioners of dentistry,
including measures to facilitate
the effective exercise of the
right of establishment and
freedom to provide services
[1978] O.J. L233/1 271
Dir.78/687 concerning the
coordination of provisions laid
down by Law, Regulation or
Administrative Action in
respect of the activities of
dental practitioners [1978]
O.J. L233/10 271
Dir.78/855 based on Article
54(3)(g) of the Treaty
concerning mergers of public
limited liability companies
[1978] O.J. L295/36 278
Dir.78/1026 concerning the
mutual recognition of
diplomas, certificates and

other evidence of formal
qualifications in veterinary
medicine, including measures
to facilitate the effective exer
cise of the right of
establishment and freedom to
provide services [1978]
O.J. L362/1 271

Dir.78/1027 concerning the
coordination of provisions laid
down by Law, Regulation or
Administrative Action in
respect of the activities of
veterinary surgeons [1978]
O.J. L362/7 271

1979 Dir.79/7 on the progressive
implementation of the
principle of equal treatment of
men and women in matters of
social security [1979]
O.J. L6/24 . . . . 477, 479

Dir.79/112 on the approximation
of the laws of the Member
States relating to the labelling,
presentation and advertising of
foodstuffs for the sale to the
ultimate consumer [1979]
O.J. L33/1 499

Dir.79/267 on the coordination
of laws, regulations and
administrative provisions
relating to the taking up and
pursuit of the business of
direct life assurance [1979]
O.J. L63/1 296

Dir.79/279 coordinating the
conditions for the admission of
securities to official stock
exchange listing [1979]
O.J. L66/21 280

Dir.79/409 on the conservation
of wild birds [1979] O.J.
L103/1 546

Dir.79/581 on consumer
protection in the indication
of the prices of foodstuffs
[1979] O.J. L158/19 499

Dir.79/695 on the harmonization
of procedures for the release of
goods for free circulation
[1979] O.J. L205/19 224

Dir.79/923 on the quality
required of shellfish waters
[1979] O.J. L281/47 545

Dir.79/1071 amending Directive
76/308/EEC on mutual

assistance for the recovery of
claims resulting from operations
forming part of the system of
financing of the European
Agricultural Guidance and
Guarantee Fund, and of
agricultural levies and
customs duties [1979]
O.J. L331/10 428

1980 Dir.80/68 on the protection of
groundwater against pollution
caused by certain dangerous
substances [1980]
O.J. L20/43 545

Dir.80/154 concerning the
mutual recognition of
diplomas, certificates and
other evidence of formal
qualifications in midwifery
and including measures to
facilitate the effective exercise
of the right of establishment
and freedom to provide
services [1981]
O.J. L33/1 271

Dir.80/155 concerning the
coordination of provisions laid
down by Law, Regulation or
Administrative Action relating
to the taking up and pursuit
of the activities of midwives
[1980] O.J. L33/8 271

Dir.80/390 coordinating the
requirements for the drawing
up, scrutiny and distribution of
the listing particulars to be
published for the admission of
securities to official stock
exchange listing [1980]
O.J. L100/1 280

Dir.80/723 on the transparency of
financial relations between
Member States and public
undertakings [1980] O.J.
L195/35 . . . . 114, 348, 378, 392
Art.2 377
Art.5 378

Dir.80/778 relating to the quality
of water intended for human
consumption [1980]
O.J. L229/11 545

Dir.80/779 on air quality limit
values and guide values for
sulphur dioxide and
suspended particulates
[1980] O.J. L229/30 546

Dir.80/987 on the approximation of the laws of the Member States relating to the protection of employees in the event of the insolvency of their employer [1980] O.J. L283/23 .... 473, 473

Dir.80/1107 concerning the protection of workers from the risks related to exposure to chemical, physical and biological agents [1980] O.J. L327/8 472

1982 Dir.82/121 on information to be published on a regular basis by companies the shares of which have been admitted to official stock-exchange listing [1982] O.J. L48/26 280

Dir.82/470 on measures to facilitate the effective exercise of freedom of establishment and freedom to provide services in respect of activities of self-employed persons in certain services incidental to transport and travel agencies (ISIC Group 718) and in storage and warehousing [1982] O.J. L213/1 267

Dir.82/501 on the major-accident hazards of certain industrial activities [1982] O.J. L230/1 546

Dir.82/891 based on Article 54(3)(g) of the Treaty, concerning the division of public limited liability companies [1982] O.J. L378/47 279

1983 Dir.83/182 on tax exemptions within the Community for certain means of transport temporarily imported into one Member State from another [1983] O.J. L105/59 269

Dir.83/189 laying down a procedure for the provision of information in the field of technical standards and regulations [1983] O.J. L109/8 234

Dir.83/349 based on the Article 54(3)(g) of the Treaty on consolidated accounts [1983] O.J. L193/1 .... 279, 280, 292

Dir.83/477 on the protection of workers from the risks related to exposure to asbestos at work [1983] O.J. L263/25 472

Dir.83/515 concerning certain measures to adjust capacity in the fisheries sector [1983] O.J. L290/15 420

1984 Dir.84/5 on the approximation of the laws of the Member States relating to insurance against civil liability in respect of the use of motor vehicles [1984] O.J. L8/17 296

Dir.84/253 based on Article 54(3)(g) of the Treaty on the approval of persons responsible for carrying out the statutory audits of accounting [1984] O.J. L126/20 279

Dir.84/360 on the combating of air pollution from industrial plants [1984] O.J. L188/20 546

Dir.84/450 relating to the approximation of the laws, regulations and administrative provisions of the Member States concerning misleading advertising [1984] O.J. L250/17 496

Dir.84/467/Euratom as regards the basic safety standards for the health protection of the general public and workers against the dangers of ionizing radiation [1984] O.J. L265/4 182

1985 Dir.85/337 on the assessment of the effects of certain public and private projects on the environment [1985] O.J. L175/40

Art.1(2) 32
Art.2(1) 32
Art.4(2) 32

Dir.85/374 on the approximation of the laws, regulations and administrative provisions of the Member States concerning liability for defective products [1985] O.J. L210/29 .... 497, 498

Dir.85/384 on the mutual recognition of diplomas,

certificates and other evidence
of formal qualifications in
architecture, including
measures to facilitate the
effective exercise of the right
of establishment and freedom
to provide services [1985]
O.J. L223/15 271

Dir.85/432 concerning the
coordination of provisions laid
down by Law, Regulation or
Administrative Action in
respect of certain activities
in the field of pharmacy
[1985] O.J. L254/34 271

Dir.85/433 concerning the mutual
recognition of diplomas,
certificates and other evidence
of formal qualifications in
pharmacy, including measures
to facilitate the effective
exercise of the right of
establishment relating to
certain activities in the field
of pharmacy [1985]
O.J. L253/37 271

Directive 85/577 to protect the
consumer in respect of
contracts negotiated away
from business premises [1985]
O.J. L372/31 497
Art.5(1) 497

Dir.85/611 on the coordination
of laws, regulations and
administrative provisions
relating to undertakings for
collective investment in
transferable securities [1985]
O.J. L375/03 294

1986 Dir.86/613 on the application of
the principle of equal treatment
between men and women
engaged in an activity,
including agriculture, in a self-
employed capacity, and on the
protection of self-employed
women during pregnancy and
motherhood [1989]
O.J. L359/56 . . . . 474, 479

Dir.86/635 on the annual
accounts and consolidated
accounts of banks and other
financial institutions [1986]
O.J. L372/1 . . . . 279, 280

Dir.86/653 on the coordination of
the laws of the Member States

relating to self-employed
commercial agents [1986]
O.J. L382/17 . . . . 267, 370

1987 Dir.87/22 on the approximation
of national measures relating
to the placing on the market
of high-technology medicinal
products, particularly those
derived from biotechnology
[1987] O.J. L15/38 195

Dir.87/102 for the approximation
of the laws, regulations and
administrative provisions of
the Member States concerning
consumer credit [1987]
O.J. L42/48 498

Dir.87/217 on the prevention
and reduction of environmental
pollution by asbestos [1987]
O.J. L85/40 492

Dir.87/344 on the coordination
of laws, regulations and
administrative provisions
relating to legal expenses
insurance [1987]
O.J. L185/77 296

1988 Dir.88/182 amending Directive
83/189/EEC laying down a
procedure for the provision of
information in the field of
technical standards and
regulations [1988]
O.J. L81/75 234

Dir.88/301 on competition in the
markets in telecommunications
terminal equipment [1988]
O.J. L131/73 . . . . 345, 510

Dir.88/303 on competition in the
markets in telecommunications
terminal equipment [1988]
O.J. L131/73 510

Dir.88/314 on consumer
protection in the indication
of the prices of non-food
products [1988]
O.J. L142/19 498

Dir.88/357 on the coordination of
laws, regulations and
administrative provisions
relating to direct insurance
other than life assurance and
laying down provisions to
facilitate the effective exercise
of freedom to provide services
and amending Directive
73/239 [1988] L172/1 296

Dir.88/361 for the implementation of Article 67 of the Treaty [1988] O.J. L178/5 298
Annex I 298, 299
Dir.88/378 on the approximation of the laws of the Member States concerning the safety of toys [1988] O.J. L187/1 496

1989   Dir.89/48 on a general system for the recognition of higher-education diplomas awarded on completion of professional education and training of at least three years' duration [1989] O.J. L19/16 .... 272, 275, 276, 277
Dir.89/104 to approximate the laws of the Member States relating to trade marks [1989] O.J. L40/1 305
Art.7 305
Dir.89/117 on the obligations of branches established in a Member State of credit institutions and financial institutions having their head offices outside that Member State regarding the publication of annual accounting documents [1989] O.J. L44/40 .... 279, 292
Dir.89/299 on the own funds of credit institutions [1989] O.J. L124/16 .... 279, 292
Dir.89/391 on the introduction of measures to encourage improvements in the safety and health of workers at work [1989] O.J. L183/1 .... 251, 472
Art.16(1) 251
Dir.89/459 on the approximation of the laws of the Member States relating to the tread depth of tyres of certain categories of motor vehicles and their trailers [1989] O.J. L226/4 446
Dir.89/552 on the coordination of certain provisions laid down by Law, Regulation or Administrative Action in Member States concerning the pursuit of television broadcasting activities [1989] O.J. L298/23 513

Dir.89/629 on the limitation of noise emission from civil subsonic jet aeroplanes [1989] O.J. L363/27 451
Dir.89/646 on the coordination of laws, regulations and administrative provisions relating to the taking up and pursuit of the business of credit institutions and amending Directive 77/780 [1989] O.J. L386/1 .... 293, 294
Dir.89/647 on a solvency ratio for credit institutions [1989] O.J. L386/14 292
Dir.89/654 concerning the minimum safety and health requirements for the workplace [1989] O.J. L393/1 472
Dir.89/656 on the minimum health and safety requirements for the use by workers of personal protective equipment at the workplace [1989] O.J. L393/18 472
Dir.89/665 adopting a specific research and technical development programme for the European Atomic Energy Community in the field of management and storage of radioactive waste [1989] O.J. L 395/28 472
                                314, 316
Art.2(1)(a) 316
          (b) 316
          (c) 316
Dir.89/666 concerning disclosure requirements in respect of branches opened in a Member State by certain types of company governed by the law of another State [1989] O.J. L395/36 280

1990   Dir.30/232 on the approximation of the laws of the Member States relating to insurance against civil liability in respect of the use of motor vehicles [1990] O.J. L129/33 .... 32, 296
Dir.90/269 on the minimum health and safety requirements for the manual handling of loads where there is a risk particularly of back injury to workers [1990] O.J. L156/9 472

Dir.90/270 on the minimum safety and health requirements for work with display screen equipment [1990] O.J. L156/14 472

Dir.90/314 on package travel, package holidays and package tours [1990] O.J. L158/59 .... 451, 498
Art.5 498
Art.7 498

Dir.90/364 on the right of residence [1990] O.J. L180/26 247

Dir.90/365 on the right of residence for employees and self-employed persons who have ceased their occupational activity [1990] O.J. L180/28 .... 247, 269

Dir.90/387 on the establishment of the internal market for telecommunications services through the implementation of open network provision [1990] O.J. L192/1 .... 345, 510

Dir.90/388 on competition in the markets for telecommunications services [1990] O.J. L192/10 345

Dir.90/434 on the common system of taxation applicable to mergers, divisions, transfers of assets and exchanges of shares concerning companies of different Member States [1990] O.J. L225/1 ..... 281, 431, 432

Dir.90/435 on the common system of taxation applicable in the case of parent companies and subsidiaries of different Member States [1990] O.J. L225/6 .... 281, 431
Art.4(1) 281, 431

Dir.90/496 on nutritional labelling for foodstuffs [1990] O.J. L276/40 499

Dir.90/547 on the transit of electricity through transmission grids [1990] O.J. L313/30 515

Dir.90/684 on aid to shipbuilding [1990] O.J. L380/27 385

1991 Dir.91/67 on measures governing the placing on the market of aquaculture animals and products [1991] O.J. L46/1 418

Dir.91/250 on the legal protection of computer programs [1991] O.J. L122/42 301

Dir.91/296 on the transit of natural gas through grids [1991] O.J. L147/37 555

Dir.91/308 on prevention of the use of the financial system for the purpose of money laundering [1991] O.J. L166/77 .... 52, 293, 299, 432

Dir.91/440 on the development of the Community's railways [1998] O.J. L237/25 ..... 120, 345, 387, 447, 449
Art.10 345

Dir.91/414 concerning the placing of plant protection products on the market [1991] O.J. L230/1 .... 197, 545

Dir.91/439 on driving licences [1991] O.J. L237/1 445

Dir.91/477 on control of the acquisition and possession of weapons [1991] O.J. L256/51 499

Dir.91/533 on an employer's obligation to inform employees of the conditions applicable to the contract or employment relationship [1991] O.J. L288/32 474

Dir.91/671 on the approximation of the laws of the Member States relating to compulsory use of safety belts in vehicles of less than 3,5 tonnes [1991] O.J. L373/26 445

Dir.91/674 on the annual accounts and consolidated accounts of insurance undertakings [1991] O.J. L374/7 ...... 279, 280, 296

Dir.91/680 supplementing the common system of value added tax and amending Directive 77/388 with a view to the abolition of the fiscal frontiers [1991] O.J. L376/1 428

Dir.91/689 on dangerous waste [1991] O.J. L377/20 .... 542, 546

1992   Dir.92/6 on the installation and use
of speed limitation devices for
certain categories of motor
vehicles in the Community
[1992] O.J. L57/27 445

Dir.92/12 on the general
arrangements for products subject
to excise duty and on the holding,
movement and monitoring
of such products [1992]
O.J. L76/1 . . . . 429, 430

Dir.92/13 coordinating the laws,
regulations and administrative
provisions relating to the
application of Community rules
on the procurement procedures
of entities operating in the water,
energy, transport and
telecommunications sectors
[1992] O.J. L 76/14 316

Dir.92/22 on safety glazing and
glazing materials on motor
vehicles and their trailers
[1991] O.J. L129/11 445

Dir.92/29 on the minimum safety
and health requirements for
improved medical treatment on
board vessels [1992]
O.J. L113/19 456

Dir.92/30 on the supervision of
credit institutions on a
consolidated basis [1992]
O.J. L110/52 292

Dir.92/43 on the conservation of
natural habitats and of wild
fauna and flora [1992] O.J.
L206/7 546

Dir.92/44 on the application of
open network provision to
leased lines [1992]
O.J. L165/27 . . . . 347, 510

Dir.92/49 on the coordination of
laws, regulations and
administrative provisions
relating to direct insurance other
than life assurance and
amending Directives 73/239/EEC
and 88/357/EEC [1992]
O.J. L228/1 . . . . . 294, 295, 296

Dir.92/50 relating to the
coordination of procedures for
the award of public service
contracts [1992]
O.J. L209/1 . . . . 297, 311
Art.14 311
Art.16 311

Annex IV 311

Dir.92/51 on a second general
system for the recognition of
professional education and
training to supplement
Directive 89/48/EEC [1992]
O.J. L209/25 272,
276, 277

Dir.94/55 on the approximation of
the laws of the Member States
with regard to the transport of
dangerous goods by road
[1994] O.J. L319/7 445

Dir.92/57 on the implementation
of minimum safety and health
requirements at temporary or
mobile construction sites
[1992] O.J. L245/6 472

Dir.92/58 on the minimum
requirements for the provision of
safety and/or health signs at work
[1992] O.J. L245/23 472

Dir.92/59 on general product
safety (Product Safety Directive)
[1992] O.J. L228/24 235

Dir.92/77 supplementing the
common system of value added
tax and amending Directive
77/388/EEC [1992]
O.J. L316/1 428

Dir.92/79 on the approximation of
taxes on cigarettes [1992]
O.J. L316/8 429

Dir.92/80 on the approximation of
taxes on manufactured tobacco
other than cigarettes [1992]
O.J. L316/10 429

Dir.92/84 on the approximation of
the rates of excise duty on alcohol
and alcoholic beverages
[1992] O.J. L319/29 429

Dir.92/85 on the introduction of
measures to encourage
improvements in the safety and
health at work of pregnant
workers and workers who have
recently given birth or are
breastfeeding [1992]
O.J. L348/1 472

Dir.92/91 concerning the
minimum requirements for
improving the safety and health
protection of workers in the
mineral-extracting industries
through drilling [1992]
O.J. L348/9 472

Dir.92/96 on the coordination of laws, regulations and administrative provisions relating to direct life assurance and amending Directives 79/267/EEC and 90/619/EEC [1992] O.J. L360/1 . . . . . . 294, 295, 296

Dir.92/100 on rental right and lending right and on certain rights related to copyright in the field of intellectual property [1992] O.J. L346/61 301
Art.2(1) 301
Art.8(2) 301

Dir.92/101 amending Directive 77/91/EEC on the formation of public limited-liability companies and the maintenance and alteration of their capital [1992] O.J. L347/64 278

Dir.92/104 on the minimum requirements for improving the safety and health protection of workers in surface and underground mineral-extracting industries [1992] O.J. L404/10 472

Dir.92/106 on the establishment of common rules for certain types of combined transport of goods between Member States [1992] O.J. L368/38 447

Dir.92/114 relating to the external projections forward of the cab's rear panel of motor vehicles of category N [1992] O.J. L409/17 446

Dir.92/121 on the monitoring and control of large exposures of credit institutions [1993] O.J. L29/1 292

1993 Dir.93/6 on the capital adequacy of investments firms and credit institutions [1993] O.J. L141/1 292

Dir.93/7 on the return of cultural objects unlawfully removed from the territory of a Member State [1993] O.J. L74/74 488

Dir.93/13 on unfair terms in consumer contracts [1993] O.J. L95/29 . . . . 451, 498

Dir.93/16 to facilitate the free movement of doctors and the mutual recognition of their

diplomas, certificates and other evidence of formal qualifications [1993] O.J. L165/1 271

Dir.93/22 on investment services in the securities field [1993] O.J. L197/58 293

Dir.93/38 coordinating the procurement procedures of entities operating in the water, energy, transport and [1993] O.J. L199/84 314

Dir.93/39 amending Directives 65/65/EEC, 75/318/EEC and 75/319/EEC in respect of medicinal products [1993] O.J. L214/22 195

Dir.93/40 amending Directives 81/851/EEC and 81/852/EEC on the approximation of the laws of the Member States relating to veterinary medicinal products [1993] O.J. L214/31 195

Dir.93/41 repealing Directive 87/22/EEC on the approximation of national measures relating to the placing on the market of high-technology medicinal products, particularly those derived from biotechnology [1993] O.J. L214/40 195

Dir.93/42 concerning medical devices [1993] O.J. L169/1 495

Dir.93/53 on measure for the control of certain fish diseases [1993] O.J. L175/28 418

Dir.93/96 on the right of residence for students [1993] O.J. L317/59 . . . . . . 265, 270

Dir.93/103 concerning the minimum safety and health requirements for work on board fishing vessels [1993] O.J. L307/1 472

Dir.93/102 relating to the labelling, presentation and advertising of foodstuffs for sale to the ultimate consumer [1993] O.J. L291/14 499

Dir.93/104 concerning certain aspects of the organisation of working time [1993] O.J. L307/18 476

Dir.93/109 laying down detailed arrangements for the exercise of

the right to vote and stand as a
candidate in elections to the
European Parliament for citizens
of the Union residing in a
Member State of which they are
not nationals [1993]
O.J. L329/34 240

1994   Dir.94/19 on deposit-guarantee
schemes [1994]
O.J. L135/5 292
Dir.94/22 on the conditions for
granting and using
authorisations for the
prospection, exploration and
production of hydrocarbons
[1994] O.J. L164/3 557
Dir.94/31 amending Directive
91/689/EEC on hazardous waste
[1994] O.J. L168/28 542
Dir.94/33 on protection of young
people at work [1997]
O.J. L 215/12 472
Dir.94/45 on the establishment of a
European Works Council or a
procedure in Community-scale
undertakings and Community-
scale groups of undertakings for
the purposes of informing and
consulting employees [1994]
O.J. L254/64 . . . . 282, 474
Dir.94/46 amending Directive
88/301/EEC and Directive
90/388/EEC in particular with
regard to satellite
communications [1994]
O.J. L268/15 . . . . 345, 510
Dir.94/54 concerning the
compulsory indication on the
labelling of certain foodstuffs of
particulars other than those
provided for in Council
Directive 79/112/EEC [1994]
O.J. L300/14 499
Dir.94/55 on the approximation of
the laws of the Member States
with regard to the transport of
dangerous goods by road
[1994] O.J. L319/7 448
Directive 94/57 [1994]
O.J. L319/20 456
Dir.94/80 laying down detailed
arrangements for the exercise of
the right to vote and to stand as a
candidate in municipal elections
by citizens of the Union residing
in a Member State of which they

are not nationals [1994]
O.J. L368/38 . . . . 4, 240

1995   Dir.95/18 on the licensing of
railway [1995]
O.J. L143/70 . . . . . . 387, 448
Dir.95/19 on the allocation of
railway infrastructure capacity
and the charging of
infrastructure fees [1995]
O.J. L143/75 387
Dir.95/21 concerning the
enforcement, in respect of
shipping using Community ports
and sailing in the waters under
the jurisdiction of the Member
States, of international standards
for ship safety, pollution
prevention and shipboard living
and working conditions
[1995] O.J. L157/1 456
Dir.95/46 on the protection of
individuals with regard to the
processing of personal data and on
the free movement of such data
[1995] O.J. L281/31 501
Dir.95/51 amending Directive
90/388/EEC with regard to the
abolition of the restrictions on the
use of cable television networks
for the provision of already
liberalized telecommunications
services [1995]
O.J. L256/49 . . . . 346, 510
Dir.95/62 on the application of
open network provisions to
voice telephony [1995]
O.J. L321/6 . . . . 347, 510

1996   Directive 96/2 amending Directive
90/388/EEC with regard to
mobile and personal
communications [1996]
O.J. L20/59 . . . . 346, 510
Dir.96/9 on the legal protection of
databases [1996] O.J. L77/20
Dir.96/19 amending Directive
90/388/EEC with regard to the
implementation of full
competition in
telecommunications markets
[1996] O.J. L74/13 . . . . 346, 510
Dir.96/48 on the interoperability of
the trans-European high-speed
rail system, [1996]
O.J. L235/6 . . . . 447, 515
Dir.96/49 on the approximation of
the laws of the Member States

with regard to the transport of dangerous goods by rail [1996] O.J. L235/25 .... 445, 448

Dir.96/67 on access to the groundhandling market at Community airports [1996] O.J. L272/36 451

Dir.96/71 concerning the posting of workers in the framework of the provision of services [1997] O.J. L18/1 476

Dir.96/96 on the approximation of the laws of the Member States relating to roadworthiness tests for motor vehicles and their trailers [1996] O.J. L46/1 445

Dir.96/75 on the systems of chartering and pricing in national and international inland waterway transport in the Community [1996] O.J. L304/12 388

Dir.96/92 concerning common rules for the internal market in electricity [1997] O.J. L27/20 552

1997 Dir.97/5 on cross-border credit transfers [1997] O.J. L43/25 292

Dir.97/7 on the protection of consumers in respect of distance contracts [1997] O.J. L144/19 497

Dir.97/13 on a common framework for general authorisations and individual licences in the field of telecommunications services [1997] O.J. L117/15 510

Dir.97/33 on interconnection in telecommunications with regard to ensuring universal service and interoperability through application of the principles of Open Network Provision (ONP) [1997] O.J. L199/32 510

Dir.97/57 establishing Annex VI to Directive 91/414/EEC concerning the placing of plant protection products on the market [1997] O.J. L265/87 197

Dir.97/67 on common rules for the development of the internal market of Community postal

services and the improvement of quality of service [1998] O.J. L15/14 .... 248, 349

Dir.97/70 setting up a harmonised safety regime for fishing vessels of 24 metres in length and over [1998] O.J. L34/1 456

Dir.97/74 extending, to the United Kingdom of Great Britain and Northern Ireland, Directive 94/45/EC on the establishment of a European Works Council or a procedure in Community-scale undertakings and Community-scale groups of undertakings for the purposes of informing and consulting employees [1998] O.J. L10/22 474

Dir.97/80 on the burden of proof in cases of discrimination based on sex [1998] O.J. L14/6 .... 474, 479

Dir.97/81 concerning the Framework Agreement on part-time work concluded by UNICE, CEEP and the ETUC – Annex: Framework agreement on part-time work [1998] O.J. L14/9 .... 476, 479

1998 Dir.98/5 to facilitate practice of the profession of lawyer on a permanent basis in a Member State other than that in which the qualification was obtained [1998] O.J. L77/36 275

Dir.98/6 on consumer protection in the indication of the prices of products offered to consumers [1998] O.J. L80/27 498

Dir.98/8 concerning the placing of biocidal products on the market [1998] O.J. L123/1 545

Dir.98/18 on safety rules and standards for passenger ships [1998] O.J. L144/1 456

Dir.98/24 on the protection of the health and safety of workers from the risks related to chemical agents at work [1998] O.J. L131/11 472

Dir.98/27 on injunctions for the protection of consumers' interests [1998] O.J. L166/51 496

Dir.98/34 laying down a procedure for the provision of information

in the field of technical
standards and regulations
[1998] O.J. L204/37 234,
531

Dir.98/37 on the approximation
of the laws of the Member
States relating to machinery
[1998] O.J. L207/1 497

Dir.98/59 on the approximation of
the laws of the Member States
relating to collective
redundancies [1998]
O.J. L225/16 473

Dir.98/70 relating to the quality
of petrol and diesel fuels and
amending Council Directive
93/12/EEC [1998]
O.J. L350/58 547

Dir.98/71 on the legal protection
of designs [1998]
O.J. L289/28 .... 305, 307

Dir.98/84 on the legal protection of
services based on, or consisting
of, conditional access [1998]
O.J. L320/54 288,
307, 508

1999   Dir.1999/5 on radio equipment
and telecommunications terminal
equipment and the mutual
recognition of their conformity
[1999] O.J. L91/10 510

Dir.1999/29 on the undesirable
substances and products in
animal nutrition [1999]
O.J. L6/45 418

Dir.1999/31 on the landfill
of waste [1999]
O.J. L182/1 546

Dir.99/35 on a system of
mandatory surveys for the safe
operation of regular ro-ro
ferry and high-speed passenger
craft services [1999]
O.J. L138/1 456

Dir.99/36 on transportable
pressure equipment approved
for the inland transport of
dangerous goods by road
and by rail [1999]
O.J. L138/20 .... 445, 448

Dir.99/42 establishing a mechanism
for the recognition of
qualifications in respect of the
professional activities covered by
the Directives on liberalisation
and transitional measures and

supplementing the general
systems for the recognition of
qualifications [1999]
O.J. L201/77 .... 272, 276
Arts 24–33 272
Art.50 272
Art.52 272
Art.53 272
Art.54 272
Art.55 272

Dir.99/44 on certain aspects of
the sale of consumer goods
and associated guarantees
[1999] O.J. L171/12 497
Art/3 497

Dir.1999/62 on the charging of
heavy goods vehicles for the
use of certain infrastructure
[1999] O.J. L187/42 444

Dir.99/92 on minimum
requirements for improving the
safety and health protection of
workers potentially at risk from
explosive atmospheres [200]
O.J. L23/57 472

Dir.1999/93 on a Union
framework for electronic
signature [1999]
O.J. L13/12 511

2000   Dir.2000/12 relating to the
taking up and pursuit of the
business of credit institutions
[2000] O.J. L126/1 292

Dir.2000/13 relating to labelling,
presentation and advertising
of foodstuffs [2000]
O.J. L109/29 .... 493, 494

Dir.2000/26 on the approximation
of the laws of the Member
States relating to insurance
against civil liability in respect
of the use of motor vehicles and
amending Council Directives
73/239/EEC and 88/357/EEC
(Fourth Motor Insurance
Directive) [2000]
O.J. L181/65 296

Dir.2000/31 on certain legal
aspects of information society
services, in particular
electronic commerce, in the
Internal Market [2000]
O.J. L178/1 .... 497, 511
Art.5(1)(c) 497

Dir.2000/30 on the technical
roadside inspection of the

roadworthiness of commercial
vehicles circulating in the
Community [2000]
O.J. L203/1 446

Dir.2000/35 on combating late
payment in commercial
transactions [2000]
O.J. L200/35 498

Dir.2000/43 implementing the
principle of equal treatment
between persons irrespective of
racial or ethnic origin [2000]
O.J. L180/22 479
Art.2(2)(a) 479

Dir.2000/46 on the taking up,
pursuit of and prudential
supervision of the business of
electronic money institutions
[2000] O.J. L275/39 293

Dir.2000/53 on end-of life vehicles
[2000] O.J. L269/34 546

Dir.2000/54 on the protection of
workers from risks related to
exposure to biological agents
at work [2000]
O.J. L262/21 472

Dir.2000/59 on port reception
facilities for ship generated
waste and cargo residues
[2000] O.J. L332/81 455

Dir.2000/69 relating to limit
values for benzene and carbon
monoxide in ambient air
[2000] O.J. L313/12 546

Dir.2000/70 as regards medical
devices incorporating stable
derivates of human blood or
human plasma [2000]
O.J. L313/22 495

Dir.2000/78 establishing a
general framework for equal
treatment in employment and
occupation [2000]
O.J. L303/16 .... 474, 479

Dir.2000/81 amending the
Annexes to Council Directives
86/362/EEC, 86/363/EEC and
90/642/EEC on the fixing of
maximum levels for pesticide
residues in and on cereals,
foodstuffs of animal origin
and certain products of
plant origin, including
fruit and vegetables,
respectively [2000]
O.J. L326/56 546

2001

Dir.2000/331 relating to the
labelling, presentation and
advertising of foodstuffs
[2000] O.J. L109/29 499

Dir.2001/12 amending Council
Directive 91/440/EEC on the
development of the
Community's railways
[2001] O.J. L75/1 .... 447, 448

Dir.2001/13 amending Council
Directive 95/18/EC on the
licensing of railway
undertakings [2001]
O.J. L75/26 .... 447, 448

Dir.2001/14 on the allocation of
railway infrastructure capacity
and the levying of charges for
the use of railway infrastructure
and safety certification
[2001] O.J. L75/29 345,
                        447, 448

Directive 2001/16 [2001]
O.J. L110/1 448

Dir.2001/17 on the reorganisation
and winding-up of insurance
undertakings [2000]
O.J. L110/28 .... 292, 296

Dir.2001/18 on the deliberate
release into the environment of
genetically modified organisms
and repealing Council
Directive 90/220/EEC
[2001] O.J. L106/1 .... 198, 410

Dir. 2001/19 amending Council
Directives 89/48/EEC and
92/51/EEC on the general
system for the recognition of
professional qualifications
and Council Directives
77/452/EEC, 77/453/EEC,
78/686/EEC, 78/687/EEC,
78/1026/EEC, 78/1027/EEC,
80/154/EEC, 80/155/EEC,
85/384/EEC, 85/432/EEC,
85/433/EEC and 93/16/EEC
concerning the professions of
nurse responsible for general
care, dental practitioner,
veterinary surgeon, midwife,
architect, pharmacist and doctor
[2001] O.J. L206/1 273

Dir.2001/21 on the harmonisation
of certain aspects of copyright
and related rights in the
information society [2001]
O.J. L167/10 511

Dir.2001/23 on the approximation
of the laws of the Member States
relating to the safeguarding of
employees' rights in the event of
transfers of undertakings,
businesses or parts of
undertakings or businesses
[2001] O.J. L82/16 473
Dir.2001/24 on the reorganisation
and winding up of credit
institutions [2000]
O.J. L125/15 292
Dir.2001/25 on the minimum level
of training of seafarers [2001]
O.J. L136/17 456
Dir.2001/29 on the harmonisation
of certain aspects of copyright
and related rights in the
information society [2001]
O.J. L167/10 .... 303, 308
Dir.2001/34 on the admission of
securities to official stock
exchange listing and on
information to be published on
those securities [2001]
O.J. L184/1 .... 280, 281
Dir.2001/37 on the approximation
of the laws, regulations and
administrative provisions of the
Member States concerning the
manufacture, presentation and
sale of tobacco products [2001]
O.J. L194/26 493
Dir.2001/78 amending Annex IV
to Council Directive 93/36/EEC,
Annexes IV, V and VI to
Council Dir.93/37/EEC,
Annexes III and IV to Council
Directive 92/50/EEC, as amended
by Directive 97/52/EC, and
Annexes XII to XV, XVII and
XVIII to Council Directive
93/38/EEC, as amended by
Directive 98/4/EC [2001]
O.J. L 285/1 315
Dir.2001/82 on the Community
code relating to veterinary
medicinal products [2004]
O.J. L311/1 195
Dir.2001/83 on the Community
code relating to medicinal
products for human use [2004]
O.J. L311/67 .... 195, 495
Dir.2001/86 supplementing the
Statute for a European company
with regard to the involvement

of employees [2001]
O.J. L294/22 282
Dir.2001/95 on general product
safety [2001] O.J. L11/4 ... 497,
498
Dir.2001/96 establishing
harmonised requirements and
procedures for the safe loading
and unloading of bulk carriers
[2002] O.J. L13/9 456
Dir.2001/110 relating to honey
[2001] O.J. L10/47 409
2002 Dir.2002/14 establishing a general
framework for informing and
consulting employees in the
European Community – Joint
declaration of the European
Parliament, the Council and the
Commission on employee
representation [2002]
O.J. L80/29 282
Art.3(1) 282
Dir.2002/15 on the organisation of
working time of persons
performing mobile road
transport activities [2006]
O.J. L102/1 446
Dir.2002/18 amending Annex I to
Council Directive 91/414/EEC
concerning the placing of
plant-protection products on
the market to include
isoproturon as an active
substance [2002]
O.J. L55/29 456
Directive 2002/19 on access to,
and interconnection of,
electronic communications
networks and associated
facilities (Access Directive)
[2002] O.J. L108/7 346,
509
Dir.2002/20 on the authorisation
of electronic communications
networks and services
(Authorisation Directive)
[2002] O.J. L108/21 346,
509, 517
Art.5(2) 346
Art.7(3) 345, 346
Art.9(1) 346
Dir.2002/21 on a common
regulatory framework for
electronic communications
networks and services
(Framework Directive) [2002]

O.J. L108/33 . . . . 345, 346,
509, 511, 517
Art.6(5) 346
Art.9(1) 345
Art.14(2) 511
Art.27(1) 509
Dir.2002/22 on universal service
and users' rights relating to
electronic communications
networks and services (Universal
Service Directive) [2002]
O.J. L108/51 346,
509, 517
Art.31(1) 509
Dir.2002/38 amending and
amending temporarily Directive
77/388/EEC as regards the value
added tax arrangements
applicable to radio and
television broadcasting services
and certain electronically
supplied services [2002]
O.J. L128/41 427
Dir.2002/44 on the minimum
health and safety requirements
regarding the exposure of
workers to the risks arising from
physical agents [2002]
O.J. L177/13 472
Dir.2002/49 relating to the
assessment and management
of environmental noise –
Declaration by the Commission
in the Conciliation Committee
on the Directive relating to the
assessment and management of
environmental noise [2002]
O.J. L189/12 546
Dir.2002/58 concerning the
processing of personal data
and the protection of
privacy in the electronic
communications sector
(Directive on privacy and
electronic communications)
[2002] O.J. L201/37 512
Dir.2002/59 establishing a Union
vessel traffic monitoring and
information system [2002]
O.J. L203/10 456
Dir.2002/65 concerning the
distance marketing of financial
services [2002]
O.J. L271/16 511
Dir.2002/73 amending Council
Directive 76/207/EEC on the

implementation of the principle
of equal treatment for men and
women as regards access to
employment, vocational
training and promotion, and
working condition [2002]
O.J. L269/15 479
Dir.2002/77 on competition in the
markets for electronic
communications networks
and services [2002]
O.J. L249/21 345,
347, 510
Art.4 . . . . 345, 346
Dir.2002/92 on insurance
mediation [2003]
O.J. L9/3 296
Dir.2002/95 on the restriction of
the use of certain hazardous
substances in electrical and
electronic equipment [2003]
O.J. L37/19 541
Dir.2002/96 on waste electrical
and electronic equipment
(WEEE) [2003]
O.J. L37/24 541
Dir.2002/98 setting standards of
quality and safety for the
collection, testing, processing,
storage and distribution of
human blood and blood
components and amending
Directive 2001/83/EC [2003]
O.J. L33/30 495
2003 Dir.2003/4 on public access to
environmental information
[2003] O.J. L41/26 543
Dir.2003/6 on insider dealing and
market manipulation [2003]
O.J. L96/16 . . . . 281, 295
Dir.2003/8 to improve access to
justice in cross-border disputes
by establishing minimum
common rules relating to
legal aid for such disputes
[2003] O.J. L26/41 259
Dir.2003/10 on the minimum
health and safety requirements
regarding the exposure of
workers to the risks arising from
physical agents (noise) [2003]
O.J. L42/38 . . . . 251, 472
Dir.2003/25 on specific stability
requirements for ro-ro
passenger ships [2003]
O.J. L123/22 456

Dir.2003/33 on the approximation
of the laws, regulations and
administrative provisions of the
Member States relating to the
advertising and sponsorship of
tobacco products [2003]
O.J. L152/16 493
Dir.2003/43 laying down the
animal health requirements
applicable to intra-Community
trade in and imports of
semen of domestic animals of
the bovine species [2003]
O.J. L143/23 431
Dir.2003/48 on taxation of
savings income in the form of
interest payments [2003]
O.J. L157/38 295,
430, 431
Dir.2003/54 concerning common
rules for the internal market in
electricity and repealing
Directive 96/92/EC [2003]
O.J. L176/37 209,
552, 557
Dir.2003/55 concerning common
rules for the internal market in
natural gas and repealing
Directive 98/30/EC [2003]
O.J. L176/57 .... 209, 555,
557, 559
Dir.2003/542003/59 on the initial
qualification and periodic
training of drivers of certain
road vehicles for the carriage of
goods or passengers [2003]
O.J. L226/4 444
Dir.2003/87 establishing a scheme
for greenhouse gas emission
allowance trading within the
Community and amending
Council Directive 96/61/EC
[2003] O.J. L275/32 547
Dir.2003/88 on certain aspects
of the organisation of
working time [2003]
O.J. L299/9 .... 446, 476
Dir.2003/96 restructuring the
Community framework for the
taxation of energy products
and electricity [2003]
O.J. L283/51 429
Dir.2003/71 on the prospectus to be
published when securities are
offered to the public or admitted
to trading and amending Directive

2001/34/EC [2003]
O.J. L345/64 .... 281, 295
Dir.2003/72 supplementing the
Statute for a European
Cooperative Society with
regard to the involvement
of employees [2003]
O.J. L207/25 283
Dir.2003/94 laying down the
principles and guidelines
of good manufacturing
practices in respect of
medicinal production for
human use and investigational
medicinal products for
human use [2003]
O.J. L262/22 495
Dir.2003/108 amending Directive
2002/96/EC on waste electrical
and electronic equipment
(WEEE) [2003]
O.J. L345/106 546
Dir.2003/124 implementing
Directive 2003/6/EC of the
European Parliament and of
the Council as regards the
definition and public disclosure
of inside information and the
definition of market
manipulation [2003]
O.J. L339/70 281
Dir.2003/125 implementing
Directive 2003/6/EC of the
European Parliament and of the
Council as regards the fair
presentation of investment
recommendations and the
disclosure of conflicts of
interest [2003]
O.J. L339/73 281
Dir.2003/965 on waste electrical
and electronic equipment
(WEEE) [2002]
O.J. L37/24 546
2004 Dir.2004/16 laying down the
sampling methods and the
methods of analysis for
the official control of the levels
of tin in canned foods
[2004] O.J. L42/16
Art.35 313
Art.36 313
Dir.2004/17 coordinating the
procurement procedures of
entities operating in the water,
energy, transport and postal

services sectors [2004]
O.J. L134/1 .... 310, 314, 315
Art.1(6) 313
Art.12 315
Art.14 314
Art.15 314
Art.26 315
Art.30 315
Art.55 315
Art.59 315
Dir.2004/18 on the coordination of
procedures for the award of
public works contracts, public
supply contracts and public
service contracts [2004]
O.J. L134/114 ...... 310, 314
Art.1(5) 312
(6) 312
(7) 312, 313
(10) 312
Art.5 315
Art.7 312
Art.8 312
Art.13 310
Art.15 312
Art.16 314
Art.19 313
Arts 20–22 314
Art.23 313
Art.29 312
Art.30 312
Art.31 312
Art.32 312
Art.33 312
Art.42 314
Art.53 313
Art.55 313
Arts 56–62 314
Dir.2004/23 on setting standards
of quality and safety for the
donation, procurement, testing,
processing, preservation, storage
and distribution of human
tissues and cells [2004]
O.J. L102/48 495
Dir.2004/25 on takeover bids
[2004] O.J. L 142/1 280,
295
Dir.2004/33 implementing
Directive 2002/98/EC of the
European Parliament and
of the Council as regards
certain technical requirements
for blood and blood
components [2004]
O.J. L91/25 495

Dir.2004/36 on the safety of
third-country aircraft using
Community airports [2004]
O.J. L143/76 ...... 199, 451
Dir.2004/37 on the protection
of workers from the risks
related to exposure to
carcinogens or mutagens
at work [2004]
O.J. L158/50 ...... 251, 472
Dir.2004/38 on the right of citizens
of the Union and their family
members to move and reside
freely within the territory of the
Member States amending
Regulation (EEC) No.1612/68
and repealing Directives
64/221/EEC, 68/360/EEC,
72/194/EEC, 73/148/EEC,
75/34/EEC, 75/35/EEC,
90/364/EEC, 90/365/EEC
and 93/96/EEC [2004]
O.J. L158/77 .... 239, 243,
247, 250, 253,
266, 269, 270,
276, 284, 287, 288
Preamble (17) 240
Dir.2004/39 on markets in
financial instruments amending
Council Directives 85/611/EEC
and 93/6/EEC and Directive
2000/12/EC of the European
Parliament and of the Council
and repealing Council Directive
93/22/EEC [2004]
O.J. L145/1 295
Dir.2004/40 concerning risks
arising from physical agents
(electromagnetic fields)
[2004] O.J. L184/1 .... 251, 472
Dir.2004/48 on the enforcement of
intellectual property rights
[2004] O.J. L195/16 307
Dir.2004/49 on safety on the
Community's railways and
amending Council Directive
95/18/EC on the licensing of
railway undertakings and
Directive 2001/14/EC on the
allocation of railway
infrastructure capacity and
the levying of charges for the
use of railway infrastructure
and safety certification
(Railway Safety Directive)
[2004] O.J. L164/44 448

Dir.2004/50 amending Council
    Directive 96/48/EC on the
    interoperability of the trans-
    European high-speed rail system
    and Directive 2001/16/EC of the
    European Parliament and of the
    Council on the interoperability
    of the trans-European
    conventional rail system
    [2004] O.J. L164/114 448
Dir.2004/51 amending Council
    Directive 91/440/EEC on the
    development of the
    Community's railways
    [2004] O.J. L164/164 448
Dir.2004/72 as regards accepted
    market practices, the definition
    of inside information in relation
    to derivatives on commodities,
    the drawing up of lists of
    insiders, the notification of
    managers' transactions and the
    notification of suspicious
    transactions [2004]
    O.J. L162/70 282
Dir.2004/76 amending Directive
    2003/49/EC as regards the
    possibility for certain Member
    States to apply transitional
    periods for the application of a
    common system of taxation
    applicable to interest and royalty
    payments made between
    associated companies of different
    Member States [2004] O.J.
    L157/106 431
Dir.2004/77 amending Directive
    94/54/EC as regards the labelling
    of certain foods containing
    glycyrrhizinic acid and its
    ammonium salt [2004] O.J.
    L162/76 253
Dir.2004/80 relating to
    compensation to crime victims
    [2004] O.J. L261/15 290
Dir.2004/83 on minimum
    standards for the qualification
    and status of third country
    nationals or stateless persons as
    refugees or as persons who
    otherwise need international
    protection and the content of the
    protection granted [2004]
    O.J. L304/12 257
Dir.2004/109 on the harmonisation
    of transparency requirements in
    relation to information about
    issuers whose securities are
    admitted to trading on a
    regulated market and amending
    Directive 2001/34/EC [2004]
    O.J. L390/38 .... 280, 295
2005 Dir.2005/29 concerning unfair
    business-to-consumer
    commercial practices in the
    internal market and amending
    Council Directive 84/450/EEC,
    Directives 97/7/EC, 98/27/EC
    and 2002/65/EC of the
    European Parliament and of the
    Council and Regulation (EC)
    No.2006/2004 of the European
    Parliament and of the Council
    [2005] O.J. L149/22 496
    Art.5(5) 496
Dir.2005/35 on ship-source
    pollution and on the
    introduction of penalties for
    infringement [2005] O.J.
    L255/1 455
Dir.2005/36 on the recognition of
    professional qualifications
    [2005] O.J. L255/22 269,
                            271, 276
    Art.5 276
    Art.6 274
    Art.7 274
    Art.8 274
    Art.9 274
    Art.10 276
    Arts 10–15 274
    Art.15 277
    Arts 16–20 274
    Arts 21–49 274
    Arts 24–37 273
    Arts 38–39 273
    Arts 40–43 273
    Arts 44–45 274
    Arts 46–49 274
    Annex II 269
    Annex III 269
    Annex V.1 272
    Annex V.2 273
    Annex V.3 273
    Annex V.4 273
    Annex V.6 274
    Annex V.7 274
Dir.2005/56 on cross-border
    mergers of limited liability
    companies (Market Abuse
    Directive) [2005] O.J.
    L310/1 281

Dir.2005/60 on the prevention of the use of the financial system for the purpose of money laundering and terrorist financing [2007] O.J. L309/15 . . . . 432, 433

Dir.2005/85 on minimum standards on procedures in Member States for granting and withdrawing refugee status [2005] O.J. L326/13 257

2006 Dir.2006/1 on the use of vehicles hired without drivers for the carriage of goods by road [2006] O.J. L33/86 444

Dir.2006/25 on the minimum health and safety requirements regarding the exposure of workers to risks arising from physical agents [2006] O.J. L114/38 472

Dir.2006/32 on energy end-use efficiency and energy services and repealing Council Directive 93/76/EEC [2006] O.J. L114/64 554

Dir.2006/46 amending Council Directives 78/660/EEC on the annual accounts of certain types of companies, 83/349/EEC on consolidated accounts, 86/635/EEC on the annual accounts and consolidated accounts of banks and other financial institutions and 91/674/EEC on the annual accounts and consolidated accounts of insurance undertakings [2006] O.J. L224/1 292

Dir.2006/48 relating to the taking up and pursuit of the business of credit institutions [2006] O.J. L177/1 292

Dir.2006/49 on the capital adequacy of investment firms and credit institutions [2006] O.J. L177/201 292

Dir.2006/67 imposing an obligation on Member States to maintain minimum stocks of crude oil and/or petroleum products [2006] O.J. L217/8 553

Dir.2008/68 on the inland transport of dangerous goods [2008] O.J. L260/13 440

Dir.2006/87 laying down technical requirements for inland waterway vessels and repealing Council Directive 82/714/EEC [2006] O.J. L389/1 454

Dir.2006/94 on the establishment of common rules for certain types of carriage of goods by road [2006] O.J. L374/5 . . . 444

Dir.2006/105 adapting Directives 73/239/EEC, 74/557/EEC and 2002/83/EC in the field of environment, by reason of the accession of Bulgaria and Romania [2006] O.J. L363/368 422

Dir.2006/112 on the common system of value added tax [2006] O.J. L347/1 427

Dir.2006/115 on rental right and lending right and on certain rights related to copyright in the field of intellectual property [2006] O.J. L376/28 304

Dir.2006/116 on the term of protection of copyright and certain related rights [2006] O.J. L372/12 304

Dir.2006/123 on services in the internal market [2006] O.J. L376/36 297

Directive 2006/126 [2006] O.J. L403/18 445

2007 Dir.2007/14 laying down detailed rules for the implementation of certain provisions of Directive 2004/109/EC on the harmonisation of transparency requirements in relation to information about issuers whose securities are admitted to trading on a regulated market [2007] O.J. L69/27 . . . . 280, 295

Dir.2007/16 implementing Council Directive 85/611/EEC on the coordination of laws, regulations and administrative provisions relating to undertakings for collective investment in transferable securities (UCITS) as regards the clarification of certain definitions [2007] O.J. L79/11 294

Dir.2007/46 establishing a framework for the approval of motor vehicles and their trailers,

and of systems, components and
separate technical units intended
for such vehicle [2007] O.J.
L263/1 445
Dir.2007/58 amending Council
Directive 91/440/EEC on the
development of the Community's
railways and Directive
2001/14/EC on the allocation of
railway infrastructure capacity
and the levying of charges for the
use of railway infrastructure
[2007] O.J. L315/44 449
Dir.2007/64 on payment
services in the internal market
amending Directives 97/7/EC,
2002/65/EC, 2005/60/EC and
2006/48/EC and repealing
Directive 97/5/EC [2007]
O.J. L319/1 . . . . 292, 433,
                          497, 511
Dir.2007/69 on the certification of
train drivers operating
locomotives and trains on the
railway system in the Union
[2007] O.J. L315/51 449
2008   Dir.2008/6 amending Directive
97/67/EC with regard to the
full accomplishment of the
internal market of Community
postal services [2008]
O.J. L52/3 349
Dir.2008/7 concerning indirect
taxes on the raising of capital
[2008] O.J. L46/11 428
Dir.2008/8 amending Directive
2006/112/EC as regards the
place of supply of services
[2008] O.J. L.44/11 428
Dir.2008/9 laying down detailed
rules for the refund of value
added tax, provided for in
Directive 2006/112/EC, to
taxable persons not established
in the Member State of refund
but established in another
Member State [2008]
O.J. L44/23 428
Dir.2008/18 amending Council
Directive 85/611/EEC on the
coordination of laws, regulations
and administrative provisions
relating to undertakings for
collective investment in
transferable securities (UCITS),
as regards the implementing

powers conferred on the
Commission [2008] O.J.
L76/42 115
Dir.2008/31 amending Directive
98/8/EC concerning the placing
of biocidal products on the
market, as regards the
implementing powers conferred
on the Commission [2008]
O.J. L81/57 499
Dir.2008/34 amending Directive
2002/96/EC on waste electrical
and electronic equipment
(WEEE), as regards the
implementing powers conferred
on the Commission [2008]
O.J. L81/65 546
Dir.2008/46 amending Directive
2004/40/EC on minimum health
and safety requirements
regarding the exposure of
workers to the risks arising from
physical agents [2008]
O.J. L114/88 472
Dir.2008/48 on credit
agreements for consumers and
repealing Council Directive
87/102/EEC [2008]
O.J. L133/66 . . . . 497, 498
Dir.2008/50 on ambient air quality
and cleaner air for Europe
[2008] O.J. L152/1 . . 541, 545
Dir.2008/52 on certain aspects of
mediation in civil and
commercial matters [2008]
O.J. L136/3 259
Dir.2008/55 on mutual assistance
for the recovery of claims
relating to certain levies,
duties, taxes and other
measures [2008] O.J.
L150/28 428
Dir.2008/56 establishing a
framework for community
action in the field of marine
environmental policy [2008]
O.J. L164/19 515
Dir.2008/57 on the interoperability
of the rail system within the
Community [2008] O.J.
L191/1 447
Annex VII 447, 448
Dir.2008/63 on competition in the
markets in telecommunications
terminal equipment [2008]
O.J. L162/20 348

Dir.2008/68 on the inland
transport of dangerous
goods [2008] O.J.
L260/13 . . . . 445, 448
Dir.2008/94 on the protection of
employees in the event of the
insolvency of their employer
[2008] O.J. L283/36 473
Dir.2008/95 to approximate the
laws of the Member States
relating to trade marks
[2008] O.J. L299/25 305
Dir.2008/98 on waste and
repealing certain Directives
[32008] O.J. L312/3 541,
545
Dir.2008/101 amending Directive
2003/87/EC so as to include
aviation activities in the scheme
for greenhouse gas emission
allowance trading within the
Community [2008] O.J.
L8/3 547
Dir.2008/104 on temporary
agency work [2008] O.J.
L327/9 370
Dir.2008/105 on environmental
quality standards in the field of
water policy [2008] O.J.
L348/84 545
Dir.2008/118 concerning the
general arrangements for excise
duty and repealing Directive
92/12/EEC [2009] O.J.
L9/12 . . . . 429, 430
2009 Dir.2009/111/EC of the European
Parliament and of the Council of
16 September 2009 amending
Directives 2006/48/EC,
2006/49/EC and 2007/64/EC as
regards banks affiliated to
central institutions, certain own
funds items, large exposures,
supervisory arrangements, and
crisis management [2009]
O.J. l302/97 292
Dir.2009/22 on injunctions for the
protection of consumers'
interests [2009] O.J.
L110/30 496
Dir.2009/24 on the legal
protection of computer
programs [2009] O.J.
L111/16 301
Dir.2009/30 amending Directive
98/70/EC as regards the

specification of petrol, diesel and
gas-oil and introducing a
mechanism to monitor and
reduce greenhouse gas emissions
and amending Council Directive
1999/32/EC as regards the
specification of fuel used by
inland waterway vessels and
repealing Directive 93/12/EEC
[2009] O.J. L140/88 547
Dir.2009/33 on the promotion of
clean and energy-efficient road
transport vehicles [2009]
O.J. L120/5 444
Dir.2009/38 on the establishment
of a European Works Council or
a procedure in Community-scale
undertakings and Community-
scale groups of undertakings for
the purposes of informing and
consulting employees [2009]
O.J. L122/28 . . . . 282, 474
Dir.2009/45 on safety rules and
standards for passenger ships
[2009] O.J. L163/1 456
Dir.2008/46 amending Directive
2004/40/EC on minimum health
and safety requirements
regarding the exposure of
workers to the risks arising from
physical agents [2008] O.J.
L114/88 472
Dir.2009/48 on the safety of toys
[2009] O.J. L170/1 499
Dir.2009/50 on the conditions of
entry and residence of third-
country nationals for the
purposes of highly qualified
employment [2009] O.J.
L155/17 254
Dir.2009/52 providing for
minimum standards on
sanctions and measures against
employers of illegally staying
third-country nationals
[2009] O.J. L168/24 257
Dir.2003/54 concerning common
rules for the internal market in
electricity and repealing
Directive 96/92/EC – Statements
made with regard to
decommissioning and waste
management activities
[2003] O.J. L176/37 555
Dir.2009/72 concerning common
rules for the internal market in

electricity and repealing
Directive 2003/54/EC [2009]
O.J. L211/55 . . . . 552, 555
Dir.2009/73 concerning common
rules for the internal market in
natural gas and repealing
Directive 2003/55/EC
[2009] O.J. L211/94 555
Dir.2009/103 relating to insurance
against civil liability in respect of
the use of motor vehicles, and
the enforcement of the
obligation to insure against
such liability [2009]
O.J. L263/11 . . . . 296, 445
Dir.2009/136/EC of the European
Parliament and of the Council of
25 November 2009 amending
Directive 2002/22/EC on
universal service and users'
rights relating to electronic
communications networks and
services, Directive 2002/58/EC
concerning the processing of
personal data and the protection
of privacy in the electronic
communications sector and
Regulation (EC) No 2006/2004
on cooperation between national
authorities responsible for the
enforcement of consumer
protection laws [2009]
O.J. L337/11 . . . . 346, 512
Dir. 2009/140/EC of the European
Parliament and of the Council of
25 November 2009 amending
Directives 2002/21/EC on a
common regulatory framework
for electronic communications
networks and services,
2002/19/EC on access to, and
interconnection of, electronic
communications networks and
associated facilities, and
2002/20/EC on the authorisation
of electronic communications
networks and services [2009]
O.J. L337/37 . . . . 346, 512

Regulations

1958 Reg.1/58 determining the
languages to be used by the
European Economic
Community [1958] O.J.
L17/385 37

1960 Reg. 11/60 concerning the
abolition of discrimination in
transport rates and conditions,
in implementation of Art.79(3)
of the Treaty establishing the
European Economic
Community [1960]
O.J. L52/1121 . . . . . . 113, 444
Art.18 132
1961 Reg.7a/61 adding certain products
to the list in Annex II to the
Treaty establishing the European
Economic Community
[1961] O.J. 7/71 400
1962 Reg.17/62 First Regulation
implementing Articles 85 and 86
of the Treaty [1962] O.J.
L13/204 . . . . 37, 327,
342, 350, 351,
353, 360, 363, 443
Art.3 353
Reg.26/62 applying certain
rules of competition to
production of and trade in
agricultural products [1962]
O.J. L30/993 . . . . 342, 388
Recital (1) 342
Art.2 342
Reg.27/62 First Regulation
implementing Council Regulation
No.17 of February 6, 1962
[1962] O.J. 35/1118 353
Reg.141/62 exempting transport
from the application of Council
Regulation No.17 [1962]
O.J. L124/2751 443
1963 Reg.99/63 on the hearings
provided for in Article 19 (1)
and (2) of Council
Regulation No.17 [1963]
O.J. 127/2268 110
1965 Reg.19/65 on application of
Article 85(3) of the Treaty to
certain categories of
agreements and concerted
practices [1965] O.J.
L36/533 . . . . 329, 334, 363
1968 Reg.950/68 on the common
customs tariff [1968] O.J.
L172/1 225
Reg.1017/68 applying rules of
competition to transport by rail,
road and inland waterway
[1968] O.J. L175/1 . . . 113, 342,
343, 363,
438, 443, 446

Art.22 52
Art.24 132
Reg.1612/68 on freedom of
movement for workers within
the Community [1968]
O.J. L257/2 . . . . 245, 246,
248, 253
Recital, para.6 245
Art.10(1) 249
Art.12 249

1969 Reg.1191/69 on action by Member
States concerning the obligations
inherent in the concept of a public
service in transport by rail, road
and inland waterway [1969]
O.J. L56/1 . . . . 443, 447
Reg.1192/69 on common rules for
the normalisation of the
accounts of railways
undertakings [1969] O.J.
L156/8 446
Reg.1630/69 on the hearings
provided for in Article 26(1)
and (2) of Council Regulation
(EEC) No.1017/68 [1969]
O.J. L209/11 342

1970 Reg.1107/70 on the granting of
aids for transport by rail, road
and inland waterway [1970]
O.J. L130/1 . . . . 387, 443
Reg.1251/70 on the right of
workers to remain in the
territory of a Member State
after having been employed
in that State 250
Reg.2141/70 laying down a
common structural policy for the
fishing industry [1970]
O.J. L236/1 420

1971 Reg.1182/71 determining the
rules applicable to periods,
dates and time limits
[1971] O.J. L124/1 395
Reg.1408/71 on the application of
social security schemes to
employed persons and their
families moving within the
Community [1971]
O.J. L149/2 . . . . 245, 250,
265, 267, 477
Art.1(a)(i) 245
Art.46(2) 251
Arts 80–83 251
Art.81(a) 251
Reg.2821/71 on application of
Article 85(3) of the Treaty to

categories of agreements,
decisions and concerted
practices [1971] O.J.
L258/46 . . . . 329, 363

1972 Reg.574/72 fixing the procedure
for implementing Regulation
(EEC) No.1408/71 on the
application of social security
schemes to employed persons
and their families moving within
the Community [1972]
O.J. L74/1 250

1974 Reg.2988/74 concerning limitation
periods in proceedings and the
enforcement of sanctions under
the rules of the European
Economic Community relating
to transport and competition
[1974] O.J. L319/1 342,
353, 363
Arts 4–6 353

1975 Reg.337/75 establishing a
European Centre for the
Development of Vocational
Training [1975] O.J.
L39/1 . . . . 192, 476, 483
Reg.724/75 establishing a
European Regional
Development Fund
[1975] O.J. L73/1 . . . 519, 521
Reg.1365/75 on the creation of a
European Foundation for the
improvement of living and
working conditions [1975]
O.J. L139/1 . . . . 192, 473
Reg.2771/75 on the common
organization of the market
in eggs [1075] O.J.
L282/49 408

1976 Reg.101/76 laying down a
common structural policy for
the fishing industry [1976]
O.J. L20/19 420

1977 Reg.355/77 on common measures
to improve the conditions under
which agricultural products are
processed and marketed
[1977] O.J. L51/1 420
Reg.1778/77 concerning the
application of the anti-dumping
duty on ball bearings and
tapered roller bearings,
originating in Japan [1977]
O.J. L196/1 163
Reg.2892/77 implementing in
respect of own resources

accruing from value added tax
the Decision of April 21, 1970
on the replacement of financial
contributions from Member
States by the Communities'
own resources [1977] O.J.
L336/8 215
Reg.3023/77 on certain measures
to put an end to abuses resulting
from the sale of agricultural
products on board ship
[1977] O.J. L358/2 37
Financial Regulation of 21
December 1977 applicable to the
general budget of the European
Communities [1977] O.J.
L356/1 216
    Art.15 216
    Art.16 216

1979   Reg.214/79 amending Regulation
(EEC) No.724/75 establishing a
European Regional Development
Fund [1979] O.J. L35/1 61
Reg.954/79 concerning the
ratification by Member States
of, or their accession to, the
United Nations Convention on
a Code of Conduct for Liner
Conferences [1979] O.J.
L121/1 455

1980   Reg.2744/80 establishing
supplementary measures in
favour of the United Kingdom
[1980] O.J. L284/4 215

1983   Reg.56/83 concerning the
implementation of the
Agreement on the international
carriage of passengers by road
by means of occasional coach
and bus services (ASOR)
[1983] O.J. L10/1 443
Reg.170/83 establishing a
Community system for the
conservation and management of
fishery resources [1983] O.J.
L24/1 416
Reg.1983/83 on the application of
Article 85(3) of the Treaty to
categories of exclusive
distribution agreements
[1983] O.J. L173/1 329
Reg.1984/83 on the application of
Article 85(3) of the Treaty to
categories of exclusive
purchasing agreements
[1983] O.J. L173/5 329

Reg.2908/83 on a common
measure for restructuring,
modernizing and developing the
fishing industry and for
developing aquaculture
[1983] O.J. L290/1 420
Reg.2909/83 on measures to
encourage exploratory fishing
and cooperation through joint
ventures in the fishing sector
[1983] O.J. L290/9 420
Reg.3166/83 on applications for
aid from the Guidance Section of
the European Agricultural
Guidance and Guarantee Fund
for investment projects in
fisheries and aquaculture
L316/1 420

1984   Reg.2349/84 on the application of
Article 85(3) of the Treaty to
certain categories of patent
licensing agreements [1984]
O.J. L219/15 .... 304, 334

1985   Reg.2137/85 on the European
Economic Interest Grouping
[1985] O.J. L199/1 283
Reg.3820/85 on the harmonising
of certain social legislation
regarding to road transport
[1985] O.J. L370/1 446
Reg.3821/85 on recording
equipment in road transport
[1985] O.J. L370/8 ... 442, 445

1986   Reg.4028/86 on Community
measures to improve and adapt
structures in the fisheries and
aquaculture sector [1986]
O.J. L376/7 420
Reg.4055/86 applying the principle
of freedom to provide services to
maritime transport between
Member States and between
Member States and third
countries [1986] O.J.
L378/1 455
Reg.4056/86 laying down detailed
rules for the application of
Articles 85 and 86 of the Treaty
to maritime transport
[1986] O.J. L378/4 343,
                        363, 438
Reg.4057/86 on unfair pricing
practices in maritime transport
[1986] O.J. L378/14 455
Reg.4058/86 concerning
coordinated action to safeguard

free access to cargoes in
ocean trades [1986] O.J.
L378/21 455

1987 Reg.1761/87 amending Regulation
(EEC) No.2176/84 on protection
against dumped or subsidized
imports from countries not
members of the European
Economic Community
[1987] O.J. L167/9 584
Reg.2241/87 establishing certain
control measures for fishing
activities [1987] O.J.
L207/1 417
Reg.3975/87 laying down the
procedure for the application
of the rules on competition to
undertakings in the air
transport sector [1987]
O.J. L374/1 . . . . 344, 450
Art.14 132
Reg.3976/87 on the application of
Article 85(3) of the Treaty to
certain categories of agreements
and concerted practices in the air
transport sector [1987]
O.J. L374/9 344,
363, 450

1988 Reg.1988/2006 amending
Regulation No.2424/2001 on
the development of the second
generation Schengen
Information System [1988]
O.J. L411/1 242
Reg.4073/88 amending Regulation
No.1975/82 on the acceleration
of agricultural development in
certain regions of Greece
[1988] O.J. L359/1 329
Reg.4253/88 laying down
provisions for implementing
Regulation (EEC) No.2052/88 as
regards coordination of the
activities of the different
Structural Funds between
themselves and with the
operations of the European
Investment Bank and the other
existing financial instruments
[1988] O.J. L374/1 421
Reg.4261/88 on the complaints,
applications and hearings
provided for in Council
Regulation (EEC) No.3975/87
laying down the procedure for
the application of the rules on

competition to undertakings in
the air transport sector
[1988] O.J. L376/10 344

1989 Reg.1101/89 on structural
improvements in inland
waterway transport [1989]
O.J. L116/25 388
Reg.556/89 on the application of
Article 85 (3) of the Treaty to
certain categories of know-how
licensing agreements [1989]
O.J. L61/1 . . . . 340, 335
Reg.2299/89 on a code of conduct
for computerized reservation
systems [1989] O.J.
L220/1 451
Art.17 132
Reg.3906/89 on economic aid to the
Republic of Hungary and the
Polish People's Republic [1989]
O.J. L375/11 . . . . 198, 612
Reg.4058/89 on the fixing of rates
for the carriage of goods by road
between Member States
[1989] O.J. L390/1 444
Reg.4060/89 on the elimination of
controls performed at the
frontiers of Member States in the
field of road and inland
waterway transport [1989]
O.J. L390/18 445
Annex I 445
Annex III 445
Annex IV 445
Annex VI 445
Annex VII 445
Annex XI 445
Annex XV 445
Reg.4064/89 on the control of
concentrations between
undertakings [1989]
O.J. L395/1 . . . . 367, 373

1990 Reg.1152/90 instituting a system
of aid in favour of small
cotton producers [1990]
O.J. L116/1 407
Reg.1210/90 on the establishment
of the European Environment
Agency and the European
Environment Information and
Observation Network [1990]
O.J. L120/1 . . . . 192, 550
Reg.1360/90 establishing a
European Training
Foundation [1990]
O.J. L131/1 . . . . 193, 483

1991 Reg.1534/91 on the application
of Article 85(3) of the Treaty
to certain categories of
agreements, decisions and
concerted practices in the
insurance sector [1991]
O.J. L143/1 . . . . 329, 349
Reg.1994/91 fixing the minimum
selling prices for the purposes of
the standing invitation to tender
issued by Regulation (EEC)
No.1993/91 [1991] O.J.
L1/422 363
Regulation 2092/91 on organic
production of agricultural
products and indications
referring thereto on agricultural
products and foodstuffs
[1991] O.J. L198/1 410
Reg.3922/91 on the harmonisation
of technical requirements and
administrative procedures in the
field of civil aviation [1991]
O.J. L373/4 451
1992 Reg.479/92 on the application of
Article 85(3) of the Treaty to
certain categories of agreements,
decisions and concerted practices
between liner shipping
companies [1992] O.J.
L55/3 . . . . 343, 455
Reg.684/92 on common rules for
the international carriage of
passengers by coach and bus
[1992] O.J. L71/1 443
Reg.880/1992 on a Community
eco-label award scheme
[1992] O.J. L99/1 . . . . 500, 541
Reg.881/92 on access to the
market in the carriage of goods
by road within the Community
to or from the territory of a
Member State or passing across
the territory of one or more
Member States [1992]
O.J. L95/1 444
Reg.1762/92 on the
implementation of the Protocols
on financial and technical
cooperation concluded by the
Community with Mediterranean
non-member countries
[1992] O.J. L181/1 593
Reg.1763/92 concerning
financial cooperation in
respect of all Mediterranean

non-member countries
[1992] O.J. L181/5 593
Reg.1764/92 amending the
arrangements for the import into
the Community of certain
agricultural products originating
in Algeria, Cyprus, Egypt, Israel,
Jordan, Lebanon, Malta,
Morocco, Syria and Tunisia
[1992] O.J. L181/9 593
Reg.1973/92 establishing a
financial instrument for the
environment (LIFE) [1992]
O.J. L206/1 550
Reg.2075/92 on the common
organization of the market in
raw tobacco [1992] O.J.
L215/70 406
Reg.2081/92 on the protection of
geographical indications and
designations of origin for
agricultural products and
foodstuffs [1992] O.J.
L208/1 308
Annex II 308
Reg.2407/92 on licensing of
air carriers [1992] O.J.
L240/1 450
Reg.2408/92 on access for
Community air carriers to
intra-Community air routes
[1992] O.J. L240/8 . . . . 344, 450
Reg.2409/92 on fares and rates
for air services [1992]
O.J. L240/15 450
Reg.2455/92 concerning the
export and import of certain
dangerous chemicals
[1992] O.J. L251/13 546
Regulation 2719/92 on the
accompanying administrative
document for the movement
under duty suspension
arrangements of products
subject to excise duty
[1992] O.J. 276/1 430
Reg.3577/92 applying the principle
of freedom to provide sevices to
maritime transport within
Member States [1992]
O.J. L364/7 455
Reg.3759/92 on the common
organisation of the market in
fishery and aquaculture
products [1992] O.J.
L388/1 414

Reg.3911/92 on the export of cultural goods [1992] O.J. L395/1 488

Reg.3927/92 laying down certain conservation and management measures for fishery resources in the Regulatory Area as defined in the Convention on Future Multilateral Co-operation in the North-West Atlantic Fisheries [1992] O.J. L397/78 420

Reg.3932/92 on the application of Article 85(3) of the Treaty to certain categories of agreements, decisions and concerted practices in the insurance sector [1992] O.J. L398/7 .... 349, 420

1993 Reg.95/93 on common rules for the allocation of slots at Community airports [1993] O.J. L14/1 451

Reg.259/93 on the supervision and control of shipments of waste within, into and out of the European Community [1993] O.J. L30/1 546

Reg.302/93 on the establishment of a European Monitoring Centre for Drugs and Drug Addiction [1993] O.J. L36/1 194

Reg.752/93 laying down provisions for the implementation of Regulation 3911/92 [1993] O.J. L77/24 488

Reg.1617/93 on the application of Article 85 (3) of the Treaty to certain categories of agreements and concerted practices concerning joint planning and coordination of schedules, joint operations, consultations on passenger and cargo tariffs on scheduled air services and slot allocation at airports [1993] O.J. L155/18 .... 344, 451

Reg.1836/93 allowing voluntary participation by companies in the industrial sector in a Community eco-management and audit scheme [1993] O.J. L168/1 547

Reg.2080/93 laying down provisions for implementing Regulation 2052/88 as regards the financial instrument of fisheries guidance [1993] O.J. L193/1 421

Reg.2083/93 amending Regulation (EEC) No.4254/88 laying down provisions for implementing Regulation (EEC) No.2052/898 as regards the European Regional Development Fund [1993] O.J. L193/34 515

Reg.2186/93 on Community coordination in drawing up business registers for statistical purposes [1993] O.J. L196/1 110

Reg.2309/93 laying down Community procedures for the authorization and supervision of medicinal products for human and veterinary use and establishing a European Agency for the Evaluation of Medicinal Products [1993] O.J. L214/1 ... 194, 495
  Art.12 194
  Art.34 194

Reg.2454/93 laying down provisions for the implementation of Council Regulation (EEC) No.2913/92 establishing the Community Customs Code [1993] O.J. L253/1 226

Reg.2847/93 establishing a control system applicable to the common fisheries policy [1993] O.J. L261/1 418

Reg.3118/93 laying down the conditions under which non-resident carriers may operate road haulage services within a Member State [1993] O.J. L279/1 444

Reg.3464/93 amending Regulation (EEC, Euratom) No.1552/89 implementing Decision 88/376/EEC, Euratom on the system of the Communities' own resources [1993] O.J. L317/1 215

1994 Reg.40/94 on the Community trade mark [1994] O.J. L11/1 .... 195, 197, 305

Regulation 519/94 on common rules for imports from certain

thirdworld countries [1994]
O.J. L67/89 583
Regulation 792/94 laying down
detailed rules for the
application of Regulation
3118/93 to road haulage
operators on own account
[1994] O.J. L92/13 444
Reg.1164/94 establishing a
Cohesion Fund [1994]
O.J. L130/1 . . . . 522, 551
Reg.1796/94 amending, for the
fifteenth time, Regulation
(EEC) No.3094/86 laying
down certain technical
measures for the conservation
of fishery resources [1994]
O.J. L187/1 416
Reg.2062/94 establishing a
European Agency for Safety and
Health at Work [1994]
O.J. L216/1 . . . . 197, 472
Reg.2100/94 on Community
plant variety rights [1994]
O.J. L227/1 197
Reg.2965/94 setting up a
Translation Centre for bodies
of the European Union
[1994] O.J. L 314/1 196
Reg.3286/94 laying down
Community procedures in the
field of the common commercial
policy in order to ensure the
exercise of the Community's
rights under international
trade rules, in particular those
established under the auspices of
the World Trade Organization
[1994] O.J. L349/71 585
Reg.3385/94 on the form, content
and other details of applications
and notifications provided for in
Council Regulation No.17
[1994] O.J. L377/28 360
1995   Reg.297/95 on fees payable to the
European Agency for the
Evaluation of Medicinal
Products [1995] O.J.
L35/1 195
Reg.870/95 on the application of
Article 85 (3) of the Treaty to
certain categories of agreements,
decisions and concerted practices
between liner shipping
companies (consortia) pursuant
to Council Regulation (EEC)

No.479/92 [1995] O.J.
L89/7 343
Reg.1238/95 establishing
implementing rules for the
application of Council
Regulation (EC) No.2100/94
as regards the fees payable to
the Community Plant Variety
Office [1995] O.J.
L121/31 197
Reg.1239/95 establishing
implementing rules for the
application of Council Regulation
(EC) No.2100/94 as regards
proceedings before the
Community Plant Variety Office
[1995] O.J. L121/37 197
Reg.1768/95 implementing rules
on the agricultural exemption
provided for in Article 14 (3) of
Council Regulation (EC) No
2100/94 on Community plant
variety rights [1995] O.J.
L173/14 197
Reg.2236/95 laying down general
rules for the granting of Union
financial aid in the field of
trans-European networks
[1995] O.J. L228/1 515
Reg.2610/95 amending Regulation
(EC) No.2965/94 setting up a
Translation Centre for bodies
of the European Union
[1995] O.J. L268/1 196
Reg.2744/95 on statistics on
the structure and distribution
of earnings [1995] O.J.
L287/3 476
Reg.2868/95 amending
Regulation (EC) No.2965/94
setting up a Translation
Centre for bodies of the
European Union [1995]
O.J. L303/1 . . . . 197, 305
Reg.2869/95 on the fees payable to
the Office for Harmonization in
the Internal Market (Trade
Marks and Designs) [1995]
O.J. L303/33 196
Reg.3051/95 on the safety
management of roll-on/roll-off
passenger ferries (ro-ro ferries)
[1995] O.J. L320/14 456
Reg.3094/95 on aid to
shipbuilding [1995] O.J.
L332/1 382

1996 Reg.216/96 laying down the
rules of procedure of the
Boards of Appeal of the Office
for Harmonization in the
Internal Market (Trade
Marks and Designs) [1996]
O.J. L28/11 . . . . 196, 305

Reg.240/96 on the application of
Article 85 (3) of the Treaty to
certain categories of technology
transfer agreements [1996]
O.J. L31/2 334

Reg.384/96 on protection against
dumped imports from countries
not members of the Union
[1996] O.J. L56/1 583

Reg.1107/96 on the registration of
geographical indications and
designations of origin under the
procedure laid down in Article
17 of Council Regulation
(EEC) No.2081/92 [1996]
O.J. L148/1 499

Reg.1256/96 applying multiannual
schemes of generalized tariff
preferences from July 1, 1996 to
30 June 1999 in respect of
certain agricultural products
originating in developing
countries [1996] O.J.
L160/1 602

Reg.1257/96 concerning
humanitarian aid [1996]
O.J. L163/1 601

Reg.1488/96 on financial and
technical measures to
accompany (MEDA) the reform
of economic and social
structures in the framework of
the Euro-Mediterranean
partnership [1996] O.J.
L189/1 594

Reg.1610/96 concerning the
creation of a supplementary
protection certificate for plant
protection products [1996]
O.J. L198/30 197

Reg.2185/96 concerning
on-the-spot checks and
inspections carried out by
the Commission in order to
protect the European
Communities' financial
interests against fraud and
other irregularities [1996]
O.J. L292/2 433

Reg.2200/96 on the common
organization of the market in
fruit and vegetables [1996]
O.J. L297/1 405

Reg.2201/96 on the common
organization of the markets
in processed fruit and
vegetable products [1996]
O.J. L297/29 405

Reg.2202/96 introducing a
Community aid scheme for
producers of certain citrus fruits
[1996] O.J. L297/49 405

Reg.2400/96 on the entry of
certain names in the 'Register of
protected designation of origin
and protected geographical
indications' provided for in
Council Regulation (EEC)
No.2081/92 on the protection
of geographical indications and
designations of origin for
agricultural products and
foodstuffs [1996] O.J.
L327/11 499

1997 Reg.338/97 on the protection of
species of wild fauna and flora
by regulating trade therein
[1997] O.J. L61/1 546

Reg.535/97 amending Regulation
(EEC) No.2081/92 on the
protection of geographical
indications and designations
of origin for agricultural
products and foodstuffs
[1997] O.J. L83/3 308

Reg.701/97 amending a
programme to promote
international cooperation in the
energy sector – Synergy
programme [1997] O.J.
L104/1 554

Regulation 894/87 laying down
transitional provisions and
detailed rules for the application,
as regards measures for the
modernization of the fishing
fleet, of Council Regulation
(EEC) No.4028/86 [1997]
O.J. L88/1 416

Reg.1103/97 on certain
provisions relating to the
introduction of the euro
[1997] O.J. L162/1 459

Reg.1221/97 laying down general
rules for the application of

measures to improve the
production and marketing
of honey [1997] O.J. L
173/1 408
Reg.1310/97 amending Regulation
(EEC) No.4064/89 on the
control of concentrations
between undertakings
[1997] O.J. L180/1 364
Reg.1466/97 on the strengthening of
the surveillance of budgetary
positions and the surveillance and
coordination of economic policies
[1997] O.J. L209/1 466
Art.6(3) 467
Reg.1467/97 on speeding up and
clarifying the implementation of
excessive deficit procedure
[1997] O.J. L209/6 466
Art.2(1) 467
Reg.1667/97 amending Council
Regulation (EC) No.1981/94
opening and providing for the
administration of Community
tariff quotas for certain products
originating in Algeria, Cyprus,
Egypt, Israel, Jordan, Malta,
Morocco, the West Bank and the
Gaza Strip, Tunisia and Turkey,
and providing detailed rules for
extending and adapting these
tariff quotas [1997] O.J.
L236/3 466
Reg.2026/97 on protection against
imports from countries not
members of the Union
[1997] O.J. L288/1 583
Reg.2027/97 on air carrier liability
in the event of accidents
[1997] O.J. L285/1 452
Reg.2300/97 on detailed rules to
implement Council Regulation
(EC) No.1221/97 laying down
general rules for the application of
measures to improve the
production and marketing of
honey [1997] O.J. L319/4 ... 409
1998 Reg.12/98 laying down the
conditions under which
non-resident carriers may
operate national road passenger
transport services within a
Member State [1998]
O.J. L4/10 .... 443, 444
Reg.447/98 on the notifications,
time limits and hearings

provided for in Council
Regulation (EEC) No.4064/89
on the control of concentrations
between undertakings
[1998] O.J. L61/1 ... 367, 368
Annex 366
Reg.974/98 on the introduction
of the Euro [1998] O.J.
L139/1 459
Reg.994/98 on the application of
Articles 92 and 93 of the Treaty
establishing the European
Community to certain categories
of horizontal State aid
[1998] O.J. L142/1 389
Reg.1659/98 on decentralised
cooperation [1998] O.J.
L213/6 602
Reg.2121/98 laying down detailed
rules for the application of
Council Regulations (EEC)
No.684/92 and (EC) No.12/98
as regards documents for the
carriage of passengers by
coach and bus [1998] O.J.
L268/10 443
Reg.2135/98 amending Regulation
(EEC) No.3821/85 on recording
equipment in road transport and
Directive 88/599/EEC
concerning the application of
Regulations (EEC) No.3820/84
and (EEC) No.3821/85
[1998] O.J. L274/1 445
Reg.2532/98 concerning the
powers of the European Central
Bank to impose sanctions
[1998] O.J. L318/4 178
Reg.2679/98 on the functioning of
the internal market in relation to
the free movement of goods
among the Member States
[1998] O.J. L337/8 235
Reg.2818/98 on the application of
minimum reserves [1998]
O.J. L356/1 465
Reg.2819/98 concerning the
consolidated balance sheet
of the monetary financial
institutions sector [1998]
O.J. L356/7 465
Reg.2842/98 on the hearing of
parties in certain proceedings
under Articles 85 and 86 of
the EC Treaty [1998] O.J.
L354/18 360

Reg.2843/98 on the form, content and other details of applications and notifications provided for in Council Regulations (EEC) No.1017/68, (EEC) No.4056/86 and (EEC) No.3975/87 applying the rules on competition to the transport sector [1998] O.J. L354/22 . . . . 344, 360

Reg.2848/98 laying down detailed rules for the application of Council Regulation (EEC) No.2075/92 as regards the premium scheme, production quotas and the specific aid to be granted to producer groups in the raw tobacco sector [1998] O.J. L358/17 406

1999 Reg.307/1999 amending Regulation (EEC) No.1408/71 on the application of social security schemes to employed persons, to self-employed persons and to members of their families moving within the Community and Regulation (EEC) No.574/72 laying down the procedure for implementing Regulation (EEC) No.1408/71 with a view to extending them to cover students [1999] O.J. L38/1 265

Regulation 659/99 laying down detailed rules for the application of art.108 [88] [1999] O.J. L83/1 . . . . 394, 395, 397, 427
  Art.8 . . . . 337, 396

Reg.718/1999 on a Community-fleet capacity policy to promote inland waterway transport [1999] O.J. L90/1 454

Reg.1073/99 concerning investigations conducted by the European Anti-Fraud Office [1999] O.J. L136/1 . . . . . 79, 219

Reg.1074/1999 concerning investigations conducted by the European Anti-Fraud Office [1999] O.J. L136/8 79

Reg.1085/99 fixing the minimum selling prices for beef put up for sale under the invitation to tender referred to in Regulation (EC) No.837/1999 [1999] O.J. L131/33 522

Reg.1225/99 concerning the definitions of characteristics for insurance services statistics [1999] O.J. L154/1 296

Reg.1226/99 concerning the derogations to be granted for insurance services statistics [1999] O.J. L154/46 296

Reg.1227/99 concerning the technical format for the transmission of insurance services statistics [1999] O.J. L154/75 296

Reg.1228/99 concerning the series of data to be produced for insurance services statistics [1999] O.J. L154/91 296

Reg.1254/99 on the common organisation of the market in beef and veal [1999] O.J. L160/21 407

Reg.1255/99 on the common organisation of the market in milk and milk products [1999] O.J. L160/48 407

Reg.1257/99 on support for rural development from the European Agricultural Guidance and Guarantee Fund (EAGGF) and amending and repealing certain Regulations [1999] O.J. L 160/80 411

Reg.1263/99 on the Financial Instrument for Fisheries Guidance [1999] O.J. L161/54 417

Reg.1267/1999 establishing an Instrument for Structural Policies for Pre-accession [1999] O.J. L161/73 . . . . 611, 612

Reg.1268/1999 on Community support for pre-accession measures for agriculture and rural development in the applicant countries of central and eastern Europe in the pre- accession period [1999] O.J. L161/87 612

Reg.1493/99 on the common organisation of the market in wine [1999] O.J. L179/1 405

Reg.1783/99 on the European Regional Development Fund [1999] O.J. L213/1 522

Reg.1784/1999 on the European
Social Fund [1999] O.J.
L213/5 . . . . 479, 522
Reg.1804/1999 supplementing
Regulation (EEC) No.2092/91
on organic production of
agricultural products and
indications referring thereto on
agricultural products and
foodstuffs to include livestock
production [1999] O.J.
L222/1 410
Reg.2157/99 on the powers of the
European Central Bank to
impose sanctions [1999]
O.J. L264/21 178
Reg.2790/99 on the application of
Article 81(3) of the Treaty to
categories of vertical agreements
and concerted practices
[1999] O.J. L336/21 329
Art.2(2) 330
Art.9 330
Reg.2792/99 laying down the
detailed rules and arrangements
regarding Community structural
assistance in the fisheries sector
[1999] O.J. L337/10 388,
417, 419

2000   Reg.70/2001 on the application of
Articles 87 and 88 of the EC
Treaty to State aid to small
and medium-sized enterprises
[2001] O.J. L10/33 393
Reg.2000/78 establishing a general
framework for equal treatment in
employment and occupation
[2000] O.J. L303/16 248
Reg.823/2000 on the application of
Article 81(3) of the Treaty to
certain categories of agreements,
decisions and concerted practices
between liner shipping companies
(consortia) [2000]
O.J. L100/24 . . . . 343, 455
Reg.1009/2000 concerning capital
increases of the European
Central Bank [2000] O.J.
L115/1 178
Reg.1010/2000 concerning further
calls of foreign reserve assets by
the European Central Bank
[2000] O.J. L115/2 178
Reg.1227/2000 laying down
detailed rules for the application
of Council Regulation (EC)

No.1493/1999 on the common
organisation of the market in
wine, as regards production
potential [2000] O.J.
L143/1 405
Reg.1346/2000 on insolvency
proceedings [2000] O.J.
L160/1 260
Reg.1347/2000 on jurisdiction and
the recognition and enforcement
of judgments in matrimonial
matters and in matters of
parental responsibility for
children of both spouses
[2000] O.J. L160/19 259
Reg.1348/2000 on the service in
the Member States of judicial
and extrajudicial documents in
civil or commercial matters
[2000] O.J. L160/37 259
Reg.1980/2000 on a revised
Community eco-label award
scheme [2002] L237/1 500
Reg.1921/2000 amending
Regulation (EC) No.2818/98 of
the European Central Bank on
the application of minimum
reserves (ECB/1998/15) and
amending Regulation (EC)
No.2819/98 of the European
Central Bank concerning the
consolidated balance sheet
of the monetary financial
institutions sector [2000]
O.J. L229/34 178
Reg.2037/2000 on substances that
deplete the ozone layer
[2000] O.J. L244/1 541
Reg.2658/00 on the application of
Article 81(3) of the Treaty to
categories of specialisation
agreements [2000] O.J.
L304/3 332
Reg.2659/00 on the application of
Article 81(3) of the Treaty to
categories of research and
development agreements
[2000] O.J. L304/7 333
Reg.2666/2000 on assistance for
Albania, Bosnia and
Herzegovina, Croatia, the
Federal Republic of Yugoslavia
and the Former Yugoslav
Republic of Macedonia,
repealing Regulation (EC)
No.1628/96 and amending

Regulations (EEC) No.3906/89 and (EEC) No.1360/90 and Decisions 97/256/EC and 1999/311/EC [2000] O.J. L306/1 .... 612, 614, 615
Reg.2698/00 amending Regulation (EC) No.1488/96 on financial and technical measures to accompany (MEDA) the reform of economic and social structures in the framework of the Euro- Mediterranean partnership [2000] O.J. L311/1 594
Reg.2725/00 concerning the establishment of 'Eurodac' for the comparison of fingerprints for the effective application of the Dublin Convention [2000] O.J. L316/1 256
Regulation 2887/00 on unbundled access to the local loop [2000] O.J. L336/4 .... 347, 509
2001　Reg.44/2001 on jurisdiction and the recognition and enforcement of judgments in civil and commercial matters [2001] O.J. L12/1 .... 258, 260
Art.5(3)(b) 258
Art.6(1) 258
Art.9 258
Art.22(2) 258
Art.34(2) 258
Reg.45/2001 on the protection of individuals with regard to the processing of personal data by the Community institutions and bodies and on the free movement of such data [2001] O.J. L8/1 189
Reg.68/2001 on the application of Articles 87 and 88 of the EC Treaty to training aid [2001] O.J. L10/20 .... 390, 394
Reg.69/2001 on the application of Articles 87 and 88 of the EC Treaty to de minimis aid [2001] O.J. L10/30 443
Reg.70/2001 on the application of Articles 87 and 88 of the EC Treaty to State aid to small and medium-sized enterprise [2001] O.J. L10/33 391
Reg.79/2001 setting up the Military Committee of the

European Union [2001] O.J. L27/4 578
Reg.381/2001 creating a rapid-reaction mechanism [2001] O.J. L57/5 568
Reg.390/2001 on assistance to Turkey in the framework of the pre-accession strategy, and in particular on the establishment of an Accession Partnership [2001] O.J. L58/1 611
Reg.466/2001 setting maximum levels for certain contaminants in foodstuffs [2001] O.J. L77/1 418
Reg.539/2001 listing the third countries whose nationals must be in possession of visas when crossing the external borders and those whose nationals are exempt from that requirement [2001] O.J. L81/1 243
Reg.1206/2001 [2001] O.J. L 174/1 259
Reg.1049/2001 of Parliament and the Council regarding public access to Parliament, Council and commission documents, [2001] O.J. L145/43 ..... 104, 124, 544
Reg.2157/2001 on the Statute for a European company (SE) [2001] O.J. L294/1 ... 282
Reg.2415/01 amending Regulation (EC) No.2666/2000 on assistance for Albania, Bosnia and Herzegovina, Croatia, the Federal Republic of Yugoslavia and the Former Yugoslav Republic of Macedonia and Regulation (EC) No.2667/2000 on the European Agency for Reconstruction [2001] O.J. L 327/3 198
Reg.2423/2001 concerning the consolidated balance sheet of the monetary financial institutions sector [2001] O.J. L333/1 279
Reg.2424/2001 on the development of the second generation SIS [2001] O.J. L328/4 242
Reg.2560/2001 on cross-border payments in euro [2001] O.J. L344/13 300

2002   Reg.6/2002 on Community designs
[2002] O.J. L3/1 305
Reg.63/2002 concerning statistics
on interest rates applied by
monetary financial institutions
to deposits and loans vis-à-vis
households and non-financial
corporations [2002] O.J.
L10/24 279
Reg.178/2002 laying down the
general principles and
requirements of food law,
establishing the European Food
Safety Authority and laying
down procedures in matters of
food safety [2002] O.J.
L31/1 198,
493, 494
Art.1 494
Reg.254/02 establishing measures
to be applicable in 2002 for
the recovery of the stock of
cod in the Irish Sea [2002]
O.J. L41/1 . . . . 416, 463
Reg.332/2002 establishing a
facility providing medium-term
financial assistance for Member
States' balances of payments
[2002] O.J. L53/1 461
Reg.417/2002 on the accelerated
phasing-in of double hull or
equivalent design requirements
for single hull oil tankers and
repealing Council Regulation
(EC) No.2978/94 [2002]
O.J. L64/1 456
Reg.1047/02 on aid to the coal
industry [2002] O.J.
L329/12 557
Reg.1105/02 as regards
consultations on passenger
tariffs and slot allocation
at airports [2002] O.J.
L167/6 344
Reg.1150/02 opening an
autonomous quota for imports
of high-quality beef [2002]
O.J. L170/14 596
Reg.1177/02 concerning a
temporary defensive mechanism
to shipbuilding [2004] O.J.
L2/1 385
Reg.1400/2002 on the application
of Article 81(3) of the Treaty to
categories of vertical agreements
and concerted practices in the

motor vehicle sector [2002]
O.J. L203/30 331
Reg.1406/2002 establishing a
European Maritime Safety
Agency [2002] O.J.
L208/1 456
Reg.1407/02 on State aid to the
coal industry [2002]
O.J. L205/1 . . . . 385, 386
Reg.1592/02 on common rules in
the field of civil aviation and
establishing a European Aviation
Safety Agency [2002]
O.J. L240/1 . . . . 199, 452
Reg.1606/02 on the application
of international accounting
standards [2002] O.J.
L243/1 . . . . 279, 280,
292, 296
Reg.2204/2002 on the application
of Articles 87 and 88 of the EC
Treaty to State aid for
employment [2002]
O.J. L337/3 . . . . 390, 394
Reg.2182/02 laying down
detailed rules for the application
of Council Regulation (EEC)
No.2075/92 with regard to the
Community Tobacco Fund
[2002] O.J. L 331/16 406
Reg.2195/2002 on the Common
Procurement Vocabulary [2002]
O.J. L 340/1 316
Reg.2245/2002 implementing
Council Regulation (EC)
No.6/2002 on Community
designs [2002] O.J. L
341/28 306
Reg.2246/02 on the fees payable
to the Office for Harmonization
in the Internal Market (Trade
Marks and Designs) in respect
of the registration of
Community designs [2002]
O.J. L341/54 . . . . 305, 307
Reg.2304/2002 on the association
of the overseas countries and
territories with the European
Community [2002] O.J.
L348/82 608
Reg.2320/2002 establishing
common rules in the field of civil
aviation security [2002]
O.J. L355/1 451
Reg.2347/02 on specific access
requirements and associated

conditions for deep-sea stocks [2002] O.J. L351/28 416
Reg.2369/02 amending Regulation (EC) No.2792/1999 laying down the detailed rules and arrangements regarding Community structural assistance in the fisheries sector [2002] O.J. L 358/49 421
Reg.2371/02 on the conservation and sustainable exploitation of fish stocks under the common fisheries policy [2002] O.J. L358/59 416
Reg.2320/02 establishing common rules in the field of civil aviation security [2002] O.J. L355/1 .... 20 452
Reg.2342/02 laying down detailed rules for the implementation of Council Regulation (EC, Euratom) No.1605/2002 on the Financial Regulation applicable to the general budget of the European Communities [2002] O.J. L357/1 216

2003 Reg.1/2003 on the implementation of the rules on competition laid down in Articles 81 and 82 of the Treaty [2003] O.J. L1/1 ...... 37, 52, 319, 327, 334, 342, 343, 350, 351, 354, 363, 373, 438, 443, 455
    Recital (6) 351
    Recital (8) 320
    Art.1(1) 327
      (2) 320, 328
    Art.4 110
    Art.3 110
    Art.5 .... 110, 320
    Art.6 352
    Art.7 .... 353, 356
      (1) 353
    Art.8 353
    Art.9 353
    Art.10 353
    Art.11 351
    Art.12 352
    Art.13 352
    Art.14 359
    Art.15 .... 113, 352
    Art.16(2) 351
    Art.18(2) 353
      (3) 353

Art.19 353
Art.20 354
  (2)(a) 354
    (b) 354
  (6) 355
Art.21 355
Art.22 355
Art.23 .... 52, 132, 355
Art.24 52
Art.25 358
  (1)(b) 358
Art.27 358
  (1) 358
  (2) 359
Art.28 359
Art.32 360
Art.33(1) 360
Art.35(1) 351
  (3) 352
  (4) 352
Reg.16/2003 laying down special detailed rules for implementing Council Regulation (EC) No.1164/94 as regards eligibility of expenditure in the context of measures part-financed by the Cohesion Fund [2003] O.J. L2/7 551
Reg.58/2003 laying down the statute for executive agencies to be entrusted with certain tasks in the management of Community programmes [2003] O.J. L11/1 .... 191, 492
Reg.343/2003 establishing the criteria and mechanisms for determining the Member State responsible for examining an asylum application lodged in one of the Member States by a third- country national [2003] O.J. L50/1 256
Reg.358/2003 on the application of Article 81(3) of the Treaty to certain categories of agreements, decisions and concerted practices in the insurance sector [2003] O.J. L53/8 349
Reg.622/2003 laying down measures for the implementation of the common basic standards on aviation security [2003] O.J. L89/9 .... 200, 452
Reg.1059/2003 on the establishment of a common classification of territorial units

for statistics [2003] O.J.
L154/1 525
Art.19 525
Art.21 525
Art.37 527
Reg.1228/2003 on conditions
for access to the network for
cross-border exchanges in
electricity [2003] O.J.
L176/1 555
Reg.1382/2003 on the granting of
Community financial assistance
to improve the environmental
performance of the freight
transport system [2003]
O.J. L196/1 457
Reg.1435/2003 on the Statute
for a European Cooperative
Society [2003] O.J.
L207/1 . . . . 283, 436
Reg.1452/2003 maintaining the
derogation provided for in
Article 6(3)(a) of Council
Regulation (EEC) No.2092/91
with regard to certain species of
seed and vegetative propagating
material and laying down
procedural rules and criteria
relating to that derogation
[2003] O.J. L206/17 410
Reg.1438/2003 laying down
implementing rules on the
Community Fleet Policy as
defined in Chapter III of Council
Regulation (EC) No.2371/2002
[2003] O.J. L204/21 418
Reg.1461/2003 laying down
conditions for pilot projects for
the electronic transmission of
information on fishing activities
and for remote sensing
[2003] O.J. L208/14 418
Reg.1518/2003 laying down
detailed rules for implementing
the system of export licences in
the pigmeat sector [2003]
O.J. L217/35 408
Reg.1560/2003 laying down
detailed rules for the application
of Council Regulation (EC)
No.343/2003 establishing the
criteria and mechanisms for
determining the Member State
responsible for examining an
asylum application lodged in
one of the Member States by a

third-country national
[2003] O.J. L222/3 256
Reg.1702/2003 laying down
implementing rules for the
airworthiness and environmental
certification of aircraft and
related products, parts and
appliances, as well as for the
certification of design and
production organisations
[2003] O.J. L243/6 451
Reg.1725/2003 on the application
of international accounting
standards [2003] O.J. L
261/1 280
Reg.1782/2003 establishing
common rules for direct support
schemes under the common
agricultural policy and
establishing certain support
schemes for farmers and
amending Regulations (EEC)
No.2019/93, (EC)
No.1452/2001, (EC)
No.1453/2001, (EC)
No.1454/2001, (EC) 1868/94,
(EC) No.1251/1999, (EC)
No.1254/1999, (EC)
No.1673/2000, (EEC)
No.2358/71 and (EC)
No.2529/2001 [2003] O.J.
L270/1 403
Reg.1798/2003 on administrative
cooperation in the field of value
added tax and repealing
Regulation (EEC) No.218/92
[2003] O.J. L264/1 . . . . 427, 428
Reg.1830/2003 concerning the
traceability and labelling of
genetically modified organisms
and the traceability of food and
feed products produced from
genetically modified organisms
and amending Directive
2001/18/EC [2003] O.J.
L268/24 410
Reg.1882/2003 adapting to
Council Decision 1999/468/EC
the provisions relating to
committees which assist the
Commission in the exercise of its
implementing powers laid down
in instruments subject to the
procedure referred to in Article
251 of the EC Treaty
[2003] O.J. L284/1 116

Reg.1946/2003 on transboundary movements of genetically modified organisms [2003] O.J. L287/1 410

Reg.2004/2003 on the regulations governing political parties at European level and the rules regarding their funding [2003] O.J. L297/1 81

Reg.2042/03 on the continuing airworthiness of aircraft and aeronautical products, parts and appliances, and on the approval of organisations and personnel involved in these tasks O.J. L315/1 452

Reg.2201/2003 concerning jurisdiction and the recognition and enforcement of judgments in matrimonial matters and the matters of parental responsibility, repealing Regulation (EC) No.1347/2000 [2003] O.J. L338/1 259

Regulation 2244/03 laying down detailed provisions regarding satellite-based Vessel Monitoring Systems [2003] O.J. L333/17 418

Reg.2273/2003 implementing Directive 2003/6/EC of the European Parliament and of the Council as regards exemptions for buy-back programmes and stabilisation of financial instrument [2003] O.J. L336/33 282

2004   Reg.139/2004 on the control of concentrations between undertakings (the EC Merger Regulation) [2004] O.J. L24/1 . . . . . 133, 319, 320, 364, 367, 368, 369, 370, 372
  Art.1 365
  Art.2(1) 366, 368
    (3) 364
  Art.3 . . . . 364, 366
    (4) 364
  Art.4 366
    (1) 366
    (3) 366
  Art.5(3) 355
  Art.6(1)(b) 369
    (2) 367, 368
  Art.7 368

Art.8(2) 368, 369
Art.9(3)(b) 368
Art.10 368
Art.13 368
Art.14 368
Art.15 368
Art.16 132
Art.17 369
Art.19 368
Art.20a 368
Art.21(1) 369

Reg.261/2004 vent of denied boarding and of cancellation or long delay of flights, and repealing Regulation (EEC) No.295/9 [2004] O.J. L46/1 451

Reg.364/04 amending Regulation (EC) No.70/2001 as regards the extension of its scope to include aid for research and development [2004] O.J. L63/22 390

Reg.411/2004 repealing Regulation (EEC) No.3975/87 and amending Regulations (EEC) No.3976/87 and (EC) No.1/2003, in connection with air transport between the Community and third countries [2004] O.J. L68/1 . . . . 344, 363, 438, 443, 450

Reg.423/2004 establishing measures for the recovery of cod stocks [2004] O.J. L70/8 416

Reg.460/2004 establishing the European Network and Information Security Agency [2004] O.J. L77/1 200

Reg.533/2004 on the establishment of European partnerships in the framework of the stabilisation and association process [2004] O.J. L86/1 . . . . 612, 613

Reg.549/2004 laying down the framework for the creation of the single European sky (the Framework Regulation) [2004] O.J. L96/1 452

Reg.550/2004 on the provision of air navigation services in the single European sky (the Service Provision Regulation) [2004] O.J. L96/10 452

Reg.551/2004 on the organisation and use of the airspace in the single European sky (the Airspace Regulation) [2004] O.J. L96/20 452

Reg.552/2004 on the interoperability of the European Air Traffic Management network [2004] O.J. L96/26 . . . . 451, 452

Reg.639/2004 on the management of fishing fleets registered in the Union outermost regions [2004] O.J. L102/9 422

Reg.723/2004 amending the Staff Regulations of officials of the European Communities and the Conditions of Employment of other servants of the European Communities [1968] O.J. L124/1 124

Reg.725/2004 on enhancing ship and port facility security [2004] O.J. L129/6 456

Reg.726/2004 laying down Community procedures for the authorisation and supervision of medicinal products for human and veterinary use and establishing a European Medicines Agency [2004] O.J. L136/1 194
Art.84(3) 52

Reg.770/2004 amending Regulation (EC) No.2791/1999 laying down certain control measures applicable in the area covered by the Convention on future multilateral cooperation in the north-east Atlantic fisheries [2004] O.J. L123/4 419

Reg.773/2004 relating to the conduct of proceedings by the Commission pursuant to Articles 81 and 82 of the EC Treaty [2004] O.J. L123/18 . . . . . . 342, 356, 360, 363, 450, 455
Art.5(1) 362
Arts 5–9 361

Reg.785/2004 on insurance requirements for air carriers an aircraft operators [2004] O.J. L138/1 452

Reg.794/2004 implementing Council Regulation (EC) No.659/1999 laying down detailed rules for the application of Article 93 of the EC Treaty [2004] O.J. L140/1 395

Reg.802/2004 implementing Council Regulation (EC) No.139/2004 on the control of concentrations between undertakings [2004] O.J. L133/1 368

Reg.805/2004 creating a European Enforcement Order for uncontested claims [2004] O.J. L143/15 260

Reg.809/2004 implementing Directive 2003/71/EC of the European Parliament and of the Council as regards information contained in prospectuses as well as the format, incorporation by reference and publication of such prospectuses and dissemination of advertisements [2004] O.J. L149/1 295

Reg.811/2004 establishing measures for the recovery of the Northern hake stock [2004] O.J. L150/1 416

Reg.812/2004 laying down measures concerning incidental catches of cetaceans in fisheries and amending Regulation (EC) No.88/98 [2004] O.J. L150/12 . . . . 416, 417

Reg.813/2004 as regards certain conservation measures relating to waters around Malta [2004] O.J. L150/32 416

Reg.831/2004 amending Regulation (EC) No.973/2001 laying down certain technical measures for the conservation of certain stocks of highly migratory species [2004] O.J. L127/33 416

Reg.881/2004 establishing a European Railway Agency [2004] O.J. L164/1 201

Reg.851/2004 [2004] O.J. L142/1 201

Reg.930/2004 on temporary derogation for the Maltese language [2004] O.J. L196/1 37

Reg.1321/2004 on the establishment of structures for the management of the European satellite radio-navigation programmes [2004] O.J. L246/1 201

Reg.1655/2000 concerning the Financial Instrument for the Environment [2000] O.J. L192/1 550

Reg.1682/2004 amending Regulation (EC) No.1655/2000 concerning the Financial Instrument for the Environment (LIFE) [2004] O.J. L308/1 550

Reg.1860/2004 on the application of Articles 87 and 88 of the EC Treaty to de minimis aid in the agriculture and fisheries sectors [2004] O.J. L325/4 388

Regulation 2006/2004 on cooperation between national authorities responsible for the enforcement of consumer protection laws [2004] O.J. L364/1 451

Reg.2007/2004 establishing a European Agency for the Management of Operational Cooperation at the External Borders of the Member States of the European Union [2004] O.J. L349/1 202

Reg.2086/04 amending Regulation (EC) No.1725/2003 on the adoption of certain international accounting standards in accordance with Regulation (EC) No.1606/2002 of the European Parliament and of the Council as regards the insertion of IAS 39 [2004] O.J. L363/1 .... 279, 296

Reg.2104/04 laying down detailed implementing rules for Council Regulation (EC) No.639/2004 on the management of fishing fleets registered in the Community outermost regions [2004] O.J. L365/19 422

Reg.2181/2004 amending Regulation (EC) No.2423/2001 (ECB/2001/13) concerning the consolidated balance sheet of the monetary financial institutions

sector and Regulation (EC) No.63/2002 (ECB/2001/18) concerning statistics on interest rates applied by monetary financial institutions to deposits and loans vis-à-vis households and non-financial corporation [2004] O.J. L371/42 279

Reg.2230/04 laying down detailed rules for the implementation of European Parliament and Council Regulation (EC) No.178/2002 with regard to the network of organisations operating in the fields within the European Food Safety Authority's mission [2004] O.J. L379/64 198

Reg.2236/04 amending Regulation (EC) No.1725/2003 adopting certain international accounting standards in accordance with Regulation (EC) No.1606/2002 of the European Parliament and of the Council as regards International Financial Reporting Standards (IFRSs) Nos 1, 3 to 5, International Accounting Standards (IASs) Nos 1, 10, 12, 14, 16 to 19, 22, 27, 28, 31 to 41 and the interpretations by the Standard Interpretation Committee (SIC) Nos 9, 22, 28 and 32 [2004] O.J. L392/1 280

Reg.2237/04 amending Regulation (EC) No.1725/2003 adopting certain international accounting standards in accordance with Regulation (EC) No.1606/2002 of the European Parliament and of the Council, as regards IAS No.32 and IFRIC 1 [2004] O.J. L393/1 280

Reg.2238/04 amending Regulation (EC) No.1725/2003 adopting certain international accounting standards in accordance with Regulation (EC) No.1606/2002 of the European Parliament and of the Council, as regards IASs IFRS 1, IASs Nos 1 to 10, 12 to 17, 19 to 24, 27 to 38, 40 and 41 and SIC Nos 1 to 7, 11 to 14, 18 to 27 and 30 to 33 [2004] O.J. L394/1 280

Table of Secondary Legislation

Reg.2265/04 on trade in certain steel products between the Union and the republic of Kazakhstan [2004] O.J. L395/1 587

Reg.2267/04 on trade in certain steel products between the EC and the Russian Federation [2004] O.J. L395/38 591

2005 Reg.211/2005 amending Regulation (EC) No.1725/2003 adopting certain international accounting standards in accordance with Regulation (EC) No.1606/2002 of the European Parliament and of the Council as regards International Financial Reporting Standards (IFRS) 1 and 2 and International Accounting Standards (IASs) No.12, 16, 19, 32, 33, 38 and 39 [2005] O.J. L41/1 280

Reg.768/2005 establishing a Community Fisheries Control Agency and amending Regulation (EEC) No.2847/93 establishing a control system applicable to the common fisheries policy [2005] O.J. L128/1 202

Reg.781/2005 amending Regulation (EC) No.622/2003 laying down measures for the implementation of the common basic standards on aviation security [2005] O.J. L131/24 200

Reg.884/2005 laying down procedures for conducting Commission inspections in the field of maritime security [2005] O.J. L 148/25 456

Reg.1055/2005 amending Regulation (EC) No.1466/97 on the strengthening of the surveillance of budgetary positions and the surveillance and coordination of economic policies [2005] O.J. L174/1 . . . . 466, 467

Regulation 1056/2005 [2005] O.J. L174/5 467
Art.1(2) 467
(3) 468

Reg.1290/2005 on the financing of the common agricultural policy [2005] O.J. L209/1 413

Reg.1698/2005 on support for rural development by the European Agricultural Fund for Rural Development [2005] O.J. L277/1 412

Reg.1751/2005 amending Regulation (EC) No.1725/2003 adopting certain international accounting standards in accordance with Regulation (EC) No.1606/2002 of the European Parliament and of the Council, as regards IFRS 1, IAS 39 and SIC 12 [2005] O.J. L282/3 280

Reg.1775/05 on conditions for access to the natural gas transmission [2005] O.J. L289/1 . . . . 555, 557

Reg.1905/2005 amending Regulation (EC) No.297/95 on fees payable to the European Medicines Agency [2005] O.J. L304/1 195

Reg.1927/06 on establishing the European Globalisation Adjustment Fund [2006] O.J. L406/1 252

Reg.2049/2005 laying down, pursuant to Regulation (EC) No.726/2004 of the European Parliament and of the Council, rules regarding the payment of fees to, and the receipt of administrative assistance from, the European Medicines Agency by micro, small and medium-sized enterprises [2005] O.J. L329/4 195

Reg.2083/2005 amending Directives 2004/17/EC and 2004/18/EC of the European Parliament and of the Council in respect of their application thresholds for the procedures for the award of contracts [2005] O.J. L333/28 . . . . 311, 314

Reg.2096/2005 laying down common requirements for the provision of air navigation services [2005] O.J. L335/13 451

Reg.2111/2005 on the establishment of a Community list of air carriers subject to an operating ban within the Community and on informing air transport passengers of the identity of the operating air carrier, and repealing Article 9 of Directive 2004/36/EC [2005] O.J. L344/15 . . . . 451, 453

2006 Reg.66/2006 exempting the transfer of small quantities of ores, source materials and special fissile materials from the rules of the chapter on supplies [2006] O.J. L11/6 182

Reg.269/2006 amending Regulation (EC) No.533/2004 on the establishment of European partnerships in the framework of the stabilisation and association process [2006] O.J. L47/7 612

Reg.336/2006 on the implementation of the International Safety Management Code within the Community and repealing Council Regulation (EC) No.3051/95 [2006] O.J. L64/1 456

Reg.474/2006 establishing the Community list of air carriers which are subject to an operating ban within the Community referred to in Chapter II of Regulation (EC) No.2111/2005 of the European Parliament and of the Council [2006] O.J. L84/14 . . . . 451, 453

Reg.561/2006 on the harmonisation of certain social legislation relating to road transport and amending Council Regulations (EEC) No.3821/85 and (EC) No.2135/98 and repealing Council Regulation (EEC) No.3820/85 [2006] O.J. L102/1 . . . . 442, 446

Reg.562/2006 establishing a Community Code on the rules governing the movement of persons across borders [2006] O.J. L105/1 242

Reg.736/2006 on working methods of the European Aviation Safety Agency for conducting standardisation inspections [2006] O.J. L129/10 199

Reg.742/2006 adapting certain fish quotas for 2006 pursuant to Council Regulation (EC)

No.847/96 introducing additional conditions for year-to-year management of TACs and quotas [2006] O.J. L130/7 416

Reg.768/2006 implementing Directive 2004/36/EC of the European Parliament and of the Council as regards the collection and exchange of information on the safety of aircraft using Community airports and the management of the information system [2006] O.J. L134/16 199

Reg.871/2006 determining for the 2005/06 marketing year actual production of unginned cotton and the ensuing guide price reduction [2006] O.J. L164/3 416

Reg.1049/2001 regarding public access to European Parliament, Council and Commission documents [2001] O.J. L145/43 544

Reg.1080/2006 on the European Regional Development Fund and repealing Regulation (EC) No.1783/1999 [2006] O.J. L210/1 522

Reg.1081/06 on the European Social Fund and repealing Regulation (EC) No.1784/1999 [2006] O.J. L210/12 522

Reg.1082/2006 on a European grouping of territorial cooperation [2006] O.J. L210/19 522

Reg.1083/2006 laying down general provisions on the European Regional Development Fund, the European Social Fund and the Cohesion Fund and repealing Regulation (EC) No.1260/1999 [2006] O.J. L 210/25 . . . . 522, 524, 530
Title V 528
Art.45 528
Art.47 528
Ar.52 528
Art.55 528
Annex I 527

Reg.1084/2006 establishing a Cohesion Fund and repealing

Regulation (EC) No.1164/94
[2006] O.J. L210/79 522
Reg.1085/2006 establishing an
Instrument for Pre-Accession
Assistance [2006] O.J.
L210/82 610
Reg.1198/06 on the European
Fisheries Fund [2006] O.J.
L223/1 . . . . 417, 420,
                          421, 422, 522
Reg.1367/2006 on the application
of the provisions of the Aarhus
Convention on Access to
Information, Public Participation
in Decision-making and Access
to Justice in Environmental
Matters to Community
institutions and bodies
[2006] O.J. L264/13 544
Reg.1419/2006 repealing
Regulation (EEC) No.4056/86
laying down detailed rules for
the application of Articles 85
and 86 of the Treaty to
maritime transport, and
amending Regulation (EC)
No.1/2003 as regards the
extension of its scope to include
cabotage and international
tramp services [2006] O.J.
L269/1 . . . . 443, 455
Reg.1459/2006 on the application
of Article 81(3) of the Treaty to
certain categories of agreements
and concerted practices
concerning consultations on
passenger tariffs on scheduled air
services and slot allocation at
airports [2006] L272/3 451
Reg.1628/06 on the application
of Articles 87 and 88 of the
Treaty to national regional
investment aid [2006]
O.J. L302/29 . . . . 384, 394
Reg.1638/2006 laying down
general provisions establishing
a European Neighbourhood and
Partnership Instrument [2006]
O.J. L310/1 . . . . 573, 574
Reg.1692/2006 establishing the
second Marco Polo programme
for the granting of Community
financial assistance to improve
the environmental performance
of the freight transport system
(Marco Polo II) and repealing

Regulation (EC) No.1382/2003
[2006] O.J. L328/1 457
Reg.1717/06 establishing an
Instrument for Stability
[2006] O.J. L327/1 577
Reg.1828/06 setting out rules for
the implementation of Council
Regulation (EC) No.1083/2006
laying down general provisions
on the European Regional
Development Fund, the
European Social Fund and the
Cohesion Fund and of
Regulation (EC) No.1080/2006
of the European Parliament and
of the Council on the European
Regional Development Fund
[2006] O.J. L371/1 524
Reg.1891/06 amending Regulations
(EC) No.6/2002 and (EC)
No.40/94 to give effect to the
accession of the European
Community to the Geneva Act of
the Hague Agreement concerning
the international registration
of industrial designs [2006]
O.J. L386/14 307
Reg.1896/2006 creating a
European order for payment
procedure [2006] O.J.
L399/1 . . . . 260, 498
Reg.1907/2006 concerning the
Registration, Evaluation,
Authorisation and Restriction of
Chemicals (REACH), establishing
a European Chemicals Agency,
amending Directive 1999/45/EC
and repealing Council Regulation
(EEC) No.793/93 and
Commission Regulation (EC)
No.1488/94 as well as
Council Directive 76/769/EEC
and Commission Directives
91/155/EEC, 93/67/EEC,
93/105/EC and
2000/21/EC [2006]
O.J. L396/1 . . . . 203, 492
Annex XVII 203
Reg.1908/2006 laying down the
rules for the participation of
undertakings, research centres
and universities in action under
the Seventh Framework
Programme of the European
Atomic Energy Community
and for the dissemination of

research results [2006]
O.J. L400/1 533

Reg.1922/2006 on establishing
a European Institute for
Gender Equality [2006]
O.J. L403/9 203

Reg.1927/2006 on establishing the
European Globalisation
Adjustment Fund [2006]
O.J. L406/1 480

Reg.1974/2006 laying down
detailed rules for the application
of Council Regulation (EC)
No.1698/2005 on support for
rural development by the
European Agricultural Fund for
Rural Development [206]
O.J. L368/15 412

2007 Reg.71/2007 setting up the Clean
Sky Joint Undertaking [2008]
O.J. L30/1 . . . . 533, 535

Reg.134/2007 fixing the A1 and B
export refunds for fruit and
vegetables (tomatoes, oranges,
lemons, table grapes and apples)
[2007] O.J. L42/16 . . . 405, 406

Reg.168/2007 establishing a
European Union Agency for
Fundamental Rights [2007]
O.J. L 53/1 204

Reg.498/2007 laying down detailed
rules for the implementation of
Council Regulation (EC)
No.1198/2006 on the European
Fisheries Fund [2007]
O.J. L120/1 . . . . 417, 421

Reg.593/2007 on the fees and
charges levied by the European
Aviation Safety Agency [2007]
O.J. L140/3 199

Reg.614/2007 concerning the
Financial Instrument for the
Environment (LIFE+) –
Commission statement [2007]
O.J. L149/1 551

Reg.680/2007 laying down general
rules for the granting of
Community financial aid in the
field of the trans-European
transport and energy networks
[2007] O.J. L162/1 210

Reg.717/2007 on roaming on
public mobile telephone
networks within the
Community and amending
Directive 2002/21/EC

[2007] O.J.
L171/32 . . . . . . 346, 509, 517

Reg.718/2007 implementing Council
Regulation (EC) No.1085/2006
establishing an instrument for
pre-accession assistance
[2007] O.J. L170/1 610

Reg.834/2007 on organic
production and labelling of
organic products and repealing
Regulation (EEC) No.2092/91
[2007] O.J. L189/1 410

Reg.861/2007 establishing a
European Small Claims
Procedure [2007] O.J.
L199/1 260
Art.3 260
(1) 260
Art.16 260

Reg.863/2007 establishing a
mechanism for the creation of a
Rapid Border Intervention Team
[2007] O.J. L199/30 202

Reg.864/2007 on the law
applicable to non-contractual
obligations [2007] O.J.
L199/40 260

Reg.875/2007 on the application of
Articles 87 and 88 of the EC
Treaty to de minimis aid in the
fisheries sector and amending
Regulation (EC) No.1860/2004
[2007] O.J. L193/6 . . . . 387, 422

Reg.876/2007 amending
Regulation (EC) No.2245/2002
implementing Council Regulation
(EC) No.6/2002 on Community
designs following the accession
of the European Community to
the Geneva Act of the Hague
Agreement concerning the
international registration of
industrial designs [2007]
O.J. L193/13 . . . . 306, 307

Reg.877/2007 amending
Regulation (EC) No.2246/2002
concerning the fees payable to
the Office for Harmonization in
the Internal Market (Trade
Marks and Designs) following
the accession of the European
Community to the Geneva Act of
the Hague Agreement concerning
the international registration
of industrial designs [2007]
O.J. L193/16 306

Reg.951/2007 laying down
implementing rules for
cross-border cooperation
programmes financed under
Regulation (EC) No.1638/2006
of the European Parliament and
of the Council laying down
general provisions establishing a
European Neighbourhood and
Partnership Instrument
[2007] O.J. L210/10 574
Regulation 1234/2007 establishing
a common organisation of
agricultural markets and on
specific provisions for certain
agricultural products (Single
CMO Regulation) [2007]
O.J. L299/1 .... 404, 405,
406, 407
Reg.1298/2007 amending
Regulation (EC) No.900/2007 in
order to distinguish between
third countries and territories of
European Union Member States
not forming part of the customs
territory of the Community
[2007] O.J. L289/3 12
Reg.1370/2007 on public passenger
transport services by rail and by
road and repealing Council
Regulations (EEC) Nos 1191/69
and 1107/70 [2007]
O.J. L315/1 .... 345, 443,
446, 447, 449
Reg.1371/2007 on rail passengers'
rights and obligations [2007]
O.J. L315/4 449
Reg.1393/2007 on the service in
the Member State of judicial and
extrajudicial documents in civil
and commercial matters
[2007] O.J. L324/79 259
Reg.1580/07 laying down
implementing rules of Council
Regulations (EC) No.2200/96,
(EC) No.2201/96 and (EC)
No.1182/2007 in the fruit and
vegetable sector [2007]
O.J. L350/1 405
2008   Reg.72/2008 setting up the ENIAC
Joint Undertaking [2008]
O.J. L30/21 533
Reg.73/2008 setting up the Joint
Undertaking for the
implementation of the Joint
Technology Initiative on

Innovative Medicines
[2008] O.J. L30/38 533
Reg.110/2008 on the definition,
description, presentation,
labelling and the protection of
geographical indications of spirit
drinks and repealing Council
Regulation (EEC) No.1576/89
[2008] O.J. L39/16 409
Reg.143/2008 amending
Regulation (EC) No.1798/2003
as regards the introduction of
administrative cooperation and
the exchange of information
concerning the rules relating to
the place of supply of services,
the special schemes and the
refund procedure for value
added tax [2008] O.J.
L44/1 428
Reg.199/2008 concerning the
establishment of a Community
framework for the collection,
management and use of data in
the fisheries sector and support
for scientific advice regarding
the Common Fisheries Policy
[2008] O.J. L60/1 417
Regulation 215/2008 on the
Financial Regulation applicable
to the 10th European
Development Fund [2008]
O.J. L78/1 606
Reg.216/2008 on common rules in
the field of civil aviation and
establishing a European Aviation
Safety Agency, and repealing
Council Directive 91/670/EEC,
Regulation (EC) No.1592/2002
and Directive 2004/36/EC
[2008] O.J. L79/1 199
Reg.241/2008 on the conclusion of
the Fisheries Partnership
Agreement between the
European Community and the
Republic of Guinea-Bissau
[2008] O.J. L75/49 419
Reg.242/2008 on the conclusion of
the Fisheries Partnership
Agreement between the
European Community and the
Republic of Côte d'Ivoire
[2008] O.J. L75/51 419
Reg.246/2008 amending
Regulation (EC) No.1043/2005
implementing Council

Regulation (EC) No.3448/93 as regards the system of granting export refunds on certain agricultural products exported in the form of goods not covered by Annex I to the Treaty, and the criteria for fixing the amount of such refunds [2008] O.J. L75/64 409

Reg.274/2008 amending Regulation (EEC) No.918/83 setting up a Community system of relief from customs duty [2008] O.J. L85/1 227

Reg.275/2008 amending Council Regulation (EEC) No.2658/87 on the tariff and statistical nomenclature and on the Common Customs Tariff [2008] O.J. L85/3 227

Reg.294/2008 establishing the European Institute of Innovation and Technology [2008] O.J. L97/1 188

Reg.300/2008 on common rules in the field of civil aviation security and repealing Regulation (EC) No.2320/2002 [2008] O.J. L97/72 . . . . 200, 451

Reg.248/2008 amending Regulation (EC) No.1234/2007 as regards the national quotas for milk [2008] O.J. L76/6 407

Reg.446/2008 adapting certain bluefin tuna quotas in 2008 pursuant to Article 21(4) of Council Regulation (EEC) No.2847/93 establishing a control system applicable to the Common Fisheries Policy [2008] O.J. L134/11 418

Reg.450/2008 laying down the Community Customs Code [2008] O.J. L145/1 . . . . 226, 227

Reg.452/2008 concerning the production and development of statistics on education and lifelong learning [2008] O.J. L145/227 482

Reg.470/2008 amending Regulation (EC) No.1782/2003 as regards the transfer of tobacco aid to the Community Tobacco Fund for the years 2008 and 2009 and Regulation (EC)

No.1234/2007 with regard to financing of the Community Tobacco Fund [2008] O.J. L140/1 406

Reg.556/2008 amending Regulation (EC) No.2505/96 opening and providing for the administration of autonomous Community tariff quotas for certain agricultural and industrial products [2008] O.J. L160/1 227

Reg.593/2008 on the law applicable to contractual obligations [2008] O.J. L177/6 260
Art.24 260

Reg.595/2008 amending Regulation (EC) No.1255/96 temporarily suspending the autonomous common customs tariff duties on certain industrial, agricultural and fishery products [2008] O.J. L164/1 227

Reg.615/2008 amending Regulation (EC) No.1405/2006 laying down specific measures for agriculture in favour of the smaller Aegean islands and amending Regulation (EC) No.1782/2003 establishing common rules for direct support schemes under the common agricultural policy and establishing certain support schemes for farmers [2008] O.J. L168/1 403

Reg.622/2008 amending Regulation (EC) No.773/2004, as regards the conduct of settlement procedures in cartel cases [2008] O.J. L171/3 356

Reg.637/2008 amending Regulation (EC) No.1782/2003 and establishing national restructuring programmes for the cotton sector [2008] O.J. L178/1 407

Reg.683/2008 on the further implementation of the European satellite navigation programmes [2008] O.J. L196/1 440

Reg.689/2008 concerning the export and import of dangerous chemicals [2008] O.J. L204/1 541

Reg.732/2008 applying a scheme of generalised tariff preferences for the period from 1 January 2009 to 31 December 2011 and amending Regulations (EC) No.552/97, (EC) No.1933/2006 and Commission Regulations (EC) No.1100/2006 and (EC) No.964/2007 [2008] O.J. L211/1 602

Reg.744/2008 instituting a temporary specific action aiming to promote the restructuring of the European Community fishing fleets affected by the economic crisis [2008] O.J. L202/1 . . . . 417, 422

Reg.755/2008 amending Annex II to Directive 2005/36/EC of the European Parliament and of the Council on the recognition of professional qualifications [2008] O.J. L205/10 269

Reg.764/2008 laying down procedures relating to the application of certain national technical rules to product lawfully marketed in another Member State [2008] O.J. L218/21 . . . . 195, 236

Reg.767/2008 concerning the Visa Information System (VIS) and the exchange of data between Member States on short-stay visas [2008] O.J. L218/60 256

Reg.800/2008 declaring certain categories of aid compatible with the common market in application of Articles 87 and 88 of the Treaty (General block exemption Regulation) [2008] O.J. L214/3 393

Reg.889/2008 laying down detailed rules for the implementation of Council Regulation (EC) No.834/2007 on organic production and labelling of organic products with regard to organic production, labelling and control [2008] O.J. L250/1 410

Reg.1005/2008 establishing a Community system to prevent, deter and eliminate illegal, unreported and unregulated fishing, amending Regulations (EEC) No.2847/93, (EC) No.1936/2001 and (EC) No.601/2004 and repealing Regulations (EC) No.1093/94 and (EC) No.1447/1999 [2008] O.J. L286/1 417

Reg.1006/2008 concerning authorisations for fishing activities of Community fishing vessels outside Community waters and the access of third country vessels to Community waters, amending Regulations (EEC) No.2847/93 and (EC) No.1627/94 and repealing Regulation (EC) No.3317/94 [2008] O.J. L286/33 417

Reg.1007/2008 amending Regulation (EC) No.460/2004 establishing the European Network and Information Security Agency as regards its duration [2008] O.J. L293/1 200

Regulation 1008/2008 on common rules for the operation of air services in the Community [2008] O.J. L293/3 451

Reg.1033/2008 [2008] O.J. L279/3 368

Reg.1100/2008 on the elimination of controls performed at the frontiers of Member States in the field of road and inland waterway transport [2008] O.J. L304/63 445

Reg.1102/2008 on the banning of exports of metallic mercury and certain mercury compounds and mixtures and the safe storage of metallic mercury [2008] O.J. L304/75 541

Reg.1126/2008 adopting certain international accounting standards in accordance with Regulation (EC) No.1606/2002 of the European Parliament and of the Council [2008] O.J. L320/1 279

Reg.1179/2008 laying down detailed rules for implementing certain provisions of Council Directive 2008/55/EC on mutual assistance for the recovery of claims relating to certain levies, duties, taxes and other measures [2008] O.J. L319/21 428

Reg.1272/2008 on classification, labelling and packaging of substances and mixtures, amending and repealing Directives 67/548/EEC and 1999/45/EC, and amending Regulation (EC) No.1907/2006 [2008] O.J. L353/1 .... 492, 546

Reg.1339/2008 establishing a European Training Foundation [2008] O.J. L354/82 .... 193, 483

Reg.1272/2008 on classification, labelling and packaging of substances and mixtures, amending and repealing Directives 67/548/EEC and 1999/45/EC, and amending Regulation (EC) No.1907/2006 [2008] O.J. L353/1 540

2009 Reg.43/2009 fixing for 2009 the fishing opportunities and associated conditions for certain fish stocks and groups of fish stocks, applicable in Community waters and, for Community vessels, in waters where catch limitations are required [2009] O.J. L22/1 415

Reg.69/2009 amending Regulation (EC) No.1126/2008 adopting certain international accounting standards in accordance with Regulation (EC) No.1606/2002 of the European Parliament and of the Council as regards amendments to International Financial Reporting Standard (IFRS) 1 and International Accounting Standard (IAS) 27 [2009] O.J. L21/10 292

Reg.70/2009 as regards improvements to international Financial Reporting Standards (IFRSs) [2009] O.J. L21/16 .... 279, 292

Reg.73/2009 of 19 January 2009 establishing common rules for direct support schemes for farmers under the common agricultural policy and establishing certain support schemes for farmers, amending Regulations (EC) No 1290/2005, (EC) No 247/2006, (EC) No 378/2007 and repealing Regulation (EC) No 1782/2003 [2009] O.J. L30/16 403

Reg.99/2009 establishing the standard import values for determining the entry price of certain fruits and vegetables [2009] O.J. L341/1 202

Reg.169/2009 applying rules of competition to transport by rail, road and inland waterway [2009] O.J. L61/1 .... 342, 343, 439, 443

Reg.272/2009 supplementing the common basic standards on civil aviation security laid down in the Annex to Regulation (EC) No.300/2008 of the European Parliament and of the Council [2009] O.J. L91/7 200

Reg.297/2009 amending Regulation (EC) No.1277/2005 laying down implementing rules for Regulation (EC) No.273/2004 of the European Parliament and of the Council on drug precursors and for Council Regulation (EC) No.111/2005 laying down rules for the monitoring of trade between the Community and third countries in drug precursors [2009] O.J. L95/13 279

Reg.325/2009 on the adoption of a common safety method on risk evaluation and assessment as referred to in Article 6(3)(a) of Directive 2004/49/EC of the European Parliament and of the Council [2009] O.J. L108/4 448

Reg.401/2009 on the European Environment Agency and the European Environment Information and Observation Network [2009] O.J. L126/13 192

Reg.407/2009 amending Council Regulation (EC) No.338/97 on the protection of species of wild fauna and flora by regulating trade therein [2009] L123/3 546

Reg.443/2009 setting emission performance standards for new passenger cars as part of the Community's integrated approach to reduce CO2 emissions from light-duty vehicles [2009] O.J. L140/1 544

Reg.473/2009 amending Regulation (EC) No.1698/2005 on support for rural development by the European Agricultural Fund for Rural Development (EAFRD) and Regulation (EC) No.1290/2005 on the financing of the common agricultural policy [2009] O.J. L144/3 412

Reg.479/2008 on the common organisation of the market in wine, amending Regulations (EC) No.1493/1999, (EC) No.1782/2003, (EC) No.1290/2005, (EC) No.3/2008 and repealing Regulations (EEC) No.2392/86 and (EC) No.1493/1999 [2008] O.J. L335/32 . . . . 405, 462

Reg.480/2009 establishing a Guarantee Fund for external actions [2009] O.J. L145/10 567

Reg.483/2009 amending Regulation (EC) No.820/2008 laying down measures for the implementation of the common basic standards on aviation security [2009] O.J. L 145/23 . . . . 200, 452

Reg.487/2009 on the application of Article 81(3) of the Treaty to certain categories of agreements and concerted practices in the air transport sector [2009] O.J. L148/1 . . . . 344, 363, 450

Reg.496/2009 amending Council Regulation (EC) No.872/2004 concerning further restrictive measures in relation to Liberia [2009] O.J. L149/60 116

Reg.713/2009 establishing an Agency for the Cooperation of Energy Regulators [2009] O.J. L211/1 208

Reg.714/2009 on conditions for access to the network for cross-border exchanges in electricity and repealing Regulation (EC) No.1228/2003 [2009] O.J. L211/15 555

Reg.715/2009 on conditions for access to the natural gas transmission networks and repealing Regulation (EC) No.1775/2005 [2009] O.J. L211/36 555

Reg.790/2009 amending, for the purposes of its adaptation to technical and scientific progress, Regulation (EC) No.1272/2008 of the European Parliament and of the Council on classification, labelling and packaging of substances and mixtures [2009] O.J. L235/1 492

Reg.1070/2009 of the European Parliament and of the Council of 21 October 2009 amending Regulations (EC) No 549/2004, (EC) No 550/2004, (EC) No 551/2004 and (EC) No 552/2004 in order to improve the performance and sustainability of the European aviation system [2009] O.J. L300/34 452

Reg. 1136/2009 Commission Regulation (EC) of 25 November 2009 amending Regulation (EC) No 1126/2008 adopting certain international accounting standards in accordance with Regulation (EC) No 1606/2002 of the European Parliament and of the Council as regards International Financial Reporting Standard (IFRS) 1 (Text with EEA relevance) [2009] O.J. L311/6 280

Reg.1140/2009 of 20 November 2009 amending Regulation (EC) No 1234/2007 establishing a common organisation of agricultural markets and on specific provisions for certain agricultural products (Single CMO Regulation) [2009] O.J. L312/4 404

Reg.1163/2009 of 30 November 2009 amending Regulation (EC) No 417/2002 of the European Parliament and of the Council

on the accelerated phasing-in
of double-hull or equivalent
design requirements for
single-hull oil tankers [2009]
O.J. L314/13 456
Reg.1164/2009 Commission
Regulation (EC) of 27 November
2009 amending Regulation (EC)
No 1126/2008 adopting certain
international accounting
standards in accordance with
Regulation (EC) No 1606/2002
of the European Parliament and
of the Council as regards
International Financial Reporting
Interpretations Committee's
(IFRIC) Interpretation 18 [2009]
O.J. L314/15
Reg.1224/2009 of 20 November
2009 establishing a Community
control system for ensuring
compliance with the rules of the
common fisheries policy,
amending Regulations (EC) No
847/96, (EC) No 2371/2002,
(EC) No 811/2004, (EC) No
768/2005, (EC) No 2115/2005,
(EC) No 2166/2005, (EC) No
388/2006, (EC) No 509/2007,
(EC) No 676/2007, (EC) No
1098/2007, (EC) No 1300/2008,
(EC) No 1342/2008 and
repealing Regulations (EEC)
No 2847/93, (EC) No 1627/94
and (EC) No 1966/2006 [2009]
O.J. L343/1 . . . . 202, 416
Reg.1250/2009 of 30 November
2009 amending Regulation (EC)
No 73/2009 establishing
common rules for direct support
schemes for farmers under the
common agricultural policy and
establishing certain support
schemes for farmers [2009]
O.J. L338/1
2010 Reg.18/2010 of 8 January 2010
amending Regulation (EC) No
300/2008 of the European
Parliament and of the Council
as far as specifications for
national quality control
programmes in the field of civil
aviation security are concerned
[2010] O.J. L7/3 451
Reg.23/2010 of 14 January 2010
fixing for 2010 the fishing

opportunities for certain fish
stocks and groups of fish stocks,
applicable in EU waters and, for
EU vessels, in waters where
catch limitations are required
and amending Regulations (EC)
No 1359/2008, (EC) No
754/2009, (EC) No 1226/2009
and (EC) No 1287/2009
[2010] O.J. L21/1 415
Reg.66/2010 of the European
Parliament and of the
Council of 25 November 2009
on the EU Ecolabel [2010]
O.J. L27/1 500

DECISIONS

1960 Dec.60/912 on speeding up the
pace at which the objectives of
the Treaty are achieved
[1960] O.J. L58/1217 16
1962 Dec.62/528 on additional
measures to speed up the pace
at which the objectives of the
Treaty are achieved [1962]
O.J. L41/1284 16
1968 Dec.68/183 authorising certain
management measures to be taken
within the framework of the
common organisation of the
agricultural markets (SOCEMAS)
[1968] O.J. L89/13 . . . . 115, 326
1969 Dec.69/494 concerning progressive
uniformisation of existing
trade agreement [1969]
O.J. L326/39 581
1970 Dec.70/243 on the replacement of
financial contributions from
Member States by the
Communities' own resources
[1970] O.J. L94/19 . . . . 16, 214
Dec.70/333 ASPA [1970]
O.J. L148/1 322
Decision creating the
Communities' own resources
April 21, 1970 9
1976 Dec.76/787 concerning the
election of the representatives
of the Assembly by direct
universal suffrage [1976]
O.J. L278/1 62
1980 Dec.80/45 on the introduction and
implementation of technical
regulations and standards
[1980] O.J. L14/36 234

1982 Dec.82/534 adopting the fifth
medium-term economic policy
programme [1982] O.J.
L236/10 41

1987 Dec.87/305 setting up an advisory
committee on the opening-up of
public procurement [1987]
O.J. L152/32 316
Dec.87/327 adopting the European
Community Action Scheme for
the Mobility of University
Students (Erasmus) [1987]
O.J. L166/20 481
Dec.87/560 setting up an advisory
committee on the opening-up of
public procurement [1987]
O.J. L338/37 316

1988 Dec.88/376 on the system of the
Communities' own resources
[1988] O.J. L185/24 215
Dec.88/568 relating to a
proceeding under Article 85 of
the EEC Treaty (IV/32.437/8 -
Eurotunnel) [1988] O.J.
L311/36 340
Dec.88/591 establishing a Court of
First Instance of the European
Communities [1988] O.J.
L319/1 165

1989 Dec.89/489 establishing an action
programme to promote foreign
languages competence in the
European Union [1989] O.J.
L239/24 481
Dec.89/631 on a Community
financial contribution towards
expenditure incurred by Member
States for the purpose of
ensuring compliance with the
Community system for the
conservation and management
of fishery resources [1989]
O.J. L364/64 417

1990 Dec.90/233 establishing a trans-
European mobility scheme for
university studies (Tempus)
[1990] O.J. L131/21 481

1991 Dec.91/169 authorizing extension
or tacit renewal of certain trade
agreements concluded between
Member States and third
countries [1991] O.J.
L83/13 581
Dec.3855/91 establishing Union
rules for aid to the steel industry
[1991] O.J. L362/57 385

1993 Dec.1/93 amending Appendix III
to the Convention of 20 May
1987 on a common transit
procedure [1994] O.J.
L12/32 20
Dec.93/631 concerning the grant
of assistance from the cohesion
financial instrument to the
following project in Ireland
[1993] O.J. L308/1 515
Dec.93/731 on public access to
Council documents [1993]
O.J. L340/43 104
Dec.3632/93/ECSC establishing
Community rules for State aid to
the coal industry [1993]
O.J. L329/121 ...... 555, 557

1994 Dec.1/94 adopting the Rules of
Procedure of the EEA Council
[1994] O.J. L138/39 20
Dec.94/19 relating to a proceeding
pursuant to Article 86 of the EC
Treaty (IV / 34.689 – Sea
Containers v Stena Sealink –
Interim measures) [1994]
O.J. L15/8 341
Dec.94/262 on the regulations and
general conditions governing the
performance of the
Ombudsman's duties [1994] O.J.
L113/15 72
Dec.94/375 on Community
membership of the European
Investment Fund [1994] O.J.
L173/12 186
Dec.94/663 relating to a
proceeding pursuant to Article
85 of the EC Treaty and Article
53 of the EEA Agreement (IV /
34.600 – Night Services)
[1994] O.J. L 259/20 340
Dec.94/819 establishing an action
programme for the
implementation of a
European Community
vocational training policy
[1994] O.J. L340/8 483
Dec.94/800 as regards matters
within its competence, of the
agreements reached in the
Uruguay Round multilateral
negotiations [1994] O.J.
L336/1 308

1995 Dec.95/167 on the detailed
provisions governing the exercise
of the European Parliament's

right of inquiry [1995] O.J.
L113/2 72

Dec.95/260 setting up a
Consumer Committee [1995]
O.J. L162/37 499

Dec.95/364 relating to a
proceeding pursuant to Article
90(3) of the Treaty (Landing
fees at Zaventem) [1995]
O.J. L218/8 . . . . 341, 378

Dec.95/468 on a Community
contribution for telematic
interchange of data between
administrations in the
Community (IDA) [1995]
O.J. L269/23 141

Dec.95/489 on a set of guidelines
for the development of the
EURO-ISDN (Integrated
Services Digital Network) as
a trans- European network
[1995] O.J. L282/16 516

Dec.95/547 giving conditional
approval to the aid granted by
France to the bank Crédit
Lyonnais [1995] O.J.
L308/92 389

Dec.95/553 regarding protection
for citizens of the European
Union by diplomatic and
consular representations
[1995] O.J. L314/73 5

Dec.819/95 establishing an action
programme SOCRATES
[1995] O.J. L87/10 482

Dec.3052/95 of Parliament and
Council establishing a
procedure for the exchange of
information on national measures
derogating from the principle of
the free movement of goods
within the Union [1995]
O.J. L321/1 . . . . 195, 234

1996 Dec.96/39 laying down a series of
measures aimed at creating a
more favourable context for the
development of trans-European
networks in the energy sector
[1996] O.J. L161/154 515

Dec.96/537 defining the
specifications of projects of
common interest identified by
Decision No.1254/96/EC of the
European Parliament and of the
Council laying down a series of
guidelines for trans-European

energy networks [1996]
O.J. L230/16 516

Dec.97/606 of the EC Treaty on
the exclusive right to broadcast
television advertising in Flanders
[1997] O.J. L244/18 377

Dec.96/1025 renewing the
Management Board of the
European Centre for the
Development of Vocational
Training [1996] O.J.
C316/1 483

Dec.96/1692 on Community
guidelines for the development
of the trans-European transport
network [1996] O.J.
L228/1 516

Dec.645/96 programme of
Union action on health
promotion, information,
education and training
[1996] O.J. C95/1 491

Dec.646/96 on action plan to
combat cancer [1996]
O.J. L95/9 491

Dec.647/96 setting up a Union
programme on the prevention of
AIDS and certain other
communicable diseases
[1996] O/J L95/16 491

Dec.1254/96 laying down a series
of guidelines for trans-European
energy networks [1996]
O.J. L161/147 515

Dec.1692/96 on Union guidelines
for the development of the
trans-European transport
network [1996] O.J.
L228/1 442

1997 Dec.97/126 concerning the
conclusion of an Agreement
between the EC and the
Government of Denmark and
the Home Government of the
Faeroe Islands [1997] O.J.
L53/1 12

Dec.97/292 on a specific measure
to encourage Italian fishermen
to diversify out of certain
fishing activities [1997] O.J.
L121/20 421

Dec.97/416 abrogating the
decision on the existence of an
excessive deficit in the
Netherlands [1997] O.J.
L177/23 462

Dec.102/97 on a programme of
Union action on the prevention
of drug dependence [1997]
O.J. L19/25 491

Dec.210/97 adopting an action
programme for customs in the
Union (Customs 2000)
[1997] O.J. L33/24 226

Dec.1336/97 on a series of
guidelines for trans-European
telecommunications networks
[1997] O.J. L183/12 516,
516

Dec.1400/97 on a programme for
healthy monitoring [1997] O.J.
L193/1 491

1998 Dec.98/489 concerning the
conclusion of the International
Cocoa Agreement 1993, on
behalf of the Union [1998]
O.J. L220/1 585

Dec.98/537 approving the text of
the amendment to the trade-
related provisions of the Energy
Charter Treaty and its
provisional application agreed
by the Energy Charter
Conference and the International
Conference of the Signatories of
the Energy Charter Treaty
[1998] O.J. L252/21 554

Dec.98/743 on the detailed
provisions concerning the
composition of the Economic
and Financial Committee
[1998] O.J. L358/109 465

Dec.98/2119 setting up a network
for the epidemiological
surveillance and control of
communicable diseases in the
Community [1998] O.J.
L268/1 492

Dec.576/98 amending Decision
No.819/95/EC establishing
the Community action
programme Socrates [1998]
O.J. L77/1 482

1999 Dec.99/25 Euratom adopting a
multi-annual programme
(1998–2002) of actions in the
nuclear sector, relating to the
safe transport of radioactive
materials and to safeguards and
industry co-operation to
promote certain aspects of safety
of nuclear installations in the

countries currently participating
in the TACIS programme
[1999] O.J. L7/31 559

Dec.99/311 adopting the third
phase of the trans-European
cooperation scheme for
higher education (Tempus III)
(2000-2006) [2002] O.J.
L195/34 594
Art.3 219

Dec.99/382 establishing the second
phase of the Community
vocational training action
programme 'Leonardo da Vinci'
[1999] O.J. L146/33 483

Dec.99/435 concerning the
definition of the Schengen acquis
for the purpose of determining, in
conformity with the relevant
provisions of the Treaty
establishing the European
Community and the Treaty on
European Union, the legal basis
for each of the provisions or
decisions which constitute the
acquis [1999] O.J. L176/1 . . 243
Art.1(2) 243

Dec.99/468 laying down the
procedure for the exercise of
implementing powers conferred
on the Commission [1999]
O.J. L184/23 . . . . 71, 116, 413
Art.5a 422

Dec.1999/493 on the composition
of the Commission [1999]
O.J. L192/53 108

Dec.99/569 on the basic
parameters for the command-
and-control and signalling
subsystems relating to the
trans-European high-speed
rail systems [1999]
O.J. L216/23 515

Dec.1295/99 on Union action on
rare diseases [1999] O.J.
L155/1 491

Dec.1296/1999 action programme
on pollution related diseases
[1999] O.J. C200/1 492

Council Decision of April 27,
1999 62

2000 Dec.2000/44 on the settlement of
the Bangemann case [2000]
O.J. L16/73 108

Dec.2000/427 in accordance with
Article 122(2) of the Treaty on

the adoption by Greece of
the single currency on
January 1, 2001 [2000] O.J.
L167/19 459

Dec.2000/761 defining the
specifications of projects of
common interest identified in the
sector of trans-European energy
networks by Decision 1254/96
[2000] O.J. L305/22 515

Dec.508/2000 establishing the
Culture 2000 programme
[2000] O.J. L63/1 490

Dec.647/2000 of Parliament and
the Council adopting a
multi-annual programme for the
promotion of energy efficiency
[2000] O.J. L79/6 554

Dec.2000/749 Decision No 178 of
9 December 1999 on the
interpretation of Article 111(1)
and (2) of Regulation (EEC)
No.574/72 [2000] O.J.
L302/71 251

Dec.2000/1987 [2007] O.J.
L90/58 535

Decision of December 8, 2000 on
the signing, on behalf of the
Union, of the UN Convention
against trans-national organised
crime and its Protocol on
combating trafficking in persons,
especially women and children,
and the smuggling of migrants
by land, air and sea [2000]
O.J. L30/44 257

2001   Dec.2001/220/JHA on the standing
of victims in criminal
proceedings [2001] O.J.
L82/1 261
Art.2 261
Art.3 261

Dec.2001/271 imposing fines on
Deutsche Post/trans-o-flex
[2001] O.J. L97/1 354

Dec.2001/431 on a financial
contribution by the Community
to certain expenditure incurred
by the Member States in
implementing the control,
inspection and surveillance
systems applicable to the
common fisheries policy
[2001] O.J. L154/22 417

Dec.2001/470 establishing a
European Judicial Network in

civil and commercial matters
[2001] O.J. L174/25 259

Dec.2001/781 adopting a manual of
receiving agencies and a glossary
of documents that may be served
in the Member State [2008]
O.J. L173/17 259

Dec.2001/822 on the association
of the overseas countries and
territories with the European
Community ("Overseas
Association Decision")
[2001] O.J. L314/1 608

Dec.2001/462 on the terms of
reference of hearing officers in
competition procedures
[2001] O.J. L162/21 358

Dec.2001/539 on the conclusion
by the EC of the Convention for
the Unification of Certain Rules
for International Carriage by Air
(the Montreal Convention)
[2001] O.J. L194/38 453

Dec.1/2001 concerning the
adoption of the Rules of
Procedure of the Council
[2001] O.J. L43/20 607

Dec.2/2001 concerning the
adoption of the Rules of
procedure of the Committee
[2001] O.J. L43/24 607

2002   Dec.2002/158 on the mobilisation
of the flexibility instrument
[2002] O.J. L53/28 79

Dec.2002/187 setting up Eurojust
with a view to reinforcing the
fight against serious crime
[2002] O.J. L63/1 ... 186, 207

Dec.2002/494/JHA setting up a
European network of contact
points in respect of persons
responsible for genocide, crimes
against humanity and war crimes
[2002] O.J. L167/1 263

Dec.2002/584/JHA on the
European arrest warrant and the
surrender procedure between
Member States [2002] O.J.
L190/3 263
Art.4(6) 263

Dec.2002/620 of the institutions,
the Committees and the
Ombudsman [2002]
O.J. L197/53 .... 124, 211

Dec.2002/621 of the same on the
organisation and operation of

EPSO [2002] O.J.
L197/56 124

Dec.2006/702 on Union strategic
guidelines on cohesion
[2006] O.J. L291/11 519

Dec.2002/772 amending the Act
concerning the election of the
representatives of the European
Parliament by direct universal
suffrage, annexed to Decision
76/787/ECSC, EEC, Euratom
[2002] O.J. L283/1 62

Dec.2002/818 concerning trade
practices maintained by
Korea affecting trade in
commercial vessels [2002]
O.J. L281/15 595

Dec.2002/836 on structuring the
European Research Area
[2002] O.J. L294/44 534

Dec.2002/838 adopting a specific
programme (Euratom) for
research and training on nuclear
energy (2002–2006) [2002]
O.J. L294/74 537

Dec.2002/835 adopting a specific
programme for RTD and
demonstration: "Integrating and
strengthening the European
Research Area" (2002–2006)
[2002] O.J. L294/1 532

Decision of June 3, 2002
concerning the Euratom
programme 534

Dec.1145/2002 on Community
incentive measures in the field
of employment [2002] O.J.
L170/1 486

Dec.1513/2002 15/13/02
concerning the sixth framework
programme of the European
Community for research,
technological development and
demonstration activities,
contributing to the creation of
the European Research Area and
to innovation (2002 to 2006)
[2002] O.J. L232 534

Dec.1786/2002 adopting a
programme of Community
action in the field of public
health (2003-2008) [2002]
O.J. L271/1 .... 211, 492, 493

Dec.2235/2002 adopting a
Community programme to
improve the operation of

taxation systems in the
internal market [2002] O.J.
L341/1 429

Dec.676/2002 on a regulatory
framework for radio spectrum
policy in the European
Community (Radio Spectrum
Decision) [2002] O.J.
L108/1 509

2003   Dec.2003/80/JAI on the protection
of the environment through
criminal law [2003] O.J.
L 29/55 548

Dec.2003/93 authorising the
Member States, in the interest of
the Community, to sign the 1996
Hague Convention on
jurisdiction, applicable law,
recognition, enforcement and
cooperation in respect of
parental responsibility and
measures for the protection
of children [2003] O.J.
L48/1 260

Dec.2003/535/JHA on the
investigation and prosecution of
genocide, crimes against
humanity and war crimes
[2003] O.J. L118/12 263

Dec.2003/564 on the application
of Directive 72/166 relating to
checks on insurance against civil
liability in respect of the use of
motor vehicles [2003]
O.J. L192/23 .... 296, 445

Dec.2003/577 on the execution in
the European Union of orders
freezing property or evidence
[2003] O.J. L196/45 259

Dec.2003/641 on the use of colour
photographs or other
illustrations as health warnings
on tobacco packages [2003]
O.J. L226/24 493

Dec.2003/796 on establishing the
European Regulators Group for
Electricity and Gas [2003]
O.J. L296/34 555

Dec.1152/2003 on computerising
the movement and surveillance
of excisable products [2003]
O.J. L162/5 430

Dec.1229/2003 laying down a
series of guidelines for trans-
European energy networks and
repealing Decision

No.1254/96/EC [2003]
O.J. L176/11 .... 516, 555
Dec.1230/2003 adopting a
multiannual programme for
action in the field of energy:
"Intelligent Energy – Europe"
(2003 – 2006) [2003] O.J.
L176/29 210
2004 Dec.2004/20 setting up an
executive agency, the "Intelligent
Energy Executive Agency", to
manage Community action in
the field of energy in application
of Council Regulation (EC)
No.58/2003 [2004] O.J.
L5/85 .... 210, 553
Dec.2004/134 declaring a
concentration to be incompatible
with the common market and the
EEA Agreement Case COMP /
M.2220 – General Electric/
Honeywell [2004]
O.J. L48/1 374
Dec.2004/566 amending Decision
2000/820/JHA establishing a
European Police College
(CEPOL) [2004] O.J.
L251/19 206
Dec.2004/567 amending Decision
2000/820/JHA establishing a
European Police College
(CEPOL) [2004] O.J.
L251/20 207
Dec.2004/575 laying down
minimum provisions on the
constituent elements of criminal
acts and penalties in the field of
drug trafficking [2004] O.J.
L335/8 262
Dec.2004/676 concerning the Staff
Regulations of the European
Defence Agency [2004] O.J.
L310/9 206
Dec.2004/677 concerning the
Rules applicable to national
experts and military staff on
secondment to the European
Defence Agency [2004] O.J.
L310/64 206
Dec.2004/752 establishing the
European Union Civil Service
Tribunal [2004] O.J.
L333/7 170
Art.7(4) 171
(5) 171
Art.9 171

Art.10 171
Art.12 171
Dec.2004/858 setting up an
executive agency, the 'Executive
Agency for the Public Health
Programme', for the
management of Community
action in the field of public
health – pursuant to Council
Regulation (EC) No 58/2003
[2004] O.J. L369/73 493
Dec.2004/919 on tackling vehicle
crime with cross-border
implications [2004] O.J.
L389/28 263
Dec.792/2004 establishing a Union
action programme to promote
bodies active at European level
in the field of culture [2004]
O.J. L138/40 489
2005 Dec.2005/49 concerning the
operating rules of the committee
provided for in Article 3(3) of
Annex I to the Protocol on the
Statute of the Court of Justice
[2005] O.J. L21/13 170
Dec.2005/56 on the State aid
granted by France to EDF and
the electricity and gas industries
[2007] O.J. L49/21 210
Dec.2005/150 concerning the
conditions and arrangements
governing the submission and
processing of applications for
appointment as a judge of the
European Union Civil Service
Tribunal [2005] O.J.
L50/7 170
Dec.2005/214/JHA on the
application of the principle of
mutual recognition to financial
penalties[2005 O.J.
L76/16 263
Dec.2005/600 on Guidelines for
the employment policies of the
Member States [2005] O.J.
L205/21 526
Dec.2005/681/JHA establishing a
European Police College
(CEPOL) and repealing Decision
2000/820/JHA [2005] O.J.
L256/63 206
Dec.2005/696 amending the
Protocol on the Statute of the
Court of Justice, in order to lay
down the conditions and limits

for the review by the Court
of Justice of decisions given by
the Court of First Instance
[2005] O.J. L266/60 154
Dec.2005/720 establishing an
association between the
European Communities and
their Member States and the
republic of Tunisia [2005]
O.J. L278/1 593
Dec.854/2005 establishing a multi-
annual Union programme on
promoting safer use of the
Internet and new online
technologies [2005] O.J.
L149/1 508

2006   Dec.2006/356 concerning the
conclusion of the Euro-
Mediterranean Agreement
[2006] O.J. L143/1 593
Dec.2006/512 introducing the
regulatory procedure with
scrutiny [2006] O.J.
L200/11 116
Dec.2006/595 drawing up the list
of regions eligible for funding
from the Structural Funds under
the Convergence objective for
the period 2007-2013
[2006] O.J. L343/44 525
Dec.2006/580 concerning the
signing of the Interim Agreement
on trade and trade-related
matters between the Albania
[2006] O.J. L 112/1586
Dec.2006/609 fixing an indicative
allocation by Member State of
the commitment appropriations
for the European territorial
cooperation objective for the
period 2007-2013 [2006] O.J.
L347/26 525
Dec.2006/636 fixing the annual
breakdown by Member State of
the amount for Community
support to rural development for
the period from January 1,
2007 to December 31, 2013
[2006] O.J. L261/32 413
Dec.2006/702 on Community
strategic guidelines on cohesion
[2006] O.J. L291/11 522
Dec.2006/972 concerning the
specific programme: 'Ideas'
implementing the Seventh
Framework Programme of the

European Community for
research, technological
development and demonstration
activities [2007] O.J.
L54/81 532
Dec.2006/973 concerning the
specific programme 'People'
implementing the Seventh
Framework Programme of the
European Community for
research, technological
development and demonstration
activities (2007 to 2013)
[2007] O.J. L54/91 532
Dec.2006/974 on the specific
programme: 'Capacities'
implementing the Seventh
Framework Programme of the
European Community for
research, technological
development and demonstration
activities [2007] O.J.
L54/101 532
Dec.2006/769 drawing up the list
of regions and areas eligible for
funding from the European
Regional Development Fund
under the cross-border and
transnational strands of the
European territorial
cooperation objective for the
period 2007 to 2013
[2006] O.J. L312/47 525
Dec.2006/594 fixing an indicative
allocation by Member State of
the commitment appropriations
for the Convergence objective
for the period 2007–2013
[2006] O.J. L243/37 525
Dec.2006/954 approving the
accession of the European
Community to the Geneva Act
of the Hague Agreement
concerning the international
registration of industrial
designs, adopted in Geneva on
July 2, 1999 [2006]
O.J. L386/28 307
Dec.1639/2006 establishing a
Competitiveness and Innovation
Framework Programme
[2006] O.J. L310/15 506
Dec.1719/06 establishing the
Youth in Action programme for
the period 2007 to 2013
[2006] O.J. L327/30 484

2007   Dec.2007/60 establishing the
       Trans-European Transport
       Network Executive Agency
       pursuant to Council
       Regulation (EC) No.58/2003
       [2007] O.J. L32/88 209
       Dec.2007/134 establishing the
       European Research Council
       [2007] O.J. L57/14 532
       Dec.2007/247 on the Union
       participation in the capital
       increase of the EIF [2007]
       O.J. L107/5 186
       Dec.2007/339 on the signature and
       provisional application of the
       Air Transport Agreement
       between the European
       Community and its Member
       States, on the one hand, and
       the United States of America,
       on the other hand [2007] O.J.
       L134/1 453
       Dec.2007/372 amending Decision
       2004/20/EC in order to transform
       the Intelligent Energy Executive
       Agency into the Executive Agency
       for Competitiveness and
       Innovation [2007]
       O.J. L140/52 553
       Dec.2007/383 fixing the annual
       breakdown by Member State of
       the amount for Union support to
       rural development for the period
       from January 1, 2007 to
       December 31, 2013 [2007]
       O.J. L147/21 412
       Dec.2007/384 establishing a
       mechanism to administer the
       financing of the common costs
       of European Union operations
       having military or defence
       implications [2007]
       O.J. L152/14 578
       Dec.2007/470 on the signing and
       provisional application of the
       Agreement between the
       European Community and the
       Government of the Kyrgyz
       Republic on certain aspects of
       air services [2007] O.J.
       L179/38 453
       Dec.2007/491 [2007] O.J.
       L205/21 526
       Dec.2007/500 amending Decision
       2001/781/EC adopting a manual
       of receiving agencies and a

       glossary of documents that may
       be served under Council
       Regulation (EC) No 1348/2000
       on the service in the Member
       States of judicial and
       extrajudicial documents in
       civil or commercial matters
       [2007] O.J. L185/24 259
       Dec.2007/533 on the
       establishment, operation and use
       of the second generation
       Schengen Information System
       [2007] O.J. L205/63 242
       Dec.2007/1350 establishing a
       second programme of
       Community action in the
       field of health (2008-13)
       [2007] O.J. L301/3 493
       Dec.435/2007 amending
       Regulation (EC) No 1010/2006
       on certain exceptional market
       support measures in the eggs
       and poultry sector in certain
       Member States [2007] O.J.
       L104/13 258
       Dec.573/2007 establishing the
       European Refugee Fund for the
       period 2008 to 2013 as part of
       the General programme
       Solidarity and Management of
       Migration Flows and repealing
       Council Decision 2004/904/EC
       [2007] O.J. L144/1 257
       Dec.575/2007 establishing the
       European Return Fund for the
       period 2008 to 2013 as part of
       the General Programme
       Solidarity and Management of
       Migration Flows [2007]
       O.J. L144/45 258
       Dec.779/2007 establishing for the
       period 2007–2013 a specific
       programme to prevent and
       combat violence against
       children, young people and
       women and to protect victims
       and groups at risk (Daphne III
       programme) as part of the
       general programme
       "Fundamental Rights and
       Justice" [2007] O.J.
       L173/19 262
2008   Dec.2008/67 on taking account of
       convictions in the Member States
       of the European Union in the
       course of new criminal

proceedings [2008] O.J.
L220/32 261

Dec.2008/294 on harmonised
conditions of spectrum use for
the operation of mobile
communication services on
aircraft (MCA services) in
the Union [2008] O.J.
L98/19 452

Dec.2008/370 on the mobilisation
of the European Globalisation
Adjustment Fund in accordance
with point 28 of the
Interinstitutional Agreement of
May 17, 2006 between the
European Parliament, the
Council and the Commission
on budgetary discipline and
sound financial management
[2008] O.J. L128/6 252

Dec.2008/372 on the signing and
provisional application of a
Protocol to the Euro-
Mediterranean Agreement
establishing an association
between the European
Communities and their Member
States, of the one part, and the
State of Israel, of the other part,
on a framework Agreement
between the European
Community and the State of
Israel on the general principles
governing the State of Israel's
participation in Community
programmes [2008] O.J.
L129/39 594

Dec.2008/375 concerning the
conclusion of the Agreement
between the European
Community and the Republic of
Turkey on the participation of
the Republic of Turkey in the
work of the European
Monitoring Centre for Drugs
and Drug Addiction [2008]
O.J. L128/48 194

Dec.2008/381 establishing a
European Migration Network
[2008] O.J. L131/7 258

Dec.2008/386 concerning the
technical specification for
interoperability relating to
the control-command and
signalling sub-system of the
trans-European conventional

and high-speed rail system
[2008] O.J. L136/11 447

Dec.2008/457 laying down rules
for the implementation of
Council Decision 2007/435/EC
establishing the European
Fund for the Integration of
third-country nationals for the
period 2007 to 2013 as part of
the General programme
Solidarity and Management of
Migration Flows as regards
Member States' management
and control systems, the rules
for administrative and financial
management and the eligibility
of expenditure on projects
co-financed by the Fund
[2008] O.J. L167/69 258

Dec.2008/458 laying down rules
for the implementation of
Decision No .75/2007/EC of the
European Parliament and of the
Council establishing the
European Return Fund for the
period 2008 to 2013 as part of
the General programme
Solidarity and Management of
Migration Flows as regards
Member States' management
and control systems, the rules
for administrative and financial
management and the eligibility
of expenditure on projects
co-financed by the Fund
[2008] O.J. L167/135 258

Dec.2008/544 amending Decision
2004/858/EC in order to
transform the Executive Agency
for the Public Health Programme
into the Executive Agency for
Health and Consumers
[2008] O.J. L173/27 493

Dec.2008/593 amending Decision
No.2007/60/EC as regards the
modification of the tasks and
the period of operation of the
Trans-European Transport
Network Executive Agency
[2008] O.J. L190/35 210

Dec.2008/618 on Guidelines
for the employment policies
of the Member States [2008]
O.J. L198/47 485

Dec.2008/675 on taking account
of convictions in the Member

States of the European Union
in the course of new criminal
proceedings [2008] O.J.
L220/32 261
Dec.2008/841 on the fight against
organised crime [2008] O.J.
L300/42 260
Dec.2008/909 on the application
of the principle of mutual
recognition to judgments in
criminal matters imposing
custodial sentences or measures
involving deprivation of liberty
for the purpose of their
enforcement in the European
Union [2008] O.J.
L327/27 261
Dec.2008/947 on the application
of the principle of mutual
recognition to judgments and
probation decisions with a view
to the supervision of probation
measures and alternative
sanctions [2008] O.J.
L337/102 258
Dec.2008/976 on the European
Judicial Network [2008]
O.J. L348/130 264
Dec.2008/978 on the European
evidence warrant for the purpose
of obtaining objects, documents
and data for use in proceedings
in criminal matters [2008]
O.J. L350/72 264
Dec.70/2008 on a paperless
environment for customs
and trade [2008] O.J.
L23/21 227
Dec.1065/2008 repealing Council
Decision 85/368/EEC on the
comparability of vocational
training qualifications between
the Member States of the
European Community [2008]
O.J. L288/4 483
Dec.1352/2008 amending
Decision No.1855/2006/EC
establishing the Culture
Programme (2007 to 2013)
[2008] O.J. L348/128 490
Decision N560/2008 of
November 10, 2008 389
Decision N528/2008 of
November 12, 2008 389
Decision NN68/2008 of
November 25, 2008 389

2009 Dec.2009/102 providing
Community medium-term
financial assistance for Hungary
[2009] O.J. L57/5 463
Dec.2009/117 on the signing and
provisional application of the
Agreement between the
European Community and the
Government of Nepal on certain
aspects of air services [2009]
O.J. L41/3 453
Dec.2009/299 amending
Framework Decisions
2002/584/JHA, 2005/214/JHA,
2006/783/JHA, 2008/909/JHA
and 2008/947/JHA, thereby
enhancing the procedural rights
of persons and fostering the
application of the principle
of mutual recognition to
decisions rendered in the
absence of the person
concerned at the trial [2009]
O.J. L81/24 . . . . 261, 263
Art.32 263
Dec.2009/321 [2009] O.J.
L123/37 208
Dec.2009/377 adopting
implementing measures for the
consultation mechanism and the
other procedures referred to in
Article 16 of Regulation (EC)
No.767/2008 of the European
Parliament and of the Council
concerning the Visa Information
System (VIS) and the exchange
of data between Member States
on short-stay visas (VIS
Regulation [2009] O.J.
L117/3 256
Dec.2009/409 establishing, in
accordance with Article 104(8)
of the Treaty, whether effective
action has been taken by the
United Kingdom in response to
the Council Recommendation
of 8 July 2008 pursuant to
Article 104(7) [2009] O.J.
L132/11 252
Dec.2009/426 on the
strengthening of Eurojust
[2009] O.J. L138/14 207
Dec.2009/430 concerning the
conclusion of the Convention on
jurisdiction and the recognition
and enforcement of judgements in

civil and commercial matters
[2009] O.J. L147/1 258
Dec.2009/434 amending
Decision 2006/493 [2009]
O.J. L144/25 412
Dec.2009/496 of Parliament,
Council, Commission, Court of
Justice, Court of Auditors, ECSC
and Committee of the Regions
[2009] O.J. L168/41 212
Dec.2009/548 establishing a
template for National
Renewable Energy Action Plans
under Directive 2009/28/EC of
the European Parliament and
of the Council [2009] O.J.
L182/33 558
Dec.2009/739 [2009] O.J.
L263/32 setting out the practical
arrangements for the exchange
of information by electronic
means between Member States
and Decision setting out
measures facilitating the use of
procedures by electronic means
through the "points of single
contact" [2009] O.J.
L274/36 297
Decision Atalanta/3/2009 on
the setting up of the Committee
of Contributors for the
European Union military
operation to contribute to the
deterrence, prevention and
repression of acts of piracy
and armed robbery of the
Somali coast [2009] O.J.
L119/40 577
Dec.2009/742 of the South
African Co-operation
Council [2009] O.J.
L265/34 597
Dec.406/2009 on the effort of
Member States to reduce their
greenhouse gas emissions to
meet the Community's
greenhouse gas emission
reduction commitments up
to 202 [2009] O.J.
L140/136 547
Dec.2009/813 authorising the
placing on the market of
products containing, consisting
of, or produced from genetically
modified maize MON 89034
(MON-89Ø34-3) pursuant to

Regulation (EC) No 1829/2003
of the European Parliament
and of the Council [2009]
O.J. L289/21 410
Dec.2009/814 authorising the
placing on the market of
products containing,
consisting of, or produced from
genetically modified maize
MON 88017 (MON-88Ø17-3)
pursuant to Regulation (EC) No
1829/2003 of the European
Parliament and of the Council
[2009] O.J. 289/25 410
Dec.2009/815 authorising the
placing on the market of products
containing, consisting of, or
produced from genetically
modified maize 59122xNK603
(DAS-59122-7>MON-ØØ6Ø3-6)
pursuant to Regulation (EC) No
1829/2003 of the European
Parliament and of the Council
[2009] O.J. L289/29 410
Dec. Council Decision of 22
December 2009 amending the
Schengen consultation network
(technical specifications) [2009]
O.J. L353/49 242
2010   Dec.2010/15 Commission Decision
of 16 December 2009 laying
down guidelines for the
management of the Community
Rapid Information System
RAPEX established under Article
12 and of the notification
procedure established under
Article 11 of Directive
2001/95/EC (the General
Product Safety Directive)
(notified under document
C(2009) 9843) [2010] O.J.
L22/1 497
Dec.2010/39 of the EIB Decision
of the Board of Governors of
30 March 2009 on the increase
in the capital of the European
Investment Bank [2009]
O.J. L10/19 . . . . 178, 427
Dec.2010/51 of the Secretaries-
General of the European
Parliament, the Council and the
Commission, the Registrar of the
Court of Justice, the Secretaries-
General of the Court of
Auditors, the European

Economic and Social Committee,
the Committee of the Regions
and the European Ombudsman
of 19 January 2010 amending
Decision 2002/621/EC on the
organisation and operation of
the European Communities
Personnel Selection Office
[2010] O.J. L26/24 212

Dec.2010/78 Commission Decision
of 9 February 2010 adjusting the
thresholds referred to in
Article 157(b) and Article 158(1)
of Regulation (EC, Euratom) No
2342/2002 laying down detailed
rules for the implementation of
the Financial Regulation
[2010] O.J. L37/73 216

Table of National Legislation

Belgium

1967   Law of August 6, 1967 38

Czech Republic

Constitution 27

Finland

Ministry of Justice, 1994 Act
        No.1554/94 38

France

1957   Décret No. 57/321 of March 13,
        1957 38
1958   Constitution 47, 48
        art.55 47

Germany

1961   Bundesgesetzblatt, February 3,
        1961, II, 50 38
Constitution 47
        Art.24(1) 47
        Art.25 47

Greenland

1979   Home Rule Act 18

Ireland

1972   European Communities
        (Enforcement of Community
        Judgments) Regulations
        (SI 1972/331) 38

Italy

Constitution 48
        Art.10(1) 48
1960   Decree of December 2,
        1960 38

Luxembourg

1962   Regulation of October 17, 1962
        (Memorial of October 31,
        1962, No. 58, 1028) 38

Netherlands

1953   Basic Law (Constitution) .. 47, 48
        Art.66 47
        Art.67 47
1955   Law of February 24, 1955
        StB 73 38
1960   Law of January 13, 1960,
        Stb 15 38

Portugal

1998   Law No.104/88 of August 31,
        1988 38

Spain

1986   B.O.E. No.160, July 5, 1986 .. 38

Sweden

1995   Ordonance SFS 1995:105 38

United Kingdom

1972   European Communities
        Act (c.68) 46
        s.2   47
        (1) 43, 47, 53
        (2) 47
        (4) 53
        s.3(1) 47, 143
European Communities (Enforcement
        of Union Judgments) Order
        (SI 1972/1590) 38, 39

Basic Statistics of the 27 Member States

(in alphabetical order according to national spelling)

Country	Area in KM2	Pop. in Millions[1]	GDP per inh.[2]
Belgium	30.510	10.7	35.683
Bulgaria	110.912	7.6	11.760
Czech Rep.	78.886	10.5	24.400
Denmark	43.100	5.5	36.725
Germany	356.900	82.3	34.219
Estonia	45.227	1.3	18.257
Greece	132.000	11.2	30.856
Spain	504.800	45.8	29.527
France	547.030	64.3	33.744
Italy	301.300	60	29.290
Ireland	70.300	4.5	39.445
Cyprus	9.250	0.8	29.898
Latvia	64.600	2.3	14.306
Lithuania	65.301	3.3	15.903
Luxembourg	2.600	0.5	78.723
Hungrary	93.000	10	18.728
Malta	316	0.4	23.622
Netherlands	41.526	16.4	39.273
Austria	83.900	8.3	38.896
Poland	312.685	38.1	17.989
Portugal	92.400	10.6	21.848
Romania	237.500	21.5	11.755
Slovenia	20.273	2	28.524
Slovakia	48.845	5.4	21.374
Finland	337.100	5.3	34.362
Sweden	450.000	9.2	35.934
UK	244.820	61.7	35.165
TOTAL		529.2	

[1] Dec. of 01.01.07 [2007] O.J. L1/9.
[2] International Monetary Fund 2009.

Principal Abbreviations

ACP	African, Caribbean, and Pacific countries party to the Lomé Convention.
Bull.	Bulletin of the European Communities edited by the Secretariat of the Commission; there are 11 issues per year (July-August are published together).
CAP	Common agricultural policy.
CFSP	Common Foreign and Security Policy.
CST	Civil Service Tribunal.
Competition Report	Report on the Competition Policy, published yearly, also on the Internet.
EAGF	European Agricultural Guidance and Guarantee Fund.
EAFRD	European Agricultural Fund for Rural Development.
E.C.R.	Official reports in English of most[1] cases decided by the Community Courts (Courts of Justice numbered I- . . . and General Court II– . . .) and the Civil Servant Tribunal. The numbering of the pages is the same now in all languages. They can be found on the Internet. A further distinction was established in 1994: Community personnel cases were published in a separate volume "Reports of European Community Staff Cases" E.C.R.S.C. Judgements in staff cases are no longer translated in other official languages.
EC	European Community.
ECB	European Central Bank.
EDF	European Development Fund.
EEA	European Economic Area.
EFTA	European Free Trade Association.
EIB	European Investment Bank.
E.L.Rev.	European Law Review.
EMU	European Monetary Union.
ERDF	European Regional Development Fund.
ESF	European Social Fund.
EURATOM	European Community of Atomic Energy.

[1] The executive part of the non-published judgment can be found at the end of each volume of the E.C.R.

FIFG   Financial Instrument for Fisheries Guidance.

GATT   General Agreement on Tariffs and Trade (UN).

GSP   Generalised System of Preferences.

JHA   Justice and Home Affairs; although this denomination of the so-called "third pillar" was replaced by "Provisions on Police and Judicial Co-operation in criminal matters", the logo JHA is still used.

J.O.   Journal Officiel: French edition of the Official Journal of the European Communities.

O.J.   Official Journal of the European Union.
Remarks
  1. This Journal was published under the name *Journal Officiel de la Communauté Européenne du Charbon et de l'Acler* from 1952 to April 19, 1958; on April 20, 1958, the first issue of the *Journal Officiel des Communauté Européennes* appeared, without modifying the structure of the Journal itself; this lasted until December 31, 1967.

     References to publications in the *Journal Officiel* for the period 1952 to July 1, 1967, are made by mentioning the page and the year or vice versa such as J.O. 849/65. Between July 1 and December 31, 1967, each issue is paged separately.
  2. After January 1, 1968 (see O.J. 1968, L.30), the Journal was divided into two separate editions designated by the letters "L" (legislation) and "C." (communications).

     Legislative texts are published in the edition marked "L" and are again subdivided in:

     I. Acts adopted under the EC Treaty/Euratom Treaty whose publication is obligatory;

     II. Acts whose publication is not obligatory;

     III. Acts adopted under the EU Treaty.

     All other texts are published in the edition marked "C" except "Notices and public contracts" which are published in O.J. Supplement.

     References to publication in the *Journal Officiel* after January 1, 1968, are made by mentioning the letter "L" or "C", the year, the No. of the issue and the page, e.g. J.O. 1970, 31/1.
  3. The Journal is also published in all the official languages in the union.
  4. In accordance with Article 155 of the Act of Accession, provision was made in Council Regulation 857/72 of April 24, 1972, for Special Editions of the *Official Journal* for the publication *inter alia* of the English text of acts of the institutions of the Communities adopted and published before accession. Consequently an authentic English translation now exists of the most important Community acts.

     This special edition was published in December 1972 and a subsequent edition was published in 1974 (see O.J. 1972,

L.101/1). All references to an O.J. publication prior to January 1, 1973 are necessarily in the Special Edition.

5. The numbering of pages is the same in all the languages of the Community.

OECD   Organisation for Economic Co-operation and Development.

R&TD   Research and Technological Development.

Rules   Rules of Procedure of the Court of Justice (O.J. 1975, L.102/1).

TAC   Total Allowable Catch.

TACIS   Programme for Technical Assistance to the Commonwealth of the Independent States.

TENs   Trans-European Networks.

UN   United Nations.

WEU   Western European Union.

WTO   World Trade Organisation.

PART ONE: THE EUROPEAN UNION—THE TREATIES, THE HISTORY, THE ACTS AND THE LAW

Chapter One

The European Treaties

INTRODUCTION

The reader who approaches the "European" subject for the first time will be easily forgiven if she or he feels confused by the terminology commonly used. The more so, since the expressions "European Union", "European Community", "European Communities", "Common market" and "Internal market" are often used indiscriminately to designate the same concept. The debate about the European Constitution has not been very helpful in this respect either. As this book hopes to make clear, these expressions do not cover the same realities; therefore some clarification is certainly called for at the outset. The more so since reference is also made, in this context, to the "Treaty on European Union" or "Maastricht Treaty", the "Amsterdam Treaty", the "Treaty of Nice", the "Treaty of Lisbon", the "Treaty on the Functioning of the European Union" (TFEU), the "Economic and Monetary Union" (EMU), the "European Council" and the "Council" and the "Euro", which is not even accepted in all the Member States.

Although there is no strict hierarchy among the various European Treaties, an examination of the subject "Europe" should logically start with the European Union (EU). It was established among the, at that time, 12 Member States by the Maastricht Treaty.[1] Those Member States were, according to the Preamble, "resolved to mark a new stage in the process of European integration undertaken with the establishment of the European Communities". It also shows, among other things, the resolve of these Member States to, "continue the process of creating an ever closer union among the peoples of Europe".[2] The Maastricht Treaty added new dimensions, new fields of activity to the ones provided for by the Treaties which established the three original European Communities, i.e. the European Coal and Steel Community (no longer in existence), the European Atomic Energy Community (Euratom) and what was then the European Economic Community (EEC). The EU Treaty modified those three Treaties, it did not replace them. The EU Treaty has specific features of its own and its own objectives. In addition to those features, it was founded on three elements: (1) the three European Communities; (2) a Common Foreign and Security Policy (CFSP)[3]; and (3) provisions on co-operation in the fields of justice and home affairs.[4] These three elements constituted the

---

[1] It was signed at Maastricht, the Netherlands, on February 7, 1992 and entered into force on November 1, 1993 [1993] O.J. L293/61, after having been ratified by the parliaments of the Member States, in certain cases after it was approved by referendum. It was modified by the Amsterdam, Nice and Lisbon Treaties. Consolidated version now: [2008] O.J. C115/1.

[2] art.A.2 Maastricht Treaty.

[3] Maastricht Treaty Title V.

[4] EU Title VI. This third element used to be designated "Co-operation in the field of Justice and Home Affairs" (CJH).

so-called three pillars of the European construction. They no longer exist as separate sets of provisions.

The Treaties which established the European Atomic Energy Community (Euratom) and the European Economic Community (EEC), are also referred to as the "Treaties of Rome"; it was in that city that these two Treaties were signed in March 1957. However, when reference is made in this book to the "Treaties", it is the EU Treaty and the TFEU which are generally meant. Euratom no longer plays an important independent role: for all practical purposes its activities have been absorbed into the TFEU .

The "common market", now "internal market", often confused with the Union as such, of which it is the main feature, means the so-called basic freedoms (free movement of goods, of persons, freedom of establishment, freedom to provide services and free movement of capital and of payments), together with various policies implemented by the Union itself (for instance: competition and commercial policy). The internal market does not include, for instance, external relations, except for the common commercial policy.

The internal market is defined in the TFEU as, "an area without frontiers in which the free movement of goods, persons, services and capital is ensured".[5] The completion of the internal market, at the end of 1992, was the object of the Single European Act (SEA),[6] signed in February 1986.

This book, as already indicated, is mainly about the Treaty on European Union (EU) and the Treaty on the Functioning of the European Union (TFEU); their nature will be discussed in this chapter. The internal market will be examined in detail further on but it seems necessary to start with a brief overview of the European Union.

1. The EU Treaty and the Treaty on the Functioning of the European Union (TFEU)

At the outset, the Union probably had more political, than legal significance; indeed, it constitutes the ultimate objective of European integration, the precise scope of which is, as yet, not determined in detail. However, since, as provided, amongst others, by the EU Treaty, all the nationals of the Member States are now "citizens" of that Union, which grants them certain rights, this Treaty is certainly not without significance from the legal point of view.[7]

---

[5] art.26(2) TFEU [14(2)]. It is curious, to say the least, that the freedom of establishment is not mentioned here.

[6] This Act is called "single" because it is the combination of two different instruments, which were, for practical purposes, put together into a single one. The first instrument contains modifications to the three European Treaties, while the second constitutes, in fact, an agreement among the Member States concerning co-operation in the field of external relations.

[7] Contrary to the European Communities, the Union had at first, no legal personality, but it now has: art.47 EU. For the rights granted to the citizens, see "Non-Discrimination and Citizenship of the Union" arts 20 to 25 TFEU [17 to 22]. It provides, among other things, for the right of citizens to move and reside in the territory of all the Member States (arts 20(2)(a) and 21(1) TFEU [art.18(1)]), the right to vote and to stand as a candidate in elections to the European Parliament and in municipal elections in the Member State of residence, under the same conditions as nationals of that State arts 20(2)(b) and 22 TFEU [19(1)]. See Directive 1994/80, laying down detailed arrangements for the exercise of the right to vote and to stand as a candidate in municipal elections by citizens of the Union residing in a Member State of which they are not nationals: [1994] O.J. L368/38; see *Commission v Belgium* (C-323/97) [1998] E.C.R. I-4291. In third countries where their own State

The various elements (pillars[8]) of the Union were held together by:

"[A]n institutional framework, which aims to promote its values, advance its objectives, serve its interests, those of its citizens and those of the Member States and ensure the consistency, effectiveness and the continuity of its policies and actions."[9]

This institutional framework now consists of seven institutions: The European Parliament (hereinafter "Parliament"), the European Council, the Council, the Commission, the Court of Justice, the European Central Bank and the Court of Auditors.

The objectives of the Union can be summarised as follows,[10] the Union is to:

- promote peace, its values and the wellbeing of its people;
- offer its citizens an area of freedom, security and justice: free movement of persons, but with external border controls, asylum and immigration measures, and combating of crime;
- establish an internal market;
- develop Europe based on balanced economic growth and price stability;
- establish a competitive social market economy, aiming at full employment and social progress;
- ensure a high level of protection and improvement of the quality of the environment;
- promote scientific and technological advance;
- combat social exclusion and discrimination and promote social justice and protection;
- promote equality between women and men, solidarity between generations and protection of the rights of the child;
- promote economic, social and territorial cohesion and solidarity among Member States;
- respect the rich cultural and linguistic diversity and ensure that Europe's cultural heritage is safeguarded and enhanced;
- establish an economic and monetary union whose currency is the Euro;
- and, in relation to the wider world:

    — uphold and promote its values and interests and contribute to the protection of its citizens;
    — contribute to peace, security, the sustainable development of the Earth;
    — promote solidarity and mutual respect among peoples, free and fair trade, eradication of poverty;

---

is not represented, citizens are entitled to diplomatic and consular protection from any other Member State: arts 20(2)(c) and 23 TFEU [20]; see Decision regarding protection for the citizens of the EU by diplomatic and consular representatives [1995] O.J. L314/73. The citizen also has the right to petition Parliament (art.24,2 TFEU [21]) and to apply to the Ombudsman (art.24,3 TFEU [21]). It should be noted that the Council may propose to the Member States to extend those rights (art.25,2 TFEU [22]).

[8] These pillars have now disappeared.

[9] art.13(1) EU [3]. *Acquis Communautaire* means everything that was decided and agreed upon since the establishment of the three European Communities, whatever the form in which this was done, whether legally binding or not. It refers to the body of rules which govern the Union in whatever field of activity. In other words it encompasses everything that was "acquired" by the previous Communities and the Union.

[10] art.3 EU [2].

— ensure the protection of human rights, in particular the rights of the child; and
— ensure strict observance and development of international law, including respect for the principles of the United Nations Charter.

Of great importance is the new competence of the European Council and the Council, introduced by the Treaty of Nice, concerning "serious breach of the Union's values" by a Member State. It allows, in a first phase, the Council to determine, by a majority of four-fifths of its members—after obtaining the consent of Parliament, on the basis of a reasoned proposal by one-third of the Member States, Parliament or the Commission—that there is a clear risk of a serious breach by a Member State[11] of any of the principles of human dignity, freedom, democracy, equality, the rule of law and respect for human rights; principles which are common to all Member States.[12]

In a second phase, the European Council, acting by unanimity (without taking into account the vote of the Member State in question), on a proposal by one-third of the Member States or the Commission, and after obtaining the assent of Parliament, may determine the existence of a serious and persistent breach, after inviting the Member State in question to submit its observations. The consequence of such a determination is that the Council, acting by qualified majority,[13] may suspend certain of the rights deriving from the application of the Treaties for the Member State in question, including the voting rights of its representative. The Council must take into account the possible consequences of such a suspension to the rights and obligations of natural and legal persons.[14]

The Council, acting by a qualified majority, may subsequently vary or revoke the measures taken in response to changes in the situation which led to their being imposed.[15]

The Court of Justice has jurisdiction in regard to the purely procedural stipulations of the provisions concerning a breach by a Member State of the principles of democracy.[16]

The Common Foreign and Security Policy (CFSP) shall be examined in the last part of this book; but let it be noted here that this policy could lead to a common defence, which would need to be approved by all the Member States in accordance with their constitutional requirements.[17]

As for the Police and Judicial Co-operation in Criminal Matters, now Judicial Co-operation in Criminal Matters, it will be discussed in the chapter on Free Movement of Persons.

2. ENHANCED CO-OPERATION[18]

It is provided for in Title IV of the EU Treaty and Title III of the TFEU—it was previously called Closer Co-operation.[19]

---

[11] art.7(1) EU.
[12] art.2 EU [6(1)], see also below, Ch.7: Council.
[13] The voting arrangements are laid down in art.354 TFEU.
[14] art.7(3) EU.
[15] art.7(4) EU.
[16] art.2 EU.
[17] art.7(1) EU.
[18] art.20 EU [27a to 27b, 40 to 40b] and arts 226–334 TFEU [11 and 11a].
[19] art.1(10) EU.

There are various areas of Union activity in which certain Member States are prepared to go further and faster than other Member States. This is possible under the following conditions.

Once the Council has established[20] that the objectives of such co-operation cannot be attained within a reasonable period by the Union as a whole,[21] the Member States wishing to establish enhanced co-operation between themselves in one of the areas covered by the Treaties, with the exception of the Union's exclusive competences[22] and the common foreign and security policy,[23] may, "make use of the institutions and exercise those competences by applying the relevant provisions of the Treaties".[24] Provided, however, that this co-operation:

- is aimed at furthering the objectives of the Union, at protecting its interests and at reinforcing its integration process[25];
- complies with the Treaties and Union law[26];
- does not undermine the internal market or economic, social and territorial cohesion;
- does not constitute a barrier to or discrimination in trade between Member States, nor distorts competition;
- involves at least nine Member States[27];
- respects the competences, rights and obligations of the non-participating Member States, the latter may not impede the implementation of the enhanced co-operation; and
- is open to all Member States; the Commission and the participating Member States must promote participation by as many Member States as possible.[28] Any Member State wishing to participate in enhanced co-operation in progress must notify its intention to the Council and the Commission, which must ascertain that the conditions for participation have been met and, if not, indicate the arrangements to be adopted. The Member State concerned may refer the matter to the Council.[29]

Authorisation to proceed with enhanced co-operation shall be granted by the Council acting unanimously on a proposal from the Commission and after obtaining the consent of Parliament.[30] A request for enhanced co-operation within the framework of the CFSP shall be addressed to the Council; it shall be forwarded to the High Representative of the Union for Foreign Affairs and Security Policy for an opinion on consistency with that policy and to the Commission for an opinion on consistency with other Union policies. It shall be forwarded to Parliament for information.[31]

---

[20] art.330 TFEU [arts 27, 40, 43–45 EU and arts 11 and 11a EC]: unanimity shall be constituted by the votes of the representatives of the participating Member States only and a qualified majority shall be defined in accordance with the voting procedures laid down for the Council: art.238 TFEU.
[21] art.20(2) EU.
[22] See art.3 TFEU.
[23] arts 23–46 EU [11–17].
[24] art.43 EU.
[25] art.20(1) EU.
[26] art.326,1 TFEU.
[27] art.20(2) EU.
[28] art.328(1),2 TFEU [art.43b EU].
[29] art.331(1) TFEU [arts 27, 40, 43–45 EU and arts 11, 11a EC].
[30] art.329(1), 2 TFEU.
[31] art.329(2) TFEU [arts 27, 40, 43–45 EU and arts 11 EC].

Expenditure resulting from implementation of enhanced co-operation, other than administrative costs, shall be borne by the participating Member States.[32]

3. THE TREATY ON THE FUNCTIONING OF THE EUROPEAN UNION

In 1951, the drafters of the Treaty establishing the European Coal and Steel Community (ECSC) coined the word "supranational" to describe the particular character of the functions fulfilled by the members of the High Authority, which later on became the Commission.[33] The term was from the start also used to designate the specific nature of the Union itself and of the law it embodied. It was understood to mean that the Union was more than a grouping of member nations and that its law was more than their national laws and, although the ECSC was set up by an international treaty concluded among sovereign States, the signatories were conscious of having created something very different indeed from other entities set up under the Law of Nations.

As the Court of Justice so clearly and courageously put it, back in 1962: the Contracting States were not merely accepting mutual obligations,[34] they were limiting their own sovereign rights, transferring some of them to institutions over which they had no direct control and endowing the ECSC with powers they did not always possess themselves. Furthermore, the Treaty did not only create new rights and obligations for the Member States, it also granted rights to, and directly included, their citizens, who thereby became subjects, now "citizens", of the Union.[35]

By contrast with ordinary international treaties, the European Treaties thus created their own legal system to which the term "international" does not apply, since it is not international law; the term "supranational" expressed the difference.

Furthermore, it follows from the terms and the spirit of the European Treaties that the Member States, as a corollary, may not give precedence to their national law over a legal system accepted by all of them on the basis of reciprocity. Indeed, the executive force of Union law cannot vary from one State to another in deference to domestic law without jeopardising the attainment of the objectives of the Treaties.[36] The law of the European Union cannot, therefore, be regarded as national law either. It is different, independent, it is separate, it is not national law; since it is common to 27 nations, it is truly supranational. The term "supranational" has now fallen into disrepute and was even eliminated from the ECSC Treaty.[37] This, however, does not change the specific nature of the Union and of the law it created. More importantly, the concept is now universally accepted and expressed by the words "Union Law".

---

[32] art.332 TFEU.

[33] art.9 (5 and 6) ECSC "They shall abstain from any act incompatible with the supranational character of their function", and, "Each Member State undertakes to respect this supranational character." The concept did not refer to the Union itself. Since the ECSC Treaty (1952) was concluded for 50 years, it is no longer in force.

[34] *Van Gend & Loos v Nederlandse Administratie der Belastingen* (26/62) [1963] E.C.R. 1 at 12; [1963] C.M.L.R. 105.

[35] Forty years later, the EU Treaty formally confirmed this by providing for a "citizenship" of the European Union. See now: arts 17 to 22 EU.

[36] *Costa v ENEL* (6/64) [1964] E.C.R. 585 at 594.

[37] The Merger Treaty repealed art.9 of the ECSC Treaty and replaced it with a text which is identical in the three European Treaties and, since the term "supranational" did not appear in the two Treaties of Rome, it was entirely left out.

Union law is to be found mainly in the European Treaties (also referred to as "primary" Union law) and in the implementing legislation or the "secondary" Union law, not to be confused with the *acquis communautaire*.

Primary Union law now consists of the Treaty establishing the European Atomic Energy Community (Euratom), the Treaty establishing the European Union (EU) and the Treaty on the Functioning of the European Union (TFEU), as amended over the years.[38] The first can be considered as a sectoral treaty, while the TFEU covers the economic and social fields in general. (Hereinafter, as already indicated, "Treaties" refers mainly to the EU Treaty and the TFEU.)

By "secondary legislation" is meant the legislative texts issued by the institutions, which implement, and in certain cases, complement the original Treaties. Union law has gradually evolved over the past half century, from the 100 articles of the ECSC Treaty, into an impressive body of law comprising thousands of regulations, directives, decisions, agreements and other acts and measures, and, above all, the case law of the Court of Justice.

It is impressive, not only because of its sheer volume (it covers more than 70,000 pages), but because of its specific character and its growth potential. It is worthwhile considering this particular aspect of Union law: except for the original three Treaties just mentioned, none of the Union acts finds its origin with the national institutions, bodies and organs with which lawyers and citizens were familiar and over which they exercise, through democratic elections, some sort of control. Union regulations, directives, decisions, etc. are issued outside most citizens' own countries, according to complex and remote procedures they cannot grasp and over which they have practically no say.[39] They are nevertheless directly involved. Indeed, if those measures may impose upon them obligations, they also grant them rights, which they can ask the national courts to uphold against fellow citizens, undertakings and even against their own government. Those rights arise not only where they are expressly granted by Union law, but also as a corollary to the obligations which this law, in a clearly defined way, imposes upon the Member States and the institutions of the Union.[40] Those citizens can also challenge the legality of Union measures in the Union courts, when they are directly and individually concerned: they are definitely part of the system!

---

[38] Chronologically, amendments were introduced by: the Convention on certain institutions common to the three Communities (March 25, 1957); the Treaty establishing a Single Council and a Single Commission of the European Communities (April 8, 1965); the Decision creating the Communities' own resources (April 21, 1970); the Treaty amending certain budgetary provisions (April 22, 1970); the Treaty on the accession of Denmark, Ireland and the United Kingdom (January 22, 1972); the Treaty amending certain financial provisions (July 22, 1975); the Act concerning the direct election of the European Parliament (September 20, 1976); the Treaty on the secession of Greenland (September 20, 1976); the Treaty on the accession of Greece (May 28, 1979); the Treaty concerning the accession of Portugal and Spain (March 9/30, 1985); the Single European Act (February 17/28, 1986); the Maastricht Treaty or Treaty on European Union (February 7, 1992); the Treaty concerning the accession of Austria, Finland, (Norway) and Sweden (June 24, 1994); the Treaty of Amsterdam (October 2, 1997); the Treaty of Nice (February 26, 2001); the Accession Treaty of the Czech Republic, Estonia, Cyprus, Latvia, Lithuania, Hungary, Malta, Poland, Slovenia and Slovakia (April 16, 2003); the Accession Treaty of Bulgaria and Romania (April 25, 2005), (these dates correspond to those of the signature); and, finally, the Treaty of Lisbon (2007).

[39] In order to remedy this situation, art.1, 2 of the EU Treaty provides that that Treaty marks a new stage in the process of creating an ever closer union among the peoples of Europe, "in which decisions are taken as openly as possible and as closely as possible to the citizens". It should be noted, however, that the situation of aloofness and ignorance referred to above, also prevails within the Member States.

[40] See *Van Gend & Loos* (quoted above, fn.34).

The apparent aloofness of the European authorities combined with this direct involvement might be bewildering. However, the direct election of the Members of Parliament and the increasing number of cases involving Union law introduced by private parties, both in the European and in the national courts, seems to indicate a familiarity with at least some aspects of this new system of law. But, if democratic control by the citizens of the Union is to become a reality, some knowledge of the basic rules and procedures is required. This applies not only to the law student, but also to the practitioner, the politician and the general public. Unless one realises what the Union's objectives are and what means and procedures have been provided for attaining them, no participation is possible, no criticism is justified, no suggestion can be pertinent.

The objectives of the Union were set out in detail above, and the means to attain them are analysed in detail in the chapters of the book corresponding to the various areas of Union activity.

The Treaties provide precise rules and timetables for the establishment of the internal market and of the economic and monetary union, while the other policies are, as shall be seen, described in the Treaties in rather general terms, leaving it to the institutions, and, in the first place, to the Commission, which must make proposals for the Union's legislative action, to take the initiative. However, notwithstanding this absence of a timetable, Union activities have penetrated more and more social, economic and related fields, some of which were not even, until recently,[41] explicitly provided for in the Treaties. Union law, it seems, is in the process of integrating most of the economies of the Member States.

The dynamic development of the Union is not the only proof of its vitality; notwithstanding economic recession and political turmoil, the Union not only held together, but expanded its field of activity geographically, economically and politically. This seems to indicate that it fulfils a basic need and responds to a profound aspiration of the peoples of Europe.

4. MODIFICATION OF THE TREATIES

The EU Treaty provides for three different procedures to amend the Treaties:

- the ordinary revision procedure[42] which may, inter alia, serve either to increase or reduce the competences of the Union on a proposal from a government, Parliament or the Commission to the Council which submits it to the European Council and notifies the national parliaments. After consulting Parliament and the Commission, the European Council decides by a simple majority in favour of examining the proposed amendments.

  The President of the European Council convenes a Convention composed of representatives of the national parliaments, of the Heads of State or governments, of Parliament and the Commission. The convention adopts by consensus a recommendation to a conference of representatives of the

---

[41] Education, culture, public health and industry, which were added by the EU Treaty, are examples of fields wherein the Union was active, although they were not mentioned as such. The same applies to Regional Policy, the European Monetary System, Economic and Monetary Union and Political Co-operation, that were introduced into the Treaty by the Single European Act (SEA). Activities in those fields were made possible, in the meantime, through unanimous ad hoc decisions of the Council based upon art.352 TFEU [308].

[42] art.48(2) to (5) EU.

governments of the Member States. In case the convening of the Convention is not justified by the extent of the proposed modifications, the European Council defines the terms of reference for a conference. The latter determines by common accord the amendments to be made to the Treaties, which shall enter into force after being ratified by all the Member States.

If two years after the signature of the treaty amending the Treaties, four-fifths of the Member States have ratified it and one or more Member States have encountered difficulties with ratification, the matter shall be referred to the European Council;

- the simplified revision procedure[43]: this revision procedure concerns only provisions of Part III[44] of the TFEU relating to the internal policies and action of the Union. The European Council, after consulting Parliament and the Commission, adopts an amending decision, which must be approved by the Member States. The decision may not extend the competences of the Union;
- the so-called bridging amendment[45]: where the TFEU or Title V of the EU Treaty provides for a unanimous decision of the Council, the European Council may authorise the Council to act by qualified majority, except in the area of defence. Similarly, where adoption by the Council is provided via a special legislative procedure,[46] the European Council may authorise adoption via the ordinary legislative procedure.[47] These initiatives must be notified to the national parliaments, which have six months to oppose the revision. The European Council must act by unanimity after obtaining the consent of Parliament given by a majority of its component members.

5. COUNTRIES TO WHICH THE EUROPEAN TREATIES APPLY[48] AND TERRITORIAL SCOPE OF THESE TREATIES

Broadly speaking, the Treaties apply to the 27 Member States. However, a distinction must be made between the territories (1) to which what is referred to as "the Treaties" apply, (2) to which only the Customs Union applies, and (3) referred to as the "Fiscal Territory".

As for the territory to which the Treaties apply, it is defined[49] as follows: it covers, in the first place, all the Member States; secondly—with special conditions to be laid down by the Council after consultation of Parliament—the French overseas departments, the Azores, Madeira and the Canary islands; thirdly, Part IV of the Treaty "Association of the Overseas Countries and Territories" applies to those listed in Annex II to the TFEU; and fourthly, it, "shall apply to the European territories for whose external relations a Member State is responsible". This last provision was included to cover the Saarland, that part of Germany that, after the Second World War, was occupied by France:

---

[43] art.48(6) EU.
[44] Part III "Union Policies and Internal Action" includes practically all the activities of the Union, except any external action.
[45] art.48(7) EU.
[46] art.289(2) TFEU.
[47] art.294 TFEU [251].
[48] art.52(1) EU.
[49] art.349 TFEU [299].

according to certain writers, it now applies only to Gibraltar.[50] This application
is, however, restricted by art.28 of the British Accession Act of 1972.

The territory of the "Customs Union" corresponds to that to which the
Treaties apply with the exception of Gibraltar, Ceuta, Melilla, the communes of
Livigno and Campione d'Italia, Heligoland, Greenland, Faeroe Islands and that
part of Cyprus[51] over which Cyprus does not exercise effective control. As for
Andorra, Monaco, San Marino and the Vatican, although they are independent
States, they are included in the Customs Union. In this context it is perhaps inter-
esting to note that Monaco, San Marino[52] and also the Vatican, issued their own
Euro coins when they were introduced in 2002.

The "Fiscal or VAT Territory" is identical to the territory to which the Treaties
apply excepting the Åland Islands (Finland), Heligoland Island, Büssingen
Territory (Germany), Guadeloupe, Martinique, French Guyana and Réunion
(France),[53] Mount Athos (Greece), Ceuta, Melilla and Canary Islands (Spain),
Livigno, Campione d'Italia and Lake Lugano (Italy), and Gibraltar and the
Channel islands (UK).[54]

The Treaties do not apply to:

- the Faeroe Islands[55]; and
- the United Kingdom Sovereign Base Areas of Akrotiri and Dhekelia in
Cyprus.

Further Reading

Eileen Denza, *The Intergovernmental Pillars of the European Union* (Oxford
University Press, 2002).
Koen Leanarts and Marlies Desomer, "Bricks for a Constitutional Treaty of the
European Union: values, objectives and means" (2002) E.L.Rev. 377.
Alan Dashwood, Michael Dougan, Christophe Hillion, Angus Johnston and,
Eleanor Spaventa, "Draft Constitutional Treaty of the European Union and
related documents" (2003) E.L.Rev. 3.
Fiona Muray, *EU and Member State Territories, the Special Relationship under
Community Law* (Sweet & Maxwell, 2004).

[50] Gibraltar falls outside the Customs Union, the Fiscal Territory and even the Common Agricultural Policy. See Regulation 1298/07; [2007] O.J. L289/3.
[51] art.355(5)(a) and (b) TFEU.
[52] In 2002, the EC and the Republic of San Marino concluded an Agreement on Co-operation and Customs Union, [2002] O.J. L84/43.
[53] art.349 TFEU [299].
[54] See Directive 77/388: [1977] O.J. L145/1.
[55] See Decision 1997/126 concerning the conclusion of an Agreement between the EC and the Government of Denmark and the Home Government of the Faeroe Islands [1997] O.J. L53/1 amended [2008] O.J. L212/3.

Chapter Two

History

Every institution is the product of a series of historical events, and at the same time it reflects the convictions, hopes and concerns of those who were instrumental in establishing it. The European Communities, now European Union, are no exception to this rule. For a full understanding and a correct interpretation of the European Treaties, some knowledge of the historical background seems therefore necessary.

Although the expression "United States of Europe" was already used by Victor Hugo in 1849,[1] there seems to be no need to go that far back. The end of the Second World War provides a fair starting point.

1. CHURCHILL'S SPEECH

The agreement made at Yalta in 1945 by the United Kingdom, the United States and the U.S.S.R. left Europe more divided than ever and the growing antagonism among the victorious Allies created only more tensions and catastrophes. It was on September 19, 1946, barely a year after the end of the Second World War, in a speech at Zurich University, that Winston Churchill proposed a "sovereign remedy", i.e. to, "recreate the European family, or as much of it as we can, and provide it with a structure under which it can dwell in peace, in safety and in freedom. We must build a kind of United States of Europe". He went on to, "say something that will astonish you. The first step in the recreation of the European family must be a partnership between France and Germany". At that time it needed a lot of courage and foresight to make such a suggestion about these former arch-enemies. As will be seen, it was this (British) idea that also inspired the French Government in 1950 to propose the establishment of the European Coal and Steel Community. Towards the end of his Zurich speech, Churchill also proposed to start by setting up a regional structure and to form a Council of Europe.[2]

2. MARSHALL PLAN—OEEC

If Churchill's words were well received, the European States in those days lacked the necessary stamina to proceed with such far-reaching plans, since they were preoccupied with their daily fight for economic survival. Once again, the United

---

[1] See Henri Brugmans, *L'Idée Européenne*, 1920–1970 (Bruges, 1970).
[2] The Treaty establishing the Council of Europe was signed in London on May 5, 1949.

States came to the rescue. In another famous university speech, at Harvard this time, George Marshall, United States Secretary of State, announced on June 5, 1947, that the United States would do, "whatever it is able to do, to assist in the return of normal economic health in the world". This offer was accepted by 16 European countries on July 15, 1947, and so the Marshall Plan was born; but more important for the future of European integration was the setting up of the Organisation of European Economic Co-operation (OEEC)[3] in 1948, this was in response to the American request for an agreement among Europeans about the distribution of the American aid. Within that forum, the European States re-learned to work together.

3. ROBERT SCHUMAN: MAY 9, 1950

In the meantime, Churchill's words about a partnership between France and Germany had not been forgotten and on May 9, 1950, Robert Schuman, French Foreign Minister, declared that a united Europe was essential for world peace and that a gathering of the European nations required the elimination of the century-old opposition between France and Germany. As a first practical step towards this end he proposed, "to place the whole Franco-German coal and steel production under one joint High Authority, in an organisation open to the participation of the other countries of Europe". He described this pooling of production as the "first stage of the European Federation". Germany, the Netherlands, Belgium, Luxembourg and Italy accepted in principle and negotiations started at once.

4. THE EUROPEAN COAL AND STEEL COMMUNITY (ECSC)

The negotiations progressed rapidly and were simplified by the fact that all the future partners had accepted the proposed principles; the work consisted mainly in giving them legal form. A sense of urgency was probably added to the existing goodwill by the communist invasion in South Korea. The Treaty establishing the European Coal and Steel Community (ECSC) was signed in Paris on April 18, 1951. Ratification by the national parliaments met with little opposition and on July 23, 1952 the Treaty entered into force for a period of 50 years. The ECSC therefore ceased to exist on July 23, 2002.[4] From that moment on, acts of the institutions could no longer be based upon the provisions of that Treaty.[5] The rights and obligations arising under the international agreements concluded by the ECSC were taken over by the European Community, now European Union.[6]

---

[3] In 1961, it became the Organisation for Economic Co-operation and Development (OECD), with the participation of the USA and Canada.
[4] See the Decision of the Representatives of the Governments of the Member States, meeting in Council, of February 27, 2002 on the financial consequences of the expiry of the ECSC Treaty and on the research fund for coal and steel [2002] O.J. L79/42.
[5] *SP v Commission* (Joined Cases T-27/03, etc.) [2007] E.C.R. II-4331.
[6] [2002] O.J. L194/35 and 36.

5. THE EUROPEAN DEFENCE COMMUNITY

The following two years were difficult. It has been said that the easing of the international political situation—Stalin died on March 5, 1953 and July 27, 1953 marked the end of the Korean war—diminished the necessity for "closing the ranks". In any case, two additional proposals for close co-operation among the "Six"—in the form of the European Defence Community and a European Political Community—failed miserably.

6. THE EUROPEAN ECONOMIC COMMUNITY (EEC) AND THE EUROPEAN ATOMIC ENERGY COMMUNITY (EURATOM)

Undaunted by those setbacks, the Benelux (BElgium, the NEtherlands and LUXemburg) countries proposed in 1955, to their partners in the Coal and Steel Community, to take another step towards economic integration by setting up a common market and jointly developing transportation, classical energy and atomic energy. This led to the conference of Messina in the same year, at which Mr Spaak, Belgian Foreign Minister, was asked to report on the feasibility of those plans. At that time an invitation was issued also to the British Government to join the negotiations of the Six; alas, to no avail.[7]

The Spaak Report was ready in 1956, and was discussed in Venice, where the decision was taken to start negotiations for drafting treaties that would establish a common market and an Atomic Energy Community. With incredible speed (June 1956–February 1957) these two complex Treaties were prepared for signature in Rome on March 25, 1957,[8] ratified by the six parliaments and on January 1, 1958, the European Economic Community[9] (EEC) and the European Atomic Energy Community (Euratom) became a reality. In 1961, the British Government decided to apply for negotiations to determine whether satisfactory arrangements could be made to meet the needs of the United Kingdom, of the Commonwealth and of EFTA.[10] The Government were, "baulked in their objective, so that it was not possible to determine whether satisfactory conditions of entry could be obtained".[11]

---

[7] See Hans Joachim Heiser, *British Policy with regard to the unification efforts on the European Continent* (Leyden, 1959), p.96.

[8] The story goes, however, that, since there was no time to print the full text in the four languages, the documents that were signed only contained printed first and last pages, all the others being blanks!

[9] The Treaty was modified many times, for the last times in 2005 in view of the accession of Bulgaria and Romania, the next time was the Treaty of Lisbon.

[10] The European Free Trade Association (EFTA) was set up, at the instigation of the UK, with, among others, the Scandinavian countries, to "counter" the European Communities; it never amounted to very much compared with the Communities. It still exists, however, with only Iceland, Norway, Switzerland and Liechtenstein as members.

[11] The UK and the European Communities, 1971 (Cmnd. 4715), para.6.

7. The Treaty Establishing a Single Council and a Single Commission

On April 8, 1965, the institutional set-up of the Communities, which had been "streamlined" a first time by the Convention on certain institutions common to the European Communities,[12] was simplified once again by the so-called Merger Treaty, the Treaty establishing a Single Council and a Single Commission of the European Communities. It entered into force on July 1, 1967. Until that date, there had been three Councils and three Commissions (one for each Community), while, in accordance with the above-mentioned Convention there was only a single Court of Justice and a single Assembly for the three Communities. The Convention and the Merger Treaty were repealed by the EU Treaty (1992), which, however, retained the essential elements of their provisions.

8. The Customs Union

The Customs Union provided for by the EEC Treaty became fully operational on July 1, 1968. It meant that tariffs and quotas between the Member States had, by then, been completely abolished and that the replacement of the national external tariffs by the common (external) customs tariff (CCT) had been completed. The Community was 18 months ahead of the schedule laid down in the Treaty.[13] This, however, still left differences in taxation and charges and measures with equivalent effect to tariffs and quotas as obstacles to free trade between Member States.

9. The Community's (now Union's) own Resources

The replacement of the Financial Contributions from Member States by the Union's own Resources[14] inaugurated a new era in the history of the Union. It became, in a certain way, financially independent and the Treaty amending Certain Budgetary Provisions of the ECSC, EEC and Euratom Treaties and of the Merger Treaty, conferred specific budgetary powers upon what had become the European Parliament (hereafter "Parliament"). The Union's own resources are provided by the agricultural levies, the customs duties, a percentage of the VAT collected by the Member States and, since February 1988, a rate applied to an additional base, representing the sum of the GNP at market prices.

10. The British, Danish and Irish Membership

After a debate in both Houses of Parliament, at the end of which the Government's decision was approved in the Commons by a majority of 426, the

---

[12] Signed in Rome on March 25, 1957 together with the two European Treaties.
[13] Twelve years, see art.8 EEC (abolished) and Acceleration Decisions: [1960] J.O. 1217 and [1962] J.O. 1284.
[14] Decision 70/243 of April 21, 1970: [1970] J.O. L94/19; [1970(I)] O.J. 224. It became effective on January 1, 1971, after ratification by the six national Parliaments.

British Government applied to the Council for membership of the Communities on May 10, 1967. By December of the same year it was clear, however, that the Six could not reach the unanimity necessary under the Treaties to return a reply to Britain's application. Thus ended the second endeavour of the United Kingdom to enter "Europe". The British Government, however, decided to maintain its application for membership and it was discussed at many meetings of the Council in the following two years.

At the meeting of Heads of State or Government, on December 1 and 2, 1969, at The Hague, it was finally agreed to open negotiations with Denmark, Ireland, Norway and the United Kingdom, who had applied for membership. Other important decisions taken at this "Summit" concerned the Economic and Monetary Community and the "own resources". The Treaty of Brussels relating to the accession of the United Kingdom, Ireland, Norway and Denmark was signed on January 22, 1972; this Treaty entered into force on January 1, 1973, except for Norway which, as a result of a referendum on the subject, did not ratify the Treaty. Consequently, several provisions of this Treaty and of the Act concerning the conditions of accession and the adjustments to the Treaties attached thereto were modified by the Council in the Decision of January 1, 1973, adjusting the documents concerning accession of the new Member States (hereinafter referred to as the "Adaptation Decision").

11. THE ENLARGEMENT TO GREECE, PORTUGAL AND SPAIN

On June 12, 1975, Greece applied for membership of the Union—the Treaty of Accession, together with an Act concerning the conditions of accession and the adjustments to the Treaties was signed at Athens on May 28, 1979[15]; it was ratified by the Greek Parliament on June 28, 1979. Greece became a member on January 1, 1981. On March 28, 1977, Portugal and on July 28, 1977, Spain applied for membership. Formal negotiations with Portugal started on October 16, 1978, and with Spain on February 5, 1979. They were successfully concluded at the European Council of March 29 and 30, 1985 and the third enlargement became effective on January 1, 1986, bringing the total of Member States to 12.

12. THE DIRECT ELECTION OF PARLIAMENT AND THE DECLARATION ON DEMOCRACY AND FUNDAMENTAL RIGHTS

On September 20, 1976, the Representatives of the Member States in Council agreed on the conditions for direct election and signed the Act concerning the Election of the Representatives of the Assembly by Direct Universal Suffrage,[16] which was subsequently ratified by the, at that time, nine national parliaments. The first elections were held in June 1979,[17] giving "Europe" its democratic legitimacy.

---

[15] [1979] O.J. L291/1.
[16] [1976] O.J. L278/1.
[17] See below, Ch.5: The European Parliament.

On April 5, 1977 Parliament, the Council and the Commission issued a Joint Declaration on Fundamental Rights,[18] with which the Heads of State and Government associated themselves in their Declaration on Democracy. In this declaration they confirmed their will to ensure that the values of their legal, political and moral order are respected and to safeguard the principles of representative democracy, of the rule of law, of social justice and of respect for human rights. They stated that the application of these principles implies a political system of pluralist democracy.

On June 19, 1983, the, by that time, 10 Heads of State and Government signed the "Solemn Declaration on European Community" expressing, among others, their determination, "to achieve a comprehensive and coherent common political approach" and their will to transform the whole complex of relations between their States into a European Community.

13. The Secession of Greenland

On February 1, 1985, Greenland ceased to be part of the [Union] to which it had belonged since January 1, 1973, as part of the Kingdom of Denmark. Greenland has enjoyed a special status within the Kingdom since the Home Rule Act of 1979 and the Greenland Government has exclusive competence, among others, for fishing, agriculture and stock farming.

Greenland's special features, i.e. remoteness, climatic conditions and the cultural particulars of its non-European population pleaded in favour of new arrangements after the people of the island had decided in 1982, by referendum, to withdraw from the Union and to seek a new type of relationship. The EC Treaty provisions applicable to overseas countries and territories provided an appropriate framework for these relations, although additional specific provisions were needed.[19]

In 2003, the Council decided to broaden and strengthen future relations with Greenland after 2006 and took a decision in 2006 to that effect and a Joint Declaration by the Union, on the one hand, and the Home Rule Government of Greenland and the Government of Denmark, on the other, on partnership between the Union and Greenland.[20]

14. The Completion of the Internal Market by 1992

In June 1985, the Commission sent a White Paper to the European Council entitled "Completing the Internal Market".[21] This was the beginning of "Operation 1992". It lays down a comprehensive programme and timetable for the abolition of barriers of all kinds in inter-State trade, the harmonisation of rules, the

---

[18] [1977] O.J. C103/1.
[19] See Commission opinion on the status of Greenland ([1983] E.C. Bull. 1–13) and text of amending Treaty with various Council regulations [1985] O.J. L29/1.
[20] [2006] O.J. L208/28.
[21] White Paper from the Commission to the European Council (Milan, June 28–29, 1985), COM(85) 310 final.

approximation of legislation and of the tax structures and the strengthening of monetary co-operation. To complete the internal market, the White Paper provided for removal of physical, technical and fiscal barriers. It was, among other things, to make the implementation of this comprehensive programme possible, that the Member States decided to amend the existing Treaties through the Single European Act.

15. THE SINGLE EUROPEAN ACT (SEA)

It was signed in Luxembourg on February 17, and at The Hague on February 28, 1986; it entered into force on July 1, 1987. The SEA's[22] objective is the completion of the so-called "internal market" defined as, "an area without internal frontiers in which the free movement of goods, persons, services and capital is ensured".[23] It provides, among other things, for the strengthening of the decision-making process by extending the number of decisions to be taken by qualified majority, the inclusion in the Treaty of chapters on Economic and Social Cohesion (Regional Development), Research and Technological Development and Environment. It also provides for closer involvement of Parliament in the legislative procedures. The SEA makes reference to a Treaty on an "Economic and Monetary Community" and to co-operation in the sphere of Foreign Policy.

16. THE TREATY ON EUROPEAN UNION OR MAASTRICHT TREATY (EU TREATY)

The Treaty was signed in Maastricht, the Netherlands, on February 7, 1992 and came into force on November 1, 1993. It contains seven parts. Title I provides for a European Union, sets out its objectives, among others: the establishment of an economic and monetary union ultimately including a single currency; a common foreign and security policy including the eventual framing of a common defence policy; the introduction of a citizenship of the Union for the nationals of the Member States; co-operation on justice and home affairs; the maintenance of the *acquis communautaire*; and the respect of the principle of subsidiarity.

It also "officialises" the European Council, which must provide the necessary impetus and define the general political guidelines for Union action and, it indicates that to be a Member of the Union a State's government must be founded on the principles of democracy, while the fundamental rights are considered to be general principles of Union law.

Titles II, III and IV contain amendments to the three European Treaties.

---

[22] As already indicated, the Act was designated as "Single" because, in fact, it combines two different instruments: the first one provides for modifications to the three European Treaties and the second constitutes an agreement between the Member States to jointly formulate and implement, among others, a European foreign policy.

[23] art.26(2) TFEU [14(2)].

17. The European Economic Area (EEA) and the European Free Trade Association (EFTA)

The European Economic Area (EEA) now unites the 27 Member States and three of the four EFTA States (Iceland, Liechtenstein and Norway; Switzerland having voted to stay out) into an internal market governed by the same basic rules as the Union's internal market.[24]

The Agreement establishing the EEA was signed in Oporto on May 2, 1992 between the, at that time, seven[25] EFTA countries and the "European Community" and their Member States. It entered into force in 1994. Following a referendum in Switzerland, this country dropped out of the EEA, but remained in EFTA. The signature of the EEA Agreement was held up by an Opinion delivered by the Court on the conformity of the draft agreement with the Treaty.[26] Following that Opinion the Agreement, instead of setting up an EEA Court, now provides for an EEA Joint Committee to settle disputes between the two sides and to ensure the uniform interpretation of the Agreement by keeping under permanent review the decisions of the Court and of the newly created EFTA Court.[27] The first case was introduced before that court on April 27, 1994. The latter's jurisdiction is confined to the EFTA countries. Decisions of the Committee will have no impact on the case law of the Union courts. The autonomy of the Union legal system is thus preserved. In case parties cannot agree on a uniform interpretation, they may agree to apply to the Court of Justice for an interpretation of the rules at issue.[28]

The EEA Agreement, which entered into force on January 1, 1994, establishes an integrated structure based on common rules and equal conditions of competition together with the necessary means to implement it. The free movement of goods and persons, the right of establishment and to provide services, and the free movement of capital and payments are achieved on the basis of existing Union legislation as it has evolved over the years (*acquis communautaire*). Subject to a limited number of exceptions and transitional provisions, it is now applicable in the three EEA EFTA countries. In addition to the basic freedoms, the EEA Agreement provides for co-operation in areas that are directly relevant to the economic activity, such as research and development, social policy, social security, consumer protection, the environment, statistics, and company law. It also provides for a permanent information and consultation process covering all stages of the preparation of Union instruments. It includes surveillance and enforcement rules.

The Agreement provides for an EEA Council, comparable to the European Council, an EEA Joint Committee, comparable to the European Commission,[29] and an EEA Parliamentary Committee. The EEA has its own decision-making procedure.[30]

---

[24] See below Ch.15: The Free Movement of Goods.
[25] Austria, Finland, Iceland, Liechtenstein, Norway, Sweden and Switzerland. See [1994] O.J. L1/1.
[26] Opinion 1/91 of December 14 [1991] E.C.R. I-6079 and Opinion 1/92 of April 10 [1992] E.C.R. I-2825.
[27] [1994] O.J. L344/1.
[28] Twenty-Sixth General Report (1992), p.421.
[29] See Rules of Procedure of the EFTA Surveillance Authority [1994] O.J. L113/19.
[30] See, e.g. Decisions of the EEC-EFTA Joint Committee. [1994] O.J. L12/32 and of the EFTA Surveillance Authority:[1994] O.J. C158/5 and [1994] O.J. L138/39.

The EEA Agreement was extended to include the ten new Member States on November 11, 2003 and entered into force retroactively on October 14, 2003 (date of the signature of the enlargement Treaty). The new Members enjoy the same transitional periods as those provided for in the enlargement Treaty. In order to apply on May 1, 2004, the extension was ratified by 28 States (at that time 25 Members of the EU and the three EEA EFTA members). A new extension took place on January 1, 2007 with the accession of Bulgaria and Romania to the Union.

The European Free Trade Association (EFTA) was established, as indicated above, in 1960. Most of the original EFTA members are now Union Member States; the present EFTA members are Iceland, Liechtenstein, Norway and Switzerland. EFTA is served by three institutions: the EFTA Secretariat, the EFTA Surveillance Authority and the EFTA Court.

18. THE ACCESSION OF AUSTRIA, FINLAND AND SWEDEN

At the December 1992 Edinburgh European Council meeting, it was agreed that negotiations with Austria, Finland and Sweden could start in early 1993, to be followed by similar talks with Norway once the Commission had delivered its opinion on that country's application. It will be remembered that the Treaty provides that:

> "[A]ny European State which respects the values referred to in Article 2[31] and is committed to promoting them may apply to become a member of the Union. It shall address its application to the Council, which shall act unanimously after consulting the Commission and after receiving the consent of Parliament, which shall act by a majority of its component members".[32]

The Maastricht European Council of December 1991 added a proviso to that by noting, "that any European State whose system of government was founded on the principle of democracy could apply to become a member of the [Union]".[33]

It is interesting to note that the Commission drew up a set of criteria with which applicant States should comply. First they must fulfil the three basic conditions of European identity, democratic status and respect for human rights. Secondly, they must accept the *acquis communautaire* in its entirety, but must also, subject to transitional and temporary arrangements, be able to implement it. Thirdly, this presupposes that the country in question possesses a functioning and competitive market economy and an adequate legal and administrative framework.

On the basis of the Commission's report, the Lisbon European Council of June 1992 invited the institutions to speed up preparatory work on negotiations with

[31] art.2 EU provides that the, "Union is founded on the values of respect for human dignity, freedom, democracy, equality, the rule of law and respect for human rights, including the rights of persons belonging to minorities. These values are common to the Member States in a society in which pluralism, non-discrimination, tolerance, justice, solidarity and equality between women and men prevails."

[32] art.49, 1 EU [49].

[33] Twenty-Third General Report (1992), p.249.

EFTA countries stating that official negotiations could begin as soon as the EU Treaty had been ratified[34] and the second package of financial[35] and structural[36] measures had been agreed upon. Consequently, the Commission adopted opinions on Sweden's application in July 1992, and on Finland's in November. Norway formally applied in November 1992, but withdrew following a negative referendum. The Commission's opinion on Austria's accession was delivered in July 1991. The three countries became Member States on January 1, 1995. They thereby accepted all the provisions of the European Treaties and the *acquis communautaire* in its entirety. This enlargement, which marks a significant step forward in the history of European integration, brought the number of Member States to 15 and the number of European citizens to 368 million.

19. THE TREATY OF AMSTERDAM

The intergovernmental conference (IGC), which was provided for in the EU Treaty, opened in Turin on March 29, 1996, after the agenda was adopted by the European Council. The main titles were: (1) a [Union] closer to its citizens; (2) the institutions in a more democratic and efficient [Union]; and (3) a strengthened capacity for external action by the Union. On all three accounts the conference failed miserably. The new Treaty was supposed to prepare the Union for further expansion by the inclusion of the countries of Central and Eastern Europe. This required, in the first place, a profound reform, as suggested in the "Agenda 2000" of the Common Agricultural Policy and of the structural funds, besides the long overdue reform of the institutions. Where the latter is concerned, the only progress that was achieved concerns the Parliament, which saw its direct participation in the legislative field enlarged.[37] None of the other subjects were even touched upon at Amsterdam, as if the lack of reforms were to be kept as an excuse for postponing enlargement! The difficulties encountered with the ratification of the EU Treaty had clearly shown that the citizens had to be associated with the activities of the Union institutions. One of the ways to achieve this is by more openness. And although the EU Treaty now provides that decisions must be taken, "as openly as possible and as closely as possible to the citizen", nothing much has changed. As will be seen, it is theoretically possible but still difficult to accede to the archives of the institutions, but *im*possible to get hold of preparatory documents for Union legislation, except at an early stage, in the Green papers. By refusing to communicate drafts, under the pretext that they might be amended or have not yet been approved by the hierarchy, the institutions ignore the obligations the Treaties impose upon them. What has become of the much-heralded transparency, democracy and openness?

---

[34] November 1, 1993.
[35] See below Ch.14: Financing Union Activities.
[36] See below Ch.32: Economic, Social and Territorial Cohesion/Regional Policy.
[37] See, however, the Protocol on institutions with the prospect of enlargement of the European Community, annexed to the four Treaties which provides that, on accession, the Commission shall comprise one national of each of the Member States, and that Member States which have two nationals will give up one, on the condition that the weighting of the votes in the Council has been modified in a manner acceptable to all Member States.

The Treaty also provides that one year before the EU membership exceeds 20 States, a conference of representatives of the governments of the Member States shall carry out a comprehensive review of the composition and functioning of the institutions. Nothing has come of this either.

The Treaty of Amsterdam entered into force on May 1, 1999.

20. THE TREATY OF NICE[38]

This Treaty was signed at Nice on February 26, 2001 and amends the EU Treaty, the Treaties establishing the European Communities and certain related acts.

According to one of the Recitals, the idea was to, "complete the process started by the Treaty of Amsterdam of preparing the institutions of the European Community to function in an enlarged Community". Whether they succeeded is more than questionable, and furthermore the drafters "messed up" once again the texts of the Treaties (which had been "cleaned up" by the Treaty of Amsterdam) by inserting all kinds of new provisions, so that one had, once more, articles a, b, c, etc.

21. ACCESSION OF 10 NEW MEMBER STATES

The process leading to the accession of Cyprus, Hungary, Poland, Estonia, the Czech Republic, Slovenia, Latvia, Lithuania, Malta and Slovakia was set in motion by the Luxembourg European Council in 1997; it was decided that the process would comprise a single framework, an enhanced pre-accession partnership between each candidate country and the Union, and aid for each applicant country. Although it was decided at first to proceed in two stages, this approach was later abandoned and negotiations took place with all the candidates in parallel. Association Agreements, also known as European Agreements were signed with each candidate country. The Treaty of Accession was signed in Athens on April 16, 2003. It was provided that the 10 new Member States would join the Union on May 1, 2004.

22. THE EUROPEAN CONVENTION ON THE FUTURE OF THE EUROPEAN UNION AND THE DRAFT CONSTITUTION[39]

At its meeting in Laeken (Belgium) in December 2001, the European Council convened a Convention on the future of the European [Union] (the Laeken Declaration). The task of the Convention was to pave the way for the next intergovernmental conference as broadly and openly as possible. It was to consider the key issues arising for the Union's future development, for example: what do

---

[38] See [2001] O.J. C80/1.
[39] *http://www.european-convention.eu.int/Static.asp?=EN&Content=Introduction*. See also the Decision of the Representatives of the Member States meeting within the Council of February 21, 2002 setting up a Fund for the financing of the Convention [2002] O.J. L349.

European citizens expect from the Union?; How is the division of competence between the Union and the Member States to be organised?; Within the Union, how is the division of competence between the institutions to be organised?; How can the efficiency and coherence of the Union's external action be ensured?; and How can the Union's democratic legitimacy be ensured?

The Convention opened its proceedings with a period of listening in order to find out what people wanted and expected from the Union. The second phase was a period of analysis for comparing the pros and cons of the proposals put forward for organising the Union. The third phase sought to draw together the different proposals and draft recommendations.

The Convention terminated its work on July 1, 2003 and a draft Constitution[40] was presented to the European Council of Rome by its President, Valérie Giscard d'Estaing, on July 18, 2003. An intergovernmental conference was convened in October 2003, under the Italian Presidency, to adopt a Constitution, but without success. It was finally signed in Rome in November 2004 and published in the Official Journal.[41]

Several ill-advised Member States decided to submit the ratification of the Constitution to a referendum, with the consequence, among others, that the French and Dutch voters, for reasons that more often than not had nothing to do with the content of the draft, rejected it, although Parliament (with a large majority) and 18 Member States, out of 25 at that time, had ratified the draft. The Member States decided at the European Council of June 17, 2005 that they needed a "period of reflection" to enable a broad debate in each country.[42] In July 2005 it was decided to temporarily suspend the ratification procedure, also because the European Council of June 2005 did not succeed in adopting the pluri-annual budget for 2007–2013.

23. The Accession of Bulgaria and Romania

Following the statement of the Commission of September 26, 2006, that Bulgaria and Romania, "can join the EU in 2007", these two candidates became the 26th and 27th Member States on January 1, 2007. However, the final monitoring report of the Commission indicated tough conditions for their entry. Both countries were to be closely monitored on the remaining areas of concern, such as the justice system, the fight against corruption, organised crime and agriculture. If the conditions were not met, the Commission could invoke safeguards. Under the Accession Treaty there are three types of such measures: economic, internal market and JHA (Justice and Home Affairs) that can be invoked up to three years after accession. These could affect food export bans and cuts to EU funds,[43] such as agricultural and structural funds. In addition there are transitional arrangements, such as the restriction of free movement of workers from the new Member

---

[40] Doc. No. CONV 850/03; *http//www.European-convention.eu.int/docs/Treaty/cv00850.en 03.pdf*.
[41] [2004] O.J. C310/1.
[42] Declaration by the Heads of State or Government of the Member States of the Community on the ratification of the Treaty establishing a constitution for Europe (European Council, June 16 and 17, 2005), SN 117/05.
[43] This actually happened for Bulgaria in 2008.

States. Also the Commission can take remedial measures to ensure the functioning of EU policies; this concerns the areas of food and air safety, agricultural funds, the judiciary and the fight against corruption.

24. THE TREATY OF LISBON

The rejection of the Draft Constitution by the French and Dutch voters seemingly caused nearly a two-year period of quasi-immobility in the European Union (maybe also an excuse to do nothing!) but, behind the scenes, work was carried on through diplomatic channels, to draft a new text; these efforts resulted in the adoption at the European Council of June 20 and 21, 2007 of a draft "Reform Treaty". It contained very precise indications concerning the modifications to be introduced in the existing three European Treaties (contrary to the draft Constitution that provided for one single Treaty) by a so-called intergovernmental conference. The latter was, in fact, a meeting of lawyers with the task to draft the decisions that had been taken by the European Council in June 2007.

Noteworthy are some passages of the Presidency Conclusions of that European Council: (1) "Europe is united in its resolve that only by working together can we represent our interests and goals in the World of tomorrow" and (2) ". . . secure our future as an active player in a rapidly changing World." This reference to the world rather than to Europe is remarkable since it shows an evolution from a Union centred on itself ("determined to lay the foundation of an ever closer Community among the peoples of Europe"[44]) to a player on the world scene. It constitutes an important further step in the Union's development.

Compared to the existing Treaties, as last modified by "Nice" (rather than the draft Constitution), the major changes are the following:

- Where the institutions are concerned:
  - the six-month rotating presidency of the European Council is replaced by a once-renewable period of two and a half years—it does not affect the rotating presidency of the Council;
  - a Vice-President of the Commission becomes the High Representative of the Union for Foreign Affairs and Security Policy;
  - the number of members of the Commission shall be equal to two-thirds of the number of Member States (in 2009 this means 18), instead of one member per Member State (presently 27) as it was before—however, this was modified to placate the Irish and to allow them to vote "yes" in a second referendum, after they seemingly wanted to keep an Irish "commissioner"[45];
  - the voting procedure in the Council, the so-called co-decisions procedure, becomes ordinary legislative procedure, i.e. the Parliament and Council acting jointly—Council decisions are now, except when otherwise provided, taken by qualified majority, the latter remaining unchanged until 2014, it is then slightly modified until 2017, after which a decision must be approved by 55 per cent of the Council members, representing

---

[44] Former EC Treaty, Preamble, 1st para.
[45] See Conclusions of the European Council of June 19, 2009.

15 Member States and 65 per cent of the Union population: a blocking minority must include at least four Member States, the so-called double majority;

- other modifications concern mainly:

  — the specific nature of the Foreign and Security Policy;
  — the enhanced role of the national parliaments with regard to draft Union acts;
  — the Charter of Fundamental Rights of the European Union has the same legal value as the Treaties;
  — "increased co-operation" is extended from the EMU (Euro) and Schengen to Judicial co-operation in the area of Police and Criminal Matters;
  — the competences of the Union are now clearly divided into "exclusive competences" and "competences shared with the Member States", the latter being allowed to exercise their own competences, and Union competences, "to support, coordinate or supplement the actions of the Member States"[46];
  — under "environment" reference is now made to "climate change";
  — the control of subsidiarity by the national parliaments is reinforced;

- more questionable modifications are:

  — after having been widely used for more than 50 years, the terms "European Community", "Community" and "common market" simply disappear and are replaced by "Union", "European Union" and "internal market";
  — the "EC Treaty" becomes the "Treaty on the Functioning of the European Union"(TFEU);
  — the "Court of First Instance" becomes the "General Court" and the "Judicial Panels" become "Specialised Courts";
  — voluntary withdrawal from the Union is now possible;
  — the numbering of all the articles is modified;
  — there are too many "opt-outs"!

25. IRELAND AND THE TREATY OF LISBON

In order to make it possible for the Irish people to vote in favour of the Treaty of Lisbon during a second referendum on October 2, 2009, after having rejected it by a first referendum in 2008, the following legal guarantees were agreed upon.

At the European Council meeting of June 18/19, 2009 it was mentioned that, at its meeting of December 11/12, 2008, it was agreed (in order to meet the concerns of the Irish people) that a decision would be taken, in accordance with the necessary legal procedures, to the effect that the Commission shall continue to include one national of each Member State. At the June meeting it was also agreed that other concerns of the Irish people relating to taxation policy, the right of life, education, the family and Ireland's traditional policy of military neutrality, would be addressed to the mutual satisfaction of all the Member

---

[46] art.6 TFEU.

States, by way of the necessary legal guarantees. It was also agreed that the high importance attached to a number of social issues, including workers' rights, would be confirmed.

Consequently, a decision was taken by the Heads of State or Government, meeting within the European Council, on the concerns of the Irish people on the Treaty of Lisbon and a Solemn Declaration on Workers' Rights, Social Policy and other issues.

The Decision is legally binding and took effect on the date of entry into force of the Treaty of Lisbon. At the time of the conclusion of the next accession treaty, the provisions of the Decision will be set out in a Protocol to be attached to the EU Treaty and the TFEU.

The outcome of the second Irish referendum was positive.

26. THE CZECH REPUBLIC AND THE TREATY OF LISBON

Arrangements similar to the Irish ones were made for the Czech Republic concerning the application of the Charter of Human Rights: the Czech President claimed that the Charter would allow descendants of the Germans, who were expulsed from the country after the Second World War, to reclaim their former lands. An exemption was granted.

Another obstacle to the final ratification was an appeal by 17 senators to the Constitutional Court on whether or not the Treaty of Lisbon conflicts with the Czech Constitution. The Court ruled on November 3, 2009 that there was no conflict, and the President, on the same day, signed the Treaty, which thereby was ratified by the 27 Member States in accordance with their respective constitutional requirements.

The Treaty on European Union and the Treaty on the Functioning of the European Union entered into force on December 1, 2009.

Further Reading

Lenaerts and Van Nuffel, *Constitutional Law of the European Community*, 2nd edn (Sweet & Maxwell, 2004).
Finn Laursen, *The Treaty of Nice* (Martinus Nijhoff, 2006).

Chapter Three

The Legal Acts of the Union[1]

The main lines of the Union decision-making process, i.e. the procedures for the adoption of Union acts by the institutions will be outlined in the following chapters, when analysing the role played therein by, respectively, the Parliament, the Council and the Commission.

For those who are subject to Union law, the main question with regard to the acts is to be able to determine whether or not they are binding on them and, if so, whether the institution issuing them is indeed competent to do so. According to the Court, an act is binding when it, "brings about a distinctive change in the legal position of a party".[2] Regarding the competence of the issuing institution, it is extremely important to note that, "the limits of Union competences are governed by the principle of *conferral*".[3] This is further emphasised in the TFEU as follows:

> "Under the principle of conferral, the Union shall act only within the limits of the competences conferred upon it by the Member States in the Treaties to attain the objectives set out therein. Competences not conferred upon the Union in the Treaties remain with the Member States."[4]

It must be noted that the principle of subsidiarity and the principle of proportionality also apply to the exercise by the institutions of the powers conferred upon them by the Treaties.[5]

Under the principle of subsidiarity, in areas which do not fall within its exclusive competence,[6] the Union shall act only if and in so far as the objectives of the proposed action cannot be sufficiently achieved by the Member States, either at central level or at regional and local level, or, by reason of the scale or effects of the proposed action, can be better achieved at Union level. This principle must be applied as laid down in the Protocol on the applications of the principles of subsidiarity and proportionality.[7]

Under the principle of proportionality, the content and form of Union action may not exceed what is necessary to achieve the objectives of the Treaties. This principle must be applied by the institutions as laid down in the above-mentioned Protocol.

---

[1] arts 288–292 TFEU.
[2] *IBM* (60/81) [1981] E.C.R. 21639.
[3] art.5(1) EU.
[4] art.5(2) EU.
[5] art.5(3) and (4) EU.
[6] See art.3(1) TFEU: customs union, competition, monetary policy (Euro), conservation of marine biological resources, common commercial policy and the conclusion of certain international agreements.
[7] Protocol No.2 attached to the TFEU.

Under this Protocol, the Commission must, before proposing legislative acts, "consult widely", taking into account the local and regional dimension of the act.[8] This obligation also applies to initiatives from a group of Member States, to initiatives from Parliament, to requests from the Court, to recommendations from the European Central Bank (ECB) and to requests from the European Investment Bank (EIB), for the adoption of legislative acts. For more details, see below, Ch.8: The Commission.

As for the various forms which the Union acts can take, it should be pointed out from the onset that the actual practice does sometimes differ from what the Treaty provides. As shall be seen below, the TFEU provides only for regulations, directives, decisions and agreements as binding acts.[9] However, the tendency, it seems, has been to multiply the forms of the Union acts, the procedures leading up to them[10] and the bodies issuing them. Indeed, besides those acts already mentioned, there are: joint actions,[11] common positions,[12] Communiqués, Declarations and Conclusions of the European Council. Furthermore one finds: Programmes, Resolutions, Recommendations,[13] and especially Communications.[14] Some acts are issued, for instance, not only by the Council, but also by the Representatives of the Governments of the Member States within the Council or by the Council and the Representatives of the Governments. Then there are also the Notices of the Commission by which it publishes Guidelines[15] or gives definitions[16] in the competition field. Since, generally speaking, these acts are not binding, i.e. do not create rights and obligations for those who are subject to Union law, not all of the above-mentioned measures constitute Union "acts" whose legality the Court can review. Neither are they always issued, as provided for in the Treaty, on the basis of a Commission proposal, although often there will be one. Nor is Parliament or the Social and Economic Committee or the Committee of the Regions necessarily consulted. Nonetheless these acts shape essential Union policies and consequently the development of the Union itself. They are part of the *acquis communautaire*. It sometimes appears that the more important the decision, politically speaking, the less formal the procedures that lead to them and the forms of the acts.

---

[8] Protocol No.2, art.2.

[9] art.288 TFEU.

[10] As was seen, normally the Council acts on a proposal from the Commission, there are also cases where the Council acts on a "recommendation" of the Commission: for instance art.207(3)1 TFEU [33(3)].

[11] art.14(1) EU.

[12] art.15 EU.

[13] art.126(7) TFEU [104(7)].

[14] One look at the Commission's General Reports shows that in all sectors of activity matters are dealt with mainly in the form of "communications" referred to as "COM(year) No."; see, for instance, the 2009 General Report.

[15] Some of these Guidelines are extremely important, and although they do not bind anybody except the Commission itself, no undertaking can afford to ignore them: they interpret, explain and somehow expand the provisions of binding regulations. See for instance Guidelines on the application of art.101 of the TFEU to horizontal co-operation agreements [2001] O.J. C 3/2. See *P, JCB Service v Commission* (C-167/04) [2006] E.C.R. C-9028 where the Court held that, "in adopting such rules of conduct and announcing by publishing them that they will henceforth apply to the cases to which they relate, the Commission imposes a limit on the exercise of its discretion and cannot depart from those rules under pain of being found, where appropriate, to be in breach of the general principles of law, such as equal treatment or the protection of legitimate expectations."

[16] See for instance the Commission Notice on the definition of relevant market for the purposes of Union competition law [1997] O.J. C 372/5. See comment in the previous footnote.

Nevertheless, the acts expressly provided for by the Treaties (regulations, directives, decisions, agreements) play, by far, the most important role. The conditions laid down for the decision-making process and for the contents of those acts must be seen as so many guarantees for lawfulness and judicial control and the protection of the rights of the citizens.

The Treaties invest in the Council, the Parliament and the Commission the responsibility for implementing the objectives of the Union. To carry out this task, they have empowered them to adopt regulations, directives, decisions, recommendations and opinions[17]; to those must be added, although not mentioned in the same Treaty provision, "international agreements".

Furthermore, each one of those acts fulfils a specific function in the development of Union law, and the Treaties therefore explicitly provide, in many cases, what kind of act must be adopted, by which institution and in which circumstances. Different rules apply to each category of acts and, more important, the extent of the legal protection afforded legal and natural persons varies widely from one category to another.[18]

1. BINDING ACTS PROVIDED FOR IN THE TREATIES: LEGAL ACTS/LEGISLATIVE ACTS[19]

A *regulation* has general application, it is binding in its entirety and is directly applicable in all the Member States.[20] Regulations may be adopted by the Council or by the Council jointly with Parliament under the *ordinary legislative procedure*,[21] by the Council with the participation of Parliament or by Parliament with the participation of the Council under a *special legislative procedure*,[22] by the Commission and by the European Central Bank.[23] The criterion for the distinction between a regulation and other acts, especially decisions, must be sought in its "general application". Being essentially of a, "legislative nature, a regulation is applicable, not to a limited number of persons, defined or identifiable,[24] but to categories of persons viewed abstractly and in their entirety".[25]

Secondly, a regulation is, as was mentioned, "binding in its entirety". This distinguishes it from a directive which only imposes on the Member States to which it is addressed the obligation to achieve specific results. The Court has considered that, since a regulation is binding in its entirety, it cannot be accepted that a Member State should apply provisions of a [Union] regulation in an incomplete and selective manner so as to, "render abortive certain aspects of [Union] legislation".[26]

---

[17] art.288,1 TFEU.

[18] It should be noted that it is not the name given to an act that places it in one of the above-mentioned categories, but rather the contents and objectives of its provisions. See *Chevalley v Commission* (15/70) [1970] E.C.R. 975 at 980(10). The Court has also admitted that the same act can contain provisions pertaining to different categories. See *Producteurs de fruits v Council* (Joined Cases 16/62 and 17/62) [1962] E.C.R. 471 at 479; [1963] C.M.L.R. 160.

[19] art.289(3) TFEU.

[20] art.288,2 TFEU.

[21] arts 289(1) and 294 TFEU.

[22] art.189(2) TFEU.

[23] Protocol on the Statute of the ESCB and of the ECB, art.34(1).

[24] *Calpak v Commission* (Joined Cases 789/79 and 790/79) [1980] E.C.R. 1949 at 1961(9); [1981] 1 C.M.L.R. 146.

[25] *Producteurs de fruits* (Joined Cases 16/62 and 17/62), fn.18

[26] *Commission v UK* (128/78) [1979] E.C.R. 419 at 428(9); [1979] 2 C.M.L.R. 45.

Finally, a regulation is "directly applicable" in all the Member States. This means that it does not require a national measure, such as ratification, to become binding upon institutions, States, undertakings and natural persons all over the Union. There are, however, cases where regulations provide for national administrative implementing measures.[27] Directly applicable also means that the national authorities and national legal or administrative measures, even those posterior to the Union act, cannot prevent its application.[28] By this is meant the *precedence* of Union law over national law.[29]

Direct applicability must not be confused with "direct effect". Union measures have direct effect when they create, for those who are subject to Union law, rights that the national judge is bound to uphold. This is the case every time Union rules impose, in a clear and unconditional way, an obligation (affecting a third party) upon a Member State, an institution or a natural or legal person.[30] The beneficiaries of those obligations can invoke them in the national courts and tribunals to protect the rights which result from these obligations, and those courts and tribunals are under Treaty obligation to uphold them.[31] This applies, as mentioned, even when these obligations conflict with national provisions or measures, whether anterior or posterior.

Not all Union provisions have direct effect, but the Court considers that a regulation, by reason of its very nature and its function in the system of sources of Union law, has direct effect, i.e. it is capable of creating individual rights which national courts must protect.[32]

Directives are issued by the Council, by the Council jointly with Parliament or by the Commission. They constitute the appropriate measure when existing national legislation must be modified or national provisions must be enacted, in most cases for the sake of harmonisation. Directives are binding upon the Member States to which they are addressed, as to the results to be achieved. Although this means that Member States are obliged to take the national measures necessary to achieve the results set out in the directive, they are free to decide how they "transpose" this piece of Union legislation into national law. A

---

[27] See also *Zuckerfabrik Süderdithmarschen and Zuckerfabrik Soest* (Joined Cases C-143/88 and C-92/89) [1991] E.C.R. I-415 at 540(16); [1993] 3 C.M.L.R. 1: "In cases where national authorities are responsible for the administrative implementation of [Union] regulations, the legal protection guaranteed by [Union] law includes the right of individuals to challenge, as a preliminary issue, the legality of such regulation before national courts and to induce those courts to refer questions to the Court of Justice for a preliminary ruling." But, in the absence of required implementing national measures, the regulation cannot be relied on before a national court: *Monte Arcosu* (C-403/98) [2001] E.C.R. I-103.

[28] See *Eridania v Ministry of Agriculture* (230/78) [1979] E.C.R. 2749 at 2772(35). Certain provisions contained in a regulation might need national implementing measures to become applicable, but the regulation itself does not have to be transposed into national law by a national measure.

[29] The French Conseil d'Etat only recognised this basic principle in 1989, 37 years after the first Community was established!

[30] For a more extensive analysis of direct effect, see below, Ch.4: Union Law (2. Direct effect).

[31] art.4(3),2 EU [10]: "Member States shall take all appropriate measures, whether general or particular, to ensure fulfilment of the obligations arising out of the Treaties or resulting from the acts of the institutions of the Union." In the Treaties "Member States" means all the authorities of the State: executive, legislative and judiciary.

[32] It is for the national legal system to determine which court or tribunal has jurisdiction to give this protection and, for this purpose, to decide how the individual position thus protected is to be classified. *Politi v Italy* (43/71) [1971] E.C.R. 1039 at 1048(9); [1973] C.M.L.R. 60. See also *Leonesio v Italian Ministry of Agriculture and Forestry* (93/71) [1972] E.C.R. 287 at 295, (22–23); [1973] C.M.L.R. 343.

directive is, for instance, indifferent whether the national measures are administrative, as opposed to legislative, in nature as long as they are binding and as long as they fully meet the requirements of legal certainty.[33] On the other hand, when transposing a directive into national law, Member States must take care to rely on an interpretation of the directive which allows a fair balance to be struck between the various fundamental rights protected by the Union's legal order. Furthermore, when implementing the measures transposing the directive, the authorities and courts of the Member States must not only interpret their national law in a manner consistent with the directive, but also make sure that they do not rely on an interpretation which would be in conflict with those fundamental rights or with the other general principles of Union law, such as the principle of proportionality.[34]

Although directives are not directly applicable, since they must first be transposed into national law, certain of their provisions can nevertheless have direct effect.[35] This must be ascertained on a case by case basis, taking into account their nature, background and wording.[36] According to the Court, provisions are capable of producing direct effect in the legal relationship between the addressee of the act and others, i.e. the Member State and third parties, for instance their citizens.[37] Furthermore, in the absence of full transposition, a public authority may not rely on that directive "against" an individual; this has been established in order to prevent a Member State from taking advantage of its own failure to comply with Union law.[38] As for the national judge, he may not refuse to apply a national provision contrary to a not-yet-transposed directive,[39] but, where rules of national law fall within the scope of that directive, the national courts are bound to interpret that law, as far as possible, in light of the wording and purpose of the directive so as to achieve the results it has in view.

On the other hand, an individual can, under certain circumstances, invoke the not-yet-transposed or partly-transposed directive against the Member State to which it is addressed. Indeed, although a directive imposes obligations upon a Member State, but cannot and does not impose obligations upon private parties,[40] it can confer rights upon an individual. As the Court restated recently:

> "It is clear from settled case law that, whenever the provisions of a directive appear, so far as their subject matter is concerned, to be unconditional and

[33] *Commission v Belgium* (239/85) [1986] E.C.R. 3645; [1988] 1 C.M.L.R. 248.

[34] *Promusicae* (C-275/06) [2008] E.C.R. I-271.

[35] See, for instance, *Farrell* (C-356/05) [2007] E.C.R. I-3067, where the Court found that art 1 of Directive 90/232 fulfilled all the conditions to produce direct effect and *Arcor E.A.* (Joined Cases C-152/07, C-153/07 and C-154/07) [2008] E.C.R. I-5959

[36] See, for instance, *Wells* (C-201/02) [2004] E.C.R. I-723, where the Court stated that, "In circumstances such as those in the main proceedings, an individual may, where appropriate, rely on Article 2(1) of Directive 85/337, read in conjunction with Articles 1(2) and 4(2) thereof." See also *Arcor* (Joined Cases C-152/07, C-153/07 and C-154/07) (quoted above, fn.35).

[37] *Grad v Finanzamt Traunstein* (9/70) [1970] E.C.R. 825 at 839(5); [1971] C.M.L.R. 1. The Court used as an argument the fact that art.267 TFEU [234] empowers the national courts to refer to the Court all questions regarding the validity and interpretation of all acts of the institutions, without distinction. This implies that individuals may invoke such acts before the national courts. See also *Mazzalai v Ferrovia* (111/75) [1976] E.C.R. 657 at 666; [1977] 1 C.M.L.R. 105 and *Nederlandse Ondernemingen v Inspecteur der Invoerrechten en Accijnzen* (51/76) [1977] E.C.R. 113 at 127(23). This last decision is referred to in many subsequent judgments.

[38] *FacciniDori v Recreb* (C-91/92), [1994] E.C.R. I-3325; [1994] 1 C.M.L.R. 665.

[39] *FacciniDori v Recreb*, as above, fn.38.

[40] *Arcaro* (C-168/95) [1996] E.C.R. I-4705; [1997] 1 C.M.L.R. 179.

sufficiently precise they may be relied upon before the national courts by individuals against the Member State where it has failed to implement the directive correctly."[41]

Once a directive has been properly transposed into national law, Member States are entitled to impose criminal penalties for breach of national legislation implementing that directive, even if this is not provided for by the directive.[42] However, as already mentioned, a directive cannot be relied upon as such against accused persons by a Member State within the context of criminal proceedings, in view of the fact that a directive cannot, of itself and independently of national legislation, have the effect of determining or increasing the criminal liability of the accused persons.[43]

This relationship between Member State and natural/legal persons is what is referred to as "vertical direct effect of a directive", as opposed to "horizontal direct effect". The latter would occur if private parties could claim rights under a directive, in their bilateral relationship. However, since a directive may not, of itself, impose obligations on an individual (it may only impose them on a Member State), it may not be relied upon by an individual against another private party.[44] In another instance, however, where a question concerning the interpretation of a directive was raised in a case involving two persons, the Court did not hesitate to give an answer to the preliminary question. By doing so, the Court seems to be admitting that the directive can be relied upon, at least indirectly, in the relationship between two third parties.[45]

The obligation imposed upon Member States to transpose directives into national legislation[46] makes these Member States responsible for the consequences of their failure to do so.[47] In other words, the State is liable for loss and damage caused to individuals as a result of a breach of Union law for which the State can be held responsible.[48] This obligation applies provided that three conditions are fulfilled. First, the purpose of the directive must be to grant rights to individuals.[49] Second, it must be possible to identify the content of those rights on the basis of the provisions of the directive and, finally, there must be a causal link between the breach of the State's obligation and the damage suffered.[50]

---

[41] *Arcor E.A.* (Joined Cases C-152/07, C-153/07 and 154/07) (quoted above, fn.35).

[42] *Gallotti* (Joined Cases C-58 etc./95) [1996] E.C.R. I-4345; [1997] 1 C.M.L.R. 32.

[43] *Mulliez E.A.* (Joined Cases C-23 etc./03) [2006] E.C.R. I-3923.

[44] *Marshall* (152/84) [1986] E.C.R. 723 (15, 16); [1986] 1 C.M.L.R. 688.

[45] *Beets-Proper v Van Lanschot Bankiers* (262/84) [1986] E.C.R. 773; [1987] 2 C.M.L.R. 616.

[46] This obligation follows from art.4(3) EU [10] and art.288,3 TFEU [249, 3]. It imposes upon the Member States, according to the Court, an obligation not to take any measure liable seriously to compromise the result prescribed in the directive, during the period after the adoption of the directive, but preceding the expiration of the time limit provided therein for its transposition by the Member States into national law: *Inter-Environnement Wallonie v Région Wallonne* (C-129/96) [1997] E.C.R. I-7411.

[47] *Francovich* (Joined Cases C-6/90 and C-9/90) [1991] E.C.R. I-5357; [1993] 2 C.M.L.R. 66.

[48] See *Francovich* (Joined Cases C-6/90 and C-9/90) (quoted above, fn.47) and *Brasserie du Pecheur and Factortame* (Joined Cases C-46/93 and C-48/93) [1996] E.C.R. I-1029(31); [1996] 1 C.M.L.R. 889.

[49] This is another expression of the so-called Schutznorm theory which one also finds in the Court's case law concerning reparation of damage caused by the Union's non-contractual liability. The Court explains its restrictive approach to State liability for breach of Union law, by referring to the reasons already given by the Court to justify the strict approach to non-contractual liability of Union institutions: see *HNL v Council and Commission* (Joined Cases 83 etc./76) [1978] E.C.R. 1209; [1978] 3 C.M.L.R. 566.

[50] *El Corte Ingles v Blazquez Rivero* (C-192/94) [1996] E.C.R. I-1283; [1996] 2 C.M.L.R. 507.

Recently the Court added that, "the liability of the Member State concerned is contingent on a finding of manifest and grave disregard by the State for the limits set on its discretion".[51] See below in Ch.4: Union Law (Member States' Liability for Breach of Union Law).

It should be noted that as long as a Member State has not transposed a directive into national law, it must, from the moment of entry into force of the directive, abstain from adopting measures liable seriously to compromise attainment of the objectives of the directive.[52] Also, from that date, the national courts are bound to ensure that the application of rules of national law is consistent with the principle of non-discrimination, as recognised by the Union's legal order.[53]

Furthermore, in case a directive was not timely transposed into national rules, national jurisdictions must nevertheless, from the moment the time limit for the transposition expired, interpret, as much as possible, national law in the light of the text and finality of the directive in order to achieve the results envisaged by the directive, by privileging the interpretation of the national rule most in conformity with that finality in order to find a solution compatible with the provisions of said directive.[54]

As for a *decision*, it is binding in its entirety upon those to whom it is addressed. The addressee can be a Member State or a legal or natural person. A decision can be taken by the Council, by the Council jointly with Parliament, by Parliament with the participation of the Council or by the Council with the participation of Parliament, under the *ordinary* or *special legislative procedure*,[55] by the Commission and by the ECB.

Decisions are normally of an administrative nature, implementing other Union rules, e.g. granting of an exemption or authorisation, or imposing fines.[56]

There are no requirements as to the form of a decision, so that it may, in certain cases, be doubtful whether a given act constitutes a binding decision or not. Obviously, the institutions must ensure that a decision is recognisable as a binding act by its very form.[57] Being binding in its entirety, a decision can have direct effect.[58]

The TFEU also provides for *recommendations* and *opinions*, which, however, have no binding force. Nonetheless, according to recent case law, recommendations should not be dismissed as having no legal effect whatsoever. They do not, it is true, create rights which can be invoked in the courts, but the national judges must take recommendations into consideration when solving cases submitted to them. This is especially so if the recommendations can help with the interpretation of other national or Union legal measures.[59]

There are cases where the Court annulled a recommendation, pointing out that an action for annulment is available in the cases of all measures adopted by the institutions, whatever their nature or form, which are intended to have legal

---

[51] *Robins E.A.* (C-278/05) [2007] E.C.R. I-1053.
[52] *Adeneler E.A.* (C-212/04) [2006] E.C.R. I-6057.
[53] *Navarro* (C-246/06) [2008] E.C.R. I-105.
[54] *Vassilakis E.A.* (C-364-07) [2008] E.C.R. 1–90* (only summary published, but on the Internet in the original language).
[55] art.289(1) and (2) TFEU.
[56] See *Commission v Greece* (226/87) [1988] E.C.R. 3611; [1989] 3 C.M.L.R. 569, where the Court rejected the Greek Government's contention that the Commission decision adopted pursuant to the now art.106(3) TFEU [86(3)] should merely be considered a non-binding opinion.
[57] *Hoogovens v High Authority* (28/63) [1963] E.C.R. 231 at 235; [1964] C.M.L.R. 125.
[58] *Grad v Finanzamt Traustein* (9/70) [1970] E.C.R.825 at 837 [1971] C.M.L.R. 1.
[59] *Fonds des maladies professionnelles* (322/88) [1989] E.C.R. 4407; [1991] 2 C.M.L.R. 265.

effects. This applies also to a Commission Communication which sets out to specify the manner of application of a provision of a directive.[60]

Generally speaking, recommendations aim at obtaining a given action or behaviour from the addressee. They play, however, an important role in many sectors such as Approximation of Laws,[61] Economic and Monetary Policy[62] and Education, Vocational Training and Youth.[63]

An *opinion*, on the other hand, expresses a point of view, often at the request of a third party. Having no binding effect, the legality of recommendations and opinions cannot, in theory, be reviewed by the Court. Neither can they be submitted to the Court for a preliminary ruling concerning their validity or interpretation. The Court has nevertheless agreed to examine whether recommendations had legal effect when a Member State failed to take the recommended action.[64]

The sequence in which the acts are mentioned in the Treaty does not indicate a hierarchy, it was therefore decided at Maastricht that the intergovernmental conference to be convened in 1996 would examine to what extent it might be possible to review the classification of Union acts with a view to establishing an appropriate hierarchy between the different categories of acts. This is one of the many tasks entrusted to that intergovernmental conference, which were not carried out.

A major problem exists as a result of the profusion of regulations, directives and decisions, often amending existing ones. Without even mentioning the sometimes doubtful quality and transparency of Union legislation, the citizen is confronted by an ever increasing array of measures, which it becomes impossible to understand in the absence of systematic codification. The Union institutions are aware of this and have concluded an Inter-institutional Agreement on the accelerated working method for official codification of legislative texts,[65] and one on "better law-making".[66] Unfortunately not much has been achieved so far and it seems that the method that was chosen creates, in fact, more confusion.[67] The same problem exists with the Treaties themselves: there are too many of them and too many amendments—the Amsterdam Intergovernmental Conference, therefore, adopted a Declaration on the Consolidation of the Treaties, according to which the aim is to draft a consolidation of all the relevant Treaties, including the Treaty on European Union. However, this will be done for "illustrative purposes" only and "shall have no legal value".[68]

---

[60] *France v Commission* (C-325/91) [1993] E.C.R. I-3283.
[61] art.117 TFEU [97].
[62] arts 121 and 219(2) TFEU [99 and 111(2)].
[63] art.166(4) TFEU [150(4)].
[64] *France v Commission* (C-325/91) (quoted above, fn.60).
[65] [1996] O.J. C102/2.
[66] [2003] O.J. C321/1.
[67] For instance, when an act was modified several times, the simple solution would have been to include all the amendments in the text and reissue it without further ado; unfortunately, the Council has decided that the act including all the amendments (it had previously agreed upon) has to be resubmitted and needs a new decision on the part of the institutions, at which occasion more often than not, new amendments are proposed, discussed and introduced! It so becomes a neverending process. See, however, the Declaration on the Quality of the Drafting of Union Legislation adopted by the Amsterdam Intergovernmental Conference, which provides for guidelines for improving the quality of the drafting of Union legislation and for the institutions to make best efforts to accelerate the codification of legislative texts [1997] O.J. C340/139.
[68] [1997] O.J. C340/140.

2. Regulations, Directives and Decisions must be Reasoned

Regulations, directives and decisions must state the reasons on which they are based and must refer to the proposals and opinions which were required to be obtained pursuant to the Treaties.[69]

Reasons must be understood as referring both to the Treaty provision which entitle the institution to take the measure in question and the reasons which motivated the institution to act. The mention of the provision is particularly important since, as was mentioned, the Union institutions may only exercise those powers which are explicitly conferred upon them by the Member States.

Problems may arise when the act can be based simultaneously on several treaty provisions, and a choice must be made by the legislator between them. According to the Court, it may not depend simply on an institution's conviction as to the objective pursued, but must be based on objective factors which are amenable to judicial review. Those factors include, in particular, the aim and content of the measure.[70]

As for the motives which prompted the institution to act, they must be mentioned in order to make it possible for the interested parties and for the Court to reconstruct the essential elements of the institution's reasoning,[71] thereby permitting the parties to defend their rights, the Court to exercise its control, and the Member States (and in the same way all the interested citizens) to know the conditions under which the institution has applied the Treaty.[72]

To attain those objectives, it is sufficient for the act to set out, in a concise but clear and relevant manner, the principal issues of law and fact upon which it is based and which are necessary in order that the reasoning which has led the institution to its decision may be understood.[73] The extent of this requirement depends on the nature of the measure in question. The condition can also be considered as fulfilled when reference[74] is made to the reasons developed in an earlier act.[75]

Furthermore, the question whether a statement of reasons satisfies the requirements must be assessed with reference not only to the wording of the measure but also to its context and to the whole body of legal rules governing the matter in question. If the contested measure clearly discloses the essential objective pursued by the institution, it would be excessive to require a specific statement of reasons for each of the technical choices made by the institution.[76]

If an act is not sufficiently reasoned, this constitutes an, "infringement of an essential procedural requirement"[77] that can be invoked in an action for review

---

[69] art.296(2) TFEU [253].

[70] *Commission v Council* (C-300/89) [1991] E.C.R. I-2867; [1993] 3 C.M.L.R. 359: in this case the Council could base the act on two different Treaty provisions, one of them involved the co-operation procedure with Parliament. The use of both provisions jointly would have excluded this procedure and therefore the involvement of the Parliament. In this case recourse to a dual legal basis is excluded. The Court decided that the act must be based on art.110 TFEU [90].

[71] *Hoogovens v High Authority* (14/61) [1962] E.C.R. 253 at 275; [1963] C.M.L.R. 73. *Fedesa* (C-331/88) [1990] E.C.R. I-4023 at 4066 (30); [1991] 1 C.M.L.R. 507: an effect of Council legislation must be mentioned in the latter's reasoning as one of its objectives, only if it was the genuine or main ground for the act. If it is merely a side-effect it does not have to be mentioned.

[72] *Germany v Commission* (24/62) [1963] E.C.R. 63 at 69; [1963] C.M.L.R. 347.

[73] *Germany v Commission* (24/62), as above, fn. 72. See also *Geitling v High Authority* (Joined Cases 36/59, 37/59, 38/59 and 40/59) [1960] E.C.R. 423 at 439.

[74] *Mollet v Commission* (75/77) [1978] E.C.R. 897 at 906(12).

[75] *Italy v Commission* (1/69) [1969] E.C.R. 277 at 285(9); [1970] C.M.L.R. 17. See, however, *Papiers peints v Commission* (73/74) [1975] E.C.R. 1491 at 1514 (31); [1976] 1 C.M.L.R. 589.

[76] *Arnold André* (C-434/02) [2004] E.C.R. I-11825.

[77] art.263,2 TFEU.

by the Court of the legality of the act concerned. The Court can and must of its own motion take exception to any deficiencies in the reasons which would make such review more difficult.[78]

As for the reference to the required proposals and opinions, a simple mention is considered sufficient; the institutions are not required to indicate whether or not the opinion was favourable,[79] still less must they refute dissenting opinions expressed by the consultative bodies.[80]

3. PUBLICATION AND ENTRY INTO FORCE[81]

Since regulations are of a legislative nature and therefore concern an unidentifiable group to whom they apply, they must be published in the *Official Journal of the European Union (Official Journal)*,[82] which appears in the 23 official languages[83] of the Union. The same applies to directives and decisions since they are binding acts and may concern persons other than the one(s) to whom the act is addressed. However, with regard to competition decisions, the Commission has decided no longer to publish the full texts in the *Official Journal*.

Publication must, as indicated, necessarily take place in all the official languages of the Union and cannot be replaced by electronic versions; the absence of publication precludes the obligations contained in Union legislation from being imposed on individuals, even though those persons could have learned of that legislation by other means.[84]

Acts enter into force on the day specified therein or, in the absence thereof, on the twentieth day following their publication.[85] This rule raises the question of possible retroactive effect. In this regard, the Court ruled that:

"Although in general the principle of legal certainty precludes a [Union] measure from taking effect from a point in time before its publication, it may

---

[78] art.263 TFEU [230]; *Nold v High Authority* (18/57) [1959] E.C.R. 41 at 52 and *Rewe v Hauptzollamt Kiel* (158/80) [1981] E.C.R. 1805 at 1834 (27); [1982] 1 C.M.L.R. 449, where Regulation 3023/77 was declared void for not containing a statement of the reasons on which it is based. *Silo e Mangini Martini* (C-228/99) [2001] E.C.R. I-8401(12).

[79] This, however, is no secret since both the Commission's proposals and the Parliament's opinions are published in the *Official Journal*.

[80] *I.S.A. v High Authority* (4/54) [1954–56] E.C.R. 91 at 100(6).

[81] art.297 TFEU [254].

[82] Before May 1, 2003, date of the entry into force of the Treaty of Nice, it used to be called *Official Journal of the European Communities*; art.2,38 Treaty of Nice.

[83] Regulation 1/58 [1958] O.J. B 017/385 determining the languages to be used by the Union, amended several times. The official languages of the institutions of the Union were Danish, Finnish, German, English, French, Greek, Italian, Dutch, Spanish, Swedish and Portuguese; to which are now added Estonian, Slovakian, Slovene, Hungarian, Czech, Latvian, Polish, Maltese and Lithuanian; and, since January 1, 2007, Bulgarian, Irish and Romanian. In the case of discrepancies among the languages, the requirement of a uniform interpretation across the Union excludes the consideration of one such text in isolation, obliging it to be interpreted in the light of the other versions in the other official languages: *Koschniske* (9/79) [1979] E.C.R. 2717(16); [1989] 1 C.M.L.R. 87. See Regulation 930/2004 [2004] O.J. L196/1 on temporary derogation for the Maltese language.

[84] *Skoma-Lux* (C-161/06) [2007] E.C.R. I-10841 and *Heinrich* (C-345/06) E.C.R. 10.03.09

[85] A typical example was Regulation 17 giving effect to the principles of competition (replaced by Regulation 1/2003 [2003] O.J. L1/1): the Regulation was adopted by the Council on February 6, 1962, published in the *Official Journal* on February 21, 1962 and, since it did not mention the date of entry into force, it became effective on March 13, 1962. See also *Racke v Hauptzollamt Mainz* (98/78) [1979] E.C.R. 69 at 84 (15) and *Decker v Hauptzollamt Landau* (99/78) [1979] E.C.R. 101 at 109(3).

exceptionally be otherwise where the purpose to be achieved so demands and the legitimate expectations of those concerned are duly respected."[86]

Directives and decisions concern only a limited number of persons (Member States or natural or legal persons) and must therefore be notified directly to those to whom they are addressed. However, since the Court may review the legality of decisions at the request of parties which are not addressees of such acts, when the latter are of "direct and individual concern"[87] to them, it is important that they be informed of the contents of all such decisions. The same applies to directives; as was seen, citizens may invoke them in the national courts and request the latter to ask the Court for a preliminary ruling on their validity or interpretation. Consequently, as just mentioned, directives are always published in the *Official Journal*, as are decisions which may affect the rights of third parties.[88]

4. ENFORCEMENT OF PECUNIARY OBLIGATIONS[89]

Decisions, whether of the Council, the Parliament and the Council, the Commission or the ECB, which impose a pecuniary obligation[90] on persons other than Member States and, similarly, judgments of the Courts imposing such obligations,[91] are enforceable. Enforcement of Union acts is governed by the rules of civil procedure in force within the Member State where it is to be carried out. The following steps must be taken. The institution which wants to enforce a decision presents it for verification of authenticity to the national authority that the government of each Member State has designated for this purpose[92] and made

---

[86] *SAFA* (337/88) [1990] E.C.R. I-1 at 1885(12); [1991] 1 C.M.L.R. 507. See also *Fedesa* (331/88) [1990] E.C.R. I-4023 at 4069(45), [1991] 1 C.M.L.R. 872 and *Diversinte* (Joined Cases C-260/91 and C-261/91) [1993] E.C.R. I-188.

[87] art.263 TFEU [230].

[88] See in this respect *Handelsvereniging Rotterdam v Minister van Landbouw* (Joined Cases 73/63 and 74/63) [1964] E.C.R. 1 at 14; [1964] C.M.L.R. 198 and *Salumificio di cornuda v Amministrazione delle Finanze* (130/78) [1979] E.C.R. 867; [1979] 3 C.M.L.R. 561.

[89] art.299 TFEU [256].

[90] For instance, decisions of the Commission imposing fines pursuant to Regulation 1/2003 [2003] O.J. 1/1 for violation of the competition rules.

[91] art.280 TFEU [244].

[92] Austria: Bundesministerium für Auswertige Angelegenheiten, Abteilung IV/3 "Legalisierungsbüro". The Netherlands: Law of February 24, 1955, Stb 73, modified by Law of January 13, 1960, Stb 15: Minister of Justice is addressee of request, Griffier of Hoge Raad implements. Belgium: Law of August 6, 1967: Greffier en Chef of the Court of Appeal at Brussels. Finland: Ministry of Justice, 1994 Act No.1554/94 concerning the European Union. France: Décret No. 57/321 of March 13, 1957, *Journal Officiel*, March 19, 1957, 2885, designates (1) persons who have received delegation from the Prime Minister and (2) Secrétariat Géneral du Comité Interministériel. Germany: Bundesgesetzblatt, February 3, 1961, II, 50, Minister of Justice. Italy: Decree of December 2, 1960, *Gazzetta Officiale*, February 21, 1961, No. 46, 738, Minister of Foreign Affairs. Luxembourg: Regulation of October 17, 1962, Memorial of October 31, 1962, No. 58, 1028, verification by Minister of Foreign Affairs, and order for enforcement appended by Minister of Justice. United Kingdom: European Communities (Enforcement of Union Judgments) Order 1972, SI 1972/1590, which provides for the registration in the High Court of England and Northern Ireland and the Court of Session in Scotland of Union judgments and orders to which the Secretary of State has duly appended an order for enforcement. Ireland: SI 1972/331; enforcement order appended by the Master of High Court. Denmark: by the Minister of Justice, Greece: the head of the Tribunal of First Instance at Athens. Spain: B.O.E. No.160, July 5, 1986, 17843, Minister of Justice. Portugal: Diano da Republica, Law No.104/88 of August 31, 1988, verification of authenticity, Minister of Foreign Affairs; apposition of formula through Minister of Justice, competent tribunal. Sweden: Domstolverket (National Courts Administration), Ordonance SFS 1995:105.

known to the Commission and the Court. The authority then appends to the decision an order for its enforcement.[93] The institution can then proceed to enforcement in accordance with national law, by bringing the matter directly before the competent national authorities. From that moment on, the national rules of civil procedure apply with the exception that suspension of the enforcement may only be decided by the Court.

An action brought before the Court against a decision which is being enforced has no suspensory effect.[94] However, the interested party, in case it has introduced an action against the decision, can always ask for interim measures consisting of a suspension of the enforcement.[95]

5. Binding Acts not Provided for under TFEU Article 288

As indicated at the beginning of this chapter, Union acts are not limited to regulations, directives and decisions. Judgments of the courts are also binding upon the parties and can be enforced (see previous section). As for agreements concluded by the Union with third countries or international organisations, they are binding upon the institutions of the Union and on the Member States[96] and may be invoked by persons in court.[97] The same applies to acts of bodies created by international agreements when such acts are published in the *Official Journal*.[98]

The same applies to agreements concluded by the Member States among themselves regarding matters connected with the Treaty. Somewhat different is the position of international agreements concluded by the Member States with third countries: in so far as, under the Treaty, the Union has assumed the powers previously exercised by Member States in the area governed by such international agreement, the provisions of that agreement have the effect of binding the Union.[99] These agreements can be submitted to the control of legality exercised by the Court when the Union is a party to them[100] and they constitute rules of law relating to the application of the Treaty[101]; the result being that regulations, directives and decisions can be annulled in case of infringement of these rules. These agreements can also have direct effect, which means that natural and legal

---

[93] In the UK "order for enforcement" means an order by or under the authority of the Secretary of State that the Union judgment to which it is appended is to be registered for enforcement in the UK (SI 1972/1590).

[94] When the Commission takes a decision imposing fines on a person, it usually does not seek enforcement in case an appeal has been lodged against the decision. The Court has approved this practice but only on condition that interest is paid in respect of the period of suspension and that a bank guarantee is lodged covering the amount of the fine; see *Hasselblad v Commission* (86/82 R) [1982] E.C.R. 1555; [1984] 1 C.M.L.R. 559.

[95] See below, Ch.9: The Court of Justice of the European Union (4. Special Forms of Procedure).

[96] art.300(7) TFEU. See *International Fruit Company v Produktschap voor Groenten en Fruit* (Joined Cases 21/72, 22/72, 23/72 and 24/72) [1972] E.C.R. 1219; [1975] 1 C.M.L.R. 1 and *Singer and Geigy v Amministrazione delle Finanze* (Joined Cases 290/81 and 291/81) [1983] E.C.R. 847 concerning direct effect of GATT rules.

[97] See for instance, *Cordis v Commission* (T-18/99) [2001] E.C.R. II-913; see next chapter.

[98] See for instance [2008] O.J. L72/1.

[99] *International Fruit Company* (Joined Cases 21/72, 22/72, 23/72 and 24/72) (quoted above, fn. 96); [1975] 2 C.M.L.R. 1.

[100] See for instance *Commission v Council* (22/70) [1971] E.C.R. 263; [1971] C.M.L.R. 335.

[101] art.263 TFEU [230].

persons can ask the national judge to uphold the rights that derive from these
agreements even against their own national authorities.[102]

Besides the acts already mentioned, there are the decisions of the
Representatives of the Governments of the Member States within the Council;
these cannot be submitted to the Court since they do not emanate from the
Council, the Parliament or the Commission, but they can be binding within the
whole Union.[103] However it will have to be established on a case by case basis
whether those decisions are binding only for the Member States or also for the
institutions of the Union and even for natural or legal persons. Although those
decisions constitute a flexible instrument to solve a number of questions within the
scope of the Treaties, they are not without danger for the institutional equilibrium.
Besides immunity from the Court's control, these acts do not require a
Commission proposal or an opinion of Parliament. Of course, nothing can prevent
the latter from trying to exercise its political control over these acts anyway.

6. OTHER FORMS OF UNION "ACTS"

A form often used is the Resolution, either of the Council,[104] or of the, "Council
and of the Representatives of the Governments of the Member States meeting
within the Council".[105] This latter kind of resolution was used to establish the
European Passport: "a passport of which the uniform format and scope" was
described in an annex![106] These Resolutions are not to be confused with the decision of the Representatives of the Governments of the Member States in Council
or a Resolution of Ministers within the Council.[107] In the first place the decisions
of the Representatives of the Member States are legally binding upon the latter,
while resolutions sometimes only constitute a political commitment; secondly, the
fact that the Member States act within the institutional framework is intended to
indicate that the matter directly concerns the implementation of the Treaty. On
the other hand, resolutions, generally speaking, concern matters directly connected with the Union, but not explicitly provided for under Union law.

There are, furthermore, Programmes,[108] General Action Programmes,[109]
Framework Programmes[110] and Programmes of Action,[111] which intend to lay down

---

[102] See for instance *Syndicat professionnel coordination des pêcheurs de l'étang de Berre et de la Région v EDF* (C-213/03) [2004] E.C.R. I-7357.
[103] See for instance the "acceleration" decisions by which the Member States agreed to establish the Customs Union within a shorter time limit than provided for under the EEC Treaty ([1960] J.O. 1217 and [1962] J.O. 1284). These decisions are not to be confused with decisions of the Member States such as the appointment of the Members of the Commission (art.17 EU [214(2)]) or of the Judges of the European courts (art.253 TFEU [223]).
[104] See for instance Council Resolution of February 6, 1979 concerning the guidelines for Union Regional Policy ([1979] O.J. C36/10) and the Conclusions of the Council of December 4, 1984, concerning measures necessary to guarantee the implementation of the conclusions of the European Council concerning budgetary discipline [1984] E.C. Bull. 12–24. In one case, the Court was asked to interpret a Council Resolution in a request for a preliminary ruling: *Schlüter v Hauptzollamt Lörrach* (9/73) [1973] E.C.R. 1135 at 1162—the Court interpreted the Resolution by stating that it did not impose a prohibition on the Member States.
[105] See [1991] O.J. C178/1. Another form used is the "Conclusions", [1991] O.J. C188/4.
[106] [1981] O.J. C241/1.
[107] See [1991] O.J. L188/2.
[108] For instance: Medium term economic policy programme [1982] O.J. L236/10.
[109] art.192(3) TFEU [175(3)].
[110] art.182 TFEU [166].
[111] For instance: Programme of action of the EC on the environment [1973] O.J.C112/1.

general principles for future action both by the Member States and by the institutions of the Union. Such Programmes are generally adopted by the Council, either by a Decision,[112] a Declaration[113] or a Resolution.[114]

Other matters are decided upon by decisions which are not formal binding acts[115]; they are used to settle questions related to Union affairs but do not impose rights or obligations upon the institutions of the Union nor upon natural or legal persons.[116]

Further Reading

Thomas A.J.A. Vandamme, *The invalid Directive. The legal authority of a Union Act requiring domestic law making* (Groningen, Europa Law Publishing, 2005); book review: (2006) E.L.Rev. Feb. 140.
Paul Craig, "The legal effect of Directive: policy, rules and exceptions" (2009) E.L.Rev. June.349.

---

[112] [1982] O.J. L236/10.
[113] [1973] O.J. C112/1.
[114] [1977] O.J. C139/1.
[115] Other languages such as Dutch and German use a word (Besluit; Beschluss) which clearly distinguishes this act from an art.288 TFEU [249] decision (Beschikking; Entscheidung).
[116] See for instance [1973] O.J. L207/46.

Chapter Four

Union Law

As was pointed out at the beginning of this book, the Treaties establishing what were, at the time, the European Communities, and now the Union, are more than classical international agreements creating mutual obligations between the High Contracting Parties. Indeed, by ratifying those Treaties, the Member States intended to do much more than that, though they most probably did not, at the time, foresee all the consequences which, for instance, the Court has, over the years, drawn from the specific nature of those Treaties. Hence the question: what is it that distinguishes these Treaties from other international agreements?

In the first place, they have, as the Court pointed out, created quasi-governmental bodies (the institutions), independent from the national public authorities, and endowed with legislative, administrative and judicial sovereign rights, which were transferred to them by the Member States.[1] Furthermore, the Treaties lay down basic principles that are either worked out in the Treaties themselves or defined and implemented by acts of the institutions. The Treaties and acts constitute a set of rules which directly, i.e. without interference or intervention of national authorities, impose obligations upon, and consequently create rights for, the Member States and the natural and legal persons within the Union. The Treaties therefore present many analogies with national constitutions. It can also be said that, although they started out as international treaties, these texts have become, in fact if not in law, the "Constitution" of the Union.

As was shown, the rules embodied in the Treaties (the latter being referred to as primary Union law) are constantly being expanded and implemented by new treaties, while being made more specific, interpreted and applied by the various acts and measures of the institutions, especially the courts (known as secondary Union law). The European Treaties have, therefore, as was ascertained by the Court, established a specific legal order. Indeed:

> "[B]y creating a [Union] of unlimited duration, having its own institutions, its own personality, its own legal capacity and capacity of representation on the international plane and, more particularly, real powers stemming from a limitation of sovereignty or a transfer of powers from the States to the [Union], the Member States have limited their sovereign rights, albeit within limited fields, and have created a body of law which binds both their nationals and themselves".[2]

It took years before all national courts and tribunals came to share the view that the European Treaties create a separate legal order but, at the time, several of them

---

[1] See for instance *Van Gend & Loos v Nederlandse Administratie der Belastingen* (26/72) [1963] E.C.R. 1 at 12 and *Costa v ENEL* (6/64) [1964] E.C.R. 585 at 594.

[2] *Costa v ENEL* (6/64) [1964] (quoted above, fn.1). It should be pointed out that the "unlimited duration" only applied to the EC and Euratom Treaties; the ECSC Treaty had a duration of 50 years (art.97 ECSC) and is no longer in force.

were quick to agree, as was the German Supreme Administrative Court. It stated that Union law constitutes, "a separate legal order, whose provisions belong neither to international law nor to the municipal law of the Member States".[3]

It must be clearly understood that Union law only applies in cases involving cross-border situations; in other words, purely internal occurrences do not come within the ambit of Union Law.[4]

Union law is, generally speaking, characterised by its direct applicability within the Member States, its direct effect and its primacy over national law. These concepts are briefly examined below.

1. DIRECT APPLICABILITY

Union law, being distinct from national law, is also independent from it. This means that rights can be conferred and obligations imposed, both on the Member States and on natural and legal persons, directly by Union provisions, i.e. without interference from or intervention by national authorities. There is indeed no need for Member States to intervene in order to ensure that Union decisions, regulations and, in certain cases, directives have binding effect throughout the Union.[5] Referring to regulations, the Treaty uses the words, "shall be . . . directly applicable in all Member States".[6] The latter should not be taken too literally. The territory of the Union is defined in the Treaty[7] and thereby the geographical application of Union law. However, as the Court has indicated, this does not preclude Union rules from applying outside the territory of the Union, when the activity in question retains sufficient links with the Union.[8]

In addition, Member States are committed not to interfere with the application of Union law. This also follows from the Treaties, which provide that Member States, "shall refrain from any measure which could jeopardise the attainment of the Union's objectives".[9] Furthermore, Member States are under obligation to actively support the implementation of that law by taking, "any appropriate measure, general or particular, to ensure fulfilment of the obligations arising out of the Treaties or resulting from the acts of the institutions of the Union".[10]

More important than the acceptance of the legal autonomy of the Union legal order in regard to national law, is the understanding of its raison d'être. The

---

[3] (1967) *Common Market Law Revue* (C.M.L.Rev.) 483.

[4] Some authors have suggested that, on account of the growing trend towards regional devolution and to ensure the *effet utile* of Union law, the requirement of a cross-border link should be abolished: see, for instance, (2009) E.L.Rev.433.

[5] This is what is meant by s.2(1) of the European Communities Act of 1972: these provisions, "are without further enactment to be given legal effect or use in the United Kingdom." In other words "reception" of Union law into the sphere of national law is not and cannot be required. Anyway reception is only required by those who adhere to the dualist theory, and furthermore, "if one accepts, as is logical and in one view inevitable, that Union law is sui generis then, in strictness the monist/dualist argument is excluded, since it is an argument properly limited to international law strictly so called", which is not the case with Union law. John Mitchell, "British law and British membership", Europarecht, April–June 1971, 109.

[6] art.288,2 TFEU [249,2].

[7] art.52 EU and art.355 TFEU.

[8] See *Boukhalfa v Germany* (C-214/94) [1996] E.C.R. I-2253; [1996] 3 C.M.L.R. 22: it concerned a Belgian citizen, a local resident employed in the German embassy in Algiers, who claimed the same employment conditions as the German employees.

[9] art.4(3)2 EU [10(1)].

[10] art.4(3)2 EU [10(1)].

European Treaties, it will be remembered, aim at establishing within the territories of the Member States a single market characterised by the basic freedoms (goods, persons, services, establishment, capital and payments) and constituting a geographical area wherein Union rules apply with the same force and with the same meaning and effect for all who operate therein.[11] Therefore, the very nature of the law created by the European Treaties implies uniform interpretation and application. Without those characteristics there can be no Union. Union law is either uniform in all the Member States or it simply cannot exist. This does not mean that Union rules should not take into account the specificities of the various Member States or of their regions[12]; as long as the fundamental principles are safeguarded, the way of implementing them must be adapted to local circumstance. Indeed, applying the same rule to different situations constitutes a discrimination just as much as applying different rules to comparable situations.[13]

2. DIRECT EFFECT

If the consequence of direct applicability means, for the Member States, non-interference with the implementation of Union law, for the citizens it means, in most cases, the possibility of invoking those Union rules in their national courts and tribunals to defend their rights; this is what is meant by direct effect. This allows all those who are subject to Union law to require the national judge to uphold the rights which those Union rules confer upon them.[14] Applicability of Union law must indeed be understood in two ways: on the one hand, the obligations and prohibitions (i.e. obligations to abstain) imposed upon national authorities, institutions and persons, and, on the other hand, the rights granted to those in favour of whom those obligations were imposed. Indeed, in law, every obligation imposed upon someone creates, as its corollary, a right for someone else, although this right is not always clearly specified. It is the same in Union law: obligations imposed upon Member States have, generally speaking, as their corollary, corresponding rights for the citizens of the Union. For instance, by prohibiting the Member States from hindering the free movement of goods, the Treaty grants the persons within the Union the right to move goods unhindered from one Member State to another. The same applies to the other freedoms.

It is this kind of right that the national courts and tribunals must, by virtue of the direct effect of most Union provisions, uphold in pursuance of the Treaty.[15]

---

[11] *Costa v ENEL* (6/64) (quoted above, fn 1) at 594, and *Rheinmühlen v Einfuhr-und Vorratstelle Getreide* (166/73) [1974] E.C.R. 33 at 38(2); [1974] 1 C.M.L.R. 523.

[12] See in this regard art.27 TFEU which provides that when drawing up proposals for establishing and ensuring the functioning of the internal market, "the Commission shall take into account the extent of the effort that certain economies showing differences in development will have to sustain for the establishment of the internal market and may propose appropriate provisions." These provisions may take the form of derogations.

[13] *Procureur du Roi v Debauve* (52/79) [1980] E.C.R. 833 at 858(21); [1981] 2 C.M.L.R. 362 and *Webb* (279/80) [1981] E.C.R. 3305 at 3324(16); [1982] 1 C.M.L.R. 719.

[14] This was clearly stated by the Court in *Defrenne v Sabena* (43/75) [1976] E.C.R. 455 at 474(24); [1976] 2 C.M.L.R. 98; the same was already apparent in *Reyners v Belgium* (2/74) [1974] E.C.R. 631 at 651(25); [1974] 2 C.M.L.R. 305, although less clearly stated.

[15] art.4(3) EU [10]. This provision refers to "Member States" which must be understood as covering all national authorities whether legislative, administrative or judicial. See *Rewe v Landwirtschaftskammer Saarland* (33/76) [1976] E.C.R. 1989 at 1997(5); [1977] 1 C.M.L.R. 533.

The question has been raised whether the national judge must, of his own volition, apply Union rules that have direct effect. The Court accepted the domestic law principle of "judicial passivity" in civil cases and the concomitant rule that in civil suits it is for the parties to take the initiative.[16] On the other hand, a Member State may not prevent a national judge from raising the question of the compatibility of national law with Union rules.[17] It is thus not only the directly applicable[18] regulations that are, as such, suited to, "grant to the citizens rights which the national tribunals are under obligation to protect",[19] but all binding Union acts whatever their nature or form.[20] Consequently, the question, "which provisions of Union law have direct effect"? should rather be put the other way: "which Union provisions that impose a clear and unconditional obligation upon a Member State, an institution or a person do not have direct effect?".[21] The answer is: only those which leave to the addressee of the obligation a discretionary latitude. For instance, with regard to public undertakings, the Court stated that:

> "Its application involves an appraisal of the requirements, on the one hand, of the particular task entrusted to the undertaking concerned and, on the other hand, the protection of the interests of the [Union]. This appraisal depends on the objectives of general economic policy pursued by the States under the supervision of the Commission. Consequently ... Article [106 (2)] cannot at the present stage create individual rights which the national courts must protect."[22]

In other words, this Treaty obligation is subject to a Commission appreciation and cannot therefore have direct effect.

However, the Court made it clear that in cases where the latitude is limited in time, the expiration of the time limit suffices to give direct effect to Union rules. This applies notwithstanding the absence of implementing regulations that were to be adopted by the institutions or by the national authorities. The Court found also that, even in the areas in which they have no direct effect, the Union provisions cannot be interpreted as reserving to the national legislature exclusive powers to implement those rules. Indeed, such implementation may be relieved by a combination of Union and national measures.[23]

The fact that the European Treaties have created a new legal order, directly applicable and conferring upon the citizens of the Union rights which the national courts must uphold, was not only ascertained by the Court, but also recognised from the

---

[16] *van Schijndel* (Joined Cases C-430/93 and C-431/93) [1995] E.C.R. I-4705.

[17] *Peterbroeck* (C-312/93) [1995] E.C.R. I-4599.

[18] art.288 TFEU [249]. See above Ch.3: The Legal Acts of the Union.

[19] *Leonesio v Italian Ministry for Agriculture and Forestry* (93/71) [1972] E.C.R. 287 at 293(5); [1973] C.M.L.R. 343.

[20] For instance provisions of directives, decisions or agreements; for directives, see *Delkvist v Anklagemyndigheden* (21/78) [1978] E.C.R. 2327 at 2340(21); [1979] 1 C.M.L.R. 372; for decisions see *Rewe* (33/76) (quoted above, fn.15) and for agreements see *International Fruit Company v Produktschap voor Groenten en Fruit* (Joined Cases 21/72, 22/72, 23/72 and 24/72) [1972] E.C.R. 1219 at 1227; [1975] 2 C.M.L.R. 1. Also *Kziber* (18/90) [1991] E.C.R. I-221.

[21] Originally, the question was put the other way round: see *Molkerei Zentrale Westfalen v Hauptzollamt Paderborn* (28/67) [1968] E.C.R. 143 at 153; [1968] C.M.L.R. 187. See however *Defrenne* (43/75) (quoted above, fn.14) at 471. If the acts are not clear and unconditional, the exact obligation cannot be established, neither can it, therefore, be upheld (that seems to go without saying).

[22] *Ministére Public Luxembourgeois v Muller* (10/71) [1971] E.C.R. 723 at 730 (14–16); at the time art.90 EEC.

[23] *Defrenne* (43/75) (quoted above, fn.14) at 480(68).

beginning by most national jurisdictions. Indeed, the judiciaries of all the Member States have implicitly recognised this fact for many years, by making extensive use of the possibility offered them by the Treaty to ask the Court for a preliminary ruling on questions concerning Union law raised before them.[24] By referring those questions to the Court, they accepted that Union rules do apply within the territory of their jurisdiction and may confer rights which they, as national courts, must uphold.

Under the principle of co-operation laid down in the EU Treaty,[25] it is for Member States to ensure judicial protection of an individual's rights under Union law. In the absence of Union rules governing the matter it is for the domestic legal system of each Member State to designate the courts and tribunals having jurisdiction and to lay down the detailed procedural rules governing actions for safeguarding rights which individuals derive from Union law. Those rules must be no less favourable than those governing similar domestic actions (principle of equivalence) and must not render practically impossible or excessively difficult the exercise of rights conferred by Union law. Moreover it is for the national courts to interpret the procedural rules governing actions brought before them in such a manner as to contribute to ensuring effective judicial protection of an individual's rights under Union law.[26]

The fact that Union law constitutes a new legal order was recognised explicitly, years ago, by the highest national courts and tribunals. This was the case, among others, for the Italian Corte Costituzionale, the German Bundesverfassungsgericht and the Belgian Cour de Cassation. Although of historical value only at this stage of the development of Union law, these decisions were extremely important at the time when the novelty of those issues often resulted in provoking adverse reactions from national judges. All the implications of the autonomy of the Union legal order did not always become immediately clear either. In many cases it was a lengthy process of adaptation and learning in which the Court played a decisive role.[27]

3. Precedence or Primacy of Union Law

In retrospect it might seem evident that the autonomy of the Union legal order and the necessity for its uniform interpretation and application in all the Member States, automatically imply that Union provisions have precedence over national legislation in case of conflict. Since national courts and tribunals are under obligation, as was just seen, to apply Union rules alongside the provisions of national law, it is not unlikely that conflicts will result from this simultaneous application. The European Treaties contain no explicit provisions regarding the solution to be applied in such cases.[28] Attempts were therefore made to solve such conflicts in accordance with provisions of national law. However, few national legal systems provide for conflict rules of this nature.

In the United Kingdom, for instance, the European Communities Act 1972 provides for the necessary precedence by accepting the "legal effect" of Union

---

[24] art.267 TFEU [234].
[25] art.4(3) EU.
[26] *Unibet* (C-432/05) [2007] E.C.R. I-2271.
[27] First General Report (1967), p.563.
[28] One could, however, argue that art.4(3) EU [10] constitutes a legal ground on which to base this precedence.

provisions in the United Kingdom.[29] The same applies to the decisions of the Court regarding the meaning or effect of any of the Treaties, or the validity, meaning or effect of any Union instrument.[30] In relation to statute law, this means that the directly applicable Union provisions shall prevail even over future Acts of Parliament, if the latter are inconsistent with those instruments. It also means that by ratifying the European Treaties, the United Kingdom, like any other Member State, has assented to refrain from enacting legislation inconsistent with Union law.[31]

In the Netherlands, the Basic Law (Constitution) not only provides that the provisions of international treaties have precedence over existing national laws and regulations, it also specifies that the same applies to measures enacted by the institutions set up under those treaties and adds that this precedence applies in case of conflict between an existing Union rule and subsequent national law.[32]

The French Constitution provides, in general terms, that treaties or agreements, duly ratified or approved, shall, upon their publication, have authority superior to that of laws, subject, however, for each agreement or treaty, to its application by the other party.[33]

The German Constitution provides that the Federal Republic may, by legislation, transfer sovereign powers to intergovernmental institutions[34] and refers to the precedence of the general rules of international law.[35] It is only with difficulty that one can equate Union measures with the latter.

---

[29] European Communities Act 1972 s.2(1). See *Factortame* (C-213/89) [1990] E.C.R. I-2433; [1990] 3 C.M.L.R. 1, where the Court held that, "a court [in a dispute governed by Union law] which would grant interim relief, if it were not for a rule of national law, is obliged to set aside that rule", at E.C.R. I-2474(21). See also [2005] EWCA Civ 1191; Oakley, before the English Court of Appeal: sui generis nature of s.2.

[30] European Communities Act 1972 s.3(1).

[31] European Communities Act 1972 s.2(4) provides therefore that present and future enactments shall be construed and have effect subject to s.2. See *Hansard*, February 15, 1972, Vol. 831. This basic principle derives not only from the obligations explicitly accepted by the Member States when they became members of the Union, but, as was explained, from the very nature of the Union and Union law. Indeed, as mentioned, the existence of the Union depends upon the simultaneous and uniform application throughout the Union of all the provisions of the Treaties and of the acts of the institutions. This was clearly stated over and over again by the Court. See, for instance, *Pigs Marketing Board v Redmond* (83/78) [1978] E.C.R. 2347 at 2371(56); [1979] 1 C.M.L.R. 177 and *Commission v UK* (128/78) [1979] E.C.R. 419 at 428(9); [1979] 2 C.M.L.R. 45.

[32] Articles 66 and 67 of the Dutch Constitution; these provisions were incorporated in the Constitution in 1953.

[33] Article 55 of the French Constitution of 1958. In a judgment of 1962, the French Cour de Cassation held that a contested action had been carried out under an EEC decision and regulation which were, "acts regularly published and having acquired force of international treaties" (*Gazette du Palais*, December 9 to 11 (1970) 6–7). See also *Administration des Douanes v Jacques Vabre* [1975] C.M.L.R. 336, where the French Supreme Court clearly stated that the Treaty has an authority greater than that of national acts and is binding on the national courts. See, however, the decision of the Conseil d'Etat: *Syndicat Général des Fabricants de Semoules v Direction des Industries Agricoles* [1970] C.M.L.R. 395. It was only in October 1989 (31 years after the EEC Treaty came into force) that this French highest administrative jurisdiction finally recognised the precedence of Union law over national law!

[34] Article 24(1) of the German Constitution. See, however, the German Constitutional Court on the Treaty of Maastricht, October 12, 1993, 89 BVerfGE 155, at 185. As a former German Judge of the Court of Justice wrote: "[i]n the past, after some hesitations, the German Constitutional court assented to the developing supranational power of the European Union, though with provisions for extreme situations. The judgment on the EU Treaty reversed this situation fundamentally. The [German] Court returned to a nationalistic view of democracy and opened up ways of leaving the European Union regardless of juridical bonds and declared German authorities competent to ignore Union law. It is uncertain whether this tendency to re-nationalisation will continue or whether it will be overcome by another change in the case law of the Constitutional Court." Manfred Zuleeg, "European Constitution under Constitutional Constraints: The German Scenario", (1997) 22 E.L.Rev. Feb.

[35] Article 25 of the German Constitution.

The Italian Constitution is even less precise. It only provides that, "Italy's legal system conforms with the general principles recognised by international law".[36]

These German and Italian texts, and even the French Constitution, form a rather meagre legal basis for the obligation that national courts should give precedence to Union law over national law in case of conflict between the two; and what of those Member States whose Constitution contains no provisions in this respect? Furthermore, in certain cases the above-mentioned constitutional provisions were not considered by national judges as obliging them to accept the precedence of Union provisions over national rules.[37]

Even in the case of the Dutch Constitution, that is so explicit about precedence, doubts might subsist as to the precise consequences. Furthermore, if the sole legal basis for primacy of Union law over national law were national law itself, this supremacy would be at the mercy of the next constitutional amendment.

Another ground had therefore to be found which would be accepted by all national jurisdictions without reference to their particular national legal orders. This ground was obviously in the Union legal order itself. It is indeed accepted by all the Member States which, "have adhered to the Treaty on the same conditions, definitively and without any reservations other than those set out in the supplementary protocols".[38] The Court has always considered that the wording and the spirit of the Treaty make it impossible for Member States to accord precedence to a unilateral and subsequent measure over a legal system accepted by them on the basis of reciprocity. The Court also added that:

"[T]he executive force of [Union] law cannot vary from one State to another in deference to subsequent domestic laws, without jeopardising the attainment of the objectives of the Treaty set out in Article [4(3)] and giving rise to the discrimination referred to by Article [12]".[39]

Therefore:

"[T]he law stemming from the Treaty, an independent source of law, could not, because of its special and original nature, be overridden by domestic legal provisions, however framed, without being deprived of its character as [Union] law and without the legal basis of the [Union] itself being called into question".[40]

This also applies with regard to national constitutional provisions. The Court states that the effect of a Union measure cannot be affected by allegations that it runs counter to fundamental rights as formulated by the Constitution of a State.[41]

---

[36] Article 10(1) of the Italian Constitution.
[37] By a ruling of March 1, 1968 ((1968) *Recueil Dalloz-Sirey Jurisprudence* 286) the French Conseil d'Etat ruled that a French Court is bound to ensure the application of the national *lex posterior* to an existing Union rule, whatever the meaning and scope of Union law (Second General Report (1968), 453). The Commission considered this ruling incompatible with the legal obligations deriving from the Treaty. See also Cour de Cassation, October 22, 1970, *Contributions Indirectes v Ramel* [1971] C.M.L.R. 315.
[38] *San Michele v High Authority* (Joined Cases 9/65 and 58/65) [1967] E.C.R. 1 at 30.
[39] *Costa v ENEL* (6/64) [1964] E.C.R. 585 at 594; [1964] C.M.L.R. 425. This was once again emphasised by the Court in *Commission v UK ("Tachographs")* (128/78) [1979] E.C.R. 419 at 429; [1979] 2 C.M.L.R. 45.
[40] *Costa v ENEL* (6/64), above, fn.39. See also *Internationale Handelsgesellschaft v Einfuhr-und Vorratsstelle Getreide* (11/70) [1970] E.C.R. 1125 at 1134(3); [1972] C.M.L.R. 255.
[41] *Costa v ENEL* (6/64), above, fn.39 and *Nold v Commission* (4/73) [1974] E.C.R. 491; [1974] 2 C.M.L.R. 338.

To put it simply once more: either Union law stands by itself, is uniformly applied and has precedence over all domestic law, or it does not exist. This view is now generally accepted in all the Member States.[42]

Attached to the Treaty of Lisbon is a Declaration concerning primacy, which reads as follows:

"The Conference recalls that, in accordance with well settled case law of the Court of Justice of the European Union, the Treaties and the law adopted by the Union on the basis of the Treaties have primacy over the law of Member States, under the conditions laid down by the said case law."[43]

The general principle of Union law's precedence over national law having been established, it is necessary to examine some of its more concrete consequences. As far as any national court or tribunal is concerned, the Court has described their obligations as follows. Directly applicable rules of Union law are a direct source of rights and duties for all those affected thereby. The latter also include any national court whose task it is, as an organ of a Member State, to protect, in cases within its jurisdiction, the rights conferred upon individuals by Union law. In accordance with the principle of precedence, Treaty provisions and directly applicable Union measures, by their coming into force, automatically render any conflicting provisions of current national law inapplicable.

It follows that every national court, in cases within its jurisdiction, must apply Union law in its entirety and protect the rights the latter confers upon natural or legal persons. As mentioned before, it must set aside any conflicting provision of national law, whether prior or subsequent to the Union provision. It is not necessary for the national court to request or await the prior setting aside of such national provisions by legislative or other means.[44]

As far as legislative bodies are concerned, the Court indicated that the principle of precedence precludes the valid adoption of new national legislative measures to the extent that they would be incompatible with Union provisions.[45]

Where other national authorities are concerned, it is clear that respect for the precedence of Union law and the obligations resulting for Member States from the Treaties[46] not only prevents them from enacting measures which are incompatible with existing Union provisions, but also imposes upon them the obligation to abolish all *existing* contrary measures, whatever their nature. Even where these measures are no longer applied, their maintenance gives rise to an ambiguous situation: "by maintaining, as regards those subject to the law who are concerned, a state of uncertainty as to the possibilities which are available to them of relying on [Union] law".[47]

---

[42] It might be of interest to mention some of the earliest and most important rulings of national courts since they constitute essential steps towards recognition of the Union legal order and its implications. In Belgium reference must be made to a decision of 1971 of the Cour de Cassation in the case *Belgian State v Fromagerie Franco-Suisse* [1972] C.M.L.R. 373: the primacy of the Treaty results from the very nature of international treaty law. In France, Cour de Cassation, 1975, *Administration des Douanes v Jacques Vabre et al.* ([1972] C.M.L.R. 336) and finally also the French Conseil d'Etat: *Maurice Boisdet*, September 24, 1990: [1991] 1 C.M.L.R. 3.

[43] Declaration 17 [2008] O.J. C 115/344.

[44] *Amministrazione delle Finanze dello Stato v Simmenthal* (106/77) [1978] E.C.R. 629 at 643–644 (14–18 and 21, 22, 24); [1978] 3 C.M.L.R. 263.

[45] *Simmenthal* (106/77), above, fn.44 at 17. See also *Eridania v Minister of Agriculture and Forestry* (230/78) [1979] E.C.R. 2749.

[46] art.4(3) EU [10].

[47] *Commission v France* (167/73) [1974] E.C.R. 359 at 372(41); [1974] 2 C.M.L.R. 216. See also *Commission v Italy* (159/78) [1979] E.C.R. 3247; [1980] 3 C.M.L.R. 446 and *Commission v Ireland* (61/77) [1978] E.C.R. 417 at 442; [1978] 2 C.M.L.R. 466.

The question was raised whether or not national authorities were obliged to modify a decision based on incorrect interpretation of Union law after this was established by a Court judgment clarifying Union law. The Court here made a distinction between decisions of national courts not subject to appeal or other remedies and decisions of an administrative body. In the first case, the Court ruled that the, "principle of cooperation under Art. [4 EU] does not require a national court to disapply its internal rules of procedure in order to review and set aside a final judicial decision if that decision should be contrary to Union law".[48] In the case of an administrative body, art.4(3) EU imposes an obligation to review a final administrative decision, where an application for such review is made to it, in order to take account of the interpretation of the relevant provision given in the meantime by the Court. This, however, only applies where, under national law, the body has the power to reopen its decision; in the case under review, the administrative decision became final only as a result of a national court judgment against whose decision there is no judicial remedy; that judgment was incorrect, in the light of a subsequent judgment of the Court, and without a preliminary question being asked as provided for under the Treaty; finally, the person concerned complained to the administrative body immediately after becoming aware of the preliminary decision.[49]

It follows from the preceding remarks that autonomy of the Union legal order, direct effect and precedence of Union rules over national measures all result from the particular nature of Union law.

A final aspect which needs to be mentioned in this respect is the reference by the Court to the usefulness[50] or effectiveness[51] of Union acts to justify the right of individuals to rely on obligations imposed by directives. Those acts are not directly applicable, since the choice is left to the national authorities as to the form and method of implementing the obligations imposed upon them by those acts. In other words, the implementation is left, within limits, to their discretion. Consequently, according to the present case law, directives have no direct effect and persons cannot invoke them in national courts. However, the Court admits, as was seen before,[52] that provisions of directives can have direct effect, especially after the time limit set for their transposition into national law has elapsed. Similarly, interested parties have the right to ask national courts to determine whether the competent national authorities, in exercising the choice which is left to them in transposing the directive, have kept within the limits of their discretionary powers.[53] However, whether national authorities have or have not exercised their discretionary power, for instance, to make a derogation, is a matter for the discretion of the legislative or administrative authorities of the Member State. It cannot, therefore, be subject to legal review on the basis of the provisions of the directive. "It is the duty of the national court before which the directive is invoked to determine whether the disputed national measure falls outside the margin of the discretion of the Member State."[54]

[48] *Kapferer v Schlank & Schick GmBH* (C-234/04) [2006] E.C.R. I-2585.
[49] *Kühne & Heitz* (C-453/00) [2004] E.C.R. I-837.
[50] *Nederlandse Ondernemingen v Inspecteur der Invoerrechten en Accijnzen* (51/76) [1977] E.C.R. 113 at 127(29); [1977] 1 C.M.L.R. 413.
[51] *ENKA v Inspecteur der Invoerrechten en Accijnzen* (38/77) [1977] E.C.R. 2203 at 2211(9); [1978] 2 C.M.L.R. 212.
[52] See above Ch.3: The Legal Acts of the Union.
[53] *ENKA* (38/77) (quoted above, fn.51) at 2212(10).
[54] *Nederlandse Ondernemingen* (51/76) (quoted above, fn.50) at 127(29).

But it is also the duty of the national court when it applies domestic law, and in particular legislative provisions specifically adopted for the purpose of implementing the requirements of a directive, to interpret national law, so far as possible, in the light of the wording and the purpose of the directive concerned in order to achieve the results sought by the directive and consequently comply with the obligation provided for in the Treaty and according to which, "a directive shall be binding as to the results to be achieved".[55] It might be useful to repeat once more, that this duty of the national court follows from the obligation imposed by the Treaty on the Member States, to take all appropriate measures to ensure the fulfilment of the obligations arising out of the Treaty or resulting from action taken by the institutions (here the directive) and that that obligation is binding on all the authorities of the Member States, including, for matters within their jurisdiction, the courts.[56]

In this respect it should be noted that, as will be discussed below, Member States that breach Union law, are, under given conditions, liable for the harm caused to individuals by this breach.

4. Member States' Liability for Breach of Union Law

As was pointed out in the previous chapter on Legal Acts of the Union, failure of a Member State to properly transpose a directive (which constitutes an infringement of Union law) makes that State liable for loss and damages caused to individuals by that breach, the so-called Francovich[57] liability. More generally, as is explained below in Ch.8: The Commission, Member States are not only responsible to the Union for their infringements of Union law, they are also liable for possible damage caused by their infringement to legal or natural persons. This liability of a Member State applies for acts or failures to act not only of the executive, but also of the legislature and even, in certain circumstances, of the judicature.[58]

According to the Court,[59] this liability is, "inherent in the system of the Treaty," and a, "further basis . . . is to be found in Article [4(3)] of the EU Treaty". The Court added that although the liability of the Member State to make good loss and damage caused to individuals by breaches of Union law for which it can be held responsible is required by Union law, the conditions under which there is a right to reparation depend on the nature of the breach, and whether the breached provision did confer rights upon individuals.[60]

Like the principles of direct effect and supremacy of Union law over national law, the principle of state liability for breaches of Union law, finds its origin in Union law itself, as interpreted by the Court. No other justifications are necessary, the Court being, by agreement among the Member States, the supreme arbiter. The moment one starts discussing what might have influenced the Court in reaching its conclusions, one risks bringing not only the conclusions, but even the basic principles into

---

[55] art.288,3 TFEU [249,3].

[56] *Pfeiffer and Others* (Joined Cases C-397/01, C-398/01, C-399/01, C-400/01, C-401/01, C-402/01 and C-403/01), [2004] E.C.R. I-8835.

[57] *Francovich and Others* (C-6/90 and C-9/90), [1991] E.C.R. I-5357.

[58] See, for instance, *Köbler* (C-224/01) [2003] E.C.R. I-10239 and *Traghetti v Italy* (C-173/03) [2006] E.C.R. I-5177, where the Court found Italy had infringed the Treaty by limiting the responsibility of the courts to cases of intentional fault and serious misconduct, excluding liability in connection with the interpretation of provisions of law.

[59] *Köbler* (C-224/01), above, fn.58.

[60] See *Paul* (C-222/02) [2004] E.C.R. I-9425.

question. The consequence might be that national courts, like the German Supreme Court, would decide, for instance, that their constitutions prevail over Union law. This approach risks creating tension and unsettles the Union legal order itself. These speculations find their place in political science but not in an analysis of a legal system whose acceptance by the Member States and in particular by the national judges is not always evident, although they are bound, by the obligations assumed by the States, to accept and apply the law as it is handed down by the European courts. This does not mean uncritical agreement (which is different from acceptance) with all Court decisions. Although a critical approach might lead the Court itself to modify its case law, as it did in the *Keck and Mithouard* judgment,[61] it has no place in a book that endeavours to describe the law as it stands.

5. Infringement of Union Law by Natural or Legal Persons

It follows from the Treaty provisions concerning the jurisdiction of the Court[62] that regulations adopted jointly by the Parliament and the Council or by the Council may provide for penalties to be imposed upon individuals or undertakings in case of infringement by them of provisions of said regulations.[63]

As for infringement of Union law by natural and legal person when the Union legislation does not specifically provide any penalty, the Treaty requires, according to the Court, the Member States to take all measures necessary to guarantee the application and effectiveness of Union law.[64] While the choice of penalties remains within their discretion, they must ensure that the infringements are penalised under conditions, both procedural and substantive, which are analogous to those applicable to infringements of national law of a similar nature and importance, and which in any event, make the penalty effective, proportionate and dissuasive.[65]

In order to ensure the efficacy of the rules adopted by the institutions, non-compliance with which may have serious consequences, Member States may be required to apply criminal penalties to certain forms of conduct. However, the determination of the type and level of the criminal penalties to be applied does not fall within the Union's sphere of competence.

6. Sources of Union Law

As was previously indicated, the Union legal order has its own sources, which consist not only of the European Treaties and the acts of the institutions issued in pursuance of the powers conferred upon them (regulations, directives, decisions, agreements, etc.),[66] but also of the rules relating to the application of this

---

[61] *Keck and Mithouard* (Joined Cases C-267/91 and C-268/91) [1993] E.C.R. I-6097.
[62] art.261 TFEU [229].
[63] Examples are Regulation 1/2003 [2003] O.J. L1/1, implementing the rules on competition, arts 23 and 24; Regulation 1017/68 [1968] O.J. L175/3, applying rules of competition to transport, art.22 (amended by Regulation 1/2003, above); and Regulation 726/2004 [2004] O.J. L136/1 laying down Union procedures for the authorisation and supervision of medicinal products, art.84(3). See also Directive 91/308 [1991] O.J. L166/77 on the prevention of the use of the financial system for the purpose of money laundering, as amended, accompanying statement committing the Member States to enact criminal legislation for infringement of the Directive.
[64] This obligation follows from art.4(3) EU [10].
[65] *Hansen* (326/88) [1990] E.C.R. I-2911.
[66] See above, Ch.3: The Legal Acts of the Union.

primary and secondary Union law. These rules comprise international law, in so far as applicable[67] and the general principles of law such as equal treatment (non-discrimination), proportionality, legal certainty, etc.[68] including the fundamental rights. The latter play an important role, as the Court pointed out: "respect for fundamental rights forms an integral part of the general principles of law protected by the Court of Justice", and added that, "the protection of such rights, whilst inspired by the constitutional traditions common to Member States, must be ensured within the framework . . . and objectives of the [Union]".[69] A reference to those fundamental rights is to be found in the Treaty on European Union, which provides amongst others, that the:

> "Union recognises the rights, freedoms and principles set out in the Charter of Fundamental Rights of the European Union of 7 December 2000, as adopted at Strasburg on 12 December 2007, which shall have the same legal value as the Treaties."[70]

The Treaty adds that:

> "Fundamental rights, as guaranteed by the European Convention for the Protection of Human Rights and Fundamental Freedoms and as they result from the constitutional traditions common to the Member States, shall constitute general principles of the [Union]'s law".[71]

The EU Treaty also provides that the Union shall accede to this European Convention.[72]

A Charter of fundamental rights of the European Union was "solemnly proclaimed" (whatever legal meaning that has) by the Parliament, the Council and

---

[67] Agreements concluded by the Union with third States or international organisations under art.218 TFEU [300], are governed by the rules of international law. But, according to the Court (see, e.g. *Greece v Commission* (30/88) [1989] E.C.R. 3711; [1991] 2 C.M.L.R. 169), "the provisions of an agreement concluded by the Council under [TFEU Art.218 [300] and 217 [310]], form, as from the entry into force of the agreement, an integral part of the [Union] legal system". On the other hand, as the Court pointed out, when exercising their rights to lay down Union rules, the institutions are not bound by provisions of international law, unless the Union itself has assumed the rights and obligations resulting for the Member States from international agreements to which they are parties, and unless the provisions of those agreements have direct effect within the Union: *International Fruit Company v Productschap voor Groenten en Fruit* (Joined Cases 21/72, 22/72, 23/72, 24/72) [1972] E.C.R. 1219 at 1226(8); [1975] 2 C.M.L.R. 1. See also [1972] E.C.R. 1219 at 1227(18), and *Åhlström v Commission* (Joined Cases "wood pulp" 89 etc./85) [1988] E.C.R. 5233; [1988] 4 C.M.L.R. 901, "the conduct of the Commission is covered by the territoriality principle as universally recognised by public international law". As for Treaty precedence over agreements concluded between Member States before its entrance into force, see *Commission v Italy* (10/61) [1962] E.C.R. 1 at 10; [1962] C.M.L.R. 187. The precedence of Union law over all other applicable provisions, including international law, is recognised by the European Communities Act 1972, ss.2(1) and (4).

[68] See *Verli-Wallace v Commission* (159/82) [1983] E.C.R. 2711 at 2718 (8) and below, Ch.9: The Court of Justice of the European Union.

[69] *Internationale Handelsgesellschaft v Einfuhr-und Vorratstelle Getreide* (11/70) [1970] E.C.R. 1125 at 1134 (4); [1972] C.M.L.R. 255. See also *Einfuhr-und Vorratstelle v Köster* (25/70) [1970] E.C.R. 1161 at 1176 (36); [1972] C.M.L.R. 255, where the Court found that a system of licences for import and export, involving a deposit, did not violate any right of a fundamental nature and *Hauer v Land Rheinland-Pfalz* (44/79) [1979] E.C.R. 3727; [1980] 3 C.M.L.R. 42, where the Court examined whether a Union regulation violated the right of property and the free exercise of professional activity. Also the inviolability of the domicile in *Hoechst v Commission* (46/87 R) [1987] E.C.R. 1549; [1991] 4 C.M.L.R. 410.

[70] art.6(1) EU.

[71] art.6(3) EU.

[72] art.6(2) EU.

the Commission at the end of the year 2000.[73] It refers to the above-mentioned source of Union law in addition to the Social Charters adopted by the Union and the Council of Europe and the case law of the Court of Justice and of the European Court of Human Rights. According to the EU Treaty this Charter now has, "the same legal value as the Treaties."[74]

7. APPLICATION OF NATIONAL AND INTERNATIONAL LAW BY THE EUROPEAN COURTS

The question of the applicability of the national law of the Member States by the Union institutions was raised on several occasions before the Court. The latter, however, decided that it lacked the competence to apply the internal law of the Member States.[75] Consequently, the Court cannot accept a claim that by taking a decision an institution has violated national law. Neither can the Court decide on the interpretation of a national provision.[76] However, application of national law by the Court takes place where the Treaty refers explicitly to national concepts.[77] This is the case, for instance, where reference is made to companies and firms formed in accordance with the law of a Member State.[78] Also when the Treaty provides that, in the case of non-contractual liability, the Union shall make good any damage caused by its institutions or by its servants, "in accordance with the general principles common to the laws of the Member States".[79] Similarly, when the Court is called upon to solve a question for which there are no Treaty provisions, it must solve the problem, "by reference to the rules acknowledged by the legislation, the learned writings and the case law of the member countries".[80]

In numerous cases the Court was called upon to interpret[81] and apply international law. According to the General Court (GC), it is only in case the Union intended to implement a specific obligation assumed in the framework of an international agreement, or when a Union act refers explicitly to a specific provision of an international agreement, that the Union courts are called upon to control the legality of the Union act in regard to that agreement.[82] In a recent judgement, the Court held that the validity of the Directive on ship-source

[73] [2000] O.J. C364/8.

[74] art.6(1) EU.

[75] See, e.g. *Stork v High Authority* (1/58) [1959] E.C.R. 17; *Geitling v High Authority* (Joined Cases 36/59, 37/59, 38/59, 39/59 and 40/59) [1960] E.C.R. 423. See, however, *Klöckner v High Authority* (Joined Cases 17/61 and 20/61) [1962] E.C.R. 325 and *Commission v Italy* (159/78) [1979] E.C.R. 3247.

[76] *Deutsche Grammophon v Metro* (78/70) [1971] E.C.R. 487 at 498 (3); [1971] C.M.L.R. 631.

[77] See *Wünsche v Einfuhr- und Vorratstelle Getreide* (50/71) [1972] E.C.R. 53 at 64(6); [1973] C.M.L.R. 35.

[78] art.54 TFEU [48]. See, e.g. *Nold v High Authority* (18/57) [1959] E.C.R. 41 at 48.

[79] art.340 TFEU [288].

[80] *Algera v Common Assembly* (Joined Cases 7/56, 3/57, 4/57, 5/57, 6/57 and 7/57) [1957–1958] E.C.R. 39 at 55. Another example is the definition of "misuse of power" (art.263 TFEU [230]) based on a comparative study by the Advocate-General of this concept in the municipal law of the Member States: *ASSIDER v High Authority* (3/54) [1954–1955] E.C.R. 63 at 74.

[81] See *Dior E.A.* (Joined Cases C-300/98 and C-392/98) [2000] E.C.R. I-11307, where the Court stated that when the judicial authorities of the Member States are called upon to protect rights falling within the Agreement establishing the WTO, approved on behalf of the Union, and a case is brought before the Court in accordance with art.267 TFEU [234], the Court has jurisdiction to interpret art.50 of the TRIPS Agreement set out in an annex to the WTO Agreement.

[82] *Cordis v Commission* (T-18/99) [2001] E.C.R. II-913.(45–46).

pollution[83] could not be assessed either in the light of the International Convention for the prevention of pollution from ships, nor in the light of the United Nations Convention on the Law of the Sea (Montego Bay).[84]

With regard to World Trade Organisation (WTO) agreements, the Court stated that they are, "not in principle among the rules in the light of which the Court is to review the legality," of Union measures.[85] However, the Court also stated that the WTO agreement has been signed by the Community and subsequently approved by decision; therefore the provisions of that convention form an integral part of the Community legal order. Within the framework of that legal order the Court has jurisdiction to give preliminary rulings concerning the interpretation of that agreement.[86] The same applies, for instance, to the 1999 Montreal Convention for the unification of certain rules for international carriage by air; the Court found that it was an integral part of Union law and had primacy over secondary Union legislation.[87]

Neither can the WTO rules constitute a basis for reparation of damages caused by a violation by the Union of WTO rules, despite the existence of actual and certain damage and a direct causal link between the damage suffered and the conduct of the defendant institutions.[88]

Where bilateral agreements concluded before accession are concerned, the Treaty provides[89] that the rights and obligations arising from them are not affected by the Treaty and these provisions of international law must therefore be applied by the Court. However, the Treaty adds that Member States must take all appropriate steps to eliminate the incompatibilities with the Treaties.[90] The Court also decided that even when an Union act had been declared incompatible with WTO rules by the dispute settlement body, an economic operator could not invoke this incompatibility in a national court.[91]

8. APPLICATION OF UNION LAW BY THE NATIONAL COURTS

As was seen, direct effect of Union rules means that:

"[I]t is the national courts which are entrusted with ensuring the legal protection which citizens derive from the direct effect of the provisions of [Union] law. Accordingly, in the absence of [Union] rules on the subject, it is for the domestic legal system of each Member State to designate the courts having jurisdiction and to determine the procedural conditions governing actions at law intended to ensure the protection of the rights which the citizens have from the direct effect of [Union] law, it being understood that such conditions cannot be less favourable than those relating to similar actions of a domestic nature".[92]

---

[83] Directive 2005/35 [2005] O.J. L255/1.
[84] *Intertanko and Others* (C-308/06) [2008] E.C.R. I-4057.
[85] *Portugal v Council* (C-149/96) [1999] E.C.R. I-8395.
[86] *Merck Genericos* (C-431/05) [2007] E.C.R. I-7001.
[87] *Wallentin-Hermann* (C-549/07) [2008] E.C.R. I- 22.12.08.
[88] *Fiamm and Others v European Communities* (T-69/00) [2005] E.C.R. II-5393.
[89] See art.351 TFEU [307].
[90] See *Budejovicky Budvar* (C-216/01) [2003] E.C.R. I-13617 and *Commission v Sweden* (249/06) [2009] E.C.R. 03.03.09; where the Court found that Sweden had breached art.351,2 TFEU.
[91] *Van Parys NV* (C-377/02) [2005] E.C.R I-1465.
[92] *Rewe v Landwirtschaftskammer Saarland* (33/76) [1976] E.C.R. 1989.

As was briefly pointed out above, Union law does not require national courts to raise of their own motion an issue concerning a possible breach of provisions of Union law, where examination of that issue would oblige them to abandon the passive role assigned to them by going beyond the ambit of the dispute defined by the parties.[93] However, where by virtue of domestic law, courts must raise of their own motion points of law based on binding domestic rules, which have not been raised by the parties, such an obligation also exists where binding Union rules are concerned.[94] The situation is the same, if domestic law confers on courts a discretion to apply of their own volition binding rules of law.

Indeed, pursuant to the principle of co-operation laid down in the Treaty,[95] it is for the national courts to ensure the legal protection which persons derive from the direct effect of provisions of Union law.[96] The basic rule remains, indeed, that it is the national judge who is, in the first place, responsible for the implementation, application, and interpretation of Union law when the parties refer to it in disputes brought before him.

In a 2003 judgment the Court confirmed once more that in the case of a breach of a directive by legislative provisions or by provisions of collective agreements introducing discrimination contrary to that directive:

> "[T]he national courts are required to set aside that discrimination, using all the means at their disposal, and in particular by applying those provisions for the benefit of the class placed at a disadvantage, and are not required to request or await the setting aside of the provision by the legislature, by collective negotiation or otherwise".[97]

In 1993, the Commission published a Notice on the co-operation between the Commission and the national judges according to which the national judge can, among other things, call upon the Commission for any help he might need in cases before him involving Union law.[98]

9. CONCLUSIONS

As shown by the foregoing considerations, the Union legal order grew and developed mainly at the hands of the Union judges.[99] Over the years, the Court has played an essential role in consolidating the autonomy of Union law, vis-à-vis

---

[93] *van Schijndel* (Joined Cases C-430/93 and C-431/93) [1995] E.C.R. I-4705; see also *Peterbroeck* (C-312/93) [1995] E.C.R. I-4599, where the Court held that Union law precluded the application of a national procedural rule that prevented the courts from raising of their own motion a question concerning the compatibility of a national rule with Union law, when the parties were prevented from doing so after a given period. In *Océano Grupo Editorial and Salvat Editores* (Joined Cases C-240/98, C-241/98, C-242/98, C-243/98 and C-244/98) [2000] E.C.R. I-4941, the Court went much farther and stated that, "the requirement for an interpretation in conformity with the Directive requires the national court, in particular to favour the interpretation that would allow it to decline of its own motion the jurisdiction conferred upon it by virtue of an unfair term."

[94] *Rewe* (33/76) [1976] E.C.R. 1989; [1997] 2 C.M.L.R. 1.

[95] art.4(3) EU [10].

[96] *Factortame* (C-213/89) [1990] E.C.R. I/243; [1990] 3 C.M.L.R. 375.

[97] *Kutz-Bauer* (C-187/00) [2003] E.C.R. I-2741.

[98] [1993] O.J. C39/6. See also *Tremblay* (C-91/95 P) [1996] E.C.R. I-5547; [1997] 4 C.M.L.R. 211.

[99] Of course, the Member States and the institutions did also contribute to the consolidation and development of Union law; see, e.g. the Convention on the Law applicable to Contractual Obligations ([1980] O.J. L266/1).

municipal and international law, by emphasising its originality and by imposing its precedence. It goes without saying that this task would have been impossible without the co-operation, understanding and adaptability of the national judges; for example by asking for preliminary rulings they gave the Court the opportunity to fulfil its task. Nonetheless, the Union Court was, and still is, the driving force.

It should be clear also that the task of the Court is not limited to applying, developing and interpreting Union law *stricto sensu*. According to the Treaty,[100] the Court shall ensure that "the law" is observed. The term "law" in this provision, and as it is understood by the Court, refers to the concept of what is right, much more so than to anything that is described and analysed in this book. Seen in this light, the European Union appears—beyond all the limitations, ambiguities, hesitations and conflicts—as a legal, political, social and economic system that, thanks to its balanced institutional structure and inherent potential, constitutes the only possible solution for Europe's problems and the only hope for its development.

Further Reading

René Barents, *The Autonomy of Community Law* (Kluwer Law International, 2004).

Marten Breuer, "State liability for judicial wrongs and Community law: the case *Gerbhard Käbler v Austria*" (2004) E.L.Rev. 243.

Mario Mendez, "The Impact of WTO rulings in the Community legal order", (2004) E.L.Rev. 517.

Liv Jaeckel, "The duty to protect fundamental rights in the European Community", (2003) E.L.Rev. 508.

Margot Horspool and Matthieu Humphreys, *European Union Law*, 5th edn (2008, Oxford University Press).

[100] art.19 EU [220].

PART TWO: THE INSTITUTIONS AND BODIES OF THE UNION AND THE FINANCING OF ITS ACTIVITIES

INTRODUCTION

Among the various bodies established by, or in pursuance of, the Treaties, seven are referred to as being part of the "institutional framework" of the Union: the European Parliament (Parliament), the European Council, the Council, the European Commission (the Commission), the Court of Justice of the European Union, the European Central Bank (ECB) and the Court of Auditors. The aim of this framework is to promote the values of the Union, advance its objectives, serve its interests (those of its citizens and those of the Member States) and ensure the consistency, effectiveness and continuity of its policies and actions.[1]

What distinguishes an institution from other Union bodies is the fact that the former, generally speaking, can "act", i.e. take binding decisions[2] and that its members are either elected nationally (Council and Parliament) or appointed by the governments of the Member States or by the Council. The other organs operate in specific fields and either have a purely advisory task or take decisions which are not generally binding.

Only the Union,[3] the European Investment Bank (EIB), the Supply Agency of Euratom, the ECB and a few other bodies and agencies have legal personality and capacity.[4] When the Union acquires or disposes of property or is party to legal proceedings (outside the Court of Justice) it is represented by the Commission. However, the Union is represented by each of the institutions, by virtue of their administrative autonomy, in matters relating to their respective operation.[5] With

---

[1] art.13(1) EU. Other bodies set up by the Treaties are, for instance, the Economic and Social Committee (arts 300 and 301 to 304 TFEU [7(2)]), the Committee of the Regions (arts 300 and 305 to 307 TFEU [7(2)]), a European System of Central Banks and a European Central Bank (art.8 EC), the European Investment Bank (EIB) (arts 308 and 309 TFEU [9] and Protocol on the Statute of the EIB), the Monetary Committee (art.134 TFEU [114]) and the Committee of Permanent Representatives (art.240(3) TFEU [207(1)]). For bodies/agencies set up by the institutions in pursuance of powers conferred upon them by the Treaties see, for instance, the European Environmental Agency (Regulation 1210/90 [1990] O.J. L 120/1 and below, Ch.13).
[2] This follows from the wording of art.13(2) TFEU [7]: "each institution shall act within the limits of the powers conferred on in the Treaties".
[3] art.47 TFEU [281].
[4] art.335 TFEU [281]; see *Lachmüller v Commission* (Joined Cases 43 etc. /59) [1960] E.C.R. 463 at 472: "that personality is one of public law." See also *Commission v Council* (22/70) [1971] E.C.R. 263 at 274(4); C.M.L.R. 335, where the Court decided that having this legal personality, "means that in its external relations the Union enjoys the capacity to establish contractual links with third countries over the whole field of objectives defined in Part I of the Treaty." For the EIB, see art.129 TFEU [107], and for the Supply Agency, Euratom, art.54; see also Court Ruling 1/78, [1978] E.C.R. 2151. Other organs with legal personality are, among others, the European Centre for the Development of Vocational Training, the European Foundation for the Improvement of Living and Working Conditions and the European Environment Agency; these are described below in Ch.13.
[5] art.335 TFEU [282].

the exception of the Common Foreign and Security Policy and other cases provided in the Treaties,[6] agreements with one or more States or international organisations, are negotiated by the Commission and concluded by the Council for the Union.[7]

The first European institutions, i.e. the High Authority, the Common Assembly, the Special Council of Ministers and the Court of Justice were set up by the Treaty of Paris of 1951 establishing the European Coal and Steel Community (ECSC).[8] Similar institutions: an Assembly, a Council, a Commission and a Court of Justice, were set up by the Treaties of Rome establishing the European Economic Community and the European Community for Atomic Energy (Euratom). In theory this meant 12 institutions: three of each kind. However, the Convention on certain institutions common to the European Communities[9] provided for a single Assembly and a single Court of Justice for the three Communities.

Nonetheless this left three Councils and the High Authority plus two Commissions, beside the one Assembly and the one Court; a total of eight institutions. A further rationalisation was introduced by the so-called Merger Treaty,[10] which established the "Council of the European Communities" to replace the three Councils and the "Commission of the European Communities" to replace the High Authority and the EEC and Euratom Commissions. These four institutions exercised, from then on, the powers and jurisdiction conferred by the three Treaties on the various institutions they replaced, in accordance with the provisions of the relevant Treaties.[11] A fifth institution was added by the EU Treaty that "upgraded" the Court of Auditors. As indicated above, the Treaty of Lisbon included the European Council and the ECB among the institutions.

It might be interesting to note that, according to the Preamble of the Merger Treaty, the merger of the institutions is seen as a step in the direction of the "unification of the three Communities". This "exercise" was carried out by the draft Treaty on a Constitution for Europe that amalgamates all the existing Treaty texts, as amended, into a single one. The Treaty of Lisbon maintains the three Treaties.

---

[6] art.27(1) EU; for the representation in other matters, see art.335 TFEU [282].

[7] art.218 TFEU [300(1) and (2)].

[8] art.7 ECSC (does no longer exist).

[9] This Convention was annexed to the EEC and Euratom Treaties and signed, together with these Treaties, at Rome on April 25, 1957. It was repealed by then art.9(1) EU which, however, retained its essential elements.

[10] Treaty establishing a single Council and a single Commission of the European Communities, signed at Brussels on April 8, 1965. This Treaty was also repealed by then art.9(1) EU. Its essential provisions were, however, retained, and according to its then art.11(2) there will be no change in the legal effects of the Acts in force adopted on the basis of the Treaties.

[11] arts 1 and 3 Convention; arts 1 and 9 Merger Treaty.

Chapter Five

The European Parliament[1] ("Parliament")

As indicated above, the European Treaties originally referred to this institution as the "Assembly", and for a long time there was strong opposition from the Council and from several Member States to the use of the term "Parliament" to designate this institution.

However, in 1962, the Assembly decided to call itself the European Parliament[2] and since then the other institutions, including the Court of Justice, but except for a while the Council,[3] adopted that denomination. As for the Union acts that require consultation of the Assembly, they have, except for the first few years, always referred to the "European Parliament".[4]

Finally, the name was formally changed in the Treaties, albeit in an indirect way, by the Single European Act (SEA), which refers to the institutions "designated as referred to hereafter" and all the references to this institution, further down in that Treaty, are always to the European Parliament.

Whether the Assembly was well advised in modifying its name, and having it formally changed to Parliament, can be questioned. Not so much because the institution does not, indeed, have all the powers which are characteristic of national democratic parliaments, i.e. the exclusive power to legislate and the power of taxation, but because the name Parliament has created the illusion that democratic control, as understood nationally, already existed within the Union. Although the SEA and even more so the Treaties of Maastricht, Amsterdam and Nice have extended, as shall be seen hereafter, the powers of Parliament in the legislative field, Parliament is not a parliament in the generally accepted sense of the word. Or, as the German Constitutional Court recently wrote: the European Parliament, "is not a body of representation of a sovereign European people",[5] and it shall never be.

1. THE MEMBERS OF PARLIAMENT

Parliament consists of "representatives of the Union's citizens".[6] The Nice Treaty provided that their number, "shall not exceed 732".[7] However, from January 1,

---

[1] art.14 EU and arts 223–234 TFEU [189 to 201].
[2] Resolution of March 30, [1962] J.O. 1045. On March 20, 1958 the Assembly had decided to call itself the "European Parliamentary Assembly".
[3] See, e.g. the answer to Parliamentary Question No.398/77 in which the Council stated that the denomination of any one of the institutions could only be amended by a treaty amending the existing Treaties [1977] O.J. C270/18.
[4] See, e.g. Regulation 214/79 concerning the European Regional Development Fund [1979] O.J. L35/1.
[5] BVerfG, 2vE 2/08vm 30.6.2009, *Absatz-Nr* (1–421).
[6] art.14(2) EU [189], which also provides that the number shall not exceed 750, plus the President.
[7] art.2,17 Treaty of Nice modifying the then art.189(2) of the EC Treaty, [2001] O.J. C80/20.

2007 until the end of the 2004–2009 session there were 785 members[8] and for the 2009–2014 session on there are 736 members, which means that all the Member States will see their membership numbers reduced.[9]

The exact composition is to be decided by the Council, with the Parliament's consent.[10]

(1) Election of the Members

Until the first direct elections in 1979, the members of Parliament were designated by the respective national parliaments from among their members,[11] which meant dual membership. Although the ECSC Treaty[12] already provided for election by direct universal suffrage, it was not until September 20, 1976, that the Act concerning direct election was finally adopted by the Representatives of the Member States in Council: according to this Act, elections by direct universal suffrage should be held, "in accordance with a uniform procedure in all Member States".[13] The latest version of the Rules of Procedure of Parliament (7th parliamentary term, December 2009) provided in r.1 that:

> "[T]he European Parliament is the assembly elected pursuant to the Treaties, the Act of September 20, 1976 concerning the election of the members of the European Parliament by direct universal suffrage and national legislation deriving from the Treaties".[14]

Parliament was to draw up proposals and the Council, after obtaining the assent of Parliament, was to lay down the appropriate provisions, which it shall recommend to Member States for adoption in accordance with their respective constitutional requirements. For the Member States, nothing binding, in other words. Since it was not possible to agree on such procedures, the 1979, 1984, 1989, 1994, 1999 and 2004 elections were held in accordance with the method of voting decided nationally.[15] In 2002, the Act concerning direct election was amended by a Council Decision to enable members to be elected by direct universal suffrage in accordance with principles common to all Member States, while leaving Member States free to apply their national provisions in respect of aspects not governed by the Act.[16] The latter now provides that the members of

---

[8] [2005] art.24 Act of Accession.
[9] Act of Accession art.9.
[10] art.14(2)2 EU.
[11] This was done according to a procedure laid down by each Member State. See former art.138 EC which lapsed on July 17, 1978 in accordance with art.14 of the Act concerning direct election. MEPs receive a uniform salary of €5,677 (Council Decision of April 27, 1999). However, this is not the case presently (2010).
[12] art.21(3) ECSC (no longer valid).
[13] Act concerning direct election of representatives of the European Parliament by direct universal suffrage annexed to Council Decision 76/787 of September 20, 1976, [1976] O.J. L278/1, amended: Decision 2002/772 (see below).
[14] See arts 223–234 TFEU and art.14 EU.
[15] Act concerning direct election, art.7(2): "pending the entry into force of the uniform electoral procedure and subject to other provisions of the Act [Art.9] the electoral procedure shall be governed in each Member State by its national provisions". All the Member States apply, with some variations, a proportional representation system via party lists.
[16] Decision 2002/772, [2002] O.J.L283/1; corrigendum: [2009] O.J. L.126/23.

Parliament, "shall be elected on the basis of proportional representation, using the list system or the single transferable vote", but added that, "Member States may authorise voting based on a preferential list system in accordance with the procedure they adopt."

The necessary measures are now laid down by the Council, "acting in accordance with a special legislative procedure."[17]

Citizens of the Union residing in a Member State of which they are not a national have the right to vote and to stand in elections for Parliament.[18] A Council directive lays down detailed arrangements.[19]

From January 11, 2007, the 785 seats were distributed nationally as follows: 99 for Germany; 78 for each of the other larger States (France, Italy and the United Kingdom); 54 for Poland and Spain; 35 for Romania; 27 for the Netherlands; 24 for Belgium, the Czech Republic, Greece, Hungary and Portugal; 19 for Sweden; 18 for Austria and Bulgaria; 14 for Denmark, Slovakia and Finland; 13 for Ireland and Lithuania; 9 for Latvia; 7 for Slovenia; 6 for Cyprus, Estonia and Luxembourg; and 5 for Malta. The main criteria for the allocation of seats is, very generally speaking, the population of the States concerned. As indicated, the Treaty now specifies that there may not be more than 750 members, plus the President; the "composition of the European Parliament" shall be adopted by the European Council by a unanimous decision, on the initiative of the European Parliament and with its consent.[20]

(2) The Member's Mandate

Members of the European Parliament (MEPs) are elected for a term of five years by direct universal suffrage in a free and secret ballot.[21] Anyone can stand for Parliament,[22] it being understood that, upon election, the rules concerning incompatibility[23] apply.

Before 1979, MEPs had to be members of a national parliament; presently, the Act concerning direct election simply states that there is no incompatibility between the two offices.[24] However, Belgium and Greece have created an incompatibility at national level and many political parties have done the same in their internal rules. Although it must be admitted that fulfilling two mandates is an extremely demanding task, it seems that the disjunction between the two (only very few MEPs have a double mandate) has somehow estranged the European Parliament from the national ones, thereby not only eliminating a chance for political integration, but also decreasing the political clout of the MEPs. The

---

[17] art.223(1)2 TFEU.

[18] art.22(2) TFEU. See *Spain v UK* (C-145/04) [2006] E.C.R. I-7917, where the Court stated that the right to vote is not limited to citizens!

[19] See Directive 93/109 laying down detailed arrangements for the exercise of the right to vote and to stand as a candidate in elections to the EP for citizens of the Union residing in a Member State of which they are not a national [1993] O.J. L329/34.

[20] art.14(2)2 EU.

[21] art.14(3) EU.

[22] Including, e.g. in the UK, peers and ministers of religion who are excluded from election to Westminster.

[23] Act concerning direct election, art.6(1) and (2).

[24] Act concerning direct election, art.5.

necessity of closer links between the MEPs and the national MPs is now generally recognised. To that effect a Protocol on the role of national parliaments in
the European Union was annexed to the Treaties.[25]

This Protocol provides that Commission consultation documents (Green and
White Papers and Communications), the annual legislative programme and
any other instrument of legislative planning or policy, also agendas for and the
outcome of meetings of the Council and the intention of the European Council
to allow the adoption of decisions by the Council by majority rather than the
unanimity provide for in the Treaty,[26] must be forwarded directly to national
parliaments at the same time as to the European Parliament and the Council.
The same applies to "draft legislative acts" of the Commission, of Parliament,
of a group of Member States, the Court of Justice, the European Central Bank
and the European Investment Bank. National parliaments may send to the
President of the European Parliament, the Council or the Commission a reasoned
opinion[27] on whether the draft legislative act complies with the principles of
subsidiarity.[28]

An eight-week period must elapse between the draft legislative act being made
available in the official languages of the Union and the date when it is placed on
a provisional agenda of the Council for adoption; exceptions are possible in case
of urgency.

The Protocol provides also for inter-parliamentary co-operation and a
Conference of Parliamentary Committees for Union Affairs, that may submit any
contribution it deems appropriate for the attention of the European Parliament,
the Council and the Commission; it must also promote the exchange of information and best practice between national parliaments and the European
Parliament, including their special committees.[29]

(a) Privileges and Immunity

During the sessions of Parliament, the MEPs enjoy the privileges and immunities
accorded to members of national parliaments when in their own countries, and
immunity from detention and legal proceedings when on the territory of another
Member State.[30] In an action before a national court for damages brought against
a Member in respect of opinions he has expressed, the national court, which has
not received information from that Member regarding his request to Parliament
seeking defence of his immunity,[31] is not obliged to request the Parliament to give
a decision on whether the conditions of that immunity are met. When the

---

[25] [1997] O.J. C340/113.

[26] art.48(7)1–2 EU.

[27] Protocol No. 1 to the TFEU, arts 1–2.

[28] See Protocol No. 2 to the TFEU on the application of the principles of subsidiarity and
proportionality.

[29] Protocol No. 1 to the TFEU, arts 9–10.

[30] Protocol on the Privileges and Immunities of the European Communities attached to the art.10
Merger Treaty. See, e.g. *Wybot v Faure* (149/85) [1986] E.C.R. 2403; [1987] 1 C.M.L.R. 819
from which it follows that Parliament is always "in session" and *Rothley* (T-17/00) [2000] E.C.R.
II-2085 concerning the right of the Union Antifraud Office to inspect the offices of MEPs. This
right was provided for by an amendment of Parliament's Rules, following an inter-institutional
agreement ([1999] O.J. L136/20); the amendment was contested by a number of MEPs first in the
CFI and later in the Court of Justice (*Rothley and Others v Parliament* (C-167/02) [2004] E.C.R.
I-3149); in both instances the request for annulment was rejected.

[31] Protocol on Privileges and Immunities, art. 9 and Rules, art 6(3).

national court is informed that the Member has made a request to Parliament for defence of its immunity, the national court must stay procedure and request Parliament to issue its opinion as soon as possible. Where the national court considers that the Member enjoys the immunity provided in the Protocol, it must dismiss the action brought against the Member.[32] Immunity can only be waived by Parliament.[33]

(b) Performance of Duties

Regulations and general conditions governing the performance of the duties of the members are laid down by Parliament, acting by means of regulations on its own initiative in accordance with a special legislative procedure, after seeking the opinion of the Commission and the approval of the Council. All rules or conditions relating to the taxation of Members and former Members require unanimity within the Council.[34]

The Statute for Members of the European Parliament was adopted in September 2005[35]; it covers the rules and general conditions applicable to the exercise of their mandate; it does not deal with Member's remuneration.

2. TASKS AND POWERS OF PARLIAMENT

Like all the Union institutions, Parliament, "shall act within the limits of the powers conferred on it by the Treaties",[36] the emphasis being on "conferred", since these are the only powers the institutions may exercise. Parliament exercises, jointly with the Council, legislative and budgetary functions. It also exercises functions of political control and consultation as laid down in the Treaties.[37] Previously, Parliament only had "advisory and supervisory" powers, but this changed with the SEA and even more with the Maastricht, Amsterdam and Nice Treaties. The SEA introduced the co-operation procedure, while the Amsterdam Treaty, as shall be seen, provided for the so-called co-decision power. It should be noted, however, that since 1970, Parliament exercises certain deciding powers in the budgetary field.[38] Nonetheless, as was just mentioned, Parliament does not yet fully exercise all the attributes of an elected representative body, i.e. legislation and the raising of taxes. The TFEU provides for jurisdictional control of the Court over, "acts of the European Parliament . . . intended to produce legal effects vis-à-vis third parties."[39] There are no further indications in the Treaties concerning the precise meaning of those acts. The same provision existed in the EC Treaty and one example could be a "legislative resolution".[40]

---

[32] *Marra* (Joined Cases C-200/07 and C-2001/07) [2008] E.C.R. 21.10.08.
[33] Protocol on Privileges and Immunities, Ch.III, art.18, last indent. See *Mote* (T-345/08) [2008] E.C.R. 15.10.08 request to annul decision to waive immunity rejected.
[34] art.223(2) TFEU [190(4) and (5)]
[35] [2005] O.J. L262/1. See Decision of the Bureau concerning implementing measures for the Statute of the member of the E.P. [2009] O.J. C159/1.
[36] art.13(2) EU [189].
[37] art.14(1) EU.
[38] arts 313–316 TFEU [272].
[39] art.263 TFEU [230,1]
[40] [2009] O.J. L21/7: legislative resolution with a view to adopting a Council Decision adjusting the basic salaries and allowances applicable to Europol.

The tasks and powers of Parliament, in the order in which they appear in the Treaty shall be examined hereunder.

(1) Exercise, Jointly with the Council, Legislative Functions

As mentioned already, it is in this area that the SEA, and more so the EU, Amsterdam and Nice Treaties, introduced the most far-reaching changes. The SEA increased the cases wherein Parliament must be consulted by the Council before the latter adopts an act, and introduced the co-operation procedure. The EU Treaty provided for the so-called co-decision procedure, that was extended by the Amsterdam and Nice Treaties. Presently there are, besides the simple consultation of Parliament by the Council, two different legislative procedures[41]: the "ordinary" one and the "special" one. The Treaties also provide for consultation of Parliament by the Council and the consent of Parliament for a limited number of acts to be adopted by the Council.

(a) Consultation

At the beginning, this used to be the general rule and practically all Treaty provisions dealing with acts of the Council would read: "the Council shall, on a proposal from the Commission and after consulting the European Parliament, . . .".[42]

Presently there are only a few instances where Parliament is merely "consulted".[43]

When the Council enacts regulations, directives or decisions, the consultation of Parliament is initiated by the Council on the basis of a proposal submitted to it by the Commission. This proposal may be altered by the Commission as long as the Council has not acted on it, at any time during the procedure leading to the adoption of the Act.[44] This, for example, allows the Commission, when Parliament has expressed an opinion on the proposal, to take it into account by submitting a modified proposal. In February 1990, the Commission proposed a Code of Conduct that would ensure more effective co-operation in the decision-making process, with a bigger role for Parliament in the field of external relations.[45]

Parliament's opinions have no binding force. However, mention must be made, in the relevant acts, of the fact that Parliament was consulted.[46] However,

---

[41] art.289(1) and (2) TFEU.

[42] See, e.g. former art.37(2) EC last sub-para.

[43] art.48(2) and (6) EU modification of the Treaties; art.19 TFEU [13]: combat discrimination; art.148(2) TFEU [128(2)]: guidelines on employment; art.150 TFEU [130]: establishment of an Employment Committee.

[44] art.293(2) TFEU [250(2)].

[45] [1990] EC Bull.4–81: the Code stipulates that the Commission will take care to remind the Council not to come to a "political agreement" before Parliament has given its opinion, keep the House informed of the guidelines set out by the Council and ensure that, in accordance with the principles laid down by the Court, Parliament is re-consulted should the Council substantially amend a Commission proposal. The Commission also undertakes to set up its contact with Parliament and the Council concerning the choice of the legal base to be adopted for its proposals and to take individual decisions on any amendment adopted at second reading by Parliament, which the Commission does not wish to incorporate in its proposal. Parliament, for its part, undertakes to adopt any appropriate operational and statutory measures to make the inter-institutional process more effective, and ensure in particular that opinions on the proposals linked with the creation of a frontier-free area before the end of 1992 are adopted swiftly. (Report of proceedings: [1990] O.J. Annex 3–389.)

[46] art.296,2 TFEU [253].

the Treaty does not require the Council to mention whether the opinion was favourable or not, nor to refute, in the latter case, the arguments brought forward by Parliament against the proposal.[47]

It should also be noted that where the Council acts on a proposal from the Commission, unanimity,[48] except in certain cases,[49] is required for the adoption by the Council of an act constituting an amendment to that proposal.[50] This seems to indicate that the power of the Council to adopt an act which differs from the Commission's proposal is limited to amending the latter, while respecting the essential content of the proposal. In the case where the Council introduces a modification, the question arises whether Parliament must be consulted again, this time on the amended text. According to the Court, this is only necessary when the amended text is substantially different from the one on which Parliament gave its opinion.[51]

It should be pointed out that Parliament may, acting by a majority of its component Members, "request the Commission to submit any appropriate proposal on matters on which it considers that a Union act is required for the purpose of implementing the Treaties". If the Commission does not submit a proposal it must inform Parliament of the reasons.[52] The question has been raised as to whether this right to request proposals infringes upon the "exclusive" right of initiative of the Commission. This seems unlikely since it is only a "request", and on the other hand, the Council has had the same right from the beginning,[53] and this was never considered as limiting the Commission's freedom to decide on the opportunity of making proposals. It seems that the matter rests there, unless the Commission is obliged, under the Treaty, to act; in that case, Parliament may bring an action against the Commission before the Court for failure to act.[54]

In certain cases the Treaties confer on Parliament a right of initiative.[55] The latest version of Parliament's Rules of Procedure refers to, "Rights of initiative

[47] See *Government of the Kingdom of the Netherlands v High Authority* (6/54) [1954–56] E.C.R. 103 at 111. The Commission undertook, starting with the July 1973 session of Parliament, to inform it systematically of actions taken on its opinions.

[48] However, this rule does not apply during the conciliation procedure: art.294(10) and (13) TFEU [251(4) and (5)], for the establishment of the budget (arts 310 and 314 TFEU [268 and 272]), for the adoption of the multi-annual financial framework and for authorising expenditure in excess of one-twelfth in case the budget has not been adopted at the beginning of the year (art.315,2 TFEU [273]).

[49] art.293(1) TFEU [250]. The exceptions are art.294 TFEU paras 10 [251] (Conciliation Committee) and 13 (period after approval in the Conciliation Committee), art.310 [268] (budget), art.312 (multi-annual financial framework), art.314 [272] (establishment of the budget) and art.215,2 [273] (propose expenditure in excess of one-twelfth).

[50] art.293(1) TFEU [250(1)];

[51] See *ACF Chemiefarma v Commission* (41/69) [1970] E.C.R. 661 at 689(69), *Buyl v Commission* (817/69) [1982] E.C.R. 245 and *Parliament v Council* (C-65/90) [1992] E.C.R. I-4593. Similar text in *Parliament v Council* (C-65/93) [1995] E.C.R. I-643; [1996] 1 C.M.L.R. 4.

[52] art.225 TFEU [192]. See r.42, Rules of Procedure.

[53] art.241 TFEU [208].

[54] art.265 TFEU [232].

[55] In the December 2009 Rules of Procedure, art.41 provides that, "in cases where the Treaties confer a right of initiative on Parliament, the committee responsible may decide to draw up an own-initiative report. The report shall comprise: (a) . . .; (b) where appropriate, a draft proposal; . . .Where the adoption of an act of Parliament requires the approval or the consent of the Council and the opinion or the consent of the Commission, Parliament may, following the vote on the proposal . . . decide to postpone the vote . . . until the Council or the Commission have stated their position."

conferred on parliament by the Treaties".[56] The Commission itself has pointed out that it is the Treaty which confers upon it the power to initiate legislation in the areas covered by the Treaty and that it is, therefore, legally and politically responsible for its proposals, regardless of the fact that they are drawn up at the request of another institution or of economic operators.[57]

Finally, mention must be made of the fact that, when provided for in the Treaty, consultation of Parliament constitutes an "essential procedural requirement", and failure of the Council to comply with it constitutes a ground for annulment of the relevant act by the Court.[58]

Besides the opinions given following the consultation procedure, Parliament has always formulated resolutions whenever it considered it necessary.[59] According to the Rules of Procedure, such resolutions must, however, concern matters falling within the activities of the European Union.

With a view to furthering the inclusion of Parliament in the decision-making process, a Code of Conduct has laid down, since 1990, a number of reciprocal commitments of Parliament and Commission.[60] In 2005, for instance, Parliament was consulted 113 times.

(b) The Ordinary Legislative Procedure[61]

The introduction of this co-decision procedure by the EU Treaty and the extension of its scope and of the role of Parliament in it, by the Treaties of Amsterdam, Nice and Lisbon, represents a real breakthrough for Parliament. Where, before those Treaties, its function was purely consultative, the Parliament now shares with the Council real legislative power. Consequently, most acts were no longer designated as "Council" regulations, directives or decisions, but as regulations, directives or decisions "of the European Parliament and the Council".[62] The procedure creates a kind of interplay between Parliament and Council reminiscent of that which exists between the two chambers of many national parliaments.

The rather lengthy and complex procedure can best be described on the more familiar basis of the three classical phases in Union legislation: the Commission's proposal, the role of Parliament and the role of the Council.

First Reading

1. The Commission submits a proposal to Parliament and to the Council[63];

---

[56] Rules of Procedure, r.41. General Report 2005/20, reference is made to "Own initiative procedures".
[57] See answer to written question No.3471/92: [1993] O.J. C292/22.
[58] See *Roquette Freres v Council* (139/79) and *Maizena v Council* (139/79) [1980] E.C.R. I-3149, where the Court annulled a regulation because the Council, although it had transmitted the Commission's proposal to Parliament for its opinion, adopted the regulation without having received it. However, see also *Parliament v Council* (C-65/93) [1995] E.C.R. I-643: Parliament was duly consulted, but, according to the Court, failed to meet the obligation of genuine co-operation by adjourning the last plenary session during which the draft could have been adopted. No reproach to the Council which adopted the measure without having received the opinion of Parliament, because of urgency.
[59] Rules of Procedure, r.113(1).
[60] The Code provides, e.g. for individual Commission Decisions on any amendment adopted at second reading. See [1990] EC Bull.5–80.
[61] art.294 TFEU [251].
[62] In 2005, 122 acts were adopted via this procedure.
[63] In the other procedures, the proposal is sent to the Council, which then consults the Parliament on it.

2. Parliament adopts its position in first reading and communicates it to the Council;
3. if the Council approves Parliament's position the act shall be adopted in the wording corresponding to Parliament's position;
4. if the Council does not approve Parliament's position, it shall adopt its own position at first reading and communicate it to Parliament;
5. the Council informs Parliament fully of the reasons which led it to adopt its own position. The Commission also informs Parliament of its position.

Second Reading

If, within three months of such communication, Parliament:

- approves Council's position at first reading or has not taken a decision, the act concerned shall deemed to have been adopted in the wording which corresponds to the position of the Council;
- rejects, by a majority of its component members, Council's position at first reading, the proposal shall be deemed not to have been adopted;
- proposes, by a majority of its component members, amendments to the Council's position at first reading, the text thus amended shall be forwarded to the Council and the Commission, which shall deliver an opinion on those amendments.

If within three months of receiving Parliament's amendments, the Council, acting by a qualified majority[64]:

- approves all those amendments the act shall be deemed to have been adopted (however, unanimity is required for the amendments on which the Commission has delivered a negative opinion)[65];
- does not adopt all the amendments, the President of the Council, in agreement with the President of Parliament, shall within six weeks convene a meeting of the Conciliation Committee.

Conciliation

The Conciliation Committee, which shall be composed of the members of the Council or their representatives and an equal number of members representing Parliament shall have the task of reaching agreement on a joint text by a qualified majority of the members of the Council or their representatives and by a majority of the members representing Parliament, within six weeks of being convened on the basis of the positions of Parliament and the Council at second reading.

The Commission shall take part in the Conciliation Committee's proceedings and shall take all necessary initiatives with a view of reconciling the positions of Parliament and the Council.

---

[64] For a definition of qualified majority see under Ch.6: The Council. As will be seen, there are a number of cases wherein the Council must decide unanimously throughout the whole co-decision procedure: for instance, art.21(3) TFEU [18(2)]—provisions to facilitate the exercise by the citizens of the Union of the right to move and reside freely within the territory of the Union.

[65] art.294(9) TFEU [251]. This is logical, because, where the Council acts on a proposal from the Commission and this negative opinion is equivalent to a proposal it may only amend it unanimously: art.293(1) TFEU [250(1)].

If within six weeks of it being convened, the Conciliation Committee does not approve the joint text, the proposed act shall be deemed not to have been adopted.

Third Reading

If, within that period, the Conciliation Committee approves a joint text, Parliament, acting by a majority of the votes cast, and the Council, acting by a qualified majority, shall each have a period of six weeks from that approval in which to adopt the act in question in accordance with the joint text. If they fail to do so, the proposed act shall deemed not to have been adopted.

The periods of three months and six weeks mentioned above shall be extended by a maximum of one month and two weeks respectively at the initiative of Parliament or the Council.

Special Provisions

Where in the cases provided in the Treaties, a legislative act is submitted to the ordinary legislative procedure on the initiative of a group of Member States, on a recommendation by the European Central Bank, or at the request of the Court of Justice, a proposal of the Commission is not provided for,[66] neither shall the Commission inform Parliament of its position,[67] nor can the Council act on a Commission's negative opinion.[68] However, the Parliament and Council must, in such case, communicate the proposed act to the Commission with their position at first and second reading. They may request the opinion of the Commission.

Type of Act to be Adopted

Normally the Treaties indicated what type of act can or must be adopted; when this is not the case, the Parliament, Council and Commission must select it on a case by case basis, in compliance with the applicable procedures and with the principle of proportionality.[69]

The ordinary legislative procedure described above has now become the most common way for Parliament to participate in the legislative process. However, a problem might arise when the power to legislate can be based on two different Treaty provisions. The Court has held that in such cases the act must be adopted on the basis of the two relevant provisions.[70] In case this would result in divesting the procedure of its essential element, i.e. Parliament's intervention in the legislative process, that rule is now not applicable. For instance, if one of the provisions requires the ordinary legislative procedure, and the other requires the Council to act unanimously, after merely consulting Parliament, the essential element of the ordinary legislative procedure would be undermined. Consequently, the dual legal basis is excluded. Which one should be used depends on the content of the act to be adopted.[71]

---

[66] art.294(2) TFEU [251].
[67] art.294(6) TFEU second phrase [251].
[68] art.294(9) TFEU [251].
[69] art.296,1 TFEU [253].
[70] *Commission v Council* (165/87) [1988] E.C.R. 5545; [1990] 1 C.M.L.R. 457.
[71] *Commission v Council* (C-100/89) [1991] E.C.R. I-2867 at 2897; [1991] 1 C.M.L.R. 2867.

Implementing Measures

Some acts adopted under the ordinary legislative procedure need implementing measures, which are normally adopted by the Commission. It is clear, however, that such implementing measures can be extremely important, since they often determine the actual content of the act. The Council therefore provided that such implementing regulations could only be adopted by the Commission in co-operation with a specific committee, as provided for in the basic act.[72] This "comitology" procedure is described below in Ch.8: The Commission (under "the Commission's Tasks and Powers", (3) "Exercise of powers delegated by the Council"). Furthermore, a *modus vivendi*[73] was adopted by the three institutions in 1995 containing guidelines to overcome difficulties which had arisen for reasons connected with the question of committee procedure, in order to allow a direct involvement of Parliament in the implementing procedure. It provides that drafts submitted by the Commission to the committee provided for in the basic act, shall be sent, at the same time and under the same conditions, to the appropriate committee of Parliament, which then delivers an opinion. Parliament shall be informed by the Commission when the implementing measure is not in accordance with that opinion or when the Commission must submit a proposal to the Council. The latter informs Parliament and will take due account of any unfavourable opinion. The same applies to the Commission.

(c) The Special Legislative Procedure[74]

In specific cases provided for by the Treaties, the adoption of a regulation, directive or decision, which must be done:

- by Parliament with the participation of the Council, or
- by the Council with the participation of Parliament,

constitutes a special legislative procedure.

The procedure to be adopted shall, in each case, be determined in agreement by the two institutions.

(d) Consent Procedure

The consent procedure was introduced by the SEA[75] and extended by the EU Treaty.[76] It constitutes, in fact, a veto right of Parliament,[77] rather than a right of co-decision, where Council and Parliament decide "together", as under the ordinary legislative procedure.[78] When consent is required the Council may only act after it has obtained the agreement of Parliament.

---

[72] art.290 TFEU. Decision 1999/468 laying down the procedure for the exercise of implementing powers conferred on the Commission [1999] O.J. L184/23.

[73] Regulation concerning the implementation measures for acts adopted in accordance with the procedure laid down in Article [251] of the EC Treaty [1996] O.J. C102/1, now art.290 TFEU.

[74] art.289(2) TFEU.

[75] arts 8 and 9 SEA respectively action on application for membership of the Union, and international agreements; these are the only two cases introduced by the SEA.

[76] It was reduced by the Treaty of Amsterdam and now applies in the following cases: art.7(1) EU— serious and persistent breach by a Member State; art.14(2)2 EU—composition of Parliament; art.18(7)3 EU—nomination of President and members of the Commission and of the High Representative; art.49 EU—accession of new members; art.223(1)2 TFEU [190(4)]—procedure for election of MEPs; art.218(6)(a) TFEU [300(3)]—certain international agreements.

[77] Indeed Parliament can only refuse its assent and cannot discuss the case with the Council.

[78] See above: ordinary legislative procedure.

(2) Setting up of a Temporary Committee of Inquiry

Parliament may, at the request of a quarter of its component members, set up a Temporary Committee of Inquiry to investigate, without prejudice to the powers conferred by the Treaties on other institutions or bodies, alleged contraventions or maladministration in the implementation of Union law.[79]

There are, however, a certain number of limitations. In the first place, as the name indicates, such a committee is only temporary, which means that it shall cease to exist on the submission of its report.[80] Secondly, the investigation does not supersede actions undertaken by other institutions or bodies on the basis of the powers conferred on them by the Treaty. When for example the Court of Auditors submits a special report,[81] it cannot be contradicted by the report of the Committee of Inquiry, and to avoid this Parliament must consult this institution before setting up the Committee.

The same applies, and this is the third limitation, where facts are being examined before a court and while the case is still subject to legal proceedings.[82] Detailed provisions governing the right of inquiry must be determined by Parliament, acting by means of regulations, on its own initiative, in accordance with a special legislative procedure, after obtaining the consent of the Council and the Commission.[83]

(3) Right of Petition and Appointment of an Ombudsman

The right of petition[84] is granted not only to citizens of the Union, but also to, "any natural or legal person residing or having its registered office in a Member State", individually or in association with other citizens or persons. Petitions may be sent concerning a matter which comes within the Union's field of activity by persons directly affected by them. A right of petition has been in existence for quite some time[85] and is widely used. In 2008, Parliament received over 1,000 petitions.

An *Ombudsman*, appointed by Parliament[86] after each election of Parliament for the duration of its term of office (eligible for reappointment), is empowered to receive (from the same category of persons), complaints concerning instances of maladministration in the activities of the institutions[87] or of bodies of the Union.[88] See Parliament's publication on "How to complain to the European

---

[79] art.226,1 TFEU [193]. See, for example, Decision of Parliament of July 17, 1996 setting up a temporary committee of inquiry to investigate alleged contraventions or maladministration in the implementation of Union law in relation to BSE [1996] O.J. C239/1.

[80] art.226,2 TFEU [193].

[81] art.287(4) TFEU [248(4)].

[82] art.226,1 TFEU [193].

[83] art.226,3 TFEU [193]. See Decision of the Parliament, the Council and the Commission on the detailed provisions governing the exercise of the Parliament's power of inquiry [1995] O.J. L78/1.

[84] art.227 TFEU [194].

[85] See Rules of Procedure, r.191, 2007 version.

[86] art.228 TFEU [195]. See Decision 94/262 on the Regulation and General Conditions governing the performance of the Ombudsman's duties [1994] O.J. L113/15, amended [2008] O.J. L189/25. Council Decision approving those acts [1994] O.J. L54/25 and Parliament's Resolution on the role of the Ombudsman [1995] O.J. C249/226. See also Parliament's Decision appointing an Ombudsman [2010] O.J. L37/41.

[87] [1996] O.J. C157/1.

[88] In 2008 an agreement was signed between the Ombudsman and the EIB: [2008] O.J. C244/1.

Ombudsman".[89] If the Ombudsman finds such a case, he shall refer the matter to the institution concerned, which shall inform him of its views within three months. He then sends a report to Parliament and to the institution with, if needed, suggestions for remedies. It should be noted that expenses incurred by applicants for lodging a complaint are not considered "caused" by the institutions![90]

Parliament, acting by means of regulations, on its own initiative, in accordance with a special legislative procedure,[91] must, after seeking an opinion from the Commission and with the approval of the Council, lay down the regulations and general conditions governing the performance of the Ombudsman's duties.[92]

(4) Questions to the Council, the Commission and the ECB[93]

The Treaty provides that the Commission shall reply orally or in writing to questions put to it by Parliament, i.e. by a committee, a political group or at least 37 members.[94]

Parliament's right to obtain answers to its questions constitutes an important aspect of its supervisory powers. It has been widely used.[95] This right, and the use of it, was considerably extended over the years, both as to form and as to addressees. The most important extension was probably the right to obtain answers from the Council,[96] especially when one takes into account that it was introduced in 1958 unilaterally by Parliament and accepted by the Council. It was again extended by the EU Treaty to include questions to the Councils of the Common Foreign and Security Policy[97] and of the Police and Judicial Co-operation in Criminal Matters.[98] Presently, the Treaties provide that Parliament may ask questions of the Council and make recommendations to it under the chapter concerning the Common Foreign and Security Policy and that twice a year it shall hold a debate on progress in this field, including the Common Security and Defence Policy.[99] In this field also Parliament must be consulted by the High Representative of the Union for Foreign Affairs and Security Policy ("High Representative") on the main aspects and the basic choices and be informed of how these policies evolve; the High Representative must ensure that the views of Parliament are duly taken into consideration.[100]

In other fields, the European Council and the Council "shall be heard" by Parliament in accordance with the conditions laid down in their respective rules of procedure.[101]

---

[89] *http://www.ombudsman.europa.eu.*
[90] *Internationalen-Hillfonds* (C-331/05) [2007] E.C.R. I-5475.
[91] art.289(2) TFEU.
[92] art.228(4) TFEU [195].
[93] Rules of Procedure, r.115–118.
[94] art.230,2 TFEU [197] and Rules of Procedure, r.115.
[95] For instance, during 2008 Parliament addressed, out of a total of 7,322 questions, 6,570 written questions, 659 oral questions with debate and 93 during question time to the Commission: 1,037 were addressed to the Council—547 written, 413 oral with debate and 50 during question time.
[96] Rules of Procedure, r.115,1, 2007 version. See art.197(4) EC.
[97] art.36,2 EU [21]. For the Common Foreign and Security Policy see below Ch.36.
[98] Repealed art.39(3) EU.
[99] art.36,2 EU.
[100] art.36,1 EU.
[101] art.210,3 TFEU [180].

To the questions for written and oral answers provided for in the Treaty, Parliament added, in 1962, the Oral Questions followed by a Debate.[102] This was accepted by the Commission and the Council with the proviso that, where the latter is concerned, the debate may not be concluded by a vote on a resolution concerning the debate in question.[103] This is presently the only form of questioning. Finally, in 1973, Parliament introduced the Question Time,[104] in which the Council and the Commission agreed to participate. In this case, only the answers from the Commission can give rise to a debate. Finally there are the questions for written answers, that are published in the *Official Journal of the European Union*.[105]

It is clear from the above that Parliament has succeeded in including the Council in its work, far beyond what was provided for in the Treaties. Indeed, not only the Council, as such, accepted to participate, but also the Presidency of the Common Foreign and Security Policy.[106] As indicated, there are differences in the ways the above-mentioned procedures are applied to the Council and to the Commission. This distinction reflects the particular character of the relationships existing between Parliament, on the one hand, and the other two institutions, on the other. Indeed, as far as the Commission is concerned, the relationship is one of political supervision and co-operation. The latter sometimes becomes a conspiracy against the Council which, after all, in certain cases still wields the ultimate legislative power within the Union.

Where the Council is concerned, the relationship should rather be seen as political co-operation and partnership, especially after the modifications introduced by the EU Treaty. This relationship tends to find expression in what can be considered a kind of dialogue between the two institutions. Besides the formal contacts already mentioned, each incoming President of the Council presents at the beginning of his mandate a "Programme of the Presidency", and a survey of significant developments at the end of his six-months term. Similarly, a representative of the Council presents an oral report to Parliament twice a year, on the activities of the Council.[107]

(5) The Adoption of the Rules of Procedure

The Rules of Procedure have, as seen above, played an important part in the development of Parliament's position within the Union. Parliament has used the Rules of Procedure as an instrument to increase its powers, often with success.[108] Important modifications were introduced in view of the entering into force of the EU Treaty.[109] However, as shall be seen in respect of the approval of the

---

[102] Rules of Procedure, r.115.
[103] Rules of Procedure, r.115.
[104] Rules of Procedure, r.116.
[105] Rules of Procedure, r.117.
[106] art.36,2 EU [21(1)]. Rules of Procedure, r.115.
[107] art.15(6)(d) EU [4,3].
[108] A good example is the right to put questions to (and obtain answers from) the Council. Except for the Foreign Affairs and Security policy, it is still not provided for by the Treaty (see art.230,3 TFEU [197]), but the Council does answer the questions put to it by Parliament.
[109] See minutes of the sitting of September 14, 1993, P.E. 174.510. See consolidated version, including interpretation of the rules [1997] O.J. L49/1; 14th edn of the Rules [1999] O.J. L202/1. See also Rules governing public access to Parliament's documents [1997] O.J. C289/6.

designated members of the Commission, it seems that Parliament has attributed to itself more powers than provided for under the Treaties, and, since the Rules do not bind the other institutions, it remains to be seen whether they will comply with what are, after all, only Parliament's wishes.[110]

Modifications were introduced in 2008: in case of doubt concerning the admissibility of a question, the President decides; the minimum number of members required to form a group was increased to 25, with at least seven countries participating; a new "short presentation" procedure whereby only the rapporteur and the Commission, if it so wishes, will be given the floor; only a group of 40 members will be able to table an alternative motion for non-legislative resolutions. New guidelines for the approval of the Commission were adopted: new Annex XVIb.

(6) The General Report

According to the TFEU, Parliament must, "discuss in open session the General Report" on the activities of the Union,[111] which the Commission publishes annually.[112] It is submitted to Parliament before the opening of its session, i.e. the second Tuesday in March.[113] In the old days, the discussion of the General Report gave rise to a general debate on all the facets of Union life, since the Report covers the activities of all the institutions and bodies of the Union. It should be noted that the work of the other institutions and of the EIB is described in detail in their own reports.

The General Report is supplemented by an Annual Report on the Agricultural Situation of the Union,[114] a Report on the Development of the Social Situation in the Union,[115] and a Report on Competition Policy.[116] The Commission also presents an Annual Report on the Regional Fund.

All those reports constitute an invaluable source of information on the activities of the Union, although the General Report no longer contains detailed information as it used to do. This report is less important, however, for the supervisory task of Parliament, since the latter is kept well informed through the permanent contacts it maintains, mainly with the Commission, through the work of the Parliamentary Committees in which the Commission always participates.

The discussion of the General Report no longer takes place.[117] The 2007 version of the Rules of Procedure provides, among other things, that Parliament shall work together with the Commission and the Council to determine the legislative planning of the European Union and that Parliament and the Commission shall co-operate in preparing the Commission's legislative and work

---

[110] Rules of Procedure, r.106 "Election of the Commission"! art.17 TFEU [214]: "the President and the other Members of the Commission . . . shall be subject as a body to a vote of approval by the European Parliament."

[111] art.233 TFEU [200].

[112] art.18 Merger Treaty. No longer "published" but on the Internet.

[113] art.229 TFEU [196]. The Commission has always scrupulously respected this obligation.

[114] This practice was started in 1975 at the request of Parliament.

[115] art.161 TFEU [145].

[116] Undertaking given by the Commission to Parliament on June 7, 1971.

[117] Rules of Procedure, r.119 provides that Annual Reports and other reports of other institutions, in respect of which the Treaties provide for consultation of Parliament, etc. shall be dealt with by means of a report submitted to the plenary.

programme in accordance with the timetable and arrangements agreed between the two institutions and annexed to the Rules of Procedure.[118]

(7) The Motion of Censure

Parliament has the power to dismiss the members of the Commission, as a body, by adopting a motion of censure in case it disagrees with activities of the Commission.[119] This is by far the most impressive power of control vested in Parliament; but, although motions have been tabled in the past, never yet has one been carried.[120] The procedural requirements are the following. First, the Treaty prescribes a "reflexion time": Parliament shall not vote on the motion until at least three days after it was tabled and shall decide by open vote. Secondly, the Treaty requires a two-third majority of the votes cast, representing a majority of the component Members of Parliament.

It must be underlined that the censure only affects the Commission. The Council, which is the co-legislator within the Union and therefore co-responsible for most of the activities of the Commission remains outside Parliament's reach. Furthermore, one may wonder whether such a motion can have practical effect. It shall depend, partially at least, on the reaction of the dismissed Commissioners. Indeed, they shall remain in office until they are replaced[121] and continue to exercise their functions normally.[122] Since their replacement depends on a decision of the governments of the Member States, further developments can no longer be controlled by Parliament. It would be difficult for the governments, it seems, to re-nominate the same persons, since the President and the members of the Commission, after having been nominated by the governments, must be approved as a body by Parliament before they can be appointed.

Until now, as mentioned, no motion of censure has ever been carried. It is interesting though to note that, in 1999, the fear for such a motion brought about the resignation of all the members of the Santer Commission six months before the expiration of their mandate. This most unusual and controversial act, not specifically provided for in the Treaty, brought discredit to the Commission as an institution; the misconduct—if any—of one of the members cannot justify this inglorious retreat in front of a threat.

(8) Approval of the President and Members of the Commission

"Taking into account the elections to the European Parliament and after having held the appropriated consultations",[123] the European Council, acting by a qualified majority proposes to Parliament a candidate for President of the Commission. He shall be elected by Parliament by a majority of its component

---

[118] Rules of Procedure, r.107 and Annex XIV.
[119] art.234,1 TFEU [201]. Rules of Procedure, r.107.
[120] The first motion was tabled in November 1972; it was later withdrawn. In order to avoid the motion of censure, the Commissioners can resign, as they did on March 16, 1999.
[121] arts 234 and 246 TFEU [201 and 215].
[122] art.246 TFEU [215,4]: "they shall remain in office and continue to deal with current business". Rules of Procedure, r.98(1).
[123] art.17(7) EU [214].

members, in practice, after this person has made a statement to Parliament, followed by a debate.[124] In case the candidate is not elected, the European Council must propose a new candidate within one month.

The Council, by common accord with the President-elect adopts the list of the other persons it proposes for appointment as Members of the Commission. The President, the High Representative and the other members of the Commission are then subject, as a body, to a vote of consent by Parliament.[125] In conformity with Parliament's wish, those members appear, "before the appropriate committee according to their prospective field of responsibility".[126] The problem is not only that this is not provided for by the Treaty, but that, as shall be seen, portfolios are only officially attributed by the Commission itself after it takes office. If this were to be decided beforehand, this would mean that the Council, i.e. the Member States, decide in fact on this attribution. This would violate the principle of the independence of the Commission and its members so clearly provided for in the Treaty.[127]

(9) Participation in the Budgetary Procedure

The budgetary procedure and the role of Parliament in it can best be described as follows.[128]

The annual budget of the Union is established by Parliament and the Council, acting in accordance with a special legislative procedure.[129]

1. The Commission consolidates in a "draft budget" the estimates of expenditure for the following year drawn up by the various institutions, with the exception of the European Central Bank, before July 1. The draft budget, which may contain different estimates, also contains an estimate of the revenues.
2. The Commission submits a proposal containing the draft budget to Parliament and to the Council not later than September 1 preceding the budget year. The Commission may amend the draft budget during the procedure until such time as the Conciliation Committee is convened.
3. The Council defines its position on the draft, forwards it to Parliament not later than October 1 and informs Parliament in full of the reasons which led it to adopt its position.
4. If, within 42 days of such communication, Parliament:

   (a) approves the position of the Council the budget shall be adopted;
   (b) has not taken a decision, the draft budget shall be deemed to have been adopted;
   (c) adopts amendments by a majority of its component members, the amended draft is forwarded to the Council and the Commission—the President of Parliament in agreement with the President of the Council shall immediately convene a meeting of the Conciliation Committee.

---

[124] Rules of Procedure, r.105.
[125] art.17 EU [214(2)].
[126] Rules of Procedure, r.106.
[127] art.245,1 TFEU [213(2)].
[128] arts 314–316 TFEU [272–280].
[129] art.289(2) TFEU.

However, if within ten days of the amended draft being forwarded to the Council, the latter informs Parliament that it has adopted all its amendments, the Committee shall not meet.

5. The Conciliation Committee, composed of the members of the Council or their representatives and an equal number of members representing Parliament, shall have the task of reaching agreement on a joint text, by a qualified majority of the members of the Council or their representatives and by a majority of the representatives of Parliament, within 21 days of its being convened, on the basis of the positions of Parliament and the Council. The Commission takes part in the Conciliation Committee's proceedings and must take all the necessary initiatives with a view to reconciling the positions of Parliament and the Council.

6. If, within the 21 days mentioned above, the Conciliation Committee agrees on a joint text, Parliament and the Council shall each have a period of 14 days from the date of the agreement to approve the joint text.

7. If, within that period of 14 days:

   (a) Parliament and Council both approve the joint text or fail to take a decision, or if one of these institutions approves the joint text while the other one fails to take a decision, the budget shall be deemed to be definitively adopted in accordance with the joint text;

   (b) Parliament, acting by a majority of its component members, and the Council both reject the joint text, or if one of these institutions rejects the joint text while the other one fails to take a decision, a new draft budget shall be submitted by the Commission; or

   (c) Parliament, acting by a majority of its component members, rejects the joint text while the Council approves it, a new draft budget shall be submitted by the Commission; or

   (d) Parliament approves the joint text while the Council rejects it, Parliament may, within 14 days from the date of the rejection by the Council and acting by a majority of its component members and three-fifths of the votes cast, decide to confirm all or some of the amendments referred under (c) above—where a Parliament amendment is not confirmed, the position agreed in the Conciliation Committee on the budget heading which is the subject of the amendment shall be retained, the budget shall be deemed to be adopted on this basis.

8. If, within the 21 days referred to in para.5, the Conciliation Committee does not agree on a joint text, a new draft budget shall be submitted by the Commission.

9. When the procedure provided in the article has been completed, the President of Parliament shall declare that the budget has been definitively adopted.[130]

10. Each institution must exercise the powers conferred upon it by this article, in compliance with the Treaty and the acts adopted thereunder, with particular regard to the Union's own resources and the balance between revenue and expenditure.

---

[130] art.114(9) TFEU.

It follows from this lengthy procedure, that Parliament does actually adopt the budget of the Union.[131]

In order to avoid the repetition of the numerous conflicts which arose between the Council and Parliament regarding the adoption of the Union budget, the institutions involved concluded an inter-institutional agreement[132] that covers budgetary discipline and improvements of the budgetary procedure. Its main feature was a medium-term (five years) Financial Perspective.[133] Consequently the powers of Parliament in this field were somewhat restricted. It also provides for the possible mobilisation of a "Flexibility Instrument" that allows the use of certain funds for unforeseen structural operations.[134]

Parliament's role in the budgetary field does not end with the adoption of the budget: it also exercises control over its implementation. In this task Parliament and the Council are assisted by the Court of Auditors.[135]

As shall be seen when discussing the financing of the Union's activities, the Commission is entrusted with the implementation of the budget, on its own responsibility and in accordance with the so-called financial regulations.[136]

The Commission submits annually the accounts of the preceding year, together with a financial statement of the assets and liabilities of the Union, to the Council and to Parliament.[137] The latter receives from the Court of Auditors a statement of assurance as to the reliability of the accounts and an Annual Report.[138] It is Parliament, which, on a recommendation from the Council, gives a discharge to the Commission in respect of the implementation of the budget.[139] Mention should be made here of the inter-institutional agreement between Parliament, the Council and the Commission concerning internal investigation by the European Anti-Fraud Office (OLAF).[140] This was established by the Commission Decision of April 28, 1999.[141] The investigations conducted by the Office are the subject of two Regulations.[142] Recently the Court of Justice decided that OLAF could also investigate the European Investment Bank, the European Central Bank and Parliament.[143]

(10) Procedures before the Court of Justice

Until recently, Parliament could only play a rather secondary role in the proceedings before the Union Courts. It could "intervene" in cases before the

---

[131] It could happen, of course, that the budget is not voted in time for the beginning of the financial year or is rejected by Parliament; in that case a sum equivalent to no more than one-twelfth of the budget appropriations for the preceding year may be spent each month: art.315 TFEU [273].

[132] See [1988] O.J. L185 and [1998] EC Bull.6, 112–114 and 121. The Agreement was approved by Parliament in June 1988. A new agreement on budgetary discipline and improvement of the budgetary procedure was signed on May 6, 1999 [1999] O.J. C172/1. Amended [2008] O.J. L128/8.

[133] [1988] O.J. L185. Proposals for 2000–2006, see COM(1998)164 final.

[134] See, for instance, Decision 2002/158, [2002] O.J. L53/28.

[135] See below for an analysis of this institution.

[136] art.317 TFEU [274] which refers to art.322 TFEU [279].

[137] art.318 TFEU [275].

[138] art.287 TFEU [248].

[139] art.319 TFEU [276]. In 1984, Parliament refused to give a discharge to the Commission with regard to the implementation of the 1982 budget; see Bull.11–1984, 67.

[140] [1999] O.J. L136/15.

[141] [1999] O.J. L136/20.

[142] Regulation 1073/1999 of the Parliament and Council and Regulation 1074/1999 (Euratom) of the Council (1999) O.J. L136/1 and 8.

[143] See, for instance, *Commission v ECB* (C-11/00) [2003] E.C.R. I-7147.

Courts,[144] institute third-party proceedings to contest a judgment and bring an action against the Council and/or the Commission for failure to act thereby infringing the Treaty.[145] However, its locus standi was considerably enhanced by the Treaty of Nice.[146] Presently, the Member States, Parliament, the Council and the Commission have a general right to request the Court to review the legality of Union acts.[147] The Court may also review the legality of acts when actions are brought by the Court of Auditors and by the ECB, "for the purpose of protecting their prerogatives".[148] The same applies to the right to, "obtain the opinion of the Court of Justice as to whether an agreement envisaged is compatible with the provisions of the Treaty"; this possibility is now also open to Parliament.[149]

(11) Participation in other Union Activities

Several agreements of association between the Union and third States provide for a joint Parliamentary Committee. This is the case with the EEC Turkey Association,[150] the EEA, and also with the so-called European Agreements with the candidate countries from Central and Eastern Europe.[151] These Parliamentary Committees are composed of Members of Parliament and Members of the national parliaments of the associated States. These Committees constitute discussion forums rather than decision-making bodies. Similarly, the ACP-EEC Convention provides for a Joint Assembly.[152]

3. INTERNAL ORGANISATION OF PARLIAMENT

The internal organisation of Parliament is rather different from that of any national parliament. It is based on a double structure: the political groups and the parliamentary committees.

(1) The Political Groups

These are not to be confused with national political parties; since the 2004 elections 157 national political parties were represented in Parliament and, for instance, in the PPE-DE Group, 50 members are representatives of 50 different national political parties. Indeed, representatives sit in multinational

---

[144] See, e.g. Resolution of December 14, 1979 ([1980] O.J. C4/52) to intervene in cases *Roquette Frères v Council* (138/79) [1980] E.C.R. 3333 and *Maizena v Council* (139/79) [1980] E.C.R. 3393.

[145] art.265 TFEU [232]. See, e.g. *Parliament v Council* (13/83) [1985] E.C.R. 1556; [1986] 1 C.M.L.R. 138.

[146] art.2(34) Treaty of Nice.

[147] art.263 TFEU [230]. See *Parliament v Council* (302/87) [1988] E.C.R. 5637.

[148] art.263 TFEU [230].

[149] art.218(11) TFEU [300].

[150] See art.27 of the Agreement ([1964] O.J. 3687).

[151] The first agreements were signed on December 16, 1991.

[152] The Cotonou Agreement was signed on June 23, 2000; for meetings of the Joint Assembly, see, for instance, General Report (1998).

political groups,[153] each having its own statute. The representatives are free to choose the Group to which they want to belong and unless they are a member of a political party that is a member of that group, they must ask to belong and be accepted.

However, the Act concerning direct election provides that representatives shall vote on an individual basis and that they shall not be bound by any instruction nor receive a binding mandate.[154]

According to the Rules of Procedure, a political group must comprise members, "elected in at least one-quarter of the Member States. The minimum number of members required to form a political group shall be twenty".[155] Clearly, this rule was made to encourage the formation of transnational groups, that is one of the characteristics of the European Parliament.

As for the political parties at European level, referred to in the Treaty on European Union as contributing to forming European political awareness and expressing the will of the citizens of the Union,[156] Parliament and Council must lay down, acting in accordance with the ordinary legislative procedure,[157] the regulations governing them and, in particular, the rules regarding their funding.[158] These parties[159] must satisfy a number of other conditions,[160] such as having legal personality in the Member State in which their seat is located. These conditions were laid down in 2003 by Parliament and Council, that also lays down rules regarding the funding of the parties.[161]

(2) Parliamentary Committees

The Rules of Procedure provide that Parliament can set up standing or temporary committees,[162] which in turn, may appoint one or more subcommittees. The chairmen of all the Committees form the "Conference of Committee Chairmen". Chairmen which may make recommendations to the "Conference of Presidents"[163]

---

[153] The situation in September 2009 was the following: total 736.

> European People's Party (Christian Democrats) and European Democrats (PPE-DE) 265;
> Progressive Alliance of Socialists and Democrats (S&D) 184;
> Alliance of Liberals and Democrats for Europe (ALDE) 84;
> The Greens/European Free Alliance (Greens/EFA) 55;
> European Conservatives and Reformists (ECR) 55;
> European United Left/Nordic Green Left (GUE/NGL) 35;
> Europe of Freedom and Democracy (EFD) 32;
> Non-attached Members (NA) 26.

[154] Act concerning direct elections, art.4(1); ([1976] O.J. L278/1).
[155] Rules of Procedure, r.30,2. See *Front national and Martinez v Parliament* (Joined Cases C-486/01 and C-488/01 P-R) [2002] E.C.R. I-1843.
[156] art.10(4) EU.
[157] art.294 TFEU [251].
[158] art.224 TFEU [191].
[159] Rules of Procedure, rr.208–210.
[160] See *Front National* (C-486/01 P) [2004] E.C.R. I-6289.
[161] Regulation 2004/2003 on the regulations governing political parties at European level and the rules regarding their funding [2003] O.J. L297/1; see also Decision of the Bureau of Parliament laying down the procedures for implementing said Regulation [2004] O.J. C155/1.
[162] Rules of Procedure, rr.183–192. See, for instance, Temporary Committee on policy challenges and budgetary means of the enlarged Union 2007–2013.
[163] Rules of Procedure, r.25.

about the work of the Committees. The Conference of Committee Chairmen can be instructed to carry out specific tasks.[164]

The members of the Committees are elected by Parliament after nominations have been submitted by the political groups. It is within the Committees that the real parliamentary work is carried out. When, for instance, a proposal is sent to Parliament by the Commission, it is assigned to a given Committee (that becomes the leading Committee) to examine the proposal and report on it. Such assignment may be opposed by other Committees and, eventually, the plenary shall decide. The other Committees are co-advisors. In the leading Committee each Political Group has a co-ordinator, who owns a number of points depending on the strength of his Group in Parliament; these points count when it comes to designate the rapporteur, who plays an extremely important role since he drafts the resolution that will be sent to the plenary for approval. He only can put a draft resolution on the agenda of the Committee when he thinks he has a majority in favour of it. The other Groups designate their own rapporteur—shadow-rapporteur—so there are, in fact, 1+7 rapporteurs! The leading Committee adopts a draft resolution to be submitted to Parliament in plenary session. At that point amendments may be proposed either in writing or orally by a Group or 32 MEPs. Parliament expresses its final position in the form of a legislative act.[165]

There are presently 20 committees,[166] 2 subcommittees[167] and 2 special committees.[168]

(3) The Bureau

Parliament elects its President[169] and 14 Vice-Presidents,[170] which together form the Bureau, i.e. the executive body. The Bureau drafts the agenda of the sessions, decides on matters of competence and makes the preliminary draft of Parliament's budget.[171]

The Rules of Procedure also provide for a Conference of Presidents,[172] mentioned above, consisting of the President of Parliament and the Presidents of the political groups. The Bureau constitutes the ultimate centre of decision-making for all internal matters of Parliament. The Rules of Procedure also provide for the election of Queastors; they are responsible for administrative and financial matters directly concerning Members, pursuant to guidelines laid down by the Bureau[173]—they are members of the Bureau with advisory capacity.

---

[164] Rules of Procedure, r.27.
[165] Rules of Procedure, r.180.
[166] Foreign Affairs, Development, International Trade, Budgets, Budgetary Control, Economic and Monetary Affairs, Employment and Social Affairs, Environment, Public Health and Food Safety, Industry, Research and Energy, Internal Market and Consumer Protection, Transport and Tourism, Regional Development, Agriculture, Fisheries, Culture and Education, Legal Affairs, Civil Liberties, Justice and Home Affairs, Constitutional Affairs, Women's Rights and Gender Equality and Petitions.
[167] Security and Defence and Human Rights.
[168] One on the financial crisis and the other on the financial perspective.
[169] art.14(1) EU [197(1)].
[170] Rules of Procedure, r.15.
[171] Rules of Procedure, r.75b.
[172] Rules of Procedure, r.24.
[173] Rules of Procedure, r.16.

(4) Sessions and Meeting Place(s)

Parliament holds annual sessions, i.e. lasting 12 months, but actually sits only during 12 part-time sessions, which last five days.[174] Parliament meets, without requiring to be convened, on the second Tuesday in March. Parliament may also meet in extraordinary[175] session and has instituted so-called additional sessions.

At the Edinburgh European Council in December 1992, it was decided that the:

"European Parliament shall have its seat in Strasburg, where 12 periods of monthly plenary sessions, including the budget session shall be held. The periods of additional plenary sessions shall be held in Brussels. The Committees of the European Parliament shall meet in Brussels. The Secretariat of the European Parliament and its departments shall remain in Luxemburg".[176]

This most unfortunate decision from the point of view of efficiency and costs, can only be explained by petty nationalistic and political motives. It is shocking that those considerations prevailed over common sense, which would have required Parliament to work in one single place, instead of being dispersed over three locations. This decision puts an end to the long struggle of Parliament to streamline its activities.[177]

Members of the Commission may (and do) attend all the meetings of Parliament and, on invitation, those of the Committees; the Council is represented at all the plenary sessions. The minutes of the meetings are published in the *Official Journal of the European Union* and the full debates in an annex thereto.

Except for the adoption of a motion of censure and certain decisions within the co-operation, co-decision and budgetary procedures, Parliament acts by a majority of the votes cast.[178] There is a quorum when the majority of the representatives are present; however, as long as there is no request to do so, the number of members present is not ascertained.[179]

(5) The Conference of European Affairs Committees of (National) Parliaments of the European Union (COSAC)[180]

A Protocol on the Role of National Parliaments in the European Union was annexed by the Treaty of Amsterdam to the EU Treaty and to the Treaties

---

[174] Parliament is understood to be in session even when not actually sitting, and is until the session is declared closed; see *Wagner v Fohrman* (101/63) [1964] E.C.R. 195 and *Wybot v Faure* (149/85) [1986] E.C.R. 2391.

[175] art.229,2 TFEU [196,2].

[176] Conclusions of the Presidency: Decision taken by common agreement between the Representatives of the Governments of the Member States on the location of the seats of the institutions and of certain bodies and departments of the European Communities, art.1(a): [1992] Bull.12–24. This Decision was incorporated in the Protocol on the location of the institutions and of certain bodies and departments of the EC and of Europol: [1997] O.J. C340/112.

[177] Parliament's decisions to hold its sessions wherever it decides was successfully attacked by Luxembourg: *Luxembourg v Parliament* (230/81) [1983] E.C.R. 255; [1983] 2 C.M.L.R. 726, *Luxembourg v Parliament* (108/83) [1984] E.C.R. 1945; [1986] 2 C.M.L.R. 507: Parliament has no right to decide on the location of its departments, and *France v European Parliament* (358/85) [1986] E.C.R. 2149; [1988] 3 C.M.L.R. 786 and *France v European Parliament* (C-345/95) [1997] E.C.R. I-5215.

[178] art.231 TFEU [198].

[179] Act concerning direct election, art.6(1) and (2) (quoted above).

[180] Rules of Procedure, r.124.

establishing the European Communities. It provides for Parliament to transmit to the national parliaments all the consultation documents (green books, white books and notices) and the legislative proposals of the Commission. The same applies to documents sent by the Commission to Parliament and to the Council. COSAC, which was set up in Paris on November 16/17, 1989, may submit proposals to the Union institutions and be consulted by the governments of the Member States. The Rules of Procedure of COSAC were adopted in June 2000.[181]

(6) Parliament's Secretariat

Parliament has its own staff of (end of 2008) 5,004 permanent and 127 temporary posts, grouped in a Secretariat headed by a Secretary-General. It is divided over eight Directorates-General and a legal service, mostly located in Luxembourg.[182] See also the Code of Conduct applicable to Parliament's personnel[183] and the 2002 Decision of the Secretaries-General of all the institutions, the ECSC, the Committee of the Regions and the Ombudsman on the organisation and operation of the European Communities Personnel Selection Office.[184] In 2005, they set up a European Administrative School.[185]

4. CONCLUSION

Although not fully equipped yet with all the attributes of a parliament, the European Parliament has, over the years, thanks to its determination and strongly supported by the popular claim for more democracy within the Union, succeeded in increasing its powers. It is rapidly becoming an institution with a status equal to that of the Council and the Commission. In fact, Parliament wields more power than would appear from the Treaty provisions.

Further Reading

R. Corbett, F. Jacobs and M. Schackelton, *The European Parliament*, 6th edn (John Harper Publishing, 2005).
Peter Gjerloeff Bonnor, "The European Ombudsman: a novel source of soft law in the European Union", (2003) E.L.Rev.39.
Magdalena Elisabeth de Leeuw, "The Regulation on public access to European Parliament, Council and Commission documents in the European Union: are citizens better off?", (2003) E.L.Rev. 324.
Lenaerts-Van Nuffel, *Constitutional Law of the European Union* (Sweet & Maxwell, 2005).

---

[181] [2000] O.J. C175/1 and for the European Affairs Committees [2008] O.J. C27/6. See, for instance, Conference in Brdo 7–8.05.08, [2008] O.J. C189/6.
[182] I. Presidence, II. Committees and delegations, III. Information/public relations, IV. Studies, V. Personnel, VI. Administration, VII. Translation/General services and VIII. Finances and Financial control.
[183] [2000] O.J. C97/1.
[184] [2002] O.J. L197/56.
[185] [2005] O.J. L37/17.

Chapter Six

The European Council

INTRODUCTION

To avoid confusion it must be made clear at the outset that among the seven institutions of the Union,[1] there are—besides the Parliament, the Commission, the Court of Justice, the European Central Bank and the Court of Auditors—two Councils: a "European Council" composed of Heads of State or of Government and a "Council" composed of government ministers. These two institutions shall be examined separately.

THE EUROPEAN COUNCIL

(1) History

There came a time when Council decisions were no longer taken by majority voting, although this was provided for in the Treaties, but by consensus/unanimity. Furthermore, the subjects to be decided upon became more and more political because, with the evolution towards economic and monetary union, they were of vital importance for the general economic development of the Member States themselves. Consequently, the decision-making process within the Union virtually came to a halt. It became obvious that new impetus had to be given and new methods of decision-making had to be found. Since the Council is already a gathering of high-level politicians (government ministers), the solution was sought more and more in the so-called Conferences of Heads of State or of Government.[2] At the 1974 Summit, as those Conferences were also called, the participants:

> "[R]ecognised the need for an overall approach to the internal problems involved in achieving European unity and the external problems facing Europe—consider it essential to ensure progress and overall consistency in the activities of the Communities and the work on political co-operation—and [have] therefore decided to meet, accompanied by the Ministers of Foreign Affairs, three times a year and, whenever necessary, in the Council of the Communities and in the context of Political Co-operation".[3]

---

[1] art.13(1) EU.

[2] The original idea was to organise gatherings of heads of government and the denomination "Heads of State or Government" was made necessary by the fact that in France the function of head of government is assumed by the Head of State. The first such conference was held in Paris on February 10/11, 1961; see Communiqué in [1961] EC Bull.3–13, and the second in Bonn on July 19, 1961, where it was decided to hold such meetings at regular intervals; see Communiqué in [1961] EC Bull. 7–40.

[3] General Report 1974, p. 297.

Consequently, since 1975, the Heads of State or of Government meet as the European Council, at the onset three times a year, later on twice a year, and presently (2010), twice every six months, with the possibility for the President of the European Council to convene a special meeting when the situation so requires.[4] A record of conclusions is issued on the authority of the Presidency after each meeting.[5]

(2) Composition

The European Council is composed of the Heads of State or of Government of the Member States, its President and the President of the Commission. The High Representative of the Union for Foreign Affairs and Security Policy ("High Representative") takes part in its work.

In case the agenda of the meeting requires it, the members may decide each to be assisted by a minister and, in the case of the President of the Commission, by a member of the Commission.

(3) The President of the European Council

The President is elected by the European Council, by a qualified majority, for two and a half years, renewable once. It used to be presided over by the Member State which holds the presidency of the Council on the basis of equal rotation every six months. Presently, the conditions of that rotation for Council meetings, except those concerning Foreign Affairs,[6] are established by the European Council.[7] Those conditions establish also the way these two Presidents work together.

In the event of an impediment or serious misconduct of its President, the European Council can end the President's term of office in accordance with the same procedure.[8]

The President of the European Council chairs the meetings and drives forward its work, he ensures the preparation and continuity of the work in co-operation with the President of the Commission and on the basis of the "General Affairs Council", he must endeavour to facilitate cohesion and consensus and he presents a report to Parliament after each meeting.[9] The President ensures, at his level and in that capacity, the external representation of the Union on issues concerning its Common Foreign and Security Policy, without prejudice to the powers of the High Representative. The President may not hold a national office.[10]

(4) Voting

Decisions are taken by consensus, unless the Treaties provide otherwise.[11] The latter is the case, among others, when the European Council adopts a decision

---

[4] art.15(3) EU.
[5] Those conclusions are published on the Internet: *http.//www.europa.eu/european-council/ index_eu.htm*
[6] art.16(9) EU.
[7] art.236(b) TFEU.
[8] art.15(5) EU.
[9] art.15(6) EU.
[10] art.15(6)2 and 3 EU.
[11] art.15(4) EU.

establishing the list of Council configurations, other than those of the General Affairs Council and of the Foreign Affairs Council,[12] and a decision on the Presidency of the Council configurations other than that of Foreign Affairs[13]; in those cases, the European Council acts by a qualified majority, the latter being defined in accordance with the relevant Treaty provisions.[14] The European Council shall act by simple majority for procedural questions and for the adoption of the Rules of Procedure.

Where a vote is taken, any member of the European Council may also act on behalf of not more than one other member. Abstention by members present in person or represented shall not prevent the adoption by the European Council of acts which require unanimity. Where the European Council decides by vote, its President and the President of the Commission shall not take part in the vote.[15]

(5) Tasks

The task of the European Council is defined as follows: it, "shall provide the Union with the necessary impetus for its development and shall define the general political directions and priorities thereof. It shall not exercise legislative functions".[16] The European Council has so far mostly limited itself to issuing general guidelines, which have been acted upon by the Council and the Commission. One of the tasks attributed to the European Council is to define the principles of, and general guidelines for, the Common Foreign and Security Policy (CFSP), which was provided for by the EU Treaty and modified by the Amsterdam Treaty.[17] The CFSP is the object of Ch.37.

(6) Existence of a "serious and persistent breach" by a Member State of the Union's Values

The European Council may, on a proposal by one-third of the Member States or by the Commission and after obtaining the consent of Parliament and inviting the Member State in question to submit its observations, determine the existence of a serious and persistent breach (as opposed to a "clear risk of a serious breach" which is determined by the Council[18]) by a Member State[19] of the values referred to in the Union Treaty. These values are: respect for human dignity, freedom, democracy, equality, the rule of law and human rights, including the rights of persons belonging to minorities.[20] The Treaty provides that to make this determination the European Council must be "acting by unanimity",[21] but the TFEU

---

[12] art.16(6) EU.
[13] art.16(9) EU.
[14] art.16(4) EU and art.238(2) TFEU [205(1) and (2)]. See below under "Council".
[15] art.235 TFEU.
[16] art.15(1) EU.
[17] art.26 (13) EU.
[18] art.7(1) EU where the determination is made by the Council on a reasoned proposal by one-third of the Member States, by Parliament or by the Commission.
[19] art.7(2) EU.
[20] art.2 EU.
[21] art.7(2) EU.

88 The European Council

provides that the member representing the Member State in question shall not take part in the vote.[22]

Where such a determination is made by the European Council, the Council, acting by a qualified majority, may decide to suspend certain rights deriving from the application of the Treaty, including the voting rights of the representative of the government of that Member State in the Council.[23] In doing so, the Council must take into account the possible consequences of such suspension on the rights and obligations of natural and legal persons. The Council, acting by a qualified majority, may subsequently decide to vary or revoke these measures in response to changes in the situation which led to their being imposed. Before imposing such sanctions, the European Council must obtain the assent of Parliament. The latter shall decide by a two-third majority of the votes cast, representing a majority of its members.[24]

(7) Organisation

At the Seville European Council of June 2002, agreement was reached on a series of specific measures applicable, without amendment of the Treaties, to the organisation and functioning of the European Council. The main points are the following:

- preparation: the European Council shall meet four times a year, twice every six months, and, exceptionally, it may convene a special meeting;
- the General Affairs and External Relations Council prepares its meetings and draws up the agenda—other configurations of the Council can also contribute via the former;
- an annotated agenda is drawn up distinguishing between:

  — items to be approved without debate;
  — items for discussion with a view to defining general political guidelines;
  — items for discussion with a view to adopting a "decision" (see below);
  — other items not intended to be the subject of conclusions;

- in principle the proceedings of the European Council last for one full day, but in practice they last longer;
- the Presidency may take measures to promote the best possible use of the time available, such as limiting speaking time;
- in exceptional cases, when an item is placed on the agenda for a "decision", the political conclusions drawn from the position emerging during the discussion shall be brought to the attention of the Council so that it may consider the implications for subsequent proceedings in accordance with the applicable Treaty provisions[25];

[22] art.354,1 TFEU [224]; the Treaty adds that the Member State in question shall be counted in the calculation of the one-third or four-fifths of Member States referred in paras 1 and 2 of that article.
[23] art.7(3) EU.
[24] art.354 TFEU [224].
[25] This careful language clearly indicates that the decision referred to is not a "decision" in the sense of art.288 TFEU [249] and that in order to become a decision under the Treaty all the prerequisites, such as a proposal from the Commission, must be met.

- each delegation has two seats in the meeting room, while the total size of each delegation is limited to 20 people per Member State and the Commission (that means more than 500 people!);
- the conclusions must set out policy guidelines and decisions, placing them briefly in their context and indicating the stages of the procedure to follow on from them (—since nothing is mentioned here about who is responsible for drafting and publishing them, one can assume that it still is the Presidency).

Further Reading

Jan Werts, *The European Council* (London, John Harper, 2008).

Chapter Seven

The Council

INTRODUCTION—THE OBJECTIVES OF THE TREATIES AND THE MEANS TO ACHIEVE THEM: THE ROLE OF THE COUNCIL

Although the distinction between the objectives of the Treaties and the means to attain them is not as clear as it was under the EC Treaty,[1] the present Treaties provide for several means to attain the "objectives" assigned to the Union.[2] They are: firstly, that the Union must offer its citizens an Area of Freedom, Security and Justice in which the free movement of persons is ensured[3]; secondly, the Union must establish an internal market[4]; thirdly, it must establish an Economic and Monetary Union whose currency is the Euro[5]—furthermore, the Union must define and implement a Common Foreign and Security Policy, including the progressive framing of a Common Defence Policy[6]; and, finally, it must develop a special relationship with neighbouring countries.[7]

Detailed means are provided for in the TFEU for the exercise of the Union's competences in order to implement the above-mentioned objectives. This is to be done either exclusively by the Union, or by implementing competences shared between the Union and the Member States, or by the Union carrying out actions to support, co-ordinate or supplement the actions of the Member States.[8]

Exclusive Union competence exists in the following areas: the Customs Union, competition rules, monetary policy for the Euro area, conservation of marine biological resources, the common commercial policy and the conclusion of certain international agreements.[9]

Shared competences between the Union and the Member States concern, among others: the internal market; social policy; economic, social and territorial cohesion (regional policy); agriculture and fisheries; environment; consumer protection; transport; trans-European networks; energy; area of freedom; security and justice; public health; research; technological development; and space[10] Also

---

[1] See former art.2 EC, which defined the means as, "by establishing a common market and monetary union and by implementing common policies or activities (the Community shall have as its task . . .)".

[2] art.3 EU: "promote peace, its values and the well-being of its peoples", "combat social exclusion and discrimination, etc", "promote economic, social and territorial cohesion and solidarity among Member States", "ensure that Europe's cultural heritage is safeguarded and enhanced", "in its relations with the wider world uphold and promote its values and contribute to the protection of its citizens, etc, etc.".

[3] art.3(2) EU.

[4] art.3(3) EU.

[5] art.3(4) EU.

[6] art.2(4) TFEU.

[7] art.8 EU.

[8] arts 3 to 6 TFEU.

[9] art.3 TFEU.

[10] art.4(1)–(2) TFEU.

in development of co-operation and humanitarian aid, in which area the Union may also conduct a common policy.[11]

Then there are the areas[12] where the Union has competence to carry out activities, in particular to define and implement programmes, while the Member States are not prevented from exercising their own activities: protection and improvement of human health; industry; culture; tourism; education; vocational training; youth and sports; civil protection; and administrative co-operation.[13]

All those activities shall be examined in detail in Parts Three, Four and Five of this book, but it is important at this juncture to notice the distinction the Treaty makes between the "exclusive tasks of the Union" and the, "activities of the Member States and the Union, either sharing competences or each exercising its own", both being destined to implement the Treaty objectives. This distinction indicates that certain tasks can only be accomplished by the Union institutions and the Member States acting together, each in its own sphere. It calls for closer integration of the policies of the Member States with those of the Union proper.

This is particularly relevant for the Council. Indeed, it is within this institution that the two spheres come together: the Council is an institution of the Union, but it is composed of representatives of the Member States. In other words, it is at the same time intergovernmental and supranational. This dichotomy does often create friction between the general interest of the Union and the national interests of the individual Member States, which can only be resolved by what the Treaties refer to as "solidarity among the Member States".[14] If the powers provided for in the Treaties for the establishment of the Customs Union typically come within the ambit of the Union institutions, the situation is different with regard to the activities in the economic and social policy fields. Those must necessarily be based, "on the close co-ordination of Member States' economic policies"[15] and this co-ordination necessarily takes place within the Council. Indeed, according to the EU Treaty, the Council is to, "carry out policy-making and coordinating functions".[16] On the other hand, the Council is also, together with Parliament, the Union's lawmaker, which is expressed in the Treaty by the words: it shall, jointly with Parliament, "exercise legislative and budgetary functions".[17]

1. MEMBERS OF THE COUNCIL

"The Council consists of a representative of each Member State at ministerial level,[18] who may commit the government of the Member State in question and cast its vote".[19] These last words were added by the EU Treaty to allow members of State governments in federal Member States to represent the central government, but ensures that whoever represents a government within the Council, for

---

[11] art.4(3) TFEU.
[12] art.4(3) TFEU.
[13] art.4(4) TFEU.
[14] art.3(3)3 TFEU [2 and 3].
[15] art.119(1) TFEU [4(1)].
[16] art.16(1) EU.
[17] art.16(1) EU [202, second indent].
[18] The Rules of Procedure of the Council, Annex I, last subparagraph, refer to, "the minister or State secretary of its choice" [2004] O.J. L106/22.
[19] art.16(2) EU [203]; this means 27 members as from January 1, 2007.

example a regional minister, she or he can indeed commit said central government. It is left to each government to decide which one of its members shall represent it at a given Council meeting and, although the Treaty refers to "a" representative, it sometimes happens that two or more ministers of the same Member State are present at the same Council meeting.[20]

A member of the Council who is prevented from attending a meeting may arrange to be represented.[21] Neither the Treaty, nor the Rules of Procedure of the Council specify who can represent a Council member. It is clear, however, that unless the representative is a member of a national or regional government, he or she shall not be able to cast a vote.

Being representatives of the Member States, the members of the Council act on instruction from their government. They do not, however, constitute an intergovernmental conference of ministers, nor are they in a position similar to that of their colleagues within international organisations, where decisions are practically always taken unanimously and only bind those States which afterwards ratify them.

As mentioned, the members of the Council do represent the interests of their respective States, but they must, at the same time, act as an institution of the Union and in the interest of the latter. It is not evident that this is always clearly perceived by all the members.

2. Tasks and Powers of the Council

(1) Decision-making

(a) Principles

The Council exercises, jointly with Parliament, legislative and budgetary functions. It carries out policy-making and co-ordinating functions.[22]. Those competences, however, "are governed by the principle of conferral".[23] Indeed, as indicated, the most important provision concerning the exercise of power by the institutions of the Union is to be found at the very beginning of the EU Treaty: "The Union shall act only within the limits of the competences conferred upon it by the Member States in the Treaties".[24] In other words, the Council is not endowed with a general regulatory competence; it can only act when this is specifically provided for in a Treaty provision, the reason why the latter must always be mentioned in Union acts.[25]

There may be cases, however, where action by the Union:

"[S]hould prove necessary, within the framework of the policies defined by the Treaties, to attain one of the objectives set out in the Treaties, and the Treaties have not provided the necessary powers".

---

[20] This is specifically provided for in art.15(3) EU.
[21] Rules of Procedure, art.4.
[22] art.16(1) EU.
[23] art.5(1) EU [202].
[24] art.5(2) EU.
[25] art.296(2) TFEU [253]: "Legal acts shall state the reasons on which they are based". See above, Ch.3: The Legal Acts of the Union.

In such a case, the Council, acting unanimously on a proposal from the Commission and after obtaining the consent of Parliament, shall adopt the appropriate measures.[26]

However, several stringent conditions have to be fulfilled, and this possibility may not, therefore, be considered as an unlimited opportunity for the institutions to increase their powers of decision. Indeed, the appropriate measures may only be taken when action is necessary, "to attain one of the objectives set out in the Treaties", which indicates that the powers exercised in such case are purely implementing Treaty objectives. Also, the required unanimity within the Council should provide the necessary guarantees; indeed, the extension of the Union's powers will, almost inevitably, reduce the powers of the Member States in the same proportion. Unanimity therefore constitutes a brake on a possible extension of the powers of the Union. Furthermore, the Commission's proposal and the consent of Parliament should ensure that the Union's interests are sufficiently taken into consideration— and there is always the judicial control of the Court.[27] The Treaty of Lisbon added other limitations: measures taken under this procedure may not entail harmonisation of Member States' laws or regulations where such harmonisation is excluded by the Treaties[28] and it cannot be used as a basis for attaining objectives pertaining to the foreign and security policy.[29] This procedure does, nevertheless, constitute a way of "supplementing" the Treaty provisions without going through one of the rather cumbersome procedures provided for amending it.[30]

Beside the fact that the Council (together with Parliament) may only act when this is expressly provided for in the Treaty, there is another limitation which results from the balance of powers among the Union institutions. Indeed, in practically all cases, the Council can only use its decision-making power on the basis of a proposal from the Commission. Although there are many cases where the Commission must, in pursuance of the Treaties,[31] make a proposal to the Council[32] (and to Parliament), and, although the Council (and Parliament) may, "request the Commission . . . to submit to it any appropriate proposal",[33] such a proposal for which only the Commission is responsible, remains a prerequisite for the Council's (and Parliament's) action.

It is not only the impossibility to act, in most cases,[34] without a proposal from the Commission that constitutes a limitation of the Council's decision-making

---

[26] art.352(1) TFEU [308]; at the 1972 Paris Summit it was agreed that for the purpose of carrying out the tasks laid down in the different programmes of action, "it was desirable to make the widest possible use of all the dispositions of the Treaty, including Art.[352] (308)".

[27] See *Hauptzollamt Bremerhaven v Massey-Fergusson* (8/73) [1973] E.C.R. 897 and *Commission v Council* (242/87) [1989] E.C.R. 1449, where the Court accepted the use of what is now art.308, TFEU [1991] 1 C.M.L.R. 478.

[28] See, for instance, art.149,2 TFEU [129].

[29] art.352(3) and (4) TFEU.

[30] See art.48 EU.

[31] In case the Commission were to fail to make a proposal when required to by the Treaty, the Court could be called upon to establish that this failure constitutes an infringement under art.265 TFEU [232], thereby obliging the Commission to, "take the necessary measures to comply with the judgment of the Court" (art.266 TFEU [228(1)]).

[32] This is the case each time the Treaty provides that the Council, acting on a proposal from the Commission, "shall . . .", e.g. art.31 TFEU [26], as opposed to the Council "may", on a proposal from the Commission, e.g. art.18,2 TFEU [12].

[33] arts 225 and 241 TFEU [192 and 208]

[34] As shall be seen, there are cases where the Treaties provide that other institutions and bodies and Member States may make proposals for legislative acts, such as the High Representative art.238(2) TFEU.

power, the limitation resides also, and probably more so, in the content of the Commission's proposal. Indeed, although the Council is empowered, acting unanimously, to adopt an act which constitutes an amendment to the Commission's proposal, the Council is still bound by its general content.[35] It could only adopt a content different from the original proposal if the Commission agrees to modify.[36]

Possibly also to be considered somehow as an extension of the "conferred powers" principle is the use of the "implied powers" theory as a basis for action by the institutions. In several cases the Court has admitted that, "rules established by international agreements or by law are considered to imply those rules without which the first either would have no sense or could not be reasonably or successfully applied".[37] Another example can be found in the question whether the Union has authority to enter into international commitments in the absence of explicit provisions. The Court stated that:

> "[R]egard must be had to the whole scheme of Union law no less than to its substantive provisions. Such authority arises not only from express conferment by the Treaty, but may equally flow implicitly from other provisions of the Treaty, from the Act of Accession and from measures adopted within the framework of those provisions, by the [Union] institutions".[38]

This prudent approach to a very delicate question—especially in the context of the transfer of powers from the Member States to the Union—can certainly not be considered as opening the door to extensive Treaty interpretation with regard to the powers of the institutions. Although the Court has referred in some of its decisions to the *effet utile*, or effectiveness,[39] principle to give an interpretation of Union law that seems to go beyond a strict literal meaning,[40] it does not seem possible for the Council to do likewise. The principle of "conferral" therefore stands.

As far as the decision-making powers of the Council are concerned, the built-in system of limitations, safeguards and controls constitutes a guarantee for the respect of Union law.[41]

(b) Scope

Being the Union (co)legislator, the Council's decision-making power covers the whole spectrum of the Union's activities. The Council may somehow "share" these powers with the Commission, on which it can bestow, in the acts which it adopts, powers to adopt the necessary non-legislative acts of general application

---

[35] art.293(1) TFEU [250(1)]. If the Council were to modify the proposal substantially, it would no longer be an amendment. One must apply here, by analogy, the Court's view on the requirement of renewed consultation of Parliament in case the Council modifies the proposal on which Parliament was consulted, in such a way as to affect its substance. *ACF Chemiefarma v Commission* (41/69) [1970] E.C.R. 661 at 662(3).

[36] art.293(2) TFEU [250(2)].

[37] *Fédération Charbonnière de Belgique v High Authority* (8/55) [1954–1956] E.C.R. 245 at 299 and *Commission v Council* (22/70) [1971] E.C.R. 263 at 280(72); C.M.L.R. 335.

[38] *(AETR), Commission v Council* (22/70) [1971] E.C.R. 263 at 274.

[39] This principle refers to the way Union law is enforced in the Member States in order to protect the rights which derive for legal and natural persons from Union Law. See below Ch.9: The Court of Justice of the European Union.

[40] See below under Ch.9: The Court of Justice of the European Union.

[41] art.263 TFEU [230].

to supplement or amend certain non-essential elements of the legislative act.[42] This does certainly not constitute "co-legislation" !

As was seen, most of the Council's legislative powers are now shared with Parliament. This was, from the introduction of the "own resources", already the case with the budgetary powers[43]; it now applies to most legislative acts.[44] Both were examined in some detail in the previous chapter concerning Parliament.[45]

On the other hand, the exact scope of the Council's (and Parliament's) decision-making powers in the various fields of Union activities shall be examined below in Parts Three, Four, Five and Six dealing specifically with each one of them.

(c) Voting Procedure

The voting procedure provided for under the European Treaties is one of the more interesting aspects of the Union, since it provides for the possibility of taking, by a majority vote, decisions which are nonetheless binding on all the Member States. Under the majority voting system, even under the qualified majority voting, no single Member State has a veto right.[46] It is this system that has allowed the Union to move steadily towards the implementation of its objectives. This system is unique, and it differentiates the Union from other bodies established under international law, since the latter, generally speaking, only operate on the basis of consensus or unanimous decisions.

However, according to the Rules of Procedure,[47] a vote is only taken within the Council if a majority of the members of the Council so decide, or on the initiative of its President, or on the initiative of a member of the Council or of the Commission.

The basic rule with regard to voting in the Council is that it acts, "by a qualified majority, except where the Treaties provide otherwise".[48] The same applies to the European Council which only acts by simple majority for procedural questions.[49] The presence of a majority of the members of the Council who are entitled to vote, is required in order to enable the Council to vote (= quorum).[50] Any member of the European Council[51] and of the Council may also act on behalf of not more than one other member.[52] On the other hand, there are cases in which, according to the Treaties, one or more members of the Council may not participate in the vote[53]; in such a case, "due account will be taken, in accordance with Annex III [of the Rules of Procedure] of such cases".[54]

---

[42] art.290 TFEU [202, third indent]. See consolidated version of Council "Comitology" Decision of June 28, 1999, as amended, laying down the procedures for the exercise of implementing powers conferred on the Commission [2006] O.J. C255/4. For more details see below Ch.8: The Commission, 2(4).

[43] See former art.272 EC.

[44] art.294 TFEU [251].

[45] See above Ch.5: The European Parliament.

[46] Obviously this only exists when unanimity is required; there still are a few such cases, see below.

[47] Rules of Procedure, art.7.1.

[48] art.16(3) EU [205(1)].

[49] art.235(3) TFEU.

[50] Rules of Procedure, art.11(4).

[51] art.235(1) TFEU.

[52] art.239 TFEU [206].

[53] See, for instance, art.20(3) EU [44] (provisions on enhanced co-operation).

[54] Rules of Procedure, art.16. According to a Council agreement, this does not cover the situation provided by art.7 EU: serious and persistent breach by a Member State; see 1 under art.16.

The voting procedures are: simple majority; qualified majority; and unanimity.

(i) **Simple Majority.**[55] This majority is no longer applicable for the adoption of legislative acts, but still exists in a limited number of cases.[56] When required, the Council shall act by a majority of its component members, i.e. presently 14 out of 27.

When the European Council decides to vote, the President of the Council and the President of the Commission do not take part in the vote.[57]

The simple majority does not apply unless the Treaties do specifically provide for it,[58] since the general rule is, as mentioned, that legislative acts are adopted by qualified majority.[59]

(ii) **Qualified Majority.** Three different calendar periods must be borne in mind when calculating the qualified majority, in the European Council and in the Council, for the adoption of acts requiring qualified majority:[60]

- *Until October 31, 2014*[61] Until October 31, 2014 "transitional provisions" are applicable[62]—member's votes, both in the European Council and in the Council, shall be weighted as follows,

Belgium	12	Luxembourg	4
Bulgaria	10	Hungary	12
Czech Republic	12	Malta	3
Denmark	7	Netherlands	13
Germany	29	Austria	10
Estonia	4	Poland	27
Ireland	7	Portugal	12
Greece	12	Romania	14
Spain	27	Slovenia	4
France	29	Slovakia	7
Italy	29	Finland	7
Cyprus	4	Sweden	10
Latvia	4	United Kingdom	29
Lithuania	7		

Acts shall be adopted if there are at least 255 votes in favour, representing a majority of the members (14), where, under the Treaties, they must be adopted on a proposal from the Commission. In other cases, decisions are

---

[55] art.238(1) TFEU [205(1) and (2)].
[56] See, for instance, art.240(2) and (3) TFEU [207]: organisation of the General Secretariat, adoption of the Rules of Procedure; art.241 TFEU [208] Request the Commission to undertake studies or to submit proposals; art.242 TFEU: rules governing the committees.
[57] art.235(1)2 TFEU.
[58] See, for instance, art.243 TFEU [210].
[59] art.16(3) EU.
[60] Provisions concerning these periods and the applicable rules are to be found in the EU Treaty, the TFEU and Protocol No.36, which makes the understanding of the system rather complicated!
[61] Protocol No.36 attached to the TFEU "On Transitional Provisions", art.3(1), [2008] O.J. C115/322.
[62] art.16(5) EU.

adopted if there are at least 255 votes in favour representing at least two-thirds of the members (18).

When a decision is to be adopted by a qualified majority, a member of the European Council or of the Council (as the case may be) may request that a check is made to ensure that the Member States comprising the qualified majority represent at least 62 per cent of the total population of the Union[63] (+/– 300 million); if that proves not to be the case, the act shall not be adopted.

When not all the members of the Council participate in the voting, namely in the cases where reference is made to the qualified majority as defined in the TFEU,[64] the qualified majority shall be defined as the same proportion of the weighted votes and the same proportion of the number of Council members and, if appropriate, the same percentage of the population of the Member States concerned as laid down by this Protocol No.36 on Transitional Provisions.[65]

- *Between November 1, 2014 and March 31, 2017*[66] During that period "transitional provisions" will also be applied[67]—as from November 1, 2014, a qualified majority shall be defined as at least 55 per cent of the members of the Council (15), comprising at least 15 of them and representing Member States comprising at least 65 per cent of the population of the Union (+/–325 million).

A blocking minority must include at least four Council members, failing which the qualified majority shall be deemed to be attained.[68]

When a decision is to be adopted by a qualified majority, a member of the European Council or of the Council (as the case may be) may request that the act be adopted in accordance with the rules applying before November 1, 2014.[69]

When, under the Treaties, not all the member of the Council participate in the voting, namely in the cases where reference is made to the qualified majority as defined in the TFEU,[70] the qualified majority shall be defined as at least 55 per cent of the members of the Council representing the participating Member States, comprising at least 65 per cent of the population of these States.[71]

A blocking minority must include at least the minimum number of Council members representing more than 35 per cent of the population of the participating Member States, plus one member, failing which, the qualified majority shall be deemed attained.[72]

When the Council does not act on a proposal from the Commission or from the High Representative, the qualified majority shall be defined as at

---

[63] For the population figures see Rules of Procedure, new Annex III [2006] O.J. L285/65. The population figures are recalculated and published at the end (or beginning of each year); see for instance [2008] O.J. L337/92: total EU population 501,26 million; 62 per cent 310.620 million. See also Basic Statistics at the beginning of this book.
[64] art.238(3) TFEU [205(1) and (2)].
[65] Protocol No.36, art.3(4).
[66] art.16(4)1 EU.
[67] art.16 (4) and (5) EU, art.238(2) TFEU and Protocol No.36, art.3(2).
[68] art.16(4)2 EU.
[69] Protocol No.36, art.3,2.
[70] art.238(3) TFEU [205(1) and (2)].
[71] Protocol No.36, art.3(4).
[72] art.16(4)2 TFEU [286].

least 72 per cent of the members of the Council (19), representing the participating Member States comprising at least 65 per cent of the population of these States.[73]

- *After March 31, 2017* The provisions provided for the period between November 1, 2014 and March 31, 2017 shall apply.[74] However, a member of the European Council or of the Council may no longer request that the act be adopted in accordance with the rules applying before November 1, 2014.

(iii) Unanimity. Initially, the EEC Treaty provided for unanimity in many cases until the end of the transitional period[75] and majority thereafter. Unanimity, for instance, is still required when the Council, acting on a proposal from the Commission, wants to adopt an act which constitutes an amendment to that proposal.[76] As indicated, unanimity had, in the beginning, become common practice.[77] Presently it is only required in a limited number of cases by the Treaties.[78] Abstentions by members present in person or represented do not prevent the adoption by the Council of acts which require unanimity.[79]

A final observation concerning the voting procedure of the Council is that, in case of urgency, acts may be adopted by "written procedure"; agreement of the Commission is required where the written vote is on a matter the Commission has brought before the Council.[80]

---

[73] art.238(2) TFEU [205(1)and (2)].

[74] This follows from a concurrent reading of art.16(4) and (5) EU and art.238(2) and (3) TFEU and Protocol No.36 art.3(1) and (2).

[75] The transitional period ended on December 31, 1965.

[76] art.293(1) TFEU [250(1)]—this rule does not apply in the case of art.294(10) and (13) TFEU [251(4) and (5)]; conciliation committee, art.310 TFEU [268]; financial provisions, art.312 TFEU; multiannual financial framework, art.314 TFEU [272]; budget and art.315 TFEU [273]—in case the budget is not approved at the beginning of the financial year.

[77] This practice finds its origin in the Arrangement regarding majority voting adopted by the Council at its meeting of January 28 and 29, 1966, at Luxembourg. This arrangement is sometimes improperly referred to as the "Luxembourg Agreement" or "Luxembourg Accord": it is no such thing. It is only an internal arrangement of the Council which ended the most serious crisis the Union had known and which was started by the over-nationalist government of Général De Gaulle. The arrangement provided, among others: "1. Where, in the case of decisions which may be taken by majority vote on a Commission proposal and very important interests of one or more partners are at stake, the members of the Council will endeavour, within a reasonable time, to reach solutions which can be adopted by all the members of the Council while respecting their mutual interests and those of the Union, in accordance with Article 2 of the EEC Treaty." For the French, the discussion must be continued until unanimous agreement is reached; this was not accepted by the other five and the question always remained: what happens in the event of failure to reach complete agreement? This is the reason why the Luxembourg arrangement was, in fact, an agreement to disagree. Anyway, after the SEA, EU, Amsterdam and Nice Treaties, one should be able to assume that the Luxembourg arrangement is dead. It should be remembered, however, that the arrangement only concerned cases where qualified majority voting is provided for. This means that where unanimity is required, each Member State has indeed a veto right.

[78] art.92 TFEU [72] transport; art.108(2)3 TFEU [88(2)] State aids to be considered compatible by the Council; art.203 TFEU [187] association with ACP countries; and art.346(2) TFEU [296(2)] protection of security interests.

[79] art.238(4) TFEU [205(3)].

[80] art.12 Rules of Procedure.

(2) Co-ordination of Economic Policies: Broad Guidelines of the Economic Policies of the Member States and the Union

Member States must conduct their economic policies with a view to contributing to the achievement of the objectives of the Union, as defined in the Treaty on European Union, and in the context of the broad guidelines set out by the Council. The Member States and the Union must act in accordance with the principle of an open market with free competition, favouring an efficient allocation of resources,[81] based on an economic policy founded on the close co-ordination of the Member States' economic policies, on the internal market and on the definition of common objectives.[82]

Besides having the power to take decisions in all the cases provided for by the Treaty, the Council has the task to, "adopt broad guidelines of the economic policies of the Member States and the Union".[83] To this end, the Council, on a recommendation from the Commission, formulates a draft for the broad guidelines and reports it to the European Council. The latter formulates a conclusion on the basis of which the Council adopts a recommendation setting out the broad guidelines.[84] These guidelines must be consistent with the guidelines for employment policies of the Member States.[85] Together they form the "Integrated Guidelines for growth and jobs".

As was pointed out at the beginning of this section, the Union and the Member States are also to establish an Economic and Monetary Union whose currency is the Euro and implement the common policies and activities referred to in the Treaty.[86] Mention should be made here of the fact that the "close coordination of Member States' economic policies" constitutes a necessary complement to the establishment of the internal market. As will be seen, the latter consists of the basic freedoms[87] and a number of Union policies. The list of the various policies entrusted to the Union and the Member States has grown with the SEA, the EU, Nice and Lisbon Treaties.

It now encompasses, in the order provided under the Union competences[88]: Customs Union; Competition; Monetary policy; Fisheries and conservation of marine biological resources; Common commercial policy; Conclusion of International agreements; Internal market; Social policy; Regional policy; Agriculture; Environment; Consumer protection; Transport; Trans-European networks; Energy; Area of freedom; security and justice; Research; Technological development and space; Development of co-operation and Humanitarian aid; Co-ordination of economic policies; Co-ordination of social policies; Protection of human health; Industry; Culture; Tourism; Education; Vocational training; Youth and sport; Civil protection; and Administrative co-operation and Employment policy.

It is clear from this long list that most of these activities are policies that cannot be implemented by the Union acting alone. In other words they, "do not

---

[81] art.120 TFEU [98].

[82] art.119 TFEU [4].

[83] art.121(2)3 TFEU [99].

[84] See for instance, Council Recommendation on the broad guidelines for the economic policies of the Member States and the Union (2008–2010) [2008] O.J. L137/13, updated [2009] O.J. L183/1.

[85] art.146(1) TFEU [126] and 148(2) [128].

[86] art.3 EU [3 and 4].

[87] Freedom to move goods, to accept work, to establish oneself, to provide services, to transfer capital and payments in any of the Member States.

[88] art.3 TFEU.

fall within the Union's exclusive competence".[89] In the other areas, "the Union shall share competence with the Member States"[90] or, "carry out actions to support, coordinate or supplement the actions of the Member States".[91]

In areas which do not fall within the exclusive competence of the Union, it shall take action, in accordance with the principle of subsidiarity, i.e.:

> "[O]nly if and in so far as the objectives of the proposed action cannot be sufficiently achieved by the Member States, either at central level or at regional and local level, but can rather, by reason of the scale or effects of the proposed action, be better achieved at Union level".[92]

It is important to note that the principle of subsidiarity does apply in all cases, except those where the Union has "exclusive" competence.[93]

As was pointed out, most of the above-mentioned activities of the Union require co-operation between the Union and the Member States, and it is the task of the Council to organise this co-operation. However, it is extremely difficult to describe with great precision how this task is to be carried out. Indeed, while the activities of the Union with regard to the establishment of the internal market are described in the TFEU with some precision (the Treaty indicates, for instance, whether the Council must act through regulations, directives, decisions or agreements) and contains an indication as to the timetable for their implementation (such as the EMU phases),[94] the situation is rather different when it comes to the co-ordination of the economic activities of the Member States.

Although regulations, directives and decisions are by no means excluded, the Treaty refers, as far as the Council is concerned, to "broad guidelines",[95] "multilateral surveillance",[96] "coordinated strategy",[97] "appropriate measures",[98] "general orientations",[99] "adoption of measures to contribute to the objectives referred to",[100] besides the "resolutions", "declarations", "work programmes", "multi-annual framework programmes"[101] and "general action programmes" provided for in various Treaty provisions.

Clearly, the Council's task with regard to co-ordination of economic policies is ill-defined as regards its means. And although most of these measures can only be taken on the basis of a proposal from the Commission and together with Parliament, it is not easy to determine whether or not they constitute binding acts submitted to the judicial control of the courts. Nevertheless, this loose system

---

[89] art.3(1) TFEU.

[90] art.4 TFEU.

[91] art.6 TFEU.

[92] art.5(3) EU [5(2)]. The principle of subsidiarity must also be seen in connection with art.1 EU which provides that "decisions are taken as closely as possible to the citizen".

[93] See the Protocol No.2 on the application of the principles of subsidiarity and proportionality, attached to the TFEU.

[94] art.139 TFEU [116].

[95] art.121(2–3) TFEU [99]. See, for instance, Council Recommendation of February 12, 2001, "with a view of ending the inconsistency with the broad guidelines, of the economic policies in Ireland", [2001] L69/22 and the Decision of the same day "making public" said Recommendation, [2001] O.J. L69/24. See also the Council Opinions on the updated stability programmes for various Member States, [2002] O.J. C51/1.

[96] art.121(3)2 TFEU [99].

[97] art.145 TFEU [125].

[98] art.117(1) TFEU [97].

[99] art.219(2) EC [111(2)].

[100] art.166(4) TFEU [150(4)].

[101] art.182(1) TFEU [166].

has, so far, worked in a rather satisfactorily way: to be effective, co-ordination needs to be flexible. However, one gets the impression, as mentioned before, that the more important the decisions, the more informal they sometimes are. A typical example is the setting up of the European Monetary System (EMS) which, at the time, was not even provided for in the Treaty.

As for the obligations imposed upon the Member States in the above-mentioned fields, they are often just as vague. The Treaty mentions, for example that the Member States, "shall regard their economic policies as a matter of common concern and shall coordinate them with the Council".[102] Not a very precise obligation. The question can therefore be asked whether the procedures provided in the Treaty for implementing the co-ordination of the economic policies by the Council correspond to the requirements of a democratic exercise of powers.

(3) Guidelines on Employment Policy

Under the EU Treaty,[103] the Union must, "work for the sustainable development of Europe based on balanced economic growth and price stability, a highly competitive social market economy, aiming at full employment . . .".[104]

Each year, the European Council must consider the employment situation in the Union and adopt conclusions thereon, on the basis of a joint annual report from the Council and the Commission. On the basis of these conclusions, the Council, on a proposal from the Commission and after consulting Parliament, the Economic and Social Committee, the Committee of the Regions and the Employment Committee,[105] shall draw up guidelines for the Member States.[106] These guidelines must be consistent with the Guidelines on Economic Policy mentioned above. Parliament and the Council, acting in accordance with the ordinary legislative procedure,[107] may adopt incentive measures designed to encourage co-operation between Member States and to support their action in the field of employment.[108] The Treaty also provides for the establishment of an Employment Committee with advisory status to promote co-ordination between Member States on employment and labour market policies.[109] For further details see below Ch.29: Social Policy.

3. ORGANISATIONAL ASPECTS OF THE COUNCIL

(1) Configurations of the Council

The Council meets in different configurations according to the subject matter dealt with. The list of these configurations is, according to the EU Treaty,[110] fixed by the European Council acting by qualified majority.[111]

---

[102] art.121(1) TFEU [99(1)].
[103] art.3(2) EU [2, first indent].
[104] art.3(3) EU.
[105] art.150 TFEU [130].
[106] See 2007 Guidelines [2007] O.J. L183/25.
[107] art.294 TFEU [251].
[108] art.149 TFEU [129].
[109] art.150 TFEU [130].
[110] art.2(1) Rules of Procedure.
[111] art.236 TFEU.

The various configurations of the Council are presently the following:

- General Affairs;
- Foreign Affairs;
- Economic and Financial Affairs, including budget (generally referred to as "Ecofin");
- Justice and Home Affairs, including Civil Protection;
- Employment, Social Policy, Health and Consumer Affairs;
- Competitiveness (Internal Market, Industry and Research) including Tourism;
- Transport, Telecommunications and Energy;
- Agriculture and Fisheries;
- Environment;
- Education, Youth and Culture, including Audiovisual Affairs.

Consequently, it is not unusual to have various Council meetings in session at the same time in Brussels where, according to the Rules of Procedure, the Council shall have its seat, or in Luxembourg.[112]

The office of President of the Council is held, for periods of six months, in turn by each Member State in the order decided by the European Council.[113] The same rotation applies to all the subordinate bodies of the Council, such as the Committee of Permanent Representatives (COREPER)[114] (see below), the working groups and other meetings of ministers.

However, the presidency of the Foreign Affairs Council is assumed by the High Representative.[115]

The meetings of the Council are always attended by the Commission represented by its President and/or the Commission member who is more particularly responsible for the subject under discussion. Commission officials also attend the meetings and participate in the work of COREPER (see hereunder) and other Council bodies.

(2) COREPER[116] (COmité des REprésentants PERmanents— Committee of Permanent Representatives)

The creation of this Committee stems from the fact that the Council meets no more than a few days a month and that, with the increase of Union activities, a more permanent presence of the Member States in Brussels was required. The Permanent Representatives—high-level civil servants with the rank of Ambassador—closely follow the various Union activities on a day-to-day basis. They are not deputies of the Council members, they only have very limited

---

[112] art.1(3), Rules of Procedure; see also [1997] O.J. C340/112 on the location of the seats of the institutions.

[113] art.16(9) EU, which provides that the presidency shall be held by member States' representatives on the basis of equal rotation and art.236(b) TFEU: see Decision of the European Council of December 1, 2009 on the exercise of the Presidency of the Council [2009] O.J. L315/50, and implementing Decision [2009] O.J. L322/28, corrigendum [2009] O.J. L349/56.

[114] See hereunder.

[115] art.18(3) EU. See below, Ch.35: Common Foreign and Security Policy.

[116] It is subdivided into COREPER I, composed of the deputy permanent representatives, which handle, among others the agricultural policy, and COREPER II, formed by the Ambassadors.

administrative decision-making power, since they may adopt "procedural decisions" in cases provided for in the Council's Rules of Procedure[117]; they constitute an organ within the Council structure.

Their task is to prepare the work of the Council and to carry out the tasks assigned to them by the Council.[118] They meet several days each week and, although COREPER has, as was said, no decision-making power, once it has reached agreement, for instance, on a proposal from the Commission, it can safely be assumed that the Council will decide accordingly. This is expressed by the fact that in such cases the matter is put on the agenda of the Council as an "A" point.[119] The practice is that the Council accepts the A points at the beginning of its meeting, thereby transforming them into legislative (binding) acts. It must, however, be emphasised that the Council is in no way bound to accept the A points and any Council member is free to ask for a discussion on the subject, in which case it is placed on the agenda of the next Council meeting, but this time as a "B" point. It may also happen that a member maintains a "reserve", due, for example, to the need for a national parliamentary scrutiny. This reserve can, however, be lifted in time for the next Council meeting allowing the latter to adopt the act as an "A" point. When no agreement can be reached at COREPER level, but it is thought that a solution can be found at the ministers (political) level or there is a deadline, the matter is placed on the Council's agenda as a "B" point, i.e. a subject on which discussion is needed.

COREPER is assisted in its work by a whole series of working groups, some permanent, some temporary, which prepare the work of COREPER. These working groups are composed of civil servants from the Member States and convene whenever necessary. When a Commission proposal is sent to the Council, it first comes before COREPER, which can examine it and agree on it directly, but normally sends it to one of the working groups. The latter examines it and reports to COREPER. All the meetings of COREPER and of the working groups are attended by officials of the Commission; it would be more correct to say that these Commission officials participate in their work. Indeed, real negotiations often take place inside those working groups (and at COREPER level) in order to arrive at a text which is acceptable to all Member States, or at least to enough of them to reach a qualified majority when this is provided for. This might result in the Commission modifying its proposal.[120] The meetings of the working groups are presided over by a national from the country which holds the office of President at the Council.

One great advantage of these working groups composed of national civil servants, is that the national view is clearly expressed in Brussels, while the national administrations are, in turn, directly confronted with the views of the Commission and those of the other Member States.

In the same way, it can be said that the Permanent Representatives fulfil a double function: they defend the national interests within the Union and at the same time represent the Union's point of view at home. They thus constitute an indispensable link between the national administrations and the European institutions.

---

[117] Council's Rules of Procedure [2004] O.J. L106/22.
[118] art.240(1) TFEU [207(1)].
[119] art.2(6), Rules of Procedure.
[120] art.293(2) TFEU [250(2)].

(3) The Rules of Procedure

The Rules of Procedure are adopted by the Council by a simple majority.[121] They
provide, among others, for the following:

- The adoption of a multi-annual strategic programme for the three years to
  come, on the basis of a joint proposal from the Presidency and the
  Commission and an annual operating programme. The latter shall have
  regard to relevant points resulting from the dialogue on the political priorities for the year, conducted at the Commission's initiative.
- Measures relating to co-operation between Presidencies of successive six-
  month periods and the chairing of certain working parties by a member of
  the General Secretariat of the Council.
- The Council meets in public when it deliberates and votes on draft legislative acts. To this end the each meeting shall be divided into two parts dealing respectively with Union legislative acts and non-legislative activities.[122]
- The conduct of the meetings: the Presidency is responsible for taking any
  measure required to achieve the best possible use of the time available,
  including: limiting contributors' speaking time, determining the order in
  which they speak, etc.

The present Rules of Procedure were adopted in 2006.[123] Mention should be
made here of public access to Council documents,[124] as provided for by the
Treaty: "[a]ny citizen of the Union and any natural or legal person residing or
having its registered office in a Member State, shall have the right of access to
European Parliament, Council and Commission documents".[125] See also the
Council Decision on the improvement of information on the Council's legislative
activities and the public register of Council documents.[126] It provides that
the General Secretariat shall make accessible to the public, via the Internet, the
provisional agendas of meetings of the Council and its preparatory bodies.

In 2001 the Council adopted its security regulations concerning classified
information regarding the Security and Defence Policy.[127]

---

[121] art.240(3) TFEU [207(3)].

[122] art.16(8) EU and art.15(2) TFEU [255].

[123] [2009] O.J. L325/351.

[124] See art.240(3) TFEU [207(3)]. Decision 93/731 on public access to Council documents [1993] O.J.
L340/43, art.22, Rules of Procedure amended [1993] O.J. L304/1 and Code of Conduct concerning public access to Council and Commission documents [1993] O.J. L340/41; see also *The Carvel
and Guardian Newspapers* (T-194/94), [1995] E.C.R. II-2765; [1995] 3 C.M.L.R. 359;
Netherlands v Council (C-58/94), [1996] E.C.R. I-2169; [1996] 2 C.M.L.R. 996; *Svenska
Journalist Forderbundet* (T-174/95), [1998] E.C.R. II-2289 and *Kuijer v Council* (T-188/98),
[2000] E.C.R. II-1959, where the Court found a breach of Decision 93/731.

[125] art.15(3) TFEU [255]. See Regulation 1049/2001 of Parliament and the Council regarding public
access to Parliament, Council and Commission documents, [2001] O.J. L145/43 and the Joint
Declaration relating to Regulation [2001] O.J. L173/5. See *Sweden and Turco v Council* (Joined
Cases C-39/05 P and C-52/05 P), where the Court annulled a decision of the General Court (CFI)
misinterpreting art.4(2): [2008] E.C.R. 01.07.08.

[126] [2002] O.J. L9/22.

[127] [2001] O.J. L101/1.

(4) The Secretariat

According to the Treaty, the Council is assisted by a General Secretariat, under the responsibility of a Secretary General.[128] The latter is the High Representative who is assisted by a Deputy Secretary General responsible for the running of the General Secretariat of the Council. Both are appointed by the Council, which also decides on the organisation of the Secretariat. It is, like the Commission's departments, divided in Directorates General whose competences correspond to the main activities of the Union.

At the end of 2008 the Secretariat had 3,461 permanent posts and 36 temporary ones.

Further Reading

Westlake & Gallowaay, *The Council of the European Union* (John Harper Publishing, 2004).

---

[128] art.240(2) TFEU [207(2)].

Chapter Eight

The Commission

According to the EU Treaty,[1] the Commission's task is to:

- promote the general interest of the Union and take appropriate initiatives to that end;
- ensure the application of the Treaties and of measures adopted by the institutions pursuant to them;
- oversee the application of Union law under the control of the Court of Justice of the European Union;
- execute the budget and manage programmes;
- exercise co-ordinating, executive and management functions as laid down in the Treaties;
- ensure the Union's external representation with the exception of the common foreign and security policy, and other cases provided for in the Treaties; and
- initiate the Union's annual and multi-annual programming with a view to achieving inter-institutional agreements.

The former EC Treaty provided that the Commission shall, "have its own power of decision"[2]; this has disappeared and the TFEU contains a general provision concerning the powers of all the institutions to adopt acts.[3] This, plus the fact that, as shall be seen, the Commission no longer has the exclusive monopoly of legislative proposal,[4] indicate a certain reduction in the Commission's special position among the institutions. It seems that the balance of power has somewhat shifted from the *communautaire* to the *intergovernmental*.

Nevertheless, the Commission remains the moving power of the Union's activities, and its uninterrupted presence at Brussels, the main seat of the Union institutions,[5] its competent staff and its world-wide relations create the necessary conditions for it to play a major role within the institutional system of the Union. More important, however, is the fact that it embodies and represents the common or Union interest and is responsible for ensuring that this interest prevails when decisions are taken by Member States, the Council and/or Parliament and natural and legal persons alike. The various tasks of the Commission will be examined in more detail after a short analysis of some organisational aspects.

---

[1] art.17(1) EU.
[2] art.211 EC, third indent.
[3] art.288, 1 TFEU.
[4] art.17(2) EU.
[5] See Protocol on the location of the seats of the institutions and certain bodies and departments of the European Union and of Europol annexed to the Treaty on European Union and the Treaties establishing the European Union and the European Atomic Energy Union [1997] O.J. C340/112.

1. THE MEMBERS OF THE EUROPEAN COMMISSION

(1) The Number of Commissioners

While the EC Treaty provided that the Commission, "shall include one national of each of the Member States"[6] (this means 27 members) and that that number may be altered by the Council,[7] the EU Treaty now provides that:

> "[B]etween the entry into force of the Treaty of Lisbon and 31 October 2014, the Commission shall consist of one national of each Member State, including the President and the High Representative of the Union for Foreign Affairs and Security Policy ('High Representative'), who shall be one of its Vice-Presidents"[8]

and that:

> "[A]s from 1 November 2014, the Commission shall consist of a number of members, including the president and the High Representative, corresponding to two thirds of the number of Member States, unless the European Council, acting unanimously, decides to alter this number. The members shall be chosen from among the nationals of the Member States on the basis of a system of strictly equal rotation among the Member States, reflecting the demographic and geographical range of all the Member States. This system shall be established unanimously by the European Council.[9]"[10]

The members are appointed for a period of five years.[11]

After the rejection of the Treaty of Lisbon in an Irish referendum, specific legal guarantees for Ireland were agreed upon by the European Council in order to make it possible for the Irish people to vote in favour of the Treaty in a second referendum. Among these guarantees is the number of Commission members: one from each Member State.[12]

(2) The Choice of the Members of the Commission

They are to be chosen on the ground of their competence and European commitment from persons whose independence is beyond doubt.[13]

It will be remembered that it was in connection with this "independence" that the ECSC Treaty introduced the term "supranational".[14] Although the word did

---

[6] art.213(3)4 EC.
[7] art.213(1) EC.
[8] art.17(4) EU.
[9] The system of rotation must be established on the basis of the following principles: (a) Member States shall be treated on a strictly equal footing as regards determination of the sequence of, and the time spent by their nationals as members of the Commission, and (2) each successive Commission shall reflect satisfactorily the demographic and geographic range of all the Member States.
[10] art.17(5) EU.
[11] art.17(3) EU [214(1)].
[12] See above Ch.2:History.
[13] art.17(3)2 EU.
[14] art.9 ECSC. "The members of the High Authority will refrain from any action incompatible with the supranational character of their duties. Each Member State undertakes to respect this supranational character."

not reappear in the subsequent Treaties, the substance of the concept remains. The required independence applies not only to the qualities of the candidate-commissioner, the Treaty also specifies that the members of the Commission shall, in the general interest of the Union, be completely independent, "in the performance of their duties".[15] Since the most obvious problem with regard to this independence is the relationship between the Commissioner and his own government that nominated him,[16] the Treaty explicitly imposes upon the Member State the obligation, "to respect this principle and not to seek to influence the members of the Commission in the performance of their duties".[17]

As for the members of the Commission themselves, they are bound by certain obligations both during and after their term of office.[18] In order to underline the importance of the independence and the other obligations, the Treaty provides that the members of the Commission shall, when entering upon their duties, give a solemn undertaking to respect the obligations arising from their office.[19]

A last remark concerning this all-important aspect of the duties of the members of the Commission: in the event of a breach of the above-mentioned obligations, the Court of Justice may, on application by the Council or the Commission, rule that the member concerned be, according to the circumstances, either compulsorily retired or deprived of his rights to a pension or other benefits in its stead.[20] So far there has only been one case in which this procedure was initiated by the Council against a former member of the Commission, but it ended with a settlement.[21]

(3) The Nomination Procedure of the Members of the Commission

The *President*: taking into account the elections of Parliament[22] and after having held the appropriate consultations, the European Council, acting by a qualified majority, proposes a candidate to Parliament. This candidate is elected by a majority of the component members of Parliament. In case the candidate does not obtain said majority a new candidate must be proposed within one month.

The *High Representative of the Union for Foreign Affairs and Security Policy* ("High Representative") is appointed by the European Council acting

---

[15] art.245 TFEU [213(2)].

[16] art.17 EU [214(2)].

[17] art.245 TFEU [213(2)].

[18] art.245 TFEU [213(2)].

[19] art.245,2 TFEU [213(2)]; the solemn undertaking is given before the Court of Justice during a special session. Each member undertakes to perform his duties as specified in the Treaty: complete independence in the general interest of the Union, no instructions, no action incompatible with the office, integrity and discretion; they also formally take note of the fact that the governments of the Member States have undertaken to respect their independence. One can only hope that the Commissioners strictly adhere to those obligations.

[20] art.245,2 TFEU [213(2)].

[21] See Council Decision of July 9, 1999 on the referral of the case of Mr Bangemann to the Court of Justice [1999] O.J. L192/53 and *Council v Bangemann* (C-290/99) removed from the register ([1999] O.J. C314/8) and *Bangemann v Council* (T-208/99) also removed from the register, and Council Decision of December 17, 1999 on the settlement of the *Bangemann* case: [2000] O.J. L16/73.

[22] The parliamentary elections take place in May, the Commissioner's mandate starts in October.

by a qualified majority.[23] He shall be one of the Vice-Presidents of the Commission.[24]

The *other members of the Commission*: the Council, by common accord with the President-elect shall adopt the list of the other persons it proposes for appointment; they are selected on the basis of suggestions made by the Member States.[25]

The President, the High Representative and the other members are then subject, as a body, to a vote of consent by Parliament. On the basis of this consent, the Commission shall be appointed by the European Council acting by a qualified majority.[26]

Once the members have been nominated, they form a college: they do not fulfil an individual role under the Treaty, although each one of them is put in charge of a given Commission service. They are jointly responsible to Parliament for everything the Commission does; consequently they must resign, as a body, when Parliament votes a motion of censure of the Commission,[27] except the High Representative who then resigns only from his duties in the Commission.[28]

The President of the Commission shall lay down guidelines within which the Commission is to work, decide on the internal organisation, ensuring that it acts consistently, efficiently and as a collegiate body and appoint Vice-Presidents other than the High Representative.[29] Since the President decides on the "internal organisation", he assigns the members to the different Directorates-General which compose the Commission. The President may reshuffle the allocation of those responsibilities during the Commission's term of office.[30] This allocation of responsibilities is a particular delicate task since each Member State desires the member of its nationality to be responsible for the most important services and strongly "lobbies" for it.[31]

A member of the Commission shall resign if the President so requests.[32]

From the latter it results that the position of the President of the Commission has been strengthened considerably by the Treaty of Lisbon.

2. THE COMMISSION'S TASKS AND POWERS

The Commission's tasks and powers have been enumerated at the beginning of this chapter and shall be examined in detail hereunder.

---

[23] art.18(1) EU.
[24] art.18(4) EU.
[25] art.17(7)2 EU.
[26] art.17(7)3 EU.
[27] art.234 TFEU. See above under Ch.5: The European Parliament.
[28] art.17(8) EU.
[29] art.17(6) EU.
[30] art.248 TFEU [217,2]
[31] Enormous pressure is put on the President right from the beginning of thee selection process and it is, obviously, difficult for the President to ignore the wishes of the Member States. Furthermore, Parliament, before giving its consent, subjects the candidate members to questioning on the basis of their assumed future tasks which are not supposed to be known until the Commissioners have been nominated by the European Council!
[32] art.17(6) EU last para.

(1) "Ensure the application of the Treaties, and of measures adopted by the institutions pursuant to them" and "oversee the application of Union law under the control of the Court of Justice of the European Union"[33]

The Commission is therefore often referred to as the "guardian of the Treaties", which, indeed, it is; but one should not conclude from this that it is the only body responsible for the correct application of the Union law provisions. This task belongs, as shall be seen, even more so to the national authorities and, especially to the national judge.

The measures adopted by the institutions are referred to as secondary legislation, the Treaties constituting the primary legislation. Both impose obligations upon the Member States, the institutions and the natural and legal persons operating within the Union. It is the Commission's task to ensure that they all abide by the law. For this purpose the Commission is endowed with powers consisting mainly of the right to obtain information and to institute proceedings against trespassers.

The right to obtain information is provided for, in a general way, by the Treaty[34] and by various Union acts.[35] Furthermore, the general obligation imposed upon the Member States to "facilitate the achievement of the Union's tasks"[36] should provide the necessary legal ground for the Commission to obtain all the required data. Based upon the information obtained,[37] the Commission can then, if necessary, start the following actions.

(a) With Regard to Member States[38]

When the Commission considers that a Member State has failed to fulfil an obligation under Union law:

---

[33] art.17(1) EU.
[34] art.337 TFEU [284]: "The Commission may, within the limits and under the conditions laid down by the Council. . . . collect any information and carry any checks required for the performance of the tasks entrusted to it." See for instance art.108(3) TFEU [88(3)] (plans to grant or alter aids).
[35] As for acts see, for instance, Regulation 2186/93 obliging Member States to draw up harmonised business registers and *Germany v Council* (C-426/93) [1995] E.C.R. I-3723; according to the Court, that Regulation is a measure necessary to allow the Commission to carry out its task: therefore the Regulation does not infringe the Treaty and Regulation 1/2003, arts 4 and 5 (Regulation implementing art.101 TFEU [81] and 102 [82], [2003] O.J. L1/1).
[36] art.4(3) EU [10]. See *Queen v Ministry of Agriculture* (C-5/94 R) [1996] E.C.R. I-2553; [1996] 2 C.M.L.R. 391: Member States are obliged to take all measures necessary to guarantee the application and effectiveness of Union law.
[37] The Commission can also obtain information in the course of an investigation following a complaint from a Member State or from natural or legal persons; see for instance Regulation 1/2003, art.3 ([2003] O.J. L1/1.) See *Smanor* (T-182/97) [1998] E.C.R. II-271, Order of the CFI: refusal of the Commission to start proceedings against Member States for failure to fulfil an obligation; natural or legal persons are not admissible when challenging a refusal of the Commission to start an art.258 [226] procedure and *Sateba* (T-83/97) [1997] E.C.R. II-1523; [1998] 4 C.M.L.R. 528: the procedural position of a party complaining to the Commission on the basis of Regulation 17 (now 1/2003) for violation of Regulation 99/63, [1963] O.J. 127, 2269, is fundamentally different from the one of a complainant requesting action for failure by a Member State: art.258 [226].
[38] art.258 TFEU [226].

- it shall[39] remind the government in question of its obligations and invite it to take the necessary measures or submit its observations, all within a time limit set by the Commission, usually two months;
- if no action is taken by the Member State and no observations are received, or if those that were submitted do not convince the Commission, it shall deliver a "reasoned opinion" on the matter, and lay down a time limit within which the Member State must comply;
- if the Member State does not comply, the Commission may[40] bring the matter before the Court;
- if the Court finds that the Member State has indeed failed to fulfil its obligation, "the State shall be required to take the necessary steps to comply with the judgment".[41]

What happens when the Member State fails to implement the Court's judgment? Until the entering into force of the Union Treaty, there was nothing the Union institutions could do, except start the procedure over in order to have the Court ascertain that the Member State concerned did not comply with the judgment.[42]

The Treaty now provides that, in case the Commission considers that the Member State has not taken the necessary measures to comply with the judgment, it shall, after having given the Member State the opportunity to submit its observations, issue a reasoned opinion specifying the points on which the Member State has not complied and fixing a time limit to do so. In case of non-compliance, the Commission may bring the matter before the Court and, "specify the amount of the lump sum or penalty payment to be paid", which it considers appropriate in the circumstances.[43]

If the Court finds that the Member State has, indeed, not complied with its judgment, it may impose a lump sum[44] or penalty payment. So now,[45] finally,

---

[39] The terms used here indicate that, once the Commission has determined that a Member State has indeed failed to fulfil an obligation under the Treaty (and in this determination the Commission enjoys discretionary power: it must, among other things, weigh the political implications), there is an obligation for the Commission to act. The existence of this obligation is essential within a system where the plea of *non adimpletus contractus* is inadmissible; see *Commission v Luxembourg and Belgium* (Joined Cases 90/63 and 91/63) [1964] E.C.R. 625 at 631; [1965] C.M.L.R. 58.

[40] At this point the Commission's powers are entirely discretionary.

[41] It is interesting to note that art.258 TFEU [226] refers to the judgment of the Court rather than to the Treaty obligation which was the point of departure of the whole proceedings. The Court cannot impose upon the Member States obligations which differ from what the Treaty prescribes; anyway, in its judgments based upon art.258 [226], the Court only ascertains that the Member State, "has failed to fulfil its obligation under the Treaty"; see, e.g. *Commission v Belgium* (Joined Cases 227/85, 228/85, 229/85 and 230/85) [1988] E.C.R. 12; [1989] 2 C.M.L.R. 797.

[42] See, e.g. *Commission v Belgium* (Joined Cases 227/85, 228/85, 229/85 and 230/85) quoted above, fn.41.

[43] art.258(2)1 TFEU [228(2)]. See *Commission v France* (C-304/02) [2005] E.C.R. I-6263, where the Court decided that by not controlling the fishery activities in conformity with Union law and by not insuring that violations of the fishery's provisions be prosecuted, France had not taken the measures necessary to implement the judgment of June 11, 1991 (*Commission v France* (C-64/88) [1991] E.C.R. I-2727). It therefore condemned France to pay the Commission a penalty of 57,761,250 Euros for each period of six months during which said judgment would not have been implemented.

[44] See, for instance, *Commission v France* (C-121/07) [2008] E.C.R. I-9159, where the Court imposed on France the payment of €10 million.

[45] The ECSC Treaty also provided for some kind of coercive measures (see art.88 ECSC), but they were never applied.

there exists a coercive measure against Member States that flout Union law.[46] A further slight improvement was introduced by the Treaty of Lisbon: when a case is brought against a Member State for failing to fulfil its obligation to notify measures transposing a directive, the Commission may already specify the amount of the lump sum or penalty payment to be paid by the Member State concerned.[47] This amount may not be exceeded by the Court. The payment obligation shall take effect on the date set in the judgment.[48]

As was pointed out above, the Commission enjoys a large discretionary power when deciding whether or not to pursue a Member State before the Court. It should also be noted that, in most cases, problems with the implementation of Union law by the Member States are settled out of court.

Responsibility of Member States towards private and legal persons for infringement of Union law. Member States are not only responsible towards the Union for their own infringements of Union law, there is also their responsibility for possible damages caused, by the infringement, to natural or legal persons. The responsibility of the administration (government) for damage caused by failure to correctly apply Union law was amply confirmed by the Court.[49] Less evident, maybe, is the responsibility of the Member State for infringement by the legislature or the judicature. The Court decided that where a breach of Union law by a Member State is attributable to the national legislature acting in a field in which it has a wide discretion to make legislative choices, individuals suffering loss or injury thereby, are entitled to reparation. This rule only applies, however, where the breached rule of Union law is intended to confer rights upon the said individual, the breach is sufficiently serious and there is a direct causal link between the breach and the damage sustained by the individual.[50]

Where the judiciary is concerned, the Court held that this could only be incurred in the exceptional case where the national court against whose decisions there is no judicial remedy, manifestly infringed the applicable law and the European courts' case law in the matter. In the case in question, the Court considered that the national court did not commit a manifest and thus sufficiently serious breach of Union law and that, consequently, the State in question did not incur liability for it.[51]

---

[46] No figures are published concerning art.258 TFEU [226] cases brought because of non-implementation of Court judgments. In 2005, the Commission started 2,653 infringement proceedings and brought 176 court actions against a Member State; 17 judgments ending such actions were pronounced, of which none were in favour of the Member State.

[47] art.260(3)1 TFEU.

[48] art.260(3)2 TFEU.

[49] See the following cases referred to by the Court in *Köbler* (C-224/01) [2003] E.C.R. I-10239; *Francovich* (Joined Cases C-6/90 and C-9/90) [1991] E.C.R. I-5357(35); *British Telecommunications* (C-392/93) [1996] E.C.R. I-1631(38); *Hedley Lomas* (C-5/94) [1996] E.C.R. I-2553(24); *Dillenkofer* (Joined Cases C-178/94 etc.) [1996] E.C.R. I-4845(20); *Norbrook Laboratories* (C-127/95) [1998] E.C.R. I-1531(106) and *Haim* (C-424/97) [2000] E.C.R. I-5123(43). See also *Traghetti v Italy* (C-173/03) [2006] E.C.R. I-5177.

[50] *Brasserie du Pêcheur and Factortame* (Joined Cases C-46/93 and C-48/93) [1996] E.C.R. I-1029; [1996] 1 C.M.L.R. 889. Idem. in Case *Heddley Lomas* (C-5/94) [1996] E.C.R. I-2553 and *Sutton* (C-66/95) [1997] E.C.R. I-2163; [1997] 2 C.M.L.R. 382.

[51] Case *Köbler v Austria* (C-224/01) [2003] E.C.R. I-10243.

(b) With Regard to Acts of Institutions and Other Bodies

The institutions concerned here are the Council, Parliament, the EIB[52] and the ECB.[53] The Commission and other interested parties can initiate a court action against those bodies when they are of the opinion that those acts infringe a Union provision[54] or when a failure of those bodies to act is considered by the Commission, the Member States or other institutions to be an infringement of the Treaty.[55] These actions will be examined in more detail in the chapter on the Court of Justice.

(c) With Regard to Legal or Natural Persons

The Commission has been endowed with important powers as regards undertakings both public[56] and private and natural persons. Those powers apply mainly in the competition and transport fields, where the Commission may impose fines and penalties[57] in case of violation, or order enterprises to disinvest themselves when investigating mergers and acquisitions.[58] The Commission may also start proceedings against foreign companies before national courts in third countries.[59]

(2) "Adopt regulations, directives, decisions, recommendations and opinions"

The TFEU refers, as indicated, to the "institutions" adopting regulations, directives, decisions, recommendations and opinions.[60] This is not without importance since, as pointed out, the decision-making institutions within the Union are, in principle, Parliament and Council acting jointly or the Council acting alone. The fact that the Commission also exercises a decision-making power might create the impression that the legislative power is shared by several institutions. Although all those institutions may indeed issue acts which are binding for the subjects of Union law, a distinction must be made between "legislative" powers, which are the prerogative of Parliament and Council, and "executive" and/or

---

[52] art.271(a) TFEU [237(a)]; see, for instance, *SGEEM v EIB* (C-370/89) [1992] E.C.R. I-6211.

[53] art.263,1 TFEU [230, first para]. On the other hand the ECB itself can initiate an action in the Court against a national central bank in case it is of the opinion that the latter has failed to fulfil an obligation under the Treaty.

[54] art.263 TFEU [230]. Those cases are brought either by governments, Union institutions or by individuals.

[55] art.265 TFEU [.232].

[56] art.106 TFEU [86].

[57] See Regulation 1/2003 (implementing arts 101 and 102 TFEU), art.15 ([2003] O.J. L1/1); Regulation 11/60 (implementing art.75(3))[1960] O.J. 52/1121; Regulation 1017/68 (applying the rules of competition to transport by rail, road and inland waterways) [1969], art.22, O.J. L175/1 and Regulation 139/2004 (the Merger Regulation) [2004] O.J. L24/1; see, e.g. the *Nestlé/Perrier* Decision [1992] O.J. L356/1.

[58] Regulation 139/2004, art.8(4), quoted above.

[59] See *Philip Morris v Commission* (Joined Cases T-377/00, T-379/00, T-380/00, T-260/01 and T-272/01) [2003] E.C.R. II-1 and Court (in appeal), Case C-131/03 P, [2006] E.C.R. 12.09.06: both jurisdictions confirmed the right of the Commission to start proceedings in a court in a third State.

[60] art.288,1 TFEU [249].

"implementing" powers, which befall the Commission. Although both the Legislator and the Executive may adopt binding acts, Parliament, the Council and the Commission do not operate on quite the same level, although it must be recognised that no clear-cut distinction exists between them.[61]

It should be remembered that in both cases the powers are "conferred" powers, i.e. the institutions were not endowed with a "general" decision-making power; the Treaties now refer to "conferral" of powers.[62] They only enjoy those powers which have explicitly been conferred upon them by the Treaties.[63]

As for non-binding acts, it is mostly the Commission which adopts recommendations and opinions: the many Notices and Communications of the Commission[64] fall under this category. It should be remembered that recommendations and opinions indeed have no binding force,[65] so that in fulfilling this task the Commission acts in a purely informative or advisory capacity. The most that can be said is that the Commission binds itself politically. The Treaty provides for several cases where an opinion of the Commission is required[66] and others where it is referred to as a possibility.[67]

It is in the areas where the Union exercises exclusive powers that the Commission's role comes to the fore, both in the development of the legislative procedure and in the implementation of the adopted rules. They concern the Customs Union,[68] competition,[69] the conservation of marine biological resources,[70] the common commercial policy[71] and the execution of the Union budget.[72] When exercising its right to act, the Commission has, in certain cases, a choice as to the form of the measure,[73] in other instances no form is prescribed[74] and sometimes a given act is required.[75] Decisions of the Commission are adopted, in case a vote is taken at any Member's request, "if a majority of the number of Members specified in the Treaty vote in favour"[76] and when at least, "a majority of the number of Members specified in the Treaty" are present.[77]

Such decisions must be authenticated to guarantee legal certainty[78]; failure to do so constitutes an infringement of an essential procedural requirement.[79] The

---

[61] See, e.g. Commission Directive 80/723 on the transparency of financial relations between Member States and public enterprises [1980] O.J. L195/35 and *France, Italy and United Kingdom v Commission* (Joined Cases 188/80, 189/80, 190/80) [1982] E.C.R. 2545; [1982] 3 C.M.L.R. 144, where the Court ruled that the Commission Directive in question was in conformity with the Treaty.

[62] art.5(1) EU.

[63] See above, Ch.6: The Council (3(1) Decision-making).

[64] See, e.g. Communication of the Commission following the famous *Cassis de Dijon* judgment [1980] O.J. C256/2.

[65] art.288,5 EU [249]. See, however, under Ch.3: The Legal Acts of the Union.

[66] See, e.g. art.156 TFEU [140] (opinion on problems arising at national level in the social field).

[67] art.97 TFEU [77]: reduction of charges and dues in respect of crossing of frontiers.

[68] art.3(1)(a) EU.

[69] art.101(3) TFEU [81(3)], 105(2) [85(2)], 106(3) [86(3)] and 108(2) [88(2)].

[70] art.17(1) EU.

[71] art.17(1) EU.

[72] The Commission is responsible for implementing the budget and administering the various Union funds: social fund, regional fund, cohesion fund, etc.

[73] See, e.g. art.160(3) TFEU [86(3)]: the Commission shall address "appropriate directives or decisions"; of course, the form depends on the content of the act.

[74] See, e.g. art.44 [38] TFEU: the Commission shall fix the amount of the charges.

[75] See, e.g. art.105(2) TFEU [85(2)].

[76] art.250 TFEU [219,1]. art.7 Rules of procedure, [2000] O.J. L308/26.

[77] art.8 Rules of Procedure.

[78] art.11,2 Rules of Procedure.

[79] *Commission v ICI* (C-286/95 P) [2000] E.C.R. I-2341.

Commission may, provided the principle of collective responsibility is fully respected, empower one or more of its members to take management or administrative measures on its behalf and subject to such restrictions and conditions as it shall impose. Powers conferred in this way may be sub-delegated to the Directors-General or Heads of Service, unless this is expressly prohibited in the empowering decision.[80] The Commission may not delegate its powers to autonomous bodies.[81]

It is of interest to note that the Commission is obliged to "reconsider" a decision which has become definitive when a request thereto is based on substantial new facts.[82]

The Rules of Procedure of the Commission are published in the *Official Journal of the European Union*.[83]

(3) Exercise of Powers Delegated by Legislative Act[84]

Many Commission decisions are based upon powers provided for by legislative acts.[85] Indeed, in accordance with the Treaty,[86] Parliament and the Council may delegate to the Commission the power to adopt non-legislative acts of general application to supplement or amend non-essential elements of legislative acts. This delegation of powers must necessarily be limited. As the Court indicated, the "basic elements to be dealt with" must be adopted by the Council in accordance with the procedures laid down by the Treaty. The provisions implementing the basic regulations may be adopted by the Commission (or the Council) according to a different procedure.[87] In fact and in law, it is not a "delegation of legislative power", since it only allows the Commission to, "supplement or amend certain non-essential elements of a legislative act". Furthermore, the Member States, via the committees that are part of the Commission's decision procedure, play an important, sometimes even a decisive, role in the procedure leading up to the adoption of a delegated act. As was explained above, the Council only meets a few days a month and has neither the opportunity nor the means to work out the detailed rules for implementing the Union legislation it enacts. This is, therefore, normally entrusted to the Commission. However, according to the Treaty,[88] the objectives, content, scope and duration of the delegation must be explicitly defined in the legislative act[89];

---

[80] art.213 Rules of Procedure. See, for instance, Decision 183/68 authorising certain management measures to be taken within the framework of the common organisation of the agricultural markets [1968] O.J. L89/13. See *Cementhandelaren v Commission* (8/72) [1972] E.C.R. 977; [1973] C.M.L.R. 7, concerning the legality of a document signed by a Director-General rather than by a Commissioner.

[81] See *Meroni v High Authority* (9/56) [1957 and 1958] E.C.R. 133.

[82] *INPESCA v Commission* (T-186/98) [2001] E.C.R. II-557.

[83] [2000] O.J. L 308/26. In 2001 the Commission added an Annex containing Provisions on Operational Procedures for Crisis Management [2001] O.J. L 317/1 and [2003] O.J. L92/14.

[84] art.290 TFEU.

[85] art.289 TFEU. Legislative acts are legal acts adopted by legislative procedure; there are "ordinary legislative procedures" (art.294 TFEU) and "special legislative procedures" (art.289(2) TFEU).

[86] art.83(1) TFEU.

[87] *Koster* (25/70) [1970] E.C.R. 1161(6).

[88] art.290(1)2 TFEU [202, third indent].

[89] See, for instance, Directive 2008/18 amending Directive 85/611 concerning undertakings for collective investments, "as regards the implementing powers conferred on the Commission" [2008] O.J. L76/42.

furthermore it is indicated that, "the essential elements of an area shall be reserved for the legislative act and accordingly shall not be the subject of a delegation of power".[90] The delegation to the Commission is thus limited and strictly circumscribed; in other words it does not confer on the Commission power to legislate.

The procedures to be followed by the Commission in exercising the delegated powers are laid down in the so-called *Comitology* Decision of the Council.[91] There are four different procedures and in three of them, the Commission is to co-operate with a committee; to these were added a "regulatory procedure with scrutiny" and a "safe-guard" procedure. The Council does not have to motivate the choice it makes of one of the procedures.[92]

The committees are composed of policy experts from the Member States. The Commission may only adopt a supplementing or amending act after such a committee has given its opinion on or approved the Commission's proposed measure.

The influence the opinion delivered by those committees has on the implementing powers of the Commission varies greatly from procedure to procedure:

- in the *advisory* procedure, which is normally applied, "in any case in which it is considered the most appropriate",[93] the Commission, "shall take the utmost account of the opinion delivered by the committee" by simple majority vote. The Commission must also inform the Committee of the manner in which its opinion has been taken into account;
- under the *management* procedure, normally used in the implementation of the common agricultural policy, fisheries policy and main Union programmes, the opinion of the Committee is delivered by a majority vote.[94] If the measures proposed by the Commission are in accordance with the opinion of the Committee, the Commission shall adopt measures that apply immediately. If the proposed measures are not in accordance with the Committee's opinion, they shall be communicated forthwith by the Commission to the Council. The Commission may then defer application of the measures for a period to be laid down in the basic instrument, but which may not exceed three months. Within that period, the Council may, acting by qualified majority, take a different decision;
- the *regulatory* procedure[95] should be used for measures of general scope designed to apply essential provisions. It provides that the Committee must concur with the proposed measures for the Commission to be able to adopt them. In case the Committee expresses a negative opinion or no opinion, the

[90] art.290(1)2 TFEU.
[91] Decision 1999/468, laying down the procedures for the exercise of implementing powers conferred on the Commission [1999] O.J. L 184/23, amended by Decision 2006/512 introducing the regulatory procedure with scrutiny [2006] O.J. L200/11. See Regulation 219/09 [2009] O.J. L87/109 adapting the regulatory procedure with scrutiny—Part Two and Regulation 496/09 [2009] O.J. L188/14 adapting Part Four. See also *Commission v Parliament and Council* (C-378/00) [2003] E.C.R. I-937 and Regulation 1882/2003 adapting Regulation 1999/468, [2003] O.J. L284/1; adaptation to the regulatory procedure with scrutiny—Part Three. [2008] O.J. L304/80 and to Part One [2008] O.J. L311/1.
[92] See case *Commission v Parliament and Council* (C-122/04) [2006] E.C.R.I-2001
[93] Or, according to *http://www.euractiv.commen/opinion/comitology/Article–117454*: "when the policy matters considered are not very sensitive politically".
[94] The same as for the Council, in accordance with art.16(4) and (5) EU [205(2)].
[95] See case *Commission v Parliament and Council* (C-122/04) [2006] E.C.R. I-2001, where the Commission contested the choice of the regulatory procedure, but the Court found that the measures to be adopted were not simply implementation.

Commission must make a proposal to the Council and inform Parliament. In case the proposal concerns a basic instrument adopted in accordance with the co-decision procedure and Parliament is of the opinion that the proposal exceeds the implementing powers provided for in that basic instrument, it shall inform the Council of its position. The Council then can take a decision by a majority vote within a period to be laid down in the basic instrument, but which may not exceed three months. If, on the other hand, the Council opposes the proposal, the Commission may submit an amended proposal or present a legislative proposal on the basis of the Treaty. In case the Council does not act within the set time period, the proposed implementing measure shall be adopted by the Commission;

- the *regulatory procedure with scrutiny*[96] to be followed for measures of general scope designed to amend non-essential elements of a basic instrument adopted jointly by Parliament and Council, among others, by deleting some of those elements or by adding new non-essential elements. This procedure should enable the two arms of the legislative authority to scrutinise such measures before they are adopted. This implies that Parliament should receive better information on the work of the Committees.
- the *safeguard* procedure applies where the basic instrument confers on the Commission the power to decide on safeguard measures. The Commission must notify the Council and the Member States of any decision regarding safeguard measures, unless it is stipulated that before adopting the decision, the Commission must consult the Member States in accordance with a procedure to be determined in each case.

Any Member State may refer the decision to the Council. The latter, acting by a qualified majority and within a time limit to be determined by the basic instrument, may take a different decision. Alternatively, it may be stipulated that the Council may confirm, amend or revoke the decision adopted by the Commission and that, in case the Council has not acted within the set time limit, the decision of the Commission is deemed to be revoked.

Some of the procedures described above are quite complex and lengthy, so much so that one may wonder whether one can still refer to them a, "conferring power to adopt non-legislative acts".[97] The Commission's hands are tied at every corner, and the decisions, if any are in fact taken not by the Commission, nor by the Council or Parliament, but by the representatives of the Member States which compose the various committees. Those representatives are totally anonymous within the Union framework, are not responsible to any institution and submitted to no control whatsoever [only the final implementing act is], although their work is not confidential but accessible to the public.[98] One might wonder therefore whether the procedures for the so-called supplementing powers conferred on the Commission are not to be considered as an anti-democratic deviation from the procedures laid down by the Treaties.

All this is the more surprising since the Council had received quite clear instructions from the governments for a speedy and efficient procedure. Those instructions were given at the time of the signature of the SEA. In the Declaration

---

[96] [2006] O.J. L200/11.
[97] art.290(1)1 TFEU.
[98] See *Rothmans v Commission* (T-188/97) [1999] E.C.R. II-2463, where the Court annulled a decision of the Commission refusing access to the rules of procedure and the minutes of a committee.

on the powers of implementation of the Commission attached to the SEA,[99] the Representatives of the governments of the Member States requested the Council to, "give the Advisory Committee procedure in particular a predominant place in the interest of speed and efficiency in the decision-making process, for the exercise of the powers of implementation conferred on the Commission". The question is, of course, what is to be understood by "advisory committee"? Were the Member States referring to the Consultative Committee mentioned above or to the committees in general? Whatever the answer, it can certainly not be said that the present procedures are speedy and efficient.[100]

(4) Participation in the Legislative Process

As was pointed out in the chapters on the Parliament and on the Council, the latter can, in most cases, only legislate on the basis of a proposal submitted by the Commission. The Commission no longer enjoys a complete monopoly in this respect since the Treaties now provide for initiatives from a group of Member States, initiatives from Parliament, requests from the Court of Justice, recommendations from the ECB and requests from the EIB.[101]

By submitting drafts for regulations, directives and decisions, the Commission does indeed participate directly in the shaping of measures taken by the Council and Parliament. Whenever the Commission makes such a proposal in pursuance of the Treaties; it exercises its right of initiative in the law-making process of the Union. There are cases where the Commission is required to make a proposal within a given time limit,[102] but in most cases the Commission must use its own judgment as to the suitability of making a proposal.[103] Although the Commission enjoys the near-exclusive right of initiative, the Treaty provides that both the Council[104] and Parliament[105] may "request" the Commission to submit to it any appropriate proposals. Of course, it is only a request, but it will be difficult, in many cases, for the Commission to ignore it; nonetheless, neither Council nor Parliament[106] can take legislative initiatives. When the Commission makes a proposal at the request of another institution, it remains nevertheless politically and legally[107] responsible for the proposal. The submission by the Commission of a proposal for legislation constitutes the start of the decision-making process in which

---

[99] First declaration adopted by the Conference at the time of signing the Act and annexed thereto: 1986.
[100] See *Commission v Parliament and Council* (C-378/00) [2003] E.C.R. I-937.
[101] Protocol No.2, art.3.
[102] See, e.g. arts 25 and 249 TFEU.
[103] See, e.g. art.109 TFEU [89].
[104] art.241 TFEU [208].
[105] art.225 TFEU [192]: the Treaty requires that such request be voted by a majority of the members of Parliament, and when it considers that a Union act is required for the purpose of implementing the Treaties. Although one could argue that the latter goes without saying, Parliament shall have to show, in each case, that an act is indeed required; such an obligation is not imposed on the Council.
[106] In the Parliament's Rules of Procedure reference is made to "initiative pursuant to Article 192 of the EC Treaty" (Rule 39), but it is clear from the content that it remains, even for Parliament, a request addressed to the Commission to take the initiative.
[107] *Werhahn v Council* (Joined Cases 63/72, 64/72, 65/72, 66/72, 67/72, 68/72, and 69/72) [1973] E.C.R. 1229 at 1247(8).

the three institutions, Commission, Parliament and Council each play an essential role. The roles of Parliament and of the Council have been described above in the chapters concerning those institutions, and it is therefore necessary to briefly describe the role of the Commission.

This role doesn't start with the submission of the proposal, nor does it end with it. Before drafting its proposal for a legislative act, the Commission must "consult widely".[108] Consequently, it holds informal consultations with, among others, national experts. This allows the Commission to judge the possible reactions of each of the Member States, which is essential, especially in cases of majority voting in the Council. In most cases the Commission will issue preparatory documents, such as Green Papers which contain a description of a given problem and the possible legislative solutions envisaged by the Commission. Those papers are widely distributed or sent to selected groups in order to obtain reactions and proposals.[109] The Green Paper is usually followed by a White Paper; available for anyone, it contains the broad lines of the legislation the Commission is planning to propose. Here, again, the Commission is looking for reactions from interested parties. The purpose of those consultations is, in general, to fulfil an obligation provided for in the EU Treaty, namely that decisions should be, "taken as closely as possible to the citizen",[110] but also, and for practical purpose, to allow the Commission's staff to gather the necessary information they need to draft their proposals.

Once a draft proposal has been approved by the Commission, it is, generally speaking, published in the *Official Journal*,[111] in order to allow all interested parties to comment on it. In certain cases the Commission will organise consultations of certain groups[112] and/or organise hearings. Although those consultations are quite time-consuming, they constitute, for the Commission, an invaluable source of information in view of the drafting of the definitive proposal or its modification, in case it was already submitted. It might be of interest to note that in 2008, for instance, the Commission submitted 420 proposals for directives, regulations and decisions.[113]

For the application of the principles of subsidiarity and proportionality, the Commission must also, before proposing legislative acts, forward the drafts or the amended drafts to national parliaments at the same time as to the Union legislator. Any such draft must contain a detailed statement making it possible to appreciate compliance with the above-mentioned principles. The reasons invoked must be substantiated by qualitative and, where possible, by quantitative indicators. The statement must also contain some assessment of the proposal's financial impact and, in case of a directive, of its implications for the rules to be put in place by the Member States. Any burden imposed by the envisaged act upon the Union, national governments, regional or local authorities, economic operators or citizens, must be minimised.[114]

---

[108] Protocol No.2, art.2.

[109] They are available under the reference COM, followed by the year in brackets and a number. They are always available on Internet for a limited time.

[110] art.1 EU.

[111] Proposals are published in the "C" series of the O.J. also available on the Internet, or available from the Commission and known as COM documents; the latter are also to be found in the *Official Journal*.

[112] See, e.g. [1994] O.J. C199/10.

[113] General Report 2008, p.234.

[114] Protocol No.2, art.5.

National Parliaments have eight weeks to send a reasoned opinion to the Presidents of Parliament, the Council and the Commission[115] stating why they consider that the draft does not comply with the principle of subsidiarity. In case the initiative originated with another body, the latter will be informed by the President of the Council. The drafters of the proposal shall, "take account of the reasoned opinion". Each national parliament has two votes, and if the reasoned opinion represents one third of all the votes allocated, the draft must be reviewed. This threshold is reduced to a quarter when it concerns the area of freedom, security and justice.

After such review, the drafter(s) may decide to maintain, amend or withdraw the draft. However, under the ordinary legislative procedure,[116] the Commission must review its proposal when the non-compliance reasoned opinion represents a simple majority of the allocated votes. In case the Commission then decides to maintain its proposal anyway, it must justify its position in a reasoned opinion. The two opinions are then submitted to the legislator. If 55 per cent of the members of the Council, or a majority of the votes cast by Parliament, is of the opinion that the proposal is not compatible with the principle of subsidiarity, it shall be given further consideration.[117]

The Court has jurisdiction in actions on grounds of infringement of the principle of subsidiarity in accordance with the procedure for the review of legality of acts of the institutions.[118]

All this to indicate that there is much more to the drafting of a proposal for Union legislation than the terms of the Treaty suggest: the Council or the Parliament and the Council shall decide, "on a proposal from the Commission".

The Commission's proposal constitutes, in case the consultation procedure applies, the basis for the consultation of Parliament by the Council; in practically all cases the proposal is sent directly by the Commission to both Parliament and the Council. The Commission will closely follow the work of Parliament and more particularly that of the parliamentary committees that examine the draft. Representatives of the Commission are always present when those committees meet to discuss its proposals. This allows the Commission both to explain its position in drafting the proposal and to better understand Parliament's reactions to it. The Commission is therefore fully prepared to eventually modify its proposal, which it may do as long as the Council has not acted, at any time during the procedures leading up to the adoption of a Union act.[119]

In parallel with the discussions within Parliament, the Commission is present when the proposal is discussed within the Council, either by COREPER or by the working groups set up by the latter. In many cases those groups are composed of the same national civil servants which were consulted informally by the Commission before the proposal was drafted; undoubtedly this allows for a smoother basis for the final decision of the Council.

---

[115] In 2008.

[116] See art.294 TFEU.

[117] art.7(3) Protocol No. 2.

[118] art.263 TFEU. This very complex and time-consuming procedure risks to prolong the already lengthy legislative activity, were it not that, according to some, very few national parliaments are able to react within the allocated eight weeks! This pessimistic view is belied by the facts: in 2008, for instance, the Commission sent 420 proposals and received 200 opinions; for more details see General Report 2008, p.235.

[119] art.293(2) TFEU [250(2)]. See, for instance, the amended proposal for a Council Directive amending Directive 91/440 on the development of the Union railways [1998] O.J. C321/6.

If the latter wishes to adopt an act constituting an amendment to the proposal, unanimity is required,[120] except in the conciliation procedure,[121] the budgetary procedure,[122] the establishment of the multi-annual financial framework[123] and the establishment of the Union's annual budget.[124] As pointed out before, the right of the Council to modify the proposal is certainly not unlimited: the modification may not, as the Court indicated, alter the substance of the proposal,[125] unless the Commission accepts the proposed modification. This would be the case when, during the discussion in the Council on the proposal, the Presidency makes a compromise proposal to break a deadlock; it is not unusual for the Commission itself to suggest such a compromise to the Presidency.[126] As was pointed out in the chapter on the Parliament, such modifications, even when they are accepted by the Commission, might still have to be resubmitted to Parliament for another opinion on the modified proposal.[127]

Finally, it must be noted that the Commission might be called upon to justify its proposal not only before Parliament,[128] but also before the Court, since the latter has recognised the right of applicants, in an action concerning the legality of an act, to bring proceedings not only against the Council for having adopted the act, but also against the Commission for having proposed it.[129]

(5) External Relations

The external relations of the Union will be analysed in detail in Part Six of this book, it may therefore suffice here to point out two aspects which concern the Commission in particular.

Where the Treaty provides for the conclusion of international agreements, mainly within the framework of the Union's commercial policy, the Commission makes recommendations to the Council. The latter may then authorise the Commission to open the necessary negotiations, and formulate directives for such negotiations. The Commission negotiates the international agreements in consultation with special committees appointed by the Council to assist it in this task.[130] Parliament, the Council, the Commission or a Member State may obtain the opinion of the Court as to whether an envisaged agreement is compatible with the provisions of the Treaties. Where the opinion is adverse, the agreement may not enter into force unless it is amended or the Treaties are revised.[131] As to the word "agreement", the Court held that it covers, "any undertaking entered into

---

[120] art.293(1) TFEU [250(1)].
[121] art.294(10) and (13) TFEU.
[122] art.310 TFEU.
[123] art.312 TFEU.
[124] art.314 TFEU.
[125] See, e.g. *Parliament v Council* (C-65/90) [1992] E.C.R. I-4593.
[126] *Parliament v Council* (C-65/90), above at fn. 125 at 4619(7).
[127] *Parliament v Council* (C-65/90), above at fn. 125.
[128] During the discussions in Parliament about the proposal or through parliamentary questions.
[129] *Werhahn v Council* (Joined Cases 63/72, 64/72, 65/72, 66/72, 67/72, 68/72 and 69/72) [1973] E.C.R. 1229 at 1247(8).
[130] art.218(4) TFEU [300(1)].
[131] art.118(11) TFEU [300(6)]. See, e.g. Court Opinion 1/91 on the compatibility of the Treaty establishing an European Economic Area (EEA) [1991] E.C.R. I-6079.

by a subject of international law, which has binding force".[132] Besides negotiating international agreements, the Commission:

> "[S]hall be instructed, together with the High Representative, to establish all appropriate forms of cooperation with the organs of the United Nations, and its specialised agencies, the Council of Europe, the Organisation for Security and Cooperation in Europe, the Organisation for Economic Co-operation and Development (OECD) and other international organisations".[133]

(6) Implementation of the Union Budget

The budgetary procedure and the role of the Commission in it were examined in the chapter on the Parliament.[134] The role of the Commission is formally limited to drafting its own budget and consolidating the estimates of the other institutions, except the ECB, in a draft budget to be submitted to Parliament and the Council.[135] Once the budget is adopted, it falls to the Commission to implement it in accordance with the regulations laid down by the Council.[136] Detailed rules are provided in these regulations for each institution concerning its part in effecting its own expenditure.[137] Afterwards, the Commission must seek discharge in respect of the implementation of its part of the budget. To this end, it must submit annually to the Council and to Parliament the accounts for the preceding financial year relating to the implementation of the budget, together with a financial statement of the assets and liabilities of the Union.[138] In exercising their powers of control over the Commission's implementation of the budget, the Council and Parliament are assisted by the Court of Auditors, which forwards to them an annual report after the close of each financial year.[139] The Council and Parliament examine the accounts, the financial statement and the report. Discharge is given to the Commission by Parliament on a recommendation from the Council, acting by a qualified majority.[140]

As part of the implementation of the budget, the Commission administers the European Agricultural Guarantee Fund, the European Agricultural Fund for Rural Development, the European Fisheries Fund, the European Social Fund, the European Regional Development Fund and the Cohesion Fund. The Commission is also responsible for administering the European Development Fund for the

---

[132] Opinion 2/92 concerning the competence to participate in the Third Revised Decision of the OECD on National Treatment [1995] E.C.R. I-521. The Court also decided that the fact that certain questions could be dealt with by means of other remedies, for instance art.190 TFEU [173] does not preclude the Court from being asked an opinion under art.218(11) TFEU [art.300(6) EC].

[133] art.220(1) TFEU [304].

[134] See above under Ch.5: The European Parliament (2(9)).

[135] art.314 TFEU [272(2) and (3)].

[136] art.322(1) TFEU [279]. Financial Regulation of December 21, 1977 applicable to the general budget of the EC [1977] O.J. L356/1, amended [1997] O.J. L340/1.

[137] art.317 TFEU [274].

[138] art.318 TFEU [275].

[139] art.287 TFEU [248]. See also below, Ch.11: The Court of Auditors.

[140] art.319 TFEU [276]. In 1984, Parliament refused to give discharge for the 1983 budget implementation; [1994] EC Bull. 12–67. In 1987 it deferred the discharge in respect of the implementation of the 1985 budget; Twenty-Second General Report (1988), 75.

African, Caribbean and Pacific States, financed by direct contributions from the Member States.[141]

The Commission is also empowered to borrow on the world financial markets and loan money for the financing of atomic energy projects[142] and to finance infrastructure and industrial projects.[143] The borrowing is done by the Commission, but the administration of the resources is delegated to the European Investment Bank. The Commission must carry out external administrative investigations for the purpose of strengthening the fight against fraud, corruption and any other illegal activity adversely affecting the Union's financial interests. To exercise those powers the Commission established the European Anti-Fraud Office (OLAF).[144]

(7) Publication of the Annual General Report

Each year, one month before the opening of the session of Parliament (first Tuesday in March), the Commission must publish a General Report on the activities of the European Union.[145] This report covers the activities of all the institutions and organs of the Union, and as such is an invaluable source of information. Several areas, however, are covered very summarily because they are the object of separate reports either from the Commission or from other institutions or bodies.[146]

3. Rules of Procedure and the Commission's Staff

The Commission must adopt its rules of procedure so as to ensure that both it and its departments operate in accordance with the provisions of the Treaty.[147] The departments consist of Directorates-General and Services whose responsibilities correspond more or less to the various tasks assigned to the Union by the Treaty.[148] With regard to the Union staff, two texts should be mentioned; the

---

[141] See General Report 2003, Ch.VI, ACP countries.

[142] art.172(4) Euratom and [1977] O.J. L88/9.

[143] See [1978] O.J. L298/9.

[144] For more details see hereunder Ch.14: Financing Union Activities, and [1999] O.J. L136/1.

[145] art.249(2) TFEU [212]. Since 2010, only found on the Internet.

[146] For those reports see above Ch.5: The European Parliament (Task and Powers, (5) The General Report).

[147] art.249(1) TFEU [218(2)]. See [2000] O.J. L308/26; amended [2002] O.J. L21/23 and [2004] O.J. L251/9, adding an Annex containing provisions on electronic and digitised documents; amended [2005] O.J. L347/83 replacing arts 1 to 28; amended [2006] O.J. L19/20 setting-up the ARGUS general rapid alert system. The Rules were amended in 2008 as regard detailed rules for the application of Regulation 1367/06 on the application of the provisions of the Aarhus Convention on Access to Information, Public Participation in Decision-making and Access to Justice in Environmental Matters to Community Institutions and Bodies [2008] O.J. L140/22.

[148] arts 3, 4, 5 and 6 TFEU [3 and 4]. See also the Declaration adopted by the Conference of the Representatives of the Governments of the Member States convened in Turin on March 29, 1996 to adopt the amendments to be made to the Treaties concerning the organisation and functioning of the Commission; the Conference noted the intention to undertake, in parallel with the reorganisation of the tasks within the college, a corresponding reorganisation of its departments [1997] O.J. C340/137. Presently there are, besides the Secretariat General and the Legal Service, 24 Directorates General, eight offices, two services and a group of policy advisers and Eurostat.

Protocol on the Privileges and Immunities of the European Communities[149] and the Staff Regulations of Officials of the European Communities and the Conditions of Employment of other Servants of the European Communities.[150] It might be worth mentioning at this point that the Union civil servants don't pay taxes to the Member State whose citizens they are on their Union salaries, but that they pay income tax to the Union itself and cannot, like other citizens, deduct anything, like costs or interest payments, from their taxable income.[151] Officials are recruited by the various institutions from the pool of candidates selected by the European Personnel Selection Office (EPSO)[152]; in other words, they are not seconded by the national administrations[153]—this should guarantee their independence and objectivity. Lately, however, the institutions, unable because of budgetary restraints, to recruit more personnel, have engaged, on a temporary basis, officials from the Member States (there were 1149 in 2008!); this, necessarily, creates a problem with regard to their independence and the influence the Member States can exercise. This is a highly unsatisfactory situation; but since the solution depends on the Member States, which must agree to provide more budgetary means, a solution is not in sight. At the end of 2008, the Commission had 19,796 permanent administrative posts and 366 temporary ones, and 3,828 permanent research posts. There were also 1,913 permanent posts and 177 temporary ones for offices attached to the Commission. In the agencies (see below, Ch.13: Decentralised Agencies) there were 4,163 for officials and temporary staff and 326 for temporary staff in the executive agencies.[154]

4. ACCESS TO DOCUMENTS

Access of the public to Commission documents is, as for the other institutions, provided for[155] and a refusal to grant access must, according to the Court of First Instance, state reasons for refusal.[156] Access to documents is, however, to be distinguished from access to information.[157]

Further Reading

David Spence, *The European Commission* (John Harper Publishing, 2006).

---

[149] Protocol (No.7 [34]) on the privileges and immunities of the European Union.

[150] Regulation 723/2004 [1968] O.J. L124/1.

[151] Although the income tax rate might be lower than the national ones, Union officials cannot deduct anything from their Union income: the whole income is taxed, contrary to what happens in the Member States, where one may deduct one's costs, interests payments, etc.

[152] EPSO was set up by Decision 2002/60 of the institutions, the Committees and the Ombudsman [2002] O.J. L197/53 and Decision 2002/621 of the same on the organisation and operation of EPSO [2002] O.J. L197/56.

[153] It goes without saying that when recruiting officials, the Union institutions must take the nationality of the candidates into account, and although, "no post may be reserved for a given nationality" (Staff Regulation art.27), a "geographical distribution" must exist, based upon the size of the population of the respective Member States. In 2005, there were about 17,000 permanent posts (including 1,185 for the language service).

[154] General Report 2008, p.236.

[155] Regulation 1049/2001 regarding public access to European Parliament, Council and Commission documents [2001] O.J. L145/43.

[156] [1994] O.J. L46/58 and *Interporc* (T-124/96) [1998] E.C.R. II-231. See also Notice on the internal rules of procedure for processing requests for access to files: [1997] O.J. C23/3.

[157] Case *Meyer v Commission* (T-106/99) [1999] E.C.R. II-3273.

Chapter Nine

The Court of Justice of the European Union[1]

The Court of Justice of the European Union includes the Court of Justice ("Court"), the General Court ("GC") and specialised courts.[2]

The task of those courts, is to ensure that "in the interpretation and the application of the Treaties[3] the law is observed".[4] They shall, in accordance with the Treaties, (a) rule on actions brought by a Member State, an institution or a natural or legal person, (b) give preliminary rulings, at the request of courts or tribunals of the Member States, on the interpretation of Union law or on the validity of acts adopted by the institutions, and (c) rule on other cases provided for in the Treaties.[5]

As the Court pointed out, the Union is:

> "[B]ased on the rule of law, inasmuch as neither its Member States nor its institutions can avoid a review of whether measures adopted by them are in conformity with the basic constitutional charter, the [Treaties]. The [Treaties] established the Court as the judicial body responsible for ensuring that both the Member States and the [Union] institutions comply with the law".[6]

The same applies, mutatis mutandis, to the natural and legal persons who are subjects of the law of the Union.

The above quote from one of the Court's judgments contains several essential elements. In the first place, there is the statement that the Union is, "based on the rule of law", in other words, the law prevails over all other considerations such as political and economic ones. This basic rule is not always well perceived by the Member States and there lies a particular task for the courts in ensuring the application of the law. From there the need for the judges to be totally independent,[7]

---

[1] Provisions concerning the Court of Justice of the European Union are to be found in art.19 EU, in the TFEU (art.251–281), in the Protocol on the Statute of the Court of Justice of the European Union attached to the TFEU and in the Rules of Procedure and other publications of the courts.

[2] art.19,1 EU.

[3] By Treaties is meant the Treaty on European Union (EU), the Treaty on the Functioning of the European Union (TFEU) and the Treaty establishing the European Atomic Energy Community (Euratom).

[4] art.19,1 EU.

[5] art.19,3 EU.

[6] *Les Verts v Parliament* (294/83) [1986] E.C.R. 1357 at 1365; [1987] 2 C.M.L.R. 343. See also art.6(1) EU: "The Union is founded on . . . the rule of law"; this provision was inserted by the Amsterdam Treaty.

[7] See art.253,1 TFEU [223,1]: "the Judges and the Advocates-General shall be chosen from persons whose independence is beyond doubt . . .". Before taking up his duties, "each judge shall, in open court, take an oath to perform his duties impartially and conscientiously and to preserve the secrecy of the deliberations of the Court" (art.2, Statute).

the more so since, as was explained above, the Council tends to act as an intergovernmental conference where every member fights for his country's interests, Parliament does not yet have all the required powers to exercise an effective democratic control and the Commission, which, besides its overwhelming administrative task, must also fulfil a political function, is bound to accept compromises in the implementation of Union legislation by the Member States.

The second important element in the Court's statement is the reference to the Treaties as the "basic constitutional charter". The Treaties must indeed be viewed as the constitution of the Union, i.e. the basic legal text from which all other rules derive. This is expressed, among others, by the fundamental principle that, "each institution shall act within the limits of the powers conferred upon it by the Treaties and in conformity with the procedures, conditions and objectives set out in them".[8] In other words, the Treaties are the only source of Union legislation and activities.

Finally, there is the reminder that the last word with regard to the legality of all Union acts lies with the courts. In other terms, whatever the institutions decide, whatever the natural and legal persons do, they are all, in the last resort, subject to the control of the courts.

The task of the courts is complicated by the fact that Union law is basically social and economic law, which is essentially evolutive and in constant need of adaptation. This fact is probably best rendered by the formula the Court has often used: "at the present stage in the development of [Union] law".[9] Indeed, very few of the 55 provisions of the EU Treaty and of the 358 articles of the TFEU are drafted with detailed precision; most of them only lay down general rules and the procedures necessary for their implementation. Consequently, when called upon to state what the Union law is in a given field, it is in the first place by reference to the objectives of the Union that the courts will decide. It can therefore be said that existing rules are defined and new ones are formulated via teleological interpretation. Indeed, the task of the courts is not only to interpret, but also to formulate the law in the absence of explicit provisions.

This, of course, is not particular to the Union courts, since, "wherever there are courts, the law grows at the hand of the judges".[10] But it is especially true for the Union.

Although the courts can only express themselves when called upon to do so, they have, over the years, built an impressive set of rules and principles which are of prime importance for the shaping of the law of the Union. This was done mainly through judgments interpreting the Treaties and the acts issued by the institutions, at the request of a national judge. When the latter is confronted with questions concerning the meaning of Union rules applicable in cases pending before this judge, he can, as will be seen, ask the courts for an answer (the preliminary ruling). Which also shows how important a role the national judge plays in the implementation, interpretation and development of Union law.

---

[8] art.13(2) TFEU [7(1)].
[9] See, e.g. *Fietje* (27/80) [1980] E.C.R. 3839 at (8); [1981] 3 C.M.L.R. 722.
[10] Schwarzenberger, *International Law*, p.24.

I. The Court of Justice ("Court")

1. THE JUDGES AND ADVOCATES-GENERAL

As indicated, the Court consists of one Judge per Member State, i.e. presently 27 Judges[11] and is assisted by eight Advocates-General.[12] However, the possibility of increasing that number to 11 is provided for in a Declaration annexed to the final act of the intergovernmental conference which adopted the Treaty of Lisbon.[13] These figures might also change after a next enlargement becomes effective.

The Judges and the Advocates-General shall be chosen from persons, "whose independence is beyond doubt and who possess the qualifications required for appointment to the highest judicial offices in their respective countries[14] or who are jurisconsults of recognised competence".[15]

The Judges may not hold any political or administrative office; they may not engage in any occupation, gainful or not, unless exemption is exceptionally given by the Council.[16]

The Judges and the Advocates-General are appointed for a term of six years by common accord of the Governments of the Member States,[17] after consultation of a panel set up in order to give an opinion on the candidates' suitability to perform the duties of Judge and Advocate-General of the Court and the General Court.[18]

The President of the Court is elected by the Judges from among their number, for a term of three years; he may be re-elected.[19]

The Court sits in chambers or in a Grand Chamber, in accordance with the rules laid down in the Statute of the Court ("Statute"),[20] which also provides for a full Court.

The Grand Chamber is currently composed of 11 Judges[21] and Chambers are composed of five or three Judges.[22] There are presently three Chambers of five

---

[11] art.19(2) EU [art.221 EC]: "the Court of Justice shall consist of one judge from each Member State." Every three years there shall be a partial replacement of the Judges and Advocates-General in accordance with the conditions laid down in the Statute of the Court of Justice of the European Union (art.253,2 TFEU). Retiring Judges and Advocates-General may be reappointed (art.253,4 TFEU).

[12] There are eight Advocates-General.

[13] Declaration 38 provides that if the Court so requests, the number of Advocates-General shall be increased to 11 by the Council acting unanimously and that Poland will also have a permanent Advocate-General, like Germany, France, Italy, Spain and the United Kingdom.

[14] Those qualifications are thus determined by reference to national law.

[15] art.253,1 TFEU [223,1].

[16] art.4 Statute.

[17] art.253,3 TFEU [223,1]. Several other provisions regarding the Judges and Advocates-General are to be found in the Statute of the Court, which is attached as a Protocol to the TFEU.

[18] art.255 TFEU. This panel shall comprise seven persons chosen from among former members of those courts, members of national supreme courts and lawyers of recognised competence, one of which shall be proposed by Parliament. The members of the panel are appointed by the Council which establishes its operating rules. It shall act on the initiative of the President of the Court.

[19] art.253,3 TFEU [223,3].

[20] The Protocol on the Statute of the Court of Justice of the European Union is annexed to the TFEU as Protocol No.3.

[21] For its composition see art.11b Rules of Procedure ("Rules"). A codified version of the Rules was published in [2003] O.J C193/1 and amended several times. The Grand Chamber and the full Court dealt with 13 per cent of the cases in 2005.

[22] art.251,2 TFEU [221,2]. See also the art.11(b)1 and 11(c)1 Rules on the participation of Judges in the Chambers. In 2005 the Chambers of five Judges dealt with 54 per cent of the cases and the Chambers of three Judges with 33 per cent.

Judges (the 1st, 2nd and 3rd) and three Chambers of three Judges (the 4th, 5th and 6th). To each five-Judge Chamber are assigned eight Judges and to each three-Judge Chamber are assigned seven Judges, all sitting by rotation as provided for in the Rules of Procedure ("Rules").[23] Most cases brought before the Court are heard by a Chamber. However, when a Member State or an institution that is a party to a proceeding so requests,[24] the Court must sit in a Grand Chamber.[25] The Court must sit in full Court where: Parliament requests dismissal of the Ombudsman[26]; the Council or the Commission apply for the retirement of a member of the Commission[27]; and where the Court of Auditors requests the Court to find that one of its members no longer fulfils the requisite conditions.[28] Moreover, when it considers that a case before it is of exceptional importance, the Court may decide, after hearing the Advocate-General, to refer the case to the full Court.[29]

Before taking up his duties, each Judge and Advocate-General does, in open Court, take an oath to perform his duties impartially and conscientiously and to preserve the secrecy of the deliberations of the Court.[30] The Judges and Advocates-General are immune from legal proceedings during their term of office and afterwards in respect of acts performed by them in their official capacity, including words spoken or written. The Court, sitting as a full Court, may waive the immunity.[31]

2. The Task of the Advocates-General

The position of the Advocate-General is a particularly interesting one: he is a member of the Court, but does not participate in the deliberations of the Court, although, as the Court itself stated it, he participates publicly and personally in the process leading up to the Court's decision. The Advocate-General has the same status as the Judges, particularly in so far as concerns immunity and the grounds on which he may be deprived of his office, which guarantees his full impartiality and total independence. The Advocate-General is not a public prosecutor, is not subject to any authority, in contrast to the manner in which the administration of justice is organised in certain Member States. This allows him to carry out his own examination of the case and express a personal opinion, something a Judge cannot do. The Advocate-General can also examine any related question, even if not brought forward by the parties.

Consequently, the submissions presented by the Advocate-General at the end of the oral proceedings do not reflect the Court's views, they constitute the individual reasoned opinion, expressed in open court, of a member of the Court.[32] But when the Court follows the views of the Advocate-General they often constitute a precious source of information concerning the reasoning which led to the

[23] For the Chambers see art.11c, the Rules.
[24] art.16,3, Statute.
[25] art.11a and 11b, Rules: the Grand Chamber shall be composed of the President of the Court, the Presidents of the Chambers of five Judges and other Judges designated from a list (see art.11b,2, Rules).
[26] art.228(2),2 TFEU [195(2)2].
[27] art.245(2),3 TFEU [213(2),3] and art.247 TFEU [216].
[28] art.286(6) TFEU [247(7)].
[29] art.16, last para, Statute.
[30] art.2, Statute.
[31] art.3, Statute.
[32] *Emesa Sugar* (17/98) [2000] E.C.R. I–665.

Court's decision. In many cases the Court simply refers, for certain questions, to the reasons set out by the Advocate-General in his Opinion and which the Court adopts.[33] In other cases, the Court even refers the national judge, who raised a preliminary question, to the Opinion of the Advocate-General to solve problems, which the Court itself is not empowered to consider.[34] Parties are not admitted to submit observations in response to the opinion of the Advocate-General.[35]

The Court may decide that a case shall be determined without a submission from the Advocate-General where it considers that the case raises no new points of law, and after hearing the Advocate-General.[36]

The submissions of the Advocates-General are published in the Court's reports (E.C.R.), together with the judgment, when the latter is published, which is not always the case.

3. THE COURT'S JURISDICTION

Although the task of the Court is defined in a short and sibylline text: ensure that, in the interpretation and application of the Treaties, "the law is observed", its jurisdiction is multiple. In order of appearance in the Treaties, this jurisdiction consists mainly of the following:

- "find" whether or not a Member State has failed to fulfil an obligation under the Treaties[37];
- "exercise unlimited jurisdiction" with regard to penalties provided for in regulations[38];
- "review the legality" of binding Union acts or failure of the institutions to act[39];
- "give preliminary rulings"[40];
- "has jurisdiction", in disputes relating to compensation for damage caused by the institutions or their servants[41];
- "has jurisdiction" in disputes between the Union and its servants[42];
- decide in disputes concerning obligations of Member States under the Statute of the ECB or measures adopted by the organs of the ECB and obligations of the national central banks[43];
- "give judgment" pursuant to an arbitration clause in a contract concluded by or on behalf of the Union[44];
- decide in disputes between Member States submitted under a special agreement between the parties[45];

---

[33] *Centrosteel* (C-456/98) [2000] E.C.R. I–6007 at (12).
[34] *Grzelczyk* (C-184/99) [2001] E.C.R. I–6193 at (18).
[35] *Emesa Sugar* (C-17/98) [2000] E.C.R. I–665.
[36] art.20, Statute last para.
[37] arts 258 and 260 TFEU [226 and 228].
[38] art.261 TFEU [229].
[39] arts 263 and 265 TFEU [230 and 232].
[40] art.267 TFEU [234].
[41] arts 268 and 340 TFEU [235 and 288].
[42] art.270 TFEU [236].
[43] art.271 TFEU [237].
[44] art.272 TFEU [238].
[45] art.274 TFEU [240].

- decide on the inapplicability of a regulation when the latter is at issue in a proceeding before the Court[46];
- "suspend" the application of a contested act[47];
- "prescribe" any necessary interim measures[48]; and
- "decide on appeal" against judgments of the GC.[49]

The most important aspects of this multiple jurisdiction shall be examined in some detail hereunder.

(1) Finding that a Member State has failed to fulfil an obligation under the Treaties

Both the Commission and a Member State[50] may bring such a matter before the Court. For the Commission, the possibility to initiate an action of this kind[51] constitutes its main instrument for fulfilling the task of "guardian of the Treaty".

If the Commission considers that a Member State has failed to fulfil an obligation under the Treaties, it must contact the Member State in question about the alleged failure and give it the "opportunity to submit its observations" within a given period. If these observations are not satisfactory or if the Member State fails to submit any, the Commission must deliver a reasoned opinion formally requesting the Member State to fulfil its obligations within a given time limit.

Finally, if the Member State does not comply with that opinion, the Commission may (it is not an obligation) refer the matter to the Court.

A Member State which considers that another Member State has failed to fulfil an obligation under the Treaty, must first bring the matter before the Commission. The Commission then gives each State the opportunity to submit its own case and its observations on the other party's case, both orally and in writing. The Commission must, after that, deliver a reasoned opinion within three months after the date the matter was brought before it. The absence of such an opinion cannot prevent the matter from being brought before the Court by the complaining Member State. Out of 12 cases which were brought before the Commission, only three reached the Court, and only two ended with a judgment.[52]

With regard to cases brought by a Member State against another Member State, attention must be drawn to the obligation undertaken by the Member

---

[46] art.277 TFEU [241].

[47] art.278 TFEU [242].

[48] art.279 TFEU [243].

[49] art.256(3),2 and (3),3 TFEU [225(1),2, and (3),3].

[50] Such actions by Member States are rare.

[51] In 2008, e.g. the Commission brought 103 actions against Member States before the Court; 103 judgments were pronounced, only 9 in favour of a Member State: the Annual Report 2008 of the Court, 59.

[52] *France v United Kingdom* (141/78) [1979] E.C.R. 2923; in accordance with para.3 of art.259 TFEU [227], the Commission had concluded that the UK was in breach of its obligations under the Treaty; the Court came to the same conclusion. The second example is *Belgium v Spain* (C-388/95) [2000] E.C.R. I–3123 (the Commission did not deliver an opinion and therefore Belgium went directly to court: see para.30 of judgment) and the third *Ireland v France* (58/77) was settled on 14.02.78, during the Court proceedings.

States, "not to submit a dispute concerning the interpretation or application of the Treaty to any method of settlement other than those provided for therein".[53] The principal method provided for in the Treaty being the recourse to the Court, this obligation guarantees, together with the preliminary ruling, uniformity in the interpretation and application of Union law. It should be noted that the Court also has jurisdiction in disputes between Member States that relate to the subject matter of the Treaty, when such a dispute is submitted to it under a special agreement.[54]

In cases against a Member State, the Court can only "find" that the State has failed to fulfil an obligation. However, if the State does not take the necessary measures to comply with the judgment of the Court, the Commission can again bring the case before the Court[55] after having given the State the opportunity to submit its observations. In that case the Commission must, "specify the amount of the lump sum or penalty payment to be paid by the Member State which it considers appropriate in the circumstances".[56] This possibility was introduced by the EU Treaty and put an end to an embarrassing situation in which Member States simply ignored the Court's finding. It was applied for the first time in July 2000, after the Court found that Greece had failed to comply with a 1992 judgment; it imposed a penalty payment of €20,000 for each day of delay in complying with the 1992 judgment.[57] It should be noted that the Court has jurisdiction to impose a financial penalty not suggested by the Commission.[58]

The Treaty of Lisbon added the possibility for the Commission, when it brings an action against a Member State for failing to fulfil its obligation to, "notify measures transposing a directive"[59] adopted under a legislative procedure,[60] to specify right away, in its appeal to the Court, the amount of the lump sum or penalty payment to be paid by the Member State concerned. The Court, of course, remains free to impose the amounts it considers adequate.

(2) Unlimited jurisdiction with regard to Penalties provided for in Regulations

In order to ensure compliance with the obligations laid down in the regulations they issue, Parliament and the Council acting jointly, or the Council, may make provisions for penalties to be imposed on natural and legal persons in case of infringement.[61] Those persons have, of course, the right to ask the Court to

---

[53] art. 344 TFEU [292]. See, *Commission v Ireland* (C-459/03) [2006] E.C.R. I-4635, where the Court found that Ireland had infringed the Treaty by starting an arbitration procedure against the UK in the framework of the UN.

[54] art.273 TFEU [239].

[55] art.260(2)1 [228(2)1].

[56] art.260(2)2 TFEU [228(2)2]. See, for example, *Commission v Greece* (C-568/07) [2009] E.R. I- 04.06.09, where Greece was condemned to pay the Commission a lump sum of €1 million for not having implemented the whole Court's judgment in time.

[57] *Commission v Greece* (C-387/97) [2000] E.C.R. I–5047.

[58] *France v Commission* (C-304/02) [2005] E.C.R. I-6263.

[59] art.260(3) TFEU [228].

[60] See art.294 TFEU [251].

[61] art.261 TFEU [229]. See, e.g. art.95(3)2 TFEU [75(3)2] and art.103(2)(a) [83(2)(a)]. It has been argued that art.261 TFEU [229] also attributes to the Council and Parliament acting jointly, or to the Council, a general competence to provide for penalties in the regulations they issue. This would, in my view, be contrary to the principle of conferred powers.

review the legality of the imposed penalties[62] or to reduce them but, much more important, they can also, in those proceedings, contest the validity of the regulation itself on which the penalties are based.[63]

The unlimited jurisdiction of the Court must be explicitly provided for in the regulation[64]; it allows the Court not only to annul the penalty, but also to increase or decrease it.[65]

The Treaty also attributes unlimited jurisdiction to the Court in the case of claims for damages resulting from the non-contractual liability of the Union[66] and in disputes between the Union and its servants.[67]

(3) Review of the Legality of an Act and of the Failure of an Institution to Act

(a) Appeal for Annulment[68]

In reviewing the legality of Union acts, the Court[69] gives judicial protection to all those who are subject to Union law, against arbitrary action by the institutions. It also ensures that the activities of the Union remain within the boundaries laid down by the Treaties and that institutions respect the balance of powers within the Union.

Proceedings for annulment must be instituted within two months[70] of the publication of the measure in the *Official Journal of the European Union*[71] or of its notification[72] to the claimant, or, in the absence thereof, of the day on which it came to the knowledge of the latter, as the case may be.[73]

---

[62] art.263 TFEU [230].

[63] art.277 TFEU [241].

[64] See, e.g. Regulation 11, art.18 [1960] O.J. 1121/60; Regulation 1/2003 (competition), art.23 ([2003] O.J. 1/1); Regulation 1017/68 (transport), art.24 ([1968(I)] O.J. 302); Regulation 3975/87 (air transport sector) art.14 ([1987] O.J. L374/1); Regulation 2299/89 (computerised reservation systems) art.17 ([1989] O.J. L1889/1, modified [2009] O.J. L35/47) and Regulation 139/2004 (control of concentrations) art.16 ([2004] O.J. L24/1).

[65] See, e.g. *United Brands v Commission* (27/76) [1978] E.C.R. 207; [1978] 1 C.M.L.R. 429, where the fine was reduced from one million units of account to 850,000, because part of the decision was annulled. There are no examples of the Court increasing a fine; undertakings upon which a fine has been imposed practically always go to the Court and ask for a reduction, which they do obtain very often; consequently, the Commission probably takes that into account when deciding on the importance of the fine! See, however, Guidelines on the method of setting fines [1998] O.J. C9/3.

[66] arts 268 and 340 TFEU [235 and 288], see hereunder (5) of this chapter.

[67] art.270 TFEU [236].

[68] art.263 TFEU [230].

[69] The following remarks apply also to the GC.

[70] art.263,6 TFEU [230,7]; for the calculation of this time limit, see the Rules art.80. As was seen in the chapter on The Legal Acts of the Union, to those two months must be added automatically 10 days for distance (to allow the interested parties to receive the O.J.) also when the act was notified directly to the applicant: Rules, art.81(1) and (2).

[71] art.297(3),3 TFEU [254(3)].

[72] Notification necessarily involves the communication of a detailed account of the contents of the measure notified and of the reasons on which it is based: *Socurte* (C-143/95 P) [1997] E.C.R. I-1.

[73] art.263,6 TFEU [230,5].

(i) **Acts Submitted to the Control of Legality.** The acts referred to are: legislative acts[74]; acts adopted by Parliament jointly with the Council, by the Council, the Commission and the ECB,[75] other than recommendations and opinions; and acts of Parliament and of the European Council, "intended to produce legal effects vis-à-vis third parties".[76] They also include acts of bodies, offices and agencies of the Union intended to produce legal effects vis-à-vis third parties and when this is provided for in the founding act.[77]

It follows from the case law of the courts that the form in which such acts are cast is, in principle, immaterial as regards the question whether they are open to challenge in court or not, it is the content that counts.[78] Where form is concerned, it is interesting to note, for example, that the GC accepted as admissible an action for annulment brought against an oral statement: a challengeable act needs not correspond to a written decision.

(ii) **Who may Lodge an Appeal for Annulment?** With regard to the admissibility of court actions (locus standi), all the Member States apply a principle well coined in French as *pas d'intérêt pas d'action*. The same principle applies within

---

[74] art.289(3) TFEU: acts adopted by "legislative procedure" i.e. regulations, directives and decisions jointly adopted by Parliament and Council on a proposal from the Commission, which constitutes the ordinary legislative procedure (art.289(1) TFEU). Besides this procedure there is the special legislative procedure for the adoption of legislative acts by Parliament with the participation of the Council or by the Council with the participation of Parliament (art.289(2) TFEU)

[75] art.263.3 TFEU [230]; the ECB (European Central Bank) was added by the Maastricht Treaty in art.230 EC and also in arts 232, 233, 234, 237, 241 and 288 EC.

[76] art.263,1 TFEU [230] refers to acts, "other than recommendations and opinions"; those acts are, in the first place, regulations, directives and decisions, see TFEU art.288 [249]. Since, according to that provision, recommendations and opinions "have no binding force", one must accept that the other acts do have such force. The question is whether there are other binding acts. No doubt there are, international agreements being one example. See *SFEI* (C-39/93 P) [1994] E.C.R. I-2681 at (27), where the Court stated that an institution empowered to find that there has been an infringement and to inflict a sanction in respect of it, and to which private persons may make complaints, necessarily adopts a measure producing legal effects when it terminates an investigation initiated upon a complaint by such person, and *Comité des Salines* (T-154/94) [1996] E.C.R. II-1377 at (32); [1997] 1 C.M.L.R. 943.

[77] TFEU art.263,5 [230].

[78] In *Commission v Council* (22/70) [1971] E.C.R. 263 at (42); [1971] C.M.L.R. 335, the Court ruled that: "an action for annulment must therefore be available in the case of all measures adopted by the institutions, whatever their nature or form, which are intended to have legal effect". Again, in *IBM v Commission* (60/81) [1981] E.C.R. 2639 at(9); [1981] 3 C.M.L.R. 635, the Court ruled that, "any measure the legal effects of which are binding on, and capable of affecting the interests of the applicant, by bringing about a distinctive change in his legal position, is an act . . . under Article [263]." See also *Luxembourg v Parliament* (108/83) [1984] E.C.R. 1945; [1986] 2 C.M.L.R. 507, where the Court annulled a Resolution of Parliament and *France v Commission* (C-325/91) [1993] E.C.R. I-3283, where the Court annulled a Commission Notice. On the other hand, in *Emerald Meats v Commission* (C-66/91) [1991] E.C.R. I-1143(28), the Court held that a, "communication [in this case a telex] which is from a department of the Commission and merely indicates procedures to ensure the proper administration of the system and, for the rest, announces the Commission's intention to adopt certain measures, cannot be considered to be a decision capable of having legal effects with regard to the applicant". See also *France v Commission* (C-303/90) [1991] E.C.R. I-5340, where the Court annulled a Code of conduct; *Sevince* (C-192/89) [1990] E.C.R. I-3461; [1992] 2 C.M.L.R. 57: a decision of an Association Council (EC–Turkey) forms an integral part of the Community law system; *France v Commission* (C-366/88) [1990] E.C.R. I-3595; [1992] 1 C.M.L.R. 205, where the Court annulled Commission's internal instructions. As for the GC, it declared inadmissible an action for annulment against a letter, stating that it had no influence on the

the Union. As the GC decided, "a claim for annulment is inadmissible unless that applicant has an interest in seeing the contested measure annulled" and, "such an interest can be present only if the annulment of the measure is of itself capable of having legal consequences".[79] Member States (this expression refers only to the government authorities of the Member States, and cannot include authorities of regions and autonomous communities[80]), the Council, the Commission and Parliament, and also the Court of Auditors,[81] the ECB[82] and the Committee of the Regions,[83] for the purpose of protecting their prerogatives, are considered to have an interest in the correct implementation of Union law. They therefore have, subject to a two-month time limit, the right to ask the Court or the GC to review the legality of any Union act.[84]

Where natural and legal persons are concerned, a distinction must be made between, "an act addressed to that person or which is of direct and individual concern to them" and "regulatory acts". In any case they must prove their interest in obtaining such review.[85] Obviously, they have this interest when it concerns, "an act addressed to that person" and when it concerns an act, "which is of direct and individual concern to them".[86] The following rules apply. An act is of *direct* concern when it affects somebody's legal position and when there is a causal relationship between the act and the modified legal position of the individual. The GC added that the implementation of the measure affecting the legal situation of the person concerned must be purely automatic and result from Union rules alone without the application of other intermediate rules.[87] This condition is often fulfilled.

applicant's legal position, *Nefarma v Commission* (T-113/89) [1990] E.C.R. II–797; [1991] 2 C.M.L.R. 818. But in *Italy v Commission* (Joined Cases C-138/03, C-324/03 C-431/03) [2005] E.C.R. I–10043 the Court accepted as admissible an action for annulment of a letter of the Commission.

[79] *Antilian Rice Mills* (Joined Cases T-480/93 and T-483/93) [1995] E.C.R. II–2310 at (59).

[80] *Wallonia* (C-95/97) [1997] E.C.R. I–1787, *Regione Toscana* (C-180/97) [1997] E.C.R. I–5247 and *Regione autonoma Friuli-Venezia Giulia* (T-288/97) [1999] E.C.R. II–1871.

[81] art.263,3 TFEU [230,3].

[82] art.263,3 TFEU [230,3].

[83] art.263,3 TFEU [230,3]. Added by the Treaty of Lisbon.

[84] All Member States have at one time or another appealed for annulment of an act of the Commission; appeals by Member States against Council acts are rare: *Ireland v Council* (151/73) [1974] E.C.R. 285; [1974] 1 C.M.L.R. 429. Appeals of the Commission against the Council are not uncommon: *Commission v Council* (242/87) [1989] E.C.R. 1449; [1991] 1 C.M.L.R. 478. The Court has also accepted appeals by a Member State against an act of Parliament, although this was not explicitly provided for under the Treaty: *Luxembourg v Parliament* (230/81) [1983] E.C.R. 255 at 281; [1983] 2 C.M.L.R. 726, where the Court concluded that such an appeal is provided for under the ECSC Treaty, and *Luxembourg v Parliament* (108/83) [1984] E.C.R. 1945; [1986] 2 C.M.L.R. 507. See also *Council v Parliament* (34/86) [1986] E.C.R. 2155; [1986] 3 C.M.L.R. 94 and *France v Parliament* (Joined Cases 358/85 and 51/86) [1988] E.C.R. 4846; [1990] 2 C.M.L.R. 406. The Court has also admitted appeals by Parliament against acts of the Council when that action aims at upholding Parliament's prerogatives, at a time when it was not yet provided for in the Treaty: *Parliament v Council* (C-70/88), [1990] E.C.R. I–2067; [1992] 1 C.M.L.R. 91.

[85] *BP v Commission* (77/77) [1978] E.C.R. 1513 at (13); [1978] 1 C.M.L.R. 265.

[86] TFEU art.263,4 [230,4].

[87] *DSTV v Commission* (T-69/99) [2000] E.C.R. II–4039. As far as directives are concerned, the case law provides for the admissibility of an action for annulment of measures of a legislative nature, where a superior rule of law required the body responsible for it to take into account the applicant's particular circumstances, *Rothley* (T-17/00) [2002] E.C.R. II–579.

Much more difficult is the second condition. According to established case law, "individual concern" means that the act affects the individuals:

"[B]y reason of certain attributes which are particular to them or by reason of circumstances, which are peculiar to them or by reason of circumstances in which they are differentiated from all other persons and by virtue of these factors distinguishes them individually just as in the case of the person addressed".[88]

Where "regulatory" acts are concerned (regulation, directive, agreement), it is assumed that those acts concern everybody and therefore nobody in particular. Consequently, they cannot normally, be challenged directly in court by individuals or undertakings, unless they can show that these acts contain provisions which in reality have an "individual" rather than a "general" application. This would be the case when such acts, "are of direct concern to them and do not entail implementing measures".[89] Under the EC Treaty individuals and undertakings needed to prove also that they were "individually" concerned; this is now, as will be seen, no longer required.

The GC attempted, at one point, to modify this case law by considering that the access of individuals to the courts is a constitutive element of a legal community and guaranteed by the Treaty, and that this right is based on the constitutional traditions of the Member States and on the European Convention of Human Rights. The GC added that the right to an effective court action for any person whose rights and freedoms guaranteed by the law of the Union have been infringed, was reaffirmed by the Charter of Fundamental Rights of the European Union. The GC decided that the strict interpretation which applied at the time should be revised and came to the following conclusion:

"[A] physical or moral person must be considered as individually concerned by a [Union] act having a general application which concerns it directly, when the act in question affects, in a certain and actual way, its legal position by restricting its rights or by imposing obligations on it. The number and the situation of other persons equally affected by the act or susceptible to be affected, are not in that respect pertinent considerations".[90]

However, before making this bold move, the GC had rejected the admissibility of an association, stating that it was not "individually" concerned[91]; said association appealed to the Court of Justice. The latter, implicitly rejecting[92] the innovative interpretation of the GC, reaffirmed the classical doctrine and concluded that, although individuals are entitled to effective judicial protection of the rights they derive from the Union legal order, the EC Treaty provisions did not provide

---

[88] *Plaumann v Commission* (25/62) [1963] E.C.R. 95 at 107; [1964] C.M.L.R. 29. This is not the case when the applicant is affected by the act because he belongs to a category designated abstractly and as a whole: *Nordgetreide v Commission* (42/71) [1972] E.C.R. 105 at 110(5); *Dreyfus v Commission* (C-386/86) [1998] E.C.R. I–2309, where the applicant was "individually" but not "directly" concerned; but see *Greenpeace* (C-321/95) [1998] E.C.R. I–1651. For a case where the Court ruled in appeal that the party in question was indeed individually concerned, see *Commission v Infront* (C-125/06 P) [2008] E.C.R. I–1451: decision affecting group of persons identified or identifiable at time of adoption of measure by reason of criteria specific to group members.

[89] art.263,4 TFEU [230].

[90] *Jego-Quere v Commission* (T-177/01) [2002] E.C.R. II–2365.

[91] *Union de Pequenos Agricultores v Council* (T-173/98) [1999] E.C.R. II–3357.

[92] *Union de Pequenos Agricultores v Council* (C-50/00 P) [2002] E.C R. I–6677.

for direct appeal against acts of a general nature, unless the individuals are directly and individually concerned. The Court added, after a reference to the preliminary question[93] and the possibility to invoke the "inapplicability" of a general act in proceedings where such an act is at issue,[94] that it is, "for the Member States to establish a system of legal remedies and procedures which ensure respect for the right to effective judicial protection." The Member States obliged.

Indeed, as indicated, the Treaty of Lisbon modified the situation by providing that, "any natural or legal person may . . . institute proceedings against . . . a regulatory act which is of direct concern to them and does not entail implementation measures".[95] The words "individual concern" have disappeared. However, the danger is that although a right to an effective court action is now guaranteed, it is to be seen whether this simplification is going to dramatically increase the number of appeals against regulations and directives, thereby further clogging an already overloaded Court.

It is also clear from the Court's case law that where a decision affects a group of persons who are identified or identifiable when that measure was adopted, by reason of criteria specific to members of the group, those members might be individually concerned by that measure inasmuch as they form part of a limited class of traders. That can be the case particularly when the decision alters rights acquired by the individual prior to its adoption.[96]

As for associations of undertakings, they are admissible in at least three kinds of circumstances:

- when the legal provision expressly grants a series of procedural powers to (trade) associations;
- when the association represents the interests of undertakings which would, themselves, be entitled to bring proceedings; and
- when the association is distinguished individually because its own interests as an association are affected, in particular because its negotiating position has been affected by the measure whose annulment is being sought.[97]

The interpretation of the Treaty provisions concerning the locus standi of persons is, of course, essential in determining the extent of the legal protection enjoyed by individuals and undertakings within the Union. Hence the importance of the case law of the courts in this field.[98] It can be said that without resorting to extensive interpretation, the Court has given those Treaty provisions a meaning which

---

[93] art.267 TFEU [234]. See below (4) Preliminary Ruling.

[94] art.277 TFEU [241]. See below (6) The Objection of Illegality.

[95] art.263,4 TFEU [230].

[96] *Commission v Infront WM* (C-125/06 P) [2008] E.C.R. I–1451.

[97] *Union de Pequenos Agricultores v Council* (T-173/98) [1999] E.C.R. II–3357.

[98] For an overview of the case law on this point see the opinion of the Advocate-General in, *Extramet Industries v Council* (C-358/89) [1991] E.C.R. I–2501 at 2515; [1990] 2 C.M.L.R. 406 and *Greenpeace* (C-321/95 P) [1998] E.C.R. I-1651. See also *Union Syndicale v Council* (72/74) [1975] E.C.R. 401 at (17); [1975] 2 C.M.L.R. 181. Or, as the Court put it in *Greenpeace* (C-321/95) quoted above: "where the specific situation of the appellant was not taken into consideration in the adoption of the act". See also *Dreyfus v Commission* (C-386/96) [1998] E.C.R. I–2309, where the applicant was recognised as being "individually", but not "directly" concerned. On the other hand, a region, for instance, cannot be "individually" concerned: *Regione Puglia* (T-609/97) [1998] E.C.R. II–4051.

allows private parties to contest, in some cases, the legality of acts having a general application.[99] Or, as the GC stated:

"[A]dmittedly, the Court of Justice and the [GC] have already held actions for annulment of measures of a legislative nature to be admissible where an overriding provision of law required the bodies responsible for them to take into account the applicant's particular situation".[100]

Nonetheless, the opportunities for natural and legal persons to appeal directly for annulment of a Union act are much more limited than for the Member States and the institutions.[101] However, as shown, other means exist whereby persons and enterprises can obtain a Court ruling, if not on the legality, at least on the applicability of a Union act. For the plaintiff the results will be identical if the Court finds in favour of him.[102]

(iii) **Grounds for Annulment.** There are four grounds for annulment which may be invoked by the applicant.[103]

Lack of competence. This ground embodies mainly the basic principle of conferral,[104] several times referred to above, under which the institutions of the Union may only exercise those powers which have been explicitly granted to them by the Member States in the Treaties. They enjoy conferred powers, not general powers. In case an institution were to legislate without the necessary conferred powers, the Court can annul the decision for lack of competence. Idem in case the Commission, for instance, were to adopt an act without having the necessary implementing powers.[105] For the Court this requirement is so important that it has accepted to review it, even after the time limit for instituting the proceedings has lapsed.[106]

It follows that every Union act must clearly indicate on which Union provision it is based[107]; it follows also that the choice of this provision is of essential importance.[108]

---

[99] For instance, the words "another person" in art. 263,3 TFEU [230,4] were interpreted by the Court as including also Member States, since no limitation as to the meaning of those words is to be found in the Treaty. Natural and legal persons can therefore appeal against an act of an institution addressed to a Member State, when they are directly and individually concerned by that act: *Philip Morris v Commission* (730/79) [1980] E.C.R. 2671 at 2687; [1981] 2 C.M.L.R. 321. The Court also accepted that a measure entitled by its authors a Regulation can contain provisions which are capable of being not only of direct but also of individual concern to certain natural or legal persons: *Producteurs de fruits v Council* (Joined Cases 16/62 and 17/62) [1962] E.C.R. 471 at 479. See also *Koninklijke Scholten Honig v Council and Commission* (101/76) [1977] E.C.R. 797; [1980] 2 C.M.L.R. 669, and *Cofaz v Commission* (169/84) [1986] E.C.R. 408.

[100] *Sociedade Agricula Dos Arinhos v Commission* (Joined Cases T-38/99 and T-50/99) [2001] E C.R II–585.

[101] *Producteurs de fruits* (Joined Cases 16/62 and 17/62), quoted above, fn.99 (at 478).

[102] See below "Preliminary Ruling" (see, for instance, *Kruidvat v Commission* (C-70/97 P) [1998] E.C.R. I–7183, at (48–49)), "Compensation for Damages" and "Exception of Illegality".

[103] Those grounds find their origin in French administrative law.

[104] art.5(2) EU.

[105] See, for instance, *Parliament v Commission* (C-403/05) [2007] E.C.R. I-9045.

[106] *Commission v France* (Joined Cases 6/89 and 11/89), [1969] E.C.R. 523 (11–13); [1970] C.M.L.R. 43. See however, *National Farmers Union* (C-241/01) [2002] E.C.R. I–919 at (25).

[107] See below: Infringement of an essential procedural requirement.

[108] See, for instance, *Commission v Council* (C-131/87), [1989] E.C.R. 3764; [1991] 1 C.M.L.R. 780.

Competence may also be attributed to the Commission, for instance, by acts of the Council, the so-called delegation of powers[109]; in such cases also the competence of the Commission is limited to what is explicitly conferred.

Infringement of an essential procedural requirement. If, for instance, the Council were to take a decision without a proposal from the Commission or without including Parliament[110] when this is required by the Treaties, the Council would have infringed an essential procedural requirement. The Court would have jurisdiction on that ground to annul the act. The same would apply if the Commission, for instance, were to make a proposal without asking for the opinion of the Economic and Social Committee, when this is required by the Treaties. Also, failure to mention sufficient reasons in a Union act constitutes a ground for annulment because of infringement of an essential procedural requirement.[111]

According to the Court, such an infringement, involving a matter of public policy, must be raised by the Union judicature of its own motion, contrary to an alleged infringement of a rule of law relating to the application of the Treaty [see hereunder] which can be examined by the Union judicature only if it is raised by the applicant.[112]

Infringement of the Treaties or of any rule of law pertaining to their application. It could be argued that the two grounds examined above also constitute infringements of the Treaties, since they are violations of obligations provided therein and that this ground, in fact, covers all possible illegalities.

However, the TFEU mentions four grounds[113] and those must therefore be examined separately. In the expression "infringement of the Treaties", the word "Treaties" must be understood to cover not only the three European Treaties, but also the secondary legislation, i.e. the acts of the institutions, whatever their form, as long as they are binding. When examining the meaning of "acts" submitted to the control of legality, it was pointed out that acts are binding when they bring about a distinctive change in the legal position of a party subject to Union law.[114] The word "Treaties" can, therefore, be considered here as equivalent to the *acquis communautaire*.

As for the expression "any rules relating to its application", it refers mainly to the general principles of law and to international law.[115] The general principles include those which are particular to the Member States, based on comparative studies of the 27 legal systems,[116] and those principles which the Court formulates on the basis of the wording, the contents and the systems of the Treaties. They

---

[109] art.290 TFEU.

[110] See, e.g. *Maizena v Council* (139/79), [1980] E.C.R. 3393 at (36).

[111] See above Ch.3: The Legal Acts of the Union—acts must be reasoned.

[112] *Commission v Systraval and Brink's France* (C-367/95 P) [1998] E.C.R. I–1719.

[113] art.263,2 TFEU [230].

[114] See *IBM v Commission* (60/81) [1981] E.C.R. 2639.

[115] See, e.g. *Fédération Charbonnière de Belgique v High Authority* (8/55) [1954–1956] E.C.R. 245 at 299. See also *International Fruit Company v Produktschap voor Groenten en Fruit* (Joined Cases 21/72, 22/72, 23/72 and 24/72) [1972] E.C.R. 1219 at (6); [1975] 2 C.M.L.R. 1; *Van Duyn v Home Office* (41/74) [1974] E.C.R. 1337 at (22); [1975] 1 C.M.L.R. 1 and *Racke v Hauptzollamt Mainz* (C-162/96) [1998] E.C.R. I–3655 at (25–27): "The Court is obliged to examine whether the validity might be affected by reason of the fact that it is contrary to rules of international law." However, in other cases the Court did not accept arguments based on international law; see, e.g. *Commission v Luxembourg and Belgium* (Joined Cases 90/63 and 91/63) [1964] E.C.R. 625 at 631; [1965] C.M.L.R. 58. See also above: Union Law, Ch. 4, "application of national and international law by the European courts".

[116] *Nold v Commission* (4/73) [1974] E.C.R. 491 at (13); [1974] 2 C.M.L.R. 338: "In safeguarding those rights, the Court must draw inspiration from the constitutional traditions of the Member States."

comprise also the "fundamental rights".[117] They are now explicitly mentioned by virtue of the EU Treaty:

"The Union shall respect fundamental rights, as guaranteed by the European Convention for the Protection of Human Rights and Fundamental Freedoms signed in Rome on November 4, 1950 and as they result from the constitutional traditions common to the Member States, as general principles of [Union] law".[118]

The same applies to the Charter of Fundamental Rights of the European Union, which has the same legal value as the Treaties.[119]

They often constitute an important part of the legal considerations which lead to the Court's rulings.

The following general principles, among others, have been referred to several times by the courts: the protection of legitimate expectations[120]; the right to be heard or rights of the defence[121]; freedom of trade union activity[122]; legal certainty[123]; equal treatment (non-discrimination)[124]; necessity[125]; proportionality[126];

---

[117] *Nold* (4/73), above, fn. 116, "fundamental rights form an integral part of the general principles of law".

[118] Charter of December 7, 2000, as adopted at Strasbourg on December 12, 2007.

[119] art.6(1) EU: [2007] O.J. C-303/2.

[120] In *Tea-Cegos E.A.* (Joined Cases T-376/05 and T-383/05) [2006] E.C.R. II–205, the CFI recalled that the right to claim the protection of legitimate expectation encompasses any party that finds itself in a situation from which it follows that the Union administration, by furnishing precise assurances, whatever the form in which they were communicated, created for it grounded hopes; this is the case with precise, unconditional and concordant information emanating from an authorised and trustworthy source. See, for instance, *Opel Austria* (T-115/94) [1997] E.C.R. II–39, where the Court found an infringement of applicant's legal expectation; as for an example where it was denied, see *Efisol* (T-336/94) [1996] E.C.R. II–1343: the company was issued an import quota, but was subsequently refused an import licence; according to the CFT, those are two independent stages, and the company was not justified in assuming that because it had obtained a quota, it would also obtain a licence. *Mebron v Commission* (T-216/05) [2007] E.C.R. II-1507: a person may not plead infringement of the principle of the protection of legitimate expectation unless he has been given specific assurance by the administration, but a prior administrative practice of the Commission that has been made public may give rise to legitimate expectation that the same practice will prevail again.

[121] See, for instance, *Lisrestal* (C-32/95 P) [1996] E.C.R. I–5373: the right to be heard, "in all proceedings initiated against a person and which are liable to culminate in a measure adversely affecting that person" constitutes a fundamental principle of Community law, "even in the absence of any specific rules"; this latter specification is also to be found in *Netherlands v Commission* (Joined Cases C-48/90 and C-66/90) [1992] E.C.R. I–565. As to the question when a party is "adversely affected" by a Union act, it follows from the case law that this is the case as soon as that party's interests are irremediably modified to the worse by the act in question. See also *Germany v Commission* (C-242/00) [2002] E.C.R. I–5603, where the Court concluded that the decision in question had no unfavourable implications for plaintiff, who was not, therefore, "adversely affected". See P. Mathijsen, The right to be heard in the implementation of Article 81 and 82 EC, in "Ceci n'est pas un juriste . . .", Liber Amicorum Bart De Schutter, VUBPRESS,Brussels 2003.

[122] See, e.g. *Union Syndicale, Massa et Kortner v Council* (175/73) [1974] E.C.R. 917 at (9 and 14); [1975] 1 C.M.L.R. 131.

[123] See, e.g. *Openbaar Ministerie v Bout* (21/81) [1982] E.C.R. 381 at (13); [1982] 2 C.M.L.R. 371.

[124] See, e.g. *Louwage v Commission* (148/73 R) [1974] E.C.R. 81 at (12).

[125] *BUPA* (T-289/03) [2008] E.C.R. II-81.

[126] See, e.g. *Buitoni v FORMA* (122/78) [1979] E.C.R. 677 at (16); [1979] 2 C.M.L.R. 665. However, a looser test was applied in *Henn and Darby* (34/79) [1979] E.C.R. 3795: "not manifestly inappropriate" and a more rigorous test was applied in *Commission v Germany* (178/84) [1987] E.C.R. 1227: "no less-restrictive alternative available". In *Commission v Germany* (C-131/93), [1994] E.C.R. I–3303, the Court developed three tests to determine whether or not a measure was proportional: it must be an appropriate and effective way to achieve the legitimate aim; it must be necessary, i.e. there is no less restrictive alternative and the adverse effect is not excessive when weighed against the aim of the measure.

equivalence[127]; legality of sanctions[128]; good administration[129]; effectiveness[130]; *ne bis in idem*[131]; freedom to pursue an occupation or freedom to conduct a business[132]; respect for family life,[133] etc.

Misuse of power[134] There is misuse of power when a public authority uses its lawful powers to attain an objective for which the powers were not intended. Although this ground has been invoked many times, the Court seldom accepts this as a ground for the annulment of an act.[135]

(iv) Consequences of the Annulment of an Act by the Court. Unless the Court also enjoys unlimited jurisdiction, for example in the case of penalties, it may only, when it finds that the action for annulment is well founded, declare the act void.[136] The Court may not rule *ultra petita* since that would be ultra vires, in other words, the scope of the annulment which the Court pronounces may not go further than that sought by the applicant.[137]

The institution whose act has been declared void is, "required to take the necessary measures to comply with the judgment of the Court of Justice of the European Union".[138] Since, theoretically, annulment means that the act is to be considered as never having existed—the Court's declaration has effect *ex tunc*

---

[127] *Marks & Spencer* (C-62/00) [2002] E.C.R. I-6325 at (34): national procedural rules governing actions for safeguarding rights which individuals derive from Union law may not be less favourable than those governing similar domestic actions. It is up to the Member States to designate the national courts or tribunals that must uphold the rights that the citizens draw from Union law and the procedural modalities of the recourses, in so far as these modalities are not less favourable than those of similar recourse of internal nature: principle of equivalence; see *Recheio* (C-30/02) [2004] E.C.R. I-6051.

[128] *Vandemoortele v Commission* (C-172/89) [1990] E.C.R. I-4677 at (9): a penalty, even of a non-criminal nature, cannot be imposed unless it rests on a clear and unambiguous legal basis.

[129] See, e.g. *Kuhner v Commission* (Joined Cases 33/79 and 75/79) [1980] E.C.R. 1677 at (25).

[130] The principle of effectiveness adds to the foregoing that such national recourses should not, in practice, be impossible or more difficult; see *Simmenthal* (106/77) [1978] E.C.R. 629: "a national court which is called upon to apply provisions of Community law is under a duty to give full effect to those provisions, if necessary refusing of its own motion to apply any conflicting provision of national legislation"; also *Factortame* (C-213/89) [1990] E.C.R. I-2433: application of interim relief by a national judge although this was not possible under national law, and *Delana Wells* (C-201/02) [2004] E.C.R. I-723. Also *Kühne & Heitz* (C-453/00) [2004] E.C.R. I-837, national body required to re-examine final decisions after subsequent Court judgments showed these were based on misinterpretation of Union law.

[131] For instance Convention Implementing the Schengen Agreement, arts 54–58: [2000] O.J. L239/19.

[132] *Spain and Finland v Parliament and Council* (Joined Cases C-184/02 and C-223/02) [2004] E.C.R. I-7789.

[133] Case *Parliament v Council* (C-540/03) [2006] E.C.R. I-5769.

[134] Maybe better known by its French equivalent: *détournement de pouvoir*. For more details concerning the meaning of this ground, see the comparative study of the law of the original six Member States made by the Advocate-General in his Opinion in *ASSIDER v High Authority* (3/54) [1954–1956] E.C.R. 63 at 75.

[135] One rare example is *Simmenthal v Commission* (92/78) [1979] E.C.R. 777 at (106); [1980] 1 C.M.L.R. 25. See also *Antonio Giannini v Commission* (Joined Cases T-282/97 and T-57/98) RecFP (FP stands for "Fonction Publique": staff cases) I–A-33 and II–151 and *Commission v Gianni* (C-153/99 P) [2000] E.C.R. I-2891.

[136] art.264 TFEU [231].

[137] *Commission v Assidoman Kraft Products* (C-310/97 P) [1999] E.C.R. I-5363 at (52).

[138] art.266,1 TFEU [233]. These measures involve, "the removal of the effects of the illegalities found in the judgment annulling the act" and, "the institution may thus be required to take adequate steps to restore the applicant to its original situation or to avoid the adoption of an identical measure": *Antillean Rice Mills* (Joined Cases T-480 and T-483/93) [1995] E.C.R. II-2310 at (60).

(retroactive to the moment the act was adopted)—the institution must endeavour to recreate the situation which would have existed had the act not been issued.[139] This might be impossible, especially when the nullity affects an act of general application such as a regulation. For this reason the Treaty provides that in the case of a regulation, the Court may, if it considers this necessary, "state which of the effects of the regulation which it has declared void shall be considered as definitive"[140] or that the act or the implementing measures remains valid until replaced.[141]

The annulment does not affect the validity of identical or similar acts the legality of which was not contested within the time limits provided for by the Treaty.

In certain cases where an annulment *ex tunc* would have unacceptable financial consequences for Member States, the Court has decided that the annulment will have no retroactive effect.[142] This is referred to as, "the limitation of the temporal effect of judgments".[143] In other cases, the institution may have to compensate for the irreparable damage caused by the annulled act.[144]

It should also be noted that annulment does not necessarily affect the act as a whole. If the nullity concerns only one or certain provisions and the others can remain operative, the other provisions will stand.[145]

(b) Appeal against Failure of an Institution to Act[146]

In the case of an appeal for failure to act[147] the Court is called upon to establish that, by failing to act, Parliament,[148] the Council, the Commission or the ECB have infringed the Treaties. The latter expression covers also, as already indicated, the Union's secondary legislation; whether it also covers:

---

[139] If this is not possible, compensation might have to be paid; if it concerns the annulment of an imposed penalty, interests might have to be paid; if an official was wrongly refused a promotion, he should be paid the difference in salary he would have received had he been properly promoted, etc.

[140] art.264 TFEU [231].

[141] See, e.g. *Commission v Council* (275/87) [1988] E.C.R. 259, where the act was annulled only because the legal basis chosen by the Council was not considered by the Court to be the right one. In *Parliament v Council* (C-22/96) [1998] E.C.R. I–3231, the Court annulled Decision 95/468 since it could not be adopted on the basis of art.352 TFEU [308], but the judgment, "maintains the effects of the implementing measures already adopted by the Commission on the basis of that decision".

[142] See *Defrenne v SABENA* (43/75) [1976] E.C.R. 455: the direct effect of art.143 TFEU [art.119] cannot be relied on in order to, "support pay periods prior to the date of this judgment" and *Sociale Verzekeringsbank v Cabanis-Issarte* (C-308/93) [1996] E.C.R. I–2097.

[143] For an analysis of the grounds for such limitation, see *EKW and Wein and Co* (C-437/97) [2000] E.C.R. I–1157.

[144] art.266 TFEU [233]; see below, Compensation for damage caused by an institution, and art.346 TFEU [288].

[145] See, e.g. *Société de Vente de Ciments et Bétons v Kerpen & Kerpen* (319/82) [1983] E.C.R. 4173 at (12); [1985] 1 C.M.L.R. 511.

[146] art. 265 TFEU [232].

[147] Such an appeal is admissible only if the applicant has first called upon the institution to act, and the latter has not defined its position within two months; the applicant then has another two months to bring an action. In case the institution, within those two months, defines its position by refusing to act, this position does not become an act which can only be challenged under TFEU art.263.[230], since the failure has not ceased. See *Parliament v Council* (302/87) [1988] E.C.R. 5615; this constitutes a reversal from previous case law: *Komponistenverband v Commission* (8/71) [1971] E.C.R. 705 at (2).

[148] One might wonder why the Treaty does not provide for a failure by Parliament and the Council acting jointly, as is provided for under art.263 TFEU [230].

"[A]ny rule of law relating to its application[149] has not been tested in court. It seems, however, that if acting in violation of such rules can be challenged in court, failure to act in violation of such rules should also be open to challenge.[150] The more so, since, there is no difference between the outcome of an action for annulment and an action for failure of an institution to act: in both cases the institution is required to take the necessary measures to comply with the judgment."[151]

Furthermore, the Court considers that "both provisions merely prescribe one and the same method of recourse".[152]

Actions for failure may be brought by Member States,[153] institutions[154] and the ECB, not only when an insitution fails to take a binding measure, but, in general, when an institution doesn't fulfil an obligation under the Treaties. For instance if the Commission were to fail to submit a proposal to the Council when this is required by the Treaties. On the other hand, natural and legal persons may only challenge a failure of an institution to act when it concerns a binding act of which they would have been the addressee.[155] This is not the case, for instance, when the Commission is asked to refer a matter to the Court.[156]

(4) Preliminary Ruling

The preliminary ruling[157] presupposes direct effect, i.e. the possibility for an interested party to invoke Union rules in national courts and the obligation for the national judge to uphold any rights resulting from those rules. The latter obligation is based on the principle of co-operation embodied in the Treaty.[158] The purpose of the preliminary ruling procedure is to guarantee uniformity in the interpretation and application of Union law.[159] Indeed, the responsibility for applying Union law rests, in the first place, with the national judge. For instance, when applying Union competition rules, the national courts are acting as a Union court of general jurisdiction.[160] The preliminary ruling is also looked at by

---

[149] art.263 TFEU [230].

[150] If the Union is bound by an international agreement to take some action and fails to do so, there is no reason why this failure should not be open to challenge in Court.

[151] art.266 TFEU [233].

[152] *Chevalley v Commission* (15/70) [1970] E.C.R. 975 at (6).

[153] See for instance *Assider and Italy v Commission* (Joined Cases 167/85 and 212/85) [1987] E.C.R. 1701, concerning disruption of traditional patterns of trade: according to the Court the Commission should have acted.

[154] See for instance *Parliament v Council* (13/83) [1985] E.C.R. 1315, where Parliament reproached the Council for having failed to develop a common transport policy; the Court decided that the Council had indeed failed to do so.

[155] *Mackprang v Commission* (15/71) [1971] E.C.R. 797 at (4); [1972] C.M.L.R. 52.

[156] *AITEC* (T-277/94) [1996] E.C.R. II–351.

[157] art.267 TFEU [234].

[158] art.4(3),2 and 3 EU [10]; indeed, this provision applies to all the "powers" exercised by a State: executive, legislative and also judiciary; see above under Ch.4: Union Law ((4) Member States' Liability for breach of Union law).

[159] See *Costa v ENEL* (6/64) [1964] E.C.R. 585 at 594; [1964] C.M.L.R. 425, and *Molkerei-Zentrale Westphalen v Hauptzollamt Paderborn* (28/67) [1968] E.C.R. 143 at 153; [1968] C.M.L.R. 187.

[160] *Tetra Pak* (T-51/89) [1990] E.C.R. II–309; see also *Zwartfeld* (C-2/88) [1990] E.C.R. I–3365: the judicial authorities of the Member States are responsible for ensuring that Union law is applied and respected in the national legal system.

the Court as, "an instrument of cooperation between itself and the national courts".[161]

It is in order to avoid different national judges giving different interpretations of provisions of Union law that the Court was endowed with the exclusive competence to interpret,[162] as last resort, those provisions. Indeed, as was pointed out before, in an internal market, the economic operators must be assured of being able to compete under similar conditions throughout the whole Union. This can only be ensured if they are all subjected to the same rules interpreted in the same way everywhere. This applies also to the validity of the Union's secondary legislation and therefore only the Court can decide on its validity.[163]

The preliminary ruling also constitutes, in the hands of the Court, the ideal instrument to define and develop the law of the Union. Indeed, when the Court interprets a provision of Union law, this interpretation must be accepted and applied by all national courts.[164] Furthermore, it can be assumed that parties in

---

[161] *TK-Heimdienst* (C-254/98) [2000] E.C.R. I–151 at (12).

[162] As for methods of interpretation, see, e.g. *Hoekstra v Bedrijfsvereniging Detailhandel* (75/63) [1964] E.C.R. 177 at 184; [1964] C.M.L.R. 319, and *Levin v Staatssecretaris van Justitie* (53/81) [1982] E.C.R. 1035 at (9).

[163] art.267,1(b) TFEU [234,1(b)].

[164] See 1972 European Communities Act, s.3(1) and *Rewe v Landwirtschaftskammer Saarland* (33/76) [1976] E.C.R. 1989 at (5); [1977] 1 C.M.L.R. 533, where the national judge automatically accepted an interpretation given years before. According to the Court, art.267 TFEU [234] calls for judicial co-operation between the Court and the national courts, which are required to make direct and complementary contributions to the application of Community law in a uniform manner in all the Member States: *Ministère Public and A.S.B.L. v Van Wesemael* (Joined Cases 110/78 and 111/78) [1979] E.C.R. 35 at (21); [1979] 3 C.M.L.R. 87, and *Amministrazione delle Finanze dello Stato v Ariete* (811/79) [1980] E.C.R. 2545 at (6); [1981] 1 C.M.L.R. 316: the preliminary ruling of the Court is binding on the national court as to the interpretation of the Community provision. The respective tasks of the Court and the national courts have been clarified over the years:

- the Court has no jurisdiction under art.267 TFEU [234] to apply the Treaty to a specific national case: *Costa v ENEL* (6/64) [1964] E.C.R. 585 at 592; [1964] C.M.L.R. 425; similarly, the Court is not competent to decide on the compatibility of a national provision with Community law: *Ministère Public Luxembourgeois v Muller* (10/71) [1971] E.C.R. 723 at (7). It may nonetheless furnish the national court with the interpretative criteria necessary to enable it to dispose of the dispute: *Vereniging Boekhandels v Eldi Records* (106/79) [1980] E.C.R. 1137 at (7); [1980] 3 C.M.L.R. 719, or to determine whether the national rules are compatible with Union law: *Kefer and Delmelle* (Joined Cases 95/79 and 96/79) [1980] E.C.R. 103 at (5); [1982] 2 C.M.L.R. 77; also, in cases where the domestic law of a Member State refers to a Union provision, the Court is not prevented by the Treaty to give a ruling applicable to a situation which is purely internal to that State: *ETI E.A.* (C-280/06) [2007] E.C.R. I–10893;
- the considerations which may have led a national court to its choice of questions, as well as the relevance which it attributes to such questions in the context of a case before it, are excluded from the review by the Court: *ONPTS v Damiani* (53/79) [1980] E.C.R. 273 at (5); [1981] 2 C.M.L.R. 548;
- the TFEU does not prescribe a particular form in which a national court must present its request for a ruling; the Court must derive from the wording of the request, the questions which relate exclusively to the interpretation of the Union provisions: *Volk v Vervaecke* (5/69) [1969] E.C.R. 295 at (2/4); [1969] C.M.L.R. 273; however, the reference by the national court must contain enough legal and factual information for the Court to be able to base its answer on the facts and circumstances of the case: *Banchero* (C-157/92) [1993] E.C.R. I–1085;
- it is not for the Court to appropriate for itself an assessment of the jurisdiction of the national court to refer the question or of the presence of a legal interest requiring protection on the part of the applicant in the main action: *Reina v Landeskreditbank Baden-Wuttemberg* (65/81) [1982] E.C.R. 33; [1982] 1 C.M.L.R. 744; and it is for the national court to decide at what stage in the proceedings it is appropriate to refer a question to the Court: *Campus Oil Limited v Minister for Industry and Energy* (72/83) [1984] E.C.R. 2727 at (10); [1984] 3 C.M.L.R. 544;
- the Court has jurisdiction to give a ruling only when there is a genuine dispute before the national court: *Foglia v Novello* (104/79) [1980] E.C.R. 745 at (11); [1981] 1 C.M.L.R. 45.

subsequent cases involving provisions which have been interpreted by the Court, will not lightly contest that interpretation, although they remain free to do so. In other words, even if the Court's interpretation is de jure limited to the case under review, it has de facto effect *erga omnes*.[165] It has also retroactive effect; indeed, the Court stated that a Union law thus interpreted must be applied by an administrative body within the sphere of its competence, even to legal relationships which arose or were formed before the Court gave its ruling.[166]

Besides ensuring uniform interpretation, the preliminary ruling does also provide private parties with access to the Court, when they have no locus standi to directly ask the Court to control the validity of Union acts.[167]

Requests for a preliminary ruling must emanate from a national court or tribunal.[168] When it is of the opinion that there is a genuine question, a national court "may", or when there is no judicial remedy against its judgments, "must",[169] request such a ruling. This is the first distinction to be applied: there is no obligation for the national judge to refer a question to the Court when there exists a possibility of appeal against his decision. In that case the national judge "may" decide to refer the question, or give himself the necessary interpretation of the Union rule. After all, it is the national judge who is, as was already

---

[165] See *International Chemical Corporation v Amministrazione delle Finanze dello Stato* (66/80) [1981] E.C.R. 1191 at (13); [1983] 2 C.M.L.R. 593; see also *Amministrazione delle Finanze dello Stato v Denkavit Italiana* (61/79) [1980] E.C.R. 1205 at (17); [1981] 3 C.M.L.R. 694, where the Court states that its interpretation applies even to relationships arising before the judgment.

[166] Case *Kempter* (C-02/06) [2008] E.C.R. I–411.

[167] See *International Fruit Company* (Joined Cases 21/72, 22/72, 23/72 and 24/72) (quoted above, fn. 115), [1972] E.C.R.1219 at (6): the jurisdiction of the Court to give rulings on the validity of measures adopted by the institutions extends to all the grounds capable of invalidating those measures, including the fact that they are contrary to a rule of international law and see *Roquette Frères v French Customs Administration* (145/79) [1980] E.C.R. 2917 at (52), where the Court ruled that when it declares a regulation void under an art.267 TFEU [234] procedure, it may, by analogy with art.264 TFEU [231], state which of the effects of the regulation shall be considered as definitive. In *Racke* (162/96) [1998] E.C.R. I–3655, the Court stated that art.267 TFEU [234] does not contain any limitation of the grounds on which the validity may be contested.

[168] Whether a national organ which transmits a request for a preliminary ruling is a court of law must be determined on the basis of national law: see, e.g. *Vaassen v Beambtenfonds Mijnbedrijf* (61/65) [1966] E.C.R. 261 at 273; [1966] C.M.L.R. 508. The Court has, however, laid down criteria to help in this determination: *Borker* (138/80) [1980] E.C.R. 1975 at (4); [1980] 3 C.M.L.R. 638: the Court can only be requested to give a ruling by a court which is called upon to give judgment in proceedings intended to lead to a decision of a judicial nature. Arbitrators in disputes between parties to a contract under a clause inserted in that contract cannot be considered as a "court or tribunal": *Nordsee v Reederei Mond* (102/81) [1982] E.C.R. 1095 at (13); but in *Handels-og Kontorfunktionaerernes Forbund i Danmark v Dansk Arbejdsgiverforening acting on behalf of Danfoss* (109/88) [1989] E.C.R. 3220; [1991] 1 C.M.L.R. 8, the Court ruled that an industrial arbitration board which (1) hears disputes on the application of one party without the need for the other party's agreement, (2) whose composition procedure is laid down by statute, and (3) which applies objective rules, is a "court or tribunal". Similarly, an appeals committee set up by a professional body and which may affect the exercise of rights granted by Union law is considered a "court or tribunal": *Broekmeulen v Huisarts Registratie Commissie* (246/80) [1981] E.C.R. 2311 at(17); [1991] 3 C.M.L.R. 706. In *Garofalo v Ministero della Sanità* (Joined Cases C-69–79/96) [1997] E.C.R. I–5603, the Court specified in more detail a number of factors to be taken into account in order to determine whether a body is a "court or tribunal": it depends on whether the body is established by law, is permanent, its jurisdiction is compulsory, the procedure before it is inter partes, it applies rules of law and finally, whether it is independent; in the case in question, the Court found that when it issues an opinion in the context of an extraordinary petition, the Consiglio di Stato is a court or tribunal. See Court's Information note on reference from national courts for a preliminary ruling [2005] O.J. C143/3.

[169] art.267 TFEU [234].

indicated several times, in the first place, responsible for applying and therefore also interpreting that Union rule.

However, even when there is no appeal against her/his judgment, the national judge is under no obligation to refer the question, when the national judge is of the opinion that the correct application of Community law is so evident that it does not leave room for reasonable doubt,[170] the so-called *acte clair* theory. The same applies in case the Court has previously given the necessary interpretation, the so-called *acte éclairé*.

As for the validity of Union law, the national judge may decide that it is valid and apply it; he may not, however, decide that it is invalid and consequently refuse to apply it. Only the Court may declare a Union act invalid.[171]

As for the question "when" do the TFEU's provisions concerning the preliminary ruling apply, the answer is: "where such a question is raised"[172] either by a party or by the national judge himself, i.e. if he considers that, in order to give judgment in a case pending before him, the judge needs a decision on a that question. Also, there is a question, when, when having to apply a Treaty provision, the national judge is confronted, either by himself[173] or by the parties, with a problem concerning its interpretation. The same can happen when the national judge has to apply second-ary Union law and a question is raised, by the judge or by the parties, concerning the validity or the interpretation of that rule. A second distinction must therefore be applied here between the Treaties, on the one hand, and the acts of the institutions and of the ECB, on the other. A question concerning validity may only be referred to the Court when it concerns secondary Union law; indeed, the Court itself cannot rule on the validity of the Treaties' provisions; the constitution of the Union.

The obligation for the national judge to refer a question does not apply when the national judge establishes that the question raised is irrelevant or that the Union provision in question has already been answered by the Court (*acte éclairé*). In other words, it is his decision. Neither the Court,[174] nor national law,[175] nor a Union rule[176] can deprive the national judge of this right. It is also within the national judge's discretionary power to decide whether the question has been raised in good faith, or whether it is a purely procedural move initiated by one of the parties, for instance to delay judgment.[177] There is therefore nothing automatic in the procedure of the preliminary ruling.

---

[170] *CILFIT v Ministry of Health* (283/81) [1982] E.C.R. 3415 at (8–16); [1983] 1 C.M.L.R. 472 and *TNT Traco* (C-340/99) [2001] E.C.R. I–4109 at (35).

[171] *Foto-Frost v Hauptzollamt Lübeck-Ost* (314/85) [1987] E.C.R. 4199. In *Schul* (C-461/03) [2005] E.C.R. I–10513, the Court said that a national judge could not consider illegal a Community provision when the Court had declared a similar provision illegal in an other case. However, a national judge may, under certain circumstances, grant interim measures concerning national rules based on a Community regulation which is the object of an art.267 [234] procedure concerning the validity of said act: *Atlanta* (C-465/93) [1995] E.C.R. I–3781.

[172] art.267,2 TFEU [234,2]

[173] *Salonia v Poidomani and Giglio* (126/80), [1981] E.C.R. 1563 at (7); [1982] 1 C.M.L.R. 64.

[174] *Tedeschi v Denkavit* (5/77) [1977] E.C.R. 1555 at (17); [1978] 1 C.M.L.R. 1.

[175] *Rheinmühle v Einfuhr-und Vorratstelle Getreide* (166/73) [1974] E.C.R. 33 at (4); [1974] 1 C.M.L.R. 523.

[176] *BRT v Sabam* (127/73) [1974] E.C.R. 51 at (23); [1974] 2 C.M.L.R. 238.

[177] See Opinion of the Advocate-General in *Costa v ENEL* (6/64) [1964] E.C.R. 585 at 607; [1964] C.M.L.R. 425, where mention is made of a "preliminary inquiry of legality" by the national judge concerning the relevance of the question to the solution of the dispute.

However, in case a national judge were to refuse to refer a question to the Court when there is an obligation to do so, the Member State to which the judge belongs could be held responsible for this infringement; see above in Ch.4: Union Law ("Member States' Liability for breach of Union law").

The obligation to refer a question to the Court does not exist, furthermore, "when it is raised in interlocutory proceedings and the decision to be taken is not binding on the court or tribunal, which later has to deal with the substance of the case."[178] The Court decided also that the Rules of Procedure providing for a "contentious procedure" do not apply to the preliminary ruling procedure.[179]

Once the national judge has decided to refer a question to the Court, he suspends the proceedings in the national court, and awaits the answer from the Court before resuming them. However, since it may take up to two years before an answer is received, most national judges take interim decisions to dispose temporarily of the case; however, according to the latest Court Report 2008, the average length is now 16.8 months!

In the reference, the national judge formulates a question or questions to be answered by the Court. It is then for the latter to decide whether or not this question is to be answered. Indeed, the Court does not feel under obligation to answer any question put to it. In the first place, the question must be formulated in such a way that the Court can understand the circumstances and facts of the case wherein the problem arises; if not, it might refuse to consider the question.[180] The Court may also, in case the Union law aspects are not clearly formulated in the preliminary question, "re-formulate the question to extract points of [Union] law requiring interpretation".[181] In exceptional cases, the Court can examine the conditions in which the case was referred to it by the national court, in order to assess whether it has jurisdiction. The Court may refuse to rule on a question referred for a preliminary ruling by a national court only where it is quite obvious that the interpretation of Union law that is sought bears no relation to the actual facts of the main action or its purpose.[182]

It should be noted also that the, "summary and urgent character of a procedure in the national court does not prevent the Court from regarding itself as validly seized" to give a preliminary ruling.[183] However, a national court is not required to refer to the Court (even when no judicial review is available against its decision) a question raised in interlocutory proceedings for an interim order; this only applies if each party is entitled to institute proceedings or require proceedings to be instituted on the substance of the case. Furthermore, it should be possible during those proceedings to re-examine the question provisionally decided in the summary proceedings and to refer the question to the Court.[184]

---

[178] *Morson* (Joined Cases 35/82 and 36/82) at (10).

[179] See *Dory* (C-186/01 R) [2001] E.C.R. I–7823(10).

[180] See *Telemarsicabruzzo* (Joined Cases C-320/90, C-321/90 and C-322/90) [1993] E.C.R I–393, where the Court rejected the questions as inadmissible since they did not contain sufficient information for the Court to interpret the Union competition rules in relation to a dispute which was not explained.

[181] *Inizan* (C-56/01) [2003] E.C.R. 12403 at (34).

[182] *Doulamis* (C-446/05) [2008] E.C.R. I–1377.

[183] *Hoffman-La Roche v Centrafarm* (107/76) [1977] E.C.R. 957 at (4); 2 C.M.L.R. 334.

[184] *Hoffman-La Roche v Centrafarm* (107/76), above, fn.183, at 973(5). See also *Walrave v Union Cycliste Internationale* (36/74) [1974] E.C.R. 1405; [1975] 1 C.M.L.R. 320: in a decision in summary proceedings, the President of the Arrondissementsrechtbank at Utrecht gave an interim order which was subject to the proviso that the claimant initiate proceedings in the same court within a period of six weeks so as to be able to request the Court to make a preliminary ruling, which was done.

At the request of a national court, the President of the Court may exceptionally decide, on a proposal from the Judge-Rapporteur and after hearing the Advocate-General, to apply an *accelerated procedure* derogating from the Rules, where the circumstances referred to establish that a ruling on the question is a matter of exceptional urgency.[185] Normally the procedure includes an oral part.[186] However, after written statements of case or written observations[187] have been submitted by the Union institutions, the Member State[188] or, in certain cases, a non-member State,[189] the Court, acting on a report from the Judge-Rapporteur, after informing the interested persons and after hearing the Advocate-General, may decide that the procedure shall not include an oral part. This is possible as long as none of the interested persons has submitted an application setting out the reasons for which he wishes to be heard.[190]

It is clear from the abundance of requests for preliminary rulings[191] that here lies an essential function of the Court, not only in regard to the development of Union law, but also as an instrument at the disposal of natural and legal persons confronted with Union or national measures whose legality they cannot directly challenge in the Court. Indeed, when, in a preliminary ruling, an act of the institutions or of a Member State is declared by the Court to be invalid, it becomes inapplicable because the national authorities are then under obligation to take all general and particular measures in order to ensure the application of the Court's judgment; in the meantime, the national judge may not apply the rule declared illegal or infringing Union law.[192] This has for the claimant practically the same consequences as an annulment.

The Court indicated that the preliminary ruling procedure cannot be used to have the Court examine the validity of a Union act when the interested party could have, "without any doubt[193] challenged it by virtue of Article [263][194] of the Treaty."[195]

The following should also be noted with regard to the preliminary ruling. Firstly, the competence of the Court does not apply to purely national internal

---

[185] art.104a Rules.

[186] art.104,4 Rules.

[187] art.104,4 Rules.

[188] art.104,1 Rules. Indeed, the Member States are automatically informed of every preliminary question. This requires the translation of the preliminary question in all the official languages, but art.104(1) of the Rules now permits a translation of a summary where the order for reference is particularly long.

[189] art.104,1,2 Rules: States who are parties to the EEA Agreement, and (see Council Decision amending the Protocol on the Statute of the Court, [2002] O.J. L218/1) in case this is provided for in an agreement relating to a specific subject concluded by the Council and one or more non-member States, and the question raised by the national judge falls within the scope of the agreement. art.23,4 Statute.

[190] Rules, art.104,4.

[191] In 2009, 302 preliminary questions were filed (the highest ever), 259 judgments and orders were delivered—this represented more than half of all Court decisions—and at the end of 2009, 438 references were pending: Court Report 2009.

[192] See in this regard *Jonkman E. A* (Joined Cases C-231/06 and C-233/06) [2007] E.C.R. I-5149.

[193] See *The Queen v Intervention Board for Agricultural Produce Ex p. Accrington BEEF* (C-241/95 P) [1996] E.C.R. I-6699, where a preliminary question was admitted because there were doubts as to the standing of the applicant to challenge the Regulation. Idem. *Eurotunnel v SeaFrance* (C-408/95) [1997] E.C.R. I-6315.

[194] Formerly EC art.230.

[195] *TWD Textilwerke Deggendorf* (C-188/92) [1994] E.C.R. I-833 at (24/25) and *Wiljo* (C-178/95) [1997] E.C.R. I-585.

situations; however, if the Member State has applied Union rules (provided for in a directive) also to purely internal situations, then the Court is competent to interpret the Union rules in an internal case.[196] Secondly, intervention by a private party in a preliminary ruling procedure is not admissible since those proceedings are not contentious in nature.[197] Thirdly, an application for revision of a preliminary ruling cannot be made. Only the national judge could submit to the Court new elements susceptible to provoking a different answer.[198]

The competence of the Court to give preliminary rulings is not limited to the interpretation of provisions of Union law. Indeed, this jurisdiction has been extended, by the Protocol concerning the interpretation by the Court of the Convention of February 29, 1968 on the mutual recognition of companies and legal persons and by the Protocol concerning the interpretation by the Court of the Convention of September 27, 1968 on jurisdiction and the enforcement of judgments in civil and commercial matters.[199] The competence was also extended by the First and Second Protocol on the interpretation by the Court of the Convention on the law applicable to contractual obligations.[200]

The Rules provide for a "simplified procedure" where a question for a preliminary ruling is identical to a question on which the Court has already ruled, where the answer to the question may be clearly deduced from existing case law or where the answer to the question admits of no reasonable doubt. In those cases the Court may, after hearing the national court, the persons involved and the Advocate-General, give its decision by reasoned Order in which, if appropriated, reference is made to its previous judgment or to the relevant case law.[201]

As indicated above, the Rules also provide for an "accelerated procedure"[202]; such a decision is taken exceptionally by the President, at the request of a national court, after hearing the Advocate-General, where the circumstances referred to establish that a ruling on the question put to the Court is a matter of exceptional urgency.[203]

An "urgent procedure" was added to the Rules in 2008.[204] A reference for a preliminary ruling which raises one or more questions in the area covered by Title V (Area of Freedom, Security and Justice) of the TFEU,[205] at the request of a national court or tribunal or, exceptionally, of the Court's own motion, require in certain cases, a rapid response and may therefore be dealt with under this urgent procedure. The decision concerning the request for an urgent procedure is taken by a designated chamber.[206]

---

[196] *Leur-Bloem* (C-28/95) [1997] E.C.R. I–4161.

[197] *Biogen v Smithkline* (C-181/95) [1996] E.C.R. I–717 and *Tietosuojavaltuutettu* (C-73/07) [2007] E.C.R I–7075.

[198] *Rev, Reisebüro Binder* (C-116/96) [1998] E.C.R. I–1891.

[199] The Convention was signed on June 3, 1971 by the six founding Member States and later extended to all the others, [1975] O.J. L204/28.

[200] Signed on December 19, 1988, [1989] O.J. L48/1.

[201] art.104(3) and (4) Rules. See Annual Report 2004 of the Court, 13.

[202] art.104a Rules. See, for instance, order of the President of the Court in *Metock E.A.* (C-127/08) E.C.R. I–6241. In 2009 three requests for this procedure were made; two were accepted, one was rejected: Court Report 2009.

[203] For an example of a request for an accelerated procedure which was refused, see *Plantanol* (C-201/08) [2008] E.C.R. 03.07.08.

[204] art.104b Rules. In 2009 three requests for this procedure were made; two were accepted, one was rejected: Court Report 2009.

[205] arts 67 to 89 TFEU [arts 29 to 42 EU].

[206] For an example of an urgent procedure (PU: Procédure Urgente) see *Rinau* (C-195/08 PPU) [2008] E.C.R. I–5271.

(5) Compensation for Damages Caused by Institutions

The Court has jurisdiction in disputes relating to compensation for damages resulting from the non-contractual liability of the Union.[207] Indeed, the Treaty provides that:

> "[I]n the case of non-contractual liability, the Union shall, in accordance with the general principles common to the laws of the Member States, make good any damage caused[208] by its institutions or by its servants in the performance of their duties".[209]

In one of its first judgments concerning claims for redress, the Court held that an administrative measure which had not been annulled could not constitute, on the part of the administration, a wrongful act inflicting damage upon those whom it affects.[210] In later judgments, however, the Court modified its position, indicating that actions for annulment and claims for damages are different proceedings. In providing for an appeal for damages the Treaty introduced an autonomous form of action subject to conditions on its use dictated by its specific nature. Indeed, the end of this action is not the abolition of a particular measure, but the compensation for damages inflicted by the measure or action of the administration.[211] Undoubtedly, this is true, but this action can, nevertheless, if successful, constitute a declaration on the part of the Court, that the act is illegal. Indeed, it can be argued that a measure giving rise to compensation of damages is implicitly illegal, since the Court indicated that the non-contractual liability of the Union presupposes the unlawful nature of the act, besides actual damage and a causal relationship between the act and the damage.[212] On the other hand, the unlawful nature of an act does not automatically make the Union responsible for compensation in case of damage. The cases in which compensation is granted are rather rare.[213]

In the case of legislation involving measures of economic policy, the Community does not incur non-contractual liability unless a sufficiently flagrant violation of a superior rule of law for the protection of the damaged party can be shown.[214] Furthermore, in many cases the Court has considered that the institution enjoys wide discretionary powers (e.g. in the field of agricultural policy) in

---

[207] art.268 TFEU [235].

[208] It follows that there must exist a link of causality between the act of the institution and the alleged damages; see for an absence of such link *FG Marine v Commission* (T-360/04) [2007] E.C.R. 19.07.07, not published in the Records; see E.C.R. II 2007/8, p.92*.

[209] art.336 TFEU [283].

[210] *Plauman v Commission* (25/62) [1963] E.C.R. 95 at 108; [1964] C.M.L.R. 29.

[211] *Zuckerfabrik Schöppenstedt v Council* (5/71) [1971] E.C.R. 975 at (3).

[212] *De Franceschi v Council and Commission* (51/81) [1982] E.C.R. 117 at (9).

[213] See *HNL v Council and Commission* (Joined Cases 83/76 and 94/76) [1978] E.C.R. 1209 at (4); [1978] 3 C.M.L.R. 566; *Mulder v Council and Commission* (Joined Cases C-104/89 and C-37/90) [1992] E.C.R. 3131 and *Hartmann* (T-20/94) [1997] E.C.R. II–595. See also *Eagle v Commission* (T-144/02) [2004] E.C.R. II–3381, where the GC ordered the Commission to repair the financial damage caused by its refusal to hire the plaintiff and ordered the parties to submit to the GC, within a time limit of 6 months, the amount of the damages agreed upon between them and if no agreement could be reached, their own calculations.

[214] *Ludwigshafener Walzmühle v Council and Commission* (Joined Cases 197, etc./80) [1981] E.C.R. 3211 at (19).

which case it must be shown that the institution has gone beyond the limits assigned to the exercise of its powers.[215]

As for the damage for which compensation is sought, it must be certain and have been assessed or, at least, be assessable. The Court has, however, accepted the admissibility of an action in which it was asked to declare the Union liable for imminent damage foreseeable with sufficient certainty, even if the damage cannot yet be precisely assessed.[216] The Court also admits that the damage be fixed by agreement between the parties.[217]

The Union courts have exclusive jurisdiction to hear cases concerning compensation based on the non-contractual liability of the Union.[218] This would also include compensation for moral prejudice.[219]

A problem might arise with measures taken by the Member States on the basis of a Union act. The Court has indicated that it has no jurisdiction when the application for compensation is, in fact, based on such national measures. The Member States could, of course, be sued in the national courts for faulty application of Union law if this were the case.[220] On the other hand, when the damage caused by the national implementing measure finds its origin in the underlying Union act, the liability of the Union can be established by the Court on the basis of Union law.[221]

It should be noted that actions for compensation for damage are subject to a five-year period of limitation.[222]

As was indicated above, when the Court allocates damages caused by an act of the institutions considered by the Court to be illegal, the latter becomes virtually inapplicable. The action for compensation of damages constitutes, therefore, for natural and legal persons, next to the preliminary ruling, an instrument for challenging the legality of Union acts for those who have no locus standi under the direct appeal procedure. However, the outcome of both actions cannot, as the

---

[215] See *HNL v Council and Commission* (Joined Cases 8/76 and 94/76, 4/75 and 40/77) [1978] E.C.R. 1209; [1978] 3 C.M.L.R. 566: in case of wide discretionary powers, the Community does not incur liability unless the institution concerned has manifestly and gravely disregarded the limits on the exercise of its power.

[216] See *Agraz E.A. v Commission* (C-234/05 P) [2006] E.C.R. I-10833, where the Court annulled a judgment of the GC which rejected an appeal for damages judging that the damage was not certain.

[217] *Pauls Agriculture v Council and Commission* (256/81) [1983] E.C.R. 1707 at (15) and *Biovilac v EEC* (59/83) [1984] E.C.R. 4057 at (9); also *Adams v Commission* (145/83) [1985] E.C.R. I-3539. The President of the Court referred to "serious and irreparable loss": *Netherlands v Commission* (C-110/97) [1997] E.C.R. I-1795.

[218] *Asteris v Greece* (Joined Cases 106/87, 107/87, 108/87, 109/87, 110/87, 111/87, 112/87, 113/87, 114/87, 115/87, 116/87, 117/87, 118/87, 119/87 and 120/87) [1988] E.C.R. 5531; [1990] 1 C.M.L.R. 575. The Court ruled that a question relating to the application of art.340,2 TFEU [art.288,2 EC] cannot be determined in proceedings for a preliminary ruling: *Granaria v Hoofd produktschap voor Akkerbouwprodukten* (101/78) [1979] E.C.R. 623 at (10); [1979] 3 C.M.L.R. 124.

[219] *Dreyfus* (T-485/93) [1996] E.C.R. II–1101(74); idem *Hautem v EIB* (T-11/00) [2000] E.C.R. II–4036 at (35).

[220] See *Asteris* (Joined Cases 106/87, 107/87, 108/87, 109/87, 110/87, 111/87, 112/87, 113/87, 114/87, 115/87, 116/87, 117/87, 118/87, 119/87 and 120/87) (quoted above, fn.218).

[221] *Dietz v Commission* (126/76) [1977] E.C.R. 2431; [1978] 2 C.M.L.R. 608. See also *Granaria* (101/78) quoted above, fn.218, at (3) and *EISS v Commission* (310/81) [1984] E.C.R. 1341.

[222] art.43, Statute. See *Birra Wührer v Council and Commission* (Joined Cases 256 etc./80 and 5/81) [1982] E.C.R. 85.

Court has stated, be identical and be used, for instance, to avoid the time limit[223] set by the Treaty.[224]

(6) Union Industrial Property Rights

The Council, acting unanimously in accordance with the special legislative procedure,[225] may adopt provisions to confer jurisdiction, to the extent it shall determine, on the Court of Justice of the European Union in disputes relating to the application of acts adopted on the basis of the Treaties that create industrial property rights. Those provisions of the Council will have to be adopted by the Member States in accordance with their respective constitutional requirements.[226]

The Court shall have jurisdiction in actions brought by Member States, Parliament, the Council or the Commission on the same grounds as those which can be invoked for an action for annulment, i.e. lack of competence, infringement of an essential procedural requirement, infringement of the Treaty or of any rule of law pertaining to its application, or misuse of powers. The Court shall have jurisdiction under the same conditions in actions brought by the Court of Auditors, by the ECB and by the Committee of the Regions for the purpose of protecting their prerogatives.[227]

(7) The Objection of Illegality

The objection of illegality[228] gives, according to the Court:

"[E]xpression to a general principle conferring upon any party to proceedings the right to challenge, for the purpose of obtaining the annulment of a decision of direct and individual concern to that party, the validity of previous acts of the institutions which form the legal basis of the decision which is being attacked, if that party was not entitled under Article [263][229] of the Treaty to bring a direct action challenging those acts by which it was thus affected without having been in a position to ask that they be declared void".[230]

Although the Treaty refers to a "regulation", the Court mentions "acts" in general.[231]

---

[223] art.263,6 TFEU [230,5].
[224] *Union de Pequenos Agricultores v Council* (T-173/98) [1999] E.C.R. II-3357.
[225] art.289,2 TFEU.
[226] art.262 TFEU [229].
[227] art.263 TFEU [230].
[228] art.277 TFEU [241]. See, e.g. *Rumi v Commission* (258/80) [1982] E.C.R. 487.
[229] Previously art.230 EC.
[230] *Hauts Fournaux de Chasse v High Authority* (15/57) [1957–1958] E.C.R. 211 and *Meroni v High Authority* (9/56) [1957–1958] E.C.R. 133. As was seen above, the important words are: "if that party was not entitled . . . to bring a direct action challenging those acts"; the same rule applies here as in the case of the preliminary ruling. Those indirect ways may only be used if the direct way is closed.
[231] *Simmenthal v Commission* (92/78) [1979] E.C.R. 777 at(39); [1980] 1 C.M.L.R. 162.

For the Court it is clear from the wording and the general scheme of the Treaty that, although this is not specified, a declaration of inapplicability is only possible in proceedings brought before the Court itself under some provision of the Treaty other than the one for annulment and that the plea may only be used against a measure which is the basis for the act in dispute. In other words, the objection of illegality does not constitute an independent action and may only be sought incidentally.[232] The objection of illegality constitutes, with the request for a preliminary ruling and the claim for compensation for damage, the third way for natural and legal persons to challenge a measure whose legality they cannot directly ask the Court to review.[233]

(8) Other Cases within the Court's Jurisdiction

By way of derogation from the provisions concerning the jurisdiction of the GC, jurisdiction is reserved to the Court in actions for annulment of an act of an institution,[234] or for establishing a failure of an institution to act,[235] when (with some exceptions) such action is brought by a Member State against Parliament or the Council; or those institutions acting jointly; or by an institution against Parliament, the Council or both acting jointly; or the Commission; or by an institution against the European Central Bank.[236]

Acts setting up bodies, offices and agencies of the Union[237] may lay down specific conditions and arrangements concerning actions brought by natural or legal persons against acts of those bodies, offices and agencies intended to produce legal effects in relation to them.[238]

The Court also has jurisdiction to decide on the legality of acts adopted by the European Council or by the Council concerning a serious breach by a Member State of the values on which the Union is founded,[239] solely at the request of the Member State concerned and in respect solely of the procedural stipulations contained in the EU Treaty.[240] Such a request must be made within one month from the date of the adoption of the act. The Court shall rule within one month from the date of the request.

The Court may be asked to give preliminary rulings on the validity and interpretation of framework decisions and decisions on the interpretation of conventions established under said provisions and on the validity and interpretation of the measures implementing them.

The Court has, furthermore, jurisdiction with regard to the Provisions on enhanced Co-operation[241] under the conditions laid down by the TFEU.[242] The latter provides that Member States that wish to establish closer co-operation

[232] See *CSF and CSME v Commission* (T-154/94) [1996] E.C.R. II–1377.
[233] art.263 TFEU [230].
[234] art.263 TFEU [230].
[235] art.265 TFEU [232].
[236] art.51 Statute.
[237] See below Ch.13: Decentralised Bodies of the Union.
[238] art.263,5 TFEU [230].
[239] This provision provides for the Council to determine that there is a clear risk of a serious breach by a Member State of the values on which the Union is founded (art.2 EU). The European Council, on the other hand, may determine that such a serious breach does indeed exist.
[240] art.269 TFEU.
[241] arts 326 to 334 TFEU [EU arts 43 to 45].
[242] art.326 to 334 TFEU [11].

among themselves, may be authorised, "to make use of the institutions, proce-dures and mechanisms laid down by that Treaty". There are, however, certain conditions which must be fulfilled in order to obtain such authorisation. Among other things, such co-operation may not affect Union policies, actions or pro-grammes and may not constitute a discrimination or a restriction of trade, etc.[243]

The Court's jurisdiction also applies with regard to amendments to the EU Treaty[244] and the admission of new members and consequent adjustments to the Treaty.[245]

It should be noted that the Court's jurisdiction with regard to the provisions concerning judicial co-operation in criminal matters[246] and police co-operation[247] is limited, since it has no jurisdiction to review the validity or proportionality of operations carried out by the police or other law enforcement services of the Member States or the exercise of the responsibilities incumbent upon Member States with regard to the maintenance of law and order and the safeguarding of internal security.[248]

Similar limitations are provided for with regard to the Common Foreign and Security Policy and acts adopted on the basis of those provisions.[249] In principle the Court has no jurisdiction in this field. However, the Court shall have jurisdic-tion to monitor compliance with the procedures and the extent of the powers of the institutions laid down by the Treaties, by reviewing the legality of decisions providing for restrictive measures against natural or legal persons adopted by the Council applying specific provisions concerning the Common Foreign and Security Policy.[250] Proceedings may be brought by natural and legal persons in conformity with the provisions concerning annulment of Union acts.[251]

(9) European Investment Bank (EIB) and the European Central Bank (ECB)

The Court has jurisdiction in disputes concerning the fulfilment by Member States of their obligations under the Statute of the EIB.[252]

The decisions of the Board of Governors of the EIB may be challenged in the Court by the Member States, the Commission or the Board of Directors. As for decisions of the Board of Directors, they may, in certain cases, be challenged by the Member States and the Commission.[253]

The Court has jurisdiction in disputes concerning the fulfilment by national cen-tral banks of their obligations under the Treaty and the Statute of the European Systems of Central Banks (ESCB).[254] The Governing Council of the ECB enjoys the

---

[243] art.326 TFEU.
[244] art.54 TFEU [48].
[245] art.56 TFEU [49].
[246] arts 82–86 TFEU [31].
[247] arts 87–89 TFEU [30 and 12].
[248] art.276 TFEU.
[249] art.275 TFEU.
[250] art.23 to 46 EU.
[251] art.263(4) TFEU [230].
[252] art.271 TFEU [237].
[253] See *Commission v Conseil des Gouverneurs de la EIB* (85/86) [1986] E.C.R. 2215; [1989] C.M.L.R. 103.
[254] art.271 TFEU [237].

same powers vis-à-vis the national central banks as the Commission may exercise in case of failure by a Member State to fulfil a Treaty obligation.[255] Similarly, if the Court finds that certain obligations have not been fulfilled, the national central bank concerned must take the necessary measures to comply with the judgment. There is, however, an important difference: the Governing Council of the ECB does not have the possibility to ask the Court to impose a lump sum or penalty payment in case the national central bank fails to implement the Court's judgment.[256]

On the other hand, decisions of the ECB may be challenged in court by the Union institutions.

(10) Attribution of Competence

Competence may be attributed to the Court either pursuant to an arbitration clause contained in a contract concluded by or on behalf of the Union[257] or in any dispute between Member States that relates to the subject matter of the Treaty, if the dispute is submitted to the Court under a special agreement.[258] In the case of a contract, the arbitration clause is necessary since the Treaty provides that disputes to which the Union is a party shall not, on that ground, be excluded from the jurisdiction of the courts of the Member States.[259]

(11) Appellate Jurisdiction

Since 1989, the Court also functions as court of appeal from decisions of the GC.[260] See Council Decision amending the Protocol on the Statute of the Court of Justice in order to lay down the conditions and limits for the review by the Court of decisions given by the GC.[261] An appeal may be brought before the Court within two months of the notification of the contested decision. It may concern a final decision, a decision disposing of the substantial part of the substantive issues only, or a decision disposing of procedural issues concerning a plea of lack of competence or inadmissibility.[262]

The appeal may be brought by the unsuccessful party, the interveners when the decision directly affects them, the Member States or the Union institutions.[263] Any person whose application to intervene has been dismissed by the GC may appeal within two weeks from the notification of the decision dismissing the application.[264] The parties may appeal against any decision of the GC concerning the suspension of the application of an act,[265] the prescription of interim measure[266] or the enforcement of a decision imposing pecuniary obligations.[267] An appeal to the Court shall be limited to points of law. It:

---

[255] See above, Ch.8: The Commission.
[256] art.271(d) TFEU only refers to art.258 and not to art.260(2) [228(2)].
[257] art.272 TFEU [238]. See *IDE* (C-114/94) [1997] E.C.R. I–803.
[258] art.273 TFEU [239].
[259] art.274 TFEU [240].
[260] art.256(1),2 TFEU [225].
[261] Council Decision 2005/696, [2005] O.J. L266/60, corrected [2005] O.J. L301/21.
[262] art.56,1 Statute.
[263] art.56,2 Statute.
[264] art.57.1 Statute.
[265] art.278 TFEU [242].
[266] art.279 TFEU [243].
[267] art.299 TFEU [256,4].

"[S]hall lie on the grounds of lack of competence of the GC, a breach of procedure before it, which affects the interests of the appellant as well as infringement of Union law by the GC".[268]

The Court's jurisdiction is confined to examining the assessment by the GC of the pleas argued before it. In other words, parties may not put forward for the first time before the Court a plea in law which it has not raised before the GC.[269] If the appeal is well founded, the Court shall quash the decision. It may then either give final judgment itself, if the state of the proceedings so permit—according to the Court, this is so where quashing the decision of the GC implies that the decision must be annulled[270]—or refer the case back to the GC,[271] which is then bound by the decision of the Court on matters of law. The Rules of Procedure of the Court contain special provisions for appeals against decisions of the GC.[272] The Court could, exceptionally, be called upon to act as Supreme Court, i.e. hearing an appeal from the appellate decision of the GC.[273]

A recent amendment of the Rules of Procedure provides that a special chamber shall be set up for the purpose of deciding whether a decision of the GC is to be reviewed: this chamber is composed of the President of the Court and four of the Presidents of the chambers of five Judges according to the order of precedence. A decision to review shall indicate which questions are to be reviewed. The parties and other persons to whom the decision of the Court has been notified may lodge statements or written observations on the questions which are subject to review.[274] In case the Court decides to review a decision of the GC, the language of the case shall be the language of the decision of the GC which is subject to review.[275]

4. THE PROCEDURE

The rules concerning the procedure before the Court are laid down in the Protocol on the Statute of the Court of Justice of the European Union—which may be amended by the Council[276]—annexed to the Treaties and in the Rules of Procedure of the Court of Justice (hereinafter "Rules")[277] which the Court adopts after

---

[268] art.58 Statute. Limitation to points of law, see *Hilti* (C-53/92 P) [1994] E.C.R. I–667 and *Trembla* (C-91/95 P) [1996] E.C.R. I–5547.
[269] *Hercules Chemicals NV v Commission* (C-51/92 P), [1999] E.C.R. I–4235.
[270] See *CA Pasta v Commission* (C-359/98 P), [2000] E.C.R. I–3977(38–39).
[271] art.54 Statute. However, it is not for the Court, when ruling on questions of law in the context of an appeal, to substitute, on grounds of fairness, its own assessment for that of the GC exercising its unlimited jurisdiction to rule on the amount of fines.
[272] Rules [2003] O.J. C193/1, modified on account of enlargement, [2004] O.J. L127/107 and L132/2, arts 110 to 123.
[273] art.256(2)2 TFEU [225(2)2].
[274] [2008] O.J. L200/18.
[275] [2008] O.J. L200/20.
[276] art.281 TFEU [245] 245], "acting unanimously at the request of the Court of Justice and after consulting the European Parliament and the Commission, or at the request of the Commission and after consulting the European Parliament and the Court of Justice, may amend the provisions of the Statute, with the exception of Title I." See, for instance, Rules art.29(3)6 concerning statements or written observations by non-Member States. The Protocol was amended in [2004] O.J. L132/1 and 5.
[277] The Court and the GC each have their own Rules of Procedure; those of the GC shall be designated hereinafter as "GC Rules", [2003] O.J. L193/1, amended 12 times.

having received the approval of the Council acting by a qualified majority.[278] The Rules contain, "any provisions necessary for applying and, where required, supplementing" the Statute.[279] The rules are complemented by the Instructions to the Registrar[280] and the Practice Directions relating to direct actions and appeals (and preliminary rulings).[281] Both, particularly the latter, constitute a must for lawyers and agents representing parties in court; they prescribe, for instance, that the pages of the pleadings "must be numbered consecutively in the top right-hand corner", on, "white, unlined, A4 size paper", etc. In case these instructions are not followed, the registrar will require the lawyers or agents, "to make good any irregularities of form in documents lodged which do not comply with those provisions".

The procedure before the Court, for which no fees are charged, consists of two parts: a written and an oral one. The language of the proceedings must be one of the 23 official language of the Union[282] and is determined by the applicant, except that (a) when the defendant is a Member State or a natural or legal person having the nationality of a Member State, the language of the case shall be the official language of that State; (b) at the joint request of the parties the use of another of the 23 languages may be authorised for all or part of the proceedings; and (c) at the request of one of the parties, and after the opposite party and the Advocate-General have been heard, another language may be authorised for all or part of the proceedings.[283] Requests are decided on by the President.

In the case of a preliminary ruling, the language shall be that of the national court or tribunal which has referred the question.

States other than Member States which are parties to the European Economic Area (EEA) Agreement, and also the EFTA Surveillance Authority, which may submit statements of case or written observations when one of the fields of application of that Agreement is concerned, may, in pursuance of the Statute,[284] be authorised to use one of the 23 languages other than the language of the case.[285] The same applies to third States which take part in proceedings for a preliminary ruling.[286]

(1) The Written Procedure[287]

The written procedure is defined in the Statute as follows—it:

> "[S]hall consist of the communication to the parties and to the institutions of the Union whose decisions are in dispute, of applications, statements of case,

---

[278] art.253,6 TFEU [223,6]; Parties should be aware of the fact that Annex II to the Rules providing for different extension of time limits on account of distance no longer exists. As for the Supplementary Rules concerning letters rogatory, legal aid and reports of perjury by a witness or expert, see [1974] O.J. L350/29, amended [1997] O.J. L103/4 and [2006] O.J. L72/1.

[279] art.63 Statute.

[280] [2007] O.J. L232/1.

[281] [2007] O.J. L232/7.

[282] art.29(2), Rules. The languages are: Danish, Dutch, English, Finnish, French, German, Greek, Irish, Italian, Portuguese, Spanish and Swedish; to those languages have been added Estonian, Slovakian, Slovene, Hungarian, Czech, Latvian, Polish, Maltese, Bulgarian, Romanian and Lithuanian in pursuance of the enlargement Treaties.

[283] art.29(2) Rules.

[284] art.23,3 Statute.

[285] art.37,5 Rules.

[286] art.29(3)6 Statute.

[287] art. 20 Statute and following and Rules, Title II, Chap.1 and 2.

defences and observations, and of replies, if any, as well as of all papers and documents in support or of certified copies of them".[288]

The written procedure starts with the submission to the Court of a written application addressed to the Registrar.[289] Such applications may also be transmitted by electronic means; it is up to the Court to determine the criteria for deeming a procedural document, sent in that manner, to be the original of that document.[290]

The Statute and the Rules contain various requirements as to form, content and accompanying documents of the application.[291] As already indicated, see also the very detailed Practice Directions to Parties, published by the Court.[292]

The Member States and the institutions are represented by an agent appointed for each case; the agent may be assisted by an adviser or by a lawyer[293]; non-Member States that are part of the EEA Agreement and the EFTA Surveillance Authority (the "privileged" parties[294]) are represented in the same manner. Other parties (the "non-privileged parties") must be represented by a lawyer entitled to practice before the court of a Member State or of a State which is a party to the EEA Agreement.[295] The lawyers acting for a party must lodge at the registry a certificate that they are authorised to practice before a court of a Member State or another State which is a party to the EEA Agreement.[296] Legal advisers and lawyers should carefully read in the Rules of Procedure about their rights and obligations.[297] In a recent Order the President of the GC threatened to exclude a lawyer from the proceedings in case, "new rash or vexatious requests for interim measures were filed".[298]

It is important to note that the application must state, besides the obvious, such as the applicant's name and address, etc.,[299] the subject matter of the proceedings and a, "summary of the pleads in law on which the application is based", i.e. all the grounds on which it is based, since parties may not, in the course of the

---

[288] art.20,2 Statute.

[289] art.21 Statute and art.37 Rules and following.

[290] art.37(7) Rules.

[291] art.37(7) Rules.

[292] [2007] O.J. L232/7. See, for instance, point 1 on the use of technical means of communication: e-mail address *http://www.ecj.registry@curia.europa.eu* presentation of pleadings; form and content of the principal types of pleading; annexes to pleadings; drafting and length, application for expedited procedure; application for hearing and oral argument and preparation of hearings.

[293] art.19,1 Statute.

[294] See *Valencia* (C-363/06 P) [2008] E.C.R. 20.02.08

[295] art.19,4 Statute. The application no longer needs an address for service at Luxembourg, as used to be the case, but it can state such an address and, in addition to, or instead of, state that the lawyer or agent agrees that service is to be effected on him by telefax or other technical means of communication (e-mail is mentioned in the Practice Directions, under 1: *http://www.ecj.registry@ curia.europa.eu*. [2009] O.J. L29/51; see [2003] O.J. L98/9): art.38,2 Rules. Proceedings brought by a litigant in person are inadmissible: *Lopez v Court of Justice* (C-174/96 P) [1996] E.C.R. I–6401.

[296] See *Valencia* (C-363/06 P) (quoted above, fn.295) where the Court refers to a judgment of the GC which indicates why this is required and *Valenciana v Commission* (T-357/05) [2006] E.C.R. II–2015, where the claimant was not so represented.

[297] Rules, Ch. 7 of Title I and Rules of the GC, Ch.6.

[298] *Goldstein v Commission* (T-18/01 R), [2001] E.C.R. II–1147(46).

[299] Also: description of the signatory, the name of the party or names of the parties against whom the application is made, the subject matter of the dispute, the form of order sought; where appropriate, it shall be accompanied by the measure the annulment of which is sought or documentary evidence of the date on which an institution was, in accordance with art.265 TFEU [232], requested to act. art.21,2 Statute.

proceedings, raise fresh issues, unless these are based on matters of law or of fact which come to light in the course of the written procedure, and the form of order sought.[300]

The time limit within which the application must be filed is also essential; appeals for annulment must be instituted within two months of the publication of the measures or of its notification to the applicant or, in the absence thereof, of the day on which it came to the knowledge of the latter, as the case may be.[301] This time limit is calculated, in pursuance of the Rules,[302] from the end of the fourteenth day after publication of the contested measure in the *Official Journal* (to allow the latter to arrive) and ten days for distance.[303] Furthermore, the expiry of the time limit cannot be held against a party if the latter, "proves the existence of unforeseeable circumstances or of force majeure".[304]

The date of lodgement for the purposes of compliance with time limits for taking steps in proceedings, shall be the date on which a copy of the signed original of a pleading, including the schedule of documents, is received at the Registry by telex or other technical means of communication available to the Court, provided that the signed original of the pleading, accompanied by all the required annexes, is lodged at the Registry not later than 10 days thereafter.[305] However, on the basis of a recent amendment to the Rules:

> "[T]he Court may, by decision, determine the criteria for a procedural document sent to the Registry by electronic means to be deemed to be the original of that document. That decision shall be published in the Official Journal of the European Union".[306]

The fact that an application is lodged with the Court is published in the *Official Journal*; besides the names of the parties, the subject matter of the dispute and the claims of the applicant, "a summary of the contentions and of the main arguments" is also published.[307]

The application is served on the defendant who then has one month to file a defence.[308] The plaintiff's application and the defence may (but need not) be supplemented by a reply from the applicant and a rejoinder from the defendant. The time limit within which those pleadings have to be lodged is fixed by the President of the Court. After the rejoinder has been lodged[309] the President fixes a date on which the Judge-Rapporteur is to present a Preliminary Report[310] that contains recommendations as to whether a preparatory inquiry or any other preparatory step should be undertaken, as to which chamber formation the case

---

[300] art.21 Statute and art.42,2 Rules; see *Maizena v Council* (139/79) [1980] E.C.R. 3393 at (32) and *Austria v Commission* (165/99) [2001], unpublished.

[301] art.263,3 TFEU [230,3]. If publication in the *Official Journal* allows the date to be determined with some precision (i.e. the moment it becomes available), the matter is more delicate with letters, especially when they are not registered, see *Belfiore v Commission* (108/79) [1980] E.C.R. 1769 at (7).

[302] art.81(1) Rules.

[303] art.81(2) Rules.

[304] art.45,2 Statute. See Order of 26.10.01 in *Austria v Commission* (C-165/99) unpublished.

[305] [2005] O.J. L 203/19, art.1,1.

[306] art.37(6) Rules.

[307] art.16(6) Rules.

[308] art.40(1) Rules.

[309] Unless no reply and no rejoinder were lodged, or the parties waved the right to lodge same or in the case of the expedited procedure; see Rules art.44(1).

[310] art.44(2) Rules.

should be assigned and as to whether to dispense with a hearing[311] and/or with a submission[312] of the Advocate-General.[313]

The Court, after hearing the Advocate-General, may by means of an Order, prescribe the measures of inquiry and other preparatory measure[314] that it considers appropriate, such as: personal appearance of the parties; a request for information and production of documents; oral testimony; the commissioning of experts and/or an inspection of the place or thing in question. The Advocate-General shall take part and the parties may attend. The Court may, by means of an Order also, either on its own motion or on application by a party, and after hearing the Advocate-General, order that certain facts be proven by witnesses.[315] The Rules provide for the conditions of the audition, penalties for not attending,[316] objections to a witness[317] and reimbursement of costs.[318] The Court may order that a witness be heard by the judicial authorities of his place of permanent residence[319]; for that the Court issues "letters rogatory" in accordance with supplementary rules adopted by the Court with the approval of the Council[320] and after consultation with the Governments concerned.[321]

The Statute provides that Member States must treat violation of an oath by a witness in the same manner as if the offence had been committed before one of its courts with jurisdiction in civil proceedings. The Member State shall prosecute the offender at the instance of the Court.[322] The same rules apply to experts.

After the preparatory inquiry has been completed, the President fixes the date for the opening of the oral procedure, unless the Court prescribes a period within which the parties may lodge written observations. The Judge-Rapporteur and the Advocate-General may request the parties to submit all such information relating to the facts, and all such documents and other particulars, as they may consider relevant.[323]

(2) The Oral Procedure

According to the Statute, the:

> "[O]ral procedure shall consist of the reading of the report presented by a Judge acting as Rapporteur, the hearing by the Court of agents, advisers and lawyers and of the submissions of the Advocate-General, as well as the hearing, if any, of witnesses and experts".[324]

---

[311] art.44a Rules.
[312] Please note that the Statute refers to the "submission" of the Advocate-General (art.20(5)) and the Rules to the "opinion" (art.44(2)) of the Advocate-General.
[313] art.20 Statute.
[314] arts 45 to 54a Rules.
[315] art.47 Rules.
[316] art.48(2) Rules.
[317] art.50 Rules.
[318] art.51 Rules.
[319] art.29 Statute.
[320] art.253,6 TFEU [223,6].
[321] art.125 Rules and [2006] O.J. L72/1.
[322] art.30 Statute.
[323] art.54a Rules.
[324] art.20,4 Statute.

The oral procedure,[325] which is public unless the Court decides otherwise for serious reasons,[326] starts with the reading of the report of the Judge-Rapporteur (although in practice this is no longer the case, the report being submitted to the parties before the procedure with a possibility of making remarks) and ends with the submissions of the Advocate-General[327] (in practice only the final conclusions are read). However, the Court, acting on a report from the Judge-Rapporteur and after hearing the Advocate-General, and if none of the parties has submitted (within one month from notification of the close of the written procedure) an application setting out the reasons for which he wishes to be heard, may decide to dispense with the oral pleadings.[328] The judgment[329] (i.e. the operative part) is, in turn, read in open Court, at a later date.

According to the Rules a judgment contains 12 items, among which are the grounds for the decision (which constitute its essential basis in so far as they are necessary to determine the exact meaning of what is stated in the operative part[330]) and the operative part, including the decision as to costs.[331] The judgment is published in the European Court Reports (E.C.R.). However, in 2004, the Court decided to proceed with a selective publication of the Court's judgments: in a first stage, the direct actions and the appeals will no longer be published in the Court reports when they are issued by a chamber of three Judges or by a chamber of five Judges, and when the decision was taken without submissions from an Advocate-General. In exceptional circumstances, the chamber may decide to publish the judgment or part of it. This selection does not apply to the preliminary rulings. The full text of all the judgments can be found on the Internet in the available languages.[332]

Judgments of the Court are designated with the letter "C", before the number of the case and published in part I of the E.C.R. The judgments of the GC are preceded by the letter "T" (for Tribunal) and published in part II of the E.C.R. In case of appeal from a GC judgment to the Court, the number of the case is followed by the letter "P" (Pourvoi) and summary procedures are indicated by the letter "R" (Référé), eventually followed by "-int" for interim measures. The text of the judgments that are printed in the E.C.R. is preceded by a useful summary, which refers back to the most important statements of the Court.

The duration of proceedings in 2009, concerning direct actions: 17.1 months, and for appeals: 15.4 months. In 2009, 588 cases were terminated; of those 259 were references, 215 joint actions, 97 appeals from GC decisions, 7 for interim relief, 1 request for an opinion (art.218 TFEU [300]) and 9 specific procedures.

(3) Costs

There are, generally speaking, no court costs in respect of proceedings before the European courts, except when a party has caused the Court to incur avoidable

---

[325] art.20,4 Statute and arts 55–62 Rules.
[326] art.31 Statute.
[327] art.59 Rules.
[328] art.44(2) and 44a Rules.
[329] For the prescribed content of the judgment, see art.63 Rules. The judgment always contains a decision on the costs which are normally born by the losing party; art.69 Rules and following.
[330] *Spain v Commission* (C-415/96) [1998] E.C.R. I–6993.
[331] art.63 Rules.
[332] Annual Report 2004 of the Court, 12.
[333] *http://europa.eu.int/rapid/pressReleasesAction.do?reference=CJE/06/14.*

costs and where copying and translation work is carried out at the request of a party.[334]

On the other hand, the Treaty provides that, "the Court shall adjudicate upon costs".[335] Normally,[336] the unsuccessful party shall be ordered to pay the costs incurred by the other party, if they have been applied for in the successful party's pleadings.[337]

Recoverable costs include, among others, "expenses necessarily incurred by the parties for the purpose of the proceedings, in particular the travel and subsistence expenses and the remuneration of agents, advisors and lawyers".[338] Member States and institutions that intervene bear their own costs. The Court may order other interveners to bear their own costs.[339] There is no taxation of the lawyers' costs in the judgment. In case of dispute, the courts decide by order.[340] As [Union] law does not lay down any provisions for the scales of costs, the [Union] judicature must freely assess the circumstances of the case and it does not have to take account of a national scale of costs fixing lawyers fees.

The Rules and the supplementary rules provide for a possibility of obtaining legal aid[341] for a party that is wholly or in part unable to meet the costs of the proceedings. Where legal aid is granted on the basis of an application, which need not be made through a lawyer, and on the basis of an Order from the formation of the Court the application is referred to by the Court on a proposal of the Judge-Rapporteur designated by the President and after hearing the Advocate-General. The cashier of the Court shall advance the funds necessary to meet the expenses.[342] The formation of the Court may at any time withdraw legal aid if the circumstances which led to it being granted alter during the proceedings. The sums paid shall be recovered from the party ordered to pay the costs.

(4) Special Forms of Procedure

The Statute and the Rules contain provisions for several special forms of procedure.[343]

---

[334] art.72 Rules.
[335] art.38 Statute.
[336] See *Compagnie maritime belge v Commission* (T-276/04) [2008] E.C.R. II-1277 where the Commission, although it won the case, was condemned to pay a third of applicant's costs because of the delay in handling the case.
[337] See *Svenska Journalistforbundet v Council* (T-174/95) [1998] E.C.R. II-2293, where the Court ordered the successful party to bear part of its own costs in view of the abuse of procedure committed by the applicant who had published an edited version of the defence on the Internet with an invitation to the public to send their comments to the Agents of the Council.
[338] art.73(b) Rules.
[339] art.69(4) Rules.
[340] See, for instance, Order of the GC of September 17, 1998, in *Branco v Commission, (Taxation of costs)* (T-271/94) [1998] E.C.R. II-3761: of the 2,633,319 Escudos asked for, the GC granted 1,170,000.
[341] art.76 Rules. See, for instance, Order of the Court in *AJ Schulte v Deutsche Bausparkasse Badenia AG* (C-350/03) [2005] E.C.R. I-9215.
[342] See Order of the President of the Third Chamber of the GC granting legal aid, but limiting the amount of the costs and fees of the attorneys *AJ Colin and Valerie Roberts v Commission* (T-25/99) [1999] October 29, not published in the E.C.R and *Deepak Rajani* (C-559/08) Order of 21.01.09.
[343] art.39 Statute and following and art.83 Rules and following.

Expedited Procedure[344]

This procedure may be applied by the Court where the particular urgency of the case requires a ruling to be given with the minimum of delay. On application by the applicant or the defendant, the President may exceptionally decide, on a rec-ommendation of the Judge-Rapporteur and after hearing the other party and the Advocate-General, that a case is to be determined pursuant to an expedited pro-cedure derogating from the provisions of the Rules.[345] A request thereto must be filed by separate document lodged at the same time as the application initiating the proceedings or the defence, as the case may be.

Under this procedure, reply and rejoinder may only be filed if the President so decides. The President fixes the date for the hearing and the Court shall give its ruling after hearing the Advocate-General.

Suspension of Operation or Enforcement and Other Interim Measures

As indicated, applications for annulment have no suspensory effect[346]; however, the Court may, if it considers that circumstances so require, order the application of the contested act to be suspended.[347] An application to suspend the operation of any measure adopted by the institutions shall be admissible only if the appli-cant is challenging that measure in proceedings before the Court.[348]

An application for any other interim measure is only admissible if it is made by a party to a case before the Court and relates to that case.[349]

A decision ordering a suspension or other interim measures is conditional on the existence of circumstances giving rise to urgency and of factual and legal grounds establishing a prima facie case for the interim measure.[350] According to the Court, this urgency must be assessed in relation to the need to prevent seri-ous and irreparable damage to the applicant.[351] Since interim measures may only be granted in respect of a case pending before the Court,[352] the applicant must also show that the grounds on which the substantive application is made, "appear, on first examination, not to be manifestly without foundation" or, that the application has, as the expression goes, a *fumus boni juris*.[353]

Owing to the urgency pleaded in requests for interim measures, the President was given powers to decide on them himself,[354] although, where the case is important or complex he may refer the request to the full Court.[355]

---

[344] art.62a Rules. See Resolution of the Council and of the Representatives of the Member States on the free movement of goods, inviting the Court to consider whether cases within the scope of Regulation 2679/98 on the functioning of the internal market in relation to the free movement of goods ([1998] O.J. L337/8) can be expedited.

[345] For example, see *Commission v Artegodan E.A.* (C-39/03) [2003] E.C.R. I–7885.

[346] art.278 TFEU [242].

[347] arts 278 and 279 TFEU [242 and 243]. See, for instance, Order of the President of the GC in *Oakley/OHIM* (T-116/06 R) [2006] E.C.R. II-2627.

[348] art.83(1)2 Rules.

[349] art.83(1)2 Rules.

[350] art.83(2) Rules. For suspension of an act, see *Bayer* (T-41/96 R) [1996] E.C.R. II–381.

[351] See, e.g. *NTN TOYO v Council* (113/77 R and 113/77 R-Int) [1977] E.C.R. 1721 at 1725(6); [1979] 2 C.M.L.R. 257 and *Greece v Commission* (32/89 R) [1989] E.C.R. II–985 at 989(13); [1991] 1 C.M.L.R. 377. See also *Atlantic Container Line* (C-149/95 P(R)) [1995] E.C.R. I–2169, where the appeal of the Commission against the suspension was dismissed.

[352] art.279 TFEU [243].

[353] *Johnson & Firth Brown v Commission* (3/75 R) [1975] E.C.R. 1 at 6(1); [1975] 1 C.M.L.R. 638.

[354] art.85,1 Rules.

[355] art.85 Rules.

The application is served on the opposite party that may submit written or oral observations within a short period prescribed by the President who may grant the application even before those observations have been received; it may be varied or cancelled even without any application being made by any party.[356]

Interim measures can be prescribed against persons, institutions and Member States.[357] Generally speaking, Presidents have been rather reluctant to grant interim measures and the Court considers that they should only be ordered in exceptional circumstances.[358] It must be clear, furthermore, that the decision of the President (or of the Court) in a summary procedure is, "without prejudice to the decision of the Court on the substance of the case".[359]

Decisions are made in the form of a reasoned order and no appeal against it is possible.[360]

The "other interim measures" prescribed by the Court have been extremely varied, and, indeed, the Treaty only refers to any "necessary" interim measure.[361] The Court has, for instance, ordered the parties to start negotiations to agree upon an alternative solution,[362] authorised a Member State to take temporary measures but with the consent of the Commission[363] and suspended the application of a measure on condition that a party continues to provide security.[364]

Preliminary Issues, Absence of Jurisdiction, Absolute Bar to Proceedings[365]

A party may apply to the Court for a decision on a preliminary objection or other preliminary plea not going into the substance of the case; he must make the application by separate document, indicating among others the form of order sought. The opposite party may then lodge a document. Normally, the remainder of the procedure is oral. After hearing the Advocate-General, the Court decides.

Where it is clear that the Court has no jurisdiction or where the action is manifestly inadmissible, the Court may, after hearing the Advocate-General and without taking further steps, give decision on the action.

The Court may at any time of its own motion consider that there exists an absolute bar to proceedings, and declare that the action has become devoid of purpose and that there is no need to adjudicate on it.

Intervention

The Member States, also regional entities,[366] and the institutions may always intervene in cases before the Court; legal and natural persons have the right when

[356] art.84(1) and (2) Rules.

[357] art.84(1) and (2) Rules.

[358] For persons, see *Johnson & Firth Brown* (3/75 R) (quoted above, fn.354); for institutions, see *NTN Toyo* (113/77 R) (quoted above, fn.352) and for Member States, see *Commission v UK* Joined Cases 31/77 R and 53/77 R [1977] E.C.R. 921 at 925; [1977] 2 C.M.L.R. 359.

[359] *NTN TOYO* (113/77 R) (quoted above, fn.352).

[360] art.86(4) Rules.

[361] art.279 TFEU [243].

[362] *Commission v Ireland* (61/77 R) [1977] E.C.R. 937 at (34); [1978] 2 C.M.L.R. 466.

[363] *Commission v Ireland* (61/77 R), above at fn.363.

[364] *NTN Toyo Bearing Cy v Council* (113/77 R and 113/77 R-int) [1977] E.C.R. 1721, where the Court suspended the application of Regulation 1778/77 until the final judgment and *Commission v Atlantic Container Line and others* (C-149/95) [1995] E.C.R. I-2165, where the appeal of the Commission against the suspension was dismissed.

[365] art.91 and 92 Rules.

[366] For lack of interest, see *Provincia di AscoliPiceno* (C-461/07 P(1)) [2008] E.C.R. I-11*.

they establish an interest in the result of a case—this means that anybody, whether residing within the Union or not, such as third countries or their regional authorities, are admissible from the moment they show an interest in the solution and have introduced their request for intervention in accordance with the Rules of Procedure.[367] It should be noted that the submissions made in an application to intervene must be limited to, "supporting the form of order sought by one of the parties"; in other words, the intervening party is bound to support one of the parties to the dispute, there is no other alternative.[368] However, the intervener is not precluded from advancing arguments which are new or which differ from those of the party he supports, "less his intervention be limited to restating the arguments advanced in the application, but the intervener may not modify the frame of the dispute by presenting new grounds."[369]

The application for intervention must be made within six weeks of the publication of the Notice concerning the case in the *Official Journal*. The rules concerning applications apply and the intervener must be represented. The parties in the case get an opportunity to submit their oral or written observations concerning the application. The President shall decide by Order or refer the application to the Court. If the intervention is allowed, the intervener receives a (expurgated) copy of all the documents served on the parties. The intervener may submit a statement in intervention to which the parties may reply.

Judgment by Default[370] *and Applications to Set Them Aside (OP) (Opposition),*[371] *Third Party Proceedings (TP),*[372] *Revision,*[373] *Interpretation of a Judgment*[374] *and Rectification of Judgments.*[375]

For these specific procedures, the reader is referred to the footnotes below and the corresponding provisions of the Statute and the Rules of Procedure.[376]

Stay of Proceeding[377]

In cases where both the Court and the CFI are seized, the proceedings may be stayed by decision of the President, adopted after hearing the Advocate-General,

---

[367] See *Confédération Suisse v Commission* (T-319/05) [2006] E.C.R. II–2073, where the Landkreis Waldshut was admitted to intervene.
[368] art.40 Statute and art.93 Rules.
[369] *SELEX* (T-155/04) [2006] E.C.R. II–4707.
[370] See for instance *Commission v EPE* (C-524/03) not published, but on the Internet and *Branco* (T-85/94) [1995] E.C.R. II–47, failure to file a defence.
[371] art.41 Statute and art.94 Rules. See for instance *Dresden Bank v Commission* (Joined Cases T-44/02 OP, T-54/02 OP, T-56/02 OP, T-60/02 OP and T-61/02 OP) [2006] E.C.R. II–3567: failure by the Commission to file a defence and its opposition to the judgment by default: example of a request to set aside a judgment by default (art.94(4) Rules).
[372] art.42 Statute and art.97 Rules. See *Bolognese v Scharf and Commission* (292/84 TP) [1987] E.C.R. 3563; for a rectification see Order of March 12, 1996 in *Pafitis v TKE* (C-441/93) [1996] E.C.R. I–1347; [1996] 2 C.M.L.R. 551.
[373] art.44 Statute and art.98 Rules. No revision is possible after the lapse of 10 years from date of judgment. See also *Walter Gill v Commission* (C-185/90 P Rev) [1992] E.C.R. I–993.
[374] art.43 Statute and art.102 Rules.
[375] art.66 Rules; it concerns clerical mistakes, errors in calculation and obvious slips; applications must be made within two weeks of the delivery of the judgment.
[376] For instance: *http://europa.eu./index-en.htm*. There the reader should look at: Official Documents, euro-lex European Union Law and Official Journal [2003] O.J. C193/1.
[377] art.82a Rules.

in the circumstances specified in the Statute,[378] and in all other cases, save in the case of a reference for a preliminary ruling.

(5) Time Limit[379]

Any period prescribed by the Treaties or the Rules shall be reckoned as follows:

1. for periods expressed in days, weeks, months or years after the occurrence of an event, the day during which that event occurs shall not be counted;
2. for the same periods, the end of the period shall be the same day, week, month or year, or the same date, as the one on which the event occurred; if the same day does not occur in the corresponding month, the period shall end with the expiry of the last day of that last month;
3. periods include official holidays, Sundays and Saturdays and the judicial vacation;
4. if the period ends on a Saturday, Sunday or official holiday, it shall be extended to the first following working day.

II. The General Court (GC)

As provided for in the Single European Act,[380] the Council attached to the Court of Justice[381]:

"[A] court with jurisdiction to hear and determine at first instance, subject to a right of appeal to the Court of Justice on points of law only and in accordance with the conditions laid down by the Statute, certain classes of action or proceedings brought by natural or legal persons".[382]

The GC [at the time the Court of First Instance (CFI)] started functioning in November 1989.

Under the Nice Treaty, the GC [CFI] was no longer "attached" to the Court of Justice, but constituted an independent part of the Community judicature,[383] and judicial panels could be attached to it. The Treaty now provides as follows:

"The Court of Justice of the European Union shall include the Court of Justice, the General Court and specialised courts. It shall ensure that in the interpretation and application of the Treaties the law is observed".[384]

The provisions of the Statute concerning partial replacement of the Judges every three years,[385] their residence,[386] the permanence of the sessions and the judicial

---

[378] art.54,3 Statute.
[379] arts 80 to 82 Rules.
[380] art.11 SEA.
[381] Council Decision of October 24, 1988 [1988] O.J. L319/1, modified several times.
[382] art.256(1) TFEU [225(1)].
[383] art.19 EU [220].
[384] art.19(1) EU [220,1].
[385] art.,9,1 Statute.
[386] art.14 Statute.

vacations[387] and the required number of Judges in a formation for the latter to be able to take valid decisions,[388]apply to the GC and its members.

1. MEMBERS OF THE GENERAL COURT

There are currently 27 judges as the Treaty provides, "that the General Court shall include at least one judge per Member State",[389] chosen from persons whose independence is beyond doubt and who possess the ability required for appointment to high judicial office. They are appointed by common accord of the governments of the Member States for a term of six years. As indicated, the membership is partially renewed every three years, and retiring members are eligible for reappointment.[390] They elect their President for a period of three years.

There are presently no permanent Advocates-General attached to the GC, although according to the TFEU, "the Statute may provide for the General Court to be assisted by Advocates-General."[391] At the present time the members of the GC, with the exception of the President,[392] may be called upon to perform the function of Advocate-General[393] and make reasoned submissions in certain cases.[394] Their task is identical to that of the Advocates-General of the Court.[395] The decision to designate an Advocate-General is taken by the GC sitting in plenary session and at the request of the relevant chamber. The President designates the Judge called upon to perform the function of Advocate-General.[396] In practice this has been done only very occasionally.[397]

The GC sits in the following formations: the *full Court*, composed of all the Judges in the special cases provided for in the Treaty[398] or where the GC considers that the case before it is of exceptional importance[399]—in that case it shall be assisted by an Advocate-General designated by the President[400]; the *Grand Chamber*, composed of 13 Judges when a Member State or an institution of the Communities that is party to the proceeding so requests[401]; and, normally, in *chambers* of three or five Judges. A chamber may be assisted by an Advocate-General if it considers that the legal difficulty or the factual complexity of the case so requires.[402]

The GC establishes its Rules of Procedure[403] in agreement with the Court; those rules are practically identical to those of the Court—they require approval of the

[387] art.15 Statute.
[388] art.17,1,2,4 and 5 Statute.
[389] art.48 Statute and art.19(2)2 EU [224,3].
[390] art.254,2 TFEU [224,2].
[391] art.254,3 TFEU [224].
[392] This follows from art.19,2. Rules of Procedure ("GC Rules")
[393] art.49,1 Statute.
[394] art.252 TFEU [222,2]
[395] art.254 TFEU [224].
[396] art. 19,2 GC Rules.
[397] http://curia.europa.eu/en/instit/presentationfr/tpi.htm.
[398] art.16 Statute: art.228(2),2195(2) TFEU: dismissal of the Ombudsman, art.245,2 TFEU [.213,2]: compulsory retirement of a member of the Commission or art.247 TFEU [247(7)]: deprive a member of the Court of Auditors of his office. The same applies under the EAEC Treaty.
[399] art.16,5 Statute.
[400] art.17 GC Rules.
[401] art.16,3 Statute.
[402] art.18 GC Rules.
[403] Codified version [2003] O.J. C193/41, modified several times.

Council acting by a qualified majority.[404] Unless the Statute of the Court provides otherwise, the Treaty provisions relating to that Court apply to the GC.[405] Important also are the "Instructions to the Registrar" and "Practice Directions to Parties".[406]

2. JURISDICTION

The GC exercises at first instance the following jurisdiction[407]:

- review of the legality of:
  - legislative acts, i.e. acts adopted jointly by Parliament and Council;
  - acts of the Council, of the Commission and of the ECB;
  - acts of Parliament and of the European Council intended to produce legal effects vis-à-vis third parties; and
  - acts of bodies, offices or agencies of the Union intended to produce legal effects vis-à-vis third parties,

  at the request of a Member State,[408] Parliament, the Council or the Commission and at the request of natural or legal person.[409]
  However, actions brought by a Member State against acts or failures to act of Parliament, of the Council or of those institutions acting jointly, are reserved for the Court, except for:
  - decisions of the Council declaring a State aid compatible with the internal market[410];
  - acts of the Council adopted pursuant to a Council regulation concerning measures to protect trade as provided for under the common commercial policy[411]; and
  - acts of the Council by which the Council exercises implementing powers.[412]

  The same reservation to the Court applies to actions against an act or failure to act by the Commission in matters concerning enhanced co-operation.[413]
  Jurisdiction is also reserved to the Court when one of the above-mentioned actions (review of legality and failure to act) is brought by an institution of the Union against Parliament, the Council, or both acting jointly, the Commission or by an institution against the ECB[414];

- action for failure to act by the institutions or the ECB, the same conditions apply as for the first point[415];

---

[404] art.254,5 TFEU [224,5].
[405] art.254,6 TFEU [224,6].
[406] [2007] O.J. L232/1 and 7 respectively.
[407] art.256 TFEU [225]. See *Commission v the Translation Centre* (C-269/06) [2007] E.C.R. I-187 spelling out the GC's jurisdiction and sending a case to the GC.
[408] Generally speaking, where actions brought by a Member State are concerned, jurisdiction is reserved to the Court.
[409] art.263 TFEU [230] and Decision 2004/407 amending arts 51 and 54 of the Statute [2004] O.J. L132/5.
[410] art.108(2),3 TFEU [88(2)3].
[411] art.207 TFEU [133].
[412] art.291,2 TFEU.
[413] art.331 TFEU [arts27, 43–45 EU, and art.11 EC].
[414] art.51 Statute.
[415] art.265 TFEU [232].

- actions for compensation for damage[416];
- actions and proceedings provided for in the Euratom Treaty[417];
- following an arbitration clause[418];
- appellate jurisdiction for decisions given by specialised courts[419] on points of law only or, when provided for in the regulation establishing the specialised court, a right of appeal also on matters of fact. These decisions of the GC may exceptionally be subject to review by the Court where there is a serious risk of the unity or consistency of Union law being affected[420];
- to hear and determine questions referred for preliminary ruling[421] in specific areas laid down by the Statute[422]; where the GC considers that the case requires a decision of principle likely to affect the unity or consistency of Union law, it may refer the case to the Court for a ruling[423];
- proceedings relating to intellectual property rights.[424] It concerns proceedings brought against the Office for Harmonisation in the Internal Market (Trade Marks and Designs)[425] and against the Community Plant Variety Office[426] and concerning the application of the rules relating to an intellectual property regime. Actions must, first, be brought before a Board of Appeal.

An interesting point in this special procedure is that an intervener is not bound by the positions taken by the parties before the GC: he may, "apply for a form of order and put forward pleas in law independently of those applied for and put forward by the main parties".[427] The intervener may even, "seek an order annulling or altering the decision of the Board of Appeal on a point not raised in the application and put forward pleas in law not raised in the application".[428]

Another difference concerns the costs: in case of a decision against the Board of Appeal, the Office can only be ordered to bear its own costs, while other costs are considered recoverable.[429]

Where the GC considers that a case requires a decision of principle likely to affect the unity or consistency of Union law, it may refer the case to the Court for a ruling. However, as the Court put it:

"The [General Court] has exclusive jurisdiction, first to establish the facts except where the substantive inaccuracy of its findings is apparent from the documents submitted to it and, second, to assess those facts. When the [GC] has established or assessed the facts, the Court of Justice has jurisdiction to review the legal characterisation of those facts and the legal conclusions it has drawn from them".[430]

In other words, the Court has no jurisdiction to establish the facts.[431]

---

[416] art.268 TFEU [235].
[417] art.140a Euratom.
[418] art.272 TFEU [238].
[419] art.257 TFEU [225a].
[420] art.256(2)2 TFEU [225(2)2].
[421] art.256(3) TFEU [225(3)].
[422] art.256(3) TFEU [225(3)].
[423] art.256(3)2 TFEU [225(3)2].
[424] arts 130 to 136 GC Rules.
[425] See below, Ch.13: Decentralised Bodies of the Union.
[426] See below, Ch.13.
[427] art.134(2)2 GC Rules.
[428] art.134(3) GC Rules.
[429] art.136 GC Rules.
[430] *New Holland Ford v Commission* (C-8/95) [1998] E.C.R. I–3175(25).
[431] *New Holland Ford* (C-8/95), above, fn. 431.

3. PROCEDURE BEFORE THE GENERAL COURT

The procedure before the GC is similar to the procedure before the Court and is laid down in the Rules of Procedure of the GC (GC Rules)[432] with the exception of the provisions concerning the preliminary ruling.[433] Lawyers and agents should also be aware of the Instructions to the Registrar[434] and of the Practice Directions to Parties.[435] The latter are particularly important with regard to the transmission of procedural documents via telefax or electronic mail; this is allowed on condition that it concerns a scanned copy of the signed original and the latter is received by the Registry within 10 days following the telefax or electronic lodgement.

In 2000, the GC adopted various amendments to its Rules of Procedure with a view to expediting proceedings.[436] The amendments concern chiefly the introduction of an expedited (fast track) procedure, the possibility of the GC dispensing with a second exchange of pleadings (the emphasis being placed on the oral procedure), the shortening of the time limit for intervening and the use of modern means of communication (lodging of procedural documents in the form of a copy of the signed original sent by way of fax or attachment (scanned copy) of an e-mail[437] on condition that the signed original is received no later than 10 days thereafter) and the simplification of the rules concerning extensions of time on account of distance. The application for an expedited procedure must be made by a separate document lodged at the same time as the application or the defence. This procedure made it possible to give judgement within 11 weeks.[438]

Where a case is referred back by the Court, the GC shall be bound by the decision of the Court on points of law.[439]

III. Specialised Courts/Judicial Panels[440]—the Civil Service Tribunal (CST)

As was indicated at the beginning of this chapter, the Nice Treaty provides for the creation by the Council of judicial panels (now "specialised courts") attached to the (now) GC, to hear and determine at first instance classes of action or proceeding brought in specific cases.[441]

The members of the specialised courts are chosen from persons whose independence is beyond doubt and who possess the ability required for appointment to judicial office. They are appointed by the Council, acting unanimously.

---

[432] For a consolidated 2003 version see "curia" on the Internet [1994] O.J. L136/1, last amended [2008] O.J. L179/12 to take into account the increased role of Parliament.

[433] art.256(3) TFEU [225(3)].

[434] [2007] O.J. L232/1.

[435] [2007] O.J. L232/7.

[436] [2000] O.J. L322. The amendments entered into force on February 1, 2001.

[437] *http://www.cfi.registry@curia.europa.eu.*

[438] *Tideland Signal v Commission* (T-211/02) [2002] E.C.R. II–3785.

[439] art.61,2 Statute. The first judgment was given on January 30, 1990, only two weeks after the formal hearing: *York von Wartenburg v Parliament* (T-42/89) [1990] E.C.R. II–31.

[440] art 19 EU and art.257 TFEU [225] refer to "specialised courts", while the Statute, Title IVa and art.62c mention "Judicial Panels". The former seems to be the correct denomination.

[441] art.257 TFEU [225(A)].

The specialised courts establish their Rules of Procedure in agreement with the Court. These Rules require the approval of the Council, acting by a qualified majority.

Decisions given by specialised courts may be subject to a right of appeal on points of law only, or, when provided in the decision establishing the specialised court, a right of appeal also on matters of fact, before the GC.[442] Unless the decision establishing the specialised courts provides otherwise, the provisions of the Treaty relating to the Court and the GC and the provisions of the Statute of the Court apply to the specialised courts.[443] The first specialised court (Panel), the European Union Civil Service Tribunal (CST), was set up in 2004[444]; it started functioning on December 2, 2005 with a declaration from the President of the Court that the, "Civil Service Tribunal is duly constituted".[445] The provisions relating to the jurisdiction, composition, organisation and procedure of specialised courts are set out in an Annex to the Statute of the Court.

The CST exercises at first instance jurisdiction in disputes between the Union's institutions and their servants, including disputes between all bodies[446] or agencies[447] and their servants in respect of which jurisdiction is conferred on the Court.

The CST consists of seven Judges appointed by the Council[448] for six years on the recommendation of a Committee composed of former Judges of the Court, of the GC and lawyers of recognised competence.[449] Retiring Judges may be reappointed; any vacancies shall be filled by the appointment of a new Judge for a period of six years. This is different from the rules governing the Court and the GC, where a new Judge filling a vacancy, "shall be appointed for the remainder of his predecessor's time".[450]

The President is elected by the Judges for a term of three years.

The Rules of Procedure of the CST were issued in 2007.[451] See also the Instructions to the Registrar of the CST.[452]

The CST sits in chambers of three Judges; in certain cases it may sit in full court, a chamber of five Judges or of a single Judge.[453]

The CST is supported by the departments of the Court and of the GC. The CST appoints its registrar to whom the corresponding provisions of the Court apply. The language arrangements of the GC apply to the CST.

---

[442] art.257 TFEU [225(A)].
[443] art.257,4,5 and 6 TFEU [225(A), 4, 5 and 6].
[444] Decision establishing the European Union Civil Servants Tribunal (CST Decision) [2004] O.J. L333/7.
[445] [2005] O.J. L325/2.
[446] See below, Ch.12: Other Bodies of the Union.
[447] See below, Ch.13: Decentralised Bodies of the Union.
[448] The first Judges were appointed in July 2005 [2005] O.J. L197/28.
[449] See Decision concerning the conditions and arrangements governing the submission and processing of applications for appointment as a Judge of the EST [2005] O.J. L50/7 and Decision concerning the operating rules of such Committee [2005] O.J. L21/13.
[450] art.7 Statute.
[451] [2007] O.J. L225/1.
[452] [2007] O.J. L249/3.
[453] For the constitution and composition of the chambers, election of their Presidents and assignment of the Judges to chambers, criteria for assignment of cases to chambers, and designation of the Judge replacing the President of the tribunal as Judge hearing applications for interim measures, see [2005] O.J. L322/16.

Procedure is governed by Title III of the Statute of the Court, with the exception, among others, of the provisions concerning the preliminary question. The written procedure should normally be limited to the presentation of the application and of the statement of defence. New is that at all stages of the procedure the CST may, "examine the possibility of an amicable settlement of the dispute and may try to facilitate such settlement".[454] The unsuccessful party shall be ordered to pay the costs should the CST so decide.[455]

An *appeal* may be brought before the GC,[456] within two months of notification of the decision in question, against final decisions of the CST and decisions of the Tribunal disposing of the substantive issues in part only or disposing of procedural issue concerning a plea of lack of jurisdiction or admissibility. Such an appeal may be brought by any party who has been unsuccessful, in whole or in part of its submissions.[457]

Interveners, other than Member States and institutions, may bring such an appeal only where the decision of the CST directly affects them. A decision of the CST refusing an application to intervene may be appealed to the GC within two weeks of the notification of such decision.[458]

Appeal may also be launched against a decision of the CST concerning the suspension of the act, interim measures or enforcement. The President of the GC may, by way of summary procedure, adjudicate upon these appeals.[459] Normally, such appeals have no suspensory effect.[460] Appeals to the GC must be launched within two months of the notification of the decision. Decisions of the GC reviewing decisions of the CST may, in exceptional circumstances, be reviewed by the Court.[461] According to the Treaty this may be the case when, "there is a serious risk of the unity or consistency of Union law being affected."[462] New articles were inserted in the Statute of the Court that lay down general rules relating to the urgent nature of that procedure, to the written and oral phases of the procedure and to the possibility of its having suspensory effect.[463]

If the Court finds that the decision of the GC affects the unity or consistency of Union law, it shall refer the case back to the GC, which shall be bound by the points of law decided by the Court. The latter may decide which of the effects of the decision of the GC are to be considered as definitive in respect of the parties. For more details see the decisions referred to in footnotes above.

Further Reading

David W.K. Anderson QC and Marie Demetriou, *References to the European Court*, 2nd edn (Sweet & Maxwell, 2002).

---

[454] CST Decision art.7,4.
[455] CST Decision art.7,5.
[456] See, for instance, *Parliament v Estrup* (T-223/06) [2007] E.C.R. II-1581.
[457] CST Decision art.9.
[458] CST Decision art.9.
[459] For full details see CST Decision Art.10.
[460] See CST Decision art.12.
[461] art.256(2)2 TFEU [225(2)2]: "under the conditions and within the limits laid down by the Statute": see Decision of October 3, 2005 amending the protocol on the Statute of the Court, in order to lay down the conditions and limits for the review by the Court of decisions given by the GC [2005] O.J. L266/60.
[462] art.256(2)2 TFEU [225(2)2].
[463] art.62a and 62b Statute.

Monica Claes, *The national court's mandate in the European Union* (Hart Publishing, 2006).
Koen Lenaerts, Dirk Arts, Ignace Macelis, *Procedural law of the European Union*, 2nd edn (Sweet & Maxwell, 2006).
Anthony Arnull, *The European Union and its Court of Justice*, 2nd edn (Oxford University Press, 2006).
John Usher, "Direct and individual concern", (2003) E.L.Rev. 575.
Maria A. Teodossiou, "An analysis of the recent response of the Community to non-compliance with Court of Justice judgments: Article 228(2)", (2002) E.L.Rev. 25.
Theodor Shilling, "The Court of Justice's revolution: its effects and the conditions for its consummation", (2002) E.L.Rev. 445.
Francis J. Jacobs, "Human rights in the European Union: the role of the Court of Justice",(2001) E.L.Rev. 331.
Francis J. Jacobs, "Recent and ongoing measures to improve the efficiency of the European Court of Justice", (2004) E.L.Rev. 823.

Chapter Ten

The Court of Auditors

The Court of Auditors[1] was set up by the Treaty amending Certain Financial Provisions of the European Treaties and the Merger Treaty.[2] Previously a simple organ of the Union, it was "upgraded" to an "institution" by the EU Treaty.[3] Its task is to "carry out the Union's audit."[4] Since it is an institution, albeit without the power to issue binding acts which could be challenged in the courts, it has, nonetheless, the power to go to court, like the ECB and the Committee of the Regions, for the purpose of protecting its prerogatives.[5]

1. MEMBERS OF THE COURT OF AUDITORS

The Court of Auditors consists of one national for each Member State,[6] presently 27, appointed for a term of six years; this term is renewable. The Council, after consultation of Parliament, adopts the list of Members drawn up in accordance with the proposals made by each Member State.[7] They are chosen from among persons who belong or have belonged, in their respective countries, to external audit bodies or who are especially qualified for this office. They elect their President from among their number, for a term of three years; he may be re-elected.[8]

Their independence, like that of the members of the Commission and the Judges, must be beyond doubt. Similarly, they must be completely independent in the performance of their duties, not take any instructions, engage in no other occupation, give a solemn undertaking on beginning their duties and behave with integrity and discretion during and also after their term of office.[9]

Members may be compulsorily retired by a ruling of the Court if the latter finds, at the request of the Court of Auditors, that they no longer fulfil the requisite conditions or meet the obligations arising from their office.[10]

---

[1] art.285 TFEU [246].
[2] This Treaty was signed at Brussels on July 22, 1975, but entered into force only on June 1, 1977 ([1977] O.J. L359/10), see art.15.
[3] art.286(7) TFEU [247(7)].
[4] art 285,1 TFEU [246].
[5] arts 263,3 and 265,1 TFEU [230,3 and 232,1].
[6] art.285,2 TFEU [246(1)].
[7] art.286 (2) TFEU [247(2)].
[8] art 286(2)2 TFEU [247(2)].
[9] art.286(4) TFEU [247(4)].
[10] art.286(6) TFEU [247(6)].

2. TASKS OF THE COURT OF AUDITORS[11]

The Court of Auditors examines the accounts of all revenue and expenditure of the Union and of all bodies, offices and agencies set up by the Union,[12] in so far as their relevant constituent instrument does not preclude such examination.[13]
It must present Parliament and the Council with a:

"[S]tatement of assurance as to the reliability of the accounts and the legality and regularity of the underlying transactions which shall be published in the *Official Journal*. This statement may be supplemented by specific assessments for each major area of Union activity".[14]

It shall examine the legality and regularity of all income and expenditure and whether the financial management was sound. In doing so it must report in particular on any cases of irregularity.[15]
The auditors have the right to examine all records and visit all the premises of the other institutions and of any body, office or agency which manages revenue or expenditure on behalf of the Union; with regard to the Member States, the audit must be carried out in liaison with the national audit bodies. The other institutions, any body, office or agency managing revenue or expenditure on behalf of the Union, any natural or legal person in receipt of payments from the budget and the Member States must forward to the Court of Auditors any document and information necessary to carry out its task. In respect to the EIB managing Union expenditure and revenue, the Court of Auditors' right of access to information shall be governed by an agreement between the Court, the Bank and the Commission.[16]
The Court of Auditors draws up an annual report which is published, with the observations of the various institutions, in the *Official Journal*. Although this is not provided for in the Treaty, the Court of Auditors also publishes its own replies to those observations, which leaves the institutions at a disadvantage, since they have no possibility of making their views on those answers known. The Court of Auditors may also submit special reports on specific questions and deliver opinions at the request of another institution. It adopts its reports by a majority of its component members; it may establish internal chambers.
In a declaration adopted by the Conference which adopted the Nice Treaty, the Court of Auditors and the national audit institutions were invited to improve the framework and conditions for co-operation between them, while maintaining the autonomy of each. To that end, the President of the Court of Auditors may set up a contact committee with the chairmen of the national audit institutions.[17]
The Court of Auditors only published its Rules of Procedure in 2002 and, new rules were published in 2005.[18]

---

[11] art.287 TFEU [248].
[12] See, for instance, Reports on the financial statements and management of 10 bodies set up by the Union [2003] O.J. C319/1. While in this book I refer, in Ch.13, to Decentralised Bodies, the Court of Auditors refers to "Union satellite bodies"; it does not, however, refer to Europol.
[13] art.287 TFEU [248(1)].
[14] art.287(1)2 TFEU [248(1)2].
[15] art.287(2) TFEU [248(2)].
[16] art.287(3)3 TFEU [248(3)3].
[17] art.287(2) TFEU [248(4)2]. For a Special Report see, for instance; [1994] O.J. C13/1 concerning business and innovation centres.
[18] [2001] O.J. C 80/80.

Its role can best be summarised, in the words of the Treaty, as, "assisting the European Parliament and the Council in exercising their powers of control over the implementation of the budget".[19]

The Court of Auditors is situated in Luxembourg. It has a staff of some 300 persons of which 25 are temporary, and another 255 in joint services with the Economic and Social Committee.[20]

---

[19] [2002] O.J. L 210/1.
[20] art.287(4)4 TFEU [248(4)4].

Chapter Eleven

The European Central Bank

1. The European System of Central Banks and the European Central Bank

The European System of Central Banks (ESCB) (composed of the European Central Bank and the 27 national central banks) and the European Central Bank (ECB) were established by the EC Treaty.[1] They exercise their powers and carry out their tasks to implement the Economic and Monetary Policy of the Union that shall be examined hereafter within that framework (see below, Ch.28). The institutional aspects shall be briefly described here.

2. Institutional Provisions concerning the ESCB and the ECB

The ESCB was established, together with the ECB, at the start of the third stage of achieving the Monetary and Economic Union; its primary objective is, "to maintain price stability".[2] It must support the general economic policies in the Union with a view to contributing to the achievement of the objectives of the Union.[3] It must act in accordance with the principles of an open market economy with free competition, favouring an efficient allocation of resources, and in compliance with the principles of the Union's economic policy.[4]

The basic tasks of ESCB are:

- to define and implement the monetary policy of the Union;
- to conduct foreign exchange operations;
- to hold and manage the foreign exchange reserves of the Member States;
- to promote the smooth operation of payment systems.

The ESCB must also contribute to the smooth conduct of policies pursued by the competent authorities relating to the prudential supervision of credit institutions and the stability of the financial system.[5]

It is governed by the decision-making bodies of the ECB.[6] Its statute is laid down in a Protocol attached to the TFEU.

---

[1] art.13(1) EU, last indent and art.282 TFEU [8] and Statute of the ESCB and of the ECB annexed to the TFEU.

[2] art.127(1) TFEU [105].

[3] art.3 EU.

[4] art.119 TFEU [4].

[5] art.127(5) TFEU [127(5)]. One wonders why this "supervision" did not prevent the financial crisis of 2008; but, maybe it did reduce it.

[6] art.129(3) TFEU [107(3)].

The ECB was also established at the start of the third stage when it replaced the European Monetary Institute (EMI). (For details on the "stages" see below, Ch.28 on the Economic and Monetary Union.) As was decided by the European Council on October 29, 1993, the seat of the EMI, and consequently of the ECB, is in Frankfurt.

The ECB, which has legal personality,[7] is headed by a Governing Council and an Executive Board.[8]

The *Governing Council* consists of the members of the Executive Board and the governors of the national central banks. One of the most impressive tasks of the Governing Council is to set, for the Euro area,[9] the interest rates at which commercial banks can obtain money from their central bank. This rate practically determines the interest to be paid by anyone borrowing or investing money.

The *Executive Board* comprises the President, the Vice-President and four other members of the Governing Council. They are appointed for eight years from among, "persons of recognised standings and professional experience in monetary and banking matters", by common accord of the governments of the Member States. The appointments are decided by the latter at the level of the European Council, on a recommendation of the Council. The latter must first consult Parliament and the Governing Council. The meetings of the Governing Council may be attended, without voting right, by the President of the Council and a member of the Commission.[10] The President of the ECB shall be invited to attend meetings of the Council when the latter discusses matters relating to the objectives and tasks of the European System of Central Banks (ESCB). Clearly everything has been provided to establish close links both with the highest national monetary institutions and with the highest political decision-making authorities within the Union.

3. TASKS OF THE ECB

The ECB has the exclusive right to to authorise the issue of Euro banknotes within the Union. The ECB and the national central banks may issue such notes. The latter are the only to have the status of legal tender within the Union.

The ECB must ensure that the tasks conferred upon the ESCB under the TFEU[11] are implemented either by its own activities pursuant to the Statute or through the national central banks.[12] Its prime objective is to maintain price stability by defining the monetary policy of the Euro area so as to preserve the value of the Euro.

---

[7] art.129(2) TFEU [107(2)].

[8] art.283(1) TFEU [112(1)]. Rules of Procedure [1998] O.J. L338/28.

[9] The Euro area presently includes 16 Member States.

[10] art.294(1) TFEU [113(1)].

[11] art.105(2) Statute ESCB and ECB: the basic tasks to be carried out through the ESCB are: "to define and implement the monetary policy of the Union"; to conduct foreign exchange operations; to hold and manage the official foreign reserves of the Member States (the latter may hold and manage foreign exchange working balances (art.127(3) TFEU [105(3)])); to "promote the smooth operation of payment systems"; and art.127(5) TFEU [105(5)]: "The ESCB shall contribute to the smooth conduct of policies pursued by the competent authorities relating to the prudential *supervision* of credit institutions and the stability of the financial system."

[12] arts 12.1,3 and 14 Statute ESCB and ECB.

The ECB addresses an annual report to Parliament, the European Council, the Council and the Commission. This report is presented by the President to the Council and to Parliament, which may hold a general debate on that basis. The ECB may make regulations[13] to the extend necessary to implement a limited number of tasks[14] and to take decisions necessary for carrying out the tasks entrusted to the ESCB. Those acts are open to review and interpretation by the Court. It may also make recommendations and deliver opinions.

The ECB may institute proceedings under the conditions laid down in the TFEU.[15] Within the limits and under the conditions adopted by the Council,[16] the ECB may impose fines or periodic penalty payments on undertakings for failure to comply with obligations under its regulations and decisions.[17]

The ECB adopts its own rules of procedure[18] and it hires its own staff.[19] The capital of the ECB is established at 5 billion[20]; the national central banks are the sole subscribers to and holders of that capital, which is subscribed according to a key established by the bank on the basis of statistical data provided by the Commission.[21]

A Monetary Committee with advisory status was set up to promote co-ordination of the policies of Member States to the full extent needed for the functioning of the internal market.[22] At the start of the third stage the Monetary Committee was replaced by an *Economic and Financial Committee* with similar tasks.[23] Its tasks are:

- to deliver opinions at the request of the Council or of the Commission, or on its own initiative for submission to those two institutions;
- to keep under review the monetary and financial situation of the Member States and to report regularly thereon, especially on financial relations with third countries and international institutions;
- to contribute to the work of the Council regarding movement of capital, the guidelines for the economic policies of the Member States, guidelines on monetary policy instruments and procedures of the Eurosystem,[24] access to financial institutions, commitments of public authorities, government deficits and the transitional provisions of the economic and Monetary Union (EMU)[25];

---

[13] art.132(1) TFEU first indent [110(1)]. See for instance Regulation 1921/2000 [2000] O.J. L229/34.

[14] art.34(1) Statute ESCB and ECB.

[15] art.35 Statute ESCB and ECB.

[16] art.34.3 Statute ESCB and ECB: in accordance with the procedure laid down in art.41 of the Statute.

[17] art.34(3) Statute ESCB and ECB. See Regulation 2532/98 [1998] O.J. L318/4 and ECB Regulation 2157/99 (also referred to as ECB/1999/4) [1999] O.J. L264/21, amended [2001] O.J. L137/24.

[18] [1999] O.J. L125/34; see Rules of Procedure of the Executive Board [1999] O.J. L314/34 and of the General Council of the ECB [1999] O.J. L75/36.

[19] See conditions of employment [1999] O.J. L125/32 and Decision concerning public access to documentation and the archives [1999] O.J. L110/30.

[20] art.29 Statute ESCB and ECB; see Decision of the ECB on the percentage shares for the key [1999] O.J. L125/33. See Decision of March 30, 2009 to increase the capital [2010] O.J. L10/19.

[21] See Regulation 1009/2000 concerning capital increases of the ECB [2000] O.J. L115/1 and Regulation 1010/2000 concerning further calls of foreign reserve assets by the ECB [2000] O.J. L115/2.

[22] art.134(1) TFEU [114(1)].

[23] art.134(2) TFEU [114(2)].

[24] See, for instance, [2002] O.J. L185/1.

[25] See the EIB's Annual Report.

- to examine, at least once a year, the situation regarding the movement of capital and the freedom of payments; the Committee must report on the outcome of this examination to the Commission and to the Council.

The composition of the Committee is decided by the Council on a proposal from the Commission and after consulting the ECB and the Committee.

Chapter Twelve

Other Bodies of the Union[1]

1. THE ECONOMIC AND SOCIAL COMMITTEE (ESC)

The Economic and Social Committee[2] plays a consultative role, mainly within the decision-making process of the Union: it must be consulted by the Council or by the Commission where the Treaty so provides.[3] It may also be consulted by Parliament. If the Council or the Commission were to fail to consult it when it is provided for by the Treaties, the final act could be annulled by the courts for infringement of an essential procedural requirement.[4] The fact that consultation has taken place must be mentioned in the relevant Union act.[5]

The ESC may also be consulted, by either the Council or the Commission, in all cases where they consider it appropriate. At the 1972 Paris Summit meeting, the Heads of State or Government decided to invite, "the [Union] institutions to recognise the right of the Economic and Social Committee in future to advise on its own initiative on all questions affecting the [Union]".[6]

The number of ESC members may not exceed 350. The Committee's composition is decided unanimously by the Council on a proposal from the Commission.[7] The members are appointed for five years by the Council acting by a qualified majority, in accordance with the proposals made by each Member State and after consulting the Commission; the Council may also obtain the opinion of the various social and economic sectors and of civil society to which the Union's activities are of concern. The term of office is renewable.[8]

The members are representatives of organisations of employers, of the employed, and of other parties representative of civil society, notably the socio-economique, civic, professional and cultural areas.[9]

---

[1] These are bodies provided for in the Treaties as opposed to agencies set up by the institutions (see next chapter).

[2] art.301 TFEU [257].

[3] See, for instance, art.46 TFEU [40]: Parliament and the Council must issue a Directive or Regulation to ensure freedom of movement for workers and art.50,1 TFEU [44,1]: Directives to attain freedom of establishment.

[4] See above Ch.9: Court of Justice of the European Union (3.(3)(a)(iii) Grounds for annulment).

[5] See above Ch.3: Legal Acts of the Union (1. Regulations, Directives and Decisions must be Reasoned).

[6] Examples of own-initiative opinions in [1988] O.J. C95/12 and C134/10.

[7] art.301,1 TFEU [257].

[8] art.302 TFEU [259]: each Member State makes proposals to the Council. The number of members for each country are laid down in Protocol No.36 on Transitional Provisions: the four large countries each have 24 members; Spain and Poland 21; Romania 15; Netherlands, Bulgaria, the Czech Republic, Belgium, Greece, Hungary, Portugal, Austria and Sweden 12; Slovakia, Denmark, Lithuania, Ireland and Finland 9; Latvia, Slovenia and Estonia 7; Luxembourg and Cyprus 6; and Malta 5. See *CIDA v Council* (297/86) [1988] E.C.R. 3549; [1989] 3 C.M.L.R. 851, asking for annulment of the Council's Decision nominating the members.

[9] art.300(2) TFEU [263].

A summary of the ESC's proceedings is published in the *Official Journal*. The ESC adopts its own Rules of Procedure[10]; it has its seat in Brussels. A Decision provides for public access to ESC documents.[11]

2. THE COMMITTEE OF THE REGIONS[12]

This Committee was established by the EU Treaty and is composed of representatives of regional and local bodies who either hold a regional or local authority electoral mandate or are politically accountable to an elected assembly. The Committee has an advisory status.[13]

Like the Economic and Social Committee, the number of its members may not exceed 350, but it also has an equal number of alternate members, appointed for five years by the Council in accordance with the proposals made by each Member States. The number of seats for each country are the same as for the SEC (see above). The term of office is renewable.

The members may not be bound by any mandatory instructions, they must be completely independent in the performance of their duties, in the general interest of the Union. They may not at the same time be Members of Parliament.[14]

There are several cases where consultation of the Committee of the Regions by the Council or the Commission is provided for by the Treaties.[15] It is also consulted in all cases, in particular those that concern cross-border co-operation, in which one of those two institutions considers it appropriate.[16] It may be consulted by Parliament.[17]

The Committee of the Regions must be informed of requests for opinions from the Economic and Social Committee pursuant to the Treaty; when the Committee of the Regions is of the opinion that specific regional interests are involved it may issue an opinion on the matter.[18]

Its opinions and a record of the proceedings are forwarded to the Council and the Commission. A summary of the proceedings is published in the *Official Journal*. See Rules of Procedure, which have to be approved by the Council, and a Decision concerning public access to documents of the Committee of the Regions.[19]

---

[10] [2002] O.J. L 268/1, amended [2004] O.J. L310/77, codified version: [2007] O.J. L93/1.

[11] [1997] O.J. L339/18.

[12] art.300 and following TFEU [263 and following].

[13] arts 300 and 305 TFEU [263].

[14] arts 300 and 305 TFEU [263].

[15] See for instance, art.175 TFEU [159,2]: actions necessary outside the Regional Fund and art.192 TFEU [175(2)]: measure in the field of environment protection.

[16] Implementation of the transport policy: art.91(1) TFEU [71(1)]; the social provisions: art.153(3) TFEU [137(3)]; education, vocational training and youth: art.166(4) TFEU [150(4)]; public health: art.168(4) TFEU [152(4)]; Trans-European Networks: art.172,1 TFEU [156,1]; actions outside the structural funds: art.175,3 TFEU [159,3]; definition of tasks, priority objectives and organisation of the structural funds: art.177,1 TFEU [161,1]; implementing decisions concerning the ERDF: art.178,1 TFEU [162,1] and the environment: art.192(1) TFEU [175(1)].

[17] art.307,4 TFEU [265,4].

[18] art.307,3 TFEU [265,3].

[19] [2007] O.J. L23/10. For the Rules of Procedure see [2010] O.J. L6/14.

3. The Scientific and Technical Committee of Euratom

This Committee, set up by the Euratom Treaty,[20] is attached to the Commission; it consists of 33 members appointed for five years, in their personal capacity, by the Council after consultation with the Commission. It has an advisory status. The Commission must consult this Committee, among others, before setting up the Joint Nuclear Research Centre and before working out the basic standards for the protection of the health of workers and the general public against dangers arising from ionising radiations.[21]

4. Euratom's Supply Agency

Provided for in the Euratom Treaty, the Supply Agency has a right of option on ores, source materials and special fissile materials produced in the territories of the Member States and an exclusive right to conclude contracts relating to the supply of those materials coming from inside or outside the Union.[22] In 2006, the Commission exempted from this obligation the transfer of small quantities of ores, source materials and special fissile materials.[23]

However, the Agency is entitled to refuse to purchase material on grounds of origin of the fuel[24] and is not obliged to guarantee disposal of uranium output accumulated by Union producers.[25]

New Statutes of the Supply Agency, replacing the 1958 ones, were adopted in 2008.[26] The Agency has legal personality and is situated in Brussels.

See also Ch.35 on Energy.

5. The Group of the European Investment Bank (EIB)

The "Group" is made up of the EIB and the European Investment Fund (see below). Detailed provisions concerning the functioning of the EIB are laid down in the Statute of the Bank, which is the object of Protocol No.5 attached to the TFEU.

(1) Task

The task of the European Investment Bank (EIB)[27] is to contribute to the balanced and steady development of the common market in the interest of the Union. It does so by having recourse to the capital market and utilising its own

[20] art.134 Euratom.
[21] See, e.g. Directive 84/467/Euratom [1984] O.J. L265.
[22] art.52(2)(b) Euratom. See also arts 53 to 56.
[23] Regulation (Euratom) 66/2006 [2006] O.J. L11/6.
[24] *Lippe-EMS* (Joined Cases T-149/94 and T-181/94) [1997] E.C.R. II–161; [1997] 3 C.M.L.R. 136 and *Kernkraftwerke Lippe-Ems v Commission* (C-161/97 P) [1999] E.C.R. I–2057.
[25] *ENU* (C-357/95 P) [1997] E.C.R. I–1329; [1997] 3 C.M.L.R. 95.
[26] [2008] O.J. L41/15.
[27] art.258 TFEU [226] and Protocol EIB annexed to the Treaty.

resources on a non-profit-making basis.[28] Notwithstanding this obligation, it follows from the decision of the Board of Governors that there was, for 1996 alone for instance, a so-called operating surplus of one billion ECU.[29]

The subscribed capital of the Bank is, according to Protocol No.5, attached to the TFEU €164, 808, 169, 000[30]; it is subscribed by the Member States, which are liable only up to the amount of their share of the capital subscribed and not paid up.[31] They decided on a capital increase to €232 billion in April 2009. The subscribed capital is paid up by the Member States[32] to the extent of slightly more than 9 per cent.[33] However, instead of "paying up", the Board of Governors decided, in June 1997, that the remaining contributions would be financed using part of the proceeds of the operating surplus for 1996. The legality of this measure can be questioned.[34]

The same "solution" was applied when the capital was increased from €62 to €100 billion in 1992.

In 1998, the Board of Governors took a number of decisions laying down a Strategic Framework for the Bank.[35] This followed the invitation of the Amsterdam European Council to the Bank to step up its activities, with special reference to a number of sectors, in order to promote the creation of employment. Accordingly, the Bank introduced its Amsterdam Special Action Programme (ASAP), involving the creation of a special small and medium-size enterprise (SME) window, the development and reinforcement of EIB activities in the sectors of education, health, urban environment and environmental protection and, a new impetus to the financing of trans-European networks and other large infrastructure networks.

It is against this background that the Board of Directors has discussed the strategic framework, the main pillars of which are the following:

- concentration on "peripheral economic areas";
- continuing support to key EU policy areas such as development of Trans-European Networks (TENs), international competitiveness, SMEs, energy and the environment.

This must be viewed in the light of recent developments, i.e. recognition that the disciplines of the EMU must be accompanied by a concerted policy to reduce unemployment and the Council's decision on enlargement.[36]

The EIB grants loans and gives guarantees that facilitate the financing of:

- projects for developing less-developed region[37];
- projects for modernising and converting undertakings, under certain conditions; and

---

[28] art.309 TFEU [267].
[29] [1997] O.J. C211/6.
[30] See now: Annual Report 2008, Activity and Corporate Responsibility Report, 2.
[31] art.4 Statute EIB.
[32] art.4 Protocol No.5.
[33] art.5(1) Statute EIB.
[34] [1997] O.J. C211/16.
[35] [1998] O.J. C269/9. See also [1999] O.J. C247/6.
[36] For further details on this important document, see [1998] O.J. C269/89.
[37] The Commission finances similar projects with the European Regional Development Fund (ERDF) and other Funds, hence the need for close co-operation between the Commission and the EIB. The Director-General of "Regional Policy" is always an alternate member of the Bank's board.

- projects of common interest to several Member States which cannot be financed by individual States.

In carrying out its task the Bank must facilitate the financing of investment programmes in conjunction with assistance from the structural fund[38] and other Union financial instruments.[39]

The EIB grants loans to its members (the Member States), and private and public undertakings for investment projects to be carried out, unless authorised otherwise by the Board of Governors, in the European territories of the Member States.[40] As far as possible, loans are granted only on condition that other sources of finance are also used.[41] When granting a loan to a body other than a Member State, it is conditional on an adequate guarantee, for example, from the Member State where the project is to be carried out.[42] The necessary funds are borrowed on the international capital markets or those of the Member States.[43]

(2) Procedure for Granting Loans or Guarantees

Requests for loans are sent either directly or through the Commission or the Member State concerned. Decisions regarding applications for loans or guarantee[44] are taken by the Board of Directors on a proposal from the Management Committee. Before deciding on the financing of a project the Bank must secure the opinion of the interested Member State and of the Commission. If the latter delivers an unfavourable opinion, the Board of Directors may not grant the loan (or guarantee) unless its decision is unanimous, the Director nominated by the Commission abstaining.

Originally the Bank was mainly intended to provide financial resources for the economic development of Southern Italy, the Mezzogiorno. This is still the case today, but other regions have been added, first by the successive enlargements of the Union and secondly by the economic crisis of the 1970s. About 80 per cent of the Bank's loans go to the development regions of the Union[45] as a means of increasing economic and social cohesion.

In 2001, the governors approved the setting up of the Bank's Structured Finance Facility (SFF) that allows the EIB to finance projects with a higher degree of risk, especially in the areas of research and innovation projects and the Trans-European Networks (TENs) to be financed from the Bank's surplus. It focuses on

---

[38] The ERDF, the Social Fund and the Guidance Section of the European Agricultural Guarantee and Guidance Fund (EAGGF).

[39] e.g. the Cohesion Fund.

[40] art.18(1) Statute EIB.

[41] art.18(2) Statute EIB.

[42] art.18(3) Statute EIB. See Council Decision of December 22, 1999 granting a Union guarantee to the EIB against losses under loans for projects outside the Union: Central and Eastern European countries, Mediterranean countries, Latin American and Asian countries and South Africa [2000] O.J. L9/24.

[43] In 2008, the EIB approved loans for a total of €59,292 billion, of which 53,191 were within the member states and EFTA countries. It borrowed a total of €59,497 billion. Outstanding loans amount to €350,289 billion and borrowings to €266,989.

[44] The Bank may also guarantee loans contracted by public or private undertakings or other bodies; art.18(4) Statute EIB. Guaranties provided in 2008: €262 million.

[45] In 2005, out of €42.3 billion lent in the Union, €28 billion went in loans for regional development.

quality projects and objectives shared by the EIB and the Commission and endorsed by the European Council. Lending for the Innovation 2010 in support of the EU's Lisbon strategy increased to almost €11 billion.

In 1994 the Council established a Guarantee Fund for external operations; its main function is to shield the general budget of the Union against shocks due to defaults on loans or guaranteed loans.[46]

(3) Internal Structure of the EIB

The Bank is directed and managed by a Board of Governors, a Board of Directors and a Management Committee.

The Board of Governors consists of Ministers (of Finance) of the Member States. It lays down general directives for the credit policy of the Bank; it also decides on possible increases in the subscribed capital[47] on grants of special interest-bearing loans to the Bank to finance specific projects by Member States and on the granting of loans for investment projects to be carried out entirely or partially outside the European territory of the Member States. Decisions are taken by a majority of the members: either simple majority representing at least 50 per cent of the subscribed capital; or qualified majority (e.g. for financing outside the Union) requiring a favourable vote of members representing 68 per cent of the subscribed capital.[48]

The Board of Directors consists of 28 directors and 18 alternate[49] nominated by each Member State and the Commission and appointed by the Board of Governors for five years. Each Director has one vote. Decisions are normally taken by at least one-third of the members representing at least 50 per cent of the subscribed capital. A qualified majority shall require eighteen votes in favour and 68 per cent of the subscribed capital. The quorum is laid down in the Rules of Procedure of the Bank.[50]

The Management Committee consists of a President and eight Vice-Presidents appointed for six years by the Board of Governors. The Management Committee is responsible for the current business of the Bank under the authority of the President and the supervision of the Board of Directors. The officials and other employees of the Bank are not servants of the Union, but under contract to the Bank.

A Committee of six members verifies annually that the operations of the Bank have been conducted properly and its books kept in a proper manner. The Bank has legal personality and its members are the Member States. The EIB is submitted to the jurisdiction of the Court.[51] The Management Committee has adopted Rules on public access to document[52] and on historical archives.[53]

---

[46] [1994] O.J. 1.293/3, amended [2007] O.J. 10223/3.
[47] €100 billion.
[48] art.8 Protocol No.5.
[49] art.9(2) Protocol No.5. The Council acting unanimously, at the request of the EIB and after consultation of Parliament and the Commission, may amend those figures.
[50] art.10 Protocol No.5.
[51] See, e.g. *Commission* v EIB, [1988] E.C.R. 1281 and *SGEEM v EIB* (C-370/89) [1992] E.C.R. I–6211.
[52] [2002] O.J. C292/10.
[53] [2005] O.J. C289/12.

6. The European Investment Fund

The Fund is part of the EIB group. The Statutes of the Fund were adopted by the Board of Governors of the EIB on May 25, 1994[54] and amended in 2009.[55] The Fund has legal personality and financial autonomy. The task of the Fund is to support the development of Trans-European Networks (TENs) in the areas of transport, telecommunications and energy infrastructure[56] (2004–2008: €47 billion), and the development of small and medium-size enterprises (SMEs): close to one million SMEs received support from the EIB Group in 2008.[57] The Fund accomplishes its task by providing its guarantee for loans and by acquiring, holding or managing equity participations in any enterprise. In addition the Fund may carry out any other ancillary operations connected with its tasks.

The capital of the Fund—two billion—is provided by the EIB (since the year 2000, more than 50 per cent), the Union[58] and commercial banks. The EIB operates as manager of the Fund. By the end of 2008 the Fund had a portfolio of €15.867 billion, of which €4.754 billion was in venture capital operations and €13.017 billion in guarantees.[59]

7. The European Body for the Enhancement of Judicial Co-operation (Eurojust)

Eurojust was set up in 2002 by the Council[60] as "a body of the Union"; it has legal personality provided for in the TFEU.[61] It is composed of one national member seconded by each Member State in accordance with its legal system, being a prosecutor, judge or police officer of equivalent competence. Its objectives are, in the context of investigations and prosecutions concerning two or more Member States, of criminal behaviour in relation to serious crime, particularly when it is organised: to stimulate and improve co-ordination between the competent authorities, to improve co-operation and to support otherwise the competent authorities.

Eurojust may also assist investigations and prosecutions concerning only one Member State and a non-Member State where a co-operation agreement has been concluded with said State.

The general competence of Eurojust covers:

- the types of crime and offences in respect of which Europol[62] is at all times competent to act;

---

[54] [1994] O.J. L173/1.

[55] [2009] O.J. C216/6.

[56] See below, Ch.31: Enterprise and Industry Policy/Information Society.

[57] EIB Annual Report 18. New credit lines with financial intermediaries increased to €8.1 billion.

[58] See Council Decision 94/375 of June 6, 1994 on Union membership of the Fund [1994] O.J. L173/12 and Decision 2007/247 on the Union participation in the capital increase of the EIF: [2007] O.J. L107/5.

[59] EIB 2008 Report, 2.

[60] Council Decision of February 28, 2002 setting up Eurojust with a view of reinforcing the fight against serious crime [2002] O.J. L63/1.

[61] art.85 TFEU [EU 31].

[62] See Ch.13: Decentralised Bodies of the Union.

- the following types of crime:
  - — computer crime;
  - — fraud and corruption and any criminal offence affecting the EC's financial interests;
  - — the laundering of the proceeds of crime;
  - — participation in a criminal organisation[63];

- other offences committed together with the types of crime and offences referred to above.

Eurojust can act either through its national members or as a College; the latter consists of all the national members, each one having one vote. The Commission is also associated with the work.

An Independent Joint Supervisory body was set up to monitor collectively the activities concerning the processing of personal data.

Eurojust is assisted by a secretariat headed by an administrative director; it has its own staff of about 80 persons, subject to the rules and regulations applicable to the officials of the Union. It is situated at The Hague (the Netherlands).

8. THE EUROPEAN POLICE OFFICE (EUROPOL)

It was established in 1995 by a Council act consisting of a Convention concluded by the Member States and based on Title VI of the EU Treaty, the "Europol Convention".[64] The office is therefore financed by the Member States. (In 2008 it was decided to transform the Office into a European Agency on January 1, 2010.) It became operational on July 1, 1999, after ratification by the, at that time, 25 Member States. Some of its tasks are now provided for in the TFEU, such as:

- the collection, storage, processing, analysis and exchange of relevant information, in particular that forwarded by the authorities of the Member States or third countries or bodies;
- the co-ordination, organisation and implementation of investigative and operational action carried out jointly with the Member States' competent authorities or in the context of joint investigative teams, where appropriate in liaison with Eurojust.[65]

In 1998, a Council act laid down rules governing Europol's external relations with third States and non-European related bodies[66] and an act laying down rules governing the receipt of information from third parties.[67] Another Council act was adopted in 1999 concerning rules governing the transmission of personal data by Europol to third States and third bodies.[68] Its mandate was extended

---

[63] See Council Joint Action 98/733/JHA of December 21, 1998 on making it a criminal offence to participate in a criminal organisation in the EU [1998] O.J. L351/1.

[64] [1995] O.J. C316/2; see Rules implementing art.6a of the Convention—automatic processing of personal data: [2007] O.J. L155/78.

[65] art.88 TFEU [EU 30].

[66] [1999] O.J. C26/19. See Decision of March 27, 2000 authorising the Director of Europol to enter into negotiations on agreements with third States and non-European bodies [2000] O.J. C106/1, amended O.J. L56/14.

[67] [1999] O.J. C26/17.

[68] [1999] O.J. C88/1.

in 1999 to deal with forgery of money and means of payment.[69] A protocol on the interpretation, by way of preliminary ruling[70] by the Court of Justice of the Europol Convention was accepted by all the Member States, except the UK.

Any operational action of Europol must be carried out in liaison and in agreement with the authorities of the Member State or States whose territory is concerned. The application of coercive measures is the exclusive responsibility of the competent national authorities.

Europol is headed by a Supervisory Board and a Director and has its own staff.[71] It is situated at The Hague (the Netherlands), like Eurojust.

9. THE EUROPEAN INSTITUTE OF INNOVATION AND TECHNOLOGY (EIT)

Set up by regulation[72] in 2008 with reference to the task entrusted by the TFEU to the Union and the Member States to, "ensure that the conditions necessary for the competitiveness of the Union's industry exist."[73]

The EIT's objective is to contribute to sustainable European economic growth and competitiveness by reinforcing the innovation capacity of the Member States and the Union. It must do this by promoting and integrating higher education, research and innovation of the highest standards. The EIT operates through autonomous partnerships of higher education institutes, research organisations, companies and other stakeholders; they are designated as Knowledge and Innovation Communities (KICs).

There is a Governing Body, an Executive Committee and a Director. For more details see the above-mentioned regulation.

10. THE ECONOMIC AND FINANCIAL COMMITTEE

This Committee is provided for in the TFEU in order to promote co-ordination of the policies of the Member States to the full extent needed for the functioning of the internal market.[74] It has the following tasks:

- to deliver opinions at the request of the Council or Commission or on its own initiative;
- to keep under review the economic and financial situation of the Member States and of the Union and to report regularly thereon to the Council and the Commission, in particular on financial relations with third countries and international institutions;
- without prejudice to the work of COREPER, to contribute to the preparation of the work of the Council concerning:

---

[69] [1999] O.J. C149/16.
[70] See under Ch. 9: The Court of Justice of the European Union.
[71] See [2001] O.J. C65/1 laying down the rules on Europol personnel files and Staff Regulations applicable to Europol employees: [1999] O.J. C26/23 as amended by act of March 15, 2001 [2001] O.J. C112/1. See act of the Management Board: [2006] O.J. C68/1.
[72] Regulation 294/08: [2008] O.J. L97/1.
[73] art.173(1) TFEU [157(1)].
[74] art.134 TFEU [114].

— safeguarding measures with regard to movement of capital from and to third countries[75];
— administrative measures with regard to capital movement[76];
— guidelines of the economic policies of the Member States[77];
— Union's financial assistance to Member States in difficulties[78];
— definitions concerning overdraft facilities and privileged access to financial institutions[79];
— measures concerning excessive government deficit[80];
— conferral to ECB of tasks relating to prudential supervision of credit institutions[81];
— harmonising denominations of Euro coins[82];
— adoption of provisions concerning ESCB and ECB[83];
— establishing common positions within international financial institutions[84];
— assistance to Member States in difficulties as regards balance of payments[85];
— abolishment by Member States of protective measures[86];
— abrogation of derogation from Euro[87];
— agreement on exchange rate systems for the Euro with third States.[88]

Detailed provisions concerning the composition of the Committee are laid down by the Council after consulting the ECB and the Commission.

The Committee must keep under review the monetary and financial situation and the general payment system of the Member States with a derogation.

11. THE EUROPEAN DATA PROTECTION SUPERVISOR

The TFEU provides for rules relating to the protection of individuals with regard to the processing of personal data by the Union institutions and bodies, offices and agencies, and by the Member States when carrying out activities which fall within the scope of Union law, and the rules relating to the free movement of such data.[89] In 2001, Parliament and Council adopted a regulation[90] setting up an independent supervisory authority referred to as the Data Protection Supervisor.

---

[75] art.66 TFEU [59].
[76] art.75 TFEU [60].
[77] art.121 TFEU [99].
[78] art.143 (1)2 TFEU [119(1)2].
[79] arts 123–124 and 125 TFEU [101,102, 103].
[80] art.126 TFEU [104].
[81] art.127(6) TFEU [105(6)].
[82] art.128(2) TFEU [106(2)].
[83] art.129(4) TFEU [107(4)].
[84] art.138 TFEU [111(4)].
[85] art.143 TFEU [119].
[86] art.144 TFEU [120].
[87] art.140 TFEU [121,122,123],
[88] art.219 TFEU [111].
[89] art.16 TFEU [286(2)].
[90] Regulation 45/2001: [2001] O.J. L8/1.

His task is to monitor the application of the regulation to all processing operations carried by Union institutions or bodies.[91]

The Supervisor is located in Brussels.

Further Reading

Michael Keating, *Regions and regionalism in Europe* (Edward Elgar Publishing, 2004).

---

[91] See the Annual Reports published by the Publication Office of the Communities.

Chapter Thirteen

Decentralised Bodies of the Union

GENERAL REMARKS

It is interesting to note what the Commission wrote at the beginning of 2008: "There are two types of agency—regulatory and executive—each with different characteristics and raising different issues." "Regulatory" or "traditional" agencies have a variety of specific roles set out in their own legal basis, case by case. They are independent bodies often with their own legal personality. Most are funded by the EU budget as well as, in some cases, by the direct receipt of fees or payments. The agencies were, at the beginning, set up in successive waves in order to meet specific needs on a case by case basis. They are typified by their diversity. They are now established in accordance with a Council Regulation adopted in 2002, but published in 2003.[1] They operate under full responsibility of the Commission. The latter believes that these agencies can bring real added value to the Union's governance structure. Their work is particularly relevant in fields of shared competences where the implementation of new policies, at Union level, needs to be accompanied by close co-operation between the Member States and the EU. At present, however, this potential, "is held back by the lack of common vision about the role and function of regulatory agencies."[2]

In its General Report,[3] on the other hand, the Commission makes a distinction between Decentralised Union Agencies, Union Agencies and Executive Agencies; this grouping will be followed in this chapter.

The above-mentioned regulation lays down the statute for Executive Agencies to be entrusted with certain tasks in the management of Union programmes.[4] These Agencies are a form of "outsourcing" of Union activities.

It is important to note that the Court decided that the acts of the Agencies, not being provided for in the Treaty provisions on annulment of Union acts,[5] cannot be the subject of the Court's review of legality.[6]

---

[1] Regulation 58/03 [2003] O.J. L11/1.
[2] IP/08/412 of 12.03.08.
[3] General Report 2008, 259.
[4] Regulation 58/03: (quoted above, fn.1). See also *http://www.europa.eu/agencies/index_en.htm*, where a distinction is made between "[Union] agencies", "Common Foreign and Security Policy Agencies", "Police and Judicial Cooperation in Criminal Matters agencies" and the, above-mentioned, "Executive agencies". It mentions also Euratom agencies and bodies. This differentiation is not adopted in this book.
[5] art.263 TFEU [230].
[6] *Spain v Eurojust* (C-160/03) [2005] E.C.R. I-2077.

I. Decentralised Union Agencies[7]

1. The European Centre for the Development of Vocational Training (Cedefop)

The Centre was set up in 1975.[8] It is a scientific and technical body entrusted with promoting, at Union level, the exchange of information and experience, the distribution of documentation and the launching of research and experimental projects to facilitate the attainment of vocational training objectives set by the Treaty.[9]

The Centre is endowed with legal personality to ensure its independence. The Management Board consists of representatives of the Member States, workers' organisations, employers' organisations and the Commission. The Centre has its own budget.[10] Its seat is at Thessalonica with a staff of some 35 permanent positions and 53 temporary ones.

2. The European Foundation for the Improvement of Living and Working Conditions (Eurofound)

It was set up in 1975 with seat in Dublin.[11] The Foundation deals specifically with the following issues: men at work; organisation at work and particularly job design; problems peculiar to certain categories of workers; long-term aspects of the improvement of the environment and special distribution of human activities and their distribution in time.

It provides authoritative guidance and advice to social policy makers, assesses and analyses living and working conditions, reports on developments and trends, especially those driving change, and contributes to improving the quality of life.

The structure is similar to that of Cedefop and it has a staff of about 91 officials.[12]

3. The European Environment Agency (EEA)

The objective of the Agency and of the Information and Observation network, set up in 1990[13] and operational since 1994, is to provide the Union and the Member States with objective and reliable information at the European level in order to allow them to take the necessary measures to protect the environment, to evaluate their implementation and to ensure that correct information reaches the public on the state of the environment. A number of non-member countries participate in the work of the Agency.[14]

---

[7] The Agencies are mentioned in the chronological order of their establishment.

[8] Regulation 337/75 [1975] O.J. L39/1; modified many times; see *http://www.cedefop.europa.eu*

[9] art.156,1 TFEU third indent [140,1, third indent].

[10] See, for instance, statement of revenue and expenditure for 1994 ([1994] O.J. L35/1), which constitutes an annex to the Union budget.

[11] Regulation 1365/75 [1975] O.J. L139/1, amended several times; *http://www.eurofound.europa*.

[12] See Statement of revenue and expenditure, quoted above. See also *Ryan-Sheridan, Staff Cases* (T-589/93) [1996] E.C.R. II–77.

[13] Regulation 1210/90 [1990] O.J. L120/1, amended many times; *http://www.eea.europa.eu*. Codified version: Regulation 401/09: [2009] O.J. L126/13.

[14] See, for instance, the agreement with the Swiss Confederation: [2006] O.J. L90/36.

Its main tasks are:

- establish an Information and Observation Network;
- provide the information necessary to formulate and implement efficient environmental policies;
- register, check and evaluate environmental data;
- ensure the comparability of the data at European level;
- integrate the European information into international programmes;
- disseminate the information[15];
- precipitate the development of methods for calculating the damage caused to the environment, etc.

The agency has a Management Board, an Executive Director and a Scientific Committee. It is situated at Copenhagen, with a staff of around 115.

4. THE EUROPEAN TRAINING FOUNDATION (ETF)

The purpose of this foundation[16] is to contribute, in the context of EU external relations policy, to improving human capital development, in the following countries:

- countries eligible for support from the Instrument for Pre-accession Assistance (IPA)[17] and subsequent legal acts;
- countries eligible for support from the European Neighbourhood and Partnership Instrument[18];
- certain countries designated by decision of the Governing Board (these countries are designated as "Partner Countries").

The Foundation may provide assistance in: facilitating adaptation to industrial changes, in particular through vocational training and retraining; improving initial and continuing vocational training in order to facilitate vocational integration and reintegration into the labour market; facilitating access to vocational training; stimulating co-operation between educational establishments and firms; developing exchange of information; increasing the adaptability of workers and designing, introducing and implementing reforms in education and training systems.

The Foundation shall have the following functions:

- provide information, policy analyses and advice on human capital development;
- promote knowledge and analysis of skills;
- support relevant stakeholders in building capacity in human capital development;
- facilitate the exchange of information and experience among donors;
- support the delivery of Government assistance;
- disseminate information and encourage networking and the exchange of experience and good practice;
- contribute to the analysis of the overall effectiveness of training assistance; and
- undertake such other tasks as may be agreed between the Governing Board and the Commission.

---

[15] The EEA publishes four distinct reports, with Environmental Signals Reports being the Agency's main brand.
[16] Regulation 1360/90 [1990] O.J. L131/1, amended several times and recast by Regulation 1339/2008 [2008] O.J. L354/82.
[17] [2006] O.J. L210/82.
[18] [2006] O.J. L310/1.

It is managed by a Governing Board, a Consultative Committee and a Director. With regard to non-contractual liability it is submitted to the jurisdiction of the Court. See the Decision of the Governing Board on public access to ETF documents.[19] The Foundation has legal personality and its seat is at Turin with a staff of about 100 officials.

5. The European Monitoring Centre for Drugs and Drug Addiction (EMCDDA)[20]

The Centre's objective is to provide the Union and its Member States with objective, reliable and comparable information at European level concerning drugs and drug addiction and their consequences. Its tasks are:

- collection and analysis of existing data;
- improvement of data-comparison methods;
- dissemination of data[21]; and
- co-operation with European and international bodies and organisations and with non-Union countries. In 2008 an Agreement was concluded with Turkey for the participation of the latter in the work of the Centre.[22]

The centre works closely together with, among others, the World Health Organisation, Interpol and Europol. It has legal personality, has a Management Board, a Director and a Scientific Committee and is submitted to the jurisdiction of the Court. It became operational in December 1993, i.e. after the Member States agreed on its location: Lisbon.

6. The European Medicines Agency (EMEA)

Parliament and Council replaced the 1993 Regulation laying down Union procedures for the authorisation and supervision of medicinal products for human and veterinary use and establishing a European Agency for the Evaluation of Medicinal Product,[23] with a Regulation of March 2004,[24] that also modified the name of the Agency. Since 1995, the Union has had a twin-track approach to drug licensing. Companies are able to submit a conventional medicine either to the EMEA (the "centralised" route) or to one of the 27 national regulatory agencies (the "decentralised" route). The rule applicable in both cases is that no medicine may be put on the market without prior authorisation. The centralised route is compulsory in a certain number of cases.[25]

The new regulation corrects some of the operating procedures and makes adaptations to take account of the probable development of science and technology and the enlargement of the European Union. The general principles previously

---

[19] [1997] O.J. C369/10.
[20] Regulation 302/93 [1993] O.J. L36/1, modified [1994] O.J. L341/7. Recast [2006] O.J. L3767/3.
[21] *http://www.emcdda.europa.eu.*
[22] Decision 2008/375 [2008] O.J. L128/48.
[23] Regulation 2309/93 [1993] O.J. L214/1. See, for instance, Summary of Union decisions on marketing authorisations in respect of medicinal products, taken pursuant to art.12 or 34 of Regulation 2309/93.
[24] Regulation 726/2004 [2004] O.J. L136/1, amended [2009] O.J. L87/174.
[25] See Annex to Regulation 726/2004, quoted above fn.24.

established that govern the centralised procedure are maintained. Directives were adopted on the Union code relating to medicinal products for human use[26] and on the Union code relating to veterinary medicinal products.[27]

At the Agency's request, the Commission may impose financial penalties to holders of marketing authorisations if they fail to observe certain obligations laid down in connection with the authorisation.[28]

A centralised authorisation procedure was also set up for the placing on the market of high-technology medicinal products, particularly those resulting from biotechnical processes.[29] The same need for centralisation exists for Orphan Medicinal Products; this task is assumed by the Committee on Orphan Medicinal Products.[30] As regards Herbal Medicinal Products the responsibility is vested in the Committee on Herbal Medicinal Products.[31]

The Agency has legal personality and is situated in London with a staff of about 315 persons. Its organs are: a Director, a Council of 34 members (representatives from the Member States, from Parliament and from the Commission) and a Committee of Pharmaceutical Specialities. See also Committee for Proprietary Medicinal Products.[32]

The fees payable to the Agency are set by the Council[33]; special fees and assistance are provided for micro, small and medium-sized enterprises.[34]

7. The Office for Harmonisation in the Internal Market (Trade Marks, Designs and Models) (OHIM)

The Office was established on December 22, 1993.[35] It grants a uniform Union-wide protection which allows its owner to prohibit the use of the mark, design or model for similar goods and services.[36]

---

[26] Directive 2001/83 [2004] O.J. L311/67, amended [2009] O.J. L242/3. See *Merck Sharp and Others v Commission* (T-273/03) [2006] E.C.R. II-141: the Commission is not competent to modify the summary of the characteristics of a product and *Synthon* (C-452/06) [2008] E.C.R. I-7681: art. 28 precludes a Member State to which an application is made for mutual recognition of a marketing authorisation granted by another Member State under the abridged procedure, from refusing that application on the ground of lack of similarity with the reference product. See also *Commission v Spain* (C-88/07) marketing of herbal medicines [2009] E.C.R. 05.03.09.: herbal medicinal products produced and sold in another Member State and Decision 3052/95 on mutual recognition, repealed by Regulation 764/08 [2008] O.J. L218/21.

[27] Directive 2001/82: [2004] O.J. L311/1.

[28] art.83 TFEU [31].

[29] See Directive 87/22 [1987] O.J. L 15/38, repealed [1993]O.J. L 214/40.

[30] [2000] O.J. L18/1.

[31] Directive 2001/83 [2001] L311/67.

[32] Directive 93/39, 93/40 and 93/41 [1993] O.J. L214/22, 31 and 40.

[33] Regulation 1905/2005 [2005] O.J. L304/1. Regulation 297/95 lays down the categories and levels of the fees; amended [2009] O.J. L79/34.

[34] Regulation 2049/2005 [2005] O.J. L329/4.

[35] Regulation 40/94 on the Union Trade Mark [1994] O.J. L11/1; modified [2009] O.J. L109/3. See *Nokia* (C-316/05) [2006] E.C.R. I-12083, where the Court stated that a Union trade mark court which has issued an order prohibiting the defendant from proceeding with infringement of a Union trade mark, is required to take from among the measures provided for under national law, such as are aimed at ensuring that the prohibition is complied with, even if those measures could not be taken under national law in the case of a corresponding national infringement.

[36] *Yamanouchi* (C-110/95) [1997] E.C.R. I–3251; [1997] 3 C.M.L.R. 749.

Before granting the protection, the Office examines whether any absolute motive prevents the grant from being made; the latter can also be withdrawn, for instance, if the owner does not make use of it for five years, or if someone else proves prior claim. The protection is granted for a renewable period of 10 years, to anyone having his domicile in one of the Member States, or in one of the countries party to the Paris Convention on the Protection of Industrial Property Rights. There is a right of appeal at every stage of the procedure, before the Boards of Appeal.[37] It is possible to appeal the decisions of the Boards of Appeal in the Union courts. This gave rise to abundant case law, both in the GC[38] and on appeal in the Court.[39] In some cases national courts are competent to hear the appeals.

The Union protection does not replace the existing national protections, and the economic operators have the choice between the two. The systems have been conceived to ensure that formalities and management are kept simple:

- a single application in one of the languages of the Union;
- a single file at a single administrative centre;
- defence against opposition, cancellation and invalidity actions, in the language of application, or in German, English, French, Spanish or Italian;
- links with national registrations and the Madrid Protocol System for the International Registration of Trade Marks OAMI-ONLINE, the website of the Office offers the possibility of online filing of applications for both trade marks and designs. See also CTM-ONLINE database of trade marks and decisions of the Office. The office publishes its own monthly *Official Journal*, a weekly Union Trade Marks Bulletin and a fortnightly Union Design Bulletin.

The Office charges fees.[40] It is situated in Alicante (Spain), and started operating on April 1, 1996.

8. Translation Centre for Bodies of the European Union (CDT)

The Centre was set up in 1994[41] and its task was enlarged in 1995[42]; it is a legal person in its own right and self-financed. It was set up to meet the translation needs of other decentralised Union Agencies; it also serves the institutions and their bodies that have their own translation services, on the basis of voluntary co-operation agreements.

It participates in the Inter-institutional Committee for Translation that works to promote co-operation between the services on the basis of the principle of

---

[37] See Order of the President of the GC [CFI] of June 19, 1997, *Chaves Fonsica Ferrao v OHIM* (T-159/97 R) [1997] E.C.R. II–1049, concerning the independence of the members of the boards of appeal. See also Rules of Procedure of the Board of Appeal: Regulation 216/96 [1996] O.J. L28/11, amended [2004] O.J. L360/8.

[38] See, for instance, *Vedial v OHMI—France distribution Hubert* (T-110/01) [2002] E.C.R. II–5275.

[39] See, for instance, *DKV v OHMI* (C-104/00) [2002] E.C.R. I–7561.

[40] Regulation 2869/95 on the fees payable to the OHIM [1995] O.J. L303/1, amended [2009] O.J. L109/3.

[41] Regulation 2965/94 [1994] O.J. L 314/1, amended [2003] O.J. L245/13.

[42] Regulation 2610/95 [1995] O.J. L268/1.

subsidiarity and to achieve economies of scale in the translation field. It has a Management Board and a Director; it has over 160 staff members and is established at Luxembourg.

9. THE UNION PLANT VARIETY OFFICE (CPVO)

This Office was set up by the Regulation on Plant Variety Rights,[43] and the rules for the proceedings before the Office were published in 1995.[44] Parliament and the Council created a supplementary protection certificate for plant protection products[45] indicating that the competitiveness of the plant protection sector, by the very nature of the industry, requires a level of protection for innovation,[46] which is equivalent to that granted by the Council when creating a supplementary protection certificate for medicinal products.[47] The Office grants rights ensuring industrial property protection for eligible new varieties; these rights are valid for a duration of either 25 or 30 years. A regulation provides for the grant of compulsory licences and the rules on public inspection and access to documents held by the Union Plant Variety Office.[48] A regulation establishes the level of the annual fee and the fees relating to technical examination payable to the Office and the manner of payment.[49]

In 2005, the European Union acceded to the International Convention for the Protection of New Varieties of Plants.[50]

Every two months the Office publishes an official gazette including extracts from the registers. It also publishes an Annual Report listing valid Union plant variety rights, the names of their holders and the dates on which they were granted and will expire. The Office is situated at Angers (France) with a staff of around 37 persons.

10. THE EUROPEAN AGENCY FOR SAFETY AND HEALTH AT WORK (OSHA)

The Agency[51] started work in 1996 and is based in Bilbao, Spain. The objective of the Agency is to encourage improvements in the working environment. It shall

---

[43] Regulation 40/94 on the Union Trade Mark [1994] O.J. L11/1, implemented by Regulation 2868/95 [1995] O.J. L303/1, amended [2005] O.J. L172/4 and [2009] O.J. L109/3. Article 30 of Regulation 2100/94 on Union Plant Variety Rights [1994] O.J. L227/1, amended [2004] O.J. L162/38.

[44] Regulation 1239/95 [1995] O.J. L121/37, amended [1996] O.J. L62/3; see for recourse *Federacion v OCVV* (T-95/06) [2008] E.C.R. II-38. See also Directive 91/414 concerning the placing of plant protection products on the market [1991] O.J. L230/1; *Suède v Commission* (T-229/04) [2007] E.C.R. II-2437. where the GC annulled a Commission directive for non-application of procedural provisions; Directive 97/57 establishing Annex VI of Directive 91/44 [1997] O.J. L265/87 and Regulation 1238/95 establishing implementing rules for the application of Regulation 2100/94 as regards the fees payable to the Union Plant Variety Office [2005] O.J. L189/26.

[45] Regulation 1610/96 [1996] O.J. L198/30.

[46] See *Schulin* (C-305/00) [2003] E.C.R. I-3525, on the interpretation of Regulation 2100/94 and Regulation 1768/95. See also *Federacion de cooperativas de la Communidad Valenciana* (T-95/06) [2008] E.C.R. II-31.

[47] See above under European Medicines Agency.

[48] Regulation 2100/94 [1994] O.J. L227/1 and Regulation 1239/95 establishing implementing rules, modified [2005] O.J. L170/7.

[49] Regulation 1238/95, amended [2008] O.J. L161/7.

[50] [2005] O.J. L192/63.

[51] Regulation 2062/94 [1994] O.J. L216/1; modified [2005] O.J. L184/5.

provide the Union bodies, the Member States and those involved in health and safety at work with the technical, scientific and economic information of use in the field of occupational safety and health. The Agency is managed by a Director and has a Board, which is made up of representatives of the governments, employers and workers from the Member States and representatives of the Commission. Its staff counts about 38 people.

11. The European Agency for Reconstruction (EAR)

Set up in 1999, under a United Nations Security Council Resolution,[52] the Agency received delegation from the Commission to implement the Union assistance to Albania, Bosnia and Herzegovina, Croatia, the Federal Republic of Yugoslavia and the former Yugoslav Republic of Macedonia. In order to provide a single legal framework, a new regulation[53] set up the Union Assistance, Reconstruction, Development and Stabilisation (CARDS) programme. It confirmed the ongoing activities of the European Agency for Reconstruction and extended its mandate.[54] The objectives of the EU-funded programmes managed by the Agency are to support good governance, institution building and the rule of law; to continue supporting the development of a market economy and to invest further in critical physical infrastructure and environmental action; and to support social development and the strengthening of civil society.

The Agency is situated in Thessalonica with a staff of about 114.

12. The European Food Safety Authority (EFSA)

Set up by Parliament and the Council[55] in 2002, with legal personality and privileges. The Regulation lays down the general principles and requirements of food law and procedures in matters of food safety. It also provides the basis for the assurance of a high level of protection of human health and consumer interest in relation to food. Its purpose is to approximate the concepts, principles and procedures of the Member States so as to form a common basis for measures governing food and feed taken in the Member States and at Union level.

The Authority must provide scientific advice and scientific and technical support for the Union legislation and policies in all fields which have a direct or indirect impact on food and feed safety; it must also provide scientific opinions on other matters relating to animal health and welfare and plant health, and on products other than food and feed relating to genetically modified organisms.[56] The Authority comprises a Management Board, an Executive Director and Staff (about 140), an Advisory Forum and a Scientific Committee and Scientific Panels. It is situated at Parma.

---

[52] Resolution 1244 of June 10, 1999.
[53] Regulation 3906/89 [1989] O.J. L375/11, amended [1999] L299/1 and [2000] O.J L306/1.
[54] Regulation 2415/01 [2001] O.J. L 327/3.
[55] Regulation 178/02 [2002] O.J. L31/1. See also Regulation 2230/04 laying down detailed rules for the implementation of Regulation 178/02.
[56] See Directive 2001/18 [2001] O.J. L106/1 and *Commune de Sausheim* (552/07) [2009] E.C.R. 17.02.09 on the scope of the Directive.

13. The European Maritime Safety Agency (EMSA)

This Agency was set up by Parliament and the Council[57] in 2002, following several catastrophic maritime accidents. Its task is to assist the Commission in the preparatory works for updating and developing and, afterwards, implementing Union legislation in the field of maritime safety and prevention of pollution by ships. It shall work with the Member States and facilitate co-operation between the Member States and the Commission. For more details see the chapter on Transport.[58] The Agency is located in Lisbon.

14. The European Aviation Safety Agency (EASA)

Established in 2002 by regulation,[59] the Agency started operating in September 2003; its mission is to assist the Union in:

- establishing and maintaining a high, uniform level of civil aviation safety and environmental protection;
- facilitating the free movement of goods, persons and services;
- promoting cost efficiency in the regulatory and certification processes;
- assisting Member States in fulfilling International Civil Aviation Organisation (ICAO) obligations on a common basis; and
- promoting worldwide Union views regarding civil aviation safety standards.

The first steps concern the certification of aeronautical products and the organisations and personnel involved in the design, production and maintenance. The EASA must also assist the Commission in the monitoring of the application of the regulation; a regulation lays down the working methods of the Agency for conducting standardisation inspection.[60]

The Agency was entrusted with the management of the Safety Assessment of Foreign Aircrafts (SAFA).[61] For more information see below, Ch.27: Transport.

The revenues of the Agency consist of contributions from any European third country which has entered into an agreement under the regulation, the fees[62] paid by applicants for certificates and approvals issued, maintained or amended by the Agency, and charges for publications, handling of appeals, training and other service provided by the Agency.

The Regulation permits the association of as many European partners as possible. Parliament and Council issued a regulation establishing common rules in

---

[57] [2002] O.J. L208/1. The institutions' powers to issue this regulation are based upon art.100(2) TFEU [80(2)].
[58] See below, Ch.27: Transport.
[59] Regulation 1592/02 [2002] J.O. L240/1, amended [2003] O.J. L240/1; repealed by Regulation 216/2008 [2008] O.J. L79/1 on common rules in the field of civil aviation and establishing a European Aviation Safety Agency, the latter was amended [2009] O.J. L199/6.
[60] Regulation 736/06 [2006] O.J. L129/10.
[61] See Directive 2004/36 on the safety of third-country aircraft using Union airports [2004] O.J. L143/76, as amended, complemented by Regulation 768/06 [2006] O.J. L134/16, as regards the collection and exchange of information on the safety of aircrafts using Union airports and the management of the information system entrusted to the Agency.
[62] Regulation 593/07 on the fees and charges levied by the EASA [2007] O.J. L140/3, amended [2008] O.J. L350/46.

the field of civil aviation security.[63] It provides, amongst other things, for the Commission to adopt measures for the implementation of common basic standards for aviation security throughout the European Union.[64] It is interesting to note that the annex to said regulation, "should be secret and should not be published", "in order to prevent unlawful acts",[65] consequently the annex is non-binding in so far as it seeks to impose obligations on individuals.[66]

The Agency has a Management Board and a Director and is situated in Cologne with a staff of about 100 persons.

15. THE EUROPEAN NETWORK AND INFORMATION SECURITY AGENCY (ENISA)

The Agency was established in 2004 for five years,[67] which were extended by three years in 2008.[68] Its mission is to assist the Commission and the Member States in developing a culture of network and information security for the benefit of the citizens, consumers, enterprises and public sector organisations. ENISA will ultimately serve as a centre of expertise for Member States, the business community and the EU institutions to seek advise on matters related with network and information security. Its task is focused on:

- collecting and analysing data on security incidents and emerging risks;
- co-operating with different players notably through the establishment of public/private partnership with industry operating at EU and global level;
- raising awareness and promoting risk assessment methods and best practices for interoperable risk management solutions; and
- tracking the development of standards for products and services on Network and Information Society.[69]

The Agency is located at Heraklion in Crete, Greece.

16. THE EUROPEAN CENTRE FOR DISEASE PREVENTION AND CONTROL (ECDC)

The communicable disease outbreaks pose a significant threat to the health and wellbeing of the European citizens. Since 1999, the Commission has managed a

---

[63] Regulation 2320/02 establishing common rules in the field of civil aviation security: [2002] O.J. L355/1, repealed and replaced by Regulation 300/08 [2008] O.J. L97/72; annex supplemented by Regulation 272/09 [2009] O.J. L91/7. See now Regulation 483/09 [2009] O.J. L 145/23 laying down measures for the implementation of the common basic standards on aviation security.

[64] Regulation 622/03 [2003] O.J. L89/9, amended [2004] O.J L10/14, [2005] O.J. L143/9 [2007] O.J. L200/3 [2008] O.J. L9/12 and L111/5.

[65] See Regulation 781/05 amending Regulation 622/2003 [2005] O.J. L131/24.

[66] *Heinrich* (C-345/06) E.C.R. 10.03.09.

[67] Joint Action 2004/551 [2004] O/J/ L245/17, amended [2008] O.J. L102/34 and L293/1; Regulation 460/04 [2004] O.J. L77/1, based on art.114 TFEU [95]. The validity of this legal basis for the Regulation was contested by the UK: *UK v Parliament and Council* (C-217/04) [2006] E.C.R. I-3771, to no avail.

[68] Regulation 1007/08 [2008] O.J. L293/1

[69] *http://www. enisa/europa.eu.*

Communicable Disease Network based on ad hoc co-operation between Member States. Substantial reinforcement was needed for the Union to be in a position to control communicable diseases effectively. In 2004[70] the Centre was set up to provide a structured and systematic approach to this control and that of other serious health threats; it will also reinforce the synergies between the national centres for disease control.

The Centre is situated in Stockholm.

17. THE EUROPEAN RAILWAY AGENCY (ERA)

The Agency was set up in 2004.[71] Its objective is to contribute, on technical matters, to the implementation of the Union's legislation aimed at improving the competitive position of the railway sector by enhancing the level of interoperability of railway systems and at developing a common approach to safety on the European railway system, in order to contribute to creating a European railway area without frontiers guaranteeing a high level of safety. In pursuing these objectives, the Agency shall take full account of the process of enlargement of the EU and of the specific constraints relating to rail links with third countries.

The Agency is a body of the Union and it has legal personality; it has an Administrative Board and an Executive Director; it is located at Lille/Valencienne (France) with a staff of about 30.

18. THE EUROPEAN GNSS (GLOBAL NAVIGATION SATELLITE SYSTEM) SUPERVISORY AUTHORITY

This Authority was set up in 2004[72] given the strategic nature of the European satellite positioning and navigation programmes and the need to ensure that essential public interests in this field are adequately defended and represented. The Authority was entrusted with, among others, the following tasks:

- managing the European satellite navigation programmes such as Galileo and AGNOS and controlling the use of the funds allocated to them;
- being the licensing authority vis-à-vis the private concession holder responsible for implementing and managing the Galileo deployment and operating phases;
- all matters related to the right to use the frequencies necessary to the operation of the system;
- being the owner of the tangible and intangible assets created and developed under the Galileo and AGNOS programmes; and
- assisting the Commission in matters involving satellite radio-navigation.

It is a Union agency and is provisionally located at Brussels.

---

[70] Regulation 851/2004 [2004] O.J. L142/1.
[71] Regulation 881/2004 [2004] O.J. L161/1, amended [2008] O.J. L354/51.
[72] Regulation 1321/2004 [2004] O.J. L246/1.

19. The European Agency for the Management of Operational Co-Operation at the External Borders of the Member States of the European Union (FRONTEX)

This agency was set up in 2004[73] to improve integrated management of the Union's external borders. Although responsibility for the control and surveillance of external borders lies with the Member States, the Agency will facilitate co-ordination of existing and future Union measures relating to the management of these borders. "External borders" means land and sea borders and airports and seaports to which the provisions of Union law on the crossing of external borders by persons apply.

An agreement was concluded with Iceland and Norway on the modalities of their participation in the Agency.[74]

The main tasks of the Agency are to:

- co-ordinate operational co-operation between Member States;
- develop a common integrated risk assessment model;
- help Member States train their national border guards;
- follow up on the development of research relevant to the control and surveillance of external borders;
- assist Member States in circumstances requiring increased technical and operational assistance—a Rapid Border Intervention Team was set up in 2007[75];
- provide Member States with the necessary support in organising joint return operations.

The Agency is a Union body with legal personality and is represented by an Executive Director. It has a Management Board composed of representatives of the Member States and two of the Commission; it is situated at Warsaw.

20. The Union Fisheries Control Agency (CFCA)

The CFCA was set up in 2005[76] as a key part of the drive to improve compliance with the rules under the 2002 reform of the Common Fisheries Policy (CFP); see below, Ch.24. It should strengthen the uniformity and effectiveness of enforcement of control by pooling EU and national means of fisheries control and co-ordinating enforcement activities. It should also improve the flow of information between and among the Member States and the Commission. It should also lead to better relations between the EU and its international partners by centralising contact points and promoting more uniform control and inspection methods. To help the Agency, an EU Fisheries Monitoring Centre using satellite technology to provide information regarding the location and movements of EU vessels was established.

---

[73] Regulation 2007/2004 [2004] O.J. L349/1, amended [2007] O.J. L199/30. The validity of this Regulation was contested by the UK, but to no avail: *UK v Council* (C-77/05) [2007] E.C.R. I-11459.

[74] [2007] O.J. L188/15.

[75] Regulation 863/07 establishing a mechanism for the creation of a Rapid Border Intervention Team [2007] O.J. L199/30.

[76] Regulation 768/2005 [2005] O.J. L128/1, amended [2009] O.J. L341/1, amending Regulation 2847/93 establishing a control system applicable to the common fisheries policy [1993] O.J. L261/1, repealed [2009] O.J. L343/1.

The Agency has an Administrative Board composed of representatives of the Commission and the Member States, an Executive Director and an Advisory Board made up of representatives of the regional Fisheries Councils. It is located at Vigo, Spain.[77]

21. The European Institute for Gender Equality

Set up in 2006[78]. It became operational on January 19, 2008. The main aims of the Institute are to help:

- promote and strengthen gender equality;
- include gender mainstreaming in all Community policies and resulting national policies;
- fight discrimination based on sex; and
- raise EU citizens' awareness.

Mission and tasks are:

- collection, analysis and dissemination of information;
- promotion of dialogue at European level;
- raising of public awareness; and
- transparency.

The Institute will also raise the profile of such issues among Union citizens.

Operation: The Institute will perform its tasks within the framework of Community powers and in accordance with the EU's priorities in the field of gender equality.

The Institute will be organised in such a way as to operate independently from national authorities, civil society and the Community institutions, thereby ensuring transparency of action.

The Institute will have legal personality and comprise a Management Board, a Director and his staff, and an Advisory Forum. Its seat is in Vilnius (Lithuania).

In order to avoid duplication, the Institute will co-operate as closely as possible with all the Community programmes and agencies, notably the European Foundation for the Improvement of Living and Working Conditions, the European Agency for Safety and Health at Work, the European Centre for the Development of Vocational Training and any future agency for fundamental rights.

The Institute may enter into contractual relations, in particular subcontracting arrangements, with other organisations.

22. The European Chemicals Agency

This agency was set up together with the adoption of the regulation on the Registration, Evaluation, Authorisation and Restriction of Chemicals (REACH).[79] It is a body of the Union and has legal personality. It is composed of

---

[77] According to [2008] O.J. L278/78 it is situated at Brussels.
[78] Regulation 1922/06 [2006] O.J. L403/9.
[79] Regulation 1907/06 [2006] O.J.L396/1, amended [2009] O.J. L164/7, as regards Annex XVII and [2009] O.J. L220/1.

a Management Board, an Executive Director, a Committee for Risk Assessment, a Committee for Socio-economic Analysis, a Member State Committee, a Forum for Exchange of Information on Enforcement, a Secretariat and Board of Appeal. The regulation provides that the Agency's work may not affect the activities of the European Agency for Health and Safety at work nor those of the European Medicines Agency, or the Food Safety Authority.

The Court has jurisdiction in any dispute relating to compensation of damages caused by the non-contractual responsibility of the Agency.

The Agency shall provide the Member States and the institutions of the Community with the best possible scientific and technical advice on questions relating to chemicals which fall within its remit and which are referred to it in accordance with the provisions of the regulation.

23. THE EUROPEAN UNION AGENCY FOR FUNDAMENTAL RIGHTS

It replaced the European Monitoring Centre on Racism and Xenophobia (EUMC).[80]

The Centre was set up in 1997; it is situated in Vienna with a staff of around 34 persons—its task is to provide the Union and the Member States with objective, reliable and comparable data at European level on the phenomena of racism, xenophobia and anti-Semitism. It must study the extent, development, causes and effect of the said phenomena in the following fields:

- free movement of persons;
- information, TV and the media;
- education, vocational training and youth;
- social policy, including employment;
- free movement of goods; and
- culture.

The very core of its activities is the European Information Network on Racism and Xenophobia (RAXEN) whose objective it is to collect, co-ordinate and disseminate data at national and EU level.

The Centre was replaced by the European Union Agency for Fundamental Rights in 2007 (see hereunder).

The Agency was established[81] upon the premise that greater knowledge of, and broader awareness of, fundamental rights issues in the Union are conducive to ensuring full respect of fundamental rights. For a description of the latter, the Regulation refers to the Charter of Fundamental Rights of the European Union,[82] the constitutional traditions and international obligations of the Member States, the European Treaties, the European Convention for the protection of Human Rights and Fundamental Freedoms, the Social Charter adopted by the Union and by the Council of Europe, the case law of the Union courts and of the European Court of Human Rights.[83] The task of the Agency is to provide information and

---

[80] Replaced as from March 1, 2007 by the European Union Agency for Fundamental Rights [2007] O.J. L53/3.

[81] Regulation 168/07 [2007] O.J. L 55/1.

[82] [2000] O.J. C364/1.

[83] This reference is particularly interesting since this Court has no legal links with the Union; the Agency is to work closely with the Council of Europe.

data on fundamental rights matters. Moreover, it is considered that developing effective institutions for the protection and promotion of human rights is a common value of the international and European societies.[84]

The Agency is built upon the European Monitoring Centre on Racism and Xenophobia described above, situated in Vienna, which it succeeds.

The Agency comprises a Management Board, an Executive Board, a Scientific Committee and a Director. The Court of Justice has jurisdiction among others in disputes relating to compensation for damages caused by the Agency and its servants.

A multi-annual framework for the Agency (2007–2012) was adopted in 2008.[85] An agreement was signed between the Union and the Council of Europe on co-operation between the Agency and the Council of Europe.[86]

24. EUROPEAN INSTITUTE FOR INNOVATION AND TECHNOLOGY (EIT)

The European Institute of Innovation and Technology is to be a key driver of sustainable European growth and competitiveness through the stimulation of world-leading innovations with a positive impact on economy and society.

The mission of the EIT is to grow and capitalise on the innovation capacity and capability of actors from higher education, research, business and entrepreneurship from the EU and beyond through the creation of highly integrated Knowledge and Innovation Communities (KICs).

It is managed by a Governing Board and is situated in Budapest.

II. UNION AGENCIES

1. THE EUROPEAN DEFENCE AGENCY (EDA)

The Agency was set up by a Council Joint Action pursuant to the Treaty on European Union. It is now provided for in the EU Treaty.[87] It is subject to the authority of the Council and open to participation by all Member States. Its task is to:

- contribute to identifying the Member States' military capability objectives and evaluating observance of their capability commitments;
- promote harmonisation of operational needs and adoption of effective, compatible procurement methods;
- propose multilateral projects to fulfil the objectives in terms of military capabilities;
- support defence technology research; and
- contribute to identifying and, if necessary, implementing any useful measure for strengthening the industrial and technological base for the defence sector and for improving the effectiveness of military expenditure.

[84] Reference is made to Recommendation R (97)14 of the Committee of Ministers of the Council of Europe of 30.09.97.
[85] [2008] O.J. L63/14.
[86] [2008] O.J. L186/7.
[87] arts 42(3)2 and 45 EU.

The statute, seat and operational rules of the Agency are defined by the Council, acting by a qualified majority. It shall carry out its task in liaison with the Commission where necessary.

The Agency should contribute to the implementation of the Common Foreign and Security Policy (CFSP), in particular the European Security and Defence Policy (ESDP).

It has legal personality and has its headquarters in Brussels.[88] The Council fixed its financial rules, rules on procurement and rules on financial contributions from the operating budget of the Agency.[89] See also below Ch.37 on Common Foreign and Security Policy and the establishment of a European Security and Defence College.[90]

2. The European Union Satellite Centre (EUSC)

Established, on the basis of art.14 of the EU Treaty in July 2001, operational since January 1, 2002, the Centre has the legal personality, "necessary to perform its functions and attain its objectives".[91] The Centre supports the decision-making of the Union in the context of the Common Foreign and Security Policy (CFSP), in particular of the European Security and Defence Policy (ESDP), by providing material resulting from the analysis of satellite imagery and collateral data, including aerial imagery as appropriate.

The initial staff of the EUSC was recruited from among the staff of the West European Union (WEU) Satellite Centre, which it replaces.

It is situated at Torrejón de Ardoz, Spain.

3. The European Police College (CEPOL)

Established in 2000 by Council Decision pursuant to Title VI of the EU Treaty[92]; it was replaced by an organ with the same name and to be regarded as its successor by a Council decision[93] in 2005! It started as a network bringing together the national training institutes for senior police officers in the Member States, applicant countries and Iceland and Norway but it does not preclude the establishment of a permanent institution at a later stage. The EU has been active in this field with a common programme for the exchange and training of, and co-operation between, law enforcement authorities (OISIN).[94] It also promotes a programme for exchange, training and co-operation for persons responsible

---

[88] See Council Decision of September 24, 2004 concerning the Staff Regulation of the Agency [2004] O.J. L310/9 and Decision concerning the Rules applicable to national experts and military staff on secondment to the Agency [2004] O.J. L310/64.

[89] [2007] O.J. L269/1.

[90] Council Joint Action 2008/550 [2008] O.J. L176/20 replacing Joint Action 2005/575 [2005] O.J. L194/15.

[91] [2001] O.J. L200/5, art.6, amended [2006] O.J. L405/60, amended [2009] O.J. L297/18.

[92] [2000] O.J. L336/1 and Decision 2004/566 [2004] O.J. L251/19.

[93] Decision 2005/681/JHA establishing a European Police College (CEPOL) and repealing Decision 2000/820/JHA [2005] O.J. L256/63.

[94] O.J. L7/5.

for action to combat crime (Falcone).[95] For further details see the Council Decision.

The College is situated at Bramshill (UK).[96]

4. EUROJUST (THE EUROPEAN BODY FOR THE ENHANCEMENT OF JUDICIAL CO-OPERATION)

Eurojust was set up in 2002 by the Council as "a body of the Union"[97]; it has legal personality. It is composed of one national member seconded by each Member State in accordance with its legal system; being a prosecutor, judge or police officer of equivalent competence. Its objectives are: (in the context of investigations and prosecutions concerning two or more Member States, of criminal behaviour in relation to serious crime, particularly when it is organised) to stimulate and improve co-ordination between the competent authorities, to improve co-operation and to support otherwise the competent authorities.

Eurojust may also assist investigations and prosecutions concerning only one Member State and a non-Member State where a co-operation agreement has been concluded with said State.

The general competences of Eurojust cover:

- the types of crime and offences in respect of which Europol (see below) is at all times competent to act;
- the following types of crime:

  — computer crime;
  — fraud and corruption and any criminal offence affecting the EC's financial interests;
  — the laundering of the proceeds of crime;
  — participation in a criminal organisation;

- other offences committed together with the types of crime and offences referred to above.

Eurojust can act either through its national members or as a College; the latter consists of all the national members, each one having one vote. The Commission is also associated with the work.

An Independent joint supervisory body was set up to monitor collectively the activities concerning the processing of personal data.

Eurojust is assisted by a Secretariat headed by an Administrative Director; it has its own staff of about 80 persons, subject to the rules and regulations applicable to the officials of the Union. It is situated at The Hague (Netherlands).

5. THE EUROPEAN UNION INSTITUTE FOR SECURITY STUDIES (ISS)

Established on the basis of art.14 EU in July 2000[98] by a Council Joint Action and operational since January 1, 2002, the Institute contributes to the development of

---

[95] [1999] O.J. L99/8.

[96] Decision 2004/567 [2004] O.J. L251/20.

[97] Decision 2002/187 [2002] O.J. L63/1, setting up Eurojust with a view to reinforcing the fight against serious crime, modified by Decision 2009/426 on the strengthening of Eurojust [2009] O.J. L138/14.

[98] [2001] O.J. L200/3, amended [2006] O.J. L409/181.

the Union Foreign and Security Policy (EFSP), including the European Security and Defence Policy (ESDP), by conducting academic research and analysis in relevant fields. The Institute has the legal personality, "necessary to perform its functions and attain its objectives". The initial staff was recruited from among the staff of the West European Union (WEU) Institute for Security Studies, of which it incorporates the relevant features. It is situated in Paris. The staff regulations were published in 2005.[99]

6. THE EUROPEAN POLICE OFFICE (EUROPOL)

It was established in 1995 by a Council act consisting of a Convention concluded by the Member States and based on Title VI of the EU Treaty, the "Europol Convention". The Office is therefore financed by the Member States. (In 2008 it was decided to transform the Office into a European Agency on January 1, 2010.) It became operational on July 1, 1999, after ratification by the, at that time, 25 Member States. Some of its tasks are now provided for in the EU Treaty, such as the collection, storage, processing, analysis and exchange of relevant information including information held by law enforcement services.

The Council, on the other hand, must promote co-operation through Europol, and was given five years to:

- enable Europol to facilitate, support and encourage the co-ordination and carrying out of specific investigative actions, including operational actions of joint teams comprising representatives of Europol in a support capacity;
- allow Europol to ask the competent authorities of the Member States to conduct and co-ordinate their investigations in specific cases and develop specific expertise which may be put at the disposal of said authorities to assist them in investigating cases of organised crime; and
- promote liaison arrangements between prosecuting/investigating officials specialising in the fight against organised crime in close co-operation with Europol.

In 1998, a Council act laid down rules governing Europol's external relations with third States and non-European related bodies and an act laying down rules governing the receipt of information from third parties.

Since Europol was set up by a convention, every modification had to be ratified by all the national parliaments, which was terribly cumbersome; the convention was therefore replaced by a Council Decision.[100]

7. THE AGENCY FOR CO-OPERATION OF ENERGY REGULATORS

Established in 2009,[101] it constitutes a key measure for completing the internal markets in electricity and natural gas. It replaces the European Regulators Group for Electricity and Gas (ERGEG) established by the Commission.[102] This group

---

[99] [2005] O.J. L235/1.
[100] Decision 2009/321 [2009] O.J. L123/37.
[101] Regulation 713/09 [2009] O.J. L211/1.
[102] [2003] O.J. L296/34.

is composed of representatives of the national regulatory authorities established pursuant to Directive 303/54 concerning common rules for the internal market in electricity[103] and Directive 303/55 concerning common rules for the internal market in natural gas.[104]

It shall assist the regulatory authorities in exercising, at Union level, the regulatory tasks performed in the Member States and, where necessary, co-ordinate their action.

It is temporarily hosted on Commission premises. It has legal personality. It comprises an Administrative Board, a Board of Regulators, a Director (who represents the Agency) and a Board of Appeal.

III. EXECUTIVE AGENCIES

1. EUROPEAN RESEARCH COUNCIL EXECUTIVE AGENCY (ERC)

It is part of the Union's Seventh Research Framework Programme Set up by the Commission to support investigator-driven frontier research, with a total budget for 2007–2013 of €7.5 billion. Its main aim is to stimulate excellence in Europe by supporting and encouraging creative scientists, scholars and engineers who are invited to submit their individual proposals in any field of research.

It consists of an independent Scientific Council, which defines the strategy and methodology and an Executive Agency acting on behalf of the European Commission and which applies them.

The Executive Agency manages the following tasks:

- executing the annual work programme;
- implementing calls for proposals;
- providing information and supporting the applicants;
- organising peer review evaluation;
- establishing and managing grant agreements; and
- providing assistance to the Scientific Council.

2. TRANS-EUROPEAN TRANSPORT NETWORK EXECUTIVE AGENCY

This Agency was established in 2007[105] and the target date for it to be fully operational was the end of 2007. It manages the Union funds available for the promotion for the Trans-European Transport Network in close co-operation with the Commission's Directorate-General for Energy and Transport. Its main tasks are to ensure the technical and financial management of projects co-financed under the Trans-European Transport Network's budget,[106] to collect, analyse and transmit to the Commission all information required for the implementation of

---

[103] [2003] O.J. L176/37.
[104] [2003] O.J. L176/57.
[105] Decision 2007/60 [2007] O.J. L32/88.
[106] The Agency receives a subsidy entered in the general budget of the Union and taken from financial allocations for Union action in the field of Trans-European Transport Network and, where appropriate, other Union programmes or actions whose implementation is entrusted to the Agency.

said networks and to assist in programming and checking the conformity of projects financed by the Union with the transport policy rules and principles. Its tasks and period of operation were modified in 2008,[107] it also became responsible for projects receiving financial aid.[108]

The Agency is located in Brussels and is managed by a Steering Committee and a Director appointed by the Commission.

3. The Education, Audio-Visual and Culture Executive Agency (EACEA)[109]

It was set up in 2005 by Commission Decision[110] with a seat in Brussels; its mission is to implement and manage a number of parts of more than 15 Union-funded programmes and action in the fields of education and training, active citizenship, youth, audio-visual and culture.[111]

It operates under the supervision of its three parent Directorates-General of the Commission: Education and Culture; Information Society and Media; and the Europe Aid and Co-operation Office—it is managed by a Steering Committee and a Director appointed by the Commission.

4. The Executive Agency for Competitiveness and Innovation (EACI)[112]

This is, in fact, the new name given in 2007 to the Intelligent Energy Executive Agency[113] (which started operating in Brussels in 2004), following the integration of the Intelligent Energy programme into the Competitiveness and Innovation Framework Programme (2007–2013). The Agency is responsible for implementing the tasks concerning Union aid under the programme and it disseminates the resulting know-how and best practices. Its official lifetime is until 2015.

From 2008 on, it started managing the European Commission's SME support network and eco-innovation initiatives, which form part of the Framework Programme and the Marco Polo Programme. It reports to three Directorates-General of the Commission: Energy and Transport; Enterprise and Industry; and Environment, which remain responsible for programming and evaluation.

5. The Research Executive Agency (REA)

The Research Executive Agency, located in Brussels, was created in December 2007. Managing over €6.5 billion, it started its work in 2008, and became

---

[107] Decision 2008/593 [2008] O.J. L190/35.
[108] Regulation 680/07 [2007] O.J. L162/1.
[109] Decision 2005/56, [2007] O.J. L49/21, amended [2008] O.J. L205/47.
[110] Decision 2005/56, [2007] O.J. L49/21, amended [2008] O.J. L205/47.
[111] See *http://www.eacea.ec.europa.eu.*
[112] See *http://www.ec.europa.eu/energy/intelligent/contact/index_en.htm.*
[113] Set up by Decision 2004/20 under the Union programme "Intelligent Energy-Europe" created by Decision 1230/03.

fully independent in 2009. The REA reports to the Directorates-General for Research; Enterprise; Information Society and Media; and Energy and Transport.

The evaluation of proposals and the management of projects are at the heart of research support. The Research Executive Agency will carry out these evaluation and management processes for a large part of the current Research Framework Programme. With increasing research budgets, dedicating facilities and services to these tasks is at the core of the Framework Programme. These dedicated facilities and services will enable the Union to improve the delivery of support to the research community.

The REA will manage the following tasks:

- the Marie-Curie fellowships and related awards;
- specific research grant agreements for the benefit of small and medium-sized enterprises;
- multi-partner projects in the field of space research;
- multi-partner projects in the field of security research;
- operate the proposal reception and evaluation facility in the Covent Garden building in central Brussels;
- operate a one-stop shop helpdesk for enquiries about FP7; and
- operate the unique registration facility for project partners to reduce the amount of paperwork involved in project management.

6. THE EXECUTIVE AGENCY FOR HEALTH AND CONSUMERS (FORMERLY THE PUBLIC HEALTH EXECUTIVE AGENCY)

This Agency was established in December 2004 for a period beginning on January 1, 2005 and ending on December 31, 2010 and is situated in Luxembourg, with about 30 staff members. It is entrusted with implementing tasks concerning Union aid under the Union programme in the field of public health established by a 2002 Framework Decision.[114]

It is entrusted with the following tasks:

- managing all the phases in the lifetime of specific projects and in the work plan provided for;
- adopting the instruments of budget execution for revenue and expenditure and carrying out, where the Commission has empowered it to do so, all the operations necessary for the management of the programme, in particular those linked to the award of contracts and grants; and
- providing logistical, scientific and technical support.

The Agency is managed by a Steering Committee and a Director appointed by the Commission.

It receives a grant entered in the general budget of the Union and taken from the funds allocated to the programme on public health.

Although it does not come under any of the categories examined above, mention should be made here of the *European Personnel Selection Office* (EPSO) responsible for selecting staff for the European institutions.[115]

---

[114] Decision 1786/2002 [2002] O.J. L271/1, amended [2004] O.J. L138/7.
[115] Decision 2002/621 [2002] O.J. L197/53, amended [2010] O.J. L26/24.

IV. JOINT UNDERTAKINGS[116] AND OTHER STRUCTURES[117]

Joint Undertakings—the following were set up: Artemis Joint Undertaking (embedded computer systems); Clear Sky Joint Undertaking (air transport); ENIAC Joint Undertaking (nanoelectronics); FCH Joint Undertaking (fuel cells and hydrogen); IMI Joint Undertaking (innovative medicines); and SESAR Joint Undertaking (air traffic management).

Other structures: European Research Infrastruture Consortium (ERIC).[118]

Those joint undertakings were set up within the Seventh Framework Programme of the Union for research, technological development and demonstration activities (2007–2013),[119] which provides for a long-term public private partnership in the form of Joint Technology Initiatives, to be implemented through joint enterprises as provided for in the Treaty.[120]

For more details see below, Ch.33: Research, Technological Development and space.

V. INTER-INSTITUTIONAL OFFICE: THE PUBLICATIONS OFFICE[121]

The Publications Office of the European Union has competence for:

- publishing the *Official Journal of the European Union*;
- publishing other mandatory publications;
- publishing non-mandatory publications under the prerogative of each institution;
- publishing publications on its own initiative, the Office may procure translations by means of a service contract;
- developing, maintaining and updating electronic publishing for the public;
- all legislation and other official texts (making them available to the public);
- preserving all publications;
- allocating international standard numbers;
- managing reproduction and translation rights in respect of the institutions publications;
- proposing and selling the publications.

A Management Committee was established in which all the signatory institutions are represented.

---

[116] See General Report 2008, 261.

[117] art.187 TFEU [171]: The Union may set up joint undertakings or any other structure necessary for the efficient execution of Union research, technological development and demonstration programmes.

[118] [2009] O.J. L206/1.

[119] [2006] O.J. L.412/1.

[120] art.187 TFEU [171].

[121] Decision 2009/496 of Parliament, Council, Commission, Court of Justice, Court of Auditors, ECSC and Committee of the Regions [2009] O.J. L168/41.

Further Reading

Jan Kottmann, "Europe and the regions: sub-national entity representation at Community level", (2000) E.L.Rev. 159.)
Timothy Millett, "Community plant variety rights–Extent of the information that a holder may claim from a farmer about his use of the 'agricultural exception' ", (2004) E.L.Rev. 124.

Chapter Fourteen

Financing Union Activities

1. FINANCIAL CONTRIBUTIONS OF THE MEMBER STATES AND THE UNION'S OWN RESOURCES

The Decision to replace the Financial Contributions from the Member States (which was the original way of financing Union activities) with the Union's "Own Resources"[1] inaugurated a new era in the history of the Union. On the one hand, it made it, in a certain way, financially independent, with all the economic and political consequences this entails. On the other hand, the Treaty of April 22, 1970 Amending Certain Budgetary Provisions of the ECSC, EEC and Euratom Treaties and of the Merger Treaty, conferred at the same time certain budgetary powers upon Parliament, as a necessary complement to the transfer of national resources to the Union.[2] It is of interest to read what the Commission had to say about this transfer:

> "Own resources are a highly political issue: besides the whole question of the [Union's] financial independence, their source is a major factor in shaping the relationship between the EU's citizens, its Member States and its institutions. So the debate over the [Union's] own resources is closely linked to the wider debate over the future of European integration and the struggle between two contrasting visions, between the federal and the inter-governmental approach."[3]

In 1975 the budgetary provisions were again modified and complemented by the creation of the Court of Auditors.[4] A 2000 Decision established calculation methods for the own resources, but was repealed.

The Decision on the Union's own Resources

The main features of this Decision can be summarised as follows:

- both the agricultural levies and the Common Customs Tariff (CCT) duties constitute own resources to be entered in the budget of the Union;
- the transfer of revenue from customs duties took place progressively over a period of four years;

---

[1] Decision 70/243 of April 21, 1970 [1970] J.O. L94/19.

[2] This Treaty became effective on January 1, 1971. The budgetary powers of Parliament are analysed above in Ch.5: The European Parliament (2. (9) Participation in the Budgetary Procedure).

[3] *http://www.europa.eu.int/scadplus/leg/en/lvb/l34011.htm*. The author does not fully agree with the sharp distinction made here between "federal" and "intergovernmental": the Community is much too complex to be classified entirely in one or the other category: it necessarily has some of both. Furthermore the "own resources" decision seems irreversible so that the debate referred to above won't change its basic principle.

[4] Treaty amending Certain Financial Provisions of the Treaties establishing the European Communities and the Merger Treaty of July 22, 1975 [1977] O.J. L359/1.

- since the revenue accruing from the duties and levies did not suffice to cover the expenditures of the Union, revenue from the Value Added Tax (VAT) was also allocated.[5] It will be remembered that the revenue and expenditure shown in the Union budget must be in balance.[6]

As from January 1, 1980, the Union's expenditures were entirely financed by the revenue accruing from the agricultural levies, the customs duties[7] and a percentage of the VAT collected in the Member States.

A Decision on the system of the Union's own resources, adopted in June 1988,[8] introduced the changes adopted by the European Council at Brussels, in February 1988:

- the overall ceiling on own resources is set at 1.20 per cent of total Union GNP for payments (1.30 per cent for commitments), it was 1.27 per cent in 1999; for the "financial perspective 2007–2013" (27 Member States) it is actually 1.045 per cent, quite a reduction;
- also customs duties on ECSC products were to be paid to the Union;
- the costs of collecting the own resources was deducted from the Member States' payments (10 per cent);
- the third source (VAT) was collected at a rate of 1.4 per cent applied to a VAT base limited to 55 per cent of GNP to take account of the situation of Member States where consumption accounts for a high proportion of GNP—this was to be reduced, from 1995, to 50 per cent;
- a fourth resource, based on a GNP scale, was introduced.[9] It was meant to replace VAT as the resource for balancing the budget; it is obtained by applying a rate fixed each year under the budget procedure to a base representing the sum of the gross national products at market prices. It is calculated by reference to the difference between expenditure and the yield of the other resources.

The Brussels European Council (1998) resolved a long-standing feud about the Union's own resources which had become insufficient to cover the expenditures. This "liberated" the Union and allowed it to go ahead with the completion of the internal market by the end of 1992.[10] It should also be noted that the "budget correcting mechanism" introduced in 1976 to enable payments to be made to Member States which, due to special economic conditions, are considered to bear a disproportionate burden in financing the budget,[11] will remain applicable (this

---

[5] Directive 77/388 [1977] O.J. L145/1. The revenue results from the application of a rate not exceeding 1.4 per cent of the basis used for assessing VAT, determined in a uniform manner for the Member States. The decision to increase the rate from 1 per cent to 1.4 per cent from January 1, 1986 and to 1.6 per cent on January 1, 1988 was taken by the European Council at Fontainebleau in June 1984; see [1984] Bull. 6–11. The Decision of April 21, 1970 was implemented by Regulation 2892/77 [1977] O.J. L336; see the Commission's report on the implementation of this Regulation: COM(88) 99 final.

[6] Decision 88/376 [1988] O.J. L185 and [1988] Bull. 3–105. See Regulation 3464/93 implementing Decision 88/376 [1993] O.J. L317, and Commission proposal for replacing Decision 88/376: General Report 1993 377.

[7] In case a Member State fails to collect customs duties, it is nonetheless financially responsible for their transfer to the Community: *Commission v Denmark* (C-19/05) [2007] E.C.R. I–8597.

[8] art.210(1)3 TFEU [268,3].

[9] For details see, e.g. [1988] Bull.2, 13, and following. This resource became the most important Community resource.

[10] See below Part Three: Introduction.

[11] This means the UK: General Report 1980, 59; [1980] Bull. 5–7 and Regulation 2744/80 [1980] O.J. L284/4.

was finally modified, by the agreement of December 2005, on the 2007–2013 financial perspective). Furthermore, an adjustment was made to offset the effect of the introduction of the fourth resource. The compensation to the United Kingdom[12] was financed on the basis of a GNP scale (it gives the UK a rebate equivalent to 0.66 per cent of its net balance and is shared by the other Member States according to their share of GNP, except Germany, whose share is reduced by a third), and for Spain and Portugal abatement arrangements were applied in accordance with their Act of Accession.[13]

2. The Union Budget, Revenue and Expenditure

As the Commission remarked about the budgetary procedure of 1988: "Thanks to the new instruments governing [Union] finances the problems which have beset the budgetary procedure in the past were very largely avoided."[14] The Commission was referring to the Inter-institutional Agreement on budgetary discipline and improvement of the budgetary procedure,[15] and the Regulation amending the implementing regulation of the Decision of April 21, 1970 creating the Union's own resources.

All items of revenue and expenditure of the, at the time, three Communities were to be included in estimates to be drawn up for each financial year and be shown in the budget.[16] The revenue and expenditure shown in the budget must be in balance.[17] The financial year runs from January 1 to December 31.[18] The structure of the general budget and the form in which it is to be presented are determined by Financial Regulations.[19] The budget consists of separate sections dealing with the revenue and expenditure of each institution. The section dealing with the Commission provides for expenditure in 40 different titles corresponding more or less to the activities described in the rest of this book.[20] After giving some general indications, a few examples are given below.

---

[12] In 1980 agreement was reached on the United Kingdom's contribution to the budget: the financial correcting mechanism was modified to allow a reduction for the UK and supplementary Union expenditures were provided for to help reduce certain regional disparities in the UK. The correction for 1990 was 2,430 million ECUs.

[13] arts 187 and 374 Act of Accession.

[14] General Report 1988, p.66.

[15] This agreement came into force on July 1, 1988 [1988] O.J. C142. A novelty is the Financial Perspective 1988–92; another important aspect of the agreement is the mutual obligation to comply with the financing objectives set by the European Council for certain priority policy areas (structural funds, integrated Mediterranean programmes, framework research programme). See [1988] Bull. 6–112. A new Agreement was signed on October 29, 1993 [1993] O.J. C331 and a new financial framework laid down for 1993–1999 at the Edinburgh European Council; see General Report 1993, 375. For the latest version of the Agreement see section 3. of this chapter.

[16] One important item not covered by the Union budget is the European Development Fund (resources destined to finance aid to developing countries), because the funds for this activity are provided directly by the Member States; the activities of the European Investment Bank do not appear on the budget either.

[17] art.310(1)3 TFEU [268,3].

[18] art.313 TFEU [272].

[19] [1977] O.J. L356/1, arts 15 and 16. This regulation was amended in June 1988; see [1988] O.J. L185/3. An up-to-date version was published in [1991] O.J. C80/1. See Regulation 2342/02 laying down detailed rules for the implementation of the Financial Regulation 1605/02 applicable to the general budget of the EC [2002] O.J. L357/1, amended [2007] O.J. L343/9, more: [2010] O.J. L37/73.

[20] See [2009] O.J. L69/II/1.

The general budget for 2009 provides for the following:

- Expenditures:
  - — Commitments: €133,845,980,000
  - — Payments: €116,096,060,000
- Revenue: €116,096,060,000 composed of the following resources:
  - — VAT: 0.3278%, representing 16.90% of the revenue,
  - — GNI: 0.5847%, representing 65.39% of the revenue,
  - — own resources: 16.54% of revenue and other revenue: 1,359,720,000.

1. Common agricultural policy and rural development and accompanying measures (markets, set-aside, income aids): €53,301,727,905.
2. Fisheries and maritime affairs: €953,145,213.
3. Regional policy (cohesion fund and solidarity fund): €984,534,647.
4. External relations (European Development Fund, food aid, co-operation with third countries, Common Foreign and Security Policy, etc.): €3,919, 361,607.
5. ACP: €1,317,126,477.
6. Enlargement: €1,093,326,691.
7. Administrative expenditure of the institutions (salaries, pensions, etc.): €968,732,046.
8   Reserves: €1,824,993,050.

(1) Commitment and Payment Appropriations

The Union budget contains "non-differentiated" and "differentiated" appropriations. Under the former, commitments can be made during the financial year and the corresponding payments can be made practically at the same time, i.e. during that financial year and the next. The differentiated appropriations consist of both commitments, i.e. the maximum that may be committed during that financial year, and the corresponding payments which may be disbursed either during that same year or at any time thereafter. This system is particularly suited for medium and long-term operations such as research projects and infrastructure investments. The advantage of this method is that the total amount of the Union's financial participation can be committed at the start of the project but the payments only have to be made as the work progresses over the years.[21]

(2) Compulsory and Non-compulsory Expenditure

The Treaty of July 22, 1975 amending Certain Financial Provisions of the existing Treaties introduced the concept of, "expenditure necessarily resulting from this Treaty or from acts adopted in accordance therewith" otherwise referred to as "compulsory" expenditures. This differentiation no longer exists.[22]

---

[21] The commitment and payment appropriations are now used for all expenditures.
[22] art.313 TFEU [272].

3. Financial Framework and Inter-institutional Agreement

The Edinburgh European Council of December 1992 agreed on the resources for the financing of the Union in the period 1993–99. This allowed the Union to finance its internal and external policies. On May 6, 1999, Parliament, the Council and the Commission concluded a new Inter-institutional Agreement on budgetary discipline and improvement of the budgetary procedure. This Agreement entered into force on January 1, 2000 and replaced the (Joint) Declarations of 1982, 1995 and 1996 and the Agreements concluded previously. It was intended to ensure, besides what is indicated in the title itself, that, in the medium term, Union expenditure develops within the limits of the own resources. It covers all expenditure.

The enormous advantage of the multi-annual planning of expenditure is obvious: it gives the Union a solid base for its future planning and it eliminates the inter-institutional haggling from which the Community suffered for many years.

At the Berlin European Council of March 24–25, 1999[23] it was decided that the new financial perspective should be established for a duration of seven years covering the period 2000–2006. It should be drawn up on the basis of the working assumption of the accession of new Member States starting from 2002. The European Council also hoped that a new Inter-institutional Agreement could be established between the European Parliament, the Council and the Commission on terms ensuring strict budgetary discipline, while preserving the overall balance of powers between the institutions and clearly ring-fencing pre-accession and accession-related expenditure for the entire duration of the financial perspective.

An Agreement on budgetary discipline and sound financial management as regards the multi-annual financial framework for the 2007–2013 period was agreed by the Council, Parliament and Commission in May 2006.[24] It provides for EU spending of up to 864 billion, that represents an increase of 4 billion over the preceding agreement allowing for an increase in expenditure for, for instance: life-long learning (Erasmus and Leonardo programmes), TENs, competitiveness and innovation, future actions (Life and Natura), culture, health and consumer protection. It also allows for flexibility in allocation of spending: flexibility instrument, Solidarity Fund, Globalisation Fund and Emergency Aid Reserve. It provides—and this a recent development—for a review in 2008/2009.

The 2007–2013 financial framework was adopted, after very difficult and protracted discussions among the 25 Member States in December 2005. The figures for commitments look roughly as follows:

Year	2007	2008	2009	2010	2011	2012	2013
Total	120,601	121,307	122,362	122,752	123,641	125,055	126,646

with a grand total of 862,363 billion for seven years.

---

[23] See Presidency conclusions DN: DOC/99/1, March 26, 1999.
[24] [2006] O.J. C139/1, amended [2008] O.J. L51/7and [2009] O.J. L132/8.

4. Protection of the Union's Financial Interests

The Treaty provides that the Union and the Member States shall, "counter fraud and any other illegal activity affecting the financial interests of the Union".[25] According to the Commission this required the establishment of a European Anti-Fraud Office (OLAF).[26] This office replaced the Task Force for Co-ordination of Fraud Prevention and implements the Commission's powers to carry out external administrative investigations. Besides combating fraud, its task is, therefore, to investigate serious facts linked to the performance of professional activities by officials and servants of the institutions and other bodies of the Union. The Office is responsible for providing the Commission's support in co-operating with the Member States. It shall be in direct contact with the police and judicial authorities.

The independence of the Office is ensured by the obligation imposed upon its Director to neither seek nor take instructions from the Commission, any government or any institution or body.[27] The establishment of a Surveillance Committee is also provided for.[28] The Office became operational together with the Parliament and Council Regulation concerning investigations conducted by the Office,[29] and an Inter-institutional Agreement of Parliament, Council and Commission concerning internal investigations by the Office.[30]

---

[25] art.325(4) TFEU [280(1)].
[26] See Decision of 28.04.99 [1999] O.J. L136/20.
[27] Decision of 28.04.99 [1999] O.J. L136/20, art.3.
[28] Rules of Procedure of the Committee [2000] O.J. L41/12.
[29] Regulation 1073/99: [1999] O.J. L136/1.
[30] Inter-institutional Agreement between Parliament, Council and Commission concerning internal investigations by the European Anti-Fraud Office [1999] O.J. L136/15, with attached to it the model of an internal decision for all the institutions and bodies of the Community.

PART THREE: THE INTERNAL MARKET

INTRODUCTION

Over the past 20 years, the scope of the European Treaties has been continuously expanded, first by the Single European Act (SEA) of 1987, then by the Maastricht or EU Treaty of 1992, by the Treaty of Amsterdam (1999), by the Treaty of Nice (2001) and, finally, by the Treaty of Lisbon (2009). Indeed, each time new responsibilities were added to the list of activities of the Union.[1] This extension follows from the built-in dynamism of these Treaties and the political will of the signatories. According to the Preamble of the Amsterdam Treaty, the Member States were, "determined to lay the foundation of an ever closer union among the peoples of Europe".[2] However, the same parties deleted another recital from the previous Treaties: "[i]n view of further steps to be taken in order to advance European integration", the latter word having become politically unacceptable to certain Member States. Was this then the end of European integration, as was advocated by the so-called Eurosceptics? A few months later, even before the Amsterdam Treaty had been ratified, the greatest step towards this "integration" was taken when most Member States transferred their monetary, and partly also their economic, sovereignty to the newly set-up European Central Bank and declared themselves ready to adopt a single currency. Not only that, but in the Preamble to the Treaty on European Union, one does now again find the words: "resolved to mark a new stage in the process of European integration"! This only shows that the trend to further co-operation between the Member States is irreversible, even if the ultimate goal is not definitively fixed.[3]

Among the competences of the Union, as set out in the Treaty on the Functioning of the Union (TFEU),[4] one finds, among others, a reference to the "customs union" and to the "functioning of the internal market".[5] These shall be examined in the following chapter.

---

[1] Now, see arts 3 and 4 TFEU. The EEC Treaty provided for 11 activities, the EU Treaty increased this to 20 and the Treaty of Amsterdam added a recital on employment. The first activity, the establishment of the "customs union" corresponds to the first of the "basic freedoms": the free movement of goods, the others being the free movement of "persons" and of "self-employed persons", the latter being expressed in the Treaty by the freedom of "establishment" and the freedom to "provide services". If, furthermore, one distinguishes between the free movement of capital and the free movement of payments, one comes to a total of six basic freedoms. These freedoms constitute the "internal market", the nucleus of of the Union itself. The Treaty of Lisbon added, among others, the "conservation of marine biological resources" and "space".

[2] Preamble and first recital TFEU.

[3] This author is of the opinion that the ultimate goal can only be established in very general terms owing to the continuous evolution of the internal and external circumstances that determine the development of the Union.

[4] art.3(3) EU.

[5] art.3(1)(a) and (b) TFEU [3].

In 2007 the Commission sent three communications to Parliament, the Council, the ESC and the Committee of the Regions:

- a single market for 21st century Europe[6] containing a package of initiatives to modernise the single market and to bring more benefits to Europeans;
- services of general interest,[7] including social services of general interest: a new European commitment, reference is made here to the TFEU, which provides for the possibility for Parliament and Council to provide, to commission and to fund such services[8];
- opportunities, access and solidarity: towards a new social vision for 21st century Europe.[9]

---

[6] COM(2007) 724 final.
[7] COM(2007) 725 final.
[8] art.14 TFEU [16].
[9] COM(2007) 726 final.

Chapter Fifteen

The Free Movement of Goods

The reader is bound to still encounter the expression "common market"; this term was eliminated by the Treaty of Lisbon and, furthermore, it was nowhere described, as such, in any of the other Treaties, but it followed from their provisions, that it encompassed the "internal market" (see hereunder for a definition) and, possibly, various common policies such as the customs union, commercial policy and competition.[1]

The internal market, on the other hand, is defined in the TFEU as, "an area without internal frontiers in which the free movement of goods, persons, services and capital is ensured in accordance with the provisions of the Treaties".[2] The first of those freedoms—the free movement of goods—means that goods can circulate unimpeded across the whole Union.[3] This freedom practically constitutes the point of departure of all the other freedoms and of most, if not all, of the common policies and activities of the Union. It is important to see this, since it allows one to understand the logical link that exists between the many subjects which shall be discussed hereafter. The central idea is that the whole Union constitutes one single economic area, similar to a national market,[4] wherein trade can develop without obstacles, making, however, allowance for differences in development of certain economies.[5]

This absence of obstacles is extremely significant since it is generally admitted that free trade contributes to the creation of wealth, i.e. employment and rising standards of living that are objectives of the Union. Any producer within the Union now has a potential market of some 500 million customers, which should allow him, among others, to fully use the advantages of the economies of scale. Every consumer, on the other hand, is free to "shop" wherever he can obtain the best conditions.

The establishment of this single market required not only the elimination, between Member States, of all existing obstacles to free trade, i.e. tariff, as well as non-tariff barriers and indirect obstacles such as state monopolies, agreements

---

[1] These areas of Union activity being part of its "exclusive" competence: art.3 TFEU.

[2] art.26(2) TFEU [14(2)]. It is most surprising, to say the least, that two basic freedoms are not mentioned here: the freedom of establishment and the free movement of payments. It is therefore so surprising because the freedom of establishment not only is, from an economic point of view, at least as important as the freedom to provide services, but also because the provisions of the latter only apply, "in so far as they are not governed by the provisions relating to freedom of movement of goods, capital and persons" (art.57,2 TFEU [50,1]) and, "without prejudice to the provisions relating to the right of establishment" (art.55,3 TFEU [50,3]).

[3] For the territorial scope of the Union see art.50 EU and art.355 TFEU [299].

[4] Similar words were used by the Court with regard to the Common Agricultural Policy: *Commissionnaires Réunis v Receveur des Douanes* (Joined Cases 80/77 and 81/77) [1978] E.C.R. 927 at 946(29).

[5] art.27,1 TFEU [15], "When drawing up proposals with the aim [of establishing or ensuring the functioning of the internal market], the Commission must take into account the extend of the effort that certain economies showing differences in development will have to sustain for the establishment of the internal market and propose appropriate provisions."

between undertakings, abuses of dominant position, mergers and acquisitions, state aids and fiscal discriminations, it also called for the adoption of measures to prevent the creation of new barriers.[6]

Under the heading "free movement of goods" the Treaty provides that the:

> "Union shall comprise a customs union which shall cover all trade in goods and which shall involve the prohibition between Member States of customs duties on imports and exports and of all charges having equivalent effect, and the adoption of a common customs tariff in their relations with third countries".[7]

It also provides that, "quantitative restrictions on imports and all measures having equivalent effect shall be prohibited between the Member States".[8]

The elimination of the tariff barriers will be very briefly examined in the next section on the Customs Union, and the non-tariff barriers will be analysed in the section on the elimination of quantitative restrictions and measures having equivalent effect. The competition rules, the tax provisions and the approximation of laws, which also guarantee equal market access for all, will be examined in Part Four: Other Union Policies.

1. THE CUSTOMS UNION

The free movement of goods requires in the first place, as indicated, the creation of a customs union involving:

- the prohibition, among the Member States, of all customs duties and of all charges having equivalent effect; and
- the adoption of a common customs tariff (CCT) in relations with third countries. Without this CCT, products from third countries would all enter the Union through the country with the lowest external tariffs, since once inside, those products can circulate freely throughout the whole Union. This would "deflect" trade from the other Member States.

By "goods" must be understood, "products which can be valued in money and which are capable, as such, of forming the subject of commercial transactions".[9]

They are both industrial and agricultural[10] goods, whether originating in the Member States or imported from third countries.[11] Where imported goods are concerned, as soon as the import formalities have been complied with and all customs duties and charges have been paid, and not reimbursed, those imports are "in free circulation"[12] just like Union goods.

---

[6] art.37(2) TFEU [31(2)].

[7] art.28 TFEU [23]. The Customs Union among the original six Member States was established over a period of 10.5 years, shorter thus than the 12 years provided for in the original EEC Treaty.

[8] art.34 TFEU [28].

[9] *Commission v Italy* (7/68) [1968] E.C.R. 423 at 428. See also the definition in *Commission v Belgium* (C-2/90) [1992] E.C.R. I–4466(26): "all objects, which are being shipped across a frontier for the purpose of commercial transactions, are subject to Art.[34] whatever the nature of those transactions" (here negative value of the product).

[10] See below, Ch.23: Agriculture and Fisheries; the inclusion of agricultural products was not evident at the onset.

[11] The inclusion of imported products into the Customs Union is what distinguishes the latter from a "free trade area" (FTA) where only products originating within the participating States are included; this is because a FTA has no CCT; see art.4 EFTA Treaty.

[12] art.29 TFEU [24]. Directive 79/695 on the harmonisation of procedures for the release of goods in full circulation; see *Derudder* (C-290/01) [2004] E.C.R. I–2041.

(1) Prohibition of Customs Duties and Charges having Equivalent Effect[13]

"Charges having equivalent effect" have been defined by the Court, in its shortest judgment ever, as:

> "[A]ll charges demanded on the occasion or by reason of importation which, imposed specifically on imported products and not on similar domestic products, alter their cost price, and thus produces the same restrictive effect on the free movement of goods as a customs duty".[14]

Unless such a charge is a consideration for a benefit provided for the importer or exporter[15] it is prohibited.[16] The concept "charge having an equivalent effect" gave rise to an abundant case law and, in one of its first judgments, the Court stated that the Treaty provisions on this point create, for the citizens of the Union, individual rights which the national courts must uphold.[17] In other words, those provisions have direct effect.[18]

(2) The Common Customs Tariff (CCT)

The CCT constitutes, in the first place, a measure of commercial policy towards third countries. It is interesting to note that actions undertaken by the Union for its internal functioning have repercussions worldwide. As was pointed out, the setting up of the CCT had to coincide with the elimination of customs duties and charges among the Member States. This was necessary in order to avoid, as was mentioned already, deflection of trade, since all imports would obviously take place through the borders of the Member State with the lowest external customs duties. Consequently, it also constitutes an integral part of the Customs Union, which could not have been established without it. The CCT was adopted by a Council regulation,[19] and gradually introduced in parallel with the elimination of the customs duties. Since that time, Member States no longer have jurisdiction over the duties they levy on the goods entering their territory from third countries. They may not modify them, nor interpret[20] them, nor keep the proceeds,[21] which now belong to the Union as "own resources".[22] Modification or suspension of CCT duties is an exclusive Union matter[23] and is decided by the Council.[24] Important reductions

---

[13] art.30 TFEU [25].

[14] *Marimex v Amministrazione Finanziaria Italiana* (29/72) [1972] E.C.R. 1309 at 1318(6); [1973] C.M.L.R. 486.

[15] This is not the case, for instance, when the service is rendered in the general interest such as health inspections or charges covering the costs of customs activities: *Dubois* (C-16/94) [1995] E.C.R. I–2421; [1995] 2 C.M.L.R. 771.

[16] *Commission v Netherlands* (89/76) [1977] E.C.R. 1355.

[17] *Van Gend & Loos v Nederlandse Administratie der Belastingen* (26/62) [1963] E.C.R. 1 at 12; [1978] 3 C.M.L.R. 630.

[18] See above, Ch.4: Union Law.

[19] Regulation 950/68 O.J. L172/1; it is regularly updated.

[20] *Nederlandse Spoorwegen v Inspecteur der Invoerrechten en Accijnzen* (38/75) [1975] E.C.R. 1439 at 1449(4); [1976] 1 C.M.L.R. 167.

[21] Except for 25 percent, which they may keep to cover administrative costs; see above, Ch.14: Financing Union Activities.

[22] For "own resources" see above, Ch.14: Financing Union Activities.

[23] *Cadi Surgelés* (C-126/94) [1996] E.C.R. I–5647; [1997] 1 C.M.L.R. 795.

[24] art.31 TFEU [26].

were introduced following multilateral trade negotiations within the framework of the General Agreement on Tariffs and Trade (GATT, now World Trade Organisation WTO), such as the Kennedy Round (1964–1967), the Tokyo Round (1973–1979), the Uruguay Round (1988–1993) and the Doha Round (2001–).

Mention should also be made of the possible exception to the CCT where tariff quotas at reduced rate or zero-rate and generalised preferences are provided for.[25]

It should be noted however that, from a commercial point of view, a reduction of customs tariffs is less important than the elimination of non-tariff trade barriers, which are much more difficult to detect. This applies also to trade within the Union itself. See below.

In terms of trade, the creation of the Customs Union has resulted in shifts in the trade patterns, since industrial goods are sometimes less expensive for Union users and consumers when imported from other Member States than from third countries. Also trade among the Member States has grown much faster than trade between the Union and third countries. In relation to the latter, the Union also uses the CCT as an instrument to guarantee the effectiveness of its commercial and external policy.[26]

One should realise that setting identical tariff levels for Union's borders is only a first step towards establishing the CCT. Indeed, the latter also calls for uniform interpretation, continuing administration, harmonisation of customs rules, simplification of checks and formalities and, generally speaking, the reinforcement of the structure of the Customs Union.[27]

Parliament and Council must take measures, in accordance with the ordinary legislative procedure,[28] in order to strengthen customs co-operation between Member States and between the latter and the Commission.[29] In 2007 the Council adopted the "Customs 2013" programme modernising customs procedures.[30] The new programme aims at helping Member States to better combat customs fraud and to cut compliance costs for traders. It supports new security policy initiatives, the implementation of modernisation of the customs code and the introduction of a pan-European paperless customs environment.[31]

In 1992, the Council, wishing to assemble in a Code the provisions of custom legislation that were contained in a large number of Union regulations and directives, and which would contain the general rules and procedures which ensure the implementation of the tariffs and other measures in connection with trade in goods between the Union and third countries, adopted the Union Customs Code.[32]

An e(lectronic)-customs system was established and a Modernised Customs Code was adopted in 2008.[33]

---

[25] See below, Ch.38: Commercial Policy.

[26] See below, Ch.38: Commercial Policy (1. Commercial Policy Instruments and Import and Export Arrangements).

[27] See the Convention on the use of information technology for customs purposes and Agreement on provisional application between certain Member States [1995] O.J. C316/33.

[28] art.289 TFEU, provides, under that name, for joint action.

[29] art.33 TFEU [35]. See Decision of Parliament and Council adopting an action programme for customs in the Union (Customs 2000) [1997] O.J. L33/24.

[30] IP/07/531.

[31] IP/05/1501.

[32] Regulation 2913/92 establishing the Union's Custom Code [1992] O.J. L302/1 and Regulation 2454/93 laying down provisions for the implementation of Regulation 2913/92 [1993] O.J. L253/1, both constantly amended.

[33] Regulation 450/08 [2008] O.J. L145/1.

The decision[34] establishing electronic customs systems in Europe provides for a series of measures and deadlines with a view to replacing all customs procedures with interconnected national computerised procedures and creating a common electronic portal.

The Modernised Union Customs Code,[35] replaces the Customs Code of 1992 in order to adapt to developments in international trade; the aim is to simplify the legislation, and streamline and computerised customs procedures.

The Union system of relief from customs duties was improved[36] and customs duties on goods contained in consignments sent by one private individual to another or contained in travellers' personal luggage were amended.[37] New tariff quotas at zero rates for specified amounts of certain industrial products were opened,[38] and duties on certain industrial, agricultural and fisheries products were temporarily suspended.[39]

2. PROHIBITION OF QUANTITATIVE RESTRICTIONS[40]

As was mentioned, the elimination of customs duties and charges having equivalent effect is not sufficient to guarantee the free circulation of goods within the Union. There are indeed many other ways of hindering imports and exports; quotas are one such way, but they have since long been abolished among the Member States. The worst offenders are the so-called measures having equivalent effect to quantitative restrictions. These are all the measures which have an effect equivalent to quantitative restrictions on imports and exports, and are not covered by other provisions adopted in pursuance of the Treaties.[41] They are often referred to as "invisible trade barriers", since they are, generally speaking, difficult to detect and only discovered by their effects on trade. The latter is disrupted to the prejudice of traders and consumers alike and they must therefore be hunted down by all parties concerned.

The Court[42] has defined those measures as, "all trading rules[43] enacted by Member States[44] which are capable of hindering, directly or indirectly, actually or potentially, intra-[Union] trade". This means that the prohibition applies not only when trade is actually prevented, but already when it is simply made unnecessarily difficult.[45] Secondly, it means that the hindrance does not have to be *actual*. It suffices that it can be shown that the possibility exists that interstate trade may be hampered. In other words, one does not have to wait till the measure has produced its ill effects. It is not necessary, either, that those trading rules have an

---

[34] Decision 70/08 [2008] O.J. L23/21, on a paperless environment for customs and trade.
[35] Regulation 450/08 [2008] O.J. L145/1.
[36] Regulation 274/08 [2008] O.J. L85/1.
[37] Regulation 275/08 [2008] O.J. L85/3.
[38] Regulation 556/08 [2008] O.J. L160/1.
[39] Regulation 595/08 [2008] O.J. L164/1.
[40] arts 34 and 35 TFEU [28 and 29].
[41] See Directive 70/50 [1970] O.J. L13/29.
[42] *Procureur du Roi v Dassonville* (8/74) [1974] E.C.R. 837 at 852(5).
[43] This includes rules of a temporary nature: *Openbaar Ministerie v Van Tiggele* (82/77) [1978] E.C.R. 25 at 40(20).
[44] The prohibition also applies to measures adopted by the Union institutions: *Kieffer and Thill* (C-114/96) [1997] E.C.R. I–3629.
[45] This means that there are cases where it may or should be made difficult: *Industrie Diensten Groep v Beele* (6/81) [1982] E.C.R. 707. See also below, 4. Exceptions to the Free Movement of Goods.

appreciable effect on intra-Union trade.[46] Thirdly, the word "indirect" means that there is an infringement of the principle of the free movement of goods even when the hindrance is only indirectly attributable to the contested measure. This is the case when a measure applies to both national and imported products but, in practice, produces protective effects by favouring typical national products and, by the same token, operates to the detriment of certain types of products from other Member States.[47]

It is interesting to ascertain that the above-mentioned Court formula defining "measures with equivalent effect" has also been used in various judgements applying the Union competition rules.[48] This similarity should not surprise, since the competition rules and the provisions concerning the Customs Union have an identical objective: the free movement of goods.

The question must be asked, however, to which goods does the principle of free movement apply? According to the Court, it concerns goods which have been, "lawfully produced and marketed in one of the Member States"[49]; those goods must, "be admitted in all the other Member States". This is, because of its far-reaching implications, the most important rule concerning the free movement of goods. It means that Member States must recognise as equivalent to their own legislation concerning the production and marketing of goods, that of all the other Member States. This is referred to as the principle of "mutual recognition". Without it, free circulation of goods could only be achieved through harmonisation of all the national regulations and standards. Obviously this is impossible[50]; nonetheless, harmonisation[51] remains an essential tool for implementing the internal market. The Union chose to combine mutual recognition with a more efficient mechanism for harmonisation; and the latter only where absolutely necessary. The procedure for the approximation of the national laws and regulations was also simplified by the SEA.[52] This allowed (most of) the internal market to be completed by December 31, 1992.[53]

However, in the absence of harmonisation, even mutual recognition does not always provide the solution. Indeed, according to the Court, the basic principle of the free movement cannot yet fully be applied under all circumstances. Therefore:

"[I]n the absence of common rules relating to the production and marketing of [a given product], it is for the Member States to regulate all matters relating to the production and the marketing of [said product] on their own territory".[54]

---

[46] *Prantl* (16/83) [1984] E.C.R. 1299.
[47] *Prantl* (16/83), above, fn.46.
[48] *Consten and Grundig v Commisssion* (Joined Cases 56/64 and 58/64) [1966] E.C.R. 299 at 341.
[49] *Rewe v Bundesmonopolverwaltung für Branntwein* (the so-called *Cassis de Dijon* case) (120/78) [1979] E.C.R. 649 at 664(14); [1979] 3 C.M.L.R. 494. Of course, this rule does not apply to goods imported from third countries once they have been put into free circulation: arts 28(2) and 29 TFEU [23(2) and 24]. In *Dassonville* the Court referred to, "an authentic product which has been put into free circulation in a regular manner, in another Member State".
[50] See Commission White Paper on the Completion of the Internal Market (COM(85)510 final).
[51] See below Ch.26: Approximation of Laws.
[52] The SEA introduced the present art.114 TFEU [95], that provided that such measures could be adopted by a majority vote, rather than unanimity, as is the case under art.115 TFEU [94].
[53] art.26 TFEU [14].
[54] *Cassis de Dijon* (120/78) 662(8), quoted above, fn.49.

Consequently:

"[O]bstacles to movement [of goods] within the Union resulting from disparities between the national laws relating to marketing of the products in question, must be accepted in so far as those provisions may be recognised as being necessary in order to satisfy mandatory requirements[55] of the public interest".

Those *mandatory requirements* are, for instance, the "effectiveness of fiscal supervision", the "protection of public health",[56] the "fairness of commercial transactions" and the "defence of the consumer".[57] Others are, according to the case law: "legitimate elements of economic and social policy",[58] the "fight against inflation",[59] the "protection of the environment",[60] the "promotion of culture"[61] and the "safeguard of press diversity".[62]

The mandatory requirements are to be distinguished from the "exceptions" to the free movement of goods provided for in the TFEU.[63] The latter render the principle of the free movement inapplicable as soon as the necessary conditions are fulfilled. Those exceptions will always exist since they are provided for in the Treaty itself. The mandatory requirements are a creation of the courts and they may only be relied upon, "in the absence of common rules". Since more and more common rules are being adopted, the mandatory requirements might, in theory, cease to be applicable over time. They do not constitute exceptions to the basic principle of the free movement of goods, they only justify a temporary suspension of the total and strict applicability of that basic rule.

What is the rationale behind those mandatory requirements? The principle of the free movement of goods is embodied in the Treaty in the form of obligations imposed upon the Member States. Since every obligation implies a corresponding right for the beneficiaries of those obligations, in this case the natural and legal persons within the Union, the latter simultaneously acquired a corresponding right: the right to free trade. On the other hand, no right is unlimited and the limitations result from the necessity to protect the public interest. The Member States, as the guardians of this public interest, are entitled, even obliged, to impose the measures necessary to protect it. Those measures can, in the absence of common rules, constitute obstacles to the free movement of goods, and must be temporarily accepted.

Those measures, however, "must only be accepted in so far as [they] may be recognised as being necessary".[64] The Member State imposing them must prove that they serve a purpose which is in the general interest, and as such take precedence over the requirements of the free movement of goods, which constitutes one of the fundamental rules of the Union. They must demonstrate the need for their measures based, for instance, on international scientific research.[65] This means,

---

[55] *Cassis de Dijon* (120/78), above at fn.49.
[56] This was later withdrawn from the list by the Court, since it, finally recognised that this matter is the object of an exception under art.36 TFEU [30]!
[57] Withdrawn, as above, fn.56.
[58] *Oebel* (155/80) [1981] E.C.R. 1993 at 2008(12).
[59] *Roussel Laboratoria v Netherlands* (181/82) [1983] E.C.R. 3849 at 3870(24).
[60] *Commission v Denmark* (302/86) [1988] E.C.R. 4627.
[61] *Cinéthèque* (Joined Cases 60/84 and 61/84) [1985] E.C.R. 2605.
[62] *Familiapress v Bauer Verlag* (C-368/95) [1997] E.C.R. I–3689.
[63] art.36 TFEU [30].
[64] *Dansk Supermarked v Imerco* (58/80) [1981] E.C.R. 181.
[65] *Bellon* (C-42/90) [1990] E.C.R. I–4863.

according to the Court, that those measures must be "reasonable".[66] This is where the expression the "rule of reason" finds its origin. The latter is sometimes identified with the *Cassis de Dijon* (120/78) judgment, but wrongly so. The basic rule of that judgment is, as was mentioned, that all goods legally produced and marketed in one Member State must be admitted in all the others. Furthermore, if Member States may, under strictly limited circumstances, prohibit the marketing of such products, this prohibition must be open to appeal under a procedure, which is readily accessible and can be completed within a reasonable period.

Except in the case of mandatory requirements, all restrictions on inter-State trade, resulting from national measures having an effect equivalent to quantitative restrictions, are and remain prohibited.[67] It should be noted that a measure, "does not escape this prohibition simply because the competent authority is empowered to grant exemptions to the restriction, even if the power is freely applied to imported products". This is particularly the case with measures, which discriminate between national and non-national products. In such a case even mandatory requirements cannot justify such measures. On the other hand, even measures which apply indistinctly the domestic and imported products can, as already indicated, have restrictive effects on the latter[68] if, in practice, they produce protective effects by favouring typical national products and, by the same token, operating to the detriment of certain types of products from other Member States.[69] In such a case the (potential) effect on inter-State trade is indirect.

It might appear that the Court modified its position in the now famous *Keck* and *Mithouard* (Joined Cases C-267/91 and C-268/91) cases,[70] especially since it used the words, "contrary to what has been ruled until now". It concerned a French law, which prohibits the resale of goods at a loss. The Court stated that this law did not constitute a "trading rule"; this expression was used to define measures having equivalent effect in the *Dassonville* (8/74) case. Although it was recognised that the law could limit the sale of imported products, the Court concluded that it constituted a measure, which applies without distinction to all operators and to all products within the national territory. But, more important, it was not a measure intended to regulate "trade", it was not therefore a "trading rule" as referred to in the definition given in *Dassonville* (8/74), but rather a marketing formality, in this case, a "selling arrangement"[71];

---

[66] *Dassonville* (8/74) quoted above, fn.42.

[67] *Fietje* (27/80) [1980] E.C.R. 3839 at 3854(14). In numerous cases the Court was called upon to rule on the compatibility of national measures. For instance, prohibited are: fees charged for veterinary inspection, *Bauhuis v Netherlands* (46/76) [1977] E.C.R. 20(51); freezing all prices at a level so low that imports can only be done at a loss, *Joseph Danis* (Joined Cases 16/79, 17/79, 18/79, 19/79, 20/79) [1979] E.C.R. 3327; systematic veterinary and public health inspection, *Denkavit* (251/78) [1979] E.C.R. 3369; mandatory description on products making it necessary to modify the label, *Fietje* (quoted above); fixing of minimum and maximum limits for dry matter contained in a product, *Kelderman* (130/80) [1981] E.C.R. 527; requirement as to indication of origin, *Commission v UK* (207/83) [1985] E.C.R 1207; allowing only certain national producers to use a specific shape of wine bottle, *Prantl* (16/83) [1984] E.C.R. 1299; health checks on animal feeding-stuffs, *Denkavit* (73/84) [1985] E.C.R. 1013. On the other hand the detailed declaration of imports and exports required by a directive is not prohibited: *Kieffer and Thill* (C-114/96) [1997] E.C.R. I–3629.

[68] *Officier van Justitie v Kaasfabriek Eyssen* (53/80) [1981] E.C.R. 409, where the national measures applied only to products destined for the domestic market.

[69] *Prantl* (16/83) [1984] E.C.R. 1299; [1985] 2 C.M.L.R. 238.

[70] *Keck* and *Mithouard* (Joined Cases C-267/91 and C-268/91) [1993] E.C.R. I–6097; [1995] 1 C.M.L.R. 101.

[71] This expression was used in *Semeraro* (Joined Cases C-418/93 etc.) closing of shops on Sundays and holydays, [1996] E.C.R. I–2975; [1996] 3 C.M.L.R. 648.

it did not therefore constitute a measure having equivalent effect to quantitative restrictions.[72]

The judgment met violent criticism as being a reversal of the standing case law and accepting hindrances to intra-Union trade, rather than liberating it. On close examination this criticism seems unfounded. Indeed, the Court, when asked to interpret the expression "measures having equivalent effect to quantitative restrictions", referred to State rules regulating intra-Union trade. The word "trade" cannot be applied to the "marketing" of products and, the object of the measures in question is to regulate the way products, whatever their origin, are marketed, i.e. sold within a given Member State. Such measures have nothing to do with the prohibition of measures having equivalent effect to quotas, i.e. impeding inter-State trade.

Such measures are justified under Union law and they reflect certain choices relating to particular national or regional socio-cultural characteristics. It is for the Member States to make those choices in compliance with the requirements of Union law.[73] The latter may not be used by market operators to oppose any State measure which regulates (limits) their commercial freedom.[74]

See, however, more recent case law, where the Court seems to suggest, for the application of the prohibition of measures with equivalent effect to quantitative restrictions, a three-category test: discriminatory measures, product-related requirements and all measures that hinder market access.[75]

3. PROHIBITION OF DISCRIMINATING OR PROTECTIVE TAXATION

No Member State may impose, directly or indirectly, on the products of other Member States any internal taxation of any kind in excess of that imposed directly or indirectly on similar domestic products, nor any internal taxation of such a nature as to afford indirect protection to other products.[76] The above-mentioned prohibition supplements, within the system of the Treaty, the provisions on the abolition of customs duties and charges having equivalent effect. Their aim is to ensure free movement of goods between the Member States under normal conditions of competition by the elimination of all forms of protection which results from the application of internal taxation which discriminates against products from other Member States.[77] What distinguishes a (protective) internal taxation from a charge having an effect equivalent to a customs duty is that the first is imposed on both imported and domestic products, whilst the second is imposed exclusively on the imported product.

The Court has defined as "similar" products, those which, "have similar characteristics and meet the same needs from the point of view of the consumer".[78]

---

[72] The Court's position was clearly restated in the judgment in the case mentioned in the preceding note, at I–3004(11–13) and also in *Punto Casa and PPV* (Joined Cases C-69/93 and C-258/93) [1994] E.C.R. I–2355.

[73] *Semeraro*, (C-418/93) (quoted above, fn.71).

[74] *Keck* and *Mithouard* cases (Joined Cases C-267/91 and C-268/91) (quoted above, fn.70).

[75] *Commission v Italy* (C-110/05) [2009] 10.02.09, and *Änklagaren v Mickelson and Roos* (C-142/05) [2009] E.C.R. 04.06.09.

[76] art.110 TFEU [90].

[77] *Commission v Italy* (169/78) [1980] E.C.R. at 399(3); [1981] 2 C.M.L.R. 673.

[78] *REWE* (45/75) [1976] E.C.R. 181; [1976] 2 C.M.L.R. 1.

Similarity is not a question of strictly identical nature, but of similarity and comparability in the use of the products. For instance, spirits obtained by the distillation of cereals and sugar-cane (imports) are similar to spirits obtained from wine and marc (domestic).[79] In such a case the taxes imposed in the imported products may not be higher than the one imposed on the domestic ones.

As for protective taxation, it affects products which, without being similar, are nevertheless in competition, even partial, indirect or potential, with national products. According to the Court the prohibition applies to a national system of taxation affecting differently imported whisky and domestic production of spirits obtained from wine. Such differences affect the market in the products in question by reducing the potential consumption of imported products.[80] Although the Treaty refers explicitly only to imports, the prohibition extends, according to the Court, also to exports.[81]

4. EXCEPTIONS TO THE FREE MOVEMENT OF GOODS

Every rule has its exceptions. They can be found either in the legal provisions laying down the rule, or in the interpretation of the rule by the courts. The same applies to the basic rule concerning the free movement of goods in the Union. The Treaty provides for several exceptions to this free movement.

The most important concerns the prohibition of quantitative restrictions and measures having equivalent effects.[82] Restrictions on imports, exports and transit of goods may be justified on grounds of public morality,[83] public policy or public security,[84] the protection of health and life of humans, animals and plants,[85] the protection of national treasures possessing artistic, historic or archaeological value[86] or the protection of industrial and commercial property.[87]

---

[79] *Commission v Italy* (169/78) [1980] E.C.R. at 409; [1981] 2 C.M.L.R. 673.

[80] *Cogis* (216/81) [1982] E.C.R. at 2701(11); [1983] 1 C.M.L.R. 685.

[81] *Larsen* (142/77) [1978] E.C.R. at 1557(21); [1979] 2 C.M.L.R. 680.

[82] art.36 TFEU [30]. See *Ahokainen and Leppik* (C-434/04) [2006] E.C.R. I-917: arts 34 and 36 do not necessarily preclude a prior authorisation for import.

[83] See *Regina v Henn and Darby* (34/79) [1979] E.C.R. 3795; [1980] 1 C.M.L.R. 246; prohibition of imports of pornographic articles.

[84] See *Regina v Thompson* (7/78) [1978] E.C.R. 2247; [1979] 1 C.M.L.R. 47: export ban on silver alloy coins.

[85] The Court considers that, "health and the life of humans ranks first among the interests protected by Art.36[30]": *De Peijper* (104/75) [1975] E.C.R. 613 at 635(15); [1976] 2 C.M.L.R. 271. This ground for exception has given rise to numerous Court rulings: see, for instance, *Brandsma* (C-293/94) [1996] E.C.R. I-3159, prohibition of import of biocidal products containing dangerous substances which have not yet been the subject of Union legislation is justified even if they have already been authorised in another Member State. In *Bellon* (C-42/90) [1990] E.C.R. I-4863, the Court added that a Member State may prohibit the marketing of a foodstuffs containing certain preservatives, provided that the principle of proportionality underlying the last sentence of art.36 TFEU [30] is observed and authorisation can be obtained under a procedure which is readily accessible and which can be completed within a reasonable period, where the additive meets a genuine need and represents no danger to public health.

[86] See *Commission v Italy* (7/68) [1968] E.C.R. 423. See also Directive 93/7 on the return of cultural objects unlawfully removed from the territory of a Member State [1993] O.J. L74/74 and Regulation 3911/92 on the harmonisation of controls on the export of cultural goods [1993] O.J. L395/1, codified version [2009] O.J. L39/1.

[87] See *Keurkoop v Nancy Keen Gifts* (144/81) [1982] E.C.R. 2853; [1983] 2 C.M.L.R. 47 and *Bristol-Myers Squibb v Paranova* (Joined Cases C-427/93, C-429/93 and C-436/93) [1996] E.C.R. I-3457; [1997] 1 C.M.L.R. 1151: the exhaustion principle does not apply in the cases provided for in Directive 89/104, art.7(2).

It should be noted that, according to the relevant Treaty provision, the prohibition or restriction, "may not constitute a means of arbitrary discrimination or disguised restriction on trade between Member States".[88] The Court also considered that those exceptions are not designed to reserve certain matters to the exclusive jurisdiction of the Member States. They permit national laws to derogate from the principle of the free movement of goods to the extent to which such derogation is and continues to be justified for the attainment of the objectives referred to[89] and where Union directives provide for the harmonisation of the national measures necessary to safeguard those objectives, recourse to the exceptions will automatically be excluded.

The TFEU provides that in case difficulties arise in a Member State, the Council may decide upon "measures appropriate to the economic situation",[90] in particular if they arise in the supply of certain products. Such measures could have effects equivalent to quantitative restrictions. Although this text was introduced by the EU Treaty and has not been tested yet in court, there seems to be no doubt that it would apply in situations similar to those created by the oil crises of the 1980s.[91]

Finally, mention must be made in this context of the possibility for Member States to take such measures as they consider necessary for the protection of the essential interests of their security which are connected with the production or trade in arms, munitions and war material. A list of the products benefiting from these exceptions was drawn up by the Commission on April 15, 1958 and has never been published.[92] Similarly, Member States may be called upon to take certain measures,[93] in the event of serious internal disturbances affecting the maintenance of law and order,[94] in the event of war, serious international tension constituting a threat of war, or in order to carry out obligations they have accepted for the purpose of maintaining peace and international security.[95] In both cases, the measures taken by the Member States may limit the free movement of goods.

In the latter case the Treaty simply provides that the Member States shall consult each other with a view to taking steps together to prevent the functioning of the common market being affected. If, in both cases, the measures affect competition in the common market, the Commission shall, together with the Member State concerned, examine how those measures can be adjusted. In case the Commission or a Member State considers that another Member State is making improper use of the powers provided in the above-mentioned circumstances, they may bring the matter directly before the Court, which shall give its rule in camera.[96]

Must also be mentioned in this context the obligation imposed upon the Commission, when drawing up proposals for establishing or ensuring the functioning of the internal market, "to take into account the extent of the effort that certain, economies showing differences in development will have to sustain" and the Commission may propose appropriate provisions. The Treaty adds that, "if

---

[88] art.34 TFEU [28]. See *Commission v UK* (40/82) [1982] E.C.R. 2793.
[89] *Tedeschi v Denkavit* (5/77) [1977] E.C.R. 1555.
[90] art.122(1) TFEU [100(1)].
[91] See, for instance, *Campus Oil Ltd v Minister for Industry and Energy* (72/83) [1984] E.C.R. 2727; [1984] 3 C.M.L.R. 544.
[92] art.346 TFEU [296].
[93] art.347 TFEU [297].
[94] One could think of the situation that prevailed in Northern Ireland.
[95] Think about the intervention in former Yugoslavia.
[96] art.348 TFEU [298].

these provisions take the form of derogations, they must be of a temporary nature and must cause the least disturbance to the functioning of the internal market.[97]

5. TECHNICAL STANDARDS

Another important element with regard to the free movement of goods are technical standards; it is up to the Commission to make sure that the Member States:

> "[R]ecognise the technical specifications, standards and rules applicable in other Member States and the validity of tests carried out by approved laboratories in other Member States offering adequate guarantees of reliability and efficacy" ("mutual recognition").[98]

The Commission continues to monitor the compliance by Member States with the principle of free movement of goods, mainly through the procedure under which the Member States have to inform the Commission of technical standards and regulations which they intend to introduce.[99] In case a Member State fails to notify the Commission, the national rule may not be invoked against an individual.[100] The other institutions of the Union[101] are, of course, also involved in the fight against old and new[102] obstacles to intra-Union trade. When the Commission is of the opinion that proposed standards or regulations will infringe the principle of free trade, it issues a "detailed opinion", which is binding upon the Member States concerned.

From the above it follows that standards and technical regulations play a very important role in the functioning of the internal market. Consequently, the Council laid down provisions on the introduction and implementation of technical regulations and standard,[103] and adopted resolutions on a new approach to technical harmonisation and standard[104] and on the role of European standardisation in the European economy.[105] The Commission, on the other hand, co-operates extensively with the European standardisation bodies.

---

[97] art.27 TFEU [15].

[98] General Report 1992, 48.

[99] Directive 83/189 [1983] replaced by Directive 98/34 [1998] O.J. L204/37 amended [1998] O.J. L217/18. See *CIA* (C-194/94) [1996] E.C.R. I–2201: definition of "technical regulations" under Directive 83/189 and *Donkersteeg* (C-37/99) [2000] E.C.R. I–10223, where the Court decided that a given legal provision was not a technical standard. *Schwibbert* (C-20/05) [2007] E.C.R. I-9447: the obligation to affix a distinctive sign to compact discs constitutes a technical regulation. See also list of authorities required to notify technical regulations in addition to the central governments.

[100] *Schwibbert* C-20/05, quoted above, fn.99.

[101] See Decision 3052/95 of Parliament and Council establishing a procedure for the exchange of information on national measures derogating from the principle of the free movement of goods within the Union [1995] O.J. L321/1. This Decision applied as from January 1, 1997.

[102] See Thirteenth Annual Report Monitoring the Application of Union Law 1995 (COM(96) 600 final, 26) where the Commission points out that with regard to the notification procedure under Directive 83/189, as amended by Directive 88/182, "the Commission received 382 drafts of technical regulations . . . This figure compares with 385 in 1993 and 389 in 1994—clear evidence that, despite the completion of the internal market at the end of 1992, Member States are still adopting large numbers of technical regulations which could undermine the single market and the integrity of the benefits it has brought to all sectors of the economy".

[103] Decision 80/45 [1980] O.J. L14/36.

[104] Resolution of May 7, 1985 [1985] O.J. C136/1.

[105] Resolution of June 18, 1992 [1992] O.J. C173/1.

The Union only lays down the essential safety requirements[106] to which products placed on the market must conform in order to enjoy freedom of movement. It is for the standardisation bodies to establish the necessary technical specifications. National administrations are obliged to assume that products manufactured in conformity with harmonised standards are in conformity with the essential requirements laid down by the directives.

6. Theory and Reality of the Free Movement of Goods

What explains that 17 years after the completion of the internal market on December 31, 1992, people and undertakings still experience difficulties when moving goods within the Union? The answer, of course, is not a simple one. In the first place there are the legal exceptions just examined. Secondly there are the many remaining measures having equivalent effect and not yet (entirely) eliminated, for instance, with regard to the completion of the internal market.

Obviously, there is a task here for all the interested parties: users, consumers and traders. They are in the front line, they are the ones who experience the negative effects of those measures; it is up to them to make the necessary representations to the national authorities and to the Commission. Where the latter is concerned, the Council has defined in a regulation what constitutes an "obstacle", and what the Member States and the Commission are supposed to do when an obstacle occurs. An obstacle involves both action and inaction on the part of a Member State. Any Member State must immediately inform the Commission. When the latter considers that an obstacle has occurred, it shall notify the Member State concerned and request it to take all necessary and proportionate measures to remove the obstacle. The Commission may publish the notification in the *Official Journal*.[107]

In order to solve informally disputes between consumers and enterprises on the one hand, and public authorities on the other, the Commission created the Internal Market Problem Solving Network (SOLVIT).[108] It is an online network which helps find out-of-court solutions to complaints by consumers and enterprises regarding the misappropriation of internal market laws by public authorities. Each Member State and the EFTA EEA countries have a SOLVIT centre which networks with the other centres forming part of the public administration in which it is located. Each centre is connected to a central database, which boasts a high level of transparency and makes it possible to monitor performance and the progress made. It has been operational since November 2003. It is free of charge and attempts to find solutions within a short 10-week deadline; if a centre regards the complaint received from a customer or enterprise as justified, it forwards it to the SOLVIT centre in the country where the problem has arisen for it to be solved within 10 weeks. The solutions proposed are not binding; if the customer does not consider the proposed solution acceptable, it may recommend that the dispute be resolved through the courts. The Member State concerned is responsible for settling the dispute, but if it does not take action, the Commission reserves the right to initiate proceedings.

---

[106] See, for instance, Directive on General Product Safety (Product Safety Directive) [1992] O.J. L228/24.
[107] Regulation 2679/98 [1998] O.J. L337/8. See also the Report from the Commission to the Council and Parliament on the application of the Regulation COM(2001).
[108] [2001] O.J. L 331/79.

See also the Resolution of the Council and the Representatives of the Governments of the Member States meeting within the Council on the free movement of goods.[109] In this Resolution the Member States undertake to do all within their powers, taking into account the protection of fundamental rights, including the right or freedom to strike, to maintain the free movement of goods. This followed a judgment of the Court[110] declaring that by failing to adopt all necessary and proportionate measures in order to prevent the free movement of fruits and vegetables from being obstructed by actions of private individuals, the French Republic had failed to fulfil its obligations under the Treaty provisions concerning the prohibition of measures having an effect equivalent to quantitative restrictions.[111]

There are, however, areas where the principle of mutual recognition cannot work, mainly on account of the complexity of the required regulations. In such cases, the Commission continues to make the necessary proposals for harmonising national laws. Examples are foodstuffs, motor vehicles and the chemical sector.

In July 2005, the Commission was able to report that: "Member States have made impressive progress in transposing Internal Market directives, leading to one of the best achievements ever." Unfortunately, too often, Member States still incorrectly apply internal market rules; only four Member States have managed to reduce the number of infringements cases against them.[112]

See also the Commission Communication from 2007 The Internal Market for Goods: a cornerstone for Europe's competitiveness.[113] In it the Commission ascertains that improving the internal market is an ongoing process requiring continuous updating, taking account of recent technological progress, the constantly changing global situation and the needs of consumers. The Commission noted that, notwithstanding considerable progress, there are still two major problems: some national technical rules still constitute important barriers to free trade within the Union, particularly in sectors that have not been harmonised and several Union rules are inconsistent and a burden to trade! Small and medium-sized enterprises are the most seriously affected by this problem.

The Commission proposes four initiatives:

- mutual recognition: a proposal for a regulation laying down procedures that the national authorities must follow in applying national technical rules to products lawfully marketed in another Member State—the regulation entered into force in May 2009[114];
- accreditation and surveillance: here also the Commission mentions a proposal for a regulation to ensure that non-compliant products are quickly withdrawn from the market and make it easier to assess the conformity of goods—the certification issued by accredited laboratories and testing facilities will have to be accepted throughout the Union;
- conformity: a proposal for a decision on a common framework for the marketing of products, aiming at streamlining the various product conformity assessment procedures;
- registration of motor vehicles: an interpretative communication on the procedure for registration of vehicles originating in another Member State.[115]

---

[109] [1998] O.J. L337/10.
[110] *Commission v France* (C-265/95) [1997] E.C.R. I-6959.
[111] art.34 TFEU [28].
[112] IP/05/961 18.07.05.
[113] COM(2007) 35 final—not published in the O.J.
[114] Regulation 764/08 [2008] O.J. L218/21.
[115] See also the Enterprise and Industry Directorate-General's website on mutual recognition.

In 2008, Parliament and Council adopted a legislative package aimed, on the one hand, at facilitating the free movement of goods by removing remaining obstacles[116] and, on the other hand, at strengthening competitiveness and consumer security. In 2009 the Commission published a list of *Product Contact Points* nominated by the Member States to deal with procedures relating to the application of certain national technical rules to products lawfully produced in another Member State.[117]

Also in 2009 the Commission published a Recommendation on measures to improve the functioning of the single market, stating, among other things, that a well-functioning single market is, "crucial in the context of economic recession to facilitate the recovery of the European economy" and recommends 10 steps to be taken by the Member States.[118]

Further Reading

Lorna Woods, *Free Movement of Goods and Services within the European Union* (Aldershot, Ashgate, 2004).
Peter Oliver, assisted by Malcolm Jarvis, *Free movement of goods in the European Union*, 4th edn (Sweet & Maxwell, 2003).
Panos Koutrakos, "In search of a common vocabulary in free movement of goods: the example of repackaging pharmaceuticals" (2003) E.L.Rev. 53.
Daniel Wilsher, "Does *Keck* discrimination make any sense? An assessment of the non-discrimination principle within the European Single Market" (2008) E.L.Rev.3.

---

[116] Regulation 764/08 [2008] O.J. L218/21, laying down procedures relating to the application of certain national technical rules to product lawfully marketed in another Member State, Regulation 765/08 [2008] O.J. L218/30, setting out the requirements for accreditation and market surveillance relating to the marketing of products and Decision 768/08 [2008] O.J. L218/82, on a common framework for the marketing of products.
[117] [2009] O.J. L185/6.
[118] [2009] O.J. L176/17.

Chapter Sixteen

The Free Movement of Persons

INTRODUCTION

The free movement of persons concerns the following categories:

- Citizens of the Union ("Citizens");
- workers;
- self-employed (to be examined under right of establishment and freedom to provide services);
- nationals from third countries (these shall be examined under "area of freedom, security and justice"); and
- students.

The free movement of persons constitutes one of the fundamental freedoms guaranteed by the Treaty and the relevant provisions may not, according to the Court, be interpreted restrictively[1]; furthermore, they have direct effect.[2]

While the provisions concerning the citizens[3] are to be found in Part Two of the TFEU, the "free movement of persons, services and capital", is the subject of Part Three under Title IV, which, however, omits in its Title, to mention the freedom of establishment; this is the more surprising since, from an economic integration point of view, the right of establishment is at least as important, if not more so, than the freedom to provide services.

Part Two of the TFEU[4] provides for the rights of "citizens" of the Union and, among others, their right, "to move and reside freely within the territory of the Member States",[5] subject to certain limitations and conditions. Title V[6] sets up an "area of freedom, security and justice", which, provides also for "policies on border checks, asylum and immigration".[7] The free movement of persons is thereby enlarged to encompass persons who are not citizens of the Union, while the free movement of "citizens", of "workers" and of "self employed persons" (professionals, tradespeople, etc.) concerns only nationals of a Member State.[8] The expression self-employed also covers legal persons, but only those which are formed in accordance with the laws of a Member State.[9] For these self-employed natural and legal persons free

---

[1] *Levin v Staatssecretaris van Justitie* (53/81) [1982] E.C.R. 1035 at 1049(3); [1982] 2 C.M.L.R. 454.
[2] *Royer* (48/72) [1976] E.C.R. 497 at 51231; [1976] 2 C.M.L.R. 619.
[3] arts 20–25 TFEU [17–22].
[4] arts 20–25 TFEU [17–22].
[5] art.21(1) TFEU [18(1)].
[6] arts 67–89 TFEU [61–69].
[7] arts 77–80 TFEU [97–100].
[8] For workers see arts 45–48 TFEU [39(2)] and for self-employed, see freedom of establishment: arts 49–55 TFEU [43,3 and 48,1], and freedom to provide services: arts 56–62 TFEU [49,1].
[9] art.54 TFEU [48].

movement exists, as indicated, in "freedom of establishment" and in "freedom to provide services"; these freedoms are examined below, in Chs 17 and 18.

Consequently, the term "person" in the Treaty covers quite an array of natural and legal persons, each with their own specific rights and obligations: citizens, workers, self-employed persons, companies, nationals of third countries and students. Each category shall be examined separately hereunder, either in this chapter or in the following ones.

It should be remembered that Union law only applies when trans-frontier activities are involved. In other words, Treaty provisions cannot be invoked in purely national situations.[10]

I. THE FREE MOVEMENT OF CITIZENS

The TFEU establishes the citizenship of the Union by providing that every person holding the nationality of a Member State shall be a citizen of the Union and adds that this citizenship complements and does not replace national citizenship.[11] The Treaty furthermore provides, as already mentioned, that every citizen of the Union, "shall have the right to move and reside freely within the territory of the Member States", but that those rights, "shall be exercised in accordance with the conditions and limits defined by the Treaties and by the measures adopted there under".[12] This right is mentioned once again in the next Treaty provision.[13]

The measures referred to may be adopted by Parliament and the Council in accordance with the ordinary legislative procedure[14] with a view to facilitating the exercise of these rights.[15] Various measures were indeed "adopted to give effect" to the right of Union citizens to move and reside in the Member States.[16] Some of these measures concern also the possibility for a Member State to deport citizens for reasons of public policy, public security and public health.[17]

Under Union law applicable since 2004, Union citizens have the right of residence in the territory of another Member State:

- for a period of up to three months without any condition or formalities other than holding a valid passport or valid identity card;

---

[10] See *Regina v Sanders* (175/78) [1979] E.C.R. 1129 at 1135(10); [1979] 2 C.M.L.R. 216, where the Court held that art.45 TFEU [39] does not prevent a Member State from limiting the free movement of persons within their own territory. See also *Moser v Land Baden-Württemberg* (180/83) [1984] E.C.R. 2539; [1984] 3 C.M.L.R. 720, where it concerned a national who had never resided or worked in another Member State and could not, therefore, invoke Union law (no cross-border element).

[11] art.20(2)1(a) TFEU [17(1)].

[12] art.20(2)2 TFEU [17(1)]. The Court determined that this provision precludes legislation under which a Member State refuses to pay certain benefits granted to surviving spouses of victims of war solely because they are domiciled in certain specific Member State [2008] E.C.R. 04.12.08.

[13] art.21(1) TFEU [18].

[14] art.289(1) TFEU.

[15] art.21 TFEU [18(2)]; see *Grunkin* (C-353/06) E.C.R. I-7639: art.18 precludes a Member State, in applying national law, from refusing to recognise a child's surname, as determined and registered in a second Member State in which the child was born and has been resident since it was born.

[16] For instance Directive 2004/38 [2004] O.J. L158/77; see *Jipa* (C-33/07) [2008] E.C.R. I-5157: Member State may restrict travel to another Member State on account of "illegal residence" there, provided the personal conduct constitutes a genuine, present and sufficiently serious threat.

[17] Directive 64/221 [1964] O.J. L850, replaced by Directive 2004/38 [2004] O.J. L158/77. See *Commission v Netherlands* (C-50/06) [2006] E.C.R. I-4383, where the Court stated that the right to stay in another Member State is not limited to those citizens who reside there legally.

- for a period of longer than three months, if they:
  - — are workers or self-employed persons (see below)[18], or
  - — have sufficient resources for themselves and their family members and sickness insurance cover[19] not to become an unreasonable burden on the social assistance system of the host State, or
  - — are enrolled in an establishment accredited and financed by the host State to follow a course of study, including vocational training and have comprehensive sickness insurance cover and sufficient resources for themselves and their family not to become a burden on the social assistance system of the host State, or
  - — are family members (even when not a national of a Member State[20]) accompanying or joining a Union citizen who satisfies the above conditions;
- for permanent residence: citizens who have resided in the host Member State, in compliance with the conditions laid down in the Directive, during a continuous period of five years without becoming subject to an expulsion measure.[21]

Union citizens must be able to prove that they are indeed citizens of one of the Member States; this proof normally consists of a valid identity card or a passport, but the identity and nationality may also, according to the Court, be brought, without ambiguity, by other means.[22]

Besides the right to move and reside freely within the territory of the Member States, citizens have the right to vote and stand as candidate in municipal elections in the Member State of residence of which they are not a national, under the same conditions as nationals of that State.[23] Detailed arrangements were adopted by the Council acting unanimously in accordance with a special legislative procedure[24] and after consulting Parliament.[25] According to the Treaty, these arrangements may provide for derogations where warranted by problems specific to a Member State.

Citizens also have the right, when residing in a Member State of which they are not a national, to vote and to stand as candidate in elections to the European Parliament[26]; detailed arrangements are adopted by the Council under the above conditions.[27]

Furthermore, citizens have the right to enjoy, in the territory of a third country in which the Member State of which they are a national is not represented, the protection of the diplomatic and consular authorities of any Member State on the same conditions as the nationals of that State.[28] Member States must adopt the

---

[18] This is redundant and confusing since those persons enjoy specific rights under their own freedoms.

[19] See *Nerkowska* (C-499/06) [2008] E.C.R. I-3993 where the Court determined that residence in the country of origin may not be required under art.21 TFEU for the payment by the latter country of a disability pension to civilian victims of war or repression.

[20] See *Metock and others* (C-127/08) [2008] E.C.R. I-6241 where the Court decided that a Member State may not require that the spouse of a citizen residing in a Member State of which he is not a national, has resided legally in another Member State before entering the host State and independently of the location and date of their marriage and the way in which the citizen entered the host Member State.

[21] Directive 2004/38 [2004] O.J. L158/77, Preamble (17).

[22] *Oulane* (C-215/03) [2005] E.C.R. I-1215.

[23] arts 20(2)(b) and 22(1) TFEU [17 and 19].

[24] art.289(2) TFEU.

[25] Directive 94/80 [1994] O.J. L368/38. See *Commission v Belgium* (C-323/97) [1998] E.C.R. I-4291: failure to adopt national legislation in time.

[26] arts 20(2)(b) and 22(1) TFEU [17 and 19].

[27] Directive 93/109 [1993] O.J. L329/34.

[28] art 20(2)(C) TFEU [17].

necessary provisions and start the international negotiations to secure this protection.[29] The Council, acting in accordance with a special legislative procedure and after consulting Parliament may adopt directives establishing the co-ordination and co-operation measures necessary to facilitate such protection.[30]

Finally, citizens have the right to petition Parliament,[31] to apply to the European Ombudsman[32] and to address the institutions and advisory bodies of the Union in any of the Treaty languages and to obtain a reply in the same language.[33]

Citizens' Initiative

Not less than one million citizens who are nationals of a significant number of Member States may take the initiative of inviting the Commission, within the framework of its powers, to submit any appropriate proposal on matters where citizens consider that a legal act of the Union is required for the purpose of implementing the Treaties.[34] Provisions for the procedure and conditions required for such initiative—including the minimum number of Member States from which the citizens must come—shall be adopted by Parliament and the Council by regulation in accordance with the ordinary legislative procedure.[35]

The Council, acting unanimously, in accordance with a special legislative procedure,[36] may, following a three-yearly report by the Commission, adopt provisions to strengthen or to add to the above rights; these provisions shall enter into force after their approval by the Member States in accordance with their respective constitutional requirements.[37]

Free movement of citizens was also facilitated, in some way, by the issue of a "European Passport",[38] i.e. a passport of uniform pattern (format and colour) that replaced the national passports. Presently the passports of all citizens of the Union are "same-looking EU passports".

Although it is not limited to "citizens", mention is made here of the Schengen arrangements. Very important from a legal point of view for the free movement of persons within the Union, was the implementation of the Schengen Agreement of 1985[39] on the gradual abolition of controls at the common (inner) frontiers of the signatories and of the 1990 Convention Implementing the Schengen Agreement

---

[29] See European Union guidelines on the implementation of the consular Lead State concept [2008] O.J. C317/6.

[30] art.23 TFEU [20]. See Decision regarding protection [1995] O.J. L314/73.

[31] art.227 TFEU [194].

[32] art 228 TFEU [195].

[33] art 20(2)(d) TFEU [17].

[34] art.11(4) EU.

[35] art.24,1 TFEU [21]. For the ordinary legislative procedure see art. 294 TFEU [251].

[36] art.289(2) TFEU.

[37] art.25,2 TFEU [22].

[38] Several Resolutions were adopted by the Representatives of the Governments of the Member States meeting within the Council; [1981] O.J. C241/1, amended by [1995] O.J. C 200/1; [1982] O.J. C179/1; [1986] O.J. C185/1. See Resolution of the Representatives of the Governments of the Member States, meeting within the Council of June 8, 2004 supplementary to the resolution of June 23, 1981, June 30, 1982, July 14, 1986 and July 10, 1995 concerning the introduction of a passport of uniform pattern [2004] O.J. C245/1.

[39] Agreement of June 14, 1985; originally it fell outside the Union framework and was signed by the Benelux countries, Germany and France, which published the agreement, see for instance Moniteur Belge of April 29, 1986 (the text can also be obtained from the Benelux Secretariat in Brussels, fax 02/513.42.06), and CISA.

(CISA).[40] To this was added in 2005 the Schengen III Agreement between Belgium, Germany, Spain, France, Luxembourg, the Netherlands and Austria concerning the deepening of cross-border co-operation in the fields of the fight against terrorism, cross-border criminal activities and illegal migration, it enables the signatories to exchange all data regarding DNA fingerprints; the contracting parties having made a commitment to create and maintain national DNA analysis databases for the purpose of prosecuting criminal offences.

The Treaty of Amsterdam integrated the "Schengen *acquis*"[41] into, "the framework of the European Union".[42] The Schengen *acquis* comprises the Agreement of 1985 between the Benelux, Germany and France, the CISA, the Accession Protocols for Italy, Spain, Portugal, Greece, Austria, Denmark, Finland and Sweden, Ireland and the UK (the latter two adhered to parts of Schengen), Iceland and Norway,[43] Switzerland,[44] where the full application took place in 2008[45], Liechtenstein[46] and the 10 new Member States which adhered from the moment of their accession[47] and also the Decisions and Declarations of the Executive Committee and those of the Central Group.

In order to protect against terrorism and other crimes, the Schengen Information System (SIS) was set up; it allows the exchange of data on people's identities and description of objects stolen or lost. Later on, new functions were attributed to the SIS,[48] which became SIS II.[49] The Commission laid down the network requirements for the SIS II[50] and adopted the SIRENE manual and other implementing measures for the second generation SIS.[51] See Regulation on migration from SIS I+ to SIS II.[52] See also the Schengen Borders Code, a Union Code on the rules governing the movement of persons across borders, the Visa Information System (VIS)[53] and the Schengen consultation network.[54]

The integration of the Schengen *acquis* into the European Treaties is in itself an interesting legislative exercise worth looking at. The Treaty of Amsterdam provides that the *acquis*, which literally means everything that was acquired in the way of applicable provisions by the law of the signatories to the Schengen agreements,

[40] [2000] O.J. L239/19. See *Kretzinger* (C-288/05) [2007] E.C.R. I-6441 concerning the "*ne bis in idem*" principle. See also *Bourquain* (C-297/07) [2008] E.C.R. 11.12.08, where the Court held that the *ne bis in idem* principle also applies when a first sentence could never have been directly enforced.
[41] Definition of "Schengen *aquis*" in Annex 2 to the EU and EC Treaties [1997] O.J. C340/96 and Protocol No.19 to the TFEU on the Schengen *acquis* integrated into the framework of the Union.
[42] Consolidated version of the Treaty establishing the European Union, Protocol (No.2) integrating the Schengen *acquis* into the framework of the European Union [1997] O.J. C340/93.
[43] [1999] O.J. L176/31.
[44] [2004] O.J. L370/78; see agreement between the European Union and the Swiss Confederation of the latter's association with the implementation, application and development of the of the Schengen *acquis* [2008] O.J. L453/1
[45] [2008] 0.J. L127/15.
[46] [2008] O.J. L83/5.
[47] However, a decision of the EU Council is needed before controls at their borders are lifted.
[48] [2005] O.J. L68/44.
[49] Regulation 2424/2001 on the development of the second generation SIS [2001] O.J. L328/4, amended by Regulation 1988/2006 and Decision 2007/533 on the establishment, operation and use of the second generation Schengen Information System [2007] O.J. L205/63.
[50] [2007] O.J. L79/29.
[51] [2008] O.J. L123/1. See [2008] O.J. L149/78 on declassifying Annex IV.
[52] [2008] O.J. L299/1.
[53] Regulation 562/06 [2006] O.J. L105/1, amended [2009] O.J. L35/56 and [2009] O.J. L97/60; see List of residence permits referred to in art.2(15) [2006] O.J. C247/1. See Notification of the Swiss Confederation concerning penalties for unauthorised crossing [2009] O.J. C3/11.
[54] [2008] O.J. L328/38, the network was amended [2009] O.J. L353/49.

shall immediately apply, from the date of entry into force of the Amsterdam Treaty, as Union law in those same States.[55] However, since those provisions were not adopted in conformity with the provisions of the then applicable EC Treaty, the Council, acting unanimously, had to determine, in conformity with the relevant provisions of the EU and EC Treaties, "the legal basis for each of the provisions or decisions which constitute the Schengen *acquis*".[56] In the meantime the *acquis* was regarded as acts based on Title VI of the EU Treaty at that time: "Provisions on Co-operation in the Field of Justice and Home Affairs." This name of the so-called third pillar of the European Union was replaced, in conformity with the Treaty of Amsterdam, by "Provisions on Police and Judicial Co-operation in Criminal Matters".[57] These provisions are now to be found in Title V of the TFEU.[58]

One of the consequences of this integration of the Schengen *acquis* into the Treaty is that the Court of Justice can be called upon to interpret the Schengen Agreement via a preliminary question. This allowed the Court to determine, for instance, that when a citizen travels within the Union, his spouse who is a national of a third country is covered to a large extend by the freedom of movement, but may be refused entry on grounds of public policy or public safety. However, where such a person for whom alerts are entered into the Schengen Information System (SIS) for the purpose of refusing entry, a Member State must verify whether the presence of such person constitutes a genuine, present and sufficiently serious threat affecting one of the fundamental interests of society before refusing it entry into the Schengen area. The Court clearly stated that the Schengen Protocol confirms that the Schengen *acquis* is applicable only and in so far as it is compatible with European Union Law.[59] The Court also holds that the concept of public policy within the meaning of the 1964 Directive[60] (see below under: Exceptions to the Free Movement of Workers) does not correspond to that of the CISA. In the latter case, entry may be refused solely on the ground of a previous conviction carrying a penalty-involving deprivation of liberty of at least one year.[61]

II. THE FREE MOVEMENT OF WORKERS

The three freedoms: free movement of workers,[62] the right of establishment[63] and the right to provide services[64] do not confer unlimited rights (no right is unlimited).

---

[55] art.2(1) Treaty of Amsterdam. See Decision 99/435 of May 20 [2000] O.J. L239/1 for the purpose of determining the legal basis for each of the provisions or decisions which constitute the *acquis*, the Decision actually determining the legal basis [1999] O.J. L176/1 and 17, and the Council act on the Schengen *acquis* as referred to in art.1(2) of Decision 99/435 [1999] O.J. L176/1; see also [2000] O.J. L239/1.

[56] See Decision 99/435 [1999] O.J. L176/3 concerning the definition of the Schengen *acquis*; see *Gösütok and Brugge* (Joined Cases C-187/01 and C-385/01) [2003] E.C.R. I–1345 on the application of the *ne bis in idem* principle provided in the CISA; see also [2000] O.J. L239/3.

[57] arts 29–39 EU, consolidated text published in [1997] O.J. C340/162.

[58] arts 67–89 TFEU [69 and 29–12 EU]. See Regulation 539/2001 listing the third countries whose nationals must be in possession of visas when crossing the external borders of Member States and those whose nationals are exempted from that requirement [2001] O.J. L81/1.

[59] *Commission v Spain* (C-503/03) [2006] E.C.R. I-3969.

[60] Directive 64/221 [1964] O.J. 850, replaced by Directive 2004/38 [2004] O.J. L158/77.

[61] art.96(2)(a) CISA.

[62] arts 45–48 TFEU [39–42].

[63] arts 49–54 TFEU [43–48]

[64] arts 56–62 TFEU [49–55]

Workers' rights and the right of establishment and the freedom to provide services in other Member States exist mainly in the right for the interested person or undertaking, to be treated in the host State in the same way as the nationals of that State: the fundamental principle of equal treatment.

Without going into details, each one of those three freedoms confers, generally speaking, on the persons (and enterprises) concerned the right to enter the territory of another Member State, to reside there with their families, to exercise their activities under the same conditions as the nationals of the host Member State and to remain there afterwards. Those three freedoms must be considered, according to the Court, as based on the same principles, where entry, residence and treatment are concerned they may not be interpreted restrictively[65] and they have direct effect.[66]

However, it must be clear that for a worker, a tradesman, a professional or an undertaking to move from one place to another within their own country, is not quite the same thing as moving to and operating in another country. She or he is bound to face new administrative requirements resulting from the simple fact that each Member State has its own legal system, language and habits. Since there are differences, the implementation of the principle of equal treatment would not suffice; the Treaty therefore provides for a number of specific rights that will be examined hereunder for the corresponding freedoms.

It should be noted that discrimination occurs when two parties in the same position are treated differently, but also when the same treatment is applied to parties in different positions. Can one say that a worker, tradesman, professional or undertaking from another Member State is "in the same position" as the nationals of the host country? Doesn't the fact of being foreign constitute, necessarily, a certain difference, that might justify a slightly different treatment? This is the case, for instance, with national rules concerning the control of foreigners. Indeed, the Court found that, "the application of such legislation, where it is based upon objective factors, cannot constitute discrimination on ground of nationality" prohibited under the Treaty.[67]

The principle of freedom of movement of workers forms, according to the Court, one of the foundations of the Union and, consequently, has to be given a broad interpretation.[68] Access to employment in another Member State is a fundamental aspect of the free movement of persons within the EU. A wide area of labour mobility represents a large number of opportunities for workers to find work and for the employer to find people with adequate skills, thereby enhancing employment and economic growth. The purpose is to open European labour markets to all EU workers, which is one of the tangible aspects of European integration. As shall be seen, the right of access to national labour markets includes a right to equal treatment with respect to working conditions, as well as the right to social, economic and cultural integration of the migrant worker and her or his family in the host State.[69] Workers can be defined as "employed persons". This means that the Treaty does not know the category "employees"; consequently, a bank teller and a university professor, for instance, are both workers and so are football players[70] as far as the TFEU is concerned. There is, however, a basic condition in order

---

[65] *Levin v Staatssecretaris van Judtitie* 53/81 [1982] E.C.R. 1035.
[66] *Royer* (48/75) [1976] E.C.R. 497.
[67] art.18 TFEU [12], see *Watson and Bellemann* (118/75) [1976] E.C.R. 1185.
[68] *Commission v Belgium* (C-344/95) [1997] E.C.R. I–1035.
[69] *Royer* (48/75) (quoted above, fn.66).
[70] *Bosman* (C-415/93) [1995] E.C.R. I–4921; [1996] 1 C.M.L.R. 645.

to be recognised as a worker: the person in question must be covered by social security. There is a definite link between worker and social security and, a definition of worker is to be found in the regulation on the application of social security schemes to employed persons and their families moving within the Union.[71]

The definition of worker gave rise to an abundant case law of the Court, which has always maintained that the term, "has a Union meaning and, inasmuch as it defines the scope of one of the fundamental freedoms of the Union, must be interpreted broadly".[72] The Court furthermore indicates that the concept must be defined in accordance with objective criteria which distinguish the employment relationship by reference to the rights and duties of the persons concerned and, that, "the essential feature of an employment relationship is that for a certain period of time, a person performs services for, and under the direction of, another person, in return for which he receives remuneration".[73]

However, the Court added that freedom of movement is guaranteed only for persons pursuing or wishing to pursue an economic[74] activity and that, consequently, it only covers the pursuit of an effective and genuine activity. The latter is defined by the Court as excluding, "activities on such a small scale as to be regarded as purely marginal and ancillary".[75] Clearly, it is up to the national authorities to decide whether or not an activity fulfils those criteria. The Court also added that neither productivity nor the origin of the funds used for the remuneration can have any consequence with regard to the question whether or not the person is to be regarded as a worker. The same applies to the nature of the legal relationship between the employee and the employer.[76] Furthermore, the employment must not necessarily be full-time employment: free movement also applies to persons who pursue an activity on a part-time basis, even if, by virtue of that fact, that person obtains a remuneration lower than the minimum guaranteed wage in a given sector.[77] The Court also determined that the motives which may have prompted a worker to seek employment are of no account and must not be taken into consideration.[78]

1. OBSTACLES TO THE FREE MOVEMENT OF WORKERS AND THEIR REMEDIES

The term "obstacles"[79] is probably better than "barriers", since the latter might convey the idea that movement is prevented altogether. However, in the case of persons, the same principle applies as the one defined by the Court in the case of the free movement of goods, namely that the prohibition of the Treaty also covers actions which make the movement between Member States simply more

---

[71] Regulation 1408/71, [1971] O.J. L149/2; see art.1(a)(i) modified many times, for instance, [2008] O.J. L177/1, but still is, after 39 years, the legal basis for the application of social security to migrant workers within the Union.

[72] *Bettray v Staatssecretaris van Justitie* (344/87) [1989] E.C.R. 1621 at 1644(11); [1991] 1 C.M.L.R. 459.

[73] *Bettray* (344/87) at 1645(12), above, fn.72.

[74] See *Walrave and Koch v Association Union Cycliste Internationale* (36/74) [1974] E.C.R. at 1405(5); [1975] 1 C.M.L.R. 320, concerning the nationality of the motorcycle pacemakers and the cyclists. A minister of the Church is a typical example of a person pursuing a non-economic activity.

[75] *Levin* (53/81) (quoted above, fn.65), at 1050(17).

[76] *Sotgiu v Deutsche Bundespost* (152/73) [1974] E.C.R. 153.

[77] See also *Jenkins v Kingsgate* (96/80) [1981] E.C.R. at 911(11); [1981] 2 C.M.L.R. 24.

[78] *Levin* (53/81) (quoted above, fn.65), at 1052(22).

[79] This is the term used in Regulation 1612/68 on the freedom of movement of workers within the Union [1968] O.J. L257/2, recitals, para.6, modified [2004] O.J. L158/77.

difficult than movement within a given State. It is interesting to read what the Commission published on the Internet concerning free movement of workers.

"Historically, cross border mobility in the EU has been low. But even today[80] free movement is not yet a daily reality for Europe's citizens. Presently around five million European citizens [out of a total of about 350 million at the time] reside in another Member State. Less than two per cent of the working population in the Union consists of people from one Member State working in another, although there are considerable variations between the Member States.

While much has been achieved with regard to the free movement of workers, there is still much to be done in order to guarantee the effectiveness of the right to practice a profession in another Member State under the same conditions as nationals of that State. The way in which rules and regulations are applied raises a number of difficulties. Moreover, there is a lack of administrative flexibility towards the special situation of migrants and the level of co-operation between Member States is sometimes insufficient. There is a lack of knowledge and information about the rights and opportunities for workers moving from one Member State to another".

This sobering assessment will hopefully underline the importance of understanding the Union provisions applicable in this field.

The main obstacles to the free movement of workers within the Union are:

- discriminatory conditions of work and employment for non-nationals;
- law, regulations and administrative action, which impose on workers from other Member States obligations which are different from those governing nationals; and
- lack of co-ordination among the social security systems with harmful consequences for the migrant worker.

As shall be seen hereunder, the Treaty provides for remedies for each one of those obstacles. Those remedies have been expressed in the form of rights granted to any person who desires to exercise an economic activity as an employed person and is a national of one of the Member States.[81] Those rights have been implemented by directives and regulations issued by the Council and, since the EU Treaty, by Parliament acting jointly with the Council.[82]

With regard to the free movement of workers, the Treaty starts[83] by providing in a general way that it, "shall entail the abolition of any discrimination based on nationality between workers of the Member States as regards employment, remuneration and other conditions of work and employment".[84] This statement is followed by a list of rights, which shall be briefly examined hereafter. Before doing so it should be noted that the rights enumerated in that list are not simply examples of what is meant by non-discrimination. Indeed, equality of treatment is one thing, freedom of movement is another,[85] although it is obvious that the latter

---

[80] This text was published in September 1998.

[81] Regulation 1612/68 on freedom of movement of workers within the Union [1968] J.O. L275/2, amended [1992] O.J. L245/1. See *Martinez Sala* (C-85/96) [1998] E.C.R. I–2691.

[82] See art.46 TFEU [40] which refers to the ordinary legislative procedure [procedure referred to in art. 294 TFEU].

[83] art.45(2) TFEU [39(2)].

[84] The use of this term indicates that the list that follows is not exhaustive.

[85] See *Rutili v Minister for the Interior* (36/75) [1975] E.C.R. at 1219(27).

would have practically no meaning without the former. The TFEU provides that the worker enjoys the following rights:

1. the right, "to accept offers of employment actually made".[86] This, however, does not mean that the worker, in order to benefit from the freedom to move to another Member State, must have in his possession a duly executed employment contract. Freedom of movement also extends to persons who, "seriously wish to pursue activities as an employed person"[87];

2. the right, "to move freely within the territory of Member States".[88] This means the right to remain in any Member State[89] for the purpose of employment.

   Taking into account the fact that the right to enter and to move can also be claimed by a person looking for a job, the question was raised how long this person could go on looking. The answer given by the Court is six months, subject to appeal, unless the person in question provides evidence that she or he is continuing to seek employment and that there is a genuine chance of being engaged.[90] Workers must be admitted on the basis of an official identification,[91] i.e. an identity card or passport, showing, in particular, their nationality[92] since free movement can only be claimed by workers who are citizens of the Union; no visas may be required;

3. the right, "to stay in the Member State for the purpose of employment".[93] This requires the national authorities of the host State to deliver to the worker a residence permit in the form prescribed by Union law.[94] This permit constitutes proof of the worker's right to reside in the Member State in question; indeed, this right is not conferred by the issue of the permit, it derives directly from Union law.[95] The worker must, however, report his presence to the national authorities in conformity with national law, the Court having determined that a Member State has the right to be informed about the presence of foreigners on its territory,[96] but added that the time limit for reporting and the penalties for failing to do so had to be reasonable;

4. the right, "to employment in accordance with the provisions governing employment of nationals".[97] This is, by afar, the most important right of the migrant worker; it is the embodiment of the principle of equal treatment whatever the nationality of the worker; it applies, according to the Treaty,

---

[86] art.45(3)(a) TFEU [39(3)(a)].

[87] *Levin* (53/81) (quoted above, fn.65), at 1052(21).

[88] art.45(3)(b) TFEU [39(3)(b)].

[89] Directive 68/360 on the abolition of restrictions on movement and residence within the Union of workers of Member States and their families [1968] J.O. L257/13, [1968], replaced by Directive 2004/38 [2004] O.J. L158/77. The provisions of that Directive are directly applicable. See *Commission v Netherlands* (C-398/06) [2008] E.C.R. I-56*: requiring durable resources from pensioners infringes this Directive See also Directive 90/364 and Directive 90/365 on the right of residence for employees and self-employed persons who have ceased their occupational activity.

[90] *Queen v Immigration Appeal Tribunal* (C-292/89) [1991] E.C.R. 1745 at 1780(18); [1991] 2 C.M.L.R. 373, where the Court found that an obligation to automatically leave after three months infringes Union law.

[91] *Giagounidis* (C-376/89) [1991] E.C.R. I-1069; [1993] 1 C.M.L.R. 537.

[92] art.2(2) Directive 68/360, replaced by Directive 2004/38 [2004] O.J. L158/77.

[93] art.45(3)(c) TFEU [39(3)(c)].

[94] art.45(3) TFEU, Annex.

[95] *Royer* (48/75) [1976] E.C.R. 497; [1976] 2 C.M.L.R. 619. For the meaning of "residence", see *Reibold v Bundesanstalt für Arbeit* (C-216/89) [1990] E.C.R. I-4163.

[96] *Watson and Belmann* (118/75) [1976] E.C.R. 1185; [1976] 2 C.M.L.R. 552.

[97] art.45(3)(c) TFEU [39(3)(C)].

to, "employment, remuneration and other conditions of work and employment".[98] It means, among other things, that he must have access to all economic activities, including professional football,[99] within the territory of the host State under the same conditions as the nationals. Save exceptions, no economic activity may be reserved for nationals. And, as mentioned already, not only access, but also the conditions of employment must be the same as those which apply to nationals.[100] This concerns particularly the remuneration and other conditions of work and employment.[101] This also means that no overt or covert discriminatory criteria may be applied to workers from other Member States. Individual and collective employment agreements are subject to all the above rules.[102]

Important are the words "and other conditions of work and employment": they fulfil a role comparable to the terms used by the Treaty with regard to the free movement of goods: "and charges/measures having an equivalent effect" prohibited with regard to customs duties and quantitative restrictions. It allowed the Council in its implementing legislation and the Court in its answers to preliminary questions, to give a broad interpretation of the rights covered by the free movement of workers. They include conditions as regards dismissal, reinstatement or re-employment, social and tax advantages, access to training in vocational schools and retraining centres, membership of trade unions and the exercise of the rights attached thereto, including the right to vote, eligibility for workers' representative bodies in the undertaking. The migrant worker shall also enjoy all the rights and benefits accorded to national workers in matters of housing, including ownership;

5. the right, "to be joined by his family"; although this right is not expressly provided for in the Treaty chapter on workers, it is obvious that preventing the family from joining the migrant worker would constitute an obstacle to his freedom of movement, which it is the Council's obligation[103] to abolish.[104] It should be noted that the freedom to be joined by the family, applies irrespective of the nationality of the members of this family.[105] However, in order for a family member who is a national of a non-Member State to be allowed to join the worker, that family member must have been previously residing lawfully in the Union,[106] even if that member did not have a right of residence under the national law of the Member State of which the worker is a national.[107] In case the worker returns to his Member State of which he

---

[98] art.45(2) TFEU [39(2)].

[99] *Dona v Mantero* (13/76) [1976] E.C.R. 1333; [1976] 2 C.M.L.R. 578.

[100] See Regulation 2000/78 establishing a general framework for equal treatment in employment and occupation [2000] O.J. L303/16.

[101] art.45(2) TFEU [39(2)].

[102] Regulation 1612/68 [1968] O.J. L 257/2, on freedom of movement of workers within the Union; incorporated [1994] O.J. L1/325.

[103] art.46 TFEU [40].

[104] See, for instance, Directive 68/360, quoted above, and Regulation 1612/68, quoted above.

[105] See *MRAX* (C-459/99) [2002] E.C.R. I–6591; the case was complicated by the fact that the worker was not in possession of a valid passport or identity card. See also *Baumbast* (C-413/99) [2002] E.C.R. I–7091, where the Court had to consider whether a person continued to enjoy the protection of Union law after it ceased to qualify as a member of the family of the migrant worker; she had custody of the children. Since the children had the right of residence, the mother had to have it also on the basis of her right to respect for family life provided for in art.8 of the European Convention for the Protection of Human rights.

[106] *JIA* (C-1/05) [2007] I-1.

[107] *Minister voor vreemdelingen Zaken v Eind* (C-291/05) [2007] E.C.R. 11.12.07.

is a national, the accompanying family member who is a national of a third country has the right to accompany the worker in that Member State even if the worker does not there exercise a real and effective activity.[108]

By "family", in this context, is meant the worker's spouse and their descendants who are under the age of 21 years or are dependents,[109] and dependent relatives in the ascending line of the worker and his spouse.[110] Furthermore, the spouse and the children under the age of 21 years or dependent on him shall have the right to take up any activity as an employed person throughout the territory of the same State, even if they are not nationals of any Member State. Important here is the term "dependent"; it means the family member needs the material support of the worker or his or her spouse in order to meet their essential needs in their State of origin or in the State from which they come at the time they apply to join the worker. Proof of the need for material support may be adduced by any appropriate means, but a mere undertaking from the worker or his or her spouse to support the family member concerned need not be regarded as establishing the existence of real dependence.[111]

The worker's children shall be admitted to the host State's general educational,[112] apprenticeship and vocational training[113] courses under the same conditions as the nationals of that State, if such children are residing in its territory.[114] They must also have access to special employment programmes.[115] Generally speaking, the rights constituting the free movement of workers, especially the right of entry, movement and residence also apply to the worker's family, even if the latter are not nationals of a Member State[116];

---

[108] *Minister voor vreemdelingen Zaken v Eind* (C-291/05), above, fn. 107.

[109] *Confédération Générale du Travail E.A.* (C-1/05) [2007] E.C.R. I-1 where the Court held that, "the proof of the need for material support may be adduced by any appropriate means".

[110] art.10(1) Regulation 1612/68 [1968] 257/2.

[111] *JIA* (C-1/05) [2007] E.C.R. I-1.

[112] Directive 77/486 on the education of the children of migrant workers [1977] O.J. L199/32 and Council Conclusions concerning the implementation of Directive 77/486 [1985] O.J. C165/1.

[113] Vocational training: "Any form of education which prepares for a qualification for a particular profession, trade or employment or which provides the necessary training and skills for such a profession, trade or employment": *Gravier v City of Liege* (293/83) [1985] E.C.R. 593; [1985] 3 C.M.L.R. 1. See also art.166 TFEU [150].

[114] art.12 Regulation 1612/68 concerning education and training facilities and the rights of children of a deceased worker: *Gül v Regierungspräsident Düsseldorf* (131/85) [1986] E.C.R. 1573 at 1590(20); [1974] 2 C.M.L.R. 423, and *Forcheri v Belgium* (152/82) [1993] E.C.R. 2323 at 2336(18); [1984] 1 C.M.L.R. 334; the right only applies to vocational training, not to university level; children of migrant workers should be eligible for finance by the State on the same conditions as nationals. *Commission v Belgium* (42/87) [1988] E.C.R. 5445; [1989] 1 C.M.L.R. 457. On the other hand the obligation to pay tuition for ordinary schools is acceptable, even if it is not required from nationals, since those schools do not provide vocational training: *Belgium v Humbel* (263/86) [1988] E.C.R. 5365; [1989] 1 C.M.L.R. 393, but scholarships may not be refused: *Mattencci v Communaute Française of Belgium* (235/87) [1988] E.C.R. 5606; [1989] 1 C.M.L.R. 357.

[115] *Commission v Belgium* (C-278/94) [1996] E.C.R. I-4307; [1997] 1 C.M.L.R. 1040: tide-over allowances to young people seeking their first employment may not be subject to them having completed their secondary education in an establishment subsidised or approved by that Member State.

[116] *Christini v SNCF* (32/75) [1975] E.C.R. at 1085(19). This applies also to the member of the family from a third country when the worker returns to his country of origin after being gainfully employed in another Member State: *Eind* (C-291/05) [2007] E.C.R. I-10719.

6. the right, "to remain in the territory of a Member State after having been employed in that State",[117] subject to the conditions embodied in the implementing regulation of the Commission.[118] Those conditions are the following: the worker, at the time of termination of his activity as an employed person, must have reached the age laid down by the law of the host Member State for entitlement to an old-age pension; the worker must also have been employed in that State for, at least, the last twelve months and resided there continuously for more than three years. The latter does not apply in case of incapacity resulting from an accident at work or an occupational disease. No formalities may be required for the exercise of this right and the worker is entitled to a residence permit which shall be issued and renewed free of charge or on payment of a sum not exceeding the dues and taxes payable by nationals. If the worker has acquired the right to remain in the territory of a Member State, the members of his family shall be entitled to remain there permanently even after his death;

7. aggregation of all rights acquired anywhere in the Union under a social security system.[119]

The rights mentioned above would be useless if the migrant worker, when moving from one Member State to another would lose, even partially, the benefits acquired under social security regulations of the first Member State. The Treaty therefore provides that all the rights acquired or periods acquired under the laws of the several countries where the worker exercised his activity shall be aggregated, "for the purpose of acquiring and retaining the right to benefit and of calculating the amount of benefit of all periods taken into account under the laws of the several countries".[120] Those benefits will be paid to the worker by the Member State of residence.[121] The purpose of the Treaty therefore is not to harmonise the existing social security systems of the different Member States into a single Union social security system, but to co-ordinate them. As the Court pointed out, the Treaty allows for separate systems to exist, "creating separate claims against separate institutions against which the beneficiary has direct rights", either under national law alone or under national law supplemented by the Treaty. The Council must take such measures as are necessary to provide freedom of movement to workers and it, "shall make arrangements to secure for the migrant workers and their dependents" the aggregation and payments just mentioned.[122] Those measures gave rise to an abundance of case law, which is not surprising considering the complexity and the scope of the matter. The following branches

---

[117] art.45(3)(d) TFEU [39(3)(d)].

[118] Regulation 1251/70 on the right of workers to remain in the territory of a Member State after having been employed in the State, replaced by Directive 2004/38 on the right of the citizens of the Union and their family members to move and reside freely within the territory of the Member States [2004] O.J. L158/77, since the latter grants the beneficiaries of the right to remain, a more privileged status, namely that of the right of permanent residence.

[119] art.48 TFEU [42].

[120] art.48(a) TFEU [42(a)].

[121] art.48(b) TFEU [42(b)].

[122] Regulation 1408/71 on the application of social security schemes to employed persons and their families moving within the Union [1971] O.J. L149/71, modified [2008] O.J. L177/1 and Regulation 574/72 fixing the procedure for implementing Regulation 1408/71, both Regulations amended [2006] O.J. L114/3, [2007] O.J. L82/6 and [2009] O.J. L39/29.

of social security are covered by Council's Regulations: sickness[123] and maternity[124]; invalidity[125]; old age[126]; survivors' family benefits[127]; unemployment[128]; family allowances[129]; accidents at work and occupational disease[130]; and death grants.[131] However, social "assistance" is not included, which does not simplify matters, since it is difficult to distinguish "assistance" from "security".[132]

On the other hand, since it is better to prevent than to cure, a series of 20 directives were adopted to protect workers, whether migrant or not, against all kinds of hazards.[133] They were adopted in the social field, and since they do not pertain in particular to migrant workers, they are mentioned below in Ch.29: Social Policy (1. Union Action Supporting and Complementing Member States' Activities).

Nearly 40 years after the adoption of the first implementing measures, the Court is still called upon to interpret them, which shows how complicated the matter indeed is. To give an example, in a 1998 judgment, the Court decided that the rules concerning the free movement of "goods" preclude national rules under which social security institutions in a Member State refuse to reimburse to an insured person on a flat-rate basis the cost of a pair of spectacles purchased in another Member State, on the ground that prior authorisation is required for the purchase of medical products in other Member States, while it is not required for products purchased within that State.[134]

An Administrative Commission and an Advisory Committee on Social Security for Migrant Workers[135] were set up to help the Member States and the

---

[123] The provisions of this Regulation were extended to nationals of third countries who are not already covered by those provisions on the ground of their nationality [2003] O.J. L124/1. According to art.81(a) of that Regulation, the Administrative Commission of the European Communities on Social Security for Migrant Workers deals with questions of interpretation; see directory of Union legislation in force issued by the European Communities and, for instance Decision No. 178 on the interpretation of "recipient of benefits" in art.111 of the Regulation [2000] O.J. L302/71; *Warry* (41/77) [1977] E.C.R. 2085; [1977] 2 C.M.L.R. 783. Interesting is the interpretation given by the Court of art.46(2) of Regulation 1408/71: it requires theoretical amounts to be calculated as if the insured person had worked, "exclusively in the Member State concerned", *Koschitzki* (C-30/04) [2005] E.C.R. I–7389.

[124] *Jordens-Voster* (69/79) [1980] E.C.R. 75; [1980] 3 C.M.L.R. 412.

[125] *Murru v Caisse Regionale d'Assurance Maladies de Paris* (2/72) [1972] E.C.R. 333; [1972] C.M.L.R. 888.

[126] *Frilli v Belgium* (1/72) [1972] E.C.R. 457; [1973] C.M.L.R. 386.

[127] *Reina v Landeskreditbank Baden-Württemberg* (65/81) [1982] E.C.R. 33; [1982] 1 C.M.L.R. 744.

[128] *Di Paolo v Office National de l' Emploi* (76/76) [1977] E.C.R. 315; [1977] 2 C.M.L.R. 59.

[129] *Delbar v Caisse d' Allocations Familiales* (C-114/88) [1989] E.C.R. 4067.

[130] *Pennartz v Caisse Primaire d' Assurance Maladies des Alpes-Maritimes* (268/78) [1979] E.C.R. 2411; [1980] 1 C.M.L.R. 682.

[131] *Browning* (22/81) [1981] E.C.R. 3357; [1982] 1 C.M.L.R. 427.

[132] See *Beerens v Rijksdienst voor Arbeidsvoorziening* (35/77) [1977] E.C.R. 2249; [1978] 2 C.M.L.R. 320 where the Court found that social and medical assistance are excluded in the Netherlands from social security, while in Belgium they are included.

[133] See for instance Directive 89/391 on the introduction of measures to encourage improvements in the safety and health of workers at work [1989] O.J. L183/1 and *Commission v UK* (C-127/05) [2007] E.C.R. I–4619, on the responsibility of the employer; see also Directive 2003/10 on exposure of workers to the risks arising from physical agents (noise) [2003] O.J. L42/38, Directive 2004/37 on the protection of workers from risks related to exposure to carcinogens or mutagens, [2004] O.J. L158/50, which is the 14th individual Directive within the meaning of art.16(1) of Directive 89/391, and Directive 2004/40 concerning risks arising from physical agents (electromagnetic fields) [2004] O.J. L184/1 (18th individual Directive), amended [2008] O.J. L114/88; see Ch.29: Social Policy (1. Union Action) for complete list of individual Directives.

[134] *Decker v Caisse de Maladie des Employés Privés* (C-120/95) [1998] E.C.R. I–1831.

[135] arts 80–83 Regulation 1408/71 [1971] OJ. L149/2, as modified (quoted above). Internal Rules in [1995] O.J. C163/3.

Commission with the implementation of the measures adopted in favour of migrant workers. In order to enhance co-operation for modernising and improving social protection, the Council established a Social Protection Committee; in the same Decision the Council endorsed the four broad objectives within the overall challenge of modernising social protection systems:

1. make work pay and provide secure income;
2. make pensions safe and pension systems sustainable;
3. promote social inclusion; and
4. ensure high quality and sustainable health care.[136]

In 2006 Parliament and Council established a European Globalisation Adjustment Fund[137] to provide additional support to workers who suffer from the consequences of major structural changes in world trade patterns and to assist them to reintegrate into the labour market. It allowed the mobilisation of the Fund within the annual ceiling of €500 million; for the financial year 2008 this became €3,106,882.[138]

2. Freedom of Movement of Workers after the 2004 Enlargement

The Accession Treaty[139] signed at Athens on April 16, 2003 and applicable since May 1, 2004 sets out the conditions for freedom of movement of workers to and from the first 10 new Member States after enlargement. The above-mentioned Treaty provides for transitional arrangements that allow the EU 15 Member States to restrict for a period of seven years the free movement of workers coming from the new ones. There was an initial period of two years during which national law or bilateral agreements had to be applied; after that the EU 15 Member States had to give formal notice to the Commission of their intention to either apply in full Union law as explained above or maintain restrictive measures for a maximum of three more years, after which there will be complete freedom of movement for workers who are nationals of the EU (at that time) 25 Member States.

The Accession Treaty also provides for a "safeguard clause"[140] and a "standstill clause".[141]

Three Member States: the United Kingdom, Sweden and Finland have not applied the restrictions. It is interesting to note that a study carried out by the Commission indicates that the number of persons with the firm intention of taking advantage of mobility after May 1, 2004 accounts for just 1 per cent of

---

[136] [2004] O.J. L314/8; this Decision repealed Decision 2000/436 setting up a Social Protection Committee.

[137] Regulation 1927/06 [2006] O.J. L406/1, amended [2009] O.J. L167/26.

[138] Decision 2008/370 [2008] O.J. L128/6 and Decision 2009/409 [2009] O.J. L132/10; see also General Report 2008, 98.

[139] [2003] O.J. 326/1.

[140] Makes it possible for a Member State that has decided to no longer apply the restrictions to ask the Commission for authorisation to apply new restriction if its labour market is threatened by, or experiences, serious difficulties.

[141] The EU 15 Member States could not make access to their labour market more restrictive for workers who are nationals of the new Member States than it was on the date the Accession Treaty was signed (April 16, 2003).

the population of working age of the new Member States; so the fear of massive arrival of workers from the new Member States seemed unfounded. Similar conditions apply to Bulgaria and Romania.

3. EXCEPTIONS TO THE FREE MOVEMENT OF WORKERS

There are two exceptions to the free movement of workers: one concerns limitations to the specific rights just examined, justified on grounds of public policy, public security or public health[142]; the other excludes the "employment in the public service" from the application of the Treaty rules.[143] The meaning of the concepts "public policy", "public security" and "public health" which may limit free movement[144] was defined by a Council directive[145] and by the extensive case law of the Court on those subjects.[146]

With regard to "public policy"—but this also applies to the other two elements of this first exception—the Court stated that this concept must, in the Union context and where, in particular, it is used as a justification for derogating from the fundamental principles of equality of treatment and freedom of movement for workers, be interpreted strictly, so that its scope cannot be determined by each Member State without being subject to control by the institutions of the Union. Restrictions can only be imposed on a migrant worker if his presence or conduct constitutes a genuine and sufficiently serious threat to public policy. A Member State's decision, whether it concerns refusal of entry[147] or expulsion[148] must be based on the individual circumstances of any person under the protection of Union law, and not on general considerations. Furthermore, and this is essential, in each Member State, nationals of other Member States should have adequate legal remedies available to them in respect of the decisions of the administration based on the protection of public policy.[149]

Those remedies should be the same as are available to nationals of the State concerned in respect of acts of the administration. The remedies can have suspensive effects. In order to be able to exercise his right of appeal, the worker in question must be given a precise and comprehensive statement of the grounds for the decision.

Concerning the non-applicability of the free movement of workers to employment in the *public service*, the exception does indeed allow the Member States to

---

[142] art.45(3) TFEU [39(3)].

[143] art.45(4) TFEU [39(4)].

[144] Regulation 1612/68 (quoted above) and Directive 68/360 replaced by Directive 2004/77 [2004] O.J. L158/77.

[145] Directive 64/221 on the co-ordination of special measures concerning the movement and residence of foreign nationals which are justified on the grounds of public policy, public security or public health [1964] O.J. 850 (63–64); incorporated [1994] O.J. L 1/325, replaced by Directive 2004/38 [2004] O.J. L158/77. For failure of a government to check whether the presence of a foreign subject constitutes a real, actual and sufficiently grave menace affecting a fundamental interest of society, see *Commission v Spain* (C-503/03) [2006] E.C.R. I–1097.

[146] See for instance *Rutili v Minister for the Interior* (36/75) [1975] E.C.R. 1219; [1976] 1 C.M.L.R. 140.

[147] *Van Duyn v Home Office* (41/74) [1974] E.C.R. 1337; [1975] 1 C.M.L.R. 1.

[148] *Pecastaing v Belgian State* (98/79) [1980] E.C.R. 691; [1980] 3 C.M.L.R. 685, a person against whom an expulsion order has been issued may exercise all the remedies available to nationals in respect of acts of the administration.

[149] *the Queen v Secretary of State for the Home Department, Ex p. Singhgara and Radiom* (Joined Cases C-65/95 and C-111/95) [1997] E.C.R. I–3343; [1997] 3 C.M.L.R. 703.

refuse access of non-nationals to certain activities in the public service[150]; however, once they have been admitted into the public service, the exception cannot be invoked to justify discrimination on the ground of nationality.[151]

The Court mentions that the Commission having found that, in certain Member States, a large number of posts regarded as belonging to the public service had no connection with the exercise of authority conferred by public law or with the safeguarding of the general interests of the State, decided to implement a necessary strategy. The latter was based upon a communication on the "Freedom of movement of workers and access to employment in the public service-Commission action in respect of the application of Article 39(4)".[152]

In that communication, the Commission gave a list of commercial services carried out by entities, access to which should be open to nationals of other Member States. They concern: public transport, supply of water, electricity and gas, railways, airlines and shipping lines, post and telecommunications, radio and television, public health care services, State education and research for non military purposes conducted in public establishments. Having been informed of an opera's refusal to engage a musician on the ground of his nationality, the Commission, in letters to certain Member States, added national, municipal and local musical orchestras to the list.

The Court stated that the fact that some posts in those areas may, in certain circumstances, be covered by the exception of the Treaty, cannot justify a general prohibition of access of non-nationals in those areas.[153]

4. WORKERS FROM THIRD COUNTRIES

As indicated, the Treaty rules, generally speaking, apply only to citizens of the Union; this is the case concerning "workers". Indeed, the Treaty refers to "workers of the Member States".[154] Nonetheless, where workers from third countries are employed by an undertaking in a given Member State for more than six months on the basis of an employment contract of unlimited duration, another Member State may not make their entry and employment on its territory, by the undertaking employing them in the other Member State, more difficult than for citizens.[155]

Conditions of entry and residence of third country-nationals for the purpose of highly qualified employment, were laid down in 2009.[156]

---

[150] *Sotgiu v Deutsche Bundespost* (152/73) [1974] E.C.R. 153; [1975] 1 C.M.L.R. 91.
[151] *Commission v Hellenic Republic* (C-290/96) [1996] E.C.R. I–3285.
[152] [1988] O.J. C72/2.
[153] Practically identical judgments were delivered in *Commission v Luxembourg* (C-473/93) [1996] E.C.R. I–3207; [1996] 3 C.M.L.R. 981 and *Commission v Belgium* (C-173/94) [1996] E.C.R. I–3265.
[154] art.45(2) TFEU [39(2)].
[155] *Commission v Luxembourg* (C-445/03) [2004] E.C.R. I-10191.
[156] Directive 2009/50 [2009] O.J. L155/17.

III. An Area of Freedom, Security and Justice — The Free Movement of Third-Country Nationals

Although the provisions concerning this area form, as indicated above, a new Title separate from the articles on the free movement of persons, it is closely linked to the latter[157] (among other reasons, because it provides for the conditions under which nationals from third countries may enter, move and reside within the Union) and shall, therefore, be examined here.

The TFEU provides that the Union shall constitute an area of freedom, security and justice.[158] Concretely speaking this means: the absence of internal border controls for persons; the framing of a common policy on asylum, immigration and external border control; a high level of security through measures to prevent and combat crime, racism and xenophobia[159]; measures for co-ordination and co-operation between police and judicial authorities; the mutual recognition of judgments in criminal matters[160] (if necessary, through the approximation of criminal law); and facilitating access to justice, in particular through the mutual recognition of judicial and extra-judicial decisions in civil matters.[161] Quite a programme!

"Strategic guidelines for legislative and operational planning" in the above-mentioned areas shall be defined by the European Council,[162] which indicates the great importance of the activities provided for in this field. The Council, on the other hand, may adopt measures laying down the arrangements whereby Member States, in collaboration with the Commission, conduct objective and impartial evaluation of the implementation of the Union's policies referred to above, by Member State's authorities.[163] To this end a standing Committee will be set up within the Council,[164] which must adopt measures to ensure administrative co-operation between the relevant departments of the Member States, as well as between those departments and the Commission.[165]

---

[157] In the EC Treaty the Title under which this area of freedom, security and justice appeared, referred to "other policies related to the free movement of persons" (art.61 EC).

[158] art.67(1) TFEU [61 and EU 29].

[159] art.75 TFEU [60] complements this with a reference to "terrorism and related activities" and providing that Parliament and Council must define a framework for administrative measures with regard to capital movements and payments, such as freezing of funds, etc. Measures to implement the framework are to be taken by the Council on a proposal from the Commission.

[160] In these domains the TFEU assigns a role to the national Parliaments: ensure that the measures comply with the principle of subsidiarity: art.69 TFEU. Measures in those fields shall be adopted by the Council on a proposal from the Commission or on the initiative of a quarter of the Member States: art.76 TFEU, which constitutes a departure from the exclusive Commission's right to propose legislation.

[161] art.67 (2–4) TFEU [61 and art.29 EU].

[162] art.68 TFEU.

[163] art.70 TFEU.

[164] art.71 TFEU [36].

[165] art.74 TFEU [66].

1. Policies on Border Checks, Asylum and Immigration

The objectives of the "Policies on border checks, asylum and immigration"[166] are multiple:

- ensuring the absence of any controls on persons, whatever their nationality, when crossing internal borders;
- carrying out checks and efficient monitoring of the crossing of external borders; and
- the gradual introduction of an integrated management system for external borders.

In order to achieve these objectives, Parliament and the Council, acting in accordance with the ordinary legislative procedure,[167] must adopt measures concerning, among others: a common policy on visas and other short-stay residence permits,[168] the checks at the external borders (External Borders Fund[169]) and the conditions under which nationals of third countries shall have the freedom to travel within the Union for a short period.[170]

Where *asylum*[171] is concerned, the Union will develop a common policy in accordance with the Geneva Convention of July 28, 1951 and the Protocol of January 31, 1967 relating to the status of refugees and other relevant treaties. It is for Parliament and the Council, acting in accordance with the ordinary legislative procedure,[172] to adopt the necessary measures for a common European asylum system comprising:

- a uniform status of asylum for nationals of third countries;
- a uniform status of protection for other nationals of third countries in need of international protection;
- a common system of temporary protection for displaced persons in the event of a massive inflow;
- a common procedure for the granting and the withdrawal of the above;
- criteria and mechanisms for determining which Member State is responsible for considering corresponding applications established by the Dublin Convention[173]; EURODAC was established creating a system for comparing fingerprints of asylum seekers and illegal immigrants for the effective application of the Dublin Convention[174];
- standards concerning the conditions for the reception of applicants;

---

[166] arts 77–80 TFEU [62–63].

[167] art.294 TFEU [251].

[168] See Regulation 767/08 [2008] O.J. L218/60 concerning the visa information system (VIS) and the exchange of data between the Member States (VIS Regulation) and Decision 2009/377 [2009] O.J. L117/3, adopting implementing measures.

[169] The External Borders Fund for the period 2007 to 2013 with €1.820 million was established as part of the General Programme "Solidarity and Management of Migration Flows": [2007] O.J. L144/22.

[170] art.77(2) TFEU [62].

[171] art.78 TFEU [63–64].

[172] art.294 TFEU [251].

[173] [1996] O.J. C254/1. Regulation 343/03 [2003] O.J. L50/3 and Regulation 1560/03 [2003] O.J. L222/3 laying down detailed rules for its application; see *Migrationsverket v Petrosian* (C-19/08) [2000] E.C.R. 20.01.09.

[174] Regulation 2725/00 [2000] O.J. L316/1 concerning the establishment of EURODIAC.

- partnership and co-operation with third countries for the purpose of managing inflow of asylum seekers. In case a sudden inflow creates an emergency situation in a Member State, the Council may adopt provisional measures.

A *European Refugee Fund*[175] for the period 2008–2013 was established as part of the General Programme "Solidarity and Management of Migration Flows" (see below).

A directive was adopted on minimum standards for procedures in Member States for granting and withdrawing refugee status.[176] See also the Directive on minimum standards for the qualification and status of third-country nationals as stateless persons; as refugees or as persons who otherwise need international protection and the content of the protection granted.[177]

As for *immigration*,[178] the TFEU provides for the development of a "common immigration policy aimed at ensuring, at all stages, the efficient management of migration flows, fair treatment of third-country nationals residing legally in Member States, and the prevention of, and enhanced measures to combat, illegal immigration and trafficking in human beings". Measures are to be adopted by Parliament and Council, acting in accordance with the ordinary legislative procedure,[179] in the following areas:

- conditions of entry and residence and standards on the issue of long-term visas and residence permits; Member States remain free to determine volumes of admission of third-country nationals[180];
- the definition of the rights of third-country nationals residing legally in the Member States and their integration[181] therein;
- illegal immigration and unauthorised residence, including removal and repatriation[182]; for the latter, the Union may conclude agreements with third countries[183]; a directive provides for minimum standards on sanctions and measures against employers of illegally staying third-country nationals[184];
- combating trafficking in persons, especially women and children.[185]

The above policies must be governed by the principle of solidarity and fair sharing of responsibilities, including its financial implications,[186] between Member States.

A General Programme "Solidarity and Management of Migration Flows" was, as already indicated, set up for this purpose.[187] It provides for a fair share of

---

[175] Decision 573/07 [2007] O.J. L144/1, endowed with €628 million for the period 2007–2013; amended [2009] O.J. L179/62.

[176] Directive 2005/85 [2005] O.J. L326/13.

[177] Directive 2004/83 [2004] O.J. L304/12. See *Elgafaji* (C-465/07) [2009] E.C.R. 17.02.09.

[178] art.79 TFEU [63].

[179] art.294 TFEU [251].

[180] art.79(5) TFEU [63(5)].

[181] For this purpose an Integration Fund endowed with €825 million for the period 2007–2013 was established as part of the general programme "Solidarity and Management of Migration Flows" [2007] O.J. L168/18.

[182] A European Return Fund was established for the period 2008–2013 as part of the general programme "Solidarity and Management of Migration Flows": endowed with €676 million [2007] O.J. L144/45.

[183] art.79(3) TFEU [69(3)].

[184] Directive 2009/52 [2009] O.J. L168/24.

[185] SEE Decision of December 8, 2000 on the signing, on behalf of the Union, of the UN Convention against trans-national organised crime and its Protocol on combating trafficking in persons, especially women and children, and the smuggling of migrants by land, air and sea [2000] O.J. L30/44.

[186] See the establishment of a European Refugee Fund [2004] O.J. L381/52.

[187] COM(2005) 123 final (not published in the O.J.).

responsibility between Member States as concerns the financial burden arising from the introduction of an integrated management of the external borders of Member States and the implementation of common policies on asylum and immigration.

In 2008 the Council established a European Migration Network (EMN)[188]; the objective is to meet the information needs of Community institutions and the Member States on migration and asylum by providing up-to-date, objective reliable and comparable information with a view to supporting policymaking in the Union.

A European Fund for the Integration of third-country nationals for the period 2007–2013 was established in 2007, as part of the of the General Programme "Solidarity and Management of Migration Flows", mentioned above.[189]

A European Return Fund for the period 2008–2013 was established in 2007.[190]

2. JUDICIAL CO-OPERATION IN CIVIL AND COMMERCIAL MATTERS[191]

Of great lasting importance are the measures provided for in the TFEU on judicial co-operation in civil matters having cross-border implications. These measures include:

- the mutual recognition and enforcement between Member States of judgments and of decisions in extra-judicial cases,[192] the latter replaces the Brussels Convention[193] of 1968 and is known as Brussels 1;

---

[188] Decision 2008/381 [2008] O.J. L131/7.

[189] Decision 435/07 and Decision 2008/457 laying down rules for the implementation of Decision 435/07, amended [2009] O.J. L179/64.

[190] Decision 575/07 [2007] O.J. L144/45; see Decision 2008/458, amended [2009] O.J. L210/36, laying down rules for the implementation of Decision 575/07.

[191] art.81 TFEU [65].

[192] Regulation 44/2001 [2001] O.J. L12/1, modified [2009] O.J. L7/1 and Agreement with Denmark; see Decision 2009/430 concerning the conclusion of the Convention on jurisdiction and the recognition and enforcement of judgements in civil and commercial matters [2009] O.J. L147/1. See *Color Drack* (C-386/05) [2007] E.C.R. I-3699 for an interpretation of art.5(3)(b) when there are several places of delivery of a good within a single Member State: the principal place of delivery, *FBTO* (C-463/06) [2007] E.C.R. I-11321: art. 9 an injured party may bring an action directly against the insurer before the court in the Member State where the party is domiciled provided the insurer is domiciled in a Member State; and *Freeport* (C-98/06) [2007] E.C.R. I-8219: art.6, point 1 can be applied although the claims introduced against several defendants have different legal bases. See also *ASML* (C-283/05) [2007] E.C.R.I-12041, concerning the possibility of a defendant to proceed against a default judgment, art. 34(2). See *Hasset and Doherty* (C-372/07) [2008] E.C.R. 02.10.08, interpretation of art.22, point 2, of the Regulation *Allianz* (C-185/07) [2009] E.C.R. 10.02.09.: it is incompatible with the Regulation for a court of a Member State to make an order to restrain a person from proceeding before the court of another Member State on the ground that it would be contrary to an arbitration agreement. In *Falcon* (C-533/07) [2009] E.C.R.23.04.09, the Court found that a contract whereby the exploitation of an IPR is conceded against payment is not a service contract and in order to determine the competent jurisdiction, refers to the case law concerning art.5.1 of the Convention of September 27, 1968. With regard to art. 43(1) see (C-167/08) [2009] E.C.R. 23.04.09.

In 2007 the Union signed the Convention on jurisdiction and the recognition and enforcement of judgements in civil and commercial matters [2007] O.J. L339/1-3. See Agreement between the Union and Denmark on the service of judicial and extrajudicial documents in civil or commercial matters [2008] O.J. L331/21. In 2009 the Union signed the Convention of Choice of Court Agreements [2009] O.J. L133/1.

See Framework Decision 2008/947 on the application of the principle of mutual recognition to judgments and probation decisions with a view to the supervision of probation measures and alternative sanctions [2008] O.J. L337/102.

[193] See *Gambazzi* (C-394/07) [2009] E.C.R. 02.04.09 interpreting art.27,1.

- the cross-border service of judicial and extra-judicial documents[194]; a manual of receiving agencies and a glossary of documents that may be served was adopted[195];
- the compatibility of the rules applicable in the Member States concerning conflict of laws and of jurisdiction;
- co-operation in the taking of evidence[196]; see Council Framework Decision on the execution in the European Union of orders freezing property or evidence[197];
- effective access to justice (this includes legal aid): see Council Directive,[198] which aims at improving access to justice in cross-border disputes by establishing common rules relating to legal aid for such disputes; the Commission established a standard form for legal aid applications;
- establishment of a *European Judicial Network* in civil and commercial matters[199];
- eliminating obstacles to the good functioning of civil proceedings, if necessary by promoting the compatibility of the rules on civil procedure applicable in the Member States;
- the development of alternative methods of dispute settlement;
- support for the training of judiciary and judicial staff;
- mediation in civil and commercial matters[200];
- jurisdiction, applicable law, recognition and enforcement of decisions and co-operation in matters relating to maintenance obligations[201]; the regulation applies to maintenance obligations arising from a family relationship, parentage, marriage or affinity.

Before the Treaty of Lisbon became applicable several measures had already been taken by the Union institution concerning judicial co-operation in civil matters; they concern, among others:

- jurisdiction and the recognition and enforcement of judgments in matrimonial matters and in matters of parental responsibility.[202] See below, in this

---

[194] Regulation 1348/2000 [2000] O.J. L160/37, replaced by Regulation 1393/07 on the service in the Member State of judicial and extrajudicial documents in civil and commercial matters [2007] O.J. L324/79; Commission Decision 2001/781 adopting a manual of receiving agencies and a glossary of documents that may be served in the Member State [2008] O.J. L173/17; see *Leffler* (C-443/03) [2005] E.C.R. I–9611 on the consequences of the absence of a translation and *Weiss and Partner* (C-14/07) [2008] E.C.R. I-3367. concerning the language of the notification.

[195] Decision 2007/500 [2007] O.J. L185/24.

[196] Regulation 1206/2001 [2001] O.J. L 174/1.

[197] Framework Decision 2003/577 [2003] O.J. L196/45.

[198] Directive 2003/8 [2003] O.J. L26/41.

[199] Decision 2001/470 [2001] O.J. L174/25, amended [2009] O.J. L168/35. It's purpose is to improve, simplify and expedite effective judicial co-operation between the Member State (with the exception of DK), through the establishment of contact points, etc.

[200] Directive 2008/52 [2008] O.J. L136/3.

[201] Regulation 4/2009 [2009] O.J. L7/1.

[202] Regulation 1347/2000 [2000] O.J. L160/19 replaced by Regulation 2201/2003 [2003] O.J. L338/1, see *Sundelind Lopez* (C-68/07) [2007] E.C.R. I-10403, jurisdiction of Member State; C, (C-435/06) [2007] E.C.R. I-10106, interpretation of art.1(1) on the meaning of "civil matters"; *PPU, Inga Rinau* (C-195/08) [2008] E.C.R. I-5271, opposition to recognition of judgment; *Sundelind Lopez* (C-68/07) [2007] E.C.R. I-10403, competence in divorce matters; C (C-435/06) [2007] E.C.R. I-10141, a single decision ordering a child to be taken into care is covered by the term "civil matters"; in this case the regulation in question applies *ratione temporis*; and A (C-523/07) [2009] E.C.R. 02.04.09 interpreting "civil matter", "habitual residence", conditions for deciding a "protective measure" (taking into care of children) and obligation for the national court to inform the court of another Member State having jurisdiction.

respect, the 1996 Hague Convention on parental responsibility and protection of children[203];
- a European Enforcement Order for uncontested claim[204];
- Convention on the law applicable to contractual obligations, Rome Convention, (Rome I); a regulation of 2008[205] replaced the Rome Convention in the Member States, it concerns mainly which law is applicable to the contract;
- European contract law[206];
- insolvency proceeding[207];
- creation of a European order for payment procedure[208];
- establishment of a European Small Claims Procedure[209]; and
- law applicable to non-contractual obligations (Rome II).[210]

The implementation of the rules and measures described above also have their exceptions. They concern, for instance, the responsibility incumbent upon Member States with regard to maintenance of law and order and the safeguarding of internal security.[211]

See also, with regard to civil matters, the Hague Programme 2005–2010[212] that lists 10 key areas for priority action:

- development of policies enhancing citizenship, monitoring and promoting respect for fundamental rights;
- fight against terrorism: prevention, preparedness and response;
- migration management: developing a common EU immigration policy and countering illegal migration;
- internal and external borders, visas: integrated management of external borders and a common visa policy;
- a common asylum policy;
- maximising the positive impact of migration on society and economy;
- privacy and security in sharing information;
- fight against organised crime[213] effective access to justice for all and enforcement of judgments; and
- reviewing the effectiveness of policies and financial instruments in meeting the objectives of freedom, security and justice.

---

[203] Decision 2003/93 [2003] O.J. L48/1.The principle concerning the rights of children was laid down by art. 24 of the European Charter of fundamental rights.

[204] Regulation 805/2004 [2004] O.J. L143/15, modified [2005] O.J. L300/6, based on art.81 TFEU [65]. The same enforcement can be obtained under Regulation 44/2001 concerning jurisdiction and enforcement of judgments in civil and commercial matters [2001] O.J. L12/1, amended [2001] O.J. L307/28.

[205] Regulation 593/08 [2008] O.J. L177/6, see art. 24 and following; it is applicable since December 17, 2009.

[206] Communication from the Commission [2001] O.J. C255/1. See also Decision on the accession of the Union to the Hague Conference on Private International Law [2006] O.J. L297/3.

[207] Regulation 1346/2000 [2000] O.J. L160/1, see O.J. L121/1, amending lists of insolvency proceedings, winding-up proceedings and liquidators of annexes A, B and C, amended [2008] O.J. L213/1 Regulation 681/07 [2007] O.J. L159/1. See *Eurofood* (C-341/04) [2006] E.C.R. I-3813: interpreting art.3 and 16. *Deko Marty* (C-339/07) [2009] E.C.R. 12.02.09. according to art.3(1) the court of a Member State within which insolvency proceedings have been opened has jurisdiction to decide an action to set a transaction aside brought against a person registered in another Member State.

[208] Regulation 1896/2006 [2006] O.J. L399/1.

[209] Regulation 861/07 [2007] O.J. L199/1.

[210] Regulation 864/07 [2007] O.J. L199/40.

[211] art.72 TFEU [64(1)].

[212] [2005] O.J. L198/1.

[213] See Framework Decision 2008/841 on the fight against organised crime [2008] O.J. L300/42.

A 2002 regulation establishes a general framework for Union activities to facilitate the implementation of judicial cooperation in civil matters.[214] The plans to develop electronical Justice (*e-Justice*) would greatly facilitate the access to justice.[215]

3. JUDICIAL CO-OPERATION IN CRIMINAL MATTERS[216]

Judicial co-operation is based on the principle of mutual recognition of judgments and judicial decisions and includes the approximation of the laws and regulations of the Member States in the relevant areas. Parliament and the Council, acting in accordance with the ordinary legislative procedure[217] are to adopt measures to:

- lay down rules and procedures for ensuring recognition throughout the Union, of all forms of judgments and judicial decisions[218]; see the Framework Decision on the application of the principle of mutual recognition to judgments in criminal matters imposing custodial sentences or measures involving deprivation of liberty for the purpose of their enforcement in the European Union and a Framework Decision of 2008 on taking account of convictions in the Member States in the course of new criminal proceedings[219]; recognition of decisions rendered in the absence of the person concerned at the trial[220];
- prevent and settle conflicts of jurisdiction between Member States;
- support the training of judiciary and judicial staff; and
- facilitate co-operation between judicial or equivalent authorities of the Member States in relation to proceedings in criminal matters and the enforcement of decisions.

Parliament and Council may also, in the same way, adopt directives establishing minimum rules concerning: mutual admissibility of evidence; the rights of individuals in criminal procedure; the rights of victims of crime[221]; and any other specific aspects of criminal procedure. In case of disagreement within the Council concerning these rules, they shall be referred to the European Council.[222]

Furthermore, Parliament and the Council can, in the same way, adopt directives concerning the definition of criminal offences and sanctions in the areas of particularly serious crimes with a cross-border dimension resulting from the nature and the impact of such offences. Those areas of crimes are the following: terrorism;

---

[214] [2002] O.J. L115/1.

[215] Multi-annual European e-Justice action plan 2009–2013 [2009] O.J. C75/1. See also "E-Justice in Europe": l'Observateur de Bruxelles July 2008, p.12; *http://www.DBFBruxelles.EU*.

[216] arts 82–86 TFEU [31]. See *Advocaten voor de Wereld* (C-303/05) [2007] E.C.R. I-3633, concerning, among others, the European arrest warrant and Framework Decision 2002/584.

[217] art.294 TFEU [251].

[218] See Framework Decision 2008/67 on taking account of convictions in the Member States of the European Union in the course of new criminal proceedings [2008] O.J. L220/32 and Framework Decision 2008/909 [2008] O.J. L327/27.

[219] Framework Decision 2008/675 [2008] O.J. L220/32. Member States must take the necessary implementing measures before August 15, 2010.

[220] Framework Decision 2009/299 [2009] O.J. L81/24.

[221] See Framework Decision 2001/220/JHA on the standing of victims in criminal proceedings [2001] O.J. L82/1 and *Katz* (C-404/07) [2008] E.C.R. I-7607, arts 2 and 3 do not oblige the national judge to allow the victim to be heard as witness but must be authorised to make a deposition.

[222] art.82(3) TFEU [31].

trafficking in human beings and sexual exploitation of woman and children[223]; illicit drug trafficking[224]; and illicit arms trafficking; money laundering; corruption; counterfeiting of means of payment; computer crime; and organised crime.

In case of disagreement within the Council, reference is to be made to the European Council.[225] Parliament and the Council may establish measures to promote and support the action of Member States in the field of crime prevention.[226]

The *Daphne III Programme* to combat violence against children, young people and women and to protect victims and groups at risk, was established for the period 2007–2013 with a total budget of €30 million.[227] The funds are used to support activities submitted to and selected by the Commission.[228]

Eurojust (European Body for the Enhancement of Judicial Co-operation)[229] was set up by the Council in 2002 to improve co-operation between competent authorities.

Its mission is to support and strengthen co-operation and co-ordination between national investigating and prosecuting authorities in relation to serious crime affecting two or more Member States or requiring a prosecution on common bases, on the basis of operations conducted and information supplied by Member States' authorities and by Eurojust. It is for Parliament and Council to determine, in accordance with the ordinary legislative procedure,[230] Eurojust's structure, operation, field of action and tasks. The latter include: the initiation of criminal investigations, particularly those relating to offences against the financial interests of the Union; the co-ordination of investigations and prosecutions; and the strengthening of judicial co-operation, including by resolution of conflicts of jurisdiction and by close co-operation with the European Judicial Network.[231]

A *European Public Prosecutor's Office* from Eurojust may be established in order to combat crimes affecting the financial interests of the Union.[232] It shall be established by regulation from the Council acting unanimously after obtaining the consent of Parliament. It shall be responsible for investigating, prosecuting and bringing to judgment, where appropriate in liaison with Europol,[233] the perpetrators of, and accomplices in, offences against the Union's financial interests. This task may be extended to include serious crime having a cross-border dimension.[234]

---

[223] See Decision 779/07 establishing for the period 2007–2013 a specific programme to prevent and combat violence against children, young people and women and to protect victims and groups at risk (Daphne III programme) as part of the general programme "Fundamental Rights and Justice" [2007] O.J. L173/19.

[224] See European Union action plan for the fight against drugs and *http://www.ec.europa.eu./external.relations/drugs/index.htm*. In 2004, the European Council endorsed the EU Drug Strategy (2005–2012); see EU Drugs Action Plan (2005–2008) [2005] O.J. C168/1. See also Council Framework Decision 2004/575 laying down minimum provisions on the constituent elements of criminal acts and penalties in the field of drug trafficking [2004] O.J. L335/8.

[225] art.83(3) TFEU [31].

[226] art.84 TFEU.

[227] Decision 779/07 [2007] O.J. L173/1.

[228] art.67 TFEU [art.29 EU].

[229] See above Ch.13: Decentralised Bodies of the Union.

[230] art.294 TFEU [251].

[231] European Judicial Network in civil and commercial matters [1998] O.J. L191/4.

[232] art.86 TFEU.

[233] See Ch.13: Decentralised Bodies of the Union.

[234] art.86(4) TFEU.

It might be interesting to note that "provisions on police [below] and judicial co-operation in criminal matters" constituted Title VI of the Treaty on European Union and that the Court agreed with the GC in that no action for damages are possible under that Title.[235]

4. POLICE CO-OPERATION

The Union is to establish police co-operation involving all the Member States' competent authorities, including police, customs and other specialised law enforcement services in relation to the prevention, detection and investigation of criminal offences.[236] Parliament and the Council, acting in accordance with the ordinary legislative procedure,[237] may establish measures concerning the collection, storage, processing, analysis and exchange of relevant information, support for the training of staff and co-operation on the exchange of staff, on equipment and on research into crime-detection, and common investigative techniques in relation to the detection of serious forms of organised crime. The Council, acting in accordance with a special legislative procedure,[238] may establish measures concerning operational co-operation between national authorities.[239]

The following were set up:

- a framework for the exchange of liaison magistrates[240];
- a network of contact points in respect of people responsible for genocide and crimes against humanity[241];
- the European *arrest warrant* that, de facto, replaces the lengthy and difficult extradition procedure[242];
- surrender of procedures between Member State[243];
- mutual recognition of financial penalties[244];
- convention on driving disqualification[245];
- combating cross-border vehicle crime.[246]

---

[235] *Gestores Pro Amnistia E.A. v Council* (C-354/04 P) [2007] E.C.R. I-1579.

[236] art.87 TFEU [30].

[237] art.294 TFEU [251].

[238] art.289(2) TFEU.

[239] art.87(3) TFEU [30].

[240] Joint Action 96/277/JHA [1996] O.J. L105/1.

[241] Decision 2002/494/JHA [2002] O.J. L167/1. See also: the investigation and prosecution of genocide, crimes against humanity and war crime, Decision 2003/535/JHA [2003] O.J. L118/12; and network of contact points in respect of persons responsible for genocide and crimes against humanity, Decision 2002/494/JHA [2002] O.J. L167/1.

[242] Framework Decision 2002/584/JHA on the European arrest warrant and the surrender procedure between Member States [2002] O.J. L190/3, thereby enhancing the procedural rights of persons subject to criminal procedings and fostering the application of the principle of mutual recognition to decisions rendered in the absence of the person concerned at the trial, amended Decision 2009/299 [2009] O.J. L81/24. See (urgent procedure!) *Santesteban* (C-296/08 PPU) [2008] E.C.R. I-6307: the decision is only applicable for facts committed after the date indicated by the relevant Member State in a declaration provided for in art.32 of the Decision, see, for example, Italy's declaration [2009] O.J. L97/26. For the interpretation of the notion "staying" in a given Member State see *Kozlowski* (C-66/08) [2008] E.C.R. 17.07.08.

[243] Framework Decision 2002/584/JHA (quoted above). For an interpretation of art.4,6, European arrest warrant, see *Kozlowski* (C-66/08) [2008] E.C.R. I-6041.

[244] Framework Decision 2005/214/JHA of February 24, 2005 amended Decision 2009/299 [2009] O.J. L 2009/81.

[245] Convention [1998] O.J. C216/2.

[246] Decision 2004/919 [2004] O.J. L389/28.

In 2002, the Council established a framework programme on police and judicial co-operation in criminal matters (AGIS).[247]

All Member States signed the 1959 European Convention on Mutual Assistance in Criminal Matters.[248] The Convention regulates mutual assistance in criminal matters in a fast and efficient manner compatible with the basic principles of national laws, and in compliance with the individual rights and principles of the European Convention, signed in Rome in 1950. A network of judicial contact points was set up[249] under the name "European Judicial Network"[250]; those contact points must be active intermediaries with the task of facilitating judicial co-operation between Member States. See also a 2008 decision on the European evidence warrant for the purpose of obtaining objects, documents and data for use in proceeding in criminal matters.[251]

The fight against terrorism also became an important preoccupation for the Union, and the Council, in consultation with Parliament, adopted a Framework Decision on combating terrorism,[252] a common position on the application of specific measures to combat terrorism,[253] a decision on specific restrictive measures directed against certain persons and entities with a view of combating terrorism,[254] a decision establishing a mechanism for evaluating national legal provisions relating to the fight.

The provisions on Police and Judicial Co-operation in Criminal Matters (EU Title VI) fall under the jurisdiction of the Court of Justice in so far as the Court may be called upon, under the specific condition laid down in that Title,[255] to give preliminary rulings on the validity and interpretation of framework decisions[256] and decisions, on the interpretation of conventions established under EU Title VI and on the measures implementing them. However, the Court shall have no jurisdiction to review the validity and the proportionality of operations carried out by the national police or other law enforcement services. The same jurisdiction of the Court of Justice applies to Title VII of the Treaty on "enhanced co-operation" in the field of police and judicial co-operation[257] and, also, with regard to enhanced co-operation in the areas referred to in the EC Treaty.[258]

IV. THE FREE MOVEMENT OF STUDENTS

Based on Union law provisions and on the Belgian law of December 15, 1980, modified many times, the main conditions for free entry of students into one of the Member States, are the following:

---

[247] [2002] O.J. L203/5.
[248] Council Act adopted in accordance with art.34 EU (now repealed) [2000] O.J. C197/3. See Protocol providing additional measures for the purpose of the fight against crime, including organised crime, money laundering and financial crime; it concerns information on bank accounts held by persons subject to criminal investigation, on banking transactions, fiscal offences, etc. [2001] O.J. C326/3.
[249] Joint Action 98/428 [1998] O.J. 191/4.
[250] Decision 2008/976 [2008] O.J. L348/130.
[251] Decision 2008/978 [2008] O.J. L350/72.
[252] [2002] O.J. L164/3.
[253] Common Position 2007448 updating Common Position 2001/931 on the application of specific measures to combat terrorism [2007] O.J. L169/69.
[254] [2005] O.J. L144/59.
[255] See art.35 (3–7) EU .
[256] art. 34(2)(b) EU.
[257] arts 40, 40a and 40b EU.
[258] art.11 EU.

1. nationals of Member States:

    (a) they must be able to prove their nationality (passport or identity card);
    (b) they need a certificate of inscription in an establishment of higher education;
    (c) their rights are provided for in Union Law[259];
    (d) the student must prove that he/she has sufficient resources and is covered by sickness insurance;

2. nationals of third countries:

    (a) a certificate of inscription in an establishment of higher education; it concerns only institutions set up, recognised and financed by the authorities;
    (b) the proof of having sufficient means of existence (minimum € +/– 600 per month); any proof is acceptable; another person may provide a guarantee; a bank guarantee may be required; means may also, under given circumstances, result from work;
    (c) a medical certificate indicating that the student has none of the illnesses or handicaps mentioned in an annex to the law;
    (d) a document showing that the student has not been sentenced.

In addition, the student:

1. may not have been refused access to another Schengen country;
2. does not constitute a danger for the international relations of a Schengen country;
3. does not cause a danger for public policy, public order or public health;
4. has not been refused access in the last 10 years.

The student may be accompanied by members of his family (wife and children) if he can show that he has the necessary means to support and lodge them.

The student may be made to leave the host country in case:

- he no longer fulfils the above conditions;
- disturbs the peace;
- the studies take too long;
- the student pursues a lucrative activity which hinders the studies;
- if, without valid motive, is not present at the exams;
- stays after the end of the studies and is no longer in possession of a valid residence permit.

Further Reading

Joanna Apap, *Freedom of movement of persons* (Kluwer International 2002).
Peter J. van Krieken, *The Consolidated Asylum and Migration Acquis. The EU Directives in an Expanded Europe* (T.M.C. Asser Press by Cambridge University Press, 2004).
Rogers & Scannell, *Free Movement of Persons in the Enlarged European Union* (Sweet & Maxwell, 2005).
Steve Peers, "EU Criminal Law and the Treaty of Lisbon", (2008) E.L.R. 507.

---

[259] Directive 93/96 on the right of residence of students enrolled in a recognised educational establishment [1993] O.J. L317/59. Although the Directive refers to "vocational training" it applies also to university students, Regulation 307/1999 [1999] O.J. L38/1, amends Regulation 1408/71 on the application of social security schemes to employed and self-employed persons, with a view of extending it to cover students.

Chapter Seventeen

Freedom of Establishment/Company Law

1. INTRODUCTION: FREE MOVEMENT OF SELF-EMPLOYED PERSONS

If the free movement of workers finds its expression in the principle of equal treatment and the right to enter, move, reside and remain, with their family, in another Member State and retain their social security rights, the free movement of self-employed natural and legal persons finds its implementation both in the "right of establishment" and in the "freedom to provide services".

The expression "free movement of self-employed persons" is not used in the Treaty, which provides that the, "freedom[1] of establishment shall include the right to take up and pursue activities as a self-employed person and to set up and manage undertakings".[2]

The three basic freedoms: free movement of workers, freedom of establishment and the freedom to provide services, show great similarities in so far as they consist mainly, where the Member States are concerned, in the prohibition of discrimination in comparison with their own nationals, and the obligation to admit and let the beneficiaries of those freedoms circulate, reside and remain in their territory. See, for instance, the directive on the abolition of restriction on the movement and residence within the Union of nationals of Member States with regard to establishment and the provision of services.[3] As shall be pointed out, many implementing directives and regulations, including those concerning social security, apply without distinction to the workers and the self-employed. Even the exceptions provided for in the Treaty are practically the same for all three categories. The main differences are that free movement of workers only concern individuals, while establishment and services also apply to undertakings, and, secondly, that establishment and services require (professional) qualifications, both for legal and natural persons, in order to accede to the "regulated" professions.[4] Once they can prove they have these qualifications they are automatically admitted.

Where non-regulated professions are concerned, the Treaty provides that nationals of other Member States have a right of access to, and the right to exercise, any non-paid activity,[5] but under the same conditions as those applying to the nationals of the host Member State; whether they fulfil these conditions is the object of an individual investigation. Persons can, according to the Court, be

---

[1] As can be seen, the terms "right" and "freedom" are used indiscriminately in the Treaty: no significance may, therefore, be attached to the use of one rather than the other.

[2] art.49,2 TFEU [43,2].

[3] Directive 73/148, replaced by Directive 2004/38 on the right of citizens of the Union and their family members to move and reside freely within the territory of the Member States [2004] O.J. L158/77.

[4] See below.

[5] *Commission v Austria* (C-81/03) not published, see *http://www.curia.europa.eu/en/content/juris/*.

defined as self-employed in so far as they are voluntarily insured against sickness or old age under social security schemes organised for the benefit of workers and in so far as, in particular, they are self-employed.[6] It will be noted that, while the Treaty refers to "workers of the Member States"[7] the freedom of establishment and the freedom to provide services apply to "nationals of Member States".[8] The Court determined that this cannot be interpreted as excluding from the benefit of Union law own nationals who want to establish themselves in their own country after having resided in another Member State.[9] Self-employed persons are not only those exercising what is called the "regulated professions" such as doctors, nurses, dentists, veterinarians, midwives, pharmacists, architects and lawyers, but also trades people, for instance those engaged in personal service sectors such as hotels, restaurants and taverns,[10] transport and travel agencies,[11] commercial agents,[12] retail trade[13] and many others.[14]

For both freedoms, i.e. establishment and the provision of services, the Treaty provided earlier on for the Council to draw up "general programmes"[15] for the abolition of existing restrictions. Those programmes were indeed adopted and constituted the basis for the many directives facilitating the exercise of those two freedoms. They concern, in the first place, the harmonisation of the qualifications required from self-employed persons so that they may perform so-called regulated activities, i.e. activities subject to certain conditions. As the Court pointed out:

> "[W]hen the taking up or pursuit of a specific activity is subject to certain conditions in the host Member State, a national of another Member State intending to pursue that activity, must in principle comply with them. However, national measures liable to hinder or make less attractive the exercise of fundamental freedoms guaranteed by the Treaty, must fulfil four conditions: they must be applied in a non-discriminatory manner, they must be justified by imperative requirements in the general interest,[16] they must be suitable for securing the attainment of the objective which they pursue, and they must not go beyond what is necessary in order to attain it".[17]

---

[6] *Stöber and Piosa Pereira v Bundesanstalt für Arbeit* (Joined Cases C-4/95 and C-5/95) [1997] E.C.R. I–511 at 543(28); [1997] 2 C.M.L.R. 213. See Regulation 1408/71 on the application of social security schemes to self-employed persons [1971] O.J. L149/2, amended [2008] O.J. L177/1.

[7] art.45,2 TFEU [39(2)].

[8] arts 49,1 and 56,1 TFEU [43,1 and 49,1].

[9] See, for instance, *Knoors* (115/78) [1979] E.C.R. 399.

[10] Directive 68/368 [1968] O.J. L260/19.

[11] Directive 82/470 [1982] O.J. L213/1.

[12] Directive 86/653 [1986] O.J. L382/17 concerning the right to a commission, see *Kontogeorgas* (C-104/95) [1996] E.C.R. I–6643; [1997] 1 C.M.L.R. 1093, no right to commission in the absence of an intervention of agent; *Chevalier-Marche* (C-19/07) [2008] E.C.R. 8–159. In *Bellone v Yokohama* (C-215/97) [1998] E.C.R. I–2191, the Court held that Directive 86/653 precludes a national rule which makes the validity of an agency contract conditional upon the agent being registered in a national register. For a definition of "independent commercial agent", see *Poseidon Chartering* (C-3/04) [2006] E.C.R. I–2505.

[13] Directive 68/363 [1968] O.J. L260/496.

[14] References can be found in the "Directory of [Union] legislation in force and other acts of the [Union] institutions", Office for Official Publications of the European Union.

[15] arts 54(1) and 63(1) EEC. Those programmes are no longer mentioned in the Treaty.

[16] It will be remembered that the Court uses this expression in defining the mandatory requirements in the famous *Cassis de Dijon* (120/78) [1979] E.C.R. 649 case.

[17] *Gebhard* (C-55/94) [1995] E.C.R. I–4165; [1996] 1 C.M.L.R. 603. The last criterion is also expressed as the principle of proportionality.

The fact that one Member State imposes less strict conditions than another Member State does not mean that the rules of the latter are disproportionate and hence incompatible with Union law.[18]

The directives facilitating the exercise of the freedom of establishment of the self-employed concern, next to the harmonisation of the qualifications, the mutual recognition of diplomas, certificates and other evidence of formal qualification.

2. FREEDOM OF ESTABLISHMENT/COMPANY LAW

In accordance with Chapter Two of Title IV of the TFEU, restrictions to the freedom of establishment of nationals of a Member State in the territory of another Member State are prohibited; this prohibition also applies to the setting up of agencies, branches and subsidiaries by nationals of a Member State established in the territory of any Member State.[19] The last words "established in the territory of any Member State" refer to the Treaty requirement that in order to, "be treated in the same way as natural persons who are nationals of Member States", a company or firm must fulfil two conditions. In the first place, it must have been formed in accordance with the law of a Member State, and, in the second place, it must have its registered office, central administration or principal place of business within the Union, i.e. established in the territory of any one Member State.[20] Once these two conditions are fulfilled, the undertaking establishing itself in another Member State enjoys in that State all the rights normally exercised by undertakings, such as the possibility to appear in court[21] and acquire land and buildings.[22]

It will be noted that for an undertaking to be able to enjoy this freedom, the Treaty only requires "establishment" in one of the Member States, but not that it has the "nationality" of one of the Member States. This would have been extremely difficult, if not impossible, to establish anyway; it therefore suffices that the company or firm fulfils the two conditions referred to above. As already mentioned, the Treaty defines the freedom of establishment as including:

> "[T]he right to take up and pursue activities as a self-employed person and to set up and manage undertakings, in particular companies and firms . . . in another Member State, under the conditions laid down for its own nationals by the law of the country where such establishment is effected".[23]

Undertakings are defined as entities, "constituted under civil or commercial law, including co-operative societies, and other legal persons governed by public or private law, save for those which are non-profit-making".[24] As mentioned before, the freedoms provided for in the Treaty do not confer upon the beneficiaries absolute rights (no rights are absolute), but rights that are limited or "regulated" in the same way as the rights (and obligations) applying to the nationals of the

---

[18] *Reisebüro Broede v Sandker* (C-3/95) [1996] E.C.R. I-6511(42); [1997] 1 C.M.L.R. 224.

[19] art.49,1 TFEU [43,1].

[20] art.54,1 TFEU [48,1].

[21] *Überseering BV v NCC* (C-208/00) [2002] E.C.R. I-9919.

[22] art.50(2)(e) TFEU [44].

[23] art.49,2 TFEU [43,2]; the Treaty adds, "subject to the provisions of the chapter relating to capital." This reference has lost most of its meaning since there are no longer limitations to the free movement of capital; see the EMU.

[24] art.54,2 TFEU [48,2].

host Member State.[25] In fact, establishment in another country can mean that the person in question keeps his main interest[26] in one Member State and opens an agency, branch or subsidiary in another.

The Court expressed it as follows: "the right of establishment includes freedom to set up and maintain, subject to observance of the professional rules of conduct, more than one place of work within the [Union]."[27]

It can also mean that the legal or natural person in question moves its entire business to another Member State.[28] In the latter case, the distinction with the right to provide services is rather clear cut, since, as shall be seen, a provider of services does not move permanently to another State; in that case the separation line is rather blurred. As is the case for the free movement of workers, the Treaty explicitly provides that, besides the right to be treated without discrimination in the Member State of establishment, the beneficiary of the freedom enjoys certain specific rights. These are, for instance, to remain[29] in the territory of the host State, also after having pursued its activities[30] and to acquire and use land and buildings situated in the territory of another Member State (with some possible reservations for agricultural land).[31] There is here an evident link with the free movement of capital needed to acquire that real estate.

In order to implement the freedom of establishment, the Treaty imposes various obligations on the Council and Commission and on the Member States. The former are to act by means of directives; two legislative programmes were adopted by the Council. A first series of directives concerns the mutual recognition of diplomas and the co-ordination of the conditions of access to certain professions; from September 1, 2007 these directives were replaced by a single one that also includes provisions for the other professions.[32]

A second series of directives establishes harmonised rules for firms and companies (see below).

---

[25] art.49,2 TFEU [43,2].

[26] For taxation purposes it is sometimes important to be able to establish in which country the main interests are situated; see the rather amusing, *Ryborg* (C-297/89) [1991] E.C.R. I–1943; [1993] 1 C.M.L.R. 218, where the Court had to decide whether a person resides in the country where he works, or the one where his girlfriend lives and where he spends all his nights. The Court ruled in favour of the place where his economic interests prevailed. However, in a later judgement, concerning the interpretation of Directive 83/182 on tax exemptions for certain means of transport temporarily imported [1983] O.J. L105/59, the Court decided that in case the former rule cannot be applied, primacy should be given to the personal ties of the person in question, *Louloudakis* (C-262/99) [2001] E.C.R. I–5547.

[27] *Ordre des Avocats du Barreau de Paris v Klopp* (107/83) [1984] E.C.R. 2971 at 2987(10); [1985] 1 C.M.L.R. 99.

[28] *The Queen v Treasury and Commissioners of Inland Revenue Ex p. Daily Mail and General Trust PLC* (81/87) [1988] E.C.R. 5483 at 5510(16).

[29] Directive 73/148 on the abolition of restrictions on movement and residence within the Union for nationals of Member States with regard to establishment and the provision of services, replaced by Directive 2004/38 on the right of citizens of the Union and their family members to move and reside freely within the territory of the Member States [2004] O.J. L158/77.

[30] Directive 75/34 concerning the right of nationals of Member States to remain in the territory of another Member State after having pursued an activity in a self-employed capacity [1975] O.J. L14/10, replaced by Directive 2004/38 [2004] O.J. L158/77. See also Directive 90/365 on the right of residence for employees and self-employed persons who have ceased their occupational activity [1990] O.J. L180/28; both directives have been replaced by Directive 2004/38 (quoted above).

[31] art.50(2)(e) TFEU which refers to art.39(2) [44(2)(e)].

[32] Directive 2005/36 on the recognition of professional qualifications [2005] O.J. L255/22; corrigenda [2007] O.J. L271/18 and annexes II and III, modified [2007] O.J. L320/3. Regulation 755/08 modifying Annex II [2008] O.J. L205/10, again modified [2009] O.J. L93/11.

As for the Member States, their main obligation concerns the abolition of those administrative procedures and practices the maintenance of which would form an obstacle to freedom of establishment.[33] Reference is made both to the conditions for setting up agencies, branches and subsidiaries and the conditions governing the entry of personnel belonging to the main establishment, into managerial and supervisory posts in such agencies, branches and subsidiaries. Interesting is that this entry of personnel is not limited to nationals of the Member State[34]; this is particularly important for undertakings from third countries established in the Union. The directives referred to, were, over the years, adopted in implementation of the General Programme previously provided for in the Treaty.[35]

3. Students

One directive which might interest many readers concerns the right of residence and other rights deriving from there for students.[36] The Directive confers upon students from other Member States the right of residence under a few general conditions. They have to assure the authorities of the host State that they have sufficient resources for themselves and their families, if any, so as to avoid becoming a burden for that State; they must be enrolled in a recognised vocational training course or university and must be covered by sickness insurance.[37]

Of great importance for students are the rights this residence allows them to claim with regard to acceptance at universities or other institutes of higher education[38] and with regard to advantages offered students in the country of residence.[39]

See also the ERASMUS, TEMPUS and Leonardo da Vinci programmes destined to facilitate the mobility of university students not only within the Union, but also in regard to the candidate and the Mediterranean States.[40]

4. Required Qualifications for Natural Persons

Where the taking up of a specific activity is not subject to any rules in the host State, a national of any other Member State will be entitled to establish himself and pursue that activity there without further ado, but under the general conditions applicable to those exercising that kind of activity in the host State,

---

[33] art.50(2)(c) TFEU [art.44(2)(c)].

[34] art.50(2)(f) TFEU [44(2)(f)], where a reference is simply made to "personnel belonging to the main establishment into managerial or supervisory posts".

[35] Former art.54(1) EC; see [1962] O.J. 2/36. General Programme for the abolition of restrictions on freedom of establishment. The programme defined the persons to whom the right of establishment applies, refers to the right of entry and residence in the host Member State, and details which restrictions have to be removed (they include rules which are applicable without discrimination to nationals and others but hinder the latter more). Mention of these programmes was eliminated by the Treaty of Amsterdam, probably because they had been mostly implemented.

[36] Directive 93/96 replaced by Directive 2004/38 (quoted above).

[37] For more details see above Ch.16: Free Movement of Persons.

[38] *Commission v Austria* (C-147/03) [2005] E.C.R. I–5969.

[39] With regard to financial support offered by the State, *Bidar* (C-209/03) [2005] E.C.R. I–2119.

[40] See below Ch.29: Social Policy (under 2. The European Social Fund (ESF)).

concerning, for instance, social security and insurance. On the other hand, freedom of establishment and the right to provide services require that the natural or legal person claiming those rights has the necessary qualifications, if the latter are required in the host Member State. This is the case, in the first place, for the so-called liberal professions. These, according to the Court, concern activities:

"[W]hich involve a marked intellectual character, require a high level qualification and are usually subject to clear and strict professional regulation. In the exercise of such an activity, the personal element is of special importance, and such exercise always involves a large measure of independence in the accomplishment of the professional activities".[41]

The latter are indeed "regulated"[42] in all the Member States. The diversity of the national requirements concerning those qualifications constituted the main obstacle to the freedom of establishment and the right to provide services. Although the fact of requiring certain qualifications for the performance of professional activities is not only legitimate but constitutes a vital condition for the protection of the general interest, free movement of persons could not become effective without a minimum of harmonisation. Consequently, the Treaty provides that Council and Parliament acting (jointly)[43] in accordance with the ordinary legislative procedure,[44] issue the necessary directives. Firstly, for the, "mutual recognition of diplomas, certificates and other evidence of formal qualification".[45] Secondly, for the, "coordination of the provisions laid down by law, regulation and administrative action in Member States concerning the taking up and pursuit of activities as self-employed persons".[46]

A first series of directives adopted between 1977 and 1985 concerned the "regulated professions": doctors, nurses responsible for general care, dental practitioners, veterinary surgeons, midwifes, architects and pharmacists.[47] These directives were replaced, as mentioned, as from October 20, 2007[48] by a single directive, that shall be briefly examined for each regulated profession hereafter.

---

[41] *Urbing-Adam* (C-267/99) [2001] E.C.R. I–7467.

[42] For a definition of the notion "regulated profession", see *Fernandez de Bobadilla v Museo Nacional del Prado* (C-234/92) [1999] E.C.R. I–4773.

[43] art.53(1) TFEU [47].

[44] See art.294 TFEU [251].

[45] art.53(1) TFEU [47(1)].

[46] art.53(2) TFEU [47(2)].

[47] Since the reader might encounter references to those now repealed directives and since, "references to the repealed Directives shall be understood as references to this Directive: [2005/36] and the acts adopted on the basis of those Directives shall not be affected by this repeal", they are mentioned here. Except for doctors and architects, there were two directives for each one of the seven regulated professions: one concerning the recognition of diplomas and the second contained a very detailed description of the required training; for doctors Directive 93/16 [1993] O.J. L165/1; for nurses responsible for general care (as opposed to specialised nurses) Directive 77/452 [1977] O.J. L56/1 and Directive 77/453 [1977] O.J. L56/8; for dental practitioners Directive 78/686 [1978] O.J. L233/1 and Directive 78/687 [1978] O.J. L233/3 (see *Commission v Italy* (C-202/99) [2001] E.C.R. I–9319 maintaining a second channel for forming dentists, different from the one provided for in the Directive, is illegal), [one feels like adding of course and one may wonder why certain Member States so overtly flout Union law]; veterinary surgeons Directive 78/1026 [1978] O.J. L233/1 and Directive 78/1027 [1978] O.J. L233/10; midwifes Directive 80/154 [1981] O.J. L33/1 and Directive 80/155 [1980] O.J. L33/8; pharmacists Directive 85/432 [1985] O.J. L254/34 and Directive 85/433 [1985] O.J. L254/37; architects Directive 85/384 [1985] O.J. L223/15.

[48] Directive 2005/36 on the recognition of professional qualifications [2005] O.J. L255/22, corrigendum [2008] O.J. L93/28.

Other directives established a general system for the recognition of higher education diplomas awarded on completion of professional education and training of at least three years duration, followed by adaptation periods or an aptitude test in the Member State of establishment[49]; this was later extended to education and training of less than three years.[50] These two directives were supplemented by a third recognising the qualifications of those professional activities not covered by the other two directives.[51] These three directives were replaced also by the single directive mentioned above and shall be briefly examined after the regulated professions.

(1) The "Regulated Professions"

The recognition of regulated professional qualifications by the host Member State allows the beneficiary to gain access in that Member State to the same profession as that for which he is qualified in the home Member State and to pursue it in the host Member State under the same conditions as its nationals. When the profession is not regulated in the host Member State, the provider has to be legally established in a Member State for the purpose of pursuing the same profession there, and he must have pursued that profession there for at least two years during the 10 years preceding the provision of services. Those provisions only apply when the provider moves to the territory of the host State as opposed to a person who simply goes to another Member State for a limited period.

Further Directive provisions concern, among others, the demand by the authorities of documents and certificates,[52] the use of professional titles,[53] the required knowledge of languages,[54] the use of academic titles[55] and the approval of health insurance funds.[56]

(i) **Doctors of Medicine**.[57] The provisions concern: basic medical training, specialist medical training, acquired rights specific to specialised doctors, specific training in general medical practice, pursuit of the professional activities of general practitioners and acquired rights specific to general practitioners. Annex V.1 to the Directive (about 30 pages) sets out the "evidence of formal qualifications" and the "minimum time of training" for the various specialisations.

The Court was, on several occasions called upon to interpret the applicable provisions, and decided, for instance, that the rights provided in the Directives also apply to own nationals who have acquired the necessary qualifications in

[49] Directive 89/48, [1989] O.J. L19/16; see *Consiglio Nationale degli Ingegneri* (C-311/06) [2009] E.C.R. I-415: the Directive cannot be invoked by the holder of a certificate issued by an authority of another Member State which does not attest any education or training by the education system of that Member State.
[50] Directive 92/51 [1992] O.J. L209/25.
[51] Directive 99/42 [1999] O.J. L201/77.
[52] art.50 Directive 99/42.
[53] art.52 Directive 99/42.
[54] art.53 Directive 99/42.
[55] art.54 Directive 99/42.
[56] art.55 Directive 99/42.
[57] arts 24–33 Directive 99/42.

another Member State in accordance with Union law, and who want to establish themselves as general practitioner in their own country, even if that practice is, in the own country, subject to additional training requirements.[58] An important aspect of this judgment is the statement of the Court that the right to practice flows directly from the Directive. However, following this Court decision, the Council adopted a directive on specific training in general medical practice.[59] The latter is now included in the training provided for by the Directive.[60] It should be noted, however, that a doctor who has acquired a specialist qualification in one Member State may not automatically use his title in another Member State if the latter does not recognise it as a specialist field under the Directive.[61]

(ii) **Nurses Responsible for General Care.**[62] The Directive provides for their training, the various professional activities and acquired rights. It might be interesting to very briefly mention here the sort of training details contained in this Directive. To become a nurse one must first have a general school education of at least 10 years and secondly, have followed a full-time training programme set out in the Annex to the Directive and comprising a three-year course or 4,600 hours of theoretical and practical instruction. The Directive goes on to define where and under what supervision the instruction must have been received. In fact, this is the only way to guarantee that the nurse from another Member State is, theoretically at least, as good as the national ones. Annex V.2. sets out the details of the theoretical training and the clinical instruction.

(iii) **Dental Practitioners.**[63] The same kind of detailed training programme applies for this profession also: as for the other professions, the Directive details "basic training", "specialist dental training", the "pursuit of professional activities" and "acquired rights". See Annex V.3. to the Directive.

(iv) **Veterinary Surgeons.**[64] The Directive provides for their "training" and their "acquired rights". See also Annex V.4. to the Directive.

(v) **Midwives.** Here also, details on "training", "procedures for the recognition of formal qualifications", "pursuit of the professional activities" and "acquired rights" are to be found in the Directive.[65] See Annex V.5 to the Directive.

---

[58] *Broekmeulen v Huisarts Registratie Commissie* (246/80) [1981] E.C.R. 2311 [1982] 1 C.M.L.R. 91. See also *Garofalo v Ministero della Sanita* (Joined Cases C-69/96, C-70/96, C-71/96, C-72/96, C-73/96, C-74/96, C-75/96, C-76/96, C-77/96, C-78/96 and 79/96) [1997] E.C.R. I–5603; [1998] 1 C.M.L.R. 1087, concerning specific training in general medicine and the right to engage in general practice. See also Council Resolution on migrant doctors within the Union [1997] O.J. C241/1.
[59] See *Katharina Rinke v Artzenkammer Hamburg* (C-25/02) [2003] E.C.R. I–8349.
[60] Directive 2001/19 [2001] O.J. L206/1.
[61] See *Erpelding* (C-16/99) [2000] E.C.R. I–6821.
[62] The reference to general care distinguishes those nurses from the specialised ones such as psychiatric, child care or other nurses. The title nurse is not necessarily recognised in all the Member States and those nurses cannot therefore claim the freedom of establishment without further ado; see Notification of the Professional Title of Nurses responsible for general care [2005] O.J C123/5.
[63] art.24–37 Directive 2005/36 (quoted above). See also: Notification of evidence of formal qualifications of practitioners of dentistry and specialised dentistry [2005] O.J. C123/3.
[64] art.38–39 Directive 2005/36 (quoted above).
[65] arts 40–43 Directive 2005/36.

(vi) Pharmacists. The Directive provides for "training" and the "pursuit of professional activities"[66]; see Annex V.6. to the Directive.

In a judgment that concerned pharmacists, the Court stated that mere administrative practices which lack appropriate publicity cannot be regarded as the valid fulfilment of the obligations imposed by the Treaty on the Member States.[67]

(vii) Architects. The Directive provides for "training", "derogations from the provisions for training", "pursuit of professional activities" and "acquired rights".[68] See Annex V.7. to the Directive.

In the case of a Union national holding a diploma not listed in the Directive, the host Member State is, according to the Court, obliged to make a comparison between the specialised knowledge and abilities certified by that diploma and the qualifications required by its national legislation.[69] There is also the Council Recommendation concerning holders of a diploma in architecture awarded in a third country[70]; this is something that is not provided for with regard to the other regulated professions.

The Directive contains essential general provisions concerning, among others, membership of professional organisations and registration with a public social security body[71]; the obligation for the service provider to make a declaration in advance to the competent authorities of the host State[72]; the right of the authorities of the host State to ask the authorities of the home State to provide, for each provision of services, any information concerning the legality of the provider's establishment and good conduct, as well as the absence of any disciplinary or criminal sanctions of a professional nature[73] and the information to be given by the service provider to the recipient of the service.[74]

In case the applicant, for specific and exceptional reasons, does not satisfy the conditions laid down in the above-mentioned provisions, the Directive provides for "levels of qualification", "equal treatment of qualification", "conditions for recognition", "compensation measures" and the "waiving of compensation measures on the basis of common platforms".[75] The same apply to all activities not covered by the "recognition of professional experience"[76] or "recognition on the basis of coordination of minimum training conditions".[77]

(viii) Lawyers. (Although not part of the "regulated professions" they shall be examined here.) Until the year 2000, lawyers having obtained their qualification in their home country and wishing to practice on a permanent basis in another

---

[66] arts 44–45 Directive 2005/36 (quoted above).
[67] *Commission v Belgium* (C-167/90) [1991] E.C.R. I-2535.
[68] arts 46–49 Directive 2005/36 (quoted above).
[69] *Dreessen* (C-31/00) [2002] E.C.R. I-663.
[70] [1985] O.J. L223/28. It should be noticed that a Council "Recommendation", which, by definition, is not binding, is nonetheless published in the L series of the O.J., this is awkward, since L stands for legislation.
[71] art.6 Directive 2005/36 (quoted above).
[72] art.7 Directive 2005/36.
[73] art.8 Directive 2005/36.
[74] art.9 Directive 2005/36.
[75] arts 10–15 Directive 2005/36.
[76] arts 16–20 Directive 2005/36.
[77] arts 21–49 Directive 2005/36.

Member State had to rely on the Directive to facilitate the effective exercise by lawyers of freedom to provide services.[78] The second lawyers directive[79] became applicable on March 14, 2000. It allows a lawyer to become established in a Member State and to practice the host country's law immediately after simply proving that he is already registered as a lawyer in another Member State, without the need for either a test or an adaptation period. Moreover, after effectively and regularly pursuing, for a period of three years, an activity involving the law of the Member State in question, including Union law, a lawyer will be entitled to gain admission to the profession in the host Member State and so acquire the professional title of that Member State. For example, under the Directive, a Danish advokat could settle in Germany, practice German law immediately as an advokat and, after three years, obtain the German title of Rechtsanwalt.

In 2002, the EEA Council decided to extend the Lawyers' Establishment Directive to Iceland, Norway and Liechtenstein; the same applies to Switzerland by virtue of the EU-Swiss Accords on the Free Movement of Persons.

(2) The "Non-regulated Professions"

This profession by profession approach took years. The difficulty resides in the fact that particular education and training achievements are required in the different Member States to qualify for a regulated profession. It would have been totally impossible to achieve harmonisation for all the regulated professions and the sectors in which self-employed persons are active. As was pointed out in the chapter on free movement of goods, a similar problem was encountered with regard to the acceptance of products from other Member States. The harmonisation approach with regard to goods was partially abandoned and complemented by the principle of mutual recognition.[80] Something similar happened with the free movement of self-employed persons: as was explained above, the Council adopted, "a general system for the recognition of higher education diplomas awarded on completion of professional education and training of at least three years duration",[81] followed by adaptation periods or an aptitude test in the

---

[78] Directive 77/249 [1977] O.J. L78/17.

[79] Directive 98/5 to facilitate practice of the profession of lawyer on a permanent basis in a Member State other than that in which the qualification was obtained [1998] O.J. L77/36. See also Directive 77/249 to facilitate the effective exercise by lawyers of the freedom to provide services on a temporary basis [1977] O.J. L78/17. See *Wilson* (C-506/04) [2006] E.C.R. I-8613, the Directive precludes an appeal procedure in which the decision refusing registration must be challenged at first instance before a body composed of lawyers practising under the professional title of the host country and on appeal before a body composed for the most part of such lawyers; registration cannot be made subject to a prior examination of proficiency in the language of the host Member State and arts 3 and 4 preclude national legislation imposing penalties. See *van Leuken* (C-197/06) [2008] E.C.R. I-2627. This Directive precludes legislation by a Member State which makes the performance on its territory by a service provider established in another Member State subject to obtaining an authorisation the grant of which is conditional upon success in an aptitude test in law.

[80] See, for instance, *Cassis de Dijon* (120/78) [1979] E.C.R. 649.

[81] Directive 89/48 establishing a general system for the recognition of higher-education diplomas corresponding to education and training programmes of at least three years' duration [1989] O.J. L19/16, modified [2001] O.J. L206/1. For partial and limited recognition of professional qualifications, see *Colegio de Ingenieros* (C-330/03) [2006] E.C.R. I-801 and *Commission v Spain* (C-286/06) [2008] E.C.R. I-8025 obligation for Member State A to recognise diploma delivered by a Member State B on the basis of studies pursued in Member State A!

Member State of establishment. A second directive extended the system of mutual recognition to professional education and training of less than three years duration acquired at an establishment of higher education or at similar establishments.[82] These two directives were supplemented by a third directive for the recognition of qualifications for those professional activities not covered by the other two directives.[83]

All three directives were replaced by the 2005 Directive on the recognition of professional qualifications (see hereunder). However, the system itself was not modified in so far that professions not specifically covered by a directive (that provides automatically a right to establishment) are subject to verification and acceptance by the host Member State on an individual basis. In 2004, Parliament and Council established a, "single Union framework for the transparency of qualifications and competences" (EUROPASS). This consists of a personal, co-ordinated portfolio of documents that citizens can use on a voluntary basis to better communicate and present their qualifications and competences throughout Europe. Its purpose is to facilitate the mobility within the Union of students, persons undergoing training, volunteers, teachers and trainers. See also, a directive on the abolition of restrictions on movement and residence within the Union for nationals of Member States with regard to establishment and the provision of service.[84]

The 2005 Directive introduces a distinction between establishment[85] and provision of services.[86] Where the *provision of services* is concerned a balance is established between, on the one hand, the free movement of the qualified professional legally established in one Member State and the protection of the consumer, based upon mutual recognition and control by the host Member State.

The host Member State may require the service provider to make a declaration prior to providing any services including the details of any insurance cover or other means of personal or collective protection with regard to professional liability. The host Member State may also require that the first application be accompanied by certain documents listed in an annexe to the Directive. In case the host State requires pro forma registration with the competent professional association, this must occur automatically.

For the *right of establishment*, the Directive sets out the conditions for the recognition of the professional qualifications, and the rules governing the recognition mechanism. Three systems of recognition are provided:

- the general system: applicable to all professions that are not covered by specific rules of recognition and to situations where the migrant professional does not meet the conditions set out in other recognition schemes; in case of important differences between the training acquired by the migrant and

---

[82] Directive 92/51 on a second general system for the recognition of professional education and training to supplement Directive 89/48 [1992] O.J. L209/25, amended [1997] O.J. L184/31; annexes C and D were amended, [2000] O.J. L54/42. For an interpretation of Directive 89/48, see among others, *Isabelle Burbaud v Ministère de l'Emploi et de la Solidarité* (C-285/01) [2003] E.C.R. I–8219 and *Peros* (C-141/04) [2005] E.C.R. I–7165. See also *Dreessen* (C-31/00) [2002] E.C.R. I–663.

[83] Directive 99/42 [1999] O.J. L201/77.

[84] Directive 73/148 [1973] O.J. L172/14, replaced by Directive 2004/38 on the right of citizens of the Union and their family members to move and reside freely within the territory of the Member States [2004] O.J. L158/77.

[85] art.10 and following Directives 2005/36 (quoted above).

[86] art.5 and following, Directive 2005/36 (quoted above).

the requirements of the host State, "compensatory" measures are provided in the form of either a stage or an aptitude test (as a matter of fact the recognition mechanism established by previous directives[87] remains unchanged);

- the automatic recognition of qualifications attested by professional experience—it applies to industrial, craft and commercial activities listed in the Directive and certified by professional experience;
- the automatic recognition of qualifications for specific professions that provides for an automatic recognition of evidence of training based on a co-ordination of the minimal training conditions: it concerns the seven regulated professions referred to above.

(3) Recognition of Professional Experience

In many Member States access to, and the pursuit of, one of the activities listed in Annex IV to the Directive is contingent upon possession of general commercial or professional knowledge and aptitudes. In those cases the Member States must recognise previous pursuit of the activity in another Member State as sufficient proof of such knowledge and aptitude, if those activities have been pursued in accordance with the conditions laid down in the Directive. Such conditions may be:

- a minimum number of years on a self-employed basis or as a manager of an undertaking;
- a previous training evidenced by a certificate recognised by the Member State or judged by a competent professional body to be fully valid;
- a certain number of years in an executive position involving technical duties and responsibility for at least one department of a company, etc.

The 2005 Directive provides for "common platforms" defined as a set of criteria of professional qualifications that are suitable for compensating substantial differences as mentioned above.[88] These platforms may be submitted to the Commission by Member States or by professional associations or organisation that are representative at national or European level. If these platforms are adopted, the host State shall wave the application of compensatory measures.[89] Other directives were adopted for the production and processing activities. They concern, among others: agriculture[90]; activities in the wholesale trade and intermediaries in commerce, industry and small craft industries[91]; manufacturing and processing industries falling within Industries and Small Craft Industries (ISIC) Major groups 23 to 40[92]; mining and quarrying[93]; food manufacturing and beverage industries[94]; exploration, prospecting and drilling for petroleum and natural gas.[95]

---

[87] Directives 89/48 and 92/51 (quoted above).
[88] For more details see *http://www.europa.eu /scadplus/leg/en/cha/cl1065.htm*.
[89] Directive art.15, 2005/36.
[90] See for instance Directive 71/18 laying down detailed provisions for the attainment of freedom of establishment in respect of self-employed persons providing agricultural and horticultural services.
[91] Directive 64/222 [1964] O.J. 56/857 and Directive 64/224 [1964] O.J. 56/869.
[92] Directive 64/427 [1964] O.J. 117/1863, amended [1969] O.J. L59/8 and Directive 64/429 [1964] O.J. 117/1880.
[93] Directive 64/428 [1964] O.J. 117/1871.
[94] Directives 68/365 and 68/366 [1968] O.J. L260/505 and 509.
[95] Directive 69/82 [1969] O.J. L68/4.

5. REQUIRED QUALIFICATIONS FOR LEGAL PERSONS/COMPANY LAW

For "legal persons", i.e. undertakings, companies or firms formed in accordance with the law of a Member State and having their registered office, central administration or principal place of business within the Union,[96] the right of establishment is, according to the Court, "generally exercised by the setting up of agencies, branches and subsidiaries", as is expressly provided for by the Treaty.[97] This free movement of companies and firms obviously requires that the safeguards for the protection of the interests of the members and the public that are required by Member States, be equivalent throughout the Union. The Treaty therefore entrusts the Council and the Commission to take the necessary action, while it provides that the Council must act by means of directives.[98] Those provisions were given a wide interpretation by the institutions and the result was an ambitious legislative programme aimed at harmonising the national laws applying to undertakings, the so-called company law directives.

The *first* directive concerns the co-ordination of safeguards in the case of companies with limited liability. It provides for the protection of the interests of third parties by disclosure of information concerning such companies, the particulars of persons authorised to bind the company, restriction of the grounds on which obligations are not valid and limitation of the cases in which nullity can arise.[99]

The *second* directive deals with the formation of public liability companies and the maintenance and alteration of their capital; it restricts the right of a company to acquire its own shares.[100] This restriction was extended to the acquisition of shares by companies over which the first can exercise a dominant influence.[101]

The *third* directive concerns mergers of public limited liability companies and requires publication to the shareholders of the merger plan, accounts and reports.[102]

The *fourth* directive provides for similar legal requirements concerning the financial information that must be made public, such as annual accounts; in this respect attention must be drawn to the International Accounting Standards (IAS), the International Financial Reporting Standards (IFRS) and the International

---

[96] art.54(1) TFEU [48(1)]; see *Cartesio* (C-210/06) E.C.R. 16.12.08. Arts 49 and 54 do not preclude legislation under which a company incorporated under the law of a Member State may not transfer its seat to another Member State whilst retaining its status as a company governed by the law of the Member State of incorporation.

[97] *The Queen v Treasury and Commissioners of Inland Revenue, Ex p. Daily Mail and General Trust Plc* (81/87) [1988] E.C.R. at 5483(17).

[98] art.50(1) and (2) TFEU [44(1) and (2)].

[99] Directive 68/151 regarding disclosing requirements in respect of certain types of companies [1968] O.J. L65/8, amended [2003] O.J. L221/13, codified [2009] O.J. L258/11. See *Daihatsu-Händler v Daihatsu Deutschland* (C-97/96) [1997] E.C.R. I–6843: national legislation may not restrict to certain persons the right to apply for imposition of penalties in the event of failure of a company to disclose the annual accounts. See also *Berlusconi* (Joined Cases C-387/02, C-391/02 and C-403/02) [2005] E.C.R. I–3565, concerning false accounting.

[100] Directive 77/91 [1977] O.J. L26/3, modified [2006] O.J. L264/32, amended [2009] O.J. L259/14 as regards reporting and documentation requirements in the case of mergers and divisions. See *Pafitis v TKE* (C-44/93) [1996] E.C.R. I–1347: increase of bank capital by administrative measure not allowed; *Siemens* (C-42/95) [1996] E.C.R. I–6017: art.29 of the Directive does not prohibit the grant of a preferential right to shareholders in case of capital increase; and *Kefalas* (C-367/96) [1998] E.C.R. I–284: the right of a shareholder to invoke art.25(1) of the Directive is not annulled by successful violation.

[101] Directive 92/101 [1992] O.J. L347/64.

[102] Directive 78/855 [1978] O.J. L295/36.

Financial Reporting Interpretation Committee (IFRIC).[103] Extended to banks and other financial institutions[104] and to branches in the Union of credit or financial institutions with head offices in third countries.[105] The switch-over to the new IFRS was not an easy operation; it is now applied by the 27 Member States, Australia and South Africa and, in the coming years, by Japan, South Korea and Canada and will necessarily have to be adopted, at some point, also by the United States in view of their many subsidiaries within the Union.[106]

The *fifth* directive never passed the stage of Commission proposal.[107] It concerned the structure of public limited liability companies and the powers and obligations of their organs.

The *sixth* directive is about the division of public liability companies either by acquisition or by the formation of new companies, or both.[108] It complements the previous one on mergers.

The *seventh* directive concerns consolidated accounts,[109] and was extended to banks and other financial institutions.[110] A complementary directive concerns the annual accounts and consolidated accounts of insurance undertakings.[111]

The *eighth* directive deals with approval of persons responsible for carrying out statutory audits of accounting documents.[112]

There is no *ninth* directive, and the *tenth* never got beyond the draft stage: it was supposed to concern cross-frontier mergers of public liability companies.[113]

---

[103] Fourth Directive 78/660 [1978] O.J. L222/11, amended [1990] O.J. L317/60 and [2009] O.J. L164/42; Regulation 1126/08, amended [2009] O.J. L80/5. See *Springer* (Joined Cases C-435/02 and C-103/03) [2004] E.C.R. I–8663; see also *BIAO v Finanzamt fur Grossunternehmen* (C-306/99) [2003] E.C.R. I–1; see below, seventh Directive 83/349 [1983] O.J. L193/1, amended [2009] O.J. L164/42 and Directive 86/635 extending the seventh Directive to financial institutions [1986] O.J. L372/1 and Directive 91/674 on the annual accounts and consolidated accounts of insurance undertakings [1991]. Important is Regulation 1606/02 on the application of International Accounting Standards (IAS)/ [2002] O.J. L 243/1 (for the implementing powers conferred on the Commission, see Regulation 297/09 [2009] O.J. L97/62), and Regulation 1126/08 adopting certain international accounting standards in accordance with Regulation 1606/02 [2008] O.J. L320//32, amended [2009] O.J. L21/10 and corrigendum [2009] O.J. L68/33, amended again [2009] O.J. L139/6 as regards the IFRIC and [2009] O.J. L149/6, amended again [2009] O.J. L239/48. See also Regulation 70/09 as regards improvements to international Financial Reporting Standards (IFRSs) [2009] O.J. L21/16, amended [2009] O.J. L244/6.

[104] Directive 86/635 on the annual accounts and the consolidated accounts of banks and other financial institutions [1986] O.J. L372/1. See Regulation 1606/2002 (quoted above).

[105] Directive 89/117 [1989] O.J. L44/40. See also Directive 89/299 on the own funds of credit institutions [1989] O.J. L124/16.

[106] Financial Times April 30, 2008: Corporate finance.

[107] [1983] O.J. C240/2.

[108] Directive 82/891 [1982] O.J. L378/47, amended [2009] O.J. L259/14.

[109] See Regulation on the application of international accounting standards [2002] O.J. L243/1, Regulation 1606/2002 as regards International certain international accounting standards in accordance with Regulation 1606/2002, amended [2005] O.J. L299/45 and [2008] O.J. L320/1, modified [2008] O.J. L338/10, amended [2009] O.J. L191/5, and Regulation 2086/04 [2004] O.J.L363/1.

[110] Directive 86/635 [1986] O.J. L372/1, amended several times; see also Regulation 2423/2001 concerning the consolidated balance sheet of the monetary financial institutions [2001] O.J. L333/8 and Regulation 63/2002 concerning statistics on interest rates applied by monetary financial institutions top deposits and loans vis-à-vis households and non-financial corporations ([2002] O.J. L10/24); the latter were modified by Regulation 2181/2004 [2004] O.J. L371/42.

[111] Directive 91/674 [1991] O.J. L374/7.

[112] Directive 84/253 [1984] O.J. L126/20.

[113] [1985] O.J. C203/211.

The *eleventh* directive concerns disclosure requirements with respect to branches opened in a Member State by certain types of companies governed by the law of another State.[114]

The *twelfth* directive deals with single-member private limited liability companies.[115]

Application of the International Accounting Standards (IASs); published by the International Accounting Standards Board (IASB), interpreted by the Standing Interpretation Committee (SIC), and the International Financial Reporting Interpretations Committee (IFRICs).[116] According to the Preamble of the relevant Regulation, the reporting requirements set out in the existing Directives[117] cannot ensure the high level of transparency and comparability which is a necessary condition for building an integrated capital market. It was considered important for the competitiveness of Union capital markets to achieve convergence of the standards used in Europe for preparing financial statements, with international accounting standards that can be used globally, for cross-border transactions or listing anywhere in the world.

Mention must also be made of three directives on the admission of shares to official stock exchange listing,[118] the requirements for the drawing up, scrutiny and distribution of particulars to be published for that admission,[119] and information to be published on a regular basis by companies whose shares were admitted.[120]

In order to protect the interests of holders of the securities of companies that are the subject of takeover bids or of changes of control and whose securities or at least some of them are admitted to trading on a regulated market in a Member State, a directive on takeover bids was issued in 2004.[121] By "takeover bid" is meant, "a public offer (other than by the offeree company itself) made to the holders of the securities of a company to acquire all or some of those securities, which has as its objective the acquisition of control of the offeree company". The latter meaning, "a company, the securities of which are the subject of a bid". The Directive lays down, among other things, "general principles", defines the "supervisory authority and the applicable law", the "protection of minority

---

[114] Directive 89/666 [1989] O.J. L395/36.

[115] Directive 89/667 [1989] O.J. L395/40, codified [2009] O.J. L258/20.

[116] Regulation 1606/2002 [2002] O.J. L243/1 IFRS, modified [2009] O.J. L311/6, Regulation 1725/2003 on the application of international accounting standards [2003] O.J. L 261/1, amended [2005] O.J. L337/16 and Regulation 1606/02; Regulation 2236/04, 2237/04 and 2238/04 respectively O.J. L392/1, 393/1 and 394/1. See Regulation 211/2005 amending Regulation 1725/2003 adopting certain international accounting standards [2005] O.J. L41/1, see also Regulation 1751/05 amending Regulation 1725/03 [2005] O.J. L282/3. See also Regulation 1126/08 on IFRIC, amended [2009] O.J. L314/15 and Regulation 1171/09 [2009] O.J. L314/43.

[117] Directive 78/660 [1978], O.J. L22/11 on the annual accounts of certain types of companies, modified [2009] O.J. L164/42; Directive 83/349 on consolidated accounts [1983] O.J. L193/1, modified [2009] O.J. L164/42; Directive 86/635 on the annual accounts and consolidated accounts of banks and other financial institutions [1986] O.J. L372/1 and Directive 91/674 on the annual accounts and consolidated accounts of insurance companies [1991] O.J. L374/7.

[118] Directive 79/279 [1979] O.J. L66/21, see also Directive 2001/34 on the admission of securities to official stock exchange listing and on information to be published on those securities [2001] O.J. L184/1 amended by Directive 2004/109 on the harmonisation of transparency requirements in relation to information about issuers whose securities are admitted to trading on a regulated market [2004] O.J. L390/38, modified [2008] O.J. L76/50, and Directive 2007/14 [2007] O.J. L69/14, laying down detailed rules for the implementation of Directive 204/109. With regard to "listing particulars" (art.21 Directive 2001/34), see *Ntion et Pikoulas* (C-430/05) [2007] E.C.R. I-5835.

[119] Directive 80/390 [1980] O.J. L100/1.

[120] Directive 82/121 [1982] O.J. L48/26.

[121] Directive 2004/25 [2004] O.J. L 142/12.

shareholders, the mandatory bid and the equitable price", "information concerning bids", "time allowed for acceptance", "information for and consultation of employee's representatives", etc.

A 2003 directive[122] on the *prospectus* to be published when securities are offered to the public or admitted to trading, harmonises requirements for the drawing up, approval and distribution of the prospectus to be published. It provides that no Member State shall allow any offer of securities to be made to the public without prior publication of a prospectus, but with some exceptions. The prospectus must contain all information, which, according to the particular nature of the issuer and of the securities offered or admitting to trading, is necessary to enable the investor to make an informed assessment of the assets, liabilities, financial position, profit and losses, prospects of the issuer and rights attached. Responsibility for the information given in a prospectus shall attach, at least, to the issuer or its administrative, management or supervisory bodies, the offeror, the person asking for admission to trading or the guarantor, as the case may be. The Commission shall define the minimum information to be included. A prospectus is valid for 12 months after its publication.

Furthermore, there are directives concerning taxation in the case of mergers, divisions, transfer of assets and exchanges of shares concerning companies of different Member States[123] and in the case of parent companies and subsidiaries of different Member States.[124]

In 2005 a directive on cross-border mergers of limited liability companies[125] was adopted in order to reduce costs, while guaranteeing the requisite legal certainty and enabling as many companies as possible to benefit.

The Market Abuse Directive[126] requires Member States to amend their national legislation so that in relation to financial instruments traded on EEA regulated markets, insider dealing and market manipulation are prohibited, issuers are required to announce inside information to the public as soon as possible, issuers insure that they and those acting for them draw up "insider lists", those with managerial responsibilities for the issuer, and persons closely associated with them, are under an obligation to notify their dealings in the issuer's shares or any financial instrument linked to them, there is appropriate regulation of investment research to ensure presentation and disclosure of interest, and market professionals are required to notify the relevant competent authority of suspicious transactions. There are four sets of more detailed provisions, known as the level 2 implementing measures, which expand on the following provisions in the Directive: definition of inside information and market manipulation[127]; fair presentation of investment recommendations and disclosure of conflict of interest[128];

---

[122] Directive 2003/71 [2003] O.J L345/68, amended [2008] O.J. L76/37, also amending Directive 2001/34 [2001] O.J. L184/1 on the admission of securities to official stock exchange listing and on information to be published. See *Ntionik and Picoulas* (C-430/05) [2007] E.C.R. I-5835 establishing all the parties responsible in case of incorrect information.

[123] Directive 90/434 [1990] O.J. L225/1.

[124] Directive 90/435 [1990] O.J. L225/6. See *Crédit Mutuel* (C-27/07) [2008] E.C.R. I-2767, regarding taxable income of parent company, nature of "tax credit"; in *Cobelfret* (C-138/07) [2009] E.C.R. 12.02.09. where the Court stated that Directive 90/435, first indent of art.4(1), "is unconditional and sufficiently precise to be capable of being relied on before national courts".

[125] Directive 2005/56 [2005] O.J. L310/1.

[126] Directive 2003/6 [2003] O.J. L96/16. The description of the Directives is borrowed from Herbert Smith, corporate briefing, July 2004.

[127] Directive 2003/124 [2003] O.J. L339/70.

[128] Directive 2003/125 [2003] O.J. L339/73.

the exemptions from market abuse for buy-back programmes and stabilisa-tion[129]; and accepted market practices, definition of insider information in rela-tion to derivatives on commodities, insider lists and notification of managers' transactions and suspicious transactions.[130]

(1) The European Company: Societas Europaea (SE)

Back in 1970, the Commission made a proposal for a European Company Statute that would allow the setting up of a company according to Union law and to be recognised in all the Member States. The main difficulty was the workers' repre-sentation in such a company; this is still unacceptable for certain Member States, although rules were laid down in 1994 on the establishment of a European Work Council or a procedure for informing and consulting employees.[131] The Statute for a European Company was finally adopted by regulation in 2001.[132]

According to the recitals, the Council considered the following:

- the structures of production must be adapted to the Union dimension—companies should be able to carry out the reorganisation of their business on a Union scale;
- the necessity of cross-border mergers with their legal, psychological and fiscal problems;
- the legal framework is still largely based on national law, which forms a con-siderable obstacle to the creation of groups of companies from different Member States;
- next to the different national laws, it should be possible to form companies and carry on business under the new Statute that is directly applicable in all the Member States.

When harmonisation is impossible, reference may be made to the law governing public limited liability companies in the Member State where it has its registered office. The SE itself must take the form of a company with share capital, that being the form most suited, in terms of both financing and management, to the needs of a company carrying on business on a European scale. A minimum cap-ital is required (€120,000). Since there are presently two different systems for the administration of public limited liability companies, an SE should be free to choose between the two, the respective responsibilities of those responsible for management and those responsible for supervision must be clearly defined. The rules and general principles of private international law do apply both where the SE exercise control and where it is the controlled company.

The rules with regard to the involvement of employees in the SE are laid down in a second act, a directive[133] whose provisions form an indissociable part of the

---

[129] Regulation 2273/2003 [2003] O.J. L336/33.

[130] Directive 2004/72 [2004] O.J. L162/70.

[131] Directive 94/45 [1994] O.J. L254/64, replaced by Directive 2009/38 [2009] O.J. L122/28. See *Betriebsrat der Firma ADS v ADS Anker* (C-349/01) [2004] E.C.R. I-6803.

[132] Regulation 2157/2001 on the Statute for a European company (SE) [2001] J.O. L294/1, modified [2004] O.J. L168/1.

[133] Directive 2001/86 supplementing the Statute for a European company with regard to the involvement of employees [2001] O.J. L294/22. See also Directive 2002/14 establishing a general framework for informing and consulting employees in the European Union [2002] O.J. L80/29; see *Confédération Internationale du Travail E.A.* (C-385/05) [2007] E.C.R. I-611 art.3(1) precludes national legislation which excludes a specific category of workers from the calculation of staff members.

first act, the Regulation and must be applied concomitantly. It provides that concrete procedures of employee trans-national information and consultation, as well as, if applicable, participation, should be defined primarily by means of an agreement between parties concerned, or, in the absence thereof, through the application of a set of subsidiary rules. It is a fundamental principle to secure employees' acquired rights as regards involvement in company decisions. Employee rights in force before the establishment of SEs should provide the basis for employee rights of involvement in the SE (the "before and after" principle). Member States must lay down "standard rules" satisfying the provisions set out in the Annex to the Directive. Transposition had to take place no later than October 8, 2004.

(2) The European Co-operative Society

Similarly, the Council adopted, in 2003, a regulation on the statute for a European Co-operative Society (SCE).[134] Those societies can acquire a single legal personality and exercise their trans-national activities with a single statute and structure. Minimum capital is set at €30,000 and the responsibility is limited. It can be set up by natural or legal persons. The Regulation entered into force on August 18, 2006. The Council also adopted a directive concerning the involvement of workers in the co-operative society in order to preserve their rights such as information, consultation and participation.[135]

This was proposed in 2008 by the Commission for the small and medium-sized enterprises (SMEs).[136]

(3) The European Economic Interest Grouping

A kind of forerunner to the SE, albeit on a much more modest scale, is the European Economic Interest Grouping (EEIG),[137] which constitutes a very simple form of association between economic entities, based on Union law. When registered in one Member State, it is recognised as a legal entity in all the others. The only requirement is the drafting and registration of the bylaws; it enjoys legal personality if the Member State of registration so provides. It suffers, however, from an important drawback constituted by the fact that all the members of an EEIG are individually responsible for its debts. A problem might arise with the denomination of an EEIG, since this is done on the basis of national law.[138]

The Treaty provides that, "in order to attain freedom of establishment as regards a particular activity", the institutions must act by means of directives.[139] For more information regarding companies under Union law, see below in Ch.31: Enterprise and Industrial Policy / Information Society.

---

[134] Regulation 1435/03 [2003] O.J. L207/1, corrected [2007] O.J. L49/35.
[135] Directive 2003/72 [2003] O.J. L207/25.
[136] General Report 2008, 55.
[137] Regulation 2137/85 [1985] O.J. L199/1; incorporated [1994] O.J. L1/517.
[138] *European Information Technology Observatory (EITO)* (C-402/96) [1997] E.C.R. I–7515.
[139] art.50(1) TFEU [44(1)].

6. Exceptions to the Freedom of Establishment

A first exception might, in theory, result from the restrictions on the free movement of capital. Indeed, the Treaty provides that the freedom of establishment, which includes, as already indicated, the right to take up and pursue activities as self-employed persons and to set up and manage undertakings in another Member State, is, "subject to the provisions of the Chapter relating to capital".[140] In itself this reference to capital is not surprising since establishment implies that the beneficiary of the right moves all or part of his assets to another Member State, i.e. transfers his capital. Transfer of capital from one Member State to another used to be limited: restrictions only needed to be eliminated, "to the extent necessary to ensure the proper functioning of the common market".[141] This changed with the EU Treaty, when all restrictions on the movement of capital between Member States were prohibited.[142] Consequently, the reservation concerning capital movements, no longer has any practical significance for the freedom of establishment.

The second exception to the freedom of establishment consists in its non-applicability, so far as any given Member State is concerned, to activities which in that State are concerned, even occasionally, with the exercise of official authority.[143] (Very similar to the exception examined in the previous chapter on the free movement of workers: that freedom does not apply to "employment in the public service".[144]) According to the Court, this second exception to the freedom of establishment cannot:

> "[B]e given a scope which would exceed the objective for which the exception was inserted, having regard to the fundamental character of freedom of establishment and the rule on equal treatment with nationals in the system of the Treaty".[145]

Thirdly, there is the exception resulting from the applicability of provisions laid down by law, regulation or administrative action providing for special treatment for foreign nationals on grounds of public policy, public security or public health.[146] Those concepts were clarified by implementing legislation, which applies equally to all three freedoms: workers, establishment and services.[147]

---

[140] art.43(2) TFEU [49(2)].

[141] Former art.67 EC.

[142] art.56(1) TFEU [63(1)].

[143] art.51(1) TFEU [45,1].

[144] art.45(4) TFEU [39(4)].

[145] *Reyners v Belgium* (2/74) [1974] E.C.R. 631(43); [1974] 2 C.M.L.R. 305. The Belgian Government had argued that, since the profession of avocat is connected organically with the functioning of the administration of justice, the whole profession is excepted from the rules of the Treaty. Other governments regarded the exception limited to those activities alone, within the various professions concerned, which are actually connected with the exercise of official authority, subject to their being separable from the normal practice of the profession. In Belgium, the avocat can, for instance, be required to assume the functions of judge; it is obvious that when this is the case, the foreign lawyer will not be considered.

[146] art.52(1) [46(1)].

[147] Directive 64/221 on the co-ordination of special measures concerning the movement and residence of foreign nationals which are justified on grounds of public policy, public security or public health [1964] O.J. 56 850, replaced by Directive 2004/38 on the right of citizens of the Union and their family members to move and reside freely within the territory of the Member States [2004] O.J. L158/77.

Finally, there is the possibility for Parliament and Council, acting in accordance with the ordinary legislative procedure,[148] to rule that the provisions of this chapter shall not apply to certain activities.[149] It is not known whether any activities have been excluded.

Further Reading

Roger Blanpain, *Involvement of Employees in the European Union* (Kluwer, 2002).

Frank Dornseifer, *Corporate Business Forms in Europe* (Sweet & Maxwell, 2006).

Edith Loozen, "Professional ethics and restraints of competition", (2006) E.L.Rev. Feb.

Andrew Johnston and Phil Syrpis, "Regulatory competition in European company law after *Cartesio*", (2009) E.L Rev. June 378.

[148] art.294 TFEU [251].
[149] art.51,2 TFEU [45,2].

Chapter Eighteen

Freedom to Provide Services[1]/Financial Services

According to the TFEU, restrictions on freedom to provide services within the Union are prohibited in respect of nationals of Member States who are established in a State of the Union, other than that of the person for whom the services are intended.[2] Obviously, this means that the provider of the service may move temporarily[3] to the State of the recipient of his services. As shall be seen, the opposite also applies: the recipient of a service may freely move to another Member State to receive a service. The only requirements for being a beneficiary of the freedom to provide services, is that the provider is a citizen of the Union[4] and is "established" in a Member State different from that of the recipient party. A surgeon who moves to another Member State to perform an operation, does not "establish" himself in that other State: he remains "established" in the Member State where he resides and normally carries out his activities. For the performance of the operation in another Member State, he therefore comes under the provisions concerning the freedom to provide services, and not those providing for the right of establishment; however, according to the TFEU, the latter have priority.[5] The TFEU does, here also, explicitly refer to the basic principle of "equal treatment" or "non-discrimination.[6]

Furthermore, the Court emphasised that the Treaty does not only prohibit overt discrimination, but, "all forms of covert discrimination which, although based on criteria which appear neutral, in practice, lead to the same result".[7]

The main difference between "establishment" and "the provision of services", is that, in the first case, a national of a given Member State leaves that State to participate on a stable and continuous basis in the economic life of another Member State and profits from it, thereby contributing to economic and social interpenetration within the Union in the sphere of activities of self-employed persons. By contrast, the provider of services pursues his activity in another State on a temporary basis.

---

[1] arts 56–62 TFEU [49–55].

[2] art.56 TFEU [49].

[3] This follows from art.57,3 TFEU [50,3]: the person providing the service may, in order to do so, temporarily pursue his activity in the State where the service is provided.

[4] See however, art.56,2 TFEU [49,2]: the Council may extend the right to provide services to nationals of third countries established within the Union; this was done, among others, for architects.

[5] art.57,3 TFEU [50,3].

[6] art.57,3 TFEU [50,3]: "under the same conditions as are imposed by that State on its own nationals".

[7] *Seco v Evi* (Joined Cases 62/81 and 63/81) [1982] E.C.R. 223(8).

The Treaty describes this right as follows:

"[T]he person providing a service may, in order to do so, temporarily pursue his activity in the State where the service is provided, under the same conditions as are imposed by that State on its own nationals".[8]

This means, according to the Court, that the host State should impose on the person from another Member State who provides services on its territory, the same specific requirements based on the particular nature of the service, where they have as their purpose the application of professional rules dictated by the common interest. Those requirements concern the organisation of the profession, the qualifications, the rules of professional ethics, the supervision and the liability, which are binding upon any person providing that kind of service.[9] One would have thought that it goes without saying that requiring the service provider to be established in the country where the service is provided, would totally defeat the purpose of the freedom to provide services and, therefore, be contrary to the Treaty; however, the Court had to state this explicitly.[10] When the provider of the services temporarily moves to another Member State, he enjoys the same rights as those which are granted to the migrant worker and the person who establishes himself in another Member State. This means, among others, that he may be accompanied by his family. Indeed, practically all the directives, which implement the freedom of establishment, are also based on the Treaty provisions concerning the freedom to provide services. Consequently, the rights and obligations under both freedoms are the same.

1. REQUIRED QUALIFICATIONS

In order to exercise the right to provide services, the provider must have the required qualifications to do so. The person in question is, therefore, confronted with exactly the same problem as the person wishing to establish himself in another Member State to carry out a regulated activity. This means, for instance, that the provider of services must have the necessary diplomas. The Directives examined in the previous chapter on the right of establishment with regard to the recognition of evidence of qualification, the harmonisation of the conditions of professional education and training and the abolition of restrictions on movement and residence, also apply to those professionals who wish to avail themselves of the freedom to provide services.[11] The Court also admitted that a Member State may reserve the exercise of a given activity to a specific profession, since this rule applies without distinction to national providers of services and to those of other Member States.[12] However, the Treaty precludes the application of any national rules which have the effect of making the provision of services between Member States more difficult than the provision of services purely within a Member State.[13]

---

[8] art.57,3 TFEU [50,3].

[9] *Van Binsbergen v Bedrijfsvereniging voor de Metaalnijverheid* (33/74) [1974] E.C.R. 1299; [1975] 1 C.M.L.R. 298.

[10] *Commission v France* (220/83) [1986] E.C.R. 3663.

[11] See, for instance, Directive 73/148 on the abolition of restrictions on movement and residence within the Union for nationals of Member States with regard to establishment and the provision of services, replaced by Directive 2004/38 on the right of the citizens of the Union and their family members to move and reside freely within the territory of the Member States [2004] O.J. L158/77.

[12] *Reisebüro Broede v Sandker* (C-3/95) [1996] E.C.R. I–6511; [1997] 1 C.M.L.R. 224.

[13] See case *Commission v Italy (Private Security Guards)* (C-465/05) [2007] E.C.R. I-11091, where the Court found eight violations of art.56 TFEU [49].

Furthermore, it is up to the Member States to take the measures necessary to prohibit on their territory activities which impinge on "protected services".[14] The latter are, among others, television and radio-broadcasting and information society
services; the Directive prohibits, for instance, the manufacture, import, distribution, sale, rental or possession of "illicit devices". The latter are equipment or software designed to give access to a protected service.

Most of the directives on the freedom to provided services were adopted by the
Council (now by Parliament and the Council acting in accordance with the ordinary legislative procedure[15]), in implementation of a general programme. This
programme is no longer mentioned in the Treaty, but it was adopted and implemented and was quite similar to the general programme, which was mentioned
above, for the abolition of the obstacles to the freedom of establishment.

A question may be raised about the "recipient" of services? May he move to
another Member State to receive services? This case not being explicitly provided
for in the Treaty, the question was put to the Court, which determined that the
right to "provide" services, also means the freedom to "receive" services and, in
order to be able to do so, the recipient is just as free to move to any other
Member State to receive a service, as the provider is to provide services.[16] There
are, indeed, numerous cases where it is the receiver of the service who necessarily moves to another Member State. Examples are the patients who go and
consult a doctor, students who go to school, the businessman on the so-called
business trips and, especially, the tourists. The rights of the recipient are also
recognised in the Directive on the abolition of restrictions on movement and
residence within the Union for nationals of Member States with regard to establishment and the provision of services. Said Directive provides, "that the freedom
to provide services entails that persons providing and receiving services, should
have the right of residence for the time during which the services are being
provided".[17]

2. DEFINITION OF "SERVICES"

The Treaty gives the following definition of services: "services shall be considered
'services' within the meaning of this Treaty where they are normally provided for
remuneration".[18] The essential characteristic of remuneration lies in the fact that
it constitutes consideration for the service in question and is normally agreed upon
between the provider and the recipient of the service.[19] According to the Court,
remuneration is, for instance, absent in the case of courses provided in an establishment of higher education, that is normally financed out of public funds and
where students pay only enrolment fees.[20] The Treaty adds that the above definition only applies, "in so far as [the services] are not governed by the provisions

---

[14] Directive 98/84 on the legal protection of services based on, or consisting of, conditional access
[1998] O.J. L320/54; see also General Report 2008, 53.

[15] art.294 TFEU [251].

[16] *Luisi and Carbone v Ministero del Tesoro* (Joined Cases 286/82 and 26/83) [1984] E.C.R. 377;
[1985] 3 C.M.L.R. 52.

[17] Directive 73/148, replaced by Directive 2004/38 (quoted above).

[18] art.57,1 TFEU [50,1].

[19] *Belgium v Humbel* (263/86) [1988] E.C.R. 5365(17); [1989] 1 C.M.L.R. 393.

[20] *Belgium v Humbel* (263/86), above, fn.19.

relating to freedom of movement for goods, capital and persons".[21] This is, at first sight a rather curious addition, since one might wonder what the free movement of goods has to do with services; indeed, the Treaty also provides that, "freedom to provide services in the field of transport shall be governed by the Title relating to transport".[22] One would imagine that "services", where goods are concerned, would mainly be transport; however, one has to see that there are other ways of selling goods across a border. Those operations come, according to the Court, under the provisions concerning the free movement of goods.

The same kind of question arose with regard to television signals: are they goods or services. According to the Court, they must, in the absence of express provision to the contrary, by reason of their nature, "be regarded as provision of services".[23] The same applies to broadcasting.[24] A similar question arises with regard to the services related to movement of capital. The first service that comes to mind, in this regard, is banking. Here again, the Treaty provides that, "[t]he liberalisation of banking and insurance services connected with movement of capital shall be effected in step with the liberalization of movement of capital". From the moment the EU Treaty entered into force, capital movements across the Union were entirely free[25] and, consequently, so were services in those sectors, independently of the provisions on the freedom to provide services.

Finally, as regards "persons" whose free movement is excluded from the provisions concerning freedom to provide services, they are subject to the provisions concerning the freedom of establishment, since the Treaty provides that the right of a person providing services to temporarily pursue his activity in the State where the service is provided, is, "without prejudice to the provisions of the Chapter relating to the right of establishment".[26] According to the Court this means that the provisions of the Chapter on services, "are subordinate to those of the chapter on the right of establishment". In other words, the provisions relating to the provision of services only apply if those relating to the right of establishment do not apply; it only concerns a situation in which a person moves from one Member State to another, not for the purpose of establishment there, but in order to pursue his activity there on a temporary basis. This temporary nature has to be determined in the light of its duration, regularity, periodicity and continuity. This does not mean that the provider of services may not equip himself with some form of infrastructure in the host Member State, including an office, chambers or consulting rooms, in so far as such infrastructure is necessary for the purposes of performing the services in question.[27]

The Court gave a rather extensive interpretation of the concept "services". It determined, for instance, that a national from another Member State has the same right as the nationals from the host State to obtain the financial compensation provided for by national law in case of assault.[28] According to the Court it

---

[21] art.57,1 TFEU [50,1].

[22] art.58(1) TFEU [51(1)].

[23] *Sacchi* (155/73) [1974] E.C.R. 409(6); [1974] 2 C.M.L.R. 177. See also *Procureur du Roi v Debauve* (52/79) [1980] E.C.R. 833; [1981] 2 C.M.L.R. 362 and *Coditel v Cine Vog Films* (62/79) [1980] E.C.R. 881; [1981] 2 C.M.L.R. 362.

[24] See, for instance, *Centro Europea 7* (C-380/05) [2008] E.C.R. I-349: scope of art.46 EC finding restriction on services in the area of TV broadcasting.

[25] art.63 TFEU [56].

[26] art.57,3 TFEU [50,3].

[27] *Gebhard v Consiglio dell'Ordine degli Avvocati e Procuratori di Milano* (C-55/94) [1995] E.C.R. I-4165; [1996] 1 C.M.L.R. 603.

[28] *Cowan v Trésor Public* (186/87) [1989] E.C.R. 195; [1990] 2 C.M.L.R. 613.

concerns here a "service" provided by the State. As a consequence to that judgment, the Council issued a directive relating to compensation to crime victims.[29] The Court also stated that since the end of the transitional period, the essential requirements of the freedom to provide services are unconditionally applicable[30] and have direct effect.[31]

With regard to the kinds of services covered by the freedom, the TFEU refers to activities of an "industrial" or "commercial" character and activities of "craftsmen" and "the professions".[32] Sports are also considered by the courts as services, although the person exercising sports can also be considered as a worker whose freedom of movement is guaranteed by the Treaties. Sport is subject to Union law only in so far as it constitutes an economic activity.[33]

3. The Exceptions, the Directives and Companies and Firms

None of those subjects are explicitly mentioned in the chapter on the freedom to provide services, but the Treaty provides, as indicated, that certain provisions of the chapter on the freedom of establishment shall apply to the freedom to providing services.[34]

Those provisions concern in the first place the exceptions to the freedom to provide services. The same exceptions apply as those provided for the freedom of establishment.[35] Concretely speaking this means that Member States may prevent nationals from other Member States from exercising activities that, as far as any given Member State is concerned, are, in that State, connected, even occasionally, with the exercise of official authority.[36] It will be remembered that the Court decided that if the exercise is indeed only occasionally so connected, and can, furthermore, be separated from the main activity, then there is no justification for excluding the whole profession.[37] Freedom to provide services may also be limited on the basis of provisions laid down by law, regulation or administrative action providing special treatment for foreign nationals on grounds of public policy, public security or public health.[38] Those exceptions must, however, be interpreted restrictively and, when applied, account must be taken of the abundant case law of the Court. Exceptions can also be created by the Council: indeed, by referring to the provisions concerning the freedom of establishment,[39] the Treaty

---

[29] Directive 2004/80 [2004] O.J. L261/15. See *Dell'Orto* (C-467/05) [2007] E.C.R. T-5557 where the Court gave a definition of "victim".

[30] *Van Binsbergen* (33/74) [1974] E.C.R. 1299; [1975] 1 C.M.L.R. 298.

[31] *Ministère Public v Van Wesemael* (Joined Cases 110/78 and 111/78) [1979] E.C.R. 35; [1979] 3 C.M.L.R. 87.

[32] art.57,2 TFEU [50,2].

[33] See *Deliège* (Joined Cases C-51/96 and C-191/97) [2000] E.C.R. I–2549: a national selection for participation in international events is not a restriction on provision of services, and *Lehtonen and Castors Braine* (C-176/96) [2000] E.C.R. I–2714: the Treaty provisions concerning freedom of movement of persons do not preclude rules excluding foreign players from certain matches for reasons that are not of an economic nature, but are of sporting interest only, as in the case of matches between national teams from different countries.

[34] art.51,2 TFEU [45].

[35] art.62 TFEU [55].

[36] art.51 TFEU [45].

[37] *Reyners v Belgium* (2/74) [1974] E.C.R. 631; [1974] 2 C.M.L.R. 305.

[38] art.52 TFEU [46(1)].

[39] art. 62 TFEU [55].

also applies to the "freedom to provide services" the possibility for the Council to, "rule that the provisions of this chapter shall not apply to certain activities".[40] It is not known whether certain activities have indeed been excluded.

In the second place these provisions providing for exceptions concern the obligation, already examined above, imposed upon Parliament and the Council acting jointly to issue directives on the recognition of diplomas and the harmonisation of national provisions concerning training and conditions of access, to the regulated activities.[41]

Thirdly, there is the fact that companies and firms must be treated in the same way as natural persons that are nationals of Member States.[42] The meaning of these terms and the legislative programme implemented by the institutions of the Union, to ensure that those legal persons possess all the required qualifications in order to protect the interests of their members and of the public, were also referred to in the previous chapter on "establishment".

A final reminder: the Treaties' provisions and therefore also those concerning the freedom to provide services, only apply when a trans-national element is involved. In other words, the provisions examined in this chapter cannot be invoked by a person whose activities are confined within a single Member State.[43]

4. Financial Services (Referred to in the Treaty[44] as "Banking Services")

Of particular importance within a single market is the financial services sector, i.e. banks and the credit and financial institutions, to which should be added insurance. The free circulation of "financial products" is made constantly easier by the development of modern technology in the communications field. Those services were to be liberalised in step with the liberalisation of movement of capital and payments, in so far as those services are connected with such movement. Since the free movement of capital and payments is, as indicated, a reality since the Treaty of Amsterdam set up the Economic and Monetary Union (EMU), this does no longer constitute an obstacle for the free movement of financial services.

The problem lies with the rules concerning the operation of financial institutions in the various Member States. Free circulation of financial products needs mutual recognition by Member States of what the other States do to safeguard the interests of the public. Consequently, some harmonisation is required of such matters as licensing, financial supervision, solvency ratio, own funds, winding up, etc. It was agreed among the Member States that any harmonisation or mutual recognition must be guided by the principle of "home country control". This means assigning the primary task of supervising the financial institutions to the competent authorities of the Member State of origin; the other States would communicate to the former all the necessary information; the Member State of destination of the services would play a complementary role.

---

[40] art.51,2 TFEU [45,2].
[41] art. 53(1) TFEU [47(1)] applicable to "services" by virtue if art.62 TFEU.
[42] art.54,1 TFEU [48,1].
[43] *Procureur du Roi v Debauve* (52/79) [1980] E.C.R. 833(15); [1981] 2 C.M.L.R. 362.
[44] art.58(2) TFEU [51(2)].

The first directive adopted in this sector concerned the abolition of restrictions on freedom of establishment and freedom to provide services in respect of self-employed activities of banks and other financial institutions.[45]

A second directive co-ordinates the laws, regulations and administrative provisions relating to the taking up and pursuit of the business of credit institutions.[46] It lays down the principle of the single banking authorisation and supervision and control by the home Member State. It also enables banks to set up branches and other financial services freely throughout the Union.

Finally, there is the directive on the reorganisation and winding up of credit institutions.[47] A similar directive was adopted, for insurance undertakings.[48]

Other directives concern: the annual accounts and consolidated accounts of publicly traded banks and other financial institutions—these accounts must conform with International Accounting Standards (IAS)[49]; obligations regarding the publication of annual accounting documents of branches of credit institutions and financial institutions having their head offices outside the Member State where the branch is established[50]; the own funds of credit institutions[51]; the solvency ratio for credit institution[52]; the supervision of credit institutions on a consolidated basis[53]; the monitoring and control of large exposures of credit institution[54]; the capital adequacy of investment firms and credit institution[55]; the taking up and pursuit of the business of credit institution[56]; the deposit guarantee scheme[57]; and cross-border credit transfers.[58]

---

[45] Directive 73/183 [1973] O.J. L194/1.

[46] Directive 2000/12 [2000] O.J. L126/1; it was "recast" by Directive 2006/48 [2006] O.J. L177/1, amended by Directive 2007/64 on payment services in the internal market [2007] O.J. L319/1 and corrigendum [2009] O.J. L187/5, see, however, Directive 2009/111/[2009] O.J. L302/97 amending said Directive. Amended [2009] O.J. L267/7; according to para (3) of the Preamble, "this directive constitutes the essential instrument for the achievement of the internal market from the point of view of both the freedom of establishment and the freedom to provide financial services, in the field of credit institutions." See Regulation 69/09 adopting certain accounting standards in accordance with Directive 2006/48 [2009] O.J. L21/10 and Regulation 70/09 as regards improvements to the International Financial Reporting Standards (IFRSs) [2009] O.J. L21/16.

[47] Directive 2001 /24 [2000] O.J. L125/15.

[48] Directive 2001 /17 [2000] O.J. L110/28.

[49] Directive 78/660 on the annual accounts [1978] O.J. L22/11, amended [2009] O.J. L164/42; see *Springer* (Joined Cases C-435/02 and C-103/03) [2004] E.C.R. I–8663; Directive 83/349 on consolidated accounts [/1983] O.J. L193/1, amended [2009] O.J. L164/42 and [1991] O.J. L374/7; Directive 2006/46 on the annual accounts and consolidated accounts of insurance undertakings, all amended again [2006] O.J. L224/1 and by the Unfair Commercial Practice Directive [2005] O.J. L149/22; see Directive 1725/2003 (modified [2007] O.J. L300/32) on the adoption of certain international accounting standards in accordance with Regulation 1606/2002 as regards the insertion of "IAS 39" [2004] O.J. L363/1. For more information of IAS, see above Ch.17: Freedom of Establishment/Company Law.

[50] Directive 89/117 [1989] O.J. L44/40.

[51] Directive 89/299 [1989] O.J. L124/16, amended [1992] O.J. L110/52; see *Paul v Germany* (C-222/02) [2004] E.C.R. I-9425.

[52] Directive 89/647 [1989] O.J. L386/14, amended [1996] O.J. L85/17.

[53] Directive 92/30 [1992] O.J. L110/52, amended [1993] O.J. L141/1.

[54] Directive 92/121 [1993] O.J. L29/1.

[55] Directive 93/6 [1993] O.J. L141/1, "recast" by Directive 2006/49 [2006] O.J. L177/201, amended [2008] O.J. L76/54 and repealed [2009] O.J. L267/7.

[56] Directive 2000/12 [2000] O.J. L126/1, amended [2000] O.J. L275/37.

[57] Directive 94/19 [1994] O.J. L135/5; see *Germany v EP and Council* (C-233/94) [1997] E.C.R. I–2405, concerning the obligation imposed upon all credit institutions to join a deposit-guarantee scheme and *Pieter Paul et Alia* (C-222/02) (quoted above, fn.51) on the responsibility of the surveillance authorities.

[58] Directive 97/5 [1997] O.J. L47/25.

It is also interesting to note that the Court declared that the Directive on consumer protection in respect of contracts negotiated away from business premises was applicable to services offered by banks.[59] The Court also stated that the Harmonisation Directive[60] precludes, for instance, a Member State from requiring a credit institution already authorised in another Member State to obtain again an authorisation in order to be able to grant a mortgage loan to a person residing within its territory.[61] It also follows from the Directive[62] that if the banks must comply with an authorisation procedure, they may no longer be examined on the basis of economic needs of the market. Finally, it should be noted that in 1991 the Council adopted a directive on prevention of the use of the financial system for the purpose of money laundering.[63] The directive was accompanied by a statement committing the Member States to enact criminal legislation determining the penalties to be applied for infringement of those provisions.

Mention must also be made of a directive on the taking up, pursuit and prudential supervision of the business of electronic money institutions.[64] Generally speaking, the banking directives apply to those services. Rules concerning redeemability, capital and own funds requirements, limitations of investments, verifications by the authorities, etc. are provided for in said directive.

An Advisory Committee for banking was set up in 1977[65]; it is composed of senior officials from the Member States, whose task it is to help the Commission in implementing and completing the Union banking legislation.

5. INVESTMENT SERVICES

The Union has liberalised access to stock exchange membership and financial markets in other Member States for investment firms authorised to provide the services concerned in their home Member State. A Directive on investment services in the securities field[66] applies, generally speaking, to all investment firms. The criteria for authorisation of investment firms in their home Member State are:

- the investment firm must have sufficient initial financial resources for the proposed activities;
- the persons directing the business must have sufficient professional integrity and experience; and
- the holders of qualifying participation must be suitable persons.

The home State is responsible for the prudential supervision, while the host State is responsible for the implementation of the rules of conduct and for monitoring compliance with them.

An investment firm authorised to function in another Member State is permitted to advertise by all means of communication available in the host State. A

---

[59] *BHW v Dietzinger* (C-45/96) [1998] E.C.R. I–1199.
[60] See, for instance, Directive 89/646 amending Directive 77/780 [1989] O.J. L386/1.
[61] *Parodi v Banque H. Albert de Bary* (C-222/95) [1997] E.C.R. I–3899.
[62] Directive 89/646 [1989] O.J. L386/1, amended [1992] O.J. L110/52.
[63] Directive 91/308 [1991] O.J. L166/77, amended [2001] O.J. L344/76; see also Commission Declaration [2001] O.J. L344/82. See *Ordre des barreaux Francophones et Germanophones* (C-305/05) [2007] E.C.R. I-5305 concerning the obligation of lawyers to divulge to the competent authorities all facts that could indicate money laundering.
[64] Directive 2000/46 [2000] O.J. L275/39.
[65] Directive 77/780 [1977] O.J. L322/30.
[66] Directive 93/22 [1993] O.J. L197/58.

1995 directive reinforces the prudential supervision for investment firms, but also for credit institutions,[67] non-life insurance,[68] life insurance[69] and for undertakings for collective investment in transferable securities (UCITS).[70]

Of great importance is the Financial Services Action Plan (FSAP) that was the object of a Communication of the Commission in 1999 entitled: "Implementing the framework for financial markets: action plan".[71]

The action plan for a single financial market puts forward indicative priorities and a timetable for specific measures to achieve three strategic objectives, namely establishing a single market in wholesale financial services, making retail markets open and secure and strengthening the rules on prudential supervision.[72]

- *Wholesale markets*, i.e. securities and derivatives markets; action is planned in six areas:

  — establishing a common legal framework for integrated securities and derivatives markets;
  — removing the outstanding barriers to raising capital on a Union-wide basis;
  — moving towards a single set of financial statements for listed companies;
  — creating a coherent legal framework for supplementary pension funds;
  — providing the necessary legal certainty to underpin cross-border security trading; and
  — creating a secure and transparent environment for cross-border restructuring.

- *Retail markets*: a legal framework is in place that allows financial institutions to offer their services throughout the Union and has established a bulwark against institutional failure and systemic risk. Still, an array of legal, administrative and private law obstacles hamper the cross-border purchasing or provision of those services. The Commission has identified six areas for action to eliminate these obstacles:

  — information and transparency allowing consumers to invest in another country;
  — redress procedure: efficient and effective machinery for the amicable and judicial settlement of disputes needs to be set in place to provide the necessary confidence in cross-border activity. In 2001, the Commission launched FIN-NET, a network to facilitate out-of-court settlement of disputes in the financial field where the service provider is established in another Member State;
  — balanced application of consumer protection rules;
  — electronic: directives on electronic commerce and distant selling are in the process of being adopted;
  — insurance intermediaries: a single directive will be applicable to those intermediaries;

---

[67] Directive 89/646 [1989] O.J. L386/1.
[68] Directive 92/49 [1992] O.J. L228/1.
[69] Directive 92/96 [1992] O.J. L360/1.
[70] Directive 85/611 [1985] O.J. L375/03, amended [2008] O.J. L76/42, and the implementing Directive 2007/16 [2007] O.J. L79/11.
[71] COM(1999) 232 final (no published in the O.J.)
[72] *http://www.ec.europa.eu /internal market/financial–conglomerates/supervision/en.htm.*

— cross-border retail payments: there is a need for an integrated retail payment system providing secure and competitive small-value cross-border transfers.

- *Strengthening prudential structures:*

  — bring banking, insurance and securities prudential legislation up to higher standards;
  — supervision of financial conglomerates: these structures have developed so fast that new rules were required;
  — improve cross-sectoral discussions and co-operation between authorities: creation of a Securities Advisory Committee.

Another important issue is the elimination of tax barriers and distortions. Further progress was made by the adoption of various directives, some of which have already been mentioned:

- Directive on the taxation of the savings income in the form of interest[73];
- Directive on insider dealing and market manipulation (Market Abuse Directive)[74];
- Directive on the prospectus to be published when securities are offered to the public or admitted to trading (Prospectus Directive)[75];
- Directive on takeover bids[76];
- Directive on the harmonisation of transparency requirements in relation to information about issuers whose securities are admitted to trading on a regulated market (Transparency Directive)[77];
- Directive on markets in financial instruments (MIFID).[78] The latter constitutes a major part of the FSAP.

6. INSURANCE[79]

Similar legislation was enacted with regard to insurance. The establishment of the internal single market in that sector was completed years ago, according to the Commission,[80] with the third Council directive of 1992,[81] that introduced a single system for the authorisation and financial supervision of insurance undertakings by the Member State in which they have their head office (the home

---

[73] Directive 2003/48 [2003] O.J. L157/38.

[74] Directive 2003/6 [2003] O.J. L96/16.

[75] Directive 2003/71 [2003] O.J. L345/64 and Regulation 809/04 [2004] O.J. L149/1.

[76] Directive 2004/25 [2004] O.J. L147/12.

[77] Directive 2004/109 [2004] O.J. L390/38, amended [2008] O.J. L76/50, and Directive 2007/14 laying down the detailed rules for its implementation [2007] O.J. L69/27.

[78] Directive 2004/39 [2004] O.J. L145/1, amended [2006] O.J. L114/6 and [2008] O.J. L76/33. "MIFID is a substantial and potentially sweeping piece of Union law making. Its objective is creating efficient conditions for trading securities and other financial instruments, promoting competition and providing Union-wide standards for investor protection, serve the laudable goal of fostering economic growth in Europe through the creation of deep, liquid and well regulated financial markets on a continental scale" (*Financial Times*, November 11, 2007, p.10).

[79] See below, Ch.22: Competition Policy (3. Competition Rules Applying to Various Branches of the Economy).

[80] See Commission Interpretative Communication "Freedom to provide services and the general good in the insurance sector" [2000] O.J. C43/5.

[81] Directive 92/49 [1992] O.J. L228/1; see *Commission v France* (C-347/02) [2004] E.C.R. I–7557 and Directive 92/96 [1992] O.J. L360/1, amended several times.

Member State). Such authorisation enables an insurance undertaking to carry out its insurance business anywhere in the Union, either on the basis of the rules on establishment, i.e. by opening agencies or branches in all the Member States, or under the rules on the freedom to provide services on the basis of a single licence.[82] When carrying out business in another Member State, the insurance undertaking must comply with the conditions under which, for reasons of the general good, such business must be conducted in the host Member State.

On the other hand, the financial supervision, is a matter only for the home Member State. Laws were harmonised with regard to insurance against civil liability in respect of the use of motor vehicles,[83] direct insurance other than life insurance,[84] the activities of insurance agents and brokers,[85] co-insurance,[86] direct life insurance,[87] legal expenses insurance,[88] reorganisation and winding-up of insurance undertakings[89] and on the annual accounts and consolidated accounts of insurance undertakings.[90] In 1999, the Commission issued four regulations concerning insurance services statistics[91] and in 2001, Parliament and the Council issued a Directive on the reorganisation and winding-up of insurance undertakings.[92]

---

[82] Directive 64/225 [1964] O.J. 56.

[83] Directive 72/166, on the approximation of the laws of the Member States relating to insurance against civil liability in respect of the use of motor vehicles, and to the enforcement of the obligation to insure against such liability [1972] O.J. L103/1, several times amended; see *Farrell* (C-356/05) [2007] E.C.R. I-3067, also covers damages to persons travelling in a place of the vehicle not provided with a seat; Directive 84/5, approximation of the laws of the Member States relating to insurance against civil liability in respect of the use of motor vehicles [1984] O.J. L8/17; Directive 88/357, Directive 90/232, idem [1972] O.J. L103/1, art.1 of this Directive was considered by the Court as having direct effect and therefore providing persons with a right to invoke it directly in national courts: *Farrell* (C-356/05) (quoted above) and Directive 2000/26 (fourth motor insurance directive) [2000] O.J. L181/65. See also Decision on the application of Directive 72/166 relating to checks on insurance against civil liability in respect of the use of motor vehicles [2003] O.J. L192/23. New Directive 2009/103 [2009] O.J. L263/11.

[84] Directive 73/239 [1973] O.J. L228/3, supplemented by Directive 92/49 [1992] O.J. L228/1 and amended [2002] O.J. L77/17, Directive 73/240 on the freedom of establishment in the business of direct insurance other than life insurance [1973] O.J. L228/3, Directive 88/357, idem [1989] O.J. L166/68 and Directive 2002/87 on the supplementary supervision of credit institutions, insurance undertakings and investment firms in a financial conglomerate [2003] O.J. L35/1. See *Garcia* (C-238/94) [1996] E.C.R. I–1673 and *Forsakringsaktiebolaget Skandia* (C-241/97) [1999] E.C.R. I–1879 on restrictions on choice of assets.

[85] Directive 77/92 [1977] O.J. L26/14 on measures to facilitate the effective exercise of freedom of establishment and freedom to provide services in respect of the activities of insurance agents and brokers; see also Commission Recommendation 92/48 on insurance intermediaries [1992]O.J. L19/32. Directive 77/92 was replaced by Directive 2002/92 on insurance mediation [2003] O.J. L9/3.

[86] Directive 78/473 [1978] O.J. L151/25.

[87] Directive 79/267 [1979] O.J. L63/1, supplemented by Directive 92/96 [1992] O.J. L360/1 and amended [2002] O.J. L77/11. Directive 92/96 on the coordination of provisions relating to direct life assurance and amending Directive 79/267 and 90/619 (third life assurance directive) [1992] O.J. L360/1, amended [2000] O.J. L290/27 and [2003] O.J. L35/1. See *Forsakringsaktiebolaget* (C-241/97) (quoted above, fn.84).

[88] Directive 87/344 [1987] O.J. L185/77.

[89] Directive 2001/17 [2001] O.J. L110/28.

[90] Directive 91/674 [1991] O.J. L374/7. See Regulation 1606/02 on the application of international accounting standards [2002] O.J. L243/1 and Regulation 2086/04 [2004] OJ.J L363/1. For more information concerning the international accounting standards, see above Ch.17: Freedom of Establishment/Company Law.

[91] Regulation 1225/99 definition of characteristics, Regulation 1226/99 derogations, Regulation 1227/99 technical format for the transmission and Regulation 1228/99 series of data to be produced [1999] O.J. L154/1.

[92] Directive 2001/17 [2001] O.J. L110/28.

Restrictions on the freedom to provide services can also result from national procedures concerning public service contracts. As shall be seen in the chapter on Public procurement, several directives were adopted to achieve the opening of all national procedures to tenders from nationals of other Member States.[93]

7. FUTURE DEVELOPMENTS

Member States had until December 28, 2009 to bring into force the laws, regulations and administrative provisions to comply with it, mention must be made of the recent directive on services in the internal market.[94] Although too many sectors are excluded,[95] it constitutes a major step, although an imperfect one, on the road to liberalisation of cross-border provision of services, while at the same time increasing transparency and information for consumers giving them a wider choice and better service at lower prices.

At present numerous barriers within the internal market prevent providers, particularly small and medium-sized enterprises, from extending their operations beyond their national borders and from taking full advantage of the internal market.

The Directive establishes general provisions facilitating the exercise of the freedom of establishment for service providers and the free movement of services, while maintaining a high quality of services.

To think that the 1958 EC Treaty already provides that:

"[W]ithin the framework of the provisions set out below, restrictions on freedom to provide services within the Union shall be prohibited in respect of nationals of Member States[96] who are established in a State of the Union other than that of the person for whom the services are intended".[97]

It seems to be a repetition of what happened to the freedom of movement of goods: one had to invent the "internal market" to be established by the end of 1992 (24 years after the customs union was finalised!) in order to make the free movement of goods possible among the Member States. It does not say much about the willingness of the latter to implement their obligations under the Treaty!

Further Reading

Lorna Woods, *Free Movement of Goods and Services within the European Community*, (Aldershot, Ashgate, 2004).
Ulla Neergaard, Ruth Nielsen and Lynn M. Roseberry, *The Services Directive-Consequences for the Welfare State and the European Social Model*, (DJOF Publishing 2008).

---

[93] See, for instance, Directive 92/50 relating to the co-ordination of procedures for the award of public service contracts [1992] O.J. L209/1.

[94] Directive 2006/123 on services in the internal market [2006] O.J. L376/36, published December 27, 2006; see Decision 2009/739 [2009] O.J. L263/32 setting out the practical arrangements for the exchange of information by electronic means between Member States and Decision setting out measures facilitating the use of procedures by electronic means through the "points of single contact" [2009] O.J. L274/36, corrigendum [2009] O.J. L299/18.

[95] For example: financial service (banking, credit, insurance), electronic communication, transport, services of temporary work agencies and health care services.

[96] See also above *Further Reading* in Ch.15: Freedom of Establishment/Company Law.

[97] art.56,1 TFEU [49,1].

Chapter Nineteen

Free Movement of Capital and Payments[1]

Previously[2] the free movement of capital was only required, "to the extent necessary to ensure the proper functioning of the common market". This changed with the EU Treaty. When the European Monetary Union (EMU) was established, all restrictions on the movement of capital were abolished during the first stage of the setting up of the EMU.[3] The Treaty on the Functioning of the European Union (TFEU) now provides that, "all restrictions between Member States and between Member States and third countries shall be prohibited".[4]

The Treaty, however, starts by indicating that this prohibition applies, "within the framework of the provisions set out in this Chapter".[5] The other provisions of this Chapter on Capital and Payments, save one, refer exclusively to restrictions of the free movement of capital with third countries,[6] from which one can deduce that the prohibition applies practically without restrictions to the free movement of capital between Member States.

As for the meaning of "capital movements", Annex I to the basic Directive[7] contained a non-exhaustive list of such movements, which gives some idea of what the expression represents:

1. direct investments[8];
2. investments in real estate[9];
3. operations in securities normally dealt in on the capital market;
4. operations in units of collective investment undertakings;
5. operations in securities and other instruments normally dealt in on the money market;
6. operations in current and deposit accounts with financial institutions;
7. credits related to commercial transactions or to the provision of services in which a resident is participating;
8. financial loans and credits;
9. sureties, other guaranties and rights of pledge;
10. transfers in performance of insurance contracts;

---

[1] arts 63–66 TFEU [56–60].

[2] Former art.67 EC repealed by the Treaty of Amsterdam. However, Annex I of Directive 88/361 for the implementation of former art.67 EC is still on the books [1988] O.J. L178/5, see *Trapeza tis Ellados* (C-329/03) [2005] E.C.R. I–9341 on the interpretation of certain items of the Annex.

[3] July 1, 1990 to December 31, 1993.

[4] art.63(1) TFEU [56(1)].

[5] art.63(1) TFEU [56(1)].

[6] See art.64(1) and (2) TFEU [57(1) and (2)], art.66 [59] and art.75 [60].

[7] Directive 88/361, no longer applicable.

[8] See *Commission v Germany* (Volkswagen law) (C-112/04) [2007] E.C.R. I-8995/: is contrary to art.56, the limitation in the voting rights imposed by law, the requirement of over 80 per cent of the share capital in order to pass certain resolutions, 20 per cent of the share capital constituting a blocking minority, here held by public authorities, all constitute restrictions on the movement of capital.

[9] See *Burtscher v Stauderer* (C-213/04) [2005] E.C.R. I–10309.

11. personal capital movements;
12. physical import and export of financial assets; and
13. other capital movements.

Exceptions to the liberalisation rule concern the application of tax laws,[10] the prudential supervision of financial institutions and procedures for the declaration of capital movements for purposes of administrative or statistical information.[11] To those exceptions must be added the measures which are justified on grounds of public policy or public security. The exceptions based on the last two grounds are common to all the freedoms, as was seen above.[12] In the case of freedom to move capital, they refer, for instance, to national measures designed to ensure effective fiscal supervision and to prevent illegal activities such as tax evasion, money laundering,[13] drug trafficking or terrorism.[14] The Court considered that those aims could be attained by making movement of capital conditional on prior "declaration", but that prior "authorisation" would render the freedom of capital movement illusory.[15]

With regard to tax laws, for instance, Member States have the right to apply tax provisions distinguishing between taxpayers, which are not in the same situation with regard to their place of residence or with regard to the place where their capital is invested.[16]

The Treaty makes no distinction between movement of capital and movement of payments, both are entirely liberated. The distinction might be difficult to make anyway when it concerns, for instance, coins, banknotes or bearer cheques. The Treaty establishes a relation between capital movement and direct investment (including real estate), establishment, the provision of financial services or the admission of securities to capital markets.[17]

Another distinction has to be made with regard to means of payment such as coins: could they be considered as "goods" and consequently enjoy free movement but also be subject to limitations on that account. To take an example, the reader should try to decide whether or not gold coins such as the Krugerrands or silver alloy coins which are legal tender in a Member State are to be regarded and to be treated as "goods"?[18]

---

[10] art.65(1)(a) TFEU [58(1)(a)].

[11] art.65(1)(b) TFEU [58(1)(b)].

[12] Workers: art.45(3) TFEU [39(3)]; establishment: art.52(1) TFEU [46(1)]; and services: art.62 TFEU [55], which refers to art.52 TFEU [46].

[13] See Directive 91/308 on prevention of the use of the financial system for the purpose of money laundering [1991] O.J. L44/40, modified [2001] O.J. L344/76; see also Commission Declaration, as above, at 82.

[14] *Sanz de Lera* (Joined Cases C-163/94, C-165/94, and C-250/94) [1995] E.C.R. I-4821(22).

[15] See also *Luisi and Carbone v Ministero del Tesoro* (Joined Cases C-286/82 and C-26/83) [1984] E.C.R. 377; [1983] 3 C.M.L.R. 52 and *Criminal proceedings against Aldo Bordessa* (Joined Cases C-358/93 and C-416/93) [1995] E.C.R. I-361(25); [1996] 2 C.M.L.R. 13, where the Court already declared that the export of coins, banknotes or bearer cheques could be made conditional on prior declaration, but not on prior authorisation.

[16] art.65(1)(a) TFEU [58(1)(a)].

[17] art.64(2) TFEU [57(2)]. See *Luisi and Carbone* (Joined Cases C-286/82 and C-26/83)(quoted above, fn.15) wherein the Court refers to Directive 88/361 and its Annex I, which refers to physical imports or exports of financial assets.

[18] *R. v Thompson* (7/78) [1978] E.C.R. 2247; [1979] 1 C.M.L.R. 47: the Court decided that silver alloy coins, which are no longer legal tender, are "goods" whose export may be prohibited on the grounds of public policy within the meaning of art.36 TFEU [30]; on the other hand, silver alloy coins which are legal tender in a Member State, are by their very nature to be regarded as means of payment and the provisions concerning the free movement of goods are not applicable; the same applies to Krugerrands, since certain Member States permit dealings in these coins which are therefore to be regarded as being equivalent to currency.

It should be clear that if the free movement of capital is closely linked with the freedom of establishment, the free movement of payments is a necessary complement to the free movement of goods, workers, services and capital. Indeed, nobody would profit from those freedoms if the financial results of the activities carried out under them could not be "brought home" to wherever in the Union the operator resides. The introduction of the Euro has certainly facilitated all those transactions.

2008 saw the inception of the *Single Euro Payments Area* (SEPA), the aim of which is to create an integrated market for services in Euro, where there is genuine competition and no distinction between domestic and cross-border Euro payments.[19] The latter are the subject of a regulation.[20]

[19] General Report 2008, 51.
[20] Regulation 2560/01 [2001] O.J. L344/13.

Chapter Twenty

Intellectual Property Rights (IPR)

The first reference in the Treaty to those rights is in connection with the exceptions to the free movement of goods: prohibition or restrictions on imports, exports or transit of goods may be justified by the protection of industrial and commercial property.[1] The expression "industrial and commercial property rights" can be held to cover all the rights mentioned in the Paris Convention on the Protection of Industrial Property,[2] the Munich Convention on the European Patent[3] and the Union Patent Agreement[4] of 1989. They include: patents, utility models, industrial design, trade marks, service marks, trade names, indication of source or application of origin and copyrights. There are other similar rights that protect such property, for instance know-how.

Union law also protects databases[5] and it was decided that the expression of computer programs is protected by copyright.[6] The latter includes neighbouring rights that are protected by specific legislation.[7]

The owners of such rights enjoy a legal and absolute monopoly (but not necessarily a dominant position, this depends on the relevant market), since they can, as any property owner, claim exclusive use. But by doing so they can prevent trade between Member States since the protection is generally granted for the national territory by a Member State.[8] As the Court put it, in the absence of unification of national rules relating to such protection, industrial property rights and the differences between national rules are capable of creating obstacles to the free movement of products covered by such rights.[9] The exercise of an intellectual property right granted and guaranteed by national law can constitute an

---

[1] art.36 TFEU [30]. This chapter was revised by Katia Bodand.
[2] March 20, 1883, revised several times, last September 28, 1979.
[3] The European Patent Convention came into force in October 1977; all the Member States are party to the Convention. The European Patent Office is located in Munich. Protection can be sought in several States, with the same effect as national patents.
[4] This Union Patent Agreement was signed, but did not enter into force [1989] O.J. L401/1.
[5] Directive 96/9 on the legal protection of databases [1996] O.J. L77/20.
[6] Directive 91/250 [1991] O.J. L122/42, repealed by Directive 09/24 [2009] O.J. L111/16.
[7] See, for instance, Council Directive 92/100 on film rental rights and lending rights and on certain rights related to copyright in the field of intellectual property [1992] O.J. L346/61, amended O.J. L167/10. Art.8, para.2 was interpreted in *SENA* (C-245/00) [2003] E.C.R. I–12151 and art. 2(1) in *Commission v Portugal* (C-61/05) [2006] E.C.R. I-6779 extending those rights to videorramme producers constitutes a breach of that article. See also Council Resolution on increased protection for copyright and neighbouring rights [1992] O.J. C138/1.
[8] Except when a patent is issued under the Convention on the Union Patent that has the same effects, as regards the rights conferred by it, in all the Member States [1976] O.J. L17/1.
[9] *Parke, Davis v Centrafarm* (24/67) [1988] E.C.R. 55 at 71; [1968] C.M.L.R. 48. See also *Cicra v Renault* (53/87) [1958] E.C.R. 6067; [1990] 4 C.M.L.R. 265: the Court accepted opposition to the import of decorative parts on the basis of national law. See also the cases reported below under Union Competition Policy in Ch.22 e.g. *Terrapin v Terranova* (119/75) [1976] E.C.R. 1039; [1976] 2 C.M.L.R. 482 and *Sirena v Eda* (40/70) [1994] O.J. L11/1; [1971] E.C.R. 69; [1971] C.M.L.R. 260.

obstacle to the full application of certain fundamental Union rules. The question therefore arose of how to reconcile the use of those individual rights with the principle, for instance, of free movement of goods. The answer given by the Court is that the "existence" of the intellectual property rights is not affected by the Treaties, but that the "exercise" of such rights can, under certain conditions, be prohibited by Union law. Consequently, such exercise must be strictly limited to what is necessary to safeguard what constitutes the "specific subject-matter" of those rights.[10]

The various rules with regard to intellectual property rights and the free movement of goods were stated by the Court as follows:

1. the Treaty does not affect the existence of intellectual property rights recognised by the law of the Member States;
2. the exercise of those rights may, nevertheless, depending on the circumstances, be restricted by the prohibitions of the Treaties;
3. in as much as an exception to the fundamental principles of the Treaties is provided, it applies only to the extent necessary to safeguard rights which constitute the specific subject matter of that intellectual property;
4. the owner of the right cannot rely on national law to prevent the importation of a product which has been marketed in another Member State by the owner or with his consent;
5. it is the same when the right relied upon is the result of a subdivision, either voluntary or publicly imposed, of a trade mark which originally belonged to a single owner[11]; however, an owner can oppose the import of a product into a Member State when this product was produced in another Member State on the basis of a compulsory licence[12];

---

[10] See *Centrafarm v Sterling Drug* (15/74) and *Centrafarm v Winthrop* (16/74) both [1974] E.C.R. 1147 and 1183; [1974] 2 C.M.L.R. 480, where the Court defined what is the subject matter of a patent: the guarantee that the patentee, to reward the creative effort of the inventor, has the exclusive right to use an invention with a view to manufacturing industrial products and putting them into circulation for the first time, either directly or by the grant of licences to third parties, as well as the right to oppose infringements (*Centrafarm v Sterling drug* (15/74) (quoted above, at 1162) and of a trade mark (*Centrafarm v Winthrop* (16/74) (quoted above, at 1194); from *Parke, Davis* (24/67) (quoted above, fn.9) it follows that one can legally oppose the import and distribution of an unpatented product, otherwise one's own patent becomes useless. The same applies where the holder of a specific right prevents the import of a product from another Member State where there is no longer a protection: *EMI Electrola v Patricia In -und Export* (341/87) [1989] E.C.R. 92; [1989] 2 C.M.L.R. 413. See also *Terrapin v Terranova* (119/75) [1976] E.C.R. 1039; [1976] 2 C.M.L.R. 482: the protection of a trade mark implies also the right to prevent confusion between two products bearing similar names. It is for the national courts to determine whether a risk for confusion does in fact exist.

[11] *SA CNL-SVCAL NV v HAG GF AG* (C-10/89) [1990] E.C.R. I–3711; [1990] 3 C.M.L.R. 571: arts 34 and 36 TFEU [28 and 30] do not prevent that a national law authorises an undertaking, owner of a trade mark in a Member State, to oppose the importation from another Member State of a similar product bearing legally in that other Member State the same or confusingly similar trade mark, even if it belonged to a subsidiary and belongs now to a third party following expropriation. See also *Pall Corporation v Dahlhausen* (C-238/89) [1990] E.C.R. 4827: art.34 TFEU [28] must be interpreted as precluding the application of a national provision on unfair competition which enables a trader to obtain a prohibition in the territory of a Member State on the putting into circulation of goods bearing the letter R in a circle beside the trade mark, where the trade mark is not registered in that State but is registered in another Member State. See, however, *Hoffmann-La Roche v Centrafarm* (102/77) [1978] E.C.R. 1139; [1978] 3 C.M.L.R. 217 and *Centrafarm v American Home Products* (3/78) [1978] E.C.R. 1823; [1979] 1 C.M.L.R. 326. 10. *Pharmon v Hoechst* (19/84) [1985] E.C.R. 2298(25); [1985] 3 C.M.L.R. 775.

[12] *Pharmon v Hoechst* (19/89) [1985] (quoted above, fn.11) 3 C.M.L.R. 775.

6. even when the rights belong to different proprietors, national law may not be relied upon when the exercise of those rights is the purpose, means or result of a prohibited agreement;
7. it is compatible with the Treaty provisions concerning free trade for the owner of a trade mark to prevent the importation of products from another Member State and legally bearing a name giving rise to confusion with the trade mark. However, this does not apply when there is an agreement or link between the owner and the producer in the other Member State; their respective rights must also have arisen independently.[13]

1. EXHAUSTION

The question of the exhaustion of IPR rights arose concerning what is left of the "specific subject-matter" once the owner has used his rights in one of the Member States. The Court refers to "exhaustion of rights": the proprietor of an industrial or commercial property right protected by the legislation of a Member State may not rely on that legislation in order to oppose the importation of a product which has lawfully been marketed in another Member State by or with the consent of the proprietor of the right himself or a person legally or economically dependent on him.[14] In other words, once the owner of such a right has exercised it in the Union he can no longer claim territorial exclusivity within the internal market.[15] The situation can, however, be different in regard to products coming from third countries.[16] The Court decided that Union law[17] precludes national rules providing for exhaustion of the distribution right in respect of the original or copies of a work placed on the market outside the Union by the right-holder or with his consent.[18]

As mentioned above, the owner of an intellectual property right can occupy a dominant position and the question therefore arises whether a refusal to grant a licence can constitute an "abuse of a dominant position". The Court taking into account the danger of a wide interpretation on the "essential facility" concept, rather restricted the condition of abuse to refusing a licence on an IPR.

2. PATENTS

The Convention on the Grant of a European Patent[19] of 1973, revised in 2000, known as the European Patent Convention, is a multilateral treaty setting up the European Patent Organisation (EPO), and provides an autonomous legal system according to which a European (not a Union[20]) patent is granted. However, such a European patent is not a unitary right, but a group of essentially independent, nationally enforceable, nationally revocable patents. Those patents are granted

---

[13] *Terrapin* (119/75) (quoted above, fn.10).

[14] *Centrafarm v Sterling drug* (15/74) (quoted above, fn.10).

[15] *Keurkoop v Nancy Kean Gifts* (144/81) [1982] E.C.R. 2853 at 2873(25).

[16] See Emi Records cases: *Emi v CBS* (51/75) [1976] E.C.R. 811; *Emi Records v CBS Grammofon* (86/75) [1976] E.C.R. 871; and *Emi Records v Schallplatten* (96/75) [1976] A.C.R. 913.

[17] Directive 2001/29 on the harmonisation of certain aspects of copyright and related rights in the information society [2001] O.J. L167/10. See *Promusicae* (C-275/06) [2008] E.C.R. I-279: Directive neither compelling nor precluding obligation to disclose personal date in civil proceedings.

[18] *Laserdisken ApS* (C-479/04) [2006] E.C.R. I-8089.

[19] See *http://www.epo.org/patents/law/legal-texts/htm/epc/1973/e/ma1/htm.*

[20] There is currently no single, centrally enforceable, European Union-wide patent.

via a single harmonised procedure before the European Patent Office at Munich, at its branches at The Hague and Berlin, or at a national patent office of one of the Contracting Parties. National patents continue to exist.

As mentioned below in the chapter on competition policy, the Commission issued regulations providing block exemptions for patent licensing[21] and for know-how licensing agreements.[22] Attention must also be drawn to the Directive on the legal protection of the topographies of semi-conductor products,[23] another on the legal protection of biotechnical inventions.[24]

3. COPYRIGHTS AND RELATED RIGHTS

As far as copyrights and related rights are concerned, the principle is the same: protection[25] can only be invoked to safeguard the rights which constitute the "specific subject-matter" of this intellectual property.[26]

In 2001, Parliament and the Council adopted a directive on the harmonisation of certain aspects of copyright and related rights in the information society.[27] According to the Commission it complements the existing framework on copyright and related rights to respond to the new challenge[28] of technology and the information society. There exists presently a directive on the legal protection of computer programs[29]; on rental right and lending right and on certain rights related to copyright in the field of intellectual property[30]; on the co-ordination of certain rules concerning copyright and rights related to copyright applicable to satellite broadcasting and cable re-transmission[31]; on harmonising the term of protection of copyright and certain related rights[32]; and on the legal protection of databases.[33]

The Directive defines the scope of the acts covered by the reproduction rights with regard to the different beneficiaries. The right covers any transmission and air re-transmission of a work to the public by wire or wireless means, including broadcasting. For authors it applies to their work; for performers: to their performance; for phonogram producers: to their phonograms; for producers of the first fixation of films: to the original and copies of their films; and, for broadcasting organisations: to fixations of their broadcastings, whether transmitted by wire or over the air, including by cable or satellite. The Directive provides for exceptions and limitations, for sanctions and remedies, etc. Member States had until December 22, 2002 to transpose the Directive into their national law.

---

[21] Regulation 2349/84 [1984] O.J. L219/15, amended [1985] O.J. L113/34). See *Bayer* (65/86) [1998] E.G.R. 5249: no-challenge clause admissible under certain conditions.

[22] Regulation 556/89 [1989] O.J. L61/1.

[23] [1987] O.J. L24/36, incorporated [1994] O.J. L1/482.

[24] [1999] O.J. L213/13.

[25] For the length of the protection see Directive 2006/116 [20096] O.J. L372/12; see *Sony Music Entertainment* (C-240/07) [2009] E.C.R. 20.01.09.

[26] See *Deutsche Gramophon v Metro* (78/70) [1971] E.C.R. 487; [1971] C.M.L.R. 631 and *Musik-Vertrieb Membran v GEMA* (Joined Cases 55/80 and 57/80) [1981] E.C.R. 500; [1981] 2 C.M.L.R. 44.

[27] [2001] O.J. L167/10.

[28] Directive 2006/115 [2006] O.J. L376/28.

[29] [1991] O.J. L122/42.

[30] [1992] O.J. L346/61.

[31] [1993] O.J. L248/15.

[32] [2006] O J. L372/12.

[33] [1996] O.J. L77/20.

4. TRADE MARKS

The matter of trade mark protection finds a legal basis in the Madrid Agreement concerning the International Registration of Marks, of June 27, 1986[34] and in several Union acts. See, for instance, the first Council Directive to approximate the laws of the Member States relating to trade marks.[35] This directive can be invoked by producers to prevent parallel imports within the Union.[36] Also the Council Regulation on the Union Trade Mark[37] that provides uniform trade mark protection for the entire territory of the European Union in addition to the already existing national and international registration systems. This Regulation had to be amended in 2003 to give effect to the accession of the European Union to the Protocol relating to the Madrid Agreement concerning the international registration of marks.[38] See also the Directive on the protection of Designs.[39]

The Union trade mark is obtained by filing one single application with the Union Office[40]: the Office for Harmonisation in the Internal Market (Trade Marks, Designs and Models) (OHIM).[41] This means that only one representative has to be appointed. Furthermore, it requires use in only one Member State of the Union. The protection lasts 10 years and can be renewed. There is an implementing regulation,[42] a regulation on the fees payable to the Office, a regulation on the fees payable in respect of the registration of Union design[43] and a regulation laying down the rules of procedure of the Board of Appeal of the Office.[44] Interested parties should consult the Official Journal OHIM on evidence to be provided on claiming priority or seniority.

One of the most sensitive points is the exhaustion of trade mark rights; an exhaustive study of this question was made by the Advocate-General in one of the Court cases concerning this question.[45] In that case, the Court found that the Harmonisation Directive[46] precludes, save in given circumstances, that the reliance by a trade mark owner on his rights as owner in order to prevent an importer from marketing a product which was put on the market in another Member State by the owner or with his consent, even if that importer repackaged the product and reaffixed the trade mark to it without the owner's authorisation. On the other hand, if the importer reconditions the product and puts his own

---

[34] [1996] O.J. C293/11.

[35] Directive 89/104 [1989] O.J. L40/1, codified by Directive 2008/95 [2008] O.J. L299/25.

[36] See, for instance, *Boehringer Ingelheim E.A.* (C-348/04) [2007] E.C.R. I-3391, concerning parallel imports of pharmaceutical products.

[37] Regulation 40/94 [1994] O.J. L349/93; codified version [2009] O.J. L78/1. See *Eurohypo AG* (T-439/04) [2006] E.C.R. II-1269; appeal C-197/05.

[38] [2003] O.J. L296/1.

[39] Directive 98/71 [1998] O.J. L289/28; this Directive was completed by Regulation 6/2002 [2002] O.J. L3/1.

[40] The administration fee on application is €975 and upon registration another €1,100 is due. The protection lasts 10 years; it can be renewed at the cost of €2,500.

[41] See above, Ch.13: Decentralised Bodies of the Union.

[42] Regulation 2868/95 [1995] O.J. L303/1.

[43] Regulation 2246/02 [2002] O.J. L341/54.

[44] Regulation 216/96 [1996] O.J. L28/11.

[45] See *Bristol-Myers Squibb v Paranova* (Joined Cases C-427, etc./93) [1996] E.C.R. I-3457; [1997] 1 C.M.L.R. 1151.

[46] The Court refers to Directive 89/104, quoted above, and particularly its art.7. The latter, according to the Court in another case, regulates the question of exhaustion of trade mark rights comprehensively: *Phyteron* (C-352/95) [1997] E.C.R. I-1729; [1997] 3 C.M.L.R. 199.

name on it, the owner of the trade mark can oppose the import of a product lawfully marketed in another Member State.[47]

The basic rule, however, remains the exhaustion of rights doctrine, which provides that once an intellectual property right-holder has himself placed products, or, as a result of his consent, products have been placed, on the Union market, he is deemed to have exhausted his rights. In other words, the owner cannot after that, prevent another person from buying those products in one part of the single market and then selling them in another. In a recent case, the Court was asked whether the exhaustion doctrine also applied to products which had been put on the market, by the owner of the right, in a third country. In other words, whether the international exhaustion of rights doctrine applied in Union law. This question was particularly important, since certain Member States, like Austria, have their own rules concerning international exhaustion. The Court decided[48] that, if this were recognised, then the same product would either be subject to parallel imports in one Member State and not in another, or, as a result of the Customs Union, would be put into free circulation in the whole Union. This possibility was therefore rejected by the Court.

Another concept which gave rise to an abundant case law is that of "confusion", which according to the Court includes the notion of association between two marks.[49]

5. UNION AND INDUSTRIAL DESIGN

Its creation was decided at the end of 2001. It sets up a system for obtaining a Union design to which uniform protection is given, with uniform effect throughout the entire territory of the Union.[50] It lays down a simple and inexpensive procedure for registering designs with the Office for Harmonisation in the Internal Market.[51]

The Office registers Union designs as from April 1, 2003. The aim is to remove legal uncertainty facing industry as a result of the differences in national legislation. It also aims at encouraging creativity and innovation. The Union system coexists with the national protection systems. To qualify for protection, designs must be new and have an individual character. The regulation provides for two types of protection: without any formality—an "unregistered Union design"—protection for three years from the moment the design is made available to the public against systematic copying; and the "registered Union design", five years against both copying and development of similar design.

Only national courts are competent for dealing with infringements.

A registered design may be declared invalid by the Office; such a decision may be appealed before the Board of Appeal whose decisions are open to appeal before the Court.

The Regulation was implemented by a Commission regulation[52] supplementing the legal framework for the registration and setting the fees to be paid to the Office

---

[47] *Pharma* (C-232/94 MPA) [1996] E.C.R. I-3671.

[48] *Silhouette* (C-355/96) [1998] E.C.R. I-4799.

[49] See, for instance *Canon v Cannon* (C-37/97) [1998] E.C.R. I-5507 and *Lloyd v Klijsen* (C-342/97) [1999] E.C.R. I-3819.

[50] [2002] O.J. L3/1.

[51] See above, Ch.13: Decentralised Bodies of the Union.

[52] Regulation 2245/2002 [2002] O.J. L 341/28, amended by Regulation 876/07 [2007] O.J. L193/13 and Regulation 2246/02 [2002] O.J. L341/54 amended by Regulation 877/07 [2007] O.J. L193/16.

for registration; this regulation had to be amended following the accession of the Union to the Geneva Act of The Hague Agreement concerning the international registration of industrial designs.[53] A Council directive aims at approximating national legislations on the protection of designs.[54] The Union acceded to the Geneva Act of The Hague Agreement concerning the international registration of industrial design[55]; a regulation was adopted to give effect to this accession.[56]

6. Counterfeit Goods and Piracy

A Parliament and Council directive[57] provides for measures and procedures to be applied by the Member States to ensure the enforcement of the intellectual property rights and apply appropriate measures against those responsible for counterfeiting and piracy.

See also a directive on the legal protection of services based on, or consisting of, conditional access.[58]

7. Licensing

According to the Court, an obligation imposed upon the proprietor of a protected design to grant to third parties, even in return for a reasonable royalty, a licence for the supply of products incorporating the design would lead to the proprietor thereof to be deprived of the substance of his exclusive right and the refusal to grant such a licence cannot in itself constitute an abuse of a dominant position.[59] However, the refusal to supply spare parts by an undertaking holding a dominant position can constitute an abuse prohibited by the Treaty.[60] The Court also held that the mere fact that the owner of an intellectual property right has granted to a sole licensee an exclusive right in the territory of a Member State, while prohibiting the grant of sub-licences, is not sufficient to justify a finding that such a contract infringes competition rules.[61] The refusal to grant a licence on a copyright constitutes, according to the Court, an abuse of a dominant position where the following conditions are fulfilled: the undertaking that requests the licence intends to offer new products or services, not offered by the copyright owner and for which there is a potential consumer demand, the refusal is not justified by objective considerations and the refusal is such as to reserve to the copyright owner the supply of a service by eliminating all competition on the relevant market.[62] A similar situation was the object of a Commission decision forcing TV companies to supply a third party (Magill) with their individual advance weekly programmes listing and permitting reproduction of those listing

---

[53] Regulation 876/07 [2007] O.J. L193/13;

[54] Directive 98/71 [1998] O.J. L289/71.

[55] Decision of December 18, 2006 [2006] O.J. L386/28.

[56] Regulation 1891/06 [2006] O.J. L386/14.

[57] Directive 2004/48 [2004] OJ.J L195/16. See *Promusicae* (C-275/06) [2008] E.C.R. I-271: Directive neither compelling nor precluding obligation to disclose personal data in civil proceedings.

[58] Directive 98/84 [1998] O.J. L320/54.

[59] *Volo v Veng* (238/87) [1988] E.C.R. 6211.

[60] art.102 TFEU [82].

[61] *Tiercé Ladbroke v Commission* (T-504/93) [1997] E.C.R. II–923.

[62] *IMS Health v NDC Health* (C-418/01), [2004] E.C.R. I–5039.

that were covered by copyright.[63] This decision was confirmed by the CFI and by the Court.

8. Protected Geographical Indications and Designations of Origin[64]

There are two types of food quality names based on their geographical origin: the protected geographical indication (PGI); and the protected designation of origin (PDO). Once these names are registered, they are protected against the sale of any other competing imitation product seeking to use the reputation of the name of origin.[65]

9. International Treaties

The Treaty provisions on the Common Commercial Policy provide for the negotiation and conclusion of agreements concerning the commercial aspects of intellectual property.[66]

See Agreement on Trade Related Aspects of Intellectual Property Rights (TRIPs)[67]; a multilateral framework of minimum rules to help combat counterfeiting.

See also the World Property Organisation (WPO) and the WPO Copyright Treaty and the WPO Performance and Phonograms Treaty.[68]

Further Reading

Morag McDonald and Dr Uma Suthersanen, *Copyright: World Law and Practice* (Sweet & Maxwell, 2006).
Prof. Spyros Maniatis, *Trade marks in Europe: A Practical Jurisprudence* (Sweet & Maxwell, 2006).

---

[63] See *RTE and ITP v Commission* (Joined Cases C-241/91 P and C-242/91 P) [1995] E.C.R. I–743.
[64] Based on *http://www.europa.eu/scadplus/leg/en/lvb/121097.htm.*
[65] See Regulation 2081/92 [1992] O.J. L208/1. Annex II to that Regulation may be amended by the Commission: Regulation 535/97 [1997] O.J. L83/3.
[66] art.207 TFEU [133(5) and (7)].
[67] Decision 94/800 [1994] O.J. L336/214.
[68] Directive 2001/29 [2001] O.J. L167/10.

Chapter Twenty-one

Public Procurement[1]

The volume of public procurement contracts represents about 16 per cent of the GDP of the Union or 1,500 billion, which shows its economic importance.

The purpose of the Union legislation in this field, based on the principles of equal treatment,[2] objectivity and transparency,[3] is to open the procedures for award[4] of public contracts to competition from all undertakings situated in the Union.[5] Furthermore, competition implies the principle of non-discrimination on grounds of nationality,[6] in accordance with the Treaties,[7] which, as the Court held, cannot in this regard be interpreted restrictively. The legislation applies both to the central government authorities and to the regional and local ones.[8] The foregoing entails the application of the principle of transparency in order to enable, "the contracting authority to satisfy itself that it has been complied with".[9] Discrimination in the award of supply contracts, for instance, is contrary to the free movement of goods,[10] of persons,[11] of workers[12] and of services[13] and constitutes a measure with equivalent effect to a quantitative restriction,[14] as well as to the right of establishment provided for in the TFEU.[15]

The infringement of public contract law, brings about for the Member State responsible for it, an obligation to make reparation for the loss and damage

---

[1] This chapter was revised, a first time, by Dr. Claudio Loggi in 2007.

[2] See *Commission v France* (C-16/98) [2000] E.C.R. I–8315. For an in-depth analysis, see Paul Cassia, "Contrats publics et principe communautaire d'égalité de traitement" (2002) R.T.D.E. 413–449. As regards negotiations with a tenderer on the basis of a tender not complying with the tender conditions, see *Commission v Denmark* (C-243/89) [1993] E.C.R. I–3353.

[3] See *Commission v Belgium* (C-87/94) [1996] E.C.R. I–2043,(88), and *Universale-Bau* (C-470/89) [2002] E.C.R. I–11617, (98), and *CAS Succhi di Frutta v Commission* (T-191/96) [1999] E.C.R II–3181.

[4] For a definition of "awarding authority" see *Beentjes v Netherlands State* (31/87) [1988] E.C.R. 4635; for a definition of "contracting authority", see *Mannesmann* (C-44/96) [1998] E.C.R. I–73.

[5] See D. Batsele, Ph. Flamme et Ph Quertainmont, *Initiation aux marchés publics*, 2nd edn, (Bruxelles, Bruylant, 2001) p. 52.

[6] See *Commission v Denmark* (C-243/89) [1993] E.C.R. I–3353.

[7] art.18 TFEU [12]. See *Beentjes v Netherlands Staat* (31/87) [1988] E.C.R. 4635.

[8] *Commission v Italy* (C-360/89) [1992] E.C.R. I–3401.

[9] *Unitron Scandinavia and 3–S* (C-275/98) [1999] E.C.R. I–8291.

[10] *Eggers* (13/78) [1978] E.C.R. 1935 and *Commission v Ireland* (45/87) [1988] E.C.R. 4929.

[11] *Commission v Denmark* (C-243/89) [1993] E.C.R. I–3353.

[12] *Desquenne & Giral* (62/81) [1982] E.C.R. 223, *Rush Portuguesa v Office National d'immigration* (C-113/89) [1990] E.C.R. I–1417 and *Finalarte* (C-49/98) [2001] E.C.R. I–7831.

[13] See *Webb* (279/80) [1981] E.C.R.3305, *Transporoute v Ministère des travaux publics* (76/81) [1982] E.C.R. 417. For an analysis, see Christopher Bovis, "Recent Case Law Relating to Public Procurement: A Beacon for the Integration of Public Markets", (2002) C.M.L.R.1025–1056.

[14] *Du Pont de Nemours Italiana v USL di Carrara* (C-21/88) [1990] E.C.R. I–889.

[15] art.49 TFEU [43]. See *Commission v Italy* (3/88) [1989] E.C.R. 4035, see also *Commission v Italy* (C-272/91) [1994] E.C.R. I–1409.

caused to individuals and undertakings.[16] Exceptions to the application of the principles laid down in the Directives on public contracts shall be interpreted restrictively and defined on precise grounds, namely reasons of public health,[17] the exercise of official authority,[18] public security[19] and overriding reasons in the general interest,[20] imperative requirements and the general good.[21]

A new legislative regime became enforceable on February 1, 2006.[22] It comprises two directives: one on the co-ordination of procedures for the award of public works contracts, public supply contracts and public service contracts,[23] and one on co-ordinating the procurement procedures of entities operating in the water, energy, transport and postal services sectors,[24] the so-called public sector directive.[25]

Among many characteristics, the new directives provide for the possibility for bodies governed by public law to tender for the award of public contracts alongside private undertakings.[26] Such a possibility brought about interesting case law of the Court aimed at determining whether a contract had been concluded between two separate persons in case of a contract awarded by a contracting authority to another public authority. The Court ruled that it is sufficient that the contracting authority is a person legally distinct from that other public authority. In order to ascertain whether a local authority is a person legally distinct from the contracting authority, thus exempting, in case it is not, the latter from complying with the obligations laid down in the public contracts directives, the Court stated that that was conceivable:

"[I]n the case where the local authority exercises over the person concerned a control which is similar to that which it exercises over its own departments and, at the same time, that person carries out the essential part of its activities with the controlling local authority or authorities".[27]

The Court went even further when it stated that the condition relating to the control exercised may be fulfilled even if the control exercised by the public body concerned is more limited than that exercised over its own departments.[28] Identical control is not required, similar control suffices. Likewise, the Court held that, in respect of the delegation, by a municipality, of a public service to an inter-municipal co-operative the object of which was exclusively to provide services to

---

[16] *Francovich and Bonifaci v Italy* (C-6/90) [1991] E.C.R. I–5357, and *Brasserie du pêcheur and Factortame* (Joined Cases C-46/93 and C-48/93) [1996] E.C.R. I–1029.

[17] art.36 TFEU [30]. *Commission v Ireland* (45/87) [1988] E.C.R. 4929.

[18] art.51 TFEU [45] and art.62 [55]. *Commission v Italy* (3/88) [1989] E.C.R. 4035.

[19] arts 51 and 62 TFEU [45 and 55].

[20] *Vander Elst v Office des migrations internationals* (C-43/93) [1994] E.C.R. I–3803.

[21] *Du Pont de Nemours* (21/88) (quoted above, fn.14) and *Webb* (279/80) [1981] E.C.R. 3305.

[22] For an outlook of the path which lead to the new regime, see Richard Wainwright, "Marchés publics: Refonte des directives", R.M.C.U.E. 2001, 394–399; Alfonso Mattera, "Vers un code européen des marchés publics", Revue de droit de l'Union européenne, 2000/3, p.538; see also, Patrick Thiel, "Mémento des marchés publics", (Bruxelles, Kluwer, 2002).

[23] Directive 2004/18 [2004] O.J. L134/114, amended [2009] O.J. L216/76.

[24] Directive 2004/17 [2004] O.J. L134/1, amended [2009] O.J. L216/76.

[25] See art.13 Directive 2004/18 (quoted above): "Specific exclusions in the field of telecommunications." See *Commission v Belgium* (C-87/94) [1996] E.C.R. I–2043; [1996] 3 C.M.L.R. 671.

[26] For an analysis of the obligation to apply Union rules in such cases, see *ARGE* (C-94/99) [2000] E.C.R. I–11037, (28); see also *Teckal* (C-107/98) [1999] E.C.R. I–8121, (50) and (51).

[27] See *Teckal* (C-107/98) [1999] E.C.R. I–8121(50), and *Coname* (C-231/03) [2005] E.C.R. I–7287, (26).

[28] *Asemfo* (C-295/05) [2007] E.C.R. I-24*.

the affiliated municipalities, that they could legally take place without a call for tenders, since it considered that, notwithstanding the autonomous aspects of that co-operative's management by its board, the affiliated municipalities had to be regarded as together exercising control over it.[29] The foregoing established the principle called "in house".[30]

Finally, as far as derogations from the rules governing public contracts are concerned, the Court held constantly that:

> "[D]erogations from the rules intended to ensure the effectiveness of the rights conferred by the Treaty in relation to public (. . .) contracts, must be inter- preted strictly and that the burden of proving the existence of exceptional cir- cumstances justifying a derogation lies on the person seeking to rely on those circumstances".[31]

1. Public Works, Public Supply and Public Service[32] Contracts are Regulated in a Single Directive

It concerns the "award" of such contracts (public service contracts shall mean contracts for pecuniary interest concluded in writing between a service provider and a contracting authority[33]), not their "execution", that remains under national law. Furthermore it only concerns those contracts whose value is beyond the thresholds set in the relevant directives.

> "However, the mere fact that the Union legislature considered that the strict special procedures laid down in those directives are not appropriate in the case of public contracts of small value, does not mean that those contracts are excluded from the scope of Union law."[34]

Indeed, the contracting authorities (the State, regional or local authorities, bod- ies governed by public law, associations formed by one or more of such authori- ties or bodies governed by public law[35]), while concluding any contract, have to comply with the rules of the Treaty.[36] In this respect, the Directive concerns the most important contracts, i.e. generally speaking, public supply and service con- tracts with a value, exclusive of VAT, of more than €137,000[37]; awarded by authorities which are listed as central government authorities in Annex IV to the Directive, and €211,000 for:

---

[29] *Coditel Brabant* (C-324/07) [2008] E.C.R. 31.11.08
[30] For the application of this principle to concessions, see Joël Arnould, "Les contrats de concession, de privatisation et de services 'in house' au regard des règles communautaires", Revue française de droit administratif 1/2000.
[31] *Commission v Germany* (Joined Cases C-20/01 and C-28/01) [2003] E.C.R. I–3609,(58), see also *Commission v Germany* (C-318/94) [1996] E.C.R. I–1949, (13).
[32] Directive 92/50 relating to the co-ordination of procedures for the award of public service contracts [1992] O.J. L209/1; see *Commission v Ireland* (C-507/03) [2007] E.C.R. I-9777: arts 14 and 16 require contracting authorities to define the technical specifications by reference to national stan- dards implementing European standards, which must be given in the general or contractual docu- ments relating to each contract.
[33] *Parking Brixen* (C-458/03) [2005] E.C.R. I–8612.
[34] See Order of December 3, 2001, *Vestergaard* (C-59/00) [2001] E.C.R. I–9505(19).
[35] *Carbotermo and Consorzio Alisei* (C-340/04) [2006] E.C.R. I-4137.
[36] See *Vestergaard* (C-59/00) (quoted above, fn.34), (20).
[37] This figure and the following two were inserted by Regulation 2083/2005, [2005] O.J. L333/28.

1. supply and service contracts awarded by other public authorities;
2. supply contracts awarded by authorities listed in Annex IV; and
3. service contracts concerning telecommunications, etc.

A threshold of €5,278,000 applies for public work contracts.[38] Special rules apply when the contract is subsidised by more than 50 per cent by contracting authorities.[39]

Contracts in the water, transport and postal services sectors are excluded from this Directive; the same applies to contracts for providing or exploiting public telecommunications networks and for providing to the public one or more telecommunications services. There are a number of other "specific" exclusion[40] (see hereunder).

The Directive provides for different procedures: open (namely "national procedures whereby all interested providers may submit a tender"[41]); restricted (those national procedures whereby, "only candidates invited by the contracting entity may submit tenders"[42]); restricted procedures shall always comply with the competition principle[43]; or negotiated ("those national procedures whereby authorities consult providers of their choice and negotiate the terms of the contract with one or more of them[44] under exceptional circumstances"). As to the possibility of choosing a negotiated procedure, the Court held that:

> "[T]hose provisions, which authorise derogations from the rules intended to ensure the effectiveness of the rights conferred by the Treaty in the field of public works contracts, must be interpreted strictly and the burden of proving the actual existence of exceptional circumstances justifying a derogation lies on the person seeking to rely on those circumstances".[45]

The Court applied the same principle to the directive dealing with supply contracts.[46]

Besides these "classic" ones, new techniques for awarding contracts were introduced: the competitive dialogue,[47] the framework agreements,[48] the dynamic purchasing systems,[49] central purchasing authorities,[50] negotiated procedure with and without prior publication of a contract notice,[51] and the electronic auction.[52] The latter applies in open, restricted or negotiated procedures as well as in reopening of competition or the opening of competition for contracts to be awarded under the dynamic purchasing system. In those cases the contracting authorities may decide that the award must be preceded by an electronic auction

---

[38] art.7 Directive 2004/18.

[39] art.8 Directive 2004/18.

[40] art.15 and following, Directive 2004/18.

[41] See *Commission v Austria* (C-29/04) [2005] E.C.R. I–9705.

[42] *Strabag and Kostmann* (C-462/03) [2005] E.C.R. I–5397.

[43] *Commission v France* (C-225/98) [2000] E.C.R. I–7445.

[44] *Felix Swoboda* (C-411/00) [2002] E.C.R. I–10567.

[45] See *Commission v Italy* (199/85) [1987] E.C.R. 1039.

[46] See *Commission v Spain* (C-73/92) [1993] E.C.R. I–5997; the Court upheld those principles, see *Commission v Spain* (C-328/92) [1994] E.C.R. I–1569.

[47] art.29 Directive 2004/18.

[48] arts 1(5) and 32, Directive 2004/18.

[49] arts 1(6) and 32 and 33, Directive 2004/18.

[50] art.1(10) Directive 2004/18.

[51] arts 30 and 31, Directive 2004/18.

[52] art.1(7), Directive 2004/18

when the contract specifications can be established with precision.[53] In case of a contracting authority not complying with the obligation of publication of the call for tender as laid down in the Directive, the Commission shall bring an application for infringement[54] against the relevant State, since the Court held that:

> "[W]here a contracting authority intends to conclude a contract for pecuniary interest relating ... with a company legally distinct from it, ... the public award procedures laid down by that directive must always be applied".[55]

Generally speaking, the public procurement procedure consists of publication of "Notices", either by the public authority or by the Commission, in a special edition of the *Official Journal of the European Union*.[56] The requirements for such publication are very detailed indeed,[57] as well as the relevant obligation to publish a call for tender.[58] In this respect, following the publication of the call for tender, the contracting authority has little room for manoeuvre as to the possibility to make any change to the call for tender since any change to the notice could go against the principle of non-discrimination.[59] In fact, the publication of the call for tender imposes an, "obligation on contracting entities to apply the rules applicable to the type of procedure chosen".[60] In order to avoid discrimination references to Union norms (AFNOR, Din), rather than to national norms are required.[61]

The criteria on which the public authorities shall base the award of public contracts shall either be the lowest price only,[62] or the tender most economically advantageous[63] from the point of view of the contracting authority, taking into account various criteria such as quality, price, aesthetic, environmental, social[64] and functional characteristics.[65] Special rules apply in the case of abnormally low tenders.[66]

---

[53] art.1(7), Directive 2004/18; art.1(6), Directive 2004/17 (quoted above).The Public Sector Directive provides that an electronic auction is a repetitive process involving an electronic device for the presentation of new prices, which are revised downwards, or new values concerning certain elements of the tender (art.1(7)). The parameters for the use of electronic auction are laid down in art.54.

[54] art.258 TFEU [226]. See Alfonso Mattera, "La procédure en manquement et la protection des droits des citoyens et des opérateurs lésés", Revue du Marché Commun et de l'Union Européenne (RDUE), No.3, 1995 pp.123–166.

[55] See *Stadt Halle and RPL Lochau* (C-26/03) [2005] E.C.R. I-1,(52).

[56] For an analysis of the procedures, see P. Flamme et M.A. Flamme, "Les marchés publics de services et la coordination de leurs procédures de passation", RDUE, No.365, Février 1993, p.150; see also M. Mensi Appalti, "Servizi Pubblici e Concessioni–Procedure di gara, tutela amministrativa e processuale a livello comunitario et nazionale", CEDAM–Padova, 1999.

[57] arts 35 and 36 Directive 2004/16.

[58] See *Commission v Italy* (10/76) [1976] E.C.R. 1359, *Beentjes v Netherlands State* (31/87) [1988] E.C.R. 4635, and *Commission v Belgium* (C-323/96) [1998] E.C.R. I-5063.

[59] *ATI EAC* (C-331/04) [2005] E.C.R. I-10109.

[60] See *Commission v Belgium* (C-87/94) [1996] E.C.R. I-2043.

[61] art.23 Directive 2004/18.

[62] See *Commission v Italy* (274/83) [1985] E.C.R. 1077.

[63] For an analysis of these principles, see *Traunfellner* (C-421/01) [2003] E.C.R. I-11941; see also *SIAC Construction* (C-19/00) [2001] E.C.R. 7725.

[64] The only concession in relation to the socio-economic dimension of the award criteria is provided in art.19 of Directive 2004/18, concerning "reserved contracts" for workshops employing handicapped persons.

[65] art.53 Directive 2004/18.

[66] art.55, Directive 2004/18. See *Transporoute v Ministère des travaux publics* (76/81) [1982] E.C.R. 417, and *Fratelli Costanzo v Comune di Milano* (103/88) [1989] E.C.R. 1839; see also *Impresa Lombardini* (Joined Cases C-285/99 and C-286/99) [2001] E.C.R. I-9233.

The Directive applies also to works carried out under a concession[67] and by private persons who are, however, controlled by public authorities.[68] Special Arrangements are provided for public service contracts such as public transport.[69] An important novelty, as compared to the previous directives, is, as already mentioned, the extended use of electronics as a means of communication.[70]

A possibility to appeal concerning the awards made by public authorities for supplies, works and services is provided.[71] (See below.) Appeal to the Union courts is, of course, always possible. See in this respect a judgment of the GC [CFI], in a TACIS project case, concerning the obligation incumbent upon the Commission's Evaluation Committee.[72]

2. The Water, Energy, Transport and Postal Services Sectors

These sectors have always been considered as forming a separate sector for which different procurement procedures should apply, hence their exclusion from the Directive examined above and their implementation under the second directive.[73] The activities covered by this directive are: gas, heat and electricity, water, transport services, postal services (until January 1, 2009[74]) and exploration for, or extraction of, oil, gas, coal or other solid fuels, as well as ports and airports. Framework Agreements and dynamic purchasing systems are provided for.[75]

For supply and service, the Directive applies to contracts which have a value, excluding VAT, of no less than €422,000.[76] For works contracts it is €5,278,000.[77] Generally speaking, the rules are less strict for the water, energy, transport and postal sectors than for the public works, supply and service contracts. For instance, no obligation to publish each individual contract, they may be grouped, but it provides for more restrictive definitions of "special" and "exclusive" right[78]; the influence of the Court's case law is evident[79] and there are different possibilities: open bidding, restricted and negotiated contracts.

The Directive contains strict rules for the mutual recognition concerning required qualifications, qualification systems and criteria for qualitative selection.[80] Other provisions concern contract award criteria, use of electronic auction

---

[67] arts 56 to 62, Directive 2004/18 (quoted above).

[68] See *Commission v Italy* (C-272/91) [1994] E.C.R. I–1409, *Gemeente Arnhem and Gemeente Rheden v BFI Holding* (C-360/96) [1998] E.C.R. I–6821, *RI.SAN* (C-108/98) [1999] E.C.R. I–5219, and *Telaustria and Telefonadress* (C-324/98) [2000] E.C.R. I–10745.

[69] arts 20–22, Directive 2004/18.

[70] art.42, Directive 2004/18.

[71] Directive 89/665 [1989] O.J. L 395/33, see *Commission v Ireland* (C-507/03) [2007] E.C.R. I-9777 and for the water, energy, transport and telecommunications sectors Directive 93/38 [1993] L 199/84.

[72] *Tideland Signal v Commission* (T-211/02) [2002] E.C.R. II–3781.

[73] Directive 2004/17 [2004] O.J. L134/1. This Directive replaces Directive 93/38 [1993] O.J. L199/84, that concerned the water, energy, transport and telecommunications sectors.

[74] This transitional measures aims at the liberalisation of the postal sector.

[75] arts 14 and 15 Directive 2004/17 (quoted above).

[76] art.16 Directive 2004/18 (quoted above). This figure and the following one were inserted by Regulation 2083/2005 [2005] O.J. L 333/28.

[77] Directive 2004/18.

[78] *France v Commission* (C-202/88) [1991] E.C.R. I–1223 and *Spain v Commission* (C-271/90) [1992] E.C.R. I–5833.

[79] See *The Queen v Secretary of State for Trade and Industry, Ex p. British Telecommunications* (C-302/94) [1996] E.C.R. I–6447.

[80] Directive 2004/17 (quoted above).

(are excluded: service and work contracts having as their subject matter intellectual performances such as design of works), abnormally low tenders and relations with third countries.[81]

The Utility Directive does not apply to markets where the participants pursue an activity which is directly exposed to competition and the access to which is not limited within the relevant Member State.[82] The present directive refers to the conditions relating to agreements concluded within the World Trade Organisation.[83] Various kinds of contracts are excluded from the Directive.[84]

It will be remembered that after the conclusion of the WTO agreement, the United States protested against the Union public procurement legislation, considering it discriminatory and contrary to the GATT rules. The dispute was settled by an agreement in the form of a Memorandum of Understanding between the European Economic Union and the United States of America on government procurement.[85] Consequently, the Council adopted a decision concerning the extension of certain benefits in respect of the United States.[86] The contracts make explicit reference to, "agreements concluded within the World trade organisation".[87]

In 2001, the Commission published an interpretative Communication on the Union law applicable to public procurement and the possibilities for integrating social considerations into public procurement.[88] A similar Communication concerns the integration of environmental considerations.[89] Mention should be made of the Directive on the use of standard forms in the publication of public contract notices,[90] this directive brings about new obligations, contracting authorities must comply with. The use of these standard forms harmonises the way notices shall be published, with an aim at enhancing openness, efficiency and transparency, thus making easier the dissemination of electronic procurement. In addition, potential suppliers may use electronic search engines which make it easier for them to seek procurement notices they may be interested in. Furthermore, the standard forms cut the burden and costs contracting authorities normally bear for complying with the Directive on public procurements. The Commission released an interpretative Communication on Concessions under Union law on public contracts.[91]

---

[81] art.55 and following Directive 2004/17.

[82] art.30 Directive 2004/17.

[83] art.12, Directive 2004/17.

[84] art.26 and following, Directive 2004/17.

[85] [1993] O.J. L125/1.

[86] [1993] O.J. L125/1 at 54.

[87] art.5 Directive 2004/18 and art.59 Directive 2004/17.

[88] [2001] O.J. C 333/12. See S. Arrowsmith, *The Law of Public and Utilities Procurement* (London, Sweet & Maxwell, 1996), J.B. Auby, *Perspectives d'évolution de la concession de service public, in AA. VV., La concession de service public face au droit communautaire* (Paris, 1992); U. Bassi et A. Barone, "La communicazione interpretativa sulle concessioni nel diritto comunitario : primi spunti ricostruttivi", in Foro Italiano No.8/2000; X. Bezançon, "Les grandes étapes de la notion de service public", in Revue des Concessions et des Délégations de Service Public, 1998 No.1. C. Rangone, "La discipline législative des deux formes les plus communes de partenariat public privé in Italie : la concession et la société mixte", in Actes du Séminaire "Droit et réalité du PPP en Europe", 11, 12, 25 et 26 Janvier 1999.

[89] [2001] O.J. C 333/17.

[90] Directive 2001/78 [2001] O.J. L 285/1.

[91] [2000] O.J. C 121/2. For an analysis of this communication, see Alfonso Mattera, "La communication interprétative de la Commission sur les concessions de services d'utilité publique: un instrument de transparence et de libéralisation", Revue du droit de l'Union Européenne, No.2 (2000).

With a view to harmonising the public contracts vocabulary, the Union legislator adopted a regulation on the Common Procurement Vocabulary (CPV).[92] This Regulation should be considered as a tool that sets a single classification system applicable to public procurement. The Annexes to the regulation consist of correlation tables which permit to gather and compare a number of existing nomenclatures used in diverse countries, such as: the Statistical Classification of Products by Activity in the EEC (CPA); the Provisional Central Product Classification (CPC Prov.) of the United Nations; the General Industrial Classification of Economic Activities within the European Communities (NACE Rev. 1); and the Combined Nomenclature (CN). An Advisory Committee composed of independent experts assists the Commission in examining complaints from businesses and monitoring the functioning of the Directives and the uniform application of them in the Member States.[93]

3. THE REMEDIES DIRECTIVE[94]

This directive ensures effective implementation of the above-mentioned directives at national level and guarantees access to justice, to aggrieved contractors and interested parties against illegal or wrongful award decisions.[95] The procedure is quite defined,[96] and the Court considered that it is up to the Member States to secure a judicial system able to deal with any complaint.[97] In this respect, Member States are to take interim measures with a view to correcting an alleged infringement or preventing further damage, either set aside or ensure the setting-aside of decisions taken unlawfully, and award damages to persons harmed by an infringement.[98] As far as the scope of the remedies directives is concerned, "every decision of a contracting authority falling under the Union rules in the field of public procurement and liable to infringe them is subject to the judicial review provided for in [those] directive[s]".[99]

Furthermore, any act of a contracting authority adopted in relation to a public contract within the scope of directives producing legal effects is subject to the Remedies Directive regardless of being part of a formal award procedure.[100] As far as the possibility for any person to make use of those directives is concerned, "(. . .) review procedures are available at least to any person having or having had an interest in obtaining a public contract who has been or risks being harmed by an alleged infringement".[101]

Further Reading

Lee Digings and Prof. John Bennett, *EC public Procurement: Law and Practice* (Sweet & Maxwell, 2006).

[92] Regulation 2195/2002 [2002] O.J. L 340/1.
[93] Decision 87/305 [1987] O.J. L152/32 and Decision 87/560 [1987] O.J. L338/37.
[94] Directive 89/665 [1989] O.J. L 395/33 and Directive 92/13 [1992] O.J. L 76/14.
[95] See Boyenga-Bofala, "L'impact des directives recours sur l'organisation des voies de droit internes et les modalités d'exercice par le juge administratif français de son office" (2002) R.T.D.E. 499.
[96] See *Alcatel Austria* (C-81/98) [1999] E.C.R. I–7671.
[97] *Dorsch Consult Ingenieursgesellschaft v Bundesbaugesellschaft Berlin* (C-54/96) [1997] E.C.R. I–4961; in *Gebietskrankenkasse* [1998] E.C.R. I–5357, and *HI* (C-258/97) [1999] E.C.R. I–1405.
[98] See art.2(1)(a), (b) and (c) of Directive 89/665 (quoted above).
[99] See *HI* (C-92/00) [2002] E.C.R. I–5553,(37), and *Makedoniko Metro and Mikhaniki* (C-57/01) [2003] E.C.R. I–1091, (68).
[100] *Stadt Halle and RPL Lochau* (C-26/03) [2005] E.C.R. I–1 (34).
[101] *Stadt Halle and RPL Lochau* (C-26/03), above, fn.100 at (40); see also *Commission v Austria* (C-212/02) [2004] (unpublished), (24).

PART FOUR: OTHER UNION POLICIES

Chapter Twenty-two

Competition Policy

INTRODUCTION

Competition policy is, according to the Commission:

"[A] key driver of economic growth and sustainable jobs. The benefits of competitiveness, growth and lasting social and environmental development are mutually reinforcing. A properly managed environment for business sustains and promotes competitiveness, productivity and growth, in global, regional and national markets".[1]

The campaign against restrictive practices stays at the forefront of the Commission's competition activities. The same holds true for the application of stringent rules concerning State aids, while its activities in the field of merger control grow by the year. In order to strengthen the pursuit of its objectives in the competition field, the Commission has focused its activities on the practical implementation of the new body of rules in the field of restrictive practices and abuses of dominant positions and the merger regulation.[2] In antitrust, Regulation 1/2003[3] allows for a decentralised application of the rules by national courts and competition authorities. In the merger field, a new regulation was adopted and, with regard to state aids, the Commission launched a reform designed to simplify procedures for cases which do not raise major legal concerns.[4]

Due to the very difficult financial and economic circumstances that Europe experienced in 2008, and the way they impacted on the viability of European business, particular attention was paid to the assessment of rescue and restructuring measures.[5]

I. COMPETITION RULES APPLYING TO UNDERTAKINGS[6]

Those rules are contained mainly in three sets of provisions: the first concern what is generally referred to as "cartels", the second "abuse of dominant positions" and the third, "concentrations". The term cartel designates all forms

---

[1] XXXIVth Report on Competition Policy, 2004, introduction by Commissioner Neelie Kroes.
[2] General Report 2004, 55.
[3] Regulation 1/2003 on the implementation of the rules on competition laid down in arts 101 [81] and 102 [82] of the Treaty: [2003] O.J. L1/1.
[4] Regulation 1/2003.
[5] 2008 Report on competition policy, Introduction.
[6] arts 101–105 TFEU [81 to 85] and Merger Regulation, see below.

of co-operation among undertakings (only some of them are prohibited); the second expression refers to anti-competitive behaviour of an undertaking(s) in a dominant position; while concentrations covers limitation of competition through the creation or strengthening of a dominant position via joint ventures, mergers or take-overs. Whether or not a cartel is prohibited or whether or not there is abuse of a dominant position is decided by the national judge or by the Commission; both can grant an exemption from the prohibition or decide what measure must be taken to eliminate an abuse. As for concentrations that have a Union dimension, they must be notified to the Commission for assessment. However, a Member State can ask for the whole or part of the concentration to be assigned to it when it considers that it would affect competition on a market within that State, which, "presents all the characteristics of a distinct market".[7]

Although, according to the TFEU, "the establishing of the competition rules necessary for the functioning of the internal market"[8] falls within the exclusive competence of the Union, both the Commission and the authorities of the Member States are entrusted, in close co-operation with each other,[9] with the implementation of these rules. Both can require that an infringement be brought to an end, both can order interim measures, accept commitments and impose fines and periodic payments; national competition authorities may also impose other penalties provided for in their national law.[10]

1. Cartels (Agreements, Decisions of Associations of Undertakings and Concerted Practices)[11]

The TFEU[12] refers not only to "agreements between undertakings", but also to "decisions by associations of undertakings" and "concerted practices". They are prohibited when they may affect trade between Member States and have as their object or effect the prevention, restriction or distortion of competition. When caught by the prohibition, they are automatically void, unless they satisfy the conditions for an exemption from the prohibition.[13] Each one of these expressions needs to be clarified and interpreted.

> "The notions of agreements, decisions and concerted practices are autonomous concepts of [Union] competition law covering the coordination of behaviour of undertakings on the market as interpreted by the [Union] Courts".[14]

Hereinafter the concepts, "agreements, decisions of associations of undertakings and concerted practices" shall globally be referred to by the word "agreements", unless indicated otherwise. Will be successively examined: (a) the prohibition, (b) the nullity and (c) the exemptions from the prohibition.

---

[7] Regulation 139/2004 on the control of concentrations between undertakings, the so-called Merger Regulation [2004] O.J. L24/1.

[8] art.3(1) TFEU.

[9] See, for instance, Commission "Notice on co-operation between national competition authorities and the Commission in handling cases falling within the scope of TFEU Art.101 and 102 [[81 and [82]]" [1997] O.J. C313/3.

[10] art.5 Regulation 1/2003 (quoted above).

[11] art.101 TFEU [81].

[12] See art.101 TFEU [81].

[13] art.1(2) Regulation 1/2003 (quoted above).

[14] Eighth recital Regulation 1/2003 (quoted above).

(1) The Prohibition

Obviously only certain agreements between undertakings are prohibited; indeed, the whole economy thrives on such agreements, and the Commission has done everything to encourage undertakings to co-operate, especially across borders, in order to further European economic integration. However, such agreements are prohibited when they may affect trade between Member States, and the parties to the cartel seek to restrict competition or cause it to be restricted in the internal market. This basic rule seems simple enough, but what exactly is meant by "agreement", "undertaking", "decision by associations of undertakings", "concerted practices", "have as their object or effect", "may affect trade between Member States", and "distortion of competition"? Those terms will be successively examined hereafter.

(a) Agreements and Concerted Practices

An *agreement* is a legally binding and, therefore, an enforceable commitment.[15] According to the case law of the European courts, "there is an agreement in the sense of Article [101(1)], when the act considered by the Commission is the faithful expression of the parties' intention to conduct themselves in a certain way".[16]

The expression *concerted practice*, on the other hand, refers to an anticompetitive parallel market behaviour of several undertakings, that is caught by the prohibition when this behaviour is the result of a "concertation" among said undertakings.[17] According to the Court, concerted practice:

> "[R]efers to a form of coordination between undertakings which, without having been taken to a stage where an agreement properly so called has been concluded, knowingly substitutes for the risk of competition, practical co-operation between them."[18]

In other words, "a concerted practice implies, besides undertakings' concerting together, conduct on the market pursuant to those collusive practices, and a relationship of cause and effect between them." This applies even where competition in the market has not been actually distorted.[19]

The difference between an agreement and a concerted practice is important with regard to the conditions for the existence of a prohibition and the proof of an infringement. Indeed, in the case of an agreement, it suffices for a violation of the competition rules to occur, that the clauses of the agreement show the intention of the parties to distort competition. Whether or not competition was actually distorted is irrelevant.[20] In the case of a concerted practice, the fact that

---

[15] Such a commitment is not limited to certain forms; see *Van Landewijck v Commission* (Joined Cases 209/78–265/78 and 218/78) [1980] E.C.R. 3125; [1981] 3 C.M.L.R. 134. Also *Sandoz v Commission* (C-277/87) [1990] E.C.R. I–45: the systematic dispatching by a supplier to his customers of invoices bearing the words "exports prohibited", constitutes a prohibited agreement. Idem: Commission Decision of January 10, 1996, Adalat (Bayer): [1996] O.J. L201/1, implicit acceptance by wholesaler through continued dealing, so agreement reached.

[16] *Mayer-Melnhof* (T-347/94) [1998] E.C.R. II–1751(65).

[17] For an example of a concerted practice see *Musique Diffusion Française v Commission* (Joined Cases 100/80, 101/80, 102/80 and 103/80) [1983] E.C.R. 1825; [1983] 3 C.M.L.R. 221.

[18] *Commission v Anic* (C-49/92 P) [1999] E.C.R. I–4125 (112–138).

[19] See also *T-Mobile A.O.* (C-8/08) [2009] E.C.R. I-04.06.09.

[20] See *Société Technique Minière v Machienenbau Ulm* (56/65) [1966] E.C.R. 235 at 249; [1966] C.M.L.R. 357.

undertakings consult each other is not, in itself, prohibited; it is the market behaviour, the practice, that eventually follows the consultation, that is caught by the prohibition, even when it does not actually affect trade and distorts competition. As for the proof of the existence of a concerted practice, the Commission must show both that the intended practice violates the Treaty and that there was collusion among the parties, which led to that anti-competitive behaviour. Proof that there was prior consultation could be, for instance, the existence of a gentlemen's agreement.[21] Parallel price increases by several undertakings are not, in themselves, prohibited; they could indeed be purely coincidental or the result of a particular market situation known as oligopoly with price leadership.[22] On the other hand, such parallel price increases are prohibited when they are the result of prior consultation. Proof of such consultation will often have to be based on circumstantial evidence[23] such as the participation in meetings with an anti-competitive object.[24] According to the Court, the participation in a single meeting is sufficient proof of collusion.[25]

(b) Decisions by Associations of Undertakings

Decisions must be understood to include the constitutive act of a trade association and its internal rules,[26] decisions made in accordance with those rules and which are binding upon the members of the association,[27] and also recommendations such as the fixing of target prices by an association.[28] Whether an agreement must be regarded as one "between undertakings" or one "between associations of undertakings" is irrelevant. The same applies to the framework within which decisions of associations are taken and the classification given to that framework by the national authorities.[29] As for the term "association",[30] it is not limited to any particular form of association. It also includes associations of association[31] with

---

[21] Gentlemen's agreements and other arrangements, binding in honour only, are not, in this writer's view, prohibited by the Treaty whatever their content; it is only the resulting "practice", which can be prohibited. See *ACF Chemiefarma* Decision [1969] O.J. L192/5, where the Commission considered a gentlemen's agreement to be a binding agreement in the sense of art.101 TFEU [81] because it was concluded together with a binding agreement which referred to the former. This view was accepted by the Court: *ACF Chemiefarma v Commission* (41/69) [1970] E.C.R. 661 at 693 (113,114). See also Opinion of the Advocate-General, *ACF Chemiefarma* (41/69) at 714.

[22] In *Hoffmann-La Roche v Commission* (85/76) [1979] E.C.R. 461 at 520(39); [1979] 3 C.M.L.R. 211, the Court refers to "parallel courses of conduct which are peculiar to oligopolies".

[23] See, e.g. *ICI v Commission* (48/69) [1972] E.C.R. 619; [1972] C.M.L.R. 557 and *Suiker Unie v Commission* (Joined Cases 40, etc./73) [1975] E.C.R. 1663; [1976] C.M.L.R. 295: in both cases the Court admitted the existence of a concerted practice. Not admitted in *Cram and Rheinzink v Commission* (Joined Cases 29/83 and 30/83) [1984] E.C.R. 1679 at 1702(19); [1985] 1 C.M.L.R. 688.

[24] *SCA Holdings v Commission* (T-327/94) [1998] E.C.R. II–1374.

[25] *T-Mobile A.O.* (C-8/08) (quoted above, fn.19).

[26] *ASPA* Decision [1970] O.J. L148/1.

[27] *Bomee-Stichting* Decision [1975] O.J. L329/30.

[28] *Cementhandelaren v Commission* (8/72) [1972] E.C.R. 977 at 991(19); [1973] C.M.L.R. 7. See also *Van Landewyck* (Joined Cases 209, etc./78) [1980] E.C.R. 3125 at 3254(102); [1981] 3 C.M.L.R. 134.

[29] *BNIC v Clair* (123/83) [1985] E.C.R. 391 at 423 (17–20); [1985] 2 C.M.L.R. 430.

[30] See *Metropol Television* (Joined Cases T-528/93 etc.) [1996] E.C.R. II–649; [1996] 5 C.M.L.R. 386.

[31] A *de facto* association of associations was considered by the Commission to be an association of undertakings. See *Cecimo* Decision [1969] O.J. L69/13 and *van Landewyck* (Joined Cases 209, etc./78) (quoted above, fn.28).

or without legal personality and non-profit-making associations. According to the General Court (GC), an association representing a significant number of manufacturers in a relevant sector can be directly and individually concerned by a decision addressed to another association and is therefore admissible to challenge that Commission decision in court.[32]

(c) Undertakings

According to the Court:

"[U]nder competition law that concept covers any entity engaged in an economic activity, in particular an activity consisting in offering goods and services on a given market, regardless of its legal status and the way in which it is financed."[33]

Although the Treaty provides that companies and firms "which are non-profit making"[34] do not constitute undertakings under the Treaty, the Court decided that the fact that the offer of goods or services is made without profit motive does not prevent the entity which carries out those operations on the market from being considered an undertaking, since that offer exists in competition with that of other operators which seek to make a profit.[35]

This term also covers entities without legal personality[36]: however, in the latter case they must have some kind of recognised legal status.[37] This is necessary for them to be able to carry out economic activities.[38] In other words, they must have "legal autonomy", which they can only have when they are a legal entity. Whether or not the latter is the case, must be determined in accordance with the applicable national law.

The term "undertaking" also covers natural persons,[39] public enterprises and even the Member States[40] when they carry out commercial and economic activities.[41] Consequently, entities engaged in social,[42] religious, artistic or scientific activities are not caught by the competition rules.

---

[32] *AIUFFASS* (T-380/94) [1996] E.C.R. II–2169; [1997] 3 C.M.L.R. 542.

[33] *Commission v Italy* (C-35/96) [1998] E.C.R. I-3851.

[34] art.54,2 TFEU [48,2].

[35] *MOTOE* (C-49/07) [2008] E.C.R. I-4863.

[36] art. 49,2 TFEU [43,2] refers to "undertakings, in particular companies or firms within the meaning of the second paragraph of [art.54 TFEU]"; the latter provides that "companies or firms' means companies or firms constituted under civil or commercial law". From this it follows that when the Treaty refers to legal persons it uses the terms "company" or "firm" and that the term "undertaking" is broader and also covers entities without legal personality. See *Arbeitsgemeinschaft Deutscher Luftfahrt-Unternehmen and Hapag-Lloyd v Commission* (T-25/96) [1997] E.C.R. II-363

[37] This would be the case, e.g. with the Dutch "vennootschap onder firma", the English "partnership" and the German "offene Gesellschaft".

[38] See, e.g. *Société d'Assurance* (C-244/94) [1995] E.C.R. I–4022; [1996] 4 C.M.L.R. 536: a non-profit organisation which manages an old-age insurance scheme in keeping with the rules laid down by the authorities is an undertaking within the meaning of art.101 TFEU [81].

[39] See *Reuter/BASF* Decision [1976] O.J. L254/40.

[40] See *Pig Marketing Board v Redmonds* (83/78) [1978] E.C.R. 2347; [1979] 1 C.M.L.R. 177.

[41] See *Commission v Italy* (C-35/96) [1998] E.C.R. I-3851(36): "Constitute an economic activity, any activity which consists in offering products or services on a given market".

[42] See for instance *Cisal di Batistello* (C-218/00) [2002] E.C.R. I-691, where the Court held that an entity participating in the management of one of the traditional branches of social security, fulfils an exclusively social function and does not therefore constitute an undertaking within the meaning of art.101 TFEU [81].

Besides being a legal entity, an undertaking must also be an "economic" entity, in other words have economic independence.[43] This is not the case, under certain conditions, with undertakings belonging to the same group or concern and having the status of a subsidiary in relation to a parent company. When the subsidiary is not free to determine its market behaviour independently of the parent company,[44] and the agreements concluded between them merely constitute internal allocations of tasks, such undertakings form a single economic unit. Therefore, the agreement concluded between them is not an "agreement between undertakings". The same applies to agreements concluded between subsidiaries.[45]

On the other hand, when the market behaviour of the subsidiary is determined by the parent company and the subsidiary violates the competition rules, it is the parent company which is held responsible.[46] Whether the parent company in such a case is situated within the Union or not is irrelevant since the violation has its effects within the internal market and is therefore caught by the Union rules.[47]

(d) Which may affect Trade between Member States

This criterion serves, in the first place, to determine the field of application of the Union competition rules. Indeed, it is:

"[T]o the extent that the agreement may affect trade between Member States, that the interference with competition caused by that agreement is caught by the prohibition in [Union] law found in Article [101], while in the converse case it escapes this prohibition".[48]

In several judgments the Court held that:

"[I]n order that an agreement between undertakings may affect trade between Member States it must be possible to foresee with a sufficient degree of probability on the basis of a set of objective factors of law and fact that it may have an influence, direct or indirect, actual or potential, on the pattern of trade between Member States such as might prejudice the realisation of the aim of a single market in all the Member States."[49]

---

[43] See *Christiani and Nielsen* Decision [1969] O.J. L165/72 and confirmed in *Asia Motor France* (T-387/94) [1996] E.C.R. II–961; [1996] 5 C.M.L.R. 537.

[44] The question is whether or not the parent company controls the subsidiary; see, e.g. *Welded Steel Mesh Cartel* Decision [1989] O.J. L260/1: a 25 per cent interest held by one company in a competitor does not give rise to a parent-subsidiary relationship.

[45] See *Kodak* Decision [1970] O.J. L147/24 and *DaimlerChrysler v Commission* (T-325/01) [2005] E.C.R. II-3319.

[46] See *KNP BT v Commission* (T-309/94) [1998] E.C.R. II–1007.

[47] See, for instance, *ICI v Commission* (48/69) [1972] E.C.R. 619 at 662; [1972] C.M.L.R. 557; *Europemballage and Continental Can v Commission* (6/72) [1973] E.C.R. 215; [1973] C.M.L.R. 199; *Instituto Chemioterapico Italiano* and *Commercial Solvents v Commission* (Joined Cases 6/73 and 7/73) [1974] E.C.R. 223; [1974] 1 C.M.L.R. 309; *United Brands v Commission* (27/76) [1978] E.C.R. 207; [1978] 1 C.M.L.R. 429 and *Hoffmann-La Roche v Commission* (85/76) [1979] E.C.R. 461; [1979] 3 C.M.L.R. 211.

[48] *Société Technique Minière* (56/65) (quoted above, fn.20) at 249. See Guidelines on the effect on trade concept [2004] O.J. C101/81.

[49] *Remia v Commission* (42/84) [1985] E.C.R. 2545 at 2572(22); [1987] 1 C.M.L.R. 1. See also *Consten and Grundig v Commission* (Joined Cases 56/64, 57/64 and 58/64) [1966] E.C.R. 299 at 341; [1966] C.M.L.R. 418, where the Court added that the fact that an agreement encourages an increase, even a large one, in the volume of trade between Member States is not sufficient to exclude the possibility that an agreement "may affect" trade in the above-mentioned manner. In *Bilger v Jehle* (43/69) [1970] E.C.R. 127 at 135(5); [1974] 1 C.M.L.R. 382, the Court stated that trade may be affected even though the agreement does not concern imports or exports.

When an agreement, for instance, prevents undertakings from importing certain goods from another Member State or prohibits them from re-exporting those goods to other Member States, those agreements indisputably affect trade between Member States. Indeed, they limit the free movement of goods within the Union, which it is the object of the competition rules to guarantee. Other examples are agreements which grant an exclusive right; the Court stated that they do not necessarily, of their very nature, contain elements incompatible with the internal market. But, in such a case special attention must be given to the question whether or not the agreements are capable of partitioning the market in certain products between the Member States.[50]

It is also clear from the wording of the Treaty and the judgments of the Court that the effect on trade does not have to be actual; it suffices that the agreement is "capable of constituting a threat" to freedom of trade between Member States.[51]

(e) "Which have as their Object or Effect"

When the object of an agreement is to restrict competition, the question whether competition was indeed distorted is irrelevant. What counts, in that case, is the intention of the parties as expressed in the wording of the agreement. The intention to distort competition may result from all or some of the clauses of the agreement; only those clauses which indicate that the object of the agreement is to interfere with competition will be caught by the prohibition and are therefore automatically void, and not necessarily the whole agreement.[52] When the terms of the agreement do not disclose the intention of the parties to distort competition, the consequences of implementing the agreement must be considered. In order to be able to prove violation of the competition rules, factors must be found by the Commission or the national authorities, that show that competition was in fact distorted, or, at least that a danger of distortion existed.[53]

(f) "Prevention, Restriction or Distortion of Competition"

Competition exists when the economic operators in the common market act independently from one another and have freedom of choice.[54] Or, as the Court put it, "undistorted competition . . . can be guaranteed only if equality of opportunity is secured as between the various economic operators."[55] Operators must be understood in the broadest sense possible to include all legal and natural persons performing an economic activity; they include producers, distributors, customers and end-consumers. Most typical of the existence of competition is the free

---

[50] *Société Technique Minière* (56/65) (quoted above, fn.20).
[51] *Consten and Grundig* (Joined Cases 56/64, 57/64 and 58/64) (quoted above, fn.49) at 341.
[52] See *Consten and Grundig* (Joined Cases 56/64, 57/64 and 58/64) (quoted above, fn.49) where the Court annulled the Commission's decision because it considered the whole agreement as void. See also *Sociéteé de Vente de Ciments et Betons v Kerpen & Kerpen* (319/82) [1983] E.C.R. 4173 at 4184(12), where the Court reiterated that the consequences of the nullity of certain provisions for other parts of the agreement are not a matter for Union law, but must be determined by the national court on the basis of its own national law.
[53] See *Société Technique Minière* (56/65) (quoted above, fn.20) at 251.
[54] *Suiker Unie* (Joined Cases 40, etc./73) [1975] E.C.R. 1663, at 1942(173).
[55] *France v Commission* (C-202/88) [1991] E.C.R. I–1223(51).

choice of the consumer: one can safely say that the moment this freedom is limited in one way or another, competition is distorted. As for the producers, competition exists whenever they have to take into account the market behaviour of other producers within the relevant market.[56] The Court has further developed and specified the meaning of "distortion of competition" by indicating that in order to be prohibited, an agreement must distort competition "to an appreciable extent".[57] For instance, an, "exclusive dealing agreement, even with absolute territorial protection, may, having regard to the weak position of the persons concerned in the market and the products in question, escape the prohibition" of the Treaty.[58] In other words, the de minimis rule also applies in Union competition law. Another point emphasised by the Court is that the anticipated effect on competition may not be purely theoretical, but that, "the competition in question must be understood within the actual context in which it would occur in the absence of the agreement in dispute". It is therefore appropriate:

> "[T]o take into account the nature and quantity, limited or otherwise, of the products covered by the agreement, the position and importance of the [parties] on the market for the products concerned, the isolated nature of the disputed agreement or, alternatively, its position in a series of agreements, the severity of the clause intended to [limit trade] or alternatively the opportunities allowed for other commercial competitors in the same product by way of parallel re-exportation or importation."[59]

The Court also made clear that the prohibition only applies to anti-competitive conduct engaged in by undertakings "on their own initiative" and it is therefore necessary first to evaluate the possible impact of national regulations; that is to say that it must be determined whether or not those national regulations leave any scope for competition that may be restricted by autonomous conduct of undertakings. When it is clear that the national regulations require that undertakings engage in anti-competitive conduct, the prohibition does not apply.[60]

The TFEU gives a few examples of prohibited cartels[61] such as the fixing of purchase and selling prices and other trading conditions, the limitation or control of production, markets, technical developments or investments, the sharing of markets or sources of supply, the application of dissimilar conditions to equivalent transactions and making the conclusion of contracts subject to acceptance of supplementary conditions.

(g) "Within the Internal Market"

According to the TFEU the distortion of competition must take place within the internal market. It follows that an agreement between undertakings situated

---

[56] For the concept "relevant market" see below under "abuse of a dominant position".

[57] See *Société Technique Minière* (56/65) (quoted above, fn.20). For more details as to the meaning of "appreciable" see the Commission's Notice concerning Agreements of Minor Importance [2001] O.J. C368/13. See also Decision *SOCEMAS* [1968] O.J. L201/4.

[58] *Volk v Vervaecke* (5/69) [1969] E.C.R. 295 at 303; [1969] C.M.L.R. 273 and *Distillers Company v Commission* (30/78) [1980] E.C.R. 2229 at 2265(28); [1980] 3 C.M.L.R. 121.

[59] *Société Technique Minière* (56/65) (quoted above, fn.20) at 250 and *Lancôme v Etos* (99/79) [1980] E.C.R. 2511 at 2536(24) [1981] 2 C.M.L.R. 164. For an example of an agreement restricting competition see *Beef Industry* (C-209/07) [2008] E.C.R. 20.11.08.

[60] Case *Glaxosmithkleine Services v Commission* (T-168/01) [2006] E.C.R. II-2369.

[61] art.101(1) TFEU [81(1)].

within the Union but which limits competition exclusively in a third country is not prohibited by Union law.[62] It would be different, of course, if, as a result of this agreement, the behaviour of the parties were influenced in such a way as to cause distortion of competition and affect inter-state trade within the Union.[63] Similarly, an agreement concluded between undertakings situated outside the Union, but having effect on trade between Member States and on competition within the Union, is prohibited by, and prosecutable under, Union law.[64] The same applies when one of the parties to such an agreement is situated within the Union.[65]

Finally, it should be noted that the expression "between the Member States" does not mean that agreements must concern all the Member States or even some of them. An agreement limiting competition in one of the Member States can have distorting consequences in other Member States and affect trade within the Union. This will practically always be the case when the agreement in question covers the whole territory of one Member State, since it creates what the Court calls a "threshold effect" with regard to imports.[66]

(2) The Nullity

Prohibited cartels are automatically void.[67] Consequently, no declaration to this effect is needed.[68] For agreements caught by the prohibition, the nullity applies without a prior decision being required.[69] This nullity applied to agreements concluded after March 13, 1962[70] and not notified to the Commission[71]; different dates applied for the new Member State.[72] Since the entry into force of the new, "Regulation to give effect to the principles of TFEU Art.101 and 102",[73] agreements can only be implemented at the parties' own risks.[74]

---

[62] See, e.g. the *Rieckermann* Decision [1968] J.O. L 276/25; see, however, *Älström v Commission* (Joined Cases C-89, etc./85) [1988] E.C.R. 5193 [1988] 4 C.M.L.R. 901, concerning a concerted practice between undertakings situated in non-member countries affecting selling prices to purchasers established in the Union.

[63] Same idea in *Commercial Solvents* (Joined Cases 6/73 and 7/73) (quoted above, fn.47).

[64] This is sometimes referred to as the extra-territorial application of Union competition law. It is doubtful whether this expression is correct in the above-mentioned case since it is only in "operating within the Union", territorially speaking, that the behaviour of these undertakings is caught.

[65] See, e.g. the *Franco-Japanese Ballbearings* Decision [1974] O.J. L 343/19.

[66] See, e.g. *Cementhandelaren* (8/72) (quoted above fn.28).

[67] art.101(2) TFEU [81(2)].

[68] See art.1(1) Regulation 1/2003 where the same is provided for the prohibition [2003] O.J. L1/1.

[69] This follows from the wording of art.101(2) TFEU [81(2)].

[70] Entry into force of Regulation 17, replaced by Regulation 1/2003 [2003] O.J. L1/1.

[71] As indicated below, this notification obligation no longer exists.

[72] For the new Member States: the date of accession was substituted for the original date, January 1, 1973 for Denmark, Ireland and the UK; January 1, 1981 for Greece; January 1, 1986 for Portugal and Spain; and January 1, 1995 for Austria, Finland and Sweden; and with regard to the Czech Republic, Estonia, Cyprus, Latvia, Lithuania, Hungary, Malta, Poland, Slovenia and Slovakia, the prohibition shall not apply to cartels which were in existence at the date of accession of Austria, Finland and Sweden or at the date of accession of the 10 new Member States and which, by reason of accession, fall within the scope of art.81(1), if within six months from the date of accession, they are so amended that they comply with the conditions laid down in the various regulations.

[73] Regulation 1/2003 (quoted above, fn.70).

[74] This means that they must seek the necessary advice.

They must determine whether or not the agreement is prohibited[75] and, if so, whether an exemption applies. If an agreement is implemented anyhow, it could, later on, be found void ab initio and the parties can then be fined; furthermore, third parties that have been damaged by the agreement could also ask for redress.

(3) Exemptions from the Prohibition

Agreements caught by the prohibition but that satisfy the conditions of art.101(3) TFEU [81(3)] are not prohibited; no prior decision to that effect is required.[76] Before April 1, 2004, the exemption could only be granted by the Commission, either in individual cases notified to it, or within the framework of a so-called block exemption, that applies the exemption automatically to certain categories of agreements. The individual exemption is no longer granted by the Commission, but applies automatically and the block exemptions are still in force, as before.

(a) Individual Exemptions

No longer so called, but still in force, albeit without the intervention of the Commission. Indeed the latter was of the opinion that its intervention is no longer required, since in a mature system of antitrust enforcement all actors—undertakings, their legal advisers, the competent authorities and national courts—are well aware of the criteria that need to be fulfilled to obtain antitrust exemptions. According to the Commission: 40 years of Court of Justice and General Court case law and Commission decisional practice have established a homogeneous body of clear rules on the circumstances under which antitrust exemption is available. The Commission is, however, ready to provide guidance in case novel questions arise in individual cases by issuing an informal "guidance letter".[77]

An exemption automatically applies when, although the agreement affects trade between Member States and restricts competition, the fulfilment of the following four conditions outweighs those limitations:

- the agreement must contribute to improving the production or distribution of goods or to promoting technical or economic progress; however, the restriction of competition must be "indispensable" to the "improvement", which must in particular show appreciable objective advantages of such a character as to compensate for the disadvantages caused in the competition field[78]; this condition is referred to by the Commission as "efficiency gains";
- consumers must get a fair share of the resulting benefit;

---

[75] According to the Preamble of the new Regulation, existing practice and case law provide sufficient information for such determination.

[76] art.101(3) TFEU [81(3)] and art.1(2) Regulation 1/2003 [2003] O.J. L1/1.

[77] See Commission Guidelines on the application of art.101(3) TFEU [art.81(3) EC] [2004] O.J. C101/97 and Notice on informal guidance to novel questions concerning arts 101 and 102 TFEU [81 and 82] that arise in individual cases [2004] O.J. C101/78.

[78] *Consten and Grundig v Commission* (Joined Cases 56/64 and 58/64) (this is the official name of the cases in the ECR, but everyone always refers to them as *Grundig/Consten*) [1966] E.C.R. 299.

- the agreement may not impose on the undertakings concerned restrictions which are not indispensable to the attainment of the above objectives; and
- the agreement may not afford such undertakings the possibility of eliminating competition in respect of a substantial part of the products in question.

In fact, the four conditions overlap and constitute only different viewpoints to be considered in an evaluation of the benefits and detriments of an agreement.

(b) Exemptions for Categories of Agreements

The so-called block exemptions.[79] Those exemptions are reserved for agreements for which it can be assumed with sufficient certainty that they satisfy the conditions set by the Treaty for exemptions from the prohibition. The exemption for categories are provided by a regulation of the Commission, acting in pursuance of a Council regulation. The Council establishes the principle of the exemption and delegates to the Commission the task of working out the details. This technique was used for several categories. The first category concerns agreements to which only two undertakings are party; the "exclusive dealing agreements".[80] They concern bilateral exclusive distribution and exclusive purchasing agreements, franchise agreements and technology transfer agreements.

The second Council Regulation concerns specialisation and research and development agreements.[81]

The third concerns the insurance sector.[82]

All the regulations granting block exemptions follow, generally speaking, the same pattern. They provide in detail which restriction may be imposed upon the parties, which other restrictions do not infringe the prohibition and which restrictions are excluded from the exemption (the so-called black list). It should be noted that agreements which are not exempted under the block exemption may nonetheless be considered exempted by the parties, as indicated above.

(i) **Vertical Agreement**[83] **and Concerted Practice.**[84] This block exemption regulation applied from June 1, 2000 and expires on May 31, 2010. It replaces the Regulation on bilateral exclusive distribution (supply) agreements,[85] the Regulation on bilateral exclusive purchasing agreements[86] and the Regulation concerning franchising agreements.[87] The Regulation applies to vertical agreements for the purchase or sale of goods or services where those agreements are concluded between non-competing undertakings, between certain competitors or by certain associations of retailers of goods; it applies also to agreements containing ancillary provisions on the assignment or use of intellectual property rights.

---

[79] See also below: 3. Competition Rules Applying to Various Branches of the Economy.
[80] Regulation 19/65 [1965] J.O. 36/533 [1965–66] O.J. Spec. Ed. 35, modified [1999] O.J. 148/1 and [2003] O.J. L1/1, which repealed art.7 of Regulation 3976/87 concerning withdrawal of the benefit of a block exemption.
[81] Regulation 2821/71 [1971] J.O. L258/46; [1971–III] O.J. Spec. Ed. 1032, modified [1972] J.O. L291/144; and [2003] O.J. L1/1.
[82] Regulation 1534/91 [1991] O.J. L143/1, modified [2003] O.J. L1/1.
[83] Regulation 2790/99 [1999] O.J. L336/21.
[84] As indicated "agreements" covers also "concerted practices".
[85] Regulation 1983/83 [1983] O.J. L173/1; the literature refers to those agreements as "exclusive supply agreements".
[86] Regulation 1984/83 [1983] O.J. L173/5, no longer applicable.
[87] Regulation 4073/88 [1988] O.J. L359/46, no longer applicable.

According to the regulation, the prohibition of the Treaty does not apply to agreements between two or more undertakings operating at a different level of the production or distribution chain and relating to the conditions under which the parties may purchase, sell or resell certain goods or services. The block exemption does apply to associations and its members or between such an association and its suppliers, but only if all its members are retailers of goods, and no member, together with its connected undertakings, has a total turnover of more than 50 million.[88]

The exemption applies also to the assignment to the buyer of intellectual property rights, when those do not constitute the primary object of the agreement and are directly related to the use, sale or resale of goods and services by the buyer.

The exemption does not apply to competitors, unless they enter into a non-reciprocal vertical agreement and:

- the buyer's turnover does not exceed €100 million; or
- the supplier is a manufacturer and distributor of goods and the buyer is a distributor not manufacturing competing goods; or
- the supplier is a provider of services at several levels of trade while the buyer does not provide competing services at the level where it purchases.

The exemption provided for in the regulation applies on condition that the market share held by the supplier does not exceed 30 per cent[89] of the relevant market on which it sells the contract goods or services.

In the case of exclusive supply obligations, the exemption applies on condition that the market share held by the buyer does not exceed 80 per cent of the relevant market on which it purchases the contract goods or services.

The exemption does not apply (black list) when the object of the agreement is:

- the imposition of sales prices;
- the restriction of the territory into which the buyer may sell, except when it concerns sales:

  — into the territory allocated by the supplier to another buyer;
  — to a wholesale buyer;
  — to unauthorised distributors in a selective distribution system;
  — of components to be incorporated into other goods and supplied to customers who would use them to manufacture the same type of goods as those produced by the supplier;

- the restriction of active or passive[90] sales by the retailer end-user in selective distribution systems;
- the restriction of cross-supplies between distributors in selective distribution systems; and
- the restriction of sales of components to end-users or repairers not entrusted by buyer with repair and servicing.

The exemption does not apply either to the following contractual obligations:

- a non-compete obligation exceeding five years, except when the products are sold by the buyer from land or premises owned or leased by the supplier;

---

[88] art.2,2 Regulation 2790/99 (see above); for the calculation of the turnover see art.10.
[89] Regulation 2790/99 for the calculation of the 30 per cent; see art.9 of the Regulation.
[90] See *BASF Coating v Commission* (T-175/95) [1999] E.C.R. II–1581.

this period may, however, be renewed with the consent of both parties (this non-compete obligation must not be confused with the obligation with a similar name, but provided for after the termination of the agreement);
- obligations preventing the buyer from manufacturing, purchasing, selling or reselling unless it:
  - — relates to competing goods or services;
  - — is limited to the land or premises from which the buyer has operated during the contract period;
  - — is indispensable to protect know-how;
- obligations preventing members of selective distribution systems to sell brands of particular competing suppliers.

The exemption may be withdrawn by the Commission when vertical agreements nevertheless have effects which are incompatible with the conditions for exemption laid down by the Treaty. This could be caused by the cumulative effect of parallel networks of similar vertical restraints. Withdrawal of the exemption by a Member State is also provided when vertical agreements have effects in a Member State's territory which has all the characteristics of a distinct geographic market.

Finally, when parallel networks of similar vertical restraints cover more than 50 per cent of the relevant market, the Commission may declare the regulation not applicable.

The Commission published Guidelines on Vertical Restraints setting out, among other things, which vertical agreements fall outside the Treaty's prohibition, an analysis of the Regulation and of specific vertical restraints.[91]

(ii) **Certain Categories of Vertical Agreements and Concerted Practices in the Motor Vehicle Sector.**[92] The 2002 Regulation replaces a regulation from 1995[93] which allowed manufacturers to set up dealerships in exclusive territories. The new one represents, according to the Commission,[94] a major advance over the old one in two respects: it is based on the philosophy of the Vertical Restraints Regulation; and it no longer prescribes a single exempted system of distribution, but gives greater flexibility of choice to economic operators while laying down stricter rules. The exemption is granted for vertical agreements where they relate to the conditions under which the parties may purchase, sell or resell new motor vehicles, spare parts for motor vehicles or repair and offer maintenance services for motor vehicles and which contain vertical restraints.

In relation to the distribution of new cars, the main conditions for exemption are as follows:

- manufacturers must choose between a selective and an exclusive system;
- exemption is not granted to any restriction of passive sales, etc. in order to strengthen intra-brand competition;
- the link between selling and after-sales services is no longer exempted;
- the prohibition of multi-branding within the same showroom is no longer exempted;

---

[91] [2000] O.J. C291/1.
[92] Regulation 1400/2002 on the application of art.101(3) TFEU [art.81(3) EC] to certain categories of vertical agreements and concerted practices in the motor vehicle sector [2002] O.J. L203/30.
[93] [1995] O.J. L145/25.
[94] XXXIInd Report on Competition Policy, 175.

- limiting a distributor's right to sell motor vehicles with different specifications from those covered by the agreement are not exempted;
- intermediaries acting on behalf of consumers are no longer subject to conditions;
- the independence of vehicle distributors from their suppliers is increased by enabling them to freely represent more than one brand.

Where after-sales services are concerned, the Regulation provides for competition between authorised repairers: any operator who fulfils the qualitative selection criteria will be entitled to join the authorised repair network, establishing themselves wherever they like. Furthermore, competition between authorised members and independent repairers is enhanced by granting the latter the same rights as the former for training and access to diagnostic equipment. Finally manufacturers of automotive components and spare parts will enjoy easier access to parts distribution channels and authorised repairers.

The exemption also applies to two categories of vertical agreements: (a) those entered into between an association of undertakings and its members, or between such an association and its suppliers, on conditions that all the members are distributors and that no individual member has a total annual turnover exceeding €50 million, and (b) those which relate to the assignment to the buyer or use by the buyer of intellectual property rights as long as those provisions do not constitute the primary object of such agreements and that they are directly related to the contract goods or services.

The exemption does not apply to vertical agreements entered into by competing undertakings; there are exceptions to this rule. The exemption applies on condition that the supplier's market share does not exceed 30 per cent. In the case of agreements containing exclusive supply obligations, the market share of the buyer may not exceed 30 per cent. Another condition is the transferability of the rights and obligations to another distributor. Other conditions concern the notice given by the supplier: a minimum time period of five years or, in case of an agreement for unlimited period, that the notice has to be at least two years for both parties, and, finally, the exemption shall apply on condition that the agreement provides for each of the parties the right to refer disputes to an independent expert or arbitrator.

The Regulation provides for "hardcore restrictions" concerning the sale of new motor vehicles, repair, maintenance or spare parts, or concerning some of these activities, and "specific conditions", which exclude the application of the derogation.

The Regulation entered into force on October 1, 2002; it will expire on May 31, 2010. The Commission published an explanatory brochure which is available on the Competition Director-General's Internet site.[95]

(iii) **Specialisation Agreements.**[96] The Regulation exempting specialisation agreements from the prohibition is based on the second Council Regulation.[97] It was adopted on November 29, 2000 and shall expire on December 31, 2010. It concerns:

---

[95] "Car sector" page.
[96] Regulation 2658/00 [2000] O.J. L304/3.
[97] Regulation 2821/71 [1971] J.O. L258/46.

- unilateral specialisation agreements: one party agrees not to produce certain products and to purchase them from the competing undertaking, which agrees to produce and supply them; or
- reciprocal specialisation agreements: two or more undertakings agree on a reciprocal basis not to produce certain but different products and to purchase them from the other parties, which agree to supply them; or
- joint production agreements.

The exemption also applies when the arrangements described above are part of agreements the primary object of which is, for instance, the assignment or use of intellectual property rights.

The exemption only applies if the combined market share of the participating undertakings does not exceed 20 per cent of the relevant market. This market share is calculated on the basis of (a) the market sales value and (b) the data relating to the preceding calendar year; special rules apply for connected undertakings.

If the 20 per cent rises above 25 per cent, the exemption continues to apply for one year.

One should add that it goes without saying that the fixing of prices, the limitation of output or sales, the allocation of markets or customers are not covered by the exemption.

(iv) **Research and Development Agreements.**[98] The exempting Regulation is based on the second Council Regulation.[99] It exempts from the prohibition, agreements entered into by two or more undertakings for the purpose of:

- joint research and development of products or processes and joint exploitation of the results;
- joint exploitation of results from a prior agreement between the same undertakings; and
- joint research and development excluding joint exploitation.

There are, however, conditions:

- all the parties must have access to the results of the work; however, research institutes, academic bodies and undertakings which supply R&D as a commercial service may agree to limit the use to future research;
- when the agreement provides for R&D only, each party must be free to exploit independently the results of the joint R&D and any pre-existing know-how necessary for such exploitation, which, however, may be limited to one or more technical fields, where the parties are not competing;
- joint exploitation may only relate to results which are protected by intellectual property rights or constitute know-how which substantially contributes to technical and economic progress; furthermore, the results must be decisive for the manufacture of the product or for the application of the process; and
- the parties charged with the manufacturing by way of specialisation must fulfil orders from all the parties, except where the R&D agreement also provides for joint distribution.

---

[98] Regulation 2659/00 [2000] O.J. L304/7.
[99] Regulation 2821/71 [1971] J.O. L258/46.

The exemption is valid for a limited number of years. Where the parties to the agreement are not competing undertakings, the exemption applies for the duration of the R&D. Where the results are jointly exploited, the exemption shall continue to apply for seven years from the time the contract products are first put on the market within the internal market.

Where two or more parties are competitors, the exemption shall apply for the periods mentioned above only if, at the time the agreement is entered into, the combined market share of the participating undertakings does not exceed 25 per cent of the relevant market for the products capable of being improved or replaced by the contract products.

At the end of said periods, the exemption continues to apply as long as the combined market share of the parties does not exceed 25 per cent of the relevant market for the contract products.

The exemption does not apply to R&D agreements which have as their object;

- to restrict the freedom of the parties to carry out R&D independently or in co-operation with third parties in unconnected fields or, after completion of the R&D in connected fields;
- the prohibition to challenge after completion of the R&D the validity of intellectual property rights;
- the limitation of output or sales;
- the fixing of prices for contract products when sold to third parties;
- the restriction of customers;
- the prohibition to make passive sales of the contract products;
- the prohibition to put contract products on the market or to pursue active sales policies in territories reserved for other parties, after the end of seven years from the time the products were first put on the market;
- the requirement not to grant licenses to third parties;
- the requirement to refuse to meet demand from resellers in their respective territories who would market in other territories;
- the requirement to make it difficult for users or resellers to obtain the contract products from other resellers.

The regulation expires in December 31, 2010.

The publication of the Regulation on specialisation agreements and the R&D's block exemption was followed by a Commission Notice containing "Guidelines on the applicability of Article 81 of the EC Treaty [now art.101 TFEU] to horizontal co-operation agreements"[100] setting out the principles for assessment of horizontal co-operation agreements. This Notice replaces two previous Notices on co-operation agreement[101] and on co-operative joint ventures.[102]

(v) **Technology Transfer Agreements.** The Commission Regulation[103] granting a block exemption in this field is based upon the first Council Regulation.[104] It combines the former Regulation on patent licensing agreements[105] and the

---

[100] [2001] O.J. C3/2.
[101] [1968] O.J. C75/3.
[102] [1993] O.J. C43/2.
[103] Regulation 240/96 [1996] O.J. L31/2. Replaced [2004] O.J. L123/11; see Guidelines [2004] O.J. C101/2.
[104] Regulation 19/65 [1965] O.J. L533/65, modified by Regulation 1/2003 [2003] O.J. L1/1.
[105] Regulation 2349/84 [1984] O.J. L219/15.

Regulation on know-how licensing agreements.[106] The Commission decided that those two block exemptions ought to be combined into a single regulation covering technology transfer agreements. The object of the regulation is to facilitate the dissemination of technology and the improvement of manufacturing processes.

The Regulation applies to the Member States' patents, Union patents[107] and European patents[108] ("pure" patent licensing agreements). It also applies to agreements for the licensing of non-patented technical information such as descriptions of manufacturing processes, recipes, formulae, designs or drawings, commonly termed "know-how" ("pure" know-how licensing agreements) and, to combined patent and know-how licensing agreements ("mixed agreements"), which are playing an increasingly important role in the transfer of technology. Agreements containing ancillary provisions relating to intellectual property rights other than patents are also covered by the exemption.

The exemption applies to agreements to which only two undertakings are party and which include, among others, one or more of the following obligations:

1. the licensor undertakes not to license other undertakings in the licensed territory;
2. the licensor undertakes not to exploit himself in said territory;
3. the licensee may not exploit in the territory of the licensor;
4. the licensee accepts not to exploit in territories licensed to others;
5. the licensee accepts not to pursue an active policy of putting the licensed product in territories licensed to others, particularly no advertising aimed at those territories;
6. the licensee accepts not to sell the products in those territories in response to unsolicited order[109];
7. the licensee must use the licensor's trade mark although he may not be prevented from identifying himself as the manufacturer of the licensed product; or
8. an obligation on the licensee to limit the production to the quantities he requires in manufacturing his own products.

The Regulation exempts several other contract obligations which are generally not restrictive of competition and imposes a number of conditions for the exemption to apply. A certain number of contractual obligations are excluded from the exemption.[110]

Finally, it should be noted that the so-called opposition procedure is also provided for, i.e. that agreements which contain provisions not covered by the Regulation are exempted after the agreement is notified to the Commission and the latter does not oppose it within four months. The application of Union law to patents and know-how was further examined in the chapter on Intellectual Property Rights; however, mention must be made here of the effect the Union competition rules have on the use that can be made of intellectual property rights. Normally such rights are used by their owner to prevent third parties from

---

[106] Regulation 556/89 [1989] O.J. L61/1.

[107] Convention for the European patent for the common market (Union Patent Convention) of December 15, 1975 [1975] O.J. L17/1.

[108] Convention on the grant of European patents (European Patent Convention) of October 5, 1973.

[109] *Siemens* (T-459/93) [1995] E.C.R. II–1675.

[110] [2003] O.J. C110/21.

producing products covered by such rights, and/or by reserving the use of such rights to particular (national) territories. Although the owner acts in accordance with national law, by preventing imports and exports among the Member States, he prevents the free movement of goods within the internal market. It is in connection therewith that several cases concerning the use of intellectual property rights were submitted to the appreciation of the Court, which declared that such use is contrary to the Union competition rules.[111]

The position of the Court with regard to the use of intellectual property rights can be summarised as follows: the Treaty provisions do not affect the existence of the exclusive rights attached to patents, know-how, trade marks, copyrights, registered designs, plant breeder's rights and other similar rights. They do, however, limit their use in so far as that use restricts trade between Member States. On the other hand, the Court upholds the use of those rights when this is, "justified by the purpose of safeguarding rights which constitute the specific subject matter of such property".[112] As was seen in the chapter on IPR, the Court introduced another restriction in the form of the principle of exhaustion of intellectual and industrial property rights, when the product is put on the market in another Member State by the owner himself or with his consent.

(c) De Minimis

As mentioned above, the Court has indicated that in order to fall under the prohibition of the competition rules, the agreements must affect intra-Union trade and restrict competition in an "appreciable" manner. In a Notice on agreements of minor importance which do not appreciably restrict competition,[113] the Commission quantifies, with the help of market share thresholds what is not an appreciable restriction of competition. The notice does not quantify what does not constitute an appreciable effect on trade.

However, the Commission holds the view that agreements that affect trade between Member States do not appreciably affect competition:

- where the parties are potential or actual competitors: if the aggregate market share held by the parties does not exceed 10 per cent on any of the relevant markets;
- where the parties are not competitors: if the market share held by each of the parties does not exceed 15 per cent on any of the relevant markets;
- (in case of doubt whether the parties are competitors or not, the 10 per cent threshold applies);
- where competition is restricted by cumulative foreclosure effect of parallel networks of agreements having similar effects on the market, the above-mentioned thresholds are reduced to 5 per cent;
- where individual suppliers or distributors with a market share not exceeding 5 per cent are in general not considered to contribute significantly to a cumulative foreclosure effect, neither is there a cumulative foreclosure effect if less than 30 per cent of the relevant market is covered by parallel agreements having similar effects (these thresholds may be exceeded by two percentage points during two consecutive years).

[111] *Transacctiones Maritimas* (C-12/95 P(R)) [1995] E.C.R. I–467; [1996] 2 C.M.L.R. 580.
[112] *Pharmon v Hoechst* (19/84) [1985] E.C.R. 2281.
[113] [2001] O.J. C368/13.

The above provisions do not apply when agreements between competitors have as their object: the fixing of prices, the limitation of output or sales or the allocation of markets or consumers. As for agreements between non-competitors the de minimis does not apply when they have as their object:

- the restriction of the buyer's ability to determine its sale price (does not apply to a maximum sales price or a recommended price);
- the restriction of the territory into which the buyer may sell the contract goods or services (does not apply to restriction of active sales into other territories, restriction of sales to end-users by a wholesaler, nor to restriction of the buyer's ability to sell components for the purpose of incorporation in the same type of goods as those of the supplier);
- the restriction of active or passive sales to end-users by members of a selective distribution system;
- the restriction of cross-supplies within a selective distribution system; and
- the limitation of the supplier's ability to sell components as spare parts to end-users or to repairers.

The Notice contains various definitions and references to court cases and other Commission publications.

2. ABUSE OF A DOMINANT POSITION[114]

Competition and inter-State trade can, as was just seen, be adversely affected by cartels, i.e. agreements between undertakings, decisions of associations of undertakings and concerted practices. However, they can also be restricted by an undertaking or undertakings in a quasi-monopoly situation called "dominant position", behaving on the market in such a way that it constitutes an abuse. Such abuse is prohibited by the Treaty in so far as it affects trade between Member States.

Both the rules of competition concerning cartels and those applying to abuses have as their object to ensure that, "competition in the internal market is not distorted"[115] or, in other words, that the free movement of goods within the internal market is not hindered.

The Treaty refers to the expressions: "dominant position"; "abuse"; and "may affect trade between Member States". The latter was examined in relation with prohibited cartels; the other two concepts will be briefly analysed hereafter.

(1) Dominant Position/Joint Dominant Position

A dominant position exists, according to the Court, when the economic strength of an undertaking on a given market is such that it:

"[E]nables it to hinder the maintenance of effective competition on the relevant market by allowing it to behave to an appreciable extent independently of its competitors and customers and ultimately of its consumers".[116]

---

[114] art.102 TFEU [82].
[115] *SFEI* (C-39/94) [1996] E.C.R. I–3549; [1996] 3 C.M.L.R. 369.
[116] art.8 Regulation 659/99, [1999] O.J. L83/1; see *Scott v Commission* (C-276/03 P) [2005] E.C.R. I–8437 concerning interruption of the time limit.

An undertaking is not in a dominant position merely because of the size of its market share,[117] it can also derive from a combination of several factors which, taken separately, would not necessarily be determinative. They are, for instance, the relationship between the market share of the undertaking in question and the shares of the next largest undertaking(s), the technological lead of the undertaking in question, the existence of a highly developed sales network and the absence of potential competition.[118] An undertaking vested with a legal monopoly may be regarded as occupying a dominant position.[119]

Since the Treaty refers to one or more undertakings, a dominant position can also be held by several undertakings together, the so-called joint or collective dominance.[120] This requires, however, that there exists between the undertakings in question, "links which are sufficiently strong for there to be a collective dominant position".[121] More recently, the Court referred to, "economic links or factors which give rise to a connection between the undertakings concerned".[122] The Court added that:

> "[T]he existence of a collective dominant position may therefore flow from the nature and terms of an agreement, from the way in which it is implemented and, consequently, from the links or factors which give rise to a connection between undertakings which result from it"[123]

This applies to both horizontal and vertical relationships.[124] The concept of joint dominance was further developed by the Commission within the framework of the Merger Regulation, which will be examined below. As for the GC, it determined[125] that a collective dominant position may arise as the result of a concentration where in view of the characteristics of the relevant market and of the alterations in its structure that the transaction would entail the latter would make each member of the dominant oligopoly adopt on a lasting basis a common policy on the market. Consequently, three conditions are necessary

---

[117] Communication 2002/C 152/03 [2002] O.J. C152/5.

[118] Those criteria and others have been analysed in P. Mathijsen in "Oligopolistic Dominance under the Merger Regulation", Festschrift fur Dr Jurgen Gundich, Carl Heymans, Verlag1 KG, (1999) p.161.

[119] *Höfner and Elser* (C-41/90) [1991] E.C.R. I-1979.

[120] See *Compagnie Maritime Belge Transports and Others* (Joined Cases T-24/93, T-25/93 and T-26/93) [1996] E.C.R. II-1201(65–66); [1977] 4 C.M.L.R. 273 and Decision of May 14, 1997, in *Irish Sugar Plc* (IV/34.621) [1997] O.J. L258/1 (11–112). See also *RTE v Commission* (T-69/89) [1991] E.C.R. II-485 and *(Flat Glass) SIV v Commission* (Joined Cases T-68/89 etc.) [1992] E.C.R. II-1403; [1992] 5 C.M.L.R. 302. In Decision IV/M.1524 [2000] O.J. L93/1, the Commission indicated that, "it is not a necessary condition of collective dominance for the oligopolists always to behave as if there were one or more explicit agreements between them. It is sufficient for the oligopolists, in adapting themselves to market conditions, to act, individually, in ways which will substantially reduce competition between them".

[121] *Almelo* (C-393/92) [1994] E.C.R. I-1520(43).

[122] *Compagnie Maritime Belge Transport and others* (Joined Cases C-395/96 P and C-396/96 P) [2000] E.C.R. I-1365(41).

[123] *Compagnie Maritime Belge Transport and others* (Joined Cases C-395/96 P and C-396/96 P), above, fn.122 (45).

[124] See *Irish Sugar v Commission* (T-228/97) [1999] E.C.R. II-2969.

[125] *Airtours v Commission* (T-342/99) [2002] E.C.R. II-2585, where the GC annulled the Commission's Decision prohibiting the merger. For the existence of a joint dominant position see *Compagnie Maritime Belge and others* (Joined Cases T-24/93, T-26/93 and T-28/93) [1996] E.C.R. II-1201.

for the creation of a collective dominant position significantly impeding effective competition:

1. there must be sufficient market transparency for all members of the dominant oligopoly to be aware, sufficiently, precisely and quickly, of the way in which the other members' market conduct is evolving;
2. there must be adequate deterrents to ensure that there is a long-term incentive in not departing from the common policy; and
3. it must be established that the foreseeable reaction of current and future competitors, as well as of consumers, would not jeopardise the results expected from the common policy.

It follows, from the practice of the Commission[126] and the case law of the courts[127] that in order to determine whether an undertaking's position is dominant it must be viewed in relation to the "relevant product/service market" and to the "relevant geographic market". Indeed, logically, it is only after having defined the relevant product/service market that the Commission and the courts will be able to determine whether there does indeed exist competition, which the abuse might distort. From there the question: when does competition exist between products or services? Basically, the answer is very simple. There is competition when the end consumer has a choice between different products/services, which, because of their characteristics, their price and their intended usage, are "interchangeable". The Court defined it as follows:

"[T]he concept of relevant market, in fact, implies that there can be effective competition between the products, which form part of it and this presupposes that there is a sufficient degree of inter-changeability between all the products forming part of the same market in so far as the specific use of the product is concerned".[128]

Probably the best example of a non-interchangeable product is the banana. The Court was called upon to determine whether that product constitutes a relevant market on its own or whether it was part of the larger market of fresh fruits. It found that:

"[T]he banana has certain characteristics, appearance, taste, softness, seedlessness, easy handling, a constant level of production, which enables it to satisfy the constant needs of an important section of the population consisting of the very young, the old and the sick".[129]

The Court concluded that, "consequently, the banana market is a market which is sufficiently distinct from the other fresh fruit markets".

It follows that the Commission, when examining whether or not there has been abuse, must, in the first place determine the limits of the product/service market. With regard to services, an example of the difficulty this might present, is to be found in the definition of the banking sector. The Commission ascertained that a significant number of non-financial companies have subsidiaries involved in financial services, such as financing subsidiaries of car manufacturers, payment

---

[126] See, for instance, *BL (British Leyland)* Decision: [1984] O.J. L207/11.
[127] See, for instance *GVL v Commission*, (7/82) [1983] E.C.R. 483; [1983] 3 C.M.L.R. 645.
[128] *L'Oréal v De Nieuwe AMCK* (31/80) [1980] E.C.R. 3775; [1981] 2 C.M.L.R. 235.
[129] *United Brands v Commission* (27/76) [1978] E.C.R. 207 at 273(31); [1973] C.M.L.R. 612. Another example is to be found in *Hoffmann-La Roche* (85/76) [1979] E.C.R. 461 at 547(111).

cards or retail banking subsidiaries of big retailers. In other words, not only banks offer banking services; so, where are the limits?[130]

Besides defining the product/service relevant market, the Commission must also determine the geographic market. The larger this market, the more likelihood for competition to exist; from there its importance. The limits of this market depends on the structure of the product market, especially as far as production, supply and demand are concerned.[131] The Court did underline, "how necessary it is to define the market concerned in order that the relative strength for the undertakings in such a market might be considered".[132] The limits of the geographic market do not necessarily coincide with the territories of the Member States, nor of the Union, although they normally do, for the simple reason that statistics are generally available for those areas only. The Treaty refers to the, "internal market or a substantial part of it".[133] However, the geographic market can be very small indeed.[134] The Commission published a "Notice on the definition of the relevant market for the purpose of the [Union] competition law".[135] Market definition is a tool to identify and define the boundaries of competition between firms. It serves to establish the framework within which competition policy is applied by the Commission. The main purpose of market definition is to identify in a systematic way the competitive constraints that the undertakings involved face. The objective of defining the market is to identify the actual competitors.[136]

(2) Abuse

More difficult is the definition of "abuse". It will be remembered that cartels are prohibited when two conditions are fulfilled: trade between Member States must be affected and competition must be restricted. With regard to "abuse of a dominant position", the Treaty only refers to trade between Member States, and the term "abuse" must therefore be understood in relation to competition. According to the Court, the concept of abuse is an objective concept relating to the behaviour of an undertaking enjoying a dominant position in a given market.[137] This behaviour constitutes an abuse when it is such as to influence the structure of the relevant market. Such behaviour must have the effect, through recourse to methods different from those which condition normal competition, of hindering the maintenance or growth of existing competition.[138]

---

[130] Decision of May 20, 1998, in case no. IV/M.1016, *Price Waterhouse/Coopers & Lybrand*. See also Decision of September 21, 1994, *Night Services* [1994] O.J. L 259/20, (19l.); this Decision was annulled by the GC.

[131] See *Alsatel v Novasam* (247/86) [1988] E.C.R. 5987, where the Court did not accept the existence either of a relevant product market, nor of a national geographic market, but only of a regional one.

[132] *Hoffmann-La Roche* (85/76) quoted above, fn.129.

[133] art.102,1 TFEU [82(1)].

[134] See, e.g. Decision of December 13, 1995, *Eurotunnel* [1988] O.J. L311/36.

[135] [1997] O.J. C372/5.

[136] See also below the section on Control of Concentrations for the definition of the geographic market.

[137] For instance, an undertaking abuses its dominant position where it charges, for its services, fees which are unfair or disproportionate to the economic value of the services provided, see *TNT Traco* (C-340/99) [2001] E.C.R. I-4109.

[138] *Hoffmann-La Roche* (85/76) (quoted above, fn.29) at 541(91).

Any behaviour of an undertaking in a dominant position, which interferes with one of the basic freedoms or with the free choice of the purchaser or consumer, or with freedom of access to the market or to an essential facility,[139] constitutes an abuse.[140] The most obvious criterion is the freedom of choice left to the other participants in the market. Such a choice only exists when there is a sufficient offer to supply; this offer is practically nonexistent in the case of an undertaking which owns an essential facility and either refuses to grant access in the absence of objective justification or only against excessive prices. An essential facility can be defined as a, "facility or infrastructure, without access to which competitors cannot provide services to customers".[141] It is determined by the technical, legal or economic obstacles preventing a would-be user of the facility from competing on the relevant (downstream) market.[142] The Court, however, never uses the expression "essential facilities", but rather refers to "refusal to deal".

It should be noted that abuse can also take place on a market different from the dominated one and without effects on the latter, but the markets must be closely linked.[143] In other words, the prohibition also concerns abuses on, and affecting, associated non-dominated markets in special circumstances.

Although the Treaty refers to abuse "of" a dominant position, this does not mean that a link of causality must exist between the dominant position and the abuse. Indeed, the strengthening of the position of an undertaking may constitute an abuse and be prohibited regardless of the means and procedures by which it is achieved.

As for abuse by undertakings in a joint dominant position, the abuse does not necessarily have to be the action of all the undertakings in question. Such undertakings may engage in joint or individual abusive conduct; it suffices that that conduct relates to the exploitation of a joint dominant position which the undertakings hold on the market.[144]

3. COMPETITION RULES APPLYING TO VARIOUS BRANCHES OF THE ECONOMY

The Treaty also entrusts the Council, acting by a qualified majority on a proposal from the Commission and after consulting Parliament, to lay down appropriate regulations or directives to define, if need be, in the various branches of the economy, the scope of the competition provisions.[145]

(1) Agriculture

One of those branches is explicitly provided for in the Treaty: the, "rules on competition shall apply to production of, and trade in, agricultural products only to

---

[139] See, e.g. Decision of January 18, 1994, Case IV/34.689, *Sea Containers v Stena Seelink* [1994] O.J. L15/8.

[140] See, e.g. Decision of June 28, 1995, *Landing fees at Zaventem* [1995] O.J. L216/8 and *Job Centre* (C-55/96) [1998] E.C.R. I–7119: abuse of dominant position "unavoidable", caught by arts 101–102 TFEU [8182].

[141] Commission Decision *Sea Containers v Stena Sealink* [1994] O.J. L15/08.

[142] *Bronner v Mediaprint* (C-7/97) [1998] E.C.R. I–7791.

[143] *Tetra Pak* (T-83/91) [1994] E.C.R. II–755 and *Tetra Pak* (C-333/94) [1996] E.C.R. I–5951.

[144] See *Irish Sugar v Commission* (T-228/97) [1999] E.C.R. II–2969.

[145] art.103(2)c TFEU [83].

the extent determined by the Council".[146] In other words, the Council could, in theory, have decided that those rules do not apply to agriculture[147]; however, the Council opted for a limited application.[148]

The point of departure is that the rules of competition do apply to agriculture, but only in so far as their application does not impede the functioning of national organisations of agricultural markets—those were later replaced by the common organisations of agricultural markets—or jeopardise the attainment of the objectives of the common agricultural policy. The following cartels are exempted:

- farmers' cartels;
- farmers' associations;
- associations of such associations belonging to a single Member State, and which concern the sale of agricultural products or the use of joint facilities for the storage, treatment or processing of agricultural products and under which there is no obligation to charge identical prices.

The Commission has sole power to determine which cartels fulfil those conditions; its decisions must be published.

(2) Transport

Although, as indicated above, the Council must, if need be, define the scope of the competition rules in the various branches of the economy, there is no obligation to do so with regard to transport. In the past, the Council excluded transport services from the application of the first regulation implementing the competition rules,[149] but this exemption was repealed by the Regulation that replaced the latter in 2003.[150] This left in place rules[151] of competition for transport by rail, road and inland waterway,[152] maritime transport and air transport. These shall be briefly examined below, but more extensively in Ch.27: Transport.

Another regulation concerns the limitation periods in proceedings and the enforcement of sanctions under the Union competition rules relating to transport.[153]

(a) Maritime Transport

Reference must be made here to the Regulation laying down detailed rules for the application of the Union competition rules to maritime transport and to the block

---

[146] art.42 TFEU [36].
[147] See first recital of Regulation 26/62 [1962] J.O. 30/993: "whereas one of the matters to be decided under the common agricultural policy is whether the rules on competition . . . are to apply to production of and trade in agricultural products".
[148] Regulation 26/62 (quoted above). See *Dijkstra* (Joined Cases C-319/94, C-40/94 and C-224/94) [1995] E.C.R. I-4471; [1996] 5 C.M.L.R. 178, on the interpretation of art.2 of Regulation 26/62.
[149] Regulation 141/62 exempting transport from the application of Council Regulation No.17 [1962] O.J. 124/2750.
[150] Regulation 1/2003 [2003] O.J. L1/1.
[151] Regulation 17/62 [1962] O.J. 13/204, repealed by Regulation 1/2003 [2003] O.J. L1/1.
[152] Regulation 1017/68 [1968] O.J. L175/1, amended by Regulation 1/2003 (quoted above), replaced by codified version Regulation 169/09 [2009] O.J. L61/1. For the scope of Regulation 1017/68 see *UIC (Union Internationale des Chemins de Fer)* (C-264/95 P) [1997] E.C.R. I-1287; [1997] 5 C.M.L.R. 49. Art.26 of Regulation 1017/68 on hearings was implemented by Regulation 1630/69 [1969] O.J. L209/11; this Regulation was repealed by Regulation 773/2004 [2004] O.J. L123/18, modified [2008] O.J. L171/3.
[153] Regulation 2988/74 [1974] O.J. L319/1, amended by Regulation 1/2003 (quoted above).

exemption for Liner Conferences.[154] The Regulation supplements, among others, and makes more precise the United Nations Code of Conduct for Liner Conferences.[155] Tramp vessel services are excluded. The regulation provides for the possibility to exempt certain technical cartels and also for block exemptions of Liner Conferences under well-defined conditions and with specific obligations. The Regulation, however, recognises that its application to certain restrictive practices may result in conflicts with the laws and rules of third countries and prove harmful to important Union trading and shipping interests. Negotiations with those countries are therefore provided for. See also the 2002 interpretative judgments of the GC concerning this Regulation.[156]

The Council also adopted a regulation on the application of the competition rules to certain categories of cartels between liner shipping companies, described in shipping circles as "consortia".[157] This Regulation authorises the Commission to declare that the competition rules shall not apply to certain categories of cartels. It concerns cartels that have as their object to promote or establish co-operation in the joint operation of maritime transport services between liner shipping companies, for the purpose of rationalising their operations by means of technical, operational and/or commercial arrangements, with the exception of price-fixing consortia. The block exemption Regulation was adopted by the Commission in 1995.

In 2008 the Commission published "Guidelines on the application of Article TFEU Art. 101 [art.81] to maritime transport services".[158]

(b) Air Transport

The Treaty provides that the Title on transport shall only apply to transport by rail, road and inland waterway and that the Council may decide, "whether, to what extent and by what procedure appropriate provision may be laid down for sea and air transport".[159] Having recognised that the rules on competition form part of the Treaty's general provisions which also apply to air transport,[160] the

---

[154] Regulation 4056/86 [1986] O.J. L378/4, amended by Regulation 1/2003 [2003] O.J. L1/1. See *Compagnie Maritime Belge Transports and others v Commission* (Joined Cases T-24/93, etc.) [1996] E.C.R. II–1201.

[155] [1979] O.J. L121/1.

[156] *Atlantic Container Lines v Commission (TACA)* (T-18/97) [2002] E.C.R. II–395/94, it concern the withdrawal by the Commission of immunity; the GC ascertained that as inland price-fixing falls within the scope of the Inland Transport Regulation 1017/68, now Regulation 169/09 [2009] O.J. L61/1 which does not provide for immunity, TACA could not claim it; *Atlantic Container Line v Commission (TAA)* (T-395/94) where the GC found that the Trans-Atlantic Agreement was not a liner conference because it failed to meet the basic criterion of operating under common or uniform freight rates; and *Compagnie Générale Maritime v Commission* (T-86/95) [2002] E.C.R. II–1011.

[157] Regulation 479/92 [1992] O.J. L55/3, amended by Regulation 1/2003 (quoted above), codified version [2009] O.J. L79/1. See block exemption Regulation 870/95 [1995] O.J. L89/7, which was replaced by Regulation 823/2000 on the application of art.101(3) [81(3)] of the Treaty to certain agreements between liner shipping companies (consortia) [2000] O.J. L100/24, extended and amended 2009 IP/09/1367, arguing that consortia generally bring about improvements of productivity and service quality; it was renewed until April 25, 2010 [2005] O.J. L101/10.

[158] [2008] O.J. C245/2. For more details see below Ch.27: Transport (3.(5) Maritime Transport).

[159] art.100(2) TFEU [80(2)].

[160] This recognition only occurred after the Court had so decided, see *Ministère Public v Asjes* (Joined Cases 209/84, 210/84, 211/84, 212/84 and 213/84) [1986] E.C.R. 1425; [1986] 3 C.M.L.R. 173.

Council adopted a regulation laying down the procedure for the application of the competition rules to undertakings in the air transport sector.[161]

In that regulation the Council considered that air transport is characterised by features which are specific to this sector and that, furthermore, international air transport is regulated by a network of bilateral agreements between States. Those agreements define the conditions under which air carriers designated by the parties to the agreement may operate routes between their territories.[162] On the other hand, it is clear that practices which affect competition relating to air transport between Member States may have substantial effect on trade between Member States. It was therefore necessary to authorise the Commission to take the requisite measures for the application of the competition rules to air transport.

Consequently, the Commission adopted a regulation concerning complaints, applications and hearings in the air sector, which was replaced by a regulation generally applicable to the transport sector.[163] Subsequently, the Council adopted a regulation allowing the Commission to exclude from the prohibition provided by the Treaty, certain categories of cartels in the air sector.[164]

Altogether, the main preoccupation of the Union remains the opening of the markets, i.e. the right of access for Union air carriers to intra-Union air routes.[165]

(c) International Aviation[166]

The Commission has no effective and efficient enforcement tools to ensure that competition is preserved and promoted in the field of international air transport, i.e. between Member States and third countries.[167] The Commission sought, without success to extend the scope of regulations.[168] A recent Court judgment in the "Open Sky" cases,[169] where the Court found that the bilateral agreements concluded by several Member States were contrary to Union rules,[170] resulted in the Commission obtaining a mandate from the Council to start negotiations with the US (see below, Ch.27: Transport).

(d) Rail Transport

Until very recently, the rail transport sector was characterised by the existence in all Member States of State monopolies, with the result that national markets were

---

[161] Regulation 411/2004 [2004] O.J. L68/1.

[162] Regulation 1617/93 only applies to air transport between Member States; with regard to air transport between Member States and third countries see, among others, the "Open Sky" cases (see below); this Regulation was renewed by Regulation 1105/02 [2002] O.J. L167/6.

[163] Regulation 4261/88 [1988] O.J. L376/10, replaced by Regulation 2843/98 [1998] O.J. L354/22.

[164] Regulation 3976/87 [1987] O.J. L374/9, replaced by Regulation 487/09 [2009] O.J. L148/1 on the application of art.101(3) [81(3)] to certain categories of agreements and concerted practices in the air transport sector.

[165] See Regulation 2408/92 [1992] O.J. L240/8, and *Air Inter* (T-260/94) [1997] E.C.R. II–997.

[166] XXXIInd Report on Competition Policy, 108.

[167] Interesting also is Decision 98/710 on the Italian traffic distribution rules for the airport system of Milan [1998] O.J. L337/42. See also *Aéroports de Paris v Commission* (T-128/98) [2000] E.C.R. II–3929.

[168] Regulation 411/2004 on procedure for application of the rules of competition to undertakings in the air transport sector [1987] O.J. L374/1 and Regulation 3976/87 allowing the Commission to adopt block exemptions in that sector [1987] O.J. L374/9, amended [2004] O.J. L68/1.

[169] "Open Sky" cases (Joined Cases C-466/98, C-467/98, C-468/98, C-471/98, C-472/98, C-475/98 and C-476/98) against the UK, Denmark, Sweden, Finland, Belgium, Luxembourg, Austria and Germany [2002] E.C.R. I–9427.

[170] art.49 TFEU [43].

absolutely closed to operators from other Member States. The privatisations which have taken place lately have not changed this. Consequently, the Union has tried to pry open the national markets to operators from other Member States by providing for a "right of access".[171] Under the present Directive this right is granted only to "international groupings" and to, "railway undertakings operating international combined transport goods services".[172] Where the former are concerned they have the right of access in the Member States of establishment of their constituent railway undertakings and the right of transit in other Member States for international services between the Member States of establishment. As for the combined goods services, they have access to the infrastructure of all the Member States.

Various regulations were adopted over the years concerning the application of competition rules to the rail operators; see for instance the rules concerning aid in the form of compensation for discharging public service obligation.[173]

Further provisions concerning transport will be examined below in Ch.27: Transport.

(3) Telecommunications

Telecommunications, information industries and innovation constitute one of the most important industrial sectors for the economic development of the European Union. They will be further examined in Ch.31: Enterprise and Industrial Policy/Information Society. Full competition in the telecommunications market was only introduced in 1998, after the abolition of national monopolies for equipment[174] and value-added services.[175] But, given the fact that the infrastructure remained governed by monopoly rights, the Council introduced the Open Network Provision Directive,[176] requiring the telecommunication organisations to lease lines to new market entrants on reasonable terms and to provide open and fair access to their networks. From 1992 onwards, the satellite[177] and

---

[171] Directive 91/440 [1991] O.J. L237/25 on the development of the Union's railways, amended [2001] O.J. L75/1 and [2007] O.J. L315/44. See the landmark Decision *Ferrovie dello Stato (FS)/Georg Verkehrsorganisation (GVG)*. Press release IP/03/1183, according to which FS was required to allow new train operators to provide cross-border passenger services into Italy. See also Directive 2001/14 on the allocation of railway infrastructure capacity and the levying of charges for the use of railway infrastructure and safety certification [2001] O.J. L75/291, amended [2002] O.J. L289/30 and [2007] O.J. L315/44.

[172] art.10 Directive 91/440.

[173] Regulation 1370/07 [2007] O.J. L315/1.

[174] Directive 88/301 [1988] O.J. L131/73, incorporated [1994] O.J. L1/446, modified [1994] O.J. L268/15.

[175] Directive 2002/77 on competition in the markets for electronic communications network and services [2002] O.J. L249/21, which replaces Directive 90/388. For interpretation of art.4 of Directive 2002/77 (Competition Directive) together with art.7(3) of Directive 2002/20 (Authorisation Directive) and art.9(1) of Directive 2002/21 (Framework Directive), see *Centro Europa 7* (C-38/05) [2008] E.C.R. I-349: they preclude, in television broadcasting matters, national legislation which makes it impossible for an operator holding rights to broadcast

[176] Directive 90/387 on the establishment of the internal market for telecommunications services through the implementation of open network provision [1990] O.J. L192/1.

[177] Directive 94/46 amending Directive 88/301 and Directive 2002/77 (quoted above) in particular with regard to satellite communications [1994] O.J. L268/15.

mobile[178] services and the cable television networks[179] were progressively opened to competition.

In 1996 the Commission adopted its so-called Full Competition Directive[180] amending and extending its earlier Services Directive. The Directive's aim is at the introduction of full competition in the Union telecommunications market. It requires the Member States to abolish the last remaining areas of monopoly rights in that market.

In 2002, the liberalisation of the European telecom markets was pushed forward by the adoption of a new regulatory framework, the so-called telecom package. With regard to electronic communications networks and services, Parliament and the Council issued a series of directives on a common regulatory framework, among others on roaming charges for calls on mobile telephones within the Union, now limited to 49 cents and, for calls received, to 24 cents during the first year; respectively 46 and 22 during the second year and 43 and 19 thereafter,[181] on access and interconnection,[182] on authorisation[183] and on universal services and users' rights.[184] According to the new framework, the national regulatory authorities have to define the relevant markets. The Commission has published guidelines in which the principles for the analysis of markets and effective competition under the new regulatory framework are laid down.[185] All exclusive/special rights for the provision of public voice telephony services and the provision of the public telecommunications network were to be abolished by January 1, 1990 (with the exception of some Member States). Similarly, all exclusive/special rights regarding the self-provision of infrastructure, the use of infrastructure run by third parties and the use of shared infrastructure for the provision of services other than public voice telephony, were to be abolished by July 1, 1996 within the new regulatory framework.

The Directive also introduces the basic principles for licensing new entrants to both voice telephony and telecommunications infrastructure markets. It furthermore requires interconnection to the voice telephony service and public switched

---

[178] Directive 69/2 amending Directive 90/388 with regard to mobile and personal communications [1996] O.J. L20/59.

[179] Directive 95/51 amending Directive 90/388 with regard to the abolition of the restrictions on the use of cable television networks for the provision of already liberalised telecommunications services [1995] O.J. L256/49.

[180] Directive 96/19 amending Directive 90/388 regarding the implementation of full competition in telecommunications markets [1996] O.J. L74/13.

[181] Directive 2002/21 (Framework Directive) [2002] O.J. L108/33, amended by Regulation 717/07 on roaming on public mobile telephone networks within the Union [2007] O.J. L171/32. See *Deutsche Telekom* C-262/06 [2007] E.C.R. I-10057, provisional maintenance of obligation to obtain authorisation regarding tariffs and *Vodafone Espana* (T-109/06) [2007] E.C.R. II-5151, Commission letter under art.6(5) not binding. For interpretation of art.9(1), art.5(2) and art.7(3) of Directive 2002/20 and art.4 of Directive 2002/77 on competition in the markets for electronic communication, see *Centro Europa 7* (C-380/05) [2008] E.C.R. I-349, precludes national legislation that makes it impossible for an operator holding rights to broadcast in the absence of broadcasting radio frequencies granted on the basis of objective criteria. *Kabel* (C-336/07) [2008] E.C.R. I-22.12.08, telemedia services fall within the scope of art.31(1).

[182] Directive 2002/19 (Access Directive) [2002] O.J. L108/7, modified [2009] O.J. L337/37.

[183] Directive 2002/20 (Authorisation Directive) [2002] O.J. L108/21. See above, fn.181 *Deutsche Telekom* (C-262/06) and *Centro Europa 7* (C-380/05).

[184] Directive 2002/22 (Universal Service Directive) [2002] O.J. L108/51, modified [2009] O.J. L337/14.

[185] Commission guidelines on market analysis and the assessment of significant market power under the Union regulatory framework for electronic communications networks and services [2002] O.J. C165/6.

telecommunications networks to be granted on non-discriminatory, proportional and transparent terms, based on objective criteria.

Additional legislative action was taken to ensure a successful transition to full liberalisation. Among the most important are the extension of the Open Network Provision to leased line[186] and voice telephony.[187] The Interconnection Directive ensures to all market players the ability to obtain interconnection with the network[188] of others where this is reasonably justifiable and in accordance with the ONP principles of non-discrimination, transparency, objectivity and proportionality. See also the Notice on the application of the competition rules to access agreements in the telecommunications sector.[189]

In this field, providing unbundled access to the local loop[190] to all new entrants increases, according to the Commission, the level of competition and technological innovation in the local access network. This unbundled access was the object of a Commission Communication[191] and Recommendation.[192] In order to establish whether current commercial practices and prices in the telecommunication sector infringe Union competition rules, the Commission decided in 1999 to open inquiries related to the provision and pricing of leased lines (phase 1), mobile roaming services (phase 2) and the provision and access to and use of the residential local loop (phase 3).[193]

In 2002, the Commission also adopted a Directive on "Competition in the markets for electronic communication networks and services", amending and consolidating a similar directive from 1990[194] and in 2008 the Commission adopted a Directive on competition in the markets in telecommunications terminal equipment.[195]

(4) Postal Service[196]

Although the Court stated,[197] back in 1993, that competition rules of the Treaty (cartels, abuses of dominant positions, and also State aid provision[198]), apply also to the postal sector, the latter enjoyed a privileged position until the end of the 1990s. The application of the competition rules was carried out very progressively. This is the more surprising when one realises that the revenue of the postal sector

---

[186] Directive 92/44 on the application of open network provision to leased lines [1992] O.J. L165/27.
[187] Directive 95/62 on the application of open network provisions to voice telephony [1995] O.J. L321/6.
[188] Directive on interconnection in telecommunications with regard to ensuring universal service and interoperability through application of the principles of Open Network Provision [1997] O.J. L199/32.
[189] [1998] O.J. C265/2.
[190] "Local loop" refers to the physical circuit between the customer's premises and the telecommunications operator's local switch or equivalent facility.
[191] [2000] O.J. C272/55.
[192] Regulation 2887/00 on unbundled access to the local loop [2000] O.J. L336/4.
[193] *http://www.ec.europa.eu./competition/antitrust/others/.*
[194] Directive 2002/77 [2002] O.J. L249/21. See *Centro Europa 7* (C-380/05) [2008] E.C.R. I-349.
[195] Directive 2008/63 [2008] O.J. L162/20 (codified version).
[196] Some of the data in this section is borrowed from "La libéralisation des services postaux dans l'UE" by Stéphane Rodrigues, L'Observateur de Bruxelles, No. 63, p.II.
[197] *Netherlands and Others v Commission* (Joined Cases C-48/90 and C-66/90) [1992] E.C.R. I-565; [1993] 5 C.M.L.R. 316 and *Corbeau* (C-320/91) [1993] I-2533; [1995] 4 C.M.L.R. 621.
[198] *Banco Exterior de Espana* (C-387/92) [1994] E.C.R. I-877; [1994] 3 C.M.L.R. 473.

represents 0.9 per cent of the Union's GDP and that it provides more than five million direct and indirect jobs. The national postal services constitute, "undertakings entrusted with the operation of services of general economic interest" specifically referred to in the TFEU.[199] The Commission published a Notice[200] setting out the:

> "[G]uiding principles according to which the Commission intends to apply the competition rules to the postal sector in individual cases, while maintaining the necessary safeguards for the provision of a universal service. It also gives the enterprises and the Member States clear guidelines so as to avoid infringements of the Treaty."

The Commission also ascertains that, "the traditional structures of some services of general interest,[201] which are organised on the basis of national monopolies, constitute a challenge for European economic integration".

The Notice sets out rules concerning the duties of dominant postal operators, cross-subsidisation, public undertakings and special or exclusive rights, freedom to provide services, measures adopted by Member States, postal operators and aid, services of general economic interest and the conditions for the application of the exception provided for undertakings entrusted with the operation of such services.[202]

In 1997, Parliament and Council adopted a Directive on common rules for the development of the internal market of Union postal services and the improvement of quality of service; this Directive was modified in 2002.[203] It is based upon five elements:

- a progressive and controlled liberalisation of the postal services: different steps were taken in 2003 and 2006, the latter resulting in a liberalisation of, for instance, 43 per cent of the French postal service (outgoing trans-frontier mail and mail of more than 50g whose price is two and a half times the basic rate);
- the maintenance, in each Member State, of a universal postal service, i.e. an offer of quality service on a permanent basis at every point of the territory and at affordable prices; concretely speaking, this means at least one delivery and one clearance every weekday at the home or premises of every natural and legal person. Furthermore, it should include the following minimum facilities: the clearance, sorting, transport and distribution of postal items up to 2kg and of postal packages up to 10kg and services for registered and insured items;
- besides the obligation of affordable prices, the Directive requires transparency of the accounts; see in this respect also the obligation of transparency imposed on the relation between the State and public enterprise[204];
- the quality of the postal services: besides the quality of the internal postal service that comes under the national competences, the quality of the trans-border services is established in an Annex to the Directive and is based on the duration of the forwarding[205];

---

[199] arts 14 and 106(2) TFEU [16 and 86(2)]. The latter provides that these undertakings, "shall be subject to the rules contained in this Treaty, in particular to the rules on competition, in so far as the application of such rules does not obstruct the performance, in law or in fact, of the particular tasks assigned to them."

[200] [1998] O.J. C39/2.

[201] Communication from the Commission, Services of general interest in Europe [2001] O.J. C17/4.

[202] art.106(2) TFEU [86(2)].

[203] Directive 97/67 [1998] O.J. L15/14, amended [2002] O.J. L176/21, with regard to the further opening of Union postal services.

[204] Directive 80/723 [1980] O.J. L195/35, modified: [2005] O.J. L312/47.

[205] J+3 for 85 per cent of the deliveries and J+5 for 97 per cent of them.

- the Directive requires the Member States to establish one or more National Regulatory Authorities (NRA) that are legally distinct and functionally independent of the postal operators.

A third postal directive[206] was published in 2008 providing for abolishing legal monopolies of postal services by December 31, 2010. It provides for the accomplishment of the internal market of Union postal services via abolition of the reserved areas in all Member States, the confirmation of the scope and standard of universal service, the reinforcement of consumers' rights and upgrading of the role of national regulatory authorities and the offering of a list of measures Member States may take to safeguard and finance, if necessary, the universal service. The Directive requires Member States to continue to ensure a universal service for all customers including collection and delivery of mail at least five days per week at affordable prices throughout the territory.[207]

(5) Insurance[208]—Financial Sector

In this important sector special rules were established also. In May 1991 the Council adopted a Regulation concerning the exemption from the competition rules of certain categories of agreements in the field of insurance. It authorises the Commission to issue a regulation exempting this category from the prohibition of certain agreements.[209] On that basis the Commission issued, in December 1992, a Regulation[210] exempting four types of agreements—out of the six provided for in the Council regulation—that seek co-operation with respect to:

- the establishment of common risk-premium tariffs based on collectively ascertained statistics or on the number of claims;
- the establishment of standard policy conditions;
- the common coverage of certain types of risks; and
- the establishment of common rules on the testing and acceptance of security devices.

The Regulation was replaced, with effect of April 1, 2003.[211] The new Regulation not only provides for the two types of agreements not previously included: the settlement of claims; and registers of, and information on, aggravated risks, but also moves away from the previous approach of listing exempted clauses; it places greater emphasis on defining categories of agreements which are exempted up to a certain level of market power[212] and on specifying the restrictions or clauses which are not to be contained in such agreements.[213]

---

[206] Directive 2008/6 [2008] O.J. L52/3 modifying Directive 97/67 (quoted above).

[207] For more info. See *http://www.ec.europa.eu/internal_market/post/index_en.htm.*

[208] See also above, Ch.18. Freedom to Provide Services/Financial Services (6. Insurance).

[209] Regulation 1534/91 [1991] O.J. L143/1.

[210] Regulation 3932/92 [1992] O.J. L398/7.

[211] Regulation 358/03 [2003] O.J. L53/8, amended [2002] O.J. L168/14.

[212] In the case of co-insurance groups, the insurance products underwritten within the grouping arrangement by the participating undertakings or on their behalf, should not be more than 20 per cent of the relevant market (which may rise to 22 per cent) and in the case of co-reinsurance groups, not more than 25 per cent (which may rise to 27 per cent).

[213] This has been the new approach of the Commission with the group exemption regulations since a few years.

The Commission closely supervises the application of the Union competition rules to banks[214] and other institutions.

(6) Intellectual Property Rights

As already mentioned, such rights are used by their owner to prevent others from producing and commercialising the product covered by the right or to limit the use of this right to particular national territories. Consequently, the owner divides the Union once more into separate markets, and, although he acts in conformity with national law, he thereby prevents trade between Member States. This, of course, constitutes an infringement of the basic principle of free movement of goods and it was in relation with this principle that the Court defined the implementation of the competition rules in this important sector. This subject is discussed below in Ch.31: Enterprises and Industry Policy/Information Society.

(7) Energy

The main objective of the application of the competition rules to energy is the liberalisation of the electricity and gas sectors. The contribution of competition to the liberalisation process will increase when national legislative measures create the appropriate legal framework for the introduction of effective competition in the energy markets.[215] For more details, see below, Ch.36: Energy Policy.

(8) Coal and Steel

Until the expiry of the ECSC Treaty on July 23, 2002, these two sectors were subject to the specific competition rules of that Treaty.[216] Although, "the Commission had over the years aligned the application of the ECSC and the EC Treaties", it thought it useful, "to provide guidance for companies . . ." and consequently adopted a Communication concerning certain aspects of the treatment of competition cases resulting from the expiry of the ECSC Treaty.[217] An interesting point is that restrictive agreements which were exempted under the ECSC Treaty will not lose this exemption because of the expiry of that Treaty.

4. IMPLEMENTATION OF THE RULES ON COMPETITION[218]

Regulation 1/2003 replaced Regulation 17,[219] which was in force for just over 40 years (from March 1962 to April 30, 2004). According to the Council, it allowed

---

[214] The Commission imposed fines totalling €124,260 million on eight Austrian banks.

[215] XXXIInd Report on competition policy, 81.

[216] art.65 ECSC for agreements, art.66 for concentrations and art.67 for interference with conditions of competition by Member States. No longer in force.

[217] [2002] O.J. C152/5.

[218] [2003] O.J. L1/1, modified [2004] O.J. L68/12 (air transport) and [2006] O.J. L269/1(maritime transport).

[219] [1962] O.J. p.204/62.

a Union competition policy to develop that has helped to disseminate a competition culture within the Union. In the light of experience it had to be replaced by legislation designed to meet the challenges of an integrated market and of the enlargement of the Union.[220]

Furthermore, according to the TFEU,[221] legislation in this field must take into account the need to ensure effective supervision on the one hand, and to simplify administration to the greatest possible extent on the other. This balance could no longer be secured under Regulation 17. The Commission also realised that in order to ensure effective application of the Union competition rules, the competition authorities of the Member States had to be more closely associated with their application.[222]

(1) Role of the Member States and the European Competition Network

The role of the national competition authorities is complemented by the national courts and it was decided that these courts should be allowed to apply the competition provisions in full, including the application of exemptions from the prohibition, for certain agreements. The latter constitutes the most far-reaching change, since until then this was a Commission "monopoly".

The Commission and the competition authorities of the Member States have put in place a European Competition Network (ECN).[223] It will allow for greater co-operation and provides for an allocation of cases according to the principle of the best placed authority. The Commission will remain at the centre of the ECN. It will, as the guardian of the Treaty, ensure that decisions taken by national authorities are consistent and that the antitrust rules are applied in a uniform manner.

Several mechanisms of co-operation with the national authorities designated by the Member States[224] are provided for[225]:

1. when national competition authorities apply national competition law to agreements within the meaning of art.101(1) TFEU [81(1)] which may affect interstate trade, they must also apply art.101(3) TFEU [81(3)]; the same applies for abuses of a dominant position. This application may not lead to the prohibition of agreements which do not restrict competition in the common market, or which fulfil the conditions for an exemption or which are covered by a block exemption regulation. The latter does not apply to unilateral conduct engaged in by undertakings; neither does it apply to mergers;
2. national competition authorities may not take decisions which would run counter to decisions already adopted by the Commission[226];
3. the Commission must transmit to the competition authorities of the Member States copies of the most important documents it has collected with

---

[220] Regulation 1/2003 first recital [2003] O.J. L1/1.
[221] art.103(2)(b) TFEU [83,2(b)].
[222] Regulation 1/2003, recital 6 (quoted above).
[223] Notice on co-operation within the Network of Competition Authorities [2004] O.J. C101/43.
[224] art.35(1) Regulation 1/2003.
[225] art.11 Regulation 1/2003.
[226] art.16(2) Regulation 1/2003.

a view of finding and ordering an infringement to be terminated, ordering interim measures, accepting binding commitments, deciding the competition rules do not apply or withdraw the benefit of a block exemption;

4. the national competition authorities must inform the Commission in writing before (or without delay after) commencing the first formal investigative measure;

5. the national competition authorities must, not later than 30 days before the adoption of a decision concerning infringements, undertakings or withdrawal of the benefit of a block exemption, inform the Commission;

6. the national competition authorities may consult the Commission on any case involving the application of Union law;

7. the initiation by the Commission of proceedings shall relieve the national authorities of their competence to apply the Union competition Rules;

8. the Commission and national competition authorities may exchange and use in evidence any matter of fact or of law, including confidential information[227];

9. the Commission may reject a complaint on the ground that a national authority is dealing with the case[228];

10. as for the national courts, it is explicitly provided that they, "have the power to apply Art.101 [81] and 102 [82] of the Treaty."[229] For this purpose, they may ask the Commission to transmit information in its possession and its opinion on questions concerning the application of Union competition rules. A copy of any written judgment deciding on the application of arts 101 and 102 TFEU [81 and 82], must be forwarded to the Commission. The latter may, where the coherent application of the Union rules so require, submit written observations to the national courts; with their permission it may also submit oral observations.[230]

National courts may not take decisions running counter to decisions adopted by the Commission; they must also avoid giving decisions which would conflict with a decision "contemplated" by the Commission; it might be necessary for the national judge to stay its proceedings. National competition authorities, including courts, had to be empowered, before May 1, 2004, to apply the Union competition provisions. When the enforcement is entrusted to administrative and judicial authorities, Member States may allocate different powers and functions to those different national authorities, whether administrative or judicial. In case courts are thus designated to make decisions requiring that an infringement be brought to an end, ordering interim measures, accepting commitments or imposing fines, they shall be relieved of their competence the moment the Commission initiates proceedings for the adoption of decisions under the Regulation.[231] This, however, applies only to the prosecuting authority, when for the adoption of the above-mentioned decisions, an authority brings an action before a judicial authority that is separate and different from the prosecuting authority. That prosecuting authority shall, when the Commission opens proceedings, withdraw its claim before the judicial authority.[232]

---

[227] art.12 Regulation 1/2003.
[228] art.13 Regulation 1/2003. See also the Notice on co-operation between the Commission and the courts [2004] O.J. C101/54.
[229] art.6 Regulation 1/2003.
[230] art.15 Regulation 1/2003.
[231] art.35(3) Regulation 1/2003.
[232] art.35(4) Regulation 1/2003.

(2) Role of the Commission

Generally speaking, the Regulation provides for procedures to be followed by the Commission when it takes one of the following decisions.[233]

1. Finds, acting on a complaint from a Member State or a natural or legal person who can show a legitimate interest[234] or on its own initiative, that there is an infringement and requires undertakings or associations of undertakings to end such an infringement.[235] In this connection attention should be drawn to the limitation period of five years for enforcement procedures.[236] If these five years are interrupted by an act of the Commission, for instance asking for information; a new period of five years then starts again with a limit of a total of 10 years.[237]
2. Order interim measures in case of urgency due to the risk of serious and irreparable damage to competition, on the basis of, prima facie, finding of infringement.[238]
3. Make commitments offered by undertakings binding.[239] This is an interesting novelty since it allows the Commission to end a procedure without having to decide whether or not the Union competition rules were infringed; for the relevant undertaking(s) it creates, at least at the Union level, legal certainty and avoids statements of objections and possible fines, it being understood that the commitments must meet the concerns expressed by the Commission in its "preliminary assessment".
4. Find that the prohibition is not applicable in case the Union public interest relating to the application of the prohibitions so requires.[240]
5. To interview any natural or legal person who consents to be interviewed for the purpose of collecting information relating to the subject matter of an investigation.[241]
6. To obtain all necessary information from governments and national authorities and from undertakings, either by simple request or by decision. In both case the Commission must state the legal basis and specify what information is required, fix a time limit for providing them.[242] In case of incorrect

---

[233] Lists of decisions taken by the Commission can be found in the Annual Reports on Competition policy published in conjunction with the annual General Reports.

[234] art.7(1) Regulation 1/2003. See Regulation 27, first Regulation implementing Council regulation 17, fixing form, content and other details concerning applications [1962] J.O. 35/1118. No longer in force. See *Koelman* (T-575/93) [1996] E.C.R. II–1; [1994] 4 C.M.L.R. 636, wherein the GC ruled that the now repealed Regulation 27 fixing form, content and other details concerning complaints does not confer upon a person who lodges a complaint (application), the right to obtain from the Commission a decision within the meaning of art.288 TFEU [249]. See Notice on the handling of complaints by the Commission under arts 101 and 102 TFEU [81 and 82] [2004] O.J. C101/65.

[235] See *Camera Care v Commission* (792/79 R) [1980] E.C.R. 119 at 131(18); [1980] 1 C.M.L.R. 334: the powers which the Commission holds under art.3 (now art.7 Regulation 1/2003) include the power to take interim measures which are indispensable for the effective exercise of its function. See also *Ford Werke v Commission* (Joined Cases 228/82 R and 229/82 R) [1982] E.C.R. 3091, where interim measures were suspended.

[236] Regulation 2988/74 concerning limitation periods in proceedings and the enforcement of sanctions under the rules of the EEC relating to transport and competition [1974] O.J. L319/1, art.4–6.

[237] For more details see also *Compagnie Maritime Belge* (T-276/04) [2008] E.C.R. 01.07.08.

[238] art.8 Regulation 1/2003.

[239] art.9 Regulation 1/2003.

[240] art.10 Regulation 1/2003.

[241] art.19 Regulation 1/2003.

[242] art.18(2) and (3) Regulation 1/2003.

information or absence of information within the set time limit, the Commission may impose fines.[243] The power to ask questions is widely used by the Commission during its investigations and constitutes an indispensable means for gathering the required data. Both the Court and the GC recognised that:

"[A]n undertaking in receipt of a request for information can be recognised as having a right to silence only to the extent that it would be compelled to provide answers, which might involve an admission on its part of the existence of an infringement, which it is incumbent upon the Commission to prove".[244]

7. To undertake inspections of undertakings.[245] To this end officials authorised by the Commission to conduct an inspection (written authorisation) are empowered to:

   (a) enter any premises, land or means of transport[246];
   (b) to examine books and business records irrespective of the medium in which they are stored[247];
   (c) to take copies of or extracts from the books and business records;
   (d) to seal any business premises and books or records to the extent necessary for the inspection;
   (e) to ask for oral explanations on the spot.

Legal privilege. The confidentiality of written communications between lawyer and client is, however, protected when (i) such communications are made for the purpose and in the interest of the client's defence and (ii) they emanate from independent lawyers, i.e. lawyers who are not bound to the client by a relationship of employment.[248] If the Commission were to read documents covered by the legal privilege it could not use them nor show them to third parties. For several years undertakings' and lawyers' organisations continued to plead for inclusion of their in-house lawyers within the legal privilege; this was also rejected by the GC in 2007.[249]

Undertakings must submit to inspections ordered by Commission Decision, which shall specify the subject matter and purpose, the date on which it is to begin, the penalties provided in case of refusal and the right to have the decision reviewed by the Court. At the request of the national authorities concerned or the Commission, the Commission inspectors may be assisted by national officials. Where it is found that

---

[243] Regulation 1/2003. See, for instance, Decision 2001/271 imposing fines on Deutsche Post/trans-o-flex [2001] O.J. L97/1.

[244] *Orkem v Commission* (374/87) [1989] E.C.R. 3350(35) and *Mannesmannroehren-Werke v Commission* (T-112/98) [2001] E.C.R. II–729(67).

[245] art.20 Regulation 1/2003.

[246] art.20(a)b Regulation 1/2003. This right to enter premises was contested, but to no avail, by several undertakings: *Hoechst v Commission* (46/87 R) [1987] E.C.R. 1549 and *Dow Chemical Nederland BV v Commission* (85/87) [1987] E.C.R. 4367. See also Explanatory Notes on authorisation to investigate: Thirteenth Report on Competition policy, 1993, 270–271.

[247] art.20(2)(b) Regulation 1/2003.

[248] *AM&S* (155/79) [1982] E.C.R. 1575.

[249] *Akzo Nobel and Akcros Chemicals v Commission* (Joined Cases T-125/03 and T-253/03) Order of the President [2003] II-4771 and *Commission v Akzo and Ackros* (C-07/04) [2004] E.C.R. I-8739 and, idem [2007] E.C.R.II-3523.

an undertaking opposes an inspection, the Member State concerned shall afford the necessary assistance of the police or of an equivalent enforcement authority so as to enable the inspection to proceed.[250]

If such assistance requires authorisation from a judicial authority it shall be applied for. The national authority shall control that the Commission decision is authentic and that the coercive measures envisaged are neither arbitrary nor excessive. In the control of the proportionality the national authority may ask the Commission for detailed explanation in particular on the grounds the Commission has for suspecting infringement of the Union competition rules, the seriousness of the infringement and the nature of the involvement of the undertaking concerned. However, the national authority may not call into question the necessity for the inspection nor demand that it be provided with the Commission file. The lawfulness of the Commission decision is, of course, submitted to the review of the Court[251];

(f) inspection of other premises,[252] including the homes of directors, managers and other members of the staff. Such decision must be taken after consultation of the competent authorities of the relevant Member State. It also needs the prior authorisation of the national judicial authorities. The same conditions as set out above, apply in this case;

(g) request the relevant national authorities to undertake inspections.[253]

8. To impose fines and penalties.[254]

Fines can range up to 10 per cent of the firm's total sales in the preceding business year[255]; for credit and other financial institutions, sales may be replaced by assets.[256] For the calculation of fines see "Guidelines on the Method of Setting Fines"[257]: the combination of the value of the sales to which the infringement relates and of the duration of the infringement is regarded by the Commission as an appropriate proxy to reflect the economic importance of the infringement as well as the relative weight of each undertaking involved.[258] It is also considered appropriate to include in the fine a specific amount irrespectively, in order to deter companies from even entering into illegal practices. There are also aggravating and mitigating circumstances which may increase or decrease the basic amount.

It might be interesting to note that the amount of fines collected by the Commission in competition cases amounted to over €3.3 billion in 2007

---

[250] art.20(6) Regulation 1/2003.

[251] See *France Télécom v Commission* (T-339/04) [2007] E.C.R. II-521, where the GC examined the role of the national judge and of the national competition authorities.

[252] art.21 Regulation 1/2003.

[253] art.22 Regulation 1/2003.

[254] art.23 Regulation 1/2003. The undertakings must be told, in the statement of objections, that the Commission intends to impose fines. Fines have been imposed for submitting incomplete information ([1971] EC Bull.11–55) and periodic fines were imposed for each day an undertaking failed to fulfil an obligation imposed by the Commission: Decision MA-Statuut [1980] O.J. L318/1.

[255] art.23 Regulation 1/2003. The expression "total sales" refers to total "world" sales: see *Lafarge* (T-54/03) [2008] E.C.R. II-120*.

[256] By analogy to art.5(3) of the Merger Regulation.

[257] [2006] O.J. C210/2. In *Cheil Jedang v Commission* (T-220/00) [2003] E.C.R II-2481, the GC decided that the fact of an enterprise having been fined in the US does not give rise to a *no bis in idem*.

[258] In case of a company heading a group and owning 100 per cent of the capital of the daughter companies, that head company is responsible for the total: see *Akzo Nobel and Others v Commission* (T-112/05) [2007] E.C.R. II-5049; see appeal C-97/08.

in eight final decisions in which it fined 41 undertakings[259] and €3.2 in 2008.[260]

Settlement Procedure. The Regulation relating to the conduct of proceedings by the Commission pursuant to the cartel and dominant position rules[261] lays down rules concerning the participation of the parties concerned in such proceedings. These parties may be prepared to acknowledge their participation in a cartel violating the competition rules and their liability, if they can reasonably anticipate the Commission's findings and the fines they are likely to incur. In that case those parties might submit settlements submissions. The Commission therefore established a Settlement Procedure.[262] After the initiation of proceedings, the Commission may set a time limit within which the parties may indicate that they are prepared to engage in settlement discussions with a view to introducing settlement submissions. The Commission, on its part, may indicate the range of potential fines. A time limit for introducing the submissions may be set by the Commission. In order to be able to deal more quickly with cartel cases the Commission introduced a "fast-track" settlement system under which undertakings will be able to receive a 10 per cent reduction of their fines.[263] The co-operation covered by this Notice is different from the voluntary production of evidence to trigger or advance the Commission's investigation, which is covered by the Notice on Immunity from fines or reduction of fines in cartel cases, the "Leniency Notice", discussed below. Provided that the co-operation offered by an undertaking qualifies under both Notices, it can be cumulatively rewarded accordingly.

Like all other decisions, the one to impose fines constitutes a decision, "imposing a pecuniary obligation"[264] and is subject to the control of legality by the European courts which, can, as already indicated, lower or increase[265] a fine imposed by the Commission. In case a reduction is decided by the Court, the Commission must not only reimburse the amount on the fine exceeding the one set by the Court, but also default interests on that sum. When an appeal is filed against a decision imposing a fine, the latter does not have to be paid as long as a bank guarantee is provided for the full amount; if the decision imposing the fine is annulled, the Commission must repay not only the full amount of the fine (in case it was paid) but also the default interests; however this obligation does not extend to the guarantee cost in case the latter was provided.

The Court stated that when the GC, for instance, establishes the amount of the fine to be paid, it is not bound by a mathematical calculation method based solely on the turnover of the defendant.[266]

---

[259] XXXVII Report (2008), 1.1.2.

[260] General Report 2008, 48; see there for further details.

[261] Regulation 773/04 [2004] O.J. L123/18, amended [2006] O.J. L362/1.

[262] Regulation 622/08 [2008] O.J. L1A71/3 and Commission Notice on the conduct of settlement procedures [2008] O.J.C167/1.

[263] Commission Notice on the conduct of settlement procedures in view of the adoption of Decisions pursuant to arts 7 and 23 of Regulation 1/2003 in cartel cases.

[264] art.299 TFEU [256]. See *Commission v Ferriere Nord* (C-516/06) [2007] E.C.R. I-10685.

[265] A very rare case where a fine was increased: *BASF and UCB v Commission* (Joined Cases T-101/07 and T-111/07) [2007] E.C.R. II-4949; in the same judgment the fine imposed upon UCB was reduced by 90 per cent! See also *Tokay Carbon E.A.* (Joined Cases T-236/01, etc.) [2004] E.C.R. II-1181.

[266] *Evonik Degussa v Commission* (C-266/06) [2008] E.C.R.I-81*.

Notice on immunity from fines and reduction of fines in cartel cases: a first Notice was published in 1996,[267] a second one in 2002,[268] which was replaced in 2006.[269] This so-called Revised Leniency Notice provides as follows.

(a) Immunity.[270] Under this Notice, the Commission will grant total immunity from any fines to the first company to disclose its participation in an alleged cartel and submit contemporaneous, incriminating information and evidence on a cartel which, in the Commission's view, will enable it to carry out a targeted inspection in connection with an alleged cartel affecting the Union or to find an infringement of Union competition rules in connection with the alleged cartel. To obtain full immunity, a company must provide the Commission with the following: a detailed description of the alleged cartel—name and address of the legal entities involved, name, position, office location and home address of all individuals involved; information on other competition authorities inside or outside the Union which have been approached or are intended to be approached; and all other evidence in the possession of the applicant. The information must be contained in a corporate statement (see points 31 to 35 of the Notice concerning such statement).

Immunity shall not be granted in case the Commission was already in possession of sufficient information to adopt a decision to carry out an inspection. Is not eligible either the undertaking that took steps to coerce other undertakings to join the cartel or to remain in it.

To qualify for immunity the following conditions must also be fulfilled:

(i) the undertaking must co-operate genuinely, fully, on a continuous basis and expeditiously throughout the administrative procedure by providing the Commission with all relevant information and evidence in its possession or available to it, by remaining at the Commission's disposal to answer promptly to any request, by making current and former employees and directors available for interviews, by not destroying, falsifying or concealing relevant information or evidence and by not disclosing anything before the Commission has issued a statement of objections;

(ii) the undertaking must have ended its involvement in the alleged cartel immediately following its application, except for what would, in the Commission's view, be reasonably necessary to preserve the integrity of the inspections.

Detailed procedural rules are set out in points 14 to 22 of the Notice.

(b) Reduction of fines.[271] Reduction of fines is provided for companies that do not qualify for immunity but provide evidence that represents "significant added value" to the information in the Commission's possession and terminate their involvement in the cartel. "Added value"

---

[267] [1996] O.J. C207/4. See *Hoechst v Commission* (T-410/03) on the application of the Notice [2008] E.C.R. II-881.

[268] [2002] O.J. C45/3. However, the question of confidentiality does not seem to have been satisfactorily solved. See *SCA Holding v Commission* (T-327/94) [1998] E.C.R. II–1373, where mitigation was refused. There is one case where a fine paid was refunded. *Assidoman Kraft* (T-227/95) [1997] E.C.R. II–1189; [1997] 5 C.M.L.R. 364.

[269] [2006] O.J. C298/17.

[270] In 2007, the Commission received 20 applications for immunity.

[271] Under the 2006 Notice until the end of 2007, the Commission received 11 applications.

refers to the extent to which the evidence provided strengthens by its very nature and/or its level of detail, the Commission's ability to prove the alleged cartel.

The first company fulfilling those conditions could receive a reduction of 30 to 50 per cent of the possible fine, the second successful applicant, 20 to 30 per cent and subsequent successful applicants a reduction of up to 20 per cent.[272]

Detailed procedural rules are set out in points 27 to 30 of the Notice.

Immunity can, of course, not be granted in case the infringement is covered by the five-year limitation period.[273]

9. Impose, by decision, periodic penalty payments. Those payments which may not exceeding 5 per cent of the daily turnover, can be imposed in order to compel undertakings to (a) put an end to an infringement, (b) comply with a decision ordering interim measures, (c) comply with a binding commitment, (d) supply complete and correct information and (e) submit to an inspection.

(3) Limitation Periods

For imposing penalties, the following limitation periods apply: three years in the case of infringements concerning information or inspections and five years for all other infringements. Enforcement of penalties is subject to a limitation period of five years.[274]

(4) Hearings

Before deciding on an obligation to put an end to an infringement, on interim measures, to accept binding commitments or decide that the Union competition rules do not apply, the Commission must give the undertakings which are the subject of the proceedings the opportunity of being heard.[275] The Commission decision may only be based on objections on which the parties concerned have been able to comment. Complainants must also be associated closely with the proceedings.[276] The Commission normally informs the undertakings concerned about the points to which the Commission objects by sending a "Statement of objections" (SOs), to which the undertaking can respond.

The hearings are chaired by the Hearing Officer whose terms of reference were laid down by a Commission decision.[277] This officer is totally independent from the competition administration: he reports exclusively to the Commissioner responsible for competition. The rights of defence must be fully respected; the parties must have access to the Commission's files, subject to the legitimate interests of undertakings in the protection of their business secrets. The right of

---

[272] For an example of reduction, see Cases COMP/C–3/35.587, COMP/C–3/35.706 and COMP/C–3/36.321.
[273] art.25(1)(b) Regulation 1/2003.
[274] arts 25 and 26 Regulation 1/2003.
[275] art.27 Regulation 1/2003.
[276] art.27(1) Regulation 1/2003.
[277] Decision 2001/462 on the terms of reference of hearing officers in competition procedures [2001] O.J. L162/21.

access does not extend, among others, to confidential information and internal documents of the Commission or national authorities.[278] See, in this respect, the provisions of the regulation on professional secrecy.[279]

Nothing, however, can prevent the Commission from disclosing to other competition authorities or to the courts and from using information necessary to prove an infringement, it being understood that all authorities and officials are bound not to disclose such information, nor that covered by the obligation of professional secrecy.[280] The Commission must also invite third parties to submit their observations and therefore must publish in the *Official Journal* the essence of the decision it intends to take, and which contains a summary of the cartel or abuse, which is the object of the decision. Indeed, according to the Court, respect for the rights of the defence:

> "[R]equires that any person who may be adversely affected by the adoption of a decision should be placed in a position in which he may effectively make known his views on the evidence against him which the Commission has taken as the basis for the decision at issue."[281]

The Commission must also consult the Consultative Committee on Restrictive Practices and Dominant Positions composed of representatives of the competition authorities of the Member States, before taking a decision on: termination of an infringement; interim measures; accepting binding commitments; inapplicability of competition rules; imposition of fines or periodic penalties; and withdrawal from a block exemption.[282]

Decisions are published in the *Official Journal*[283]; they must state the name of the parties and the main content of the decision, including any penalty imposed.

Two subjects mentioned above have given rise to much discussion and several judgments of the European courts, they are the business secrets and the right of access to the Commission files by the undertakings involved in proceedings. With regard to business secrets the Court reminded the Commission of the fact that the obligation of professional secrecy is laid down in the Treaty itself.[284] Reference can also be made to the Commission Decision on the terms of reference of hearing officers[285] who have received delegation to decide that secret information may be communicated; such a decision may be challenged in court.[286]

As for the right of access to files it is generally admitted[287] and recognised by the Court[288] that due process requires that the undertakings be given access to the files held by the Commission, even when this is not explicitly provided for.

As mentioned, the Commission can act on its own initiative or on the basis of a complaint filed by a natural or legal person.[289] The question arose whether the

---

[278] art.27(2) Regulation 1/2003.
[279] art.28 Regulation 1/2003.
[280] art.28 Regulation 1/2003.
[281] *Lisrestal v Commission* (T-450/93) [1994] E.C.R. II–1177(42).
[282] art.14 Regulation 1/2003.
[283] See *Lisrestal* (T-450/93) (quoted above, fn.281).
[284] art.339 TFEU [287]. See *Pergan Hilfsstoffe* (T-474/04) [2007] E.C.R. II-4225. where the Court annulled a Commission Decision rejecting a request not to publish information concerning the applicant contained in a Decision not addressed to him.
[285] Decision 2001/462 (quoted above).
[286] art.263 TFEU [230].
[287] [1994] O.J. L330/67. See *Akzo Chimie* (53/85) [1986] E.C.R. 1965; [1987] 1 C.M.L.R. 231.
[288] XXIInd Report on Competition policy, 1992, at 38.
[289] See *Hoffmann-La Roche v Commission* (85/76) [1979] E.C.R. 461; [1979] 3 C.M.L.R. 211.

Commission could reject such a complaint. The Union courts accepted that the
Commission could reject a complaint where it finds that the case does not display
sufficient "Union interest" to justify further investigation of it.[290] According to
the Court, it is consistent with the Commission's obligations under Union law for
it to apply different degrees of priority to the cases submitted to it. In order to do
this, the Commission is entitled to refer to the Union interest, i.e. significance of
the alleged infringement as regards the functioning of the internal market, the
probability of establishing the existence of the infringement[291] and the scope of
the investigation required.[292] For more details see below, Commission Notice
on the handling of complaints.

(5) Implementing Provisions

The Commission was authorised to take measures to apply the Regulation on the
implementation of the rules on competition.[293] The following regulation, notices
and communication were adopted:

1. A Regulation relating to the conduct of proceedings by the Commission
   pursuant to the cartel and abuse provisions.[294] It concerns the initiation of
   proceedings, investigations by the Commission, the handling of complaints
   (including: the participation of complainants in proceedings, the rejection
   of complaints), statement of objections, the right to be heard, and access to
   the file. This Regulation repealed three previous regulations.[295]
2. A Notice on co-operation within the network of Competition Authorities.[296]
   Although, as the Notice mentions, "consultations and exchanges within the
   network are matters between public enforcers and do not alter any rights or
   obligations arising from Union or national law for companies", it might be of
   interest for the latter to understand how cases are allocated between the
   enforcers. Under the system of parallel competences (introduced by the new
   cartel Regulation), cases will be dealt with either by a single authority, possibly with the assistance of other Member States, or by several authorities acting in parallel, or by the Commission. In general the authority that receives
   the complaint or starts an ex-officio procedure will remain in charge of the
   case; many examples are given. Reference is also made to the position of
   applicants claiming the benefit of a leniency programme.
3. A Notice on the co-operation between the Commission and the national
   courts.[297] The term "courts" refers to those courts and tribunals of the

[290] *BEMIM (Bureau Européen des Médias de l'Industries Musicales) v Commission* (T-114/92) [1995]
E.C.R. II–147.
[291] art.32 Regulation 1/2003.
[292] *Automec* (T-24/90) [1992] E.C.R. II–2223. See, however, *Asia Motor France and Others v
Commission* (T-387/94) [1996] E.C.R. II–961; [1996] 4 C.M.L.R. 305, where the Court concluded that the Commission had made an error of assessment.
[293] art. 33(1) Regulation 1/2003 (quoted above).
[294] Regulation 773/2004 relating to the conduct of proceedings by the Commission pursuant to TFEU
Art.1001 and 102 [arts 81 and 82] [2004] O.J. L123/18, modified [2008] O.J. L171/3.
[295] Were repealed: Regulation 2842/98 on hearings, Regulation 2843/98 concerning complaints,
applications and hearings in the air transport sector and Regulation 3385/94 on the form, content
and other details of applications and notifications provided for in Regulation 17.
[296] Notice on co-operation with authorities [2004] O.J. C101/43.
[297] Notice on co-operation with courts [2004] O.J. L101/54.

Member States that have jurisdiction to apply Union competition rules and are authorised to ask a preliminary question. The national courts can apply Union competition rules without it being necessary to apply national competition rules. However, and this could be important for undertakings, when a national court applies national competition rules to agreements or abuses that may affect trade between Member States, they must, as indicated above, also apply Union competition rules. Consequently, cartels that do not infringe the Union prohibition or that fulfil the condition for an exemption may not be prohibited under national competition law. Similarly, prohibited cartels that do not fulfil these conditions cannot be upheld on the basis of national competition rules.

Generally speaking, national courts may not apply national law which contravenes a Union rule. They are bound by the case law of the Union courts and by the general principles of Union law. Where there is an infringement of Union law, national law must provide for sanctions that are effective and dissuasive; and where the infringement of Union law causes harm to an individual, the latter should, under given conditions, be able to ask the national court for damages.[298]

Finally, the rules on procedure and sanctions that national courts apply to enforce Union law must not make such enforcement excessively difficult or practically impossible (the principle of effectiveness) and may not be less favourable than the rules applicable to the enforcement of equivalent national law (principle of equivalence).

4. A Notice on the handling of complaints by the Commission under the cartel and abuse provisions.[299] As was seen above, some rules concerning complaints are to be found in the regulation concerning the conduct of proceedings by the Commission.[300] Since complaints play an essential role in the application of the Union competition rules, this Notice is a must for undertakings and lawyers. The Commission emphasises that national courts have an essential role to play and encourage undertakings to bring their complaints rather in the form of actions before the national courts. Indeed, the latter may award damages for loss suffered as a result of the infringement, something neither the Commission, nor the national competition authorities can do. Also, national courts may rule on claims for payment; it is indeed for the national court to apply the civil sanction of nullity in contractual relationships between individuals; furthermore, national courts are better placed to adopt interim measures and before national courts it is possible to combine claims under national law with claims under Union law; finally, national courts normally have the power to award legal costs to the successful applicant.

The Notice contains detailed rules concerning the making of a complaint that must be made in conformity with Form C that is annexed to the Notice and also to the above-mentioned Regulation. It should be noted that filling in the Form is no simple matter; in fact the questions asked are not very different from the information that was required in the past under Form A/B for notifications.[301]

---

[298] See, for instance, *Dillenkofer* (Joined Cases C-178/94, etc.) [1996] E.C.R. I-44845.
[299] Notice on complaints [2004] O.J. C101/65.
[300] arts 5–9 Regulation 773/2004, as modified [2008] O.J. L171/3 (quoted above).
[301] See in this respect the comments in the Notice on the "Assessment under Articles 101 and 102 [81 and 82]", points 46–52.

Only natural and legal persons who can show a "legitimate interest"[302] can be formal complainants; the Notice provides some guidance in this matter. The Commission is entitled to give differing degrees of priority to complaints based on the "Union interest" they present; if the latter is not sufficient, the Commission may reject the complaint on that ground, although it is not obliged to do so.[303]

Of great interest are the "Procedural rights of the complainant": he is entitled to receive a copy of a statement of objections, if any, he is invited to comment on them in writing and eventually orally; he may submit documents that contain business secrets, he may submit observations in case the Commission decides not to further examine the complaint, etc.

A rejection of a complaint is done in the form of a decision, that can be challenged in court.

5. Notice on informal guidance relating to novel questions concerning the cartel and abuse rules that arise in individual cases.[304] Under the previous system, undertakings would, in case of doubt about the legality of their agreements or the applicability of the exemptions, simply notify their agreements to the Commission. They would ask the Commission, for example, for a confirmation of the applicability of the exemptions. Since the new Regulation came into force, this is no longer possible. Undertakings are now on their own: it is up to them to decide whether or not their agreements are prohibited and, if so, whether or not the exemptions apply. As the Commission points out in its Notice:

"Undertakings are generally well placed to assess the legality of their actions . . . They have at their disposal the framework of block exemption regulations, case law and case practice as well as extensive guidance in Commission guidelines and notices."[305]

It could have added, "and the advice of knowledgeable lawyers and advisers"! Where despite these elements cases give rise to genuine uncertainty because they present novel or unresolved question for the application of the Union competition rules, individual undertakings may wish to seek informal guidance from the Commission.[306] The Notice contains information, among other things, on the, "framework for assessing whether to issue a guidance letter", "information on how to request guidance" and, most important, "the effects of guidance letters".

6. Guidelines on the "effect on trade" concept.[307] The criteria, "may affect trade between Member States" is an essential element for ascertaining the prohibition of cartels and abuses of dominant positions. The courts have clarified that concept by distinguishing three elements: "trade"; "may affect"; and "appreciable". The Guidelines examine these concepts on the basis of the existing case law and decisional practice of the Commission. They then apply these principles to common types of agreements and abuses. These Guidelines constitute an indispensable tool for natural and legal persons and their advisers.

---

[302] art 5(1) in the Notice on the "Assessment under Articles 101 and 102 [81 and 82]".
[303] Notice on complaints (quoted above) point 45.
[304] Guidance letter [2004] O.J. C101/78.
[305] Guidance letter point 3.
[306] Guidance letter, point 5.
[307] Guidelines on trade [2004] O.J. C101/81.

7. Guidelines on the application of the exemptions to the cartel prohibition.[308] This lengthy and impressive study of academic quality unfortunately contains few practical elements able to "guide" natural and legal persons in the application of the exemption. After analysing the prohibition itself, the document examines in detail the four conditions which must be fulfilled for the exemption to be applicable. This information might be useful to help undertakings and their advisers decide whether or not a prohibited agreement can claim an exemption.

(6) Consequences of the Entering into Force of the New Regulation for other Regulations in the Competition Field

The following regulations were modified by the entry into force of the new Regulation[309]:

1. Regulation applying rules of competition to transport by rail, road and inland waterway[310]; for details see below the chapter on Transport;
2. Regulation concerning limitation periods in proceedings and the enforcement of sanctions under the Union rules relating to transport and competition[311];
3. Regulation laying down detailed rules for the application of the competition rules to maritime transport[312]; see also Guidelines on the application of cartel rules to maritime transport[313];
4. Regulation laying down the procedure for the application of the rules of competition to undertakings in the air transport sector[314];
5. Regulations on application of the exemption to certain categories of agreement[315];
6. Regulations 17 and 141 were repealed.

5. CONTROL OF CONCENTRATIONS[316] — THE MERGER REGULATION[317]

While recognising that the dismantling of the internal frontiers of the Union results in major corporate reorganisations in the form of concentrations and that

---

[308] Guidelines on 81(3) [2004] OJ. C101/97.
[309] Regulation 1/2003. See Commission Regulation 773/2004 relating to the conduct of proceedings by the Commission pursuant to arts 101 and 102 TFEU [81 and 82] [2004] O.J. L123/18, modified [2008] O.J. L171/3.
[310] Regulation 1017/68 [1994] O.J. L1/422 and 446, modified by Regulation 1/2003. Replaced by codified version Regulation 169/09 [2009] O.J. L61/1.
[311] Regulation 2988/74.
[312] Regulation 4056/86, now repealed.
[313] SEC (2008) 2151
[314] Regulation 411/2004 [2004] O.J. L68/1.
[315] Regulation 19/65, Spec. ser.1 (65–66) p.35; Regulation 2821/71, Spec. ser. 71(III) p.1032; for the transport sector Regulation 1994/91 O.J. L1/422; for the air transport sector, Regulation 3976/87 [1987] O.J. L374/9, replaced by Regulation 487/09 [2009] O.J. L148/1; for liner shipping companies [1992] O.J. L55/3.
[316] For the concept "Concentration", see Commission Consolidated Jurisdictional Notice adopted by the Commission on 10.07.07.
[317] [2004] O.J. L24/1.

this development must be welcomed as being in line with the requirements of dynamic competition, the Council indicated that they may also seriously impede competition. The Council concluded that those concentrations must therefore be controlled.[318] This control applies to all industries, including services.

The term "Merger Regulation" is somewhat confusing since, as the title of this section mentions, what is at stake is the control of "concentrations" and that includes not only mergers, but also acquisitions and joint ventures. The Merger Regulation covers mainly two operations: mergers and acquisitions, on the one hand, and joint ventures on the other. Mergers are operations whereby two legally and economically independent companies form a single undertaking (total absorption), while acquisitions are operations whereby one undertaking takes sole control of the whole or part of another. Joint ventures are transactions whereby two or more firms (parent companies), which remain independent, acquire joint control[319] of another firm, existing or to be created. Control is constituted by rights, contracts or any other means which confer the possibility of exercising decisive influence on an undertaking and which is determined by both legal and factual considerations.[320] Full-function joint ventures that have a Union dimension and have as their object or effect the co-ordination of competitive behaviour of undertakings that remain independent—spill-over effects—were included under the Merger Regulation in 1997.[321] See Commission Notice on the Concept of Full-Function Ventures.[322] Partial-function joint ventures are not covered by the Merger Regulation.

A joint venture performing, "on a lasting basis all the functions of an autonomous economic entity", shall constitute a concentration.[323] The criteria here is independence from the "parents", since, without that, it is not autonomous. Furthermore, if the joint venture, "has as its object or effect the coordination of the competitive behaviour of undertakings, which remain independent",[324] the operation will also be examined by the Commission under the cartel provisions.[325] Mergers which would significantly impede effective competition on the internal market or in a substantial part of it, in particular as a result of the creation or strengthening of a dominant position, are prohibited.[326] "Restriction of competition" therefore become the key words of the prohibition. The definition of "dominance" under the Merger Regulation is the same as under art.102 TFEU [82] analysed above. Summarily said, an undertaking occupies a dominant position when it can operate on the market independently of its competitors, its customers and the end consumers. There are, however, important differences; indeed, the dominant position in the case of art.102 TFEU [82] refers to an existing situation, while under the Merger Regulation it concerns also a future dominant position. Furthermore, as was seen, art.102 TFEU [82] prohibits a certain behaviour, while the Merger Regulation prohibits a modification of the market structure which might impede competition. The latter, therefore, is prospective, while the former concerns the past.

---

[318] Regulation 139/2004.
[319] For the concept "joint control" see below the Commission Consolidated Jurisdictional Notice.
[320] art.3 Merger Regulation.
[321] Regulation 1310/97 amending Regulation 4064/89 [1997] O.J. L180/1.
[322] [1998] O.J. C66/1, replaced by the Commission Consolidated Jurisdictional Notice, see below.
[323] art.3(4) Merger Regulation.
[324] art.3(4) Merger Regulation.
[325] art.101 TFEU [81].
[326] art.2(3) Merger Regulation.

As the Court pointed out, "a proper definition of the relevant market is a necessary precondition for any assessment of the effect of a concentration on competition."[327] The Court refers to both the geographic and the product/service markets. With regard to the former, the Court gave the following definition:

"the relevant geographical market is a defined geographical area in which the product concerned is marketed and where the conditions of competition are sufficiently homogeneous for all economic operators, so that the effect on competition of the concentration notified can be evaluated rationally."

Joint or Collective Dominance

Although the Merger Regulation refers to a dominant position held by a single undertaking, the Commission applied the prohibition also to joint or collective dominance. This dominance includes undertakings which are not party to the merger. In other words, an undertaking operating in a given market can find itself in infringement of the Merger Regulation because other undertakings on the same market merged. The Commission's practice was challenged in the Court, which ruled that, "collective dominant positions are not excluded from the field of application of the Regulation". This put an end to a hotly disputed issue.[328] For more details see above, in the same chapter, under 2. Abuse of a Dominant Position.

The main features of the Merger Regulation are the following.

1. The Regulation applies to concentrations with a "Union dimension", i.e:

   (a) where three conditions are fulfilled:

      (i) the aggregate worldwide turnover of all the undertakings concerned is more than €5 billion;

      (ii) the aggregate Union-wide turnover of at least two of them is more than €250 million; and

      (iii) each undertaking realises at least one-third of its Union turnover in another Member State;

   (b) a concentration that does not meet the above-mentioned thresholds nonetheless has a Union dimension when:

      (i) the combined aggregate worldwide turnover of all undertakings concerned is more than €2.5 billion;

      (ii) in each of at least three Member States the combined aggregate turnover of all undertakings concerned is more than €100 million;

      (iii) in each of those three Member States the aggregate turnover of at least two of the undertakings concerned is more than €25 million; and

      (iv) the aggregate Union-wide turnover of at least two of the undertakings concerned is more than €100 million;

      (v) unless each of the undertakings concerned achieves more than two-thirds of its aggregate turnover within one and the same Member State.[329]

In other words, a concentration between two or more undertakings situated in the same Member State has no Union dimension when all of them achieve

---

[327] *France v Commission* (Joined Case C-68/94 and C-30/95) [1998] E.C.R. I–1375.
[328] *France v Commission* (C-68/94) *SCPA and EMC v Commission* (C-30/95) [1998] E.C.R. I–1375.
[329] art.1 Merger Regulation.

more than two-thirds of their turnover in that same Member State. Indeed, in that case it is an internal affair of that Member State. The Commission published a Notice on calculation of turnover.[330] The above-mentioned thresholds will be reviewed before July 1, 2009.[330a] Where the Commission finds that a notified concentration falls within the scope of the Regulation, it must publish the fact of the notification, at the same time indicating the names of the parties, the nature of the concentration and the economic sector involved.[331]

2. A "concentration" is deemed to arise where two or more previously independent undertakings merge, or where one or more persons or undertakings already controlling one or more undertakings acquire direct or indirect control of the whole or parts of one or more other undertakings; the main criteria therefore is "control".[332]

3. The above-mentioned concentrations must be notified[333] to the Commission prior to their implementation and following the conclusion of the agreement concerning the concentration, the announcement of the public bid or the acquisition of a controlling interest. Notification may also be made before that, where the undertakings involved demonstrate a good faith intention to conclude an agreement and have publicly announced an intention to make a bid.[334] It should be noted—this is very important—that the Commission encourages pre-notification contacts of the notifying parties with the Commission. The business community has found those pre-notification contacts very beneficial. In 2007 the Commission received 402 notifications (an increase of 12 per cent over 2006).

4. The Commission assesses the concentration by taking into account the need to maintain and develop competition within the internal market in view of, among other things, the structure of all the markets concerned and the actual and potential competition from undertakings located within or outside the Union. The Commission will also consider the market position of the undertakings concerned[335] and their economic and financial power, the alternatives available to suppliers and users, their access to supplies and markets, any legal or other barrier to entry, supply and demand trends for the relevant goods and services, the interests of the intermediate and ultimate consumers and the development of technical and economic progress.[336] Finally, the Commission will take into account restrictions directly related and necessary to a concentration: "ancillary restraints".[337] It concerns agreements which do not form an integral part of the concentration, but which limit the parties' freedom of action in the market. Such agreements are covered by the decision declaring the concentration compatible with the common market.

[330] [1994] O.J. C385/21.
[330a] See Communication from the Commision to the Council: SEC (2009)808/final/2.
[331] art.4(3) Merger Regulation.
[332] art.3 Merger Regulation.
[333] art.4 Merger Regulation. Notification must be made by using Form CO issued by the Commission. See Annex to Regulation 447/98 [1998] O.J. L61/1. In their notification the parties must define the relevant product market and the relevant geographic market and also any "affected market", i.e. a relevant market where two or more of the parties are engaged in business activities in the same product or individual group product market and would acquire a combined market share of more than 10 per cent; this threshold applies to both horizontal and vertical relationships.
[334] art.4(1) Merger Regulation. The Commission imposed a fine of 33,000 ECU on Samsung (South Korea) for late notification and for having put the merger into effect prematurely.
[335] See below: Commission Consolidated Jurisdictional Notice 7.
[336] art.2(1) Merger Regulation.
[337] [2001] O.J. C188/3.

It should be noted that the Commission in its assessment of a merger is not bound by decisions taken by national authorities in allegedly identical situations, having regard to the clear division of powers on which the Merger Regulation is based.[338]

5. Straightforward cases will be cleared within 25 working days from the date of notification. They shall be increased to 35 where the internal receives a request from a Member State to refer[339] the case to it or where the undertakings concerned offer commitments to render the concentration compatible (Phase I).[340] When the Commission has "serious doubts", it opens an in depth procedure which may last no more than 90 working days (Phase II).[341] Such a procedure is opened by a decision, after which the parties will receive a "statement of objections". The undertakings may contest the Commission's objections in writing and, if they so requested, during hearings.

In July 2000, the Commission introduced a, "simplified procedure for treatment of certain concentrations".[342] This procedure applies to three categories of concentrations:

(a) two or more undertakings acquire joint control of a joint venture the turnover of which and/or the turnover of the contributed activities, is less than €100 million within the EEA and the total value of assets transferred to the joint venture is less than €100 million in the territory;

(b) two or more undertakings merge, or one or more undertakings acquire sole or joint control of another undertaking, provided none of the parties do business in the same product in the same geographical market or in a product market which is upstream or downstream of the product market of another party;

(c) two or more undertakings merge, or one or more undertakings acquire sole or joint control of another undertaking and although two or more parties have a horizontal or a vertical relationship, their combined market share is not 15 per cent or more for horizontal and 25 per cent or more for vertical relationships.

The text of the Notice, and especially the footnotes, should be carefully studied before the simplified procedure is claimed.

Remedies After the notification, parties may present, during the first or second phase, modifications (remedies) to their proposed merger or acquisition in order to make it acceptable to the Commission.[343] In order to facilitate and clarify the proposal of remedies, the Commission published a Notice on acceptable remedies: how and when to cure dominance problems.[344]

---

[338] See *Cementbouw* (C-202/06 P) [2008] E.C.R. 18.12.08.

[339] See Notice on referrals [2005] O.J. C56/2.

[340] In 2007, the Commission cleared 368 merger cases without conditions, out of 402 during Phase I; another 18 transactions were cleared with conditions.

[341] In 2007 10 decisions were adopted, five without conditions; one (Ryanair Aer Lingus) was prohibited.

[342] Notice of 29.07.00 [2000] O.J. C217/32.

[343] art 6(2) Merger Regulation, which refers to, "modifications by the undertakings concerned".

[344] Commission Notice on remedies acceptable under Council Regulation 4064/89 and under Commission Regulation 447/98 [2001] O.J. C68/3. The Notice sets out the applicable general principles, the main types of commitments, such as divestiture, which have been accepted in the past, the specific requirements which proposals of commitments need to fulfil in both phases of the procedure and the main requirements for their implementation. Modifications may be proposed before the notification, together with it, or within three weeks after the date of receipt of the notification.

The rights of the defence must be fully respected and the parties directly involved will have access to the file, subject to the protection of business secrets.

After having consulted the Advisory Committee,[345] the merger must be declared either compatible or incompatible[346] with the internal market. This decision must be published in the *Official Journal*. If no decision is taken within the prescribed time limit, the merger is deemed compatible. The Commission may impose conditions and/or accept modifications to the merger agreement proposed by the parties[347] to allow it to clear the merger.

6. The Commission may order suspension of the merger until it reaches a final decision, but within given time limits.[348]

7. The Commission has powers to investigate and to impose fines or periodic penalty payments.[349]

8. The Commission has exclusive jurisdiction over mergers with a Union dimension; however, at a Member State's request, the Commission may and, under certain circumstances, must[350] refer the case, in whole or in part, to the competition authorities of that State.

A Commission Regulation[351] implementing the basic Regulation[352] and modifying an earlier regulation[353] was issued in 2008. It lays down rules for notifications, time limits and hearings provided for in the Merger Regulation.[354] It updates the notification form in particular the Form RS, relating to reasoned submissions, which deals with information requirements for pre-notification referrals; these forms are used for concentrations which require certain information based on a list of all Member States; it clarifies the procedure by which documents or statement can be considered as non-confidential. In order to ensure that the Commission is in a position to carry out a proper assessment of commitments offered by the notifying parties,[355] with a view to rendering a concentration compatible with the internal market, the notifying parties are required to submit detailed information concerning the commitments offered and, in particular, to submit specific information if the commitments offered consist in the divestiture of a business. These commitments may include details on the appropriate mechanism proposed by the parties, including the appointment of an "independent trustee", at the own expenses of the undertakings, to assist the Commission in overseeing compliance.[356] He may be appointed by the parties after the Commission has approved its identity, or by the Commission. See also Commission Notice on remedies acceptable under the above-mentioned Regulations.[357]

---

[345] art.19 Merger Regulation.

[346] art.2(1)1 Merger Regulation.

[347] art.6,2 Merger Regulation.

[348] arts 7 and 10 Merger Regulation.

[349] arts 13, 14 and 15 Merger Regulation.

[350] Those conditions are that within three weeks after having received copy of the notification, the Member State communicates to the Commission, who informs the parties, that a concentration affects a distinct market within its territory, which is not a substantial part of the internal market and that the Commission considers that such a market is indeed affected; see art.9(3)(b), last subpara.

[351] Regulation 1033/08 [2008] O.J. L279/3.

[352] Regulation 139/04 on the control of concentrations between undertakings [2004] O.J. L24/1.

[353] Regulation 802/04 [2004] O.J. L133/1.

[354] Regulation 447/98 on the notifications, time limits and hearings provided for in the Merger Regulation [1998] O.J. L61/1.

[355] Notification of commitments pursuant to art. 6(2) or 8(2) of Regulation 139/04.

[356] New art.20a.

[357] [2008] O.J. C267/1.

In 2008, more than 98 per cent of notified operations were approved.

The Commission also published several Notices to provide maximum transparency and legal certainty for all interested parties. These "Notices" are not legally binding; they reflect the Commission's decisional practice and views on key aspects concerning the meaning, implementation, practice and case law with regard to the Merger Regulation. They concern, besides the Notices mentioned above, for instance: restrictions, "*directly related and necessary to the implementation of the concentration*"[358] and Guidelines on the assessment of *horizontal mergers* under the Council Regulation on the control of concentrations between undertakings.[359] See also the Guidelines on the assessment of *non-horizontal mergers*, i.e. concentrations where the undertakings concerned are active on different relevant markets; two broad types can be distinguished: vertical mergers and conglomerate mergers.[360]

In 2008 the Commission published a "Consolidated Jurisdictional Notice under the Merger Regulation"[361]; it defines, among other things, the concept of concentration; the concept of control—acquisition of control, sole control, joint control, joint venture; Union Dimension—undertaking concerned, jurisdiction and turnover, financial institutions and insurance. This Consolidated Notice replaces four previous Notices concerning "concentration",[362] "full function joint venture",[363] "undertakings concerned"[364] and the "calculation of turnover".[365] All these aspects will be covered by the decision, if any, declaring the concentration compatible or not with the internal market.[366]

The decisions of the Commission taken under the Merger Regulation are subject to review by the courts.[367] Several decisions declaring a merger incompatible were in fact annulled.[368] A delicate problem, as with cartels, is the confidentiality of information provided to the Commission by the parties to a concentration, the so-called business secrets. It should be remembered, in the first place, that the Treaty itself requires the members of the Commission, the officials and other servants of the Union, "not to disclose information of the kind covered by the obligation of professional secrecy".[369] Furthermore, the Regulation provides that information acquired shall be used only for the purpose of the relevant request, investigation or hearing. It also specifies that neither the Commission nor the competent authorities of the Member States shall disclose information they have acquired through the application of the Regulation.[370] The protection of business

---

[358] [2001] O.J. C188/3.
[359] [2004] O.J. C31/5.
[360] [2008] O.J. C265/6.
[361] [2008] O.J. C95/1.
[362] [1998] O.J. C66/5.
[363] [1998] O.J. C66/1.
[364] [1998] O.J. C66/14.
[365] [1998] O.J. C66/25.
[366] arts 6(1)(b) and 8(2) Merger Regulation.
[367] art.21(1) Merger Regulation.
[368] See, for instance, *Schneider Electric v Commission* (T-310/01) [2002] E.C.R. I–4071 and *Tetra Laval v Commission* (T-5/02) [2002] E.C.R. II–4381.
[369] art.339 TFEU [287], which refers "in particular [to] information about undertakings, their business relations or their cost components".
[370] art.17 Merger Regulation. See detailed examination by the CFI in *Gencor v Commission* (T-106/96) [1997] E.C.R. II–879, concerning requests for confidential treatment. See also Opening to the Public of Documents and Files from the Historical Archives of the Commission, which are covered by the Obligation of professional or Business Secrecy [1997] O.J. C218/3.

secrets is further guaranteed both in the Merger Regulation and in the implementing Regulation. See below: (5) Access to the Files.

With the adoption of the Merger Regulation, the arsenal of Union instruments
at the disposal of the Union institutions and national authorities to ensure that
competition is not distorted in the internal market by undertakings, can now be
considered complete.

6. COMMISSION NOTICES OF A GENERAL NATURE

In order to clarify its competition policy, the Commission has issued several
notices; some of them, somehow, complete the block exemptions, although, contrary to the latter, they have no binding effect, except to a certain extent for the
Commission itself. They simply provide guidance and information concerning the
Commission's views on the implementation of the competition rules.

(1) Exclusive Dealing Contracts made with Commercial Agents[371]

In this Notice the Commission declares that contracts concluded with commercial agents, in which those agents undertake for a specified part of the territory
of the internal market to negotiate transactions on behalf of an enterprise, or conclude transactions in the name or on behalf of an enterprise, are not prohibited
by the Treaty.

With regard to relations between commercial agents and their principal, see the
1986 Directive on the co-ordination of laws of the Member States relating to self-
employed commercial agents.[372] Commercial agents need not be registered in the
Member State where they operate.[373] See also a directive on the co-ordination of
the laws of the Member States relating to self-employed commercial agents[374] and
another on temporary agency work.[375]

(2) Co-operation Agreements[376]

In this Notice the Commission first indicates that it encourages co-operation
between (micro) small and medium-sized enterprises (SMEs), where such co-
operation enables them to work more rationally and increases their productivity
and competitiveness on a larger market.[377] The Commission then lists eight

---

[371] [1962] O.J. 292/1.
[372] [1986] O.J. L382/17.
[373] *Centrosteel* (C-456/98) [2000] E.C.R. I–6007.
[374] Directive 86/653 [1986] O.J. L382/17. For more details see above, Ch.17: Freedom of
Establishment/Company Law (1. Introduction: Free Movement of self-employed Persons)
[375] Directive 2008/104 [2008] O.J. L327/9.
[376] Notice concerning agreements, decisions and concerted practices in the field of co-operation
between enterprises [1968] O.J. C75/3, corrected by O.J. C84/14.
[377] See Commission Recommendation 96/280 concerning the definition of SMEs [1996] O.J. L107/4.
Please note that this Recommendation was published in the L series of the O.J. normally reserved
for legislative acts. Indeed, as will be remembered, according to art.288,5 TFEU [249], recommendations, "shall have no binding force".

categories of agreements which have as their sole object the following co-operation and which, in its view, do not restrict competition.

1. Exchange of opinion or experience, joint market research, joint carrying out of comparative studies of enterprises or industries, and joint preparation of statistics and calculation models.
2. Co-operation in accounting matters, joint provision of credit guarantees, joint debt-collecting associations, and business or tax consultant agencies.
3. Joint implementation of R&D projects, joint placing of R&D contracts, the sharing-out of R&D projects among participating enterprises.
4. Joint use of production facilities and storing and transport equipment.
5. The setting-up of consortia for the joint execution of orders, where the participating enterprises do not compete with each other as regards the work to be done or where each of them by itself is unable to execute the orders.
6. Joint selling arrangements, joint after-sales and repairs service, providing the participating enterprises are not competitors with regard to the products or services covered by the agreement.
7. Joint advertising.
8. The use of a common label to designate a certain quality, where the label is available to all competitors on the same conditions.

(3) Subcontracting Agreements[378]

This form of agreement is considered by the Commission as a form of work distribution, which concerns in particular SMEs[379] and whereby technology is made available by one party to the other with restrictions as to its use. Restrictions which are not prohibited are the following.

1. Technology and equipment provided by the contractor may only be used for the purposes of the agreement, and may not be made available to third parties, and the goods and services resulting from the use of such technology may be supplied only to the contractor or used on his behalf, provided that the technology and equipment is necessary to enable the sub-contractor to carry out his obligations.
2. The above proviso is satisfied where performance of the subcontracting agreement makes necessary the use of industrial property rights of the contractor, of know-how of the contractor, of studies, plans or documents which have been prepared by the contractor or patterns or tools and accessory equipment which belong to the contractor and, which permit the manufacture of goods which differ in form, function or composition from other goods manufactured or supplied on the market.
3. The following restrictions are also authorised: an undertaking by either party not to reveal manufacturing processes or other know-how, an undertaking by the subcontractor not to make use, even after expiration of the agreement, of the above, and an undertaking by the subcontractor to pass to the contractor on a non-exclusive basis any technical improvement which he has made during the execution of the subcontracting agreement.

---

[378] [1979] O.J. C1/2.
[379] See Commission Recommendation concerning the definition of SMEs (quoted above, fn.377).

4. The contractor may forbid the use by the subcontractor of trademark, trade names and get-up in the case of goods, which are not to be supplied to the contractor.

(4) Agreements of Minor Importance[380]

There used to be two thresholds—turnover and market share—below which undertakings were considered as not in a position to distort competition. There is no longer a turnover threshold, so that large firms with small shares in given markets can also benefit from the exemption provided by this Notice. A distinction is made with regard to the market share threshold between horizontal agreements (for which a threshold of a market share of 10 per cent applies) and vertical agreements (15 per cent).

There is a blacklist of restrictions which, because of their nature, are regarded as typically incompatible with art.101(1) TFEU [81(1)]. These are caught by the prohibition even when they are below the above-mentioned thresholds. The restrictions in question are the following:

1. agreements between competitors having as their object price-fixing, limitation of output or sales, allocation of markets or customers; and
2. agreements between non-competitors having as their object restriction of the buyer's ability to determine its sale prices, restriction of the territory into which the buyer may sell the contracts goods or services, restriction on active or passive sales to end-users or restriction of cross-supplies between distributors within a selective distribution system.

Below the thresholds it is primarily for the national authorities and courts to intervene. The Commission will examine such agreements only if, in its opinion, this is necessary in the Union interest and, in particular, if such agreements hinder the smooth functioning of the internal market.

(5) Access to the Files

The right of access to the files is laid down in a Notice on the internal rules of procedure for processing of requests for access to the file of cases pursuant to arts 101 and 102 TFEU [81 and 82][381] and Regulation 139/2004.[382] Among other things, this Notice defines "non-communicable" and "communicable" documents; the former are "internal documents" and "business secrets and other confidential information". These definitions are clarified in the revised Notice.[383]

The Notice was updated in 2005 in order to increase the transparency of competition procedures and underline the Commission's commitment to due process and parties rights of defence. The access is granted only to addressees of a Statement of Objection; limited access to specific documents is provided for complainants in antitrust cases and other involved parties in merger cases.

---

[380] [2001] O.J. C368/13.
[381] [1997] O.J. C23/3.
[382] [2004] O.J. L24/1.
[383] IP/05/1581.

7. RELATIONSHIP BETWEEN UNION AND NATIONAL COMPETITION RULES

In one of its early judgments,[384] the Court had to answer the question of whether or not Union competition law and national competition rules could be applied simultaneously to the same cartel. The Court found that Union law and national rules consider cartels from different points of view. The former regards them in the light of the obstacles which may result for trade between Member States, while the latter proceeds on the basis of considerations which are particular to it. It follows that one and the same agreement may, in principle, be the object of two parallel proceedings.

However, if the ultimate general aim of the Treaty is to be respected, the parallel application of the national system can only be allowed in so far as it does not prejudice the uniform application throughout the internal market of the Union rules on cartels, and the full effect of the measures adopted in implementation of those rules.

The Court concluded that: "consequently, conflicts between the rules of the [Union] and national rules, in the matter of the law on cartels, must be resolved by applying the principle that [Union] law takes precedence".

As long as this rule is applied, national authorities may take action in accordance with their national law, even when an examination of the same cartel is pending before the Commission.

As indicated above, national authorities may not take decisions which run counter to decisions already adopted by the Commission. On the other hand, when applying national competition law to agreements within the meaning of art.101(1) TFEU [81(1)], which may affect interstate trade, national authorities are obliged to apply Union law, as long as the Commission has not opened proceedings. Furthermore, nothing prevents those authorities from prohibiting, under national law, agreements which are void under Union law. Neither are they prevented from imposing fines upon the undertakings concerned, even if fines have been already imposed by the Commission. Similarly, the Commission is not prevented from imposing fines after an undertaking has been fined under national law. However, according to the Court, the Commission must take account of the penalties which have already been borne by the same undertaking for the same action, where penalties have been imposed in a Member State. The situation is different when penalties have been imposed in a third country.[385]

The co-operation between the Commission, on the one hand, and the national judge[386] and national competition authorities,[387] on the other, must, since the entry into force of the new Regulation concerning the application of the Union competition rules[388] and the new Merger Regulation[389] be viewed in that context, as was described above.

---

[384] *Wilhelm v Bundeskartellamt* (14/68) [1969] E.C.R. 1; [1969] C.M.L.R. 100.

[385] *Boehringer v Commission* (7/72) [1972] E.C.R. 1281 at 1289.

[386] See, e.g. *Delimitis* (C-234/89) [1991] E.C.R. I–991; [1992] 5 C.M.L.R. 210.

[387] [1997] O.J. C313/3.

[388] Regulation 1/2003 [2003] O.J. L1/1; see above under 4. Implementation of the Rules on Competition.

[389] Regulation 4064/89 [1989] O.J. L 395/1, corrected version [1990] O.J. L 257/13, amended [2004] O.J. L24/1.

8. INTERNATIONAL CO-OPERATION

An agreement was concluded between the Commission and the United States Government regarding the implementation of their competition laws.[390] This agreement contains provisions on exchange of information, consultation, notification and other procedural aspects. It also provides for co-operation in cases where the parties to the agreement apply their competition rules to identical or related situations. They agree to take into account the important interests of the other party, referred to as "comity".

This co-operation has allowed the competition authorities of both parties to harmonise, for instance, the content and timing of their final decisions in identical cases,[391] thereby avoiding discrepancies, which might create embarrassing situations when the object of the investigations concerns cases with worldwide ramifications, as is more and more the case in this period of globalisation.[392] This first agreement was complemented by another agreement between the European Union and the Government of the United States of America[393] on the application of positive comity principles in the enforcement of their competition laws. In 2002, the European and US competition authorities issued a set of best practices on co-operation in reviewing mergers that require approval of both sides of the Atlantic with a view to enhancing the good relationship developed over the last decade.[394] The document defines objectives and provides indications concerning co-ordination on timing, collection and evaluation of evidence, communication between the two reviewing agencies and remedies and settlement.

An agreement similar to the first EU-US agreement was signed with Canada in 1999[395]: it provides for:

1. the reciprocal notification of cases under investigation where they affect the important interests of the other party;
2. the co-ordination of the enforcement activities and the rendering of reciprocal assistance;
3. the possibility to request the other party to take enforcement action (positive comity)[396] and for a party to take into account the interests of the other in the enforcement procedure; and
4. the exchange of information.

An agreement was signed in 2004 between the EU and China on a structured dialogue on competition.[397] A Memorandum of Understanding on a structured dialogue on competition between the European Union and Korea was signed in 2004. The primary objective is to establish a permanent forum of consultation, transparency and co-operation.[398]

---

[390] Exchange of letters [1995] O.J. L95/45.
[391] See, e.g. *Boeing v McDonnell Douglas* (IV/M 877) [1997] O.J. L 336/16 and *Price Waterhouse v Coopers & Lybrand* [1999] O.J. L50/27.
[392] This was the case with *General Electric/Honeywell* (Case M.2220, Decision of July 3, 2001) and *Microsoft*.
[393] [1998] O.J. L173/28.
[394] *http://www.ec.europa.eu.t/rapid/start/cgi/guesten.ksh?p<EL3>—<RV3>action.gettxt=gt&doc=IP: 02/1591/O/RAA.* Case M.2220, Decision of July 3, 2001.
[395] [1999] O.J. L175/5.
[396] [2001] O.J. C363/10.
[397] IP/04/595.
[398] IP/04/1325.

On a broader front mention must be made of a Communication from the Commission to the Council: "Towards an international framework of competition rules"[399] and a Recommendation of the Council concerning "co-operation between Member Countries on Anti-Competitive Practices Affecting International Trade".[400]

II. Competition Rules Applying to Member States

1. State Monopolies

Member States are required by the TFEU to "adjust" their monopolies of a commercial[401] character, so as to ensure that, by the end of the transitional period[402] no discrimination regarding the conditions under which goods are procured and marketed, exists between nationals of the Member States.[403] However, the:

> "[A]rticle does not apply to national provisions which do not concern the exercise by a public monopoly of its exclusive right, but apply in a general manner to the production and marketing of goods, whether or not they are covered by the monopoly in question".[404]

This reference to the application, in a general manner, of national legislation to the marketing of goods is particularly interesting in view of the interpretation given by the Court of the concept "measures having [an] effect equivalent [to quantitative restrictions]"[405]; it is, in fact, an application of the principle developed in the famous *Keck and Mithouard* judgment.[406]

According to the Commission, "liberalisation of the traditionally monopolised sectors is a crucial step in the establishment of a real single market."[407] Nevertheless, the Commission is aware that the particular way those sectors are organised very often reflect legitimate concerns to ensure social cohesion. In its Notice on services of general interest in Europe (see next section), the Commission advocated a pragmatic and gradual approach which respects the special characteristics of each sector. The Commission tries to reach a consensus

---

[399] COM(96) 284 final, [1996] EC Bull. 6–125.

[400] COM(95) 130 final.

[401] The term "commercial" indicates that production monopolies are not affected by the Treaty. Indeed, in an internal market, production monopolies do not constitute an obstacle to free trade between Member States, this freedom being the test for the existence of competition. Neither are the common agricultural organisations affected by art.43 TFEU [37], since, under art.38(2) [32(2)], the the rules laid down for the establishment and functioning of the internal market apply, "save as otherwise provided in Articles 39 to 44". See *Pigs Marketing Board v Redmond* (83/78) [1978] E.C.R. 2347; [1979] 2 C.M.L.R. 573. The same applies to service monopolies, see *Gervais and Others* (C-17/94) [1995] E.C.R. I-4353.

[402] For the original six Member States this was the December 31, 1969; other dates were, of course, provided by the different Accession Treaties.

[403] art.37(1) TFEU [31(1)].

[404] *Banchero* (C-387/93) [1995] E.C.R. I-4663; [1996] 1 C.M.L.R. 829.

[405] art.34 TFEU [28].

[406] *Keck and Mithouard* (Joined Cases C-267/91 and C-268/91) [1993] E.C.R. I-6097; [1995] 1 C.M.L.R. 101. See under Free movement of Goods.

[407] XXVIth Report on Competition policy, 1996, 53.

with other Union institutions, the Member States and the parties concerned by a parallel approach of liberalisation measures and the harmonising directives of Parliament and the Council. One can only subscribe to this implementation of the Union competition rules in a less exclusive and strict legal way. Indeed, this means that, although the Commission intends to make use of all the legal instruments available to it, it is of the view that the objectives of liberalisation and of public service can be kept fully compatible.

At the time the EEC Treaty came into force, about a dozen monopolies existed within the Union. The timetable provided for in the Treaty was not respected and although most monopolies were either simply abolished or adapted, it was only in 1993 that the Commission could report that the measures taken by the various governments were adequate,[408] thereby overlooking that certain sectors, like energy, were, in most Member States, in the hands of monopolies which also control imports and exports.[409]

The successive accessions brought new monopolies into the Union; this was particularly the case with Greece, Portugal and Spain and, lately, the accession of Austria, Finland and Sweden extended the list and created problems due, for example, to the extremely strict rules concerning the sales of alcohol in the Nordic countries. Interestingly enough the Swedish monopoly was not considered as being in breach of the monopoly rules, since it was not discriminatory, but rather as constituting an obstacle to trade contrary to the free movement of goods. As for the Swedish and Finish retail monopolies they were not considered contrary to Union law, taking account of the objectives pursued as long as there is no discrimination between national and imported goods.[410]

Presently, it can be said that, with certain important exceptions, the monopolies of a commercial nature existing in the former 15 Member States have been "adapted" in conformity with the Treaty rules. However, there still exist monopolies in the public service sector, which have not yet been adapted.[411] They concern sectors such as telecommunications, energy, postal service and transport. These were examined above under I3. Competition Rules Applying to Various Branches of the Economy.

2. Public Undertakings/Services of General Economic Interest

A public undertaking is any undertaking, whatever its public or private status, whose economic behaviour the State can influence. This influence could be based, for instance, on the State's direct or indirect financial participation or on legal provisions governing the establishment of the undertaking in question. In other words, the criteria for determining whether an undertaking is a "public" one, in

---

[408] XXIInd Report on Competition policy, 1992, 149.

[409] See, however, *Commission v The Netherlands, Italy, France and Spain* (C-157/94, etc.) [1997] E.C.R. I-5699, I-5789, I-5815 and I-5851, where the Court concluded that the Commission did not prove that the existing monopolies were disproportionate or contrary to Union interest.

[410] See *Franzén* (C-189/95) [1997] E.C.R. I-5909 and *Rosengren e.a. v Riksaklagaren* (C-170/04) [2007] E.C.R. I-4071.

[411] See hereafter the corresponding chapters.

the sense of the Treaty, depends on whether the public authority can and, in fact, does exercise control over it.[412]

The logical consequence of the subordinate position of the public undertaking in relation to the public authority which controls it, is that the latter is responsible for the market behaviour of said undertaking. The object of the Treaty provisions examined here, is to prevent that a Member State could exercise, through a public undertaking, an activity which it is prohibited from exercising itself. This would constitute a circumvention of the Treaty rules by that public authority to which these rules apply in the first place. Indeed, very few Treaty rules apply directly to undertakings, the most important ones being the competition rules. On the other hand, when a public undertaking infringes rules applying to undertakings, it can be held directly responsible by the Commission notwithstanding the fact that it might have been induced to do so by a public authority. The same applies when national legislation imposes an anti-competitive behaviour on a public undertaking. Indeed, such legislation does not excuse the public undertaking from its obligation to implement the Union competition rules.[413]

However, these competition rules only apply when the public undertaking is in competition with undertakings not controlled by the State.[414] Neither do they apply when the public undertaking acts for the State in the exercise of an activity which is connected by its nature, its aim and the rules to which it is subject, with the exercise of powers relating, for instance, to the protection of the environment, which, typically, constitute powers of a public authority.[415] However, in the case of infringement by a public undertaking of these competition rules, the State and its legislation can also be challenged by the Commission.[416] Indeed, the Treaty on EU[417] provides that the Member States shall neither enact, nor maintain in force any measure contrary to the rules of the Treaty, in particular to the rules on competition. This means that the State is under obligation to ensure that the undertakings it controls abide by the Treaty rules.

According to the Court, the Commission is empowered to determine that a given State measure is incompatible with the Union competition rules. Such powers are essential to allow the Commission to discharge the duty imposed upon it to ensure the application of the rules on competition and to contribute to the institution of a system of undistorted competition in the internal market. It would be impossible for the Commission to discharge its duty completely if it could impose penalties only in respect of anti-competitive conduct of undertakings and could not take action directly against Member States enacting or maintaining in force measures having the same anti-competitive effect.[418]

---

[412] See art.2 Directive 80/723 on the transparency of financial relations between Member States and public undertakings as well as on financial transparency within certain undertakings [1980] O.J. L195/35, amended [2005] O.J. L312/47 and *Commission v Italy* (118/85) [1987] E.C.R. 2599 at 2621(8).

[413] See *Commission and France v Ladbroke Racing* (Joined Cases C-359/95 P and C-379/95 P) [1997] E.C.R. I–6265; [1998] 4 C.M.L.R. 27. See also Commission Decision 97/606 [1997] O.J. L244/18: breach of arts 106 and 49 TFEU [86 and 43].

[414] *Luxembourg* (10/71) [1971] E.C.R. 723.

[415] *Cali & Figli v SEPG* (C-343/95) [1997] E.C.R. I–1547.

[416] This challenge would be based on art.4 EU [10] and arts 101 and 106(3) TFEU [81 and 86(3)].

[417] art.4 EU [10].

[418] *The Netherlands v Commission* (Joined Cases C-48/90 and C-66/90) [1992] E.C.R. I–565.

Services of General Economic Interest

An exception is, however, provided for undertakings entrusted with the operation of "services of general economic interest". The Union rules, in particular the rules on competition, only apply, "in so far as the application of those rules does not obstruct the performance, in law or in fact, of the particular tasks assigned to them".[419] The Commission published a Methodological Note for the Horizontal Evaluation of Services of General Economic Interest.[420] For the application of this exception to State aids, see next section, under (2) Aids Compatible or Declared Compatible with the Internal Market.

The GC reiterated that since the exception concerning services of general economic interest permits, in certain circumstances, derogation from the rules of the Treaties, it must be strictly interpreted. It is therefore not sufficient that the application of the Treaties' provision in question simply would hinder or make the performance of the public service more difficult: "obstruction" must be proved. The GC added that the application of the exception is not left to the discretion of the Member States.[421] In order to ensure the application of the provisions concerning public undertakings, the Commission shall, where necessary, address appropriate directive[422] and decision[423] to Member States. This provision clearly shows that the Member State is indeed responsible for the market behaviour of the public undertaking.

Individuals may challenge decisions taken by the Commission in this context.[424] However, according to the Court, the Commission enjoys a broad discretion in the application of this Treaty provision. And since this discretion involves complex economic and social appraisals, the Court must confine itself to verifying whether the Commission complied with the rules governing procedure and the statement of reasons, whether the facts, on which the contested decision was based, have been accurately stated and whether there has been any manifest error of assessment or misuse of power. But the Court cannot substitute its own economic assessment to that of the Commission.[425]

Owing to the very important role played by the public undertakings in the economy as producers of goods and services, it is to be expected that the provisions of art.106 TFEU [86] will continue to be applied with increasing vigour.[426]

---

[419] art.106(2) TFEU [86(2)]. See Communication on services of general interest COM(96)443 final and *Labrandi v Cuttic (Autotrasporti)* (C-38/97) [1998] E.C.R. I–5955.

[420] COM (2007)724 at *http://www.eur-lex.europa.eu/LexUriSer/site/en/com/2007/com2007_0724en01.pdf*.

[421] *Air Inter* (T-260/94) [1997] E.C.R. II–997; [1997] 5 C.M.L.R. 851.

[422] See Directive 80/723 on the transparency of financial relations between Member States and public undertakings [1980] O.J. L195/35.

[423] See Decision with regard to the landing fees at Zaventem [1995] O.J. L218/8.

[424] *Bundesverband der Bilanzbuchhalter* (C-107/95 P) [1997] E.C.R. I–947; [1997] 3 C.M.L.R. 1189; [1997] 5 C.M.L.R. 432. See also *The Netherlands v Commission* (Joined Cases C-48/90 and C-66/90) [1992] E.C.R. I–565 on the rights of the defence.

[425] *British Airways and British Midlands v Commission* (Joined Cases T-371/94 and T-394/94) [1998] E.C.R. II–2405.

[426] See Commission Communication to the Member States—Application of Art.[87] and [88] and of Art.5 of Dir.80/723 to public enterprises in the manufacturing sector [1993] O.J. C273/2. It is particularly interesting to note that this communication, which in theory is a non-binding act, was challenged in Court by the French government; the Commission was obliged to modify it: *France v Commission* (C-325/91) [1993] E.C.R. I–3393.

3. AIDS GRANTED BY STATES[427]

(1) The Notion of Aid

To start with, let it be noted that there is no, "binding and general definition of the concept of State aid" and the Court stated that the Commission has no power to lay down such a definition.[428] However, it is safe to say that any aid granted by a Member State or through State resources in any form whatsoever which distorts competition by favouring certain undertakings or the production of certain goods is, in so far as it affects trade between Member States, incompatible with the internal market.[429]

In other words, for a measure to be regarded as an aid that is subject to the principle of incompatibility with the common market, it must satisfy four conditions, which are cumulative. The measure must: "advantage" an undertaking; the aid must be granted by a "Member State or through State resources"; it must favour "certain" undertakings or the production of "certain" goods; and it must "distort competition" and "affect trade between Member States".

(a) "advantage an undertaking"

According to the Court[430] and the Commission, a measure constitutes an aid when it confers upon an undertaking an economic or financial advantage, which it would not have enjoyed in the normal course of events and which reduces the charges it would otherwise have born.[431] On the other hand, compensation for the extra costs connected, for instance, with public service obligations does not constitute a State aid.[432] Similarly, the public financing of infrastructure at certain industrial sites does not involve State aid on condition that the infrastructure is open to all the firms in those areas without discrimination.[433] In this context, see the Commission communication on State aid elements in sales of land and buildings by public authorities: when the sale is the result of an open and sufficiently advertised auction, the Commission will assume that no aid was involved.[434] As regards privatisations, the Commission continues to apply the principle that there is no aid when the shares are sold to the highest bidder following an open and unconditional bidding procedure.

(b) "granted by a Member State or through State resources"

The latter must be taken in the broadest possible sense.[435] It embraces not only positive benefits, such as subsidies, but also measures which, in various forms,

---

[427] arts 107–109 TFEU [87–89]. Parts of the section are based upon the Reports on Competition policy.

[428] *Belgium v Commission* (C-110/03) [2005] E.C.R. I-2801.

[429] art.107(1) TFEU [87(1)].

[430] See, for example, *Amministrazione delle Finanze dello Stato v Denkavit Italiana* (61/79) [1994] E.C.R. 709; [1981] 3 C.M.L.R. 694.

[431] See, for instance, *Banco Exterior de Espana* (C-387/92) [1994] E.C.R. I-877 (12, 13); [1994] 3 C.M.L.R. 473.

[432] Commission Decision Financing of Portuguese radio and television of 07.11.96 and *SIC v Commission* (T-46/97) [2000] E.C.R. II-2125.

[433] XXVIth Report on Competition Policiy, 1996, 72.

[434] [1997] O.J. C209/3.

[435] See, for instance, *Italy v Commission* (C-305/89) [1991] E.C.R. I-1603 and *Belgium v Commission* (234/84) [1986] E.C.R. 2263; [1988] 2 C.M.L.R. 331.

mitigate the charges which are normally included in the budget of an enterprise and therefore have the same effect.[436] As the Commission has indicated, cross-subsidisation, for instance, between a public company operating in a non-competitive market and one of its subsidiaries operating in a market where there is free competition, may constitute aid granted through State resources.[437] As for State participation in undertakings, the Commission applies the "market investor" principle. It allows the Commission to determine whether the transfer of public funds to public or private undertakings partially owned by the State constitutes an aid. This is the case if a private investor, operating under normal market conditions, would provide the funds on less favourable conditions or would not provide them at all.[438]

Particular attention was paid to fiscal aids by both the Council and the Commission which issued a "notice"[439] and "conclusions"[440] on the subject. Several court cases have also clarified the concept of fiscal aid.[441]

(c) "specificity": Favour "certain" Undertakings or the Production of "certain" Goods

This is the case when the measure concerns a well-defined category of undertakings, such as "road haulers operating for hire or reward".[442] Another element for this specificity is the discretion enjoyed by the subsidising authority in choosing the beneficiaries. Specificity does not exist in the case of general economic, fiscal or social measures, which grant an advantage to firms in the Member State implementing them but it does exist when the measure is:

"[S]ubject to a series of objective criteria pursuant to which it may be granted, within the framework of a predetermined overall budget allocation, to an indefinite number of beneficiaries, who are not initially individually identified."[443]

The distinction between those measures and State aids is difficult to establish, according to the Commission. It seems, however, that from the moment a measure only benefits certain undertakings in a given economic sector, as opposed to a measure applying indiscriminately to all undertakings in that sector, there can be little doubt about it constituting an aid. A good example, already mentioned, is national legislation intended to reduce the tax burden on road hauliers operating for hire or reward. According to the Court, "that legislation

---

[436] *Ecotrade v AFS* (C-200/97) [1998] E.C.R. I–7907(34).
[437] See Commission Decision in *Société Française de Messageries Chronopost and Securitpost* I.P.(96) 126. See also *SFEI* (C-39/94) [1996] E.C.R. I–3547; [1996] 3 C.M.L.R. 369.
[438] XXVIIth Competition Report on Competition policy, 1997, 78.
[439] Commission Notice on the application of state aid rules to measures relating to direct business taxation [1998] O.J. C384/3.
[440] Council Conclusions concerning the establishment of the Code of Conduct Group for business taxation [1998] O.J. C99/1. See also Council Conclusions of the ECOFIN meeting of 01.12.97 [1998] O.J. C2/1.
[441] See, for instance, (all five cases) *Diputacion Foral de Alava v Commission* (Joined Cases T-129/99, T-129/99 and T-148/99 and Joined Cases T-92/00 and T-103/99) [2002] E.C.R. II–1275 and II–1423.
[442] *Italy v Commission* (C-6/97) [1999] E.C.R. I–2981(17).
[443] *CETM v Commission* (T-55/99) [2000] E.C.R. II–3207(40).

meets the condition that it should relate to specific undertakings."[444] As for distortions resulting, in the internal market, from advantages granted by general measures to the undertakings of one Member State, as compared to the undertakings of other Member States, they can only be eliminated through approximation of legislation.[445] General State measures are therefore excluded from the incompatibility with the common market.

According to the Court, for a measure to be described as "general", it is necessary, in particular, that the State should have no discretionary power enabling it to vary the application of the measure according to such considerations as the choice of recipient, the amount, or the conditions of the intervention.[446]

See also the Commission Notice on Monitoring of State Aid and Reduction of Labour Costs,[447] where the Commission clarified the distinction between general measures and aids.

(d) "distort competition and affect trade between Member States"

It seems difficult to imagine measures favouring certain undertakings in one Member State which are trading across inter-State borders, that would not distort competition and trade between Member States.[448] However, incompatibility of aid with the internal market is "neither absolute, nor unconditional".[449] The distortions must therefore be proved.

Aids which fulfil the four above-mentioned criteria are incompatible with the internal market, unless they belong to the small category of compatible aids or are declared compatible by the Commission. However, according to the Court:

"[T]he characterization of a measure as State aid, which, according to the Treaty, is the responsibility of both the Commission and the national courts, cannot in principle justify the attribution of a broad discretion to the Commission".

It is only in cases where art.107(3) TFEU [87(3)] fails to be applied, and where accordingly the Commission must rely on complex economic, social, regional and sectoral assessments, that a "broad discretion is conferred on that institution".[450]

---

[444] See *Italy v Commission* (C-6/97) [1999] E.C.R. I-2981.
[445] See below, Ch.26: Approximation of Laws and arts 114, 115 116 TFEU [94, 95 and 96].
[446] *France v Commission* (C-241/94) [1996] E.C.R. I-4551; [1997] 1 C.M.L.R. 983. For a measure declared general although favouring one undertaking, but justified by the nature or the general economy of the system, see *Netherlands v Commission* (T-233/04) [2008] E.C.R. II-591.
[447] [1997] O.J. C1/5. See the "Mirabel" Decision where the Commission declared incompatible the Belgian increased reduction in social security contributions, in respect of manual workers, granted to employers in one of the sectors most exposed to international competition [1997] O.J. L95/25.
[448] In *Philip Morris v Commission* (730/79) [1980] E.C.R. 2671; [1981] 2 C.M.L.R. 321, the Court rejected the applicant's argument that in order to show that an aid falls within the terms of art.107(1) 87(1) TFEU, the Commission must apply the tests, which determine the existence of restriction of competition under arts 101 and 102 TFEU [81 and 82] (relevant markets, market structure, etc.). The Court held that simpler grounds (a more favourable treatment of certain undertakings affects inter-State trade) are adequate. See, however, *Intermills v Commission* (323/82) [1984] E.C.R. 3809; [1986] 1 C.M.L.R. 614 the granting of aid cannot be regarded as automatically contrary to the Treaty.
[449] *Iannelli v Meroni* (74/76) [1977] E.C.R. 557(11); [1977] 2 C.M.L.R. 688.
[450] *France v Ladbroke Racing and Commission* (C-83/98 P) [2000] E.C.R. I-3271.

(2) Aids Compatible or Declared Compatible with the Internal Market

State aids can also constitute an instrument of structural development policy when certain legitimate objectives of economic growth cannot be attained solely by the interplay of market forces, or not within an acceptable time limit, or not without unacceptable social frictions. The Treaty, therefore, having stated the principle of the incompatibility of State aids with the internal market, provides for certain categories of aid, which either are, or may be considered by the Commission[451]—or in exceptional cases by the Council[452]—as being compatible with the internal market.

Compatible aids are: (1) those having a social character, granted to individual consumers, provided it is granted without discrimination related to the origin of the products concerned; (2) aids to make good the damage caused by natural disasters or exceptional occurrences; and (3) aids granted to certain areas of Germany and required to compensate for the economic disadvantages caused by the previous division of that country; this point may be repealed by the Council, acting on a proposal from the Commission, five years after the entry into force of the Treaty of Lisbon.

Among these compatible aids, are those provided as compensation for services of general economic interest[453]: they are subject to the Treaties' rules, in particular those on competition, in so far as their application does not obstruct the performance, in law or in fact, of the particular tasks assigned to them. This compensation may not, however, exceed the extra costs assumed by the provider of the public service.[454]

The Court[455] formulated four conditions which must be fulfilled in order for such compensation not to constitute State aid. First the recipient undertaking is actually required to discharge clearly defined public service obligations; second, the parameters on the basis of which the compensation is calculated have been established beforehand in an objective and transparent manner; third, the compensation does not exceed what is necessary to cover all or part of the costs incurred in discharging the public service obligations, taking into account the relevant receipts and a reasonable profit for discharging those obligations; and fourth, where the undertaking in question is not chosen in a public procurement procedure, the level of compensation needed has been determined on the basis of an analysis of the costs which a typical undertaking, well run and adequately provided with means of transport, would have incurred, taking into account receipts and a reasonable profit.[456]

---

[451] This category of aids can be extended by the Council pursuant to art.107(3)(e) TFEU [87(3)(e)]. See, for instance, aid to shipbuilding: Regulation 3094 [1995] O.J. L332/1, amended [1996] O.J. L251/5; pending the entry into force of the Agreement respecting normal competitive conditions in the commercial shipbuilding and repair industry, Regulation 90/684 continued to apply [1994] O.J. C375/3, amended [1997] O.J. L351/18 until July 1, 2005.

[452] art.108(2) TFEU [88(2)]. On application by a Member State, the Council may, acting unanimously, decide that an aid which that State is granting or intends to grant shall be considered to be compatible. This application suspends the Commission procedure. See for instance Council Decision of May 3, 2002 on the granting of national aids by the Netherlands in favour of road transport undertakings [2002] O.J. L131/12.

[453] art.106(2) TFEU [86(2)].

[454] *Ferring* (C-53/00) [2001] E.C.R. I–9067.

[455] *Altmark Trans* (C-28/00) [2003] I-7747.

[456] See also *Chronopost SA, La Poste and French Republic v Commission* (Joined Cases C-83/01 P, C-93/01 P and C-94/01 P) [2003] I-6993.

The de minimis rule for State aids sets a threshold figure below which the incompatibility can be said not to apply, so that a measure needs no longer to be notified in advance to the Commission. An aid is considered too small to be of interest for Union vetting, when it does not exceed €200,000 over a period of three years.[457]

Aids which can be "declared" compatible with the internal market by the Commission pursuant to a procedure which will be examined hereafter. The TFEU provides for five categories of such aids: aids to promote the economic development of less-developed areas; aids for important projects of common European interest or to remedy a serious disturbance in the economy of a Member State; aids to certain economic activities or economic areas; aids to promote culture and heritage conservation, where such aid does not affect trading conditions and competition in the Union to an extent contrary to the common interest; and other categories of aids specified by the Council on a proposal from the Commission.[458] The following aids will be examined hereunder: regional, sectoral and others.

(a) Regional Development Aids

The TFEU provides for two kinds of regional development aids, which may be considered by the Commission to be compatible with the common market.[459] They are, firstly, the aids to promote the economic development of areas where the standard of living is abnormally low or where there is serious underemployment and of regions where development is severely restrained in view of their structural, economic and social situation.[460] Secondly, the aids to promote the development of certain economic areas, where such aid does not adversely affect trading conditions to an extent contrary to the common interest. The first concerns areas in general, while the second ones concern "economic" areas, which are areas economically developed, but subject to acute and temporary difficulties.

As the Commission indicated in its 1998 Guidelines,[461] regional aid is designed to develop the less-favoured regions by supporting investment and job creation in a sustainable context. It promotes the expansion, modernisation and diversification of the activities of establishments located in those regions and encourages new firms to settle there. The granting of such aid must be conditional on the maintenance of the investment and the jobs created during a minimum period. In exceptional cases those aids might have to be supplemented by operating aids. These Guidelines were applicable until December 31, 2006 and replaced by new Guidelines applicable indefinitely, but to be reviewed within five years.[462] Those guidelines provide for the selection of the most disadvantaged regions and the maximum aid intensities that Member States can allow, the definition

---

[457] [2006] O.J. L379/5.
[458] art.107(3) TFEU [87(3)].
[459] art.107(3)(a) and (c) TFEU [87(3)(a) and (c)].
[460] art.107(3)(a) TFEU refers to art.349 TFEU which mentions: Guadeloupe, French Guiana, Martinique, Réunion, Saint Barthélemy, Saint Martin, the Azores, Madaira and the Canary Islands.
[461] [1998] O.J. C74/9, amended [2000] O.J. C258/5. See also the new multi-sectoral framework on regional aid to large investment projects [1998] O.J. C107/7.
[462] [2003] O.J. C110/11.

of eligible costs, the incentive effect, the rules on large investment projects, operating aid, cumulation and transparency.[463] The new guidelines were accepted by all the Member States except Germany; consequently the Commission carried out a formal investigation procedure against all the existing German regional aid schemes to ensure identical application of Union rules in all the Member States.

A block exemption regulation for regional investment aid was issued in 2006.[464]

The distortions of competition resulting from the granting of these regional aids must be accepted if the equilibrium between those distortions and the advantages of the aid in terms of development of the less-favoured regions can be guaranteed. Another requirement is that the aid adheres to certain principles and obeys certain rules.[465] Furthermore, it must be neutral towards the allocation of resources between the various economic sectors and activities. In 2002, the Commission published a new "Multisectoral framework on regional aid for large investment projects".[466] Under this framework, no advance notification of aid below certain thresholds is required provided that aid is granted in accordance with an aid scheme approved by the Commission.

The Commission considers that the total extent of the assisted regions must remain smaller than that of the non-assisted regions, i.e. less than 50 per cent of the Union population. Approval of the "regional maps", i.e. description of the regions eligible for aid and the intensity of aids, are decided by the Commission. The conditions of abnormally low standard of living or serious underemployment[467] are fulfilled when a level II geographical unit[468] has a per capita GDP, measured in purchasing power standards, of less than 75 per cent of the Union average, based on the average of the last three years.

As for the second exception, aids to facilitate the development of certain economic activities or of certain economic areas, it allows greater latitude. It also gives the Commission power to authorise aid for the development of areas which are disadvantaged in relation to national rather than Union average.

The object of regional aid is to secure either productive investment or job creation which is linked to investment. To ensure that the investment is viable and sound, the recipient's contribution must be at least 25 per cent. The form of aid is variable: grant, low-interest loan or interest rebate, government guarantee, tax exemption, reduction of social security contributions, supply of goods and services at concessionary prices, etc. Eligible expenditure can also include transfer of technology through the acquisition of patents or know-how. Operating aid, i.e. aid aimed at reducing the firm's current expenses, is normally prohibited, but there are exceptions for the outermost regions of the Union. More details on the grant of aids, by the Union, will be found below in Ch.32: Regional Policy/Economic, Social and Territorial Cohesion.

---

[463] IP/06/851.

[464] Regulation 1628/06 [2006] O.J. L302/29.

[465] See the Communication from the Commission to the Member States on the links between regional aid and competition policy [1998] O.J. C90/3.

[466] [2002] O.J. C70/8.

[467] For a definition of those concepts see *Germany v Commission* (248/84) [1987] E.C.R. 4013(19); [1989] 1 C.M.L.R. 591.

[468] Nomenclature of Statistical Territorial Units.

(b) Sectoral Aids[469]

See also the Multisectoral Framework on regional aid for large investment projects, mentioned above.[470] The aim of this framework is to limit aid for large-scale projects, of whatever sector of industry, to a level which avoids as much as possible adverse effects on competition between regions, but which at the same time maintains the attraction of the assisted areas. The framework provides for the prior notification of all projects with a total cost of at least €50 million and an aid intensity of at least 50 per cent of the regional aid ceiling, or where the total aid is at least €50 million. Specific rules were drawn up by the Union institutions for the following sectors.

(i) **Shipbuilding.** In 1998, the Council established new rules on aid to shipbuilding[471] and in 2003 the Commission published a Framework on State aid to shipbuilding[472] and a Communication on the submission of individual notification of all regional investment aid.[473] See also a Council Regulation concerning a temporary defensive mechanism to shipbuilding.[474] It was directed against what was considered unfair practices by South Korea.[475] The validity of the Regulation was extended until March 31, 2005; it is no longer in force.

(ii) **Steel.** In 1996, the Commission adopted the sixth and last steel aid code,[476] which covered the period up to the expiration of the ECSC Treaty in July 2002. It contains rules on State aids for R&D and on aid for environmental protection. The Commission also allows aids for partial closures and aligns the procedural rules of the steel aid code on new developments in the Union. In 2002, the Commission published a Communication on "Rescue and restructuring aid and closure aid for the steel sector".[477] Those aids must be notified to the Commission. As for the consequences of the expiry of the ECSC Treaty, the Commission published a Communication stating that, "the ban on regional investment aid and rescue and restructuring aid to the steel sector will continue after the expiry of the ECSC Treaty", and, "aids granted . . . under the schemes authorized by the Commission will no longer be subject to the prior notification requirement established in the current Steel Aid Code".[478]

(iii) **Coal.** A new framework has applied since 2002 to State aid granted in the coal sector.[479] On that basis the Commission authorised various Member States:

[469] art.107(3)(c) TFEU [87(3)(c)]: "development of certain economic activities". A list of sectors facing structural problems was published in a Commission Communication modifying the Multisectoral Framework on regional aids.
[470] [2002] O.J. C70/4.
[471] [1998] O.J. L202/1, replaced Directive 90/684 [1990] O.J. L380/27.
[472] [2003] O.J. C317/11; the validity was extended to December 31, 2008 [2006] O.J. C260/7.
[473] [2003] O.J. C263/1.
[474] Regulation 1177/02 [2004] O.J. L2/1.
[475] See General Report 2003, 291.
[476] Decision 3855/91 ECSC establishing Union rules for aid to the steel industry [1991] O.J. L362/57. See also *Salzgitter v Commission* (C-210/98) [2000] E.C.R. I–5843.
[477] [2002] O.J. C70/21.
[478] [2002] O.J. C70/21.
[479] Regulation 1407/02 [2002] O.J. L205/1, amended.

Germany, the United Kingdom, France, Spain and Portugal to grant financial assistance to cover, among other things, operating losses, inherited liabilities resulting from modernisation, rationalisation and restructuring, exceptional welfare aid paid to workers who lose their jobs as a result of restructuring, the technical costs of closing down mining installations, R&D projects and the protection of the environment. From July 24, 2002 on such aids are examined by the Commission on the basis of a new regulation laying down substantive rules and procedures.[480]

(iv) **Motor Vehicle Industry.** In 2001, the Commission published a new "Union framework for State aid to the motor vehicle industry".[481] In 2002 the Commission approved the recasting of the rules applicable to regional aids for large investment projects and the motor vehicle sector was included.[482] The previous framework contains a most interesting footnote on aids granted by Member States: in the period 1977 to 1987, State aid to the motor vehicle industry, essentially in the form of capital injections or extensive debt write-offs, is estimated at 26 billion ECUs. Between 1989, when the framework entered into force, and July 1996, the Commission approved 5.4 billion ECUs of aid. The framework is presented as an "appropriate measure" under art.108(1) TFEU [88(1)] and proposes to the Member States that, pursuant to art.108(3) TFEU [88(3)], they give prior notification of the most significant aid cases, i.e. when it concerns an aid under authorised aid schemes, and that either of the following thresholds is reached: total cost of the project—€50 million; or total gross aid for the project—€5 million. On the other hand, any ad hoc aid must be notified. The framework also establishes guidelines for the assessment of aid, based on a cost-benefit analysis.[483]

The motor vehicle sector continues to be affected by structural over-capacity in Europe; the task of the Commission here is to prevent surplus production capacity from further distorting competition.

Most aids to the motor vehicle industry are granted in the form of regional aids. In practice, a "top-up" of 3 per cent of the eligible regional investment is authorised where the recipient of the aid does not create extra capacity in a saturated market segment.[484]

(v) **Synthetic Fibres Industry.** Since 1977, the conditions under which aid may be awarded to this industry have been laid down in a Code whose terms and scope have been revised periodically. See here also the Communication of the Commission concerning a Multisectoral Framework on regional aid for large investment projects—Code on aid to the synthetic fibres industry—etc.[485]

---

[480] Regulation 1407/02 [2002] O.J. L205/1, amended.

[481] [1997] O.J. C279/1.

[482] [2003] O.J. C263/1.

[483] It should be noted that such a framework is addressed to the Member States and must be approved by all of them. See *Spain v Commission* (C-135/93) [1995] E.C.R. I–1651.

[484] In the case of MCC–Swatch a top-up was allowed because the special characteristics of the new Smart car will create a new production segment on the vehicle market. See XXVIst Report on Competition Policy, 1996, 77.

[485] [2003] O.J. C263/3.

(vi) Transport. The basic regulation[486] provides, in the first place, that the Treaty provisions, and among others the competition rules, do apply to transport by rail, road and internal waterway. Secondly, since the Treaty also provides that authorisation should be given to aid that meets the needs for co-ordination of transport or that represents reimbursement of the discharge of certain obligations inherent in the concept of public service[487]; the Regulation sets out in detail those cases and conditions where such aid is authorised. See also below Ch.27: Transport. The number of aid cases to transport have increased with the constant opening up of the transport market and the resulting increase in competition, together with the progress of the single market for transport. As the Commission points out, "under those circumstances the control of State aid is of particular importance to ensure that fair conditions of competition are maintained between public and private enterprises".[488]

Similarly, the Commission published a Communication setting out guidelines for the application of State aid provisions for aid granted in the civil aviation field,[489] and pays particular attention to the aids granted by the Member States to their national airlines. This was the case for Iberia, Olympic Airways, Air France and TAP.[490] However, the Commission decisions in this field are not always appreciated by the competitors and it was at the request of several European Airlines that the Court annulled the decision authorising, once again, the recapitalisation of Air France.[491] Following the events of 9/11, the Commission authorised the governments of Denmark, Spain, Finland, France, Greece, Ireland, the Netherlands, Sweden and the UK to grant aid to their air transport sector. This authorisation was prolonged several times.

With regard to the maritime transport sector, the Commission admitted in its Communication "Towards a New Maritime Strategy", that support measures may be required to maintain and to develop the Union's shipping industries. In 1997, the Commission adopted new Union guidelines for State aid in the maritime transport sector.[492] Aids may only be granted to ships registered in a Member State.

In the *ports* sector, the Commission acts, often on the basis of complaints about public assistance, to check on the possible grant of aids.[493] The same applies to road transport.

As for rail transport the Commission is endeavouring to have the Member States implement the basic Directives on the development of the Union's railways, on the licensing of railway undertakings and on the allocation of railway infrastructure capacity and the charging of infrastructure fees.[494] The aim is to arrive at a system where the only public financing of railways will be for infrastructure or compensation for public service obligations. Altogether the institutions issued 15 directives or regulations for the railway sector.[495]

---

[486] Regulation 1107/70 [1970] O.J. L130/1, supplemented in 1982 by provisions on combined transport [1982] O.J. L184/1, repealed by Regulation 1370/07, on public passenger transport by rail and by road [2007] O.J. L315/1.

[487] art.93 TFEU [73].

[488] XXVIst Report on Competition policy, 1996, 80.

[489] [1997] O.J. C350/5.

[490] XXVIst Report on Competition policy, 1996, 80.

[491] *British Airways and British Midland v Commission* (Joined Cases T-371/94 and T-394/94) [1998] E.C.R. II-2405.

[492] See also Union Guidelines on State aid to maritime transport [1997] O.J. C205/5.

[493] XXXIInd Report on Competition policy, 2002, 501.

[494] Directive 91/440 [1991] O.J. L237/25, modified [2007] O.J. L315/44; Directive 95/18 [1995] O.J. L143/77 and 95/19 [1995] O.J. L143/75.

[495] See Europa/competition/state aid legislation: provisions of the Treaty.

Finally, in the area of inland waterways, the Union will part-finance the structural reorganisation aimed at reducing over-capacity. Measures were provided on structural improvements in inland waterway transport[496] and on the systems of chartering and pricing in national and international inland waterway transport in the Union.[497]

(vii) **Agriculture and Fisheries.** Since the Treaty provides that the competition rules, "shall apply to production of and trade in agricultural products only to the extent determined by the Council,"[498] the latter adopted a regulation to that effect, back in 1962.[499] In 2000, the Commission adopted a new version of the Union Guidelines for rescue and restructuring aid to agricultural undertakings[500]; they involve a substantive change in policy. The former specific criteria have been replaced by criteria similar to those contained in the guidelines applicable to all sectors, i.e. a quid pro quo for the aid is needed in the surplus sectors in the form of an irreversible reduction or closure of capacity; derogations are provided to take into account the particular features of agriculture. The Commission also published guidelines for State aid in connection with investments in the processing and marketing of agricultural products[501] and a communication sets out the Commission's philosophy of its policy in this field.[502] The guidelines for the examination of State aid to fisheries and aquaculture[503] were based to a large extent on a Council Regulation laying down the criteria and arrangements regarding Union structural assistance in those sectors.[504] In 2001 the Commission issued Guidelines for State aid for advertising of agricultural products[505]; the Commission indicates that, providing certain conditions are met, it takes a favourable view of such aids.[506] It should be noted that the Guidelines for aids to employment and training, R&D, rescue and restructuring, examined elsewhere in this section, generally also apply to the agricultural and fisheries sectors. In 2004, the Commission published Guidelines for the examination of State aids to Fisheries and aquaculture[507] and a Regulation on the application of State aid rules to small and medium-sized enterprises active in the production, processing and marketing of fishery products.[508] Guidelines for subsidised short-term loans were published in 2001.[509]

See also the Regulation concerning de minimis aids for the fisheries sector.[510]

---

[496] Regulation 1101/89: [1989] O.J. L116/25, amended [1996] O.J. L304/1 and implemented [1989] OJ. L116/30.

[497] Directive 96/75 [1996] O.J. L304/12.

[498] art.42 TFEU [36].

[499] Regulation 26/62 O.J. B 30 of April 24,1962.

[500] [2000] O.J. C28/2, corrigendum [2000] O.J. C232/17.

[501] [1995] O.J. C29/4.

[502] [1994] O.J. C189.

[503] [2004] O.J. C84/10.

[504] Regulation 2792/1999 [1999] O.J. L337/10.

[505] [2000] O.J. C28/2.

[506] [2001] O.J. C252/5.

[507] [2004] O.J. C229/5.

[508] [2004] O.J. L291/3.

[509] [2001] O.J. C.252/5.

[510] Regulation 875/07 on the application of arts 87 and 88 to de minimis aid in the fisheries sector and amending Regulation 1860/04 [2004] O.J. L325/4 concerning de minimis aid in the agriculture and fisheries sector.

(viii) **Financial Sector.** No specific rules governing the granting of aid in this particularly sensitive sector existed until the disastrous financial upheaval which occurred towards the end of 2008. However, mention must be made here of the massive aids accepted by the Commission for the restructuring of the Credit Lyonnais[511] and fines imposed upon eight Austrian banks.[512]

Following the financial crash of the end of 2008, the Commission issued a communication ("the banking communication") on, "The application of State aid rules to measures taken in relation to financial institutions in the context of the current global financial crisis"[513] in which the Commission recognised that recapitalisation schemes are one of the key measures that Member States can take to preserve the stability and proper functioning of the financial markets. Consequently, the Commission approved *Financial Support Measures to the banking Industry in the UK*,[514] *Support measures for financial institutions in Germany*,[515] *Support measures for the credit institutions in Greece*,[516] *Aid to the ING Group in the Netherlands*[517] *and Latvian State support to JSC Parex Banka*.[518]

A new Communication was published in December 2008: "The recapitalisation of financial institutions in the current financial crisis: limitation of aid to the minimum necessary and safeguards against undue distortion of competition". It provides guidance for new recapitalisation schemes and open the possibility for adjustment of existing recapitalisation schemes.[519] This second communication provides criteria, on the one hand, for temporary recapitalisation of fundamentally sound banks in order to foster financial stability and lending to the real economy and, on the other hand, for rescue recapitalisation of other banks.

(ix) **Broadcasting.** See Commission Communication on the application of State aid rules to public service broadcasting. It sets out the principles to be followed by the Commission in the application of the rules to states funding public service in broadcasting.[520]

The Commission monitors the switchover from analogue to digital broadcasting; it considers that financing of public service broadcasting by means of budgetary contributions or license fee financing constitutes State aid.[521]

(c) Horizontal Aids

Those are aids that apply across the board to all sectors. The Council adopted a Regulation[522] on the application of the Union rules to certain categories of horizontal State aids; this Regulation allows the Commission to adopt regulations

---

[511] XXVIst Report on Competition Policy, 1996, 84(211). See Decision 95/547, conditional approval on State aid granted by France to the bank Credit Lyonnais [1995] O.J. L308/92.
[512] See IP/02/844: Commission fines eight Austrian banks for a price cartel.
[513] [2008] O.J. C270/8.
[514] [2008] O.J. C290/4.
[515] [2008] O.J. C293/2.
[516] Decision of 10.11.08 in case N560/2008.
[517] Decision of 12.11.08 in case N528/2008.
[518] Decision of 25.11.08 in case NN68/2008.
[519] C(2008) 8259 final. (05.12.08)
[520] [2001] O.J. C320/5.
[521] See *Altmark Trans* (C-280/00) [2003] E.C.R. I-7747 and Competition Report 2007, 15.
[522] Regulation 994/98 [1998] O.J. L142/1; this Regulation is based on art.109 [89].

exempting certain categories of aid from the obligation to notify. No implementation regulations have been issued yet. The Commission, on the other hand,
published a number of guidelines, setting out the way in which it applies the
Treaty provisions on aid in various sectors.

(i) **R&D.** A Framework for State Aid for Research and Development was
published in 1996; it allows the Member States to give financial support under
well-defined conditions.[523] Fundamental research is not concerned as it is always
considered "compatible" with the internal market. It applies to industrial
research and development activities. The Commission examines each individual
case and determines the eligible funding as a percentage of total costs with
increases for SMEs, poorer regions, etc. The Regulation concerning SMEs (see
below) was extended to include R&D.[524]

(ii) **Employment and Training.** Regarding aid to employment, the Commission
makes a distinction between aid to create jobs and aid to maintain existing jobs.
Clearly, the preference of the Commission goes to the former. Those aids do not have
to be notified. However, the Commission let it be known that it had an a priori negative position with regard to employment aid targeted at certain sectors in a Notice
on the monitoring of State aid and reduction of labour costs.[525] See the Regulation
on the application of the Treaty rules to aid for employment[526]; it creates a block
exemption system for certain types of State aid up to certain ceilings.

As for aid for training, the Commission published Guidelines[527] and a
Framework on training aid.[528] They were the object of interpretation by the
Court.[529] A distinction is made between specific and general training; in the
Commission's opinion, the latter effectively improves the worker's employability
and adaptability and thus makes a larger contribution in the field of employment
and human resource development. The framework also establishes a list of reim-
bursable costs and the authorised intensity of aid for training. The Commission
later issued a regulation on the application of the Treaty rules to training aid.[530]

(iii) **Environment.** Union Guidelines on State aid for environmental protection were published in 2008.[531] The guidelines apply to aid to protect the environment in all sectors governed by the Treaties, including those mentioned above
under "Sectoral Aids". The Commission distinguishes between investment aid,
operating aid to promote waste management and energy saving, and aid to SMEs

---

[523] [1996] O.J. C45/5.
[524] Regulation 364/04 [2004] O.J. L63/22.
[525] [1997] O.J. C1/10.
[526] Regulation 2204/2002 [2002] O.J. L337/3; the legality of this Regulation was contested—*Belgium
v Commission* (C-110/03) [2005] E.C.R. I–2801 and *Lodato* (C-14/07) [2009] E.C.R. 02.04.09,
notion of "job creation".
[527] [1995] O.J. C334/4. See also the Commission Communication concerning the guidelines on State
aid for employment [2000] O.J. C371/12.
[528] [1998] O.J. C343/10.
[529] See, for instance, *Italy v Commission* (C-310/99) [2002] E.C.R. I–2289.
[530] Regulation 68/2001 [2001] O.J. L10/20, amended [2004] O.J. L 63/.
[531] [2008] O.J. L82/1.

for services in the environmental field; these are special aids to help SMEs to adapt to new Union standards (maximum 15 per cent gross of eligible costs) and for improving on Union standards (in that case aids may be increased by as much as 10 percentage points). Other provisions concern renewable energy sources, combined production of electricity and heat and policies, measures and instruments for reducing greenhouse gases. See also Ch.34: Environment.

Guidelines on State aid subsidies for environmental protection were adopted by the Commission in 2008.[532]

(iv) **Small and Medium-Sized Enterprises.** The first Guidelines were published in 1992[533] and last revised in 2001.[534] The definition of an SME is interesting[535]: an enterprise with fewer than 250 salary-earners employed full-time for a whole year, with part-time or seasonal work being counted as fractions of a unit. The turnover is about the amount derived from the sale of products and the provision of services, after deduction of rebates and taxes.[536] Are considered compatible, aids for investment in tangible and intangible assets; the gross aid intensity may not exceed 15 per cent in the case of small enterprises and 7.5 per cent in the case of medium-sized ones. There are different ceilings for these aids granted in regional development areas. Aids for consultancy and other service activities are also covered; large individual aid grants are subject to a ceiling. Finally the relevant Member State must have adopted legal provisions establishing a legal right to aid according to objective criteria.[537] The Commission also considers acceptable aid for the transfer of SMEs.[538] See also the Communication of the Commission to the Member States on the accelerated clearance of aid schemes for SMEs[539] and aid to SMEs active in the production of agricultural products.[540]

(v) **Rescue and Restructuring.** Guidelines on State aids for rescuing and restructuring firms in difficulties were published in 2004,[541] including specific rules for agriculture and fisheries.[542] It must be regarded as exceptional. The "one time, last time" principle was strengthened in order to stop repeated calls for rescue and restructuring aid. They are authorised for no more than six months. Only loans or loan guaranties are acceptable and they must be reimbursed within 12 months.

(vi) **Aid to Firms in Under-privileged Urban Areas.** The Commission takes a favourable view of certain aid measures aimed at encouraging investment

---

[532] [2008] O.J. C82/1.
[533] [1992] O.J. C213/2.
[534] Regulation 70/2001 [2001] O.J. L10/33, amended [2004] O.J. L63/22.
[535] When it is necessary to distinguish between small and medium-sized undertakings, a small one is an undertaking of fewer than 50 employees, a turnover not exceeding €7 million and conforms to the criterion of independence defined by the Commission in its guidelines.
[536] See fourth Company Law Directive 1978] O.J. L222/11, amended [2001] O.J. L283/28.
[537] [2001] O.J. L10/33.
[538] Recommendation on the transfer of SMEs [1994] O.J. L385/14 and Commission Communication [1994] O.J. C400/1.
[539] *http://www.ec.europa.eu./competition/state-aid/legislation/legislation.html.*
[540] [2006] O.J. L358/3.
[541] [2004] O.J. C244/2.
[542] [1999] O.J. C288/1.

and job creation through the development of small businesses in run-down neighbourhoods.[543]

(vii) General Aid Schemes. These general measures do not fall within one of the categories provided for in the Treaty as being suitable to be declared compatible with the common market. Consequently, the Commission is unable to take a definitive position on such aid schemes, but grants a general acceptance. It requires the Member States, when implementing those schemes, to notify in advance the regional or sectoral programmes envisaged, or the significant cases of aid to be granted under those schemes. However, according to the Court, such aids constitute "existing aids", which must not be notified unless otherwise provided by the Commission Decision accepting the aid scheme. Such individual aids are covered by the Commission approved general scheme, and the Commission has no further power to adopt a decision on individual aid. However, such aids may be challenged in national courts.[544] On the other hand, when the Commission authorises a general aid scheme on condition that individual significant cases be notified with a view to an assessment of their impact on intra-Union trade and commerce, it cannot constitute blanket approval of all aid granted pursuant to that scheme, since the obligation to notify significant cases must be interpreted as a reservation on the approval contained in the decision itself.[545]

(viii) Financial Transfers to Public Undertakings. See: Directive on the transparency of financial relations between Member States and public undertakings.[546] Commission Communication concerning aid elements in land sale by public authorities[547] and Communication concerning short-term export-credit insurance.[548] See also above: 2. Public Undertakings.

(ix) Direct Business Taxation. See Communication of the Commission on the application of the State aid rules to measures relating to direct business taxation.[549]

(x) State Guarantees. See Commission Notice on the application of the State aid rules to State aid in the form of guarantees.[550] A recent case concerned the guarantees granted in Germany to State-owned banks and saving banks and in Austria to public Credit institutes. In the latter case agreement was reached on the gradual elimination of these guarantees[551] in April 2003. A similar agreement

---

[543] SEC(96) 1706/2.

[544] *Comité des Salines* (C-278/96) [1996] E.C.R. 2410. See also *Siemens* (C-278/95 P) (on the qualification of aids) [1997] E.C.R. I-2507.

[545] *AITEC v Commission* (Joined Cases T-447/93, etc.) [1995] E.C.R. II-1971.

[546] Directive 80/723 [1980] O.J. 195/35, amended [2000] O.J. L193/75.

[547] [1997] O.J. C209/3.

[548] [1997] O.J. C281/4, amended [2001] O.J. C217/2.

[549] [1998] O.J. C384/3.

[550] [2000] O.J. C71/1.

[551] See IP/03/476 of April 1, 2003. Later on eight Austrian bank were fined €124,25 million; see IP/02/844.

that entered into force on July 19, 2005, had previously been reached between the finance ministers of the relevant German States and the Commission.[552]

See Commission Notice on the application of the competition rules to State aid in the form of guarantees.[553] It describes all types of guarantees (it does not apply to export credit guarantees), provides for special rules for SMEs and concludes that when guarantees do not comply with the market economy investor principle, it is deemed to entail State aid. See also Commission Communication.[554]

(xi) **The State Aid Action Plan.** In 2005 the Commission launched the State Aid Action Plan[555] outlining the guiding principles for a comprehensive reform of State aid rules and procedures over the following five years.[556] The Commission hoped to encourage Member States to focus aid on improving the competitiveness of Union industry and creating sustainable jobs (aid for R&D, innovation and risk capital for small firms), ensuring social and regional cohesion and improving public services. The Commission also aimed at rationalising and streamlining procedures, so that the rules are clearer and less aid has to be notified, and to accelerate decision-making.

The Action Plan is based on the following elements:

- less and better targeted state aid;
- a more refined economic-based approach so that less distorting aid, particularly where money is less readily available, can be approved more easily and quickly;
- more streamlined and efficient procedures: the Commission intends to exempt more planned subsidies from the obligation to notify; and
- a shared responsibility between the Member States and the Commission who cannot improve State aid rules and practice without their co-operation.

The Commission adopted a new method for setting reference and discount rates more aligned with market principle.[557]

(xii) **General Block Exemption Regulation**[558] The Regulation defines general compatibility criteria as regards aids:

- in favour of SMEs, in the form of investment aid in and outside assisted areas, in the form of risk capital schemes and in the area of research, development and innovation, in particular in the context of the implementation on the regulation on the application of the competition rules to SMEs[559];

---

[552] IP/01/1007 of July 17, 2001 and IP/03/49. See also *Commission v Germany* (C-209/00) [2002] E.C.R. I–11695 and *Westduitsch Landesbank and Land Nordrhein-Westphalen v Commission* (Joined Cases T-228/99 and T-233/99) E.C.R. II–435, where the CFI annulled the Commission's Decision imposing a fine, for insufficient reasoning.

[553] [2008] O.J. C155/10.

[554] IP/08/764.

[555] 2005 Report on competition policy, 119.

[556] *http://www.ec.europa.eu/competition/state_aid/reform.htm*.

[557] Competition Report 2007, 5.

[558] Regulation 800/2008 declaring certain categories of aid compatible with the common market in application of Articles 87 and 88 [now 107 and 108] [2008] O.J. L214/3.

[559] Regulation 70/2001 [2001] O.J L10/33, amended [2006] O.J. L368/85.

- training aid, employments aid, environmental aid, research and development and innovation aid and regional aid with regard to both SMEs and large enterprises, in particular in the context of the implementation of the Regulation on the application of the competition rules to training aid,[560] of the Regulation concerning State aid for employment,[561] the Regulation concerning national regional investment aid,[562] the Community Framework for research and development,[563] the Community Framework for State aid for research and development,[564] the 2001 Community Guidelines for State aid for environmental protection[565] and the Guidelines on national regional aids for 2007–2013.[566]

The Regulation exempts any aid that fulfils all the conditions of the Regulation. Member States must inform the Commission concerning the measures implemented under the Regulation; if not, the Commission may withdraw the Regulation or parts of it for the future as regards the Member State concerned. State aid not covered by the Regulation remains subject to notification.

(xiii) **Special Measures to Combat the 2008/2009 World Crisis.**[567] See for instance the Commission Communication concerning a "Temporary framework for State aid measures to support access to finance in the current financial and economic crisis".[568] Member States are able to grant, without notification of individual cases, subsidised loans, loan guarantees at a reduced premium, risk capital for SMEs and direct aids of up to €500,000.[569]

(d) Procedural Rules

In order to allow the Commission to supervise the implementation of the competition rules in the aid sector and to declare certain aids compatible with the common market, Member States must notify the Commission of any plans to grant or alter aid.[570] Those notifications are published in the *Official Journal* to give interested parties the opportunity to make their comments known to the Commission.[571] Until the Commission has decided on the compatibility, the Member State may not put the measure into effect. However, failure to notify is not in itself enough to enable aid to be declared incompatible with the internal

---

[560] Regulation 68/2001 [2001] O.J. L10/20.
[561] Regulation 2204/2002 [2002] O.J. L337/2002, amended [2006] O.J. L368/85.
[562] Regulation 1628/2006 [2006] O.J. L302/29.
[563] [1996] O.J. L45/5.
[564] [2006] O.J. C232/1.
[565] [2008] O.J. 82/1.
[566] [2006] O.J. C54/13.
[567] See General Report 2008, Ch.1, Section 4.
[568] [2009] O.J. L83/1.
[569] General Report 2008, 47.
[570] art.108(3) TFEU [88(3)]. During the year 2008, the Commission received 660 notifications of new schemes or amendments to existing ones; it took 616 final decisions, it approved aid in 96 per cent of cases. General Report 2008, 47. See Regulation 659/99 laying down detailed rules for the application of art.108 [88] [1999] O.J. L83/1.
[571] The entries into the O.J. are accompanied by the indication "notified under number C . . ."; this indicates the number of the aid in the Register of the Commission; see: *http://www.ec.europa.eu/ competition/state–aid/register/about–en.html#ii–ca* with the indication of the number, in order to get all the information on the case.

market.[572] However, if an interested third party files a complaint with the Commission concerning a non-notified aid, the institution is obliged to examine such complaint, and even examines elements which have not been raised by the complainant.[573] The Commission published a Form for the submission of complaints concerning alleged unlawful State aid.[574] The Commission has the exclusive competence to find that an aid is illegal. The Commission is, therefore, obliged to take one of the following decision[575]: either that the measure does not constitute an aid; or that it constitutes an aid but is compatible; or, to open the procedure as provided in the Treaty. The Commission is obliged to do the latter when it meets with serious difficulties in appreciating whether the aid is compatible with the common market or not.[576] Such "serious difficulties" are presumed, by the GC, to exist when, for instance, the Commission has requested supplementary information several times and has taken several months to reach a decision.[577]

However, Member States must notify the Commission, "in sufficient time to enable it to submit its comments".[578] In order to facilitate the preparation of State aid notifications and their assessment by the Commission, the Council adopted a compulsory notification form and rules regarding the Annual Reports referred to in a former regulation.[579] After having received the notification, the Commission has two months to take a decision.[580] A regulation determines the rules applicable to periods, dates and time limits.[581] This time limit applies even when the Member State has not answered the Commission's questions with due diligence.[582] The Commission is under obligation to keep, in co-operation with Member States, under constant review all systems of aid existing in those States.[583]

See Regulation laying down detailed rules for the application of the Treaty rules on State aid[584] and the Notice on co-operation between national courts and the Commission in the State aid field.[585]

(e) Recovery of Aid

When State aids have been granted illegally, the Commission can require the national authorities to recover the aid.[586] The same applies to Union aids. The

[572] *SIDE* (T-49/93) [1995] E.C.R. II–2501, where the GC based itself on the case law of the Court of Justice; *France v Commission* (C-301/87) [1990] E.C.R. I–307 and *FNCE (Salmon Processor)* (C-354/90) [1991] E.C.R. I–5505(84).
[573] *Commission v Sytraval and Brink's France* (C-367/95 P) [1998] E.C.R. I–1719.
[574] [2003] O.J. C116/3. See also Commission Notice on the determination of the applicable rules for the assessment of unlawful State aid [2002] O.J. L119/22.
[575] *Gestevision v Commission* (T-95/96) [1998] E.C.R. II–3407.
[576] *SIC v Commission* (T-46/97) [2000] E.C.R. I–2125(71).
[577] *Prayon-Rupel v Commission* (T-73/98) [2001] E.C.R. II–867.
[578] art.108(3) TFEU [88(3)].
[579] Regulation 659/99 laying down detailed rules for the application of art.113 TFEU [93] [1999] O.J. L83/1 and implementing Commission Regulation 794/2004, amended [2008] O.J. L82/1.
[580] This time limit was set by the Court in *Nordsee v Germany* (122/73) [1973] E.C.R. 1511 at 1522(4).
[581] Regulation 1182/71 [1971] O.J. L124/1.
[582] *Austria v Commission* (C-99/98) [2001] E.C.R. I–1101.
[583] art.108 TFEU [88].
[584] Regulation 659/1999 [1999] O.J. L83/1 and Regulation 794/2004 implementing Regulation 659 [2004] O.J. L140/1, amended [2006] O.J. L302/10, amended [2006] O.J. L407/1, amended [2008] O.J. L82/1.
[585] [1995] O.J. C312/8.
[586] See Commission Communication on aids granted illegally [1983].

Commission can even seek the payment of interests on the sums recovered,[587] and published a Communication on the interest rates to be applied when aid granted unlawfully is being recovered.[588]

In the event the beneficiary or the public authority which granted the aid obtains an interim order from the Court to suspend the repayment, a suspension will be conditional upon the provision of a bank guarantee; the judge is entitled to take into account the overall financial resources of the applicant and the Union interest in securing effectiveness of the judgment to be given.[589] The Commission may also authorise an aid that a Member State is planning to give to an undertaking, but prohibit payment thereof until the undertaking has repaid previously received aid which has been found to be unlawful by a decision of the Commission, which has become final.[590]

In case of unforeseen and unforeseeable difficulties encountered by the Member State in the recuperation of the aid, the Commission and the Member State must work together in good faith with a view to overcoming the difficulties whilst fully observing the Treaty provisions and especially those on aid.[591] However, non-recovery is acceptable in certain circumstances, and under condition that the beneficiary's good faith is established, and the same applies to the recovery of purely national payments.[592]

In any case, there is little, it seems, the beneficiary of the illegal aid can do to prevent repayment of the aid. In the first place, the Court has decided that, under certain circumstances, a prudent operator should make sure, before accepting an aid, that it is being granted legally.[593] Therefore, "negligence" on the part of the beneficiary might be held against him. In the second place, the only possibility for the recipient who has paid back the aid is to start an action against the Member State which granted the aid, for damage caused by a breach of Union law by said Member State. In case the Commission has attached conditions to the authorisation to grant an aid and the beneficiary was not informed of those conditions:

> "[I]t is not contrary to Union law to apply the principle of legal certainty so as to preclude repayment by that beneficiary of the amounts wrongly paid, provided that it is possible to establish the beneficiary's good faith."[594]

Besides this problem, the beneficiary who is asked to pay back the aid, must demonstrate, as was also indicated in relation with the responsibility of Member States for breach of Union law, that three conditions are fulfilled. In the first place the Union rule breached must provide a right for the plaintiff; in the second place, the Member States must be guilty of an infringement, and, finally, the damage sustained must have been caused by the said breach.

The right of the Commission to claim repayment of illegally granted aid expires after 10 years.[595]

[587] *Siemens* (T-459/93) [1995] E.C.R. II–1675.
[588] [2003] O.J. C110/21.
[589] *Transacctiones Maritimas* (C-12/95 P(R)) [1995] E.C.R. I–468; [1996] 2 C.M.L.R. 580.
[590] *TWD v Commission* (Joined Cases T-244/93 and T-486/93) [1995] E.C.R. II–2265; [1996] 1 C.M.L.R. 332.
[591] *Commission v Italy* (C-349/93) [1995] E.C.R. I–343.
[592] *Oelm Ühle* (C-298/96) [1998] E.C.R. I–4767.
[593] *SFEI* (C-39/94) [1996] E.C.R. I–3549; [1996] 3 C.M.L.R. 369.
[594] *Stichting ROM-Projecten* (158/06) [2007] E.C.R. 21.06.07.
[595] art.8 Regulation 659/99 [1999] O.J. L83/1; see *Scott v Commission* (C-276/03 P) [2005] E.C.R. I–8437 concerning interruption of the time limit.

In 2007 the Commission published a Notice "towards an effective implementation of Commission decisions ordering Member States to recover unlawful and
incompatible State aid".[596] The Commission indicated that it is prepared to take
strong action against unlawful aid ever since the entry into force of Regulation
659/1999 ("the Procedural Regulation").[597] In its Notice the Commission noted
that, "Recent editions of the State aid Scoreboard also show that 45% of all
recovery decisions adopted in 2000–2001 had still not been implemented by June
2006."!

See Communication regarding the obsolescence of certain State aid policy
documents.[598]

4. COMPETITION RULES OF THE EUROPEAN COAL AND STEEL COMMUNITY (ECSC)

Although, as was mentioned at the beginning of this book, the ECSC Treaty no
longer exists, mention was made, in several sections of this chapter, of the
competition rules of the ECSC Treaty. They concern antitrust, merger control
and State aids. The ECSC Treaty expired on July 23, 2002, and a solution had to
be found for the competition cases provided for under that Treaty. Consequently,
the Commission indicated, in a Communication,[599] that the sectors previously
covered by the ECSC Treaty became subject to the rules of the then existing
EC Treaty, as well as the procedural rules and other secondary legislation
derived from that Treaty. The Communication indicates which rules apply in
which cases.

Further Reading

Alison Jones & Brenda Sufrin, *EC Competition Law*, 2nd edn (Oxford
University Press, 2004).
Alister Lindsay, *EC merger regulation: Substantive Issues*, 2nd edn (Sweet &
Maxwell, 2006).
Andrea Biondi, Piet Eeckhout and James Flynn, *The Law of State Aid in the
European Union* (Oxford University Press, 2004).
Christopher Kerse and Nicholas Kahn, *EC Antitrust Procedure*, 5th edn (Sweet
& Maxwell, 2005).
Christopher Jones and Marc van der Wouden, *EC Competition Law Handbook*,
published annually (Sweet & Maxwell, 2007).
F. Wijckmans, F. Tuytschaever, A. Vandererlst, *Vertical Agreements in EC
Competition Law* (Oxford University Press, 2006).
Frauke Henning-Bodewig, *Unfair Competition law, European Union and
Member States* (Kluwer Law International, 2006).
Gerhard Dannecker & Oswald Jansen, "Competition Law Sanctioning in the
European Union", European Monographs 46, 2004.

---

[596] [2007] O.J. C272/4.
[597] Regulation laying down detailed rules for the application of art.113 TFEU [93] [1999] O.J. L83/3.
[598] [2004] O.J. C115/1.
[599] Communication 2002/C 152/03 [2002] O.J. C152/5.

John Cook and Riccardo Celli, *EC merger Control*, 4th edn (Sweet & Maxwell, 2005).

Joanna Goyder, *EU Distribution Law* (Hart Publishing, 2005).

Lennart Ritter, W. David Braun, *E.C. Competition Law. A Practitioner's Guide*, 3rd edn (Kluwer, 2004).

Luis Ortiz Blanco, *EC Competition procedure*, 2nd edn (Oxford Unversity Press, 2006).

Leigh Hancher, Tom Ottervanger and Piet Jan Slot, *EC State Aids* (Sweet & Maxwell, 2006).

Nihoul P. & Rodford P., *EU Electronic Commuinications Law. Competition and Regulation in the European Telecommunications Market* (Oxford University Press, 2004).

Robert O'Donoghue-George Padilla, *The Law and Economics of Article 82 EC* (Hart Publishing, 2006).

Thomas Hays, *Parallel Importation under European Union Law* (Sweet & Maxwell, 2004).

Valentine Korah, *An Introductory Guide to EC Competition Law and Practice*, (Hart Publishing, 2004).

Van Bael & Bellis, *Competition Law of the EC*, 4th edn (Kluwer Law International, 2004).

Chapter Twenty-three

Agriculture and Fisheries[1]

According to the Commission, the Common Agricultural Policy (CAP) is:

"[F]undamental to the strength and competitiveness of EU farming and the agri-food sector as a whole, with its 19 million jobs. The policy ensures that farming and preservation of the environment go hand in hand. It helps develop the economic and social fabric of rural communities. It plays a vital role in confronting new challenges such as climate change, bioenergy and biodiversity."[2]

As will be briefly shown below:

"EU agricultural policy is constantly evolving. In the earliest days, 50 years ago, the emphasis was on providing enough food for a Europe emerging from a decade of war-induced shortages. Subsidising production on a large scale and buying up surpluses in the interest of food security are now largely a thing of the past. The focus of EU policy is to get food producers—of all forms of food from crops and livestock to fruit and vegetables, or wine—to be able to stand on their own feet on EU and world markets."[3]

"Agriculture" in the Union is no longer centred around agricultural markets, i.e. production and marketing of agricultural products, but now rests on two so-called pillars: the CAP, on the one hand, and Rural Development, on the other. Until the beginning of the 1990s, the main content of the CAP, which on its own devoured nearly 70 per cent of the Union budget, was agriculture per se. However, as the Commission indicated, new challenges appeared in the form of globalisation of world trade (especially trade in agricultural products), consumer-led quality requirements and Union enlargement. These changes affected not only the agricultural markets (see hereunder), but also local economies in rural areas. The Commission underlined that the future of agriculture itself is closely linked to a balanced development of rural areas that account—few European citizens realise this—for 80 per cent of the European territory (before accession of the 10 new Member States). Consequently, not only "agriculture", but also "rural policy" have an important role to play in the cohesion of the Union's territorial, economic and social policies. This double approach is also reflected in the Union budgets and in the Financial Perspectives,[4] where the amounts for agriculture are divided between the Common Agricultural Policy (CAP) and Rural

---

[1] The term "Fisheries" was added in the denomination of Title III of Part Three of the TFEU by the Treaty of Lisbon; the fisheries policy will be examine in the next chapter of this book, but it should be noted that the TFEU provides that, "Reference to the common agricultural policy or to agriculture and the use of the term 'agricultural', shall be understood as also referring to fisheries, having regard to the special characteristics of that sector." (art.33(1)2 TFEU).

[2] EUROPA. Activities of the European Union. Agriculture.

[3] EUROPA. Overviews of European Union activities Agriculture.

[4] See above Ch.14: Financing Union Activities.

Development and accompanying measures. The amounts for these two Union activities still represent today around 46 per cent of Union expenditures.

The TFEU,[5] now provides that the, "internal market shall extend to agriculture,[6] fisheries and trade in agricultural products",[7] and that, "save as otherwise provided in Articles 39 to 44, the rules laid down for the establishment and functioning of the internal market shall apply to agricultural products"[8]. The latter are defined as the products of the soil, of stockfarming and of fisheries and products of first-stage processing directly related to those products.[9]

The Treaty also provides that the, "operation and development of the internal market for agricultural products must be accompanied by the establishment [of a common agricultural policy".[10] In other words, an unqualified application, for instance, of the Union competition rules to agricultural products was, from the start, deemed impossible. Special complementary rules, known as agricultural policy, were needed. The more so, since agriculture has always represented, due to its particular nature,[11] difficult problems in all the Member States. Elaborate and costly national measures to aid agriculture existed (and still exist) practically everywhere. Consequently, the inclusion of agriculture in, what was then called the common market, was agreed upon, but on special terms, i.e. via, "the establishment of a common agricultural policy"[12] and the, "need to effect the appropriate adjustments by degree".[13]

Consequently, the provisions relating to the CAP have precedence, in case of conflict, over the rules relating to the establishment of the internal market, such as those on the free movement of goods.[14] On the other hand, it means that, in the absence of specific provisions, the general rules of the Treaties fully apply to the agricultural sector since the end of the transitional period.[15] As for the national measures existing at the time of the establishment of the CAP, they were replaced by a, "common organization of agricultural markets"[16] that took the form of various European Market Organisation[s][17], now replaced by a single Common Market Organisation (see below).

---

[5] art.38(1) TFEU [32(1)].

[6] One could, in theory, have established a internal market without agricultural products [today, agriculture only represents 1.3 per cent of Union GDP], but in the 1950s agriculture constituted, in all the Member States, a sector closely linked with the economy as a whole (see art.39(2)(c) TFEU), and could therefore not be left out of the internal market. The food industry, which processes more than three-quarters of the agricultural products of the Union, also constitutes its most important industrial sector in terms of turn over and employment.

[7] art.38(1)2 TFEU [32].

[8] art.38(2) TFEU [32(2)].

[9] They are listed in Annex II to the Treaty. In pursuance of old art.32(3) EC a number of products were added to this list in 1960. See Regulation 7a [1961] J.O. 71/61 and [1959–1962]68.

[10] art.38(4) TFEU [32(4)].

[11] art.39(2)(a) TFEU [33(2)(a)] refers to the, "particular nature of agricultural activity which results from the social structure of agriculture and from structural and natural disparities between the various agricultural regions".

[12] art.38(4) TFEU [32(4)].

[13] art.39(2)(b) TFEU [33(2)(b)].

[14] *Pig Marketing Board v Redmond* (83/78) [1978] E.C.R. 2347; [1979] 1 C.M.L.R. 177.

[15] *Charmasson v Minister for Economic Affairs and Finance* (48/74) [1974] E.C.R. 1383; [1975] 2 C.M.L.R. 208.

[16] art.40(1) TFEU [34(1)].

[17] art.40(1)(c) TFEU [34(1)(c)].

1. THE COMMON AGRICULTURAL POLICY (CAP)

It is important to mention the objectives assigned by the TFEU to the CAP, since, as the Court stated, taken separately, they appear to conflict with one another and it is up to the Union Institutions to allow, where necessary, temporary priority to one of them.[18] The objectives of the common agricultural policy still are, after all those years the following:

"(a) to increase agricultural productivity by promoting technical progress and by ensuring the rational development of agricultural production and the optimum utilisation of the factors of production, in particular labour;
(b) thus to ensure a fair standard of living for the agricultural community, in particular by increasing the individual earnings of persons engaged in agriculture;
(c) to stabilise markets;
(d) to assure the availability of supplies;
(e) to ensure that supplies reach consumers at reasonable prices."[19]

Looking back over the past 50 years or so, it is easy to ascertain that only some of those objectives were actually attained. There is no doubt that agricultural productivity and production increased dramatically; it could be said, out of all proportion to the internal and external needs. However, one should not forget that the CAP was established by people who had lived through World War II and that the memories about the scarcity of food during that period and about those who died of hunger, were still very vivid at the time. What was more natural than the strong desire, "to assure the availability of supplies",[20] preferably home-grown to avoid dependency upon outside suppliers? One has to add to that the claim of the farmers' organisations, which have long enjoyed and exercised an excessive influence[21] on political decisions concerning agriculture. They pretended that the, "increase of individual earnings of persons engaged in agriculture"[22] was guaranteed to them by the Treaty, ignoring the other objectives. The result was the impossibility to, "stabilise the markets"[23] and, "to ensure that supplies reach consumers at reasonable prices".[24]

These above-mentioned Treaty objectives were complemented under "Agenda 2000" by a reform whose purpose was:

"[T]o preserve the European model of agriculture by insuring that farming throughout the Union, even in the regions with special problems, is sustainable and competitive, capable of maintaining the landscape, conserving nature, contributing to the vitality of the countryside and responding to the concerns and demands of consumers in terms of food quality and safety, environmental protection and animal welfare."[25]

---

[18] *Balkan-Import-Export v Hauptzollamt Berlin-Packhof* (5/73) [1973] E.C.R. 1091.
[19] art.39(1) TFEU [33(1)].
[20] art.30(1)(d) TFEU [33(1)(d)].
[21] This influence, fortunately, has waned with the years, together with the decline of the number of farmers (which before enlargement represented less than 2 per cent of the working population), and the economic importance of farm products in the GNP of the Member States.
[22] art.39(1)(b) TFEU [33(1)(b)].
[23] art.39(1)(c) TFEU [33(1)(c)].
[24] art.39(1)(e) TFEU [33(1)(e)].
[25] General Report 1999, 494.

The basic principles which determined the orientation of the CAP were adopted by the Council in 1960 and still apply to-day:

1. free movement of agricultural products within the Union;
2. a common price level for all agricultural products;
3. fair earnings for those employed in agriculture (i.e. price support);
4. a uniform system of levies imposed on all imported products and export restitutions;
5. co-ordination of national measures for structural reform.

(1) A Bit of History: Mixed Results of the Successive Reforms of the CAP

After several decades of operation, with outstanding positive results, the problems created by appalling overproduction in some sectors and the resulting unbearable costs to the Union, among others, for storing them, made a revision of the CAP mandatory.[26] A first reform of the CAP took place in 1984.[27] Although it was considered by the Commission as, "a milestone in the development of the [agricultural] policy",[28] the Union faced a major crisis a few years later due to a combination of accumulated surplus stocks and acute budgetary difficulties. A turning point came at the meeting of the European Council in Brussels, in February 1988. The Council approved a Commission Communication entitled "The Single European Act: a new Frontier for Europe". At that meeting the Union endowed itself with the political and financial resources it needed to finally complete the internal market.

Notwithstanding all those efforts, the CAP continued to suffer from a fundamental deficiency: agricultural production was guided by price-setting rather than by demand. Farmers continued to produce huge quantities of products for which the Union offered the highest guaranteed prices, irrespective of the need for those products. So, once again the Council approved, in May 1992, a number of measures redirecting agriculture in the Union. This so-called Mac Sharry re-orientation was prolonged by the above-mentioned Agenda 2000 and was restructured in the course of 2003 (see below).

On June 26, 2003 EU farm ministers adopted a new fundamental reform of the CAP: it completely changed the way the EU supports its farm sector. The new CAP is geared towards consumers and taxpayers, while giving EU farmers the freedom to produce what the market wants. One can only deeply regret that after all those years of subsidised wild overproduction geared at support rather than demand, that sentence doesn't read as follows, "while forcing farmers to produce only what the market demands". [That would finally have introduced some

---

[26] See the Communiqué of the European Council of June 1983 [1983] Bull.6 at 19.
[27] [1983] EC Suppl. Bull. 4 at 19. The following adaptations were proposed:

1. co-responsibility principle, guaranteed thresholds and delivery quotas for milk;
2. a prudent and, in certain cases, restrictive price policy, and for cereals a reduction of the gap between Union and World prices;
3. existing aids and premiums to be discontinued;
4. promotion of agricultural exports; and
5. dismantlement of the monetary compensatory amounts. See General Report 1983, 172.

[28] General Report 1984, 64.

economic common sense into the CAP.] However, since then, the vast majority of subsidies have been paid independently from the volume of production; this makes farmers more competitive and market-orientated, while providing the necessary income stability. Exceptions are possible. These new "single farm payments"[29] or "single payment scheme (SPS)" are also linked to the respect of environmental, food safety and animal welfare standards.

The two pillars of the 2003 reform are the decoupling of direct aid to producers (cutting the link between support and production) and introduction of the single payment scheme. Direct aid no longer depends on the type of production.

Cross-compliance: farmers may receive direct payments provided that they maintain their land in good agricultural condition and comply with the standards of public health, the environment and animal welfare.

Degressivity, modulation and financial discipline: between 2005 and 2012, direct payments (other than in the outermost regions[30] and the Aegean Islands[31]) are to be reduced each year (3 per cent in 2005, 4 per cent in 2006 and afterwards 5 per cent each year).

They entered into force in 2005 for those Member States that decided to start on January 1, 2005: Austria, Belgium, Denmark, Germany, Ireland, Italy, Luxembourg, Portugal, Sweden and the United Kingdom. The five other old Member States applied the SPS in 2006, while two new Member States, Malta and Slovenia, started in 2007. The other new Member States will apply the new system in 2009 at the latest. The reform also provides for a revision of the tobacco, olive oil, cotton and sugar sectors.

The key elements of the reformed CAP can therefore be summarised as follows[32]:

- Single Payment Scheme for EU farmers, independent from production;
- payment is linked to the respect of environmental, food safety, animal and plant health and animal welfare standards, as well as the requirement to keep all farmland in good agricultural and environmental condition (cross-compliance);
- a strengthened rural development policy with more EU money, new measures to promote the environment, quality and animal welfare and to help farmers to meet Union production standards starting in 2005;
- a reduction in direct payments ("modulation") to bigger farms to finance the new rural development policy;
- a "financial discipline" mechanism to prevent spending exceeding the ceiling agreed upon, until 2013.

Hopefully these changes will give consumers what they want, offer taxpayers more transparency and contribute towards more market-orientated world trade. It is important to note that farmers are no longer paid just to produce food. Today's CAP is, according to the Commission,[33] demand driven.

---

[29] Regulation 1782/03 establishing common rules for direct support schemes and establishing certain support schemes for farmers [2003] O.J. L270, amended many times.

[30] For details, see below in Ch.32 Regional Policy/Economic, Social and Territorial Cohesion.

[31] See Regulation 615/08 [2008] O.J. L168/1 providing for two support schemes.

[32] See IP/04/1540 23.12.04. Direct support for Farmers Regulation 73/09 [2009] O.J. L30/16, amended [2009] O.J. L338/1.

[33] See under *http://www.ec.europa.eu/agriculture*: agriculture explained.

(2) The Single Common Market Organisation (CMO)[34]

As was indicated, the Treaty provides for the establishment of "common organisations of agricultural markets" in order to attain the objectives of the CAP.[35] Some kind of organisation exists for the following products classified in: on the one hand, "plant products", also referred to as "crop products"[36]—arable crops, wine, olive oil, fruit and vegetables, sugar, tobacco, cotton and hops; and, on the other hand, "animal products", also referred to as "livestock products"—milk and milk products, beef and veal, sheep-meat and goat-meat, pig-meat, poultry-meat, eggs and honey. These markets will be briefly examined hereunder. In addition, the Council adopted three regulations with specific rules for ethyl alcohol of agricultural origin,[37] on measures improving general conditions for the production and marketing of agricultural products[38] and special measures to encourage silkworm rearing.[39]

The 21 existing common market organisations were replaced in 2008 by the Single Common Market Organisation (Single CMO).[40] According to the Commission it constitutes the most significant technical simplification of the CAP yet undertaken; it allows the repeal of almost 50 Council acts and replaces more than 650 legal articles in the Regulations.[41] However, all the existing policies remain unchanged and, consequently, it has no financial impact. It does not include those parts of CMOs which are subject to policy reforms; this was the case with regard to most parts of the fruit and vegetables, processed fruit and vegetables and the wine sector; the substantive provisions of the relevant Regulations will be incorporated in the CMO once the respective reforms have been enacted.

It is important to note the possibility under the TFEU[42] to change existing price levels with regard to all sectors covered by the Regulation.

(a) Plant Products

(i) **Cereals.**[43] They cover a wide range of annual crops of primary importance, such as wheat, barley, maize, rye, colza, sunflower, peas, etc. They cover 40 per cent of the EU's utilised agricultural area, and are found in all the Member States. Since 1992, they have been eligible for a hectare-based aid scheme, which also includes set-aside measures. In the cereals sector, Union prices are, on average, still higher than world prices; to allow for exports, "refunds" are granted covering the difference between those two prices. The subsidised exports are limited each year in terms of volume and value, as part of the Union's international commitments to the WTO. A solution is to be found in aligning the Union prices with those of the world market.

---

[34] Some of the following text has been borrowed from *http://www.ec.europa.eu/agricultur/markets/index_en.htm*.

[35] art.39 TFEU [34].

[36] This is the expression used in the General Report 2004, 116.

[37] [2003] O.J. L97/6.

[38] [2004] O.J. L125/1.

[39] [2006] O.J. L286/1.

[40] Regulation 1234/2007 "Single CMO Regulation", establishing a common organisation of agricultural markets and on specific provisions for certain agricultural products [2007] O.J. L299/1, amended [2008] O.J. L121/1, [2009] O.J. L154/1 and [2009] O.J. L312/4.

[41] European Commission "Agriculture and Rural Development" simplifying the CAP.

[42] art.43(2) TFEU [49].

[43] See CMO, Annex I, Part I, which applied to cereals on July 1, 2008 [2007] O.J. L299/1.

As for oil seeds, the alignment of payments per hectare on those of cereal, should eliminate their specific character.

(ii) **Wine.**[44] The Union occupies a leading position in the world wine market, accounting for 45 per cent of wine-growing areas, 65 per cent of production, 57 per cent of global consumption (although this is now declining) and 70 per cent of exports in global terms. The Union wine market went through several transformations including a serious structural surplus, a ban on planting, the obligation to distil the surplus, incentives to giving up vineyards, etc. Following the GATT agreements, demand being in constant decline, the necessity to develop towards a qualitative level that the vineyard could not always guarantee, the introduction of a new CMO became necessary.[45] It simplified the legislation in this field, recognised the role of producers and inter-branch organisations, provided for restructuring of the vineyards and was supposed to put an end to intervention, except in special circumstances. See financial transfer of the common organisation of the market in wine to rural development.[46] Now replaced by the Single Common Market Organisation. The common organisation for the market in wine was reformed in 2008.[47]

(iii) **Olive oil and table olives.** The Union is the leading world producer, accounting for 80 per cent and consuming 70 per cent of the world's olive oil. World demand is steadily increasing to the benefit of many Union regions in whose economies it plays an important role. The Union encourages production of a high quality product for the benefit of growers, processors, traders and consumers. It is based on a single payment system. 40 per cent of the funding is an area aid for the upkeep of olive groves of environmental and social value. Since July 1, 2008 it is part of the single CMO.[48]

(iv) **Fresh fruit and vegetables.** There are three categories: fresh fruit and vegetables,[49] processed fruit and vegetables[50] and certain citrus fruits.[51] The CMO was modified in 2000 including the special arrangements for certain types of fruits and vegetables, like tomatoes, peach, pear and citrus fruit processing. The changes aim at boosting support for the sector in a resolutely market-orientated way;

---

[44] Regulation 1493/99 [2008] O.J. L148/1, amended [2008] O.J. L335/32, and Regulation 1227/00 detailed rules for the application of Regulation 1493/99 now CMO, Annex I, Part XII; applicable since August 1, 2008. See *Schneider* (C-285/06) [2008] E.C.R. I-1501 interpreting art.47 of Regulation 1493/99.

[45] Regulation 1493/1999 [1999] O.J. L179/1. No longer applicable. See CMO Regulation 134/2007 [2007] O.J. L299/1.

[46] Regulation 479/08 [2008] O.J. L335/32.

[47] Regulation 479/08 [2008] O.J. L148/1.

[48] Regulation 1234/07 [2007] O.J. L299/1.

[49] Regulation 2200/96 [1996] O.J. L297/1, modified [2004] O.J. L106/10, implemented by Regulation 1580/07 [2007] O.J. L350/1, amended [2008] O.J. L336/1. Since January 1, 2008 Single CMO, Regulation 1234/07 [2007] O.J. L299/1.

[50] Regulation 2201/96 [1996] O.J. L297/29, modified [2004] O.J. L64/25. Since January 1, 2008 Single CMO, Regulation 1234/07 (quoted above).

[51] Regulation 2202/96 [1996] O.J. L297/49, modified [2001] O.J. L262/6. Now Single CMO Regulation 1234/07 (quoted above).

simplification of aid schemes increased their transparency. Of interest here is the fact that aid is paid directly to producer organisations, which make the scheme more flexible and increase producers responsibility. Since January 1, 2008 replaced by Single CMO.[52]

(v) **Processed fruit and vegetables.** The provisions governing this market organisation are now, without modification, included in the single Market Organisation, which became applicable for these agricultural products, on January 1, 2008.[53]

(vi) **Raw tobacco.** The CMO was set up in 1992[54] and amended in 1998 and 2002.[55] It comprises a premium system, a system of production orientation and limitation and measures to convert production (including the Union Tobacco Fund[56] and a quota buy-back programme). Detailed rules were laid down for the implementation of the system[57] and with regard to the Fund.[58]

(vii) **Sugar.**[59] The CMO for sugar was set up in 1968 to ensure fair income for producers and self supply for the Union. Import levies provided protection against external competition and export refunds allowed for sales to third countries. A major reform became effective on July 1, 2006; the key to the reform is a 36 per cent cut in the guaranteed minimum price, generous compensation for farmers and a Restructuring Fund as an incentive to uncompetitive sugar producers to leave the industry.

(viii) **Rice.** The common organisation was based on a 1995 regulation.[60] It provides for intervention on the internal market, including the fixing of an intervention price and certain support measures for European products when they are traded on international markets. In addition it is heavily influenced by certain international agreements under the WTO. It is part of the Single CMO since September 1, 2008.

(ix) **Cotton.** This agricultural sector suffers from overproduction and severe competition from third countries. The CMO has undergone several changes; since the 2000/2001 marketing year, the price reduction mechanism has been significantly strengthened above certain production thresholds in order to respect budgetary discipline, the main concern, and to avoid the environmental problems caused by extreme intensification and the spread of cotton growing. There is a

---

[52] Since January 1, 2008 Regulation 1234/07 (quoted above).
[53] Regulation 1234/07 (quoted above).
[54] Regulation 2075/92 [1992] O.J. L215/70, amended [2003] O.J. L345/17 and [2005] O.J. L271/1. Since July 1, 2008 Single CMO, Regulation 1234/07 (quoted above).
[55] Regulation Fixing the premiums and guarantee thresholds for leaf tobacco by variety group and Member State [2002] O.J. L84/4. Now Single CMO.
[56] See Regulation 470/08 [2008] O.J. L140/1.
[57] Regulation 2848/98 [1998] O.J. L358/17. Now Single CMO [2007] O.J. L.299/1.
[58] Regulation 2182/02 [2002] O.J. L 331/16. Now Single CMO (quoted above).
[59] See single CMO, Regulation 1234/07 (quoted above).
[60] Regulation 370/95.

special aid scheme for small producers.[61] A 2008 regulation[62] established national restructuring programmes for the cotton ginning industry and to enhance the quality and marketing of the cotton produced.

(x) Hops.[63] The CMO covers three products: cones, powder and extracts. Aid is granted to producers at 480 per hectare. From January 1, 2005, the sector was integrated into the single farm payments system (see above). With enlargement, the Union areas under hops increased by almost 50 per cent. The trend is, however, towards area reduction as a consequence of increased yields of the bitter constituent of hops that gives beer its bitter taste. There are practically no unsold stocks within the Union, which is traditionally a net exporter.

(xi) Bananas. This CMO was based on a 1993 regulation and should allow the Union market to receive satisfactory supplies of quality bananas at fair prices for producers and consumers and ensure a balance between the various sources of supply. It was based on a tariff-only system. It was reformed in 2006 and is absorbed in the Single CMO[64] since January 1, 2008.

(b) Animal Products

(i) Milk and milk products. The CMO is based on a 1999 regulation.[65] It refers to the additional levy which was introduced in 1992 for the purpose of reducing the imbalance between supply and demand. In order to stimulate consumption within the Union and improve competitiveness on the international markets, the level of market support was reduced, through a gradual reduction of the target prices and the intervention prices, starting of July 1, 2005. Milk production was increased by 2 per cent from April 2008.[66]

Besides the intervention in respect of butter and fresh cream, the regulation provides for:

1. buying-in of skimmed milk powder with a minimum protein content;
2. defraying part of the costs for supplying milk to pupils in schools;
3. the introduction of individual income support;
4. import duties and export refunds based on the undertakings accepted under the Uruguay Round; and
5. application of the Treaty provisions concerning the granting of State aid to this sector. Several other measures are provided for in case of difficulty in implementing the above-mentioned regulation.

(ii) Beef and veal. The CMO is based on a 1999 regulation.[67] To rebalance supply and demand, market support was gradually reduced by 20 per cent,

---

[61] Regulation 1152/90 [1990] O.J. L116/1. Now Single CMO (quoted above).
[62] Regulation 637/08 [2008] O.J. L178/1.
[63] Since July 1, 2008 Single CMO (quoted above).
[64] Regulation 1234/07 [2007] O.J. L299/1.
[65] Regulation 1255/99 [1999] O.J. L160/48, amended several times. Since July 1, 2008 Single CMO [2007] O.J. L299/1.
[66] Regulation 248/08 [2008] O.J. L76/6.
[67] Regulation 1254/99 [2000] O.J. L263/34, amended several times. Since July 1, 2008 Single CMO [2007] O.J. L199/1.

farmers being compensated by direct payments set up under Agenda 2000. One of them is to encourage producers to adopt extensive grazing methods ("extensification payment"); these were not very successful and the Commission proposed measures to curb the tendency towards intensive production.

(iii) **Sheep-meat and goat-meat.**[68] This CMO was based on a 2001 regulation brought into effect on January 1, 2002. A fixed premium for producers has replaced a price-dependent variable compensatory payment. The main components of the regulation are: rules on direct payments, rules on trade with third countries and market monitoring.

(iv) **Pig-meat.**[69] Measures were provided to ensure that supply is in line with market demand. It provides for (1) a basic price and the possibility of intervention (not used in the last 20 years), (2) rules concerning trade with third countries: possibly import and export licences, additional import duties in case of risk to destabilise the Union market, export refunds; prohibition of taxes equivalent to customs duties and quotas and application of Treaty rules on State aids. Many other regulations were adopted concerning, for instance, export licences.[70]

(v) **Poultry-meat.**[71] This CMO was established by a 1975 regulation still in force but amended many times. It covers: cocks, hens, ducks, geese, turkeys and guinea-fowl. Marketing standards related to grading by category, quality and weight and to labelling are mandatory. The Regulation contains rules on trade with third countries: import and export licences, customs tariffs, additional import duties, tariff quotas, export refunds, safeguard measures, trade barriers, animal diseases and State aid.

(vi) **Eggs.** This market was based on a 1975 regulation[72] amended several times. It covers eggs of domestic fowl, eggs not in shell and egg yolks however preserved. Union measures in support of trade or joint trade initiatives may be taken. Marketing standards related to grading by category and weight and to labelling are mandatory. Rules on trade with third countries refer to import and export licences, the common customs tariff, quotas, safeguard measures, animal diseases and State aids.

(vii) **Honey.** The legal basis for this CMO was a 1997 regulation.[73] This Regulation gives Member States the chance to lay down national annual programmes, in close co-operation with trade organisations and co-operatives. May

---

[68] Since July 1, 2008 Single CMO Regulation 1234/07 [2007] O.J. L299/1.
[69] Since July 1, 2008 Single CMO (quoted above).
[70] Regulation 1518/03 [2003] O.J. L320/07 now Single CMO (quoted above).
[71] Since July 1, 2008 Single CMO (quoted above).
[72] Regulation 2771/75 [1075] O.J. L282/49. Since July 1, 2008 Single CMO Regulation 1234/77 [2007] O.J. L199/1.
[73] Regulation 1221/97 [1997] O.J. L 173/1. Now Single CMO (quoted above).

be included in those programmes: technical assistance, control of varroasis, ratio-nalisation of transhumance, support for laboratories carrying out analyses of honey and applied research to improve the quality of honey. Details for these pro-grammes were laid down in a Commission regulation.[74] See also a directive relat-ing to honey, which establishes a definition of honey and rules concerning labelling in order to inform the consumer of the country of origin of the honey and possible mixtures.[75]

A very important point is that all decisions to be taken in the various fields briefly described above, are proposed by the Commission and need the agreement of the Management Committee set up for each variety.

The market organisations for floriculture (since January 1, 2007), dried fodder (since April 1), seeds (since July 1), flax and hemp[76] (since July 1), were all replaced at various dates in 2008 by the Single CMO.[77]

There also is an organisation for "spirit drinks": their definition, description, presentation, labelling and protection of geographical indication.[78]

(3) The Structural Measures

They concern, among others, the protection of the environment and forestry. The former provides for agricultural production methods compatible with the require-ments of the protection of the environment and the maintenance of the countryside. Its object is to reduce the harmful effects and pollution caused by agriculture, while ensuring recognition of the fundamental function performed by farmers in terms of management of the countryside and protection of natural resources. The latter introduces an Union aid scheme for forestry, measures in agriculture, intended to enable farmers to adjust to the changes arising from the adjustments to the market organisations, particularly by providing economically viable alternatives to the agricultural use of land. In the context of the protection of forests against atmos-pheric pollution and fire, the Council adopted measures to ensure the extension, improvement and reinforcement of the mechanisms set up previously.

(a) Organic Farming[79]

"Organic farming" implies that the farmers use only organically produced seed. It differs from other farming systems in a number of ways. It favours renewable resources and recycling, returning to the soil nutrients found in waste products. Where livestock is concerned, meat and poultry production is regulated with par-ticular concern for animal welfare and by using natural foodstuffs. Organic farm-ing respects the environment's own systems for controlling pests and diseases in raising crops and livestock and avoids the use of synthetic pesticides, herbicides, chemical fertilisers, growth hormones, antibiotics and gene manipulation. Instead organic farmers use a range of techniques that help sustain ecosystems and reduce pollution.

---

[74] Regulation 2300/97 [1997] O.J. L319/4. Now Single CMO (quoted above).
[75] Directive 2001/110 [2001] O.J. L10/47. Now Single CMO (quoted above).
[76] Regulation 246/08 [2008] O.J. L76/1.
[77] See *http://www.ec.europa.eu/agriculture/simplification/cmo/index_en.htm*.
[78] Regulation 110/08 [2008] O.J. L39/16.
[79] See General Report 2004, 111 and *http://www.ec.europa.eu/agriculture/food/index_en.htm*.

Increased consumer awareness of food safety issues and environmental concerns have contributed to the growth of organic farming developing into one of the most dynamic agricultural sectors. It has to be understood as part of a sustainable farming system and a viable alternative to the more traditional approaches in agriculture. Union rules came into force in 1992.[80] For organic farming to enjoy the confidence of consumers, stringent regulations covering production and quality were necessary, as well as measures to prevent fraudulent claims to organic status. Present regulations have evolved into a comprehensive framework for the organic production of crops and livestock and for the labelling, processing and marketing of organic products.[81]

(b) Genetically Modified Food and Feed[82]

Modern biotechnology has many applications in the pharmaceutical and agri-food industries. One example is the use of genetically modified organisms (GMOs) in the food production chain. GMOs are organisms such as plants, animals and micro-organisms (bacteria, viruses, etc.) the genetic characteristics of which have been modified artificially in order to give them a new property (a plant's resistance to a disease or insect, improvement of food's quality or nutritional value, increased crop productivity, a plant's tolerance of a herbicide, etc.). In order to ensure that this development of modern biotechnology, and more specifically of GMOs, takes place in complete safety, the EU has established a legal framework comprising various acts. In this field, the Union issued a Directive on the contained use of genetically modified micro-organisms,[83] a Directive on the deliberate release into the environment of genetically modified organisms,[84] a Regulation on genetically modified food and feed, a Regulation on trans-boundary movements of genetically modified organisms[85] and a Regulation concerning the traceability and labelling of genetically modified organisms and traceability of food and feed products produced from genetically modified organisms.[86]

See, for instance, Commission decisions authorising the placing on the market of products containing consisting of, or produced from genetically modified maize.[87]

(c) Food Safety

According to the Commission,[88] the food safety policy is based on a series of principles established or updated at the beginning of 2000. These principles, applied in

---

[80] Regulation 2092/91 on organic production of agricultural products and indications referring thereto on agricultural products and foodstuffs [1991] O.J. L198/1, supplemented by Regulation 1804/1999 [1999] O.J. L219/1; corrigendum [2000] O.J. L83/35. See also Regulation 1452/2003 [2003] O.J. L206/17, maintaining the derogations provided in Regulation 2092/91 with regard to certain species of seed and vegetative propagating material and laying down procedural rules and criteria relating to that derogation.

[81] See, for instance, Regulation 834/07 [2007] O.J. L189/1 on organic production and labelling of organic products with regard to organic production; labelling and control and implementing detailed rules: Regulation 889/08 [2008] O.J. L250/1, modified [2008] O.J. L337/80.

[82] *http://www.ec.europa.eu./food/food/biotechnology/index_en.htm.*

[83] Directive 90/219 [1990] O.J. L117/1.

[84] Directive 2001/18 [2001] O.J. L106/1, modified [2003] O.J. L268/24; see *Commune de Sausheim* (C-552/07) [2009] E.C.R. 17.02.09 on scope of Directive.

[85] Regulation 1946/03 [2003] O.J. L287/1.

[86] Regulation 1830/03 [2003] O.J. L268/24.

[87] Decisions of October 30, 2009 [2009] O.J. L289/ 21, 25 and 29.

[88] *http://www.europa.eu/scadplus/leg/en/s805000.htm.*

line with the integrated approach "From the Farm to the Fork", specifically include transparency, risk analysis and prevention, the protection of consumer interests and free circulation of safe and high quality products. A certain number of bodies, in particular the European Food Safety Authority[89] are responsible for helping to guarantee food safety. More details below in the chapter on Health Protection.

2. RURAL DEVELOPMENT

As indicated at the beginning of this chapter, rural development has become the second pillar of the Union's agricultural policy. In 1999, the Council adopted a "Framework for [Union] support for sustainable rural development"[90] to accompany and complement other instruments of the CAP. The new rural development policy aims at providing for the improvement of agricultural holdings, to guarantee safety and quality of foodstuffs, to ensure fair and stable incomes for farmers, to ensure that environmental issues are taken into account, to develop complementary and alternative activities, to improve living and working conditions, etc. Rural development is based on the following principles:

- the multi-functionality of agriculture over and above the production of foodstuffs; it recognises and encourages the range of services provided by farmers;
- a multi-sectoral and integrated approach to the rural economy in order to diversify activities, create new sources of income and employment and protect the rural heritage;
- flexible aids for rural development based on subsidiarity and promoting decentralisation, consultation at regional, local and partnership level;
- simplified and more accessible legislation.

The main features are:

- strengthening the agricultural and forestry sector;
- improving the competitiveness of rural areas; and
- preserving the environment and rural heritage.

The Union set up a new Union initiative for rural development: LEADER. It was designed to help rural actors consider the long term potential of their rural region. A total of €5,046.5 million was available for the period 2000–2006.

3. FINANCING THE CAP AND RURAL DEVELOPMENT

As was also mentioned at the beginning of this chapter, one of the basic principles adopted at the onset for the CAP was the financial responsibility of the Union for all the expenses, or "financial solidarity". The European Agricultural Guarantee and Guidance Fund (EAGGF), maybe better known by its French abbreviation, FEOGA, was a Union household name since the very beginning. It was set up in 1962,[91] but it no longer exists as such. It consisted of a guarantee

[89] See above Ch.13: Decentralised Bodies of the Union.
[90] Regulation 1257/99: [1999] O.J. L 160/80, amended [2004] O.J. L 91/11.
[91] [1962] O. J. 991. Spec. Ed. O.J. 1959–1962, 126.

section (expenditures for the price system) and a guidance section (for financing the socio-structural measures). The EAGGF was replaced in 2005 by two Funds: the European Agricultural Guarantee Fund (EAGF) and the European Agricultural Fund for Rural Development (EAFRD).[92] It will be remembered that the European Council approved a European Economic Recovery Plan (EERP) which envisages the initiation of priority action to enable Member States' economies to adjust rapidly to the current challenges and based on a figure amounting to around €200 billion. Of this amount, €1.020 billion is made available to all the Member States via the EAFRD, with a view to developing broadband Internet in rural areas and to strengthen the operations related to priorities laid down in the regulation on support for rural development.[93]

A little history seems called for here to be able to understand references made left and right to the way the CAP was financed. Long acclaimed as the first and only totally integrated economic sector of the Union, the EAGGF grew over the years to absorb nearly 70 per cent of the total Union budget. It not only became a financial burden but a danger for the Union itself. Some Member States were no longer prepared to contribute to the open-ended system that benefited only some Member States, mainly France. The ever-increasing agricultural expenditures were one of the reasons, if not the main one, for the various reforms referred to above and especially the 1992 one. However, outside pressures also played a role. As mentioned, the multilateral trade negotiations within the GATT, the Uruguay Round, forced the Union to strengthen its negotiation position by making some of the required adaptations to its policy with the ensuing reductions in agricultural expenditure.

It resulted, as was explained above, in a shift from market price support to direct payments to farmers. It has ensured transparency and somewhat allowed restoring of market balance.

This however applied only to the Guarantee Section. As described above, the guaranteed price system has been severely curtailed by the latest reform and expenditures were from then on fixed in advance in order to avoid overspending; this was one of the main results of Agenda 2000, adopted in Berlin, and that put a ceiling on the Communities expenditures for a period of seven years. A new reform became inevitable when the Union decided to enlarge to the countries of Central and Eastern Europe. The latter are still overwhelmingly agricultural and the application of the present CAP to those countries would, as the Commission expresses it mildly, "create difficulties".

A reorientation of the CAP with less focus on price support and more on direct income support, as well as on rural development and environment policy helped to reduce the price gap and provided support for the structural adjustment process of acceding countries. Finally, adequate implementation and enforcement of the Union acquis in the candidate countries was essential for the protection of plant, animal and public health in an enlarged Union as a whole. It must be

---

[92] Regulation 1698/05 on support for rural development by the EAFRD, amended [2009] O.J. L30/100 and L144/3, and Regulation 1974/06 lying down detailed rules for the application of Regulation 1698/05 [2006] O.J. L368/15, amended and corrected [2008] O.J. L318/6, amended [2009] O.J. L111/5 and [2009] O.J. L145/17; also Decision 2007/383 fixing the annual breakdown by Member State of the amount for Union support to rural development for the period from January 1, 2007 to December 31, 2013 [2007] O.J. L147/21, amended [2009] O.J.L181/49 and Decision 2009/434 amending Decision 2006/493 [2009] O.J. L144/25 on the minimum amount to be concentrated in the regions eligible under the Convergence Objective.

[93] Regulation 473/09: [2009] O.J. L144/3.

accomplished before the movement of agricultural products without border control can be established.

The Fund is administered by the Commission and the Member States, co-operating within the EAGF Committee, which consists of representatives of the Member States and the Commission.[94] The EAGF finances, among others, refunds for export, intervention measures to regulate agricultural markets, direct payments to farmers and contribution to information and promotion for agricultural products. The EAFRD finances contributions to rural development programmes.

Payments are made by paying agencies accredited by the Member States since only they offer reasonable assurance that the necessary controls have been carried out before granting Union aid to beneficiaries. Maximum expenditure for the EAGF and the EAFRD for each year is laid down by the budgetary authorities by reference to the amounts fixed by the Interinstitutional Agreement and the Financial Perspective set out in Annex 1 to that Agreement.[95] The annual breakdown by Member State of the amount for Union support to rural development for the period 2007–2013, and the minimum amount to be concentrated in regions eligible under the Convergence Objective, was fixed by Council decision.[96]

It can only be hoped that the latest reform will allow an improvement of the market equilibrium and of the internal and international competitiveness of Union agriculture, as well as ensuring a greater stability in farm incomes and a more equitable distribution of the Union's resources. The reform also aimed at helping to secure quality production which is more respectful of the environment and at lower prices for the consumer. It should also mark a new approach to the developing countries, especially in Africa. Agriculture on that continent has suffered over the years a very important reduction in agricultural production because of the competition from subsidised agricultural products from the Union, both within it and in the world. Here more than anywhere else the Union should head the African request of "no aid, but trade": the African countries could produce at much lower cost and equal quality, if given a chance to compete on equal ground with Union producers.

Further Reading

B. Sheridan, *EU Biotechnology Law and Practice. Regulating Genetically Modified and Novel Food Products* (Palladian Law Publishing, 2001).

J. A. Usher, E. C., *Agricultural Law*, 2nd edn (Oxford University Press, 2002).

Melaku Geboye Desta, *The law of international trade in agricultural products* (Kluwer, 2002).

Naomi Salmon, "A European perspective on the precautionary principle. Food safety and the free trade imperative of the WTO" (2003) E.L.Rev. 138.

O'Rourke, *European Food Law* (Palladian Law Publishing, 2002).

Yearly Report of the European Commission, *The Agricultural Situation in the European Union* (Office for Official Publications of the European Communities, Luxembourg).

---

[94] See Decision 1999/468 [1999] O.J. L184/23, modified several times; see above Ch.8: The Commission, laying down procedures for the exercise of powers conferred by the Council.

[95] [2003] O.J. L147/25. See Regulation 1290/05 on the financing of the common agricultural policy [2005] O.J. L2009/1.

[96] Decision 2006/636 [2006] O.J. L261/32, amended [2009] O.J. L8/22.

Chapter Twenty-four

The Common Fisheries Policy (CFP)[1] and Marine Policy

As the Commission indicated:

"[F]ishing and aquaculture are two of the most important uses of the sea. As well as providing a healthy and enjoyable source of food, they create much-needed jobs in costal areas and promote the social and economic well-being of the European Union's fishing regions."[2]

The Commission sees it as its task, among others in this field, to ensure sustainable, i.e. responsible, fishing and aquaculture and secure the future of the fishing industry through the Common Fisheries Policy. Fishing and aquaculture activities are regulated also through international co-operation in order to allow for the continuous renewal of stocks and the protection of the marine ecosystem. The competence of the Union in regard to fisheries is based on the same Treaty provisions as those for agriculture[3] of which they are a part: there are no specific provisions regarding fisheries and/or maritime policies—the TFEU specifies that:

"[R]eference to the common agricultural policy or to agriculture, and the use of the term agricultural shall be understood as also referring to fisheries having regard to the specific characteristics of this sector".[4]

Nevertheless, fisheries acquired a momentum of their own and developed into an autonomous policy, which is examined below.

Since the Second World War, fishery products have become an important food resource, and although this sector only provides a few hundred thousand jobs, compared with millions in agriculture, the industry is also of crucial economic importance to many otherwise disadvantaged coastal areas. It was not until 1970 that the first decisions concerning fisheries were taken by the Union, which used its powers in the following fields. The CFP is based on the principle of common access to all fishing grounds in the Union, monitoring fishing activities, the common organisation of the market,[5] agreements with third countries and structural measures. It came into being in 1983 and takes account of the biological,

---

[1] arts 38–44 TFEU [32–38].

[2] *http://www.ec.europa.eu/fisheries/cfp_en.htm*; some of the data in this chapter has been borrowed from this website.

[3] See *France v United Kingdom* (141/78) [1979] E.C.R. 2923; [1990] 1 C.M.L.R. 6. The shared powers of the Union and the Member States in fishing matters are provided for in art.4(1)(d) TFEU [3(1)(d)] and art.38(3) [32(3)] and Annex I to the Treaty, which includes fisheries within the sphere of the common agricultural policy.

[4] art.38(1)2 TFEU [32].

[5] Regulation 3759/92 on the common organisation of the market in fishery and aquaculture products [1992] O.J. L388/1. The establishment of a common market organisation is based on producer organisations, a price support mechanism and protection for the Union market, a structural policy, conservation and administration of resources, and relations with third countries.

social and economic dimension of fishing. Its main aspects will be briefly examined hereunder, they are: conservation of fish stocks; the common market organisation; agreements with third countries; and structural measures. The Union has a new CFP since 2003 (date of the reform of the PAC); indeed, a new policy was needed to ensure conservation of resources, protection of the marine environment, economic viability of the fishing fleets and good quality food to consumers. As the Commission put it: too many fish had been taken from the sea by fishing, leaving too few adult fish to reproduce and rebuild the stocks. Today, several important fish stocks, such as cod, are on the verge of collapse. Beyond the damage done to fish stocks, such a situation has a significant negative effect on fisherman's income, the balance of the marine ecosystem and the supply of fish to the market.

1. Access to Fishing Grounds

Access to coastal waters, i.e. coastal bands 6 to 12 miles deep, is reserved for fishermen from local ports to protect their fishing rights and help ensure that fishing remains an essential part of the local economy. However, the restriction was not absolute: small fishing boats from a given Member State, which have traditionally operated in the coastal waters of another continued to do so.

Outside the 12-mile band, the general principle of free access to fishing grounds still applies, except for predetermined protected areas where the right to fish is restricted or completely withdrawn. Corresponding decisions are based on biological advice and implemented to protect rich breeding grounds of fish for human consumption.

In 1995, a new system of fishing licences—a kind of identity paper—was introduced for Union fishing boats operating in and outside Union waters. Moreover, a system of fishing permits provides a management mechanism to limit the fishing effort of individual vessels having access to certain fisheries.

2. Conservation of Fish Stocks

Fish stocks need to renew themselves as fish die through natural causes and fishing: to have enough mature fish to renew stocks, small fish must be left to grow and reproduce. It is most surprising, however, that this evidence is not understood and often not accepted by those most closely connected with these products of the sea, i.e. the fishermen. Indeed, in many cases they oppose, by all possible means, the limitations necessarily imposed on their catches to allow renewal of stocks.

To limit the capture of small fish, a number of technical rules have been adopted by the Union: minimum mesh sizes, certain areas are closed, some fishing gears are banned, selective techniques are imposed, minimum fish sizes are imposed and catches and landings have to be recorded in special log books. Conservation was ensured by the annual fixing of Total Allowable Catches (TACs)[6] for all species threatened because of overfishing,[7] taking into account the

---

[6] *Commission v Council* (C-25/94) [1996] E.C.R. I–1469: exclusive competence of the Union in matters relating to conservation of the biological resources of the sea.

[7] For 2009 see Regulation 43/09 fixing for 2009 the fishing opportunities and associated conditions for certain fish stocks and groups of fish stocks, applicable in Community waters and, for Community vessels, in waters where catch limitations are required [2009] O.J. L22/1, corrigendum [2009] O.J. L124/75; for 2010, Regulation 23/2010 [2010] O.J. L21/1.

international agreements and arrangements made with interested third countries. This was complemented by the setting of long-term objectives for attaining and/or maintaining safe levels of adult fish.[8]

Various regulations were adopted in specific sectors and places, such as: measures to reduce incidental catches of cetaceans in fisheries,[9] transposition of the new technical recommendations of the International Commission for the Conservation of Atlantic Tunas,[10] establishment of a definitive plan for the recovery of cod stocks,[11] idem for Northern hake stock.[12] The importance of Mediterranean fisheries was recognised by an ambitious Action Plan and conservation measures relating to waters around Malta.[13]

The TACs are divided among the Member States, in the form of quotas, in pursuance of the principle of relative stability that allows for a global equilibrium among the fishing fleets. Concretely speaking, each Member State concerned keeps a fixed percentage for each stock as originally established.[14]

The accession of new Member States required, of course, an adaptation of the existing quotas especially in so far as they concerned also non-Union waters.[15] After accession, Spain and Portugal, for instance, contested the principle of relative stability before the Court, which however, rejected most of their complaints.[16] Another problem resulted from the so-called quota hopping. This was the transfer of fishing boats from one Member State to the flag of another in order to use the quota allocated to the latter. Certain Member States therefore restricted access to their quotas. The Court has admitted that conditions be imposed in the sense that the boat in question should have some economic ties with that country; it did not admit, however, restrictions based on the nationality or residence of the crew, limitations to the right to land the captures in other Member States or restrict normal fishing activities.[17]

At the end of 2002, the Council adopted various regulations on conservation measures.[18] On that basis, the Council established financial measures for the implementation of the common fisheries policy and in the area of the Law of the Sea.[19]

In 2008 the Council adopted a dozen regulations fixing, for instance, fishing opportunities for certain fish stocks, cod fishing quotas in the Baltic sea, in the Black sea, for certain deep-sea fish, etc.[20]

---

[8] See Regulation 2371/2002 on the conservation and sustainable exploitation of fisheries resources under the CFP [2002] O.J. L358/59, modified [2009] O.J. L343/1.

[9] Regulation 812/04 O.J. L150/12.

[10] Regulation 831/04 O.J. L127/33.

[11] Regulation 423/04 O.J. L70/8, modified [2009] O.J. L343/1.

[12] Regulation 811/04 O.J. L185/1.

[13] Regulation 813/04 O.J. L150/32.

[14] Regulation 894/87 relating to technical measures for the conservation of fisheries resources [1997] O.J. L132/1, modified [1998] O.J. L171/17.

[15] Regulation 170/83 no longer in force. See Regulation 1796/94 [1994] O.J. L187/1.

[16] *Portugal and Spain v Council* (Joined Cases C-63/90 and C-67/90) [1992] E.C.R. I–5073.

[17] *Agegate* (C-3/87) [1989] E.C.R. 4459; [1990] 1 C.M.L.R. 366 and *Jaderow* (216/87) [1989] E.C.R. 4509; [1991] 2 C.M.L.R. 556; *Commission v United Kingdom* (C-246/89) [1991] E.C.R. I–4585; *R. v Secretary of State for Transport Ex p., Factortame* (C-221/89) [1991] E.C.R. I–3905.

[18] Regulation 2371/02 on the conservation and sustainable exploitation of fish stocks under the common fisheries policy [2002] O.J. L358/59 and Regulation 742/2006 adapting certain fish quotas pursuant to Regulation 847/96 introducing additional conditions for year-to-year management for TACs and quotas [2006] O.J. L130/7, modified [2009] O.J. L343/1. Regulation 2347/02 on specific access requirements and associated conditions for deep-sea stocks [2002] O.J. L351/28 and Regulation 254/02, measures to be applicable in 2002 for the recovery of the stock of cod in the Irish sea [2002] O.J. L41/1.

[19] Regulation 871/2006 [2006] O.J. L160/1.

[20] See General Report 2008, 118.

3. MONITORING FISHING ACTIVITIES

The Member States are in charge of implementing the preservation measures taken on their territory and in their waters and, for the vessels flying their flag, outside their territorial waters. The task of the Commission was to monitor their correct application until the end of 2005, when the Union inspection system became operative.[21] The Commission also monitors compliance with TACs (Total Acceptable Catches) and quotas in Union and in certain international waters; the same applies to fishery agreements with third countries and international agreements. The Commission also contributes to the financing of programmes presented by Member States for the acquisition and improvement of means of monitoring and inspection.[22] Satellite technology to check vessel movements is used for all over 15 metre-vessels.[23]

In 2008 a regulation was adopted establishing a Union system to prevent, deter and eliminate illegal, unreported and unregulated fishing.[24] This Regulation aims to ensure the viability of the fish stocks and improve the situation of Union fishermen facing unfair competition from illegal products. Another regulation updates the system of authorisation for fishing activities of Union fishing vessels outside Union waters and of third-country vessels in Union waters.[25] It is intended to better align Union authorisation procedures with international obligation. A new Union framework for the collection, management and use of data in the fisheries sector and support for scientific advice was also issued[26]; it covers the whole process from the collection of data at ports or at sea to their use by the end-users. Another regulation provides a temporary specific action aiming to promote the restructuring of the fishing fleets affected by the economic crisis.[27]

4. AQUACULTURE[28]

Aquaculture means the rearing or culture of aquatic organisms using techniques designed to increase the production of the organisms in question beyond the natural capacity of the environment; the organisms remain the property of a natural or legal person throughout the rearing or culture stage, up to and including harvesting.[29] The principal aquaculture products of the EU are fish (trout, salmon, sea bass, sea bream) and molluscs (mussels, oysters and clams). Aquaculture constitutes 17 per cent of the volume and 27 per cent of the value of the total fishery production of the EU. It is essentially made up of three sub-sectors: freshwater fish

---

[21] Regulation 2241/87 establishing certain control measures for fishing activities [1987] O.J. L207/1.

[22] Council Decision 89/631 [1989] O.J. L364/64, modified [1992] O.J. L213/35 extending the programme to include the Mediterranean. It was extended by Decision 2001/431 [2001] O.J. L154/22.

[23] From: *http://www.ec.europa.eu/fisheries/publications/reform_en.htm.*

[24] Regulation 1005/08 [2008] O.J. L286. Borrowed from General Report 2008, 117.

[25] Regulation 1006/08 [2008] O.J. L286.

[26] Regulation 199/08 [2008] O.J. L60.

[27] Regulation 744/08: [2008] O.J. L202.

[28] Based on, among others, *http://www.ec.europa.eu/fisheries/studies_reports_en.htm.*

[29] Regulation 1263/99 [1999] O.J. L161/54 and Regulation 2792/99 laying down the detailed rules and arrangements regarding Union structural assistance in the fishery sector [1999] O.J. L337/10 were replaced by Regulation 1198/06 (the basic Regulation) which was implemented by Regulation 498/07 [2007] O.J. L120/1 laying down detailed rules for the implementation of Regulation 1198/06 on the European Fisheries Fund.

farming—unfortunately there is limited demand for fresh water fish; marine mollusc farming—locally extremely important in economic terms and for job creation; marine fish farming—the most recent development and the most complex, it suffers from over-production and environmental problems since fish are fed with industrial feed.

Aquaculture is spread widely over the EU and often in rural areas which depend on fishing. The EU has a vast legal armour[30] on aquaculture; it has to cope with problems in the context of health protection, environment and market instability.

5. THE COMMON ORGANISATION OF THE MARKET

The common organisation of the market in fishery and aquaculture products was set up in 1970 with the following objectives:

- applying common marketing standards;
- establishing producers' organisations;
- instituting a price support system based on intervention mechanisms or compensation mechanisms; and
- establishing a regime for trade with non-member countries.

It was, as was the rest of agriculture, reformed in 1992. In 1993, a new regulation[31] strengthened the controls and extended monitoring beyond the catching of fish, to other aspects of the CFP, such as structures, fish marketing and aquaculture. In addition all links in the fishery chain from producer to consumer, whether catches themselves, landings, transport or actual sales, are now monitored and documented. This provides for much more detailed checks of the data recorded in the fishermen's logbooks. Penalties are decided by national courts. They may range from heavy fines, confiscation of fishing nets, of fish caught and even of the boat itself to temporary suspension or permanent withdrawal of fishing licences.

Various regulations were adopted to tighten the control on fishing activities: for instance, electronic transmission of information on fishing activities and for remote sensing,[32] implementing rules on the Union fleet policy,[33] detailed provisions regarding a satellite-based vessel monitoring system.[34]

The Union also encourages research with various programmes such as the Fisheries and Aquaculture Research (FAR) and AIR, an integrated programme in agriculture and agro-industry.

---

[30] See, for instance, Directive 1999/29 on the undesirable substances and products in animal nutrition [1999] O.J. L6/45, modified [2001] O.J. L115/32; Regulation 466/2001 setting maximum levels for certain contaminants in foodstuffs [2001] O.J. L77/1, amended [2001] O.J. L321/1; Directive 91/67 on measures governing the placing on the market of aquaculture animals and products [1991] O.J. L46/1, amended [2003] O.J. L122/1; and Directive 93/53 on measure for the control of certain fish diseases [1993] O.J. L175/28, amended [2001] O.J. L99/11.

[31] Regulation 2847/93 establishing a control system applicable to the common fisheries policy, adapted for bluefin tuna by Regulation 446/08 [2008] O.J. L134/11. See *Commission v Italy* (C-249/08) [2009] E.C.R. 29.10.09.

[32] Regulation 1461/03 [2003] O.J. L208/14.

[33] Regulation 1438/03 [2003] O.J. L204/21.

[34] Regulation 2244/03 [2003] O.J. L333/17 implementing Regulation 2371/02 on the conservation and sustainable exploitation of fisheries resources under the CFP [2004] O.J. L240/17.

A new Common Organisation for the Markets in fishery and aquaculture products was adopted in 2000 and entered into force in 2001. It aims to:

- encourage fisherman to fish only what can be sold;
- strengthen industry organisations, particularly Producers' Organisations, and make them more competitive;
- enable consumers to know what they are buying;
- ensure a better match between supply and demand; and
- protect employment in the catching sector as well as in the processing industry.

To achieve these aims, new measures were introduced:

- obligation for the Producers' Organisations to set up fishing programmes to adapt supply to demand;
- support for the development of inter-professional organisations;
- updating the intervention mechanism[35];
- the obligation for retailers to provide better information to consumers; and
- improving supply conditions for the processing industry.

6. Agreements with Third Countries and International Conventions

Since 1976, the Union has been exclusively competent to handle international fishing negotiations. Fishing agreements were signed with a number of third countries[36] in order to safeguard traditional fishing rights of Union vessels or to seek new opportunities.

Indeed, without those agreements the general extension of fishing zones to 200 miles and the resulting substantial reduction in fishing opportunities would have had serious repercussions for Union fishermen. Furthermore, in the present circumstances of surplus capacity in Union waters, these agreements represent a means of reducing fishing efforts in those waters. Multilateral agreements have also been concluded with a view to the Union's participation in the international agreements covering the North-West,[37] North-East, East, Central and South-East Atlantic: the North-Atlantic Salmon Conservation Organisation (NASCO), the North-East Atlantic Fisheries[38] Commission (NEAFC), The Southern Indian Ocean Fisheries Agreement,[39] the International Commission for the South East Atlantic Fisheries (ICSEAF), the Fishery Committee for the Eastern-Central Atlantic (CECAF), the International Whaling Commission, etc.[40]

To date, the Union has concluded several dozen agreements with countries from Africa[41] and the Indian Ocean and from the North Atlantic area. In the latter area problems developed mainly with Canada, which forced the Council to

---

[35] Regulation 2792/1999 (quoted above).

[36] See various General Reports.

[37] See Regulation 1386/07 laying down conservation and enforcement measures applicable in the Regulatory Area of North-West Atlantic Fisheries Organization [2007] O.J. L318/1, modified [2008] O.J. L157/1, amended [2008] O.J. L157/1.

[38] See, for instance, Regulation 770/04 [2004] O.J. L123/4.

[39] [2006] O.J. L196/14.

[40] See General Report 1989, 270.

[41] See, for instance, fishery partnership agreements with Côte d'Ivoire: Regulation 242/08 [2008] O.J. L75/51; and Guinea-Bissau: Regulation 241/08 [2008] O.J. L75/49.

regulate access and catches for the North-West Atlantic Fisheries Organisation (NAFO) Convention area.[42]

Different categories of fisheries agreements exist, which are distinguished according to the type of concession offered: reciprocal arrangements; access to surplus stock; access to stocks in return for market access; access to stocks in return for financial compensation; and access to stocks in return for payment and market access. For more details see the annual General Reports published by the Commission in February of each year.[43]

7. STRUCTURAL MEASURES—THE EUROPEAN FISHERIES FUND[44]

These measures help the fishing sector to adapt to present needs. Funding is available for projects in all branches and for market and development research, for modernisation of fishing fleets as well as getting rid of excess fishing capacity. The first rules laying down a common structural policy for the fishing industry were enacted in 1970.[45] Following enlargement, a new regulation was adopted in 1976.[46] Those provisions enabled the Union to support financially, through the agricultural fund, fish processing and marketing development projects, building of inshore fishing vessels, refitting of vessels and extension of fish farming schemes. In 1977, common measures were adopted to improve the conditions under which agricultural and fishery products are processed and marketed[47] and in 1983 the Council adopted common measures for restructuring, modernising and developing the fishing industry and for developing aquaculture[48] and measures to encourage exploratory fishing.[49] Once again new structural aspects of the fisheries policy were adopted, this time in 1986,[50] to finance the construction of fishing vessels, aquaculture and structural work in coastal waters, modernisation of fishing vessels and exploratory fishing voyages, while at the same time financing programmes to reduce the capacity of the Member States' fishing fleets to bring them into line with the available fish stocks.[51]

The actions relating to the transformation and the commercialisation of products of fishery and aquaculture have as their objective the modernisation and the rationalisation of the factories, mainly sanitary conditions. Following the reform of the Structural Funds, the Union established, within that framework, a

[42] Regulation 3927/92 laying down certain conservation and management measures for fishery resources in the Regulatory Area as defined in the Convention on Future Multilateral Co-operation in the North-West Atlantic Fisheries [1992] O.J. L397/67 and Regulation 3928/92 establishing a NAFO pilot observer scheme applicable to Union fishing vessels operating on the Regulatory Area of the North-West Atlantic Fisheries Organisation (NAFO) [1992] O.J. L397/78.
[43] General Report 2002, 442 and 443. See for instance Council Regulation 1765/03 on the conclusion of an agreement with the government of the republic of Guinea setting out the fishing opportunities and financial contribution [2003] O.J. L256/1.
[44] Regulation 1198/06 [2006] O.J. L223/1 on the European Fishery Fund.
[45] Regulation 2141/70 [1970] O.J. L236/1.
[46] Regulation 101/76 [1976] O.J. L20/19.
[47] Regulation 355/77 [1977] O.J. L51/1.
[48] Regulation 2908/83 [1983] O.J. L290/1 and Regulation 3166/83 L316/1.
[49] Regulation 2909/83 [1983] O.J. L290/9.
[50] Regulation 4028/86 [1986] O.J. L376/7.
[51] General Report 1988, 297 and Directive 83/515 [1983] O.J. L290/15).

Financial Instrument for Fisheries Guidance (FIFG).[52] This permitted a doubling of the available resources. The Union adopted a regulation in 2002 lying down the detailed rules and arrangements regarding Union structural assistance in the fisheries sector.[53]

The Union fisheries suffer from overcapacity of fleets in comparison to diminishing resources; it is essential to re-establish an equilibrium. This can only be achieved through several activities: the Union must increase the effectiveness of the TACs—reinforce the monitoring, reduce the fishing capacity; compensate the socio-economic consequence with accompanying measures; and, at the same time, guarantee a constant supply at reasonable prices. Important changes are required while the Union, on the other hand, needs to import huge quantities to satisfy the internal demand.

Mention must also be made of the adoption of the PESCA Union initiative[54] that seeks to generate clearly focused projects to help the fishing sector to adapt and coastal areas to diversify their economic activities[55] and of the Multi-annual Programme to restructure the Union fishing industry providing for cuts in fleet tonnage and engine power. Member States finally accepted the need for a common set of vessel measurements and agreed on the creation of a Union register of vessels to make the information on fishing capacity more open and easy to check. This had been lacking due to Member States' reluctance to accept the inevitable. However, cuts are now expressed in "fishing efforts" calculated by multiplying the capacity of a fishing vessel expressed in tonnage and engine power by the number of days spent at sea. Furthermore, to protect depleted stock from overfishing, the totality of fish stocks was divided into three groups and Union vessels were also split into groups or "segments", according to the main fisheries. These measures were designed to match stocks and vessels.

On the basis of a scientific study (the Gulland Report), the Commission made recommendations for cuts and the Council agreed to reduce fishing efforts for fish living at the bottom of the sea (demersal) by 20 per cent (the Commission had recommended 30 per cent) and flat fish (benthic) by 15 per cent (the Commission had recommended 20 per cent). Fishing efforts can also be reduced, of course, by scrapping vessels or keeping them in port for set periods of time. The choice was left to the Member States; all chose to eliminate excess capacity and, as a result, overall fleet was cut by 7 per cent.[56]

The Multi-annual Guidance Programme (MAGP) IV (1997–2001) further reduced fishing efforts. The validity of this MAGP was prolonged by the Council.[57] Actions for the fisheries sector outside Objective 1 region[58] will be supported,

---

[52] Regulation 2080/93 laying down provisions for implementing Regulation 2052/88 as regards the financial instrument of fisheries guidance [1993] O.J. L193/1 and Regulation 4253/88. See *Vereniging Nationaal Overlegorgaan Sociale Werkvoorziening A.O.* (Joined Cases C-383/06, C-384/06, C-385/06 and C-386/06) [2008] E.C.R. I–1597, concerning obligations of Member States to recover any amount lost as a result of irregularity or negligence.

[53] Regulation 2369/02 [2002] O.J. L 358/49. See also Regulation 498/2007 laying down detailed rules for the implementation of the European Fisheries Fund [2007] O.J. L120/1.

[54] See below, Ch.32: Regional Policy / Economic, Social and Territorial Cohesion, for the Union Initiatives.

[55] In 1997, this initiative was endowed with 21,456 million ECUs. See also Decision 97/292 on a specific measure to encourage Italian fishermen to diversify out of certain fishing activities [1997] O.J. L121/20.

[56] See General Report 2002, 435.

[57] See below, Ch.32: Regional Policy / Economic, Social and Territorial Cohesion.

[58] Regulation 1198/2006 [2006] O.J. L223/1.

according to the decisions taken by the Berlin European Council of March 24–25, 1999, by the Financial Instrument for Fisheries Guidance (FIFG) with an amount of €1.1 billion over the period 2000–2006. A new European Fisheries Fund (EFF) was established in 2006[59] establishing a framework for Union support for a sustainable development of the fisheries sector, fisheries areas and inland fishing.

With regard to State aids to the fisheries sector, see the de minimis Regulation.[60]

In 2004, the Council introduced special arrangements for the management of the fishing fleets of the outermost regions in order to take account of their structural, social and economic situation.[61]

The European Fisheries Fund (EFF) was set up in 2002 and renewed in 2006[62]; it forms part of the Structural Funds; for more information see below, Ch.32: Regional Policy/Economic, Social and Territorial Cohesion.

8. MARINE ENVIRONMENTAL POLICY[63]

In line with the Decision of Parliament and the Council of 2002 laying down the Sixth Community Environment Action Programme,[64] a thematic strategy for the protection and conservation of the marine environment was developed with the overall aim of promoting sustainable use of the seas and conserving marine ecosystems.

The establishment of marine protected areas, including areas already designated or to be designated under the Directive on the conservation of natural habitats and of wild fauna and flora (Habitats Directive),[65] and under the Directive on the conservation of wild birds (Birds Directive)[66] and also under international and regional agreements to which the Union[67] or Member States concerned are Parties, constitute an important contribution to the achievement of good environmental status under the 2008 Directive establishing a framework for Union action in the fields of marine environmental policy (Marine Strategy Framework Directive).[68]

The Directive only applies to Member States with coastal waters.

The Commission is empowered[69] to lay down criteria and methodological standards to be used by the Member States and to adopt specifications and standardised methods for monitoring and assessment.

---

[59] Regulation 639/2004 on the management of fishing fleets registered in the Union outermost regions [2004] O.J. L102/9 and Regulation 2104/04 laying down detailed implementation rules [2004] O.J. L365/19, corrected [2005] O.J. L 252/6, amended [2008] O.J. L327/1.

[60] Regulation 875/07 [2007] O.J. L193/6.

[61] This section is partly taken from *http://www.ec.europa.eu./fisheries/cfp/control_enforcement/ reform_control_control_ en.htm.*

[62] Regulation 1198/06 [2006] O.J. L223/1,

[63] Regulation 744/08 [2008]O.J. L202/1.

[64] [2002] O.J. L242/1.

[65] [1992] O.J. L206/7, amended by Directive 2006/105 [2006] O.J. L363/368.

[66] [1979] O.J. L103/1, amended by Directive 2006/105 (quoted above).

[67] Convention on the Protection of the Marine Environment in the Baltic Sea Area [1994] O.J.L73/19; idem for the North-East Atlantic [1998] O.J. L104/1, Convention on the Protection of the Marine Environment and the Coastal Region of the Mediterranean [1977] O.J. L240/1, [1999] O.J. L322/32, [1983] O.J. L67/1; and [1999] O.J. L322/18.

[68] [2008] O.J. L164/19. The above passage is quoted from that Directive.

[69] Since those measures are of general scope and are designed to amend non-essential elements, the measures must be adopted in accordance with the regulatory procedure with scrutiny (Decision 1999/468, art.5a).

PART FIVE: POLICIES OF THE UNION AND THE MEMBER STATES

Chapter Twenty-five

Taxation

Title VII of the TFEU provides for, "common rules on competition, taxation and approximation of laws." All of them aim at guaranteeing the fundamental principles of the Treaty, among which is "equal treatment", which forms the basis of the internal market. It seems evident, that, for instance, cartels, abuses of dominant positions, State aids and monopolies can restrict the basic freedoms, for instance, the free movement of goods. Similarly, a different tax treatment by a Member State of products coming from another Member State, risks preventing the commercialisation of those products in the first State. Finally, as shall be seen, differences between the provisions laid down by laws, regulations and administrative provisions of Member States may directly affect the freedom of establishment and the functioning of the internal market, thereby rendering more difficult the free flow of goods within the Union.

In order to remove tax obstacles, discriminatory taxation is prohibited, except where there exists a specific justification for it, and disparities between tax provisions of the Member States should be eliminated by approximation. The Treaty prohibits the direct or indirect imposition of tax on products from other Member States[1] or of "any internal taxation of any kind" in excess of that imposed on similar domestic products.[2] This basic Treaty provision gave rise to an abundance of case law. There is, in the first place, the definition of the term "taxation". The fact that the Treaty refers to "any kind", indicates that it must be interpreted widely. This was confirmed by the Court.[3] Even an import surcharge, which, at first sight, might be viewed as a charge having an equivalent effect to a customs duty, must, according to the Court, be assessed in the light of the tax provisions, where the surcharge is added to a general duty that forms part of a general system of internal dues.[4] Obviously, stamp duties[5] and fees for a mark on precious metal[6] constitute internal taxation. A distinction between the latter and customs duties and charges having equivalent effect should be possible on the simple basis, that the latter are levied, as was seen, at the occasion of a product crossing a border between Member States. Taxes, on the other hand, are levied once the products are inside the territory. The distinction, however, is not always that easy.

---

[1] The expression "other Member States" includes products from third countries in free circulation; see *Co-Frutta* (193/85) [1987] E.C.R. 2085.

[2] art.110,2 TFEU [90,2] has direct effect, see *Finck-Frucht v Hauptzollamt München-Landsbergerstrasse* (27/67) [1968] E.C.R. 223; [1968] C.M.L.R. 187.

[3] *Schottle v Finanzamt Freudenstadt* (20/76) [1977] E.C.R. 247; [1977] 2 C.M.L.R. 98: taxation imposed indirectly on products must be interpreted as including a charge imposed on international transport of goods by road according to the distance covered on the national territory and the weight of the goods.

[4] *Haahr Petroleum v Abenra Havn* (C-90/94) [1997] E.C.R. I–4085; [1998] 1 C.M.L.R. 771.

[5] *Commission v Belgium* (77/69) [1970] E.C.R. 237; [1974] 1 C.M.L.R. 203: the rate was the same, but the basis on which it was applied resulted in heavier taxes for the imported products.

[6] *Statens Kontrol v Larsen* (142/77) [1978] E.C.R. 1543; [1979] 2 C.M.L.R. 680.

As for the term "indirect", the Court decided that it must also be widely interpreted.[7] For instance, although Member States are free to subject cars to a road tax that increases progressively depending on an objective criterion, the Treaty prohibits the charging on cars exceeding a given power of a special fixed tax, where the only cars subject to the special tax are imported cars, in particular from other Member States.[8] On the other hand, in a later judgment, the Court decided that a progressive tax is not prohibited solely because only imported products come within the most heavily taxed category. Such taxation only breaches the prohibition of the Treaty if it may deter consumers from purchasing the more heavily taxed imported cars, to the benefit of products of domestic manufacture of which there are practically none in the most heavily taxed category.[9]

The term "similar" refers, according to the Court, to products having the same characteristics and meeting the same needs from the point of view of the consumer.[10] It is therefore necessary to determine the scope of the prohibition on the basis, not of the criterion of the strictly identical "nature" of the products, but on that of their similar and comparable "use".

The Treaty also prohibits the imposition on the products from other Member States of any internal taxation of such a nature, as to afford indirect protection to other products.[11] This provision covers all forms of indirect taxation that protects products which, without being similar, are nevertheless in competition, even partial, indirect or potential, with certain imported products.[12]

As mentioned already, every rule has its exceptions, and this applies also in the case of the tax provisions. As was just mentioned in the example concerning cars, not every tax that penalises imported products heavier than national products, is prohibited. The Court has developed a theory according to which discrimination can be accepted on the basis of "objective criteria", such as the nature of the products used or the production process employed, as long as it pursues "economic policy objectives" that are compatible with Union law and are not discriminatory or protective in their nature.[13] The Court considered that, although the taxation resulted in restraining imports, it had an equivalent economic effect in the State itself. The reader will remember that with regard to the prohibition of measures having an effect equivalent to a quantitative restriction with regard to the free movement of goods, the Court adopted a similar position. It considered that a national measure prohibiting the sale of a product at a loss, could indeed restrict imports, but pursued an acceptable economic objective and was applicable without discrimination to all products.[14] The same principle applies if the object is to protect the environment.

For the sake of completeness, mention must be made of the prohibition imposed on the Member States to repay internal taxation exceeding that taxation

---

[7] *Molkerei-Zentrale Westfalen v Hauptzollamt Paderborn* (28/67) [1968] E.C.R. 143; [1968] C.M.L.R. 187.

[8] *Humblot* (112/84) [1985] E.C.R. 1367; [1986] 2 C.M.L.R. 338.

[9] *Jacquier v Directeur Général des Impots* (C-113/94) [1995] E.C.R. I–4203.

[10] *Commission v France* (168/78) [1979] E.C.R. 855.

[11] art.110,2 TFEU [90.2].

[12] See the cases mentioned above.

[13] *Chemial Farmaceutici v DAF* (140/79) [1981] E.C.R. 1, concerned taxation which favoured the production of alcohol from agricultural products rather than from petroleum derivatives, and, although it results in restraining the importation of synthetic alcohol, it has an economic policy justification.

[14] *Keck and Mithouard* (Joined Cases C-267/91 and C-268/91) [1993] E.C.R. I–6097; [1995] 1 C.M.L.R. 101.

imposed directly or indirectly, where products are exported to any Member State.[15] The same prohibition applies to remissions or repayments, in respect of exports to other Member States, of charges other than turnover taxes, excise duties and other forms of indirect taxation, unless the measures contemplated have been previously approved for a limited period by the Council.[16] The same prohibition applies to the imposition of countervailing charges in respect of imports from Member States.

The Council's power to harmonise national tax laws is limited to the legislation on turnover taxes, excise duties and other forms of indirect taxation.[17] And the Council may only act by unanimity, in accordance with a special legislative procedure,[18] after having consulted Parliament and the SEC, and, "to the extent that such harmonisation is necessary to ensure the establishment and the functioning of the internal market and to avoid distortion of competition".[19] Notwithstanding those limitations, an impressive and exceedingly important legislative programme has been implemented over the years.

1. INDIRECT TAXATION

(1) Value Added Tax (VAT)

VAT is a general tax on the consumption of goods and services and any exclusion of it requires a specific provision. The legal basis for this cumulative multi-stage turnover tax was adopted in 1977 by the Sixth VAT Directive that was replaced in 2006 by a new directive.[20] The Directive established a uniform VAT coverage. Currently there is a standard rate of 15 per cent and an optional "reduced rate" at 5 per cent (only for supplies of goods and services referred to in an exhaustive list). However, there are still a great number of derogations to this Directive, especially for new Member States or special services. The scope of the Directive has been extended to electronically delivered services.[21]

The importance of VAT for the Union derives, inter alia, from the fact that since 1970 a percentage of VAT collected by Member States belongs to the Union as "own resource".[22] With the entering into force of the internal market at the end of 1992, that implied the elimination of the fiscal frontiers within the Union,

---

[15] art.111 TFEU [91].

[16] art.112 TFEU [92].

[17] art.113 TFEU [93]. See Regulation 659/99 [1999] O.J. L83/1 laying down detailed rules for the application of [TFEU Article 113], implemented by Regulation 794/04 [2004] O.J. L140/1 establishing compulsory comprehensive State aid notification form, amended as regards Part III.10 of its Annex I [2008] O.J. L313/1.

[18] See art.289,2 TFEU.

[19] art.289,2 TFEU.

[20] The Sixth Council Directive 77/388 on the harmonisation of the laws of the Member States relating to turnover taxes—Common system of value added tax: uniform basis of assessment [1977] O.J. L145/1 was repealed by Directive 2006/112 on a common system of VAT [2006] O.J. L347/1, amended [2009] O.J. L.14/7, amended [2010] O.J. L10/19. See Regulation 1798/03 on administrative co-operation on VAT [2003] O.J. L.264/1, modified [2009] O.J. L.14/1. See *Welcome Trust v Commissioners of Customs and Excise* (C-155/94) [1996] E.C.R. I–3013; [1996] 2 C.M.L.R. 909.

[21] E-commerce Directive, Directive 2002/38 [2002] O.J. L128/41, as amended. The validity for special VAT arrangements for those products have been extended until end 2008 by the Council at its 2774th Council Meeting (see 16325/06 [Press 354]).

[22] See above Ch.14: Financing Union Activities.

new rules had to be adopted concerning the collection of VAT. Agreement was reached on a Transitional VAT System, which is still applicable. All tax checks and formalities at intra-Union frontiers have been abolished. For private persons the current system provides for VAT to be paid in the country of origin of the product or service, whereas for transactions between taxable persons VAT is still collected in the country of destination of the product or service in question. At the end of the transitional period, the definitive VAT system will be based on payment in the Member State in which the goods or services originated.[23] See below: the VAT package.

Products or services sold on markets outside the Internal Market are not subject to VAT. In order to combat VAT evasion and avoidance a framework for co-operation between the national tax authorities of the Member States was set up; it provides in particular for closer co-operation and mutual assistance.[24] In addition, in 1993 a VAT information exchange system (VIES) was established.[25] The co-operation was recently simplified, decentralised and reinforced.

In 2008 the Council (Ecofin) adopted the so-called VAT package[26]: place of supply rules changed January 1, 2010. The package contains substantial changes affecting the place of supply for business to consumer (B2C) and business to business (B2B) services, the rules on cross-border refunds, and administrative co-operation and exchange of information among Member States. The final adoption of the package entails a major revolution for businesses engaged in cross-border trade. It will oblige companies to rethink how their services flow is planned as well as their compliance and reporting obligations. The general rule for B2B services will be the place where the customer is established, whereas for B2C it remains the place where the supplier is established, except for electronically provided services, telecom and broadcasting services: the place of supply will be the place where the customer is established. Exceptions to these rules will be introduced and maintained (e.g. cultural, catering and services connected to immovable property).

Several other directives were adopted in 2008: concerning indirect taxes on the raising of capital[27]; on mutual assistance for the recovery of claims relating to certain duties, levies, taxes; and certain other measures.[28]

(2) Excise Duties

Excise duties are indirect taxes on the consumption or the use of certain products. A basic directive was adopted in 1992, before the establishment of the internal

---

[23] Directive 91/680 supplementing the common system of value added tax and amending Directive 77/388 with a view to the abolition of the fiscal frontiers [1991] O.J. L376/1. The rates of VAT to be applied were established by Directive 92/77 [1992] O.J. L316/1.

[24] Directive 77/799 on mutual assistance by the competent authorities of the Member States in the field of direct taxation [1977] O.J. L336/15 and Directive 76/308 were extended to VAT by Directive 79/1071 [1979] O.J. L331/10.

[25] Now under a single legal framework, Regulation 1798/2003 on administrative co-operation in the field of value added tax [2003] O.J. L264/1.

[26] Directive 2008/8 [2008] O.J. L.44/11 and Directive 2008/9 [2008] O.J. L44/23 and Regulation 143/08 [2008] O.J. L44/1. See General Report 2008, 44.

[27] Directive 2008/7 [2008] O.J. L46/11.

[28] Directive 2008/55 [2008] O.J. L150/28. See detailed implementing rules: Regulation 1179/08 [2008] O.J. L319/21.

market.[29] It is based on the principles that the imposition of excise duties should be identical in all Member States; that products subject to excise duties that are bought and transported by private people for their own use are to be taxed in the Member State of origin[30] and that for commercial traffic, the excise duty on goods is imposed by the Member State of destination. However, the rates are still laid down by Member States; in other words no harmonisation has yet been accepted by them, except for some products[31] with the consequence that trade is distorted to the advantage of those Member States with low rates. That is why for travellers there exist some limitations on quantities.[32] The Mutual Assistance Directive[33] applies also to excise duties. The fact that it has not been possible yet to achieve a harmonised common system of excise duties within the Union means that the internal market cannot function properly.

Union law relating to excise duties can be divided into three main groups:

- the structure of the tax to be applied to a particular group of products;
- the rates; and
- the movement and storage of goods subject to excise duties.

The most commonly applied excise duties are those on manufactured tobacco products,[34] energy products[35] and alcoholic beverages.[36] The rates for those products have been the object of approximation by the Council.[37]

In 1998, Parliament and the Council established a programme of Union action to ameliorate the internal taxation systems on the internal market, the FISCALIS programme.[38] Originally established for four years it was extended to 2007[39] and subsequently to 2013. The programme has a budget of €157 million and started in 2008. The programme is intended to improve the operation of the indirect taxation systems in the internal market. It is designed to:

- improve the taxation officials' knowledge of Union law;
- secure wide-ranging and effective co-operation among the Member States as well as between them and the Union;
- reduce the costs born by economic operators in complying with Union VAT and excise legislation; and

---

[29] Directive 2008/118 [2009] O.J. L9/12, on the general arrangements for excise duty. Repealing Directive 92/12 [1992] O.J. L76/1.

[30] See *Joustra* (C-5/05) [2005] E.C.R. I-11075.

[31] But see, for instance, Directive 92/84 on the approximation of the rates of excise duty on alcohol and alcoholic beverages [1992] O.J. L316/29.

[32] See *http://www.ec.europa.eu/taxationcustoms/common/travellers/withineu/indexen.htm*.

[33] Directive 77/799 concerning mutual assistance by the competent authorities of the Member States in the field of direct taxation [1977] O.J. L336/15, amended many times, the title is now "concerning mutual assistance by the competent authorities of the Member States in the field of direct taxation, certain excise duties and taxation of insurance premiums".

[34] [1995] O.J. L291/40, amended [2002] O.J. L46/26.

[35] Directive 2003/96 restructuring the Union framework for the taxation of energy products and electricity [2003] O.J. L283/51, as amended.

[36] [1992] O.J. L316/21.

[37] For tobacco products: Directive 92/79 and Directive 92/80 [1992] O.J. L316/8, amended several times; for energy products: Directive 2003/96 [2003] O.J. L283/51, as amended; and for alcoholic beverages Directive 92/84 [1992] O.J. L319/29.

[38] [1998] O.J. L126/1.

[39] Decision 2235/2002 [2002] O.J. L2341/1, amended [2004] O.J. L138/12. See the ex post evaluation by the Commission: COM(2008) 623.

- improve the efficiency of administrative proceedings. It will also contribute towards the development of trans-European computerised systems in the fiscal area.

One of the main reasons for setting up the programme was to fight against fiscal fraud.

In order to replace the current Administrative Accompanying Document[40] (AAD) for duty suspended excise goods transported between Member States, an Excise Movement and Control System (EMCS) will in future monitor their movement.[41]

General arrangements were agreed upon to strengthen the fight against tax fraud and to simplify the procedures applicable to the movement of products subject to excise tax.[42]

2. DIRECT TAXES

Direct taxes, such as taxes on income or wealth, remain within the exclusive competence of the Member States. However, the Court has consistently held that, in the absence of harmonisation, the taxation by Member States must respect the fundamental Treaty principles on the free movement of goods, persons, services and capital. In particular, there may not be any direct or indirect discrimination on the basis of nationality, nor may there be any unjustified restrictions to the basic freedoms.[43] Nonetheless, the Council and the Representatives of the Governments of the Member States adopted in 1998 a resolution on a Code of Conduct for Business Taxation and Taxation of Saving.[44] The aim was to tackle tax obstacles to cross-border activities within the internal market, prevent significant losses of tax revenue and to help tax structure to develop in a more employment-friendly way. In order to avoid harmful tax competition between the Member States, to avoid double taxation and to safeguard the Treaty freedoms, the Commission proposed, in 2001, a "Tax Package" consisting of:

- a code of conduct to eliminate harmful business tax regimes;
- a measure to ensure an efficient minimum level of taxation of savings income; and
- a measure to eliminate source taxes on cross-border payments on interests and royalties between associated companies.[45]

Today there exist several legislations concerning personal income and company tax.

As for taxes on personal income the Council adopted a Directive on the taxations of saving income in the form of interest payments.[46] Although the

---

[40] Regulation 2719/92 on the accompanying administrative document for the movement under duty-suspension arrangements of products subject to excise duty [1992] O.J. 276/1.

[41] Decision 1152/2003 on computerising the movement and surveillance of excisable products [2003] O.J. L162/5.

[42] Directive 2008/118 [2008] O.J. L9/12, repealing Directive 92/12.

[43] See, for instance, *Commission v France* (270/83) [1986] ECR 273.

[44] [1998] O.J. C99/1 and C2/6.

[45] See for more details Communication of May 23, 2001 on "Tax policy in the European Union-Priorities for the years ahead" (COM(2001) 260) and IP/03/787.

[46] Directive 2003/48 [2003] O.J. L157/38, it is applicable since January 1, 2005; it established an automatically information exchange system of information reporting, except for Belgium, Luxembourg and Austria because of their banking secrecy but as well because of their fear of losing bank clients

Commission had wanted to also eliminate obstacles to the taxation of pensions,[47] the Council did not come to an agreement. Also for dividend income of individuals, there is no intention of harmonisation at Union level[48] and therefore tax obstacles can only be tackled by referring to the principles of Union law. The Commission has also issued a recommendation concerning the taxation of cross-border workers,[49] which has been largely confirmed by the Court. It ruled that direct taxes must be levied in a way that is in consistency with Union law.[50] The Court pointed out that non-residents should not be taxed more heavily than residents, if they derive most of their income from the State of employment.[51]

Concerning company tax, several rules were adopted: first of all, in 1969, a Directive concerning indirect taxes on the raising of capital[52] that gives the Member State the right, but not the obligation to impose such taxes, secondly, to impose capital duty at a minimum level of 1 per cent on the creation of a company in that Member State, thirdly a 1990 Directive on cross-border mergers[53] and, finally, a Parent-Subsidiary Directive.[54]

In 1993 followed a Directive on a common system of taxation applicable to interest and royalty payments made between associated companies of different Member States (I + R Directive).[55] This Directive abolishes the withholding tax on royalty payments and interest payments made in a Member State, provided that the beneficial owner of the payments is a company established in another Member State. In order to combat harmful tax competition, the Council adopted in 1997 a Code of Conduct that requires the Member States to refrain from introducing any new harmful tax measures and to phase out existing harmful tax measures.[56] Harmful tax measures have been identified in a report[57] and the Commission has published a notice on State aid guidelines relating to direct business taxation.[58] Multinational companies can allocate their profits by transfer

---

to other countries with a banking secrecy such as Switzerland, the Principalities of Andorra, Liechtenstein and Monaco and the Republic of San Marino. For this reason, the EC has negotiated special agreements in order to ensure that those countries adopt measures equivalent to those provided for in Directive 2003/48 (see [2004] O.J. L385/28, L385/50; L359/32; L379/83; L381/32 and [2005] O.J. L19/53).

[47] See IP/01/575.
[48] See COM/2003/810.
[49] [2004] O.J. L39/22.
[50] See *Schumacker* (C-279/93) [1995] E.C.R. I-225; [1996] 2 C.M.L.R. 450.
[51] *Wielockx* (C-80/94) [1995] E.C.R. I-2493, applying the same principle to the self-employed.
[52] Directive 69/335 [1969] O.J. L245/25.
[53] Directive 90/434 [1990] O.J. L225/1, amended [2005] O.J. L58/19, which has extended the scope to new legal entities and to new types of transactions.
[54] Directive 90/435 [1990] L225/6, amended [2004] O.J. L7/41, extending the benefits of the Merger Directive to a greater number of legal entities, including the European Company and the European Co-operative Society and providing for a transition period for accession countries. The Directive removes the double taxation of dividends and provides a common tax regime. See *Crédit Mutuel* (C-27/07) [2008] E.C.R. I-2767: taxable income of parent company; nature of "tax credit"; in *Cobelfret* (C-138/07) [2009] E.C.R. 12.02.09, the Court found that art.4(1) had direct effect.
[55] Directive 2003/43 [2003] O.J. L157/49, amended [2004] O.J. L157/106, that extended the scope to new types of companies; and by Directive 2004/76, which provides for a transitional period for some new Member States. A survey on the implementation of this Directive was been published in 2006, see *http://www.ec.europa.eu/taxation-customs/resources/documents/common/publications/studies/surveydir.pdf.*
[56] [1998] O.J. C2/1.
[57] *http://www.ec.europa.eu/taxation<EL3>—<RV3>customs/resources/documents/primarolo<EL3>—<RV3>en.pdf.*
[58] [1998] O.J. C384/3.

pricing, the Council has therefore adopted a Code of Conduct on that subject.[59] However, it only reflects a political commitment without limiting the competences of the Member States. In 2001 the Commission established a strategy for providing companies with a consolidated corporate tax base for their Union-wide activities in order to reduce the compliance costs, administrative burden, the lack of cross-border loss-relief and of transparency.[60] Since the end of 2004 a working group deals with this subject and in 2006 the Commission issued a Communication on the Progress to date and next steps towards a Common Consolidated Corporate Tax Base (CCCTB).[61]

A system for the exchange of information between the competent authorities of the Member States, in the field of direct taxation, similar to the one mentioned above for indirect taxes, was set up by the so-called Mutual Assistance Directive.[62] See also the Merger Directive on a common system of taxation applicable to mergers, divisions, transfers of assets or exchanges of shares concerning companies of different Member States.[63]

Within the framework of this chapter on Taxation, a word must be said about so-called "duty free". This system of turnover tax and excise duty exemption was set up in 1969 in order to allow travellers crossing a border between two Member States to be exempted from reclaiming taxes already paid when leaving one Member State, and paying new taxes on arrival in the other Member State. The traveller was therefore allowed to purchase goods to be transported in his personal luggage at a price which does not include VAT, nor excise duty; the amounts of goods, which the traveller could thus purchase were strictly limited. To put this system into practice, vendors at airports and on board ships and planes were allowed to purchase those goods at "duty free" prices in order to sell them at those same prices to the traveller. Unfortunately, the system was perverted and abused, since the vendors kept for themselves most of the profit which the Council had intended for the traveller. The vendors made huge profits that, in addition, distorted competition. Furthermore, the system discriminated between categories of travellers. Notwithstanding the entry into force of the internal market at the end of 1992, and the elimination of the fiscal frontiers, which were the origin of the whole system, the Council, in 1992, extended the duty free exemption to June 30, 1999. This system has now disappeared for intra-Union travellers but still applies to travellers leaving or entering the EU.

A last word in this chapter on taxation ought to be said about the prevention of tax evasion and tax avoidance. On this subject the Council has, over the years, issued several acts. A first directive was already mentioned above: it concerns mutual assistance by the competent authorities of the Member States in the field of direct taxation.[64] The second, a regulation on prevention of the use of the

---

[59] [2006] O.J. C176/1.
[60] COM/2001/582.
[61] COM/2006/157.
[62] Directive 77/799 [1977] O.J. L336/15, amended several times; and Directive 76/308 [1976] O.J. L73/18 concerning the agricultural fund, agricultural levies and customs duties, amended [2001] O.J. L175/17.
[63] Directive 90/434 [1990] O.J. L225/3.
[64] Directive 77/799 [1977] O.J. L336/15, amended several times.

financial system for the purpose of money laundering,[65] was also mentioned above in Ch.15 on The Freedom of Establishment for financial institutions. It concerns on-the-spot checks and inspections carried out by the Commission in order to protect the Union's financial interests against fraud and other irregularities.[66] It followed a Resolution on the legal protection of the financial interests of the Union[67] and Conclusions concerning the fight against fraud.[68] The first Council Resolution is from 1975 and concerns the measures to be taken by the Union in order to combat international tax evasion and tax avoidance.[69] There also is the Resolution of the Council and of the Representatives of the Governments of the Member States, meeting within the Council, concerning the protection of the financial interests of the Union.[70] Important is a directive on the prevention of the use of the financial system for the purpose of money laundering and terrorist financing.[71]

Further Reading

Ben Terra and Peter Waddell, *European Tax Law*, 3rd edn (Kluwer, 2001).
Pascal Pistone, *The Impact of Community Law on Tax Treaties*, (Kluwer, 2002).
Pinto Carlo, *Tax competition and EU law* (Kluwer, 2003).
Servaas van Thiel, "Removal of income tax barriers to market integration in the EU litigation by the Community citizens instead of harmonisation by the Community legislation?", EC Tax Review 2003, Vol.12, No.1, pp.4–19.

---

[65] Directive 91/308 [1991] O.J. L166/77, replaced by Directive 2005/60: see below.
[66] Regulation 2185/96 [1996] O.J. L292/2.
[67] [1994] O.J. C355/2.
[68] [1994] O.J. C292/1.
[69] [1975] O.J. C35/1, also Directive 77/799 (quoted above).
[70] [1991] O.J. C328/1.
[71] Directive 2005/60 [2007] O.J. L309/15, modified by the Directive on payment services in the internal market [2007] O.J. L319/1 and [2008] O.J. L76/46, amended [2009] O.J. L267/7.

Chapter Twenty-six

Approximation of Laws[1]

"Approximation", which is the name given in the TFEU to this activity,[2] refers to the objective to be attained: harmonisation of the provisions laid down by law, regulation and administrative action in the Member States and the method to be used to attain this objective consists of "harmonisation" measures. It is clear that the many differences existing between the laws, etc. of the Member States impede the development and functioning of the internal market on which the Union is based. As indicated in the chapter on the free movement of goods, the differences between the, "laws, regulations or administrative provisions of the Member States"[3] can be bridged either by "mutual recognition" of existing national provisions of other Member States or, when that is not desirable or possible, through harmonisation of existing provisions of all the Member States.

As far as "mutual recognition" is concerned, the chapter on free movement of goods contained a most interesting provision, which was repealed since it referred only to the year 1992. It provided that the Council, on the basis of an inventory drawn up by the Commission of national provisions that have not been harmonised, could decide that, "the provisions in force in a Member State must be recognised as being equivalent to those applied by another Member State".[4] It is unfortunate that a similar, more general, provision was not kept in the Treaty. It would have greatly facilitated the indispensable approximation activity.

Harmonisation consists of replacing existing national provisions by rules whose content is common to all the Member States. Those are not exactly "common rules", if by that is understood identical rules. Indeed, as was indicated, the instrument to achieve the objective of approximation is the directive, and the latter, as was seen in the chapter on Union acts, is only binding as to the results to be achieved. It leaves to the national authorities the choice of form and methods.[5]

The Treaty made a distinction between national provisions that, "directly affect the establishment or functioning of the internal market",[6] and rules which have as their "object" the establishment and functioning of the internal market.[7] Although the expression "common market" no longer exists, it might be useful for the reader (who will necessarily still be confronted with it) to understand what it meant. The words "common market", which were not defined in the EC Treaty, cover the basic freedoms and some policy areas such as those where the

---

[1] arts 114–118 TFEU [95–97].
[2] This activity is no longer mentioned among the, "categories and areas of Community competence": arts 3,4 and 5 TFEU [3(1)(h)].
[3] art.114(1) TFEU [95(1)].
[4] Former art.100b(1)(2) EC.
[5] art.288 TFEU [249].
[6] art.115 TFEU [94].
[7] art.114(1) TFEU [95(1)].

Union exercises exclusive competence.[8] Since the establishment of the internal market was bound by a time limit—the end of 1992[9]—a method more rapid than the one applying to approximation in general, had to be devised to achieve this objective. The EU Treaty introduced it.

As regards national rules that "directly affect" the establishment or functioning of the common market, the Treaties provided and still, now, provide for directives issued by the Council, acting unanimously in accordance with a special legislative procedure,[10] on a proposal from the Commission and after consulting Parliament and the ESC. The requirement of unanimity makes the implementation of this provision extremely time-consuming, if not practically impossible. Many directives were nonetheless adopted pursuant to this method, especially in those areas of Union activity where harmonising directives were provided for by the Treaty. This was the case, for instance, for the implementation of the freedom of movement of workers and self-employed persons.

It became clear, however, that another solution had to be found to expedite the establishment and functioning of the "internal market" before the end of 1992.[11] Consequently, the Commission in its White Book on the "Completion of the Internal Market", proposed a new approach consisting both of simplifying the harmonisation procedure and replacing it, whenever possible, by "mutual recognition" (acceptance by Member States of the national rules of the other Member States as equivalent to theirs). The latter is as basic to the functioning of the internal market as is the principle of "equal treatment" (no distinction between goods, originating in another Member State, persons, workers, self-employed and companies established in another Member State and their national equivalent).

The simplification of the harmonisation procedure consisted in replacing the required unanimity by qualified majority. To this end the EU Treaty introduced a new provision for "the achievement of the objectives set out in Article 14" (the latter defined the internal market). The TFEU now provides that Parliament and the Council, "acting in accordance with the ordinary legislative procedure,[12] after consulting the ESC, shall adopt the measures for the approximation . . . which have as their object the establishment and functioning of the internal market",[13] as distinct from national measures which "directly affect" the establishment and functioning of the internal market.[14] By this wording, according to the Court,[15] the authors of the Treaty intended to confer on the Union legislature a discretion, depending on the general context and the specific circumstances of the matter to be harmonised, as regards the harmonisation technique most appropriate for achieving the desired results, in particular in fields that are characterised by complex technical features. The harmonisation measures provided for in the Treaty also cover the establishment of a Union body,[16] responsible for contributing to the implementation of a process of harmonisation.[17]

---

[8] art.3 TFEU.

[9] Former art.14(1) EC.

[10] See art.189(2) TFEU.

[11] Former art.14 EC.

[12] art. 294 TFEU [251].

[13] art 114(1) TFEU [95].

[14] art.94 TFEU [115].

[15] Former art.100a(1) EC which was identical to art.95(1) EC.

[16] See above, Ch.13: Decentralised Bodies of the Union (I 15. The European Network and Information Security Agency (ENISA)).

[17] *United Kingdom v Parliament and Council* (C-217/04) [2006] E.C.R. I-3771.

The Court also stated that, in the case of an harmonisation process in stages, two conditions had to be fulfilled. First, the basic act must determine the essential elements of the harmonising measure and, second, the mechanism for implementing these elements must be designed in such a way that it leads to a harmonisation within the meaning of the relevant Treaty provision.

It is clear, however, that the harmonisation measures may only be used when the result is the replacement of existing national laws or regulations by Union rules. This is not the case when Union rules are created while the national rules remain unchanged.[18]

The Treaty empowers the Council to issue directives and Parliament and the Council to adopt measures for approximation, (except for fiscal provisions, those relating to the free movement of persons and those relating to the rights and interests of employed persons) and also confers upon the Commission powers to adopt harmonisation measures.[19] According to the Court, an act adopted by the Union legislature may be limited to defining the provisions that are essential for the achievement of the objectives in connection with the establishment and functioning of the internal market, while conferring power on the Commission to adopt the harmonisation measures needed for the implementation of the legislative act in question.[20]

There are, of course, exceptions, such as health, food safety, environmental protection and consumer protection where approximation still has its place.[21] In those areas the Treaty provides that the Commission, when it makes its proposals, must take as a base a high level of protection, "taking account, in particular, of any new development based on scientific facts".[22]

The Treaty also provides for exceptions in the case of protection of the environment or of the working environment.[23] These exceptions allow Member States, after the adoption of a harmonisation measure, and under the supervision of the Commission,[24] either to maintain national provisions, or to introduce national provisions based on new scientific evidence, "on grounds of a problem specific to [a given] Member State".[25] As stated by the Court, the supervision by the Commission implies that the Member State may not apply unilateral rules, derogating from the Union harmonised measures, without the prior authorisation of the Commission.[26] The Treaty also provides that in case the Commission or any Member State considers that another Member State is making improper use of the exception, they can bring the matter directly before the Court, without going through the normal procedures.[27] The Chapter on approximation also

---

[18] Regulation 1435/2003 lays down a single statute for the European Cooperative Society (SCE) on the basis of art.352 TFEU [art.308 EC]; this was contested by Parliament, which proposed art.114 TFEU [art.95 EC]; since the national provisions remained unchanged, the Court ruled that this did not constitute a harmonisation: *Parliament v Council* (C-436/03) [2006] E.C.R. I-3733.

[19] art.114(1) TFEU [95(1)].

[20] *UK v Parliament and Council* (C-66/04) (quoted above, fn.17).

[21] See the famous *Dassonville* (8/74) ([1974] E.C.R. 837(5) and *Cassis de Dijon* (20/78) [1979] E.C.R. 649(14) cases.

[22] art.114(3) TFEU [95(3)].

[23] art.114(4) and (5) TFEU [95(4) and (5)].

[24] art.114(4) TFEU [95(4)].

[25] art.114(5) TFEU [95(5)].

[26] *France v Commission* (C-41/93) [1994] E.C.R. I-1829; [1995] 3 C.M.L.R. 733.

[27] art.114(9) TFEU [95(9)]. A Member State must first bring the matter before the Commission, which gives each of the States concerned the opportunity to submit its own case and its observation on the other party's case. The Commission can then deliver a reasoned opinion; if the Commission has not done so within three months, the Member State which considers that another Member State has failed to fulfil a Treaty obligation, may bring the matter before the Court.

contains provisions concerning a difference between a national provision that, "is distorting the conditions of competition" and that, that according to the Commission, "needs to be eliminated".[28]

In that case, the Commission must first consult the Member States concerned. It is only if such consultation does not result in an agreement eliminating the distortion of competition, that Parliament and the Council, acting in accordance with the ordinary legislative procedure[29] must issue the necessary directives or any other appropriate measure provided for in the Treaties.[30]. This provision seems to indicate that differences between national provisions that distort competition are more urgent than differences that, "directly affect the establishment or functioning of the common market"; indeed, only qualified majority is required in the first case.

The Treaty furthermore provides that, where there is fear that the adoption or amendment of existing provisions might distort the conditions of competition, the Member State wishing to proceed therewith, must first consult the Commission.[31] The latter may make recommendations, and if the Member State does not comply therewith, other Member States are not required to amend their own provisions in order to eliminate the distortion. However, when the distortion is only detrimental to the Member State which has introduced the provision and not followed the Commission's recommendation, the Treaty does not apply.[32] Since, as indicated at the beginning of this chapter, harmonisation[33] is but a method to arrive at, "approximation of the national provisions applicable in the various areas of activity of the Union as defined in the Treaty",[34] the many harmonisation directives issued by the institutions are, in this book, examined in the chapters corresponding to those activities. For instance, the directives harmonising the conditions of access to the regulated professions are examined in the chapter on the freedom of establishment.[35]

Finally, it should be noted that, as indicated above, there are certain subjects that are excluded from the approximation process. One example is to be found in the field of employment. The Treaty provides that the Council may adopt, "incentive measures designed to encourage co-operation between Member States and to support their action in the field of employment", but adds that those, "measures shall not include harmonisation of the laws and regulations of the Member States".[36] Other fields, namely those relating to fiscal provisions, the free movement of persons and the rights and interests of employed persons, are excluded from the harmonisation procedure provided for the establishment and functioning of the internal market.[37] They are not, however, excluded from the "normal" harmonisation procedure.[38] On the other hand, vocational training policy,[39] culture,[40] public health[41] and education[42] are excluded from any harmonisation process.

---

[28] art.116 TFEU [96].
[29] See art.294 TFEU [251].
[30] art.116,2 TFEU [96,2].
[31] art.117 TFEU [97].
[32] art.117 TFEU [97].
[33] Former art.100c and 100d EC.
[34] arts 4 and 5 TFEU [3].
[35] See above, Ch.17.
[36] art.149 TFEU [129].
[37] art.114(2) TFEU [95(2)].
[38] art.115 TFEU [94].
[39] art.166(4) TFEU [150(4)].
[40] art.167(5) TFEU first indent [151(5) first indent].
[41] art.168(5) TFEU [152(4)(c)].
[42] art.165(4) TFEU first indent [149(4) first indent].

Chapter Twenty-seven

Transport

INTRODUCTION

The importance of transport for the Union follows from the fact that the implementation and functioning of the internal market with its fundamental freedoms, provided for in the Treaties, depends on interconnected and interoperable regional and national transport networks, as well as on access to such networks. The TFEU therefore provides that shared competence between the Union and the Member States also applies to transport,[1] and that the objectives of the Treaty are to be pursued within the framework of the Common Transport Policy.[2] It is the task of Parliament and the Council, acting in accordance with the ordinary legislative procedure,[3] and after consulting the ESC and the Committee of the Regions and taking into account the distinctive features of transport,[4] to provide for:

- common rules applicable to international transport to or from the territory of a Member State or passing across the territory of one or more Member States;
- the conditions under which non-resident carriers may operate transport services within a Member State;
- measures to improve transport safety; and
- any other appropriate provision.[5]

In adopting the Common Transport Policy (or any other policy for that matter), the Union has to take into consideration the obligation to ensure a high level of human health protection,[6] to contribute to the protection of the health, safety and economic interests of consumers[7] and to integrate environmental protection requirements.[8] Until the above-mentioned provisions had been laid down by the Union, the Member States were to observe a standstill with regard to similar national provisions, in the sense that they were not allowed to adopt provisions less favourable, in their direct or indirect effect, on carriers of other Member

---

[1] art.4(2)(G) TFEU [3(f)].

[2] arts 90–100 TFEU [70–80].

[3] art.294 TFEU [251]. Account must be taken of cases where their application might seriously effect the standards of living and level of employment in certain regions and the operation of transport facilities: art.91(2) TFEU [71(2)].

[4] Regulation 1017/68 applying rules of competition to transport by rail, road and inland waterway [1968] O.J. L175/10, codified version Regulation 169/09 [2009] O.J. L61/1; Regulation 411/2004 laying down the procedure for the application of the rules on competition to undertakings in the air transport sector [2004] O.J. L68/1; and Regulation 4056/86 laying down detailed rules for the application of arts 101 and 102 TFEU [arts 81 and 82] to maritime transport [1986] O.J. L378/4; all three amended by Regulation 1/2003 [2003] O.J. L1/1.

[5] art.91(1) TFEU [71(1)].

[6] See art.168(1) TFEU [152].

[7] arts 12 and 169(1) TFEU [153].

[8] art.11 TFEU [6] and art.191 [174].

States as compared with carriers of their own State. This prohibition applies unless the Council has unanimously adopted a measure granting a derogation.[9]

Although mentioned at the very end of Title VI of the TFEU on Transport, the provisions of that Title only apply to transport by rail, road and inland waterways.[10] However, Parliament and the Council acting in accordance with the ordinary legislative procedure,[11] may lay down appropriate provisions for sea and air transport, after consulting the ECS and the Committee of the Regions.[12] That was done and, as will be seen, many Union acts have been adopted concerning those latter means of transport. The *acquis communautaire* supporting the Common Transport Policy has become an impressive law compilation.

1. NEW EUROPEAN TRANSPORT POLICY: ADAPT THE MOBILITY SYSTEM TO NEW CHALLENGES

At the beginning, the aim of the Common Transport Policy was to open up the transport market and to support the construction of new infrastructure in order to promote the economic competitiveness and economic and cultural exchanges within the Union. Today, this is considered to be insufficient to meet the problems[13] of the increasing demand of mobility as a result of the economic growth, globalisation, the enlarged internal market and the increasing shortage of adequate transport supply due to major bottlenecks in the European infrastructure.

In September 2001 the Commission adopted a White Paper, "European Transport Policy for 2010: time to decide",[14] that sets out steps towards a transport policy which meets the demands of enlargement and sustainable development. The new objectives aim at restoring the balance between modes of transport and developing inter-modality, combating congestion, improving safety and the quality of services, while maintaining the right to mobility. In this new Transport Policy Paper, the Commission proposed an action plan including 60 measures based on the following objectives:

- revitalise the railways by opening up the national and international market both in terms of freight and passengers;
- improve the quality of road transport by harmonising inspection procedures and penalties as well as ensuring satisfactory working conditions;
- improve road safety and reduce the number of accident victims by half;
- promote short sea and inland waterway transport to combat road congestion and deficiencies in railway infrastructure by building "sea motorways" as part of the Trans-European Network (TEN), and also developing a European maritime traffic management system to improve maritime safety;
- increase air transport while respecting the environment by adopting new regulations to reduce noise and pollution, introducing a "single sky" in order to manage the air traffic better and by 2004, implement Union legislation on air traffic to increase EU co-ordination in air transport;

---

[9] art.92 TFEU [72].

[10] art.100 TFEU [80].

[11] art.294 TFEU [251]

[12] art.100(2) TFEU [80(2)].

[13] For instance: congestion, environmental nuisance, accidents, isolation of outlying regions.

[14] See COM (2001) 370; see as well mid-term review of the European Commission's 2001 Transport White Paper COM (2006) 314.

- increase inter-modality by integrating the modes of transport, harmonise and promote interoperability between systems, and promote alternative solutions to road transport[15];
- develop the Trans-European Networks by removing the bottlenecks in the railway network; completing the routes defined as priorities for absorbing the traffic flows generated by enlargement and improving access to outlying areas;
- adopt a policy on effective charging for transport so that each mode of transport pays for the costs it generates,[16] harmonise fuel taxation for commercial users, particularly in road transport, introduce an infrastructure-charging system and allowing cross-financing by channeling revenues into specific funds;
- recognise the rights and obligations of users by extending measures to improve the quality of service[17];
- develop quality urban transport by making better use of public transport and the existing infrastructure in order to meet the international commitments to reduce CO_2 emissions (Kyoto Protocol); in 2008 a directive was adopted on the inland transport of dangerous goods, which includes provisions for the protection of the environment[18];
- use research and technology to develop clean and efficient transport[19];
- manage the effects of globalisation by opening transport markets while continuing to maintain quality and safety in transport by reinforcing the position of the Union in international organisations[20]; and
- develop a European satellite navigation system, "Galileo", a global navigation satellite system (GNSS) and European satellite radionavigation system EGNOS (European Geostationary Navigation Overlay Service).[21] In 2009 Parliament and Council adopted a regulation on the future of these European satellite radionavigation programmes.[22] The budgetary resources were set at €3.4 billion for the period 2007–2013. It also provides for improving the governance of these programmes.

2. SPECIAL FEATURES OF TRANSPORT

As already mentioned, transport has several characteristics which distinguish it from other services.[23] One is the fact that it extends inevitably beyond the geographic borders of the Union and is thus subject to many international agreements and conventions. It suffices to think about sea and air transport.[24] Furthermore, most kinds of

---

[15] See the Marco Polo programme below.
[16] See also the Commission White Paper, "Fair Payment for Infrastructure Use: A phased approach to a common transport infrastructure charging framework in the EU" COM (1998) 466.
[17] For example transparency of information to passengers, special contract conditions.
[18] Directive 2008/68 [2008] O.J. L260/13.
[19] See the 7th RTD Framework Programme for 2007–2013 and the European Research Area below, in Ch.33: Research and Technological Development.
[20] For instance: the International Civil Aviation Organisation (ICAO), the International Maritime Organisation, the Rhine Navigation Commission, the Danube Commission and Eurocontrol.
[21] See General Report 2007, 81.
[22] Regulation 683/08 [2008] O.J. L196/1.
[23] art.91 TFEU [71].
[24] art.100(2) TFEU [80(2)] and, for instance, the Chicago Convention of December 7, 1944 (see *http://www.iasl.mcgill.ca/airlaw*).

transport infrastructure require high investments, which, due to varying demand, remain temporarily unproductive. In addition, there exists an enormous difference between the infrastructures needed for the various modes of transport. Some, like railways and inland shipping, need heavy and very specific infrastructures, which are only intermittently used by a limited number of carriers. Therefore, the offer exceeds the demand most of the time. On the other hand, the road infrastructure is used by millions of people which do not contribute directly to its cost. Another characteristic is that some means of transport have been until recently (or still are) in the hands or under the control of the States, either through public undertakings or undertakings to which they grant special or exclusive rights. This is due, among others, to the fact that they are obliged to offer (public) services which are not justified from a purely economic point of view. Finally, all forms of transport, especially public transport, are subject to strict safety requirements.

In order to understand the challenges the Union faces in developing its Common Transport Policy, a few basic facts should be kept in mind.

The first important fact is the constant increase in demand for transport, because of, among others things, the increased standard of living, which allows people to travel more and farther, changing lifestyles and consumer habits. Looking at the development in passenger transport, the continuing growth becomes obvious: the number of cars has tripled in the last 30 years and in the enlarged Union this growth continues.

Secondly, the creation of the internal market has led to substantial changes in the European economy and its system of production: the economic activities are no longer concentrated in urban areas but geographically spread, depending on the production costs (especially labour costs). The same applies to the population in general: suburbia has inevitably increased the demand for transport due to longer distances between home and work.

Thirdly, the different modes of transport have not grown equally—for reasons of unequal adaptation to the needs of modern economy and society, because of unequal regulations and other factors. Contrary to 20 years ago, inland waterways amount to 3.3 per cent of the EU goods transport market, air 0.1 per cent, railways 9.6 per cent, while maritime transport amounts to 39.3 per cent and road transport to 44.5 per cent (referring to 2005).

Looking at the passenger transport, the predominance of road transport becomes obvious (referring to 2008): road transport, 77 per cent; railways, including tram and metro, 7 per cent; air transport, 8 per cent; sea, 1 per cent.[25] Bearing those figures in mind it is clear that, if nothing is done, road transport will continue to grow to the detriment of the other modes of transport, but also, taking into account the problems with regard to the environment and congestion that creates significant external costs, to the detriment of the population and the economy of the Union.

Looking back at the development of the Common Transport Policy, one ascertains that, although the former EC Treaty did from the beginning provide for a "common transport policy", the Council failed, for many years, to materialise it.[26]

---

[25] See "Energy & Transport in Figures 2006; Part 3: Transport", European Commission, Director-General of Transport in co-operation with Eurostat; *http://www.ec.europa.eu/dgs/energy-transport/figures/pocketbook/doc/2006/2006-transport-en.pdf.*

[26] At that time, unanimity was needed for a Council decision related to transport and only a few dispersed provisions had been adopted.

It took an action in the Court,[27] lodged by Parliament and supported by the Commission, against the Council for failure to implement the Treaty provisions in this field to get things moving. The Court ruled that, "there is not yet a set of rules which may be regarded as a common transport policy" and consequently concluded that:

> "[I]n breach of the Treaty, the Council had failed to ensure freedom to provide services in the sphere of international transport and to lay down the conditions under which non-resident carriers may operate transport services in a Member State".[28]

In the light of this Court judgement, the Council finally adopted a policy approach to transport, rather than the piecemeal one used before. Subsequently, the Treaties reinforced the political, institutional and budgetary foundations for a transport policy. For instance, the unanimity requirement for Council decisions was replaced by qualified majority.[29] Furthermore the Union became responsible for transport safety,[30] which is in line with the new obligations to ensure human health protection[31] and consumer protection.[32]

Also very important was the introduction of the Trans-European Networks (TENs),[33] among others, in the field of transport and the setting up of a Cohesion Fund to provide financial contributions to projects in the fields of environment and the TENs and in order to built the necessary transport infrastructure in less-developed regions.[34] Community financial aid is provided in the field of the trans-European transport and energy networks.[35]

Another new feature was the necessity to integrate environmental protection requirements into the definition and implementation of other Union policies, and therefore, also into the Common Transport Policy.[36] If one adds to that the necessary international aspects, the conclusion can only be that there was a need for a global Union transport policy. As mentioned, such a policy is based on the free movement of goods, the free movement of persons, the freedom to provide services and the right of establishment, while also taking into account other policies such as social policy.[37] The object remains to provide the carriers with the greatest possible choice while at the same time harmonising technical characteristics.[38]

---

[27] art.265 TFEU [232].

[28] *Parliament v Council* (13/83) [1985] E.C.R. 1513; [1986] 1 C.M.L.R. 138.

[29] See art.91 TFEU [71].

[30] art.91(1)(c) TFEU [71(1)(c)].

[31] art.168(1) TFEU [152(1)].

[32] arts 12 and 169 TFEU [153].

[33] TFEU Title XVI (arts 170–172), see Decision 1692/96 on Union guidelines for the development of the trans-European transport network [1996] O.J. L228/1, as amended, and see below Ch.31: Enterprise and Industrial Policy/ Information Society.

[34] art.177 EFDC and TFEU [161], see also below Ch.32: Regional Policy/Economic, Social and Territorial Cohesion.

[35] Regulation 680/07 [2007] O.J. L162/1.

[36] art.11 TFEU [6].

[37] See, for instance, Regulation 561/2006 on the harmonisation of certain social legislation relating to road transport [2006] O.J. L102/1 and Regulation 3821/85 on recording equipment in road transport [1985] O.J. L370/8, amended for the ninth time [2009] O.J. L21/3 and [2009] O.J. L29/45. See *Raemdonck* (C-128/04) [2005] E.C.R. I-2445: definition of "material or equipment".

[38] Numerous directives were adopted relating, for instance, to the type-approval of motor vehicles and their trailers, [1970] O.J. L42/1, several times amended [2006] O.J. L65/27.

3. APPLICATION OF COMPETITION RULES TO TRANSPORT

This subject was examined in some detail above in the chapter on Competition, with special reference to maritime, air and rail transport. It was also pointed out that transport is subject to specific competition rules,[39] but that in 2004 the implementing system was harmonised,[40] which has affected also the transport sector.[41] Furthermore, the specific State aid rules applicable to the transport sector have to be kept in mind. State aid is only considered to be compatible with the common market if it meets the needs of co-ordination of transport or if it represents reimbursement for the discharge of certain obligations inherent in the concept of public service.[42] In 2004, the Commission decided to apply the de minimis rules[43] to the transport sector, i.e. it will no longer examine small amounts, i.e. less than €100.000, of State aid to the transport sector.[44]

As mentioned above, the Treaty entrusts the Union institutions with laying down common rules applicable to international transport, conditions for market access, measures to improve transport safety and any other appropriate provisions.[45] The main provisions will be examined below for the various modes of transport.

4. ROAD TRANSPORT

Road transport can be subdivided into transport of passengers and transport of goods. For the former, a regulation laid down common rules for the international carriage of passengers by coach and bus,[46] and another lays down the conditions under which non-resident carriers may operate national road passenger transport services within a Member State.[47] The Union signed the Agreement on the International Carriage of Passengers by Road by means of Occasional Coach and

---

[39] See Regulation 1017/68 (quoted above), most articles were repealed by Regulation 1/2003 [2003] O.J. L1/1, replaced by Regulation 169/09, codified version [2009] O.J. L61/1. See Regulation 773/2004 relating to the conduct of proceedings by the Commission pursuant to arts 101–102 TFEU [81 and 82] [2004] O.J. L123/18; Regulation 1419/2006 [2006] O.J. L269/1 (maritime transport); and Regulation 411/2004 [2004] O.J. L68/1 (air transport).

[40] Regulation 1/2003 [2003] O.J. L1/1.

[41] Regulation 1/2003 [2003] O.J. L1/1 on the implementation of the rules on competition laid down in arts 101–102 TFEU [81 and 82] has repealed Regulation 141/62 exempting transport from the application of Regulation 17 [1962] O.J. 124/2751 and amended Regulation 1017/68 [1968] O.J. L175/10 (transport by rail, road and inland waterway), replaced by codified version Regulation 169/09 [2009] O.J. L61/1.

[42] art.93 TFEU [73]. See Regulation 1191/69 on action by Member States concerning the obligations inherent in the concept of a public service in transport by rail, road and inland waterway [1969] O.J. L56/1, repealed by Regulation 1370/07 on public passenger transport services by rail and by road [2007] O.J. L315/1; Regulation 1107/70 on the granting of aids for transport by rail, road and internal waterway [1970] O.J. L130/1, amended [1997] O.J. L84/6, repealed by Regulation 1370/07 on public passenger transport by rail and road [2007] O.J. L315/1.

[43] See Regulation 69/2001 on the application of arts 106 and 107 TFEU [86 and 87] to de minimis aid [2001] O.J. L10/30.

[44] IP/04/290.

[45] art.91 TFEU [71].

[46] Regulation 684/92 [1992] O.J. L74/1, amended [1998] O.J. L4/1 and [2006] O.J. L363/1.

[47] Regulation 12/98 [1998] O.J. L4/10.

[48] [1982] O.J. L230/39. See also Regulation 56/83 concerning the implementation of the Agreement [1983] O.J. L10/1 and Regulation 684/92 on common rules for the international carriage of passengers by coach or bus [1992] O.J. L74/1, as amended, and implemented as regards documents by Regulation 2121/98 [1998] O.J. L268/10.

Bus Services (ASOR),[48] and the Agreement on the international occasional carriage of passengers by coach and bus (Interbus Agreement).[49] The ASOR provides for harmonised liberalisation measures and simplified inspection measures by introducing a single document. The aim of the Interbus Agreement is to harmonise rules and thus to facilitate tourism between the contracting parties. For non-resident carriers conditions have been adopted for the right to operate national road passenger transport services within a Member State (cabotage transport operations).[50]

Where the carriage of goods is concerned, common rules for international transport of goods by road for hire or reward are provided for.[51] The conditions for market access are laid down in a basic regulation,[52] while a regulation concerning the right of non-resident carriers with regard to road haulage services within a Member State, has introduced progressively the free road cabotage for freights.[53] A directive regulates the use of vehicles hired without drivers for the carriage of goods by road[54] and another establishes common rules for certain types of carriage of goods by road.[55] In order to ensure the freedom to provide transport services, the Treaty explicitly provides that:

> "[D]iscrimination which takes the form of charging different rates and imposing different conditions for the carriage of the same goods over the same transport links on grounds of the country of origin or of destination of the goods in question must be abolished".[56]

It is up to the Council to lay down the necessary rules for implementing this principle.[57] Nevertheless, the Member States remain free to charge tolls on roads, provided they are in line with the Treaty provisions.[58] Charges will become more important in order to meet the "polluter pays" principle and the realisation of a fair principle, some of the objectives set out in the White Paper.[59] A 2009 directive provides measures to promote clean and energy-efficient road transport vehicles.[60]

---

[49] [2002] O.J. L321/11.

[50] Regulation 12/98 [1998] O.J. L4/10.

[51] Directive 62/2005 [1962] O.J. 70/2005, as amended. See also Directive 2003/59 on the initial qualification and periodic training of drivers of certain road vehicles for the carriage of goods or passengers [2003] O.J. L226/4, adapted by reason of the accession: [2004] O.J. L168/35; it applied as from September 10, 2008 to drivers of vehicles for the carriage of passengers by road, and as from September 10, 2009 to drivers of vehicles for the carriage of goods by road; and Directive 2006/1 on the use of vehicles hired without drivers for the carriage of goods by road [2006] O.J. L33/82; see *Bourrasse and Perchicot* (Joined Cases C-228/01 and C-289/01) [2002] E.C.R. I-10213.

[52] Regulation 881/92 [1992] O.J. L95/1, as amended.

[53] Regulation 3118/93 laying down the conditions under which non-resident carriers may operate road haulage services within a Member State [1993] O.J. L279/1, as amended and Regulation 792/94 laying down detailed rules for the application of Regulation 3118/93 to road haulage operators on own account [1994] O.J .L.92/13.

[54] Directive 2006/1 [2006] O.J. L33/86.

[55] Directive 2006/94 [2006] O.J. L374/5.

[56] art.95(1) TFEU [75(1)].

[57] Regulation No.11 concerning the abolition of discrimination in transport rates and conditions [1960] O.J. 52/1121, as amended, and Regulation 4058/89 on the fixing of rates for the carriage of goods by road between Member States [1989] O.J. L390/1. The Court accepted that road haulage tariffs are approved and brought into force by the State: *Autotrasporti Librandi* (C-38/97) [1998] E.C.R. I-5955.

[58] Directive 1999/62 on the charging of heavy goods vehicles for the use of certain infrastructure [1999] O.J. L187/42 contains only a framework and did not harmonise the national systems nor included the environmental costs.

[59] White Paper "European transport policy for 2010: time to decide", COM(2001)370.

[60] Directive 2009/33 [2009] O.J. L120/5.

For both road haulage and passenger transport, the Council laid down the conditions for admission to the occupation and the mutual recognition of diplomas in order to facilitate the freedom of establishment. Member States shall issue national driving licences, which shall be mutually recognised, based on a Union model driving licence.[61] In 2008 the Commission issued a decision on equivalence between categories of driving licences.[62]

Other subjects, such as insurance against liability in respect of the use of motor vehicles,[63] the installation and use of speed limitation devices for certain categories of motor vehicles,[64] recording equipment in road transport[65] and elimination of controls performed at the frontiers of Member States,[66] are the subject of several Union rules. See also rules concerning a framework for the approval of motor vehicles and their trailers, and of systems, components and separate technical units intended for such vehicles.[67]

The fact that in 2007 more than 40,000 (in 1990: 70,628) people were killed and more than 1.3 million were injured (in 1990: more than 1.45 million)[68] in road accidents in the Union shows that the implementation of road safety measures is very important.[69] Consequently, legislation concerning roadworthiness tests for motor vehicles and their trailers,[70] the minimum level of training for some road transport drivers,[71] the transport of dangerous goods,[72] the weights and dimension for heavy good vehicles,[73] and technical conditions were adopted. Where the latter are concerned, Union legislation is very detailed indeed. They concern, for instance, the use of safety belts,[74] safety glazing on motor vehicles and their trailers,[75] the technical

---

[61] Directive 91/439 on driving licences [1991] O.J. L237/1, amended [2009] O.J. L223/26. See *Wiedemann* (Joined Cases C-329/06 and C-343/06) [2008] E.C.R. I-4635: withdrawal of driver's licence in one Member State and issue of new licence in another Member State: mutual recognition, but possibility of art.227 EC action. See also Directive 2006/126 [2006] O.J. L403/18, amended [2009] O.J. L223/31.

[62] [2008] O.J. L270/31.

[63] Decision 2003/564 on the application of Directive 72/166 relating to checks on insurance against civil liability in respect of the use of motor vehicles [2003] O.J. L192/23, now Directive 2009/103 [2009] O.J. L263/11; see *Farrell* (C-356/05) [2007] E.C.R.I-3067 concerning damages to a person without a seat in a car.

[64] Directive 92/6 [1992] O.J. L57/27, as amended; *Elbertsen* (C-449/08) [2009] E.C.R. 22.10.09.

[65] Regulation 3821/85 [1985] O.J. L370/8, amended [2009] O.J. L2945. Regulation 2135/98: [1998] O.J. L274/1.

[66] Regulation 4060/89 [1989] O.J. L390/18, codified by Regulation 1100/08 [2008] O.J. L304/63.

[67] Framework Directive 2007/46 [2007] O.J. L263/1. Replacement of Annexes I, III, IV, VI, VII, XI and XV [2008] O.J. L 292/1.

[68] Based on CARE figures (see below). See, "Energy & Transport in Figures 2006; Part 3: Transport", European Commission, Director-General Transport in co-operation with Eurostat; *http://www.ec.europa.eu/dgs/energy-transport/figures/pocketbook/doc/2006/2006-transport-en.pdf*.

[69] See also CARE (Community data base on road accidents) Decision 93/704 [1993] O.J. L329/63.

[70] Directive 96/96 [1996] O.J. L46/1, as amended.

[71] Directive 76/914 [1976] O.J. L357/36, repealed [2003] O.J. L226/4, which applied as from September 10, 2008 to drivers of vehicles for the carriage of passengers by road, and as from September 10, 2009 to drivers of vehicles for the carriage of goods by road.

[72] Directive 94/55 [1994] O.J. L319/7, replaced together with Directive 96/49 (see below) by Directive 2008/68 [2008] O.J. L260/13; see also Directive 99/36 on transportable pressure equipment approved for the inland transport of dangerous goods by road and by rail [1999] O.J. L138/20, as amended.

[73] Directive 96/53 laying down for certain road vehicles circulating within the Union the maximum authorised dimensions in national and international traffic and the maximum authorised weights in international traffic [1996] O.J. L235/59, as amended.

[74] Directive 91/671 [1991] O.J. L373/26, as amended.

[75] Directive 92/22 [1991] O.J. L129/11, as amended.

roadside inspection of the roadworthiness of commercial vehicles circulating in the Union,[76] the tread depth of tyres,[77] the external projections forward of the cab's rear panel of motor vehicles of category N,[78] etc. The list seems unending.[79]

The Union also adhered to the European Agreement concerning the work of crews of vehicles engaged in international road transport (AETR),[80] which was the object of a famous judgment establishing the international competence of the Union in a field where no specific powers were granted by the Treaty.[81] Several pieces of legislation were adopted to improve safety and working conditions in the road transport sector.[82] Transport has its competition rules,[83] but certain sectors have their own.[84]

See also the regulation on public passenger transport service by rail and by road applying the concept of "services of general economic interest" to this mode of transport.[85]

5. RAIL TRANSPORT

Rail transport requires extremely heavy expenditure on infrastructure, which in addition is only used intermittently, with the consequence that railway companies risk being in deficit[86] and, were in the past all nationalised. While road and air transport, both for passengers and freight, have increased their market share, railway transport has seen its own constantly reduced, not only in relative, but also in absolute terms. This, in turn, deprived it of the sorely needed income to modernise its infrastructure and rolling stock. Nevertheless, rail transport is needed, it is more environmentally friendly and safer than other means of transport. How to explain this decline? The railways themselves are, of course, partly to blame: inefficiency (except for a few remarkable achievements), corporatism, lack of co-operation with other railway companies[87] and conservatism. The real

---

[76] Directive 2000/30 [2000] O.J. L203/1, as amended.

[77] Directive 89/459 [1989] O.J. L226/4.

[78] Directive 92/114 [1992] O.J. L409/17.

[79] As mentioned already the complete list of all the Union acts in force can be found in the Directory of Union Legislation, published by the Official Journal, in Luxembourg, or under *http://www.eur-lex/europa.eu*.

[80] [1978] O.J. L95/1.

[81] *Commission v Council* (22/70) [1971] E.C.R. 263; [1971] C.M.L.R. 335.

[82] Directive 2003/88 on certain aspects of the organisation of working time [2003] O.J. L299/9; see concerning annual sick leave and compensation (Joined Cases C-350/06 and C-520/06): Member State not allowed to make existence of right subject to any precondition E.C.R [2009] 20.01.09; Regulation 3820/85 on the harmonising of certain social legislation regarding to road transport [1985] O.J. L370/1, adapted by reason of the accession [2004] O.J. L168/35, amended [2009] O.J. L29/45. See also Regulation 561/2006: [2006] O.J. L102/1. Directive 2002/15 on the organisation of working time of persons performing mobile road transport activities [2006] O.J. L102/1; see *Spain and Finland v Parliament and Council* (Joined Cases C-184/02 and C-223/02) [2004] E.C.R. I-7789, where the Court rejected a request for annulment of said Directive.

[83] Regulation 1017/68 [1988] O.J. L 175/1, amended [2003] O.J. L1.

[84] See below: (3) Air Transport and (5) Maritime Transport.

[85] Regulation 1370/07 [2007] O.J. L315/1.

[86] Regulation 1192/69 on common rules for the normalisation of the accounts of railways undertakings [1969] O.J. L156/8, as amended.

[87] Council Resolution on co-operation between railway undertakings [1971] O.J. C5/1; for a long time, no "international" trains existed; indeed, when crossing a border, a train, besides changing locomotive, acquired the nationality of the host country and was submitted to all the rules and regulations applying to "national" trains.

cause, however, was their monopoly position and the market fragmentation. In other words, there was no competition and therefore closed-off and protected markets. This could only partly be explained by the obligations of public service[88] generally imposed on the railways by the national governments.

More than a decade after liberalising road and air transport in the Union, steps have been taken to develop an internal market for railways. This includes the creation of a high-speed rail network[89] and freight transport "freeways" across the Union. A series of measures aiming to ensure the development of a Union's international railways freight market have been adopted. In 2007, the Commission adopted a communication "Towards a rail network giving priority to freight", which aims to make freight transport more competitive, in particular by reducing transit times and improving the reliability of rail and its responsiveness to customers' demands.[90]

The first important piece of legislation required the Member States to manage railway undertakings in a competitive manner, to make railway undertakings independent by giving them a separate budget and system of accounts, to guarantee rights of access for rail transport operators on specific terms in other Member States to international combined transport services, and to have separate accounting for railway infrastructure (track and related equipment) and the operation of transport services as such as from January 1, 1993.[91] Important is as well the "combined" transport, which the Union tries to encourage and regulate.[92]

The *first railway package* (also called rail infrastructure package) aimed to enable rail companies to provide competitive European services to meet the demands of industry and forwarders. It consists of three Directives on the further development of the Union's railways,[93] on the licensing of railway undertakings[94] and on the allocation of railway infrastructure capacity and the levying of charges for the use of railway infrastructure and safety certification.[95]

The first package also provides for an extension of fair and non-discriminatory access for licensed railway undertakings to the entire network for a transitional period of up to seven years. This includes access to, and supply of, services in major terminals and ports, better organisation of frontier crossings, elimination

---

[88] Regulation 1191/69 on action by Member States concerning the obligations inherent in the concept of public service in the transport by rail, road and inland waterway [1969] O.J. L156/1, amended several times. See also art.93 TFEU [73], which refers to the discharge of certain obligations inherent in the concept of public service.

[89] Directive 96/48 on the interoperability of the trans-European high-speed rail system, [1996] O.J. L235/6, amended [2007] O.J L141/63, repealed by Regulation 1370/07 on public passenger transport by rail and by road [2007] O.J. L315/1 and the Commission Recommendation on the basic parameters of this system [2001] O.J. L100/17; see Decision concerning a technical specification for interoperability relating to the "infrastructure" sub-system of the trans-European high-speed rail system [2008] O.J. L77/1. See also Decision 2008/386 concerning the technical specification for interoperability relating to the control-command and signalling sub-system of the trans-European conventional and high-speed rail system [2008] O.J. L136/11 and Directive 2008/57 on the interoperability of the rail system within the Union [2008] O.J. L191/1, Annex VII modified [2009] O.J. L273/12.

[90] COM(2007) 608.

[91] Directive 91/440 on the development of the Union's railways [1991] O.J. L237/25, amended [2007] O.J. L315/44.

[92] Directive 92/106 on the establishment of common rules for certain types of combined transport of goods between Member States [1992] O.J. L368/38, as amended; and Council Resolution on the development of rail transport and combined transport: [1995] O.J. C169/1.

[93] Directive 2001/12 [2001] O.J. L75/1, amending [1991] O.J. L237/25; see *Commission v Germany* (C-477/03) [2004] E.C.R. 17.11.04, unpublished.

[94] Directive 2001/13 [2001] O.J. L75/28, amending [1995] O.J. L143/70.

[95] Directive 2001/14 [2001] O.J. L75/29, amended [2007] O.J. L315/44.

of the main bottlenecks in the system, independent regulatory bodies qualified to issue safety certificates and allocation of train paths as well as the interoperability of the trans-European conventional rail system.[96] The "Trans European Rail Freight Network" (TERFN) provided for in this package had to be implemented by Member States by March 15, 2003. To the detriment of the liberalisation of the rail freight transport sector, several Member States have failed to implement the first rail infrastructure package within the time limit set.[97] The delays in transposition have had repercussions on the ability of the actors to assert themselves on the European stage due to the resulting uncertainty surrounding the national regulatory situation.[98] In 2008 the Commission launched infringement proceedings against 24 (!) Member States for incorrect transposition of the directives making up the first railway package.[99] As from March 15, 2008, the entire European Rail Network is open to international freight services. The situation for passenger transport, however, remains unchanged.[100]

Safety does, of course, play an important role. For instance, a general licensing system for railway undertakings was set up,[101] as mentioned, a Directive on transportable pressure equipment approved for the inland transport of dangerous goods by road and by rail,[102] rules regarding the transport of dangerous goods by rail have been adopted[103] and a European Rail Traffic Management System was backed by the Union to enhance cross-border interoperability and signalling procurement by creating a single European-wide standard for railway signalling.[104] In order to complement the first package and to revitalise the railways by rapidly building an integrated European Railways Area, the Commission published, in 2001, a White Paper[105] concerning a second package.

The *second railways package* was adopted by Parliament and the Council in 2004. It covers the opening of the market for international freight transport to the entire European rail network as of January 1, 2006, the liberalisation of the market for national freight transport (cabotage) as of January 1, 2007, the interoperability of trans-European rail systems,[106] the development of the Union's railways,[107] safety rules[108] and the establishment of an European Railway

[96] Directive 2001/16 [2001] O.J. L110/1, amended [2007] O.J. L141/63, replaced by Directive 2008/57 on the interoperability of rail systems within the Community [2008] O.J. L191/1.

[97] Court cases (unpublished, but on the Internet under "Curia"): *Commission v Greece* (C-550/03); *Commission v United Kingdom* (C-483/03) and *Commission v Germany* (C-447/03): non-notification implementation measures for Directives 2001/12, 2001/13 and 2001/14 as well as: *Commission v Luxembourg* (C-481/03): non-notification implementation measures for Directives 2001/12 and 2001/13.

[98] Report from the Commission on the implementation of the first railway package of May 3, 2006; COM (2006) 189 final.

[99] General Report 2008, 83.

[100] But see Commission Decision of August 28, 2003 (COMP/37.685 GVG/FS) which concerned cross-border passenger service.

[101] Directive 95/18 [1995] O.J. L143/70, as amended.

[102] Directive 99/36 [1999] O.J. L138/20, as amended.

[103] Directive 96/49 on the approximation of the laws of the Member States with regard to the transport of dangerous goods by rail [1996] O.J. L235/25, replaced, together with Directive 94/55 (see above), by Directive 2008/68 [2008] O.J. L260/13.

[104] For more information see the Internet.

[105] White Paper, "European transport policy for 2010: time to decide", COM (2001) 370.

[106] Directive 2004/50 [2004] O.J. L164/114.

[107] Directive 2004/51 [2004] O.J. L164/164.

[108] Directive 2004/49 [2004] O.J. L164/44 (Railway Safety Directive), modified [2008] O.J. L345/62. See Regulation 352/2009 on the adoption of a common safety method on risk evaluation and assessment [2009] O.J. L108/4.

Agency[109] to steer the technical work on safety and interoperability. With regard to the latter, Parliament and the Council adopted a directive which establishes a legislative framework aimed at reducing barriers to bringing railway vehicles into service. Cross-acceptance between Member States should be improved through the application of the principle of mutual recognition and the harmonisation of national authorisation procedures.[110]

In March 2004, the Commission proposed a *third railway package* of measures. The *third package* of railway measures was adopted by Parliament and the Council in 2007[111]; it consists of one regulation and two directives:

- a Regulation on the rights and obligations of rail passengers, which is intended to enhance and improve these passengers' rights. It covers all journeys and rail services provided throughout the Union by one or more railway undertakings;
- a Directive[112] providing for the opening-up to competition of the international rail passenger transport service market by 2010 and includes the right for international trains to provide cabotage services, i.e. to take up and set down passengers at stations in the same Member State;
- a Directive on the certification of train drivers operating locomotives and trains on the railway system in the Union.[113]

In 2007, Parliament and the Council adopted the public service obligation regulation on public passengers transport service by rail and by road,[114] similar, in part, to the one adopted in 2004 establishing common rules on compensation and assistance to passengers in the event of denied boarding and of cancellation or long delays of flights,[115] and a Regulation on Public Service Obligations.[116] In 2007, the Commission published a Communication on monitoring development of the rail market providing for: statistical analysis, regular reporting and presenting the the regulatory and institutional framework established for the purpose of liberating this market.[117]

See also above the chapter on Competition for rules applying to transport, e.g. Guidelines for State aid to rail undertakings.[118]

6. Air Transport

As indicated, air transport was at the beginning not covered by the provisions on Transport of the EC Treaty, which, according to the Court does not mean that the

---

[109] See above, Ch.13: Decentralised Bodies of the Union.
[110] General Report 2008, 83.
[111] General Report 2007, 76.
[112] Directive 2007/58 [2007] O.J. L315/44, amending Directive 91/440 on the development of the Community railways [1991] O.J. L237/25.
[113] Directive 2007/69 on the certification of train drivers operating locomotives and trains on the railway system in the Union [2007] O.J. L315/51.
[114] Regulation 1370/07 [2007] O.J. L315/1 and Regulation 1371/07 on rail passengers' rights and obligations [2007] O.J. L315/14..
[115] [2004] O.J. L46/1.
[116] Regulation 1370/07 [2007] O.J. L315/1.
[117] COM(2007) 609.
[118] [2008] O.J. C 184/13 and Directive 91/440 [1991] L237/25.

general provisions of the Treaty did not apply either.[119] From the beginning, these two modes of transport were indeed subject to the general rules of the Treaty.[120]

Air transport, although in full expansion, suffered from the same drawback as rail transport, namely its monopoly position, and was therefore a protected national market. However, because of reciprocal traffic rights, some competition from foreign carriers had to be accepted on international routes, but for a long time, there were no competing national ones. Although the national airlines, the so-called Flag Carriers, desperately fought to keep foreign airlines from providing air service within their territory, i.e. from flying passengers from one city to another within the same country (so called cabotage), the situation has changed completely in the last years due to successive liberalisation packages adopted by the Union.

The *first liberalisation package* was adopted in December 1987. It limited, for example, the right of governments to object to the introduction of new fares and enabled airlines of two different states having a bilateral air transport agreement with each other, to share seating capacity. It was in the same year that the Council laid down the procedure for the application of the competition rules to undertakings in the air transport sector and for exemptions by category for agreements and concerted practices.[121] Those measures have been supplemented in June 1990 by the *second liberalisation package*, which opened up the market further. It gave the carriers a greater flexibility over the setting of fares and capacity-sharing and opened up the routes between Member States to all Union carriers.[122]

The *third liberalisation package* was adopted in July 1992 and is applicable since January 1993. It introduced gradually the freedom to provide air transport services within the Union and led, in April 1997, to the freedom to provide services within another Member State (cabotage).[123] This package provides for a Union air carrier's licence,[124] freedom of access to the market[125] and the freedom to set fares and rates for air services.[126] However, this freedom only applies to Union air carriers; where air carriers from third countries operating on intra-Union routes are concerned, the Union has acquired exclusive competence to enter into commitments with non-Member States concerning fares and rates to be charged (external competence of the Union).[127] This was followed by various other regulations: on exemption for agreements and concerted practices concerning

---

[119] art.100 TFEU [80].

[120] In *Commission v France* (167/73) [1974] E.C.R. 359, 24–25; [1974] 2 C.M.L.R. 216, where the Court ruled that the very first words of the Title on Transport: "The objectives of this Treaty shall be pursued . . .". refer to the provisions of arts 2 and 3 EC, and since the fundamental provisions applicable to the whole complex of economic activities are of prime importance for the attainment of those objectives, the object of the rules relating to the common transport policy, far from involving a departure from those fundamental rules, is to implement and complement them by means of common action; see as well *Nouvelles Frontiéres* (Joined Cases 209/84, 210/84, 211/84, 212/84 and 213/84) [1986] E.C.R. 1425.

[121] Regulation 3975/87 which was repealed by Regulation 411/2004 [2004] O.J. L68/1 and Regulation 3976/87 on the application of art.101(3) [81(3)] of the Treaty to certain categories of agreement and concerted practices in the air transport sector, replaced by Regulation 487/09 [2009] O.J. L148/1. See also Regulation 773/2004 [2004] O.J. L123/18, as amended.

[122] Regulation 2408/92 on access for air carriers to scheduled intra-Union air service routes [1992] O.J. L240/8, as amended.

[123] In 2003, the Commission announced the revision of the third liberalisation package in order to adapt the current rules to the recent changes.

[124] Regulation 2407/92 [1992] O.J. L240/1.

[125] Regulation 2408/92 [1992] O.J. L240/8, as amended.

[126] Regulation 2409/92 [1992] O.J. L240/15.

[127] See *Commission v Netherlands* (C-523/04) [2007] E.C.R. I-3267.

consultations on passenger tariffs on scheduled air services and slot allocation at airports,[128] code of conduct for computerised reservation systems,[129] common rules for the allocation of slots at Union airports,[130] access to the ground-handling market at Union airports,[131] and the limitation of noise emission.[132] See also a regulation laying down common requirements for the provisions of air navigation services, as regarding working methods and operating procedure,[133] and a regulation on common rules for the operation of air service in the Union—Public service obligations in respect of scheduled air services.[134]

In order to strengthen passengers' rights, a regulation establishing common rules for a denied-boarding compensation system in scheduled air transport,[135] a directive on unfair terms in consumer contracts[136] and a directive on package travel, package holidays and package tours[137] have been adopted.

Safety, of course, plays a very important role and several regulations and directives have been adopted,[138] including one on protection of the European sky against unsafe airlines[139] and on a restriction of liquids in carry-on baggage.[140]

(1) Single European Sky

In 2009, Parliament and the Council adopted the second *Single European Sky* package in order to improve and reinforce safety, to restructure European airspace as a function of air traffic flow, to create additional capacity and to increase

[128] Regulation 1617/93 [1993] O.J. L155/18, ended June 30, 2005. It was followed by Regulation 1459/2006 [2006] L272/3, whose validity ended October 31, 2006. Presently, Regulation 95/93 [1993] O.J. L14/1 on common rules for the allocation of slots at Union airports applies, modified [2009] O.J. L167/24.

[129] Regulation 2299/89 [1989] O.J. L220/1, amended [2009] O.J. L35/47.

[130] Regulation 95/93 [1995] O.J. L14/1, as amended. See Communication of April 30, 2008 (IP/08/672) clarifying a number of issues in order to ensure a better implementation COM (2008) 227.

[131] Directive 96/67 [1996] O.J. L272/36, as amended. See *Commission v Italy* (C-460/02) [2004] E.C.R. I-7335.

[132] Directive 89/629 [1989] O.J. L363/27. See *Commission v Spain* (C-70/03) [2004] I-7999.

[133] Regulation 2096/05 [2005] O.J. L335/13, amended [2008] O.J. L188/5.

[134] Regulation 1008/08 [2008] O.J. L293/3.

[135] Regulation 261/2004 [2004] O.J. L46/1. The Court determined that this Regulation only applies for travels within the Union: *Emirate Airlines* (C-173/07) [2008] E.C.R. I-5237. See *IATA and ELFAA* (C-344/04) [2006] E.C.R. I-403, as well as Regulation 2006/2004 on co-operation between national authorities responsible for the enforcement of consumer protection laws [2004] O.J. L364/1.

[136] Directive 93/13 [1993] O.J. L95/29. See *Oceano Grupo Editorial and Salva Editores* (Joined Cases C-240/98 and C-244/98) on the role of the national courts [2000] E.C.R. I-4941 and *Commission v Spain* (C-70/03) [2004] E.C.R. I-7999.

[137] Directive 90/314 [1990] O.J. L158/59.

[138] See, for instance, Regulation 300/08 on common rules in the field of civil aviation security [2008] O.J. L97/72, amended [2010] O.J. L7/3, and repealing Regulation 2320/02; also Regulation 552/2004 on the interoperability of the European Air Traffic Management network [2004] O.J. L96/26; Regulation 3922/91 on the harmonisation of technical requirements and administrative procedures in the field of civil aviation [1991] O.J. L373/4, amended [2008] O.J. L10/1 and [2008] L254/1. In 2007 the Council established a Joint Undertaking to develop the new generation European air traffic management system (SESAR) [2007] O.J. L64/1, amended [2008] O.J. L352/12.

[139] Regulation 2111/2005 on the establishment of a Union list of air carriers subject to an operating ban ("Airlines black list") within the Union and on informing air transport passengers of the identity of the operating air carrier [2005] O.J. L344/15; Regulation 474/2006 establishing the Union list of air carriers which are subject to an operating ban within the Union referred to in Ch.II of Regulation 2111/2005 [2006] O.J. L84/14, amended [2008] O.J. L102/3; Directive 2004/36 on the safety of third-country aircraft using Union airports [2004] O.J. L143/76, as amended.

[140] See IP/06/1313.

the overall efficiency of the Air Traffic Management system (ATM). It comprises four regulations[141] covering the essential elements for a seamless ATM. The actions defined in the regulations reinforces as well the integration of the civil and military air traffic control.

In order to achieve the objectives of the Single European Sky Initiative, the Commission is working closely together with the European Organisation for the Safety of Air Navigation (Eurocontrol). The co-operation should avoid duplication of efforts and will also be extended to other areas like Galileo, research and development, support to States and co-ordinated actions in international organisations.[142] The Union will become a member of Eurocontrol[143] and its membership has been implemented on a provisional basis in order to enable it participation during the ratification process.

Other safety rules have established common rules in the field of civil aviation security,[144] or regulate air carrier liability in the event of accidents.[145] Insurance requirements for air carriers and aircraft operators have been established,[146] while measures for the implementation of the common basic standards on aviation security have also been issued.[147] The principal objective is to establish and maintain a high uniform level of civil aviation safety in Europe.

A European Aviation Safety Agency (EASA), briefly described above in Ch.13, was established in 2002.[148] This Regulation applies to the design, production, maintenance and operation of aeronautical products, parts and appliances, and to the personnel and organisations involved in the operation of aircraft. Essential requirements for airworthiness are laid down in an annex, and products, parts and appliances must comply with the environmental protection requirements contained in the Chicago Convention of December 7, 1944. Several regulations were adopted.[149]

In 2008 the Commission authorised mobile communication services on aircraft (MCA services) in the Union.[150] When authorising MCA services, Member States must comply with the common regulatory framework for electronic

---

[141] Regulation 1108/09 laying down the framework for the creation of the single European sky (the Framework Regulation) [2009] O.J. L309/51; Regulation 550/2004 on the provision of air navigation services in the single European sky (the Service Provision Regulation) [2004] O.J. L96/10; Regulation 551/2004 on the organisation and use of the airspace in the single European sky (the Airspace Regulation) [2004] O.J. L96/20 and Notice implementing art.5 [2009] O.J. C46/26; Regulation 552/2004 on the interoperability of the European Air Traffic Management network (the Interoperability Regulation) [2004] O.J. L96/26. All modified [2009] O.J. L300/34.

[142] Memorandum of Co-operation between the Commission and EUROCONTROL of December 22, 2003, which governs the relationship between the two organisations and points the way for future co-operation.

[143] Council Decision concerning the conclusion by the European Union of the Protocol on the accession of EUROCONTROL, Council Document 5565/1/04.

[144] Regulation 2320/2002 [2002] O.J. L355/1, amended: see Regulation 483/09 [2009] O.J. L145/23.

[145] Regulation 2027/97 [1997] O.J. L285/1, as amended in order to align it with the Montreal Convention of May 28, 1999 [2001] O.J. L194/38. *Bogiatzi* (C-301/08) [2009] E.C.R. 22.10.09.

[146] Regulation 785/2004 [2004] O.J. L138/1.

[147] Regulation 622/2003 [2003] O.J. L89/9, amended [2008] O.J. L9/12 and L111/5; since the Annex was not published in the O.J., for security reasons, it is non-binding on individuals: *Heinrich* (C-345/06) E.C.R. 10.03.09.

[148] Regulation 1592/2002 [2002] O.J. L240/1, as amended.

[149] See for instance Regulation 1702/03 [2003] O.J. L243/6, amended [2006] O.J. L122/16 and [2007] O.J. L94/3 and Regulation 2042/03 O.J. L315/1, amended [2007] O.J. L94/18 and [2008] O.J. L283/5.

[150] Decision 2008/294 on harmonised conditions of spectrum use for the operation of mobile communication services on aircraft (MCA services) in the Union [2008] O.J. L98/19 and Recommendation 2008/295 [2008] O.J. L98/24.

communications network and services (Framework Directive)[151] and with the Directive on authorisation of electronic communications network and services (Authorisation Directive).[152]

(2) Safety Assessment of Foreign Aircraft (SAFA)[153]

In 2005 Parliament and Council decided that a Community list would be established of air carriers subject to an operating ban within the Community and on informing air transport passengers of the identity of the operating air carriers.[154] The list was established by the Commission in 2006.[155]

Details about this programme can be found above in Ch.13: Decentralised Bodies of the Union (I 14. The European Aviation Safety Agency).

(3) International Agreements

More than any other mode of transport, air transport extends beyond international borders, from there the necessity for agreements with third countries and International Organisations and Conventions.[156] Following the so called "open skies" decisions of the Court, in which agreements of eight Member States with the United States were found to partly infringe Union Law,[157] the Commission requested a negotiation mandate.

It contains first, a mandate for the Commission to open negotiations with the United States on the creation of an Open Aviation Area, consequently an air transport agreement was signed with the United States.[158] As a result all EU airlines can fly direct to the US from any airport in Europe and no longer only from their own country of origin. The agreement does away with all restrictions affecting connections, fares or the number of flights per week. An agreement was also signed on co-operation in the regulation of civil aviation safety.

Second, a mandate for the Commission to negotiate with third countries the replacement of certain provisions in existing bilateral agreements with a Union agreement, and third, a proposal for a regulation on the negotiation and implementation of air service agreements between Member States and third countries; an agreement was signed with Russia on the utilisation of the trans-Siberian routes, with the Kyrgys Republc,[159] Jordan,[160] the United Arab Emirates,[161] Panama, New Zealand, Armenia, Nepal,[162] Mongolia.[163] Decisions were adopted

---

[151] [2002] O.J L108/33, amended [2007] O.J. L171/32.

[152] [2002] O.J L108/21.

[153] See report from the Commission on the European Community SAFA programme [2008] O.J. L42/1.

[154] Regulation 2111/05 [2005] O.J. L344/15.

[155] Regulation 474/06 [2006] O.J. L84/14, amended [2008] O.J. L197/36 and [2009] O.J. L95/16 and [2009] O.J. L182/4.

[156] See, for instance, Decision on the conclusion by the EC of the Convention for the Unification of Certain Rules for International Carriage by Air (the Montreal Convention) [2001] O.J. L194/38.

[157] See *United Kingdom, Denmark, Sweden, Finland, Belgium. Luxembourg, Austria et Germany v Commission* (C-466/98, C-467/98, C-469/98, C-471/98, C-472/98, C-475/98 and C-776/98) [2002] E.C.R. I-9427.

[158] Decision 2007/339 [2007] O.J. L134/1.

[159] Decision 2007/470 [2007] O.J. L179/38.

[160] [2009] O.J. L173/6.

[161] [2009] O.J. L173/6.

[162] Decision 2009/117 [2009] O.J. L41/3.

[163] General Report 2007, 82.

concerning the conclusion of agreements with Croatia, Macedonia, Georgia, Kyrgyzstan, Lebanon, Malaysia, the Maldives, Moldova, Panama, Paraguay, Singapore, Uruguay,[164] Morocco,[165] Azerbaijan, Australia,[166] India, Pakistan.

An agreements exists between the Union and the Swiss Confederation[167] and the State of Israel[168] on air transport. An agreement on civil aviation safety was signed with Canada.[169]

Decisions on the signing and provisional application of agreements were also adopted for Australia, Nepal, Pakistan, Israel, India and Armenia.[170]

In order to protect the European air carriers against distortion of competition by non-European carriers, a regulation concerning protection against subsidisation and unfair pricing practices causing injury to Union air carriers in the supply of air services from countries not members of the European Union has been adopted.[171] Mention must also be made of the Agreement between the Union and the USA concerning the application of the "GATT Agreement on Trade in Civil Aircraft" to trade in large civil aircraft.[172] The purpose was to put an end to the financial support granted on both sides of the Atlantic to the constructors of large aircrafts (Boeing v Airbus). From the complaints recently filed by both parties with the WTO it appears that this endeavour was not successful.

7. INLAND WATERWAY TRANSPORT

Europe is known for its canals and natural waterways used for transport, not only of goods but also of passengers. The Union legislation in this field is particularly extensive, but of interest to only a small group of people. Let it be sufficient to mention a Regulation[173] on a Union-fleet capacity policy to promote inland waterway transport, which aimed to reduce overcapacity in that sector by introducing an "old-for-new" rule and a recent directive laying down technical requirements for inland waterway vessels.[174] No further mention will be made here of the rules applying to this mode of transport. As already mentioned, the *Official Journal Repertory of Union Legislation in force*, contains most of the needed information.[175]

8. MARITIME TRANSPORT

This mode of transport has, by definition, an international aspect. There is no question, therefore, of treating this field exclusively at Union level. As an example,

---

[164] [2008] O.J. L60/22 and L106/6.
[165] [2008] O.J. L87/9.
[166] [2009] O.J. L173/4.
[167] Agreement of December 16, 2008. See Decision of the Joint Community/Switzerland Air Transport Committee [2009] O.J. L40/38.
[168] [2009] O.J. L90/10.
[169] [2009] O.J. L153/10.
[170] General Report 2008, 86.
[171] [2004] O.J. L162/1.
[172] [1992] O.J. L301/32.
[173] Regulation 718/1999 [1999] O.J. L90/1, as amended, concerning the scope of application, see, e.g. *Josanne E.A. v Commission* (T-82/01) [2003] E.C.R. II-2013.
[174] Directive 2006/87 [2006] O.J. L389/3, modified [2006] O.J. L399/3, [2008] O.J. L255/5 and [2009] O.J. L32/1 and L109/14, correction [2009] O.J. L150/5.
[175] Office for Official Publications of the European Union, L-2985 Luxembourg.

at the international level the Union has ratified[176] the UN Convention on the Law of the Sea.[177] Within the Union this applies, in the first place, to the rules of competition. Special rules have therefore been adopted: first concerning the application of the competition rules to maritime transport[178] and a Regulation on unfair pricing practices in maritime transport.[179] Since liner shipping companies (consortia) play an important role in shipping, an exemption for certain categories of agreements was also provided for.[180] The same applies to Liner Conferences: the Council adopted a Regulation on the ratification by the Member States of the United Nations Convention on a Code of Conduct of Liner Conferences.[181] Market access is crucial, both within the Union and outside of it, for which adequate rules have been adopted granting freedom to provide maritime transport services within Member States (maritime cabotage),[182] or providing for coordinated action to safeguard free access to cargoes in ocean trades.[183] In 2008 the Commission published Guidelines on the application of Articles 101 and 102 [81 and 82] to maritime transport Services.[184] The latter cover liner shipping services, cabotage and tramp services. The guidelines define their relevant market. With regard to horizontal agreements in the maritime transport sector, certain technical agreements, information exchange between competitors in liner shipping and pool agreements in tramp shipping are acceptable from a competition point of view, under certain conditions set out in the Guidelines.

Understandably, environmental safety and safety at sea was a major preoccupation. In order to ensure the uniform and compulsory application of environmental standards as, for example, provided for in the International Convention for the Prevention of Pollution from Ships (so-called MARPOL 73/78),[185] adopted by the International Maritime Organisation and signed by all Member States, a directive has been adopted.[186] The Council recommended the ratification of several

---

[176] See *http://www.un.org/Depts/los/reference-files/status2006.pdf*; The United Nations Convention on the Law of the Sea.

[177] See *http://www.unclos.com*.

[178] Regulation 1419/2006 [2006] O.J. L269/1.

[179] Regulation 4057/86 [1986] O.J. L378/14, codified version [2009] O.J. L79/1.

[180] See Regulation 479/92 [1992] O.J. L55/3, as amended, and Regulation 823/2000 on the application of art.101(3) TFEU [81(3)] to certain categories of agreements, decisions and concerted practices between liner shipping companies (consortia) [2000] O.J. L100/24, amended and prolonged [2005] O.J. L110/10. New Regulation: IP/09/1367.

[181] Regulation 954/79 [1979] O.J. L121/1, repealed as from the end of the transition period provided in Regulation 1419/06 [2006] O.J. L269/1. See Commission Decision imposing fines on the Trans-Atlantic Conference Agreement for abuse of a dominant position: press release IP/98/811 of September 16, 1998.

[182] Regulation 3577/92 [1992] O.J. L364/7. Regulation 1419/2006 [2006] O.J. L269/1 extended the scope of Regulation 1/2003 and of Regulation 773/2004 conduct of proceedings by the Commission pursuant to arts 101 and 102 [81 and 82] [2004] O.J. L123/18) to include cabotage and tramp vessel services.

[183] Regulation 4055/86 applying the principle of freedom to provide services to maritime transport between Member States and between Member States and third countries: [1986] O.J. L378/1, as amended, and Regulation 4058/86 [1986] O.J. L378/21.

[184] [2008] O.J. C245/2.

[185] See *http://www.imo.org/home.asp?topic-idz161*.

[186] Directive 2005/35 on ship-source pollution and on the introduction of penalties for infringement [2005] O.J. L255/1, modified [2009] O.J. L280/52; see also Directive 2000/59 on port reception facilities for ship generated waste and cargo residues [2000] O.J. L332/81, amended with regard to the former Directive; the Court ascertrained that its validity cannot be assessed either in the light of the International Convention for the prevention of pollution from ships or inthe light of the UN Convention on the law of the Sea (Montego Bay, December 10, 1982).

international conventions concerning safety at sea,[187] laid down rules for a vessel traffic monitoring and information system with a view to enhancing the safety and efficiency of maritime traffic, improving the response of authorities to incidents, accidents or potentially dangerous situations at sea, including search and rescue operations, and contributing to a better prevention and detection of pollution by ships[188] and ruled on the accelerated phasing-in of double hull or equivalent design requirements for single-hull oil tankers. Since 2008 no oil tanker carrying heavy grades of oil is allowed to enter or leave ports or off-shore terminals or to anchor in areas under the jurisdiction of a Member State, unless it is a double-hull tanker.[189]

Following several catastrophic accidents with ferries, rules have been adopted on the safety management of roll-on/roll-off passenger ferries[190]; on safety rules and standards for passenger ships[191]; on specific stability requirements for ro-ro passenger ships[192]; requirements and procedures for the safe loading and unloading of bulk carriers[193]; the setting up of a harmonised safety regime for fishing vessels of 24 metres in length or over[194]; on common rules and standards for ship inspection[195]; on the minimum safety and health requirements for improved medical treatment on board vessels[196]; on the minimum level of training of seafarers[197]; concerning enforcement, in respect of shipping using Union ports[198] and sailing in the waters under the jurisdiction of the Member States; of international standards for ship safety, pollution prevention and shipboard living and working conditions (port State control).[199] Furthermore, a European Maritime Safety Agency (EMSA),[200] and a specialised expert body assisting the

[187] Convention on safety in shipping [1978] O.J. L194/17; Convention on standards of training, certification and watch-keeping for sea-farers [1979] O.J. L33/31; Convention for safe containers [1979] O.J. L125/18; and the Convention for the safety of fishing vessels, see Council Resolution [1985] O.J. L72 /110; Convention for the safety of life at sea; Convention for the prevention of pollution from ships [1993] O.J. L194/5; and the Convention on maritime Search and Rescue (SAR) [1983] O.J. L237/34. It will be noticed that all those Council Recommendations were published in the L (Legislation) series of the *Official Journal*, although they do not constitute binding acts.
[188] Directive 2002/59 establishing a Union vessel traffic monitoring and information system [2002] O.J. L203/10, amended [2009] O.J. L131/101 and by Directive 2002/18 establishing the fundamental principles governing the investigation of accidents in the maritime transport sector [2009] O.J. L131/114, amended [2009] O.J. L314/13.
[189] Regulation 417/2002 [2002] O.J. L64/1, after the Prestige and Erika accidents, amended [2007] O.J. L113/1.
[190] Regulation 3051/95 [1995] O.J. L320/14, which has been repealed by Regulation 336/2006 on the implementation of the International Safety Management Code within the Union [2006] O.J. L64/1, and Directive 99/35 on a system of mandatory surveys for the safe operation of regular ro-ro ferry and high-speed passenger craft services [1999] O.J. L138/1, amended by Directive 2009/18 establishing the fundamental principles governing the investigation of accidents in the maritime transport sector [2009] O.J. L131/114.
[191] Directive 98/18 [1998] O.J. L144/1, recast by Directive 2009/45 [2009] O.J. L163/1.
[192] Directive 2003/25 [2003] O.J. L123/22, as amended.
[193] Directive 2001/96 [2002] O.J. L13/9, as amended.
[194] Directive 97/70 [1998] O.J. L34/1, as amended.
[195] Directive 94/57 [1994] O.J. L319/20, as amended.
[196] Directive 92/29 [1992] O.J. L113/19, as amended.
[197] Directive 2001/25 [2001] O.J. L136/17, as amended.
[198] See Regulation 725/2004 on enhancing ship and port facility security [2004] O.J. L129/6, modified [2009] O.J.L29/53.
[199] Directive 95/21 [1995] O.J. L157/1, as amended. See also Regulation 725/2004 on enhancing ship and port facility security [2004] O.J. L129/6 and Regulation 884/2005 laying down procedures for conducting Commission inspections in the field of maritime security [2005] O.J. L 148/25.
[200] Regulation 1406/2002 [2002] O.J. L208/1, amended [2004] O.J. L129/1.

Commission in its task and facilitating the co-operation within the Union, have been established.[201]

In 2007 the Commission adopted an action plan for an integrated maritime policy[202] and in 2008 presented a communication on "Guidelines for an integrated approach to maritime policy: Towards best practice in integrated maritime governance and stakeholder consultation".[203]

An agreement on maritime transport was signed with China in 2002 and entered into force in 2008[204]; it was amended in 2009.[205]

9. INTERMODALITY

Intermodality plays a major role in the Commission's objectives for the transport policy in order to shift the congestion of road transport to other modes.[206] The concept of intermodal freight transport involves the easy and efficient movement of goods using more than one mode of transport to exploit the advantages of multiple means of transport. The so-called Marco Polo Programme[207] was designed to achieve modal shifts from road transport to transport by sea, rail, and inland waterway. This programme has been replaced in 2006 by the *second* Marco Polo Programme, which started as from January 1, 2007.[208] The program has a budget of €400 million for the period 2007–2013; it includes new actions such as motorways of the sea and traffic avoidance measures and has been extended to countries bordering the EU.

10. TRANS-EUROPEAN TRANSPORT NETWORKS

A Trans-European Transport Network Executive Agency was set up to manage the Union funds for the promotion of the trans-European transport network.[209] The funds allocated to railway projects under the 2007–2013 programme exceed €1.7 billion. Exploratory talks took place regarding co-operation in the field of transport with neighbouring countries. Discussions with the Western Balkans have been concluded and the Commission has proposed negotiating directives to establish a transport community in the region.[210]

---

[201] For more details see above, Ch.13 Decentralised Bodies of the Union.
[202] COM(2007) 575.
[203] COM(2008) 395.
[204] [2008] O.J. L46/25.
[205] [2009] O.J. L144/20.
[206] White Paper "European transport policy for 2010: time to decide", COM(2001) 370.
[207] Regulation 1382/2003 [2003] O.J. L196/1, as amended.
[208] Regulation 1692/2006 establishing the second Marco Polo (Marco Polo II) programme for granting of Union financial assistance to improve the environmental performance of the freight transport system [2006] O.J. L328/1, amended [2009] O.J. L266/1.
[209] See Ch.13, Part III.
[210] General Report 2008, 87.

11. Conclusion with Regard to a "Common Transport Policy"

As was seen, transport in the Union is the subject of an impressive array of rules and regulations. The question is, however, whether this constitutes a "common policy". As was seen above, important steps were taken to liberalise transport within the Union, cabotage is now possible; another important step was the creation of the Trans-European Networks (TENs) by the EU Treaty, which should help to integrate the national networks into a single system. This aim has been practically achieved with regard to the road system, but is still an ongoing process as far as rail transport is concerned. Nevertheless, as is clearly stated in the White Paper, there is now a global approach to the various sectors of transport aiming to tackle the existing imbalance in the different modes of transport and to enhance the environmental problems. The objective remains the establishment and functioning of an Internal Transport Market, which can only be attained through liberalisation, integration and harmonisation. It is to be seen how the Union will manage the challenges of the transport issues in the enlarged internal market. Much has been achieved, much remains to be done.

Further Reading

Liz Heffernan and Conor McAuliffe, "External relations in the air transport sector. The Court of Justice and the open sky agreements", (2003) E.L.Rev. 601.

Chapter Twenty-eight

Economic and Monetary Union (Policy)[1]

The most tangible aspect of European integration and more particularly of the Economic and Monetary Union (EMU) was, for the European citizens, the introduction of the single currency, called the Euro.[2] The introduction of the Euro on January 1, 2002, in replacement[3] of the national currencies of the Member States participating in this aspect of EMU[4] constitutes a major event not only from an economic and monetary point of view, but foremost from the point of view of European integration. Indeed, a corollary of the introduction of the Euro, is the setting up of the European Central Bank (ECB)[5] to which the Member States have surrendered, as shall be seen, the definition of their monetary policies. It can be said, without exaggeration, that through this transfer of sovereignty, the process of European integration has reached the point of no return. None of the preceding achievements, including the internal market, were secure in the absence of a single currency. Politically speaking, it was *the* decisive step on the way to European Union. At the risk of incurring the disfavour of some readers, it is submitted that this fact alone stands out as the most important decision taken by and for Europe since the end of WWII.

The introduction of the Euro was the result of a rather short—10 years—but complex procedure with economic, monetary and institutional aspects. Those shall be briefly described in the following sections. The introduction was an unprecedented success thanks to meticulous preparation and to the enthusiastic welcome given to it by a large majority of the public. Title VIII of the TFEU on "Economic and Monetary Policy" is divided into five chapters: "Economic policy"; "Monetary policy"; "Institutional provisions"; "Provisions specific to Member States whose currency is not the euro"; and "Transitional provisions".

It is interesting to note that "Economic and Monetary Policy" is not mentioned among the "Categories and Areas of Union Competence"[6], only "monetary policy for the Member States whose currency is the euro"[7] is; but the Treaty also provides

---

[1] arts 119–144 TFEU [98–124].

[2] Regulation 1103/97 [1997] O.J. L162/1 and *Berthu v Council* (T-207/97) [1998] E.C.R. II-509. See also Council Regulation 974/98 on the introduction of the Euro [1998] O.J. L139/1, modified [2005] O.J. L346/1 and [2007] O.J. L186/3 (Malta) and [2007] O.J. L 186/1 (Cyprus) and Slovakia [2008] O.J. L195/24.

[3] National currencies ceased to exist on June 30, 2002.

[4] Practically all of the Member States (Belgium, Germany, Ireland, Spain, France, Italy, Luxembourg, the Netherlands, Austria, Portugal and Finland), except Denmark, Greece (which joined later on, see Decision 2000/427 [2000] O.J. L167/19), Sweden, which has a derogation, art.139(1) TFEU and the UK, which decided not to move to the third stage; as indicated, Slovenia joined in 2007, Malta and Cyprus in 2008 and Slovakia in 2009. The 10 new Member States also have a derogation: see [2007] O.J. L186/32, (4) and have yet to meet the conditions for adopting the single currency.

[5] See above Ch.12: Other bodies of the Union.

[6] arts 3, 4, 5 and 6 TFEU.

[7] art.3(1)(c) TFEU.

that, "the Member States shall coordinate their economic policies within the Union"[8] and that the Council shall adopt measures, in particular broad guidelines, for these economic policies.[9] See above, Ch.6: The Council. This economic policy is based upon "common objectives", which are not further defined.[10] The Treaty, however, makes clear that the economic policy envisaged, must be conducted, "in accordance with the principle of an open market economy with free competition".[11] At least the basic economic philosophy is here unequivocally affirmed. The TFEU adds that,

> "[T]hese activities shall include a single currency, the euro, and the definition and conduct of a single monetary policy and exchange rate policy the primary objective of both of which shall be to maintain price stability, and, without prejudice to this objective, to support the general economic policies in the Union"[12].

Furthermore, "these activities of the Member States and the Union shall entail compliance with the following principles: stable prices, sound public finances and monetary conditions and a sustainable balance of payments."[13] As for the monetary policy, as shall be seen, the Treaty provides that the primary objective is to maintain price stability and to support the general economic policies in the Union.[14] Here again the principle of an open market economy with free competition is asserted.[15] Those principles correspond more or less to the famous four criteria[16] that must be fulfilled by the Member States, "for the adoption of a single currency".[17]

The above constitutes, in a nutshell, the economic and monetary policy of the Union; its various aspects will, as already mentioned, be examined in some more detail below.

1. ECONOMIC POLICY[18]

Although no mention is made of social policy in the context of the economic and monetary policy, it is quite obvious that the social aspects cannot be dissociated from either policies, even if this is more obvious with regard to economic policies as such.

The chapter on economic policy covers the following subjects:

- the conduct of economic policies by the Member States in the context of the broad guidelines set out by the Council[19];
- the monitoring of economic developments in each of the Member States by the Council[20];

---

[8] art.5(1) TFEU [4(1)].
[9] art.5(1) TFEU [4].
[10] art.121(2) [99(2)] TFEU provides that on the basis of a conclusion of the European Council, the Council shall adopt a recommendation setting out broad guidelines of the economic policies of the Member States and of the Union.
[11] art.119(1) TFEU [4(1)].
[12] art.119(2) TFEU [4(2)].
[13] art.119(3) TFEU [4(3)].
[14] art.127(1) TFEU [105(1)].
[15] art.119 TFEU [4(2)].
[16] art.140(1) TFEU [121(1)].
[17] art.140(1) TFEU [121(1)].
[18] arts 120–126 TFEU [98 to 104].
[19] art.121(2) TFEU [99(1)].
[20] art.121(3) TFEU [99(3)].

- Union financial assistance to Member States in difficulties[21];
- the prohibition of overdraft or any other type of credit facility with the ECB or with central banks of the Member States for public bodies, except public-owned credit institutions[22] and of privileged access to financial institutions[23];
- mutual financial guarantees for the joint execution of a specific project[24]; and
- the avoidance of excessive government deficits.[25]

The first and the last items are, from an economic policy point of view, by far the most important.

(1) Co-ordination of the Economic Policies of the Member States[26]

Member States must conduct their economic policies in the context of "broad guidelines". These are drafted by the Council on a recommendation from the Commission and submitted to the European Council. The latter discusses a "conclusion" on the guidelines, after which the Council adopts a "recommendation" setting out these guidelines.[27]

The implementation of the broad guidelines forms the object of a "multilateral surveillance" by the Council. In order to ensure closer co-ordination of the economic policies and sustained convergence of the economic performances of the Member States, the Council monitors the implementation of the guidelines on the basis of reports submitted by the Commission on the economic developments in each Member State.[28] The latter must forward all relevant information to the Commission.[29] When it is established that the economic policies of a Member State are not consistent with the broad guidelines, the Council may, on recommendation from the Commission, make by qualified majority the necessary recommendations to the Member State concerned.[30] It is worthwhile noting here that none of the binding Union acts provided for in the Treaty, i.e. regulations, directives and decisions, are mentioned here; the terms "report" and "conclusion", in such a context, were novelties in the text of the Treaty. Furthermore, the setting out of "broad guidelines" for the economic policies of the Member States via a non-binding "recommendation" seems to minimise their importance. This is surprising since great weight is attached to the consistency between the economic policies of the Member States and those guidelines and since Parliament and the Council, acting by means of regulations, in accordance with the ordinary legislative procedure,[31] may adopt detailed rules for the multilateral surveillance procedure.[32]

---

[21] art.122 TFEU [100]. See Regulation 332/2002 establishing a facility providing medium-term financial assistance to Member States' balance of payments [2002] O.J. L53/1, amended [2008] O.J. L352/11.

[22] art.123 TFEU [101].

[23] art.124 TFEU [102].

[24] art.125 TFEU [103].

[25] art.126(1) TFEU [104].

[26] art.121 TFEU [99].

[27] See, for instance, Council Recommendation on the broad guidelines 2008–2010 [2008] O.J. L137/13.

[28] art.121(3), 1 TFEU [99(3)].

[29] art.121(3), 2 TFEU [99(3)].

[30] art.121(4) TFEU [99(4)]. See for instance Council Recommendation of February 12, 2001.

[31] art.294 TFEU [251].

[32] art.121(6) TFEU [99(6)].

(2) Excessive Government Deficits[33]

The Treaty introduces the notion of "budgetary discipline" in order to avoid excessive government deficits.[34] Two criteria are provided that allow the Commission to monitor the development of the budgetary situation and the stock of government debt. The ratio of deficit, on the one hand, and of the government debt, on the other, to gross domestic product, may not exceed a reference value specified in the Protocol on the excessive deficit procedure annexed to the Treaty.[35] The application of the Protocol is the object of a regulation.[36]

In case those criteria are not observed by a Member State, the Commission prepares a report which is submitted to the Economic and Financial Committee,[37] that formulates an opinion thereon. If the Commission considers that an excessive deficit exists or may occur, it addresses an opinion to the Member State concerned and informs the Council accordingly.[38] The latter shall, on a proposal from the Commission, after having considered the observations of the Member State concerned, decide, after an overall assessment, whether an excessive deficit does indeed exist.[39] The Council must then adopt, on a recommendation from the Commission, "recommendations" addressed to the Member State in question with a view to bringing the situation to an end within a given period. These recommendations shall not be made public, unless the Council establishes that there has been no effective action in response to its recommendations. If the latter fails to put the recommendations into practice, the Council may decide to give notice to that Member State, "to take, within a specified time limit, measures for the deficit reduction".[40] Although failure by the Member State in question to abide by the notice does not constitute a failure, "to fulfil an obligation under this Treaty",[41] that can be brought before the Court, the Treaty provides for some measures which can be taken against the recalcitrant Member State.

These measures are the following[42]:

- require the Member State to publish additional information before issuing bonds and securities;
- invite the EIB to reconsider its lending policy towards said State;
- require a non-interest-bearing deposit of an appropriate size with the Union; and/or
- impose fines of an appropriate size.

---

[33] art.126 TFEU [104].

[34] art.126(2) TFEU [104(2)].

[35] Protocol No.12. The ratios are respectively 3 and 60 per cent. This Protocol shall be replaced by "appropriate provisions" adopted by the Council, acting unanimously on a proposal from the Commission and after consulting Parliament and the ECB: art.126(14)2 TFEU [104(14)2].

[36] Regulation 479/09 [2009] O.J. L145/1.

[37] This Economic and Monetary Committee was set up, under a different name (Economic and Financial Committee), at the start of the third stage; at the time, it replaced the Monetary Committee. Its task is to "promote coordination of the policies of the Member States to the full extend needed for the functioning of the internal market." art.126(4) TFEU [114(4)].

[38] art.126(5) TFEU [114(5)].

[39] art.126(6) TFEU [104(6)]. See, for instance, Council Decision of June 30, 1997 abrogating the decision on the existence of an excessive deficit in the Netherlands [1997] O.J. L177/23. See Council Decision of November 5, 2002 on the existence of an excessive deficit in Portugal [2002] O.J. L322/30 and decisions concerning the existence of an excessive deficit in France, Greece, Italy and Spain [2009] O.J. L135/19, 21, 23 and 25.

[40] art.126(9) TFEU [104(9)].

[41] art.126(10) TFEU [104(10)].

[42] art.126(11) TFEU [104(11)].

The President of the Council informs Parliament.

All decisions are taken by the Council, on a recommendation from the Commission, by qualified majority, weighted as for normal Council decisions.[43] The last time the Commission made such a recommendation was in October 2003 in respect of France.[44]

When the excessive deficit has been corrected, the Council abrogates some or all of its decisions and recommendations.

(3) Prohibition of "overdraft facilities"[45] and "privileged access to financial institutions"[46]

Overdraft facilities with the Central Banks and privileged access to financial institutions for governments, regional, local or other public authorities have always been a simple means to finance deficits. They had, therefore, to be abolished in order to help eliminate those deficits and their recurrence. On the other hand, the Treaty provides for mutual assistance, where a Member State is in difficulties or seriously threatened with difficulties as regards its balance of payments, and where those difficulties are liable to jeopardise the functioning of the internal market or the progressive implementation of the common commercial policy.[47] In 2002 the Council established a facility providing medium-term financial assistance for Member States, outside the Euro area. In 2009, the scope and intensity of the international financial crisis required raising the ceiling of outstanding loans from €25 billion to €50 billion.[48]

2. MONETARY POLICY[49]

Expanding on the task of the European System of Central Banks (ESCB) (described in Ch.13), it can be noted, once again, that the primary objective of the Union monetary policies is to maintain price stability. In order to make this possible a vast programme for achieving economic and monetary union, of which a part was just described, was devised. It had to be implemented in three stages.[50]

---

[43] See above Ch.7: The Council.

[44] IP/03/1353.

[45] art.123 TFEU [101].

[46] art.124 TFEU [102].

[47] arts 122(2) and 143 TFEU [119(2)].

[48] Regulation 332/02 [2002] O.J. L53/1, modified [2009] O.J. L128/1. See, for instance, Decision 2009/102 providing Community medium-term financial assistance for Hungary [2009] O.J. L57/5.

[49] arts 127–133 TFEU [105 to 111].

[50] The *first stage* started on July 1, 1990 and ended on December 31, 1993. It consisted essentially in an attempt at greater convergence of the national economies and the strengthening of the co-operation between the central banks. During that stage, all restrictions on the free movement of capital and payments between Member States, and between Member States and third countries, were abolished and so were the overdraft facilities and the privileged access to financial institutions, mentioned above. Furthermore, the Council was to assess the progress made with regard to economic and monetary convergence, in particular with regard to price stability and sound public finances, and progress made with regard to Union law concerning the internal market. Governments also had to avoid excessive deficits and start the process leading to the independence of their central bank. The *second stage* for achieving economic and monetary union started on January 1, 1994. On that date the European

3. Provisions Specific to Member States whose Currency is the Euro[51] — the Euro Group

The Council is to adopt measures specific to the Member States whose currency is the Euro in order to strengthen the co-ordination and surveillance of their budgetary discipline and to set out economic policy guidelines for them, while ensuring that they are compatible with those adopted for the whole of the Union and are kept under surveillance.

Monetary Institute (EMI) was established (in Frankfurt) and took up its duties. It was replaced, five years later, by the European Central Bank (ECB), at the start of the *third stage*. The EMI's task was to prepare the third stage; details can be found in the corresponding Treaty provisions. In particular it should be noted that the EMI had to specify the regulatory, organisational and logistical framework for the European System of Central Banks (ESCB). The latter's task is to define and implement the monetary policy of the Union. The most important decision to be taken during the second stage was which Member States could participate in the single currency system. Since no other date had been set for the beginning of the third stage, it was decided that it would start on January 1, 1999. The Council, meeting in the composition of Heads of State or Government had to confirm, before July 1, 1998, which Member States fulfilled the necessary conditions for the adoption of the single currency and whether a majority of the Member States fulfilled the necessary conditions. Although this is now history, it is of interest to note that this decision was taken on the basis of a report from the Commission and the EMI on, among other things, the achievement of a high degree of sustainable convergence. The latter was judged by reference to the fulfilment by each Member State of four criteria, i.e. inflation, budgetary deficit, exchange-rate fluctuations within the European Monetary System and long-term interest rate levels. Those criteria were further developed in a Protocol annexed to the Treaty. The *third stage*. The decision was taken by the Heads of State and Government on May 1, 1998, and as indicated above, all the Member States, except Denmark, Greece, Sweden and the UK, were found to fulfil the necessary conditions for the adoption of a single currency. Denmark, Greece (which joined later on) and Sweden became "Member States with a derogation", which assume certain obligations, and will integrate the single currency system, as soon as their economic policies allow. On that date also financial transactions could be carried out in Euros; anyone could open a bank account in that currency. However, the Euro did not become legal tender for current transactions. That had to wait for the issuing of Euro banknotes and coins. The Treaty confers upon the ECB the, "exclusive right to authorise the issue of banknotes within the Union". Both the ECB and the national central banks may issue such notes. Those banknotes are the, "only such notes to have the status of legal tender within the Union". With regard to coins, the Treaty provides that they may be issued by the Member States, subject to approval by the ECB of the volume of the issue. As indicated above, measures were adopted by the Council to harmonise the denominations and technical specifications of all coins intended for circulation to the extent necessary to permit their smooth circulation within the Union. These coins and banknotes were issued on January 1, 2002; on that date the citizens of the participating Member States carried two different currencies: the Euro and their national currency for a period of six months: until June 30, 2002 at midnight. This date was modified to the last day of February. Until then, both currencies were legal tender at the same time but after that date only the Euro was accepted as current payment. The Treaty also provides that the Council may conclude formal agreements on an exchange-rate system for the euro in relation with non-Union currencies. From the start of the third stage, the value of the Euro was irrevocably fixed, the composition of the Euro basket was not changed from that of the ECU. From that date on also, the Member States participating in the single currency did no longer implement their own monetary policy. This role was transferred to the European System of Central Banks (ESCB). The latter is composed of the ECB and the national central banks, including those of the Member States which do not participate in the single currency. The ESCB has no legal personality (only the ECB has) and its Statute, together whith that of the ECB, is the object of Protocol No. 4 annexed to the TFEU. Its primary objective is to maintain price stability and to support the general economic policies in the Union. Its basic tasks are described as follows: to define and implement the monetary policy of the Union, to conduct foreign exchange operations, to hold and manage the official foreign reserves of the Member States and to promote the smooth operation of payments systems.

[51] arts 136–138 TFEU.

Interesting and important are the, "arrangements for meetings between finance ministers of those Member States" as laid down by the Protocol on the Euro Group.[52] The latter provides that the Ministers "with responsibility for finance" of those Member States shall "meet informally", when necessary, to discuss questions related to the specific responsibilities they share with regard to the single currency. The Commission takes part and the ECB shall be invited. The president is elected for two and a half years.

This not-very-well-known body plays a role much more important than it appears at first sight.

4. INSTITUTIONAL PROVISIONS

The most interesting institutional provision is the one conferring upon the ECB, the power to make regulations, take decisions, and make recommendations and deliver opinions.[53] The fact that the ECB has the power to make regulations,[54] which have general application and are binding in their entirety and directly applicable in all Member States,[55] might explain why the Treaty of Lisbon conferred upon the ECB the status of an "institution" of the Union.[56] Like all binding acts of the institutions, the regulations and decisions of the ECB must be reasoned and published in the *Official Journal of the European Union*.[57] They must be made available to the citizens of the Union and when they impose a pecuniary obligation[58] on persons other than States, they shall be enforceable. The binding acts of the ECB are also submitted to the control of legality by the European courts.[59] The composition of the ECB was described above in Ch.12: Other Bodies of the Union. As indicated above, an Economic and Financial Committee was set up,[60] among others, to keep under review the economic and financial situation of the Member States.[61]

5. TRANSITIONAL PROVISIONS

Most of the transitional provisions provided for under this Treaty Title have been incorporated in the three stages described above in a footnote. They concerned, among others, the EMI, which no longer exists.

---

[52] Protocol No. 14.

[53] See for instance, Regulation 2818/98 of the ECB on the application of minimum reserves and Regulation 2819/98 concerning the consolidated balance sheet of the monetary financial institutions sector [1998] O.J. L356/1 and 7.

[54] art.132(1) TFEU [110(1)].

[55] See art.287 TFEU [249], which contains an identical definition of a regulation.

[56] art.13(1) EU.

[57] This is provided for in art.297 TFEU [254] to which art.132 TFEU [110] indirectly refers, when it provides that the ECB shall make regulations, "in accordance with the provisions of the Treaties".

[58] The ECB may be entitled by the Council to impose fines or periodic penalty payments on undertakings for failure to comply with obligations under its regulations and decisions: art.132(3) TFEU [110(3)].

[59] art.354 TFEU [230].

[60] art.134 TFEU.

[61] art.134(2) TFEU [114(2)]. See Decision 98/743 on the detailed provisions concerning the composition of the Economic and Financial Committee [1998] O.J. L358/109.

6. STABILITY AND GROWTH PACT[62]

This agreement consists of a Resolution and two Council Regulations[63] and aims at safeguarding sound Government finances as a means to strengthen the price stability and strong sustainable growth conducive to employment creation. It is also considered necessary that national budgetary policies support stability oriented monetary policies. According to the Resolution, adherence to the objective of sound budgetary positions close to balance or in surplus will allow all Member States to deal with normal cyclical fluctuations while keeping the government deficit within the *reference value of 3 per cent of GDP*. The Resolution contains firm political guidelines issued to the Member States, the Council and the Commission, in order to implement the Growth and Stability Pact.[64] Unfortunately, the economic crises in the first years of the twenty-first century, coupled with demagogic policies and bad public management, brought several of the larger Member States (the same ones that had insisted on the necessity for this Pact!) to flout their obligations under the Pact.

This behaviour raised the question whether it would be possible, in the future, to maintain this indispensable link in the chain of measures on which the EMU is based. The solution was found in modifications to the two above-mentioned regulations. The first one[65] provides for the strengthening of budgetary surveillance and co-ordination of economic policies (the "preventive arm" of the Pact), while the second regulation[66] concerns the excessive deficit procedure (the "corrective arm" of the Pact).

These regulations implement the Treaty provisions concerning mutual surveillance, i.e. the monitoring of "the economic developments in each of the Member States and the Union" by the Council and the obligation for the Member States to "avoid excessive government deficits".[67] They can be briefly described as follows.

(1) The Strengthening of Budgetary Surveillance and Co-ordination of Economic Policies

Under this Regulation, Member States are required to submit to the Council and to the Commission a Stability Programme and yearly updated programmes; these programmes are made public. These programmes must present, among others, the "medium-term budgetary objectives" (MTOs). Under the changes introduced in 2005,[68] these MTOs are differentiated to take into account the diversity of economic and budgetary positions and their sustainability. They now range from a deficit of 1 per cent of GDP to a balance or surplus for Euro area and ERM II countries. In case they have not yet reached their MTO, these countries will have

---

[62] Resolution of the European Council on the Stability and Growth Pact, Amsterdam, June 17, 1997 [1997] O.J. C236/1.

[63] Regulation 1466/97 on the strengthening of the surveillance of budgetary positions and the surveillance and co-ordination of economic policies [1997] O.J. L209/1, and Regulation 1467/97 on speeding up and clarifying the implementation of excessive deficit procedure [1997] O.J. L209/6.

[64] See point (2) of Regulation 1466/97 (quoted above).

[65] Regulation 1466/97 [1997] O.J. L209/1.

[66] Regulation 1467/97 [1997] O.J. L209/6.

[67] art.126 TFEU [104].

[68] Regulation 1055/2005 [2005] O.J. L174/1. Details borrowed from the Internet.

to pursue an annual improvement of 0.5 per cent of GDP as a benchmark of their cyclically-adjusted balance, net of one-off measures. A higher effort must be pursued in good times. Member States having implemented major structural reforms, with a verifiable impact on the long-term sustainability of public finances, will be allowed to temporarily deviate from the MTO or the adjustment path toward it.

On the basis of an assessment of the Stability Programme by the Commission and the Economic and Financial Committee,[69] the Council examines whether the medium-term budget objective provides for a safety margin to ensure the avoidance of an excessive deficit, whether the economic assumptions are realistic and whether the measures taken or proposed are sufficient to achieve the targeted adjustment path towards the medium-term budgetary objective.[70] The Council delivers an "opinion" and, in case it considers that the objectives and contents should be strengthened, the Council must, in its opinion, invite the Member State to adjust the programme.

Furthermore, the Council must monitor the implementation of the stability programmes, and, in case it identifies significant divergence of the budgetary position from the MTO, it must, with a view to giving early warning in order to prevent the occurrence of an excessive deficit, address a recommendation to the Member State concerned to, "take prompt corrective measures and may ... make its recommendation public".[71] The above described procedure applies to so-called participating Member States, i.e. those that adopt the single currency. A similar procedure applies to "non-participating Member States".

(2) Speeding-up and Clarifying the Implementation of the Excessive Deficit Procedure

This Regulation provides for the Council to decide that an "excessive deficit" exists in a Member State.[72] The Council must do this on the basis of an assessment by the Commission after consultation of the Economic and Financial Committee. The Council must at the same time make recommendations with a view to bringing that situation to an end within a given period. However, the excessive deficit shall be considered, "exceptional and temporary when resulting, for instance, from a "severe economic downturn",[73] the latter being defined as, "an annual fall of real GDP of at least 2%". This definition was modified in 2005 and now refers to a "negative annual GDP volume growth rate" or an, "accumulated loss of output during a protracted period of very low annual GDP volume growth relative to its potential".[74]

If a Member State persists in failing to put into practice the recommendations of the Council, the latter may decide to give notice to the Member State to take, within a specified time limit, measures for the deficit reduction. Under the modifications introduced in 2005, the deadlines for taking measures to correct excessive deficits are extended to give more time to take effective and more permanent action; also, the Council shall now request the Member State to achieve a minimum annual

---

[69] art.134 TFEU [114].
[70] Regulation 1055/2005 [2005] O.J. L174/1.
[71] art.6(3) Regulation 1466/97.
[72] art.126(6) TFEU [104(6)].
[73] art.2(1) Regulation 1467/97.
[74] art.1(2) Regulation 1056/2005 [2005] O.J. L174/5.

improvement of at least 0.5 per cent of GDP and, in case of unexpected adverse economic events with major unfavourable consequences for government finances, the Council may now adopt a "revised notice".[75] In case the Member State fails to comply, the Council may, among other measures, "impose fines of an appropriate size".[76] The regulation also provides for various sanctions.

It is to be hoped that with the more relaxed Stability and Growth Pact, the objectives of price stability and strong sustainable growth conducive to employment creation will finally be implemented.

(3) Global Financial Crisis and the Stability and Growth Pact

The annual review of the situation in each Member State was conducted as usual and the Council adopted its opinions based on the updated stability and convergence programmes of the EU–27.[77] Various actions were taken with regard to excessive deficit procedures.[78] In response to the exceptional circumstances caused by the financial crisis, the European Council decided that budget policies should continue to come under the revised Stability and Growth Pact.

See also the Commission's Communications: "Public finances in EMU 2008— The role of quality public finances in the EU governance framework",[79] and "EMU at 10: Successes and challenges after ten years of Economic and Monetary Union".[80]

(4) The European Response to the Financial Crises

The Commission wrote the following in its 2008 General Report.

> "The financial crisis which unfolded on the American subprime mortgage market in 2007 led to major turmoil and uncertainty in the entire global financial system. In response to this situation, in October 2007, the Council adopted a number of conclusions to address the main weaknesses in the financial system highlighted by the crisis. The areas to be given priority treatment were set out in the Ecofin roadmap, focussing on four key areas: improving transparency, the valuation of financial products,, strengthening prudential requirements, and improving the functioning of the markets by means of tighter credit rating policy."[81]

Several statements were made and various measures were adopted. For instance, the 27 Union Heads of State or Government declared that they would take the necessary measures to ensure the stability of the financial system by means of enhanced bank deposit guarantees, cash injections from the central banks and measures targeted at particular banks. The Commission published guidelines for the Member States on measures taken for financial institutions in crisis. These

---

[75] art.1(3)1 Regulation 1056/2005 [2005] O.J. L174/5.
[76] art.126(11) TFEU [104(11), last indent].
[77] [2008] O.J. C49, 73, 74, 75 and 182.
[78] For details see General Report 2008, 41–42.
[79] COM(2008) 387 [2008] O.J. C10.
[80] COM(2008) 204 [2008] O.J. C202.
[81] General Report 2008, 30.

guidelines are based on the treaty rules authorising aid to remedy a serious disruption in the economy of a Member State.[82] The Commission also adopted the "European economic recovery plan" to tackle the economic slowdown.[83] A package of measures was adopted to facilitate the implementation of the plan.[84] For further details see the 2008 and the 2009 General Report of the Commission.

Further Reading

C. Zilioli and M. Selmayr, *The Law of the European Central Bank* (Hart Publishing, 2001).

---

[82] art.107(3)(b) TFEU [87(3)(b)].
[83] General Report 2008, 35 and 2009, 10.
[84] General Report 2008, 37 and following.

Chapter Twenty-nine

Social Policy[1] and Education

Under this heading will be examined the social provisions of the TFEU,[2] the European Social Fund (ESF),[3] education, vocational training, youth and sport,[4] and also, although it is not mentioned under the same heading in the TFEU, employment.[5] The latter was added to the EC Treaty by the Treaty of Amsterdam.

The Union has been accused of giving priority to the economic and monetary developments, forgetting the social aspects, or even at their cost. It suffices, however, to look at the first of the European Treaties establishing the now defunct European Coal and Steel Community, to realise that, from the beginning, the social preoccupations were present; as for the European Economic Community, it not only contained a Title III on Social Policy with social provisions and a Social Fund, but the free movement of workers was considered as requiring measures in the field of social security. Similarly, the Euratom Treaty contains several provisions on the health and safety of workers.[6] The Court underlined this importance of the "social" by stating that the Union has, "not only an economic but also a social purpose".[7] However, only the social provisions of the TFEU shall be examined here.

One of the reasons why the Union is viewed as neglecting the social aspects is because social policy remains largely within the exclusive competence of the Member States. Indeed, the role of the Union is limited: the TFEU provides that social policy, but then only, "for the aspects defined in the Treaty",[8] is part of the competences the Union shares with the Member States.[9] This means that both the Member States and the Union are to take implementing measures that take account of the diverse forms of national practices, in particular in the field of contractual relations,[10] and having regard to the conditions and technical rules pertaining to those in each Member State.[11]

The Treaty also refers to the, "need to maintain the competitiveness of the Union economy"[12]; maybe this is a hidden way of reminding the workers and their organisations of the fact that, besides all the rights mentioned in the various charters (see hereunder), workers also have "obligations" with regard, for instance, to productivity and wage-restraint.

[1] arts 151–164 TFEU [136–150].
[2] arts 151–161 TFEU [136–145]
[3] arts 162–164 TFEU [146–148].
[4] arts 165, 166 TFEU [149–150].
[5] arts 145–150 TFEU [125–130].
[6] EAEC, Title Two, Ch.3.
[7] *International Transport Workers Association v Viking Line* (C-438/05) [2007] E.C.R. I-10779.
[8] art.4(2)(b) TFEU.
[9] arts 4(2) and 153(1) TFEU [137(1)].
[10] art.151,2 TFEU [136,2].
[11] art.155(2)(b) TFEU [139(2)(b)].
[12] art.151,2 TFEU [136,2].

1. Social Provisions

The social provisions of the TFEU[13] start with a reference to the European Social Charter of 1961 and the 1989 [Union] Charter of the Fundamental Social Rights of Workers (Social Charter). The former was signed at Turin in 1962 within the framework of the Council of Europe. It provides for 19 "rights", such as the rights to work, to just conditions of work, to safe and healthy working conditions, to fair remuneration, to organise, to bargain collectively, to social security, to medical assistance, etc. As for the Social Charter, it was adopted at the Strasbourg European Council, on December 8 and 9, 1989. Although referred to in many Union publications, it was never published officially; only the Agreement on social policy between the Member States, with the exception of the UK, was annexed to the EU Treaty[14]; it no longer is. The purpose of that Agreement was to implement the 1989 Social Charter. This led to the adoption of several directives, that were later accepted by the UK, which also adhered to the Charter and the Agreement with the entry into force of the EU Treaty. Most of the rights provided for in the Charter and the Agreement are now to be found in the social provisions of the TFEU.[15]

It is interesting to note that the Union and the Member States included a "credo" in the Treaty (something that is normally done in the recitals), by affirming that they "believe"[16] that the implementation of the objectives outlined above will ensue, among others, "from the functioning of the common market", which will favour the harmonisation of the social systems.[17] The Treaty procedures and the approximation of laws are other means to achieve the objectives set out in this chapter.

The social provisions refer to four different Union activities:

1. the Union is to "support and complement"[18] the activities of the Member States in various fields[19];
2. the Commission has the task of promoting the consultation of management and labour[20];
3. the Commission must encourage co-operation between the Member States in given fields[21]; and
4. Member States must ensure the principle of equal pay for male and female workers.[22]

These activities will be briefly examined below.

---

[13] art.151 TFEU [136].
[14] Former EC Protocol 14.
[15] art.151,1 TFEU [136,1].
[16] art.151,3 TFEU [136,3].
[17] It will be remembered that with regard to the free movement of workers and self-employed persons, a harmonisation of the social security systems was not envisaged.
[18] This expression is confusing because it is similar to the one used in art.6 TFEU to describe the third category of Union competences, besides the exclusive and the shared ones: "The Union shall have competence to carry out actions to support, coordinate or supplement the actions of the Member States."
[19] art.153 TFEU [137].
[20] art.154 TFEU [138].
[21] art.156 TFEU [140].
[22] art.157 TFEU [141].

(1) Union Action Supporting and Complementing Member States' Activities

In the social field also, one of the first tasks of the Union is, as mentioned, to "support and complement" the activities of the Member States in the 11 areas below. This is to be done by adopting measures to encourage co-operation between Member States through various initiatives[23] and by means of directives setting out minimum requirements for gradual implementation, having regard to the conditions and technical rules restraining in each of the Member States. These requirements relate to:

- improvement in particular of the working environment to protect workers' health and safety; with regard to the latter, several directives on the protection of workers from certain risks at work[24] were adopted by the Council, and the Agency for Safety and Health at Work was set up[25];
- working conditions; the European Foundation for the improvement of living and working conditions[26] was created to help achieve this objective;

[23] For more details see art.153(2)(a) TFEU.

[24] The basic Directive 80/1107 concerning the protection of workers from the risks related to exposure to chemical, physical and biological agents [1980] O.J. L327/8, see [1998] O.J. L131/11, was implemented through a number of "individual" directives. The basic Directive and some of the implementing Directives were repealed [1998] O.J. L131/11. Still applicable are: Directive 83/477, exposure to asbestos [1983] O.J. L263/25, amended [2003] O.J. L97/48; Directive 80/1107 was replaced by Directive 89/391, on the introduction of measures to encourage improvements in the safety and health of workers at work [1989] O.J. L183/1; see *Lewen v Denda* (C-333/97) [1999] E.C.R. I-7243. This Directive was implemented by a series of individual directives as provided for in its art.16(1): Directive 89/654 (1st Directive), concerning the minimum safety and health requirements for the workplace [1989] O.J. L393/1; Directive 89/655 (2nd Directive), idem for the use of equipment [1989] O.J. L393/13, amended [2001] O.J. L195/46; Directive 89/656 (3rd Directive) idem for the use of protective equipment [1989] O.J. L393/18; Directive 90/269 (4th Directive), idem for the manual handling of loads where there is a risk of back injury [1990] O.J. L156/9; Directive 90/270 (5th Directive), idem for work with display screen equipment [1990] O.J. L156/14; Directive 2004/37 (6th Directive) codified version, risks related to exposure to carcinogens [2004] O.J. L158/50; Directive 2000/54 (7th Directive), idem at temporary or mobile construction sites [2000] O.J. L262/21; Directive 2000/54 (8th Directive), risks related to exposure to biological agents [2000] O.J. L262/21; Directive 92/57 health and safety at temporary and mobile construction sites [1992] O.J. L245; see Communication on practical implementation COM(2008)698; Directive 92/58 (9th Directive), minimum requirements for the provisions of safety and/or health signs [1992] O.J. L245/23; see idem Directive 92/85 (10th Directive), pregnant workers or who have recently given birth or are breastfeeding [1992] O.J. L348/1, see *Paquay* (C-460/06) art.10 prohibits not only the notification of a decision to dismiss but also the taking of preparatory steps for such a decision before the end of the period of protection; Directive 92/91 (11th Directive), workers in the mineral-extracting industries through drilling [1992] O.J. L348/9; Directive 92/104 (12th Directive), workers in the surface and underground mineral-extracting industries [1992] O.J. L404/10; Directive 93/103 (13th Directive), work on board fishing vessels [1993] O.J. L307/1; Directive 98/24 (14th Directive), risk related to chemical agents [1998] O.J. L131/11; Directive 99/92 (15th Directive) risks from explosive atmosphere [1999] O.J. L23/57; Directive 2002/44 (16th Directive) risks arising from physical agents (vibration) [2002] O.J. L177/13; Directive 2003/10 (17th Directive) risks arising from physical agents (noise) [2003] O.J. L42/38; Directive 2004/40 (18th Directive) risks from electromagnetic fields [2004] 159/1, transposition postponed, see below, Directive 2008/46; Directive 2006/25 (19th Directive) risks arising from physical agents (artificial optical radiation), [2006] O.J. L114/38. See also Directive 94/33 on protection of young people at work [1997] O.J. L 215/12; Directive 08/46 minimum health and safety requirements regarding the exposure of workers to the risks arising from physical agents (electromagnetic fields) [2008] O.J. L114/88.

[25] Established by Regulation 2062/94 [1994] O.J. L216/1. See above Ch.13: Decentralised Bodies of the Union.

[26] Regulation 1365/75 [1975] O.J. L139/1, amended [1993] O.J. L181/13. See above Ch.13: Decentralised Bodies of the Union.

- social security and social protection of workers; the Nice Treaty provided for the establishment of a Social Protection Committee[27] with advisory status to promote co-operation on social protection policies between the Member States. The task of this Committee is to monitor the social situation and the development of social protection, promote exchanges of information and prepare reports, formulate opinions or undertake other work within its field of competence. In fulfilling its mandate the Committee must establish appropriate contacts with management and labour[28];
- protection of workers where their employment contract is terminated; several directives were adopted concerning, among others, collective redundancies,[29] safeguarding employees rights in the event of transfers of undertakings,[30] the protection of workers in the event of the insolvency of their employer,[31] and the obligation of the employer to notify an employee of the

---

[27] art.160 TFEU [144].

[28] art.160 TFEU [144].

[29] Directive 75/129 [1975] O.J. L48/29 and Directive 98/59 [1998] O.J. L225/16, modified [2007] O.J. L59/84. See *Rockfon v Specialarbejderforbundet i Danmark* (C-449/93) [1995] E.C.R. I-4291: collective redundancies, definition of "establishment", company forming part of a group. See also for the notion of "redundancy"; *Junk* (C-188/03) [2005] E.C.R. I-885 and *Cofédération Internationale du Travail E.A.* (C-385/05) [2007] E.C.R. I-611: art.1(1)(a) of Directive 98/59 precludes national legislation which excludes a specific category of workers from the calculation of staff members.

[30] Directive 2001/23 on the approximation of the laws of the Member States relating to the safeguarding of employees' rights in the event of transfer of undertakings, business or parts of undertakings or business [2001] O.J. L82/16 (codified version of Directive 77/187, several times amended and repealed). An "employee" is defined as any person who, in the Member State concerned, is protected as an employee under national employment law (art.2(1)(d)). See *Henke v Gemeinde Schierke and Verwaltungsgemeinschaft'Brocken'* (C-298/94) [1996] E.C.R. I-4989; [1997] 1 C.M.L.R. 373, does not apply to the transfer of administrative functions from a municipality to an administrative collectivity. *Rotsart de Hertaing* (C-305/94) [1996] E.C.R. I-5927; [1997] 1 C.M.L.R. 329; the contracts of employment and the employment relationships existing on the date of the transfer of an undertaking, between the transferor and the workers employed in the undertaking transferred, are automatically transferred from the transferor to the transferee by the mere fact of the transfer of the undertaking, despite the contrary intention of the transferor or the transferee. The Directive does not apply in case of termination of a cleaning contract with an independent contractor: *Süzen v Zehnacker Gebäudereinigung* (C-13/95) [1997] E.C.R. 1259; [1997] 1 C.M.L.R. 768; *Francovich v Italian Republic* (C-497/93) [1995] E.C.R. I-3843, gives a definition of insolvency under Directive 80/987: employers who are subject to proceedings, involving their assets, to satisfy collectively the claims of creditors. *Merckx and Neuhuys* (Joined Cases C-171/94 and C-172/94) [1996] E.C.R. I-1253, concept of transfer: the criterion is whether the entity in question retains its economic identity, as indicated, among others, by the fact that the operation is actually continued or resumed and *Dethier Equipement v Dassy and Sovam* (C-319/94) [1998] E.C.R. I-1061, workers illegally made redundant by the transferor can turn to the transferee on the basis of art.4.1 of Directive 77/187. *Liikene* (C-172/99) [2001] E.C.R. I-745: Directive 77/187 does not apply in the absence of transfer of tangible assets. *Collino and Chiappero* (C-343/98) [2000] E.C.R. I-6659: the Directive also applies when a body managed by a public entity is transferred in the form of an administrative concession to a private company set up by a public body which owns all of its capital. As for the date of the transfer, see *Celtec* (C-478/03) [2005] E.C.R. I-4389. In *Klarenberg* (C-466/07) [2009] E.C.R. 12.02.09. The Directive may also apply, under certain conditions, where part of an undertaking is transferred. The Directive does not require the preservation of a commercial lease even if the termination of the lease is likely to entail the termination of contracts of employment transferred to the transferee: *Kirtruna* (C-313/07) [2008] E.C.R. I-7907.

[31] Directive 80/987 on the approximation of the laws of the Member States relating to the protection of employees in the event of the insolvency of their employer [1980] O.J. L283/23, amended [2002] O.J. L270/10, codified by Directive 08/94 [2008] O.J. L283/36; art.4 has direct effect. *AGS Assedic* (C-235/95) [1998] E.C.R. I-4531; see also *José Vicente v Fondo di Garantia Salarial* (C-520/03) [2004] E.C.R. I-12065: are indemnities for irregular discharge included in "remuneration"?; to be determined by the national judge on the basis of national law and for arts 3(1) and 10 see *Maria Nunez* (C-498/06) [2008] E.C.R. I-921. Another Directive was adopted in 2008 providing a minimum degree of protection for employees in case of insolvency of their employer: Directive 08/94: [2008] O.J. L283/36.

essential aspects of the contract or employment relationship by written declaration not later than two months after the commencement of employment.[32] (A landmark judgment in this field is *Francovich*[33] where the Court held that a Member State is required to make good loss and damage caused to individuals by its failure to transpose a directive.)

The Treaty provisions do not apply, however, to pay, the right of association, the right to strike or the right to impose lock-outs[34];

- the information and consultation of workers; the Council adopted a directive on the establishment of a European Works Council or a procedure for informing and consulting employees[35];
- representation and collective defence of the interests of workers and employers, including co-determination;
- conditions of employment of third-country nationals legally residing in Union territory;
- the integration of people excluded from the labour market; social protection and inclusion[36];
- equality between men and women with regard to the labour market opportunities and treatment at work[37] (not to be confused with equal pay for male and female workers for equal work or work of equal value,[38] which shall be examined below);
- the combating of social exclusion;
- the modernisation of social protection systems; see MISSOC (Mutual Information System on Social Protection in the Member States and the EEA).

---

[32] Directive 91/533 [1991] O.J. L288/32; see *Kampelmann and Others v Landschaftverband Westfalen-Lippe and Others* (Joined Cases C-253/96, C-254/96, C-255/96, C-256/96, C-257/96 and C-258/96) [1997] E.C.R. I-6907: the burden of proving correctness of details notified must be determined by national law.

[33] *Francovich and Others* (Joined Cases C-6/90 and C-9/90) [1991] E.C.R. I-5357.

[34] art.153(5) TFEU [137(5)].

[35] Directive 94/45 on establishment of a European Works Council or a procedure in Union-scale undertakings and Union-scale groups of undertakings for the purpose of informing and consulting employees [1994] O.J. L254/64; extended to the UK by Directive 97/74 [1998] O.J. L10/22; replaced by Directive 2009/38 [2009] O.J. L122/28. See *Bofrost* (C-62/99) [2001] E.C.R. I-2579 and *ADS Anker* (C-349/01) [2004] E.C.R. I-6803.

[36] General Report 2008, 98 and 99.

[37] See, for instance, Directive 76/207 on the implementation of the principle of equal treatment for men and women as regards access to employment, vocational training and promotion, and working conditions (the "equal treatment directive") [1976] O.J. L39/40. See *Draehmpaehl* (C-180/95) [1997] E.C.R. I-2195; [1997] 3 C.M.L.R. 1107, *Coote* (C-185/97) [1998] E.C.R. I-5199, refusal of employer to provide references, and *Kachelmann* (C-322/98) [2000] E.C.R. I-7505, where the Court held that part-time workers and full-time workers are not comparable when a part-time job must be eliminated for economic reasons. The Directive also applies after the work relationship was terminated. See also *Paquay* (C-460/06) [2007] E.C.R. I-851, dismissal on the ground of pregnancy or child birth is contrary to arts 2(1) and 5(1); Council Recommendation on the promotion of positive action for women [1984] O.J. L331/34; Council Directive 86/613 on the application of the principle of equal treatment between men and women engaged in an activity, including agriculture, in a self-employed capacity, and on the protection of self-employed women during pregnancy (see *McKenna* (C-191/03) [2005] E.C.R. I-7631) and motherhood [1986] O.J. L359/56; Resolution on the promotion of equal opportunities for women [1986] O.J. C203/2; Council Recommendation on the balanced participation of women and men in the decision-making process; and Directive 97/80 on the burden of proof in cases of discrimination based on sex [1998] O.J. L14/6, extended to the UK [1998] O.J. L205/66. This Directive applies to any kind of discrimination. Directive 2000/78 establishing a general framework for equal treatment in employment and occupation [2000] O.J. L303/16.

[38] art.157 TFEU [141].

In those areas Parliament and the Council may adopt measures in accordance with the ordinary legislative procedure,[39] after consulting the ESC and the Committee of the Regions.[40] However, in some fields the Council must act alone and unanimously, in accordance with a special legislative procedure,[41] after consulting Parliament and the said committees: this is the case for social security, social protection of workers where their employment contract is terminated, representation and collective defence of the interests of workers and employers, and conditions of employment for third-country nationals legally residing within the Union[42] (it will be remembered that in those fields the Member States are particularly jealous of their independence).

The Council may also adopt measures designed to encourage co-operation between Member States through initiatives aimed at improving knowledge, developing exchanges of information and best practices, but, here again, excluding any harmonisation of the laws and regulations of the Member States. Furthermore, the Council may, with regard to the nine first activities mentioned above, adopt directives for gradual implementation.

It should also be noted that the above-mentioned directives do not prevent any Member State from maintaining or introducing more stringent protective measures compatible with the Treaty.[43] A similar provision exists in different other fields, where the policy in question is the joint responsibility of the Member States and the Union, for instance "Environment"[44], "Public Health"[45] and "consumer protection"[46]. Neither do the Treaty provisions affect the right of the Member States to define the fundamental principles of their social security systems and may not significantly affect the financial equilibrium thereof.[47]

(2) Consultation of Management and Labour

With regard to management and labour, the Treaty provides that a Member State may entrust them, at their joint request, with the implementation of the above-mentioned directives.[48] The Commission, on the other hand, has the task of promoting the consultation of management and labour, by doing that before submitting proposals in the social policy field, and following that, consulting them on the content of the envisaged proposals.[49] On that occasion management and labour may inform the Commission that they wish to initiate a dialogue at Union level, which may lead to contractual relations, including agreements. Implementation of such agreements can be done by a Council decision.[50] Of

---

[39] art.294 TFEU [251].
[40] art.153(2)2 TFEU [169 and 12].
[41] art.189. TFEU.
[42] art.153(2)5 TFEU [169 and 12].
[43] art.153(4) TFEU second indent [137(4) second indent].
[44] art.172 TFEU [156].
[45] art.168 TFEU [152(4)(a)]; however, this possibility was provided for in art.154 TFEU [138].
[46] art.169(4) TFEU [185].
[47] art.153(4) TFEU [137(4)].
[48] art.153(4) TFEU [137(4)].
[49] art.154 TFEU [138].
[50] art.155 TFEU [139].

interest in this context is the Commission Communication on the "European social dialogue, a force for innovation and change".[51] It puts forward concrete measures aimed at strengthening the different levels and forms of social dialogue. This approach to social dialogue is based on the social partner's contribution to the Laeken European Council and the reflections of the High Level Group on Industrial relations.

(3) Encouraging Co-operation Between the Member States and Facilitating Co-ordination of their Action

This is the task of the Commission and is to take place particularly in matters relating to:

- employment[52]; a Standing Committee on Employment in the European Communities was set up,[53] special measures of Union interest were introduced granting financial assistance[54];
- labour law and working conditions; various measures were taken concerning, for instance, the organisation of working time,[55] safety at work,[56] wages, income and working hours,[57] industrial relations, etc;
- basic and advanced vocational training[58]; it suffices to mention here that the Commission is helped in this task by the European Centre for the Development of Vocational Training[59]; vocational training will be examined below;

---

[51] COM (2002) 341 final.

[52] In December 1993, the Commission forwarded to the European Council, at its request, a White Paper entitled "Growth, Competitiveness, Employment: the Challenge and Ways forward into the 21st Century".

[53] [1970] O.J. L273/25, amended [1975] O.J. L21/17.

[54] [1984] O.J. L177/1.

[55] Directive 93/104: [1993] O.J. L307/18, this Directive was amended to cover sectors and activities that were excluded at first, [2000] O.J. L195/41; see *Michaeler and Subito GmbH* (Joined Cases C-55/07 and C-56/07) [2008] E.C.R. I-3135, on equal treatment of part-time and full-time workers; see also Directive 2003/88 concerning certain aspects of the organisation of the working time [2003] O.J. L299/9. For both Directives see cases concerning annual leave, compensation and sick leave (Joined Cases C-350/06 and C-520/06) [2009] E.C.R.20.01.09. Directive 96/71 concerning the "posting" (temporary employ in another Member State) of workers in the framework of the provision of services [1996] O.J. L18/1. See *Rüffert* (C-346/06) [2008] E.C.R. 8-1989: the Directive precludes a legislative measure requiring contracting authorities to designate as contractors for public works only those undertakings which agree in writing to pay their employees at least the remuneration prescribed by collective agreement; see Communication from the Commission (COM(2006)159 final): "Guidance on the posting of workers in the framework of the provision of services" and *Robinson-Steel and Clarke* (Joint Cases C-131/04 and C-257/04) [2006] E.C.R. I-2531. See also Directive 97/81 concerning the framework agreement on part-time work concluded by UNICE, CEEP and ETUC [1998] O.J. L14/9, amended [1998] O.J. L131/10.

[56] Quoted above.

[57] See, for instance, Directive 93/104 concerning certain aspects of the organisation of working time [1993] O.J. L307/18 and Regulation 2744/95 on statistics on the structure and distribution of earnings [1995] O.J. L287/3.

[58] Vocational training was, from the beginning, part of the activities of the Union.

[59] The Centre was set up in 1975, Regulation 337/75 [1975] O.J. L39/1, amended several times [2004] O.J. L355/1; see above, Ch.13: Decentralised Bodies of the Union.

- social security[60]; since the task of the Union in this field is limited to encouraging co-operation between Member States, the Commission and the Council only issue Recommendations and Resolutions[61];
- prevention of occupational accidents and diseases[62];
- occupational hygiene;
- the right of association and collective bargaining between employers and workers.

As mentioned already, the role of the Union in those fields is rather limited: the Commission, acting in close contact with the Member States, may only act, "by making studies, delivering opinions and arranging consultations"[63]; not very much indeed!

(4) The Principle of Equal Opportunity and Equal Treatment of Men and Women[64]

The directive on the implementation of the principle of equal treatment of men and women as regards access to employment, vocational training and promotion, and working conditions[65] was interpreted by the Court as meaning that absolute priority to women in case of equivalent qualifications is not provided. The Court ruled that the Directive does not preclude a rule of national case law under which a candidate belonging to the under-represented sex may be granted preference over a competitor of the opposite sex, provided that the candidate possesses equivalent or substantially equivalent merits, where the candidates are subjected to an objective assessment that takes account of the specific personal situations of all the candidates.[66] The Court also ruled that the Directive precludes a refusal to appoint a pregnant women to a post for an indefinite period on the ground of a national statutory prohibition.[67]

[60] It will be remembered that this subject was broached above under Ch.16: The Free Movement of Persons, the Treaty secures for workers, for the purpose of acquiring and retaining the right to social security benefits, aggregation of all the periods taken into account under the laws of the several Member States and the payment of those benefits in whatever Member State the beneficiary resides. Furthermore, many regulations were adopted on the application of social security schemes to employed persons and their families moving within the Union, see, for instance, Regulation 1408/71 [1971] O.J. L149/2, modified [2008] O.J. L177/1.
[61] Council Recommendation 92/441 on common criteria concerning sufficient resources and social assistance in social protection systems [1992] O.J. L245/46 and Recommendation 92/442 on the convergence of social protection objectives and policies [1992] O.J. L245/49; it will be noticed that those non-binding acts were published in the L series of the O.J. normally reserved for Legislative acts; see also Council Resolution on flexible retirement arrangements [1993] O.J. C188/1.
[62] Commission Recommendation 90/326 concerning the adoption of a European schedule of occupational diseases [1990] O.J. L160/39.
[63] art.156 TFEU [140].
[64] art.157 TFEU [141]. See, for instance, Directive 79/7 on the progressive implementation of the principle of equal treatment of men and women in matters of social security [1979] O.J. L6/24 and *Züchner v Handelskrankenkasse (Erztskasse) Bremen* (C-77/95). [1996] E.C.R. I-5689; [1997] 3 C.M.L.R. 263: not applicable to persons not engaged in an economic activity. Also *Dietz v Stichting Thuiszorg Rotterdam* (C-435/93): right to payment of a retirement pension, Part-time workers [1996] E.C.R. I-5223.
[65] Directive 76/207 [1976] O.J. L39/40. *Kalanke v Bremen* (C-450/93): promotion, equal qualifications, priority to women [1995] E.C.R. I-3051.
[66] *Abrahamsson and Anderson* (C-407/98) [2000] E.C.R. I-5539.
[67] *Mahlburg* (C-207/98) [2000] E.C.R. I-549.

Equal Pay

The principle of "equal opportunity" also includes the principle of "equal pay-ment" for male and female workers; it only applies, of course, "for equal work or work of equal value". It concerns here an obligation imposed upon the Member States; Parliament and the Council must, acting in accordance with the ordinary legislative procedure,[68] adopt the necessary measures. Reference to "equal opportunity" was made above, the focus here is on equal "pay". The lat-ter is defined as, "ordinary basic or minimum wage or salary and any considera-tion, whether in cash or in kind, which the worker receives directly or indirectly, in respect of his employment, from his employer".[69] As for "equal pay", it means that, "the pay for the same work at piece rates shall be calculated on the basis of the same unit of measurement" and that, "pay for work at time rates shall be the same for the same job".[70] It should be noted that this Treaty provision has direct effect. Several directives[71] were adopted by the Council to implement the above-mentioned principles and many Court judgments have clarified the various concepts.[72] Although the Treaty, in the context of its social provisions, refers only to equality between women and men, the Treaty provisions concerning the "Principles" of the Union provide that the Council, acting unanimously, on a proposal from the Commission and after consulting Parliament, may take appro-priate action to combat discrimination based on sex, racial or ethnic origin, religion or belief, disability, age or sexual orientation.[73] On that basis, the

---

[68] art.294 TFEU [251].
[69] art.157 TFEU [141(2)].
[70] Protocol No.33 attached to the TFEU provides that, "for the purpose of Art.157 [141] of the TFEU, benefits under occupational schemes shall not be considered as remuneration if and in so far as they are attributable to periods of employment prior to May 17, 1990 (date of the Barber judgment, see below), except in the case of workers or those claiming under them who have before that date initi-ated legal proceedings or introduced an equivalent claim under applicable national law".
[71] See, for instance, Directive 75/117 on the approximation of the laws of the Member States relating to the application of the principle of equal pay for men and women [1975] O.J. L45/19; in *Rummler v Dato-Druck* (237/85) [1986] E.C.R. 2101 the use of the criterion of muscular demand is not prohibited; Directive 76/207 on the implementation of the principle of equal treatment for men and women as regards access to employment, vocational training and promotion and work-ing conditions [1976] O.J. L39/40.
[72] *Barber* (C-262/88) [1990] E.C.R. I-1889; [1990] 2 C.M.L.R. 513 on the notion of "remuneration", on the fact that the benefits paid by an employer to a worker on the latter's redundancy, constitutes a form of pay, also that, unlike the benefits awarded by national statutory social security schemes, retirement pensions paid under private occupational schemes constitute consideration paid by the employer in respect of his employment and consequently fall within the scope of art.157 TFEU [141]—furthermore, it is unlawful to discriminate between the sexes by providing for their respec-tive pension benefits to be payable at different ages; also *Larsson v Fotex Supermarked* (C-400/95) [1997] E.C.R. I-2757; [1979] 2 C.M.L.R. 915: outside periods of maternity leave, women are not protected against dismissal of ground of absence due to illness attributable to pregnancy. Famous cases are the *Defrenne* cases: *Defrenne v Belgium* (80/70) [1971] E.C.R. 445 and *Defrenne v Sabena* (43/75) [1976] E.C.R. 455. See also *Commission v UK* (61/81) [1982] E.C.R. 2601 and *Commission v UK* (165/82) [1983] E.C.R. 3431; [1984] 1 C.M.L.R. 44. However, the Court admitted that, although a "bridging allowance" falls under the concept of "pay", there are situa-tions where art.157 TFEU [141] and Directive 75/117 do not preclude the application of a social plan providing for a difference in the treatment of male and female workers in terms of the age at which they are entitled to the bridging allowance, since under national law they are in different sit-uations with regard to the factors relevant to the grant of that allowance: *Hlozek* (C-19/02) [2004] E.C.R. I-11491. The Court also held that when there are important differences between the pay of men and that of women, and they cannot be explained, it is up to the employer to prove that there is no discrimination: *Handelsverband v Danfoss* (109/88) [1989] E.C.R. 3199.
[73] art.19 TFEU [13].

Council adopted two directives in 2000,[74] and in 2002 amended the basic Directive ensuring equal treatment between women and men to update its provisions in the light of evolving case law and to ensure consistency with the two Directives just mentioned.

See also "Framework Strategy on gender Equality (2001–2005)".[75] To summarise, directives exist in the following fields:

- equal treatment for men and women as regards access to employment; vocational training and promotion and working conditions[76];
- equal pay[77];
- equal treatment at the workplace;
- equal treatment with regard to statutory social security schemes[78];
- equal treatment with regard to occupational social security systems;
- equal treatment for self-employed[79] and their assisting spouses;
- maternity leave (see *Sass* (C-284/02) [2004] E.C.R. I-11143);
- organisation of working time;
- parental leave;
- burden of proof in sexual discrimination cases[80]; and
- Framework Agreement on part-time work.[81]

In January 2008 the Commission adopted its Annual Report on equality between men and women[82]: it shows that gender gaps remain substantial, especially differences concerning working arrangements, labour market segregation still exists and is on the rise in certain countries, and the pay gap is not diminishing. Numerous challenges still had to be taken up.

2. THE EUROPEAN SOCIAL FUND[83]

The European Social Fund (ESF)[84] was set up by the EC Treaty in 1958: its objectives were not modified, neither by the Single European Act, nor by the Treaties of Amsterdam, Nice or Lisbon. Those objectives are to:

---

[74] Directive 2000/43 implementing the principle of equal treatment between persons irrespective of racial or ethnic origin [2000] O.J. L180/22; see *Feryn* (C-54/07) [2008] E.C.R. I-5187, an employer's public statement that it will not recrut employees of a certain ethnic or racial origin constitutes direct discrimination within the meaning of art.2(2)(a), it is then for the employer to prove that there is no breach of the principle of equal treatment—art.15 requires that national sanctions be effective, proportionate and dissuasive even when there is no identifiable victim. See also Directive 2000/78 establishing a general framework for equal treatment in employment and occupation [2000] O.J. L303/16. See *Palacios de la Villa* (C-411/05) [2007] E.C.R. I-853, discrimination based on age justified; see also *Maruko* (C-267/06) [2008] E.C.R. I-1757, application to survivor of same sex partners. In *Coleman* (C-303/06) [2008] E.C.R. I-5603 the Court held that the prohibition of direct discrimination and harassment is not limited to people themselves disabled—in this case the child was disabled and was the origin of harassment by the law firm!

[75] COM (2000) 335.

[76] Directive 2002/73 [2002] O.J. L269/15.

[77] Directive 75/117 [1975] O.J. L45/19.

[78] Directive 79/7 [1979] O.J. L6/24.

[79] Directive 86/613 [1986] O.J. L359/56.

[80] Directive 97/80 [1998] O.J. L14/6.

[81] Directive 97/81 [1998] O.J. L128/71. See *Wippel* (C-313/02) [2004] E.C.R. I-9483; part-time workers, sex discrimination, working time.

[82] COM(2008) 10 [2008] O.J. C118/9.

[83] See Regulation 1784/1999 [1999] O.J. L213/5.

[84] arts 162–164 TFEU [146–148].

"[I]mprove employment opportunities for workers in the internal market and to contribute thereby to the raising of the standards of living; it shall aim to render the employment of workers easier and to increase their geographical and occupational mobility within the Union, and to facilitate their adaptation to industrial changes and to changes in production systems, in particular through vocational training and retraining".[85]

In other words, the ESF is clearly linked to employment (see hereafter), to the free movement of workers (which was examined above in Ch.16) and to vocational training (see below).

Of great interest is the addition introduced by the EU Treaty concerning the necessary adaptations of the working force to economic changes; from that it follows that social policy is not only about granting rights to workers and protecting them, but also about helping them to accept the consequences of a changing economic environment, i.e. globalisation. It was pointed out earlier on that the Treaty enjoined the Union and the Member States to implement measures that take account of the, "need to maintain competitiveness of the Union economy".[86] Although in a rather indirect way, those two provisions give a clear hint as to the obligations which rest on the workers and their organisations to help achieve the objectives of the Union.

As is explained below in Ch.32: Regional Policy/Economic, Social and Territorial Cohesion, the ESF, together with the European Agricultural Guidance and Guarantee Fund, the Fisheries Fund, the Rural Development Fund and the European Regional Development Fund, are now grouped within the "Structural Funds", which, with the European Investment Bank and the other existing financial instruments, support the achievement of the objective of overall harmonious development.[87] The EFS is examined in that context. Let it, however, be mentioned here that a reform of the ESF was undertaken in order to redefine the framework and political priorities of the Fund for the period 2000–2006 to support the European Employment Strategy as part of the Agenda 2000 reform of the structural funds. It might be of interest to note that, according to the Court, using ESF assistance in breach of the conditions set out in the relevant Union acts does not constitute a criminal act, but should be penalised by the Member States.[88]

A European Globalisation Adjustment Fund was set up to provide additional support for workers who suffer the consequences of major structural changes in world trade patterns.[89]

3. EDUCATION, VOCATIONAL TRAINING, YOUTH AND SPORTS

(1) Education

Education in this context refers to general education, i.e. grammar school, high school and university, while vocational training refers to the teaching of specific

---

[85] art.162 TFEU [146].
[86] art.151,2 TFEU [136,2].
[87] arts 174 and 175 TFEU [158 and 159].
[88] *Nunes and de Matos* (C-186/98) [1999] E.C.R. I-4883.
[89] Regulation 1927/06 [2006] O.J. L406/1. For more details see Ch.16: II The Free Movement of Workers.

trades, corresponding to the distinction between workers and professionals, the latter, as was seen above in Ch.16: The Free Movement of Persons, being only a part of the "self-employed".

Education remains the sole responsibility of the Member States, where the content of teaching and the organisation of education systems are concerned—except for the professions.[90] As the Commission indicated: "There is no common education policy". The main task of the Union in this field is therefore to, "contribute to the development of quality education".[91] The means at its disposal to fulfil this task are: encouraging co-operation between Member States and, if necessary, supporting and supplementing their action. It is probably to be considered as normal that, even where it is their exclusive responsibility, Member States do not hesitate to ask for the (financial) support of the Union. Indeed, the Treaty provides that the Union may "supplement" the action of the Member States. However, the Treaty adds immediately that, while doing this, the Union must not only respect the responsibility of the Member States just mentioned, but also their cultural and linguistic diversity.

Furthermore, the incentive measures to be adopted by Parliament and the Council acting jointly, may not lead to harmonisation of the laws and regulations of the Member States.[92]

The Union action shall, according to the Treaty, be aimed at:

- developing the European dimension in education,[93] particularly through the teaching and dissemination of the languages of the Member States. (The reader might wonder about this objective: with 23 official languages is this a viable proposition? Surely, everyone will want to learn or improve English, since, for all practical purposes, that is the "common" language (lingua franca), but such an idea is, of course, anathema in all the non-English-speaking capitals. Anyway, the Union set up the LINGUA programme[94] to promote the teaching and learning of all the languages[95] of the Union); see also Council's conclusions on multilinguism[96] and the Commission communication on "Multilinguism, an asset for Europe and a shared commitment"[97];
- encouraging mobility of students and teachers; for this purpose the Union Action Programme for the Mobility of University Students (ERASMUS)[98] and the Trans-European Mobility Scheme for University Students (TEMPUS)[99] were established; these programmes now also apply to the Mediterranean States; the mobility should be facilitated, among others, by encouraging the academic recognition of diplomas and periods of study.[100]

---

[90] See above, Ch.17: Freedom of Establishment/Company Law.

[91] art.165(1) TFEU [149(1)].

[92] art.165(4) TFEU.

[93] See Resolution of the Council and the Ministers of Education meeting within the Council on the European dimension in education [1988] O.J. C177/5; idem for higher education [1992] O.J. C336/4.

[94] Council Decision 89/489 establishing an action programme to promote foreign languages competence in the European Union [1989] O.J. L239/24.

[95] Council Resolution on the early teaching of European Union languages [1998] O.J. C1/2.

[96] [2008] O.J. C140/14.

[97] General Report 2008, 80.

[98] Decision 87/327 [1987] O.J. L166/20. In 2008, the Commission implemented the first phase of the Erasmus Mundus programme (2004–2008) and negotiated the second phase (2009–2013).

[99] Decision 90/233 [1990] O.J. L131/21.

[100] See above, Chs 16 and 17, The Free Movement of Persons and Freedom of Establishment/Company Law. See also [1974] O.J. C98/1, Resolution on mutual recognition of diplomas, certificates and other evidence of formal qualifications.

These programmes, together with the SOCRATES, ORION and EURYDICE programmes are now grouped in the "Lifelong Learning programme".[101]

The Lifelong Learning Programme (LLP)[102] supports learning opportunities from childhood to old age in every single life situation. It has a budget of €7 billion for the period 2007–2013. It is composed of four sectoral sub-programmes: COMENIUS (action for schools); ERASMUS (higher education); LEONARDO DA VINCI (vocational education and training); and GRUNDTVIG (adult education).

There are activities in four themed areas across all sectors: (1) policy co-operation and innovation in education and training; (2) language and language learning; (3) development of ICT-based content and services; and (4) dissemination and exploitation of the results of the programmes.

A regulation on the production and development of statistics on education and lifelong learning was adopted in 2008.[103] The European qualification framework (EQF) for lifelong learning was approved in order to improve mobility by making qualifications obtained in all areas of education across the Union, more transparent.[104] A Commission communication on schools intends to support Member States' efforts to improve the quality of their education systems.[105]

There also is a Jean Monet programme which supports institutions and actions in favour of European integration;

- promoting co-operation between educational establishments[106]; this constitutes one of the objectives of the Union action programme SOCRATES,[107] which was endowed with €1.85 billion for the period 2000–2005;
- developing exchanges of information and experience on issues common to the education systems of the Member States; see the EURYDICE network (part of SOCRATES) concerning quality assurance in teachers education in Europe and the ARION programme[108];
- encouraging the development of youth[109] exchanges and the exchange of socio-educational instructors and encouraging the participation of young people in democratic life in Europe;
- encouraging the development of distance education.[110]

---

[101] *http://www.eacea.ec.europa.eu/llp/index_en.htm.*
[102] [2006] O.J. L327/45.
[103] Regulation 452/08 [2008] O.J. L145/227.
[104] [2008] O.J. C111/1.
[105] COM(2008) 425.
[106] Conclusion of the Council and the Ministers of Education meeting within the Council concerning a pilot action for multilateral school partnership in the European Union [1991] O.J. C321/3.
[107] Decision 819/95 establishing an action programme SOCRATES [1995] O.J. L87/10 with the objective of contributing to the development of quality education and training and the creation of an open European area for co-operation in education, including Erasmus for higher education and Comenius for school education; amended by Decision 576/98 [1998] O.J. L77/1.
[108] See EURYDICE: [1992] O.J. C336/7, *http://www.eurydice.org* and Arion programme on study visits for education specialists and administrators; Eur-lex database, Section 16.30.
[109] See the "Youth in Action" programme for the period 2007–2013 [2008] O.J. L348/113.
[110] Conclusions on the development of open and distance learning [1992] O.J. C151/3 and on criteria for actions for open and distant learning [1992] O.J. C336/6.

(2) Vocational Training

The Treaty provides for the Union to implement its own vocational training policy, which, however, must, "support and supplement the action of the Member States", the latter remaining responsible for the content and organisation of vocational training.[111] In 2008, a decision was adopted on the comparability of vocational training qualifications between the Member States.[112]

Like in the field of education, measures are to be adopted jointly by Parliament and Council to achieve the objectives referred to in the Treaty, with the exclusion, however, of any harmonisation of the laws and regulations of the Member States. Once again, Member States accept Union support, but are not ready yet for an approximation of their national rules.

Vocational training was provided for by the Treaties from the very beginning; it was referred to as one of the actions of the Member States which could be financed at 50 per cent by the ESF. It has become an activity on its own: see the Leonardo da Vinci action programme for the implementation of a Union vocational training policy,[113] which received €1.15 billion for the period 2000–2006 and, as mentioned in Ch.13 above, the setting up of the European Centre for the Development of Vocational Training.[114] The latter is a scientific and technical body entrusted with promoting, at Union level, the exchange of information and experience, the distribution of documents and the launching of research and experimental projects to facilitate the attainment of the vocational training objectives. As for the European Training Foundation, its purpose is to help the countries of Central and Eastern Europe with professional training.[115]

The aims of the Union action in the field of vocational training are the following:

- facilitate adaptation to industrial changes;
- improve initial and continuing vocational training;
- facilitate access to vocational training and encourage mobility of instructors and trainees and, particularly, young people;
- stimulate co-operation on training between training establishments and firms; and
- develop exchanges of information and experience.

In the field of vocational training also, the Union and the Member States are to foster co-operation with third countries and international organisations.[116] No reference is made here to the Council of Europe.

---

[111] art.166 TFEU [150].
[112] Decision 1065/08 [2008] O.J. L288/4.
[113] Decision 94/819 [1994] O.J. L340/8 and Decision 1999/382 establishing the second phase of the Union vocational training action programme [1999] O.J. L146/33.
[114] Regulation 337/75 [1975] O.J. L39/1, amended several times [2004] O.J. L355/1; see also Decision 96/1025 [1996] O.J. C316/1.
[115] Regulation 1360/90 establishing the European Training Foundation for Central and Eastern Europe [1990] O.J. L131/1, replaced by Regulation 1339/2008 establishing a European training Foundation (recast) [2008] O.J. L354/82.
[116] Quoted above.

(3) Youth

The Union's youth policies[117] aim to meet young people's changing expectations, while encouraging them to contribute to society by concrete action in the form of a specific programme for young people called "Youth in Action". In 2005, the European Council established a framework programme, now made up of three main strands:

- young people's active citizenship with the following instruments: "Youth in Action" programme,[118] "Youth Portal", adopted in 2005, and the "European knowledge centre on youth policy";
- social and occupational integration via the European Youth Pact;
- youth dimension in other Union policies.

See also mobility of young volunteers across the European Union[119] and a renewed framework in the youth field (2010–2018).[119a]

(4) Sports

The aim here is to: developing the European dimention of sport, by promoting fair-ness and openness in sporting competitions and co-operation between bodies responsible for sports, and by protecting the physical and moral integrity of sports-men and sportswomen, especially the youngest ones.[120]

The TFEU also provides for the Union and the Member States to foster co-operation with third countries,[121] and the competent international organisations in the field of education and sports, in particular the Council of Europe.[122] 35 new joint projects were launched in 2008 with the United States (16), Canada (5), Australia (4) and New-Zealand (1); these projects are co-financed with the part-ner countries.[123] A China-EU language exchange programme, sponsored by the Chinese Government, was also launched.

In order to contribute to the achievement of these objectives, Parliament and the Council, acting in accordance with the ordinary legislative procedure,[124] after consulting the ESC and the Committee of the Regions, shall adopt "incentive measures" (no further defined), excluding any harmonisation, and the Council, on a proposal from the Commisssion, shall adopt recommendations (not very binding!).[125]

---

[117] Borrowed from: *http://www.ec.europa ;eu/youth/youth-policies/doc23_en.htm.*
[118] Decision 1719/06 for the period 2007–2013 with a budget of €855 million.
[119] Council Recommendation [2008] O.J. C319/8.
[119a] [2009] O.J. C31/11.
[120] art.165(2) TFEU last indent [181].
[121] See Agreement between the EU and the US establishing a co-operation programme in higher education and vocational education and training [1995] O.J. L279/13; idem with Canada [1995] O.J. L300/19; also Association in this field with Romania [1997] O.J. L229/5.
[122] art.165(3) TFEU [149(3)].
[123] General Report 2008, 80.
[124] art.294 TFEU [251].
[125] art.165 TFEU (4).

4. EMPLOYMENT

Employment is the object of TFEU Title IX,[126] which was introduced by the Treaty of Amsterdam. It is not part of Title X on Social Policy, where it probably belongs; it was inserted into the EC Treaty immediately after the Title on "Economic and Monetary Policy", to function as the social "counterpart", to prevent the Treaty from looking too one-sided in favour of economic preoccupations.

The set-up of this Title is similar to the various parts of Social Policy, i.e. shared responsibility of the Union and the Member States for achieving the objectives; the task of the Union is limited to encouraging co-operation between the Member States. This is accomplished through the drawing up by the Council, on the basis of the conclusions of the European Council and after consulting Parliament and the SEC, the Committee of the Regions and the Employment Committee, of Guidelines, which the Member States "shall take into account".[127] The TFEU also provides for the adoption by Parliament and Council of incentive measures, after consulting the above-mentioned Committees. Harmonisation measures are, however, excluded here also.

Furthermore, the Treaty only refers to "coordinated strategy", "promotion" of a skilled, trained and adaptable workforce, "employment policy", promoting employment as a "matter of common concern", the "objective of a high level of employment", the European Council, which must "each year consider the employment situation" and adopt "conclusions thereon", the Council and the Commission making a "joint annual report on the employment situation in the Union",[128] "exchange of information and best practice", providing "comparative analysis and advice" and promoting "innovative approaches", "evaluating experiences" and an Employment Committee. One can only hope that all this "soft" action will indeed create jobs.

Clearly, it is up to the Member States to take the necessary measures and implement their own employment policy, the Union can only encourage co-operation between Member States and support their action in the field of employment. The danger of providing for the kind of Union activity described above, is that it might create the illusion that the Union is actively engaged in combating unemployment. This is not its task; it is not equipped to do this; the principle of subsidiarity applies here to the full. The only action the Union can undertake, besides trying to co-ordinate the actions of the Member States, is to help in training and retraining the workforce in order to make it responsive to economic change. Nonetheless the Union publishes "Employment Guidelines",[129] and at the

---

[126] arts 145 to 150 TFEU [125–130].

[127] art.148(2) TFEU [128,2]. The Employment Guidelines for 1998, agreed upon at the Luxembourg Job Summit of November 1997, were built on four main pillars: employability, entrepeneurship, adaptability and equal opportunity. Every year, a set of guidelines is adopted for each of the pillars, which set out a number of specific targets for Member States, to achieve in their national employment policies. Those Guidelines are then transposed into concrete and administrative measures by each Member State, through their National Action Plans for Employment (NAPS). See Council Decision on guidelines for Member State, employment policies and Recommendation on the implementation [2004] O.J. 326/45.

[128] In fact there are two reports: the Joint Employment Report, the objective of which is to present the employment situation in the Member States and to assess the quality of the efforts being undertaken by them to implement their national Action Plans, and the Employment Rates Report on employment performance in the Member States.

[129] See Decision 2008/618 on Guidelines for the employment policies of the Member States [2008] O.J. L198/47.

Barcelona European Council it was made clear that the European Employment Strategy had to be reinforced with continuing emphasis on reform of employment and labour-market policies.[130] Incentive measures were adopted to bolster the Union strategy with activities geared to analysis, research and co-operation between Member States.[131]

Unemployment is the most crucial problem facing the Union. The hope is that the Economic and Monetary Union, with its single currency, may play a decisive role in helping to create the necessary jobs, thanks to the greater flexibility it will generate in the exchanges and trade between Member States. Mention must also be made of the European Employment Services (EURES), which is a European labour market network aiming at facilitating the mobility of workers in the European Economic Area. It links more than 450 Euroadvisers—specialists in employment matters—throughout Europe. The Luxembourg European Council in 1997 had initiated the European Employment Strategy (EES), also known as the Luxembourg Process. It is designated as the main tool to give direction to, and ensure co-ordination of, the employment policy priorities to which the Member States should subscribe at Union level. It is the basis for the Employment Guidelines, the National Action Plans, the Joint Employment Report and Council country-specific Recommendations.

5. The Social Agenda (2005–2010)[132]

Launched by the Commission in 2005, it aims at:

> "[M]odernising Europe's social model under the revised Lisbon Strategy for growth and jobs. It focuses on providing jobs and equal opportunities for all and ensuring that the benefits of the Union's growth and job drive reach every- one in society. By modernising labour markets and social protection systems, it will help people seize the opportunities created by international competition, technological advance and changing population patterns while protecting the most vulnerable in society."

The Agenda develops a two-pronged strategy: the first is to strengthen citizens' confidence and, secondly, it presents key measures under two headings: employ- ment and equal opportunity and inclusion.

Further Reading

Van den Bogaert, Stefaan and Vermeersch, "Sport and the EC Treaty: a tale of uneasy bedfellows", (2006) E.L.Rev. 821.
Elise Muir, "Enhancing the effects of Ciommunity law on national employment policies: the *Mangold* case", (2006) E.L.Rev. 879.
Henk Overbeek, *The political economy of European employment* (Routledge, 2003).
Marc Bell and Lisa Waddington, "Reflecting on inequalities in European equal- ity law", (2003) E.L.Rev. 349.
Roger Blanpain, *European labour Law*, 10th edn (Kluwer Law International, 2006).
Tamara Herbey and Jeff Kenner, *Economic and Social Rights under the EU Charter of Fundamental Rights* (Hart Publishing, 2003).

---

[130] General Report 2003, 150.
[131] Decision 1145/02 [2002] O.J. L170/1.
[132] COM (2005) 33 final: Comminication from the Commission. See also the Internet.

Chapter Thirty

Culture, Public Health, Consumer Protection

Those three subjects are treated here together because they have much in common, although they form separate titles in Part Three of the TFEU: "Union policies and Internal actions". In a previous edition, I wrote that, "Compared to subjects like the basic freedoms or competition, they constitute 'minor' Union activities". As will be seen hereunder, this is no longer true. Public health, is an example, as the Commission puts it: "the 'mad cow' and 'dioxin' crisis and the emergence or re-emergence of certain diseases such as tuberculosis have highlighted the need for a genuine Union-level policy."[1]

However, in accordance with the TFEU provisions, the above-mentioned policies merely tend to "complement", "supplement" or "support" the Member States' actions in those fields. This means that the emphasis is on the Member States, not on the Union's activities. The Treaty, furthermore, contains very few provisions (one single article for each subject), and those are, most of the time, couched in general terms: "the Union shall contribute to", "shall complement national policies", etc. These activities could be called what the Treaty of Amsterdam refers to as "directly related flanking measures".[2] However, are these actions directly related to other activities? For other areas, such as "Trans-European Networks", the Treaty itself indicates that they are to, "help achieve the objectives referred to in Articles 26 [14] [internal market] and 174 [158] [regional policy]".[3] Other subjects such as Education and Vocational Training, obviously are indispensable for the free movement of workers and the self-employed. Nothing of the sort is provided for the subjects examined here and, one could indeed wonder why the EU Treaty inserted them into the Treaty. Nevertheless, as is so often the case, even in the absence of specific provisions, the Member States are ready, when a crisis occurs, to endow the Union with the necessary powers to act. This is especially so when the crisis affects several Member States and its solution requires heavy expenditure. However, a question remains concerning the limits of the activities which genuinely belong to the Union level. It seems that the fact that certain Treaty rules, such as those on competition, apply to various human activities, like sports, means the Union must be endowed with competences in those fields. It is not simply because the Union is no longer referred to as the "Economic" Union, that, therefore, "non-directly related" fields may be legitimately included. What about the principle of subsidiarity[4] and the famous slogan "let's do less, but do it better"? Anyway, the activities are in the Treaty, and they will therefore be examined.

---

[1] *http://www.europa.eu/scadplus/leg/en/sz03000.htm.*
[2] Former art.61(a) EC.
[3] art.170(1) TFEU [154(1)].
[4] art.5 EU.

1. CULTURE[5]

Even before the insertion of the present Title into the Treaty, there were references to activities which can be classified under the heading "culture": to start with the, "protection of national treasures possessing artistic, historic or archaeological value", which justifies prohibitions or restrictions on imports, exports or transit.[6] Other provisions were adopted, for instance, for the return of cultural objects unlawfully removed from the territory of a Member State[7]; the harmonisation of controls on exports of cultural goods[8]; besides more mundane arrangements like the application of the Social Fund to "cultural workers",[9] special conditions of admission of young people to museums and cultural events[10] and the protection of Europe's architectural heritage.[11] Since the entry into force of the EU Treaty, the Union has a task with regard to both the cultures of the Member States, whose national and regional diversities must be respected, and the "common cultural heritage"[12]; access for everyone to the latter was facilitated by the creation of the European digital library EUROPEANA.[13] The heritage will be brought "to the fore", while the Union must "contribute to the flowering"[14] of the former. However, the Union is not to develop its own independent activity, but simply to encourage co-operation between the Member States and, if necessary, to support and supplement their action in the following areas[15]:

- improvement of the knowledge and dissemination of the culture and history of the European peoples;
- conservation and safeguarding of cultural heritage of European significance;
- non-commercial cultural exchanges; and
- artistic and literary creation, including the audio-visual sector.

---

[5] art.167 TFEU [151].

[6] art.36 TFEU [30].

[7] Directive 93/7 [1993] O.J. L74/74, amended [1996] O.J. L60/59 and Regulation 3911/92 on the harmonisation of controls on the export of cultural goods [1993] O.J. L 395, codified [2009] O.J. L39/1.1. See also Council Resolution on the implementation of Directive 93/7 [2002] O.J. C 32/3 and list of central authorities nominated by the Member States to deal with the return of cultural objects unlawfully removed [2006] O.J. C123/4.

[8] Regulation 3911/92 [1992] O.J. L395/1, amended [1996] O.J. L335/9; see also Regulation 752/93 laying down provisions for the implementation of Regulation 3911/92 [1993] O.J. L77/24.

[9] Resolution of the Council and of the Ministers responsible for Cultural Affairs meeting within the Council [1985] O.J. L2/2.

[10] Resolution of December 20, 1985 [1985] O.J. C348/2.

[11] Resolution of November 13, 1986 [1986] O.J. C320/1.

[12] art.167(1) TFEU [151(1)].

[13] Council Conclusion of November 20, 2008 [2008] O.J. C319/18.

[14] See art.6(c) TFEU [3(1)(q)]: "The Union shall have competence to carry out actions to support, coordinate or supplement the actions of the Member States. The areas of such actions shall, at European level, be: . . . (c) culture".

[15] See however Council Resolution on the role of culture in the development of the European Union [2002] O. J. C32/2.

The "supporting and supplementing" will be done by Parliament and the Council[16] in accordance with the ordinary legislative procedure,[17] after consulting the Committee of the Regions. The Council must also adopt recommendations on a proposal from the Commission. All this clearly shows that this field remains solidly in the hands of the Member States, which only consent to receiving (financial) "support" from the Union!

The TFEU also provides that the Union and the Member States (acting together), shall foster co-operation with third countries and the competent international organisations, in particular the Council of Europe.[18] Interesting is that the cultural aspects must be taken into account by the institutions in all actions under other provisions of the Treaty, in particular in order to respect and to promote the diversity of its cultures.[19] Other activities referred to are audiovisual policy, regional development, employment and training, research and technological development, agriculture, the information society, tourism and business.

Culture and Audio-visual Media. Following the adoption of the Television without frontiers Directive in 1989, the Commission runs two programmes: the Media Plus programme (2001–2006)[20] and the Multilingual Radio and Television Initiatives.[21]

Culture and Regional Development. Funds available for regional development make up the lion's share of the European budget for culture. The Commission establishes guidelines on the basis of which the Member States adopt programmes.

Culture and Research and Technological Development. This co-operation at Union level reflects its cultural choices. Some research programmes of the Seventh Framework Programme (2007–2013) focus their resources on projects relating directly to cultural activities.

Culture and agriculture. Agriculture is part of European culture. The Treaty provisions promote traditional forms of production, preservation of the cultural heritage and the creation of jobs relating to culture.

---

[16] See, for instance, Decision of Parliament and Council establishing a programme to support artistic and cultural activities having a European dimension (Kaleidoscope) [1996] O.J. L99/20 and Decision 792/2004 establishing a Union action programme to promote bodies active at European level in the field of culture [2004] O.J. L138/40; idem to support, including translation, in the field of books and reading (Ariane) [1997] O.J. L291/26; Decision on cross-border fixed book prices in European linguistic areas [1997] O.J. L305/2; idem in the field of cultural heritage (Raphaël) [1997] O.J. L305/31; there are also at least two dozen Resolutions and Conclusions (none of them binding) of the Council, or of the Council and the Ministers responsible for Cultural Affairs meeting within the Council, or of those Ministers alone, concerning electronic publishing, a European sculpture competition, the European Foundation, etc. Special mention must be made of the Decision establishing a Union action for the Europe capital of Culture event for the years 2005 to 2019 [1999] O.J. L166/1.

[17] art.294 TFEU [251].

[18] art.167(3) TFEU. As shall be seen, the Union is to establish all appropriate forms of co-operation with the Council of Europe: art.220(1) TFEU [303].

[19] art.167(4) TFEU [151(4)].

[20] [2000] O.J. L336/82. See General Report 2008/74 for the Commission's final assessment report on the implementation and results of the MEDIA Plus and MEDIA Training programmes.

[21] See Council Resolution on the development of the audiovisual sector [2002] O.J. C32/4.

Culture and the Information Society. The emergence of new information technologies brings with it new methods of work in the cultural sphere. The Commission thus encourages the application of these new instruments to culture. See for instance the User-friendly Information Society programme.[22]

Culture and the Environment. The preservation of natural habitats as cultural heritage is encouraged by the environment financial instruments LIFE III and by European environmental regulations. See the Energy, Environment and Sustainable Development programme.[23]

It should also be noted that the Treaty authorises Member States to provide aid for economic operators in order to promote culture and heritage conservation, provided such aid does not affect trading conditions and competition in the Union to an extent that is contrary to the common interest.[24] Mention must be made of the Decision of Parliament and Council establishing the Culture 2000 programme supporting artists and cultural projects with a European dimension.[25] The aim of the programme, which combines the Raphaël, Kaleidoscope and Ariane programmes, is to develop a common cultural area by promoting cultural dialogue, knowledge of the history, creation and dissemination of culture, the mobility of artists and their works, European cultural heritage, new forms of cultural expression, the socioeconomic role of culture, co-operation between creative artists and the cultural institutions of the Member States. With this programme, the Union is taking a new approach to its cultural action. Besides the aims just mentions, it promotes the international distribution of European culture and history, development of heritage sites and collections of European importance as well as intercultural dialogue integration.

The financial framework for the implementation of the Culture 2000 programme for the period 2000–2006 was set at €236 million. The programme was open to participation by the countries of the European Economic Area and Romania and Bulgaria. The 2007–2013 Culture programme was established at the end of 2008.[26] The Commission is in charge of implementing the programme and addresses a report[27] to the Council, Parliament, the ESC and the Committee of the Regions.

Finally, cultural activities throughout the Union are facilitated by the implementation of the basic freedoms: free movement of workers and of the self-employed, i.e. the freedom of establishment and the freedom to provide services and the free movement of (cultural) goods. Similarly the protection of copyright and related rights encourages creativity in the cultural field.

In July 2002, the Council adopted a Resolution on a new work plan on European co-operation in the field of culture.[28] This plan was later implemented, among others, by a Resolution concerning "European added value and mobility of persons and circulation of works in the cultural sector".[29]

According to the Commission's website the Union's fields of activity are: architecture, visual arts, cinema and audiovisual media, dance, education and training

[22] [1999] O.J. L64/20.
[23] [1999] O.J. L64/58.
[24] art.107(3)(d) TFEU [87(3)(d)], that defines aid "which may be considered [by the Commission] to be compatible with the common market".
[25] Decision 508/2000 [2000] O.J. L63/1, modified [2004] O.J. L99/3.
[26] Decision 1352/08 [2008] O.J. L348/128.
[27] See for the years 2000–2001 COM(2003) 722.
[28] [2002] O.J. C162/5.
[29] [2003] O.J. C13/5.

in fine arts, books, music, cultural heritage and theatre. On the other hand, the Union is active via cultural co-operation, cultural industries, access to culture, the culture professionals, cultural facilities, linguistic diversity, regulatory aspects and international relations. Where the latter are concerned, the Union approved the Unesco Convention on the Protection and Promotion of the Diversity of Cultural Expressions.[30]

2. PUBLIC HEALTH[31]

In pursuance of the TFEU, the Union must, whenever it defines or implements any of its policies and activities, ensure a high level of human health protection; it shall also complement national policies. The field of action is circumscribed as follows: improving public health, preventing human illness and diseases and obviating sources of danger to physical and mental health, that includes the fight against the "major health scourges",[32] by promoting research into their causes, their transmission and their prevention, as well as health information and education.[33] Reference is also made to the reduction of drug-related health damage, including information[34] and prevention[35] and monitoring, early warning of and combating serious cross-border threats to health. Although in this field like in that of culture, the first task of the Union is to, "encourage co-operation between Member States" and, if necessary, lend support to their action, it is also to develop its own activity. The latter came into the limelight when, as pointed out above, the "mad cow" and "dioxine" crises and the emergence or re-emergence of certain diseases such as tuberculosis showed the need for a genuine Union-level health policy. This is to be done by Parliament and the Council, acting in accordance with the ordinary legislative procedure,[36] and after consulting the ESC and the Committee of the Regions, adopting, in order to meet common safety concerns, measures with regard to the quality and safety of organs and substances of human origin, blood and blood derivatives, the protection of human health in the veterinary and phytosanitary fields and setting high standards of quality and safety for medicinal products and devices for medical use. Parliament and Council may also, in the same way, adopt incentive measures to protect and improve human health and, in particular, to combat the major cross-border health scourges, measures concerning monitoring, early warning of and combating serious cross-border threats to health and measures having as their direct objective the protection of public health regarding tobacco and the abuse of alcohol.[37]

[30] [2006] O.J. L2001/15.

[31] art.168 TFEU [152].

[32] See, for instance, Decision 646/96 on action plan to combat cancer [1996] O.J. L95/9 and [2001] O.J. L79/1; Decision 647/96 setting up a Union programme on the prevention of AIDS and certain other communicable diseases [1996] O/J L95/16 and [2001] O.J. L79/1; see also Decision 1295/99 on Union action on rare diseases [1999] O.J. L155/1.

[33] Decision 645/96 programme of Union action on health promotion, information, education and training [1996] O.J. C95/1 and [2001] O.J. L79/1.

[34] Decision 1400/97 on a programme for healthy monitoring [1997] O.J. L193/1 and [2001] O.J. L79/1.

[35] Decision 102/97 on a programme of Union action on the prevention of drug dependence [1997] O.J. L19/25 and [2001] O.J. L79/1.

[36] art.294 TFEU.

[37] art.168(7) TFEU.

The Treaty makes clear that the Union will not tread on national toes: harmonisation is excluded and the, "responsibilities of the Member States for the definition of their health policy and the organisation and the delivery of health services and medical care" must be respected. In particular, adds the Treaty, the above measures, "shall not affect national provisions on the donation or medical use of organs and blood".[38]

Obviously, many aspects of health protection overlap with Consumer Protection which is analysed in the next section and Environment (Ch.32) the object of which is also to protect human health.[39] This applies, for instance, to the classification, packaging and labelling of dangerous substances,[40] restrictions on the marketing and use of certain dangerous substances and preparations,[41] pesticides,[42] asbestos,[43] biotechnology, the quality of drinking[44] and bathing[45] water. Human health is, of course, dependent also on animal health. In this field the Union has been very active, mainly within the framework of the agricultural policy.

Mention must be made of a Parliament and Council Decision setting up a Network for Epidemiological Surveillance and Control of Communicable Diseases in the Union[46] and the Decision on the common diseases to be progressively covered by this Union network.[47] It should also be noted that health protection projects may be co-financed in certain regions by the European Regional Development Fund (ERDF) and the European Social Fund (ESF).

On May 16, 2000, the Commission sent a Communication[48] to the Council, Parliament, the ESC and the Committee of the Regions on the Health Strategy of the European Union. This strategy consisted of two main elements: (1) a public health framework, including an action programme in the field of public health (2003–2008)[49] and, (2) the development of an integrated health strategy; it contained specific measures to address the obligation to incorporate health protection into all Union policies.

An "Executive Agency for the Public health programme" was set up; like other agencies, it is to be entrusted with certain tasks in the management of Union programmes.[50] In addition to the Public Health programme, the framework provided for other legislative measures. These included:

- prevention and monitoring of communicable diseases; an international network of epidemiological surveillance and control of communicable diseases was set up in 1999[51];

[38] art.168(5) TFEU [152(5)].
[39] See, for instance, Decision 1296/1999 action programme on pollution related diseases [1999] O.J. C200/1 and [2001] O.J. L79/1.
[40] Directive 67/548 [1967] O.J. 196/1, amended for the 31st time [2009] O.J. L11/6 [1997] O.J. L343/19 and [2007] O.J. L136/281, in order to adapt it to Regulation 1907/2006 concerning the Registration, Evaluation, Authorisation and Restriction of Chemicals (REACH) [2006] O.J. L396/1. Amended again for the 31st time [2009] O.J. L11/6, modifying Annex 1. Repealed by Regulation 1272/08 [2008] O.J. L353/1, amended by Regulation 790/09 [2009] O.J. L235/1.
[41] Directive 76/769 [1976] O.J. L262/201, amended [1997] O.J. L315/13.
[42] Directive 78/631 [1978] O.J. L206/13, amended [1992] O.J. L154/1.
[43] Directive 87/217 [1987] O.J. L85/40.
[44] Directive 75/440 [1975] O.J. L194/26.
[45] Directive 76/160 [1976] O.J. L31/1, amended several times.
[46] Decision 98/2119 [1998] O.J. L268/1.
[47] [2000] O.J. L28/50.
[48] COM (2000) 285 final.
[49] Decision 02/1786 [2002] O.J. L271/1; see [2007] O.J. L46/237.
[50] Regulation 58/2003 [2003] O.J. L11/1.
[51] [1999] O.J. L268/1.

- prevention of drug dependence: action plan to combat drugs;
- Union action programme on injury prevention (1999–2003)[52];
- Union action programme on health monitoring (1997–2001)[53];
- Daphne, action programme to combat violence against children, young persons and women (2000–2003)[54];
- Union action programme on pollution-related diseases (1999–2001)[55];
- Union action programme on rare diseases (1999–2003).[56] The list of health problems which the Union helps to cure seems endless:
- Cancer: Europe against Cancer action plan (1996–2000); action against smoking; ban on smoking in places open to the public; advertising and sponsorship of tobacco products[57]; health warning on tobacco packages[58]; manufacturing, presentation and sales of tobacco products[59];
- Aids: several actions and programmes: "Europe against Aids" programme[60];
- Bovine spongiform encephalopathy (BSE): identification and labelling of beef and veal;
- Drugs, see Action Plan to Combat drugs[61];
- Doping: Union support plan to combat doping in sport;
- Alcohol abuse: maximum authorised level of alcohol in the blood of motor-vehicle drivers;
- Food: food law in the EU[62]; genetically modified organisms;
- Etc, etc.[63]

As mentioned before, in September 2002, Parliament and Council adopted a programme of Union action in the field of public health (2003–2008).[64] An Executive Agency for the Public Health programme was set up by the Commission.[65] A second programme for Union action in the field of Health (2008–2013) was adopted in 2007,[66] its objectives are to improve citizens health, to promote health in order to improve prosperity and solidarity and to generate and disseminate health knowledge. The Executive Agency for the Public Health Programme was renamed Executive Agency for Health and Consumers.[67]

---

[52] [1999] O.J. L46/1.
[53] [1997] O.J. L193/1.
[54] [2000] O.J. L34/1.
[55] [1999] O.J. L155/7.
[56] [1999] O.J. L155/1.
[57] Directive 2003/33 [2003] O.J. L152/16.
[58] Decision 2003/641 [2003] O.J. L226/24.
[59] Directive 2001/37 [2001] O.J. L194/26.
[60] [1995] O.J. L168/1.
[61] COM (1999) 239 final.
[62] See Directive 2000/13 relating to labelling, presentation and advertising of foodstuffs [2000] O.J. L109/29 and Regulation 178/2002 laying down the general principles and requirements of food law, establishing the European Food Safety Authority (see above, Ch.11) and laying down procedures in matters of food safety [2002] O.J. L31/1.
[63] Consult for more information *http://www.europa.eu.int/scadplus/leg/en/s03000.htm* on which most of the above is based.
[64] Decision 1786/2002 [2002] O.J. L271/1.
[65] Decision 04/858 [2004] O.J. L369/73.
[66] Decision 07/1350 [2007] O.J. L301/3.
[67] Decision 08/544 [2008] O.J. L173/27.

The objectives of this second programme are:

1. to improve citizens' health security: developing Union and Member States' capacity to respond to health threats, for example with health emergency planning and preparedness measures and actions related to patient safety;
2. to promote health, including the reduction of health inequalities: action on health determinants, such as nutrition, alcohol, tobacco and drug consumption, as well as social and environmental determinants, measures on the prevention of major deseases and reducing health inequalities across the Union, and increasing healthy life years and promoting healthy ageing;
3. health information and knowledge: action on health indicators and ways of disseminating information to citizens and focus on Union added-value action to exchange knowledge in areas such as gender issues, childrens' health or rare deseases.

(1) Food Safety

It is one of the major preoccupations of the European citizens and 2000 was not too soon for the Union to develop activities in this field. Indeed, food is a prime example of products which circulate widely across the whole Union and therefore need to be regulated at Union level. The directive issued in 2000 on the approximation of the laws of the Member States relating to the labelling, presentation and advertising of foodstuffs[68] is a first major step to provide assurance of a high level of protection of human health and consumers' interest in relation to food. It takes into account in particular the diversity in the supply of food, including traditional products, while ensuring the effective functioning of the internal market. Among others, the following particulars are compulsory on the labelling: the name under which the product is sold, the list of ingredients, the quantity of certain ingredients, in the case of prepackaged foodstuffs the net quantity, the date of minimum durability, any special storage conditions or conditions of use, the name or business name and address of the manufacturer or packager, or of a seller established within the Union.

The Directive was complemented by a regulation[69] with a very broad scope; indeed, it, "establishes common principles and responsibilities, the means to provide a strong science base, efficient organisational arrangements and procedures to underpin decision making in matters of food and feed safety". It applies at all stages of production, processing and distribution of food and feed.[70] An essential element is constituted by the traceability of food; all operators in this sector are, since January 1, 2005, obliged to put into place a traceability system allowing, for each one of their products, the identification of the provider of the ingredients and to whom they were delivered, to register this data in a given system allowing to keep them for a period longer than the life of the product and, finally, to provide the data quasi-immediately on demand by the competent authorities. Traceability allows the authorities to withdraw from the market products that present a danger to public health. The Union now has a General Food Law providing for risk analysis, precautionary principle, protection of

---

[68] Directive 2000/13, (quoted above, fn. 62).
[69] Regulation 178/2002, (quoted above, fn. 62).
[70] art.1 Regulation 178/2002 (quoted above, fn. 62).

consumers interests, public consultation, public information, obligations for food trade, food and feed safety requirements, responsibilities, among others, of the food business operators, traceability and liability.

Finally, mention must be made of the Precautionary Principle, which allows Member States to take measures when the potentially dangerous effects of a phenomenon, product or process have been identified by a scientific and objective evaluation, which does not, however, allow the risk to be determined with sufficient certainty. The Treaty contains only one reference to this principle, namely in the Title on the environment,[71] but it is generally accepted that it also covers human, animal and plant health and consumer policy. Since the principle is not defined in the Treaty nor in secondary Union law, the Council requested the Commission to develop clear and effective guidelines for its application. This was done by a Communication of February 2, 2000,[72] which is examined hereafter in Ch.34: Environment.

(2) Medicinal Products

A major role in the field of health protection is played by medicinal products. The latter to be distinguished from "medicinal devices" and "cosmetics". In those three fields, the institutions have adopted numerous directives and regulations.[73]

The basic principle is that no medicinal product may be placed on the market without a prior authorisation either from a Member State[74] or from the Union.[75] For the latter see above, Ch.13: Decentralised Bodies of the Union (6. The European Medicines Agency). See also the Directive on the Union code relating to medicinal products for human use.[76]

Mention should be made also of a Directive setting standards of quality and safety for the collection, testing, processing, storage and distribution of human blood and blood components.[77] A similar Directive concerns human tissues and cells.[78]

In 1976 the Council issued a Directive on the approximation of the laws of the Member States relating to *cosmetic* products,[79] defined as:

"[A]ny substance or preparation intended for placing in contact with the various parts of the human body or with the teeth . . . with a view to cleaning

---

[71] art.191(2) TFEU [174(2)].
[72] COM (2000)1 final.
[73] See, for instance: Directive 2000/70 amending Directive 93/42 as regards medical devices incorporating stable derivates of human blood or human plasma and Directive 2003/94 laying down the principles and guidelines of good manufacturing practices in respect of medicinal production for human use and investigational medicinal products for human use [2003] O.J. L262/22.
[74] Directive 65/65 on the approximation of provisions relating to proprietary medicinal products [1965] O.J. p.369, incorporated [1994] O.J. L1/263 and Directive 319/75 [1975] O.J. L147/1, incorporated [1994] O.J. L1/263, amended [2000] O.J. L139/28.
[75] Regulation 2309/93, laying down a Union procedure for the authorisation and supervision of medicinal products for human and veterinary use and establishing a European Medicines Agency [1993] O.J. L214/1. See above Ch.13 (6. The European Medicines Agency). See also Directive 2001/83 on the Union code relating to medicinal products for human use [2003] O.J. L159/46, amended [2009] O.J. L242/3.
[76] Directive 2001/83 [2001] O.J. L311/67; for more details see above, Ch.13: Decentralised Bodies of the Union (6. The European Medicines Agency).
[77] Directive 2002/98 [2003] O.J. L33/30, implemented by Directive 2004/33 [2004] O.J. L91/25.
[78] Directive 2004/23 [2004] O.J. L102/48.
[79] [1976] O.J. L262/169.

them, perfuming them or protecting them in order to keep them in good condition, change their appearance or correct body odours."

The marketing of cosmetics containing certain substances listed in the Directive is prohibited.

In 1993, the Council issued a directive on *medical devices*, defined as:

"[A]ny instrument, apparatus, appliance, material or other article . . . to be used for human beings for the purpose of diagnosis . . . investigation . . . or control of conception, and which does not achieve its principal intended action by pharmacological . . . means."[80]

3. CONSUMER PROTECTION[81]

What the Commission wrote many years ago[82] still applies today for the more than 500 million consumers in the European Union.

"The Member States and the [Union] have adopted policies designed to protect the specific interests of consumers, who play a key economic and political role in society. Investing them with a certain number of fundamental rights, the Member States have put in place policies designed to reduce inequalities, abolish unfair practices, promote safety and health and improve living standards in general."

The history of consumer protection starts with the Council Resolution of April 14, 1975 concerning a preliminary programme for a protection and information policy of the consumer, followed by an action programme on consumer policy.[83] It referred to a large number of areas, some of which were introduced into the EC Treaty by the EU Treaty. They are, the protection of the health, safety[84] and economic interests of the consumer, and the right to information and education and to organise in order to safeguard their interests.[85] Other areas not explicitly referred to in the Treaty are, under the heading protection of the economic interests: misleading advertising,[86] unfair commercial practices,[87] the protection in respect of distance contracts—the customer has a

[80] [1993] O.J. L169/1.
[81] art.169 TFEU]153].
[82] *http://www.europa.eu/scadplus/leg/en/s16300 .htm.*
[83] [1975] O.J. C92/1.
[84] See, for instance, Directive 88/378 on the safety of toys [1988] O.J. L187/1, amended [1993] O.J. L220/1.
[85] art.169 TFEU [153]. See Directive 98/27 on injunctions for the protection of consumers' interests [1998] O.J. L166/51, amended by the Unfair Commercial Practice Directive, (quoted below, fn. 86) and repealed by Directive 09/22 [2009] O.J. L110/30, protection of the collective interests of consumers. See Commission Communication concerning art.'(3) [2009] O.J. C 135/1.
[86] Directive 84/450 concerning misleading advertisement and comparative publicity [1984] O.J. L250/17, modified by the Unfair Commercial Practice Directive [2005] O.J. L149/23. See *Lidi Belgium* (C-356/04) [2006] E.C.R. I-8501: comparison may be "misleading" where omissions are likely to deceive significant numbers of consumers.
[87] Directive 2005/29 [2005] O.J. L149/22, based on art.114 TFEU [95] provides for a complete harmonisation; it increases the legal protection of both the consumer and the undertakings. It provides for a single general prohibition of unfair commercial practices that modify the commercial behaviour of the consumer. It concerns both the misleading and the aggressive practices. Also explicitly prohibited is the lack of necessary information. The Directive contains a black list of commercial practices that are always prohibited (art.5,5); it also contains a list of aggressive practices. Directive 84/450 approximation of laws concerning misleading advertising [1984] O.J. L250/18, amended, see below. See *VTB and Galatea* (Joined Cases 261/07 and 299/07) [2009] E.C.R. 23.04.09. The Directive precludes a national regulation prohibiting joined offers.

time limit of at least seven days to annul the purchase[88]—sale of consumer goods and associated guarantees,[89] electronic commerce[90] and, furthermore, advice, help and redress.[91] A regulation was issued in 2004 on co-operation between national authorities responsible for the enforcement of consumer protection laws: the "Regulation on consumer protection co-operation"[92]; a Union Action Programme in the field of consumer policy (2007–2013) was adopted at the end of 2006.[93] See also a Directive promoting the establishment and operation of the internal market in the field of consumer credit and securing a high level of protection for consumers throughout the Union.[94]

Product Liability. Of great importance for consumers, distributors and producers are the directives on general product safety[95] and liability for defective products,[96] under which only the producer can be held responsible, except in certain well defined cases where responsibility is shifted to the supplier.[97] The Court determined that, in order for a producer to incur liability for defective products, the victim does not have to prove that the producer was at fault; that, however, in accordance with the principle of fair apportionment of risk between

---

[88] Directive 97/7 [1997] O.J. L144/19, amended by the Unfair Commercial Practice Directive, (quoted above, fn.86), corrigendum [2009] O.J. L187/5; see, *Gysbrechts* (C-205/07) [2008] E.C.R. 16.12.08: not allowing supplier to request consumer to provide his payment card number constitutes infringement, and modified by Directive 2007/64 on payment services in the internal market [2007] O.J. L319/1. See also Directive 85/577 to protect the consumer in respect of contracts negotiated away from business premises [1985] O.J. L372/31; see *Hamilton* (C-412/06) [2008] E.C.R. I-2383 concerning the right to cancel provided for in art.5(1) and *Gysbrecht* (C-205/07) (quoted above), concerning the right of the seller to ask for a downpayment in the case of a trans-frontier transaction; with regard to its application to sales of immovable property, see *Schulte* (C-350/03) [2005] E.C.R. I-9215.

[89] Directive 99/44 [1999] O.J. L171/12. See *Quelle* (C-404/06) [2008] E.C.R. I-2685, art.3 precludes national legislation under which a seller who has sold consumer goods which are not in conformity, may require the consumer to pay compensation for the use of those defective goods until their replacement with new goods, since the seller is responsible for having supplied a defective good; however, in case the consumer makes use of the goods in a manner incompatible with the principles of civil law, such as those of good faith and unjust enrichment, he may be required to make compensation for the use of the good, *Messner* (C-489/07) E.C.R. 03.09.09.

[90] Directive 2000/31 [2000] O.J. L178/1 on certain legal aspects of information society services, in particular electronic commerce, in the internal market ("Directive on electronic commerce"). See *Promusicae* (C-275/06) [2008] E.C.R. 8-271, the Directive neither compels nor precludes obligation to disclose personal data in civil procedure and *Deutsche Internet Verziecherung* (C-298/07) [2008] E.C.R. I-7841, interpreting art.5(1)(c), obligation of service provider to supply recipient with information before the conclusion of the contract.

[91] See European Network for Out-of-Court Settlement of Consumer Disputes or European Extra Judicial Network (eej-net) Europa, Consumer Affairs, eej.net, IP/00/445.

[92] [2004] O.J. L 364/1.

[93] [2006] O.J. L404/39.

[94] Directive 2008/48 on credit agreements for consumers [2008] O.J. L133/66.

[95] Directive 2001/95 with a view of ensuring a high level of protection of safety and health of persons as required by art.168 TFEU [152] [2001] O.J. L11/04, Commission Communication [2006] O.J. L171/23 and Decision on compliance of certain standards with the general safety requirements [2006] O.J. L200/35. See Rapid Information System [2010] O.J. L22/1.

[96] Directive 85/374 [1985] O.J. L210/29, amended O.J. L141/20 in order to include non-transformed agricultural products; it is also stated that "product" includes electricity. For an interpretation of "put into circulation" see case *Declan O'Byrne* (C-127/04) [2006] E.C.R. I-1313; on what constitutes sufficient prove of damage caused by a product, *Commission v Greece* (C-285/08) [2009] E.C.R. 04.06.09. See also Directive 98/37 on the approximation of the laws of the Member States relating to machinery [1998] O.J. L207/1 and Commission communication [2009] O.J. C22/1.

[97] art.3(3) Directive 87/374.

the injured person and the producer,[98] the latter has a defence if he can prove certain facts exonerating him from liability, including that, "the state of scientific and technical knowledge at the time when he put the product into circulation, was not such as to enable the existence of the defect to be discovered".[99] The Court determined that national law may establish liability of the supplier without restriction for producer's fault-based liability.[100] The Court also determined that the producer and the distributor may be bound only by obligations imposed on them respectively by directive.[101] There is a time limit of three years. It should also be noted that this liability does not exclude the possibility for the injured party to claim also damage under other liabilities.[102]

The protection of the economic interests covers, besides the ones mentioned already, various other areas such as consumer credit,[103] the indication of the prices on non-food products,[104] unfair terms in consumer contracts,[105] package travel, package holidays and package tours,[106] combating late payments in commercial transactions.[107] The latter is particularly important for undertakings (it does not apply to natural persons); "late" payment means more than 30 days following the date of receipt of the invoice by the debtor (for certain categories of contracts, the Member States may fix the period at 60 days). The interest to be paid in case of late payment is the sum of at least seven percentage points (the "margin") plus the interest rate applied by the ECB to its most recent main refinancing operations (the "reference rate").

In order to facilitate cross-border payments, a European Order for payment procedure was set up.[108] It is worthwhile noting that with regard to consumer protection, the Court decided that the term "consumer" refers exclusively to physical persons.[109]

---

[98] Preamble of Directive 85/374.

[99] *Commission v UK* (C-300/95) [1997] E.C.R. I-2649.

[100] *SKOV and Bilka* (C-402/03) [2006] E.C.R. I-199.

[101] Directive 2001/95; *Lidl* (C-132/08) E.C.R. 30.04.09.

[102] *Gonzalez Sanchez* (C-183/00) [2002] E.C.R. I-3901.

[103] Directive 87/102 [1987] O.J. L42/48, modified [1998] O.J. L101/17, repealed by Directive 2008/48 [2008] O.J. L133/66, corrigendum [2009] O.J. L207/14. See *Rampion and Godard* (C-429/05) [2007] E.C.R. I-8017, concerning the interpretation of arts 11 and 14 and where the Court stated that the Directive allows the national courts to apply of their own motion the provisions transposing art.11(2) of Directive 87/102 into national law. For the same art. see also *Scarpelli* (C-509/07) [2009] E.C.R. 23.04.09.

[104] Directive 88/314 [1988] O.J. L142/19 and Directive 98/6 on consumer protection in the indication of the prices of products offered to consumers [1998] O.J. L80/27.

[105] Directive 93/13 [1993] O.J. L95/29; see *Commission v Spain* (C-70/03) [2004] E.C.R. I-7999: abusive clauses in a contract—rules of interpretation—rules of conflict of laws and *Mostaza Claro* (C-168/05) [2006] E.C.R. I-10421, an arbitration award must be annulled by the national court where the agreement contains an unfair term even if the consumer has not pleaded that invalidity in the course of the arbitration. For an example of an abusive contract term, see *Pannon GSM* (C-243/08) [2009] E.C.R. I- 04.06.09.

[106] Directive 90/314 [1990] O.J. L158/59. See *Verein für Konsumenteninformation* (C-364/96) [1998] E.C.R. I-2949, art.7 protects travellers who have already paid their hotel and who must pay it a second time following the bankruptcy of the travel organisation, and *Leitner* (C-168/00) [2002] E.C.R. I-26321, art.5 confers on consumers a right in principle to compensation for non-material damage.

[107] Directive 2000/35 on combating late payment in commercial transactions [2000] O.J. L200/35. See *Telecom v Deutsche Telkom* (C-306/06) [2008] E.C.R. I-1923, defining at which date a payment is considered made and *Caffaro* (C-265/07) [2008] E.C.R. I-7095. Directive does not prevent national law providing a time limit of 120 days for forced execution against a public authority.

[108] Regulation 1896/06 [2006] O.J. L399/1.

[109] *Cape and Ideal Service MN RE* (Joined Cases C-541/99 and C-542/99) [2001] E.C.R. I-9049.

Great emphasis was put on foodstuffs following the publication by the Commission of what is sometimes referred to as the "White Paper bis" on the completion of the internal market for foodstuffs, wherein the Commission points out four areas in which it will continue to propose legislation, leaving the others to mutual recognition. It concerns mainly labelling[110] and nutritional labelling. (See above, "Food Safety".) As with public health, consumer protection requirements must be taken into account in defining and implementing other Union policies and activities.

To help therewith a Consumer Committee was set up.[111] Here also, the Union must take measures to attain the objectives stated above[112] and to support, supplement and monitor the policy pursued by the Member States. The latter measures must be adopted by Parliament and Council in accordance with the ordinary legislative procedure,[113] after consulting the ESC. In 2009, the Commission set up a European Consumer Consultative Group[114] to be consulted on all issues relating to consumer interest at Union level.

Under the Treaty, Union actions must, as pointed out, help protect the health, safety[115] and economic interests of consumers and promote their rights to receive information and education and to join forces in order to protect their interests.[116] A General Framework Decision covered a five-year period (1999–2003) and was allocated an amount of €2.5 million. It was open to the associated countries of Eastern and Central Europe, as well as Cyprus and the countries of the EEA. The activities cover measures (1) taken by the Commission to supplement the policies of the Member States, (2) in support of activities of European consumer organisations and (3) in support of external initiatives to promote consumers' interests. The Decision identifies four areas requiring action at Union level:

- the health and safety as regards products[117] and services;
- protecting the economic and legal interests, including access to dispute resolution;
- educating and informing about protection and rights; and
- promotion and representation of the interests of consumers.

---

[110] Directive 79/112 on the approximation of the laws of the Member States relating to the labelling, presentation and advertising of foodstuffs for the sale to the ultimate consumer [1979] O.J. L33/1, modified [1997] O.J. L4/21; Directive 79/581 on consumer protection in the indication of the prices of foodstuffs [1979] O.J. L158/19; Directive 90/496 on nutritional labelling for foodstuffs [1990] O.J. L276/40; Directive 93/102 relating to the labelling, presentation and advertising of foodstuffs for sale to the ultimate consumer [1993] O.J. L291/14; and Directive 94/54 [1994] O.J. L300/14. See *Diageme* (C-85/94) [1995] E.C.R. I-2955, the requiring of the language of the "Taalgebiet" goes too far and *Goerres* (C-385/96) [1998] E.C.R. I-4431, the language must be on the label in a comprehensible language. Regulation on the protection of geographical indications and designations of origin for agricultural products and foodstuffs [1992] O.J. L208/1, amended [1997] O.J. L156/10 and Regulation 1107/96 [1996] O.J. L148/1, amended [1998] O.J. L87/8 and Regulation 2400/96 [1996] O.J. L327/111; Directive 76/796, approximation of laws relating to the marketing and use of certain dangerous substances and preparations [1976] O.J. L262/201, amended [1997] O.J. L315/13. See also Directive 2000/13 relating to the labelling, presentation and advertising of foodstuffs [2000] O.J. L109/29, amended [2001] O.J. L310/19.

[111] Decision of June 13, 1995 [1995] O.J. L162/37.

[112] See Council Resolution on Union consumer policy 1999 to 2001 [1999] O.J. C206/1.

[113] art.294 TFEU [251].

[114] [2009] O.J. L244/21.

[115] See, for instance, Directive 2008/31 modifying Directive 91/477 [1991] O.J. L256/51, on control of the acquisition and possession of weapons [2008] O.J. L179/5.

[116] art.169(1) TFEU.

[117] See, for instance, Directive 2009/48 on the safety of toys [2009] O.J. L170/1.

The Commission is responsible for evaluating and monitoring the various measures and must submit an annual report.

In 2002 the Commission issued the "Consumer policy strategy 2002–2006"[118] with three objectives:

- a high common level of consumer protection;
- effective enforcement of consumer protection rules; and
- proper involvement of consumer organisations in Union policies, and the follow-up actions proposed therein.

This policy strategy was endorsed by the Council.[119] It is clear that consumer policy has grown from a minor flanking measure to a full-fledged Union policy indicating thereby that the citizens' interests now constitute a major part of the Union's responsibilities and activities.

Mention should also be made here of the Union *Eco-label* award scheme, although the measures concerning this scheme were adopted[120] on the basis of the Treaty provisions concerning "Environment".[121] The scheme is intended to promote the design, production, marketing and use of products which have a reduced environmental impact during their entire life cycle, and to provide consumers with better information on the environmental impact of products. The Regulation does not apply to food, drink and pharmaceuticals. The decision to award the eco-label is taken by competent bodies designated by each Member State.

It might be of interest to note what the Commission refers to as the "Ten Basic Principles of consumer protection"[122]:

"1. Buy what you want, where you want
2. If it doesn't work, send it back
3. High safety standard for food and other consumer goods
4. Know what you are eating
5. Contracts should be fair to consumers
6. Sometimes consumers can change their mind
7. Making it easier to compare prices
8. Consumer should not be misled
9. Protection while you are on holiday
10. Effective redress for cross-border disputes."

The European Consumer Centres Network (ECC-Net) is a EU-wide network to promote consumer confidence.

Protection of personal data. Although not directly connected with "consumers" as such, a Directive on the protection of individuals with regard to the

---

[118] [2002] O.J. C137/2.
[119] [2003] O.J. C11/1.
[120] Regulation 880/1992 [1992] O.J. L99/1, amended by Regulation 1980/2000 on a revised Union eco-label award scheme [2002] L237/1. Now see Regulation 66/2010 [2010] O.J. L27/1.
[121] art.192(1) TFEU [175(1)]; see below Ch.34: Environment.
[122] *http://www.ec.europa.eu./consumers/cons_info/10principles/en.pdf.*

processing of personal data and on the free movement of such data, should be mentioned here.[123]

Further Reading

Raymond O'Rourke, *European Food Law*, 3rd edn (Sweet & Maxwell, 2005).
Gerazint Howells and Thomas Wilhelmsson, "EC consumer law: has it come of age?", (2003) E.L.Rev. 370.
Nicolas Moussis, *Access to Social Europe* (European Study Service 2004).
Evangelia Psychoglopoulos, *The Integration of Cultural Consideraztions in EU Law and Policies* (Martinus Nijhof 2008).

---

[123] Directive 95/46 [1995] O.J. L281/31. See *Österreichischer Runfunk E.A.* (Joined Cases C-465/00, C-138/01 and C-139/01) [2003] E.C.R. I-4989, where the Court stated that art.6(1)(c) and art.7(c) and (e) had direct effect, i.e. could be invoked by the citizens in their national courts. See also *Parliament v Council and Commission* (Joined Cases C-317/04 and C-318/04) [2006] E.C.R. I-4721, where the Court annulled an agreement with the US for failure to protect personal data. See also *Huber* (C-524/06) E.C.R. 16.12.08. where the Court determined that this Directive precludes the putting in place, for the purpose of fighting crime, of a system for processing personal date specific to non-nationals and *Rijkeboer* (C-553/07) E.C.R. 07.05.09: balance between interest in access and obligation to provide access.

Chapter Thirty-one

Enterprise and Industrial Policy/Information Society

In this chapter, besides general policies, several specific aspects such as the information society, small and medium-sized enterprises and the Trans-European Networks, will also be examined. However, it should be borne in mind that Union legislation in this domain[1] covers another 16 to 20 sectors, which shall not be examined here in detail.[2]

General Remarks

Enterprise policy aims at creating a favourable environment for enterprises and businesses in Europe, thus creating productivity growth and the jobs and wealth necessary to achieve the objectives of the March 2000 "Lisbon Strategy".[3] Enterprise policy comprises a number of policy actions related to industrial policy, framework conditions favourable to SMEs, multi-annual programmes for enterprise and entrepreneurship and a better business environment.

1. The Lisbon Strategy/Programme

The European Council held a special meeting in March 2000, "to agree a new strategic goal for the [Union] in order to strengthen employment, economic reform and social cohesion as part of a knowledge-based economy".[4]

It constitutes a lofty programme with far-reaching objectives: "to become the most competitive and dynamic knowledge-based economy in the world, capable of sustainable economic growth with more and better jobs and greater social cohesion." It sounds more like a political election programme than a serious new strategic goal. That this could not be achieved must have been clear already for everyone at the time. Furthermore, the absence of incentives left the implementation to the political will of the Member States and, thereby, deprived it of all

---

[1] art.173 TFEU [157].

[2] Iron and steel industry, shipbuilding, aeronautical industry, textiles, leather, hides, skins and footwear, information technology, telecommunications and data processing, motor vehicles, agricultural and forestry tractors, metrology, electrical material, foodstuffs, proprietary medicinal products, cosmetics, dangerous substances, fertilisers and other industrial sectors. Information about those sectors can be found on *http://www.eur-lex.europa.eu./en/legis/latest/ chap13.htm*.

[3] For the 2000 Lisbon Strategy, see the Presidency Conclusions of the Lisbon European Council, *http://www.consilium.europa.eu/ueDocs/cms_Data/docs/oressData/en/ec/00100-rl.en0.htm*; see also: *http://www.ec.europa.eu/enterprise/policy_en.htm*.

[4] See fn.3.

realism. It was therefore inevitable that, in February 2005, the Commission proposed a new start for the Lisbon Strategy focusing the European Union's efforts on two principal tasks: delivering stronger, lasting growth and more and better jobs.[5] Even this is vague and suffers from the absence of a concrete implementation programme with dates and especially means.

The Presidency Conclusions of the Lisbon European Council were divided in four sections, each sub-divided in several sub-sections. The titles are mentioned hereunder.

1. Preparing the transition to a competitive, dynamic and knowledge-based economy by: (a) establishing a European area of research and innovation; (b) creating a friendly environment for starting up and developing innovative businesses, especially SMEs; (c) economic reforms for a complete and fully operational internal market; (d) efficient and integrated financial markets; and (e) co-ordinating macro-economic policies: fiscal consolidation, quality and sustainability of public finances.
2. Modernising the European social model by investing in people and building an active welfare State, by (a) education and training for living and working in the knowledge society; (b) more and better jobs for Europe: developing an active employment policy; (c) modernising social protection; and (d) promoting social inclusion.
3. Putting decisions into practice: a more coherent and systematic approach by (a) improving the existing approach; (b) implementing a new open method of co-ordination; and (c) mobilising the necessary means. (The latter, unfortunately, was, as indicated, not done.)

As mentioned above, the failure of the Member States to implement this Lisbon Strategy, forced the Commission to propose, in February 2005, a new start focusing the EU's efforts on two tasks: delivering (1) stronger, lasting growth; and (2) more and better jobs.[6] This led to a Communication from the Commission to the Council and Parliament on "Common Action for growth and Employment: The Union Lisbon programme".[7]

An important element of the re-launch was the overhaul of its governance structure to define more clearly the respective responsibilities at the national and the Union level: the Commission is to complement the efforts of the Member States; consequently, policy actions at Union and Member State level have been split into complementary, but separate agendas. The European Council of June 2005 endorsed the Integrated Guidelines for Growth and Jobs, whose policy measures fall under three main areas:

- knowledge and innovation for growth;
- making Europe a more attractive place to invest and work;
- creating more and better jobs.

The European Council invited the Commission to present, as counterpart to the national programmes, a Union Lisbon Programme. The Union is to contribute by completing the internal market[8] and by implementing common policies and

---

[5] COM (2005) 24, of February 2, 2005.
[6] COM (2005) 24.
[7] COM (2005) 330 final.
[8] And to think that, according the former art.14(2) EC, the internal market had to be established on December 31, 1992! Fourteen years later the Union still talks about "completing the internal market".

activities that support and complement national policies. It constitutes the first three-year cycle (2005–2007) and concentrates in particular on a number of key actions with high value: the support of knowledge and innovation; the reform of the State aid policy; the improvement and simplification of the regulatory framework in which business operates; the completion of the internal market for services; the completion of an ambitious agreement in the Doha round; the removal of obstacles to physical labour and academic mobility; the development of a common approach to economic migration; and the support of efforts to deal with the social consequences of economic restructuring.[9]

A second three-year cycle (2008–2010) was launched by the European Council in March 2008,[10] with four priority areas of action: knowledge and innovation, business environment, employment, energy and climate change—€230 billion has been allocated to investment in those four priority areas.[11] In December the Commission adopted a package of measures designed to facilitate the implementation of the *European economic recovery plan*,[12] which was endorsed by the European Council at its meeting on December 11/12, 2008 and to strengthen the Lisbon Strategy.

2. INDUSTRIAL POLICY

As the Commission indicated,[13] industrial policy today is vastly different from what it was 30 years ago when some national authorities believed that barriers to shield their companies from competition from abroad was the key to prosperity. Other Member States questioned the need for an industrial policy altogether, arguing that industrial policy had no place in an open market. Now it is widely accepted that insularity can only lead to stagnation and that it is liberalisation of markets that offers the greatest benefits to both consumer and supplier, and that it will help industry to remain profitable in an increasingly global and increasingly competitive market. Unfortunately some traditional governments still believe that shielding industry is the solution to their economic and social problems. Thus the key question that industrial policy now seeks to address is, what needs to be done to help business and industry to compete in the global marketplace. Inevitably, this is a multi-faced issue and one that cuts across many other policy areas. The response to that question will have implications for education and training, research and development, competition and environment, to name only a few.

The Union's industrial policy is presently determined by the modifications that were introduced in the EC Treaty by the EU Treaty and maintained unchanged by the Treaties of Amsterdam and Nice. The sole objective of the TFEU in this area is to ensure that the, "conditions necessary for the competitiveness of the Union's industry exist".[14] This is the task of both the Union and the Member States, but the latter remain so to say "in the lead". Indeed the Treaty provides

---

[9] For full list of measures see SEC (2005) 981 of July 20, 2005.
[10] General Report 2008, 37.
[11] General Report 2008, 38.
[12] General Report 2008, 35 and COM (2008) 800.
[13] *http://www.europa.eu/scasplus/leg/en/lvb/n26109 .htm*; parts of this chapter are based on, or have been taken from, this publication.
[14] art.173(1) TFEU [157(1)].

that they must "consult" each other, in liaison with the Commission, and where necessary, "co-ordinate" their action. Nothing very concrete. The Union, on the other hand, may only, "take any useful initiative to promote such coordination". The aim of the action of the Union and the Member States, in view of the competitiveness of the industry, and in accordance with a system of open and competitive markets, is described as follows in the Treaty:

- speeding up the adjustment of industry to structural changes (this clearly indicates that the drafters of the Treaty were aware of the new market conditions mentioned above);
- encouraging an environment favourable to initiative and to the development of undertakings throughout the Union, particularly small and medium-sized undertakings (a clear indication that the action is to consist in flanking measures and not in direct intervention in favour of undertakings); in this context it is noteworthy that the Treaty explicitly indicates that it does, "not provide a basis for the introduction by the Union of any measure which could lead to distortion of competition"[15]; important also are the words "throughout the Union", that can also be found in the introductory provisions of the Treaty,[16] they indicate that the less-developed regions must not be forgotten, but they don't get priority, that being the task of other policies; finally, the reference to the small and medium-sized enterprises (SMEs) should be underlined: it is universally recognised that they are the principal creators of jobs and, as was seen in other places in this book, for instance under competition, they are the object of special measures (see below);
- encouraging an environment favourable to co-operation between undertakings (this must be seen in relation with Union competition policy, that, as was seen, exempts from the cartel prohibition various forms of co-operation);
- fostering better exploitation of the industrial potential of policies of innovation, research and technological development (those policies will be examined below). Although, as was indicated at the beginning of this chapter, the initiative in this area lies, according to the Treaty provisions, with the Member States, the Union is entrusted with the task to, "contribute to the achievement of the objectives set out [above] through the policies and activities it pursues under other provisions of the Treaty".[17] In other words, no specific "industrial" actions. However, the Treaty also provides that the Council may decide on specific measures, but then only, "in support of action taken in the Member States" to achieve the objectives set out above.[18]

Promotion of intangible investment: with the growth in information-based competition, investment training and R&D have become vital. The drafters of the Single European Act were well aware of R&D's importance when they introduced it in the Treaty. It was kept practically unchanged, as already mentioned,

---

[15] art.173(3,2) TFEU [157(2)].

[16] art.173(3,2) TFEU [157(2)], last para.

[17] art.173(3) TFEU [157(3)]. Under the heading "economic, social and territorial cohesion", the Treaty refers to "overall" harmonious development: art.174 TFEU [158].

[18] It seems to be the same old story: Member States want to do it each in their own way, at the most consult each other, but gladly accept the (financial) support of the Union; see what was said about education, vocational training and youth, culture, health protection, consumer protection and Trans-European networks.

by the EU Treaty and the Treaties of Amsterdam and Nice. Since it forms a separate Title in the TFEU it will be examined below. As for the internal market, the removal of the many hidden barriers to trade continue to boost the competitiveness of Union companies, while the emergence of a continent-wide market should enable them to reduce unit costs, forge links and partnerships across borders and innovate more rapidly and successfully.

Nevertheless, as the Commission recognises[19] the internal market remains incomplete in a number of areas, including company law, public procurement and fiscal harmonisation. One must add to that, unfortunately, the refusal of many a Member State to implement the rules governing the internal market, especially with regard to the free movement of goods, services (transport, for instance), the right of establishment and more generally speaking the refusal of their administrations to view the territory of the 27 Member States as one single economic entity, where the same rules apply to all. With regard to the free movement of goods, which after all is the cornerstone, so to say, of the European construction, standards, for instance, play an extremely important role. In other areas it is the telecommunication and information industries, the intellectual and industrial property rights and public procurement, which greatly influence the competitiveness of the industry.

The manufacturing industry still plays a key role in Europe's prosperity and the Commission has felt the need to put industry back at the heart of policy concerns. It has done this by launching, at the end of 2005, a new, more integrated industrial policy in order to create better framework conditions for manufacturing industries.[20]

Some industrial sectors have been briefly examined elsewhere in this book, among others, in the chapter on competition to which the reader is referred.

The competitiveness and innovation framework programme (2007–2013)[21] aims to encourage the competitiveness of European enterprises. With small and medium-sized enterprises as its main target, the programme supports innovation activities (including eco-innovation), provides better access to finance and delivers business support services in the regions. It will encourage a better take-up and use of information and communication technology (ICT) and help to develop the "information society". It also promotes the increased use of renewable energies and energy efficiency. It is divided into three operational programmes: "Entrepreneurship and Innovation Programme" (EIP), Information Communication Technologies-Policy Support Programme" (ICT PSP) and "Intelligent Energy Europe" (IEE). It is financed mainly by the European Investment Fund.[22]

In July 2008 the Commission adopted an action plan on sustainable consumption and production and sustainable industry policy.[23] The core of the action plan is a dynamic framework to improve the energy and environmental performance of products and foster their uptake by consumers.[24]

---

[19] See above.
[20] *http://www.europa.eu./pressReleaseActio.do?reference=IP/05/1225.*
[21] Decision 1639/2006 [2006] O.J. L310/15.
[22] See Ch.12: Other Bodies of the Union.
[23] COM (2008) 397.
[24] General Report 2008, 62.

Promoting Open Standards

The application of standards by the industry presupposes three related issues:

- regulations, i.e. mandatory rules adopted and enforced by governments, widely misrepresented as a weapon for imposing uniform European regulations for their own sake! They are in fact the result of the approximation of laws which aim to remove those discrepancies between existing national regulations that hinder trade. The objective is to ensure that a product accepted for sale in one Member State has free access to the whole European market, with advantages for both the consumer and the competitiveness of the industry;
- standards, i.e. voluntary specifications prepared by autonomous standardisation bodies made up of representatives of industry, consumer groups and administrations, i.e. CEN (for general standards), CENELEC (for electronic standards) and ETSI (for telecommunications standards); equipment and appliances need to be capable of working together in the different Member States without sacrificing quality, safety or environmental principles[25];
- certification, i.e. a means by which manufacturers can declare that their products conform to the appropriate quality and technical requirements. The Commission's role is to reinforce and ensure the mutual equivalence and recognition of the testing, certification and accreditation bodies in Europe.

In 2008 the Commission adopted a communication "Towards an increased contribution from standardisation to innovation in Europe".[26] Several directives[27] and regulations[28] were adopted to bring various fields into line with the regulatory procedure with scrutiny.

3. INFORMATION SOCIETY

One of the EU objectives is to make sure that Europe's business, government and citizens continue to play a leading role in shaping and participating in the global knowledge and information-based economy. To achieve this the following methods are employed:

- stimulating research into the development of new information and communication technologies;
- establishing and maintaining a framework of regulations and standards designed to generate competition; and
- stimulating the development of applications and supporting initiatives that encourage and enable all citizens to benefit from the information society.

The main components and legal bases of this policy are:

- for telecommunications: internal market harmonisation,[29] competition[30] and the right of establishment and the freedom to provide services.[31] See in the

---

[25] One highly successful example is the GSM (Global System for Mobile communication) standard that allows mobile telephones to work in most of the Union.
[26] COM (2008) 133 [2008] O.J. C202/17.
[27] See [2008] O.J. L76 and L81, General Report 2008, 63.
[28] See [2008] O.J. L97.
[29] art.114 TFEU [95].
[30] arts 101–102 TFEU [81 and 82].
[31] arts 53 and 62 TFEU [47 and 55].

respect the Directive on legal protection of services based on, or consisting of, conditional access[32];

- support for technological development in information and communication technologies: research and development provisions[33];
- contribution to creating conditions for the competitiveness of the Union's industry: the provisions on industry[34];
- telecommunications: the TENs.[35]

(1) Implementation of the Information Society Policies

(a) The Internet

The Internet is the key driver of the information society and the Commission's strategy aims:

- to bring every citizen, home, school, business and administration "on-line" by making Internet access faster, cheaper and more secure;
- to create a digital literate and entrepreneurial Europe via the Internet;
- to build a socially inclusive information society for all.

A Safer Internet Plus programme (2005–2008) was adopted to promote safer use of the Internet and protect end-users against undesirable content.[36] With a budget of €45 million it aims to promote safer use of the Internet particularly for children, and to fight against illegal content and content unwanted by the end-user.

The creation of the EU top-level domain gave Europe its own Internet identity. The register is open to applications from the general public since April 7, 2006.

(b) The i2010

A European Information Society for growth and employment.[37] Launched in 2005, it is the Commission's new strategic framework for the information society and the media. The eEurope 2005 Action Plan is focused essentially on the deployment of broadband access at competitive prices,[38] the security of the networks and the development and use of information technology by public authorities (eGovernment). It is build around three priorities:

- completion of a Single European Information Space;
- stepping up innovation and investment in ICT research;
- achieving an inclusive European information Society.

---

[32] Directive 98/84 [1998] O.J. L320/54.
[33] arts 179–190 TFEU [163–172].
[34] art.173 TFEU [157].
[35] arts 170–172 TFEU [154–156].
[36] Decision 854/2005 establishing a multi-annual Union programme on promoting safer use of the Internet and new online technologies [2005] O.J. L149/1.
[37] See *http://www.europa.eu.int/information-society/eeurope/i2010/index-en.htm.*
[38] See the Commission's report of 2008 stressing that the penetration of broadband in Europe continues to improve, with gaps narrowing between the Member States, General Report, 2008, 73

(c) Telecommunications

In the field of telecommunications, a very intensive programme of legislation was undertaken by the Commission, that has led to complete liberalisation of most of the European telecommunications market, since January 1, 1998. This was achieved by gradually abolishing the exclusive rights traditionally held by Europe's state-owned telecommunications organisations. For instance, in 2000 Parliament and the Council provided for unbundled access to the local loop (the last chain in the transmission to the final user).[39] In 2002 the liberalisation of the European telecom markets was pushed forward by the adoption of a new regulatory framework, the so-called telecom-package, which comprises five directives and one regulation. With regard to electronic communications networks and services, the European Parliament and the Council issued a series of directives on a common regulatory framework,[40] on access and interconnection,[41] on authorisation[42] and on universal service and users' rights.[43] Simultaneously, Parliament and the Council took a decision on a regulatory framework for radio spectrum policy.[44] European policy on the deregulation of telecommunications must be seen in the wider context of economic integration in Europe, initiated by the Treaty.

The liberalisation of the EU telecommunications market proceeded in three phases. A first phase covers the period from 1987 until the publication by the Commission of its 1992 review.[45] The second phase covers the remaining period until the introduction of full competition in 1998. The third phase commenced in November 1999 with the Commission's electronic communications review[46] and was completed in July 2003, when the new regulatory framework entered into force.[47] The progress of the European telecoms regulation and markets 2002 is analysed in the "Eighth Report on the Implementation of the Telecommunications Regulatory Package".[48] See the Decision Parliament and the Council promoting the development of a competitive internal market for mobile satellite services.[49]

---

[39] Regulation 2887/2000 [2000] O.J. L336/4. See the lengthy judgment in *Arcor* (C-55/06) [2008] E.C.R. I-2931, on the calculation of the tariffs for access to the local loop.

[40] Directive 2002/21 [2002] O.J. L108/33 (Framework Directive) amended by Regulation 717/07 on roaming on public mobile telephone networks within the Union [2007] O.J. L171/07, for calls: 49 cents, the second year: 46 and third: 43; for calls received: 24, 22 and 19. See *Deutsche Telekom* (C-262/06) [2007] E.C.R. I-10057, concerning art.27(1) and *Vidafone Espana* (T-109/06) [2007] E.C.R. II-5151, Commission letter under art.7 not binding.

[41] Directive 2002/19 [2002] O.J. L108/7 (Access Directive).

[42] Directive 2002/20 [2002] O.J. L108/21 (Authorisation Directive).

[43] Directive 2002/22 [2002] O.J. L108/51 (Universal Service Directive). See *Deutsche Telekiom* (C-262/06) (abve, fn.40) concerning art.16(1)(a) and *Kabel* (C-336/07) [2008] E.C.R. I-22.12.08, telemedie falls within scope of art.31(1).

[44] Decision 676/02 [2002] O.J. L108/1.

[45] 1992 review of the situation in the telecommunications services sector: Communication by the Commission, SEC (92) 1048, October 21, 1992.

[46] COM (1999) 539.

[47] The directives entered into force on July 25, 2003. The documents and other related information can be found on the Internet at *http://www.europa.eu.int/information-society/topics/telecoms/regulatory/new-rf/index-en.htm.*

[48] Commission Communication of December 3, 2002 on the Eighth report on the implementation of the telecommunications regulatory package—European telecoms regulation and markets 2002 COM (2002) 695 final.

[49] General Report 2008, 73.

Within the first five years following the 1987 Green Paper, legislation was introduced to liberalise the telecommunications equipment[50] and value-added services markets.[51] Given the fact that the infrastructure remained governed by monopoly rights, the Commission introduced the Open Network Provision Directive (ONP)[52] requiring the telecommunication organisations to lease lines to new market entrants on reasonable terms and to provide open and fair access to their networks. During the second phase, from 1992 onwards, the satellite[53] and mobile[54] services, and the cable television networks,[55] were progressively opened up to competition. On March 13, 1996, the Commission adopted its so-called Full Competition Directive,[56] amending and extending its earlier Services Directive. This Directive also introduces the basic principles for licensing new entrants to both voice telephony and telecommunications infrastructure markets, and requires interconnection to the voice telephony service and public switched telecommunications networks to be granted on non-discriminatory, proportional and transparent terms, based on objective criteria. Additional legislative action was taken to ensure a successful transition to full liberalisation.

Among the most important are the extension of the open network provision (ONP) to leased lines[57] and voice telephony.[58] The Interconnection Directive[59] ensures to all market players the ability to obtain interconnection with the networks of others where this is reasonably justifiable and in accordance with the ONP principles of non-discrimination, transparency, objectivity and proportionality. Finally, a common framework was set up for general authorisations and individual licenses in the field of telecommunications.[60] See in this respect the recommendation of the Commission on, among others, interconnection pricing.[61]

---

[50] Directive 88/301 on competition in the markets of telecommunications terminal equipment [1988] O.J. L131/73. See Directive 1999/5 on radio equipment and telecommunications terminal equipment and the mutual recognition of their conformity [1999] O.J. L91/10. See also Directive 88/303 on competition in the markets in telecommunications terminal equipment [1988] O.J. L131/73.

[51] Directive 2002/77 on competition in the markets for electronic communications networks and services [2002] O.J. L249/21.

[52] Directive 90/387 on the establishment of the internal market for telecommunications services through the implementation of open network provision [1990] O.J. L192/1.

[53] Directive 94/46 amending Directive 88/301 and Directive 90/388 in particular with regard to satellite communications [1994] O.J. L268/15.

[54] Directive 96/2 [1996] O.J. L20/59 amending Directive 90/388 with regard to mobile and personal communications.

[55] Directive 95/51 amending Directive 90/388 with regard to the abolition of the restrictions on the use of cable television networks for the provision of already liberalised telecommunications services [1995] O.J. L256/49.

[56] Directive 96/19 amending Directive 90/388 regarding the implementation of full competition in telecommunications markets [1996] O.J. L74/13.

[57] Directive 92/44 on the application of open network provision to leased lines [1992] O.J. L165/27.

[58] Directive 95/62 on the application of open network provision (ONP) to voice telephony [1995] O.J. L321/6.

[59] Directive 97/33 on interconnection in telecommunications with regard to ensuring universal service and interoperability through application of the principles of Open Network Provision (ONP) [1997] O.J. L199/32. See *Telefonica de Espana* (C-79/00) [2001] E.C.R. I-10075.

[60] Directive 97/13 on a common framework for general authorisations and individual licences in the field of telecommunications services [1997] O.J. L117/15. See *Germany v ISIS and Firma 02* (Joined Cases C-327/03 and C-328/03) on the interpretation of art.11 concerning payments for authorisations [2005] E.C.R. I-8877. Idem in *i-21, Germany* and *Arcor* (Joined Cases C-392/04 and C-422/04) [2006] E.C.R. I-8559, the application of a fee calculated by taking into account general administration costs is precluded. .

[61] Recommendation 98/195 on Interconnection in a liberalised telecommunication market, last amended [2000] O.J. C651/1.

Beyond 1998, the European telecommunications policy focused on the effective implementation of the 1998 regulatory framework and maintained it under constant review in order to take account of future changes, such as the increasing convergence between telecommunications, information and audio-visual sectors.

The third phase takes into account the rapid technological changes in the area of electronic communications and defines the competences of the National Regulatory Authorities and the European Competition administration. Furthermore, the markets to be regulated are defined in accordance with the principles of European competition law.[62]

The Framework Directive foresees that the new definition of Significant Market Power (SMP) will be based on the notion of "dominance" under EC competition rules.[63]

(d) Electronic Commerce

The take-up of e-commerce by customers and businesses depends upon the creation of an EU-wide framework that provides substantial legal guaranties for commercial transactions carried out electronically and allows for the free movement of services. EU legislation focuses on essential areas with directives on "legal aspects of e-commerce",[64] the "protection of copyrights in the information society",[65] "distance marketing of financial services",[66] etc. The Commission also encourages industry self-regulation.

(e) Information Society Technology (IST)

Information and Communication Technologies (ICT) are a key component of the Union's framework programmes for research. In the Seventh Framework Programme (2007–2013) ICT is one of the nine themes of the specific Co-operation programme. Activities are designed to strengthen Europe's scientific and technology base in ICT, help stimulate innovation through ICT use and ensure that ICT progress is rapidly transformed into benefits for Europe's citizens, businesses, industry and governments

For the latest developments, see the 2008 General Report.

(f) Protection of Personal Data

New technologies call for specific requirements to ensure that users have a right to privacy. The EU has adopted a legal framework in this respect: a directive ensuring the legal and mutual recognition of electronic signatures,[67] a regulation liberalising intra-Union trade in encryption products and a directive concerning

---

[62] Commission Guidelines on market analysis and the assessment of significant market power under the Union regulatory framework for electronic communications networks and services (2002/C165/03).

[63] art.14(2) of the Framework Directive.

[64] Directive 2000/31 on certain legal aspects of information society services in particular electronic commerce in the internal market (Directive on electronic commerce) [2000] O.J. L178/1. See *Promusicae* (C-275/06) [2008] E.C.R. I-271, Directive neither compelling nor precluding obligation to disclose personal data in civil proceedings.

[65] Directive 2001/21 on the harmonisation of certain aspects of copyright and related rights in the information society [2001] O.J. L167/10.

[66] Directive 2002/65 concerning the distance marketing of financial services [2002] O.J. L271/16, modified by Directive 2007/64 on payment services in the internal market [2007] O.J. L319/1, corrigendum [2009] O.J. L187/5.

[67] Directive 1999/93 on a Union framework for electronic signature [1999] O.J. L13/12.

processing of personal data and the protection in the electronic communications sector.[68] It concerns, among others; the preservation of connection data by the Member Sates for police surveillance purposes, the sending of unsolicited emails and the inclusion of personal data in directories.[69]

(g) Network Security

This concerns measures to tackle cyber crime and penalise attacks against information systems. To ensure the highest level of security the EU set up a European Network and Information Security Agency (ENISA) that acts as an advisory and co-ordinating body.[70]

(h) International Dimension

The Commission is involved in the work of several multilateral organisations such as the International Communication Union (ITU), World Trade Organisation (WTO), General Agreement on Trade in Services (GATS), the World International Property Organisation (WIPO) and the Organisation of Economic Co-operation and Development (OECD). Mention should be made of the Joint Committee established under the Agreement on Mutual Recognition between the European Union and the United States of America. This Committee is empowered to take decisions concerning telecommunications equipment, electromagnetic compatibility, pharmaceutical GMPs and medical devices.[71]

(2) Framework Programmes

As mentioned, the Framework Programmes play an important role with regard to the information industries. The Fourth Framework Programme for research and development was adopted by Parliament and the Council in 1994 and covers the period 1995–1998. Under this framework, an important role had been attributed to information technologies. They can be divided into three sections: the telematic applications (Telematics programme), the advanced telecommunications technologies (Acts programme), and information technologies (former Esprit programme). One of the four thematic programmes under the Fifth Framework Programme (1998–2002) concerned "users friendly information society". The Sixth Framework Programme (2003–2006) set out the priorities—including the Information Society Technologies (IST) priority—for the period 2003–2006. In addition to the IST Thematic Priority, Information Society related activities can be funded in the following parts of the Sixth Framework Programme: Research infrastructures—GEANT and GRIDs, research activities involving SMEs (CRAFT), Marie Curie actions—human resources and mobility, co-ordination of research activities (ERA-NET), nanotechnologies and nano-sciences, knowledge-based multifunctional materials and new production processes and devices. Most of these activities were continued under the Seventh Framework Programme (2007–2013).[72]

Many sectors are directly interested in the further development of information technology, e.g. commerce (among others, electronic commerce); transport;

---

[68] Directive 2002/58 [2002] O.J. L201/37, modified [2009] O.J. L337/11.
[69] All this information is taken from *http://www.europa.eu.int/scadplus/leg/en/lvb/l24100.htm.*
[70] See above Ch.13: Decentralised Bodies of the Union.
[71] [2001] O.J. L43/55.
[72] See in Ch.33: Research and Technological Development

health care; flexible and distant learning; the rural areas; linguistic research; engineering and libraries. A special aspect of this further development consists in computerised communication of data, information and documents, standardisation, dissemination and exploitation of the results of Union and national research programmes and of an information services market.

It should be noted that one of the most important means of conveying information is television broadcasting; the Union has co-ordinated certain provisions laid down by the Member States in this field.[73] The Directive is based on the Treaty provisions concerning the taking-up and pursuit of activities as self-employed persons.[74]

4. ENTERPRISE POLICY—(MICRO) SMALL AND MEDIUM-SIZED ENTERPRISES (SMEs)

Activities in this area include the improvement of the business environment and administrative simplification. To this end the Commission set up an Enterprise Policy Group, consisting of high-level experts from the enterprise community and representatives of the Member States to assist the Commission in the identification and dissemination of good practice.[75]

More specifically with regard to the supply of business services, mention must be made of the Euro-Info-Centres, the Business Co-operation Network and the Business Co-operation Centre and the Business Support Network,[76] that aim to be vehicles for promoting business contacts of a non-confidential nature. As for the small and medium-sized enterprises (SMEs), it is generally recognised that SMEs are the principal creators of jobs, but often lack the knowledge, experience, means and tools for competitive and sustainable investments. However, both at national and Union level innumerable initiatives have been developed to help the SMEs to remedy these shortcomings through publications, seminars, meetings, conferences, etc. For instance, the Union established many programmes such as: experimental training schemes, Euro management, participation in public procurement, the setting up of seed capital, etc. See, for instance, a Council Decision on measures of financial assistance for innovation and job-creating by small and medium-sized enterprises and the Growth and Employment Initiative.[77]

Furthermore, and this is important, the SMEs enjoy numerous privileges in the form of exceptions to many rules that normally condition the economic activities of large enterprises; this applies, among others, in regard to competition rules, State aids, financing by Structural Funds, etc. Obviously the qualification of "small" or "medium-sized" plays an important "access" role for all those programmes. Consequently, the Commission issued a Recommendation concerning the definition of small and medium-sized enterprises:

---

[73] Directive 89/552 [1989] O.J. L298/23, amended [2007] O.J. L332/27. See *Infront v Commission* (T-33/01) [2005] E.C.R. II-5897, *Östereichischer Rundfunk* (C-195/06) [2007] E.C.R. I-8817, interpretation of art.1 and *UTECA* (222/07) E.C.R. 05.03.09, Directive does not preclude measures which require television operators to earmark 5 per cent of their revenue for the production of works in one of the official languages of that Member State.

[74] art.53 TFEU [47(2)].

[75] [2000] O.J. L285/24.

[76] COM (2003) 680 of 05.03.03.

[77] [1998] O.J. L155/43.

- a "small" enterprise is when:
  - — it has fewer than 50 employees;
  - — a turnover not exceeding €7 million or an annual balance sheet total of less than €5 million;
  - — it is independent;
- an enterprise is "medium-sized" when:
  - — it has fewer than 250 employees;
  - — a turnover of less than €40 million, or a balance sheet total of less than €27 million; and
  - — it is independent.

Lately the Commission has, in a recommendation, added the concept of "micro" enterprises, defined as an enterprise (that includes self-employed persons and family businesses) that employs fewer than 10 persons and whose annual turnover and/or annual balance sheet total does not exceed €2 million. See also the Council Resolution of 1996 on the co-ordination of Union activities in favour of small and medium-sized enterprises and the craft sector.

Also the Decision on the Multi-annual programme for enterprises and entrepreneurship and in particular for small and medium-sized enterprises 2001–2005. It was followed by the Notice of implementation of the EFT start-up facilities, the SME guarantee facility and the seed capital action under the multi-annual programme. Those facilities applied also, since the beginning of 2003, to the candidate countries, including Bulgaria and Romania.

In 2008 the Commission launched the "Enterprise Europe Network" the aim of which is to give SMEs assistance in respect of Union policies, innovation and technology transfer. The Network provides businesses with integrated support services and support for innovation thanks to over 550 partners in 44 countries. A large number of third countries are taking part in the network. The Executive Agency for Competitiveness and Innovation[78] was entrusted with managing the network.[79]

To support SMEs that are active in the field of research and development, Parliament and the Council established the "Eurostar's Joint Programme",[80] aimed at SMEs for developing technologies, production processes and advanced services in their fields and those carrying out market-based research.[81]

An important measure, already mentioined, that does apply to all undertakings, but especially to SMEs, was adopted in 2000 on, "combating late payment in commercial transactions". It provides that, unless a payment date is provided for in the contract, interest shall become payable automatically without the necessity of a reminder 30 days after the date of receipt by the debtor of the invoice or, in case that date is uncertain, 30 days after the receipt of the goods or services. The level of interest for late payment shall be the sum of the interest rate applied by the ECB, plus at least seven percentage points, unless otherwise specified in the contract.

In the chapter on freedom of establishment (Ch.17), mention was made of "company law" that is to say, among others, a series of directives harmonising the legal requirements for Union companies to operate in all the Member States. These Directives form the basis for equal treatment throughout the internal market of companies and firms formed in accordance with the law of one of the

---

[78] See above Ch.13: Decentralised Bodies of the Union.
[79] General Report 2008, 61.
[80] Decision 743/08 [2008] O.J. L201/58.
[81] General Report 2008, 62.

Member States and having their registered office, central administration or principal place of business within the Union.[82]

Enterprise policy was also the subject of various Commission Communications, such as "Challenges for enterprise policy in the knowledge-driven economy" and the "EU Enterprise policy for the New Economy".

5. TRANS-EUROPEAN NETWORKS

The concept of Trans-European Networks (TENs) was introduced by the EU Treaty. It is closely associated with Regional Policy and with the achievement of the internal market. It expressly refers to both Union activities where the Treaty provides that the TENs are intended to help achieve the objectives of both those policies.[83] As can be seen in the chapter on Regional Policy, the European Regional Development Fund may contribute to the financing of the TENs.[84]

By "networks" is meant the interconnection and interoperability of national networks as well as access to such networks in the areas of transport,[85] telecommunications[86] and energy infrastructures.[87] The regional development preoccupation clearly appears when the Treaty provides that account shall be taken in particular of the need to link island and landlocked areas and peripheral regions with the central regions of the Union. Union activity in the TENs field consist of:

- establishing guidelines covering objectives, priorities and broad outlines of envisaged measures;
- implementation of measures that may prove necessary to ensure the interoperability of the networks, in particular in the field of standardisation;
- support for the financial efforts made by Member States for projects of common interest[88]; the Union may also contribute to specific projects in the area of transport infrastructure through the Cohesion Fund.[89]

As for the Member States, they must co-ordinate among themselves the policies used at national level that may have an impact on the achievement of the

---

[82] art.54 TFEU [48]

[83] art.170(1) TFEU [154(1)].

[84] art.1(b) former Regulation 2083/93 first indent [1993] O.J. L193/34.

[85] Decision on Union guidelines for the development of trans-European transport networks [1996] O.J. L228/1, amended [2001] O.J. L185/1; Directive 96/48 on the interoperability of trans-European high-speed rail system [1996] O.J. L235/6, amended [2007] O.J. L141/63 and Decision concerning a technical specification for interoperability to the "infrastructure" subsystem of the trans-European high-speed railway system [2008] O.J. L77/1, replaced by Directive 2008/56 on the interoperability of the rail system within the Community [2008] O.J. L191/1; Decision on the basic parameters for the command-and-control and signalling subsystems relating to the trans-European high-speed rail systems [1999 6] O.J. L216/23; Directive on the interoperability of the trans-European conventional rail systems [2001] O.J. L110/1.

[86] Decision 1336/97 on a series of guidelines for trans-European telecommunication networks [1997] O.J. L194/5.

[87] See, for instance, Directive 90/547 on the transit of electricity through transmission grids [1990] O.J. L313/30; Decision 96/39 laying down a series of measures aimed at creating a more favourable context for the development of trans-European networks in the energy sector [1996] O.J. L161/154; Decision 1254/96 of Parliament and the Council laying down a series of guidelines for trans-European energy networks [1996] O.J. L161/147; Decision 2000/761 defining the specifications of projects of common interest identified in the sector of trans-European energy networks by Decision 1254/96 [2000] J.O. L305/22.

[88] Regulation 2236/95 laying down general rules for the granting of Union financial aid in the field of trans-European networks [1995] O.J. L228/1, amended [2005] O.J. L191/16.

[89] See Commission Decisions concerning projects to be co-financed [1993] O.J. L308/1.

above-mentioned objectives.[90] The Union may also co-operate with third countries to promote projects of mutual interest.

Wide powers have been attributed, in the TENs field, to Parliament since the
guidelines to be established shall be adopted by the Council together with
Parliament and after consultation of the Economic and Social Committee and the
Committee of the Regions.[91]

In the case of common projects which relate to the territory of a Member State,
the latter's approval shall, of course, be required. As was seen, one of the first
tasks of the Union was to establish guidelines. Following the modifications introduced by the Treaty of Amsterdam, all the measures concerning the TENs are
adopted according to the co-decision procedure,[92] and after consultation of the
ESC and the Committee of the Regions. The first ones were adopted in 1995,
according to the co-operation procedure, and concerned the telecommunications
field of Euro-ISDN,[93] they were followed by guidelines for the development of
energy,[94] transport[95] and telecommunications[96] networks. On the basis of those
guidelines, the Commission determines which projects are of common interest,[97]
after having consulted the Member State where the project is to be carried out.
However, a first list of 10 priority projects in the energy field and 14 in the transport area was established by the European Council at Essen.[98] To think that it
needs Heads of State or Government to select individual projects!

During the years following the Essen European Council, steady progress
was made in implementing some of the selected projects in the transport sector.
These are of course large infrastructure projects that take years to construct. The
Commission adopted a communication seeking to clarify the application of the
competition rules to new rail infrastructure projects.[99] Where telematics and
telecommunications are concerned, the Parliament and the Council adopted a
decision on guidelines for trans-European telecommunication networks.[100]

Those guidelines cover all telecommunication networks, including satellites
and mobile networks; they incorporate the guidelines adopted in 1995 for integrated services digital networks (ISDN). They also identify projects of common
interest eligible for financial aid from the Union; those projects concern the basic
networks, namely ISDN and IBC (integrated broadband communications)
generic services and sectoral applications. To assist with the completion of the
single market, the eTEN programme is part of the Trans-European Networks
policy of the Union.[101] It is a key instrument of the eEurope Action Plan 2005
and supports the establishment of operational services of common interest based
on electronic data transmission networks.

[90] art.171(2) TFEU [155(2)].
[91] art.172 TFEU [156].
[92] art.172 TFEU [156].
[93] Decision 95/489 [1995] O.J. L282/16.
[94] Decision 1229/2003 [2003] O.J. L176/11.
[95] Decision 96/1692 [1996] O.J. L228/1.
[96] Decision 97/1336 [1997] O.J. L183/12.
[97] See, for instance, for the energy sector, Decision 96/537 [1996] O.J. L230/16 and 97/548 [1997]
    O.J. L225/25.
[98] See General Report 1994, 112 and 113.
[99] COM (98) 480.
[100] Decision 1336/97 [1997] O.J. L183/12, amended [2002] O.J. L200/1.
[101] eTEN Work Programme 2003, "Deploying Services for an Information Society for All", June 2,
    2003, *http://www.ec.europa.eu/information_society/activities/eten/index_en.htm*.

"The main focus of eTEN in 2003 was the practical realisation of eEurope general interest services objectives–addressing a broad set of applications and generic services in the area of eGovernment (eAdministration), eHealth (eHealthcare), eInclusion, eLearning, eBusiness, advanced mobile services and trust and confidence services."

In 2002 a new regulatory framework for electronic communications networks and services was established in accordance with Parliament and Council directives on a common regulatory framework.[102] As for energy, Parliament and the Council supplemented the list of projects of common interest, in order to take account of the rapidly changing market, especially for natural gas, the acceleration towards the extension of the interconnected network across the European continent and the prospects of Union enlargement.[103] Guidelines were laid down by decision of Parliament and the Council.[104]

6. JUDICIAL CO-OPERATION IN CIVIL AND COMMERCIAL MATTERS

This subject was already examined above, in Ch.16: Free Movement of Persons (2. An Area of Freedom, Security and Justice); it can have a direct bearing on commerce; the reader is referred to the above-mentioned chapter.

Further Reading

Alexander Layton & Hugh Mercer, *European Civil Practice* (Sweet & Maxwell, 2004).
Arwel Devies, "Electronic public procurement initiatives within the European Community", (2003) E.L.Rev. 632.
Christa Tobler, " 'Women's Clauses' in public procurement under Community law", (2003) E.L.Rev. 618.
David Gillies & Roger Marschall, *Telecommunication Law*, 2nd edn. (Butterworths).
David Musker, *The Community Design Handbook*, (Sweet & Maxwell, 2005).
Dominique Kaesmacher and Lionel Duez, "Le nouveau règlement 6/2002 sur les dessins ou modèles communautaires", *Journal des Tribunaux, Droit Européen*, No.92, October 2002.
Farr & Oakley, *EU Communication Law* (Palladian Law Publishing).
Guy Tritton, *Intellectual Property in Europe*, 2nd edn (Sweet & Maxwell, 2002).
Keith Beresford, *Patenting Software under the European Patent Convention*, 2nd edn (Sweet & Maxwell, 2005).

---

[102] Directive 2002/21 [2002] O.J. L108/33 on access to, and interconnection of, electronic communications and associated facilities (Access Directive) [2002] O.J. L108/7, amended by Regulation 717/07 on roaming charges on public telephone networks within the Union [2007] O.J. L171/07, amended [2009] O.J. L337/37, on the authorisation of electronic communications networks and services (Authorisation Directive) [2002] O.J. L108/21 and on the universal services and users' rights related to electronic communication networks and services (Universal Service Directive) [2002] O.J. L108/51. See *Deutsche Telekom* (C-262/06) (quoted above, fn.40).
[103] Further details on the various projects can, as always, be found in the yearly General Reports of the Commission and in the Bulletin.
[104] See amending Decision [1999] O.J. L207/1.

Koenig, Bartosch, Braun, *EC Competition and Telecommunications Law*, (Kluwer, 2002).
Nihoul P.& Rodford P., *EU Electronic Communications Law: Competition and Regulation in the European Telecommunications Market* (Oxford University Press, 2004).
Sebastian Farr and Vanessa Oakley, *EU Communications Law* (Sweet & Maxwell, 2006).
Singer and Staunder, *The European Patent Convention*, 3rd edn (Sweet & Maxwell, 2003).

Chapter Thirty-two

Regional Policy/Economic, Social and Territorial Cohesion

GENERALITIES

As the Commission wrote[1]: "The European Union's regional policy seeks to reduce disparities between EU regions, foster balanced development throughout the EU and promote real equal opportunities for all." Based on the concept of solidarity and economic and social cohesion, it achieves this in practical terms by means of a variety of financing operations, principally through the Structural Funds and the Cohesion Fund. For the period 2007–2013 the European Union's regional policy is the EU's second largest budget item, with an allocation of €348 billion. The objective of economic and social cohesion was introduced in 1986 with the adoption of the Single European Act. The policy was finally incorporated in what was then the EC Treaty[2] in 1992.

It is interesting and useful, at the start of this chapter, to get an idea about the disparities between the levels of development of the various regions.[3] In its Third progress report on cohesion,[4] the Commission ascertains that the economic and social disparities between the, at that time, 25 Member States, in per capita GDP (based on purchasing power parity (ppp)), are considerable. In Latvia, GDP per capita is 41 per cent of the Union average, as against 215 per cent in Luxembourg. 41 per cent of the Union population lives in 64 regions whose per capita GDP is less than 75 per cent of the Union average. And although regional disparities have been decreasing since 1995, the employment rate was 62.99 per cent in 2003 and productivity 30 per cent of the Union average.

These are the facts; regional policy's objective is to further reduce the disparities. When the Title on Economic and Social Cohesion was added to the EC Treaty, regional policy had already been an important Union activity since 1975.[5] This is acknowledged by the wording of the Treaty which provides that the Union must develop and, "pursue its actions leading to the strengthening of its economic, social and territorial cohesion."[6] It was assumed from the moment the internal market was established that it could not function as an economic entity

---

[1] *http://www.ec.europa.eu/regional_policy/index _en.htm.*
[2] arts 174–178 TFEU [158–162].
[3] There are now 268 regions in the Union.
[4] COM (2005) 192 final.
[5] The Regulation setting up the European Regional Development Fund (ERDF) was adopted in March 1975: Regulation 724/75 [1975] O.J. L73/1. The Social Fund and the Agricultural Fund have been in existence practically since the very beginning; they were provided for in the EEC Treaty.
[6] art.174 TFEU [158]. See Decision 2006/702 on Union strategic guidelines on cohesion [2006] O.J. L291/11.

if the differences in economic development of the composing regions were excessive. That there are and will be differences is inevitable, due, among others, to great differences in geography, climate, tradition and population, but, without some similarity of the levels of economic and social development the internal market simply cannot function. If, for instance, the purchasing power in one part of the Union does not allow its inhabitants to acquire the goods they need, the producers in the richer parts will not be able to sell them their products. Furthermore, since economic integration of the Union is based, in the first place, on inter-State trade, such a situation not only jeopardises the development of the internal market itself, but makes it practically impossible to pursue the economic and monetary convergence which is required for the smooth functioning of the EMU.[7]

As indicated, economic, social and territorial cohesion is the objective primarily of "regional policy", but other policies such as Social Policy, Agricultural Policy[8] and Fisheries are also involved in the attainment of the objectives of regional policy. Those objectives are clearly set out in the Treaty as, "reducing disparities between the levels of development of the various regions and the backwardness of the leastfavoured regions". According to the TFEU, among the regions concerned, particular attention must be paid, "to rural areas, areas affected by industrial transition, and regions which suffer from severe and permanent natural or demographic handicaps, such as the northernmost regions with very low population density and island, cross-border and mountain regions."[9]

The Treaty established three basic principles for the implementation of economic, social and territorial cohesion. In the first place, as with many Union activities, the responsibility for attaining the objectives rests both on the Union and on the Member States: indeed, according to the TFEU, it is part of the principal areas of "shared competence".[10] Furthermore, the Member States must conduct their economic policies and co-ordinate them, "in such a way as . . . to attain the objectives" set out in the Treaty.[11] Secondly, the Treaty provides that these objectives must be taken into account by the institutions when formulating and implementing other Union policies and actions and the implementation of the internal market, and that those policies and actions must support the achievement of these objectives. A similar obligation is imposed by the Treaties with regard to other policies.[12] In other words, the formulation and implementation of all Union policies must be achieved in a coherent and co-ordinated manner, with special attention given to the so-called horizontal policies.[13] A third point is the indication in the Treaty that the various existing funds, among others the so-called Structural Funds, the Cohesion Fund and the European Investment Bank (EIB) must all be used to attain these objectives. If specific actions prove necessary outside the Funds, such actions may be adopted by the Council, acting

---

[7] According to art.3 EU, among the means to achieve the objectives of the Treaty figure the internal market and Economic and Monetary Union.

[8] See art.175,1 TFEU where reference is made to the Structural Funds which includes the Agricultural Fund.

[9] art.174,3 TFEU [158]. The words "rural areas" were added by the EU Treaty.

[10] art.4(2)(B) TFEU.

[11] art.175 TFEU [159].

[12] For instance, the protection of the environment: art.4(2)(e) TFEU [6].

[13] See, for instance, Communication from the Commission to the Member States on the links between regional and competition policy [1998] O.J. C90/3.

in accordance with the ordinary legislative procedure,[14] after consulting the ESC and the Committee of the Regions.[15]

Besides the provisions concerning economic, social and territorial cohesion, there are several other Treaty provisions which refer to underdeveloped regions[16]; this shows that, from the very beginning and even in the absence of specific provisions, the regional problems were taken into account.[17] However, it appears that the signatories of the Treaty were convinced (or rather, hoped) that the functioning of the internal market, with the resulting development of economic activity throughout the Union, would more or less automatically reduce regional disparities. The functioning of the internal market did, indeed, achieve spectacular results in the most depressed areas, as is evidenced by the doubling, even trebling of their per capita income over the years. Nevertheless, this was not enough for achieving the necessary coherence among the regions in a Union where similar developments took place in the well-developed areas. The result was that, although the gap between the richest and poorest regions might not have widened, it was not reduced significantly. It goes without saying that the existing discrepancies are no longer socially and politically acceptable and create a major problem for the Union as a whole. Even worse, it becomes very difficult, if not impossible, to achieve the economic convergence which is required for the functioning of the EMU. Indeed, as long as some Member States (and their number increases with each enlargement), have to devote large proportions of their limited resources to the development of their less favoured regions, they will remain subject to inflation, balance of payment problems and excessive budget deficits.

It was at the October 1972 Paris "Conference of Heads of States or of Governments" (as the European Council was then called), that it was agreed to give a high priority to the aim of correcting the structural and regional imbalances that might affect the realisation of the Economic and Monetary Union.[18] The Member States undertook to co-ordinate their regional policies and invited the Union institutions to create a European Regional Development Fund (ERDF).[19] However, it was not until March 1975 that the Council adopted the Regulation setting up the ERDF,[20] and a Decision creating a Regional Policy Committee.[21] It is interesting to note that no reference was made to a Union regional "policy". This had to wait till February 1979, when amendments to the above-mentioned Regulation were made,[22] together with the adoption of a Resolution concerning guidelines for such a policy.[23] Finally in 1984 a regulation was adopted concerning both a Union Regional Policy and the ERDF.[24]

---

[14] See art.294 TFEU [215].

[15] art.175,3 TFEU [159,3].

[16] The European Investment Bank (EIB), for instance, was set up to facilitate the financing, among other things, of "projects for developing less-developed regions" art.309(a) TFEU [267(a)].

[17] See, for instance, art.137(3)(a) TFEU [87(3)(a)].

[18] Bull.10 [1972] 9. This was the first "summit" in which Denmark, Ireland and the UK participated.

[19] See the Commission's "Report on Regional Problems in the Enlarged [Union]", 1973 Bull. suppl.8.

[20] Regulation 724/75 [1975] O.J. L73/1. It was based on what is now art.352 TFEU [308] (action is necessary but required powers that are not provided for in the Treaties). Initially the ERDF was endowed with the equivalent of €375 million; in 2004 it was, together with the other funds, for the period 2000–2006, more than €195 billion and now, as indicated above, for the period 2007–2013, €348 billion.

[21] [1975] O.J. L73/47.

[22] [1979] O.J. L35/1.

[23] [1979] O.J. C36/10.

[24] [1984] O.J. L169/1.

Over the past years, the ERDF Regulation was amended several times and one of the novelties was its inclusion into the Structural Funds. This allowed for far-reaching co-ordination of objectives and procedures with other funds: the EIB,[25] the European Agricultural Guidance and Guarantee Fund (EAGGF) Guidance Section,[26] the European Social Fund (ESF),[27] the Financial Instrument of Fisheries Guidance (FIFG)[28] (now the European Fisheries Fund (EFF)),[29] that were also included in the Structural Funds, and, finally, the Cohesion Fund.[30]

The latest revision of the ERDF Regulation was completed, together with the revision of the ESF, EAGGF and Cohesion Fund in 2006. The provisions concerning the Structural Funds are now embodied in five regulations: a "Framework" regulation laying down general provisions on the ERDF, ESF and the Cohesion Fund.[31] This Framework Regulation is accompanied by four "sectoral" regulations: regional,[32] social,[33] grouping of territorial co-operation[34] and the Cohesion Fund.[35]

The Structural Funds Principles

As indicated above in Ch.23: Agriculture and Fisheries, Agenda 2000 concerned, besides the Union financing for the next seven years (2000–2006) and the reform of the agricultural policy, the reform of the existing structural funds: ESF, ERDF, the structural part of FEOGA, the Fisheries Fund and the Cohesion Fund. As was mentioned, all those funds were merged so to speak, within the Structural Funds, and the expenditure of the available amounts under those different funds was closely co-ordinated.

See Council Decision on Union strategic guidelines on cohesion.[36]

1. STRUCTURAL OPERATIONS

Improving the effectiveness of the structural and cohesion funds in achieving the goal of economic, social and territorial cohesion enshrined in the Treaty was a central plank of the Agenda 2000 reforms. This goal was maintained even as priorities continued to evolve in a more diverse Union, taking account of the aim of achieving greater concentration of structural assistance, improving the financial management of the structural funds, as well as simplifying their operation and administration. Greater concentration of structural fund assistance in the areas of greatest need was achieved by reducing to three the number of objectives of the funds. In fostering economic, social and territorial cohesion by pursuing these objectives, the Union contributes to the harmonious, balanced and sustainable

---

[25] art.308 TFEU [266].
[26] See above, Ch.23: Agriculture and Fisheries.
[27] See above, Ch.29: Social Policy and Education.
[28] See above, Ch.24: The Common Fisheries Policy (CFP).
[29] Regulation 1198/06 [2006] O.J. L223/1.
[30] See below in this chapter.
[31] Regulation 1083/06 [2006] O.J. L 210/25, corrigendum [2008] O.J. L301/40, amended [2008] O.J. L348/19 and [2009] O.J. L25/1, corrigendum [2009] O.J. L33/49, amended [2009] O.J. L94/10 and L250/1
[32] Regulation 1080/06 [2006] O.J. L210/1, repealing Regulation 1783/99.
[33] Regulation 1081/06 [2006] O.J. L210/12, repealing Regulation 1784/99.
[34] Regulation 1082/06 [2006] O.J. L210/19, repealing Regulation 1085/99.
[35] Regulation 1084/06 [2006] O.J. L210/79, repealing Regulation 1164/94.
[36] Decision 2006/702 [2006] O.J. L291/11.

development of economic activities, the development of employment and human resources, the protection and improvement of the environment, the elimination of inequalities and the promotion of equality between men and women. The Commission and the Member States must ensure that the operations financed by the funds are in conformity with the provisions of the Treaties, the instruments adopted under it, and are consistent with other Union policies and operations. In view of the continued priority accorded to economic, social and territorial cohesion and as a result of more targeted concentration of structural expenditure in line with the Treaties' objectives, it was decided that the overall amounts for the structural and cohesion funds should, in the future, enable the Union to maintain the existing average aid intensity levels, thereby consolidating the overall effort in this field.

2. OBJECTIVES OF THE STRUCTURAL FUNDS[37]

The financial support from the Structural Funds for the period 2007–2013 is provided for three objectives:

- the *"Convergence"* objective: assistance on supporting sustainable integrated economic development and the creation of sustainable jobs. Operational programmes are aimed at modernising and diversifying regional economic structures, particularly in the following fields:

  — research and technological development, innovation and entrepreneurship,
  — information society,
  — environment,
  — risk prevention,
  — tourism,
  — investment in culture,
  — investment in transport,
  — energy,
  — investment in education,
  — investment in health and social structures,
  — direct assistance for investment in SMEs.

  60 per cent of the fund goes to the poorest Member States and regions. The other regions come under the second objective;

- the *"Regional Competitiveness and Employment"* objective, intended to support:

  — innovation and the knowledge economy, including the improvement of regional R&TD and innovation capacities (see "implementing the broad-based innovation strategy"[38]), entrepreneurship and creation of new financial instruments for businesses,
  — environment and risk prevention, included restoring contaminated land, encouraging energy efficiency, promoting the use of clean technology in public transport, and formulating plans to anticipate and manage natural and technology-related risks,

[37] Most of the information is borrowed from SCADPlus: European Regional Development Fund.
[38] General Report 2008, 60.

— access to transport and telecommunications services of general economic interest, especially by improving secondary networks and encouraging access to information and communication technologies for SMEs.

16 per cent of the fund is devoted to this objective. A list of regions eligible for funding under this objective was drawn up by the Commission,[39] and thirdly;

- the *"European Territorial Co-operation"* (ETC) objective: provided for a new legal instrument with the aim to facilitate cross-border, transnational and/or inter-regional co-operation between regional and local authorities. It is to support:

  — development of cross-border economic, social and environmental activities through joint strategies for sustainable territorial development. This involves, for example, encouraging entrepreneurship, protection and management of natural and cultural resources, and the development of collaboration, capacities and the joint use of infrastructures,
  — establishing and developing transnational co-operation, including bilateral co-operation between maritime regions. This co-operation would be invested with legal personality—the "European Grouping for Territorial Cooperation"—for the implementation of territorial co-operation programmes based on a convention agreed between the participating national, regional, local and other public authorities. The priorities are innovation, the environment, better accessibility and sustainable urban development,
  — reinforcing the effectiveness of regional policy by encouraging regional and local authorities to form networks and exchange experience.

Under this objective, the Commission established the ESPON 2013 programme to provide comparable information, evidence, analyses and scenarios on framework conditions for the development of regions, cities and larger territories.

3. ALLOCATION OF FINANCIAL SUPPORT

The objectives to which the funds are to contribute, the criteria for Member States and regions to be eligible under the funds, the financial resources and the criteria for their allocation are defined in the already mentioned Regulation laying down general provisions for the Structural Funds.[40]

The three objectives: "Convergence", "Regional competitiveness and employment" and "European territorial co-operation" were briefly described above. They constitute the basis for determining the eligibility of regions and Member States for funding under the Structural Funds.

---

[39] [2006] O.J. L243/49.
[40] Regulation 1083/06 [2006] O.J. L210/25, amended [2008] O.J. L 348/19; Regulation 1828/06 laying down general provisions on the various Funds [2006] O.J. L371/1.

(1) Convergence Objective

Eligible are regions corresponding to NUTS[41] level 2, whose gross domestic product (GDP) per capita, measured in purchasing power parity (ppp) and calculated on the basis of Union figures for the period 2000–2002, is less than 75 per cent of the average GDP of the EU-25 for the same reference period. As for Member States, are eligible those whose Gross Domestic Income (GDI) per capita, measured in ppp, and calculated on the basis of Union figures for the period 2001–2003, is less than 90 per cent of the average GNI of the EU-25 and which have a programme for meeting the convergence conditions of the Treaty.[42] Overall resources for the Convergence objective are, for the period 2007–2013, €251,163,134,221.[43] See Commission Decision drawing up the list of the eligible regions[44] and indicative allocation by Member States of the commitment appropriations.[45]

(2) Regional Competitiveness and Employment Objective

Regions eligible under this objective are those not covered by the Convergence objective. Member States must present the NUTS level 1 and NUTS level 2 regions for which they will present a programme for financing by the ERDF. Overall resources for this objective amount to €49,127,784,318. See Commission Decision allocating by Member State the commitment appropriations.[46]

(3) European Territorial Co-operation Objective

Eligible for financing NUTS level 3, are regions along all internal and certain external land borders and all NUTS level 3 regions along maritime borders, separated by a maximum of 150km. Overall assistance for this objective is €7,750,081,461.[47]

For each of these objectives, the Council must establish, at Union level, strategic guidelines on economic, social and territorial cohesion defining an indicative framework for the intervention of the Funds.[48] See Commission Decision drawing up the list of eligible regions and areas[49] and the decision allocating commitments appropriations per Member State.[50]

---

[41] Common classification of territorial units for statistics within the meaning of Regulation 1059/03 [2003] O.J. L154/1.
[42] art.126 TFEU [104].
[43] For a breakdown among the various actions see art.19 of the Regulation.
[44] Decision 2006/595 [2006] O.J. L343/44. List valid until December 31, 2013 shall be reviewed in 2010.
[45] Decision of August 4, 2006 [2006] O.J. L243/37.
[46] [2006] O.J. L243/32.
[47] For further details see art.21 of the Regulation.
[48] These Guidelines were to be adopted before February 1, 2007 in accordance with art.177 TFEU [161].
[49] Decision 2006/769 [2006] O.J. L312/47.
[50] Decision 2006/609 [2006] O.J. L347/26.

(4) Specific Types of Areas

Areas are:

- urban areas: they are incorporated in operational programmes and aim at resolving economic, environmental and social problems in towns and cities;
- rural areas and areas dependent on the fishing industry: the action concentrates on diversification such as, infrastructure to improve accessibility, telecommunications networks and services in rural areas, development of new economic activities, improving of links between urban and rural areas, and development of tourism and regeneration of rural areas;
- areas with natural handicaps: the ERDF helps finance investment in the improvement of accessibility, economic activities linked to cultural heritage, the sustainable use of resources and tourism development;
- outermost regions: the Azores, Madeira, the four French overseas departments and the Canaries—subsidising freight transport services and the start-up of transport services, operations linked to storage constraints, the maintenance of production tools and lack of human capital in the local market. See Commission Communication "Strategy for the outermost regions: achievements and future prospects".[51]

4. ELIGIBILITY

(i) **Additionality.** The funds shall provide assistance that complements national actions, including actions at the regional and local levels, integrating them into the priorities of the Union. In other words contributions from the Funds may not replace public or equivalent structural expenditure by a Member State; it is the Commission's task to verify the additionality.

(ii) **Consistency.** The Commission and the Member States must ensure that assistance from the Funds is consistent with activities, policies and priorities of the Union and complementary to other financial instruments of the Union.

The assistance co-financed by the Funds must target the EU priorities of promoting competitiveness and creating jobs, including meeting the objectives of the Integrated Guidelines for Growth and Jobs (2005–2008) set out by Council Decision[52]; consequently 60 per cent of expenditure for the Convergence objective and 75 per cent of expenditure for the Regional competitiveness and employment objective is set for the above-mentioned priorities.

(iii) **Co-ordination.** Co-ordination must be ensured between the assistance from the Funds, the ERDF,[53] the EFF[54] and the intervention of EIB and other existing financial instruments.

---

[51] [2007] O.J. C138/36. See Communication from the Commission "The outermost regions: an asset for Europe" COM (2008) 642 final of October 17, 2008.

[52] Decision 2005/600 [2005] O.J. L205/21; these guidelines were maintained for 2007, Decision 2007/491: [2007] O.J. L205/21.

[53] European Agricultural Fund for Rural Development.

[54] European Fisheries Fund.

(iv) **Programmes.** The objectives of the Funds are to be pursued in the framework of a multi-annual programming system organised in several stages comprising the identification of the priorities, the financing and a system of management and control.[55] As part of an operational programme, the ERDF and the Cohesion Fund may also finance major projects. Management and implementation of a part of an operational programme may be entrusted to one or more intermediate bodies.

The Commission approved the national strategic reference frameworks established by the 27 Member States in line with the Community strategic guidelines for 2007. This paved the way for the adoption of the operational programmes financed by the Structural Funds: 302 such programmes were formally adopted at the end of December 2007.[56]

(v) **Partnership.** These objectives must be pursued in the framework of close partnership between the Commission and each Member State and, if possible, with competent regional, local and other public authorities, the economic and social partners and any other appropriate body representing civil society, environmental partners, NGOs and bodies responsible for promoting equality between men and women. The partnership shall cover the preparation, implementation, monitoring and evaluation of operational programmes.

(vi) **Global Resources.** The resources available for commitment from the Funds for the period 2007–2013 are €398 billion at 2004 prices. This amount is indexed at 2 per cent per year. A breakdown is to be found in Annex I to the Regulation.[57]

As already mentioned, the Treaty provides that if specific actions prove necessary outside the Funds, such actions may be adopted by the Council acting in accordance with the ordinary legislative procedure[58] and after consulting the ESC and the Committee of the Regions.[59] The Council, on that basis, established in 2006 the European Globalisation Adjustment Fund which provides specific, one-off support to facilitate the reintegration into employment of workers in areas, sectors, territories, or labour marker regions suffering the shock of serious economic disruption. The Fund is to promote entrepreneurship, for example through micro-credits or for setting up co-operative projects.[60]

Mention must be made of the Joint European Resources for Micro to medium Enterprises (JEREMIE) an initiative of the Commission and the EIB Group; it uses Union financial know-how to support small businesses in Europe. It provides the framework for a series of coherent financial actions to improve the financial environment for medium, small and micro enterprises at national, regional and local level, increasing small businesses' access to finance and risk capital. The JEREMIE initiative offers new opportunities for Member States and Regions to invest and reinvest. Structural Funds using a range of financial

---

[55] See art.37 of the Regulation.
[56] General Report 2007, 93.
[57] [2006] O.J. L.210/70.
[58] art.294 TFEU [251].
[59] art.175,3 TFEU [159,3].
[60] [2006] O.J. L406/1.

instruments instead of grants, notably guaranties, venture capital, securitisation and loans. JEREMIE operates on market terms to encourage the participation of private as well as public financial institutions, which is of key importance.[61]

In 2006 Parliament and the Council set up the European Globalisation Adjustment Fund,[62] with the aim of stimulating economic growth and creating more jobs in the Union; the fund provides support for workers made redundant as a result of major structural changes in world trade patterns due to globalisation, where those redundancies have a significant adverse effect on the regional or local economy.[63]

(vii) **Reporting.** Member States are to report on the contribution of the operational programmes co-financed by the Funds; these reports are to be summarised by the Commission in its Annual Progress report to the Spring European Council. The Commission, as provided in the Treaty,[64] must submit a report every three years on the progress made towards achieving economic and social cohesion. In 2007 the Commission adopted its fourth report,[65] which describes the situation in the enlarged Union of 27 Member States and 268 regions. It contains a detailed analysis of the position of the regions in terms of GDP, productivity and employment. It provides a first assessment of the impact of European Cohesion policy in the 2000–2006 programming period. The fifth progress report on economic, social and territorial cohesion was adopted in 2008.[66]

In 2008 the Commission presented the "Regions 2020" report,[67] putting forward a prospective analysis of the probable regional impact of the four key challenges facing Europe: globalisation, demographic change, climate change and the energy challenge.

The Regulation laying down general provisions for the Funds also provides for technical assistance[68] and evaluation linked to the monitoring of operational programmes.[69]

(viii) **Rates of Assistance.** For details see Title V of the general Regulation.[70] The rates are lower for contributions of the Funds to revenue generating infrastructure investment and investment in firms.[71]

(ix) **Administration and Financial Management of the Structural Funds.** The administration of the structural funds was substantially simplified by giving practical effect to decentralising decision-making and striking a balance between

---

[61] See "Jeremie—Regional Funding".
[62] [2005] O.J. L406/1.
[63] The fund was mobilised for a total of €3.8 million for redundancies in the suppliers of Peugeot and Renault: Decision 2007/726 [2007] O.J. L6/9.
[64] art.175(2) TFEU [159,2].
[65] General Report 2007, 92 and COM (2007) 273 [2007] O.J. C191/17.
[66] General Report 2008, 94 and COM (371) [2009] O.J. C10/18: "growing regions, growing Europe".
[67] General Report 2008, 94 and SEC (2008) 2868.
[68] art.45 of Regulation 1198/06 [2006] O.J. L223/1.
[69] art.47 of Regulation 1198/06 [2006] O.J. L223/1.
[70] art.52 of Regulation 1198/06 [2006] O.J. L223/1.
[71] art.55 of Regulation 1198/06 [2006] O.J. L223/1.

simplification and flexibility, so as to ensure that funds are disbursed quickly and effectively. To achieve this, responsibilities of Member States, their partners and the Commission were clarified, bureaucracy reduced and monitoring, evaluation and control strengthened, thereby ensuring improved and sound financial management.

5. THE COHESION FUND

The basic objective of the Cohesion Fund is to strengthen the economic and social cohesion in the Union in the interest of promoting sustainable development. It is governed by the general Regulation referred to above.[72] Assistance from the Fund is to be given to actions in the following areas, considering an appropriate balance to be agreed in partnership between the Member States and the Commission, and according to the investments and infrastructure needs specific to each Member State receiving assistance:

- trans-European transport networks;
- the environment within the priorities assigned to the Union environmental protection policy, in areas closely related to sustainable development that clearly represent environmental benefits and in the transport sector outside the trans-European networks.

Not eligible for assistance are: interest on debt; the purchase of land for an amount exceeding 10 per cent of the total eligible expenditure; housing; decommissioning of nuclear stations; and recoverable VAT.

Assistance is conditioned on the following rules: in the case of excessive government deficit[73] the Council may suspend the totality or part of the commitment; it shall be lifted as soon as the Member State in question has taken the necessary corrective action.

Since this Regulation repealed a previous one, the latter's provision remain applicable under given conditions. For the period 2007–2013 the following Member States were eligible on January 1, 2007: Czech Republic, Estonia, Greece, Cyprus, Latvia, Lithuania, Hungary, Malta, Poland, Portugal, Slovenia, Slovakia and, on a transitional and specific basis, Spain.[74] In the event of a Member State becoming ineligible, resources for the Cohesion Fund are reduced accordingly.

Finally, it must be noted that each Fund has its own characteristic which must be respected; their individual scope can be described as follows:

- the ERDF can finance productive investments, infrastructure, local development and SMEs, pilot projects, investment in education and health, Trans-European Networks and R&D;
- the ESF may give financial assistance for vocational training, start-up aid, innovation measures, training and education schemes and R&D.

The Treaty envisages the possibility of grouping the Funds.[75]

---

[72] Regulation 1083/06 [2006] O.J. L210/25, modified [2009] O.J. L25/1 and [2009] O.J. L33/49 and L250/1.
[73] art.126(6) and (7) TFEU [104(6) and (7)].
[74] [2006] O.J. L243/47.
[75] art.177 TFEU [161].

Chapter Thirty-three

Research and Technological Development and Space

1. INTRODUCTION

The Union adopted a policy for Research and Technological Development (R&TD) with the establishment of the European Atomic Energy Community (Euratom) and the Single European Act, which introduced a new Title in what was then the EC Treaty. In 1984, the European Strategic Programme for Research in Information Technologies (ESPRIT) added a new level of sophistication to the R&TD policy.

R&TD comprises one of the lengthier chapters of the TFEU.[1] The EU Treaty and Treaty of Amsterdam left the policy practically untouched; the latter only modified the unanimity required, among other things, for setting up joint undertakings, in qualified majority and the co-operation procedure or "co-decision", for the other measures. With the level of worldwide competition in the field of research, in addition to security threats faced by the public today, R&TD has become a prominent policy of the Union. It is interesting and worrying to read what the Commission wrote at the beginning of 2000 (with reference to the Union Lisbon Programme[2]):

> "[T]he range of [Union] economic activities exposed to external competition has widened, now including the production of both high-tech and labour intensive goods and services. R&D investment in the EU has become close to stagnation. If current trends continue, R&D investments will be at 2.2 per cent[3] of GDP in 2010, considerably lower than the agreed objective of 3 per cent.[4] Against this background important decisions need to be taken which will determine Europe's economic and social future."

Contrary to other fields examined in the previous chapters, with regard to R&TD, the Union was assigned its own task, mainly through the implementation of the multi-annual framework programmes, while, on the other hand, complementing the activities of the Member States. To avoid wasteful duplication, co-ordination is therefore essential and the Treaty does, indeed, provide for it:

> "[T]he Union and the Member States shall co-ordinate their research and technological development activities so as to ensure that the national policies and the Union policy are mutually consistent".[5]

---

[1] arts 179 to 190 TFEU, Title XIX [163 to 173].
[2] See COM (2005) 330 final or SEC (2005) 981.
[3] According to another Commission publication, it presently represents only 1.8 per cent of GDP! See the website quoted below.
[4] The 3 per cent figure is the expenditure on RDT in the US and Japan; see website quoted below.
[5] art.181(1) TFEU [165(1)].

It is therefore sad to read the following statement of the Commission:

"At the present time, however, it cannot be claimed that there is a European research policy. The research policies of the Member States and that of the Union are conducted in parallel, but do not constitute a coherent whole".[6]

It is interesting to note that the objective of R&TD is not research for its own sake or for scientific purpose, but for:

"[S]trengthening the scientific and technological bases by achieving a 'European research area',[7] in which researchers, scientific knowledge and technology circulate freely and encouraging it to become more competitive, including in its industry, while promoting all the research activities deemed necessary by virtue of other chapters of the Treaty",[8]

one of the main Lisbon Objectives.[9] The whole activity of the Union in this field, is industrially orientated, whether it is carried out in the undertakings themselves, including small and medium-sized ones, or in research centres and at universities. The task of the Union is to encourage such research and to support the efforts of co-operation among all the actors. This is made easier by the establishment of the internal market,[10] the opening of national public contracts,[11] the definition of common standards[12] and the removal of legal[13] and fiscal obstacles to the co-operation. The importance of co-operation between undertakings, research centres and universities is further underlined by the tasks entrusted to the Union.[14]

The means to achieve the objectives are, firstly, the implementation of the multi-annual programmes,[15] secondly co-operation with third countries and international organisations,[16] thirdly, the dissemination and optimisation of the results of activities in Union research, technological development and demonstration,[17] and, fourthly, stimulation of the training and mobility of researchers in the Union.[18] It will be noticed, however, that there are, in the R&TD sector, very few binding acts: practically all the activities are regulated by "Communications".

2. THE SEVENTH FRAMEWORK PROGRAMME (2007–2013)[19]

The Seventh Framework Programme for Research, Technological Development and Demonstration Activities is adapted to the EU's needs in terms of growth and employment. It includes the Seventh Framework Programme of Euratom and

---

[6] *http://www.europa.eu/scadplus/leg/en/lvb/i23010.htm.*
[7] See "The European research area: new perspectives" [2007] O.J. C181/17.
[8] art.179 (1) TFEU [163(1)].
[9] Bull. 3, 2004, points 1–10.
[10] See above, Ch.15: Free Movement of Goods.
[11] See above, Ch.31: Enterprise and Industrial Policy/Information Society.
[12] See above, Ch.15: Free Movement of Goods (6. Theory and Reality of the Free Movement of Goods). See Directive 98/34 laying down a Procedure for the Provision of Information in the Field of Technical Standards and Regulations [1998] O.J. L204/37, amended [1998] O.J. L217/18.
[13] See above, Ch.22: Competition Policy.
[14] art.180 TFEU [164].
[15] arts 182 to 186 TFEU [166 to 170].
[16] art.180(b) TFEU [164(b).
[17] art.180(c) TFEU [164(c)].
[18] art.180(d) TFEU [164(d)].
[19] Taken from: *http://www.europa.eu/scadplus/leg/en/lvb/i23022.htm.*

centres on four specific programmes which correspond to the four main objectives of European research policy:

1. the *"Co-operation" programme*[20]: promoting co-operation between industry and university to achieve greater leadership in key technological areas; this programme[21] aims to stimulate co-operation and improve links between industry and research within a transnational framework. The programme has nine themes that are to be managed autonomously, but will be complementary in terms of implementation:

    (a) health;
    (b) food, agriculture and biotechnology;
    (c) information and communication technologies;
    (d) nanosciences, nanotechnologies, materials and new production technologies;
    (e) energy;
    (f) environment (including climate changes);
    (g) transport (including aeronautics);
    (h) socioeconomic sciences and the humanities;
    (i) security and space;

2. the *"Ideas"*[22] *programme*: intended to enhance exploratory research in Europe, i.e. research aimed at discovering new knowledge that fundamentally changes our vision of the world and our way of life. A new European Research Council (ERC) will support the most ambitious and innovative research projects. A Commission decision[23] defines its structure, which comprises the Scientific Council, the ERC's Secretary-General and the dedicated implementation structure. The Scientific Council will identify priorities and scientific strategies;

3. the *"People"*[24] *programme*: mobilises significant funds that can be used to improve the career prospects of researchers in Europe and attract more high-quality researchers. The programme will reinforce the existing Marie Curie actions;

4. the *"Capacities"*[25] *programme*: intended to give researchers powerful tools that will enable them to enhance the quality and competitiveness of European research.

Furthermore, .the Seventh Framework Programme finances the direct actions of the Joint Research Centre (JRC) and the actions covered by the Euratom Framework Programme in the fields of:

- research into fusion energy;
- nuclear fission and radiation protection.

The duration of the programme was extended from four to seven years; it is placed within the context of the European Research Area. The seventh programme introduces new measures designed to improve the coherence and effectiveness of the Union's research policy; the main innovations are: simplification of

[20] [2006] O.J. L400/86.
[21] Decision 2006/974 [2007] O.J. L54/101.
[22] Decision 2006/972 [2007] O.J. L54/81.
[23] [2006] O.J. L400/243 and Decision 2007/134 [2007] O.J. L57/14.
[24] [2006] O.J. L400/272 and Decision 2006/973 [2007] O.J. L54/91.
[25] [2006] O.J. L400/299 and Decision 2006/974 [2007] O.J. L54/101.

the procedures for participation; implementation of the programme and its budget by themes instead of by instruments; creation of the European Research Council; improved co-operation with industry via the Joint Technology Initiatives, which will combine private investment and public funding (see below); the support of a European research infrastructure policy; and the creation of Risk Sharing Finance Facility to facilitate access to EIB loans. This facility is endowed with €1 billion each from the EIB and the Framework Programme.[26] It is an innovation scheme to improve access to debt financing for private companies or public institutions promoting activities in the field of research, technological development, demonstration and innovation investments. It is built on the principle of credit risk sharing between the Union and the EIB and extends thereby the ability of the Bank to provide loans and guarantees with a low and sub-investment grade risk profile.

Rules were laid down for the participation of undertakings, research centres and universities in actions under the programme.[27]

Some actions under the Seventh Framework Programme are to be carried out by the Joint Research Centre.[28]

Joint Technology Initiatives—Joint Undertakings

The programme provides for a long-term public-private partnership in the form of Joint Technology Initiatives, which can be implemented through Joint Undertakings, as provided for in the TFEU.[29] These enterprises are, generally, bodies of the Union, with legal personality and funded 50/50 by the Union and the private sector. The following joint undertakings were set up.

- ARTEMIS Joint Undertaking: embedded computer systems.
- Clear Sky Joint Undertaking: air transport[30] set up for the period up to December 31, 2017, to ensure the appropriate management of research activities, including exploitation of the results by the member of the joint enterprise.
- The ENIAC Joint Undertaking[31]: nanoelectronics—it is a Community body and has legal personality and located in Brussels. It will ensure and promote a safe, integrated and responsible approach to nanoelectronics in keeping with the high safety standards already established in the industry and in accordance with public health, safety, environmental and consumer Union policies.
- IMI, the Joint Undertaking for the implementation of the Joint Technology Initiative on Innovative Medicine.[32]
- FCH Joint Undertaking[33]: fuel cells and hydrogen. Budget 2008–2017: 1 billion.

---

[26] See *http://www.eib.org:products/loans/special/rsff/*.
[27] Regulation 1908/2006 [2006] O.J. L400/1, corrigendum [2007] O.J. L54/4.
[28] [2007] O.J. L54/126, 139 and 149.
[29] art.187 TFEU [171]: "The Union may set up joint undertakings or any other structure necessary for the efficient execution of the research, technological development and demonstration programmes."
[30] Regulation 71/07 [2007] O.J. L30/1, amended [2009] O.J. L175/14.
[31] Regulation 72/08 [2008] O.J. L30/21.
[32] Regulation 73/08 [2008] O.J. L30/38.
[33] General Report 2008, 261.

- SESAR Joint Undertaking: air traffic management.[34] The Commission has proposed a budget of €70 billion for the period 2007–2013. The detailed implementation of the programme was published in December[35] 2006.

In a communication "Competitive European regions through research and innovation: a contribution to more growth and more and better jobs",[36] the Commission describes the synergies of design of the European research, innovation and cohesion policies and calls on Member States and regions to make more effective use of European Union research, innovation and cohesion policies and instruments: greater effort could be made at the national and regional level to improve information about the instruments and their use.[37]

3. THE EUROPEAN RESEARCH AREA[38]

The primary focus of the Sixth Framework Programme was the creation of the European Research Area (ERA),[39] an integrated science and technology complement to the internal market. While previous framework programmes have aimed to enhance co-operation among Member States, the Sixth Framework Programme went much further to create focused research at the Union level. Designed to improve competitiveness and innovation, the ERA will promote increased co-ordination among the relevant actors to produce integrated projects with clear objectives. To this end, the Sixth Framework Programme simplified procedures, reduced priorities, established new support mechanisms, and promoted collaboration and integration. These measures were intended to increase efficiency through more precise, focused and progressively integrated projects, and in turn create a broader, more lasting impact on scientific and technological development within the Union, that will enhance economic growth across the internal market. The ERA is the next step towards funding coherent Union-wide projects.

Framework funds are allocated based, not on national quotas, but on several criteria, among which, that projects must involve partners from multiple Member States; projects follow the "calls for proposals" guidelines of the Commission meaning they are competitive and in line with the Commissions priorities; the scientific excellence, quality and relevance of the project is approved by five independent experts; and the funds allocated to a project must be applied to specific work, and may not be subsidies for broad research or companies. In order to ensure that the Commission's research priorities match those of the scientific

---

[34] General Report 2008, 261.

[35] [2006] O.J. L400/1; the whole issue (more than 400 pages) concerns the implementation of the Seventh Programme, for instance: rules for the participation of undertakings, research centres and universities.

[36] COM (2007) 474.

[37] General Report 2007, 64.

[38] Decision 15/13/02 of Parliament and the Council concerning the Sixth Framework Programme of the EC for research, technical development and demonstration activities contributing to the creation of the European Research Area and to innovation (2002–2006) [2002] O.J. L232/1 and Decision of June 3, 2002 concerning the Euratom programme, ibid. at 34.

[39] Decision 2002/835 adopting a specific programme for RTD and demonstration: "Integrating and strengthening the European Research Area" (2002–2006) [2002] O.J. L294/1; see also Decision 2002/836 on "structuring the European Research Area" [2002] O.J. L294/44.

community, the Commission published a "call for expression of interest" in March 2002 and successfully received 15,000 proposals from the scientific and industrial community. These proposals will influence the official "calls for proposals" that the Commission will publish when the new framework comes into effect. The "calls for proposals" not only invite teams to submit project ideas, but they provide transparent and equal access to funding for all applicants.

It is clear from the previous remarks that the multi-annual framework programmes play an important role in the implementation of the research and technological development activities of the Union. Those programmes are adopted by Parliament and the Council acting in accordance with the ordinary legislative procedure[40] after consulting the ESC.[41] They establish the scientific and technological objectives, fix the relevant priorities, indicate the broad lines of each activity and fix the maximum overall amount for Union financial participation. Those programmes are to be implemented through specific programmes developed for each activity. The rules for the participation of undertakings, research centres and universities in those programmes, and the dissemination of the results, are determined by Parliament and the Council in accordance with the ordinary legislative procedure[42] and after consulting the ESC.

The Treaty also provides that supplementary programmes may be financed by certain Member States only; this will, of course, influence the dissemination of the results of such programmes.[43] Also, the Union may participate in programmes carried out by several Member States,[44] while in its own programmes it may make provisions for co-operation with third countries or international organisations.[45]

It is also provided that the Union may set up joint undertakings or any other structure necessary for the execution of its research, technological development and demonstration programmes.[46] As indicated previously, R&TD programmes may be co-financed by the European Regional Development Fund and the European Social Fund in specific regions.[47]

4. THE EUROPEAN SPACE POLICY[48]

The Treaty of Lisbon introduced "space" into the Union's activities. Based on the peaceful exploitation of outer space by all the Member States, the space policy is intended to promote scientific and technical progress, industrial competitiveness and the implementation of the Union's policies. To this end it may promote joint

---

[40] art.294 TFEU [251].
[41] art.183 TFEU [167].
[42] art.294 TFEU [251].
[43] art.184 TFEU [168].
[44] art.185 TFEU [169].
[45] art.186 TFEU [170].
[46] art.187 TFEU [171]. See, for instance, Regulation 71/2007 setting up the Clean Sky Joint Undertaking [2008] O.J. L30/1 and Decision 2000/1987 [2007] O.J. L90/58 setting up the Joint Undertaking for the international thermonuclear experimental reactor and the development of fusion energy; it will manage the contribution of Euratom to the International Fusion Energy Organisation of €1.717 billion.
[47] See above Ch.32: Regional Policy/Economic, Social and Territorial Cohesion.
[48] art.189 TFEU.

initiatives, support research and technological development and co-ordinate the efforts needed for the exploration and exploitation of space.

Parliament and the Council, acting in accordance with the ordinary legislative procedure,[49] must establish the necessary measures, which may take the form of a European Space Programme. The Union is to establish any appropriate relations with the European Space Agency.[50]

In 2008, the Council adopted a resolution "Taking forward the European Space policy".[51] It refers to Galileo, which constitutes the first flagship space pro- gramme of the Union and GMES (Global Monitoring for Environment and Security), which is a user-driven initiative that should maximise the use of existing space and non-space Earth Observation centres, capacities and services in Europe. The resolution defines new priorities within the European Space pol- icy: Space and climate change, contribution of Space to the Lisbon Strategy, Space and security and Space exploration. In 2007 the Commission adopted a Communication on European space policy.[52]

See also a directive which lays down general rules for the establishment of the infrastructure for Spacial Information in the Union (INSPIRE)[53] and the implementing regulation.[54]

5. Co-operation with Third Countries

The implementation of the R&TD tasks is also carried out through the promotion of co-operation with third countries and international organisations. Supporting the objective of integration in the Sixth Framework Programme, the Commission established a separate international scientific co-operation policy. This policy aims at enhanced international co-operation in R&TD to allow for greater political and economic relations with non-EU countries. The European Research Advisory Board (EURAB) was established by the Commission in June 2001[55] to provide independent advice on the implementation of EU research policy. This board is enti- tled to present opinions and advice about policy as well as form working groups with other research groups or experts as it deems necessary. The 45 members nom- inated by academics and industrialists represent both Union and non-Union nation- als providing a decisive point of influence for non-Union interests.

In this context mention must be made of certain special agreements concluded with third countries, namely Union participation in the following organisations: European Science Foundation (ESF), the European Space Agency (ESA), the European Molecular Biology Organisation (EMBO), the European Molecular

---

[49] art.294 TFEU [251].
[50] Established in 1975, it is an intergovernmental organisation dedicated to the exploration of space, currently with 18 members. Its mission is to shape the development of Europe's space capability and ensure that investment in space continues to deliver benefits for the citizens of Europe and the world. Its headquarters are in Paris and it has centres in Germany, Spain, Italy and the Netherlands. It employs about 1,900 people and has a budget for 2009 of €9.3 billion. See the Agreement between the European Space Agency and the Union on the security and exchange of classified information.
[51] [2008] O.J. C 268/1.
[52] [2007] O.J. C181/17.
[53] [2007] O.J. L108/1.
[54] [2009] O.J. L274/9.
[55] [2001] O.J. L192/21.

Biology Laboratory (EMBL), the European Organisation for Nuclear Research (CERN), the European Southern Observatory (ESO), the European Synchrotron Radiation Facility (ESRF), the Institute Laue-Langevin (ILL), and the European Co-operation in the Field of Scientific and Technical Research. Furthermore, the Union participates in the International Science and Technology Centre with the USA, Japan, and the Russian Federation. This list is far from exhaustive and the Union has concluded agreements with countries around the world.

For instance, an agreement was concluded with Japan for the joint implementation of broader approach activities in the field of fusion energy research. A scientific and technology co-operation agreement was signed with South Korea, Switzerland, Israel and India. The Former Yugoslav Republic of Macedonia, Serbia and Turkey are eligible to participate in the Seventh Framework Programme on the same terms as the Member States.

6. DISSEMINATION OF RESULTS

One of the most important aspects of an efficient R&TD program, is that the results of the Union activities in this field must be disseminated and optimised. If results are not immediately and properly communicated to the undertakings which need them, such programmes will not fulfil the objectives set out in the Treaty. With the Sixth Framework Programme in mind, the Commission proposed new, "rules for the participation of undertakings, research centres and universities and for the dissemination of research results for the implementation of the European Union Framework Programmes 2002–2006".[56] These rules adopted under the co-decision procedure are one mechanism towards the implementation of the new framework programme and are meant to simplify provisions for dissemination and make them more accessible. The decision lays down general rules on dissemination and protection of knowledge and provides for the implementation of centralised dissemination and exploitation measures.

One further task of the Union is to stimulate the training and mobility of researchers. This should be made easier by the Union activities with regard to education and training examined elsewhere in this book and, of course, the free movement of persons.[57]

7. THE JOINT RESEARCH CENTRE

Some of the above-mentioned research is carried out by the Union itself in the Joint Research Centre (JRC) which was set up in pursuance of the Euratom Treaty.[58] The JRC carries out its work in the Centre's four areas of activity: specific research programmes under the framework programme, support for Commission departments, work under contract for outside bodies and exploratory research. It is composed

[56] [2006] O.J. L 400/1.
[57] See above Ch.16: Free Movement of Persons.
[58] art.8 (1) Euratom. See for instance Decision 2002/838 adopting a specific programme (Euratom) for research and training on nuclear energy (2002–2006) [2002] O.J. L294/74.

of seven institutes: reference materials and measurement (IRMM: Geel, Belgium), trans-uranium elements (ITU: Karlsruhe, Germany), energy (IE: Petten, Netherlands), protection and the security of the citizen (IPSC: Ispra, Italy), environment and sustainability (IES: Ispra, Italy), health and consumer protection (IHCP: Ispra, Italy), and prospective technological studies (IPTS: Seville, Spain).

The JRC Work Programme[59] provides that the JRC should be competitive to maintain high-level research as well as being flexible to adjust to the evolving research priorities of the Commission.[60] Considerable research is devoted to support the European Chemicals Bureau, the European Integrated Pollution Prevention and Controls Bureau, and the European Laboratory for Air Pollution. With the implementation of the Framework Programmes, the JRC will focus on research in the areas of food, chemical products, and health; environment and sustainability; nuclear safety[61] and security; and dependability of information systems and services. Furthermore, the JRC provides horizontal support with the:

"[P]roduction of reference materials and measurements, and the development of risk management tools for increased safety and public security, including fight against fraud. Technology foresight activities will be concentrated on networks of national institutes in this field, allowing for synergies and economies of scale".[62]

The JRC also plays an important role in research training through both courses and work experience as well as providing the ERA with access to its extensive facilities and networks.

Under the Union's Seventh Framework Programme and the Seventh Framework Programme of Euratom, the JRC's programme is organised into five themes:

1. prosperity in a knowledge intensive society;
2. solidarity and the responsible management of resources;
3. security and freedom;
4. Europe as a world partner;
5. the Euratom programme.

These five themes are subdivided into 17 policy agendas.[63] In 2009 the Commission concluded a Memorandum of Understanding with the European Organisation for Nuclear Research (CERN).[64]

The non-nuclear part of the Euratom research programme now represents about three-quarters of the Centre's activities; it has, for instance, adopted a medical intelligence system "MedSys" to identify public health threat by gathering and processing information published on the Internet. It also contributes to monitoring the forest fires which occur during the summer by providing satellite imaging and information generated by the European forest fire information service.

---

[59] The multi-annual work programme is based on a Council decision.

[60] For further information, see the Commission's Communication on "Fulfilling the JRC's Mission in the European Research Area", COM (2001) 215.

[61] The JRC provides national authorities with expertise on combating and tracing illicit nuclear materials General Report 2007,67.

[62] See JRC website: *http://www.jrc.cec.eu.int/index.asp*.

[63] For more details see *http://www.ec.europa.eu/dgs/jrc/indew.cfm?id=&1590&lang=en*.

[64] [2009] O.J. L161/13.

A supplementary research programme to be carried out by the JRC was adopted in 2009.[65]

Finally, the Commission must each year send a report to Parliament and the Council on its R&TD activities, the dissemination of results and the work programme for the current year.[66]

[65] [2009] O.J. L132/13.
[66] art.190 TFEU [173].

Chapter Thirty-four

Environment

1. THE TREATY PROVISIONS[1]

The first Union environmental legislation emerged in the 1970s. The Union and the Member States started to realise that—especially over the long term—the promotion of economic growth within the Union and the establishment of a single market economy required an underlying cross-border environmental protection regime. However, before the Single European Act of 1987, the Treaty did not explicitly provide for the adoption of environmental measures. Consequently, the early legislation[2] was founded either on the internal market harmonisation provisions[3] or on the possibility for the Council to adopt the appropriate measures when action proved to be necessary, within the framework of the policies defined in the Treaties, to attain one of the objectives of the Treaties and the Treaties have not provided the necessary powers.[4] In both cases, a unanimous decision by the Council is required, on a proposal from the Commission and after obtaining the consent of Parliament. The Court, on the other hand, relied on the Preamble to the Treaty and on the tasks assigned to the Union to justify such measures. As mentioned, the SEA introduced environmental provisions into the Treaty: Title VII "Environment" and into the harmonisation provisions.[5] Furthermore, one of the Union tasks was described as the promotion of a, "sustainable and non-inflationary growth respecting the environment".

The Treaty of Amsterdam of 1997 slightly modified the description of those tasks, focusing on:

> "[A] harmonious, balanced and sustainable development of economic activities, . . . sustainable and non-inflationary growth, . . . a high level of protection and improvement of the quality of the environment, the raising of the standard in living and quality of life".

---

[1] arts 191–193 TFEU [174–176].

[2] For instance: Directive 67/548 [1967] O.J. L196/1 on classification, packaging and labelling of dangerous substances, modified for the 31st time [2009] O.J. L11/6, repealed by Regulation 13272/08 [2008] O.J. L353/1, amended [2009] O.J. L235/1; Directive 70/157 [1970] O.J. L42/16 on noise levels; Directive 70/220 [1970] O.J. L76/1 on automobile emissions.

[3] *Commission v Italy* (91/79) [1980] E.C.R. I-1099; [1981] 1 C.M.L.R. 331 and *Commission v Italy* (92/79) [1980] E.C.R. 1115; [1981] 1 C.M.L.R. 331.

[4] art.352 TFEU [308]. Since the Treaty did not refer to environmental protection as one of its objectives, the Court relied on an interpretation of art.2 EC, which defines as a task of the Union, "a harmonious development of economic activities, a continuous and balanced expansion, . . . (and) an accelerated raising of the standard of living", and of the Preamble stating that Union goals include, "the constant improvement of living and working conditions". In 1985, the Court finally held that environmental protection is one of the Union's "essential objectives": *Procureur de la République v Association de défense des bruleurs d'huiles usagèes* (240/83) [1985] E.C.R. I-531(549).

[5] Former art.100a(3) EC granted the right to adopt measures progressively establishing the internal market and concerning health, safety, environmental protection and consumer protection.

This objective was given even more weight by the inclusion, under the "activities" of the Union, of a, "policy in the sphere of the environment".[6]

The Treaty of Amsterdam significantly enhanced the scope of environmental responsibility within the Union by "democratising" the decision-making process; this was achieved by conferring more power upon Parliament in this sector also. The Union's objectives for environmental protection are listed as follows[7]:

- preserving, protecting and improving the quality of the environment;
- protecting human health; see, for instance, the Air Quality Directive,[8] the Regulation on conditions for the export and import of certain dangerous chemicals,[9] and a Regulation on the banning and export of metallic mercury[10];
- prudent and rational utilisation of natural resources; see Framework Directive on waste,[11] and a Directive on reducing the environmental impact of waste electrical and electronic equipment,[12] and a Directive on the reduction of certain hazardous substances in those equipments[13];
- promotion of measures at international level to deal with regional or world-wide environmental problems and (added by Lisbon) in particular combating climate change.[14]

The first of these objectives had also received some implementation with the establishment of a Union eco-label award system,[15] which is intended to promote the design, production, marketing and use of products which have a reduced environmental impact during their entire life cycle and provide consumers with better information on the environmental impact of products. Some of these products contain ozone-depleting substances and their destruction is regulated.[16] The system does not apply to food, drink and pharmaceuticals. The conditions for awarding the eco-label are defined by product groups. The decision to award is made by a "competent body" designated by each Member State. A revised eco-label award system was adopted by Parliament and the Council in 2002.[17]

2. GUIDING PRINCIPLES

While aiming at a "high level of protection", the Union policy must take into account the diversity of situations in various regions of the Union. It shall be based on the *precautionary principle*[18] and on the principles that preventive

---

[6] arts 3–6 TFEU [3(1)].
[7] art.191 TFEU [174].
[8] Directive 2008/50 [2008] O.J. L152/1, on ambient air quality and cleaner air for Europe: it sets standards and deadlines for the reduction of concentrations of fine particulate matter.
[9] Regulation 689/08 [2008] O.J. L204/1.
[10] Regulation 1102/08 [2008] O.J. L304/75.
[11] Directive 2008/98 [32008] O.J. L312/3, repealing certain Directives.
[12] Directive 2002/96 [2003] O.J. L37/24.
[13] Directive 2002/95 [2003] O.J. L37/19.
[14] art.191,1 TFEU last indent.
[15] Regulation 880/1992 [1992] O.J. L99/1.
[16] Regulation 2037/2000 [2000] O.J. L244/1.
[17] [2000] O.J. L237/1.
[18] Although not expressly defined in the Treaty, this principle entails that, despite scientific uncertainty concerning the likelihood of harm, certain measures should be taken before the environmental risk can be clearly evidenced. See Communication of the Commission of February 2, 2003 COM (2000) 1 and *National Farmers' Community* (C-157/96) [1998] E.C.R. I-2211(63), that, however, does not give a definitive answer.

action should be taken, that environmental damage should, as a priority, be rectified at source: *proximity principle* and the *polluter pay principle.*[19]

In preparing its policy on the environment, the Union must take account of available scientific and technical data, environmental conditions in the various regions, the potential benefits and costs of action or lack of action and the economic and social development of the Union as a whole and the balanced development of its regions.

[The reader shall have noticed that in this single Treaty provision there are three references to the "regions", which seems to indicate that regional policy, i.e. economic, social and territorial cohesion, must be taken into account when implementing environmental policy.]

By requiring that, "environmental protection requirements shall be a component of the Union's other policies", this so-called *integration principle* led to a general obligation for Union institutions to seek to conciliate other Treaty objectives (e.g. single market economy) with environmental protection, determining the wide scope of environmental responsibility.[20]

Finally, the *principle of subsidiarity*, first mentioned in the SEA in relation with the environment, was generalised by the EU Treaty: the Union is only to legislate if and in so far as the objectives stated above, "cannot be sufficiently achieved by the Member States and can, therefore, by reason of the scale or effects of the proposed action, be better achieved by the Union".[21] But even where protective measures are adopted by the Union, the Treaty allows Member States to maintain or introduce stricter protective measures, as long as they are, "compatible with the Treaty and notified to the Commission".[22] The latter will only approve them if it is satisfied that they are based on "grounds of major needs", or on new scientific evidence relating to the protection of the environment or the working environment. The Commission must also be convinced that those measures are neither means of arbitrary discrimination nor disguised restrictions on Union inter-State commerce or other obstacles to the functioning of the internal market.[23]

As mentioned before, the EU Treaty substantially enhanced the decision-making power of Parliament in the area of environmental legislation. Where unanimous decisions of the Council, after prior consultation of Parliament, were required, the Treaty now provides for a decision of Parliament and Council, acting in accordance with the ordinary legislative provision[24] and after consulting the ESC and the Committee of the Regions.[25] Acting unanimously, the Council can, in accordance with a specific legislative procedure,[26] and after consulting Parliament, the ESC and the Committee of the Regions, adopt provisions primarily of a fiscal

---

[19] This polluter pays principle is regarded as the cornerstone of Union environmental policy. References to it are made, among others, in Directive 75/439 on the disposal of waste oils [1975] O.J. L194/23 and Directive 91/689 on dangerous waste [1991] O.J. L377/20, amended by Directive 94/31 [1994] O.J. L168/28.

[20] The Treaty provides for the integration principle in art.11 TFEU [6]: "environmental protection requirements must be integrated into the definition and implementation of the Union policies and activities referred to in Art. 3, 4, 5 and 6, in particular with a view to promoting sustainable development."

[21] Protocol No.2 on the application of the principles of subsidiarity and proportionality annexed to the TFEU.

[22] art.193 TFEU [176].

[23] art.114(5) and (6) TFEU [95(5) and (6)]. See *Deponietzweckverband Eiterköpfe* (C-6/03) [2005] E.C.R. I-2753.

[24] See art.294 TFEU [251].

[25] art.192,1 TFEU [175], which refers to art.191 TFEU [174].

[26] See art.289,2 TFEU.

nature, measures affecting town and country planning, quantitative management of water resources or land use with the exception of waste management and measures significantly affecting Member States' choices between different energy sources and the general structure of its energy supply.[27]

3. ENVIRONMENTAL ACTION PROGRAMMES

Since 1973, the Union environmental policy has been developed through the enactment by Parliament and the Council of a series of non-binding "Environmental Action Programmes",[28] after consultation of the ESC and the Committee of the Regions.[29] Serving as an orientation for future Union action, the Fifth Programme was entitled "Towards Sustainability". It addressed the need for a greater use of market forces through market instruments and incentives (e.g. taxes, eco-labelling, liability schemes, eco-audits, voluntary agreements, deposit/refund systems, etc.). It also introduced the notion of shared responsibility between public authorities (see below), public and private enterprises and the general public, emphasising the need for their wider involvement in environmental affairs.

In 1992, a Directive on the freedom of public access to environmental information came into force; the aim is to trigger public participation in the decision-making and in the monitoring process by disseminating environmental information held by public authorities.[30] Most significant, though, is the shift among Member States to accept the concept of "sustainable development",[31] as being fundamental to future economic Union policy leading to the prudent use of resources and to profound changes in current patterns of development, production, consumption and behaviour. In 2008, the Commission adopted a communication "Towards a Shared Environmental Information System" (SEIS), proposing to modify and modernise the existing Union system.[32]

4. THE SIXTH ENVIRONMENT ACTION PROGRAMME (2001–2012)

Entitled "Environment 2010: Our Future, Our Choice", it sets the following priorities:

- climate change;
- nature and biodiversity;

---

[27] art.192,2 TFEU [175,2]
[28] Passed either as resolutions or decisions: First Action Programme (1973–77) [1973] O.J. C112/1; Second Action Programme (1977–83) [1977] O.J. C139/1; Third Action Programme (1983–87) [1983] O.J. C46/1; Fourth Action Programme (1987–93) [1987] O.J. C328/1; Fifth Action Programme (1993–2000) [1993] O.J. C138/1; and Sixth Action Programme (2001–2012) [2002] O.J L242/1.
[29] art.192(3) TFEU [175(3)].
[30] Directive 2003/4 on public access to environmental information [2003] O.J. L41/26.
[31] Following the Report of the World Commission on Environment and Development (Brundtland Commission), the term "sustainable development" can be defined as, "development which meets the needs of the present, without compromising the ability of future generations to meet their own needs".
[32] COM (2008) 46 [2008] O.J. C118/10.

- environment and health and quality of life; and
- natural resources and waste.

A report on the main developments in those four main policy areas was adopted by the Commission in 2008.[33]

Measures to achieve these priorities are outlined:

- improving the application of environmental legislation necessary to set a common baseline for all Union countries;
- integration of environmental concerns: environmental problems have to be tackled where their source is and this is frequently in other policies[34];
- use of a blend of instruments: all types have to be considered, the criteria for choice being that they offer the best efficiency and effectiveness;
- stimulation of participation and action of all actors, from business to citizens, NGOs and social partners through better and more accessible information on the environment and joint action on solutions. The Sixth Programme stresses the importance of providing adequate information and effective opportunities for public participation in environment decision-making. This increases accountability and transparency of decision-making and contributes to public awareness and support for the decisions taken. A regulation[35] applies the Aarhus Convention on Access to Information, Public Participation in Decision-making and Access to Justice in Environmental matters to Community institutions and bodies. The Union signed in 1998 the United Nations Economic Commission for Europe (UNECE) Convention; it was approved in 2005![36] Where public access to Parliament, the Council and Commission documents are concerned, the Aarhus Convention makes an exception for judicial and legislative acts; this would, however, be in contradiction with the rules applicable within the Union.[37] Access under Aarhus had therefore to be extended to legislative acts by the above-mentioned Regulation.

An innovation worth mentioning is the *integrated product policy*. Its aim is to develop a more ecological product market by making products more environmentally sustainable throughout their life cycle.[38]

A Commission Communication of May 2000 sets out long-term objectives for *sustainable development* and essentially concerns climate change, transport, health and natural resources.[39] The new programme provides the environmental

---

[33] COM (2008) 409.

[34] See, for instance, Regulation 443/09 setting emission performance standards for new passenger cars as part of the Union's integrated approach to reduce CO2 emissions from light-duty vehicles [2009] O.J. L140/1.

[35] Regulation 1367/2006 [2006] O.J. L264/13.

[36] [2005] O.J. L124/1.

[37] Regulation 1049/2001 [2001] O.J. L145/43.

[38] [1992] Bull.12, 93 in accordance with this realisation process, the Treaty of Amsterdam includes the concept of sustainable development into various provisions, namely the Preamble of the Treaty on the European Union (in connection with the promotion of environmental protection) and art.2 EU stating that one of the objectives of the Union shall be, "to achieve balanced and sustainable development". Nevertheless, in the latter case, specific reference to environmental protection was not made. Furthermore, former art.2 EC stresses "sustainable development" as a Union task, whereas art.11 TFEU [6] combines the integration principle with the accompanying promotion of sustainable economic development.

[39] COM (2001) 264 final.

component of the Union's strategy for sustainable development. It also makes the link between environment and the European objective for growth and competitiveness. Seven thematic strategies were developed according to a common approach independently of the specific content requirements relating to their subject matter:

- Clean Air For Europe (CAFE)[40];
- soil protection: concerns erosion, organic matter, contamination, monitoring and research;
- sustainable use of pesticides: the EU has defined strict rules for the authorisation of plant protection products (PPPs) requiring prior risk assessment and rules defining maximum residue limits[41];
- protect and conserve the marine environment[42];
- waste prevention and recycling[43];
- sustainable use of natural resources;
- urban environment.[44]

Noticeably, almost all of the more than 300 Union legislative acts aiming at environmental protection are in the form of directives, leaving room for each Member State to implement them taking into account its own economic, social and cultural background. Thus, due to the diversity of situations within the various regions of the Union, Union environmental policy focuses rather on the harmonisation than on the unification of environmental standards.[45] In this context, the major sectors of environmental Union concern have been the protection of fresh and seawater,[46]

---

[40] See COM (2005) 447 and Directive 2008/50 on ambient air quality and cleaner air for Europe [2008] O.J. L152/1.

[41] Directive 91/414 [1991] O.J. L230/1. See also the Biocidal Product Directive 98/8 [1998] O.J. L123/1.

[42] COM (2002) 539 final.

[43] See the Waste Management Directive 08/98 [2008] O.J. L312/3.

[44] See COM (2004) 60.

[45] In terms of national environmental legislation within the Member States, substantial differences exist due to diverse social, cultural and economic realities. Unification of standards would often neglect the respective socio-economic situation of a Member State. Therefore, the use of Directives leaves room for each Member State to adjust its laws accordingly. At present, for example, Member States such as Denmark, the Netherlands, Sweden, Austria and Germany are far more concerned about environmental protection than, for instance, Greece, Spain or Italy.

[46] Many Directives in this area are concerned with quality standards of water for specific uses, e.g. Directive 75/440 [1975] O.J. L194/26 to help ensure clean drinking water by protecting those rivers, lakes and reservoirs used as drinking water sources: See Directive 2008/105 on environmental quality standards in the field of water policy [2008] O.J. L348/84; Directive 76/160 [1976] O.J. L31/1 to safeguard the health of bathers and to maintain the quality of bathing water; Directive 78/659 [1978] O.J. L222/1 to protect freshwater bodies capable of supporting fish life; Directive 79/923 [1979] O.J. L281/47 to protect coastal and brackish waters to support shellfish populations; Directive 80/778 [1980] O.J. L229/11 to safeguard human health by imposing strict quality standards for water intended for direct or indirect human consumption. Various amendments and modifications have followed. Other legislation introduced emission standards for discharges to surface waters and groundwater, for instance, Framework Directive 76/464 [1976] O.J. L129/23 on the discharge of dangerous substances into the aquatic environment; Directive 80/68 on the protection of groundwater against pollution caused by certain dangerous substances [1980] O.J. L20/43), it established a system of information exchange on river water quality between the Member States.

the monitoring of atmospheric pollution,[47] the prevention of noise,[48] the conservation of wild flora and fauna,[49] waste management,[50] the control of chemicals[51] and energy policies. With regard to atmospheric pollution, the Union set itself targets under the Kyoto Protocol; to this end it has approved a Programme on climate change and a Communication on its implementation.[52] In recent years, particular attention has been paid to a shift from "command and-control"

[47] In the 1980s, especially under the impression of acid rain pollution, various Directives on air quality standards were enacted, for instance, Directive 80/779 [1980] O.J. L229/30 setting up quality standards for sulphur dioxide and suspended particulates; other Directives for lead and nitrogen dioxides followed. For new industrial plants prior authorisation schemes were developed verifying, among others, the use of "green" technologies and the compliance with certain air quality standards to prevent excessive air pollution: Framework Directive 84/360 [1984] O.J. L188/20; see *Commission v Greece* (C-364/03) [2005] E.C.R. I-6159, atmospheric pollution by electrical plant. Various "daughter" directives flowed from this, as well as legislation setting up emission standards for industrial plants and motor vehicles. See also Directive 2000/69 relating to limit values for benzene and carbon monoxide in ambient air [2000] O.J. L313/12 and Directive 2000/81 on national emission ceilings for certain atmospheric pollutants [2001] O.J. L309/22. An information exchange system was established by a Council decision concerning atmospheric pollution in each Member State.

[48] In order to give fresh impetus to the campaign against noise, a Directive was adopted in 2002, it defines a Union approach for the management and evaluation of ambient noise in order to protect public health, Directive 2002/49 [2002] O.J. L189/12 and Commission Recommendation [2003] O.J. L212/49.

[49] For instance, Directive 92/43 [1992] O.J. L206/7 on the conservation of European wildlife and natural habitats; Directive 79/409 [1979] O.J. L103/1 on the conservation of wild birds; other legislation banned the import of sea pup skins or the use of leg-hold traps within the Union and established common rules for the imports of whales and other cetacean products. See also Regulation 338/97 on the protection of species of wild fauna and flora by regulating trade therein [1997] O.J. L61/1, modified [2001] O.J. L209/14, amended by Regulation 407/09 and corrigendum [2009] O.J. L.139/35.

[50] For instance, Framework Directive 75/442 [1975] O.J. L194/39 on waste management, modified [1991] O.J. L78/32, see *Commune of Mesquer v Total* (C-188/07) [2008] E.C.R.I-4501, on the definition of waste and where the Court declared the International Convention on Civil Liability for Oil Pollution Damage non applicable. See also [1996] O.J. L135/32; Directive 75/439 [1975] O.J. L194/23, on the elimination of used oils, modified [1987] O.J. L42/43; Directive 91/689 [1991] O.J. L377/20 on waste management in hazardous waste; Regulation 259/93 [1993] O.J. L30/1, on the supervision and control of shipments of waste within, into and out of the EU (legislation implementing the obligations under the Basel Convention (1989) and the Lomé IV Convention (1991)); see *EU-Wood-Trading GmbH v Sonderabfall-Management* (C-277/02) [2004] E.C.R. I-11957; other Directives focused on landfill waste, Directive 1999/31 [1999] O.J. L182/1, packaging and packaging waste, waste disposal installations or the encouragement of the production of recyclable/refillable products (for instance, containers of liquid); see *ASA* (C-6/00) [2002] E.C.R. I-1961. A Directive of September 2000 on end-of-life vehicles provides for the introduction of a system for collecting such vehicles at the manufacturer's expense, Directive 00/53 [2000] O.J. L269/34. Similarly, Directive 2003/965 on waste electrical and electronic equipment (WEEE) [2002] O.J. L37/24 and restricting the use of certain dangerous substances in such equipment, Directive 2003/108 [2003] O.J. L345/106 and Directive 2008/34 [2008] O.J. L81/65.

[51] For instance, Framework Directive 67/548 [1967] O.J. L196/1 on the classification, packaging and labelling of dangerous chemical substances especially in the area of agriculture (use of pesticides and artificial fertiliser, etc.), amended for the 31st time [2009] O.J. L11/6, repealed by Regulation 1272/08 [2008] O.J. L353/1, amended [2009] O.J. L235/1; the so-called Seveso-Directive 82/501 [1982] O.J. L230/1, on the prevention of major accident hazards of chemical industrial activities trying to set up a better control mechanism concerning actions entailing potential risk; Regulation 2455/92 [1992] O.J. L251/13, establishing a prior informed consent procedure for exports and imports of substances that are already severely restricted within the Union.

[52] Green Paper, COM (2000) 87 final and COM (2000) 88 final.

measures (e.g. fines, imprisonment, etc.) to market-based incentives,[53] as well as to the above-mentioned improvement of public participation and information. An eco-audit regime allows for voluntary registration of private industrial companies in eco-management and audit schemes aiming at the improvement of the companies' environmental performance. They provide, e.g. for the introduction of environmental reviews, programmes and management systems, audits and the publication of "environmental statements", while exposing them to public scrutiny.[54]

As regards greenhouse gas emissions,[55] an allowance trading scheme was established[56]; aviation was brought within the remit of this scheme.[57] A Commission decision provided guidelines for the monitoring and reporting of greenhouse gas emissions.[58] Guidance to this end was given by Intergovernmental Panel on Climate Change (IPCC), the International Standardisation organisation (ISO), the Greenhouse Gas Protocol Initiative of the World Business Council on Sustainable Development (WBCSD) and the World Resource Institute (WRI).

In 2008, the Commission issued a series of regulations establishing minimum requirements and the conditions for mutual recognition of companies and personnel as regards items containing fluorinated greenhouse gases.[59]

The efforts of Member States to reduce their greenhouse gas emissions to meet the Union's greenhouse gas emission reduction commitments up to 2020, was the object of a decision of Parliament and the Council in 2009.[60] See also the Directive regarding the specifications of petrol, diesel and gas-oil and introducing a mechanism to monitor and reduce greenhouse gas emissions.[61]

The Seventh Annual Survey on the implementation of the Union's environmental law (some 633 acts),[62] shows serious shortcomings in the implementation. This deprives citizens of the high level of environmental protection that they expect. It shows also that Member States are late in transposing environmental directives: in 2005 the Commission issued 141 reasoned opinions[63] and brought 42 cases against Member States before the Court. The Commission also issued 21 letters of formal notice and 11 reasoned opinions for failure by a Member State to comply with a judgment of the Court.[64]

---

[53] In 1992, the proposal of a combined CO_2/energy tax failed by not reaching the necessary unanimous consent [1992] O.J. C196/1. The negotiations appear to steer toward a voluntary system of national energy tax regimes.

[54] Regulation 1836/93 [1993] O.J. L168/1; by 1997 some 700 sites had been registered which are, in return, allowed to use a logo on their correspondence papers indicating their participation in the system.

[55] See Directive 2003/87 [2003] O.J. L275/32, amended [2004] O.J. L338/18. See *Germany v Commission* (C-374/04) [2006] E.C.R. I-11673.

[56] Directive 98/70, amended [2009] O.J. L140/88.

[57] Directive 08/101 [2008] O.J. L8/3.

[58] [2004] O.J. L59/1, replaced by [2007] O.J. L229/1.

[59] [2008] O.J. L92/1–25.

[60] Decision 406/09 [2009] O.J. L140/136.

[61] Directive 2009/30 [2009] O.J. L140/88.

[62] *http://www.ec.europa.eu/en/legis/latest/chap1540.htm.*

[63] See art.258,1 TFEU [226].

[64] See art.260(2) TFEU [228(2)].

5. Civil Liability

In 1989, the proposal of a civil liability scheme for damage caused by waste calling for a system of unlimited strict liability on the waste producer,[65] was heavily criticised and eventually not further approached.[66] In 1993, the Council of Europe initiated the Lugano Convention establishing a civil liability scheme for activities dangerous to the environment[67] and the same year, the Commission published a Green Paper[68] addressing the usefulness of a general liability system. This Green Paper was followed in February 2000 by a White Paper on environmental liability, and following its publication, the need for Union action on liability for damage caused to the environment and on making good such damage has been gaining ground.[69] The paper sets out objective principles. For the principle of liability to be effective polluters must be identifiable, the damage must be quantifiable and there must be a link between the polluter and the damage. In addition, the principle of liability cannot be applied for dealing with pollution of a widespread character (climate change).

In most of the Member States, there exist laws on liability for damage caused by activities that are hazardous to the environment, but these laws only apply with respect to damage to human health or property. What is needed is an environmental liability regime which covers damage to natural resources. The White Paper contains a proposal for the main features of a Union liability regime, such as a definition of the types of liability and the possible options for Union action. In conclusion, the Commission believes that the optimum solution would be to have a framework directive, which would invoke strict liability on the part of persons performing an activity and authorise certain defences as regards traditional environmental damage, and provide for fault-based liability in the case of damage caused to biodiversity by non-hazardous activities.

Certain Member States have introduced economic incentives (taxes) for undertakings to implement strict environmental rules, but civil liability for damage caused to the environment still does not exist. The Council adopted in 2003 a framework decision concerning the protection of the environment through criminal law.[70] It defines a number of infringements to the environment and invites the Member States to provide for penal sanctions.[71] However, this Framework Decision was annulled by the Court,[72] at the request of the Commission, which was of the opinion that the decision was based on the wrong provisions.[73]

---

[65] See amended proposal [1991] O.J. C192/6; this approach was based on the preventive action and polluter pays principles and entailed provisions for a compulsory insurance by producers and disposers of waste.

[66] Mainly the industrial and insurance lobby as well as France, Germany and the United Kingdom argued that the establishment of a civil liability regime should be left to each Member State and that the subsidiarity principle did not call for Union action in this area.

[67] This Convention set up an unlimited strict, joint, several and retroactive liability scheme in which access to justice was granted to individuals and non-governmental organisations. But at the end, only eight of the 27 participants signed the document.

[68] Green Paper on remedying environmental damage, COM (93) 47 final.

[69] COM (95) 624 and COM (2000) 66 final.

[70] Framework Decision 2003/80/JAI on the protection of the environment through criminal law [2003] O.J. L 29/55.

[71] This Decision was based on arts 29, 31,e) and 34(2),b), EU Title VI, as they were drafted before Nice.

[72] *Commission v Council* (C-176/03) [2005] E.C.R. I-7879.

[73] According to the Commission the act should be based upon art.175(1) EC.

6. PROTECTION OF THE ENVIRONMENT THROUGH CRIMINAL LAW

Where criminal penalties are concerned, as a general rule, neither criminal law nor the rules of criminal procedure fall within the competence of the Union, but when the application of effective, proportional and dissuasive criminal penalties by the competent national authorities is an essential measure for combating serious environmental offences, the Community legislature might require the Member States to introduce such penalties for violation of Union environmental rules, here ship-source pollution and transport rules.[74]

Concern grew at the rise in environmental offences and their effects, which are increasingly extending beyond the borders of the States in which the offences are committed. In 2008 a directive was adopted, which provides that, among other activities, the following acts can be considered criminal offences:

- illegal disposal of radioactive substances and illegal waste management, in particular waste transport when harmful;
- illegal operation of production plants pursuing hazardous activities likely to have harmful effects;
- illegal slaughter or destruction of protected animals or plants as well as any illegal action resulting in deterioration of habitat within a protected district;
- illegal production and use of substances that deplete the ozone layer.

Addressing both natural and legal persons, the Directive also provides that the criminal penalties must be effective proportionate and dissuasive

7. EXTERNAL CO-OPERATION

Externally, the Union has become party to numerous international Conventions and related Protocols for the protection of the environment.[75] These international Treaties have without exception, the form of joint agreements between the Union and its Member States. This is due to the fact that their respective subject matters usually fall partly within the competence of the Union and partly within that of the Member States (shared competence).[76] In 2005, the European Union

---

[74] *Commission v Council* (C-176/03) [2005] E.C.R. I-7879; for an overview of the case law regarding penal sanctions, see Conclusions (34), and *Commission v Council* (C-440/05) [2007] E.C.R I-9097. .

[75] For instance, Rio de Janeiro Convention on Biological Diversity [1993] O.J. L309/1; Vienna Convention on the Protection of the Ozone Layer and the Montreal Protocol on Substances that Deplete the Ozone Layer, both in [1988] O.J. L297/8; Basel Convention on the Control of Transport of Hazardous Waste [1993] O.J. L39/1; New York Convention on Climate Change [1994] O.J. L33/11; Bonn Convention on the Conservation of Migratory Species of Wild Animals [1982] O.J. L210/10; Paris Convention for the Prevention of Marine Pollution from Land-Based Sources: [1975] O.J. L194/5.

[76] art.191(4) TFEU [174(4)]; this provision reserves, again, strong rights for the Member States to conclude international agreements individually and limits the power of the Union accordingly. However, the Treaty only refers in this respect to, "their respective fields of competence" without further specification. Therefore, future disputes over the respective limits of each side's competence cannot be excluded until clear-cut criteria for such a distinction—similar to the "Protocol on the application of the principles of subsidiarity and proportionality" added by the Treaty of Amsterdam—will be established. See in this respect Opinion 2/00 of the Court, December 6, 2001 concerning the Cartagena Protocoll 1997 on Living Modified Organisms [2001] E.C.R. I-9713; [1998] O.J. L127/11.

concluded the so-called Aarhus Convention on access to information, public participation in decision-making and access to justice in environmental matters, which aims at granting the public certain rights and imposes on parties and public authorities obligations regarding access, participation and justice. According to the Decision on the conclusion[77] of the Convention, its objective is consistent with the objectives of the Union's environmental policy listed in the Treaties.[78]

8. THE EUROPEAN ENVIRONMENTAL AGENCY[79]

The establishment of the European Environmental Agency and the European Environment Information and Observation Network[80] in 1990, created an organisational basis for an independent, objective, comparative collection, screening and evaluation network of environmental data and information. Although it is a Union Agency, Norway, Iceland and Switzerland are members and so were the 12 candidate countries before accession.[81]

9. FINANCIAL INSTRUMENTS

In 1993, the Commission set up a European Environmental Forum with general consultative functions.[82] However, the fact that about 90 per cent of Union environmental legislation is in the form of directives, means that the major problem with the environmental law of the Union resides in the too prudent and often insufficient implementation by the Member States.[83] Therefore, in 1992, a financial instrument for the environment (LIFE) was created, the main objective of which is the development and implementation of Union environmental policy by granting financial assistance.[84] Under the Financial perspectives 2007–2013, the

---

[77] [2005] O.J. L124/1.

[78] art.191 TFEU [174].

[79] See also above Ch.13: Decentralised Bodies of the Union.

[80] Regulation 1210/90 [1990] O.J. L120/1, amended [1999] O.J. L117/1. The Agency is located in Copenhagen.

[81] [2001] O.J. L213/1. See above Ch.13: Decentralised Bodies of the Union.

[82] The Forum consists of 32 members elected from the sectors of economics and of environmental protection.

[83] From the start of the environmental legislation there has been a steady increase in the number of Court actions initiated by the Commission about lack of proper implementation by the Member States, particularly in the fields of drinking water quality, environmental impact assessments and the protection of wild birds. Finally, a new legal procedure was introduced to enable the Union to exert stronger influence on each Member State's implementation activities. Now, where a Member State does not comply with a judgment of the Court, although it has been previously found in breach of Union law by not implementing appropriately directives, the Commission can propose and specify to the Court the amount of a lump sum or penalty payment to be paid by the Member State concerned: art.260 TFEU [228]. The Court may then impose such penalty. In 1997, the first two environmental cases were submitted to the Court both against Germany asking for penalty payments of €26,400 and €158,000, per day respectively (both *Commission v Germany* (C-121/97) [1997] O.J. C166/7 [1990] E.C.R. I-272).

[84] Regulation 1973/92 [1992] O.J. L206/1; its annual budget is about €100 million. See also Regulation 1655/2000 concerning the Financial Instrument for the Environment [2000] O.J. L192/1. Concerning the implementation of the LIFE programme see *Commission v Parliament and Council* (C-378/00) [2003] E.C.R. I-937. See Regulation 1682/2004 amending Regulation 1655/2000 concerning the Financial Instrument for the Environment [2004] O.J. L308/1.

budget for LIFE is €2.1 billion.[85] The new programme is divided in LIFE+ Nature and Biodiversity, LIFE+ Environment policy and governance and LIFE+ Information and communication.[86]

In 2007, Parliament and the Council adopted a Regulation on the LIFE+ financial instruments.[87] This new instrument merges a wide range of existing environmental programmes and instruments into a single mechanism and has a budget of €1.9 billion for the period 2007–2013.

In 1993, the establishment of the Cohesion Fund which was designed to finance environmental and transport infrastructure projects in Member States whose gross domestic product is less than 90 per cent of the Union average, made even more financial support available.[88] Union pre-accession aid in the environment sector to the candidate countries has been stepped up considerably since 2000, using the pre-accession structural instrument (PASI), which concerns the environment and transport. Finally, the European Investment Bank funds environmental projects that pass a prior environmental assessment procedure.

10. COMPETITION

The Commission has, among others, adopted guidelines for State aid subsidies for environmental protection.[89] For more details see above Ch.22 on Competition Policy.

Further Reading

L. Kramer *EC Environmental Law*, 5th edn (Sweet & Maxwell, London, 2003).
Marco Onida "Europe and the Environment", *Legal Essays in honour of Ludwig Kramer*, (Europa Law Publishing, 2004).
Nerle Dhondt, *Integration of Environmental Protection into other EC policies*, (Europa Law Publishing, 2003).

---

[85] In 2008 the Commission approved funding of €186 million for 143 new projects.
[86] IP/06/856. See Regulation 614/07 concerning LIFE+ [2007] O.J. L149/1.
[87] Regulation 614/07 [2007] O.J. L149/1.
[88] Regulation 1164/94 [1994] O.J. L130/1 and Regulation 16/2003 [2003], rules concerning eligibility; its budget for the period of 1993 to 1999 contains €15.15 billion. Currently, only Greece, Ireland, Portugal and Spain are eligible for financial assistance. Union pre-accession aid in the environment sector has been increased substantially since 2000, using pre-accession structural instruments such as PASI which relates to environment and transport [2000] O.J. L72/21.
[89] [2008] O.J. C82/1.

Chapter Thirty-five

Energy Policy

There was no Title on "Energy" in the EC Treaty, neither after nor before the modifications introduced by the EU Treaty and the Treaties of Amsterdam and Nice.[1] However, a Chapter with a single article was introduced by the Treaty of Lisbon.[2] As is well known, coal, previously the main source of energy, has been the object of Union measures since 1952 under the now extinct European Community for Coal and Steal Treaty and the development of nuclear energy is the objective of Euratom since 1958, but a concerted effort in the energy field is required, especially now, from the Member States and the Union, as much as in the areas of agriculture, transport or commercial policy.

Notwithstanding the above-mentioned absence of Treaty provisions concerning an energy policy, the Union has developed over the years and is still expanding and implementing, in close co-operation with the Member States, a Union energy policy. This, however, raises the question of the competence of the Union to do so, since, as has been explained several times in the foregoing pages, the Union may only exercise those powers which have been explicitly conferred upon it. As shall be seen, the institutions adopted directives, regulations and decisions in the energy field and it is interesting to examine at the onset what empowered the Union to do so.

A typical example is the Directive of Parliament and the Council concerning common rules for the internal market in electricity.[3] The institutions indicate, as legal bases for their acts, in the first place, the Treaty provisions concerning the right of establishment, among them, the obligation of the Council to, "issue directives for the co-ordination of provisions laid down by law, regulation or administrative action in the Member States concerning the taking-up and pursuit of activities as self-employed persons".[4] Secondly they indicate the Treaty provisions concerning the freedom to provide services,[5] and, thirdly, the Treaty provisions concerning the harmonisation measures necessary for the establishment and functioning of the internal market.[6] Although an energy policy as such was not, as mentioned, provided for in the Treaties, the references to the above-mentioned provisions are ample justification for the Union to act in this domain.[7]

---

[1] This might explain why, until the end of 2008, there was no Energy Directorate-General at the Commission.

[2] art.194 TFEU.

[3] Directive 96/92 [1997] O.J. L27/20, replaced by Directive 2003/54 [2003] O.J. L176/37, repealed by Directive 2009/72 [2009] O.J. L211/55, see *Citiworks A.G.* (C-439/06) [2008] E.C.R. I-3913 interpreting art.20(1) Directive 2003/54.

[4] art.53(1) TFEU [47(1)].

[5] art.62 TFEU [55] which refers back to several provisions concerning the right of establishment, including the above-mentioned art.53(2) TFEU [47(2)].

[6] art.114(1) TFEU [95(1)].

[7] The absence of an explicit reference to Energy in the Treaty has nothing to do with the Commission's Communication to the Parliament and the Council concerning the repeal of several Union legislative texts in the field of energy policy [1996] O.J. C221/3.

In December 1998, the Council adopted a multi-annual framework pro-gramme for actions in the energy sector (1998–2002) and connected measures. This programme was primarily to contribute to the balanced pursuit of security of supply, competitiveness and protection of the environment. The Council also adopted a multi-annual programme of studies, analyses, forecasts and other related work in the energy sector (1998–2002).[8] This multi-annual programme was followed by another one referred to as "Intelligent Energy-Europe" (2003–2006).[9] As a first step the Commission had to define, in consultation with the Programme Committee, the priority areas, the criteria for selection of proj-ects, the funding arrangements, etc. The Commission then launched a call for proposals and a call for tenders. The "Intelligent Energy Europe II" programme (IEE II) was launched in 2007 together with the work programme for implement-ing it[10]; it now forms an integral part of the competitiveness and innovation framework programme.[11] In association with this programme, the Commission established the Executive Agency for Competitiveness and Innovation, with responsibility, in particular, for implementing IEE II.[12]

According to the Commission,[13] the overall objective of the Union's energy policy is to provide Europe with competitive and sustainable energy, the main thrust of which are the fight against climate change, boosting competitiveness with a regulatory framework conducive to it and limiting the Europeans Union's dependence on gas and oil imports.[14]

At the European Council of March 2007, the foundations for a European energy policy, including commitments, binding targets and procedures were adopted:

- with regard to climate change, an independent commitment by the Union to reduce greenhouse gas emissions by at least 20 per cent by 2020 compared with 1990, and a commitment to a 30 per cent reduction if other developed countries undertake to make comparable emissions reductions;
- as regards the single market for gas and electricity, effective separation of supply and production activities from network operations (unbundling);
- as regards renewable energies, the binding target of 20 per cent by 2020 with a minimum share of bio-fuels of 10 per cent of overall petrol and diesel con-sumption in the Union.

In order to be able to implement its energy policy, the Union pursues different objectives—see below.

1. SECURITY OF ENERGY SUPPLY AND INTERNATIONAL CO-OPERATION

Besides the obligation imposed on the Member States to maintain minimum stocks of crude oil and/or petroleum products,[15] this includes the development of relations

[8] [1999] O.J. L7/16 and 20; the Decision were based upon art.352 TFEU [308] and art.203.
[9] [2003] O.J. L176/29; it entered into force on August 4, 2003.
[10] General Report 2007, 85.
[11] See below, Ch.31: Enterprise and Industrial Policy/Information Society.
[12] Decision 2007/372 [2007] O.J. L140/52 amending Decision 2004/20 in order to transform the Intelligent Energy Executive Agency into this new agency. See above, Ch.13: Decentralised Bodies of the Union.
[13] See *http://www.europa.eu.int/comm/dgs/energy-transport/index-en.html*, on which much of this chapter is based and from which some parts are reproduced here.
[14] Communication "An energy policy for Europe" [2007] O.J. C138/14.
[15] Directive 2006/67 [2006] O.J. L217/8.

with the supplier countries through bilateral and multilateral agreements such as the Energy Charter. The Energy Charter Treaty[16] was adopted in 1997 and is designed to develop new relations between the main European countries and most of the independent States of the former Soviet Union and Central and Eastern Europe, Canada, the USA and Japan, covering trade, investment and energy co-operation. The main aim is to meet the challenge of developing the energy potential of the independent States of the former Soviet Union and Eastern Europe while helping to improve security of supply for the European Union.[17] Another aspect of those relations is the external interconnection of Trans-European Networks.[18] A series of guidelines for Trans-European Energy Networks were laid down by Parliament and the Council[19]; the latter also laid down general rules for the granting of Union financial aid,[20] and the Commission set out the specifications for projects of common interest identified in respect of those networks.[21] The actions also aim at the more efficient use of existing resources; a multi-annual programme was set up to promote energy efficiency in the Union (SAVE II),[22] the diversification of energy resources through the promotion of new energy sources,[23] the use of renewable sources[24] (hydroelectric, solar, wind, geothermal and bio-fuels), and the implementation of provisions concerning the supply of nuclear materials and safeguard measures.[25]

Other actions focus on energy demand, which include the promotion of energy saving and the development of a culture of energy-saving behaviour and rational energy consumption. A directive was adopted on end-use efficiency and energy services.[26]

International Co-operation[27]

In December 1998, the Council adopted a multi-annual programme to promote international co-operation in the energy sector (1998–2002).[28] These include actions in the context of general technical assistance programmes: PHARE, TACIS[29] and MEDA.[30] These programmes finance international co-operation

[16] See also the Decision with regard to the ECT, the Energy Charter Protocol on energy efficiency and related environmental aspects, and the amendments to the ECT [1998] O.J. L252/21, amended [2001] O.J. L209/32.

[17] [1997] Bull. 9, 26.

[18] arts 170 and 171 TFEU [154 and 155]. See above Ch.31: Enterprise and Industrial Policy/Information Society, and the Communication from the Commission to Parliament and Council: "The external dimension of Trans-European Networks" COM(97) 125.

[19] [1996] O.J. L161/147, amended [1999] O.J. L207/1.

[20] [1995] O.J. L228/1, amended several times.

[21] [2000] O.J. L305/1.

[22] Decision 647/2000 of Parliament and the Council adopting a multi-annual programme for the promotion of energy efficiency (SAVE) 1998–2002.

[23] See, for instance, Communication from the Commission on a Union strategy to promote combined heat and power (CHP) and to dismantle barriers to its development COM(97) 514 final.

[24] See the White Paper on energy for the future: renewable sources of energy COM(97) 599 final.

[25] See Communication from the Commission on the nuclear industries in the EU COM(97) 401 final.

[26] Directive 2006/32 [2006] O.J. L114/64.

[27] See General Report 2008, 90.

[28] [1999] O.J. L7/23.

[29] See Decision adopting a multi-annual programme (1998–2002) of actions in the nuclear sector, relating to the safe transport of radioactive materials and safeguards and industrial co-operation to promote certain aspects of the safety of nuclear installations in the countries currently participating in the TACIS programme [1999] O.J. L7/31.

[30] Regulation 701/97 amending a programme to promote international co-operation in the energy sector—Synergy programme [1997] O.J. L104/1.

projects with third countries for developing, formulating and implementing their energy policy in fields of mutual interest. Those projects have to contribute to accomplishing the objectives defined in the Commission's White Paper on "An energy policy for the European Union". In 2004 the Council adopted a directive concerning measures to safeguard security of natural gas supply.[31] Also included are actions for the preparation of the accession of new States, co-operation with international organisations—IEA, IAEA, OECD, ERBD—and the World Bank, and the definition of crisis-management measures to be implemented for each type of energy source, if needed. In 2006 the Union concluded an Energy Community Treaty with the view of establishing an Integrated Energy Market Organisation in South-East Europe.[32]

2. INTEGRATING ENERGY MARKETS

The main objective of this action is the completion of the Internal Energy Market, especially in the fields of electricity and gas. A directive was adopted by Parliament and the Council in 2009 concerning common rules for the internal market in electricity.[33] It concerns electrical energy, electricity supply, energy production, energy transport and the internal market. These institutions also adopted a regulation on conditions for access to the network for cross-border exchanges of electricity[34] and a decision laying down a series of guidelines for Trans-European Energy Networks.[35] During the same year, a directive was adopted regarding natural gas,[36] followed by a regulation on the conditions of access to the gas transport network.[37]

To clarify this legislation, the Commission published "interpretative notes" on various subjects such as "unbundling", "public service obligations", "distribution", "labelling", "gas storage", etc.[38] In order to consolidate the internal energy market, the Commission established the European Regulators Group for Electricity and Gas; it shall facilitate consultation, co-ordination and co-operation of national regulatory authorities contributing to a consistent application of the above-mentioned provisions.[39] The Court reinforced the legislative framework by stipulating that existing long-term contracts could not deprive newcomers from access to existing facilities.[40] Other actions include the implementation of competition rules, including State aids,[41] the establishment of networks for the transport of energy throughout Europe,[42] taxation of energy

---

[31] [2004] O.J. L127/92.

[32] [2006] O.J. L198/15.

[33] Directive 2009/72 [2009] O.J. L176/37 concerning common rules for the internal market in electricity, repealed by Directive 2009/72 [2009] O.J. L211/55.

[34] Regulation 1228/03 [2003] O.J. L176/1 repealed by Regulation 714/09 [2009] O.J. L211/15.

[35] Decision 1229/03 [2003] O.J. L176/11.

[36] Directive 2003/55 [2003] O.J. L176/57, repealed by Directive 2009/73 [2009]O.J. L211/94.

[37] Regulation 1775/05 [2005] O.J. L289/1, repealed [2009] O.J. L229/29. See Regulation 715/09 [2009] O.J. L211/36, corrigendum [2009] O.J. L229/29.

[38] These notes can be found *http://www.europa.eu.int/comm./energy/electricity/legislation/notes-for-implementation-en.htm.*

[39] Decision 2003/796 [2003] O.J. L296/34.

[40] *VEMV* (C-17/03) [2005] E.C.R. I-49831.

[41] See, for instance, Decision 3632/93 establishing Union rules for State aids to the coal industry [1993] O.J. L329/12.

[42] See, for instance, Directive 91/296 on the transit of natural gas through grids [1991] O.J. L147/37.

products[43] and the promotion of standards for energy products. Those actions are closely linked with Union action in the field of regional policy.[44] The Commission sent a communication on energy and social and economic cohesion in the Union to the other institutions[45] and contributions for energy are provided for in the Structural Funds. Energy investments are also financed by the TENs, the EIB, the ECSC (until July 23, 2002) and Euratom aids and loans. The 2003 Directives had to be transposed by July 1, 2004 and since not all Member States had complied with this obligation, several court actions were introduced by the Commission. The Directives provide also for an annual report on the implementation of the Directives; according to the 2008 report, despite some encouraging improvements, especially with respect to the development of best practice solutions on a regional level, the overall analysis of progress shows that major barriers to the efficient functioning of the internal market still exist.[46] At the end of 2007, the Commission had to sound the alarm on the state of the internal gas and electricity market[47]: the final report on the sectoral inquiry on competition[48] demonstrated that numerous restrictions on free competition, and, in particular, obstacles to infrastructure access, lack of investment in interconnections[49] and excessive market concentration, have not yet allowed a truly competitive gas and electricity market to be created.

3. Promoting Energy Technology Development

This is carried out in the context of the Research, Development and Demonstration programme, JOULE-THERMIE,[50] and Euratom programmes. In 2008 the Council set out fundamental principles, objectives and actions for a European policy on energy technology; it should improve synergies at Union level and take account of existing structures for co-operation on research, development, demonstration and development in the field of energy technology; the private sector must be fully involved.[51] See also the European strategic energy technology (SET).[52]

A programme to aid economic recovery by granting Union financial assistance to projects in the field of energy was adopted in 2009.[53]

4. Sectoral Aspects

Coal was within the ambit of the European Coal and Steel Community that ceased to exist, as mentioned, on July 23, 2003 since it was concluded for a

---

[43] In October 2003 the Council adopted a directive concerning taxation of energy and electricity; it extends to all the energy products, including coal and natural gas, the minimum tax rates, thereby reducing competition between various energy sources.

[44] See above, Ch.32: Regional Policy/ Economic, Social and Territorial Cohesion.

[45] COM (93) 645 final.

[46] General Report 2008, 89.

[47] [2007] O.J. C138/14.

[48] [2007] O.J. C138/14.

[49] As regards interconnections see Communication "Priority interconnection plan".

[50] A non-nuclear research, development and research programme designed to encourage the development of new, economically viable and environmental safe energy options.

[51] General Report 2008, 89.

[52] COM (2007) 723.

[53] [2009] O.J. L200/31.

period of 50 years from its entry into force,[54] i.e. July 23, 1952. From 2003 on, coal is considered as a "good" in the sense of the EC Treaty, and subject to its rules; it now comes under the TFEU. The main problem with this solid fuel is the uneconomical extraction conditions prevailing in all the Member States.[55] Coal mines are still maintained in operation in four Member States: Germany, France, Spain and the UK. State aid to coal was governed by an ECSC Decision[56] until the expiry of that Treaty. On that day the Council adopted a regulation[57] providing for minimum coal production, which will help maintain an indigenous primary energy source. In December 1998, the Council adopted a multi-annual programme of technological actions promoting the clean and efficient use of solid fuels (1998–2002).[58] After the expiry of the ECSC Treaty, the Union activities in this field were, as indicated, taken over by the EC Treaty.[59]

In a 2007 communication the Commission stressed that the future use of coal must be made compatible with sustainable objectives and climate-change policy.[60]

Oil and petroleum products are, as mentioned, mainly imported from third countries; consequently, the Union attaches great importance to prospecting, exploration and production within the Union itself.[61]

As for *natural gas*, which is also produced in limited quantities within the Union, the Union has established conditions for access to the natural gas transmission networks[62] and common rules for the internal market in gas,[63] which are similar to those for electricity.

The common rules for *electricity* entered into force in February 1997.[64] They are based on a balanced approach to public service obligations and competition rules and on the broad application of the subsidiarity principle, in order to take account of the different gas and electricity systems existing in the Member States. They provide for the opening-up of the market over a period of 10 years.[65]

Nuclear energy is submitted to the rules of the Euratom Treaty, which shows great similarities with the EC Treaty and now the TFEU. One of the main particularities consists of the fact that nuclear fissile materials are the property of the Union. This property right is exercised, among others, by the right of option of Euratom's Supply Agency on all fissile material.[66] Furthermore, all operations concerning nuclear material must be handled by said Agency. The latter will be examined hereafter. Another important aspect is the necessity to safeguard the use of the fissile material for non-military purposes, when they have been declared to be destined for peaceful purposes.[67] Bilateral agreements exist with

---

[54] art.97 ECSC.

[55] Coal imported from Australia is cheaper on arrival in Rotterdam than European coal.

[56] Decision 3632/93/ECSC [1993] O.J. L205/1 and Regulation 1047/02 [2002] O.J. L329/12.

[57] Report on Competition 2002/474.

[58] [1999] O.J. L7/28.

[59] See, for instance, Regulation 1047/02 on aid to the coal industry [2002] O.J. L329/12.

[60] [2007] O.J. C138/14.

[61] See Directive 94/22 on the conditions for granting and using authorisations for the prospection, exploration and production of hydrocarbons [1994] O.J. L164/3.

[62] Regulation 1775/2005: [2005] O.J. L289/1, replaced [2009] O.J. L211/36.

[63] Directive 2003/55 [2003] O.J. L76/57, repealed [2009] O.J. L211/94.

[64] [1997] O.J. L27/20.

[65] See, for instance, Directive 2003/54 concerning common rules for the internal market in electricity [2003] O.J. L176/37. For third-party access to the transmission and distribution systems see *Sabatauskas A.O.* (C-239/07) [2008] E.C.R. I-7523.

[66] See *ENU v Commission* (Joined Cases T-458/93 and T-523/93 [1995] E.C.R. II-2459.

[67] See the Agreement for co-operation in the peaceful use of nuclear energy between Euratom and the US [1996] O.J. L120/1.

Australia, Canada and the United States; supply agreements were also signed with Uzbekistan (2004), Kazakhstan, Ukraine, Japan (2006) and Russia (2007).

Renewable Energy

Renewable sources of energy—wind power, solar power (thermal and photo-voltaic), hydroelectric power, tidal power, geothermal energy and biomass—are an essential alternative to fossil fuels. See Commission Communication "Renewable energy in the 21st century: building a more sustainable future".[68] In it the Commission proposed establishing a legal binding target of 20 per cent for renewable energy's share of energy consumption in the Union by 2020, and a new legislative framework for the promotion and use of renewable energy in the Union. A Directive establishing National Renewable Energy Action Plans was adopted in 2009.[69]

A specific programme was put in place: ALTENER. The development concerns energy from wind, water, solar power and biomass. Renewable energy has indeed an important role to play in reducing carbon dioxide; it enhances sustainability and helps to improve the security of energy supply by reducing the Union's growing dependence on imported energy sources. It is expected to become competitive with conventional energy in the medium- to long-term. It is, by definition local, and therefore can create new business, bring employment and encourage economic and social cohesion in regions that otherwise lack industrial development. ALTENER II applied until December 2002. It was replaced by the ALTENER programme for which a budget of €77 million is provided.

5. Nuclear Energy—Euratom's Supply Agency and Safeguards

Nuclear power stations currently produce around a third of the electricity and 15 per cent of the energy consumed in the Union. The sector represents a source of energy with low carbon levels and relatively stable costs, which makes it attractive from the point of view of security of supply and fighting climate change. It is up to each Member State, however, to decide whether or not to pursue the option of nuclear power.[70]

The main function of Euratom consists in furthering co-operation in the field of research, protecting the public by establishing common safety standards, ensuring an adequate and equitable supply of ores and nuclear fuel, monitoring the peaceful use of nuclear material, and co-operating with other countries and international organisations.[71]

The property of all special fissionable material within the territory of the Member States is, as indicated, vested in the Union,[72] in so far as this material is subject to Euratom's safeguard control. The latter does not extend to materials "intended to meet defence requirements".[73] The Treaty provides for the creation

---

[68] [2007] O.J. C.138/14.
[69] [2009] O.J. L140/16 and Commission Decision establishing a template for it [2009] O.J. L182/33.
[70] Taken from EUROPA > Summaries of EU legislation > Energy > Nuclear energy.
[71] Taken from EUROPA. See there for further information on Euratom.
[72] art.86 Euratom.
[73] art.85 Euratom.

of a Supply Agency[74] having a right of option on all ores, source materials and special fissile materials produced in the territories of the Member States. It also has the exclusive right to conclude contracts relating to the supply of ores, source material and special fissile materials coming from inside or outside the Union.[75] New Statutes of the Agency were laid down by the Council in 2008[76] and various regulations have specified the conditions under which nuclear materials can be acquired, sold or transferred.[77] Currently, the supply of natural uranium, special fissile material and enrichment services to Union users and the provisions of services for the whole fuel cycle do not present any problems.[78] The Union depends on imports for some 94 per cent of its supplies of natural uranium.[79] Canada (18.15 per cent), Russia (24.65 per cent), Niger (16.92 per cent) and Australia (15.38 per cent) are the main suppliers of nuclear materials to the Union.[80]

The Council decided to support the creation of a nuclear fuel bank under the control of the International Atomic Energy Agency (IAEA). The Union contributes €25 million to this project. It is part of a wider effort aimed at establishing multilateral fuel supply mechanisms.[81]

In this context must also be mentioned the Euratom safeguards. In pursuance of the Euratom Treaty:

"[T]he Commission must satisfy itself that, in the territories of the Member States, ores, source materials and special fissile materials are not diverted from their intended uses as declared by the users, and that the provisions relating to supply and any particular safeguarding obligation assumed by the Union, under an agreement concluded with a third State or an international organisation, are complied with".[82]

To fulfil those obligations, the Commission must carry out inspections and its inspectors have access to all places and data and all persons who, by reason of their occupation, deal with materials, equipment or installations which are subject to the Euratom safeguards. If serious irregularities are discovered, the Commission imposes sanctions.[83]

---

[74] art.52(2)(b) Euratom.

[75] art.52(2)(b) Euratom. In 2007, e.g. the Agency concluded or was notified of, 58 contracts for natural uranium and 18 for special fissile material (Euratom Supply Agency, 2007 Report). See *Commission v France* (7/71) [1971] E.C.R. 1003; [1972] C.M.L.R. 453. See also *Kernkraftwerke Lippe-Ems v Commission* (C-161/97 P) [1999] E.C.R. I-2057, concerning, among other things, the conclusion of contracts and the powers of the Agency to refuse to do so.

[76] [2008] O.J. L41/15.

[77] See J.O. 777/60 [1959–1962] (manner in which demand is to be balanced against supply); J.O. 4057/66 (implementation of supply provisions) and J.O. 1460/60 and 240/64 (communications of the Agency). For the Rules of the Agency see [160] O.J. No. 60 and [1975] O.J. L 123/37.

[78] Directive 2003/55 concerning common rules for the internal market in natural gas [2003] O.J. L76/57, corrigendum [2004] O.J. L16/74.

[79] Directive 2003/55, above, fn. 78.

[80] Euratom Supply Agency 2007 Annual Report.

[81] General Report 2008, 89.

[82] art.77 Euratom.

[83] See General Report 1992, 236. See also Decision 99/25, Euratom adopting a multi-annual programme (1998–2002) of actions in the nuclear sector, relating to the safe transport of radioactive materials and to safeguards and industry co-operation to promote certain aspects of safety of nuclear installations in the countries currently participating in the TACIS programme [1999] O.J. L7/31. See Bull. 12, 2003, 1.4.73: report on safeguards.

As far as the International Atomic Energy Agency (IAEA) is concerned, joint IAEA-Euratom safeguards are applied in certain Union installations in compliance with the Verification Agreement in force since 1973.[84] Safeguard provisions are an essential element in all the agreements which the Union has concluded with third-world countries.[85]

6. NUCLEAR SAFETY

Various international conventions concern nuclear safety. The Council authorised the Member States, which are contracting parties to the 1960 Paris Convention on Third Party Liability in the field of Nuclear Energy, to ratify, in the interest of the Union, a Protocol amending that Convention, or to accede to it.[86] The Council also called on the Member States to accede to the 1994 Vienna Convention on Nuclear Safety and the Joint Convention on the Safety of Spent Fuel Management and on the Safety of Radioactive Waste Management. The Council has also approved the 1986 Convention on Early Notification of a Nuclear Accident and on Assistance in the Case of Nuclear Accident or Radiological Emergency.[87]

Further Reading

Christiane Trüe, "Legislative competences of the European Community in the energy sector: the 'Nuclear Package' of the Commission", (2003) E.L.Rev. 664.
Christopher W, "EU Energy Law in Europe", in Vol.2, *EU Competition law and Energy markets* (Jones-Claeys & Casteels, 2005).
Martha M. Roggenkamp, Catherine Redgwell, Inigo del Guayo and Anita Ronne, *Energy Law in Europe* (Oxford University Press, 2007).

---

[84] See amendment to Council Declaration attached to the Decision approving the accession to the Vienna Convention, following a Court's ruling: *Commission v Council* (C-29/99) [2002] E.C.R. I–11221.
[85] Decision approving the accession to the Vienna Convention following *Commission v Council* (C-29/99) above, fn. 84. See also General Report 2003, 659.
[86] [2004] O.J. L97/53.
[87] General Report 2004, 176.

PART SIX: EXTERNAL ACTION BY THE UNION, THE COMMON FOREIGN AND SECURITY POLICY AND ENLARGEMENT

INTRODUCTION

Contrary to the old EU and EC Treaties, both the actual Treaty on European Union and the TFEU contain extensive and co-ordinated provisions concerning the external activities of the Union. While the EU Treaty provides for general provisions concerning this action[1] and specific provisions on the Common Foreign and Security Policy (CFSP),[2] the TFEU[3] contains a new Part V "External action by the Union" consisting of:

- "General provisions",
- "Common Commercial Policy",[4] and
- "Co-operation with third Countries and Humanitarian Aid", this last Title, furthermore, encompasses:
  - "Development Co-operation",[5]
  - "Economic, Financial and Technical Co-operation with Third Countries",[6]
  - "Humanitarian Aid",[7]
  - "Restrictive Measures",[8]
  - "International Agreements",[9]
  - "The Union's Relations with International Organisations and Third Countries and Union's Delegations"[10] and
  - "Solidarity Clause".[11]

From these various provisions of the EU Treaty and the TFEU it follows that a distinction must be made between the Union's "common foreign policy", which covers, "all areas of foreign policy"[12] and the Union's "external action" which refers to a series of specific activities. Both must, "be guided by the principles, pursue the objectives and be conducted in accordance with the general provisions laid down"[13] in the Treaty on European Union.[14]

---

[1] arts 21 and 22 EU.
[2] arts 23 to 46 EU.
[3] arts 205 to 222 TFEU.
[4] arts 206 and 207 TFEU. See below, Ch.38.
[5] arts 208 to 211 TFEU. See below Ch.39.
[6] arts 212 and 213 TFEU.
[7] art.214 TFEU.
[8] art.215 TFEU.
[9] arts 216 to 219 TFEU.
[10] arts 220 and 221 TFEU.
[11] art.222 TFEU.
[12] art.24(1) EU.
[13] Both art.23 EU and art.205 TFEU contain exactly the same text.
[14] EU Ch.I, Title V, arts 21 and 22.

All these provisions will be briefly examined hereafter, together with the Union's "Neighbouring Policy", however, not necessarily in the order they are mentioned above: the Common Foreign and Security Policy, the Common Commercial Policy and Development Co-operation are examined separately, respectively in Chs 37, 38 and 39. Enlargement will be examined in the last chapter of this book.

Chapter Thirty-six

General Provisions Concerning the Union's External Action[1]

The EU Treaty provides, under the Title "General provisions on the Union's external action" that:

"[T]he Union's action on the international scene, shall be guided by the principles which have inspired its own creation, development and enlargement, and which it seeks to advance in the wider world: democracy, the rule of law, the universality and indivisibility of human rights and fundamental freedoms, respect for human dignity, the principle of equality and solidarity, and respect for the principles of the United Nations Charter and international law."[2]

The Union must seek to develop relations and build partnerships with third countries and international, regional and global organisations which share the above principles.[3]

As will appear, the means provided to achieve those lofty objectives do not seem to be sufficient; this is probably due to the opposition from those Member States which resent any encroachment on their so-called national sovereignty, of which foreign affairs and defence are symbols. Nonetheless, over the years, the external competences of the Union were enlarged in several ways; first, by the simple fact that its internal competences were increased and these constitute the basis for external action,[4] and secondly, by the inclusion in the former EC Treaty of a new external policy: "Development Co-operation"[5] and finally, by the addition to the EU Treaty of "Provisions on a Common Foreign and Security Policy".[6] With regard to the competences of the Union that existed previously under the EC Treaty, except for the provisions concerning the conclusion of international agreements,[7] not much was changed however, and the CFSP remained under different institutional arrangements.

The Union must define and pursue common policies and actions and work to a high degree of co-operation in all fields of international relations, in order to:

1. safeguard its values, fundamental interests, security, independence and integrity;

---

[1] arts 21 and 22 EU.
[2] art.21(1)1 EU.
[3] art.21(1)2 EU.
[4] As pointed out at the beginning of this book, the Union's competences were enlarged with Education, Culture, Public Health, Consumer Protection, Trans-European Networks, etc. Another example is the possibility for the Union to conclude agreements concerning monetary and foreign exchange regime matters, art.219(3) TFEU [111(3)].
[5] arts 208–211 TFEU [177 to 181].
[6] art.24 EU [11].
[7] art.218 TFEU [300].

2. consolidate and support democracy, the rule of law, human rights and the principles of international law;
3. preserve peace, prevent conflicts and strengthen international security, in accordance with the purposes and principles of the United Nations Charter, with the principles of the Helsinki Final Act and with the aims of the Charter of Paris, including those relating to external borders;
4. foster the sustainable economic, social and environmental development of developing countries with the primary aim of eradicating poverty[8];
5. encourage the integration of all countries into the world economy, including the progressive abolition of restrictions on international trade;
6. help develop international measures to preserve and improve the quality of the environment and the management of natural resources;
7. assist populations, countries and regions confronting natural or man-made disasters[9];
8. promote an international system based on stronger multilateral co-operation and global governance.[10]

The Council and the Commission, assisted by the High Representative of the Union for Foreign Affairs and Security Policy ("High Representative"), must ensure consistency between the different areas of the Union's external action and between these and its other policies.

It is the task of the European Council to identify the strategic interests and objectives of the Union; its decisions may concern relations with a specific country or region or may be thematic in approach. They must define their duration, and the means to be made available by the Union and the Member States. The European Council must act unanimously on a recommendation from the Council or joint proposals from the High Representative and the Commission.[11]

One should realise that the absence, in the former EC Treaty, of provisions conferring upon the "Community", as it was then called, a general competence with regard to foreign policy, has not prevented it from developing a particularly active one. This was made possible, as will be seen, with the help of the Court. According to the latter the Union is a body created by an international treaty concluded between sovereign States with the task, among others, of exercising activities in the international field. This body enjoys international legal personality and participates in activities which come within the ambit of international law.[12]

However, it is only to the extent that other subjects of international law recognise the Union as a member of the international community, that it can take initiatives and play an active role in the international sphere. This recognition was never a problem. It was rather, among the Member States, that some disagreement existed as to the extent of the Union's jurisdiction in international affairs. The question was raised mainly with regard to the Union's treaty-making power; in other words, how much of the Member States' treaty-making power was transferred to the Union? That some powers were transferred was not questioned, but it was not clear whether those powers were to be exercised exclusively by the Union or in conjunction with the Member States. As far as the first question is concerned, the views of the Court

---

[8] See below, Ch.39: Development Co-operation.
[9] See below, Ch.39: Development Co-operation (II. Humanitarian Aid).
[10] art.21(2) EU.
[11] art.22 EU.
[12] *Commission v Council* (22/70), [1971] E.C.R. 263.

were clearly formulated in 1971[13] and repeated in later judgments. They were based on the former EC Treaty that provides that, "the Community shall have legal personality".[14] According to the Court, this provision, placed at the head of Part Six of the Treaty devoted to "General and Final Provisions", means that in its external relations, the Union enjoys the capacity to enter into international commitments over the whole field of objectives defined in Part One of the Treaty, which Part Six supplements. The following statement is also important:

> "[T]o establish in a particular case whether the [Union] has authority to enter into international commitments, regard must be had to the whole scheme of [Union] law no less than to its substantive provisions. Such authority arises not only from express conferment by the Treaty but may equally flow implicitly from other provisions of the Treaty, from the Act of accession and from measures adopted within the framework of those provisions, by the [Union] institutions."[15]

In other words, whenever Union law has created powers for the institutions, within the internal system, for the purpose of attaining a specific objective, the Union has authority to enter into the international commitments necessary for the attainment of that objective, even in the absence of an express provision in that connection.[16] This is particularly so in all cases where internal power has already been used by the Union institutions in order to adopt measures which come within the attainment of common policies.[17]

With regard to the second question (exclusive or shared jurisdiction) the Court admits a "mixed procedure", i.e. both the Union and the Member States are the contracting parties when an agreement covers matters for which the Union is competent and others coming within the ambit of the Member States.[18] However:

> "[E]ach time the [Union], with a view to implementing a common policy envisaged by the Treaty, adopts provisions laying down common rule, whatever form these may take, the Member States no longer have the right, acting individually

---

[13] *Commission v Council* (better known as the *AETR* case: Accord Européen de Transport (European Transport Agreement)) (22/70) [1971] E.C.R. 263 at 274(14); [1971] C.M.L.R. 335. See also the Opinions of the Court given under former art.300(6) EC (now 218(11)): Opinion 1/75 [1975] E.C.R. 1355, compatibility with the EEC Treaty of a draft "Understanding on a Local Cost Standard" drawn up under the auspices of the OECD; Opinion 1/76 [1977] E.C.R. 741, compatibility of a draft agreement establishing a European lying-up Fund for inland waterway vessels; Opinion 1/78 [1979] E.C.R. 2871 compatibility of the draft International Agreement on Natural Rubber negotiated in the UNCTAD; *Commission v Council* (C-25/94) [1996] E.C.R. I-1469; *Kramer* (Joined Cases 3/76, 4/76 and 6/76) [1976] E.C.R. 1279; [1976] 2 C.M.L.R. 440; Opinion 2/91, [1993] E.C.R. I-1061; [1993] 3 C.M.L.R. 800 concerning the compatibility of the ILO Convention 170 on safety in the use of chemicals at work; and Opinion 1/94, [1994] E.C.R. I-5267.

[14] Former art.281 EC.

[15] *Commission v Council* (22/70) (quoted above, fn.27) at 274 (17–18). In its Opinion of 2/91 the Court expressed it as follows: "Whenever [Union] law created for the institutions of the [Union] powers within its internal system for the purpose of attaining a specific objective, the [Union] has authority to enter into the international commitments necessary for the attainment of that objective even in the absence of an express provision in that connection."

[16] Opinion 1/76: Lying-up Fund (quoted above, fn.27), at 755.

[17] Opinion 1/76: Lying-up Fund, above, fn.27.

[18] Opinion 1/76: Lying-up Fund, above, fn.27 at 756(7). In Opinion 2/91 (quoted above, fn.27) the Court came to the conclusion that the ILO Convention 170 is a matter which falls within the joint competence of the Member States and the Union. As the Court mentioned in its Opinion 3/94 [1995] E.C.R. I-4577, with regard to the Uruguay Round multilateral negotiations, the Council adopted Decision 94/800 concerning the conclusion, on behalf of the European Union, "as regards matters within its competence". The other matters were adopted by the Member States.

or even collectively, to undertake obligations with third countries which affect those rules".[19]

However, as long as the Union has not exercised its right to conclude agreements, the Member States retain the power to do so.[20] Nonetheless, this authority is only of a transitional nature and Member States are bound by Union obligations in their negotiations with third countries: they may not enter into or renew any commitment which could hinder the Union in the carrying out of the tasks entrusted to it by the Treaties.[21]

The emergence of a Union competence should not, however, be seen as a sudden break; Union law being "evolutive", the transfer of power from the Member States to the Union is necessarily gradual.[22] There is also the question of the consequences for the Union and Union law of collective international commitments undertaken by the Member States before the establishment of the Union. Here the Court has, through various judgments, formulated the basic principles. For instance, with regard to tariffs and trade policy the Member States have progressively transferred to the Union their jurisdiction. By doing so they have also conferred upon the Union the international rights and obligations connected with the exercise of this jurisdiction, particularly with regard to the General Agreement on Tariffs and Trade (GATT), now World Trade Organisation (WTO). It follows that the Union itself is bound by that agreement.[23] This constitutes a clear case of substitution of the Union for the Member States in the implementation of multilateral treaties bearing on the subject matter of the Treaty.

As for the rights which derive for the Union from those agreements, their exercise depends on recognition of the Union by the other contracting parties; as mentioned, this was never a problem. The internal problems of the Union in this field may not, of course, obliterate the interests of third countries. In the various Court statements referred to above, this principle was underlined several times.[24] However, third States may not intervene in internal matters of the Union and, more particularly, in the determination of the very complex and delicate relationship between the Union and its own Member States.[25]

---

[19] *AETR* (22/70) (quoted above, fn.27) at 274(17).

[20] See answer to Parliamentary question no.173/77 [1978] O.J. C72/1.

[21] *Kramer* (Joined Cases 3/76, 4/76 and 6/76) (quoted above, fn.27), at 1310(40). See also art.351 TFEU [307] agreements concluded, before January 1, 1958 or before accession, between one or more Member States and one or more third countries are not affected by the entry into force of the Treaty. art.267 TFEU [234] (preliminary ruling) takes effect only if the agreement imposes on a Member State an obligation that is incompatible with the Treaty: *Evans Medical and MacFarlan Smith* (C-324/93) [1995] E.C.R. I-563.

[22] *AETR* (22/70) (quoted above, fn.27) at 281(81–92).

[23] *International Fruit Company v Produktschap voor Groenten en Fruit* (Joined Cases 21/72, 22/72, 23/72 and 24/72) [1972] E.C.R. 1219 at 1227(18); [1975] 2 C.M.L.R. 1. The Union has assumed those powers in pursuance of arts 206 and 207 TFEU [131 and 133]. See also *Nederlandse Spoorwegen v Inspecteur der invoerrechten en accijnzen* (38/75) [1975] E.C.R. 1439 at 1450(21); [1976] 1 C.M.L.R. 1; *Amministrazione delle Finanze dello Stato v SPI and SAMI* (Joined Cases 267/81, 268/81 and 269/81) [1983] E.C.R. 801; [1984] 1 C.M.L.R. 334; and *Singer and Geigy v Amministrazione delle Finanze dello Stato* (Joined Cases 290/81 and 291/81) [1983] E.C.R. 847.

[24] See, e.g. Opinion 1/75: Local Cost Standards (quoted above, fn.27) and Opinion 1/76, Laying-up Fund (fn.27).

[25] Ruling 1/78 [1978] E.C.R. 2151, compatibility with the Euratom Treaty of a draft Convention of the IAEA on the Physical Protection of Nuclear Materials, Facilities and Transport.

I. Economic, Financial and Technical Co-operation with Third Countries[26]

This action of the Union concerns third countries other than developing countries. It must carry out economic, financial and technical co-operation measures, including assistance, including financial assistance. Those measures must be consistent with the Union's "development policy" examined below and with the principles and objectives of its external action, described above.

Since this Union activity concerns a, "shared competence between the Union and the Member States", it has competence to carry out activities and conduct a common policy, which may not, however, result in Member States being prevented from exercising theirs.[27] The Union's operations and those of the Member States must complement and reinforce each other.[28] Parliament and the Council, acting in accordance with the ordinary legislative procedure,[29] must adopt the necessary measures.

Within their respective spheres of competence, the Union and the Member States co-operate with third countries and the competent international organisations (see point 5 below). The arrangements for such co-operation may be the subject of agreements between the Union and the third parties concerned (see point 4 below) but, the Member States retain the right to negotiate in international bodies and to conclude international agreements on their own, except, of course, in matters that have been dealt with already by the Union, since it is not possible for Member States to assume obligations which might affect Union rules or alter their scope.[30]

As already indicated, Member States consider these relations with third countries and international organisations as important symbols of what is left, according to them, of their "sovereignty",[31] and refuse to include these relations within common Union actions. This dichotomy enfeebles the Union's external influence, since it is not only unable to speak with one voice in the world bodies, but presents to the rest of the world a very divided image,[32] which does not correspond to its economic weight as the largest economic unit in the world.

The TFEU also provides that when the situation in a third country requires urgent financial assistance from the Union, the Council shall adopt the necessary decisions on a proposal from the Commission.[33] It is interesting to note that no legislative procedure is prescribed in this case. A Guarantee Fund for external action was established.[34]

---

[26] arts 212 and 213 TFEU [181a].
[27] art.4(4) TFEU.
[28] art.212(1) TFEU [181a].
[29] See art.294 TFEU [251].
[30] See *Commission v Greece* (C-45/07) [2009] E.C.R. 12.02.09.
[31] I do hope that the reader realises that in the present world the freedom of countries to operate in total independence (= sovereignty) is extremely limited: their inter-dependence with other countries and international institutions, in every field, indeed dictates most of their actions.
[32] Remember what Henry Kissinger, US Foreign Secretary said: "the EU lacks a single telephone number for foreign leaders to call when they want to speak to "Europe""; maybe that will change when the High Representative appears.
[33] art.213 TFEU.
[34] Regulation 480/09 [2009] O.J. L145/10.

II. Humanitarian Aid[35]

Under the former EC Treaty, Humanitarian Aid was part of "Development Co-operation", but now constitutes an independent Union activity. It is intended to provide ad hoc assistance and relief and protection for people in third countries who are victims of natural or man-made disasters, in order to meet the humanitarian needs resulting from these different situations. Here again the TFEU provides that the, "Union's measures and those of the Member States shall complement and reinforce each other"[36]; the Commission may take any useful initiative to promote co-ordination between actions of the Union and those of the Member States in order to enhance the efficiency and complementary nature of each other's measures. The TFEU also provides that, "humanitarian aid operations shall be conducted in compliance with the principles of international law and with the principle of impartiality, neutrality and non-discrimination".[37] The TFEU also provides that:

> "[I]n the areas of development cooperation and humanitarian aid, the Union shall have competence to carry out activities and conduct a common policy; however the exercise of the competence shall not result in Member States being prevented from exercising theirs."[38]

Parliament and the Council are to establish the measures defining the framework within which the Union's humanitarian aid operations are to be implemented.

The principal objectives of the humanitarian aid operations are, according to existing provisions, the following:

- save and preserve life during emergencies and their immediate aftermath and natural disasters;
- provide assistance and relief to people affected by longer-lasting crises;
- help finance the transport of aid;
- carry out short-term rehabilitation and reconstruction work;
- cope with the consequences of population movements;
- assure preparedness for risks of natural disasters;
- support civil operations to protect the victims of fighting and comparable emergencies.

To carry out those tasks, the European Office for Emergency Humanitarian Aid (ECHO) was set up in 1996. In recent years, assistance has been granted, among others, to victims of the war in the former Yugoslavia and victims of conflicts in Afghanistan, Armenia, Azerbaijan and Tajikistan.

In order to underpin existing Union policies and programmes (such as development aid, macro-financial aid, aid for economic, regional and technical co-operation, aid for reconstruction, for refugees and displaced persons, etc.) and to enable the Union to take urgent action to help re-establish or safeguard normal conditions, a Rapid Reaction Fund was set up. It is referred to as "the Rapid Reaction Mechanism".[39]

---

[35] art.214 TFEU.
[36] art.214(1) TFEU.
[37] art.214(2) TFEU.
[38] art.4(4) TFEU.
[39] Regulation 381/2001 [2001] O.J. L57/5.

A very interesting novelty introduced by the Lisbon Treaty is the setting up of a European Voluntary Humanitarian Aid Corps: a framework for joint contributions from young Europeans to the humanitarian aid operations of the Union.[40] Parliament and the Council, acting by means of regulations in accordance with the ordinary legislative procedure,[41] will determine the rules and procedures for the operation of the Corps.

The Union may conclude with third countries and competent international organisations any agreement helping to achieve the objectives of humanitarian aid. It must ensure that its humanitarian aid operations are co-ordinated and consistent with those of international organisations and bodies, in particular those forming part of the United Nations system.

III. RESTRICTIVE MEASURES[42]

When a decision adopted under the Special Provisions on the Common Foreign and Security Policy[42] provides for the interruption or reduction, in part or completely, of economic and financial relations with one or more third countries, the Council, acting by a qualified majority on a joint proposal from the High Representative and the Commission, shall adopt the necessary measures. The Council must inform Parliament. Such measures were already provided for under the previous EU Treaty.[44]

Under the same conditions, the Council may adopt restrictive measures against natural or legal persons and groups and non-State entities.

The TFEU adds that those acts shall, "include necessary provisions on legal safeguards."[45]

IV. INTERNATIONAL AGREEMENTS[46]

The TFEU provides for four cases in which the Union may conclude an agreement with one or more third countries or international organisations:

- where the Treaties so provide,[47]
- where the conclusion of an agreement is necessary in order to achieve, within the framework of the Union policies, one of the objectives referred to in the Treaties,
- where it is provided for in a legally binding Union act, and
- where it is likely to affect common rules or alter their scope.

It should be noted that such agreements constitute, "acts of the institutions of the Union" and as such can be challenged in the courts as to their compatibility with

---

[40] art.214(5) TFEU.
[41] art.294 TFEU [215].
[42] art.215 TFEU [301].
[43] arts 23 to 46 EU.
[44] Title IV of the former EU Treaty. See, for instance, restrictive measures against the Democratic Republic of the Congo [2009] O.J. L106/60.
[45] art.215(3) TFEU [301]
[46] arts 216 to 219 TFEU [310 to 111(1)].
[47] See, for instance, point II above.

the Treaties.[48] In the second place, provisions of international agreements concluded by the Union in conformity with the procedures provided for in the Treaties (see below), "are binding upon the institutions of the Union and on its Member States".[49] Such provisions are directly applicable in the Union. They can also have direct effect. Indeed, an agreement concluded by the Union with third countries must be considered as having direct effect when, taking into account its provisions and the object and nature of the agreement, it contains a clear and precise obligation, which is not submitted, in its implementation or effects, to a subsequent act. International agreements also override conflicting provisions of Member States' domestic law.[50]

The Union may conclude with one or more third countries or international organisations agreements establishing an association involving reciprocal rights and obligations, common action and special procedure.[51]

Procedures for the Adoption of International Agreements by the Union

Taking into account that special procedures are provided for the conclusion of international agreements within the framework of the common commercial policy,[52] agreements between the Union and third countries or international organisations shall be negotiated and concluded in accordance with the following procedure,[53] under which it is the Council, acting by a qualified majority,[54] that authorises the opening of negotiations, adopts negotiating directives, authorises the signing of agreements and concludes them. Parliament must be fully and immediately informed at all the stages of the procedure.

- The Commission (or the High Representative when the agreement relates exclusively or principally to the Common Foreign and Security Policy) submits recommendations to the Council;
- the Council adopts a decision authorising the opening of negotiations and,
- depending on the subject of the agreement, nominating the Union negotiator or the head of the Union's negotiating team;

---

[48] arts 263 and 267 TFEU [230 and 234].

[49] art.216(2) TFEU [300(2)]. See also Opinion 1/76, Laying-up Fund (quoted above, fn.27), at 6 and 7. See especially *Kupferberg* (104/81) [1982] E.C.R. 3641: according to art.216(2) TFEU [300(2)], Member States are bound in the same manner as the institutions of the Union, by the international agreement which the latter are empowered to conclude. When they ensure respect for commitments arising from an agreement concluded by the Union institutions, they fulfil an obligation, not only in relation to the non-member country concerned, but also and above all in relation to the Union, which has assumed responsibility for the due performance of the agreement. That is why the provisions of such an agreement form an integral part of the Union legal system. It follows from the Union nature of such provisions that their effect in the Union may not be allowed to vary according to whether this application is in practice the responsibility of the Union institutions or of the Member States. Violation by a Member State of obligations resulting from such an international agreement engages the responsibility of said Member State.

[50] *Bresciani v Amministrazione Italiana delle Finanze* (87/75) [1976] E.C.R. 129 at 141(23); [1976] 2 C.M.L.R. 62. See also *Razanatsimba* (65/77) [1977] E.C.R. 2229; [1978] 1 C.M.L.R. 246; *Demuel* (12/86) [1987] E.C.R. 3719(14).

[51] art.217 TFEU [310].

[52] See art.207 TFEU [133].

[53] art.218 TFEU [300].

[54] Unanimity is required where it is required for the adoption of a Union act, for instance: association agreements.

- the Council may address directives to the negotiator and designate a special committee in consultation with which the negotiations must be conducted;
- the Council, on a proposal by the negotiator, adopts a decision authorising the signing of the agreement and, if necessary, its provisional application before entry into force;
- except where the agreement relates exclusively to the Foreign and Security Policy, the Council, on a proposal by the negotiator, adopts a decision concluding the agreement, either, after obtaining the consent of Parliament in the following cases:

  — association agreement;
  — agreement on the Union accession to the European Convention for the Protection of Human Rights and Fundamental Freedoms[55];
  — agreement establishing a specific institutional framework by organising co-operation procedures;
  — agreements with important budgetary implications for the Union;
  — agreements covering fields to which either the ordinary legislative procedure[56] applies, or the special legislative procedure,[57] where consent by Parliament is required, in the latter case the Council and Parliament may agree upon a time limit for consent,

  or, after consulting Parliament in other cases; Parliament must deliver its opinion within a time limit set by the Council depending on the urgency of the matter; in the absence of an opinion the Council may act.

When concluding an agreement, the Council may authorise the negotiator to approve, on behalf of the Union, modifications to the agreement where it provides for them to be adopted by a simplified procedure or by a body set up by the agreement. The Council may attach specific conditions to such authorisation.[58] However, when a body set up by an agreement is called upon to adopt acts having legal effects, the Council, on a proposal from the Commission or the High Representative, shall adopt a decision suspending the application of an agreement and establishing the position to be adopted on the Union's behalf in said body.[59]

Member States, Parliament, the Council and the Commission may obtain an opinion of the Court as to whether the envisaged agreement is compatible with the Treaties. Where the opinion is adverse, the agreement may not enter into force unless it is amended or the Treaties revised.[60]

Special rules are provided for agreements on an exchange-rate system or concerning monetary or foreign exchange regime matters.[61]

The TFEU also provides that Member States may negotiate in international bodies and conclude international agreements without prejudice to Union competence and Union agreements, as regards economic and monetary union.[62]

---

[55] In this case the Council must act unanimously and the decision must be approved by the Member States: art.118(8) TFEU.
[56] art.294 TFEU [215].
[57] art.189 TFEU.
[58] art.118(7) TFEU.
[59] art.118(9) TFEU.
[60] art.218(11) TFEU [300].
[61] art.219(1),(2),(3) TFEU [111].
[62] art.219(4) TFEU [300].

V. The Union's Relations with International Organisations and third Countries and the Union's Delegations[63]

Under the EC Treaty it was for the Commission to, "ensure the maintenance of all appropriate relations with the organs of the United Nations",[64] it is now the Union, acting via the High Representative and the Commission,[65] which establishes:

"[A]ll appropriate forms of cooperation with the organs of the United Nations and its Specialised Agencies, the Council of Europe, the Organisation for Security and Cooperation in Europe and the Organisation for Economic Cooperation and Development."

The Union is to maintain also such relations as are appropriate with other international organisations.

The Union's Right of Passive and Active Legation

With regard to diplomatic representation with the Union, the only relevant Treaty provisions are to be found in the Protocol on the Privileges and Immunities.[66] The Member States in whose territory the Union has its seats, shall accord the customary diplomatic immunities and privileges to missions of third countries accredited to the Union.[67] Reference can also be made to the Statement issued after the extraordinary meeting of the Council in January 1966, held in Luxembourg. It provides that the credentials of the Heads of Missions of non-Member States accredited to the Union will be submitted jointly to the President of the Council and the President of the Commission, meeting together for this purpose.

The Union Delegations/The European External Action Service[68]

The representatives of the Union in third countries enjoy the same diplomatic immunities and privileges. This is the case also for the Commission delegations to various third countries and International Organisations such as the WTO, the OECD, the United Nations and its Specialised Agencies.

The TFEU now provides that the Union is represented in third countries and at international organisations by "Union delegations",[69] which are placed under the authority of the High Representative and that they shall act in close co-operation with Member States' diplomatic and consular missions. The European External Action Service[70]: this service somehow constitutes in all aspects but name, the

---

[63] arts 220 and 221 TFEU [302–304].
[64] Former art.302 EC.
[65] art.220(2) TFEU [302–304].
[66] Annexed to the Merger Treaty. Another mention is to be found, but in a different context, in Part Two of the TFEU concerning "Citizenship": every citizen of the Union shall, in the territory of a third country in which the Member State of which he is a national is not represented, be entitled to protection by the diplomatic or consular authorities of any Member State, art.23 TFEU [20]
[67] TFEU Protocol No.7, art.10 [17]. For a list of the accredited missions, see "Corps diplomatique accredité auprés des Communautés Européennes", Directorate-General External Relations.
[68] art.27(3) EU.
[69] art.221(1) TFEU.
[70] art.27(3) EU.

"diplomatic corps" of the Union. The Service works in co-operation with the diplomatic services of the Member States and comprises officials from relevant departments of the General Secretariat of the Council and of the Commission as well as staff seconded from national diplomatic services of the Member States.

The organisation and functioning of the Service is established by a decision of the Council which acts on a proposal from the High Representative after consulting Parliament and after obtaining the consent[71] of the Commission.

Without it being more explicitly provided for in the Treaty, the Union thus exercises the right of active and passive legation.

VI. SOLIDARITY CLAUSE[72]

Under this title the TFEU provides for joint action by the Union and the Member States in case a Member State is the object of a terrorist attack or the victim of a natural or man-made disaster. If this happens, the Union must mobilise all the instruments at its disposal, including the military resources made available by the Member States, in order to:

- prevent the terrorist threat,
- protect democratic institutions and the civilian population, and
- assist a Member State in its territory, at the request of its political authorities.

Similarly, the other Member States must assist it and co-ordinate their action within the Council.

The arrangements for the implementation of the Solidarity Clause shall be defined by a Council decision acting on a joint proposal from the Commission and the High Representative. Where this decision has defence implications the Council must act unanimously and legislative acts are excluded.[73] The Council shall be assisted, as always, by COREPER, but also by the Political and Security Committee (PSC)[74] and by the standing committee set up within the Council to ensure that operational co-operation on internal security is promoted and strengthened within the Union.[75]

The European Council must regularly assess the threats facing the Union in order to enable the Union and the Member States to take effective action.[76]

VII. THE EUROPEAN NEIGHBOURHOOD POLICY (ENP)[77]

This policy was developed in 2004 with the object of avoiding the emergence of new dividing lines between the enlarged EU and its neighbours, and instead,

---

[71] This term is normally used in relation to the involvement of Parliament in the legislative procedure: it confers what amounts to a veto right.

[72] art.222 TFEU.

[73] art.31(1) EU.

[74] The PSC is the permanent body in the field of foreign and security policy; see below, Ch.37: Common Foreign and Security Policy.

[75] art.71 TFEU [36].

[76] art.222(4) TFEU.

[77] Regulation 1638/06 [2006] O.J. L310/1, laying down general provisions establishing a European Neighbourhood and Partnership Instrument. See General Report 2009, 59.

strengthening the prosperity, stability and security of all concerned. The EU offers its neighbours a privileged relationship based upon a mutual commitment to common values: democracy and human rights, the rule of law, good governance, market economy principles and sustainable development. It goes beyond existing relationships; it remains distinct from the process of enlargement. It applies to the Union's immediate neighbours by land and sea: Algeria, Armenia,[78] Azerbaijan,[79] Belarus, Egypt,[80] Georgia,[81] Israel (associated), Jordan,[81] Lebanon,[83] Libya, Moldavia,[84] Morocco,[85] Occupied Palestina Territory,[86] Syria, Tunisia[87] and Ukraine.[88]

The central element of the ENP is the bilateral ENP Action Plans agreed between the Union and each partner. The Action Plans are built upon existing agreements such as Partnership and Co-operation Agreements or Association Agreements in the framework of the Euro-Mediterranean Partnership. Those action plans or individual country programmes support cross-border contacts and co-operation between regional actors and civil society.[89]

The European Neighbourhood and Partnership Instrument (ENPI),[90] which from January 1, 2007 replaced the MEDA, TACIS and various other instruments, was established in 2006 and a Regulation laying down implementing rules, for cross-border co-operation programmes financed under the ENP, was issued in 2007.[91]

Further Reading

Panos Koutrakos, "Primary law and policy in EU external relations—moving away from the big picture" (2008) 33 E.L.Review 666.
Marise Cremona and Bruno De Witte, *EU Foreign Relations Law: Constitutional Fundamentals* (Oxford, Hart Publishing, 2008).
Rass Holdgaard, *External Relations Law of the European Community* (Kluwer Law International, 2009).

---

[78] The overall allocation for 2007–2010 for Armenia: €964 million.
[79] Idem for Azerbaijan: €92 million.
[80] Idem for Egypt: €558 million.
[81] Idem for Georgia: €170 million.
[82] Idem for Jordan: €265 million
[83] Idem for Lebanon: €187 million.
[84] Idem for Moldavia: €250 million.
[85] Idem for Morocco: €654 million.
[86] Idem for Palestine: €664 million.
[87] Idem for Tunisia: €300 million.
[88] Idem for Ukraine: €500 million.
[89] See ENPI Cross-Border Co-operation Strategic Paper.
[90] Regulation 1638/06 [2006] O.J. L310/1. For the period 2007–2013 approximately €12 billion in Union funding is available, of which each cross-border co-operation programme receives €1 billion.
[91] Regulation 951/07 [2007] O.J. L210/10, corrigendum [2009] O.J. L221/7.

Chapter Thirty-seven

The Common Foreign and Security Policy[1] (CFSP)

The Preamble to the EU Treaty refers, among others, to the implementation of:

"[A] common foreign and security policy including the progressive framing of a common defence policy, which might lead to a common defence in accordance with the provisions concerning the common security and defence policy,[2] thereby reinforcing the European identity and its independence in order to promote peace, security and progress in Europe and in the world".[3]

The Union's competences in this field cover all areas of foreign policy and all questions relating to the Union's security, including the progressive framing of a defence policy that might lead to a common defence.[4]

The CFSP is subject to specific rules and procedures: it is defined by the European Council and the Council acting unanimously, unless otherwise provided in the Treaties. The adoption of legislative acts is excluded; it shall be put into effect by the High Representative and by Member States; there is a specific role for Parliament and the Commission. The Court has no jurisdiction with respect to the provisions relating to the CFSP and the acts adopted under it.[5] However, the Court has jurisdiction to monitor compliance with the strict separation of the procedures and the extent of the powers of the institutions laid down by the Treaties for the exercise of the competences referred to in Articles 3 to 6 of the TFEU and the implementation of the CFSP,[6] and to review the legality of certain "decisions providing for restrictive measures against natural or legal persons".[7]

The development of CFSP is to be based on the development of mutual political solidarity among Member States, the identification of questions of general interest and the achievement of an ever increasing degree of convergence of the Member States' actions.[8]

The CFSP is conducted by:

1. defining the general guidelines;
2. adopting decisions defining

   (a) actions to be undertaken by the Union,[9]

---

[1] arts 23–41 EU.
[2] art.42 EU.
[3] EU Preamble, para.11.
[4] art.24(1) EU.
[5] art.24(1)2 EU.
[6] art.40 EU.
[7] art.275 TFEU.
[8] art.24(2) EU.
[9] See, for instance, Joint Action 2008/124/CFSP on the European Union rule of law mission in Kosovo [2008] O.J. L42/22 and the agreement with the Swiss Confederation on its participation in it [2008] O.J. L217/23.

(b) positions to be taken by the Union, and
(c) arrangements for the implementation of these decisions;

3. strengthening systematic co-operation between Member States in the conduct of policy.[10]

The European Council indentifies the Union's strategic interests, determines the objectives and defines general guidelines, while the Council takes the necessary decisions for defining and implementing the CFSP; the latter and the High Representative ensure the unity, consistency and effectiveness of actions by the Union.[11]

Where the international situation requires operational action, the Council adopts the necessary decisions that lay down the objectives, scope, the means to be made available to the Union, if necessary their duration and the conditions of their implementation. Those decisions shall commit the Member States in the positions they adopt and in the conduct of their activity.[12] These operational actions correspond to the "joint actions"[13] previously provided for in the EU Treaty.

The Council also adopts decisions that shall define the approach of the Union to a particular matter of a geographical or thematic nature.[14] They correspond to the former "common positions".

As indicated, decisions with regard to the CFSP are taken by the European Council and the Council acting unanimously; however, there are exceptions.[15]

Member States must consult one another within the European Council and the Council on any matter of foreign and security policy of general interest in order to determine a common approach.[16] The latter may be defined by the European Council or the Council. Member States must co-ordinate their action in international organisations and conferences. Member States that are also members of the United Nations Security Council must concert and keep the other Member States and the High Representative fully informed.[17]

A Special Representative may be appointed by the Council with a mandate in relation to particular policy issues.[18]

Diplomatic and consular missions of the Member States and the Commission Delegations in third countries and international conferences, and their representations to international organisations, shall co-operate in ensuring that decisions defining Union positions and actions adopted pursuant to the EU Chapter on CFSP are complied with and implemented.[19]

The Treaty provides that the Union may conclude international agreements in implementation of the CFSP.[20]

A Political and Security Committee[21] was set up to monitor the international situation in the areas covered by the CFSP and to contribute to the definition of

[10] art.25 EU.
[11] art.26 EU.
[12] art.28 EU
[13] In 2008, more than 30 Joint Actions and more than 20 Common Positions concerned the Balkans, South Caucasus, Asia, Africa, Indian Ocean, the Middle East and Eastern Europe, the European Security Strategy and the European Security and Defence Policy; see General Report 2008, 201.
[14] art.29 EU.
[15] See art.31(2) EU.
[16] art.32 EU.
[17] art.34(2)2 EU.
[18] art.33 EU.
[19] art.35 EU [16].
[20] art.37 EU.
[21] art.38 EU.

policies by delivering opinions to the Council, at the request of the Council or of the High Representative, or on its own initiative. The Committee exercises, under the responsibility of the Council and of the High Representative the political control and strategic direction of crisis management operations provided for under the Common Security and Defence Policy.[22] The Committee may be authorised by the Council to take the relevant decisions[23] concerning political control and strategic direction of the operations.

It should be noted that the implementation of the CFSP does not affect the application of the procedures and the extent of the powers of the institutions laid down by the Treaties for the exercise of the Union competences refered to in the TFEU.[24]

All expenditures following from the implementation of the CFSP are charged to the Union's budget, unless they are financed by a "start-up" fund made up of Member States' contributions.[25]

An Instrument for Stability[26] with a total budget for 2007–2013 of €2 billion was set up to respond urgently to the needs of countries threatened with or undergoing severe political instability or suffering from the effects of a technological or natural disaster. (It replaces the Rapid Reaction Mechanism.) In short, it is a mechanism for preventing crises and conflicts, managing crises and emerging conflicts, and restoring peace. It may also be deployed to address trans-border challenges including nuclear safety and non-proliferation, the fight against trafficking, organised crime and terrorism. It can only finance operations where other financial instruments cannot respond within the timeframe necessary; it cannot, for instance, finance humanitarian assistance. A simplified decision process is used: the Commission may adopt measures which apply immediately, it is assisted by a committee and if the Commission's action is not in accordance with the opinion of the committee, the Council will immediately be informed and may overrule the Commission within 30 days. Parliament is kept informed.

1. THE COMMON SECURITY AND DEFENCE POLICY (CSDP)[27]

The CSDP is an integral part of the Common Foreign and Security policy (CFSP). It provides the Union with an operational capacity drawing on civilian and military assets. The Union may use them on missions outside the Union for peacekeeping, conflict prevention and strengthening international security in accordance with the principles of the United Nations Charter. The performance of those tasks is undertaken using capabilities provided by the Member States.[28] The latter must make civilian and military capabilities available to the Union for the implementation of the CSDP and to contribute to the objectives defined by the Council. Multinational forces may also be made available.[29]

---

[22] art.42 EU.
[23] See, for instance, Decision Atalanta/3/2009 on the setting up of the Committee of Contributors for the European Union military operation to contribute to the deterrence, prevention and repression of acts of piracy and armed robbery of the Somali coast [2009] O.J. L119/40.
[24] art.40 EU with reference to arts 3–6 of the TFEU.
[25] art.41 EU.
[26] Regulation 1717/06 [2006] O.J. L327/1. It became fully operational in 2008. See General Report 2008, 200.
[27] arts 42–46 EU.
[28] art.42(1) EU.
[29] art.42(3)1 EU.

The CSDP includes the progressive framing of a Common Defence Policy, which will lead to a common defence, when the European Council, acting unanimously, so decides. The Council shall then recommend the Member States adopt such a decision in accordance with their respective constitutional requirements. Decisions relating to the CSDP are adopted by the Council acting unanimously on a proposal from the High Representative or an initiative from a Member State. The High Representative may propose the use of both national resources and Union instruments, together with the Commisssion where appropriate.[30]

The Member States undertake progressively to improve their military capabilities. A European Defence Agency is provided for in the Treaty.[31] A European Security and Defense College (ESDC) was established in 2005.[32]

At the Helsinki European Council, the Member States decided to establish, within the Council, new permanent political and military bodies enabling the EU to assume its responsibilities for the full range of conflict prevention and crisis management, tasks defined in the EU Treaty, the "Petersberg tasks".[33] These tasks concern humanitarian and rescue tasks, peacekeeping tasks and tasks of combat forces in crisis management, including peacemaking.[34] The implementation of those tasks may be entrusted, by the Council, to a group of Member States which are willing and have the necessary capabilities.[35] The defence policy of the Union may not prejudice the defence policy of certain Member States and respects the obligations of certain Member States, which see their common defence realised in the North Atlantic Treaty Organisation (NATO), under the North Atlantic Treaty.[36]

In 2001, the Council set up a Military Committee and established a Military Staff of the European Union (EUMS).[37] This was decided within the framework of the strengthening of the CFSP and in particular of the Common Security and Defence Policy (CSDP).[38] In accordance with this decision, military personnel is seconded from Member States to the General Secretariat of the Council, of which the EUMS is part. The Mission and functions of the Military Staff are reproduced in the Annex to the decision: "within the Council structures [to] provide[s] military expertise and support to the CSDP, including the conduct of EU-led military crisis operations." A mechanism was established in 2004 to administer the financing of the common costs of European Union operations having military or defence implication (Athena).[39]

The military staff is to perform, "early warning, situation assessment and strategic planning for 'Petersberg tasks' including identification of European national and multinational forces" and implement policies and decisions as directed by the European Union Military Committee (EUMC).

---

[30] art.42(4) EU.

[31] art.42(3)2 EU. See above, Ch.13: Decentralised Bodies of the Union.

[32] Joint Action 2005/575 [2005] O.J. L194/15, replaced by [2008] O.J. L176/20.

[33] These tasks were set out in the Petersberg Declaration adopted at the Ministerial Council of the Western European Union (WEU) in June 1992, are an integral part of the ESDP and were explicitly included in art.17 of the EU Treaty, now art.42.

[34] art.43 EU. Decisions relating to those tasks shall be adopted by the Council and will define their objectives, scope and the general conditions for their implementation (art.43(2) EU).

[35] art.44 EU.

[36] art.42(2)2 EU.

[37] Regulation 79/2001 [2001] O.J. L27/4 and 7, amended [2008] O.J. L102/25.

[38] art.42 EU [17].

[39] Decision 2007/384 [2007] O.J. L152/14.

A permanent structure of co-operation within the Union framework can be established by those Member States whose military capabilities fulfil higher criteria and which have made more binding commitments to one another with a view to the most demanding missions.[40] Member States that wish to participate, fulfil the criteria and have made the commitments on military capabilities, shall notify their intention to the Council and the High Representative. The Council shall adopt the necessary decisions.[41]

If a Member State is the victim of armed aggression on its territory, the other Member States shall have towards it an obligation of aid and assistance by all the means in their power in accordance with the United Nations Charter.[42]

None of the actions taken under the CSDP may prejudice the specific character of the security and defence policy of certain Member States. Commitments and co-operation in this area shall be consistent with commitments under the North Atlantic Treaty Organisation, which for its members remains the foundation of their collective defence and the forum for its implementation.[43] The tasks, in the course of which the Union may use civilian and military means, include disarmament operations, humanitarian aid and rescue tasks, military advice and assistance tasks, conflict prevention and peacekeeping, tasks of combat forces in crisis management, including peacekeeping and post-conflict stabilisation. All these tasks may contribute to the fight against terrorism, including by supporting third countries in combating terrorism in their territories. The Council will adopt the necessary decisions defining their objective and scope and the general conditions for their implementation. Co-ordination is ensured by the High Representative under the authority of the Council and in close contact with the Political and Security Committee.[44] The Council may entrust the implementation of those tasks to a group of Member States who are willing and have the capabilities for such tasks. They must keep the Council regularly informed of their progress.

2. THE HIGH REPRESENTATIVE[45]

The High Representative chairs the Foreign Affairs Council, contributes, through his proposals, towards the preparation of the CFSP and ensures the implementation of the decisions adopted by the European Council and the Council. He represents the Union in matters relating to the CFSP. He conducts political dialogue with third parties on the Union's behalf and expresses the Union's position in international organisations and at international conferences. He is assisted by the European External Action Service (see below).

The High Representative must regularly consult Parliament on the main aspects and the basic choices of the CFSP and inform it of how these policies evolve. He must ensure that the views of Parliament are duly taken into consideration. Parliament may ask questions of the Council or make recommendations to it and the High Representative.[46]

[40] art.42(6) EU.
[41] art.46 EU.
[42] art.42(7) EU. Similar provisions are to be found in the "Solidarity Clause" in the art.222 TFEU.
[43] art.42(7)2 EU.
[44] art.43 EU.
[45] art.27 EU.
[46] art.36 EU.

Chapter Thirty-eight

Common Commercial Policy[1] and Relations with Third Countries

General Principles

The European Union is now the largest trading group in the world, accounting for just over 20 per cent of total global trade in goods. This gives the Union the capacity, for instance, to play a leadership role in global negotiations to liberalise world trade; indeed it is one of the tasks imposed upon the Union by the TFEU:

> "[B]y establishing a customs union in accordance with Articles 28 to 32 the Union shall contribute, in the common interest, to the harmonious development of world trade, the progressive abolition of restrictions on international trade and on foreign direct investment, and the lowering of customs and other barriers."[2]

The TFEU also provides that, when establishing the Customs Union, the Commission shall be guided, among others things, by, "the need to promote trade between Member States and third countries".[3] Furthermore, free trade has traditionally been one of the main aims of the Union, because it is heavily dependent on international commerce, more so than, for example, the US. This broad objective has been pursued multilaterally first in the GATT, now in the World Trade Organisation (WTO), through regional agreements, and in bilateral relations with other countries.

As previously indicated, the Union has sole responsibility for commercial trade policy. Indeed, one of the first TFEU articles provides that, the Union shall have exclusive competence in the area of "common commercial policy".[4] Further on, it is stated that the Union is based upon a Customs Union which involves, "the adoption of a common customs tariff in their relations with third countries".[5] As was pointed out above in Ch.15: Free Movement of Goods, the elimination of internal customs tariffs does indeed require the adoption of a common customs tariff with regard to third countries since, without it, trade from third countries would be deflected towards the Member State with the lowest external tariffs. Customs tariffs, furthermore, are one of the main instruments of commercial policy, i.e. in the relations with third countries.

Since the external customs tariffs had to be "common", the commercial policy itself must be a policy common to the 27 Member States. The TFEU, consequently, provides that:

---

[1] arts 206–207 TFEU [131–134].
[2] art.206 TFEU [131].
[3] art.32 TFEU [27(a)].
[4] art.3(1)(e) TFEU [3(1)(b)].
[5] art.28(1) TFEU [23(1)].

"[T]he common commercial policy must be based on uniform principles, particularly with regard to changes in tariff rates, the conclusion of tariff and trade agreements relating to trade in goods and services, and the commercial aspects of intellectual property, foreign direct investment, the achievement of uniformity in measures of liberalisation, export policy and measures to protect trade such as those to be taken in the event of dumping or subsidies".[6]

As the Court indicated, commercial policy was thus transferred by the Treaty from the national ambit to the Union's jurisdiction.[7] Unfortunately, this evidence is not always fully accepted by all the national governments; this can maybe be explained by the fact that commercial policy formed part of external relations in general, and the latter, until recently were strictly reserved to the Member States themselves. Theoretically, national measures of commercial policy are no longer possible, but can still be taken with the Union's authorisation.[8] This situation is necessarily detrimental to the conduct of a coherent commercial policy towards third countries. It is to be hoped therefore, that the Treaties' provisions concerning the external action of the Union, introduced by the Treaty of Lisbon, will "communitarise" the whole spectrum of relations with third countries. Indeed, the TFEU provides for the achievement of, "an ever-increasing degree of convergence of Member States' action."[9]

However, where customs tariffs are concerned, it was accepted from the beginning by all the Member States that they can only be modified by the Council, as provided for in the Treaty.[10] Changes in tariff rates and the conclusion of tariff agreements must, as was just pointed out, be based on uniform principles. The Treaty provides for two procedures in this field: first, the so-called "autonomous" modification of tariffs, where the Union acts on its own,[11] but that is now very limited, since most duties have been "consolidated" under the WTO; and, secondly, those that take place pursuant to agreements with third countries.

Those agreements are negotiated in the same way as those described above in Ch.36: General Provisions concerning the Union's External Action, i.e. by the Commission, in consultation with a Special Committee on the basis of a mandate that it proposes to, and receives from, the Council, and within the framework of such directives as the Council may issue to it. These agreements are concluded by the Council.[12]

For the negotiation and conclusion of international agreements in the area of the Common Commercial Policy, the Council acts by qualified majority.[13] However, when it concerns trade in services and the commercial aspects of intellectual property, as well as foreign direct investment, the Council must act unanimously, where

---

[6] art.207 TFEU [133(1)].
[7] Court Opinion 1/75 [1975] E.C.R. 1355.
[8] *Donckerwolcke v Procureur de la République* (41/76) [1976] E.C.R. 1921 at 1937(32); [1977] 2 C.M.L.R. 535. See Council Decision of March 27, 1991 authorising prorogation or tacit renewal of commercial agreements concluded by the Member States [1991] O.J. L83/13. Art.207 TFEU [133] and Council Decision 69/494 concerning progressive uniformisation of existing trade agreement [1969] O.J. L326/39. See [1991] O.J. L82/52.
[9] art.24(2) EU [11]. Progress was recently made with regard to the so-called open sky agreements with the US, following a judgment of the Court. See, for instance, *Commission v Sweden* (C-468/98) [2002] E.C.R. I-9575, affirming the exclusive competence of the Union.
[10] arts 31 and 207 TFEU [26 and 133].
[11] art.31 TFEU [26].
[12] art.207 TFEU [133(3)]. This Committee is composed of national officials appointed by the Council.
[13] art.207(4) TFEU [133(4)].

such agreements include provisions for which unanimity is required for the adoption of internal rules.[14]

Furthermore, the TFEU specifies that the Council must also act unanimously for agreements in the field of trade in cultural and audio-visual services, where those agreements risk prejudicing the Union's cultural and linguistic diversity. Unanimity is also provided for trade in the field of social, education and health services, where these agreements risk seriously disturbing the national organisation of such services and prejudicing the responsibility of Member States to deliver them.

Finally, the TFEU provides that the competences conferred in the area of the common commercial policy may not affect the delimitation of competences between the Union and the Member States and shall not lead to harmonisation unless this is provided for by the Treaties.[15]

1. COMMERCIAL POLICY INSTRUMENTS AND IMPORT AND EXPORT ARRANGEMENTS

It will be noted that the specific Treaty provisions concerning commercial policy refer to, "the achievement of uniformity in measures of liberalisation, export policy and measures to protect trade such as those to be taken in the event of dumping or subsidies."[16]

(1) Liberalisation and Export Policy

Member States must harmonise the systems whereby they grant aid for export to third countries, to the extent necessary to ensure that competition between enterprises is not distorted. In this context reference must be made to the OECD Arrangement on Guidelines for Officially Supported Export Credits "Consensus". The application of the agreement was made compulsory for the Member States.[17] Generally speaking, exports from the Union are free, although the Council is empowered to impose restrictions in certain cases. For instance, in 1992, the Council adopted a regulation requiring prior authorisation for the export of eight chemical products. This authorisation may not be given if there is reason to believe that the products in question will be used for the development or the production of chemical weapons or that there is a risk of their being delivered directly or indirectly to belligerent countries or to areas of serious international tension.[18]

On the other hand, the Commission supplements Member States' export promotion efforts with a programme based on fairs, trade forums and co-ordinated Union initiatives; it gave, for instance, priority to promoting exports to the Gulf and Asian countries. See Council Decision on the implementation by the

---

[14] art.207(4)2 TFEU [133(5)2.

[15] art.207(6) TFEU [133(6)].

[16] art.207(1) TFEU [133(1)].

[17] [1997] O.J. L216/77, amended [2001] O.J. L32/1.

[18] General Report 1992, 311. See, for instance, the suspension of trade concession to former Yugoslavia: *Racke* (C-162/96) [1998] E.C.R. I-3655 concerning the EEC/Yugoslavia Co-operation Agreement and the Vienna Convention on the Law of Treaties: application of the rule *rebus sic stantibus*.

Commission of activities relating to the Union market access strategy.[19] See the 2009 regulation establishing common rules for exports, accepting as a Union principle that exports to third countries are not subject to any quantitative restrictions, subject to certain exceptions and measures as Member States may take in conformity with the TFEU.[20]

(2) Measures to Protect Trade

The instruments concerning imports consist mainly of anti-dumping and anti-subsidy measures.[21] The purpose of the anti-dumping measures is to eliminate the prejudice suffered by Union producers of a given product because of imports of a similar product being "dumped". Dumping exists when an exporter applies to exported products a price that is lower than the so-called normal value. The latter is the price asked for that product on the exporter's home market.[22] In case the products were sold domestically for a loss, then the normal value would be construed by adding a profit margin to the production costs, the so called constructed value.

Union action, generally speaking, takes the form of provisional anti-dumping duties imposed on the imported product causing injury. This is followed either by an undertaking from the exporter concerning his export price to the Union or by definitive duties. Such action is taken at the end of a procedure which starts with a complaint containing sufficient proof, submitted to the Commission, by a majority of the European producers of a given branch or by a Member State. The Commission can then initiate proceedings and an investigation, after consultation of a consultative committee. The initiation of proceedings is announced in the *Official Journal*. The Commission could also open proceedings on its own initiative, but never does so, deeming the industry better placed to gather the necessary proofs. The complaint should be submitted by producers of a similar product that, furthermore, must be "communautaire".

Next, the existence of dumping and of a prejudice must be ascertained by the Commission. The Commission's investigation covers a period of six months following the submission of the complaint. To conduct the investigation the Commission needs the full co-operation of all interested parties. The Commission cannot however impose coercive measures, but in case of a refusal to furnish the

---

[19] [1998] O.J. L265/31. See General Report 2003, 799.

[20] [2009] O.J. L291/1.

[21] See, for instance, Regulation 384/96 [1996] O.J. L56/1 on protection against dumped imports from countries not members of the European Union and Regulation 2026/97 [1997] O.J. L288/1 on protection against subsidised imports from countries not members of the European Union, modified [2004] O.J. L77/13.

[22] Regulation 384/96 on protection against dumped imports from countries not members of the Union [1996] O.J. L56/1, amended [2004] O.J. L77/12, which also amended Regulation 2026/97 on protection against imports from countries not members of the Union [1997] O.J. L.288/1. See Guide to the European Communities' anti-dumping and countervailing legislation and questionnaires on lodging complaints, one intended for producers and exporters and one intended for importers. See also Guidelines for the calculation of the amount of subsidy in countervailing duty investigations [1998] O.J. C394/6. Also of interest is Regulation 519/94 on common rules for imports from certain third-world countries [1994] O.J. L67/89, amended [2009] O.J. L37/4, codified [2009] O.J. L185/1. See also *BEUC v Commission* (T-256/97) [2000] E.C.R. II-101, where it was decided that consumer organisations could not be "interested parties" in proceedings involving products not commonly sold at retail level.

requested information, the Commission may, in pursuance of the WTO Anti-Dumping Code, decide on the basis of the existing evidence. Indeed, mention should be made of the fact that the Union rules in this field are based upon the General Agreement for Tariffs and Trade (GATT), now WTO.

The proceedings are closed either by a decision that there is no need for protective measures, by the expiration or abrogation of the anti-dumping measures or by the nullity of the price undertaking. This means that, as long as one of these three events has not occurred, the Council can take a new measure without opening proceedings again.

Measures can only be imposed by the Union after it has ascertained that there is dumping and that it causes injury to Union producers. This may be a lengthy procedure and reactions to a complaint cannot therefore be immediate. There is however, a further requirement namely that the interest of the Union does require such measures. In practice, injury to a Union industry is considered as constituting an Union interest. As for the undertaking made by an exporter, it consists in applying a price which will eliminate the dumping effect and the injury to the Union producers. The implementation of the undertaking is verified by periodical reports from the exporter to the Commission.

The anti-dumping duties are established for five years and are levied when the product is put in free circulation. The proceedings and measures described above are similar for anti-subsidy measures; in order to offset any subsidy bestowed, directly or indirectly, in the country of origin or export, upon their manufacture, production, export or transport of any product whose release in the free circulation in the Union causes injury, a countervailing duty may be imposed.[23]

Finally, it should be pointed out that it was established that the regulation could be circumvented by importing spare parts and assembling them within the Union. Indeed, those products would have been subject to anti-dumping duties had they been imported in a finished state. To prevent this deflection, the Union adopted a regulation concerning the so-called screwdriver plants.[24]

Anti-dumping or countervailing duties imposed by the Union are subject to the judicial control of the Court; this control has given rise to an abundant case law.

"Many trading partners, many commercial agreements." Those are the words of the Commission[25] to indicate that, in addition to full participation in the multilateral negotiation and management activities of the WTO, the Union also has a broad range of commercial agreements of differing types with its many partners; these are, for instance:

- agreements creating Customs Unions with Turkey, Malta and Cyprus;
- free trade agreements with the three members of the European Economic Area;
- "Europe" agreements (also known as association agreements), which were concluded before accession, with Central and Eastern European countries. Those aimed to integrate their economies with the Union in view of their accession;
- preferential agreements with Mediterranean countries and, through the Lomé Convention, with more than 70 African, Caribbean and Pacific countries. These arrangements give their exports privileged access to the EU as well as financial and technical assistance;

---

[23] See General Report 2003, 792.
[24] Regulation 1761/87 [1987] O.J. L167/9.
[25] Parts of this chapter are based on, or borrowed from, *http://www.europa.eu.int/pol/comm/infoen.htm.* (December 1998).

- non-preferential commercial and economic co-operation agreements with many countries of Latin America and Asia;
- sectoral agreements, such as in textiles and clothing, guaranteeing third-world producers access to the Union market;
- international commodity agreements, such as the Cocoa Agreement 1993; and[26]
- generalised system of preferences[27] (see below, Ch.39: Development Co-operation).

A regulation lays down Union procedures in the field of the common commercial policy, in order to ensure the exercise of the Union's rights under international trade rules, in particular those established under the auspices of the World Trade Organisation.[28]

2. RELATIONS WITH OTHER EUROPEAN COUNTRIES

(1) The European Economic Area (EEA)

The European Economic Area was born on January 1, 1994; it joins together the three remaining members of the EFTA—Iceland, Liechtenstein and Norway[29]—with the Union in one single market. Among other things, it grants those countries the basic freedoms of goods, services, capital and persons, and requires them to adopt most EU policies on mergers, State aids, consumer protection, labour markets and the environment. The agreement gives the three States the right to be consulted by the Commission during the formulation of Union legislation, although they have no say in the decision-making.[30] All new Union legislation, in the areas covered by the EEA, is integrated into the Agreement through a Joint Committee decision and subsequently made part of the national legislation of the EEA States. From an institutional point of view, it might be interesting to note that the EEA has a Council, a Joint Committee and a Consultative Committee, which meet either in Brussels or in the capital of one of the member countries. Members of the EEA do actually participate in several Union activities: Norway and Iceland, for instance, participate in the European Medicines Agency, in the European Environment Agency and in other schemes. It should be noted that those three countries and Switzerland do apply, for instance, the Union Directive on the right of establishment of lawyers.

Relations with Switzerland, that in a referendum rejected membership of the EEA, will continue to be governed by the existing co-operation agreements.[31] An agreement on scientific and technological co-operation was signed in 2007[32] and one on trade in agricultural products in 2009.[33]

---

[26] Decision 98/489 concerning the conclusion of the International Cocoa Agreement 1993, on behalf of the Union [1998] O.J. L220/1.

[27] See Scheme for the period January 1, 2009 to December 31, 2011 [2008] O.J. L211/1. General Report 2008, 171.

[28] Regulation 3286/94 [1994] O.J. L349/71, modified [2008] O.J. L40/1; see *FICF v Commission* (T-317/02) [2004] E.C.R. II-4325.

[29] See, for instance, bilateral free trade Agreement [1973] O.J. L171/2 and [2004] O.J. L370/70.

[30] General Report 1997, 305.

[31] See [2002] O. J. L11k/1 and [2004] O. J. L368/26 (Schengen). See Agreement on Scientific and Technological Co-operation [2007] O.J. L189/24.

[32] [2008] O.J. L86/25.

[33] [2009] O.J. L136/1.

(2) Other European Countries

A co-operation and Customs Union Agreement was concluded and entered into force with San Marino.[34] A co-operation agreement exists with Andorra, in respect of the environment, communications, education, transport, and regional and trans-frontier co-operation and veterinary matters. A monetary agreement with Monaco was signed by France on behalf of the Union.[35] For more information on those various subjects the reader is referred to the Commission's General Reports, published yearly.[36]

(3) Central and Eastern European Countries (CEECs)

The collapse of communism led to a surge in the relations between the Union and most of the CEECs, including the signing of association agreements, the so-called Europe Agreements. These relations have been further deepened since the European Council meeting in Copenhagen in June 1993, which established that those countries that had signed Europe Agreements with the Union could be eligible for membership. There were 13 such agreements with each one of the candidate countries. These agreements gave the signatories associate status and covered both political and economic relations. They established regular and intensive political dialogue, progressive economic integration and financial assistance. They are of unlimited duration and allow the CEECs up to 10 years to remove economic and commercial barriers, while Union restrictions on the import of their industrial goods were removed by January 1, 1995, with some exemptions for textiles and steel. These exemptions had to be removed by the end of 1997. Total aid from the Union and its Member States to the CEECs (plus Albania[37] and the former Yugoslav Republic of Macedonia) was €33.8 billion between 1990 and 1994, 45 per cent of the total assistance they received.

Some €5.3 billion was committed under PHARE, which was the Union's main technical assistance programme for the CEECs for the period 1990–1995; it was replaced by ITA (see below). The European Union's PHARE programme, of its own inception, was a technical assistance programme given the task of supporting the pre-accession strategy as a structural assistance programme. Set up in 1998, PHARE was originally intended to support the transition to democracy of Poland and Hungary; it became the main channel of assistance to Albania, Bosnia Herzegovina, Bulgaria, the Czech Republic, Estonia, the former Yugoslav Republic of Macedonia, Latvia, Lithuania, Romania, Slovakia and Slovenia. Between 1990 and 2006, the amounts provided or to be provided under the PHARE programme were in the order of €21 billion. Within the context of enlargement, an amount of €36 million from the 2002 PHARE budget was earmarked for a new instrument developed by the EIB: the Municipal Infrastructure Facility, which is designated to facilitate small investments (less than €5 million) in municipal infrastructure in seven, at the time, candidate countries bordering the Union.

---

[34] [1991] O.J. C302/10.
[35] [2002] O.J. L142/59.
[36] [1989] O.J. L54/1.
[37] See Decision 2006/580 concerning the signing of the Interim Agreement on trade and trade-related matters with Albania [2006] O.J. L 112/1.

Another facility was established for encouraging banks to extend their municipal infrastructure financing operations. It was set up jointly by the Commission, on the one hand, and the EIB, EBRD and the Council of the European Development Bank, on the other; these three sponsors provided a total of at least €220 million.[38]

(4) The New Independent States (NIS)

Relations with these republics of the former Soviet Union are regulated by partnership and co-operation agreements whose scope is political, economic, commercial and cultural. They aim to pave the way for the integration of these countries into the wider European economy. Such agreements and others have been signed with Ukraine,[39] Moldova,[40] Kyrgyz Republic,[41] Belarus,[42] Kazakhstan,[43] Georgia,[44] Armenia,[45] Azerbaijan,[46] Turkmenistan,[47] Tajikistan[47a] and Uzbekistan.[48]

Substantial allocations—€132.5 million, including Russia—were committed over the period 1996–2000, which represents approximately 5 per cent of the total the TACIS budget. The purpose of the programme is to aid the NIS in their transition to a market economy and to entrench democracy. In 2002, €440 million was allocated for assistance to Armenia, Azerbaijan, Georgia, Mongolia, Russia, Ukraine[49] and the countries of central Asia. It covered six fields of co-operation: institutional, judicial and administrative reform; support for the private sector; social consequences from transition to market economy; infrastructure networks; protection of the environment and management of natural resources; development of rural economy.

3. RELATIONS WITH MAJOR INDUSTRIALISED COUNTRIES[50]

(1) The United States

The relations between the United States and the Union are rather ambiguous. On the one hand, both sides claim to attach great importance to closer co-operation and to a strengthening of their relations, and on the other hand they are involved

---

[38] General Report 2002, 83.
[39] [2000] O.J. L283/27. See also the Agreement on trade in certain steel products [2004] O.J. L384/23 and General Report 2004, 253.
[40] [2000] O.J. L283/27 at 36 and General Report 2004, 251.
[41] [1999] O.J. L196/46.
[42] See *http://www.europa.eu.int*. Relations of the EU with Belarus, General Report 2004, 250.
[43] [1999] O.J. L196/1. See also Regulation 2265/04 on trade in certain steel products between the Union and the Republic of Kazakhstan [2004] O.J. L395/1.
[44] See, for instance, [1999] O.J. L343/1 and General Report 2004, 251.
[45] [1999] O.J. L343/1.
[46] [1999] O.J. L343/1 and General Report 2004, 250.
[47] [1999] O.J. L343/1.
[47a] [2009] O.J. L350/1.
[48] [1999] O.J. L343/1.
[49] With regard to some of those countries see also the "Neighbourhood Policy", above, in Ch.36: General Provisions concerning the Union's External Action.
[50] Information in this section is based on *http://www.europa.eu.int/comm/trade/issues/bilateral/countries/usa/index-en.htm*. See same for more details.

in several disputes[51] (threats, retaliation measures, counter-retaliations, WTO panels, Boeing/Airbus, etc.). These two economic powers are, however, bound to co-operate very closely in the economic and political fields. This they successfully do, for example, within the Western Economic Summits held every year and recently with joint proposals for the new WTO multilateral round, which unfortunately, did not get very far, and also in the G8 and G20. The EU and the US form a global partnership, covering not only trade and economics but also co-operation on a whole range of foreign issues and global challenges.

The economic relationship between the two is characterised by close economic interdependence. Together the EU and the US produce 57 per cent of the world GDP and are responsible for about two-fifths of world trade. The EU and the US are each others most important partners in trade and in investment. The total amount of two-way investments amounts to over €1.5 trillion, with each partner employing about six million people in the other. In 2005 the EU exported goods to the US for €260 billion and imported from the US for €180 billion.

Where services are concerned, in 2004, from the Union to the US €139 billion and the US to the Union €127.9.

Agreements were signed between the parties concerning mutual recognition of technical norms and certificates,[52] establishing a co-operation programme in higher education and vocational education and training,[53] on sanitary measures to protect public and animal health in trade in live animals and animal products,[54] for scientific and technological co-operation[55] and on trade in wine.[56] Notwithstanding the above-mentioned disputes, the bilateral dialogue and consultations are increasing both in the economic and political fields.[57] Examples are the already mentioned Transatlantic Business Dialogue, the Transatlantic Environment Dialogue, the Transatlantic Consumers Dialogue, the Transatlantic Labour—Legislators'—and Development Dialogue.[58] In 2003 an EU-US Agreement was signed on extradition and mutual assistance in criminal matters.[59] An agreement was signed on extradition between the Union and the United States and one on mutual legal assistance,[60] and another on the processing and transfer of Financial Messaging Data.[60a]

Mention should also be made of the Bilateral Positive Economic Agenda concerning financial markets dialogue, the launch of regulatory co-operation in four priority sectors (cosmetics, automobile, nutritional labelling and metrology) and the conclusion of an agreement on marine safety equipment.

---

[51] For details about those disputes, consult the General Reports published by the Commission each February; see, for instance General Report 2004, 210. General Report 1997, 333, where mention is made, among other things of the US legislation with an extraterritorial effect like the Cuban liberty and democratic solidarity (Helms-Burton) Act and the Iran and Libya Sanctions Act (d'Amato), about which the EU and the US reached an understanding in April 1997; see also General Report 1996, point 878, and lately the banana dispute.

[52] Under this Agreement a Joint Committee was established and empowered to take decisions; see, for instance, [2001] O.J. L306/34, listing of Conformity Assessment Bodies under the Sectoral Annex on Telecommunication Equipment and on Electromagnetic Compatibility, and concerning medical devices [2002] O.J. L302/30.

[53] [1995] O.J. L279/13, renewed [2001] O.J. L71/7.

[54] [1998] O.J. L118/3.

[55] [1998] O.J. L284/37, renewed [2004] O.J. L335/5 and amended [2009] O.J. L90/20.

[56] [2006] O.J. L87/1.

[57] [1996] Bull.12, 171.

[58] http://www.europa.eu.int/comm/external-relations/us/intro/index.htm.

[59] [2003] O.J. Ll81/25.

[60] [2009] O.J. L291/40.

[60a] [2010] O.J. L8/9.

An Air Transport Agreement was signed and provisionally applied in 2007[61] and an Agreement was concluded the same year on the security of classified information.[62]

(2) Canada

Links between Europe and Canada have traditionally been close.

> "What started out in 1950 as a purely economic relationship has evolved over the years to become a close strategic alliance. The EU and Canada now work together on a great range of diverse issues ranging from research into alternative energy sources to providing police officers for Bosnia."[63]

The Union is Canada's second trade partner, while Canada ranks 11th in terms of Union trade. The first co-operation agreement ever signed by the Union with an industrialised country was with Canada in 1976, the Framework Agreement for Commercial and Economic Co-operation. This provided for closer business and commercial links, economic co-operation and joint undertakings between industries and companies.

The Union and its Member States and Canada adopted a Joint Declaration in 1996 and an Action Plan on relations between the Union and Canada. Less tense than with the United States, the economic and trade relations between Canada and the Union were clouded by numerous disagreements. The worst concerned fish and lasted many years.

At the summit held in Ottawa in March 2004 the Union and Canada adopted the Framework for the Canada-EU Trade and Investment Enhancement Agreement (TIEA), the key element of which is co-operation between Union and Canadian regulators. In addition the agreement addresses issues such as: mutual recognition of professional qualifications; E-commerce; financial services; government procurement; trade and investment facilitation; intellectual property rights; science and technology, etc. In addition, the Union and Canada adopted the EU-Canada Partnership Agenda.

Trade in goods to Canada in 2008 amounted to €26.1 billion and imports from Canada to €23.8 billion.[64] Trade in services, respectively €11.3 and €9.5

In order to facilitate trade between the two partners, they signed an Agreement on mutual recognition,[65] and an Agreement establishing a Co-operation programme in higher education and vocational education and training,[66] an agreement for Scientific and Technological Co-operation,[67] a 1997 Agreement on Customs Co-operation and Mutual Assistance, another in 1998 on Mutual Recognition of Conformity Assessments, a 1999 Veterinary Agreement and a Competition Agreement in view of the increasing number of cases reviewed both by the Commission Directorate-General for Competition and the Canadian Bureau of Competition Policy. (See above, Ch.22: Competition Policy.)

---

[61] [2007] O.J. L134/4.
[62] [2007] O.J. L115/29.
[63] *http://www.europa.eu.int/comm/external-relations/canada/intro/index.htm.*
[64] See Internet.
[65] [1998] O.J. L280/3.
[66] [1995] O.J. L300/19, renewed [2001] O.J. L71/15.
[67] [1996] O.J. L74/25, amended [1999] O.J. L156/23.

In 2004 the EU and Canada adopted a Partnership Agenda for joint action in foreign and security policy, in the field of justice and home affairs, multilateral trade talks and tackling global challenges such as climate change and poverty in developing countries.

Summit meetings are held yearly, the last one in October 2007.[68]

(3) Japan

Japan and the EU together represent nearly 40 per cent of world GDP (2001) and Japan is the EU's third largest export market (after the US and Switzerland) and the third largest source of imports. Relations with Japan were strained for a long time due to the Japanese trade surplus and the difficulties encountered by exporters in Japan. The latter has, however, especially since its "financial bubble" collapsed, began to accept that it has to make special efforts to open its economy to international competition and embark on structural reforms for its own good and for the benefit of the international economy. Relations improved after the EC-Japan Political Declaration of 1991[69] on relations between the EC and its Member States and Japan. It established common principles and shared objectives in the political, economic, co-operation and cultural areas and established a consultation framework including annual summit meetings.[70]

The co-operation covers various fields such as trade, the environment, industry, scientific research, social affairs, competition policy and energy. However, the commercial relations with Japan were a constant worry for the Union, as shown in the Commission Communication entitled "A consistent and global approach: a review of the Union's relations with Japan".[71] The Council therefore asked the Commission to analyse, on a regular basis, statistically, the development of trade with Japan in goods and services.[72] The Union's trade balance with Japan started to improve in April 1993 and this trend continued, albeit rather slowly. In 2007, Union exports to Japan were €1.238 billion and imports from Japan were €1.424 billion. Japan is also a major investor in the Union.

Co-operation between the Union and Japan now takes place across a wide range of areas, including, besides those already mentioned, development assistance, macroeconomic and financial affairs and transport. An Agreement on mutual recognition was concluded in 2001.[73] The Commission operates an executive training programme that takes young European business people to Japan for 12 months of in-house training in a Japanese company. Important agreements were signed. The EU-Japan Mutual Recognition Agreement (MRA), which entered into force on January 1, 2002, permits acceptance of conformity assessments conducted in one party according to the regulations of the other for telecommunication terminal equipment and radio equipment, electrical products, Good Laboratory Practice for chemicals and Good Manufacturing Practice for pharmaceuticals. Agreements on Co-operation on Anti-competitive Activities,[74] on custom co-operation (2008) and an assistance in criminal matters (2010) were signed.

---

[68] General Report 2008, 175.
[69] General Report 1991, 272.
[70] The 14th Summit meeting took place in Luxembourg in June 2004.
[71] COM (92) 219; [1992] Bull.5-1992.
[72] [1992] Bull.6, 95. General Report 1993, 257.
[73] [2001] O.J. L284/1.
[74] [2003] O.J. L183/111.

(4) Russia

The EU is Russia's largest trading partner by far, accounting for close to 52 per cent of the latter's foreign trade. Political and economic relations are governed by a Partnership and Co-operation Agreement (PCA)[75] that entered into force on December 1, 1997[76] and was extended to the 10 new Member States.[77] The agreement establishes a political dialogue at all levels, regulates the trade in nuclear fuels, allows free EU investment in Russia with full repatriation of profits, liberalises the activities of foreign banks in Russia, removes all EU quotas on Russian exports apart from certain textile and steel products[78] and allows temporary Russian quotas on some EU imports. After enlargement, Russia and the EU became direct neighbours[79]; hence the interest of both parties in maintaining and strengthening solid, predictable, transparent and open trade relations.

In 2008, bilateral trade in goods amounted to €180 billion, with Union exports of €105 billion, and imports of €173.2 billion. Services were €18 billion as against €11.5 in favour of the Union. Foreign direct investments were of €17 billion to Russia and €1 billion from Russia.

The relationship is based on a Partnership and Co-operation Agreement (PCA); a new agreement is under negotiation.

An Agreement on co-operation in science and technology was renewed in March 2009.[80]

(5) China

In 1995, China became the Union's 4th largest export market and its 4th largest supplier, with the EU's imports exceeding its exports. In 2004 China had become the second largest trade partner of the EU (after the US) with a total trade of €175 billion and an EU deficit of €78.5 billion (the greatest trade deficit).

China is the EU's largest supplier of textiles and clothing (see General Report 2005, 145). The legal framework for commercial relations and a programme of co-operation and development are provided by the EC-China Trade and Co-operation Agreement signed in 1985. At the end of 1995, the Council issued guidelines for a EU strategy towards China, whose objectives emphasised the, "smooth and gradual integration of China into the world economy, together with the promotion of democracy, structures based on the rule of law and respect for human rights". As the Commission writes, "two of the biggest markets in the world have everything to gain from deepening their commercial ties."

Trade in goods represented, in 2008, for the Union €247.6 billion in imports and only €78.4 billion in exports; trade in services was slightly better with exports of €20.1 billion and imports of €154.4 billion. Union investments in China reached €4.5 billion, while Chinese investments in the Union were €0.1 billion.

---

[75] *Simuntenkov* (C-265/03) [2005] E.C.R. I-2581 gave the Court an opportunity to rule, for the first time, on the effects of a partnership agreement between the EC and a non-Member State.
[76] *http://www.europa.eu.int/comm/external-relations/ceeca/pca/pca-russia.pdf.*
[77] IP/04/549.
[78] See Regulation 2267/04 on trade in certain steel products between the EC and the Russian Federation [2004] O.J. L395/38.
[79] See European Neighbourhood Policy on the Internet.
[80] [2009] O.J. L92/3.

A High Level Economic and Trade Dialogue was launched in Beijing in 2008.

EU-China Co-operation

The current strategy for EC co-operation with China is defined in the Country Strategy Paper 2002–2006 (CSP), which proposes a concentration of activities in three areas:

1. support for the social and economic reform process;
2. prevention of environmental degradation, conservation of the natural environment, integration of environmental considerations into other policy areas and improved balance between environmental protection and social development;
3. support for the transition to an open society based on the rule of law and respect for human rights.

Financing for the CSP 2002–2006 amounted to €250 million.

Other agreements are a Science and Technology agreement, an agreement on co-operation in EU's Galileo satellite navigation programme, joint research in the peaceful use of atomic energy, maritime transport,[81] and customs co-operation.

Political dialogue and human rights dialogue: a political dialogue was formally established in 1994; it has grown into regular, structured series of meetings at several levels. The sixth summit meeting took place in 2003.

(6) Australia

The Union is Australia's main trading partner; trade between the two continues to grow: Australia's exports to the EU in 2008 rose to €11.2 billion, while Union exports to Australia amounted to €25.2 billion. Trade in services is, from Australia, €6.2 billion and to Australia, €10.7 billion.

In 2008 an Agreement was signed between the Union and Australia on certain aspects of air service.[82]

The Union is still Australia's second largest supplier and its 11th export market. It is its leading partner for services while the Union is also the chief source of cumulative investment and the second home for Australian overseas investments.[83]

(7) New Zealand

Co-operation between the EU and New Zealand is based on preferential agreements largely focused on agricultural products. Thus, butter and lamb imports into the EU from New Zealand have enjoyed preferential access for many years. Total trade between the two is about €3 billion with a small balance in favour of New Zealand. In 1991, the two sides signed a scientific and technical co-operation agreement covering agriculture, biomass, biotechnology, environment, forest, renewable sources of energy and information technology. Other agreements cover, for instance, sanitary

---

[81] See Agreement on maritime transport [2008] O.J. L46/23, modified [2009] O.J. L294/10.
[82] [2008] O.J. L14965.
[83] General Report 1992, 278.

measures applicable to trade in live animals and animal products,[84] mutual recognition in relation to conformity assessments.[85]

4. RELATIONS WITH MEDITERRANEAN COUNTRIES

Implementation of a new Mediterranean policy started in 1992 with three regulations. One concerning financial co-operation in respect of all the non member countries of the area,[86] the second concerns the detailed implementation of financial co-operation under the existing protocols with all those countries[87] and the third, improving the arrangements for the import into the Union of certain agricultural products originating in Algeria, Cyprus, Egypt, Israel, Jordan, Lebanon, Malta, Morocco, the Palestine Authority, Syria, Tunisia and Turkey.[88] An Association Agreement exists with Turkey. Agreements exist also with the Maghreb Countries, Algeria,[89] Morocco and Tunisia,[90] the Mashreq countries, Egypt, Jordan,[91] Lebanon[92] and Syria, and with Israel, the West Bank and the Gaza Strip ("occupied territories"). Those agreements cover agriculture, energy, industry, distribution trades, infrastructure, education and training, health and environment and scientific co-operation. Those activities are financed by the resources provided for in the financial protocols. In 1992, the Council adopted the 4th Financial Protocols with Algeria, Israel, Jordan and Lebanon in the context of the new Mediterranean policy. Similar protocols with the other countries were already concluded or on the point of being concluded. In December 1994, the Essen European Council endorsed a strategy set out by the Commission in the framework of a Euro-Mediterranean partnership with a view of strengthening the Union's policy for peace, security and welfare of the Mediterranean. The long-term goal was the creation of an extensive trade area, backed up by substantial financial aid.[93]

A Euro-Mediterranean ministerial conference took place in Barcelona in November 1995.[94] The EU and its 12 Mediterranean partners[95] adopted a Declaration[96] in which they decided to put their relations on a multilateral and durable footing based on a spirit of partnership and on a work programme. Reinforced and regular political dialogue, enhanced economic and financial co-operation in support of the creation of a free trade area and a further strengthening of the social, cultural and human dimension are the partnerships' three

---

[84] [2003] O.J. L214/36.

[85] [1998] O.J. L229/61.

[86] Regulation 1763/92 [1992] O.J. L181/5.

[87] Regulation 1762/92 [1992] O.J. L181/1.

[88] Regulation 1764/92 [1992] O.J. L181/9.

[89] A Euro-Mediterranean Agreement establishing an Association between the Union and its Member States, of the one part, and the People's Democratic republic of Algeria, of the other part, was concluded in July 2005 [2005] O.J. L265/1. In 2005, a Euro-Mediterranean Agreement established an association with Algeria [2005] O.J. L292/10.

[90] See Decision of September 20, 2005 establishing an association between the European Communities and their Member States and the republic of Tunisia [2005] O.J. L278/1.

[91] Agreement establishing an Association [2002] O.J. L129/1, modified [2006] O.J. L41/1. See also signing of a protocol [2005] O.J. L283/2, Association Agreement amended [2008] O.J. L207/16.

[92] Decision concerning the conclusion of the Euro-Mediterranean Agreement [2006] O.J. L143/1.

[93] General Report 1995, 327.

[94] [1995] Bull.11, point 1.4.56 and Suppl.2/95.

[95] Algeria, Cyprus, Egypt, Israel, Jordan, Lebanon, Malta, Morocco, Syria, Tunisia, Turkey and the Palestinian Authority.

[96] The full text of the Declaration and the work programme can be found in [1995] Bull.11.

key components. Those three facets are being implemented and the process was spurred on by a second Euro-Mediterranean ministerial[97] conference in 1997, in Malta.[98] The concrete implementation is carried out through Euro-Mediterranean Association Agreements. The existing association or co-operation agreements were "re-launched" on the basis of the Barcelona Declaration. The latter also sets the ambitious target of a free zone by 2010 between the Union and the 12 countries from the Southern and Eastern Mediterranean. A Euro-Mediterranean Conference of Foreign Ministers took place in Valencia in April 2002,[99] followed by a series of Euro-Mediterranean sectoral ministerial conferences.[100] Financial and technical measures were provided to accompany the reform of economic and social structures. Euro-Mediterranean co-operation in higher education was considered an indispensable instrument to achieve the key objectives set out in the Barcelona declaration (MEDA).[101] On the other hand, it will be remembered that the Union set up a Trans-European Co-operation Scheme for Higher Education (TEMPUS). The geographical scope of the TEMPUS III programme was enlarged to the Mediterranean non-member countries and territories.[102] The financial envelope for MEDA for the period 2000–2006 was set at €5.35 billion. Taken together with loans, which are available from the EIB, this means the EU funding for the region during the seven-year period could reach some €13 billion. Under MEDA II,[103] the Commission committed €2.5 million in 2002.

Following the Laeken European Council the Euro-Mediterranean Investment Facility was set up within the EIB. The latter also manages technical assistance and venture capital projects financed from the Union budget. Current agreements give duty-free access into the EU to all, or most, of the Mediterranean industrial products, will some concessions for agricultural produce and financial aid in the form of grants and loans. Mention must also be made of the Co-operation Agreement between the EEC, on the one part, and the countries party to the Charter of the Co-operation Council for the Arab States of the Gulf (the State of the United Arab Emirates, the State of Bahrain, the Kingdom of Saudi Arabia, the Sultanate of Oman, the State of Qatar and the State of Kuwait), on the other part, signed in 1988.[104]

In 2008 a framework agreement was concluded between the Union and Israel on the general principles governing the State of Israel's participation in Union programmes.[105]

5. Relations with Asia

In 2004 €272 million was committed under financial and technical co-operation with the countries of Asia.[106] Afghanistan received €18 million to cover rehabil-

---

[97] 27 foreign ministers met in April 1997.

[98] General Report 1997, 315.

[99] General Report 2002, 880 and *http://www.europa.eu.int/comm./external-relations/euromed/conf/val/index.htm*.

[100] General Report 2002, 880.

[101] Regulation 1488/96 [1996] O.J. L189/1, amended [2000] O.J. L311/1.

[102] Decision amending Decision 1999/311 adopting the third phase of TEMPUS (2000 to 2006) [2002] O.J. L195/34.

[103] Regulation 2698/00 [2000] O.J. L311/1.

[104] See below, Ch.40: Enlargement, [1989] O. J. L54/1.

[105] Decision 2008/372 [2008] O.J. L129/39.

[106] General Report 2004, 264.

itation and reconstruction schemes.[107] Operations to support uprooted people amounted to €25 million, while €3.4 million was allocated under the heading of political, economic and cultural co-operation.

Mention must be made of the Asia-Europe Meetings (ASEM) comprising the seven members of the ASEAN (Association of South-East Asian Nations) plus China, Japan and South Korea.[108]

(1) South Korea

A Framework Agreement for Trade and Co-operation and its attached political declaration was signed in October 1996 in South Korea. It aims at promoting closer economic relations and exchanges of information and mutually beneficial investment.[109] Total trade increased to €46 billion in 2004, the EU becoming the second most important export area for South Korea. With registered investment stock of €24 billion (March 2005) the EU remains the largest investor in South Korea.

In addition, the EU is contributing to the Korean Peninsula Energy Development Organisation in support of the search for peace and stability in the region. The EU supports the inter-Korean reconciliation process. From a commercial point of view there are a certain number of regulatory and access issues that remain unresolved.[110]

(2) India

The current 1994 co-operation agreement goes well beyond trade and economic co-operation. The EU is India's largest trading partner. Total trade in 2005 was €40 billion (imports €19 billion, exports €21 billion). India benefits from the Generalised Preferential System. Overall high tariff levels and non-tariff trade barriers remain an obstacle for European industry. Various agreements have been concluded: on sugar cane, on trade in textiles, on science and technology and customs co-operation.

A Framework Agreement on Trade and Co-operation is in force since 2001. Back in 1997 two Agreements were concluded on Co-operation and Mutual Administrative Assistance in Customs matters and on Telecommunications Procurement. EU-India relations were upgraded to a "strategic partnership" in 2004[111] and in 2005 India decided to participate in the European satellite radio navigation programme "Galileo"; it ensures the availability of the highest quality Galileo services in India as well as co-operation to establish regional augmentation systems based on EGNOS and Galileo.[112]

---

[107] General Report 2004, 260.
[108] General Report 2004, 259.
[109] See [2005] O.J. L332/1.
[110] See, for instance, Commission Decision of October 8, 2002 concerning trade practices maintained by Korea affecting trade in commercial vessels [2002] O.J. L281/15.
[111] General Report 2004, 262.
[112] *http://www.europa.eu.int/comm/external-relations/india/news/ip05-1105.htm.*

(3) Other Asian Countries

Where other Asian Countries are concerned, the 25-nation summit in Bangkok between European and Asian leaders in March 1996, was a major step towards widening and deepening the dialogue between the two regions. The meeting brought together the 15 EU members with the seven members of ASEAN as well as China, Japan and Vietnam.

Co-operation agreements were signed with Cambodia and Laos, while Myanmar (Burma) was withdrawn from the GSP.

Co-operation agreements exist with Bangladesh, Pakistan and Sri Lanka in the fields of rural development, food aid, scientific and technical co-operation and industrial and trade promotion. Under a system of compensation for loss of export earnings for least-developed countries not signatories to the Lomé Convention,[113] Nepal, Bangladesh and Haiti have received Union financial aid. Diplomatic relations with Vietnam were established in 1990. Relations were established with Singapore, Indonesia, Bhutan, Cambodia and Pakistan.[114] The main activities covered a programme to protect EC-Asian patents and registered trade marks, education, environmental technology, energy co-operation, medical co-operation, refugee aid, etc.[115]

6. LATIN-AMERICA

Agreements exist with Mexico[116] (Global Agreement 2000), Brazil (1995), Paraguay (Framework Co-operation Agreement 1992), Uruguay (Framework Cooperation Agreement 1992), Chile (1996 Framework Co-operation Agreement) and Argentina (1990 Framework Co-operation Agreement). The EU is the main trading partner, after the US, of most of these countries. Details can be found on the Commission website. The Union has established relations with the Rio Group Countries (Argentina,[117] Bolivia, Brazil,[118] Chile,[119] Columbia, Ecuador, Panama, Paraguay, Peru, Uruguay and Venezuela), the countries of Central America and Mercosur[120]

---

[113] [1987] O.J. L43/1.

[114] For information concerning the relations of Europe with these countries, see the Bulletin and the General Reports.

[115] General Report 1992, 299. See Decision of December 2, 1993; Agreement on trade in textiles with Hong Kong, Singapore, Macao, Indonesia, the Philippines, China, Bangladesh, Korea, India, Malaysia, Pakistan, Sri Lanka and Thailand [1994] O.J. L110/1.

[116] An Economic Partnership, political Co-ordination and Co-operation Agreement was signed in 1997 with the Community and its Member States [2000] O.J. L276/45 and a Joint Council was set up; see [2008] O.J. L198/55.

[117] See Regulation 1150/02 opening an additional autonomous quota for imports of high-quality beef [2002] O.J. L170/14.

[118] In 2002 the EC and Brazil signed a Memorandum of Understanding on Co-operation. It reflected the priorities for bilateral EC-Brazilian co-operation until the end of 2006. It foresees an indicative budget of close to €64 million and include the possibility of adjustments when the parties considered this necessary, IP/02/1707. In 2005, an Agreement was concluded for scientific and technological co-operation [2005] O.J. L295/37.

[119] An agreement establishing an association between the European Union and its Member States, of the one part, and the Republic of Chile, of the other part, was concluded at the end of 2002 [2002] O.J. L352/1 and 3; it entered into force on March 1, 2005. In 2005, the EU concluded an aviation agreement with Chile; it is the first of its kind, it allows EU airlines to fly between Chile and the EU Member States.

[120] General Report 1993, 271. The Association Agreement contained an Agreement on trade in Wines (Annex V [2002] O.J. L352/1083), the latter was amended [2006] O.J. L 54/23.

and the Andean Group. There is also the San José Group composed of Costa Rica, El Salvador, Guatemala, Honduras, Nicaragua and Panama; with all those groups the Union holds regular meetings at ministerial level.

Besides those multilateral relations the Union has bilateral relations with a number of Latin-American countries.

Following the establishment of the common organisation of the banana market a five-year diversification and development programme was established for the Latin-American banana-producing countries: Panama, Costa Rica, Nicaragua, Honduras, El Salvador, Guatemala, Columbia, Venezuela, Ecuador, Peru and Bolivia.

The main economic co-operation activities were geared to trade promotion, training, regional integration, energy co-operation, investment promotion, development of democracy in the region, refugee aid, etc.[121]

7. AFRICA

Africa has always been the main playground for European colonialists and their influence is still very great. As was seen under the ACP agreement, most of the partners are African.

South Africa is an important trade partner: an Agreement on trade, development and co-operation between the Union and its Member States and South Africa has been in existence for some time.[122]

8. EURATOM'S EXTERNAL RELATIONS

Contrary to the EC Treaty, the Euratom Treaty contains a Chapter concerning the "External Relations" of that Union. It explicitly provides for the necessary powers and jurisdiction to, "enter into obligations by concluding agreements or contracts with a third State, an international organisation or a national of a third State".[123] Such agreements are negotiated by the Commission in accordance with the directives of the Council, and are concluded by the Commission with approval of the Council.[124] However, agreements and contracts whose implementation does not require action by the Council and can be effected within the limits of the relevant budget, are negotiated and concluded solely by the Commission, which must keep the Council informed.

Furthermore Member States must communicate to the Commission the draft agreements or contracts with third State, an international organisation or a national from a third State when such agreements or contracts concern matters within the ambit of the Euratom Treaty.[125] The Commission can oppose the conclusion of such acts and the Court of Justice must decide when called upon by the Member States in question.

---

[121] EEC-Central America Co-operation Agreement [1986] O.J. L172/1.
[122] See Decision of the South African Co-operation Council of 2009 [2009] O.J. L265/34.
[123] art. 101, Euratom.
[124] Several such agreements were concluded right from the beginning for the purchase of nuclear material, among others with the US and the UK. See also Agreement between the EEC and Euratom and the USSR of 1990 [1990] O.J. L68/2 and a similar Agreement with the republic of Tajikistan [2004] O.J. L340/21.
[125] art. 103, Euratom.

9. MULTILATERAL RELATIONS

(1) GATT[126]

The negotiations for the Uruguay Round started on September 20, 1986 at Punte del Este and ended in Geneva on December 15, 1993. The final text was signed on April 15, 1994.

(2) The World Trade Organisation (WTO)

The Uruguay Round agreement established the World Trade Organisation (WTO), providing for the attainment of the following objectives. Thanks to the institutional framework of the WTO it makes possible the establishment the rules of world trade on a stable basis and on a commitment of the participants to all the results of the negotiation, without exception. As mentioned, it encompasses an effective system for the settlement of disputes and, finally, it allows for a better co-ordination with the International Monetary Fund (IMF) and the Bank for Industrial Reconstruction and Development (BIRD). The institutions of the WTO consist of the Ministerial Conference which meets at least once every two years and takes the basic decisions and a General Council, which oversees the functioning of the WTO and the implementation of the ministerial decisions. It is, at the same time, the Organ for the Settlement of Disputes and the Organ for the Examination of the Commercial Policies. Councils for goods, services and TRIPs (Trade Related Intellectual Property Rights) were set up. The functioning of the WTO, like that of the GATT, is based on consensus, and when a vote is necessary, decisions are, save exceptions, taken by a majority of the votes cast. However, decisions concerning the interpretation of the Agreement and the granting of exemptions must be taken by a two-third majority of the members. Specific rules are provided for amendments to the Agreement.

The Agreement contains one binding provision concerning the conformity of the national legislations with the rules of the WTO. Special attention is also given to the tandems "trade and environment" and "trade and competition". The WTO permits a reduction of the trade obstacles resulting in an improvement of the free "market access". It should also put an end to the bilateral and unilateral trade measures, which, particularly, the United States has a tendency to prefer above the agreed-upon multilateral arrangements. The final results of the Uruguay Round were put in the form of various agreements: on trade in goods, in services, trade related to intellectual property rights (TRIPS), dispute settlement regarding anti-dumping and anti-subsidy, trade policy review mechanisms and plurilateral trade agreements.

The Uruguay Round Agreement ended with a Declaration on the Functioning of the GATT which, among other things, aims at establishing a link between trade, monetary and financial policies.

(3) The Doha Negotiations for a New Round

On November 14, 2001, the WTO members agreed on a Declaration providing for a new round of global trade negotiations. Special attention was to be given to

---

[126] This summary is based on the Commission's weekly reports.

the "Least Developed Countries", social development, services, market access for non-agricultural products, competition, investment, simplifying customs and related procedures, government procurement, trade-related aspects of intellectual property (TRIPS), environment, public health, etc.[127] This list is very long indeed, and was so at the insistence of the EU; one might wonder whether the EU did not thereby overplay its hand.

Further Reading

Dr Robert Maclean, *EU Trade Barrier Regulation: Tackling Unfair Foreign Trade Practices*, (Sweet & Maxwell, 2005).
Mistuo Matsushita, Thomas J. Schoenbaum, Petros C. Mavroidis, *The World Trade Organisation* (Oxford University Press, 2003).
Van Bael & Bellis, *Anti-dumping and other trade protection laws of the E.C.*, (Kluwer Law International, 2004).

---

[127] *http://www.wto.org/english/thewto-e/minist/min01-e/mindecl-e.htm.*

Chapter Thirty-nine

Development Co-operation

1. GENERAL REMARKS

According to the TFEU, Union policy in the field of development co-operation must be conducted within the framework of the principles and objectives of the Union external action (see above, Ch.36). The Union's development co-operation and that of the Member States must complement and reinforce each other. The TFEU provides that:

> "[I]n the area of development cooperation and humanitarian aid, the Union shall have competence to carry out activities and conduct a common policy; however, the exercise of that competence shall not result in Member States being prevented from exercising theirs."[1]

The Union's development co-operation has, as its primary objective, the reduction, and, in the long-term the eradication of, poverty.

This policy must comply with the international commitments of the Union.[2] More specifically the TFEU provides that the Union and the Member States must comply with the commitments and take account of the objectives they have approved in the context of the United Nations and other competent international organisations.[3] In this regard, account must be taken of the Millennium Development Goals (MDGs), which 192 United Nations Member States and at least 23 international organisations have agreed to achieve by 2015. They are:

- eradicate extreme poverty and hunger,
- achieve universal primary education,
- promote gender equality and empower women,
- reduce child mortality,
- improve maternal health,
- combat HIV/AIDS, malaria and other diseases,
- ensure environmental sustainability, and
- develop a global partnership for development.[4]

Related to these targets is the pledge of the participating countries to contribute 0.7 per cent of the GDP towards poverty reduction. The European Union has reaffirmed its commitment to the 0.7 per cent target. In 2008 the Council stated its belief that all MDGs could be achieved in all regions provided that immediate,

---

[1] art.5(4) TFEU.
[2] art.208(2) TFEU [177(3)].
[3] art.208(2) TFEU.
[4] For more information of the Union's activities in some of these areas, see General Report 2008, 183–184.

concerted action was taken and sustained for the seven years that remained for attaining them.[5]

In 2008, the Commission confirmed the European Union's status as the world's leading donor, contributing 60 per cent of total official development assistance.[6]

The development policy must, furthermore, be integrated into all the activities of the Union: it must be taken into account when implementing other policies that are likely to affect developing countries.[7] This is, of course, the real test of a development policy. The best example for an area where there clearly are conflicts with this development policy is the Union's agricultural policy.[8] It cannot be said, unfortunately, that the Union has adjusted that policy to allow the third world to develop what often is its unique source of income. The same reproach must be made to all other developed countries and, in the first place, to the US.

Development co-operation also allows the Union to help 79 African, Caribbean and Pacific (ACP) States (see below), 20 overseas countries and territories, and all other developing countries. A financial instrument for development co-operation was established at the end of 2006.[9] Food aid and food security operations are just one example (see humanitarian aid); the Union also co-operates with Development Non-Governmental Organisations (NGOs). Presently, the Commission pursues the following targets:

- improve the coherence in the Union's approach between all different policies involved with development;
- improve the collaboration between the policies of the Union and those of the Member States[10];
- strengthen the ACP-EU relations; and
- prepare for the after-Lomé (Cotonou).

Despite growing pressure on public budgets, the Commission was able to report[11] that the European Union and its members remain at the centre of global efforts to promote aid and development in the South or Third World. They are committing up to €26 billion a year (2001) for this purpose (of which 5.96 billion is from the EC proper) and account for between 45 and 50 per cent of all public aid for development. All Member States[12] are committed to increasing their collective development aid from 0.32 per cent in 2000 to 0.39 per cent of GNI by 2006, as a step towards reaching the 0.7 per cent target. This compares with around 0.2 per cent from the US (11.4 billion or barely 0.11 per cent of its Gross National Income, but not counting private donations that amounts to several billion US $) and 18 per cent from Japan (9.8 billion, or 0.23 per cent of GNI). The Union itself is responsible for around 15 per cent of the total aid given by Member States whose national interests—let us not forget—are served by helping developing countries, which both supply them with raw material and offer markets on which Member States can sell their products. On the other hand, the Union is also a vital market

---

[5] General Report 2009, 67.
[6] General Report 2009.
[7] art.208(1)2 TFEU.
[8] See, e.g. below, under relations with Latin-American countries, the measures taken to counteract the effects of the Union's banana policy.
[9] [2006] O.J. L378/41.
[10] Indeed, the Member States, each on their own, continue to grant aid to a certain number of developing countries.
[11] *http://www.europa.eu/pol/dev/index_en.htm.*
[12] Regulation 1257/96 [1996] O.J. L163/1.

for developing countries, absorbing more than 21 per cent of their total exports. It offers free access without offsetting concessions to the products of 79 African, Caribbean and Pacific countries. Virtually all developing countries enjoy special trade provisions of one kind or other.

The EU's aid and development initiatives take two forms:

- regional agreements such as the Cotonou Convention examined in the next section, and
- worldwide action, i.e. humanitarian aid, food aid, Generalised System of Preferences (GSP), Project Co-financing and Decentralised Co-operation.

The Generalised System of Preferences gives developing countries duty-free or reduced-duty access the Union market for their finished and semi-finished products.[13] In 1996, the Council adopted a revised scheme of agricultural preferences based on the same principles as the scheme for the industrial sector and covering a much greater number of products; the scheme came into force on July 1, 1996,[14] and in 2008 a regulation applied the GSP for the period January 1, 2009 to December 31, 2011.[15] For that period 16 beneficiary countries have qualified to receive the additional preferences under the GSP+ incentive arrangements; these countries must be considered "vulnerable" in terms of their size or the limited diversification of their exports. They must also have ratified and implemented 27 specific international conventions in the fields of human rights, core labour standards, sustainable development and good governance.[16]

Many more schemes exist through which the Union helps underdeveloped countries; (to name but a few) the International Commodity Agreements, the North-South Co-operation on drugs and drug abuse, the North-South Co-operation on health issues, the Co-operation on Eradicating Anti-personnel Mines, Co-operation through Non-Governmental Organisations, Rehabilitation Aid, etc.[17] In 2009 the Commission signed a €4 million contribution agreement towards the Enhanced Integrated Framework (EIF), which is a partnership to support the sustainable developments of least-developed countries. A regulation was adopted on the introduction of a special facility worth €1 billion aiming to save the 2009 and 2010 harvests of the worst-hit countries by providing them with, for instance, seed or fertilisers.[18]

Contrary to other new policies introduced by the EU Treaty where the powers of the Union are strictly limited, the EC Treaty provided for measures to be adopted jointly by the Council and Parliament.[19]

In order to help bring about a real change of the Union's development co-operation procedures in the long term the Union introduced the "decentralised co-operation".[20] Reference is made in the Treaty to multi-annual co-operation

---

[13] Regulation 732/08 [2008] O.J. L211/1 applying a scheme of generalised tariff preferences for the period January 1, 2009 to December 31, 2011. See General Report 2008, 171.

[14] Regulation 1256/96 applying multi-annual schemes of generalised tariff preferences from July 1, 1996 to June 30, 1999 in respect of certain agricultural products originating in developing countries [1996] O.J. L160/1, amended [1998] O.J. L80/1.

[15] Regulation 732/08 [2008] O.J. L211/1.

[16] European Commission: Trade: General System of Preferences (GSP) Windows Internet Explorer.

[17] The reader will find the necessary information concerning those multiple forms of intervention in the yearly General Reports of the Commission and on the Internet.

[18] Regulation 1337/08 [2008] O.J. L354/62 establishing a facility for rapid response to soaring food prices in developing countries.

[19] Similar provisions now in art.209(1) TFEU [179].

[20] Regulation 1659/98 [1998] O.J. L213/6, extended and amended [2002] O.J. L148/1.

programmes with developing countries or programmes with a thematic approach.[21] Those programmes will have to be financed, and for this purpose the EIB is also instructed to participate.[22]

The Union may also conclude agreements with third countries and international organisations[23] helping to achieve the objectives of development co-operation and those referred to in the general provisions on the Union's external action.[24]

All this, of course, without prejudice to the co-operation with the ACP countries.[25] The latter is in any case financed by the European Development Fund (EDF), which draws its resources not from the Union budget but from direct contributions from the Member States.[26]

The Union's development co-operation policy is not an exclusive one, the Member States retain the necessary powers to continue to carry out their own development policy. Consequently, the Treaty provides for co-ordination of those policies and instructs the Union and the Member States to consult each other on their aid programmes, including in international organisations and during international conferences.[27] They may also undertake joint action and Member States shall contribute, if necessary, to the implementation of the Union aid programmes.[28] In other words, the Union policy is complementary to those of the Member States and the "division of labour" in this field shall necessarily be based on the principle of subsidiarity,[29] which means that the Union will implement its policy only if the Member States, on their own, cannot attain the objectives set out in the Treaty.

The Union's co-operation with third countries and international organisations may be the subject, as indicated, of agreements which are concluded in accordance with the Treaty provisions on the conclusion of international agreements.[30]

Europe Aid Co-Operation Office[31]

This office was set by the Commission on January 1, 2001, as part of its effort to reform the management of external aid; its task is to implement all the external aid instruments of the Commission. It is responsible for all phases of the project cycle: identification and appraisal, preparation of financing decisions, implementation and monitoring and evaluation. It handles the devolution, to

---

[21] art.209(1) TFEU [181]

[22] art.209(3) TFEU [179(2)].

[23] art.209(2) TFEU [181]

[24] art.21 EU [36].

[25] art.198 TFEU [182]. For ACP co-operation see next section.

[26] Following are the contributions from the Member States to the 9th EDF in millions of Euros: Belgium: 940,96; Denmark: 295,32; Germany: 3,223,68; Greece: 172,50; Spain: 805,92; France: 3,353,40; Ireland: 85,56; Italy: 1,739,52; Luxembourg: 40,02; Netherlands: 720,36; Austria: 365,70; Portugal: 133,86; Finland: 204,24; Sweden: 376,74; United Kingdom: 1,751,22. Total: 1,3800,00. See the Internal Agreement between the Representatives of the Member States, meeting within the Council, on the financing of Union aid under the multi-annual financial framework for the period 2007 to 2013 in accordance with the ACP-EC Partnership Agreement and on the allocation of financial assistance for the Overseas Countries and territories to which Part IV of the Treaty applies [2006] O.J. L247/32.

[27] art.210(1) TFEU [180].

[28] art.210(1) TFEU [180].

[29] art.5(3) EU [5].

[30] art.209(2) TFEU [181] and art.218 [300].

[31] *http://www.ec.europa.eu/europeaid/who/index_en.htm.*

Commission delegations, in the developing countries, of all operations that can be better managed locally.

In February 2006, the Council and the representatives of the governments of the Member States meeting within the Council, the European Parliament and the Commission issued a joint statement on European Union Development Policy: "The European Consensus".[32] This lengthy document sets out the Union's vision on development and the Union development policy. The same year, the Union created a Financial Instrument for Development Co-operation.[33]

2. RELATIONS WITH THE AFRICAN, CARIBBEAN AND PACIFIC COUNTRIES (ACP)

The main feature of the Union policy towards developing countries is the ACP–EEC Agreement, initially known as the Yaoundé Convention, until recently as the Lomé Convention (there was Lomé I, Lomé II, Lomé III and Lomé IV), and presently as the Cotonou Agreement, signed on June 23, 2000.[34] It is officially designated as: "Partnership Agreement between the members of the African, Caribbean and Pacific group of States of the one part, and the European [Union] and its Member States, of the other part."[35] The new agreement entered into force on April 1, 2003 (when Belgium, as last country to ratify, deposited the instruments). The objective is to:

"[P]romote and expedite the economic, cultural and social development of the ACP States, with a view of contributing to peace and security and to promote a stable and democratic political environment."[36]

It establishes commercial, industrial and financial relations between the Union on the one hand, and now 79 African, Caribbean and Pacific countries,[37] on the other. It is therefore a bilateral agreement, both sides being designated as "party".

This relationship grew out of a quite different set of links which existed when the first Union was established. Most of the countries now "associated" with the Union were colonies at the time and the Member States had special responsibilities towards them. The EEC Treaty provided for the association of "overseas countries and territories", in order to increase trade and to promote jointly economic and social development.[38] Consequently, countries which had special relations with

---

[32] [2006] O.J. C46/1. Note that in a footnote it is mentioned that, "the EU includes both Member States and the European [Union]."

[33] [2006] O.J L378/41, modified [2009] O.J. L270/8, which added and deleted beneficiary States.

[34] [2000] O.J. L317/1, amended [2005] O.J. L209/26.

[35] See [2000] O.J. L317/1.

[36] art.1 Agreement, para.2.

[37] Angola, Antigua and Barbuda, the Commonwealth of the Bahamas, Barbados, Belize, Benin, Botswana, Burkina Faso, Burundi, Cameroon, Cape Verde, Central African Republic, Chad, Cape Verde, Comoros, Congo (Democratic Republic of the), Congo (Republic of the), Cook Islands, Cote d'Ivoire, Cuba, Djibouti, the Commonwealth of Dominica, Dominican Republic, East Timor, Equatorial Guinea, Eritrea, Ethiopia, Fiji, Gabon, the Gambia, Ghana, Grenada, Guinea, Guinea-Bissau, the Republic of Guyana, the Republic of Haiti, Jamaica, Kenya, Kiribati, Lesotho, Liberia, Madagascar, Malawi, Mali, Marshall Islands, Mauritania, Mauritius, Micronesia (Federated States of), Mozambique, Namibia, Nauru, Niger, Nigeria, Niue, Palau, Papua New Guinea, Rwanda, Saint Christopher and Nevis, Saint Lucia, Saint Vincent and the Grenadines, Samoa, Sao Tomé & Principe, Senegal, Seychelles, Sierra Leone, Solomon Islands, Somalia, South Africa, Sudan, the Republic of Surinam, Swaziland, Tanzania, Cape Verde Togo, Tonga, the Republic of Trinidad and Tobago, Tuvalu, Uganda, Vanuatu, Zambia, Zimbabwe.

[38] art.198 TFEU [182].

Belgium, France, Italy and the Netherlands and, after accession, Denmark, the United Kingdom, Portugal and Spain were associated with the Union. The Treaty provisions were drafted at a time when most of these overseas countries were still dependent but the principle of a special relationship was maintained after they gained independence.

For a first period of five years, the details and the procedures of the association were determined by an implementing convention[39] annexed to the Treaty.[40] This convention was replaced by an agreement negotiated between the Union and the emerging African and Malgasy States. Known as the Yaounde Convention,[41] it still bears the marks of the paternalistic approach most European countries nourished towards their former colonies. A second Yaounde Convention, similar to the first, came into force on January 1, 1971.[42] It did not apply to the United Kingdom, Ireland and Denmark until January 1, 1975.[43] An entirely new agreement was signed at Lomé (Togo) on February 28, 1975, between the Union of 10 and 46 countries situated in Africa, the Caribbean and the Pacific.[44] It came into force on April 1, 1976,[45] and expired on March 1, 1980. The Lomé II expired in 1985 and the Lomé III in 1990.

The Lomé Conventions differ from the Yaounde Conventions in that they aim to establish a kind of partnership between the developing countries and the Union and its Member States. The latter was emphasised in the Cotonou Agreement[46] that, as indicated, is officially designated as a "Partnership Agreement". The main features of the latter concern "co-operation strategies" and "development finance co-operation". The strategies put the emphasis on private investment and the development of a dynamic, viable and competitive private sector, the improvement of the quality, availability and accessability of financial and non-financial services to private enterprises and the promotion of business development through the provision of finance, guarantee facilities and technical support for the creation, establishment, expansion, diversification, rehabilitation, restructuring, modernisation or privatisation of dynamic, viable and competitive enterprises in all economic sectors.[47] Clearly, the emphasis is on private business and thereby, away from the "State", which, until recently, was the only actor in this so-called partnership between the ACP States and the Union. The agreement also provides for economic sector development,[48] tourism, social, youth and culture. Assistance is also provided for "regional co-operation and integration". Next comes economic and trade co-operation: its purpose is to replace the non-reciprocal trade preferences, still applied under the 4th ACP/EC Convention, by new trade arrangements within the framework of the WTO. Economic Partnership Agreements[49] are to be

---

[39] This was a convention concluded between the Member States themselves, not with the overseas countries.
[40] art.203 TFEU [187].
[41] [1964] O.J. 1431 and 1490.
[42] [1970] O.J. L282/1; O.J. Spec. Ser. I(2) 7.
[43] arts 109 and 115(1) Act of Accession.
[44] [1976] O.J. L25/1.
[45] [1976] O.J. L25/1. Since it expired before the Lomé II Agreement became effective, transitional measures were adopted [1980] O.J. L55/1. The Lomé III, see [1984] Bull. 11, 7 and General Report 1984, 275.
[46] [2005] O.J. L209/1.
[47] art.21 Agreement.
[48] art.23 and following Agreement.
[49] art.37 Agreement; see *http://www.acpsec.org/gb/press/jtacpeu.htm*, on the ACP and EU joint declaration and report on phase 1 of negotiations of the Economic Partnership Agreements.

negotiated and new trading arrangements were to enter into force on January 1, 2008. Parties recognise the need to ensure a better operation of the international commodity market and to increase market transparency. The same applies to services, information and communication technology, the information society and trade-related areas.[50] Also need to be considered the protection of intellectual property rights, standardisation and certification, sanitary and phytosanitary measures, environment, labour standards and consumer protection and health.

Most important for the ACP is the development of finance co-operation.[51] Operations finance is implemented by the Parties in close co-operation. The ACP States are responsible for defining the objectives and priorities, choosing projects and programmes, preparing and presenting dossiers, preparing, negotiating and concluding contracts, implementation and management and maintaining the projects and the programmes. The Union is responsible for taking the financing decisions.[52] Eligible for financial support are: ACP States, regional and inter-State bodies and joint bodies set up by the ACP States and the Union. Private companies, firms and other private organisations and private operators are also eligible, subject to the agreement of the ACP State or States. This constitutes a very important novelty and is the logical consequence of the emphasis put on private investment.[53] The latter can also profit from the Centre for Development of Enterprise (CDE).[54]

The scope of financing may include measures to attenuate the debt burden of an ACP country, macroeconomic reforms, mitigation of instability of export earnings, sectoral policies, institutional development, technical co-operation and, humanitarian and emergency assistance. The overall amount and the method of financing are decided jointly by the ACP State and the Union.[55] The Agreement also contains special provisions for the least-developed, landlocked and island ACP States.[56]

The Agreement is concluded for 20 years, having commenced on March 1, 2000; financial Protocols are defined for five years. The financial resources are the Tenth European Development Fund (EDF)[57] for the period 2008–2013: €22.7 billion.[58]

Finally, there are the provisions on consultation procedure and appropriate measures as regards human rights, democratic principles and the rule of law. In case of presumed violation of these provisions, consultation may be requested, which may not last more than 60 days. If no solution acceptable to both Parties is found or if consultation is refused, "appropriate measures" may be taken in

---

[50] art.44 Agreement.

[51] art.55 and following Agreement.

[52] See Internal Agreement of July 17, 2006 between the Representatives of the Member States on the financing of Community aid under the multi-annual financial framework for the period 2008–2013 in accordance with the ACP-EC Partnership Agreement and the allocation of financial assistance to the Overseas Countries and territories [2007] O.J. L202/35 and the Financial Regulation applicable to the 9th European development Fund [2003] O.J. L83/1, amended [2007] O.J. L82/1.

[53] art.74 and following Agreement.

[54] This centre is a joint institution of the Union and the ACP Countries; its is endowed with €110 million from the EDF; it operates to complement the Commission, the ACP Secretariat and the EIB.

[55] arts 62 and 63 Agreement.

[56] arts 84 to 90 Agreement.

[57] [2007] O.J. L314/1; see also Regulation 215/2008 on the Financial Regulation applicable to the 10th EDF [2008] O.J. L78/1 and Decision adopting the rules of procedure of the EDF Committee [2008] O.J. L78/35.

[58] See Regulation 215/2008 on the Financial Regulation applicable to the 10th EDF [2008] O.J. L78/1.

accordance with international law, and proportional to the violation. It is under-stood that suspension would be a measure of last resort.[59] It was, however, applied in 2002 against a few ACP countries: Haiti, Zimbabwe, Ivory Coast, Fiji and Comoros.[60] The Partnership Agreement was modified in 2008 to allow the Union to take appropriate measures, including partial suspension, where an ACP State fails to fulfil an obligation under the Agreement on non-proliferation of weapons of mass destruction.[61]

Institutional Aspects of the ACP Convention

The Convention provides for three common institutions: the Council of Ministers (Council),[62] the Committee of Ambassadors (Committee)[63] and the Joint Assembly (Assembly). The Council is composed of the members of the Council of the Communities and members of the Commission and, on the other side, of a member of the government of each ACP State. Its function is to conduct the political dialogue, adopt the policy guidelines and take the decisions necessary for the implementation of the Agreement, settle disputes,[64] and ensure the smooth functioning of the political dialogue. Decisions are taken by common agreement. Proceedings are valid when half of the members of the Council and one member of the Commission and two-thirds of the members representing the ACP States are present; members may be represented. The Committee is composed of the Permanent Representatives of the Member States of the Union, a member of the Commission and, on the other hand, of the Heads of Mission of the ACP coun-tries to the Union. It assists the Council in the implementation of its tasks and follows the application of the Convention.[65] The Assembly is composed in equal numbers of members of the European Parliament and members of the ACP par-liaments; failing this, the persons designated must first be approved by the Assembly. It is a purely consultative body.

In 2008 the Union signed and provisionally applied the Economic Partnership Agreement between certain ACP countries: the CARIFORUM States and the Union and its Member States.[66] These ACP countries are: Antigua and Barbuda, the Commonwealth of the Bahamas, Barbados, Belize, the Commonwealth of Dominica, the Dominican Republic, Grenada, the Republic of Guyana, the Republic of Haiti, Jamaica, Saint Christopher and Nevis, Saint Lucia, Saint Vincent and the Grenadines, the Republic of Suriname and the Republic of Trinidad and Tobago. The Agreement provides for a CARIFORUM-EC Council and a Trade and Development Committee.

The main parts of this Agreement concern trade partnership and sustainable development, trade-related matters, competition, environment, investment and trade-related services, e-commerce, etc, etc.

---

[59] art.96 Agreement.
[60] General Report 2002, 1004.
[61] [2008] O.J. L129/44.
[62] art.15 Agreement of Decision 1/2001 concerning the adoption of the Rules of Procedure of the Council [2001] O.J. L43/20.
[63] Decision 2/2001 concerning the adoption of the Rules of Procedure of the Committee [2001] O.J. L43/24.
[64] art.98 Agreement.
[65] art.16 Agreement.
[66] [2008] O.J. L289/1/1.

In 2009 the Union and its Member States signed and provisionally applied an Economic Partnership Agreement (EPA) with the South African Development Community (SADC) comprising Botswana, Lesotho, Namibia, Swaziland and Mozambique.[66a]

3. ASSOCIATION OF THE OVERSEAS COUNTRIES AND TERRITORIES (OCT)[67]

These countries and territories, the list of wich is to be found in Annex II to the TFEU, are "associated" with the European Union.[68] They concern entities which have special relations with Denmark, France, the Netherlands and the UK. In 2001, the Council decided to extend the association. It deals with the politics, general relations and co-operation between the EC and the OCTs. The Council decision transfers, in fact, the results of the Cotonou Convention to the OCTs in order to strengthen their economic structures. Major fields of co-operation are environment, agriculture, fisheries, industrial development, services, tourism and trade. The declared aim of the decision is to promote and accelerate economic, cultural and social development.

The TFEU provisions also apply to Greenland subject to the specific arrangements set out in Protocol No.34 annexed to the TFEU.

Non-associated Third Countries

The Union also contributes to the development of "non-associated" third countries; India has been the main recipient of the allocated financial aid. The aid programme is intended mainly for the most underprivileged sections of the population in the poorest countries. It has been running since 1976; the emphasis is on the rural sector and improving supplies of foodstuffs.[69]

Further Reading

Online Publications Catalogue of the Directorate General for Development: *http://www.ec.europa.eu/development/icenter/publication_en.cfm*
O. Barbarinde & G. Faber, *The European Union and the Developing Countries, The Cotonou Agreement* (Martinus Nijhoff, 2006).

[66a] [2009] O.J. L319/1.
[67] arts 198–204 TFEU [182–188].
[68] Decision 2001/822 on the association of the OCTs with the European Union [2001] O.J. L314/1; General Report 2001, 1129 and Regulation 2304/2002 implementing the Decision [2002] O.J. L343/1.
[69] See Council Regulation on the implementation of the programme [1981] O.J. L48/8. See Annual Report on the EC Development Policy COM (2003) 527.

Chapter Forty

Enlargement[1]

It might be useful, at the onset of one of the most important transformations the EU has undergone, to recall what has happened before 2010. The Union was founded in 1957, in Rome, by six States: Belgium, Germany, France, Italy, Luxembourg, and the Netherlands. In 1973 it was enlarged a first time to Denmark, Ireland and the United Kingdom. In 1981 Greece joined, followed in 1986 by Portugal and Spain and, in 1995, the Union was enlarged to Austria, Finland and Sweden, bringing the number of Member States to 15. The possibility of such enlargements was provided for by the various European Treaties, right from the beginning, since the objective has always been to unite Europe. See above, Ch.2: History, where it is mentioned that already in 1946, barely a year after the end of the Second World War, Churchill proposed to, "recreate the European family" by "building a kind of United States of Europe". The reader will therefore also understand that the unprecedented enlargement which took place in 2004 will be followed by several more, until all the States from Western, Central and Eastern Europe are "united" in the Union.

Any European State which respects the principles of liberty, democracy, respect for human rights and fundamental freedoms, and the rule of law,[2] may apply to become a member of the Union. It must address its application to the Council, which shall act unanimously, after consulting the Commission and receiving the assent of Parliament.[3]

In November 2008 the Commission adopted its annual strategy paper for the EU enlargement policy. It gives an updated overview of the enlargement policy and a summary of progress made by each of the candidate and potential candidate countries.[4]

Once negotiations with a candidate country have started, the Commission issues Regular Reports on the process towards accession. The Commission uses objective economic and political criteria to assess each applicant's ability to fulfil, in the medium term, the obligations arising out of accession. These criteria were defined by the European Council in Copenhagen in 1993[5]; they ensure equal treatment of all applicants. An applicant country must have:

- stable institutions guaranteeing democracy, the rule of law, human rights and respect for and protection of minorities;
- a functioning market economy and the capacity to cope with competitive pressure and market forces within the Union;

---

[1] The content of this chapter is partly based on *http://www.ec..europa.euenlargementindex_en.htm* and on the 2008 General Report.

[2] arts 49 and 6(1) EU.

[3] art.49 EU.

[4] COM (2008) 674.

[5] EC Bull. 1993–6, 1013.

- the ability to take on the obligations of membership, including adherence to the aims of political, economic and monetary union.

The Commission seeks to evaluate the progress each applicant might reasonably be expected to make in the years ahead, bearing in mind that the *acquis commu-nautaire* (existing Union law and practice acquired over the years) would con-tinue to evolve. Without prejudice to the actual date of accession, the Commission's opinion is, therefore, based on the foreseeable economic situation in the relevant country and its probable capacity to apply existing Union rules in the medium term.

1. FINANCIAL AND ECONOMIC ASSISTANCE

In order to help the countries that applied to become members of the Union to carry out the required reforms, the Union provides financial assistance in various areas: institutional building through the PHARE[6] programme, environment and transport investment through the ISPA[7] (Instrument for Structural policies for Pre-Accession) programme and agriculture[8] and rural development by means of the SAPARD (Special Accession Programme for Agriculture and Rural Development) programme. In 2006 the Council established an instrument for pre-accession assistance (IPA),[9] which was implemented by a Commission regu-lation in 2007.[10] In 2008 the Commission adopted the multi-annual financing framework document for all candidate and potential candidate countries, estab-lishing the 2010–2012 financial framework with indicative allocation for each beneficiary.[11] Over that period the amount of assistance is €5.334 billion.

A donor conference was organised aimed at raising pledges of funding for Kosovo's socioeconomic development; participants pledged €1.2 billion including 70 percent from the Union and the Member States.

2. CANDIDATE COUNTRIES

(1) Turkey

The history of the accession of Turkey to the Union is a long one and has known many ups and downs. For instance, a Customs Union between Turkey and the Union was established in 1995, and in 2006 Turkey became the 7th largest trad-ing partner of the Union. In 1999, at the Helsinki European Council, Turkey was officially recognised as a candidate State, on an equal footing with other States; negotiations for accession finally started on October 3, 2005 and are expected to last at least 10 years!

The attitude of certain Member States to Turkey joining the Union is, to say the least, ambiguous. Nevertheless, the European Council always formally acted

---

[6] See PHARE programme Annual Report.
[7] Regulation 1085/06 [2006] O.J. L210/82.
[8] In 2008, Croatia was the only remaining beneficiary.
[9] Regulation 1085/06 [2006] O.J. L210/82.
[10] Regulation 718/07 [2007] O.J. L170/1, amended [2010] O.J. L25/1.
[11] COM (2008) 705.

as if there were no doubts about starting negotiations. The conclusions of one of the European Councils read as follows.

"The European Council welcomes the commitments of the Turkish government to carry forward the reform process, in particular the remaining legislative work by the end of 2003, and supports its ongoing effort to fulfil the Copenhagen political criteria for opening access negotiations with the Union. Taking into account progress achieved, significant further efforts to this end are required."

With a view to helping Turkey achieve this objective, the Council adopted recently a revised accession partnership,[12] which sets out the priorities which Turkey should pursue, supported by substantially increased pre-accession financial assistance. In accordance with the Helsinki conclusions, fulfilment of these priorities will assist Turkey towards EU membership. The Accession Partnership[13] constitutes the cornerstone of EU/Turkey relations. In January 2006, the Council decided on the principles, priorities and conditions contained in the Accession partnership.[14] Union assistance: between 1996 and 2004, Turkey received around €1.5 billion for different projects; €300 million in 2005 and €500 in 2006. From 2007 on Turkey, with other candidates will be a beneficiary of the Instrument for Structural Policy for pre-Accession (IPA)[15]; the annual allocation for Turkey in the 2007–2013 period will be €1 billion.

During 2008, the accession negotiations continued and by the end of that year negotiations had been opened on 10 of the 31 Chapters[16] and provisionally closed on one! According to the monitoring report,[17] Turkey continued to fulfil the Copenhagen political criteria sufficiently, although progress on reform was limited in 2008, but it had made progress on alignment with the Union's legal order and, as regard the economic criteria, was a functioning market economy.

(2) Croatia

This Balkan country applied for membership on the February 21, 2003. The Commission gave its opinion on Croatia's application in April 2004.[18] The European Council of June 2004 decided that Croatia was a candidate country for membership. Accession negotiations started on October 3, 2005. This fits in with

---

[12] [2003] O.J. L 145/40.

[13] See Regulation 390/2001 on assistance to Turkey in the framework of the pre-accession strategy, and in particular on the establishment of an Accession Partnership [2001] O.J. L58/1.

[14] [2006] O.J. L22/34.

[15] Regulation 1267/1999 [1999] O.J. L161/73. IPA replaces PHARE, ISPA, SAPARD and CARDS.

[16] The negotiations concern the following 31 chapters: 1. free movement of goods, 2. free movement of persons, 3. freedom to provide services, 4. free movement of capital, 5. company law [which includes the basic freedom of establishment], 6. competition policy, 7. agriculture, 8. fisheries, 9. transport, 10. taxation, 11. economic and monetary union, 12. statistics, 13. social policy and employment, 14. energy, 15. industrial policy, 16. small- and medium-sized enterprises, 17. science and research, 18. education and training, 19. telecommunications and information technology, 20. culture and audio-visual policy, 21. regional policy and co-ordination of structural instruments, 22. environment, 23. consumer and health protection, 24. co-operation in the field of justice and home affairs, 25. customs union, 26. external relations, 27. common foreign and security policy, 28. financial control, 29. financial and budgetary provisions, 30 institutions and 31. others.

[17] COM (2008) 674.

[18] COM (2004) 257.

what was indicated above, namely that all the Balkan countries will necessarily, one day, become Members of the Union. As part of the stabilisation and association process, an Accession Partnership was established in February 2006.[19]

Croatia continues to meet the Copenhagen political criteria and is a functioning market economy. It has improved its ability to take on the obligations of membership. Nevertheless Croatia needs to sustain its reform efforts, particularly as regards the judicial system and public administration, fighting organised crime and corruption, promoting minority rights, the prosecution of war crimes and access to the International Tribunal for the former Yugoslavia for certain documents.[20]

As a candidate country, Croatia benefited from all pre-accession financial instruments: the Programme of Community Aid to Countries of Central and Eastern Europe (PHARE),[21] for institution-building and economic and social cohesion, the Instrument for Structural Policy for pre-Accession (ISPA),[22] for environments and transport infrastructure, and the Special Accession Programme for Agriculture and Rural Development (SAPARD).[23] This assistance amounted to €105 million in 2005 and €140 million in 2006. Croatia was also eligible for the Community Assistance for Reconstruction, Development and Stabilisation (CARDS)[24]: €257 between 2001 and 2004. PHARE, ISPA, SAPARD and CARDS were replaced by IPA. The Multi-annual Indicative Financial Framework (MIFF) for 2009–2011 provides €749.8 million (including 2007 and 2008).

(3) Macedonia (former Yugoslav Republic of)

A Stabilisation and Association Agreement (SAA)[25] was signed in April 2001; it entered into force in April 2004. Macedonia applied for membership in March 2004. In June 2004 the Council decided on the European partnership[26] and on the principles, priorities and conditions contained in the European Partnership.[27] Macedonia benefited from a total EC assistance of about €728 million between 2002 and 2004. In addition, the former Yugoslav Republic of Macedonia benefited from the Community Assistance for the Reconstruction, Development and Stability (CARDS)[28] regional programme, macroeconomic assistance and humanitarian assistance. Several agreements were concluded with the Union on wine, trade in agricultural and fisheries products, on the participation in Union programmes, on transport, on the presence of the European Union Monitoring Mission and on the EU Police Mission and the Status of Force (SOFA).[29]

The country does not yet meet the Copenhagen criteria and the key priorities of the Accession Partnership, in particular it needs to guarantee free and fair

---

[19] Regulation 269/2006 [2006] O.J. L47/7.
[20] General Report 2008, 153.
[21] Regulation 3906/89 [1989] O.J. L375/11.
[22] Regulation 1267/1999 [1999] O.J. L161/73.
[23] Regulation 1268/1999 [1999] O.J. L161/87.
[24] Regulation 2666/2000 [2000] O.J. L306/1.
[25] [2004] O.J. L86/1.
[26] Regulation 533/2004 [2004] O.J. L86/1.
[27] [2004] O.J. L222/20, replaced [2006] O.J. L35/57.
[28] Regulation 2666/2000 [2000] O.J. L306/1.
[29] For further information consult, *http://www.ec.europa.eu./enlargement/candidate-countries the _former_yugoslav_republic_of_macedonia-_relations_ en.htm.*

elections, and to strengthen the dialogue between key political parties and actors to allow an effective functioning of political institutions and speed up the pace of reform.[30]

(4) Iceland

The Icelandic Parliament voted on July 16, 2009 to seek membership of the European Union and a formal request for membership was filed with the Union on July 23, 2009.

3. POTENTIAL CANDIDATE COUNTRIES

The Western Balkans: Albania, Bosnia and Herzegovina, [Croatia], [the former Yugoslav Republic of Macedonia] Serbia and Montenegro. The Union grants autonomous trade preferences to the Western Balkans. They have been key instruments in the revitalisation of that area's economies by providing privileged access to the Union market. In 2000 the Union granted exceptional unlimited duty-free access for nearly all products originating in the countries and territories benefiting from the Stabilisation and Association Process: Albania, Bosnia and Herzegovina, Croatia, the former Yugoslav Republic of Macedonia, Serbia and Montenegro, including Kosovo. The preferences were originally adopted for a period until the end of 2005. The country has moved closer towards becoming a functioning market economy.

The EU's policy framework for the countries of the Western Balkans is the Stabilisation and Association Process (SAP). It supports the countries' development and preparations for future Union membership by combining three main instruments:

- the Stabilisation and Association Agreements,
- autonomous trade measures, and
- substantial financial assistance.

Regional co-operation constitutes a cornerstone of the SAP. The European perspectives of the countries in question were confirmed by the European Council of Thessaloniki in June 2003.[31]

(1) Albania

In March 2004 the Council adopted a Regulation on the establishment of European Partnerships in the framework of the Stabilisation and Association Process,[32] while in 2003, the Thessaloniki European Council endorsed the "Thessaloniki Agenda for the Western Balkans: moving towards European integration", which mentioned European Partnerships as one of the means to intensify the Stabilisation and Association Process (SAP).

---

[30] General Report 2008, 154.
[31] See the Internet.
[32] Regulation 533/2004 [2004] O.J. L86/1.

The June 2000 European Council stated that all the SAP countries are "potential candidates" for Union membership. The principles, priorities and conditions contained in the European Partnership with Albania were laid down by the Council in June 2004[33] and revised in February 2006.[34]

Albania profited from autonomous trade preferences, national and regional financial assistance under Community Assistance for Reconstruction, Development and Stabilisation (CARDS).[35] A Stabilisation and Association Agreement (SAA) like the one signed with Croatia (see above) was signed on June 12, 2006 and entered into force on April 1, 2009.[36] The EC/Albania readmission Agreement was signed on April 14, 2005.

According to the monitoring report,[37] Albania continued to make headway on key judicial and electoral reforms, but the rule of law and guarantees as to the proper functioning of state institutions require further consolidation to allow the political system to function effectively. Further efforts are required in the justice sector and on combating corruption and organised crime.

(2) Bosnia and Herzegovina

In 1999, the Union proposed the Stabilisation and Association Process (SAP) for five countries of South-East Europe, including Bosnia and Herzegovina. Since all the SAP countries are "potential candidates" for Union membership, negotiations for the conclusion of a Stabilisation and Association Agreement (SAA) ware opened in November 2005.

From 2001 on the Community Assistance for Reconstruction, Development and Stability (CARDS)[38] is applied to Bosnia and Herzegovina; €312 million was allocated for the period 2001–2004 and €100 for 2005–2006. In addition the EC has provided macro-financial assistance in 1999 and 2002. In 2008, a stabilisation and association agreement and an Interim Agreement on trade and trade-related matters were signed with the Union.[39] The former is aimed at supporting efforts to strengthen democracy and the rule of law and to complete the transition to a market economy. A regulation was adopted laying down procedures for the adoption of detailed rules for the implementation of both agreements.

Although there are no contractual links between Bosnia and Herzegovina and the EC, the latter is their main trade partner, thanks to an autonomous preferential regime adopted by the Union in 2000. Bosnia and Herzegovina urgently need to achieve the necessary political consensus and to proceed with reforms; it also needs to set out a shared vision of its future in order, amongst other things, to speak with one voice on matters relating to the Union.

---

[33] [2004] O.J. L223/20.
[34] [2006] O.J. L35/1.
[35] Regulation 2666/2000 [2000] O.J. L306/1. It was replaced by the Instrument for Pre-Accession Assistance (IPA).
[36] [2009] O.J. L104/57.
[37] COM (2008) 674.
[38] Regulation 2666/2000 [2000] O.J. L306/1. CARDS was replaced by IPA, as indicated above.
[39] [2008] O.J. L233/6.

(3) Serbia and Montenegro[40]

These two countries were covered in 1999, when they were still one country, by the new Stabilisation and Association Process. November 2000: Framework Agreement between the Former Republic of Yugoslavia and the Union for the provision of Assistance and Support; Serbia and Montenegro also benefit from autonomous trade preferences. In April 2005, the Commission adopted a Feasibility Report concluding that Serbia and Montenegro is prepared to negotiate a Stabilisation and Association Agreement with the Union. Negotiations were to be held with the State, Union or the Republics in their respective fields of competence. Since 2001 the Union provides policy advice through an Enhanced Permanent Dialogue (EPD), which monitors and drives reforms on the basis of the European Partnership. The authorities have been advised to pay special attention and make further significant progress concerning the following issues:

- constitutional issues: the distribution of powers between the State Union and the Republics must be clarified and implemented (this is now "*dépassé*");
- strengthening of the democratic functioning of the parliaments and the executives;
- efforts need to be made as regards human rights and the protection of minorities;
- efforts with regard to the reform of the public administration.

The principles, priorities and conditions contained in the European Partnership with Serbia and Montenegro, including Kosovo, as defined by the United Nations Security Council Resolution 1244 of June 10, 1999, are laid down in a Council Decision.[41]

Union assistance was provided through the Community Assistance for Reconstruction, Development and Stability (CARDS),[42] macro-financial and humanitarian assistance. Although there are no formal contractual relations between the Union and Serbia and Montenegro, the Union granted generous trade conditions.

The recent declaration of independence by Montenegro that was recognised by the international community, has created a new situation that will necessarily result in separate further negotiations between the two countries.

(a) Montenegro

The interim agreement on trade and trade-related matters entered into force on January 1, 2008 and its implementation is proceeding satisfactorily. It has made significant progress in addressing the political criteria in improving its legal framework and in strengthening its institutional infrastructure. Efforts are needed to continue reforming the judicial system, consolidating the rule of law and stepping up the fight against corruption and organised crime.[43]

---

[40] Borrowed from *http://www.ec.europa.eu/enlargement/serbia/eu_serbia_and_montenegro_relations_en.htm.*
[41] [2006] O.J. L35/32.
[42] Regulation 2666/2000 [2000] O.J. L306/1.
[43] General Report 2008, 155 and 2009, 58.

(b) Serbia

Serbia has made progress in its effort to meet the political criteria. It has the capacity to make progress towards membership. Efforts are needed to reform the judicial system and measures to prevent corruption. Candidate status could be granted in 2009, according to the Commission.[44] An Interm Agreement on Trade and trade related matters was signed.[45]

Further Reading

"Enlargement of the Union", *http://www.europa.eu/scadplus/leg/en s40000.htm.*
Marise Cremona, *The Enlargement of the European Union* (Oxford University Press, 2003).
Giandomenico Majone, "Unity in diversity: European integration and the enlargement process", (2008) E.L.Review 457.
Hurbert Isak, *A European perspective for the Western Balcans* (Neuer Wissenschaftilicher Verlag, Vienna, 2008)

---

[44] General Report 2008, 156 and 2009, 58.
[45] [2010] O.J. L28/1 and 2.

Index

This index has been prepared using Sweet and Maxwell's Legal Taxonomy. Main index entries conform to keywords provided by the Legal Taxonomy except where references to specific documents or non-standard terms (denoted by quotation marks) have been included. These keywords provide a means of identifying similar concepts in other Sweet & Maxwell publications and online services to which keywords from the Legal Taxonomy have been applied. Readers may find some minor differences between terms used in the text and those which appear in the index. Suggestions to *taxonomy@sweetandmaxwell.co.uk*.

Aarhus Convention
environmental policy, and
external co-operation, 550
generally, 544
Abuse of dominant position
'abuse', 340–341
agriculture, 341–342
air transport, 343–345
coal and steel, 350
'dominant position', 337–340
energy, 350
generally, 337
implementation of rules
Commission's role, 353–358
European Competition Network, 351
hearings, 358–360
implementing provisions, 360–363
introduction, 350–351
legal privilege, 354–355
limitation periods, 358
member states' role, 351–352
modified regulations, 363
settlement procedure, 356
insurance, 349–350
intellectual property rights, 350
international aviation, 344
introduction, 319–320
maritime transport, 342–343
'may affect trade between member states'
generally, 324–325
introduction, 337
motor vehicle sector, 331–332
postal service, 347–349
rail transport, 344–345
research and development agreements, 333–334
specific economic sectors
agriculture, 341–342
air transport, 343–345

coal and steel, 350
energy, 350
insurance, 349–350
intellectual property rights, 350
international aviation, 344
maritime transport, 342–343
postal service, 347–349
rail transport, 344–345
telecommunications, 345–347
transport, 342–345
specialisation agreements, 332–333
technology transfer agreements, 334–336
telecommunications, 345–347
transport
air transport, 343–345
international aviation, 344
introduction, 342
maritime, 342–343
rail, 344–345
vertical agreements
generally, 329–331
motor vehicles, 331–332
Abuse of power
actions for annulment, and, 140
Access to documents
European Commission, and, 124
Access to information
Court of Auditors, and, 174
environmental policy, and
external co-operation, 550
generally, 544
structural funds, and, 524
"Access to the files"
competition policy, and, 372
Accession
Austria, Finland and Sweden, 21–22
Bulgaria and Romania, 24–25

eastern European states, 23
Greece, Portugal and Spain, 17
UK, Ireland and Denmark, 16–17
Accreditation
free movement of goods, and, 236
ACP states
development co-operation, and, 604–607
Acquis communautaire
accession of Austria, Finland and
Sweden, and, 21
EEA Agreement, and, 20
enlargement, and, 610
jurisdiction of the ECJ, and, 138
legal Acts of the EU, and, 29
Schengen Agreement, and 242–243
Treaty on the European Union, 19
Treaty on the Functioning of the
European Union, 9
transport policy, and, 439
Acquisitions
generally, 363–365
introduction, 319–320
joint or collective dominance, 365–370
Actions for annulment
acts submitted to the control of
legality, 133
consequences, 140–141
appellants, 133–137
generally, 132
grounds, 137–140
infringement of essential procedural
requirement, 138
infringement of treaties or rule of law,
138–140
lack of competence, 137–138
legislative acts, 133
misuse of power, 140
Adaptation Decision
generally, 17
"Additionality"
structural funds, and, 526
Advisory procedure
European Commission, and, 116
Advocates-General
duties, 128–129
generally, 127–128
Africa
development co-operation, and,
604–607
external relations, and, 597
**Agency for the Co-operation of Energy
Regulators**
generally, 208–209
Agriculture
animal products
beef, 407–408

eggs, 408
goat-meat, 408
honey, 408–409
milk and milk products, 407
pig-meat, 408
poultry-meat, 408
sheep-meat, 408
veal, 407–408
bananas, 407
beef, 407–408
cereals, 404–405
Common Agricultural Policy
basic principles, 402
cross-compliance, 403
degressivity, modulation and financial
discipline, 403
financing, 411–413
generally, 399
introduction, 401–402
objectives, 401
reforms, 402–404
Single Common Market
Organisation, 404–409
structural measures, 409–411
competition policy, and, 341–342
cotton, 406–407
crops
bananas, 407
cereals, 404–405
cotton, 406–407
fruit and vegetables, 405–406
hops, 407
olive oil, 405
processed fruit and vegetables, 406
raw tobacco, 406
rice, 406
sugar, 406
table olives, 405
wine, 405
cross-compliance, 403
degressivity, modulation and financial
discipline, 403
eggs, 408
financing, 411–413
food safety, 410–411
fruit and vegetables, 405–406
genetically modified food and feed, 410
goat-meat, 408
honey, 408–409
hops, 407
introduction, 399–400
milk and milk products, 407
olive oil, 405
organic farming, 409–410
pig-meat, 408
plant products

bananas, 407
cereals, 404–405
cotton, 406–407
fruit and vegetables, 405–406
hops, 407
olive oil, 405
processed fruit and vegetables, 406
raw tobacco, 406
rice, 406
sugar, 406
table olives, 405
wine, 405
poultry-meat, 408
processed fruit and vegetables, 406
raw tobacco, 406
regional policy, and, 520
rice, 406
rural development
    financing, 411–413
    generally, 411
sheep-meat, 408
Single Common Market Organisation
    animal products, 407–409
    introduction, 404
    plant products, 404–407
single payment scheme, 403
state aid, and, 388
structural measures
    food safety, 410–411
    genetically modified food and
        feed, 410
    introduction, 409
    organic farming, 409–410
sugar, 406
table olives, 405
veal, 407–408
wine, 405
Agreements of minor importance
See **De minimis**
Air transport
competition policy, and
    generally, 449–451
    international agreements, 453–454
    introduction, 343–344
    safety assessment of foreign aircraft,
        453
    Single European Sky, 451–453
external relations with US, and, 589
joint undertakings, and
    generally, 533
    introduction, 212
sectoral state aid, and, 387
Albania
enlargement, and, 613–614
ALTENER
renewable energy, and, 558

Amsterdam Treaty
generally, 22–23
introduction, 3
Ancillary restraints
concentrations, and, 366
Animal products
And see **Common Agricultural Policy**
beef, 407–408
eggs, 408
goat-meat, 408
honey, 408–409
milk and milk products, 407
pig-meat, 408
poultry-meat, 408
sheep-meat, 408
veal, 407–408
Annual reports
Community Plant Variety Office,
    and, 197
consumer protection, and, 500
Court of Auditors, and, 174
employment policy, and, 101
energy policy, and, 556
equal pay, and, 479
EU budget, and, 122
European Central Bank, and, 178
European Commission, and, 123
European Parliament, and, 75–76
Annulment
EU acts, and
    acts submitted to the control of
        legality, 133
    consequences, 140–141
    appellants, 133–137
    generally, 132
    grounds, 137–140
    infringement of essential procedural
        requirement, 138
    infringement of treaties or rule of law,
        138–140
    lack of competence, 137–138
    legislative acts, 133
    misuse of power, 140
Anti-competitive practices
'agreements', 321–322
agriculture, 341–342
agreements of minor importance
    Commission Notice, 372
    generally, 336–337
air transport, 343–345
block exemptions
    introduction, 329
    motor vehicles, 331–332
    research and development
        agreements, 333–334
    specialisation agreements, 332–333

technology transfer agreements,
334–336
vertical agreements, 329–331
coal and steel, 350
'concerted practices', 321–322
de minimis, 336–337
'decisions by associations of
undertakings', 322–323
effect, 327–327
energy, 350
exclusive dealing agreements, 329–330
exemptions from prohibition
block, 329–336
de minimis, 336–337
individual, 328–329
introduction, 328
general prohibition
'agreements', 321–322
'concerted practices', 321–322
'decisions by associations of
undertakings', 322–323
introduction, 321
'may affect trade between member
states', 324–325
'prevention, restriction of distortion
of competition', 325–326
'undertakings', 323–324
'which have as their object or effect',
325
'within the internal market',
326–327
generally, 320
implementation of rules
Commission's role, 353–358
European Competition Network, 351
hearings, 358–360
implementing provisions, 360–363
introduction, 350–351
legal privilege, 354–355
limitation periods, 358
member states' role, 351–352
modified regulations, 363
settlement procedure, 356
individual exemptions, 328–329
insurance, 349–350
intellectual property rights, 350
international aviation, 344
introduction, 319–320
maritime transport, 342–343
'may affect trade between member
states', 324–325
motor vehicle sector, 331–332
nullity, 327–328
postal service, 347–349
'prevention, restriction of distortion of
competition', 325–326

rail transport, 344–345
research and development agreements,
333–334
specific economic sectors
agriculture, 341–342
air transport, 343–345
coal and steel, 350
energy, 350
insurance, 349–350
intellectual property rights, 350
international aviation, 344
maritime transport, 342–343
postal service, 347–349
rail transport, 344–345
telecommunications, 345–347
transport, 342–345
specialisation agreements, 332–333
technology transfer agreements,
334–336
telecommunications, 345–347
transport
air transport, 343–345
international aviation, 344
introduction, 342
maritime, 342–343
rail, 344–345
'undertakings', 323–324
vertical agreements
generally, 329–331
motor vehicles, 331–332
'which have as their object or effect',
325
'within the internal market',
326–327
Anti-dumping duties
commercial policy, and, 583–584
WTO dispute resolution, and, 598
Anti-subsidy duties
See **Countervailing duties**
Approximation of laws
generally, 434–437
harmonisation, 434
mutual recognition, 434
qualified majority voting, 435
Aquaculture
And see **Fisheries**
generally, 417–418
Architects
freedom of establishment, and, 274
Area of freedom, security and justice
asylum policy, 256–258
border controls, 256–258
generally, 255
immigration policy, 256–258
judicial co-operation, 258–263
police co-operation, 263–264

Asia
  external relations, and
    India, 595
    introduction, 594–595
    other, 596
    South Korea, 595
Association of the Overseas Countries
    and Territories
  See Overseas countries and territories
Asylum policy
  free movement of persons, and, 256–258
Audiovisual aids
  culture, and, 489
Australia
  external relations, and, 592
Austria
  accession, and, 21–22
Aviation
  competition policy, and, 344

Banking services
  freedom to provide services, and,
    291–293
Block exemptions
  introduction, 329
  motor vehicles, 331–332
  research and development agreements,
    333–334
  specialisation agreements, 332–333
  state aid, and, 393–394
  technology transfer agreements,
    334–336
  vertical agreements, 329–331
Border controls
  free movement of persons, and, 256–258
Bosnia and Herzegovina
  enlargement, and, 614
Broadcasting
  state aid, and, 389
Budget
  See EU budget
Bulgaria
  accession, and, 24–25
Bureau of the European Parliament
  generally, 82

Cabotage
  air transport, and, 450
  common transport policy, and, 458
  maritime transport, and, 455
  rail transport, and, 448
  road transport, and, 444
Canada
  external relations, and, 589–590
Caribbean
  development co-operation, and, 604–607

Cartels
  And see Anti-competitive practices
  exemptions from prohibition, 328–337
  general prohibition, 321–327
  generally, 320
  implementation of rules, 350–363
  introduction, 319–320
  nullity, 327–328
  specific economic sectors, 341–350
CEDEFOP
  See European Centre for Development
    of Vocational Training
Censure
  powers of European Parliament,
    and, 76
CEPOL
  See European Police College
Charges having equivalent effect
  free movement of goods, and, 225
Charter of Fundamental Rights of the
    European Union
  generally, 26
Charter of the Fundamental Social Rights
    of Workers
  social policy, and, 471
China
  external relations, and, 591–592
Civil Service Tribunal
  See European Union Civil Service
    Tribunal
"Clean Air for Europe (CAFE)"
  environmental policy, and, 545
Climate change
  environmental policy, and, 546–547
  Treaty of Lisbon, and, 26
Closer co-operation
  See Enhanced co-operation
Coal
  competition policy, and, 350
  energy policy, and, 556–557
  state aid, and, 385–386
Co-decision procedure
  See Ordinary legislative procedure
Cohesion Fund
  generally, 529
  introduction, 519
Comity
  competition policy, and, 374
Commercial agents
  exclusive dealing agreements, and, 370
Commission
  See European Commission
Commission Notices
  access to the files, 372
  agreements of minor importance, 372
  co-operations agreements, 370–371

exclusive dealing contracts made with
  commercial agents, 370
introduction, 370
subcontracting agreements, 371–372
Committee of Permanent Representatives
See **COREPER**
Committee of the Regions
generally, 181
Common agricultural policy
And see **Agriculture**
animal products
  beef, 407–408
  eggs, 408
  goat-meat, 408
  honey, 408–409
  milk and milk products, 407
  pig-meat, 408
  poultry-meat, 408
  sheep-meat, 408
  veal, 407–408
bananas, 407
basic principles, 402
beef, 407–408
cereals, 404–405
cotton, 406–407
cross-compliance, 403
degressivity, modulation and financial
  discipline, 403
eggs, 408
financing, 411–413
food safety, 410–411
fruit and vegetables, 405–406
generally, 399
genetically modified food and feed, 410
goat-meat, 408
honey, 408–409
hops, 407
introduction, 401–402
milk and milk products, 407
objectives, 401
olive oil, 405
organic farming, 409–410
pig-meat, 408
plant products
  bananas, 407
  cereals, 404–405
  cotton, 406–407
  fruit and vegetables, 405–406
  hops, 407
  olive oil, 405
  processed fruit and vegetables, 406
  raw tobacco, 406
  rice, 406
  sugar, 406
  table olives, 405
  wine, 405

poultry-meat, 408
processed fruit and vegetables, 406
raw tobacco, 406
reforms, 402–404
rice, 406
sheep-meat, 408
Single Common Market Organisation
  animal products, 407–409
  introduction, 404
  plant products, 404–407
structural measures
  food safety, 410–411
  genetically modified food and feed, 410
  introduction, 409
  organic farming, 409–410
sugar, 406
table olives, 405
veal, 407–408
wine, 405
Common commercial policy
export policy, 582–583
general principles, 580–582
instruments, 582–585
introduction, 561
liberalisation, 582–583
measures to protect trade, 583–585
Common Customs Tariff
free movement of goods, and, 225–227
**Common European Security and Defence
  Policy**
generally, 577–579
Common fisheries policy
access to fishing grounds, 415
aquaculture, 417–418
common organisation of the market,
  418–419
conservation of fish stocks, 415–416
environmental policy, 422
European Fisheries Fund, 422
Fisheries and Aquaculture Research, 418
fishing licences, 415
international conventions, 419–420
introduction, 414–415
marine environmental policy, 422
monitoring fishing activities, 417
overfishing, 415–416
research, 418
state aid, and, 388
structural measures, 420–422
third country agreements, 419–420
total allowable catches, 415–416
Common foreign and security policy
adopting decisions, 575–576
co-operation between member states, 576
defining general guidelines, 575
diplomatic missions, 576

generally, 3
High Representative, 579
Instrument for Stability, 577
introduction, 575–577
Political and Security Committee,
    576–577
Security and Defence, 577–579
Special Representatives, 576
Common transport policy
And see **Transport**
acquis communautaire, 439
conclusion, 458
generally, 438
new approach, 439–440
Common market
See **Internal market**
Common positions
legal Acts of the EU, and, 3
"Communiqués"
legal Acts of the EU, and, 3
Community Acts
See **EU Acts**
Community agencies
See **EU agencies**
Community bodies
See **EU agencies**
Community designs
intellectual property, and, 306–307
Community Fisheries Control Agency
generally, 202–203
Community Plant Variety Office
generally, 197
Company law
freedom of establishment, and,
    268–270
Community trade marks
intellectual property, and, 305–306
Companies
freedom of establishment, and
    company law, 268–270
    exceptions, 284
    introduction, 266–268
    qualifications required for legal
        persons, where, 278–283
    qualifications required for natural
        persons, where, 270–277
tax, and, 431–432
Compensation
jurisdiction of European Court of
    Justice, and, 149–151
Competence
introduction, 6
jurisdiction of European Court of
    Justice, and, 154
Competition policy
abuse of dominant position

'abuse', 340–341
'dominant position', 337–340
generally, 337
implementation of rules, 350–363
introduction, 319–320
'may affect trade between member
    states', 337
specific economic sectors, 341–350
agriculture, 341–342
air transport, 343–345
anti-competitive practices
    And see **Anti-competitive practices**
    exemptions from prohibition,
        328–337
    general prohibition, 321–327
    generally, 320
    implementation of rules, 350–363
    introduction, 319–320
    nullity, 327–328
    specific economic sectors, 341–350
application of rules to member states
    European Coal and Steel
        Community, 397
    monopolies, 375–376
    public undertakings, 376–377
    services of general economic interest,
        378
    state aid, 379–397
application of rules to undertakings
    abuse of dominant position,
        337–341
    cartels, 320–337
    concentrations, 319
    introduction, 319–320
block exemptions, 329–336
cartels
    And see **Anti-competitive practices**
    exemptions from prohibition,
        328–337
    general prohibition, 321–327
    generally, 320
    implementation of rules, 350–363
    introduction, 319–320
    nullity, 327–328
    specific economic sectors, 341–350
coal and steel, 350
comity, 374
Commission Notices
    access to the files, 372
    agreements of minor importance, 372
    co-operations agreements,
        370–371
    exclusive dealing contracts made with
        commercial agents, 370
    introduction, 370
    subcontracting agreements, 371–372

concentrations
    ancillary restraints, 366
    generally, 363–365
    introduction, 319–320
    joint or collective dominance,
        365–370
concerted practices
    And see **Anti-competitive practices**
    generally, 321–322
decisions by associations of
        undertakings
    And see **Anti-competitive practices**
    generally, 322–323
energy, 350
environmental policy, and, 551
European Coal and Steel Community,
        397
European Competition Network, 351
implementation of rules
    Commission's role, 353–358
    European Competition Network, 351
    hearings, 358–360
    implementing provisions, 360–363
    introduction, 350–351
    legal privilege, 354–355
    limitation periods, 358
    member states' role, 351–352
    modified regulations, 363
    settlement procedure, 356
insurance, 349–350
intellectual property rights, 350
international aviation, 344
international co-operation, 374–375
introduction, 319
maritime transport, 342–343
mergers
    generally, 363–365
    introduction, 319–320
    joint or collective dominance, 365–370
monopolies, 375–376
postal service, 347–349
public undertakings
    generally, 376–377
    services of general economic interest,
        378
rail transport, 344–345
relationship between Union and
        national rules, 373
services of general economic interest, 378
state aid
    'advantage an undertaking', 379
    'affect trade between member
        states', 381
    aids compatible with the internal
        market, 382–397
    'distort competition', 381

'favour certain undertakings or the
        production of certain goods',
        380–381
'granted by a member state or
        through the state resources,
        379–380
notion of aid, 379–381
'specificity', 380–381
state monopolies, 375–376
telecommunications, 345–347
transport
    air transport, 343–345
    international aviation, 344
    introduction, 342
    maritime, 342–343
    rail, 344–345
Computer programs
See **Software**
Concentrations
    ancillary restraints, 366
    generally, 363–365
    introduction, 319–320
    joint or collective dominance, 365–370
Concerted practices
    And see **Anti-competitive practices**
    generally, 321–322
**Conference of European Affairs
        Committees**
See **COSAC**
Conferral
See **Principle of conferral**
Conformity
    free movement of goods, and, 236
Consent
    powers of European Parliament, and, 71
Consultation procedure
    legislative procedure, and, 66–68
Consumer protection
    data protection, 500–501
    generally, 496–497
    introduction, 487
    product liability, 497–500
**Convention on the Future of the European
        Union**
    generally, 23–24
"Convergence"
    Common Agriculture Policy, and, 413
    common foreign and security policy,
        and, 575
    economic policy, and, 461
    freedom of establishment, and, 280
    regional policy, and
        generally, 525
        introduction, 523
    stability and growth pact, and, 468
    telecommunications, and, 511

Co-operation agreements
competition policy, and, 370–371
Copyright
culture, and, 490
generally, 304
COREPER
generally, 102–103
Corporation tax
generally, 431–432
COSAC
generally, 83–84
Costs
jurisdiction of European Court of
Justice, and, 160–161
Council of the European Union
competence, 6
configurations, 101–102
co-ordination of economic policy,
99–101
COREPER, 102–103
decision-making
principles, 92–94
scope, 94–95
voting procedure, 95–98
employment policy guidelines, 101
European Parliament, and, 73
generally, 3
introduction, 90–91
membership, 91–92
organisation
configurations, 101–102
COREPER, 102–103
rules of procedure, 104
Secretariat, 105
powers and duties
co-ordination of economic policy,
99–101
decision-making, 92–98
procedural rules, 104
qualified majority voting, 96–98
Secretariat, 105
Treaty of Lisbon, and, 25
voting procedures
introduction, 95–96
qualified majority, 96–98
simple majority, 96
unanimity, 98
Council Secretariat
generally, 105
Counterfeits
intellectual property, and, 307
Countervailing duties
commercial policy, and, 583–584
Court of Auditors
annual reports, 174
duties, 174–175

introduction, 173
location, 175
membership, 173
rules of procedure, 174
staff, 175
Court of Justice of the European Union
European Court of Justice
And see **European Court of Justice**
Advocates-General, 127–129
appellate jurisdiction, 154–155
compensation for damages,
149–151
failure to fulfil obligations, 130–131
introduction, 125–126
judges, 127–128
jurisdiction, 129–155
preliminary rulings, 142–148
procedure, 155–165
General Court
And see **General Court**
introduction, 165–166
jurisdiction, 167–168
membership, 166–167
introduction, 125–126
"Credit crunch"
economic and monetary union, and
European response, 468–469
generally, 468
state aid, and, 394
Croatia
enlargement, and, 611–612
Crops
And see **Common Agricultural Policy**
bananas, 407
cereals, 404–405
cotton, 406–407
fruit and vegetables, 405–406
hops, 407
olive oil, 405
processed fruit and vegetables, 406
raw tobacco, 406
rice, 406
sugar, 406
table olives, 405
wine, 405
Culture
audio-visual media, and, 489
copyright, and, 490
environment, and, 490
EUROPEANA, 488
'four freedoms', and, 490
generally, 488–489
Information Society, and, 490
introduction, 487
regional development, and, 489
· research and development, and, 489

state aid, and, 490
technological development, and, 489
Currencies
Euro
economic and monetary union, 459
introduction, 3
Customs Union
charges having equivalent effect, 225
Common Customs Tariff, 225–227
generally, 16
introduction, 224
Czech Republic
accession, and, 23
Treaty of Lisbon, and, 27
Cyprus
accession, and, 23

Damages
jurisdiction of European Court of
Justice, and, 149–151
Data protection
consumer protection, and, 500–501
Information Society, and, 511–512
Databases
intellectual property, and, 304
De minimis
Commission Notice, 372
generally, 336–337
Decision-making
Council of the European Union, and
principles, 92–94
scope, 94–95
voting procedure, 95–98
Decisions
entry into force, 37–38
European Commission, and,
113–115
generally, 34–35
introduction, 28–30
publication, 37–38
reasoning, 36–37
"Decisions by associations of undertakings"
And see **Anti-competitive practices**
generally, 322–323
Declaration on Democracy
generally, 18
Declaration on Fundamental Rights
generally, 18
Default judgments
European Court of Justice, and, 164
Delegated powers
European Commission, and
advisory procedure, 116
generally, 115–118
management procedure, 116
regulatory procedure, 116–117

safeguard procedure, 117
scrutiny procedure, 117
Denmark
accession, and, 16–17
Dentists
freedom of establishment, and, 273
Designs
intellectual property, and, 306–307
Development co-operation
ACP-EEC Agreement, 604–607
Association of the Overseas Countries
and Territories, 608
Europe Aid Co-operation Office,
603–604
general, 600–603
Generalised System of Preferences, 602
introduction, 561
Millennium Development Goals, 600
Direct applicability
generally, 43–44
introduction, 31
supremacy of EU law, and, 50
Direct effect
application of EU law by national
courts, and, 55
charges having equivalent effect,
and, 225
decisions, and, 33
directives, and, 32–33
equal pay, and, 478
free movement of persons, and, 238
freedom to provide services, and, 290
generally, 44–46
international agreements, and
generally, 570
introduction, 39
preliminary rulings, and, 142
regulations, and, 31
supremacy of EU law, and, 50
Direct taxes
generally, 430–433
Directives
entry into force, 37–38
European Commission, and, 113–115
generally, 31–34
introduction, 28–30
publication, 37–38
reasoning, 36–37
Discriminatory taxation
free movement of goods, and,
231–232
Doctors
freedom of establishment, and, 272–273
Dominant position
And see **Abuse of dominant position**
generally, 337–340

Duty free
tax, and, 432

Eastern Europe
accession, and, 23
external relations, and, 586–587
EC Treaty
See **Treaty on the Functioning of the European Union**
Economic and Financial Committee
generally, 188–189
Economic and monetary policy
budgetary surveillance, 466–467
co-ordination of economic affairs, 466–467
co-ordination of economic policies of member states, 461–462
'credit crunch', and
European response, 468–469
generally, 468
economic policy
co-ordination of policies of member states, 461–462
excessive government deficits, 462–463
introduction, 460–461
overdraft facilities with central banks, 463
privileged access to financial institutions, 463
Euro, 459
'Euro group', 464–465
European Central Bank, 459
excessive government deficits
generally, 462–463
stability and growth pact, 467–468
generally, 3
global financial crisis, and
European response, 468–469
generally, 468
institutional provisions, 465
introduction, 459–460
medium-term budgetary objectives (MTOs), 466
monetary policy, 463
overdraft facilities with central banks, 463
privileged access t financial institutions, 463
stability and growth pact
budgetary surveillance, 466–467
co-ordination of economic affairs, 466–467
excessive deficit procedure, 467–468
global financial crisis, and, 468
introduction, 466
transitional provisions, 465

Economic and monetary union
Council of the European Union, and
co-ordination of economic policy, 99
generally, 90
employment, and, 486
enlargement, and, 610
European Central Bank, and
duties and powers, 178
generally, 177
freedom to provide services, and, 291
generally, 459
international agreements, and, 571
monetary policy, 463
Economic and social cohesion
And see **Regional policy**
generally, 519–520
Economic and Social Committee
generally, 180–181
Economic policy
co-ordination of policies of member states, 461–462
Council of the European Union, and, 99–101
excessive government deficits, 462–463
introduction, 460–461
overdraft facilities with central banks, 463
privileged access t financial institutions, 463
Education, Audi-Visual and Culture Executive Agency
generally, 210
Educational policy
ERASMUS, 481
generally, 480–482
Lifelong Learning Programme, 482
LINGUA programme, 481
sports, 484
TEMPUS, 481
vocational training, 483
young persons, 484
EEA Agreement
generally, 20–21
Electronic commerce
Information Society, and, 511
Emissions trading
environmental policy, and, 547
Employment policy
Council of the European Union, and, 101
generally, 485–486
state aid, and, 390
EMU
See **Economic and monetary union**
Energy policy
ALTENER, 558
coal, 556–557

competition policy, and, 350
Framework Programmes, 553
integration of markets, 555–556
International Atomic Energy Agency, 559–560
international co-operation, 554–555
introduction, 552–553
natural gas, 557
nuclear energy
  Euratom Supply Agency, 559
  generally, 557–558
  safeguard controls, 558–560
  safety, 560
oil and petroleum, 557
renewable energy, 558
sectoral aspects
  coal, 556–557
  natural gas, 557
  nuclear energy, 557–558
  oil and petroleum, 557
  renewable energy, 558
security of supply, 553–555
technological development, 556
Enforcement
pecuniary obligations, 38–39
Enhanced co-operation
free movement of persons, and, 264
generally, 6–8
jurisdiction of European Court of Justice, and, 152
jurisdiction of General Court, and, 167
police co-operation, and, 264
ENISA
generally, 200
Enlargement
Albania, 613–614
Bosnia and Herzegovina, 614
candidate countries, 610–616
Croatia, 611–612
financial and economic assistance, 610
Iceland, 613
introduction, 609–610
Macedonia, 612–613
Montenegro, 615
Serbia, 615–616
Turkey, 610–611
Enterprise policy
Euro Info Centres, 513
industrial policy, 504–506
Information Society, and, 506
introduction, 502
judicial co-operation in civil and criminal matters, 517
Lisbon Strategy (2000), 502–504
promotion of open standards, 507

small and medium-sized enterprises, 513–515
Trans-European Networks, 515–517
Environmental policy
action programmes
  generally, 543
  Sixth (2001–2012), 543–547
civil liability, 548
Clean Air for Europe, 545
climate change, 546–547
competition policy, and, 551
criminal sanctions, 549
culture, and, 490
emissions trading, 547
European Environmental Agency, 550
external co-operation, 549–550
financial instrument for the environment, 550–551
greenhouse gas emissions, 547
guiding principles, 541–543
integrated product policy, 544
integration principle, 542
introduction, 540–541
marine environment, 545
pesticides, 545
polluter pays principle, 542
precautionary principles, 541
proximity principle, 542
Shared Environmental Information System, 543
soil protection, 545
state aid, and, 390–391
subsidiarity, 542
sustainable development, 544–545
Treaty of Lisbon, and, 26
urban environment, 545
waste prevention and recycling, 545
Equal opportunities
equal pay, 478–479
generally, 477
gender equality, 479
Equal pay
social policy, and, 478–479
Equal treatment
generally, 477–479
sources of EU law, and, 53
ERASMUS
educational policy, and, 481
Estonia
accession, and, 23
EU Acts
actions for annulment
  acts submitted to the control of legality, 133
  consequences, 140–141
  appellants, 133–137

generally, 132
grounds, 137–140
infringement of essential procedural
requirement, 138
infringement of treaties or rule of law,
138–140
lack of competence, 137–138
legislative acts, 133
misuse of power, 140
conferral, 28
decisions, 34–35
direct applicability, 31
direct effect, 31
directives, 31–34
entry into force, 37–38
generally, 30–31
introduction, 28–30
opinions, 35
other forms, 40–41
proportionality, 28
publication, 37–38
reasoning, 36–37
regulations, 30–31
review of legality
appeals against failure of institution
to act, 141–142
appeals for annulment, 132–141
subsidiarity, 28
EU agencies
See also **EU executive agencies**
See also **EU institutions**
Agency for Co-operation of Energy
Regulators, 208–209
capacity, 59
CEDEFOP, 192
CEPOL, 206–207
Community Fisheries Control Agency,
202–203
Community Plant Variety Office, 197
ECDC, 200
EMCDDA, 194
ENISA, 200
EUROFOUND, 192
Eurojust, 207
European Agency for the Management
of Operational Co-operation, 202
European Agency for Reconstruction,
198
European Agency for Safety and Health
at Work, 197–198
European Aviation Safety Agency,
199–200
European Body for the Enhancement of
Judicial Co-operation, 207
European Centre for Development of
Vocational Training, 192

European Centre for Disease Prevention
and Control, 200–201
European Chemicals Agency, 203–204
European Defence Agency, 205–206
European Environment Agency, 192–193
European Food Safety Authority, 198
European Foundation for the
Improvement of Living and
Working Conditions, 192
European GNSS Supervisory Authority,
201
European Institute for Gender Equality,
203
European Institute for Innovation and
Technology, 205
European Maritime Safety Agency, 199
European Medicines Agency, 194–195
European Monitoring Centre for Drugs
and Drug Addiction, 194
European Network and Information
Security Agency, 200
European Police College, 206–207
European Police Office, 208
European Railways Agency, 201
European Training Foundation, 193–194
European Union Satellite Centre, 206
European Union Agency for
Fundamental Rights, 204–205
European Union Institute for Security
Studies, 207–208
Europol, 208
FRONTEX, 202
generally, 191
GNSS Supervisory Authority, 201
introduction, 59
ISS, 207–208
Office for Harmonisation in the Internal
Market, 195–196
OHIM, 195–196
OSHA, 197–198
Translation Centre for Bodies of the
European Union, 196–197
EU budget
commitment and payment
appropriations, 217
compulsory expenditure, 217
European Commission, and, 122–123
introduction, 216
non-compulsory expenditure, 217
summary, 217
EU executive agencies
See also **EU agencies**
See also **EU institutions**
Competition and Innovation, 210
Education, Audi-Visual and Culture, 210
European Research Council, 209

Health and Consumers, 211
Public Health, 211
Research, 210–211
Trans-European Transport Network,
209–210
EU institutions
See also **EU agencies**
capacity, 59
Civil Service Tribunal, 169–171
Committee of the Regions, 181
Council of the European Union
And see **Council of the European Union**
configurations, 101–102
co-ordination of economic policy,
99–101
COREPER, 102–103
decision-making, 92–98
employment policy guidelines, 101
introduction, 90–91
membership, 91–92
organisation, 101–105
powers and duties, 92–101
procedural rules, 104
Secretariat, 105
Court of Auditors
And see **Court of Auditors**
duties, 174–175
introduction, 173
membership, 173
Economic and Financial Committee,
188–189
Economic and Social Committee,
180–181
Euratom Supply Agency, 182
Eurojust, 186–187
European Central Bank
duties, 177–179
establishment, 177
Executive Board, 177
Governing Council, 177
introduction, 176
European Commission
And see **European Commission**
access to documents, 124
introduction, 106
membership, 107–109
powers and duties, 109–123
procedural rules, 123–124
European Council
And see **European Council**
composition, 86
duties, 87
historical background, 85–86
introduction, 85
organisation, 88–89
President, 86

'serious and persistent breach', 87–88
voting, 86–87
European Court of Justice
And see **European Court of Justice**
Advocates-General, 127–129
appellate, 154–155
compensation for damages, 149–151
competence, and, 154
costs, 160–161
ECB, 153–154
EIB, 153–154
failure to fulfil obligations, 130–131
illegality, 151–152
industrial property rights, 151
introduction, 125–126
judges, 127–128
jurisdiction, 129–155
oral procedure, 159–160
penalties, 131–132
preliminary rulings, 142–148
procedure, 155–165
review of legality of Acts, 132–142
written procedure, 156–159
European Data Protection Supervisor,
189–190
European Institute of Innovation and
Technology, 188
European Investment Bank
duties, 182–184
internal structure, 185
introduction, 182
procedure for grant of loans or
guarantees, 184–185
subscribed capital, 183
European Investment Fund, 186
European Parliament
And see **European Parliament**
conclusion, 84
internal organisation, 80–84
introduction, 61
Members of Parliament, 61–65
powers and duties, 65–80
European Police Office, 187–188
European System of Central Banks
duties, 176
establishment, 176
introduction, 176
European Union Civil Service Tribunal,
169–171
Europol, 187–188
General Court
And see **General Court**
introduction, 165–166
jurisdiction, 167–168
membership, 166–167
procedure, 169

introduction, 59–60
Scientific and Technical Committee of
Euratom, 182
EU law
application by national courts, 55–56
conclusions, 56–57
direct applicability, 43–44
direct effect, 44–46
European Commission, and
introduction, 110
with regard to acts of institutions and
other bodies, 113
with regard to legal persons, 113
with regard to member states, 110–112
with regard to natural persons, 113
introduction, 42–43
liability for breach
legal persons, 52
member states, 51–52
natural persons, 52
precedence, 46–51
primacy, 46–51
sources, 52–54
supremacy, 46–51
EU legislative process
consent procedure, 71
consultation, 67–68
introduction, 67
ordinary legislative procedure
conciliation, 69–70
first reading, 68–69
implementing measures, 71
introduction, 68
second reading, 69
special provisions, 70
third reading, 70
type of Act to be adopted, 70
special legislative procedure, 71
EU Treaty
See **Treaty on European Union**
Euratom
See **European Atomic Energy
Community**
Euratom Supply Agency
capacity, 59
energy policy, and, 559
generally, 182
introduction, 59
EURES
generally, 486
"Euro"
economic and monetary union, and,
459
introduction, 3
EUROCONTROL
generally, 452

EUROFOUND
generally, 192
Euro Info Centres
enterprise policy, and, 513
Eurojust
generally, 186–187, 207
EuropeAid Co-operation Office
development co-operation, and,
603–604
European Administrative School
generally, 84
**European Agency for the Management of
Operational Co-operation**
See **FRONTEX**
European Agency for Reconstruction
generally, 198
**European Agency for Safety and Health at
Work**
generally, 197–198
**European Agricultural Guidance and
Guarantee Fund**
regional policy, and, 522
European Anti-Fraud Office
generally, 219
European Atomic Energy Community
establishment, 4
external relations, and, 597
generally, 15
introduction, 3
Scientific and Technical Committee,
182
social policy, and, 470
Supply Agency, 182
European Aviation Safety Agency
generally, 199–200
intrroduction, 452
**European Body for the Enhancement of
Judicial Co-operation**
See **Eurojust**
European Central Bank
annual reports, 178
capacity, 59
duties, 177–179
Economic and Financial Committee, 178
economic and monetary union,
and, 459
establishment, 177
EU Acts, and, 29
European Parliament, and, 73
Executive Board, 177
Governing Council, 177
introduction, 176
jurisdiction of European Court of
Justice, and, 153–154
legal personality, 177
Monetary Committee, 178

European Centre for Development of Vocational Training
generally, 192
European Centre for Disease Prevention and Control
generally, 200–201
European Chemicals Agency
generally, 203–204
European Coal and Steel Community
generally, 14
introduction, 3
European Commission
access to documents, 124
adoption of regulations, directives, decisions, recommendations and opinions, 113–115
advisory procedure, 116
competition policy, and, 353–358
duties
  adopt measures, 113–115
  ensure application of treaties and measures adopted, 110–113
  exercise delegated powers, 115–118
  external relations, 121–122
  generally, 109
  implementation of EU budget, 122–123
  introduction, 106
  oversee application of EU law, 110–113
  participate in legislative process, 118–121
  publication of annual general report, 123
ensuring application of treaties and measures adopted
  introduction, 110
  with regard to acts of institutions and other bodies, 113
  with regard to legal persons, 113
  with regard to member states, 110–112
  with regard to natural persons, 113
European Parliament, and, 73
exercise of delegated powers
  advisory procedure, 116
  generally, 115–118
  management procedure, 116
  regulatory procedure, 116–117
  safeguard procedure, 117
  scrutiny procedure, 117
external relations, 121–122
High Representative of the Union for Foreign Affairs and Security Policy, 108–109
implementation of EU budget, 122–123
introduction, 106
management procedure, 116

members
  choice, 107–108
  nomination procedure, 108–109
  number, 107
overseeing application of EU law
  introduction, 110
  with regard to acts of institutions and other bodies, 113
  with regard to legal persons, 113
  with regard to member states, 110–112
  with regard to natural persons, 113
participation in legislative process, 118–121
powers and duties
  adopt measures, 113–115
  ensure application of treaties and measures adopted, 110–113
  exercise delegated powers, 115–118
  external relations, 121–122
  generally, 109
  implementation of EU budget, 122–123
  introduction, 106
  oversee application of EU law, 110–113
  participate in legislative process, 118–121
  publication of annual general report, 123
President of the Union, 108
procedural rules, 123–124
publication of annual general report, 123
regulatory procedure, 116–117
safeguard procedure, 117
scrutiny procedure, 117
staff, 123–124
Treaty of Lisbon, and, 25
European Community
historical background, 15
European companies
freedom of establishment, and, 282–283
European Competition Network
competition policy, and, 351
European co-operative societies
freedom of establishment, and, 283
European Council
competence, 6
composition, 86
duties, 87
generally, 3
historical background, 85–86
introduction, 85
organisation, 88–89
President, 86
'serious and persistent breach', 87–88

Treaty of Lisbon, and, 25
voting, 86–87
European Court of Justice
actions for annulment
acts submitted to the control of
legality, 133
consequences, 140–141
appellants, 133–137
generally, 132
grounds, 137–140
infringement of essential procedural
requirement, 138
infringement of treaties or rule of law,
138–140
lack of competence, 137–138
legislative acts, 133
misuse of power, 140
Advocates-General
duties, 128–129
generally, 127–128
appeals
annulment, for, 132–141
failure of institution to act, against,
141–142
annulment
acts submitted to the control of
legality, 133
consequences, 140–141
appellants, 133–137
generally, 132
grounds, 137–140
infringement of essential procedural
requirement, 138
infringement of treaties or rule of law,
138–140
lack of competence, 137–138
legislative acts, 133
misuse of power, 140
appellate jurisdiction, 154–155
attribution of competence, 154
compensation for damages caused by
institutions, 149–151
competence, and, 154
costs, 160–161
ECB, 153–154
EIB, 153–154
European Parliament, and, 79–80
expedited procedure, 162
failure of institution to act, 141–142
failure to fulfil obligations, 130–131
General Court, and, 154–155
illegality, 151–152
intellectual property rights, 151
interim measures, 162–162
interpretation of judgments, 164
introduction, 125–126

judges, 127–128
judgment by default, 164
jurisdiction
annulment, 132–141
appellate, 154–155
attribution of competence, 154
compensation for damages caused by
institutions, 149–151
failure to act, 141–142
failure to fulfil obligations, 130–131
illegality, 151–152
industrial property rights, 151
introduction, 129–130
member state obligations to ECB and
EIB, 153–154
other, 152–153
penalties, 131–132
preliminary rulings, 142–148
review of legality of Acts, 132–142
member state obligations to ECB and
EIB, 153–154
oral procedure, 159–160
penalties, 131–132
preliminary rulings, 142–148
procedure
costs, 160–161
expedited, 162
generally, 155–165
interim measures, 162–162
interpretation of judgments, 164
judgment by default, 164
oral, 159–160
powers of European Parliament, and,
79–80
rectification of judgments, 164
revision of judgments, 164
setting aside judgments, 164
special forms, 161–165
stay of proceedings, 164–165
suspension of operation or
enforcement, 152
third party proceedings, 164
time limits, 165
written, 156–159
rectification of judgments, 164
review of legality of Acts
appeals against failure of institution
to act, 141–142
appeals for annulment, 132–141
revision of judgments, 164
setting aside judgments, 164
special forms, 161–165
stay of proceedings, 164–165
suspension of operation or enforcement,
152
third party proceedings, 164

time limits, 165
written procedure, 156–159
European Data Protection Supervisor
generally, 189–190
European Defence Agency
generally, 205–206
European Economic Area
external relations, and, 585
generally, 20–21
European Economic Community
See **European Community**
European economic interest groupings
freedom of establishment, and, 283
European Employment Services
See **EURES**
European Environment Agency
environmental policy, and, 550
generally, 192–193
European Fisheries Fund
generally, 422
regional policy, and, 522
European Food Safety Authority
generally, 198
European Foundation for the Improvement
of Living and Working Conditions
See **EUROFOUND**
European Free Trade Association
generally, 20–21
European Geostationary Navigation
Overlay Service
See **Satellite navigation**
European GNSS Supervisory Authority
generally, 201
European Institute for Gender Equality
generally, 203
European Institute of Innovation and
Technology
generally, 188, 205
European Investment Bank
capacity, 59
duties, 182–184
EU Acts, and, 29
generally, 59
internal structure, 185
introduction, 182
jurisdiction of European Court of
Justice, and, 153–154
procedure for grant of loans or
guarantees, 184–185
regional policy, and, 520
subscribed capital, 183
European Investment Fund
generally, 186
European Maritime Safety Agency
generally, 199
introduction, 456

European Medicines Agency
generally, 194–195
European Monitoring Centre for Drugs
and Drug Addiction
generally, 194
European Monitoring Centre for Racism
and Xenophobia
generally, 204
European Neighbourhood Policy
external relations, and, 573–574
European Network and Information
Security Agency
See **ENISA**
European Ombudsman
appointment, 72–73
European Organisation for the Safety of
Air Navigation
See **EUROCONTROL**
European Parliament
adoption of procedure rules, 74–75
appointment of Ombudsman, 72–73
approval of President and Members,
76–77
Bureau, 82
censure motion, 76
conclusion, 84
Conference of European Affairs
Committees, 83–84
consent procedure, 71
duties and powers
adoption of procedure rules, 74–75
appointment of Ombudsman, 72–73
approval of President and Members,
76–77
general report, 75–76
introduction, 65–66
joint exercise of legislative functions,
66–71
motion of censure, 76
participation in budgetary procedure,
77–79
participation in other Union
activities, 80
procedures before Court of Justice,
79–80
questions to the Council, Commission
and ECB, 73–74
right of petition, 72
temporary committee of inquiry, 72
elections, 17–18
general report, 75–76
internal organisation
Bureau, 82
COSAC, 83–84
introduction, 80
meeting places, 83

Parliamentary committees, 81–82
political groups, 80–81
Secretariat, 84
sessions, 83
introduction, 61
joint exercise of legislative functions
consent procedure, 71
consultation, 66–68
introduction, 66
ordinary legislative procedure,
68–71
special legislative procedure, 71
meeting places, 83
Members of the European Parliament
election, 62–63
immunity, 64–65
introduction, 61–62
mandate, 63–64
performance of duties, 65
privileges, 64–65
motion of censure, 76
Ombudsman appointment, 72–73
ordinary legislative procedure
conciliation, 69–70
first reading, 68–69
implementing measures, 71
introduction, 68
second reading, 69
special provisions, 70
third reading, 70
type of Act to be adopted, 70
Parliamentary committees, 81–82
participation in budgetary procedure,
77–79
participation in other Union activities, 80
political groups, 80–81
powers and duties
adoption of procedure rules, 74–75
appointment of Ombudsman, 72–73
approval of President and Members,
76–77
general report, 75–76
introduction, 65–66
joint exercise of legislative functions,
66–71
motion of censure, 76
participation in budgetary procedure,
77–79
participation in other Union
activities, 80
procedures before Court of Justice,
79–80
questions to the Council, Commission
and ECB, 73–74
right of petition, 72
temporary committee of inquiry, 72

procedures before Court of Justice, 79–80
questions to the Council, Commission
and ECB, 73–74
right of petition, 72
Secretariat, 84
sessions, 83
special legislative procedure, 71
temporary committee of inquiry, 72
European Parliament Secretariat
generally, 84
European Police College
generally, 206–207
European Police Office
See **Europol**
European Railway Agency
generally, 201
European Regional Development Fund
public health, and, 492
regional policy, and
Cohesion Fund, 529
generally, 521–522
structural funds, 525
research and technological development,
and, 535
European Research Advisory Board
research and technological development,
and, 536
European Research Area
generally, 534
introduction, 532
European Research Council
generally, 209
**European Research Infrastructure
Consortium**
generally, 212
European Security and Defence College
See **Common European Security and
Defence Policy**
European Social Charter
social policy, and, 471
European Social Fund
generally, 479
introduction, 470
public health, and, 492
regional policy, and
Cohesion Fund, 529
generally, 521–522
research and technological development,
and, 535
European Space Agency
research and technological development,
and, 536
European System of Central Banks
duties, 176
establishment, 176
introduction, 176

European territorial co-operation
  generally, 525
  introduction, 524
European Training Foundation
  generally, 193–194
European treaties
  See **Treaties**
European Union
  accession
    Austria, Finland and Sweden, 21–22
    Greece, Portugal and Spain, 17
    UK, Ireland and Denmark, 16–17
  historical background
    accession of Austria, Finland and
      Sweden, 21–22
    accession of Bulgaria and Romania,
      24–25
    accession of Greece, Portugal and
      Spain, 17
    access of eastern European states, 23
    accession of UK, Ireland and
      Denmark, 16–17
    Adaptation Decision, 17
    Churchill's speech, 13
    Customs Union, 16
    Declaration on Democracy, 18
    Declaration on Fundamental Rights, 18
    direct election of Parliament, 17
    European Atomic Energy
      Community, 15
    European Coal and Steel
      Community, 14
    European Defence Community, 15
    European Economic Area, 20–21
    European Economic Community, 15
    European Free Trade Association,
      20–21
    Financial Contributions, 16
    internal market, 18–19
    introduction, 13
    Laeken Declaration, 23–24
    Marshall Plan, 13–14
    Merger Treaty, 16
    OEEC, 14
    own resources, 16
    Schuman declaration, 14
    secession of Greenland, 18
    Single European Act, 19
    Treaty of Amsterdam, 22–23
    Treaty of Brussels, 16–17
    Treaty of Lisbon, 25–27
    Treaty of Nice, 23
    Treaty on European Union, 19
  legal acts
    enforcement of pecuniary obligations,
      38–39
    entry into force, 37–38
    introduction, 28–30
    legislation, 30–35
    non-TFEU acts, 29–40
    other forms, 4041
    publication, 37–38
    reasoning, 36–37
  objectives, 5
  secession of Greenland, 18
**European Union Agency for Fundamental
  Rights**
  generally, 204–205
European Union Civil Service Tribunal
  generally, 169–171
**European Union Institute for Security
  Studies**
  generally, 207–208
European Union Military Staff
  external relations, and, 578
European Union Satellite Centre
  generally, 206
"EUROPEANA"
  culture, and, 488
Europol
  generally, 187–188, 208
Excise duty
  generally, 428–430
Exclusive dealership agreements
  competition policy, and, 331–332
Exclusive distribution agreements
  commercial agents, and, 370
  generally, 329–330
Exclusive purchasing agreements
  competition policy, and, 329–330
**Executive Agency for Competition and
  Innovation**
  generally, 210
**Executive Agency for Health and
  Consumers**
  generally, 211
  introduction, 492
Exhaustion of rights
  intellectual property, and, 303
Expedited procedure
  jurisdiction of European Court of
    Justice, and, 162
Exports
  external relations, and, 582–583
External relations
  Africa, with, 597
  Asia, with
    India, 595
    introduction, 594–595
    other, 596
    South Korea, 595
  Australia, with, 592

Canada, with, 589–590
central European countries, with,
   586–587
China, with, 591–592
Common Commercial Policy
   export policy, 582–583
   general principles, 580–582
   instruments, 582–585
   introduction, 561
   liberalisation, 582–583
   measures to protect trade,
      583–585
Common Foreign and Security Policy
   adopting decisions, 575–576
   co-operation between member
      states, 576
   defining general guidelines, 575
   diplomatic missions, 576
   High Representative, 579
   Instrument for Stability, 577
   introduction, 575–577
   Political and Security Committee,
      576–577
   Security and Defence, 577–579
   Special Representatives, 576
Common Security and Defence Policy,
   577–579
co-operation with third countries
   development co-operation, 561
   economic, financial and technical
      co-operation, 567
   humanitarian aid, 568
   international agreements, 569–571
   introduction, 561
   restrictive measures, 569
   solidarity clause, 573
development co-operation
   ACP-EEC Agreement, 604–607
   Association of the Overseas Countries
      and Territories, 608
   Europe Aid Co-operation Office,
      603—604
   general, 600–603
   introduction, 561
economic, financial and technical
   co-operation, 567
eastern European countries, with,
   586–587
enlargement
   Albania, 613–614
   Bosnia and Herzegovina, 614
   candidate countries, 610–616
   Croatia, 611–612
   financial and economic assistance, 610
   Iceland, 613
   introduction, 609–610

   Macedonia, 612–613
   Montenegro, 615
   Serbia, 615–616
   Turkey, 610–611
Euratom, and, 597
European Commission, and, 121–122
European Economic Area, with, 585
European Neighbourhood Policy,
   573–574
European Security and Defence
   College, 578
export policy, 582–583
GATT, and
   Doha round, 598–599
   Uruguay round, 598
general provisions
   generally, 563–566
   introduction, 561
High Representative, 579
humanitarian aid, 568
India, with, 595
international agreements, 569–571
international organisations, with,
   572–573
introduction, 561–562
Japan, with, 590
Latin-America, with, 596–597
major industrialised countries, with
   Australia, 592
   Canada, 589–590
   China, 591–592
   Japan, 590
   New Zealand, 592–593
   Russia, 591
   United States, 587–589
measures to protect trade, 583–585
Mediterranean countries, with,
   593–594
Military Staff of the European
   Union, 578
new Independent States, with, 587
New Zealand, with, 592–593
other European countries, with, 596
Political and Security Committee,
   576–577
restrictive measures, 569
Russia, with, 591
solidarity clause, 573
South Korea, with, 595
Special Representatives, 576
United States, with, 587–589
World Trade Organisation, and, 598

Failure to act
   jurisdiction of European Court of
      Justice, and, 141–142

Failure to fulfil obligations
jurisdiction of European Court of
Justice, and, 130–131
Finance
EU budget
commitment and payment
appropriations, 217
compulsory expenditure, 217
introduction, 216
non-compulsory expenditure, 217
summary, 217
European Anti-Fraud Office, 219
financial framework, 218
Inter-institutional Agreement, 218
own resources, 214–216
protection of interests, 219
Financial Contributions
See **Own resources**
**"Financial instrument for the environment
(LIFE)"**
environmental policy, and, 550–551
Financial services
freedom to provide services, and,
291–293
state aid, and, 389
Finland
accession, and, 21–22
First reading
ordinary legislative procedure, and, 68–69
Fisheries
access to fishing grounds, 415
aquaculture, 417–418
common organisation of the market,
418–419
conservation of fish stocks, 415–416
environmental policy, 422
European Fisheries Fund, 422
Fisheries and Aquaculture Research, 418
fishing licences, 415
international conventions, 419–420
introduction, 414–415
marine environmental policy, 422
monitoring fishing activities, 417
overfishing, 415–416
regional policy, and, 520
research, 418
state aid, and, 388
structural measures, 420–422
third country agreements, 419–420
total allowable catches, 415–416
Food safety
public health, and, 494–495
Framework programmes
economic policy, and, 100
energy policy, and, 553
executive agencies, and

Competitiveness and Innovation,
for, 210
European Research Council, 209
Research, 211
industrial policy, and, 506
Information Society, and, 512–513
joint undertakings, and, 212
legal Acts of the EU, and, 40
police co-operation, and, 264
research and technological development,
and
culture, 489
dissemination of results, 537
European Research Area, 534
generally, 531–534
introduction, 530
Joint Research Centre, 537–538
third country co-operation, 536
youth policy, and, 484
"Francovich liability"
breach of EU Law, and, 51
Free movement of capital
generally, 298–300
Free movement of goods
accreditation, and, 236
conformity, and, 236
culture, and, 490
Customs Union
charges having equivalent effect, 225
Common Customs Tariff, 225–227
introduction, 224
discriminatory taxation, 231–232
exceptions, 232–234
introduction, 223–224
motor vehicle registration, and, 236
mutual recognition, and, 236
prohibitions
discriminatory taxation, 231–232
duties and charges having equivalent
effect, 225
protective taxation, 231–232
quantitative restrictions, 227–231
protective taxation, 231–232
quantitative restrictions, 227–231
surveillance, and, 236
technical standards, 234–235
theory and reality, 235–237
vehicle registration, and, 236
Free movement of persons
area of freedom, security and justice
asylum policy, 256–258
border controls, 256–258
generally, 255
immigration policy, 256–258
judicial co-operation, 258–263
police co-operation, 263–264

asylum policy, 256–258
border controls, 256–258
citizens
    Citizens' Initiative, 241–243
    generally, 239–241
culture, and, 490
immigration policy, 256–258
introduction, 238–239
judicial co-operation
    civil and commercial matters,
        258–261
    criminal matters, 261–263
police co-operation, 263–264
self-employed persons
    culture, and, 490
    generally, 238
students, 264–265
third country nationals, 255–264
workers
    exceptions, 253–254
    introduction, 243–245
    obstacles, 245–252
    post-2004 enlargement, 252–253
    third countries, from, 254
    'worker', 245
Freedom of establishment
company law, 268–270
culture, and, 490
European companies, 282–283
European co-operative societies, 283
European economic interest groupings,
    283
exceptions, 284
introduction, 266–268
non-regulated professions, 275–277
professional experience, 277
qualifications required for legal persons,
    where
    European companies, 282–283
    European co-operative societies, 283
    generally, 278–282
    private European company, 283
qualifications required for natural
    persons, where
    introduction, 270–272
    non-regulated professions,
        275–277
    recognition of professional
        experience, 277
    regulated professions, 272–275
regulated professions
    architects, 274
    dental practitioners, 273
    doctors of medicine, 272–273
    introduction, 272
    lawyers, 274–275

midwives, 273
nurses responsible for general care,
    273
pharmacists, 274
veterinary surgeons, 273
self-employed persons, 266–268
students, 270
Freedom of movement for workers
culture, and, 490
exceptions, 253–254
introduction, 243–245
obstacles, 245–252
post-2004 enlargement, 252–253
third countries, from, 254
'worker', 245
Freedom to provide services
banking services, 291–293
culture, and, 490
exceptions, 290–291
financial services, 291–293
future developments, 297
insurance, 295–297
introduction, 286–287
investment services, 293–295
required qualifications, 287–288
'services', 288–290
FRONTEX
generally, 202

"Galileo"
generally, 440
space policy, and, 536
Gas
energy policy, and, 557
"General action programmes"
legal Acts of the EU, and, 40
General Agreement on Tariffs and Trade
Doha round, 598–599
Uruguay round, 598
General Court
introduction, 165–166
jurisdiction, 167–168
members, 166–167
procedure, 169
"General Report"
European Parliament, and, 75–76
Generalised System of Preferences
See **Tariff preferences**
Genetically modified organisms
common agricultural policy, and, 410
**"Global Monitoring for Environment and
    Security (GMES)"**
space policy, and, 536
GNSS Supervisory Authority
See **European GNSS Supervisory
    Authority**

Greece
 accession, and, 17
Greenhouse gas emissions
 environmental policy, and, 547
Greenland
 secession, 18
Guarantees
 state aid, and, 392–393
Guidelines
 legal Acts of the EU, and, 29

Harmonisation
 And see **Approximation of laws**
 Common Customs Tariff, and, 226
 copyright, and, 304
 Council of the European Union, and, 93
 culture, and, 488
 directives, and, 31
 educational policy, and, 481
 employment policy, and, 485
 energy policy, and, 552
 environmental policy, and, 540
 European company, and, 282
 European Defence Agency, and, 205
 excise duties, and, 429
 financial services, and, 291
 free movement of goods, and
  Common Customs Tariff, 226
  exceptions, 233
  quantitative restrictions, 228
  technical standards, 234
 free movement of persons, and
  introduction, 267–268
  non-regulated professions, 275
  required qualifications, 271
 free movement of self-employed
  persons, and, 267–268
 freedom of establishment, and, 282
 freedom to provide services, and
  exceptions, 291
  financial services, 291
  investment services, 295
  required classifications, 287
 generally, 434–437
 industrial policy, and, 506
 internal market, and, 18
 investment services, and, 295
 public health, and, 492
 quantitative restrictions, and, 228
 rail transport, and, 449
 social policy, and, 471
 sports, and, 484
 tax, and
  direct taxes, 430
  excise duties, 429
  generally, 427

 telecommunications, and, 507
 trade marks, and, 305
 vocational training, and, 483
**High Representative of the Union for
 Foreign Affairs and Security Policy**
 external relations, and, 579
 generally, 108–109
 Treaty of Lisbon, and, 25
"Horizontal aid"
 'credit crunch' measures, 394
 direct business taxation, 392
 employment, 390
 environment, 390–391
 financial transfers to public
  undertakings, 392
 firms in under-privileged urban areas,
  391–392
 general aid schemes, 392
 General Block Exemption Regulation,
  393–394
 introduction, 389–390
 rescue and restructuring, 391
 research and development, 390
 small and medium-sized enterprises,
  391
 State Aid Action Plan, 393
 state guarantees, 392–393
 training, 390
Humanitarian aid
 external relations, and, 568
Hungary
 accession, and, 23

Iceland
 enlargement, and, 613
Illegality
 jurisdiction of European Court of
  Justice, and, 151–152
Immigration policy
 free movement of persons, and,
  256–258
Income tax
 generally, 430–433
India
 external relations, and, 595
Indirect taxes
 excise duty, 428–430
 value added tax, 427–428
Industrial designs
 See **Designs**
Industrial policy
 generally, 504–506
Information Society
 culture, and, 490
 enterprise policy, and, 506
 Framework Programmes, 512–513

implementation of policies
  data protection, 511–512
  electronic commerce, 511
  i2010, 508
  information society technology, 511
  international dimension, 512
  internet, 508
  network security, 512
  telecommunications, 509–511
  introduction, 507–508
  Safer Internet Plus programme, 508
Infrastructure for Spacial Information in the Union
See **INSPIRE**
Inland waterways
  competition policy, and, 454
"INSPIRE"
  space policy, and, 536
Insurance
  competition policy, and, 349–350
  freedom to provide services, and, 295–297
Intellectual property
  Community designs, 306–307
  competition policy, and, 350
  computer programs, 304
  copyright and related rights, 304
  counterfeits, 307
  databases, 304
  designs, 306–307
  exhaustion, 303
  industrial designs, 306–307
  international treaties, 308
  introduction, 301–303
  jurisdiction of European Court of Justice, and, 151
  know-how, 301
  lending rights, 304
  licensing, 307–308
  neighbouring rights, 301
  patents, 303–304
  piracy, 307
  protected designations of origin, 308
  protected geographical indications, 308
  rental rights, 304
  trade marks, 305–306
"Interbus Agreement"
  transport, and, 444
Interim measures
  European Court of Justice, and, 162–162
Intermodality
  See **Multimodal transport**
Internal market
  Communications, 222
  completion, 18–19

free movement of capital, 298–300
free movement of goods
  And see **Free movement of goods**
  Customs Union, 224–227
  discriminatory taxation, 231–232
  exceptions, 232–234
  introduction, 223–224
  protective taxation, 231–232
  quantitative restrictions, 227–231
  technical standards, 234–235
  theory and reality, 235–237
free movement of persons
  And see **Free movement of persons**
  citizens, 239–243
  introduction, 238–239
  students, 264–265
  third country nationals, 255–264
  workers, 243–254
free movement of self-employed persons, 266–267
freedom of establishment
  And see **Freedom of establishment**
  company law, 268–270
  European companies, 282–283
  European co-operative societies, 283
  European economic interest groupings, 283
  exceptions, 284
  introduction, 266–268
  non-regulated professions, 275–277
  professional experience, 277
  qualifications required for legal persons, where, 278–283
  qualifications required for natural persons, where, 270–277
  regulated professions, 272–275
  self-employed persons, 266–268
  students, 270
freedom of movement for workers
  exceptions, 253–254
  introduction, 243–245
  obstacles, 245–252
  post-2004 enlargement, 252–253
  third countries, from, 254
freedom to provide services
  And see **Freedom to provide services**
  exceptions, 290–291
  financial services, 291–293
  future developments, 297
  insurance, 295–297
  introduction, 286–287
  investment services, 293–295
  required qualifications, 287–288
  'services', 288–290
generally, 4
intellectual property rights

And see **Intellectual property**
Community designs, 306–307
copyright and related rights, 304
counterfeits, 307
designs, 306–307
exhaustion, 303
international treaties, 308
introduction, 301–303
licensing, 307–308
patents, 303–304
piracy, 307
protected designations of origin, 308
protected geographical indications, 308
trade marks, 305–306
introduction, 221–222
meaning, 4
public procurement
And see **Public procurement**
introduction, 309–311
regulated contracts, 311–314
remedies. 316
water, energy, transport and postal
services sectors, 314–316
International accounting standards
freedom of establishment, and, 280
International agreements
See **Treaties**
International co-operation
competition policy, and, 374–375
energy policy, and, 554–555
fisheries, and, 414
research and technological development,
and, 536
International organisations
external relations, and, 572–573
International trade
GATT, and
Doha round, 598–599
Uruguay round, 598
Internet
And see **Information Society**
generally, 508
Investment management
freedom to provide services, and,
293–295
Ireland
accession, and, 16–17
Treaty of Lisbon, and, 27
ISS
See **European Union Institute for
Security Studies**

Japan
external relations, and, 590
Joint actions
legal Acts of the EU, and, 29

Joint Research Centre
generally, 537–539
introduction, 532
"Joint Technology Initiatives"
generally, 212
research and technological development,
and, 533
Joint undertakings
generally, 212
research and technological development,
and, 533
Joint ventures
generally, 363–365
introduction, 319–320
joint or collective dominance, 365–370
Judges
European Court of Justice, and, 127–128
Judgments by default
See **Default judgments**
Judicial co-operation
enterprise policy, and, 517
Eurojust, and, 186–187
free movement of persons, and
civil and commercial matters,
258–261
criminal matters, 261–263
introduction, 6
jurisdiction of Court of Justice, and,
153
Treaty of Lisbon, and, 26
Judicial panels
General Court, and, 165
generally, 169
Treaty of Lisbon, and, 26
Jurisdiction
European Court of Justice, and
annulment, 132–141
appellate, 154–155
attribution of competence, 154
compensation for damages caused by
institutions, 149–151
failure to act, 141–142
failure to fulfil obligations, 130–131
illegality, 151–152
industrial property rights, 151
introduction, 129–130
member state obligations to ECB and
EIB, 153–154
other, 152–153
penalties, 131–132
preliminary rulings, 142–148
review of legality of Acts, 132–142
General Court, and, 167–168

Know-how
intellectual property, and, 301

Laeken Declaration
generally, 23–24
Latin America
See **South America**
Latvia
accession, and, 23
Lawyers
freedom of establishment, and, 274–275
Legal acts of the Union
See **EU Acts**
Lending right
intellectual property, and, 304
Licensing
intellectual property, and, 307–308
"Lifelong Learning Programme"
educational policy, and, 482
Limitation periods
competition policy, and, 358
Liner conferences
competition policy, and, 343
"LINGUA programme"
educational policy, and, 481
Lithuania
accession, and, 23

Maastricht Treaty
introduction, 3
Macedonia
enlargement, and, 612–613
Majority voting
generally, 95
Malta
accession, and, 23
Management procedure
European Commission, and, 116
Marine environments
environmental policy, and, 545
Maritime transport
See **Shipping**
"MARPOL Convention"
transport, and, 455
Marshall Plan
generally, 13–14
Measures having equivalent effect
free movement of goods, and, 225
Medicinal products
See **Pharmaceuticals**
Mediterranean countries
See **Southern Europe**
"Medium-term budgetary objectives"
economic and monetary union, and, 466
Members of the European Parliament
election, 62–63
immunity, 64–65
introduction, 61–62
mandate, 63–64

performance of duties, 65
privileges, 64–65
Merger Treaty
EU institutions, and, 60
generally, 16
Mergers
ancillary restraints, 366
generally, 363–365
introduction, 319–320
joint or collective dominance, 365–370
Midwives
freedom of establishment, and, 273
Military staff
See **European Union Military Staff**
"Millennium Development Goals"
development co-operation, and, 600
Misuse of power
actions for annulment, and, 140
Monetary policy
economic and monetary union, and, 463
Monopolies
See also **Competition policy**
generally, 375–376
Montenegro
enlargement, and, 615
Motions of censure
See **Power of censure**
Motor vehicles
competition policy, and, 331–332
state aid, and, 386
Multimodal transport
transport, and, 457
Mutual recognition principle
free movement of goods, and, 236

Natural gas
energy policy, and, 557
Neighbouring rights
intellectual property, and, 301
New Zealand
external relations, and, 592–593
Notices
legal Acts of the EU, and, 29
Nuclear energy
Euratom Supply Agency, 559
generally, 557–558
safeguard controls, 558–560
safety, 560
Nurses
freedom of establishment, and, 273

"Occasional Coach and Bus Services Agreement"
transport, and, 443–444

OECD
generally, 14
Office for Harmonisation in the Internal Market
designs, and, 306
generally, 195–196
jurisdiction of Court of Justice, and, 168
trade marks, and, 305
Official Journal of the European Union
legal Acts of the EU, and, 37
OHIM
See **Office for Harmonisation in the Internal Market**
Oil
energy policy, and, 557
Ombudsman of the European Union
See **European Ombudsman**
Opinions
European Commission, and, 113–115
generally, 35
"Oral procedure"
European Court of Justice, and, 159–160
Ordinary legislative procedure
approximation of laws, and, 435
conciliation, 69–70
consumer protection, and, 499
Council of the European Union, and
employment policy, 101
culture, and, 489
economic policy, and, 461
employment policy, and, 101
environment, and, 542
equal pay, and, 478
European Commission, and
exercise of delegated powers, 117
participation in legislative process, 120
European Parliament, and
internal organisation, 83
introduction, 65
joint exercise of legislative functions, 66
political groups, 81
European Research Area, and, 535
European Space Policy, and, 536
external action, and
economic, financial and technical co-operation, 567
humanitarian aid, 569
international agreements, 571
first reading, 68–69
free movement of goods, and, 226
free movement of persons, and
border checks, 256–257
Citizen's Initiative, 241

introduction, 239
judicial co-operation in criminal matters, 261–262
police co-operation, 263
freedom of establishment
exceptions, 285
qualifications for natural persons, 271
freedom to provide services, 288
generally, 25
implementing measures, 71
introduction, 68
modification of treaties, and, 11
product liability, and, 499
public health, and, 491
regional policy, and
general, 521
global resources, 527
regulations, and, 30
research and technological development, and
co-operation with third countries, 537
generally, 530
second reading, 69
social policy, and, 475
special provisions, 70
sports policy, and, 484
third reading, 70
Trans-European Networks, and, 516
transport, 438–439
type of Act to be adopted, 70
Organisation for Economic Co-operation and Development
See **OECD**
OSHA
See **European Agency for Safety and Health at Work**
Overseas countries and territories
development co-operation, and, 608
Own resources
generally, 214–216
introduction, 16

Parliamentary committees
generally, 81–82
Parliamentary privilege
Members of the European Parliament, and, 64–65
Passports
free movement of persons, and, 241
Patents
intellectual property, and, 303–304
Penalties
European Court of Justice, and, 131–132
Pesticides
environmental policy, and, 545

Petrol
energy policy, and, 557
Pharmaceuticals
public health, and, 495–496
Pharmacists
freedom of establishment, and, 274
Piracy
intellectual property, and, 307
Plant products
See **Crops**
Poland
accession, and, 23
Police co-operation
free movement of persons, and,
263–264
Political groups
European Parliament, and, 80–81
Polluter pays
environmental policy, and, 542
Portugal
accession, and, 17
Postal services
competition policy, and, 347–349
Power of censure
European Parliament, and, 76
Precautionary principle
environmental policy, and, 541
food safety, and, 494–495
Precedence
See **Supremacy of EU law**
Preliminary rulings
European Court of Justice, and,
142–148
President of the European Union
European Commission, and, 108
Primacy of EU law
See **Supremacy of EU law**
Principle of conferral
Council of the European Union, and, 92
Court of Justice, and, 137
Economic and Financial Committee,
and, 189
European Commission, and, 114
generally, 28
introduction, 3
Privilege
competition policy, and, 354–355
Product liability
consumer protection, and, 497–500
Programmes
legal Acts of the EU, and, 40
Proportionality
competition rules, and
Commission's role in implementation,
355
telecommunications, 347

generally, 28–29
jurisdiction of European Court of
Justice, and
action for annulment, 139
other cases, 153
legislative role of European
Commission, and, 119
ordinary legislative procedure, and, 70
police co-operation, and, 264
sources of EU law, and, 53
telecommunications, and
competition rules, 347
implementation of Information
Society policy, 510
Protected designations of origin
intellectual property, and, 308
Protected geographical indications
intellectual property, and, 308
Protective taxation
See **Discriminatory taxation**
Proximity
environmental policy, and, 542
Public health
ERDF, and, 492
European Social Fund, and, 492
food safety, 494–495
generally, 491–494
introduction, 487
legislative framework, 492–493
medicinal products, 495–496
pharmaceuticals, 495–496
Public Health Executive Agency
See **Executive Agency for Health and
Consumers**
Public procurement
introduction, 309–311
public sector services, 314–316
regulated contracts, 311–314
remedies. 316
water, energy, transport and postal
services sectors, 314–316
"Public undertakings"
competition policy, and, 376–377
**Publications Office of the European
Union**
generally, 212

Qualified majority voting
generally, 96–98
Quantitative restrictions
free movement of goods, and, 227–231

Railways
competition policy, and
generally, 446–449
introduction, 344–345

European Railway Agency, and, 201
state aid, and, 387
Trans-European Networks, and, 457
transport policy, and, 439–440
Recommendations
European Commission, and, 113–115
generally, 29
Rectification
European Court of Justice judgments,
and, 164
Recycling
environmental policy, and, 545
Regional development
culture, and, 489
state aid, and, 383–384
Regional policy
agriculture, and, 520
basic principles, 520
Cohesion Fund
generally, 529
introduction, 519
convergence
generally, 525
introduction, 523
European Agricultural Guidance and
Guarantee Fund, 522
European Fisheries Fund, 522
European Investment Bank, 520
European Regional Development Fund,
521–522
European Social Fund, 522
European territorial co-operation
generally, 525
introduction, 524
fisheries, and, 520
general, 519–522
objective, 519
regional competitiveness and
employment
generally, 525
introduction, 523–524
sectoral regulations, 522
social policy, and, 520
structural funds
additionality, 526
administration and management, 528
allocation, 524
consistency, 526
convergence, 525
co-ordination, 526
eligibility, 524–529
financial management, 528–529
fishing-dependent areas, 526
global resources, 527–528
introduction, 519
objectives, 523–524

outermost regions, 526
partnership, 527
principles, 522
programmes, 527
rates of assistance, 528
regional competitiveness and
employment, 525
reporting, 528
rural areas, 526
specific areas, 526–529
territorial co-operation, 525
urban areas, 526
structural operations, 522
Regulations
entry into force, 37–38
European Commission, and, 113–115
generally, 30–31
introduction, 28–30
publication, 37–38
reasoning, 36–37
Regulatory procedure
European Commission, and, 116–117
Regulatory procedure with scrutiny
European Commission, and, 117
Renewable energy
energy policy, and, 558
Rental rights
intellectual property, and, 304
Reports
European Parliament, and, 75–76
Rescue aid
state aid, and, 391
Research and development
competition policy, and, 333–334
co-operation with third countries,
536–537
culture, and, 489
dissemination of results, 537
energy policy, and, 556
European Regional Development Fund,
535
European Research Advisory Board, 536
European Research Area
generally, 534
introduction, 532
European Social Fund, 535
European Space Agency, 536
introduction, 530–531
Joint Research Centre
generally, 537–539
introduction, 532
Joint Undertakings, 533
Seventh Framework Programme
(2007–2013)
Capacities programme, 532
Co-operation programme, 532

Euratom, and, 532
  generally, 531–533
  Ideas programme, 532
  Joint Technology Initiatives,
    533–534
  People programme, 532
  space, and, 535–536
  state aid, and, 390
  third country co-operation, 536–537
Research Executive Agency
  generally, 210–211
Resolutions
  legal Acts of the EU, and, 40
Restructuring aid
  state aid, and, 391
Right of petition
  European Parliament, and, 72
Roads
  competition policy, and, 443–446
Romania
  accession, and, 24–25
Rules of procedure
  Council of the European Union, and,
    104
  Court of Auditors, and, 174
  European Commission, and, 123–124
Russia
  external relations, and, 591

Safeguard procedure
  European Commission, and, 117
Safer Internet Plus programme
  Information Society, and, 508
Satellite navigation
  European Organisation for the Safety of
    Air Navigation, 452
  Galileo
    generally, 440
    space policy, 536
  generally, 440
Schengen Agreement
  generally, 241–242
  Treaty of Lisbon, and, 26
"Schengen Information System"
  generally, 242
"Schuman declaration"
  generally, 14
Scientific and Technical Committee of
    Euratom
  generally, 182
Scrutiny procedure
  See Regulatory procedure with scrutiny
"Sea motorways"
  transport, and, 439
Second reading
  ordinary legislative procedure, and, 69

Self-employed workers
  free movement of persons, and, 238
  freedom of establishment, and,
    266–268
Serbia
  enlargement, and, 615–616
"Serious and persistent breach"
  European Council, and, 87–88
Services of general economic interest
  generally, 378
  state aid, and, 382
Setting aside
  European Court of Justice judgments,
    and, 164
Settlement
  competition policy, and, 356
Sex discrimination
  social policy, and, 479
"Shared Environmental Information
    System"
  environmental policy, and, 543
Shipbuilding
  state aid, and, 395
Shipping
  competition policy, and
    generally, 454–457
    introduction, 342–343
Single currency
  economic and monetary union, and, 459
  introduction, 3
Single European Act
  economic and social cohesion, and, 519
  environmental policy, and, 540
  European Parliament, and, 61
  General Court, and, 165
  generally, 19
  industrial policy, and, 505
  internal market, and, 221
  introduction, 4
  regional policy, and, 519
  research and technological development,
    and, 530
"Single European Sky"
  transport, and, 451–453
Single market
  See Internal market
Slovakia
  accession, and, 23
Slovenia
  accession, and, 23
Small and medium-sized enterprises
  enterprise policy, and, 513–515
  state aid, and, 391
Social policy
  Charter of the Fundamental Social
    Rights of Workers, 471

consultation of management and labour, 475–476
co-operation between member states, 476–477
equal opportunity
  equal pay, 478–479
  generally, 477
  gender equality, 479
Euratom Treaty, 470
European Social Charter, 471
European Social Fund
  generally, 479
  introduction, 470
facilitating co-ordination of member state actions, 476–477
introduction, 470
regional policy, and, 520
Social Agenda (2005 – 2010), 486
support and complement member state activities, 472–475
Societas Europaea
See **European companies**
Software
intellectual property, and, 304
"Solidarity clause"
external relations, and, 573
SOLVIT
free movement of goods, and, 235
Sources of law
generally, 53
South America
external relations, and, 596–597
Southern Europe
external relations, and, 593–594
South Korea
external relations, and, 595
Space industry
generally, 535–536
Infrastructure for Spacial Information in the Union, 536
Spain
accession, and, 17
Special legislative procedure
European Parliament, and, 71
Specialisation agreements
competition policy, and, 332–333
Specialised courts
Civil Service Tribunal, 170–171
General Court, and, 165
generally, 169–170
Treaty of Lisbon, and, 26
Sports
educational policy, and, 484
Stability and growth pact
And see **Economic and monetary union**
budgetary surveillance, 466–467

co-ordination of economic affairs, 466–467
excessive deficit procedure, 467–468
global financial crisis, and, 468
introduction, 466
Stamp duty
generally, 425
Standards
industrial policy, and, 507
State aid
Action Plan, 393
'advantage an undertaking', 379
'affect trade between member states', 381
agriculture, 388
aids compatible with the internal market
  'compatible aids', 382
  horizontal aids, 389–394
  introduction, 382–383
  procedural rules, 394–395
  recovery of aid, 395–397
  regional development aids, 383–384
  sectoral aids, 385–389
broadcasting, 389
coal, 385–386
'compatible aids', 382
'credit crunch' measures, 394
culture, and, 490
direct business taxation, 392
'distort competition', 381
employment, 390
environment, 390–391
'favour certain undertakings or the production of certain goods', 380–381
financial services, 389
financial transfers to public undertakings, 392
firms in under-privileged urban areas, 391–392
fisheries, 388
general aid schemes, 392
General Block Exemption Regulation, 393–394
'granted by a member state or through the state resources, 379–380
guarantees, 392–393
horizontal aids
  'credit crunch' measures, 394
  direct business taxation, 392
  employment, 390
  environment, 390–391
  financial transfers to public undertakings, 392
  firms in under-privileged urban areas, 391–392
  general aid schemes, 392

General Block Exemption Regulation, 393–394
  introduction, 389–390
  rescue and restructuring, 391
  research and development, 390
  small and medium-sized enterprises, 391
  State Aid Action Plan, 393
  state guarantees, 392–393
  training, 390
motor vehicles, 386
notion of aid, 379–381
procedural rules, 394–395
recovery of aid, 395–397
regional development aids, 383–384
rescue and restructuring, 391
research and development, 390
sectoral aids
  agriculture, 388
  broadcasting, 389
  coal, 385–386
  financial services, 389
  fisheries, 388
  introduction, 385
  motor vehicles, 386
  shipbuilding, 395
  steel, 385
  synthetic fibres, 386
  transport, 387–388
services of general economic interest, and, 382
shipbuilding, 395
small and medium-sized enterprises, 391
'specificity', 380–381
State Aid Action Plan, 393
state guarantees, 392–393
steel, 385
synthetic fibres, 386
training, 390
transport
  generally, 387–388
  introduction, 443
Stay of proceedings
European Court of Justice, and, 164–165
Steel
competition policy, and, 350
state aid, and, 385
Structural funds
additionality, 526
administration and management, 528
allocation, 524
consistency, 526
convergence, 525
co-ordination, 526
eligibility, 524–529

financial management, 528–529
fishing-dependent areas, 526
global resources, 527–528
introduction, 519
objectives, 523–524
outermost regions, 526
partnership, 527
principles, 522
programmes, 527
rates of assistance, 528
regional competitiveness and employment, 525
reporting, 528
rural areas, 526
specific areas, 526–529
territorial co-operation, 525
urban areas, 526
Students
free movement of persons, and, 264–265
freedom of establishment, and, 270
Sub-contracts
competition policy, and, 370–371
Subsidiarity
development co-operation, and, 603
economic policy, and, 100
employment, and, 485
energy policy, and, 557
environmental policy, and, 542
European Commission, and, 119–120
generally, 28
members of the European Parliament, and, 64
rural development, and, 411
Translation Centre, and, 197
Treaty on European Union, and, 19
Treaty of Lisbon, and, 26
Supremacy of EU law
generally, 46–51
introduction, 31
Surveillance
free movement of goods, and, 236
Sustainable development
environmental policy, and, 544–545
Sweden
accession, and, 21–22
"Synthetic fibres"
state aid, and, 386

Tariff preferences
development co-operation, and, 602
Tax
company taxes, 431–432
direct taxes, 430–433
duty-free, 432
excise duty, 428–430

income tax, 430–433
indirect taxes
excise duty, 428–430
value added tax, 427–428
introduction, 425–427
personal taxes, 430–431
stamp duties, 425
value added tax, 427–428
wealth taxes, 430–433
Technical standards
free movement of goods, and,
234–235
Technology
See also **Research and development**
culture, and, 489
energy policy, and, 556
Technology transfer
competition policy, and, 334–336
Telecommunications
competition policy, and, 345–347
Information Society, and, 509–511
"TEMPUS"
educational policy, and, 481
Third country nationals
free movement of persons, and,
255–264
Third country relations
See **External relations**
Third party proceedings
European Court of Justice, and, 164
Third reading
ordinary legislative procedure, and, 70
"Three pillars"
introduction, 4
Time limits
European Court of Justice, and, 165
Trade marks
intellectual property, and, 305–306
**Trade Related Aspects of Intellectual
Property Rights**
See **TRIPs**
Training
state aid, and, 390
Trans-European Networks
enterprise policy, and, 515–517
transport, and
conclusion, 458
generally, 457
introduction, 439
rail freight, 448
**Trans-European Transport Network
Executive Agency**
generally, 209–210
introduction, 457
Translation Centre
generally, 196–197

Transport
air transport (competition policy)
generally, 449–451
international agreements, 453–454
introduction, 343–344
safety assessment of foreign aircraft,
453
Single European Sky, 451–453
approach of new policy, 439–440
Common Transport Policy
acquis communautaire, 439
conclusion, 458
generally, 438
new approach, 439–440
competition policy, and
air transport, 449–454
generally, 443
inland waterways, 454
introduction, 342–345
maritime transport, 454–457
railways, 446–449
road transport, 443–446
shipping, 454–457
Eurocontrol, 452
European Aviation Safety Agency, 452
European Geostationary Navigation
Overlay Service, 440
European Maritime Safety Agency,
456
Galileo, 440
inland waterways, 454
Interbus Agreement, 444
intermodality, 457
international aviation, 344
introduction, 438
maritime transport (competition
policy)
generally, 454–457
introduction, 342–343
MARPOL Convention, 455
Occasional Coach and Bus Services
Agreement, 443–444
pollution from ships, 455
railways (competition policy)
generally, 446–449
introduction, 344–345
road transport, 443–446
'sea motorways', 439
shipping (competition policy)
generally, 454–457
introduction, 342–343
Single European Sky, 451–453
special features, 440–442
state aid, and
generally, 387–388
introduction, 443

Trans-European Network
  conclusion, 458
  generally, 457
  introduction, 439
  rail freight, 448
UN Convention on The Law of the
  Sea, 455
Treaties
  enhanced co-operation, 6–8
  external relations, and, 569–571
  intellectual property, and, 308
  introduction, 3–4
  membership, 11
  modification, 10–11
  territorial scope, 11–12
  Treaty of Amsterdam, 22–23
  Treaty of Brussels, 16–17
  Treaty of Lisbon, 25–27
  Treaty of Nice, 23
  Treaty on European Union, 4–6, 19
  Treaty on the Functioning of the
    European Union, 8–10
Treaties of Rome
  introduction, 4
Treaty of Amsterdam
  generally, 22–23
  introduction, 3
Treaty of Brussels
  generally, 16–17
Treaty of Lisbon
  Czech Republic, and, 27
  generally, 25–26
  introduction, 3
  Ireland, and, 26–27
Treaty of Nice
  generally, 23
  introduction, 3
Treaty on European Union
  enhanced co-operation, 6–8
  generally, 4–6
  introduction, 3
  membership, 11
  modification, 10–11
  overview, 19
  territorial scope, 11–12
**Treaty on the Functioning of the European
  Union**
  enhanced co-operation, 6–8
  generally, 8–10
  introduction, 3
  membership, 11
  modification, 10–11
  territorial scope, 11–12

TRIPs
  commercial policy, and, 598
  generally, 308
Turkey
  enlargement, and, 610–611

UN Convention on The Law of the Sea
  transport, and, 455
Union Acts
  See EU Acts
Union law
  See EU law
United Kingdom
  accession, and, 16–17
United States
  external relations, and, 587–589

Value added tax
  generally, 427–428
Vehicle registration
  free movement of goods, and, 236
Vertical agreements
  generally, 329–331
  motor vehicles, 331–332
Veterinary surgeons
  freedom of establishment, and, 273
"Visa Information System"
  generally, 242
Vocational training
  educational policy, and, 483
Voting
  Council of the European Union, and
    introduction, 95–96
    qualified majority, 96–98
    simple majority, 96
    unanimity, 98

Waste minimisation
  environmental policy, and, 545
Workers
  free movement of persons, and
    exceptions, 253–254
    introduction, 243–245
    obstacles, 245–252
    post-2004 enlargement, 252–253
    third countries, from, 254
World Trade Organisation
  external relations, and, 598
"Written procedure"
  European Court of Justice, and, 156–159

Young persons
  educational policy, and, 484